Exploring Our World: People, Places, and Cultures
Western Hemisphere, Europe, and Russia

Features and Benefits

Dynamic Instructional Structure	**. . . presents clear and comprehensive coverage of geography and world cultures.** • Co-author National Geographic created the **Reference Atlas, Geography Skills Handbook,** the **Unit Regional Atlases,** and every in-text map and chart. • Each engaging section introduction includes **Guide to Reading, Content and Academic Vocabulary,** and a motivating **Picture This** feature. • Big Ideas for each section help students organize important geographical concepts and make it easier to understand patterns and relationships. • The **Visual Summary** at the end of each chapter presents the major concepts in a bulleted list complete with maps and photographs.
A Strong Reading Strand	**. . . encourages active reading and learning for students of all reading levels.** • **Main Idea** and **Geography and You** at the beginning of each main heading give students a focus and a reason for reading, and **Reading Checks** assess comprehension. • The **Reading Social Studies** feature at the beginning of each unit allows students to learn and practice new content-area reading skills. • The **Reading Essentials and Note-Taking Guide** ancillary benefits all students by combining a concise version of the text, at a lower reading level, with a 2-column note-taking guide.
Differentiated Instruction	**. . . makes *Exploring Our World* accessible to students of all learning levels.** • Differentiated Instruction activities and strategies can be found in the **Teacher Wraparound Edition,** the **Unit Resource** ancillaries, the **Teacher's Guide to Differentiated Instruction** ancillary, and online at **glencoe.com.** • **Reading and Study Skills Foldables™** are 3-D kinesthetic exercises that help students organize and process key concepts as they read. • ***Exploring Our World* in Graphic Novel** is one of many motivating tools for differentiating instruction and engaging all learners in geography.
Standardized Test Preparation	**. . . gives students the opportunity to practice for state and national exams.** • **Chapter Assessments** are now in standardized test format to provide truly useful standardized test preparation. • Prescriptive prompts on each chapter assessment page guide students to where they can revisit the material.
A Variety of Motivational Activities and Features	**. . . are essential for student success and to get students excited about geography and world cultures.** • The **National Geographic Regional Atlas** provides a preview of the land, climates, economies, and people that will be presented in the unit. • The **National Geographic Geography and History** feature shows students how geography and history are intertwined. • The **TIME Perspectives, TIME Journal,** and **TIME Global Citizens** features enlist the expertise of TIME Magazine journalists to bring current and relevant information into your classroom. • **World Literature** and **You Decide** features help develop critical thinking skills while making the connection between geography and other disciplines.
Teacher Resources	**. . . provide convenient strategies to help both new and experienced teachers.** • The **Teacher Wraparound Edition** now contains the **Brackets and Letters System,** identifying reading, differentiated instruction, writing support, critical thinking, and skill practice activities and strategies at the *exact* point-of-use. • ***TeacherWorks Plus*™ DVD** contains the Interactive Teacher Edition, all ancillaries and transparencies, *editable* blackline masters, and the most powerful and easy-to-use lesson planner in the business.
Technology	**. . . provides time-saving aids to help you reduce preparation time and engage students creatively.** • ***StudentWorks Plus*™ DVD** includes the Interactive Student Edition, all student workbooks, and *full audio of the entire text* in English, with a Spanish audio summary. • ***ExamView® Assessment Suite*** allows you to make customized tests using a huge databank of questions, including DBQs, that can be modified for all students. • ***Exploring Our World*** at **glencoe.com** provides chapter-based, interactive activities and Web-based resources that will engage your students. • ***Study Central*™** is an online, section-based homework helper that offers additional content, skills practice, and vocabulary development. • ***Study-To-Go*™** provides content and vocabulary review activities for portable electronic devices. • ***Presentation Plus! with MindJogger Checkpoint* DVD** contains a PowerPoint™ presentation of the textbook, all program transparencies, and the interactive **MindJogger** quiz game. • The ***Exploring Our World* Video Program** offers interesting and diverse content extension. There is one video per section.

Glencoe

New York, New York Columbus, Ohio Chicago, Illinois Woodland Hills, California

About the Authors

NATIONAL GEOGRAPHIC

The National Geographic Society, founded in 1888 for the increase and diffusion of geographic knowledge, is the world's largest nonprofit scientific and educational organization. Since its earliest days, the Society has used sophisticated communication technologies, from color photography to holography, to convey geographic knowledge to a worldwide membership. The School Publishing Division supports the Society's mission by developing innovative education programs—ranging from traditional print materials to multimedia programs including CD-ROMs, videos, and software.

Senior Author

Richard G. Boehm

Richard G. Boehm, Ph.D., was one of seven authors of *Geography for Life,* national standards in geography, prepared under Goals 2000: Educate America Act. He was also one of the authors of the *Guidelines for Geographic Education,* in which the Five Themes of Geography were first articulated. Dr. Boehm has received many honors, including "Distinguished Geography Educator" by the National Geographic Society (1990), the "George J. Miller Award" from the National Council for Geographic Education (NCGE) for distinguished service to geographic education (1991), and "Gilbert Grosvenor Honors" in geographic education from the Association of American Geographers (2002). He was President of the NCGE and has twice won the *Journal of Geography* award for best article. He has received the NCGE's "Distinguished Teaching Achievement" award and presently holds the Jesse H. Jones Distinguished Chair in Geographic Education at Texas State University in San Marcos, Texas.

Francis P. Hunkins

Francis P. Hunkins, Ph.D., is Professor of Education at the University of Washington. He began his career as a teacher in Massachusetts. He received his master's degree in education from Boston University and his doctorate from Kent State University with a major in general curriculum and a minor in geography. Dr. Hunkins has written numerous books and articles.

David G. Armstrong

David G. Armstrong, Ph.D., served as Dean of the School of Education at the University of North Carolina at Greensboro. A social studies education specialist with additional advanced training in geography, Dr. Armstrong was educated at Stanford University, University of Montana, and University of Washington.

Dinah Zike

Dinah Zike, M.Ed., is an award-winning author, educator, and inventor known for designing three-dimensional hands-on manipulatives and graphic organizers known as Foldables™. Dinah has developed educational books and materials and is the author of *The Big Book of Books and Activities,* which was awarded Learning Magazine's Teachers' Choice Award. In 2004 Dinah was honored with the CESI Science Advocacy Award. Dinah received her M.Ed. from Texas A&M, College Station, Texas.

The McGraw-Hill Companies

Send all inquiries to:
Glencoe/McGraw-Hill, 8787 Orion Place, Columbus, Ohio 43240-4027

(Teacher Wraparound Edition)
ISBN: 978-0-07-874581-2
MHID: 0-07-874581-0

(Student Edition)
ISBN: 978-0-07-874580-5
MHID: 0-07-874580-2

Printed in the United States of America.
1 2 3 4 5 6 7 8 9 079/055 14 13 12 11 10 09 08 07

Academic Consultants

Pratyusha Basu, Ph.D.
Assistant Professor of Geography
University of South Florida
Tampa, Florida

Sari Bennett, Ph.D.
Director, Center for Geographic Education
University of Maryland, Baltimore County
Baltimore, Maryland

Dennis Conway, Ph.D.
Professor of Geography
Indiana University
Bloomington, Indiana

Clifford B. Craig, Ph.D.
Professor of Geography and Earth Resources
Utah State University
Logan, Utah

Brooks Green, Ph.D.
Associate Professor of Geography
University of Central Arkansas
Conway, Arkansas

Gerald T. Hanson, Ph.D.
Professor of Cultural Geography
University of Arkansas at Little Rock
Little Rock, Arkansas

Darrell P. Kruger, Ph.D.
Professor of Geography
Illinois State University
Normal, Illinois

David A. Lanegran, Ph.D.
John S. Holl Professor of Geography
Macalester College
St. Paul, Minnesota

Elizabeth J. Leppman, Ph.D.
Adjunct Professor of Geography
Eastern Kentucky University
Richmond, Kentucky

Catherine M. Lockwood, Ph.D.
Professor of Geography
Chadron State College
Chadron, Nebraska

Paul Nagel, Ph.D.
Coordinator, Louisiana Geography Education Alliance
Northwestern State University
Natchitoches, Louisiana

Bimal Kanti Paul, Ph.D.
Professor of Geography
Kansas State University
Manhattan, Kansas

Joseph P. Stoltman, Ph.D.
Professor of Geography
Western Michigan University
Kalamazoo, Michigan

George W. White, Jr., Ph.D.
Associate Professor of Geography
Frostburg State University
Frostburg, Maryland

Teacher Reviewers

Cynthia L.N. Bloom
Comstock Northeast Middle School
Kalamazoo, Michigan

Ronda Boyd-Roberts
Spring City Middle School
Spring City, Tennessee

Melinda Clay Casey
Truman Middle School
Grand Prairie, Texas

Ann M. Christianson
John Muir Middle School
Wausau, Wisconsin

Cynthia Dabalos
Richview Middle School
Clarksville, Tennessee

Sandra Goldich
Alexandria Middle Magnet School
Alexandria, Louisiana

Julie Hill
Bob Courtway Middle School
Conway, Arkansas

Kathryn Jones
North Reading Middle School
North Reading, Massachusetts

George S. Kuhter
South Tama Middle School
Toledo, Iowa

Clark Norman
Gravelly Hill Middle School
Hillsborough, North Carolina

Robert L. O'Brian
Buffalo Public Schools
Buffalo, New York

Heather Latham Porter
Butler Junior High School
Butler, Pennsylvania

Phyllis M. Quinn
Martin J. Ryerson Middle School
Ringwood, New Jersey

Kim Roberts
University School at East Tennessee State University
Johnson City, Tennessee

Sharon L. Shelerud
Metcalf Junior High School
Burnsville, Minnesota

Sharon Sobierajski
Frederick Law Olmstead Middle School
Buffalo, New York

Melissa L. Younker-Kordish
Calkins Road Middle School
Pittsford, New York

Reading Consultant

ReLeah Lent
National Education Consultant
Alford, Florida

Contents

Farming in Manitoba, Canada

Celebration in Port-of-Spain, Trinidad

Reed boat, Lake Titicaca

Contents

The Danube River, Hungary

Contents

Breaking ice on the Arctic Ocean

Features

Geography & History

YOU Decide

Trans-Siberian Railroad train

TIME Features

Protesting in France

TIME JOURNAL

Primary Sources

Ed. = Editor	Tr. = Translator	V = Volume

UNIT 1

UNIT 2

▲ **African Americans in Harlem during the 1930s**

UNIT 3

UNIT 4

Toucan

Pan-American Highway, Panama

UNIT 5

Skills Handbook

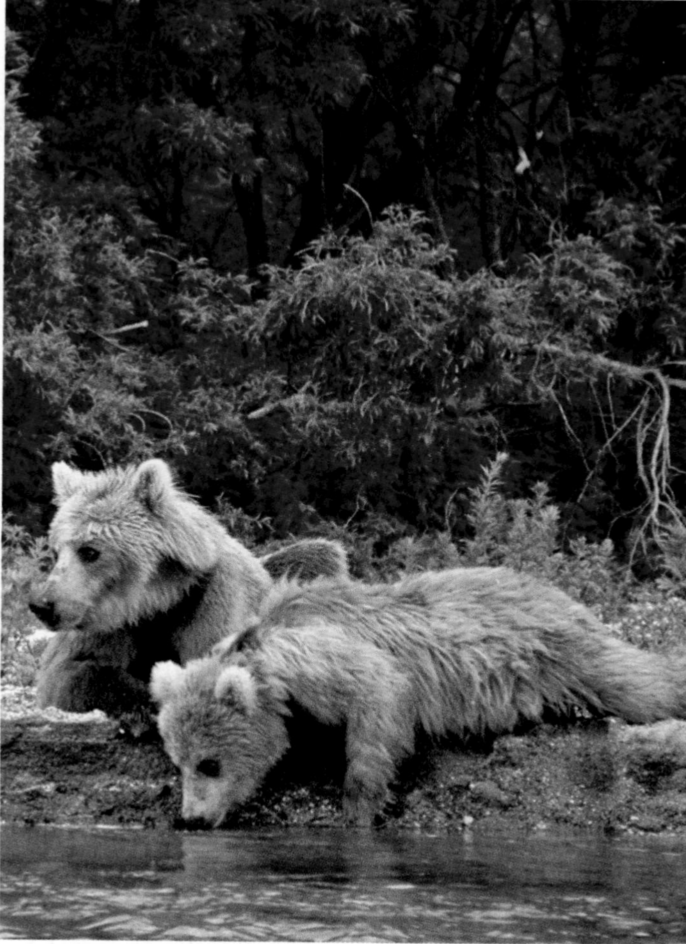

▲ **Brown bear cubs, Kamchatka Peninsula, Russia**

Maps

Reference Atlas . . . RA1

UNIT 1

The World

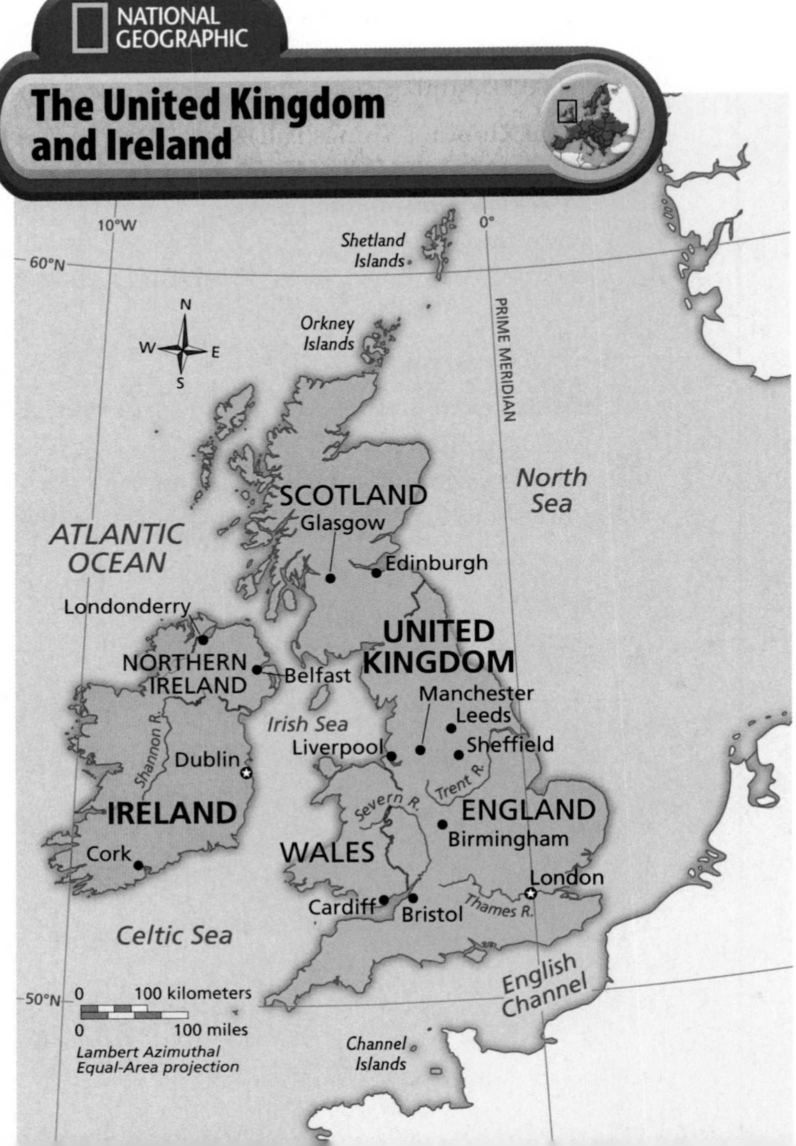

UNIT 2

The United States and Canada

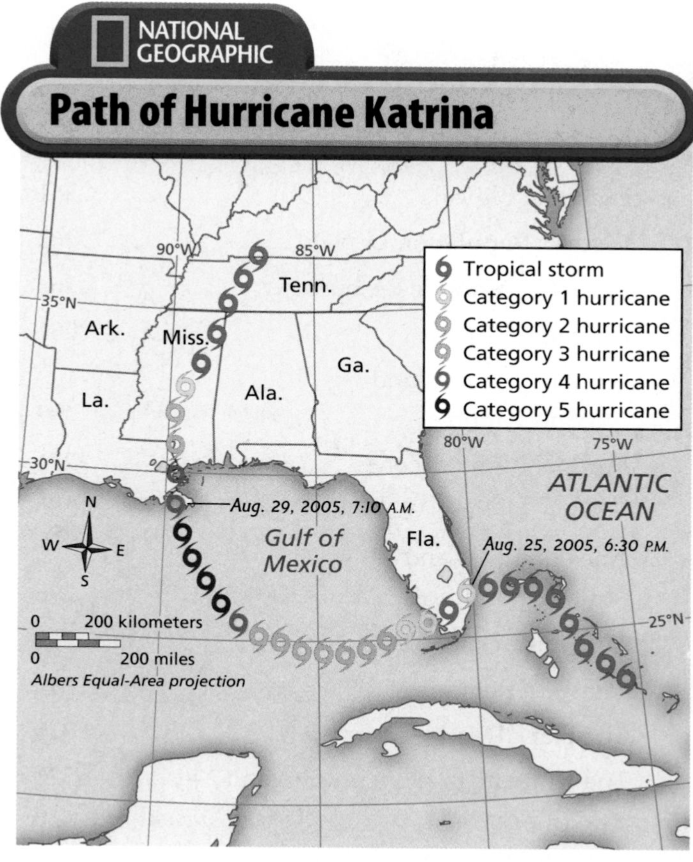

UNIT 3

Latin America

UNIT 4

Europe

UNIT 5

Russia

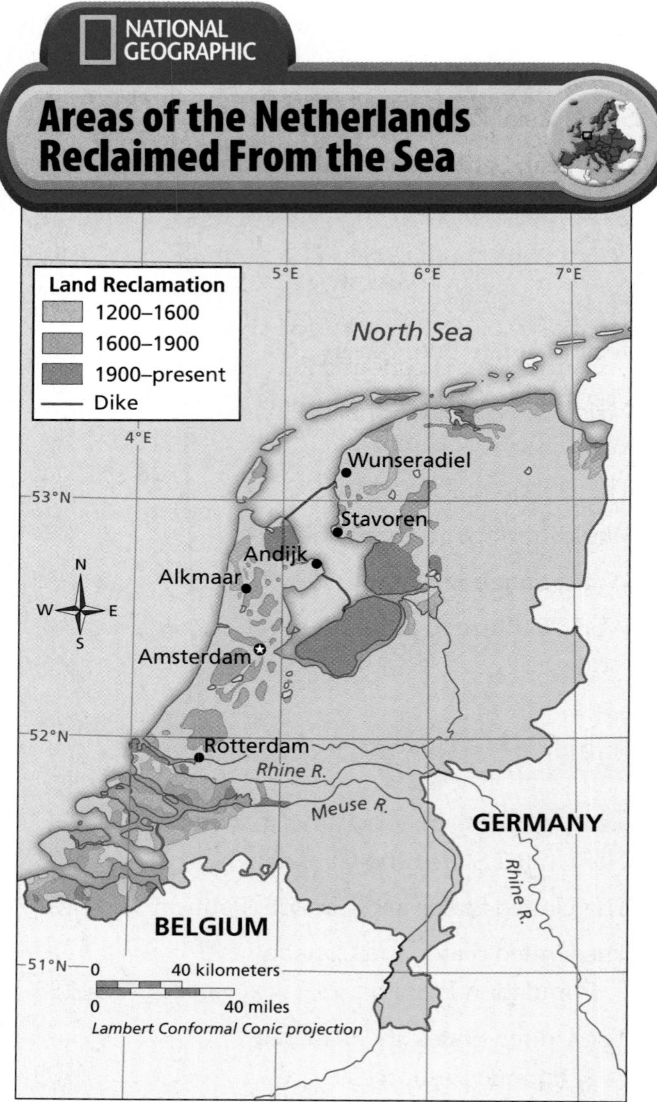

NATIONAL GEOGRAPHIC
Areas of the Netherlands Reclaimed From the Sea
Land Reclamation
1200–1600
1600–1900
1900–present
Dike
5°E
6°E
7°E
4°E
53°N
52°N
51°N
North Sea
Wunseradiel
Stavoren
Andijk
Alkmaar
Amsterdam
Rotterdam
Rhine R.
Meuse R.
GERMANY
Rhine R.
BELGIUM
N
S
E
W
0
40 kilometers
0
40 miles
Lambert Conformal Conic projection

Exploring the Eastern Hemisphere

NATIONAL GEOGRAPHIC

The Trans-Siberian Railroad

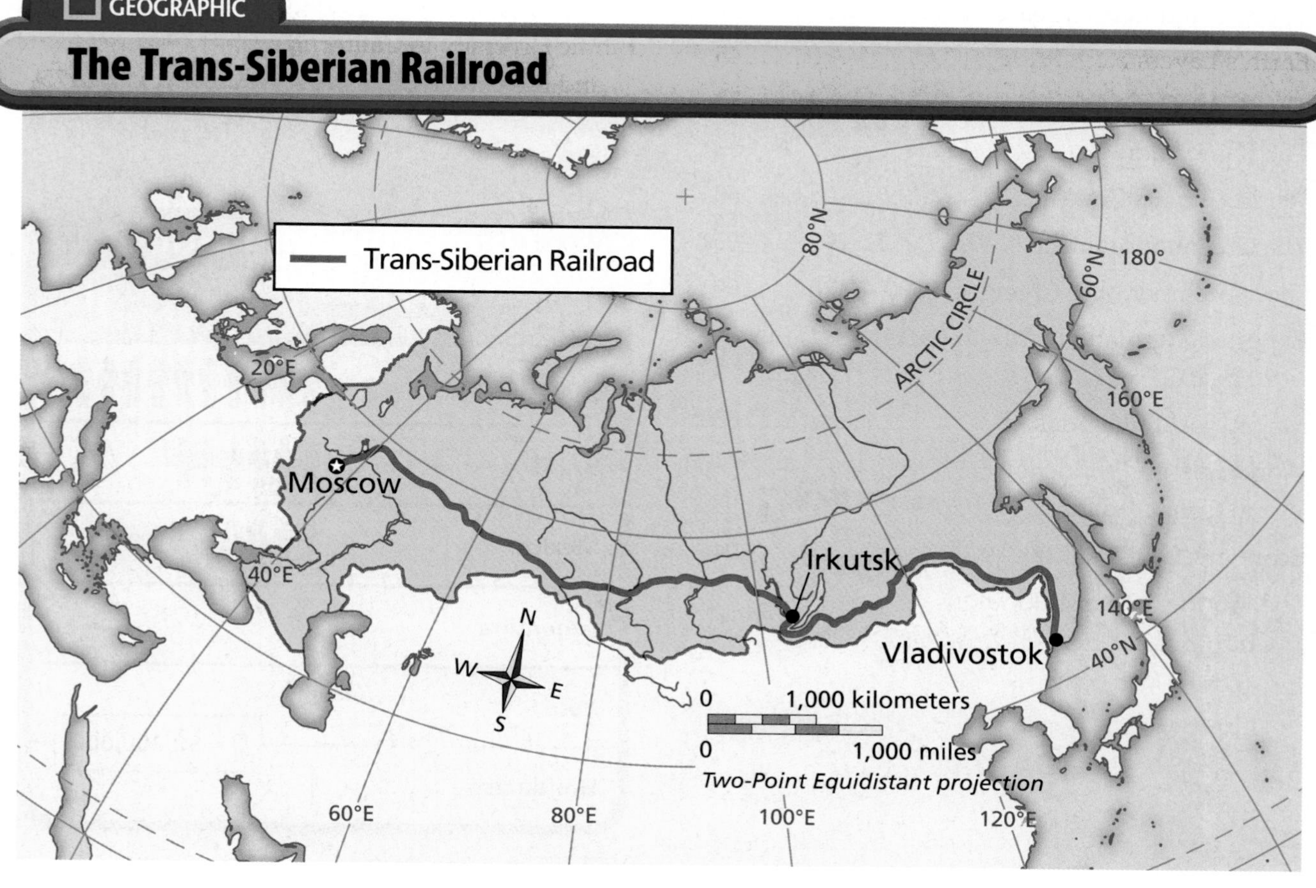

Diagrams, Charts, and Graphs

UNIT 1

The World

UNIT 2

The United States and Canada

Source: *World Population Data Sheet*, 2005.

Altitude Climate Zones

UNIT 3

Latin America

UNIT 4

Europe

UNIT 5

Russia

Exploring the Eastern Hemisphere

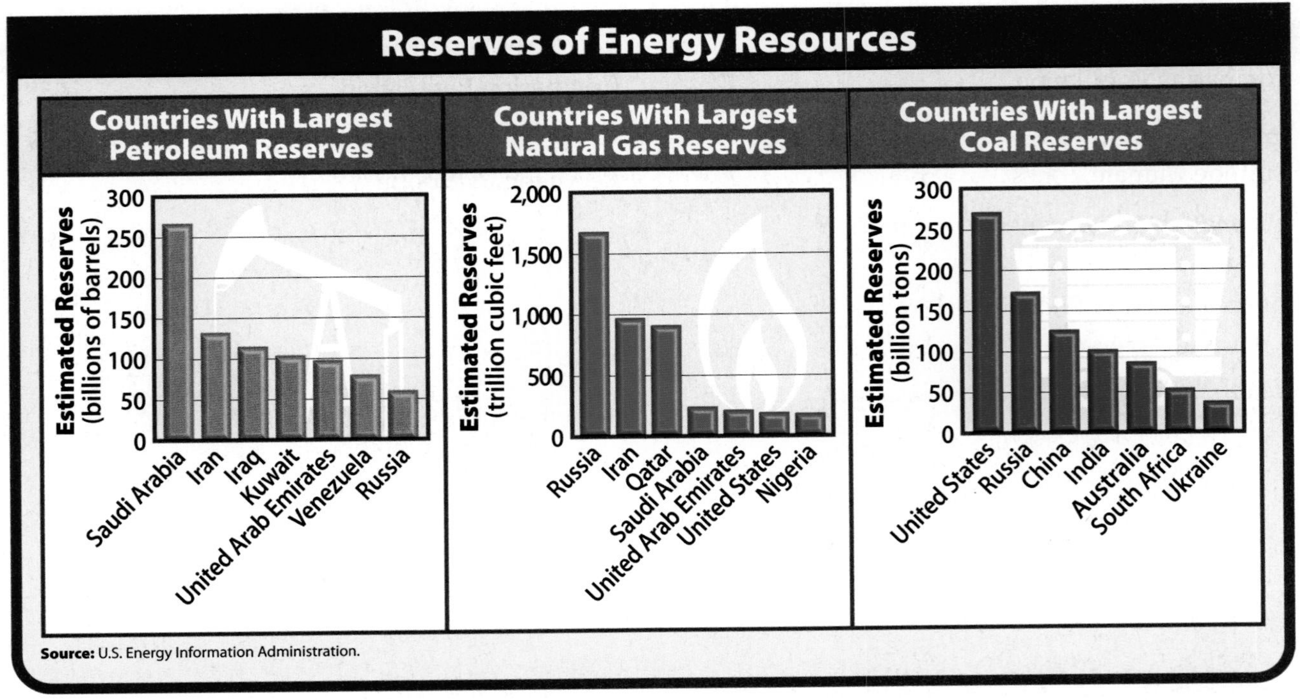

Scavenger Hunt

Exploring Our World: People, Places, and Cultures contains a wealth of information. The trick is to know where to look to access all the information in the book. If you complete this scavenger hunt exercise with your teacher or parents, you will see how the textbook is organized and how to get the most out of your reading and study time. Let's get started!

1. How many units and how many chapters are in the book?
   5 units, 15 chapters

2. What does Unit 1 cover?
   The World
3. Where can you find facts about each country in each unit?
   the chart in the Regional Atlas

4. In what three places can you learn about the Big Ideas for each section?
   Chapter Opener, Section Opener, and Section Review
5. What does the Foldables Study Organizer at the beginning of Chapter 2 ask you to do?
   make a Foldable to summarize information about the Earth's physical geography

6. How are the content vocabulary terms throughout your book highlighted in the narrative?
   highlighted yellow and boldfaced
7. Where do you find graphic organizers in your textbook?
   Section Opener: Reading Strategy and the Section Review
8. You want to quickly find all the maps in the book about the world. Where do you look?
   Reference Atlas and the Unit 1 Regional Atlas
9. Where can you practice specific social studies skills in your textbook?
   Skills Handbook at the back of the book
10. Where can you learn about the different types of map projections?
    Chapter 1 in the Geography Skills Handbook

Correlation of

Exploring Our World: People, Places, and Cultures to the National Geography Standards

Instruction in geography has been organized around the Five Themes of Geography: location, place, human-environment interaction, movement, and regions. The popularity of these content organizers set the stage for the development of two additional, more comprehensive instructional frameworks: the "Six Essential Elements" and the "Eighteen Geography Standards" within the elements.

National Geography Standards & Related Themes	Student Edition Pages
STANDARD 1 **How to use maps and other geographic representations, tools, and technologies to acquire, process, and report information from a spatial perspective** Maps are the most commonly used representations of detailed geographic information on features or places. Along with other tools such as globes, aerial photographs, satellite images, and statistical databases, they bring the whole world into focus. Maps range from simple sketch maps to complex Geographic Information Systems (GIS) analyses. **Related Themes: Location, Place**	2–3, 4–5, 6–7, 8–9, 12, 17, 22–31, 33–38, 40–41, 45–48, 50, 52, 53, 56, 58, 59, 60, 62, 65, 75, 83, 88, 93, 104–111, 120, 123, 125, 135, 160, 164, 199, 184–187, 201, 210, 224, 248, 258–264, 264–269, 281, 283, 284, 285, 296, 302, 311, 315, 321, 333, 344, 351, 354, 359, 362–367, 379, 389, 395, 417, 420, 432–437, 438–441, 444–449, 450–455, 458–463, 464, 468–473, 474–476, 480–485, 486–487
STANDARD 2 **How to use mental maps to organize information about people, places, and environments in a spatial context** A mental map exists only in the mind's eye. It represents each individual's knowledge of the location of geographic features such as countries, cities, seas, mountain ranges, and rivers. A mental map is also made up of approximate size dimensions and cultural characteristics. In scale, it may include our route to a local store or theater, or it may serve as the framework for the location of the Khyber Pass, Brasília, or the Yangtze Gorges. This map grows in complexity as experience, study, and the media bring us new geographic information. **Related Themes: Location, Place, Regions**	2–3, 4–5, 6–7, 14, 16, 23–25, 27, 29–31, 32, 35–38, 40–42, 44–48, 50, 54, 58–61, 64, 65–66, 83, 88, 104, 108–111, 116–120, 122, 123, 125–127, 128, 135, 138, 147, 159–162, 178, 180, 181, 192, 193–194, 196, 199–202, 209–210, 212, 214, 220–221, 224, 226, 233, 235, 239, 242–243, 247, 248, 249, 251, 252, 254, 258, 275–277, 280, 281, 283–288, 290, 294, 295–296, 298, 300, 303, 308, 318, 321, 324, 325, 326, 330, 337, 339, 342, 359, 374, 375, 380, 382, 385, 386, 395, 399, 417, 420, 432, 434–437, 444, 448, 458, 468, 480
STANDARD 3 **How to analyze the spatial organization of people, places, and environments on Earth's surface** Human structures organize space. Pattern, regularity, and reason are inherent in the locations of cities, factories, malls, cemeteries, and other human landscape creations. To understand the spatial patterns and processes that organize Earth's surface, it is essential to know concepts such as distance, direction, location, connections, and association. Understanding these concepts enables one to say what factors influence a locational decision for a hospital, a county seat, a sanitary landfill, or a regional shopping center. **Related Themes: Place, Human-Environment Interaction**	4–5, 6–7, 8–9, 14, 15, 22–28, 30, 35–38, 40–41, 45, 46, 48, 50, 56–60, 75–76, 104, 106–108, 110–111, 122, 125–127, 128, 149, 159–162, 178, 180, 182, 193–194, 196, 199–202, 210, 224, 227, 233, 235, 247, 251, 252, 258, 262, 275–277, 281, 283–288, 296, 302, 309, 339–342, 349, 352, 354, 355, 362–364, 366, 373, 376, 379–380, 395, 398, 400, 420, 432, 434, 436, 444, 446, 448, 458, 460–462, 468–472, 474–476, 480–485, 486–487

National Geography Standards & Related Themes	Student Edition Pages
STANDARD 4 **The physical and human characteristics of places** Places may be distinguished by their physical and human characteristics. Physical characteristics include landforms, climate, soils, hydrology, vegetation, and animal life. Human characteristics include language, religion, political and economic systems, population, and quality of life. Places change over time as new technologies, resources, knowledge, and ideologies are introduced and become part of a place's geography. Such change leads to the rise and fall of empires, may derive from shifts in climate or other physical systems, or may be generated by population expansion. **Related Themes: Place, Human-Environment Interaction**	50, 52, 56–61, 74, 83–86, 93–96, 117–122, 124–128, 135–141, 145–150, 155, 159–162, 169–172, 193–196, 199–202, 208–215, 218–221, 223–224, 229, 232–236, 237–240, 243, 246–525, 274–280, 282–288, 295–303, 306–312, 317, 321–323, 325–328, 330–337, 338–342, 343–345, 348–356, 372–375, 378–380, 382, 389–394, 396–400, 405, 409–416, 418–422
STANDARD 5 **That people create regions to interpret Earth's complexity** Regions are defined as having one or more common characteristics that give them a measure of unity and make them distinct from surrounding areas. As worlds within worlds, regions simplify geographic analysis by organizing a specific area into a unit of explicit physical and human elements. The criteria in the definition of a region can be as precise as coastline or political boundaries, or as arbitrary as the general location of people loyal to a specific athletic team. Regions are human constructs, created to facilitate the understanding of a large, varied, complex, and changing world. **Related Themes: Regions, Human-Environment Interaction**	2–3, 4–5, 8–9, 19, 25, 59–61, 88–89, 107, 110–111, 117–119, 124–127, 128, 159–162, 180–181, 184–187, 193–194, 198–202, 204, 234–235, 238–239, 239–240, 247–248, 251, 260–263, 275–277, 280, 284–288, 290, 312, 321, 325, 326, 328, 331–332, 334, 336, 337, 342, 349–350, 352–353, 355, 372–375, 378–380, 382, 384, 403, 411–412, 421, 434–435, 446–449, 460–463, 470–473, 482–485
STANDARD 6 **How culture and experience influence people's perceptions of places and regions** Perception of all places and regions depends upon personal experience, culture, age, gender, and other factors. It is sometimes said that there is no reality, only perception. In geography there is always a mixture of both. For example, a wilderness can be attractive to a camper, a source of anxiety for a child, and a nuisance to a pioneering farmer. **Related Themes: Regions, Place, Movement**	62, 77–79, 90–91, 96, 117, 134, 137, 139, 145, 147, 149, 155, 159–161, 164–166, 169–170, 197, 209–210, 214–215, 220–221, 224, 234, 239–240, 241–243, 247–249, 251–252, 276, 295–303, 306, 308–312, 317, 321–323, 325–328, 330–332, 334–337, 339, 341–342, 343, 349, 352–354, 373–375, 389–394, 397–398, 405, 412–415, 419–422

National Geography Standards & Related Themes	Student Edition Pages
STANDARD 7 **The physical processes that shape the patterns of Earth's surface** Physical processes create natural landscapes and environments arrayed across Earth's surface in spatial patterns. Understanding these forces is indispensable in daily decision-making, such as evaluating home-building sites in earthquake zones or floodplains, or building a highway along the ocean coastline. There is a systematic order in this continual remaking of Earth's surface. The geographically informed person understands the interplay of systems, forces, boundaries, thresholds, and equilibrium as they influence patterns on Earth's surface. **Related Themes: Place, Regions**	44–48, 54–61, 118, 125–128, 193–195, 198–202, 274–277, 283–288, 373–374, 379–380
STANDARD 8 **The characteristics and spatial distribution of ecosystems on Earth's surface** Ecosystems are communities of living things—plants and animals—interacting with each other and with the physical environment. Ecosystems are dynamic and ever changing. They are self-regulating, open systems that maintain flows of energy and matter that naturally move toward maturity, stability, and balance. By understanding how these systems and processes work in shaping the physical environment, students will be better able to comprehend the basic principles that guide environmental management. Such knowledge will enable them to anticipate the consequences of ongoing human effort to transform Earth's landscapes. **Related Themes: Location, Place, Regions**	2–3, 4–5, 20, 38, 53, 60, 61, 62, 64, 65–66, 108, 116, 117–120, 122, 125–127, 128, 159–162, 171–172, 193–194, 199–202, 204, 216, 241–243, 248, 259, 274, 275–277, 280, 281, 282, 284–288, 290, 321, 325, 326–327, 330, 334, 336, 339, 341–342, 352–354, 372–375, 376–377, 378–380, 382, 384–385, 433, 434, 445, 459, 469
STANDARD 9 **The characteristics, distribution, and migration of human populations on Earth's surface** The characteristics and distribution of human populations are never static. Factors such as natural increase, war, famine, disease, and rate of urbanization play decisive roles in where people live. At any one time, some populations are bound to be migrating—leaving one place, striking out for a second, or possibly settling in a third. The factors that give definition to a nation's population profile, patterns of growth or decline, and inclinations toward migration combine to be significant geographic information. **Related Themes: Human-Environment Interaction, Movement, Regions**	75–76, 94–96, 135, 145–146, 150, 165, 220–221, 224, 226, 236, 281, 300, 304, 307, 312, 323, 343–344, 389, 410–411

National Geography Standards & Related Themes	Student Edition Pages
STANDARD 10 **The characteristics, distribution, and complexity of Earth's cultural mosaics** Culture defines each group's unique view of itself and others, and includes the material goods, skills, and social behavior transmitted to successive generations. It is expressed through art, language, beliefs and institutions, the built environment, and numerous other features. Cultural patterns are never static. They change in response to human migration, diffusion, and the steady introduction of new and competing cultural traits. **Related Themes: Location, Regions, Place**	80, 83–87, 88–89, 139, 144–147, 148, 149–150, 155, 159, 175, 208, 218, 220–221, 222, 223–224, 226, 229, 233, 234, 249, 254, 294, 295–303, 307, 308–312, 314–315, 317, 323, 324, 325, 326, 327–328, 330–331, 332, 335, 336–337, 338–342, 344–346, 349–356, 358–359, 388, 389–394, 396–400, 402, 405, 416, 419, 421
STANDARD 11 **The patterns and networks of economic interdependence on Earth's surface** The goods that we need daily to make life work have sources all over the world. Economic networks at all scales, from local to global, have been developed to promote the efficient interchange of goods. Linkages of transportation, communication, language, currency, and custom have been fashioned out of the human desire to have more than what is available locally. For United States citizens, learning about the nature and significance of global interdependence is an essential aspect of being geographically well-informed. **Related Themes: Movement, Regions, Human-Environment Interaction, Location**	78–79, 81, 90–91, 109, 136, 158, 159–160, 161–162, 165, 167, 169–170, 174, 183, 211, 213–215, 234–236, 239–240, 244–245, 246, 250, 251–252, 254, 255, 263, 299, 301–302, 303, 312, 314, 318, 322, 325, 327, 328, 330, 335, 339, 341–342, 350, 352, 354, 356, 358–359, 367, 391–392, 393–394, 400, 402–403, 409–412, 414–415, 417, 420–421, 422, 424–425, 449, 463, 473, 485
STANDARD 12 **The processes, patterns, and functions of human settlement** Settlement is one of the most basic human responses to the environment. As social animals, humans achieve proximity, shared environments, and the opportunity to engage in effective economic and social interaction through settlement. Nearly half the human population has opted for city residence. However, there is a vast variety of cultural landscapes in urban settings, just as there is in village and town settings for most of the rest of the population. In all varieties of settlements, cultural landscapes reflect local resources and human preferences. **Related Themes: Place, Regions, Movement**	74, 76, 108, 135–136, 138–139, 172, 178, 182, 184–187, 209–210, 219–220, 227, 247, 258, 262, 264–269, 275, 295, 300, 307–308, 314, 323, 327, 332, 333, 340–342, 362, 365–366, 389–390, 397, 410–411, 432, 436, 438–441, 444, 448, 450–455, 458, 462, 464, 468, 472, 474–476, 480, 484, 486–487

National Geography Standards & Related Themes	Student Edition Pages
STANDARD 13 **How the forces of cooperation and conflict among people influence the division and control of Earth's surface** The tendency to divide space into segments that provide identity and a sense of security is universal. This human drive covers all scales, from individual homesteads through neighborhood and city limits to state and national boundaries. We have long declared borders, built walls, demarcated rivers and mountain ridges, and had arbitrary lines mapped across deserts. This trait relates to a wish to enclose that which we desire or perhaps exclude that which is feared. Multinational alliances as well as community interest groups are all motivated by the human capacity for expression of cooperation and conflict in the control of Earth's surface. **Related Themes: Regions, Movement, Human-Environment Interaction**	117, 122, 135–137, 139, 147, 210–212, 214, 295–297, 298, 300, 303, 325–326, 328, 334–336, 339, 352, 355–356, 388–390, 391–394, 413–415, 421
STANDARD 14 **How human actions modify the physical environment** When humans first occupied the environment, levels of technology were low enough that modifications of the physical setting were generally simple, although significant over time. However, as we have developed more powerful technology to assist us in such modifications, we have made hot areas cool, cold areas warm, dry areas garden-like, and wet areas habitable. Changing the landscape has become a signature of human use of Earth, and will be a significant theme as we see just what we have gained (and lost) in such transformations. **Related Themes: Human-Environment Interaction, Place, Regions**	15, 62, 63–66, 93, 121, 171–172, 192, 195–196, 197, 216, 230, 238, 241–243, 248, 278–280, 281, 332, 376–377, 380–382
STANDARD 15 **How physical systems affect human systems** Expanding settlement of floodplains, coastal margins, and seismic zones has brought us face-to-face with striking evidence of ways in which physical systems have profound effects on human systems. Less dramatic—but ultimately more significant—aspects of the effect of physical systems on human systems are such issues as freshwater use, ozone depletion, global warming, and soil loss. Knowledge of Earth's physical systems will be critical to the human use of Earth in the years to come and is central to *Geography for Life.* **Related Themes: Place, Regions, Human-Environment Interaction**	49, 52, 54, 61, 74, 76, 108, 119–120, 122, 123, 125–126, 128, 135, 162, 164, 192, 275, 282, 287, 288, 326–327, 375, 412

National Geography Standards & Related Themes	Student Edition Pages
STANDARD 16 **The changes that occur in the meaning, use, distribution, and importance of resources** We extract, process, market, and consume those things we value in the environment. The activity related to putting values on resources, and the subsequent demands on the environment, establish patterns of economic, political, and cultural interaction. Some natural resources we require: air, water, vegetation—and space. Others commonly used, such as oil, tin, diamonds, bananas, and coffee, have gained their value by human decisions that generally relate to levels of technology and economic development. A geographer must understand what makes an item a resource, and what the subsequent geographic implications of such an appraisal might be. **Related Themes: Human-Environment Interaction, Place, Regions**	52–53, 92–93, 119–122, 159–162, 169, 171–172, 174, 194–196, 205, 209, 238, 241–245, 247, 248, 251, 254, 277, 278–280, 281, 291, 327, 330, 334, 339, 353–355, 374–377, 382, 384–385, 412, 417
STANDARD 17 **How to apply geography to interpret the past** An understanding of spatial and environmental perspectives leads to a fuller appreciation of the human use of Earth in the past. By determining how people have assessed their own settings, and gaining understanding of why they used their settings as they did—or changed them the way they did—we can see the role that geography has played in our histories. **Related Themes: Human-Environment Interaction, Movement, Regions**	16, 34, 44, 46, 62, 123, 136–137, 164–166, 197, 209–210, 212, 275, 295, 300, 301, 321, 325, 327, 332, 336, 341–342, 349, 356, 390, 395
STANDARD 18 **How to apply geography to interpret the present and plan for the future** Geography leads people to think about spatial patterns, connections between places, integration of local to global scales, diversity, and systems. With such a scope, it is easy to see how completely geography influences the present, and how it can be significant in achieving effective planning for the future. Issues that range from resources to population to paths of movement all relate to the essence of geography. Being able to put this breadth of impact to work in planning for the future is one of the benefits of being geographically well-informed. **Related Themes: Regions, Human-Environment Interaction, Place**	12, 14, 64–66, 75, 77–79, 89, 90–91, 127–128, 165–166, 171–172, 195, 197, 200–201, 216–217, 238, 241–243, 244, 248, 278–280, 281, 288, 304–305, 308–309, 345, 352, 376–377, 380, 382, 392

Correlation of

Exploring Our World: People, Places, and Cultures to the NCSS Thematic Strands

In *Curriculum for Social Studies: Expectations of Excellence,* the National Council for the Social Studies (NCSS) identified 10 themes that serve as organizing strands for the social studies curriculum at every school level. These themes are interrelated and draw from all of the social science disciplines. Each theme provides student performance expectations in the areas of knowledge, processes, and attitudes. The 10 NCSS themes were the basis for the themes used in *Exploring Our World: People, Places, and Cultures.*

Theme and Performance Expectation	Student Pages
I. *Culture* The study of culture helps students understand similarities and differences within groups of people. By studying a culture's beliefs, values, and traditions, students begin to gain a perspective that helps them relate to different groups. In the middle grades, students begin to examine aspects of culture and how culture influences human behavior.	
A. Compare similarities and differences in the ways groups, societies, and cultures meet human needs and concerns.	85, 88, 89, 90, 91, 95, 136, 138, 141, 147, 150, 152, 157, 161, 162, 170, 171, 215, 220, 221, 223, 224, 227, 237, 255, 299, 303, 308, 309, 310, 311, 312, 319, 328, 329, 331, 332, 337, 342, 350, 356, 368
B. Explain how information and experiences may be interpreted by people from diverse cultural perspectives and frames of reference.	90, 91, 215, 300, 312, 359, 394, 400, 412, 422
C. Explain and give examples of how language, literature, the arts, architecture, other artifacts, traditions, beliefs, values, and behaviors contribute to the development and transmission of culture.	82, 83, 85, 89, 139, 144, 146, 147, 148, 149, 150, 151, 153, 168, 175, 208, 209, 210, 218, 221, 222, 223, 224, 225, 233, 234, 295, 296, 297, 298, 299, 301, 302, 303, 304, 305, 308, 310, 311, 312, 313, 315, 323, 328, 336, 337, 339, 340, 355, 381, 389, 396, 397, 398, 399, 400, 401, 402, 410, 415
D. Explain why individuals and groups respond differently to their physical and social environments and/or changes to them on the basis of shared assumptions, values, and beliefs.	89, 90, 91, 171, 211, 214, 216, 217, 280, 289, 291, 298, 299, 304, 305, 307, 308, 309, 332, 337, 349, 352, 356, 359, 376, 377, 393, 414, 415
E. Articulate the implications of cultural diversity, as well as cohesion, within and across groups.	87, 88, 89, 90, 91, 132, 145, 146, 147, 149, 150, 151, 153, 175, 207, 211, 219, 220, 221, 223, 224, 225, 302, 303, 307, 308, 309, 311, 312, 330, 332, 340, 343, 344, 345, 346, 347, 356, 394, 397, 416, 421, 424
II. *Time, Continuity, and Change* Understanding time, continuity, and change involves being knowledgeable about what things were like in the past and how things change and develop over time. Knowing how to read and reconstruct the past helps students gain a historical perspective. In the middle grades, students will continue to increase their knowledge of the past and of historical concepts. Students will also begin to learn how individual experiences, social values, and cultural traditions influence interpretations of the past.	
A. Demonstrate an understanding that different scholars may describe the same event or situation in different ways but must provide reasons or evidence for their views.	15, 16, 64, 83, 90–91, 142–143, 216–217, 288, 304–305, 359, 376–377, 415
B. Identify and use key concepts such as chronology, causality, change, conflict, and complexity to explain, analyze, and show connections among patterns of historical change and continuity.	17, 72, 73, 76, 87, 136–137, 138, 141, 145, 146, 150, 166, 167, 171, 172, 210–211, 212–213, 221, 223, 224, 227, 233, 235, 294, 295–303, 314–315, 322, 323, 326, 328, 332, 349, 350, 352, 353, 354, 355, 356, 389, 391, 393, 394, 398, 403, 404, 412, 415, 417, 419, 422, 424, 425, 426, 427, 488, 489, 490, 491
C. Identify and describe selected historical periods and patterns of change within and across cultures, such as the rise of civilizations, the development of transportation systems, the growth and breakdown of colonial systems, and others.	16, 78–79, 86, 136–137, 139, 147, 149, 209–210, 211, 212–213, 220, 227, 294, 295–303, 308, 312, 314–315, 326, 331, 334–335, 336, 343–344, 352, 353, 354, 355, 356, 389, 391–394, 412, 413–415, 426, 427, 488, 489, 490, 491
D. Identify and use processes important to reconstructing and reinterpreting the past, such as using a variety of sources, providing, validating, and weighing evidence for claims, checking credibility of sources, and searching for causality.	16, 152, 167, 209, 211, 245, 347, 389, 394, 417, 421, 426, 427, 488, 489, 490, 491

Theme and Performance Expectation	Student Pages
E. Develop critical sensitivities such as empathy and skepticism regarding attitudes, values, and behaviors of people in different historical contexts.	136–137, 145, 347, 349, 352, 353, 391, 409, 416, 424, 426, 427, 488, 489, 490, 491
F. Use knowledge of facts and concepts drawn from history, along with methods of historical inquiry, to inform decision-making about and action-taking on public issues.	62, 64, 65, 66, 69, 122, 166, 167, 172, 217, 241–245, 249, 250, 252, 254, 280, 281, 288, 337, 346, 380, 426, 427, 488, 489, 490, 491
III. *People, Places, & Environments* **The study of people, places, and environments will help students as they create their spatial views and geographic perspective of the world. Students begin to make informed and critical decisions about the relationship between humans and their environment. In the middle school years, students can relate their personal experiences to happenings in other environments. These experiences will help students increase their abstract thought when analyzing human behavior in relation to physical and cultural environments.**	
A. Elaborate mental maps of locales, regions, and the world that demonstrate understanding of relative location, direction, size, and shape.	22–27, 31, 36, 37, 44–48, 49–50, 51, 52, 54, 57, 59, 64–66, 68, 74, 104, 116–120, 125–127, 134, 135, 136, 159–162, 178, 192–196, 198–202, 204, 239, 240, 247, 249, 251, 252, 272–277, 284–288, 309, 321, 325, 326, 327, 328, 329, 330, 332, 334, 336, 341, 342, 349, 350, 352, 353, 354, 355, 362, 380, 382, 389, 390, 395, 400, 412
B. Create, interpret, use, and distinguish various representations of the earth such as maps, globes, and photographs.	2–9, 22–30, 41, 45, 47, 56, 59, 65, 75, 83, 88, 104–109, 118, 125, 131, 135, 160, 162, 178, 180–183, 184–187, 196, 198, 210, 224, 233, 248, 283, 285, 294, 295, 296, 297, 298, 302, 311, 315, 321, 333, 351, 354, 362–367, 379, 389, 395, 417, 420
C. Use appropriate resources, data sources, and geographic tools such as aerial photographs, satellite images, geographic information systems (GIS), map projections, and cartography to generate, manipulate, and interpret information such as atlases, databases, grid systems, charts, graphs, and maps.	17, 23, 25, 27, 30–33, 34, 48, 49, 55, 56, 58, 62, 63, 69, 73, 76, 78, 81, 83, 84, 88, 93, 94, 120, 124, 125, 128, 131, 134, 135, 141, 144, 147, 150, 153, 158, 162, 167, 172, 175, 192, 196, 198, 201, 202, 205, 210, 227, 240, 242, 245, 248, 252, 255, 280, 282, 283, 284, 285, 288, 291, 303, 306, 311, 320, 344, 347, 351, 359, 374–375, 378, 379, 385, 403, 411, 414, 417, 420, 425
D. Estimate distance, calculate scale, and distinguish other geographic relationships such as population density and spatial distribution patterns.	6, 27, 30–31, 35, 73, 74, 75, 76, 96, 98, 108, 128, 178, 182, 220, 227, 249, 255, 314, 362, 366, 373, 375
E. Locate and describe varying landforms and geographic features, such as mountains, plateaus, islands, rain forests, deserts, and oceans, and explain their relationship within the ecosystem.	28, 30, 31, 33, 44, 46, 47, 52, 59, 106, 107, 116–120, 122, 130, 179, 180, 196, 241–242, 248, 273–277, 280, 321–322, 325–328, 342, 363, 364, 372–375, 376–377, 380, 382, 385
F. Describe physical system changes such as seasons, climate and weather, and the water cycle and identify geographic patterns associated with them.	2, 34, 38, 40, 46–48, 53, 54, 55, 56–61, 68, 124–128, 131, 198–202, 204, 231, 282–290, 310, 375, 378–380, 382, 384, 400
G. Describe how people create places that reflect cultural values and ideals as they build neighborhoods, parks, shopping centers, and the like.	117, 122, 144, 147, 192, 193–195, 209, 210, 220, 223, 227, 233, 235, 247, 322, 398
H. Examine, interpret, and analyze physical and cultural patterns and their interactions, such as land use, settlement patterns, cultural transmission of customs and ideas, and ecosystem changes.	8, 16, 41, 54, 61, 64–66, 76, 78, 81, 86, 87, 89, 90–91, 93, 94, 98, 99, 104, 119–122, 147, 149, 150, 160, 161, 162, 175, 183, 196, 202, 219–221, 223–224, 234, 235, 236, 239, 247, 248, 279, 280, 295, 296, 303, 304–305, 306–307, 311, 312, 314, 322, 327, 328, 333, 335, 336, 340, 342, 349, 374, 375, 389, 390, 394, 396, 400, 402, 410–412, 422
I. Describe ways that historical events have been influenced by, and have influenced, physical and human geographic factors in local, regional, national, and global settings.	44, 62, 69, 72, 78, 79, 80, 81, 89, 96, 122, 135, 150, 152, 163–167, 197, 211, 214, 215, 226, 227, 241–243, 245, 250, 254, 255, 275, 279, 280, 281, 282, 290, 295–303, 308, 310, 315, 323, 326, 330, 331, 334, 343–346, 347, 356, 380, 381, 382, 388–394, 395, 408, 409, 412, 416, 420, 421, 422, 424–425
J. Observe and speculate about social and economic effects of environmental changes and crises resulting from phenomena such as floods, storms, and drought.	12, 46, 123, 126, 127, 128, 163–167, 196, 329
K. Propose, compare, and evaluate alternative uses of land and resources in communities, nations, and the world.	63, 66, 69, 172, 195, 216–217, 230, 241–245, 252, 277, 278, 280, 291, 327, 333, 358, 375–376, 382

Theme and Performance Expectation	Student Pages
IV. *Individual Development & Identity* **People and culture influence a person's identity. Examining the different forms of human behavior improves one's understanding of social relationships and the development of personal identity. The study of human behavior helps students become aware of how social processes influence a person's identity. In the middle years, issues of personal identity become important as students begin to view themselves in relation to others.**	
A. Relate personal changes to social, cultural, and historical contexts.	76, 79, 87, 220, 227, 247, 299, 300, 312, 398, 417, 425
B. Describe personal connections to place—as associated with community, nation, and world.	15, 51, 82, 128, 138, 146, 147, 149, 155, 229, 299, 307, 316, 381, 385
C. Describe the ways family, gender, ethnicity, nationality, and institutional affiliations contribute to personal identity.	140, 208, 222, 223, 224, 234, 300, 310, 339, 344, 346, 399, 404, 416
D. Relate such factors as physical endowment and capabilities, learning, motivation, personality, perception, and behavior to individual development.	141, 220, 238, 239, 243, 279, 309, 310, 392
E. Identify and describe ways regional, ethnic, and national cultures influence individuals' daily lives.	72, 80, 139, 141, 147, 153, 159, 161, 224, 233, 236, 248, 249, 298, 304–305, 314, 331, 391–392, 393, 397, 409, 410, 415
F. Identify and describe the influence of perception, attitudes, values, and beliefs on personal identity.	84–85, 136, 148, 236, 250, 296, 299, 301, 315, 345
G. Identify and interpret examples of stereotyping, conformity, and altruism.	95, 170, 214, 295, 331, 391–392
H. Work independently and cooperatively to accomplish goals.	81, 167, 245, 347, 417
V. *Individuals, Groups, & Institutions* **Institutions, such as schools, governments, and churches, influence people and often reflect a society's values. Because of the vital role that institutions play in people's lives, it is important that students know how institutions develop, what controls and influences them, and how humans react to them. Middle school students will gain experience by studying how institutions change over time. They should also be able to use their understanding to suggest ways how institutions can work for the common good.**	
A. Demonstrate an understanding of concepts such as role, status, and social class in describing the interactions of individuals and social groups.	211–213, 295, 344, 390, 403, 410, 425
B. Analyze group and institutional influences on people, events, and elements of culture.	169, 223, 233, 296, 298–299, 303, 304–305, 311, 312, 326, 350, 358, 389, 394, 410, 412, 413–417
C. Describe the various forms institutions take and the interactions of people with institutions.	84–85, 139, 140–141, 142–143, 152, 215, 233, 236, 240, 296, 322–323, 328, 349, 358, 391, 409, 420, 422, 424
D. Identify and analyze examples of tensions between expressions of individuality and group or institutional efforts to promote social conformity.	212, 240, 250, 300, 391–392, 397, 403, 415, 419, 421
E. Identify and describe examples of tensions between belief systems and government policies and laws.	171, 297, 345, 346
F. Describe the role of institutions in furthering both continuity and change.	69, 140–141, 149, 165, 167, 216, 235, 240, 345, 347, 352, 358, 398, 409
G. Apply knowledge of how groups and institutions work to meet individual needs and promote the common good.	12, 64, 95, 153, 166, 171–172, 238, 241, 243, 245, 328, 402
VI. *Power, Authority, & Governance* **Studying structures of power, authority, and governance and their functions in the United States and around the world is important for developing a notion of civic responsibility. Students will identify the purpose and characteristics of various types of government and how people try to resolve conflicts. Students will also examine the relationship between individual rights and responsibilities. During the middle school years, students apply what they have learned about rights and responsibilities in more complex contexts.**	
A. Examine persistent issues involving the rights, roles, and status of the individual in relation to the general welfare.	137, 141, 153, 240, 249, 251, 295, 296, 301, 307, 315, 343–345, 390, 393, 397, 398, 409, 410, 420
B. Describe the purpose of government and how its powers are acquired, used, and justified.	85, 86, 139, 153, 212, 215, 250, 252, 295, 296, 322–323, 335, 339, 352, 355, 356, 358, 390, 391–392, 394, 409, 420

Theme and Performance Expectation	Student Pages
C. Analyze and explain ideas and governmental mechanisms to meet needs and wants of citizens, regulate territory, manage conflict, and establish order and security.	145, 159, 161, 165, 166, 169, 205, 209, 210, 241, 243, 245, 288, 304–305, 307, 314, 328, 336, 346, 347, 349, 356, 392, 393, 402, 409, 412, 414, 417, 421, 422, 424
D. Describe the ways nations and organizations respond to forces of unity and diversity affecting order and security.	166, 175, 250, 296, 298, 339, 345, 356, 358, 390, 391, 392, 393, 414, 416, 417, 421
E. Identify and describe the basic features of the political system in the United States and identify representative leaders from various levels and branches of government.	140–141, 142–143
F. Explain conditions, actions, and motivations that contribute to conflict and cooperation within and among nations.	137, 170, 171, 172, 214, 250, 252, 302, 303, 326, 334, 352, 359, 393, 415, 422, 424
G. Describe and analyze the role of technology in communications, transportation, information processing, weapons development, or other areas as it contributes to or helps resolve conflicts.	79, 81, 96, 209, 381, 382, 393, 395, 398, 400
H. Explain and apply concepts such as power, role, status, justice, and influence to the examination of persistent issues and social problems.	137, 150, 213, 215, 233, 300, 302, 312, 331, 336, 403, 410, 412, 415, 419, 422, 425
I. Give examples and explain how governments attempt to achieve their stated ideals at home and abroad.	137–138, 153, 169, 213, 214, 235, 251, 296, 302–303, 336, 347, 390, 403
VII. *Production, Distribution, & Consumption* **Societies try to meet people's needs and wants by trying to answer the basic economic questions: What is to be produced? How should goods be produced? How should goods and services be distributed? How should land, labor, capital, and management be allocated? By studying how needs and wants are met, students learn how trade and government economic policies develop. In the middle grades, students increase their knowledge of economic concepts, principles, and reasoning.**	
A. Give and explain examples of ways that economic systems structure choices about how goods and services are to be produced and distributed.	79, 80, 81, 86, 94, 159, 235, 240, 300, 302, 303, 327, 328, 335, 342, 349, 350, 392, 410, 414, 420, 421
B. Describe the role that supply and demand, prices, incentives, and profits play in determining what is produced and distributed in a competitive market system.	94, 95, 169, 170, 209, 214, 325, 335, 349, 409, 410, 417
C. Explain the difference between private and public goods and services.	161, 243, 307, 328
D. Describe a range of examples of the various institutions that make up economic systems, such as households, business firms, banks, government agencies, labor unions, and corporations.	94, 159, 309, 322, 337, 392, 417, 421, 422
E. Describe the role of specialization and exchange in the economic process.	95, 159, 213–214, 215, 239, 252, 330, 337
F. Explain and illustrate how values and beliefs influence different economic decisions.	169, 307, 328, 350, 391–392
G. Differentiate among various forms of exchange and money.	138, 197, 211
H. Compare basic economic systems according to who determines what is produced, distributed, and consumed.	94, 240, 394, 409, 414–415
I. Use economic concepts to help explain historical and current developments and issues in local, national, or global contexts.	79, 81, 91, 96, 136, 165, 172, 235, 250, 302, 312, 340, 392, 410, 412, 418
J. Use economic reasoning to compare different proposals for dealing with a contemporary social issue such as unemployment, acid rain, or high quality education.	216–217, 243, 244, 278, 280, 377

Theme and Performance Expectation		Student Pages
VIII. *Science, Technology, & Society* The study of science, technology, and society is ever changing. It raises questions about who will benefit from it and how fundamental values and beliefs can be preserved in a technology-driven society. By the middle grades, students research the complex relationships among technology, human values, and behavior. Students will learn how technology and science have brought about change and how they have often challenged accepted societal beliefs.		
A.	Examine and describe the influence of culture on scientific and technological choices and advancement, such as in transportation, medicine, and warfare.	86, 136, 244, 309, 393, 395, 400
B.	Show through specific examples how science and technology have changed people's perceptions of the social and natural world, such as in their relationship to the land, animal life, family life, and economic wants, needs, and security.	14, 17, 34, 64, 73, 81, 158, 246, 301, 327, 398
C.	Describe examples in which values, beliefs, and attitudes have been influenced by new scientific and technological knowledge, such as the invention of the printing press, conceptions of the universe, applications of atomic energy, and genetic discoveries.	77–79, 87, 89, 398, 418
D.	Explain the need for laws and policies to govern scientific and technological applications, such as the safety and well-being of workers and consumers and the regulation of utilities, radio, and television.	281, 392
E.	Seek reasonable and ethical solutions to problems that arise when scientific advancements and social norms or values come into conflict.	64–66, 171–172, 242–243, 280, 382
IX. *Global Connections* As countries grow more interdependent, understanding global connections among world societies becomes important. Students will analyze emerging global issues in many different fields. They will also investigate relationships among the different cultures of the world. In the middle years, students analyze the interactions among states and countries and respond to global events and changes.		
A.	Describe instances in which language, art, music, belief systems, and other cultural elements can facilitate global understanding or cause misunderstanding.	80, 224, 297, 298, 299, 300, 301, 302, 303, 311, 312, 337, 344, 345, 346
B.	Analyze examples of conflict, cooperation, and interdependence among groups, societies, and nations.	69, 79, 81, 89, 96, 169, 170, 172, 288, 352, 393, 398, 421
C.	Describe and analyze the effects of changing technologies on the global community.	86, 87, 327
D.	Explore the causes, consequences, and possible solutions to persistent, contemporary, and emerging global issues, such as health, security, resource allocation, economic development, and environmental quality.	64, 65, 69, 73, 171, 241–243, 278, 279–280, 288, 291, 304–305, 344–345
E.	Describe and explain the relationships and tensions between national sovereignty and global interests in such matters as territory, natural resources, trade, use of technology, and welfare of people.	79, 81, 90–91, 96, 169, 172, 235, 288, 307, 315, 343–345, 347, 359
F.	Demonstrate understanding of concerns, standards, issues, and conflicts related to universal human rights.	315, 345, 356
G.	Identify and describe the roles of international and multinational organizations.	170, 171, 238, 303, 315, 347
X. *Civic Ideals & Practices* Understanding civic ideals and practices is crucial to complete participation in society and is the main purpose of social studies. Students will learn about civic participation and the role of the citizen within his or her community, country, and world. By the middle grades, students will broaden their understanding to analyze and evaluate relationships between civic ideals and practices.		
A.	Examine the origins and continuing influence of key ideals of the democratic republican form of government, such as individual human dignity, liberty, justice, equality, and the rule of law.	85–86, 136, 137, 140–141, 159
B.	Identify and interpret sources and examples of the rights and responsibilities of citizens.	140, 141, 153, 165, 296, 315

Theme and Performance Expectation	Student Pages
C. Locate, access, analyze, organize, and apply information about selected public issues—recognizing and explaining multiple points of view.	64, 99, 142–143, 216–217, 304–305, 359, 376–379
D. Practice forms of civic discussion and participation consistent with the ideals of citizens in a democratic republic.	81, 170, 245, 347
E. Explain and analyze various forms of citizen action that influence public policy decisions.	95, 140, 167, 236, 238, 243, 300, 331, 377, 381, 392
F. Identify and explain the roles of formal and informal political actors in influencing and shaping public policy and decision-making.	12, 17, 212, 243, 255, 393, 394, 414
G. Analyze the influence of diverse forms of public opinion on the development of public policy and decision-making.	345, 346
H. Analyze the effectiveness of selected public policies and citizen behaviors in realizing the stated ideals of a democratic republican form of government.	235–236
I. Explain the relationship between policy statements and action plans used to address issues of public concern.	69, 288, 393, 403, 415, 419
J. Examine strategies designed to strengthen the "common good," which consider a range of options for citizen action.	79, 99, 166, 243, 280, 392, 393–394, 403, 413

To Teachers:

Welcome to the Teacher Wraparound Edition of *Exploring Our World: People, Places, and Cultures*. We have created this teacher edition based on input from experienced teachers and educational consultants. Our goal is to provide you with teaching strategies and activities that are labeled for you at point-of-use. The following pages will show the structure of the Teacher Wraparound Edition.

Student-Based Instruction

Point-of-Use
Strategies and activities apply directly to student content.

Differentiated Instruction
Leveled activities and options for differentiated instruction help meet the needs of all your students, including English language learners.

Review and Reinforcement
Reading and critical thinking skills are reinforced throughout the lesson.

Assessment and Intervention
- Chapter Assessments provide standardized test practice.
- Assessments gauge student mastery of content.
- Additional resources provide intervention options.

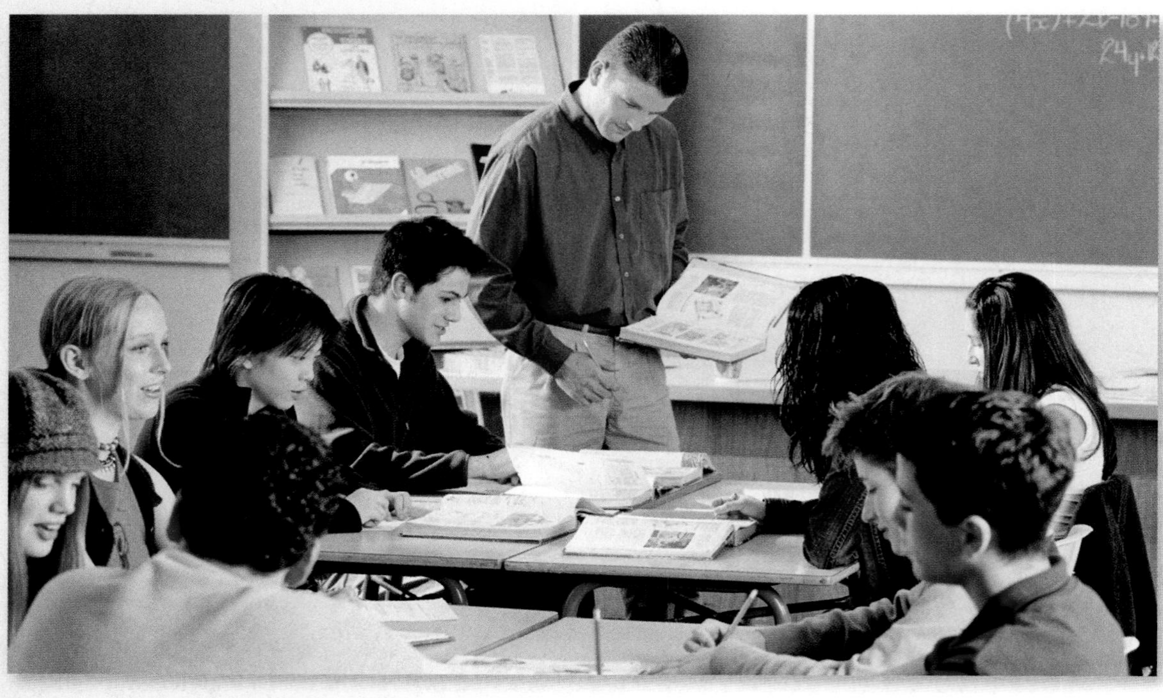

Planning and Teaching the Unit

Planning pages appear at the beginning of each unit.

Pacing Chart

Provides time management suggestions for teaching the unit

Author Note

Highlights author's ideas for teaching the region

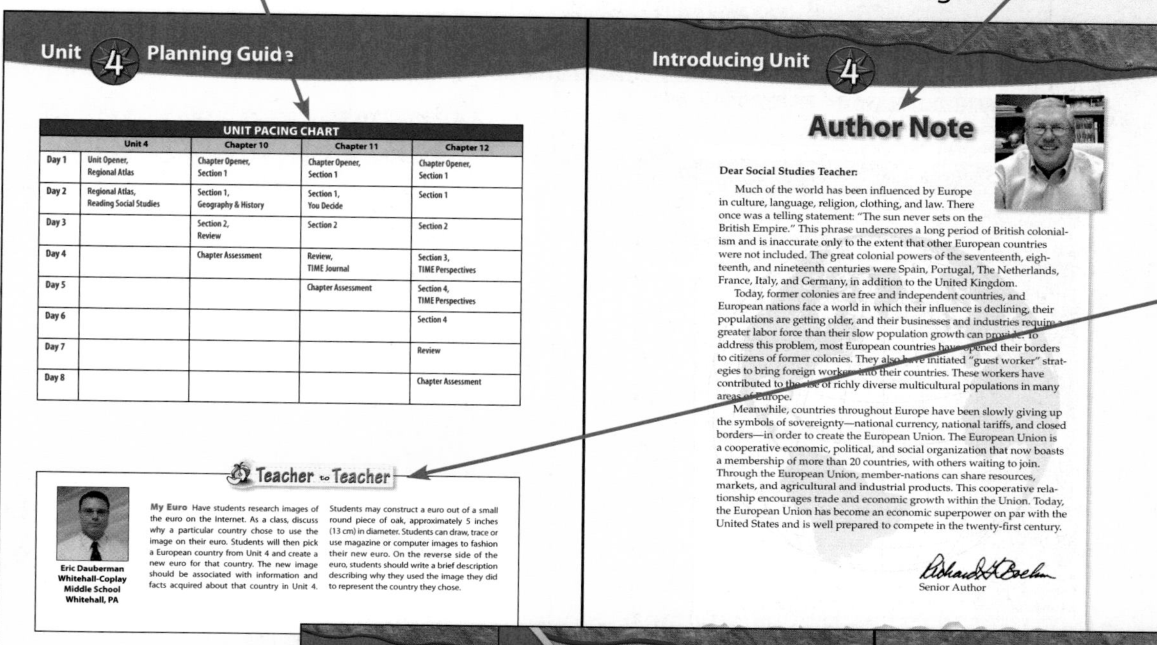

Unit 4 Planning Guide

UNIT PACING CHART

	Unit 4	Chapter 10	Chapter 11	Chapter 12
Day 1	Unit Opener, Regional Atlas	Chapter Opener, Section 1	Chapter Opener, Section 1	Chapter Opener, Section 1
Day 2	Regional Atlas, Reading Social Studies	Section 1, Geography & History	Section 1, You Decide	Section 1
Day 3		Section 2, Review	Section 2	Section 2
Day 4		Chapter Assessment	Review, TIME Journal	Section 3, TIME Perspectives
Day 5			Chapter Assessment	Section 4, TIME Perspectives
Day 6				Section 4
Day 7				Review
Day 8				Chapter Assessment

Teacher to Teacher

Eric Dauberman
Whitehall-Coplay Middle School
Whitehall, PA

My Euro Have students research images of the euro on the Internet. As a class, discuss why a particular country chose to use the image on their euro. Students will then pick a European country from Unit 4 and create a new euro for that country. The new image should be associated with information and facts acquired about that country in Unit 4. Students may construct a euro out of a small round piece of oak, approximately 5 inches (13 cm) in diameter. Students can draw, trace or use magazine or computer images to fashion their new euro. On the reverse side of the euro, students should write a brief description describing why they used the image they did to represent the country they chose.

256A

Introducing Unit 4

Author Note

Dear Social Studies Teacher:

Much of the world has been influenced by Europe in culture, language, religion, clothing, and law. There once was a telling statement: "The sun never sets on the British Empire." This phrase underscores a long period of British colonialism and is inaccurate only to the extent that other European countries were not included. The great colonial powers of the seventeenth, eighteenth, and nineteenth centuries were Spain, Portugal, The Netherlands, France, Italy, and Germany, in addition to the United Kingdom.

Today, former colonies are free and independent countries, and European nations face a world in which their influence is declining, their populations are getting older, and their businesses and industries require a greater labor force than their slow population growth can provide. To address this problem, most European countries have opened their borders to citizens of former colonies. They also have initiated "guest worker" strategies to bring foreign workers into their countries. These workers have contributed to the rise of richly diverse multicultural populations in many areas of Europe.

Meanwhile, countries throughout Europe have been slowly giving up the symbols of sovereignty—national currency, national tariffs, and closed borders—in order to create the European Union. The European Union is a cooperative economic, political, and social organization that now boasts a membership of more than 20 countries, with others waiting to join. Through the European Union, member-nations can share resources, markets, and agricultural and industrial products. This cooperative relationship encourages trade and economic growth within the Union. Today, the European Union has become an economic superpower on par with the United States and is well prepared to compete in the twenty-first century.

Senior Author

Teacher to Teacher

Includes activities from the classrooms of successful teachers

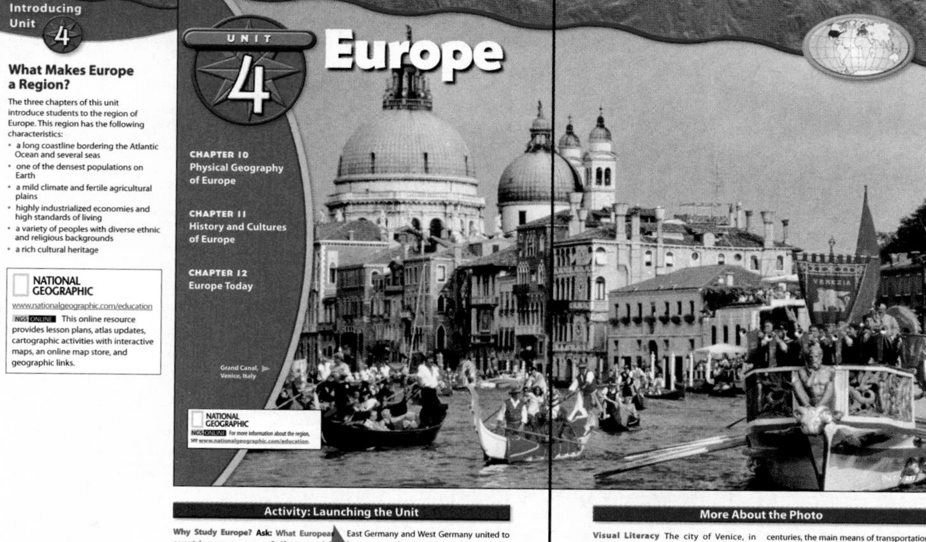

Introducing Unit 4

What Makes Europe a Region?

The three chapters of this unit introduce students to the region of Europe. This region has the following characteristics:

- a long coastline bordering the Atlantic Ocean and several seas
- one of the densest populations on Earth
- a mild climate and fertile agricultural plains
- highly industrialized economies and high standards of living
- a variety of peoples with diverse ethnic and religious backgrounds
- a rich cultural heritage

NATIONAL GEOGRAPHIC
www.nationalgeographic.com/education
NGS ONLINE This online resource provides lesson plans, atlas updates, cartographic activities with interactive maps, an online map store, and geographic links.

UNIT 4 Europe

CHAPTER 10 Physical Geography of Europe

CHAPTER 11 History and Cultures of Europe

CHAPTER 12 Europe Today

Grand Canal, Venice, Italy

NATIONAL GEOGRAPHIC
NGS ONLINE For more information about the region, see www.nationalgeographic.com/education.

Activity: Launching the Unit

Why Study Europe? Ask: What European countries can you name? *(Answers might include: United Kingdom, France, Germany, Italy, Spain, etc.)* Explain that Europe is changing politically. In 1989 communist governments in many eastern European countries were forced from power. A year later, the Berlin Wall was torn down. In 1990 East Germany and West Germany united to become one democratic state. Then, in 1991 the Soviet Union itself broke apart, and communism collapsed. Many formerly communist countries in eastern Europe have introduced free market reforms and have joined the European Union. OL

256

More About the Photo

Visual Literacy The city of Venice, in northeastern Italy, is located on more than 100 islands. These islands are connected by a system of more than 150 canals and about 400 pedestrian bridges. The Grand Canal is Venice's main thoroughfare. It is about 2 miles (3.2 km) long and follows an S-shaped course from northwest to southeast. For centuries, the main means of transportation in Venice was by gondola, a flat-bottomed boat rowed with one oar. Today, most Venetians use motor-boats for transportation. However, tourists visiting the Grand Canal can hire a gondola to view the nearly 200 palaces, built between the A.D. 1100s and 1700s, that line its banks.

Introducing Unit 4

Introduce the Region

Using Maps Have students look at the maps of physical features and political boundaries of Europe in the Regional Atlas. Point out that Europe includes more than 40 countries. **Ask: What physical region of Europe extends north of the Arctic Circle?** *(Scandinavia)* **What specific countries extend north of the Arctic Circle?** *(Norway, Sweden, and Finland)* Tell students that most areas of Europe lie within 300 miles (483 km) of an ocean or a sea. **Ask: Which ocean borders much of Europe?** *(Atlantic Ocean)* **Which seas border the countries of Europe?** *(Norwegian Sea, North Sea, Baltic Sea, Celtic Sea, Irish Sea, Mediterranean Sea, Tyrrhenian Sea, Adriatic Sea, Aegean Sea, Black Sea, Sea of Azov)* **What European countries are located on islands?** *(Iceland, United Kingdom, Ireland, Malta, Cyprus)* OL

257

What Makes This a Region?

Provides a concise explanation of how the region is thematically linked

Launching the Unit

Activates prior knowledge and stimulates discussion about unit themes

Introduce the Region

Helps students conceptualize the region's geography

Planning the Chapter

Chapter Planning Guides provide a snapshot of the scope of resources available to enhance and extend learning in each chapter.

Incorporating Resources

Utilizes a structured lesson plan to incorporate additional resources

Leveled Activities

Organizes resources by appropriate ability levels

*Spanish Resources

Indicates resources for English language learners

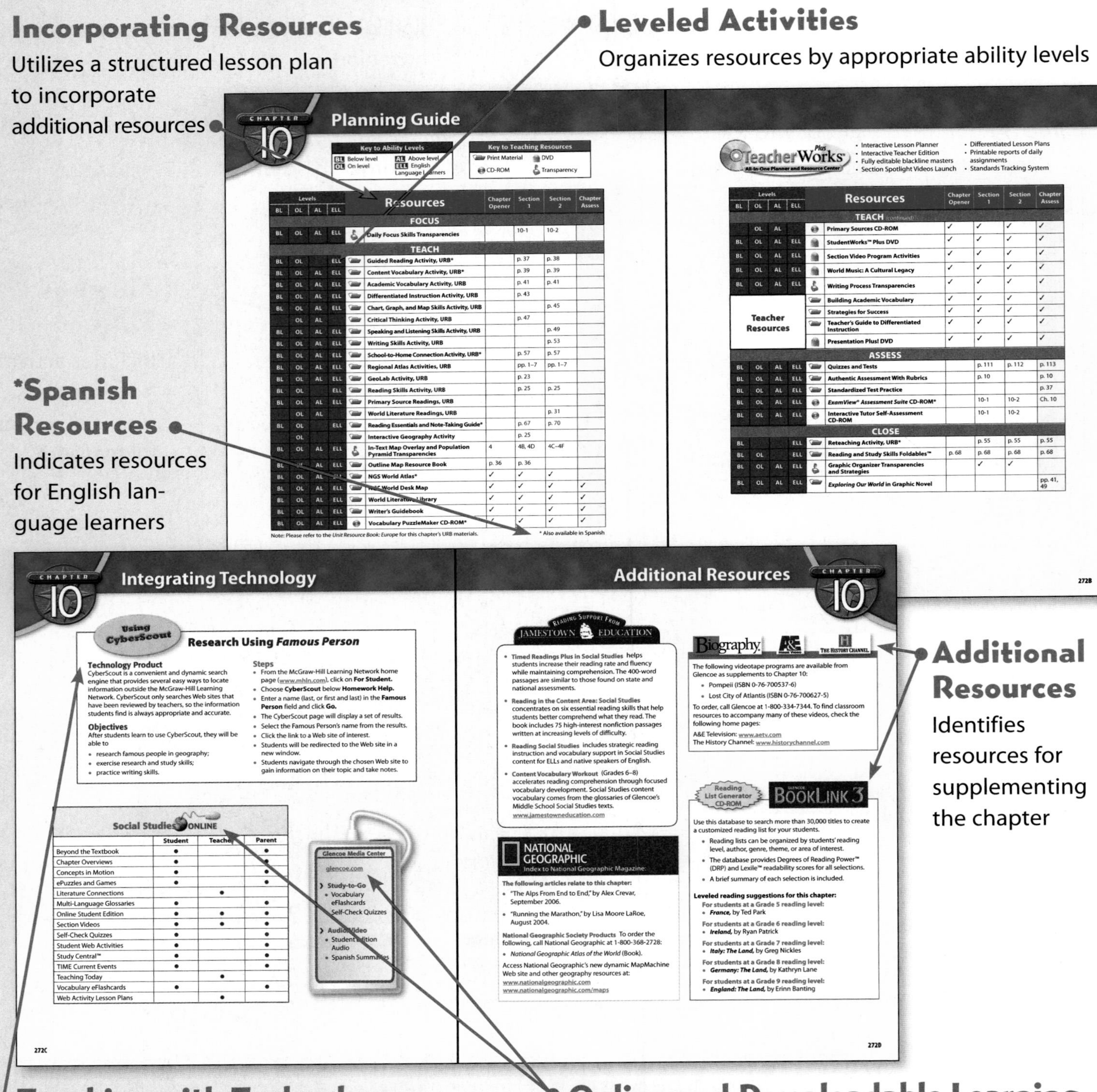

Additional Resources

Identifies resources for supplementing the chapter

Teaching with Technology

Explains how to incorporate different Glencoe technology resources in the classroom

Online and Downloadable Learning

Engages students and caregivers with online and downloadable content

Teaching the Chapter

The Big Ideas and Essential Question at the beginning of the chapter help you teach the most important chapter concepts.

The Essential Question

The Essential Question leads to an understanding of Big Ideas. These questions are broad and have no right or wrong answers. *Essential Questions* are thought-provoking, challenge old assumptions, and stimulate discussion. Student activities throughout the chapter will refer back to the *Essential Question*, leading to a greater comprehension of chapter themes.

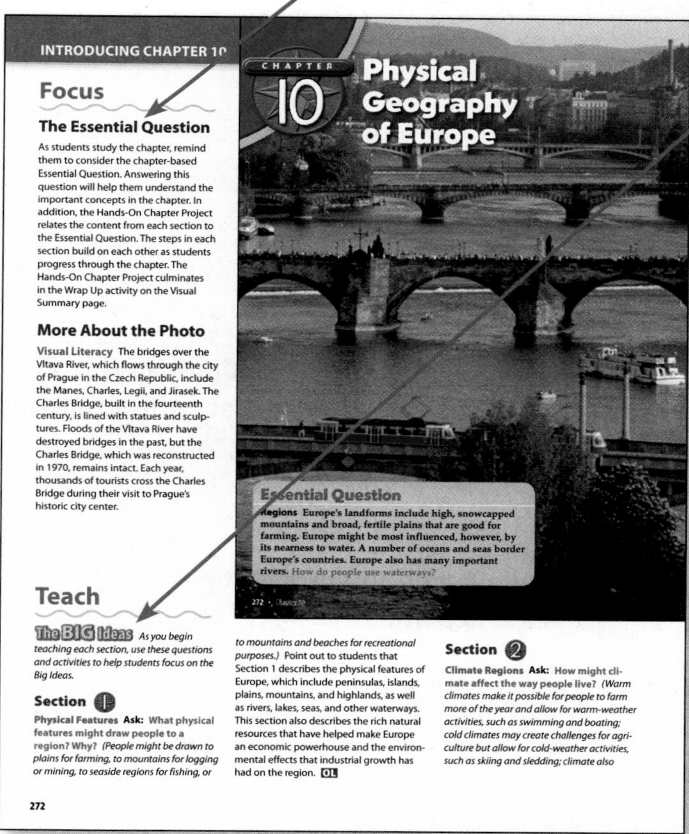

INTRODUCING CHAPTER 10

Focus

The Essential Question

As students study the chapter, remind them to consider the chapter-based Essential Question. Answering this question will help them understand the important concepts in the chapter. In addition, the Hands-On Chapter Project relates the content from each section to the Essential Question. The steps in each section build on each other as students progress through the chapter. The Hands-On Chapter Project culminates in the Wrap Up activity on the Visual Summary page.

More About the Photo

Visual Literacy The bridges over the Vltava River, which flows through the city of Prague in the Czech Republic, include the Manes, Charles, Legii, and Jirasek. The Charles Bridge, built in the fourteenth century, is lined with statues and sculptures. Floods of the Vltava River have destroyed bridges in the past, but the Charles Bridge, which was reconstructed in 1970, remains intact. Each year, thousands of tourists cross the Charles Bridge during their visit to Prague's historic city center.

CHAPTER 10 **Physical Geography of Europe**

Essential Question

Regions Europe's landforms include high, snowcapped mountains and broad, fertile plains that are good for farming. Europe might be most influenced, however, by its nearness to water. A number of oceans and seas border Europe's countries. Europe also has many important rivers. How do people use waterways?

272 • Chapter 10

Teach

The BIG Ideas *As you begin teaching each section, use these questions and activities to help students focus on the Big Ideas.*

Section 1

Physical Features Ask: What physical features might draw people to a region? Why? *(People might be drawn to plains for farming, to mountains for logging or mining, to seaside regions for fishing, or to mountains and beaches for recreational purposes.)* Point out to students that Section 1 describes the physical features of Europe, which include peninsulas, islands, plains, mountains, and highlands, as well as rivers, lakes, seas, and other waterways. This section also describes the rich natural resources that have helped make Europe an economic powerhouse and the environmental effects that industrial growth has had on the region. OL

Section 2

Climate Regions Ask: How might climate affect the way people live? *(Warm climates make it possible for people to farm more of the year and allow for warm-weather activities, such as swimming and boating; cold climates may create challenges for agriculture but allow for cold-weather activities, such as skiing and sledding; climate also*

272

The BIG Ideas

Big Ideas are major themes, issues, concepts, questions, or ideas that are tied to the *Six Essential Elements of Geography.* They help students organize information and understand geographic themes. The *Big Ideas* allow students not only to see the "big picture" but also the relevancy of what they are learning. The lesson launcher questions compel students to consider the *Big Ideas* as they relate to each section.

The BIG Ideas

The World in Spatial Terms

1. Geographers study how people and physical features are distributed on Earth's surface.

Places and Regions

2. Places reflect the relationship between humans and the physical environment.
3. Geographers organize the Earth into regions that share common characteristics.
4. Culture influences people's perceptions about places and regions.

Physical Systems

5. Physical processes shape Earth's surface.
6. All living things are dependent upon one another and their surroundings for survival.

Human Systems

7. The characteristics and movement of people impact physical and human systems.
8. Culture groups shape human systems.
9. Patterns of economic activities result in global interdependence.
10. Geographic factors influence where people settle.
11. Cooperation and conflict among people have an effect on the Earth's surface.

Environment and Society

12. People's actions can change the physical environment.
13. The physical environment affects how people live.
14. Changes occur in the use and importance of natural resources.

The Uses of Geography

15. Geography is used to interpret the past, understand the present, and plan for the future.

Lesson Structure

Each lesson in *Exploring our World: People, Places, and Cultures* is presented in a structured lesson plan: Focus, Teach, Assess, and Close.

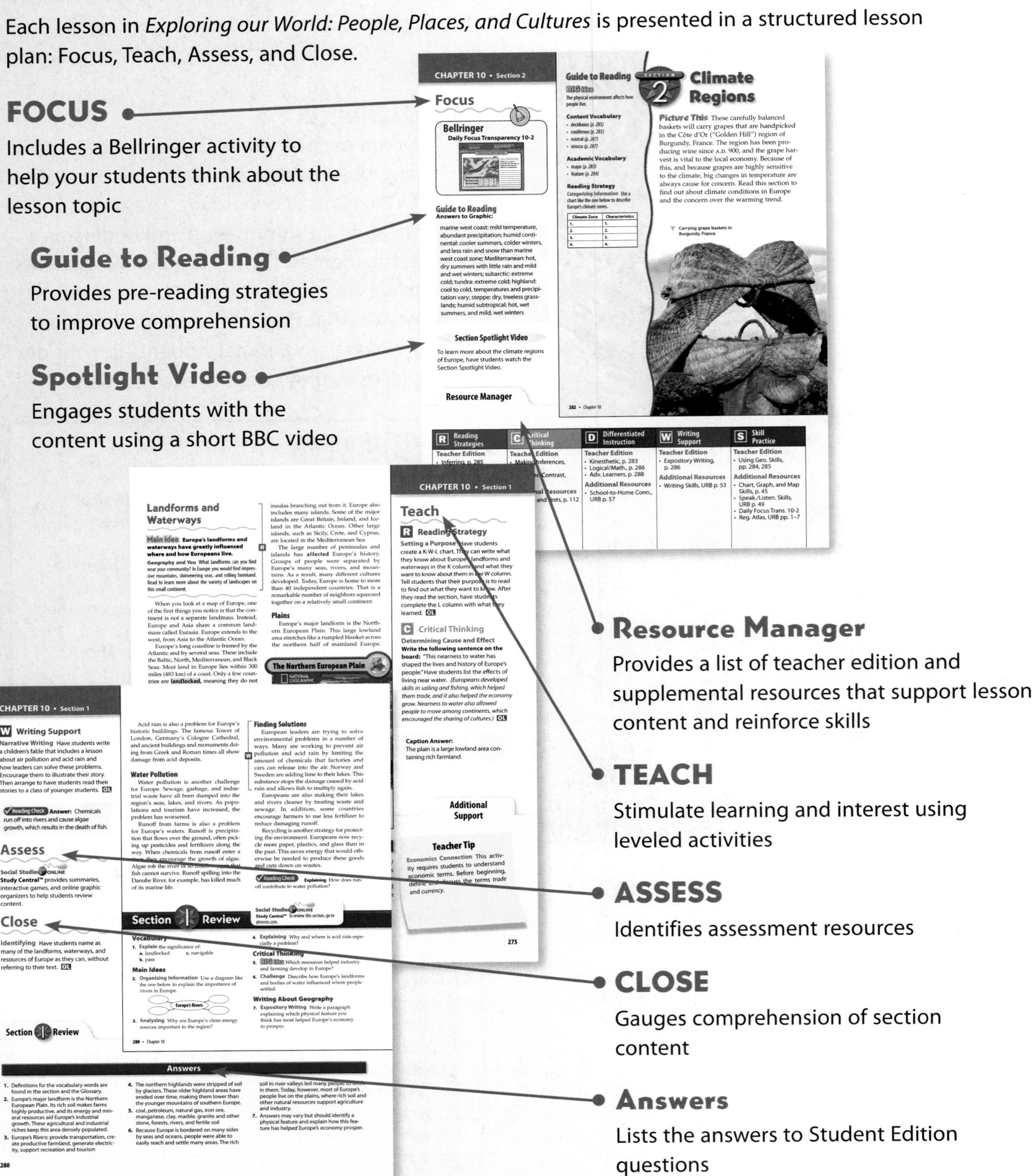

FOCUS

Includes a Bellringer activity to help your students think about the lesson topic

Guide to Reading

Provides pre-reading strategies to improve comprehension

Spotlight Video

Engages students with the content using a short BBC video

Resource Manager

Provides a list of teacher edition and supplemental resources that support lesson content and reinforce skills

TEACH

Stimulate learning and interest using leveled activities

ASSESS

Identifies assessment resources

CLOSE

Gauges comprehension of section content

Answers

Lists the answers to Student Edition questions

Understanding the Letters and Brackets

Letters*

The letters on the reduced Student Edition page identify the type of strategy or activity. See the key below to learn about the different types of strategies and activities.

Brackets

Brackets on the reduced Student Edition page correspond to teaching strategies and activities in the Teacher Wraparound Edition. As you teach the section, the brackets show you exactly where to teach these strategies and activities.

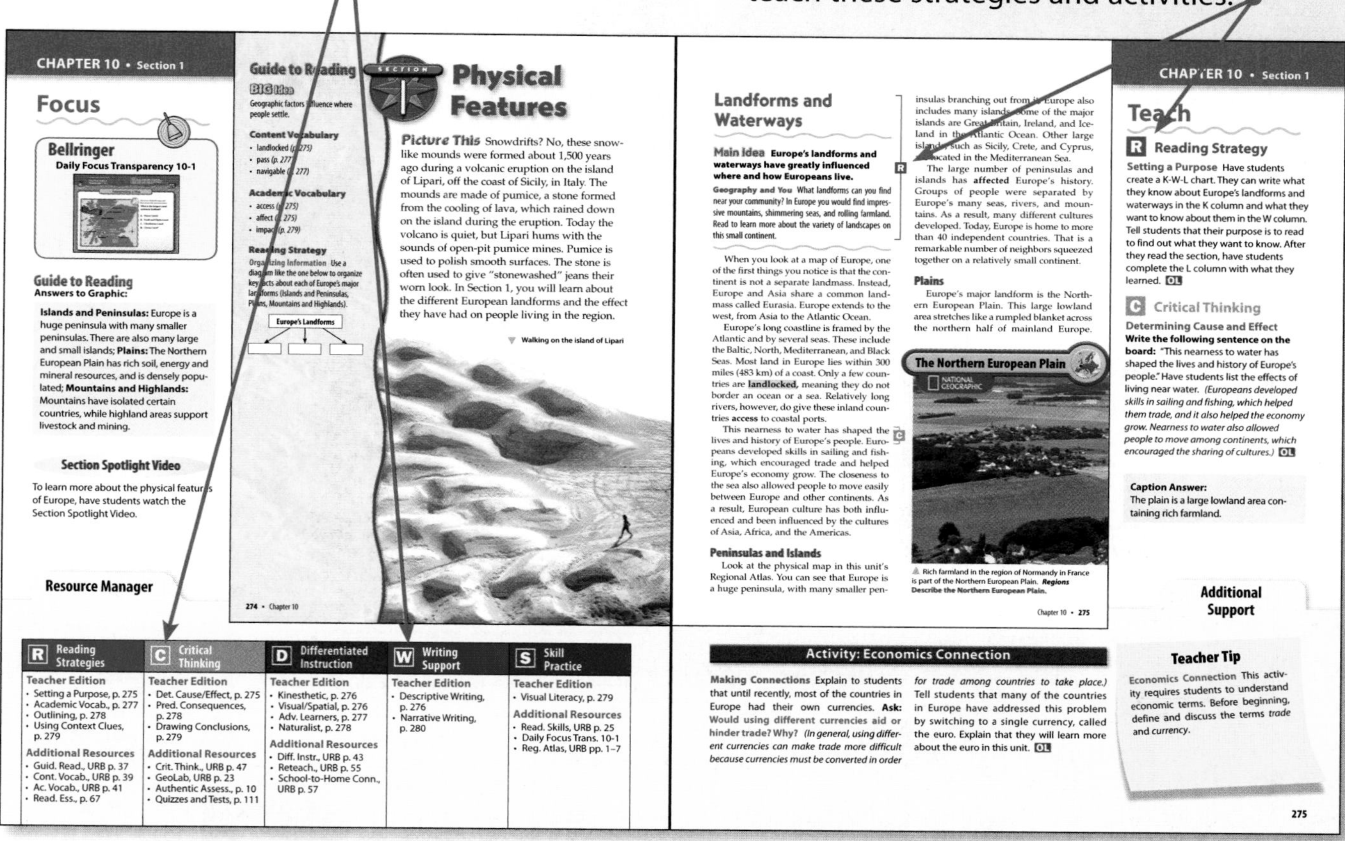

KEY for Using the Teacher Wraparound Edition

R **Reading Strategies** activities help you teach reading skills and vocabulary.

C **Critical Thinking** strategies help students apply and extend what they have learned.

D **Differentiated Instruction** activities provide differentiated instruction for students learning to speak English, along with suggestions for teaching various types of learners.

S **Skill Practice** strategies help students practice historical analysis and geography skills.

W **Writing Support** activities provide writing opportunities to help students comprehend the text.

* Letters are followed by a number when there is more than one of the same type of strategy or activity on the page.

Hands-On Chapter Projects

Extend student learning with unique and interactive Hands-On Chapter Projects. These activities allow students to take principles and put them to practical use. Projects progress through each section and culminate in a wrap-up discussion. Students conceptualize, plan, and execute their vision in a hands-on approach that makes people, places, and cultures come alive.

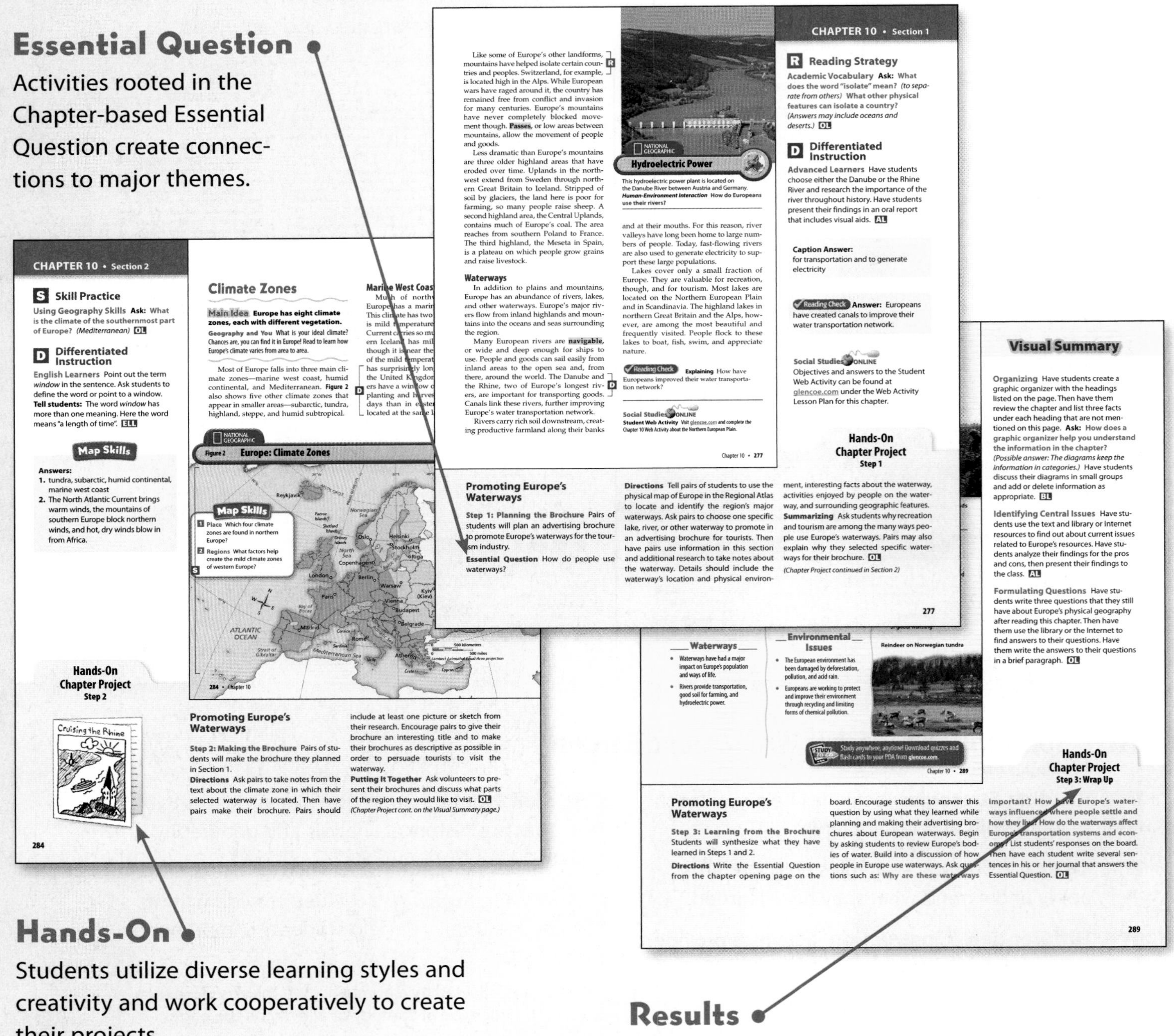

CHAPTER 10 • Section 1

R Reading Strategy
Academic Vocabulary Ask: What does the word "isolate" mean? *(to separate from others)* What other physical features can isolate a country? *(Answers may include oceans and deserts.)* OL

D Differentiated Instruction
Advanced Learners Have students choose either the Danube or the Rhine River and research the importance of the river throughout history. Have students present their findings in an oral report that includes visual aids. AL

Caption Answer: for transportation and to generate electricity

Reading Check Answer: Europeans have created canals to improve their water transportation network.

Social Studies ONLINE Objectives and answers to the Student Web Activity can be found at glencoe.com under the Web Activity Lesson Plan for this chapter.

Like some of Europe's other landforms, mountains have helped isolate certain countries and peoples. Switzerland, for example, is located high in the Alps. While European wars have raged around it, the country has remained free from conflict and invasion for many centuries. Europe's mountains have never completely blocked movement though. **Passes**, or low areas between mountains, allow the movement of people and goods.

Less dramatic than Europe's mountains are three older highland areas that have eroded over time. Uplands in the northwest extend from Sweden through northern Great Britain to Iceland. Stripped of soil by glaciers, the land here is poor for farming, so many people raise sheep. A second highland area, the Central Uplands, contains much of Europe's coal. The area reaches from southern Poland to France. The third highland, the Meseta in Spain, is a plateau on which people grow grains and raise livestock.

Waterways
In addition to plains and mountains, Europe has an abundance of rivers, lakes, and other waterways. Europe's major rivers flow from inland highlands and mountains into the oceans and seas surrounding the region.

Many European rivers are **navigable**, or wide and deep enough for ships to use. People and goods can sail easily from inland areas to the open sea and, from there, around the world. The Danube and the Rhine, two of Europe's longest rivers, are important for transporting goods. Canals link these rivers, further improving Europe's water network.

Rivers carry rich soil downstream, creating productive farmland along their banks

NATIONAL GEOGRAPHIC **Hydroelectric Power**
This hydroelectric power plant is located on the Danube River between Austria and Germany. ***Human-Environment Interaction*** How do Europeans use their rivers?

and at their mouths. For this reason, river valleys have long been home to large numbers of people. Today, fast-flowing rivers are also used to generate electricity to support these large populations.

Lakes cover only a small fraction of Europe. They are valuable for recreation, though, and for tourism. Most lakes are located on the Northern European Plain and in Scandinavia. The highland lakes in northern Great Britain and the Alps, however, are among the most beautiful and frequently visited. People flock to these lakes to boat, fish, swim, and appreciate nature.

Reading Check Explaining How have Europeans improved their water transportation network?

Social Studies ONLINE Student Web Activity Visit glencoe.com and complete the Chapter 10 Web Activity about the Northern European Plain.

Chapter 10 • 277

Hands-On Chapter Project Step 1

Promoting Europe's Waterways

Step 1: Planning the Brochure Pairs of students will plan an advertising brochure to promote Europe's waterways for the tourism industry.

Essential Question How do people use waterways?

Directions Tell pairs of students to use the physical map of Europe in the Regional Atlas to locate and identify the region's major waterways. Ask pairs to choose one specific lake, river, or other waterway to promote in an advertising brochure for tourists. Then have pairs use information in this section and additional research to take notes about the waterway. Details should include the waterway's location and physical environment, interesting facts about the waterway, activities enjoyed by people on the waterway, and surrounding geographic features.

Summarizing Ask students why recreation and tourism are among the many ways people use Europe's waterways. Pairs may also explain why they selected specific waterways for their brochure. OL

(Chapter Project continued in Section 2)

277

CHAPTER 10 • Section 2

S Skill Practice
Using Geography Skills Ask: What is the climate of the southernmost part of Europe? *(Mediterranean)* OL

D Differentiated Instruction
English Learners Point out the term *window* in the sentence. Ask students to define the word or point to a window. **Tell students:** The word *window* has more than one meaning. Here the word means "a length of time". ELL

Map Skills
Answers:
1. tundra, subarctic, humid continental, marine west coast
2. The North Atlantic Current brings warm winds, the mountains of southern Europe block northern winds, and hot, dry winds blow in from Africa.

Climate Zones

Main Idea Europe has eight climate zones, each with different vegetation.

Geography and You What is your ideal climate? Chances are, you can find it in Europe! Read to learn how Europe's climate varies from area to area.

Most of Europe falls into three main climate zones—marine west coast, humid continental, and Mediterranean. **Figure 2** also shows five other climate zones that appear in smaller areas—subarctic, tundra, highland, steppe, and humid subtropical.

NATIONAL GEOGRAPHIC Figure 2 **Europe: Climate Zones**

Map Skills
1 **Place** Which four climate zones are found in northern Europe?
2 **Regions** What factors help create the mild climate zones of western Europe?

284 • Chapter 10

Hands-On Chapter Project Step 2

Cruising the Rhine

Promoting Europe's Waterways

Step 2: Making the Brochure Pairs of students will make the brochure they planned in Section 1.

Directions Ask pairs to take notes from the text about the climate zone in which their selected waterway is located. Then have pairs make their brochure. Pairs should include at least one picture or sketch from their research. Encourage pairs to give their brochure an interesting title and to make their brochures as descriptive as possible in order to persuade tourists to visit the waterway.

Putting It Together Ask volunteers to present their brochures and discuss what parts of the region they would like to visit. OL

(Chapter Project cont. on the Visual Summary page.)

284

Visual Summary

Organizing Have students create a graphic organizer with the headings listed on the page. Then have them review the chapter and list three facts under each heading that are not mentioned on this page. **Ask:** How does a graphic organizer help you understand the information in the chapter? *(Possible answer: The diagrams keep the information in categories.)* Have students discuss their diagrams in small groups and add or delete information as appropriate. BL

Identifying Central Issues Have students use the text and library or Internet resources to find out about current issues related to Europe's resources. Have students analyze their findings for the pros and cons, then present their findings to the class. AL

Formulating Questions Have students write three questions that they still have about Europe's physical geography after reading this chapter. Then have them use the library or the Internet to find answers to their questions. Have them write the answers to their questions in a brief paragraph. OL

Waterways
- Waterways have had a major impact on Europe's population and ways of life.
- Rivers provide transportation, good soil for farming, and hydroelectric power.

Environmental Issues
- The European environment has been damaged by deforestation, pollution, and acid rain.
- Europeans are working to protect and improve their environment through recycling and limiting forms of chemical pollution.

Reindeer on Norwegian tundra

Study anywhere, anytime! Download quizzes and flash cards to your PDA from glencoe.com.

Chapter 10 • 289

Hands-On Chapter Project Step 3: Wrap Up

Promoting Europe's Waterways

Step 3: Learning from the Brochure Students will synthesize what they have learned in Steps 1 and 2.

Directions Write the Essential Question from the chapter opening page on the board. Encourage students to answer this question by using what they learned while planning and making their advertising brochures about European waterways. Begin by asking students to review Europe's bodies of water. Build into a discussion of how people in Europe use waterways. Ask questions such as: Why are these waterways important? How have Europe's waterways influenced where people settle and how they live? How do the waterways affect Europe's transportation systems and economy? List students' responses on the board. Then have each student write several sentences in his or her journal that answers the Essential Question. OL

289

Essential Question

Activities rooted in the Chapter-based Essential Question create connections to major themes.

Hands-On

Students utilize diverse learning styles and creativity and work cooperatively to create their projects.

Results

The Hands-On project culminates in an interactive discussion where students synthesize what they have learned and draw conclusions.

Differentiated Instruction

Each section of the Teacher Wraparound Edition of *Exploring Our World: People, Places, and Cultures* provides differentiated instruction activities to meet the diverse needs of every student.

Differentiated Activities

Innovative ideas meet each student's interests and learning styles through point-of-use activities

Additional Resources

Provides suggestions for incorporating additional resources based on students' different learning abilities

Leveled Activities

Extends instruction beyond the text by suggesting activities related to content on the page

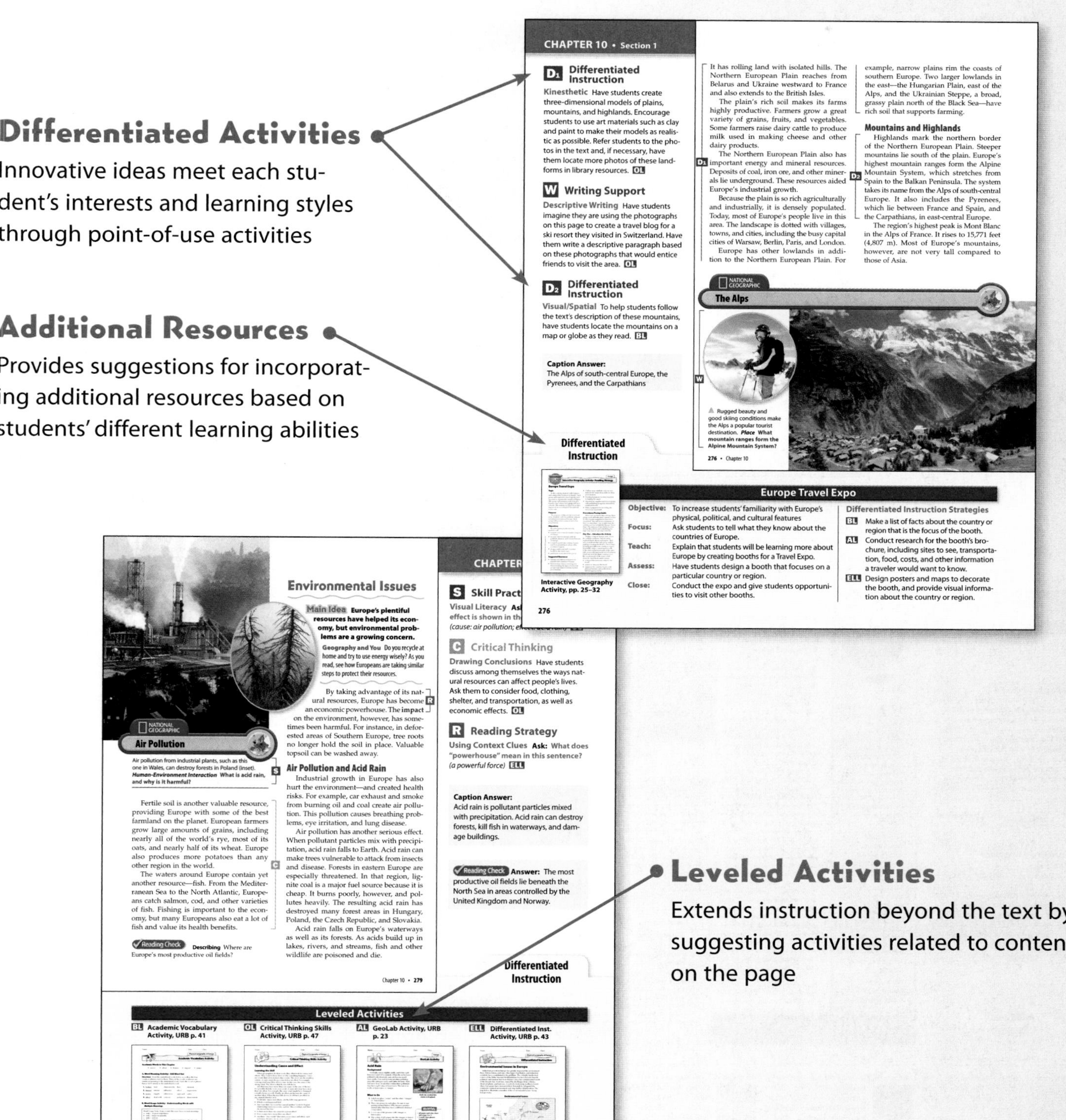

CHAPTER 10 • Section 1

D1 Differentiated Instruction

Kinesthetic Have students create three-dimensional models of plains, mountains, and highlands. Encourage students to use art materials such as clay and paint to make their models as realistic as possible. Refer students to the photos in the text and, if necessary, have them locate more photos of these landforms in library resources. OL

W Writing Support

Descriptive Writing Have students imagine they are using the photographs on this page to create a travel blog for a ski resort they visited in Switzerland. Have them write a descriptive paragraph based on these photographs that would entice friends to visit the area. OL

D2 Differentiated Instruction

Visual/Spatial To help students follow the text's description of these mountains, have students locate the mountains on a map or globe as they read. BL

Caption Answer: The Alps of south-central Europe, the Pyrenees, and the Carpathians

It has rolling land with isolated hills. The Northern European Plain reaches from Belarus and Ukraine westward to France and also extends to the British Isles.

The plain's rich soil makes its farms highly productive. Farmers grow a great variety of grains, fruits, and vegetables. Some farmers raise dairy cattle to produce milk used in making cheese and other dairy products.

The Northern European Plain also has important energy and mineral resources. Deposits of coal, iron ore, and other minerals lie underground. These resources aided Europe's industrial growth.

Because the plain is so rich agriculturally and industrially, it is densely populated. Today, most of Europe's people live in this area. The landscape is dotted with villages, towns, and cities, including the busy capital cities of Warsaw, Berlin, Paris, and London.

Europe has other lowlands in addition to the Northern European Plain. For example, narrow plains rim the coasts of southern Europe. Two larger lowlands in the east—the Hungarian Plain, east of the Alps, and the Ukrainian Steppe, a broad, grassy plain north of the Black Sea—have rich soil that supports farming.

Mountains and Highlands

Highlands mark the northern border of the Northern European Plain. Steeper mountains lie south of the plain. Europe's highest mountain ranges form the Alpine Mountain System, which stretches from Spain to the Balkan Peninsula. The system takes its name from the Alps of south-central Europe. It also includes the Pyrenees, which lie between France and Spain, and the Carpathians, in east-central Europe.

The region's highest peak is Mont Blanc in the Alps of France. It rises to 15,771 feet (4,807 m). Most of Europe's mountains, however, are not very tall compared to those of Asia.

NATIONAL GEOGRAPHIC **The Alps**

Rugged beauty and good skiing conditions make the Alps a popular tourist destination. ***Place*** **What mountain ranges form the Alpine Mountain System?**

276 • Chapter 10

Differentiated Instruction

Interactive Geography Activity, pp. 25–32

Europe Travel Expo

Objective: To increase students' familiarity with Europe's physical, political, and cultural features

Focus: Ask students to tell what they know about the countries of Europe.

Teach: Explain that students will be learning more about Europe by creating booths for a Travel Expo.

Assess: Have students design a booth that focuses on a particular country or region.

Close: Conduct the expo and give students opportunities to visit other booths.

Differentiated Instruction Strategies

BL Make a list of facts about the country or region that is the focus of the booth.

AL Conduct research for the booth's brochure, including sites to see, transportation, food, costs, and other information a traveler would want to know.

ELL Design posters and maps to decorate the booth, and provide visual information about the country or region.

276

Environmental Issues

Main Idea Europe's plentiful resources have helped its economy, but environmental problems are a growing concern.

Geography and You Do you recycle at home and try to use energy wisely? As you read, see how Europeans are taking similar steps to protect their resources.

By taking advantage of its natural resources, Europe has become an economic powerhouse. The impact on the environment, however, has sometimes been harmful. For instance, in deforested areas of Southern Europe, tree roots no longer hold the soil in place. Valuable topsoil can be washed away.

Air Pollution and Acid Rain

Industrial growth in Europe has also hurt the environment—and created health risks. For example, car exhaust and smoke from burning oil and coal create air pollution. This pollution causes breathing problems, eye irritation, and lung disease.

Air pollution has another serious effect. When pollutant particles mix with precipitation, acid rain falls to Earth. Acid rain can make trees vulnerable to attack from insects and disease. Forests in eastern Europe are especially threatened. In that region, lignite coal is a major fuel source because it is cheap. It burns poorly, however, and pollutes heavily. The resulting acid rain has destroyed many forest areas in Hungary, Poland, the Czech Republic, and Slovakia.

Acid rain falls on Europe's waterways as well as its forests. As acids build up in lakes, rivers, and streams, fish and other wildlife are poisoned and die.

NATIONAL GEOGRAPHIC **Air Pollution**

Air pollution from industrial plants, such as this one in Wales, can destroy forests in Poland (inset). ***Human-Environment Interaction*** **What is acid rain, and why is it harmful?**

Fertile soil is another valuable resource, providing Europe with some of the best farmland on the planet. European farmers grow large amounts of grains, including nearly all of the world's rye, most of its oats, and nearly half of its wheat. Europe also produces more potatoes than any other region in the world.

The waters around Europe contain yet another resource—fish. From the Mediterranean Sea to the North Atlantic, Europeans catch salmon, cod, and other varieties of fish. Fishing is important to the economy, but many Europeans also eat a lot of fish and value its health benefits.

Reading Check **Describing** Where are Europe's most productive oil fields?

Chapter 10 • 279

CHAPTER

S Skill Practice

Visual Literacy Ask ... effect is shown in th... (cause: air pollution; e...

C Critical Thinking

Drawing Conclusions Have students discuss among themselves the ways natural resources can affect people's lives. Ask them to consider food, clothing, shelter, and transportation, as well as economic effects. OL

R Reading Strategy

Using Context Clues **Ask:** What does "powerhouse" mean in this sentence? *(a powerful force)* ELL

Caption Answer: Acid rain is pollutant particles mixed with precipitation. Acid rain can destroy forests, kill fish in waterways, and damage buildings.

Reading Check **Answer:** The most productive oil fields lie beneath the North Sea in areas controlled by the United Kingdom and Norway.

Differentiated Instruction

Leveled Activities

BL Academic Vocabulary Activity, URB p. 41	OL Critical Thinking Skills Activity, URB p. 47	AL GeoLab Activity, URB p. 23	ELL Differentiated Inst. Activity, URB p. 43

279

Dynamic Features

Use these creative features to dig deep into the fascinating people, places, and cultures covered in the text.

YOU Decide

Focus

R Reading Strategy

Predicting Ask students to predict what might happen if they moved to a country in which English was not spoken. **Ask:** **How would you feel if you were not allowed to speak English at school?** *(Possible answer: I would be confused at first, because I would not understand what was going on.)* OL

For further practice on this skill (Predicting), see the **Skills Handbook**.

Teach

Have students create a T-chart with the headings "For Speaking the Same Language" and "Against Speaking the Same Language." As they read the feature, have them note arguments for and against allowing only the country's official language to be spoken in schools. OL

Additional Support

YOU Decide

Learning in School: Should All Students Speak the Same Language?

In Europe, migration between countries is common. As a result, many students do not speak the local language where they live. Some educators believe that all students should speak the nation's official language in school. For example, in Berlin, Germany, several schools allow only the German language to be spoken during class, on school property, and on school trips. However, others disagree, arguing that students should be allowed to learn in their own languages.

For: Speaking the Same Language

I believe that knowledge of the German language is the key to integration [becoming part of society] and to success both at school and in a future profession. . . . The pupils themselves are very satisfied with [this rule], because they know that speaking correct German increases their opportunities. . . .

When children start school and don't speak the language correctly, they . . . receive worse grades. That continues throughout their schooling and in the end they aren't able to get a vocational [job] training place. That's why we are in favour of introducing language tests starting from the age of four and thereby promoting language skills from kindergarten on.

—Armin Laschet
Minister for Generations, Family, Women, and Integration
North Rhine-Westphalia, Germany

Against: Speaking the Same Language

Banning pupils from speaking their [traditional] languages in the schoolyard is not the answer, even if it were workable, which it is not. Other means of developing their linguistic [language] skills, such as pre-school instruction in German, are much more likely to be effective and should be fully supported.

. . . It is perfectly acceptable to ban other languages within the classroom. But outside the classroom pupils should be free to speak whichever language they like. Banning pupils' [traditional] languages sends a message that they are somehow "second class" citizens, which is likely to promote resentment rather than integration. . . .

Many children of immigrants choose to communicate in German in any case. . . .

There also appears to be a fallacy [mistaken belief] that speaking another language somehow [takes away] from pupils' ability with German. This is not the case. Humans have an almost unlimited ability to learn languages and in general there is no reason why the average person cannot master two or more languages.

—David Gordon Smith
Editor, Expatica: Germany

You Be the Geographer

1. **Identifying** What reasons do Laschet and Smith give to support their opinions?
2. **Critical Thinking** What might be some challenges for a student who speaks a different language than that of the other students in his or her class?
3. **Read to Write** Write a paragraph that explains your own opinion about students speaking only one language at school.

Chapter 11 • 305

YOU Decide

Assess/Close

Organize the students into two groups to debate allowing only one language to be used in schools. Have students prepare by finding additional resources in the library or on the Internet. Then have each group present its arguments before another teacher at your school. Ask this teacher to explain which group was more persuasive. OL

You Be the Geographer

Answers:

1. Laschet: requiring the use of an official language will help students integrate more quickly and be more successful in school and in the future; Smith: banning students from speaking their traditional languages makes them feel inferior and that other, more effective ways can be used to develop their language skills.
2. It might be difficult for the student to make friends and to understand what is being taught.
3. Answers will vary, but students should give reasons to support their opinions.

FastFacts

Regional Languages Throughout much of Europe, various groups speak languages that are different from the official languages of their countries. In fact, it is estimated that nearly 40 million people in the European Union speak a regional or minority language. These languages are not simply dialects of the majority language of the country or foreign languages spoken by immigrants. They are distinct languages that have been passed down from generation to generation within the country itself. One example of a regional language is Catalan, a language spoken by about 7 million people in parts of Spain, France, and Sardinia; Another example is Saami, a family of languages spoken in parts of Scandinavia. Experts have identified more than 60 regional or minority languages in the European Union. Some of these languages are spoken by as little as a few hundred people.

Activity: Connecting With the United States

Language Learning in the United States Ask students if they have heard about a similar controversy in the United States. Explain that a great deal of debate takes place over how best to integrate Spanish-speaking students into American classrooms. Although people do not always agree on how best to teach English to Spanish-speaking students, many people do agree that English-speaking students could benefit from learning a second language in elementary school. Dual-immersion programs, which teach English- and Spanish-speaking students in both languages, are becoming more common. **Ask:** **Do you think dual-immersion programs would be beneficial? Why or why not?** *(Possible answer: Yes, because many students must learn a foreign language in high school, so learning a language in elementary school gives them a head start at a time in their lives when learning a second language is easier.)* OL

305

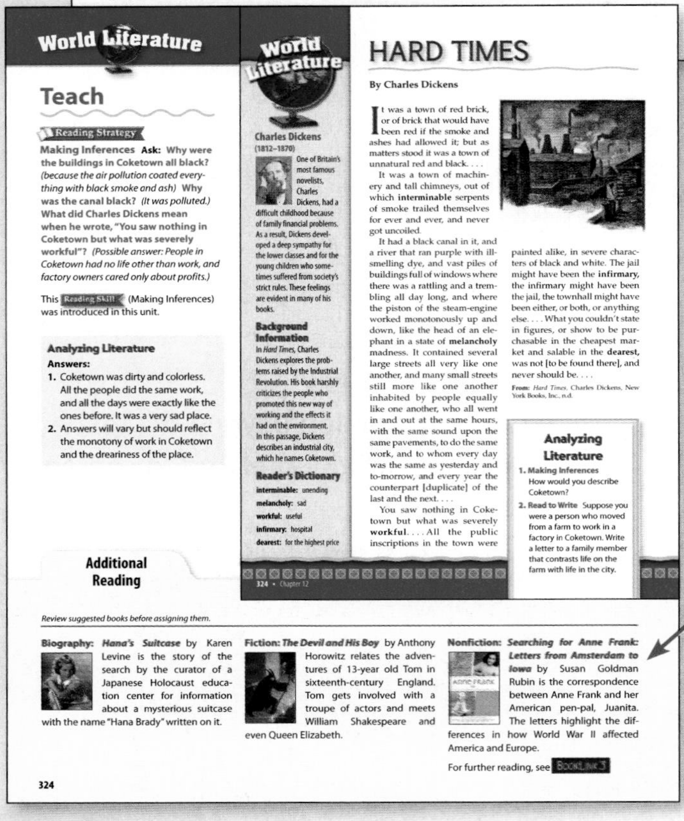

You Decide

Teaches students to analyze different points-of-view on current world issues

World Literature

Teach

Reading Strategy

Making Inferences **Ask:** **Why were the buildings in Coketown all black?** *(because the air pollution coated everything with black smoke and ash)* **Why was the canal black?** *(It was polluted.)* **What did Charles Dickens mean when he wrote, "You saw nothing in Coketown but what was severely workful"?** *(Possible answer: People in Coketown had no life other than work, and factory owners cared only about profits.)*

This Reading Skill (Making Inferences) was introduced in this unit.

Analyzing Literature

Answers:

1. Coketown was dirty and colorless. All the people did the same work, and all the days were exactly like the ones before. It was a very sad place.
2. Answers will vary but should reflect the monotony of work in Coketown and the dreariness of the place.

World Literature

Charles Dickens (1812–1870)

One of Britain's most famous novelists, Charles Dickens, had a difficult childhood because of family financial problems. As a result, Dickens developed a deep sympathy for the lower classes and for the young children who sometimes suffered from society's strict rules. These feelings are evident in many of his books.

Background Information

In *Hard Times*, Charles Dickens explores the problems raised by the Industrial Revolution. His book harshly criticizes the people who promoted this new way of working and the effects it had on the environment. In this passage, Dickens describes an industrial city, which he names Coketown.

Reader's Dictionary

interminable: unending
melancholy: sad
workful: useful
infirmary: hospital
dearest: for the highest price

HARD TIMES

By Charles Dickens

It was a town of red brick, or of brick that would have been red if the smoke and ashes had allowed it; but as matters stood it was a town of unnatural red and black. . . .

It was a town of machinery and tall chimneys, out of which **interminable** serpents of smoke trailed themselves for ever and ever, and never got uncoiled.

It had a black canal in it, and a river that ran purple with ill-smelling dye, and vast piles of buildings full of windows where there was a rattling and a trembling all day long, and where the piston of the steam-engine worked monotonously up and down, like the head of an elephant in a state of **melancholy** madness. It contained several large streets all very like one another, and many small streets still more like one another inhabited by people equally like one another, who all went in and out at the same hours, with the same sound upon the same pavements, to do the same work, and to whom every day was the same as yesterday and to-morrow, and every year the counterpart [duplicate] of the last and the next. . . .

You saw nothing in Coketown but what was severely **workful**. . . . All the public inscriptions in the town were painted alike, in severe characters of black and white. The jail might have been the **infirmary**, the infirmary might have been the jail, the townhall might have been either, or both, or anything else. . . . What you couldn't state in figures, or show to be purchasable in the cheapest market and salable in the **dearest**, was not [to be found there], and never should be. . . .

From: *Hard Times*, Charles Dickens, New York Books, Inc., n.d.

Analyzing Literature

1. **Making Inferences** How would you describe Coketown?
2. **Read to Write** Suppose you were a person who moved from a farm to work in a factory in Coketown. Write a letter to a family member that contrasts life on the farm with life in the city.

324 • Chapter 12

Additional Reading

Review suggested books before assigning them.

Biography: ***Hana's Suitcase*** by Karen Levine is the story of the search by the curator of a Japanese Holocaust education center for information about a mysterious suitcase with the name "Hana Brady" written on it.

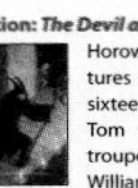

Fiction: ***The Devil and His Boy*** by Anthony Horowitz relates the adventures of 13-year old Tom in sixteenth-century England. Tom gets involved with a troupe of actors and meets William Shakespeare and even Queen Elizabeth.

Nonfiction: ***Searching for Anne Frank: Letters from Amsterdam to Iowa*** by Susan Goldman Rubin is the correspondence between Anne Frank and her American pen-pal, Juanita. The letters highlight the differences in how World War II affected America and Europe.

For further reading, see BookLink 3

324

Additional Reading

Supplemental reading suggestions provide fun and varied opportunities for students to connect with each region.

Chapter Summary and Assessment

Visual Summary

Summary activities help students to synthesize major chapter themes.

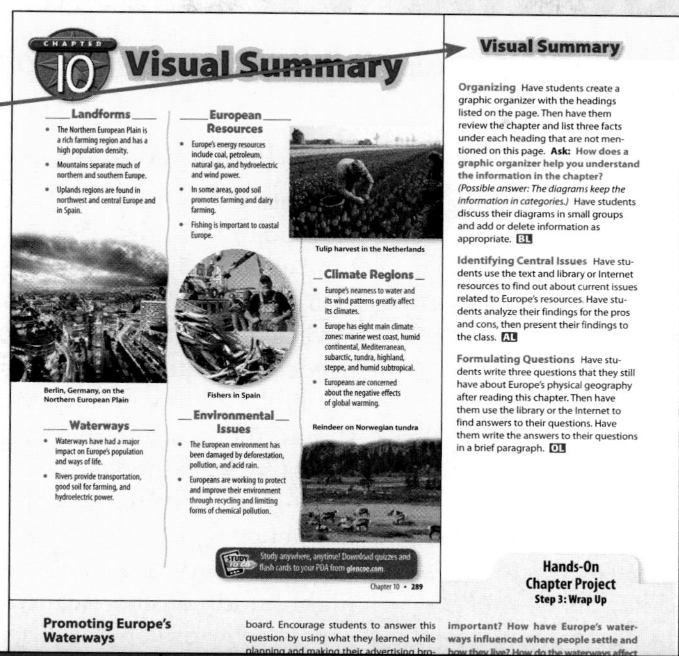

CHAPTER 10 **Visual Summary**

Landforms

- The Northern European Plain is a rich farming region and has a high population density.
- Mountains separate much of northern and southern Europe.
- Uplands regions are found in northwest and central Europe and in Spain.

Berlin, Germany, on the Northern European Plain

Waterways

- Waterways have had a major impact on Europe's population and ways of life.
- Rivers provide transportation, good soil for farming, and hydroelectric power.

European Resources

- Europe's energy resources include coal, petroleum, natural gas, and hydroelectric and wind power.
- In some areas, good soil promotes farming and dairy farming.
- Fishing is important to coastal Europe.

Fishers in Spain

Environmental Issues

- The European environment has been damaged by deforestation, pollution, and acid rain.
- Europeans are working to protect and improve their environment through recycling and limiting forms of chemical pollution.

Tulip harvest in the Netherlands

Climate Regions

- Europe's nearness to water and its wind patterns greatly affect its climates.
- Europe has eight main climate zones: marine west coast, humid continental, Mediterranean, subarctic, tundra, highland, steppe, and humid subtropical.
- Europeans are concerned about the negative effects of global warming.

Reindeer on Norwegian tundra

STUDY TO GO Study anywhere, anytime! Download quizzes and flash cards to your PDA from glencoe.com.

Chapter 10 • 289

Visual Summary

Organizing Have students create a graphic organizer with the headings listed on the page. Then have them review the chapter and list three facts under each heading that are not mentioned on this page. **Ask: How does a graphic organizer help you understand the information in the chapter?** *(Possible answer: The diagrams keep the information in categories.)* Have students discuss their diagrams in small groups and add or delete information as appropriate. BL

Identifying Central Issues Have students use the text and library or Internet resources to find out about current issues related to Europe's resources. Have students analyze their findings for the pros and cons, then present their findings to the class. AL

Formulating Questions Have students write three questions that they still have about Europe's physical geography after reading this chapter. Then have them use the library or the Internet to find answers to their questions. Have them write the answers to their questions in a brief paragraph. OL

Hands-On Chapter Project
Step 3: Wrap Up

Promoting Europe's Waterways

board. Encourage students to answer this question by using what they learned while planning and making their advertising bro-

important? How have Europe's waterways influenced where people settle and how they live? How do the waterways affect

Standardized Test Practice

Answers incorporate analysis and identify potential student pitfalls, challenges, distracters, and test-taking strategies.

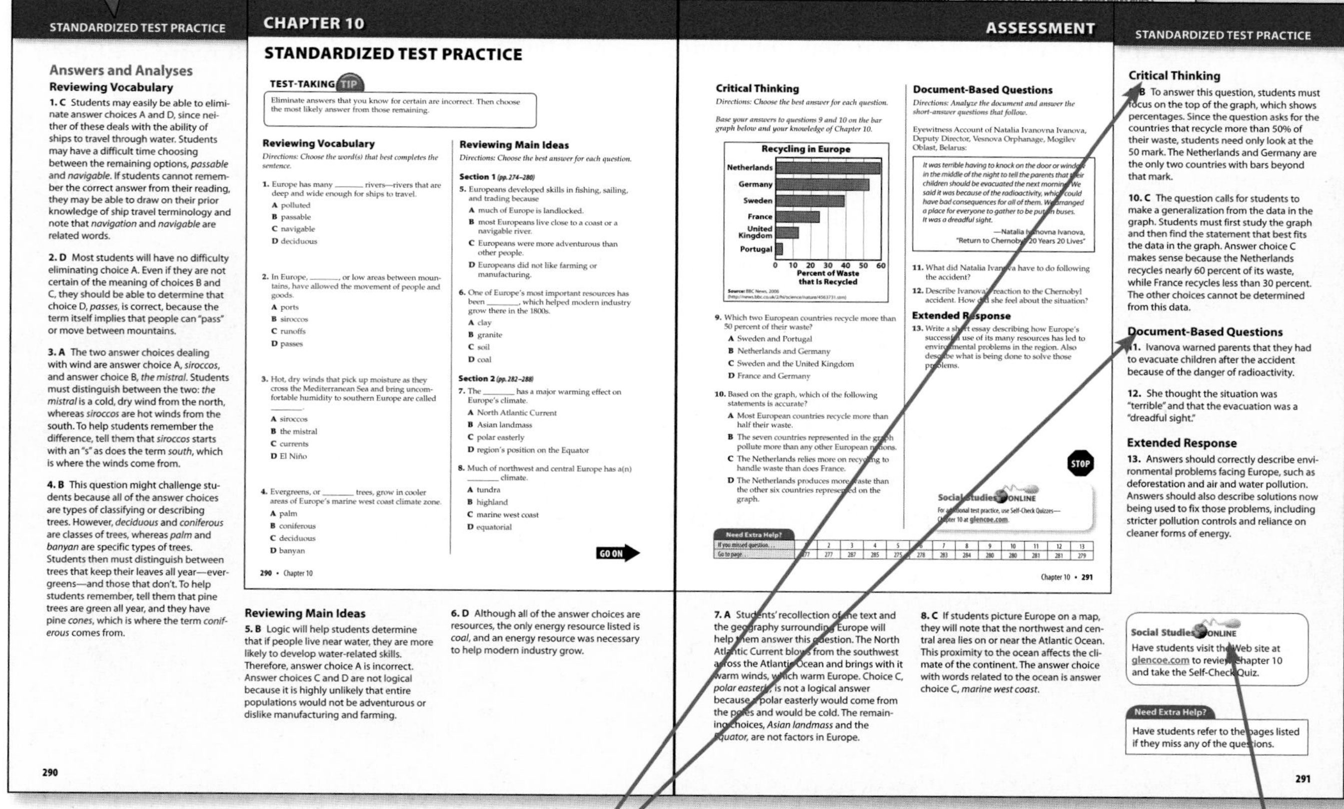

STANDARDIZED TEST PRACTICE

Answers and Analyses

Reviewing Vocabulary

1. C Students may easily be able to eliminate answer choices A and D, since neither of these deals with the ability of ships to travel through water. Students may have a difficult time choosing between the remaining options, *passable* and *navigable*. If students cannot remember the correct answer from their reading, they may be able to draw on their prior knowledge of ship travel terminology and note that *navigation* and *navigable* are related words.

2. D Most students will have no difficulty eliminating choice A. Even if they are not certain of the meaning of choices B and C, they should be able to determine that choice D, *passes*, is correct, because the term itself implies that people can "pass" or move between mountains.

3. A The two answer choices dealing with wind are answer choice A, *siroccos*, and answer choice B, *the mistral*. Students must distinguish between the two: *the mistral* is a cold, dry wind from the north, whereas *siroccos* are hot winds from the south. To help students remember the difference, tell them that *siroccos* starts with an "s" as does the term *south*, which is where the winds come from.

4. B This question might challenge students because all of the answer choices are types of classifying or describing trees. However, *deciduous* and *coniferous* are classes of trees, whereas *palm* and *banyan* are specific types of trees. Students then must distinguish between trees that keep their leaves all year—evergreens—and those that don't. To help students remember, tell them that pine trees are green all year, and they have pine *cones*, which is where the term *coniferous* comes from.

CHAPTER 10

STANDARDIZED TEST PRACTICE

TEST-TAKING TIP

Eliminate answers that you know for certain are incorrect. Then choose the most likely answer from those remaining.

Reviewing Vocabulary

Directions: Choose the word(s) that best completes the sentence.

1. Europe has many _______ rivers—rivers that are deep and wide enough for ships to travel.
   - **A** polluted
   - **B** passable
   - **C** navigable
   - **D** deciduous

2. In Europe, _______, or low areas between mountains, have allowed the movement of people and goods.
   - **A** ports
   - **B** siroccos
   - **C** runoffs
   - **D** passes

3. Hot, dry winds that pick up moisture as they cross the Mediterranean Sea and bring uncomfortable humidity to southern Europe are called _______.
   - **A** siroccos
   - **B** the mistral
   - **C** currents
   - **D** El Niño

4. Evergreens, or _______ trees, grow in cooler areas of Europe's marine west coast climate zone.
   - **A** palm
   - **B** coniferous
   - **C** deciduous
   - **D** banyan

Reviewing Main Ideas

Directions: Choose the best answer for each question.

Section 1 *(pp. 274–280)*

5. Europeans developed skills in fishing, sailing, and trading because
   - **A** much of Europe is landlocked.
   - **B** most Europeans live close to a coast or a navigable river.
   - **C** Europeans were more adventurous than other people.
   - **D** Europeans did not like farming or manufacturing.

6. One of Europe's most important resources has been _______, which helped modern industry grow there in the 1800s.
   - **A** clay
   - **B** granite
   - **C** soil
   - **D** coal

Section 2 *(pp. 282–288)*

7. The _______ has a major warming effect on Europe's climate.
   - **A** North Atlantic Current
   - **B** Asian landmass
   - **C** polar easterly
   - **D** region's position on the Equator

8. Much of northwest and central Europe has a(n) _______ climate.
   - **A** tundra
   - **B** highland
   - **C** marine west coast
   - **D** equatorial

GO ON

290 • Chapter 10

Reviewing Main Ideas

5. B Logic will help students determine that if people live near water, they are more likely to develop water-related skills. Therefore, answer choice A is incorrect. Answer choices C and D are not logical because it is highly unlikely that entire populations would not be adventurous or dislike manufacturing and farming.

6. D Although all of the answer choices are resources, the only energy resource listed is *coal*, and an energy resource was necessary to help modern industry grow.

290

ASSESSMENT

Critical Thinking

Directions: Choose the best answer for each question.

Base your answers to questions 9 and 10 on the bar graph below and your knowledge of Chapter 10.

Recycling in Europe

Source: BBC News, 2006 (http://news.bbc.co.uk/2/hi/science/nature/4563731.stm)

9. Which two European countries recycle more than 50 percent of their waste?
   - **A** Sweden and Portugal
   - **B** Netherlands and Germany
   - **C** Sweden and the United Kingdom
   - **D** France and Germany

10. Based on the graph, which of the following statements is accurate?
    - **A** Most European countries recycle more than half their waste.
    - **B** The seven countries represented in the graph pollute more than any other European nations.
    - **C** The Netherlands relies more on recycling to handle waste than does France.
    - **D** The Netherlands produces more waste than the other six countries represented on the graph.

Document-Based Questions

Directions: Analyze the document and answer the short-answer questions that follow.

Eyewitness Account of Natalia Ivanovna Ivanova, Deputy Director, Vesnova Orphanage, Mogilev Oblast, Belarus:

> *It was terrible having to knock on the door or window in the middle of the night to tell the parents that their children should be evacuated the next morning. We said it was because of the radioactivity, which could have bad consequences for all of them. We arranged a place for everyone to gather to be put on buses. It was a dreadful sight.*
>
> —Natalia Ivanovna Ivanova, "Return to Chernobyl: 20 Years 20 Lives"

11. What did Natalia Ivanova have to do following the accident?

12. Describe Ivanova's reaction to the Chernobyl accident. How did she feel about the situation?

Extended Response

13. Write a short essay describing how Europe's successful use of its many resources has led to environmental problems in the region. Also describe what is being done to solve those problems.

STOP

Social Studies ONLINE
For additional test practice, use Self-Check Quizzes—Chapter 10 at glencoe.com.

Need Extra Help?

If you missed question...	1	2	3	4	5	6	7	8	9	10	11	12	13
Go to page...	[illegible]	277	287	285	275	278	283	284	280	280	281	281	279

Chapter 10 • 291

7. A Students' recollection of the text and the geography surrounding Europe will help them answer this question. The North Atlantic Current blows from the southwest across the Atlantic Ocean and brings with it warm winds, which warm Europe. Choice C, *polar easterly*, is not a logical answer because a polar easterly would come from the poles and would be cold. The remaining choices, *Asian landmass* and the *Equator*, are not factors in Europe.

8. C If students picture Europe on a map, they will note that the northwest and central area lies on or near the Atlantic Ocean. This proximity to the ocean affects the climate of the continent. The answer choice with words related to the ocean is answer choice C, *marine west coast*.

STANDARDIZED TEST PRACTICE

Critical Thinking

9. B To answer this question, students must focus on the top of the graph, which shows percentages. Since the question asks for the countries that recycle more than 50% of their waste, students need only look at the 50 mark. The Netherlands and Germany are the only two countries with bars beyond that mark.

10. C The question calls for students to make a generalization from the data in the graph. Students must first study the graph and then find the statement that best fits the data in the graph. Answer choice C makes sense because the Netherlands recycles nearly 60 percent of its waste, while France recycles less than 30 percent. The other choices cannot be determined from this data.

Document-Based Questions

11. Ivanova warned parents that they had to evacuate children after the accident because of the danger of radioactivity.

12. She thought the situation was "terrible" and that the evacuation was a "dreadful sight."

Extended Response

13. Answers should correctly describe environmental problems facing Europe, such as deforestation and air and water pollution. Answers should also describe solutions now being used to fix those problems, including stricter pollution controls and reliance on cleaner forms of energy.

Social Studies ONLINE
Have students visit the Web site at glencoe.com to review Chapter 10 and take the Self-Check Quiz.

Need Extra Help?
Have students refer to the pages listed if they miss any of the questions.

291

Critical Thinking and Document-Based Questions

Extends answers and analysis through document and graphic assessment

Social Studies Online

Provides additional assessment opportunities

Academic Vocabulary

How Can I Help My Students Learn Academic Vocabulary?

What Is Academic English?

Academic English is the language used in academics, business, and courts of law. It is the type of English used in textbooks, and contains linguistic features associated with academic disciplines like social studies. Proficiency in reading and using academic English is especially related to long-term success in all parts of life.

By reinforcing academic English, teachers can help learners to access authentic, academic texts—not simplified texts that dummy down the content. In this way, they can provide information that will help build their students' background knowledge rapidly.

What Is Academic Vocabulary?

Academic vocabulary is based on academic English. By the time children have completed elementary school, they must have acquired the knowledge needed to understand academic vocabulary. How many words should they acquire to be able to access their textbooks? A basic 2,000-word vocabulary of high-frequency words makes up 87% of the vocabulary of academic texts. Eight hundred other academic words comprise an additional 8% of the words. Three percent of the remaining words are technical words. The remaining 2% are low-frequency words. There may be as many as 123,000 low-frequency words in academic texts.

Why Should Students Learn Academic Vocabulary?

English learners who have a basic 2,000-word vocabulary are ready to acquire most general words found in their texts.

Knowledge of academic words and general words can significantly boost a student's comprehension level of academic texts. Students who learn and practice these words before they graduate from high school are likely to master academic material with more confidence and speed. They waste less time and effort in guessing words or

consulting dictionaries than those who only know the basic 2,000 words that characterize general conversation.

How Do I Include Academic Vocabulary and Academic English in My Teaching?

Teachers can provide students with academic vocabulary and help students understand the academic English of their text.

To develop academic English, learners must have already acquired basic proficiency in the grammar of everyday English.

Academic English should be taught within contexts that make sense. In terms of instruction, teaching academic English includes providing students with access to core curriculum—in this case Social Studies.

Academic English arises in part from social practices in which academic English is used. The acquisition of academic vocabulary and grammar is necessary to advance the development of academic English.

Tips for Teaching Academic Vocabulary:

✔ **Expose Students to Academic Vocabulary** You do not need to call attention to words students are learning because they will acquire them subconsciously.

✔ **Do Not Correct Students' Mistakes When Using the Vocabulary Words** All vocabulary understanding and spelling errors will disappear once the student reads more.

✔ **Help Students Decode the Words Themselves** Once they learn the alphabet, they should be able to decode words. Decoding each word they don't recognize will help them more than trying to focus on sentence structure. Once they can recognize the words, they can read "authentic" texts.

✔ **Do Not Ignore the English Learner in This Process** They can learn academic vocabulary before they are completely fluent in oral English.

✔ **Helping Students Build Academic Vocabulary Leads to Broader Learning** Students who have mastered the basic academic vocabulary are ready to continue acquiring words from the rest of the groups. To help determine which words are in the 2,000-word basic group, refer to *West's General Service List of English Words*, 1953. The list is designed to serve as a guide for teachers and as a checklist and goal list for students. For additional information about the list, visit: http://www.vuw.ac.nz/lals/research/awl

Guidelines for Teaching Academic Vocabulary	
1. Direct and planned instruction **2.** Models—that have increasingly difficult language **3.** Attention to form—pointing out linguistic features of words	**4.** Practice **5.** Motivation **6.** Instructional feedback **7.** Assessment—on a regular basis

Classroom Activity

Writing About Modern America

Give students a brief writing assignment. Ask them to write a short essay about one of the topics listed below in the left column. Have students use as many of the academic vocabulary words in the right column as they can in their essay. When completed, ask student volunteers to share their writing. Note what academic vocabulary words they use.

Topic	Academic Vocabulary
The challenges of reducing poverty in America	sufficient
	minimum
	medical
	income
Recent technological advances	innovate
	technology
	media
	potential
	data
	transmit

Meeting the Diverse Needs of Our Students

by Douglas Fisher, Ph.D.

Today's classroom contains students from a variety of backgrounds with a variety of learning styles, strengths, and challenges. As teachers we are facing the challenge of helping students reach their educational potential. With careful planning, you can address the needs of all students in the social studies classroom. The basis for this planning is universal access. When classrooms are planned with universal access in mind, fewer students require specific accommodations.

What Is a Universal Access Design for Learning?

Universal design was first conceived in architectural studies when business people, engineers, and architects began making considerations for physical access to buildings. The idea was to plan the environment in advance to ensure that everyone had access. As a result, the environment would not have to be changed later for people with physical disabilities, people pushing strollers, workers who had injuries, or others for whom the environment would be difficult to negotiate. The Center for Universal Design at www.design.ncsu.edu/cud defines Universal Design as:

The design of products and environments to be usable by all people, to the greatest extent possible, without the need for adaptation or specialized design.

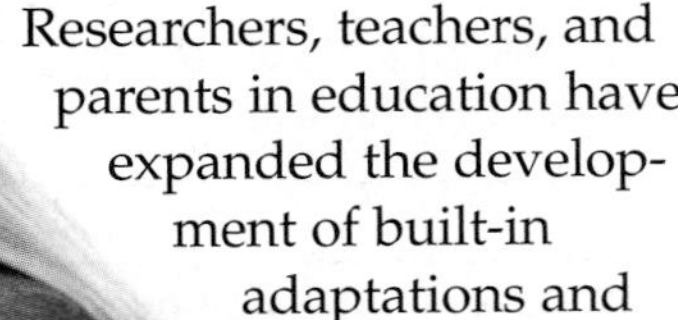

Universal Design and Access in Education

Researchers, teachers, and parents in education have expanded the development of built-in adaptations and inclusive accommodations from architectural space to the educational experience, especially in the area of curriculum.

In 1998, the National Center to Improve the Tools of Educators (NCITE), with the partnership of the Center for Applied Special Technology (CAST), proposed an expanded definition of universal design focused on education:

In terms of learning, universal design means the design of instructional materials and activities that allows the learning goals to be achievable by individuals with wide differences in their abilities to see, hear, speak, move, read, write, understand English, attend, organize, engage, and remember.

How Does Universal Design Work in Education?

Universal design and access, as they apply to education and schooling, suggest the following:

✔ **Inclusive Classroom Participation** Curriculum should be designed with all students and their needs in mind. The Glencoe/McGraw-Hill social studies texts and materials were designed with a wide range of students in mind. For example, understanding that English learners and students who struggle with reading would be using this textbook, vocabulary is specifically taught and reinforced. Similarly, the teacher-support materials provide multiple instructional points to be used depending on the needs of the students in the class. Further, the text is written such that main ideas are identified for all learners. Activating prior knowledge is also taken into consideration by the text. Connections between what students know and think about are made within the text.

- ✔ **Maximum Text Readability** In universally designed classrooms that provide access for all students, texts use direct language, clear noun-verb agreements, and clear construct-based wording. In addition to these factors, the Glencoe Social Studies text uses embedded definitions for difficult terms, provides for specific instruction in reading skills, uses a number of visual representations, and includes note-taking guides.
- ✔ **Adaptable and Accommodating** The content in this textbook can be easily translated, read aloud, or otherwise changed to meet the needs of students in the classroom. The section and end-of-chapter assessments provide students with multiple ways of demonstrating their content knowledge while also ensuring that they have practice with thinking in terms of multiple-choice questions. Critical thinking and analysis skills are also practiced.

How Is Differentiated Instruction the Key to Universal Access?

To differentiate instruction, teachers must acknowledge student differences in background knowledge and current reading, writing, and English language skills. They must also consider student learning styles and preferences, interests, and needs, and react accordingly. There are a number of general guidelines for differentiating instruction in the classroom to reach all students, including:

- ✔ **Link Assessment With Instruction** Assessments should occur before, during, and after instruction to ensure that the curriculum is aligned with what students do and do not know. Using assessments in this way allows you to plan instruction for whole groups, small groups, and individual students. Backward planning, where you establish the assessment before you begin instruction, is also important.
- ✔ **Clarify Key Concepts and Generalizations** Students need to know what is essential and how this information can be used in their future learning. In addition, students need to develop a sense of the **Big Ideas**—ideas that transcend time and place.
- ✔ **Emphasize Critical and Creative Thinking** The content, process, and products used or assigned in the classroom should require that students think about what they are learning. While some students may require support, additional motivation, varied tasks, materials, or equipment, the overall focus on critical and creative thinking allows for all students to participate in the lesson.
- ✔ **Include Teacher- and Student-Selected Tasks** A differentiated classroom includes both teacher- and student-selected activities and tasks. At some points in the lesson or day, the teacher must provide instruction and assign learning activities. In other parts of the lesson, students should be provided choices in how they engage with the content. This balance increases motivation, engagement, and learning.

How Do I Support Individual Students?

The vast majority of students will thrive in a classroom based on universal access and differentiated instruction. However, wise teachers recognize that no single option will work for all students and that there may be students who require unique systems of support to be successful.

Classroom Activity

Display a map of imperialism in Africa around 1914. Discuss with students the map's general information and have them list each country under the European power that controlled it.

To differentiate this activity:

- Have students imagine they are living in the early 1900s. Have them write a letter to a British newspaper about colonial rule in Africa.
- Have students record the number of African countries under European rule. Have them take the data and create a bar graph that shows which European powers were the most active colonizers at the time.
- Have students compose a song or poem about European rule in Africa, from an African's point of view.
- Have students choose a country of modern Africa to research. Have them write a three-page paper discussing how that country was affected by colonialism and how it has changed since the days of European rule.

Tips For Instruction

The following tips for instruction can support your efforts to help all students reach their maximum potential.

- ✔ Survey students to discover their individual differences. Use interest inventories of their unique talents so you can encourage contributions in the classroom.
- ✔ Be a model for respecting others. Adolescents crave social acceptance. The student with learning differences is especially sensitive to correction and criticism, particularly when it comes from a teacher. Your behavior will set the tone for how students treat one another.
- ✔ Expand opportunities for success. Provide a variety of instructional activities that reinforce skills and concepts.
- ✔ Establish measurable objectives and decide how you can best help students who meet them.
- ✔ Celebrate successes and make note of and praise "work in progress."
- ✔ Keep it simple. Point out problem areas if doing so can help a student effect change. Avoid overwhelming students with too many goals at one time.
- ✔ Assign cooperative group projects that challenge all students to contribute to solving a problem or creating a product.

How Do I Reach Students With Learning Disabilities?

- ✔ Provide support and structure. Clearly specify rules, assignments, and responsibilities.
- ✔ Practice skills frequently. Use games and drills to help maintain student interest.
- ✔ Incorporate many modalities into the learning process. Provide opportunities to say, hear, write, read, and act out important concepts and information.
- ✔ Link new skills and concepts to those already mastered.
- ✔ If possible, allow students to record answers on audiotape.
- ✔ Allow extra time to complete assessments and assignments.
- ✔ Let students demonstrate proficiency with alternative presentations, including oral reports, role plays, art projects, and musical presentations.
- ✔ Provide outlines, notes, or tape recordings of lecture material.
- ✔ Pair students with peer helpers, and provide class time for pair interaction.

How Do I Reach Students With Behavioral Challenges?

- ✔ Provide a structured environment with clear-cut schedules, rules, seat assignments, and safety procedures.
- ✔ Reinforce appropriate behavior and model it for students.
- ✔ Cue distracted students back to the task through verbal signals and teacher proximity.
- ✔ Set goals that can be achieved in the short term. Work for long-term improvement in the big areas.

How Do I Reach Students With Physical Challenges?

- ✔ Openly discuss with the student any uncertainties you have about when to offer aid.
- ✔ Ask parents or therapists and students what special devices or procedures are needed and whether any special safety precautions need to be taken.
- ✔ Welcome students with physical challenges into all activities, including field trips, special events, and projects.
- ✔ Provide information to assist class members and adults in their understanding of support needed.

How Do I Reach Students with Visual Impairments?

- ✔ Facilitate independence. Modify assignments as needed.
- ✔ Teach classmates how and when to serve as visual guides.
- ✔ Limit unnecessary noise in the classroom if it distracts the student with visual impairments.
- ✔ Provide tactile models whenever possible.
- ✔ Foster a spirit of inclusion. Describe people and events as they occur in the classroom. Remind classmates that the student with visual impairments cannot interpret gestures and other forms of nonverbal communication.
- ✔ Provide taped lectures and reading assignments for use outside the classroom.
- ✔ Team the student with a sighted peer for written work.

How Do I Reach Students With Hearing Impairments?

- ✔ Seat students where they can see your lip movements easily and where they can avoid any visual distractions.
- ✔ Avoid standing with your back to the window or light source.
- ✔ Use an overhead projector so you can maintain eye contact while writing information for students.
- ✔ Seat students where they can see speakers.
- ✔ Write all assignments on the board, or hand out written instructions.
- ✔ If the student has a manual interpreter, allow both student and interpreter to select the most favorable seating arrangements.
- ✔ Teach students to look directly at each other when they speak.

How Do I Reach English Learners?

- ✔ Remember, students' ability to speak English does not reflect their academic abilities.
- ✔ Try to incorporate the students' cultural experience into your instruction. The help of a bilingual aide may be effective.
- ✔ Avoid any references in your instruction that could be construed as cultural stereotypes.
- ✔ Preteach important vocabulary and concepts.
- ✔ Encourage students to preview text before they begin reading, noting headings.
- ✔ Remind students not to ignore graphic organizers, photographs, and maps since there is much information in these visuals.
- ✔ Use memorabilia and photographs whenever possible to build background knowledge and understanding. An example of this would be coins in a foreign currency or a raw cotton ball to reinforce its importance in history.

How Do I Reach Gifted Students?

- ✔ Make arrangements for students to take selected subjects early and to work on independent projects.
- ✔ Ask "what if" questions to develop high-level thinking skills. Establish an environment safe for risk taking in your classroom.
- ✔ Emphasize concepts, theories, ideas, relationships, and generalizations about the content.
- ✔ Promote interest in the past by inviting students to make connections to the present.
- ✔ Let students express themselves in alternate ways such as creative writing, acting, debates, simulations, drawing, or music.
- ✔ Provide students with a catalog of helpful resources, listing such things as agencies that provide free and inexpensive materials, appropriate community services and programs, and community experts who might be called upon to speak to your students.
- ✔ Assign extension projects that allow students to solve real-life problems related to their communities.

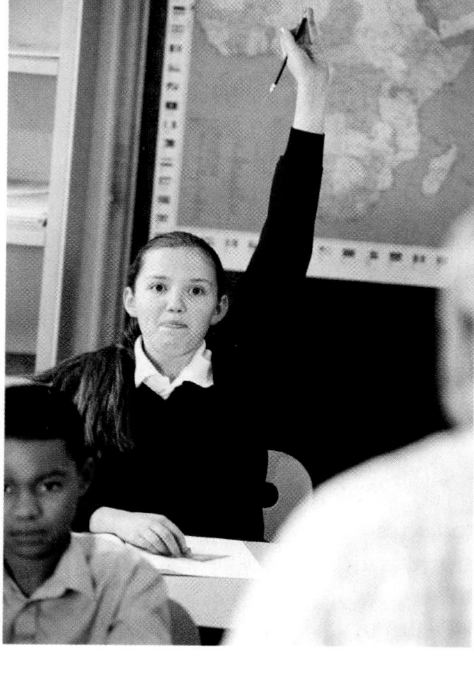

Douglas Fisher is a professor at San Diego State University, San Diego, CA.

Classroom Activity

Students respond eagerly to a subject when they can relate it to their own experiences. With the growing number of students who come from other world regions, explaining geography through a global theme (such as volcanoes) can give them a worldwide as well as a regional perspective. To develop this awareness, display a large world map. Have students use the library or the Internet to research the latitude and longitude of 15 major volcanoes around the world. Ask them to mark these locations on the map and answer the following questions:

- What patterns do you see in volcanic activity?
- What causes volcanic activity?
- Where in the world are volcanoes most active?

As a follow-up, suggest students go to http://volcano.und.nodak.edu/vwdocs/kids/legends.html to find legends about the origins of some of the world's volcanoes. Encourage students to share what they find with the class.

Classroom Solutions

Backward Mapping

How Can My Instruction Help Students Succeed in a Standards-Based System?

by Emily M. Schell, Ed.D.

Content standards articulate what students should know and be able to do in every social studies classroom. Effective instructional planning based in the standards and maximizing available resources is essential for meaningful teaching and learning of social studies. Planning instruction with educational goals in mind makes for the most effective teaching.

How Do I Map My Curriculum?

Mapping the curriculum from beginning to end, and from the end to the beginning—backward mapping—makes for solid instruction. Mapping out the curriculum allows teachers to achieve several goals. These goals include a better understanding of the standards and content-specific objectives, organization and pacing of the curriculum, and focused assessment related to specific goals and objectives.

- ✔ **Begin the Process of Curriculum Mapping** To begin, teachers analyze the body of content standards for one grade level. They then compare and contrast these standards to additional sources of information that support effective teaching and learning at that grade level and in that subject area. This process works best with same-grade colleagues who bring varying perspectives and expertise to teaching this subject. As a result of this collaboration, strengths and weaknesses of the standards become apparent. Teachers will have a better understanding of the standards and identify concerns and questions for follow-up while mapping.
- ✔ **Analyze the Organization of the Standards-Based Content** Most social studies teachers agree with researchers that history is best taught in chronological order. However, some grade-level standards either do not or cannot present the content in chronological order. Rich discussions about themes and concepts tend to emerge, and teachers identify meaningful methods for presenting complex and overlapping information. In this way students will see the connections that transcend chronology.
- ✔ **Identify the Content and Order of Teaching** A plan is developed to present certain content first, then second, then third and so on. Folding in content that is either missing from the standards or essential in building background knowledge with students enters the curriculum map as well. Outside resources brought into the classroom are good supplements.
- ✔ **Separate Overlapping Units** Identify areas of instruction for the topics, themes, big ideas, or concepts. It is at this stage that backward planning is introduced for the development of instructional units, which will support the grade-level curriculum map. The instruction must support the planned assessment.
- ✔ **Map Curriculum at Each Grade Level** Curriculum planning should be shared among grade levels. Teachers will have a better understanding of what knowledge and skills students bring to their coursework if they take into consideration what has been learned previously.

How Do I Use Backward Mapping?

After a year-long course of study is mapped out, each unit must be further developed through backward mapping. You will start with the end in mind—knowing your curricular goals and objectives at the outset, which are often found in the content standards and articulated in the curriculum maps.

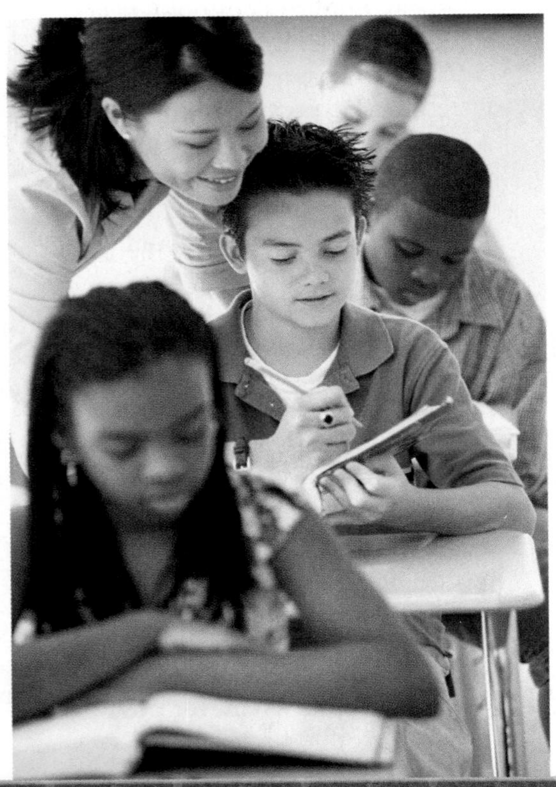

Once goals have been determined, teachers develop assessments that will show progress toward those goals and objectives. In the final step of this backward mapping process, teachers determine meaningful teaching and learning strategies and identify useful resources that support the assessment.

To use backward mapping in developing your units of instruction, consider the following steps:

Step One: Know Your Targets

First, identify exactly what students must know and do in this unit. Analyze content standards and any other resources that support curricular goals and objectives for this unit. As you plan, ask yourself:

- ✔ What do I want my students to know as a result of this unit?
- ✔ What skills will students develop during the course of this unit?
- ✔ How do I describe these goals clearly and concisely to my students so they understand where we should be at the end of this unit?
- ✔ What essential knowledge will students need to access to make sense of this information?
- ✔ Do my instructional goals align with strategies identified in the curriculum map?
- ✔ Have I introduced any Big Ideas that are pertinent to this content?

Step Two: Identify and Develop Assessments

- ✔ Second, consider the multiple forms of formal and informal assessments that will help you determine to what degree each student has achieved the stated goals and objectives seen in Step One. Some assessments are embedded throughout the instructional unit, while others come at the end of the unit. Some assessments are performance-based, while others are not. Some are authentic applications of information and skills, while others require the formal recall of information. Ask yourself:
- ✔ What do I want to know and see from each student?
- ✔ What are the best methods for students to demonstrate what they know and can do based on the goals and objectives?
- ✔ How many assessments do I need to determine what students know and can do?
- ✔ How will I balance informal and formal assessments?
- ✔ How will I assess students with diverse learning styles, skills, and abilities?
- ✔ How can I prepare and support students?
- ✔ How will these assessments promote student progress in social studies?
- ✔ At what time(s) during the unit will I administer these assessments?

Step Three: Develop Meaningful Instruction

After the assessments for the unit have been determined, consider the meaningful and effective teaching strategies that will support learning and student achievement on assessments. While developing lesson plans for instruction, ask yourself:

- ✔ How will students learn what they are expected to know?
- ✔ How will I engage students in the studies of this unit?
- ✔ In what ways might students relate or connect to this information?
- ✔ What research-based strategies will be most effective with my students and in these studies?
- ✔ How will I differentiate my instruction to meet the diverse needs of my students?
- ✔ How will I scaffold or provide access to the curriculum for my English learners?
- ✔ What vocabulary requires attention in this unit?
- ✔ How much time will I have to effectively teach this unit?
- ✔ How will I use the textbook and other resources to support the goals and objectives for this unit?
- ✔ What lessons will I develop?
- ✔ In what sequence will I teach these lessons during this unit?
- ✔ How will these lessons support the assessments from Step Two?

Step Four: Locate and Manage Resources

Effective teaching and learning of social studies requires the use of multiple forms of text and varied resources. Consider what you have available in your classroom, including your textbook, and identify resources you will add in order to teach this unit successfully. Ask yourself:

- ✔ What parts of the textbook are required for the lessons determined in Step Three?
- ✔ What ancillary materials are needed for the lessons in this unit?
- ✔ What Web sites will I recommend to students to support these lessons?
- ✔ Do I need to contact guest speakers or obtain outside resources?
- ✔ What literature resources are available to support this unit?

Emily Schell is Visiting Professor, San Diego State University; and Social Studies Education Director, SDSU City Heights Educational Collaborative, San Diego, CA

Teaching Maps, Graphs, and Charts

How Can I Use Visuals to Improve Students' Reading Comprehension?

Maps, graphs, and charts are visual tools. By using images rather than words, these tools present complex information in an easy-to-understand format. Teach students the following generalized viewing strategies, and encourage them to apply these strategies as they study each chapter.

- ✔ **Asking Questions** Students should start by looking over the graphic and asking themselves questions, such as "What is my purpose for looking at this image?" Then students can identify questions they hope to answer, such as "What is being compared?" or "What are the most important features?"
- ✔ **Finding Answers** Next, students should use the graphic's features, such as the title, labels, colors, and symbols, to help them find answers to their questions. If the source of the graphic is available, students should also determine its reliability.
- ✔ **Drawing Conclusions** After studying the visual, students should summarize its main points and draw conclusions.
- ✔ **Connecting** Students also should relate what they learned from the visual with what they gained from reading the text selection. Students can examine how the visual supports or extends the meaning of the text.

Europe: Vegetation

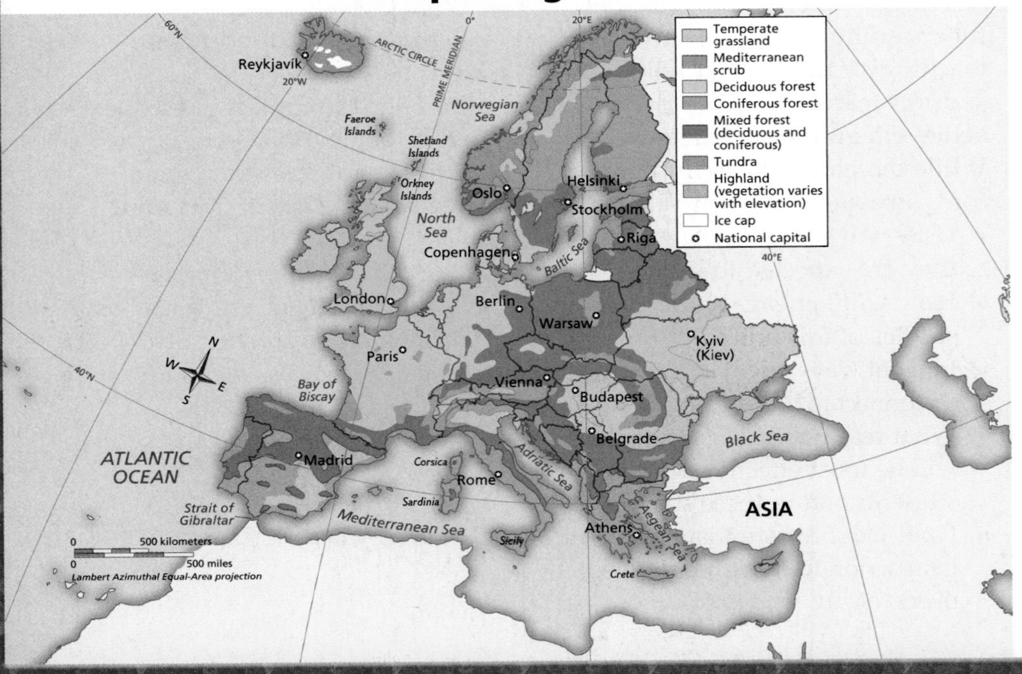

Maps

Maps show the relative size and location of specific geographic areas. Two of the most common general purpose maps are political maps and physical maps.

Parts of Maps

All maps contain parts that assist in interpreting the information. Help students learn to identify the following map parts.

- ✔ **Title** The map title identifies the area shown on the visual. The title can also identify a map's special focus.
- ✔ **Map Key** The map key, or legend, explains the symbols presented on the map, thus unlocking the map's information.
- ✔ **Compass Rose** A compass rose is a direction marker. It is a symbol that points out where the cardinal directions—north, south, east, and west—are positioned.
- ✔ **Scale** A measuring line, often called a scale bar, indicates the relationship between the distances on the map and the actual distances on Earth.
- ✔ **Latitude and Longitude** Mapmakers use lines of latitude and longitude to pinpoint exact locations on maps and globes. The imaginary horizontal lines that circle the globe from east to west are lines of latitude, also called parallels. The imaginary vertical lines are lines of longitude, also called meridians. Both parallels and meridians are measured in degrees.

Graphs

Graphs are a way of showing numbers or statistics in a clear, easy-to-read way. Because graphs summarize and present information visually, readers have an easier time understanding the data and drawing conclusions. The most common types of graphs are bar graphs, line graphs, circle graphs, and pictographs.

- ✔ **Bar Graphs** A bar graph shows how two or more subjects or statistics compare. It provides information along two sides or axes. The horizontal axis is the line across the bottom of the graph. The vertical axis is the line along the side. The bars may be either vertical or horizontal. In most cases the labels on one axis show quantity, while the labels on the opposite axis show the categories of data being compared.
- ✔ **Line Graphs** A line graph shows change over time. Like a bar graph, it organizes information along the horizontal and vertical axes. The horizontal axis usually shows passing time, such as months, years, or decades. The vertical axis usually shows quantity or amount. Sometimes more than one set of data is shown in a line graph. A double-line graph, for instance, plots data for two related quantities, which may be represented in different colors or patterns.
- ✔ **Circle Graphs** A circle graph, also called a pie graph, shows how each part or percentage relates to the whole. A circle graph enables a viewer to make comparisons between parts and to analyze the relationship of each part to the whole.
- ✔ **Pictograph** A pictograph uses rows of small symbols or pictures, each representing a parti-cular amount. Like a bar graph, a pictograph is useful for making comparisons.

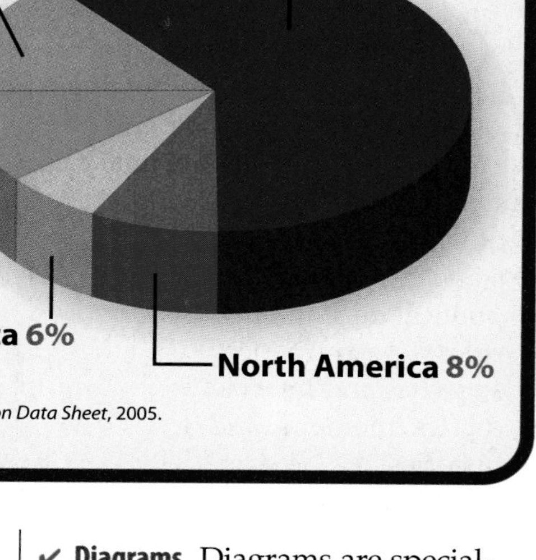

Charts

While all charts present information or data in a visual way, the type of chart is often dictated by the nature of the information and by the chartmaker's purposes.

- ✔ **Tables** Tables show information, including numerical data, in columns and rows. This organized arrangement facilitates comparisons between categories of information. Labels are usually located at the top of each column and on the left-hand side of the table.
- ✔ **Diagrams** Diagrams are specialized drawings. They can show steps in a process; point out parts of an object, organization, or idea; or explain how something works. Arrows or lines may join parts of a figure and can show relationships between parts or the flow of steps.

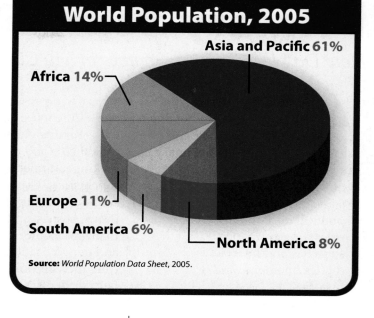

Classroom Activity

Create a Graph

Graphs can be difficult to interpret and understand. Help students by having them create their own graphs. First, separate students into small groups. Then have each group take a survey of classmates and make a graph to show their results. Suggest that students select a bar graph, line graph, circle graph, or pictograph to show their data. To prompt students' thinking, ask the following questions.

- *Do you play on a sports team? Which sport(s)?*
- *What do you plan to do after high school?*
- *About how much time do you spend watching TV each day? About how much time did you spend on TV when you were 10 years old? When you were five years old?*

After students have these graphs completed, invite each group to share its work. Discuss the types of graphs students made and their reasons for choosing them. Each group should then take the graph done by another group and transfer the information to another type of graph.

Classroom Solutions

Primary Source Strategies

How Do I Use Primary Sources in My Classroom?

A primary source is an oral or written account obtained from actual participants in an event. Examples of primary sources include the following:

- ✔ official documents (records, statistics)
- ✔ political declarations, laws, and rules for governance
- ✔ speeches and interviews
- ✔ diaries, memoirs, and oral histories
- ✔ autobiographies
- ✔ recipes and cookbooks
- ✔ advertisements and posters
- ✔ letters
- ✔ Physical objects, such as tools, dishes, fine art, photographs, maps, films, and videotapes
- ✔ songs and audio recordings

Why Use Primary Sources in Your Classroom?

Using primary sources transforms the study of social studies from a passive process to an active one. Students become investigators—finding clues, formulating hypotheses and drawing inferences, making judgments, and reaching conclusions. Using primary sources, students can think critically about events, issues, and concepts rather than just memorizing dates, names, and generalizations. Thinking critically then becomes a habit that can help students become good citizens.

How Do I Introduce Students to Primary Sources?

Carefully explain the nature of primary sources to students. Alert students to the fact that primary sources contain biases and prejudices and must be approached with caution. Every primary source reflects the creator's point of view. Students must consider the authorship and why the primary source was written.

Choosing Primary Sources

Expose students to a variety of sources, including historic photographs, folk or popular music, financial records as well as letters, journals, and historic documents.

When choosing print sources, consider the interests and reading levels of your students. Many texts contain challenging vocabulary and unfamiliar sentence structure. You may need to create a reader's guide that defines key vocabulary and paraphrases the main points of the reading.

Some documents may be too long. Decide whether using an excerpt will provide enough information for students to draw conclusions. You also may need to provide different primary sources to expose students to a variety of perspectives.

Decide how students will access the primary sources: through the Internet, the library, a museum, or other print resources. Consider the possibility of an Internet virtual field trip for students. Students can visit museum sites and other Web pages to view artifacts, interpret data, and read journals, letters, and official documents.

Interpreting a Primary Source

Before students interpret a primary source, they need to know the source's context. Then they can use guidelines, such as those below, to help them analyze and interpret the primary source.

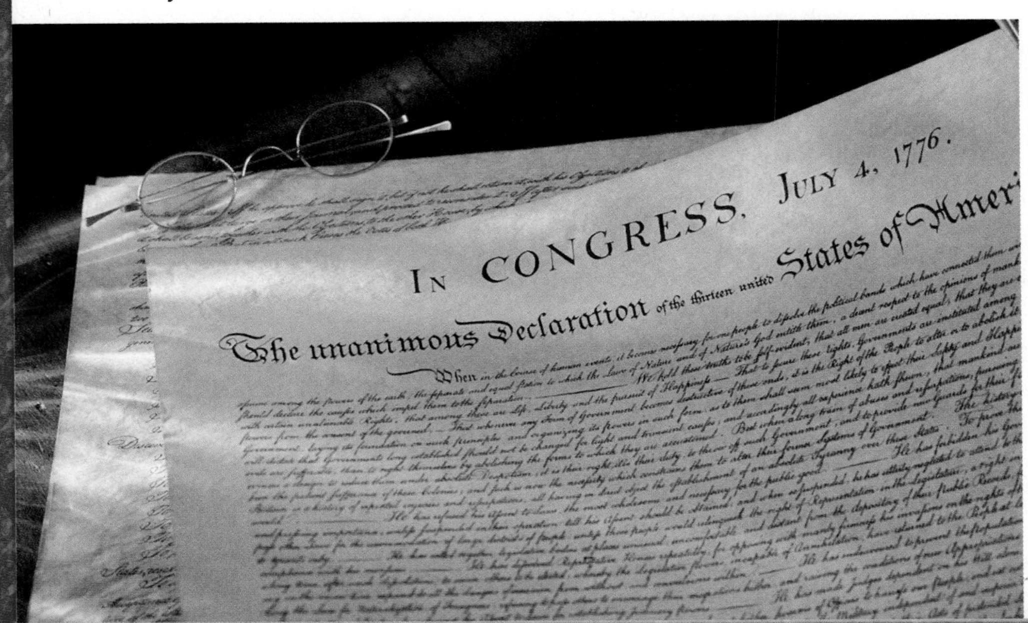

Interpreting a Primary Source

Print Sources

- Who created the source, and what was the purpose for doing so?
- Did the writer personally experience or witness the event(s)?
- Who was the intended audience?
- Was the writer trying to record facts, express an opinion, or persuade others to take action?
- What bias does it reflect?
- What information about the topic can you gather from this document?
- Compare this document with what you know about the topic. Does it confirm those ideas or introduce a new perspective?
- How might other accounts about this topic support or modify the message this source delivers?

Visual Sources

- Who created the source, and what was the purpose for doing so?
- What does the image show?
- Who or what dominates the image or catches your eye?
- How does the view impact the message?
- What is excluded from view?
- What bias does the visual reflect?
- What information about the topic can you gather from this visual?
- How might other visuals about this topic support or modify the message this one delivers?

Audio Sources

- Who created the source? What was the purpose for creating this source?
- What is the main idea of the audio?
- What bias does the audio text reflect?
- What information about the topic can you gather from this audio source?
- Compare the information in this source with what you already know about the topic. Does it confirm those ideas or introduce a new perspective?
- How might other sources about this topic support or modify the message that this one delivers?

Exploring Information

Provide a variety of primary sources related to a topic or time period. Have students compare and contrast the items, analyzing the information, making inferences, and drawing conclusions about the period.

Evaluation Activities

Have students evaluate a primary source and tell how it supports or refutes what they learned in the textbook, or have students read a primary source document that provides one perspective on a topic and have students write their own account, presenting another perspective or opinion.

Prereading Activities

Present a primary source for students to study at the beginning of a new chapter or topic. Have students analyze the source, using the questions and guidelines presented above. Then have students make predictions about what they might learn in the upcoming lessons.

Classroom Activity

Use this activity to explore the use of primary sources. This activity is especially beneficial when a less-proficient reader is paired with a more-proficient reader.

1. Before class make a list of student reading partners. Make sure one of the two is a good reader.
2. Have students read a primary source document, taking turns as they go. They should "mark" any words that they do not understand.
3. After each paragraph, the student pair should stop and restate what it says in their own words.
4. Students should look up unfamiliar words they've marked and create an illustrated dictionary entry for each term.
5. Ask student pairs to present their paraphrased primary source to the rest of the class.

Classroom Solutions

Test-Taking Strategies

How Can I Help My Students Succeed on Tests?

It's not enough for students to learn social studies facts and concepts—they must be able to show what they know in a variety of test-taking situations.

How Can I Help My Students Do Well on Objective Tests?

Objective tests may include multiple choice, true/false, and matching questions. Applying the following strategies can help students do their best on objective tests.

How Can I Help My Students Do Well on Essay Tests?

Essay tests require students to provide well-organized written responses, in addition to telling what they know. Help students use the following strategies on essay tests.

- ✔ **Analyze** To analyze means to systematically and critically examine all parts of an issue or event.
- ✔ **Classify or Categorize** To classify or categorize means to put people, things, or ideas into groups, based on a common set of characteristics.
- ✔ **Compare and Contrast** To compare is to show how things are similar, or alike. To contrast is to show how things are different.
- ✔ **Describe** To describe means to present a sketch or impression. Rich details, especially details that appeal to the senses, flesh out a description.
- ✔ **Discuss** To discuss means to systematically write about all sides of an issue or event.
- ✔ **Evaluate** To evaluate means to make a judgment and support it with evidence.
- ✔ **Explain** To explain means to clarify or make plain.
- ✔ **Illustrate** To illustrate means to provide examples or to show with a picture or other graphic.
- ✔ **Infer** To infer means to read between the lines or to use knowledge and experience to draw conclusions.
- ✔ **Justify** To justify means to prove or to support a position with specific facts and reasons.
- ✔ **Predict** To predict means to tell what will happen in the future, based on an understanding of prior events and behaviors.
- ✔ **State** To state means to briefly and concisely present information.
- ✔ **Summarize** To summarize means to give a brief overview of the main points of an issue or event.
- ✔ **Trace** To trace means to present the steps in sequential order.

Objective Texts

Multiple-Choice Questions

- Students should read the directions carefully to learn what answer the test requires—the best answer or the right answer. This is especially important when answer choices include "all of the above" or "none of the above."
- Advise students to watch for negative words in the questions, such as not, except, unless, never, and so forth. If the question contains a negative, the correct answer choice is the one that does not fit.
- Students should try to mentally answer the question before reading the answer choices.
- Students should read all the answer choices and cross out those that are obviously wrong. Then they should choose an answer from those that remain.

True/False Questions

- It is important that students read the entire question before answering. For an answer to be true, the entire statement must be true. If one part of a statement is false, the answer should be marked False.
- Remind students to watch for words like all, never, every, and always. Statements containing these words are often false.

Matching Questions

- Students should read through both lists before they mark any answers.
- Unless an answer can be used more than once, students should cross out each choice as they use it.
- Using what they know about grammar can help students find the right answer. For instance, when matching a word with its definition, the definition is often the same part of speech (noun, verb, adjective, and so forth) as the word.

Read the Question

The key to writing successful essay responses lies in reading and interpreting questions correctly. Teach students to identify and underline key words in the questions, and to use these words to guide them in understanding what the question asks. Help students understand the meaning of some of the most common key words, listed in the chart on the previous page.

Plan and Write the Essay

After students understand the question, they should follow the writing process to develop their answer. Encourage students to follow the steps below to plan and write their essays.

1. **Map out an answer.** Make lists, webs, or an outline to plan the response.

↓

2. **Decide on an order** in which to present the main points.

↓

3. **Write an opening statement** that directly responds to the essay question.

↓

4. **Write the essay.** Expand on the opening statement. Support key points with specific facts, details, and reasons.

↓

5. **Write a closing statement** that brings the main points together.

↓

6. **Proofread** to check for spelling, grammar, and punctuation.

How Can I Help My Students Prepare for Standardized Tests?

Students can follow the steps below to prepare for standardized assessments they are required to take.

- ✔ **Read About the Test** Students can familiarize themselves with the format of the test, the types of questions that will be asked, and the amount of time they will have to complete the test. Emphasize that it is very important for students to budget their time during test-taking.
- ✔ **Review the Content** Consistent study throughout the school year will help students build social studies knowledge and understanding. If there are specific objectives or standards that are tested on the exam, help students review these facts or skills to be sure they are proficient.
- ✔ **Practice** Provide practice, ideally with real released tests, to build students' familiarity with the content, format, and timing of the real exam. Students should practice all the types of questions they will encounter on the test.
- ✔ **Pace** Students should pace themselves differently depending on how the test is administered. If the test is timed, students should not allow themselves to become stuck on any one question. If the test is untimed, students should work slowly and carefully. If students have trouble with an item, they should mark it and come back to it later.
- ✔ **Analyze Practice Results** Help students improve test-taking performance by analyzing their test-taking strengths and weaknesses.

Spend time discussing students' completed practice tests. Help students identify what kinds of questions they had the most difficulty with. Look for patterns in errors and then tailor instruction to review appropriate skills or content.

Classroom Activity

Below is an example of an assessment review activity. Reviewing graded tests is a great way for students to assess their test-taking skills. It also helps teachers teach test-taking strategies and review content. As the class rereads each test question, guide students to think logically about their answer choices. Show students how to:

1. Read each question carefully to determine its meaning.
2. Look for key words in the question to support their answers.
3. Recognize synonyms in the answer choices that may match phrases in the question.
4. Narrow down answer choices by eliminating ones that don't make sense.
5. Anticipate the answer before looking at the answer choices.
6. Circle questions of which they are unsure and go back to them later. Sometimes a clue will be found in another question on the test.

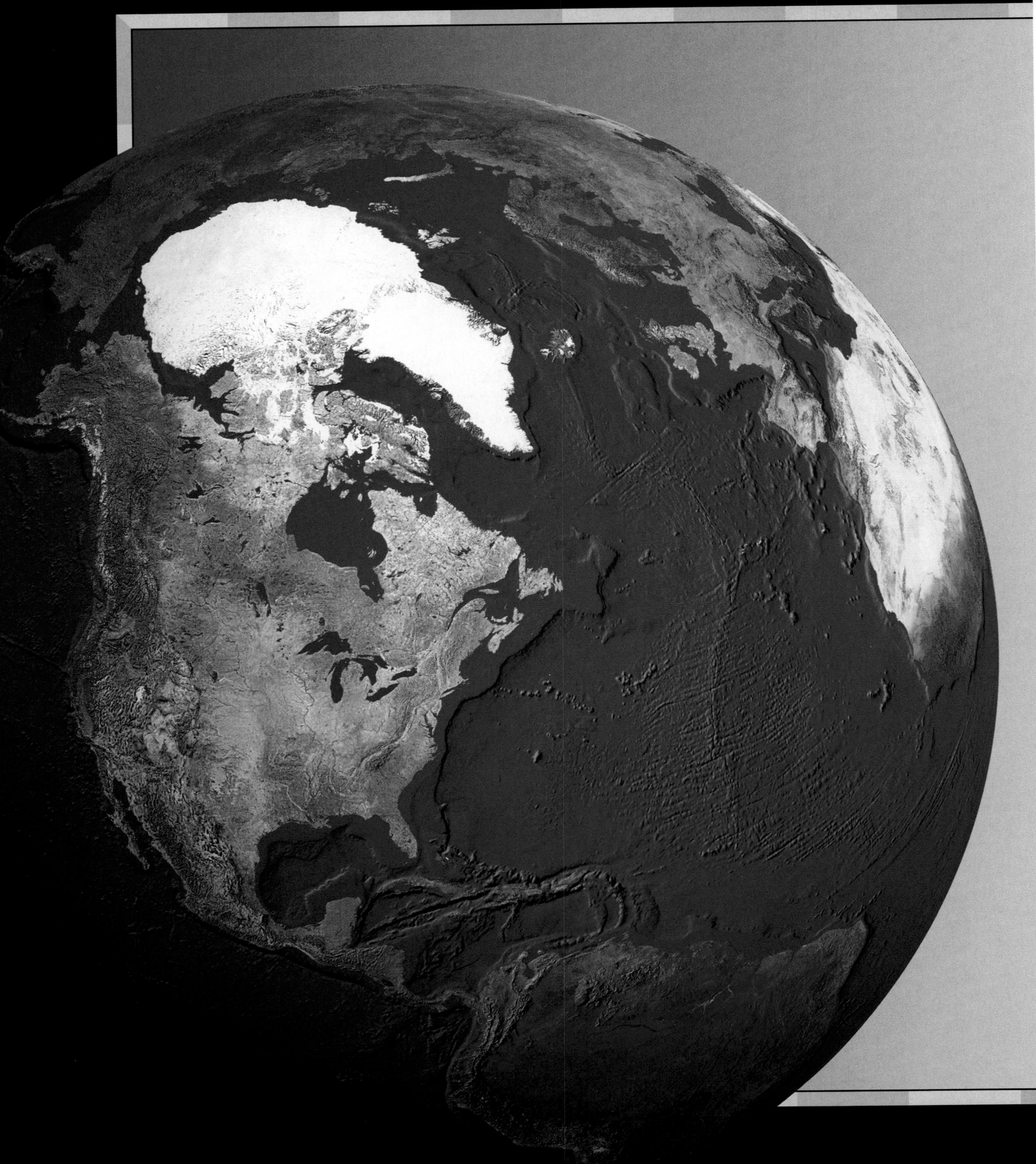

Reference Atlas

ATLAS KEY

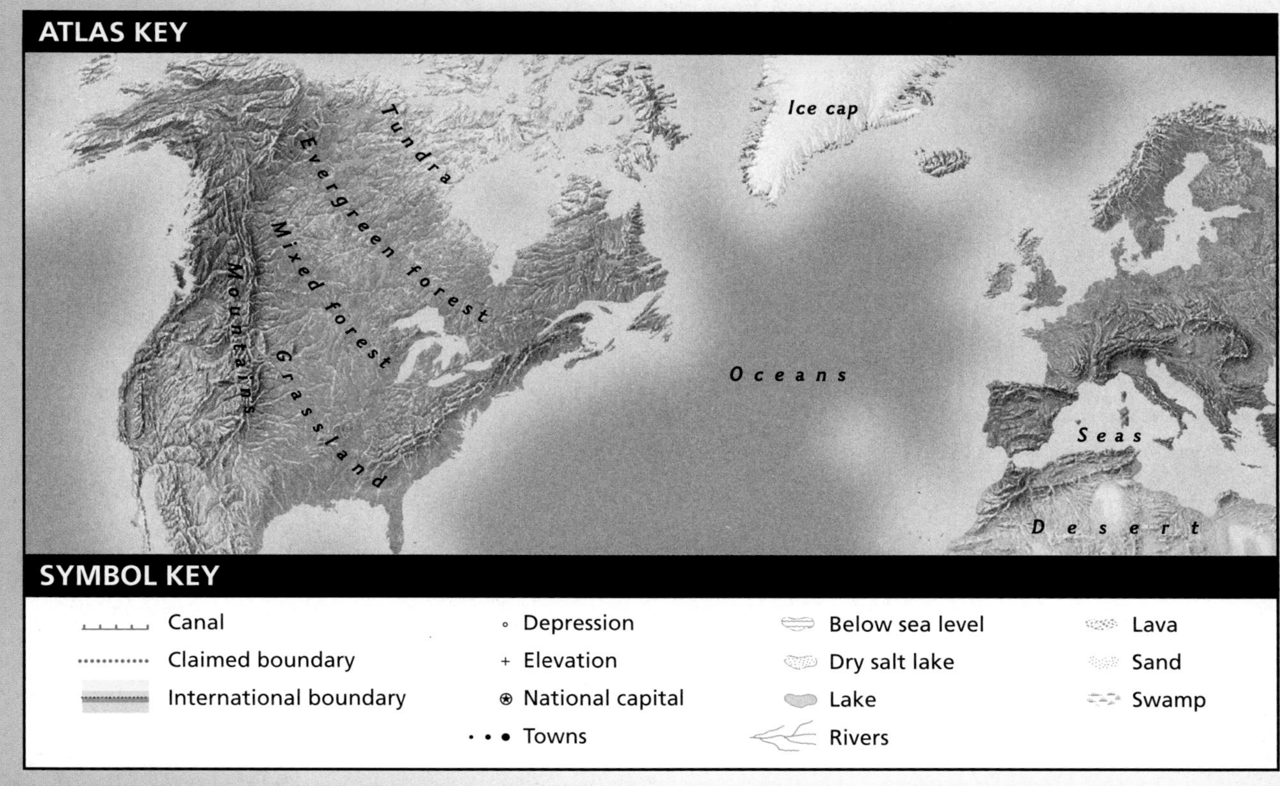

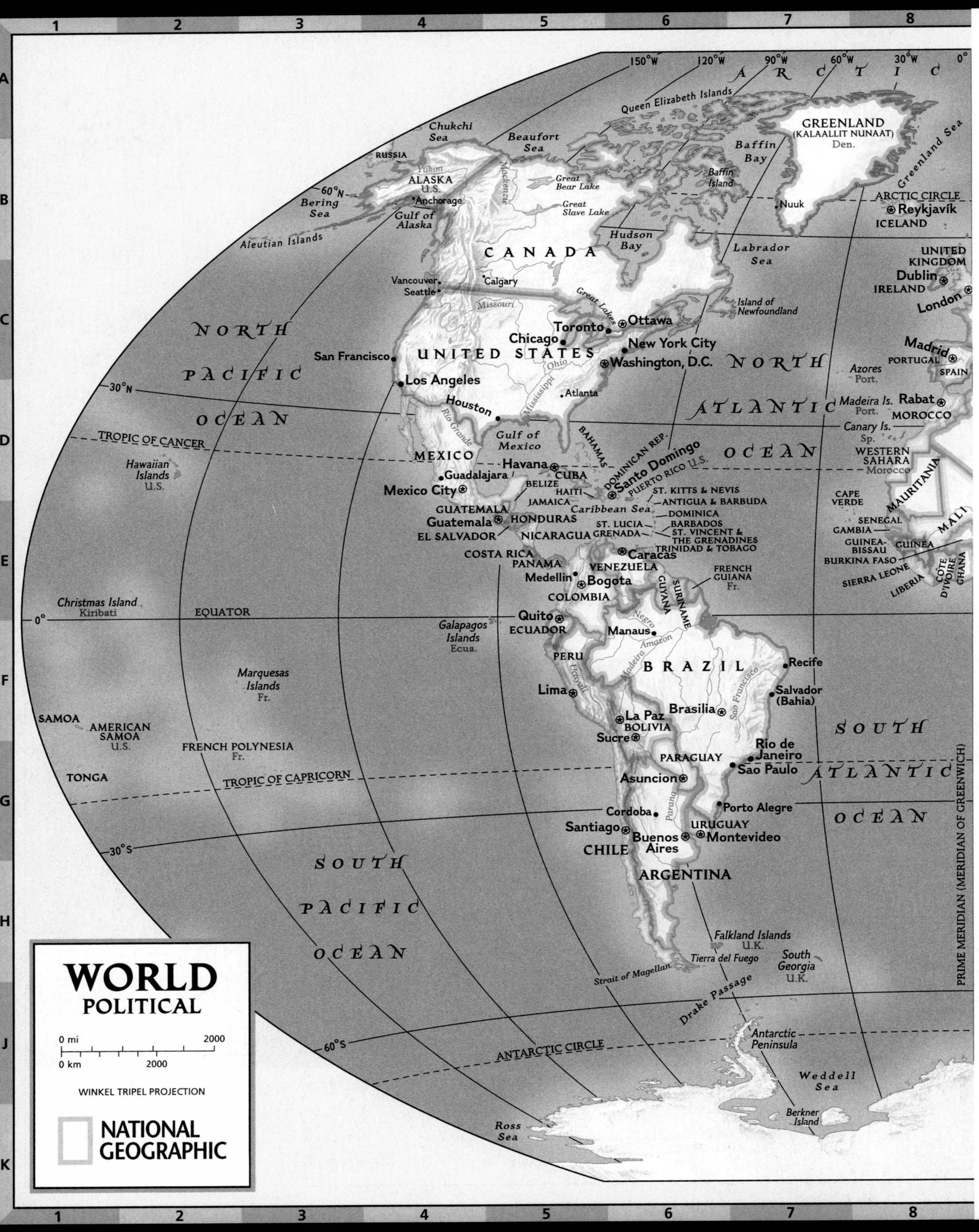

WORLD
POLITICAL
0 mi 2000
0 km 2000
WINKEL TRIPEL PROJECTION
NATIONAL GEOGRAPHIC
ARCTIC
GREENLAND (KALAALLIT NUNAAT) Den.
Queen Elizabeth Islands
Baffin Bay
Baffin Island
Greenland Sea
ARCTIC CIRCLE
Reykjavík
ICELAND
Nuuk
Chukchi Sea
Beaufort Sea
RUSSIA
ALASKA U.S.
Anchorage
Bering Sea
Gulf of Alaska
Aleutian Islands
Great Bear Lake
Great Slave Lake
Hudson Bay
Labrador Sea
CANADA
UNITED KINGDOM
Dublin
IRELAND
London
Vancouver
Seattle
Calgary
Island of Newfoundland
Ottawa
Toronto
Chicago
New York City
Washington, D.C.
San Francisco
UNITED STATES
Los Angeles
Atlanta
Houston
NORTH PACIFIC OCEAN
NORTH ATLANTIC OCEAN
Madrid
PORTUGAL
SPAIN
Azores Port.
Madeira Is. Port.
Rabat
MOROCCO
Canary Is. Sp.
WESTERN SAHARA Morocco
TROPIC OF CANCER
Hawaiian Islands U.S.
Gulf of Mexico
BAHAMAS
MEXICO
Havana
CUBA
Guadalajara
Mexico City
BELIZE
HAITI
JAMAICA
DOMINICAN REP.
Santo Domingo
PUERTO RICO U.S.
ST. KITTS & NEVIS
ANTIGUA & BARBUDA
DOMINICA
BARBADOS
ST. VINCENT & THE GRENADINES
TRINIDAD & TOBAGO
ST. LUCIA
GRENADA
Caribbean Sea
GUATEMALA
Guatemala
HONDURAS
EL SALVADOR
NICARAGUA
COSTA RICA
PANAMA
Caracas
VENEZUELA
CAPE VERDE
MAURITANIA
SENEGAL
GAMBIA
GUINEA-BISSAU
GUINEA
MALI
BURKINA FASO
SIERRA LEONE
LIBERIA
CÔTE D'IVOIRE
GHANA
FRENCH GUIANA Fr.
GUYANA
SURINAME
Medellín
Bogota
COLOMBIA
Christmas Island Kiribati
EQUATOR
Quito
ECUADOR
Galapagos Islands Ecua.
Manaus
Amazon
Negro
Madeira
PERU
BRAZIL
Recife
Salvador (Bahia)
Marquesas Islands Fr.
Lima
Brasilia
La Paz
BOLIVIA
Sucre
SAMOA
AMERICAN SAMOA U.S.
FRENCH POLYNESIA Fr.
TONGA
Rio de Janeiro
Sao Paulo
PARAGUAY
Asuncion
TROPIC OF CAPRICORN
SOUTH ATLANTIC OCEAN
Porto Alegre
Cordoba
Santiago
Buenos Aires
URUGUAY
Montevideo
CHILE
ARGENTINA
SOUTH PACIFIC OCEAN
Falkland Islands U.K.
Tierra del Fuego
South Georgia U.K.
Strait of Magellan
Drake Passage
ANTARCTIC CIRCLE
Antarctic Peninsula
Weddell Sea
Ross Sea
Berkner Island
PRIME MERIDIAN (MERIDIAN OF GREENWICH)

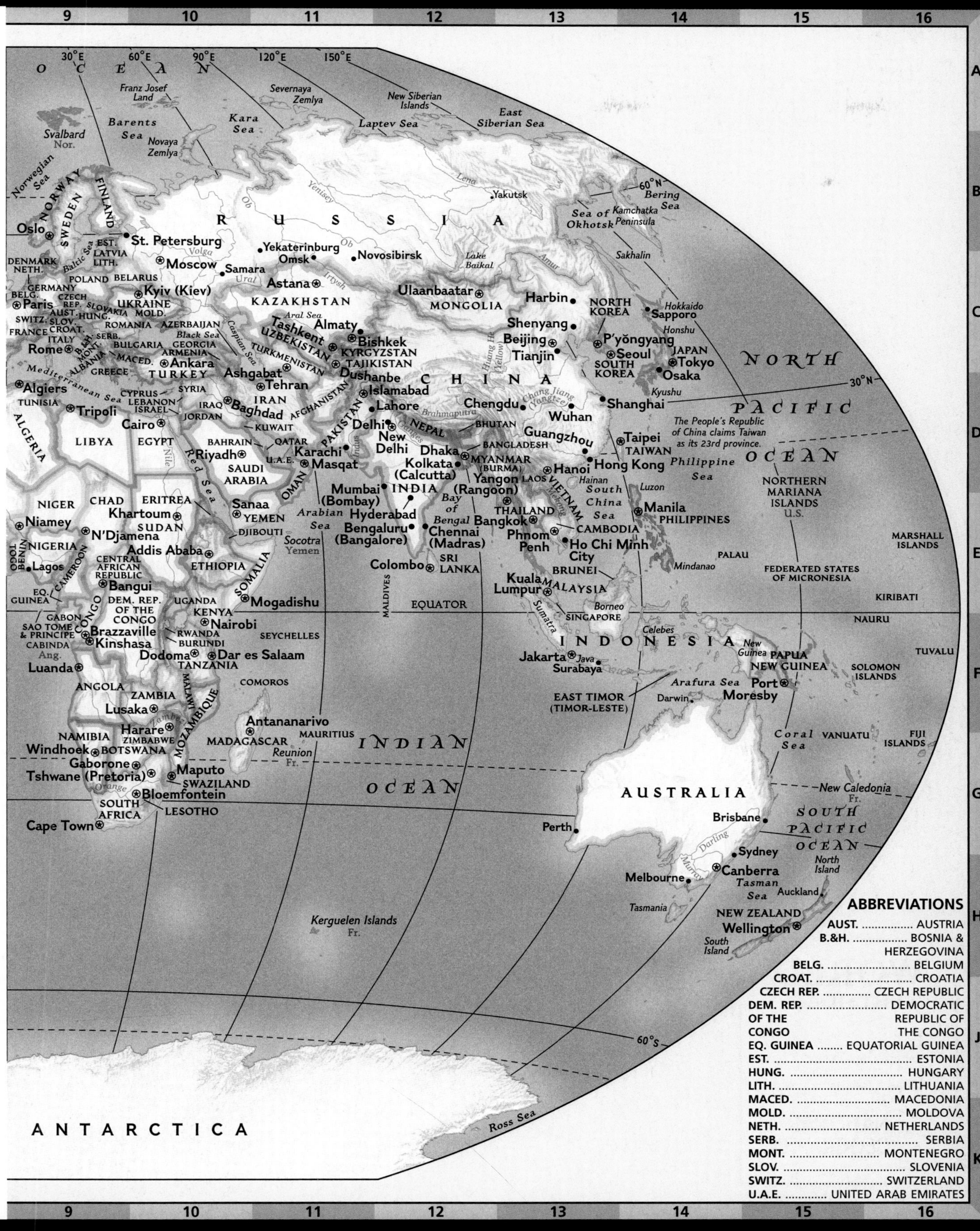

ABBREVIATIONS

AUST.	AUSTRIA
B.&H.	BOSNIA & HERZEGOVINA
BELG.	BELGIUM
CROAT.	CROATIA
CZECH REP.	CZECH REPUBLIC
DEM. REP. OF THE CONGO	DEMOCRATIC REPUBLIC OF THE CONGO
EQ. GUINEA	EQUATORIAL GUINEA
EST.	ESTONIA
HUNG.	HUNGARY
LITH.	LITHUANIA
MACED.	MACEDONIA
MOLD.	MOLDOVA
NETH.	NETHERLANDS
SERB.	SERBIA
MONT.	MONTENEGRO
SLOV.	SLOVENIA
SWITZ.	SWITZERLAND
U.A.E.	UNITED ARAB EMIRATES

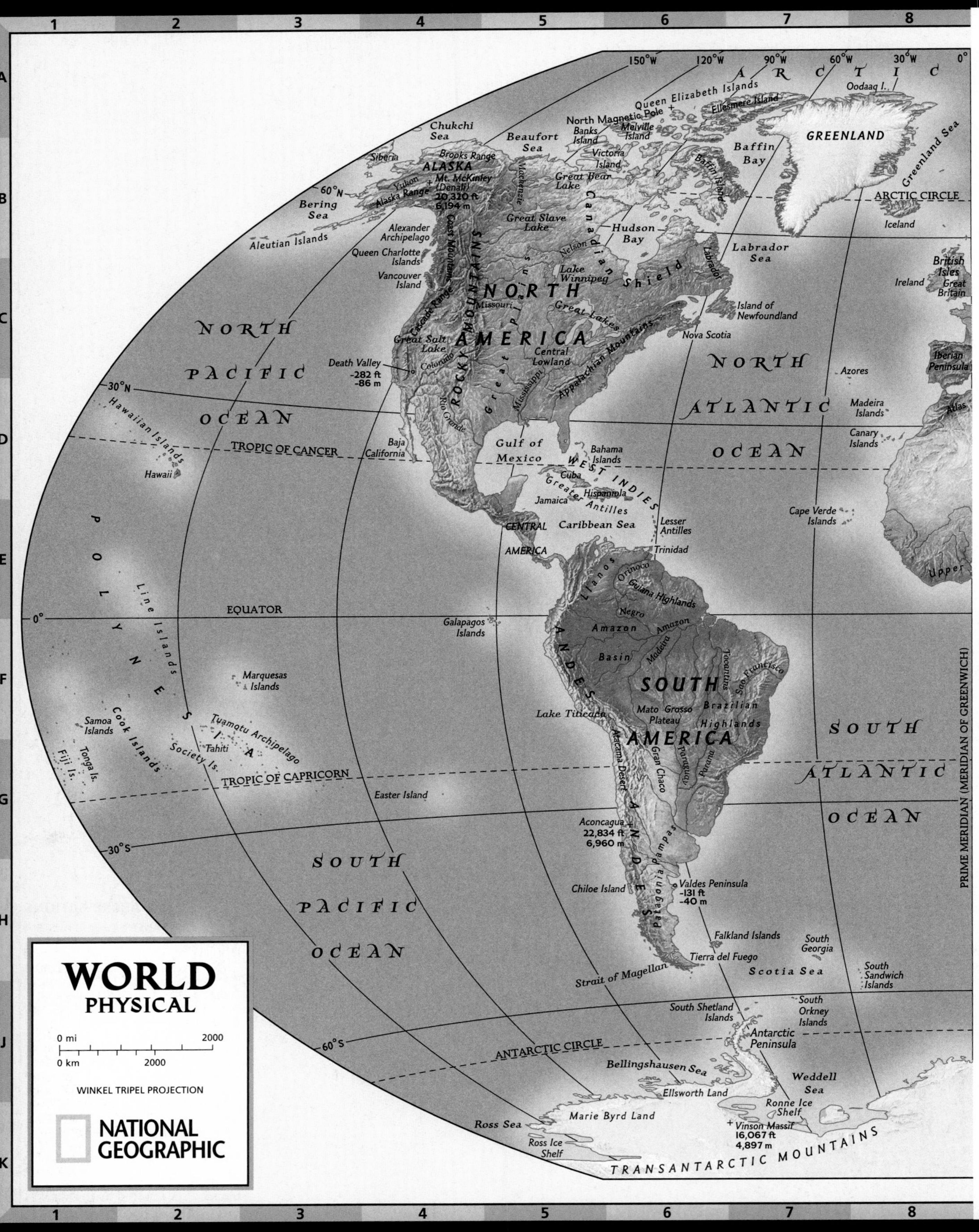

WORLD
PHYSICAL
0 mi 2000
0 km 2000
WINKEL TRIPEL PROJECTION
NATIONAL GEOGRAPHIC
1 2 3 4 5 6 7 8
A B C D E F G H J K
150°W
120°W
90°W
60°W
30°W
0°
60°N
30°N
0°
30°S
60°S
ARCTIC
Queen Elizabeth Islands
Ellesmere Island
Oodaaq I.
North Magnetic Pole
Banks Island
Melville Island
Victoria Island
Chukchi Sea
Beaufort Sea
Baffin Bay
Baffin Island
GREENLAND
Greenland Sea
ARCTIC CIRCLE
Iceland
Siberia
Brooks Range
ALASKA
Mt. McKinley (Denali) 20,320 ft 6,194 m
Yukon
Alaska Range
Mackenzie
Great Bear Lake
Bering Sea
Aleutian Islands
Alexander Archipelago
Queen Charlotte Islands
Vancouver Island
Coast Mountains
Great Slave Lake
Canadian Shield
Hudson Bay
Nelson
Labrador Sea
Labrador
Lake Winnipeg
British Isles
Ireland
Great Britain
NORTH AMERICA
ROCKY MOUNTAINS
Great Plains
Missouri
Cascade Range
Great Lakes
Island of Newfoundland
Nova Scotia
Great Salt Lake
Colorado
Central Lowland
Appalachian Mountains
Mississippi
Death Valley -282 ft -86 m
NORTH PACIFIC OCEAN
NORTH ATLANTIC OCEAN
Iberian Peninsula
Azores
Madeira Islands
Atlas
Rio Grande
Hawaiian Islands
Hawaii
TROPIC OF CANCER
Baja California
Gulf of Mexico
Bahama Islands
WEST INDIES
Cuba
Hispaniola
Greater Antilles
Jamaica
Canary Islands
Cape Verde Islands
CENTRAL AMERICA
Caribbean Sea
Lesser Antilles
Trinidad
Upper
POLYNESIA
Line Islands
EQUATOR
Llanos
Orinoco
Guiana Highlands
Negro
Amazon
Amazon Basin
Madeira
Galapagos Islands
ANDES
Tocantins
São Francisco
SOUTH AMERICA
Marquesas Islands
Lake Titicaca
Mato Grosso Plateau
Brazilian Highlands
Samoa Islands
Cook Islands
Tuamotu Archipelago
Tahiti
Society Is.
Tonga Is.
Fiji Is.
Atacama Desert
Gran Chaco
Paraguay
Paraná
SOUTH ATLANTIC OCEAN
PRIME MERIDIAN (MERIDIAN OF GREENWICH)
TROPIC OF CAPRICORN
Easter Island
Aconcagua 22,834 ft 6,960 m
Pampas
SOUTH PACIFIC OCEAN
Chiloe Island
Valdes Peninsula -131 ft -40 m
Patagonia
Falkland Islands
South Georgia
Tierra del Fuego
Scotia Sea
South Sandwich Islands
Strait of Magellan
South Shetland Islands
South Orkney Islands
Antarctic Peninsula
ANTARCTIC CIRCLE
Bellingshausen Sea
Weddell Sea
Ellsworth Land
Ronne Ice Shelf
Marie Byrd Land
Ross Sea
Vinson Massif 16,067 ft 4,897 m
Ross Ice Shelf
TRANSANTARCTIC MOUNTAINS

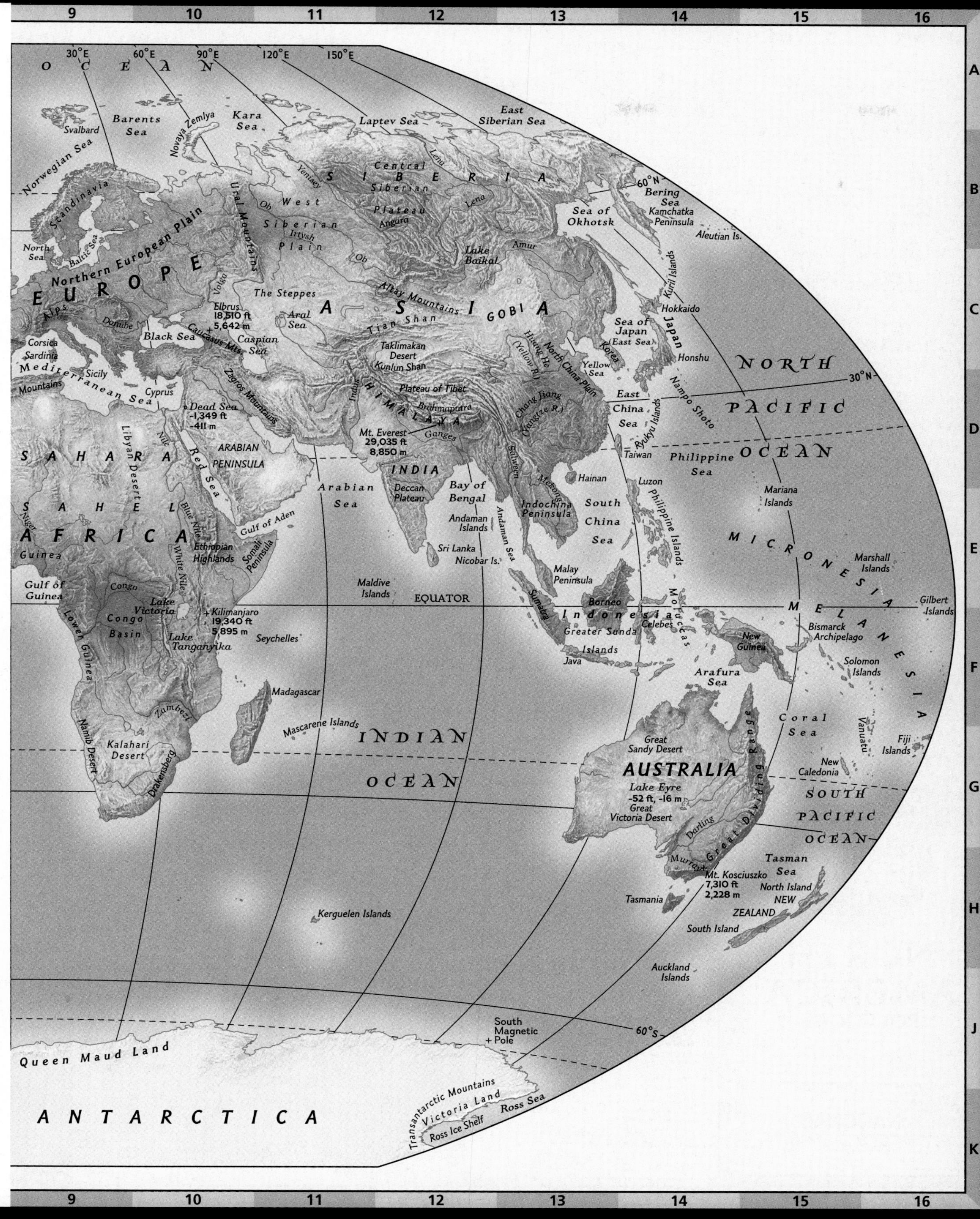

Barents Sea
Svalbard
Novaya Zemlya
Kara Sea
Laptev Sea
East Siberian Sea
Norwegian Sea
Scandinavia
North Sea
Baltic Sea
Northern European Plain
EUROPE
Alps
Danube
Ural Mountains
Volga
West Siberian Plain
Ob
Irtysh
Central Siberian Plateau
SIBERIA
Yenisey
Lena
Angara
Lake Baikal
Amur
Sea of Okhotsk
Bering Sea
Kamchatka Peninsula
Aleutian Is.
Kuril Islands
Hokkaido
Japan
Honshu
Sea of Japan (East Sea)
Korea
Yellow Sea
Nampo Shoto
The Steppes
Elbrus 18,510 ft 5,642 m
Aral Sea
ASIA
Altay Mountains
GOBI
Tian Shan
Huang He (Yellow R.)
North China Plain
Corsica
Sardinia
Black Sea
Caucasus Mts.
Caspian Sea
Taklimakan Desert
Kunlun Shan
Plateau of Tibet
Mediterranean Sea
Sicily
Mountains
Cyprus
Zagros Mountains
Indus
HIMALAYA
Brahmaputra
Chang Jiang (Yangtze R.)
East China Sea
Ryukyu Islands
NORTH PACIFIC OCEAN
Dead Sea -1,349 ft -411 m
Libyan Desert
Nile
Mt. Everest 29,035 ft 8,850 m
Ganges
SAHARA
ARABIAN PENINSULA
Red Sea
INDIA
Taiwan
Philippine Sea
SAHEL
Niger
Blue Nile
Arabian Sea
Deccan Plateau
Bay of Bengal
Salween
Mekong
Hainan
Luzon
Indochina Peninsula
South China Sea
Philippine Islands
Mariana Islands
AFRICA
Gulf of Aden
Ethiopian Highlands
Somali Peninsula
White Nile
Andaman Islands
Andaman Sea
Sri Lanka
Nicobar Is.
MICRONESIA
Marshall Islands
Guinea
Gulf of Guinea
Congo
Lake Victoria
Maldive Islands
EQUATOR
Malay Peninsula
Borneo
Moluccas
Gilbert Islands
Congo Basin
Kilimanjaro 19,340 ft 5,895 m
Lake Tanganyika
Seychelles
Sumatra
Indonesia
Celebes
Greater Sunda Islands
Java
MELANESIA
Bismarck Archipelago
New Guinea
Solomon Islands
Lower Guinea
Arafura Sea
Madagascar
Zambezi
Mascarene Islands
INDIAN OCEAN
Coral Sea
Vanuatu
Fiji Islands
Namib Desert
Kalahari Desert
Drakensberg
Great Sandy Desert
AUSTRALIA
Great Dividing Range
New Caledonia
Lake Eyre -52 ft, -16 m
Great Victoria Desert
SOUTH PACIFIC OCEAN
Darling
Murray
Tasman Sea
Mt. Kosciuszko 7,310 ft 2,228 m
North Island
NEW ZEALAND
Tasmania
Kerguelen Islands
South Island
Auckland Islands
South Magnetic Pole
Queen Maud Land
Transantarctic Mountains
Victoria Land
Ross Sea
Ross Ice Shelf
ANTARCTICA
30°E
60°E
90°E
120°E
150°E
60°N
30°N
60°S
OCEAN
9
10
11
12
13
14
15
16
A
B
C
D
E
F
G
H
J
K

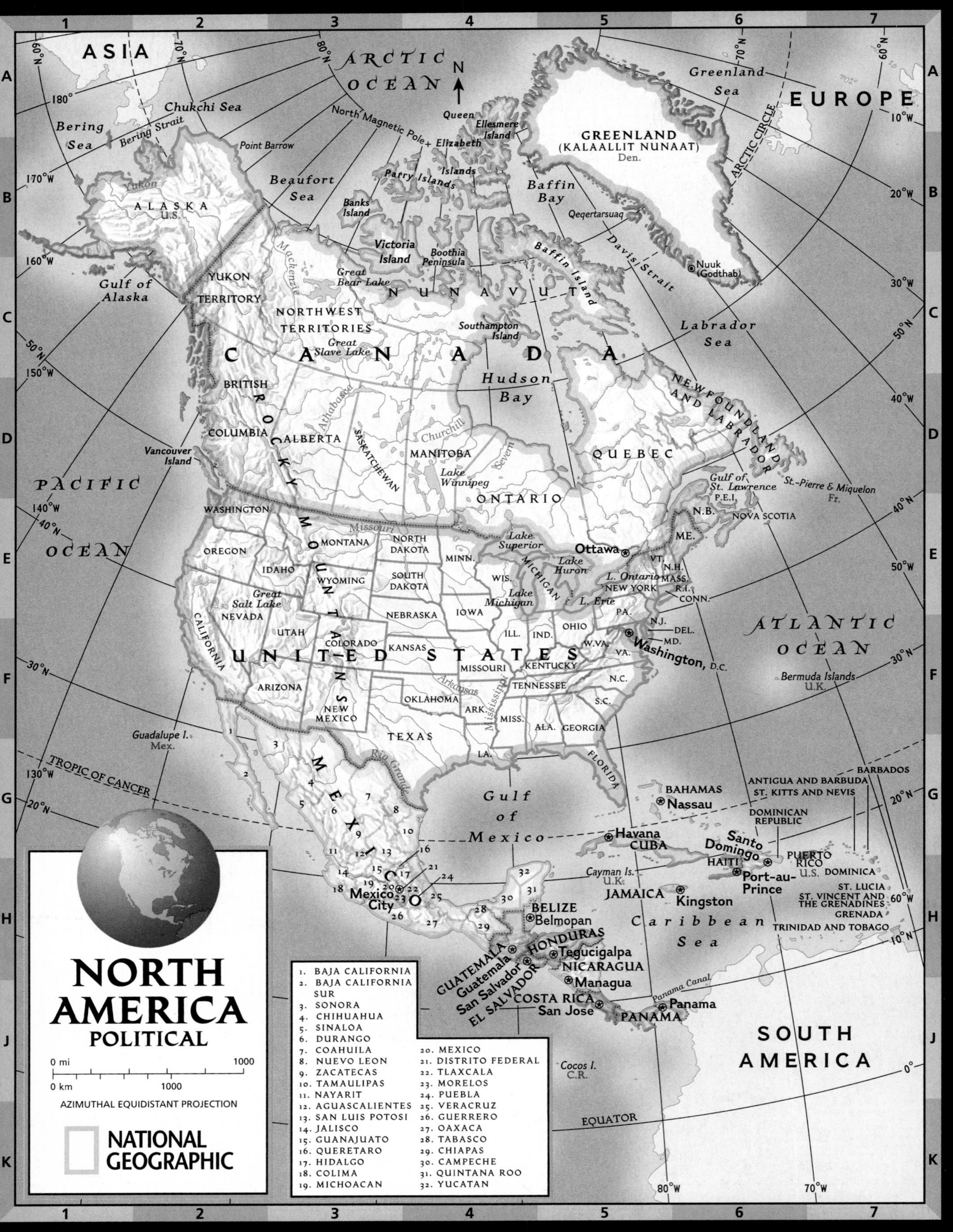
NORTH AMERICA
POLITICAL
0 mi 1000
0 km 1000
AZIMUTHAL EQUIDISTANT PROJECTION
NATIONAL GEOGRAPHIC
1. BAJA CALIFORNIA
2. BAJA CALIFORNIA SUR
3. SONORA
4. CHIHUAHUA
5. SINALOA
6. DURANGO
7. COAHUILA
8. NUEVO LEON
9. ZACATECAS
10. TAMAULIPAS
11. NAYARIT
12. AGUASCALIENTES
13. SAN LUIS POTOSI
14. JALISCO
15. GUANAJUATO
16. QUERETARO
17. HIDALGO
18. COLIMA
19. MICHOACAN
20. MEXICO
21. DISTRITO FEDERAL
22. TLAXCALA
23. MORELOS
24. PUEBLA
25. VERACRUZ
26. GUERRERO
27. OAXACA
28. TABASCO
29. CHIAPAS
30. CAMPECHE
31. QUINTANA ROO
32. YUCATAN
ASIA
ARCTIC OCEAN
N
EUROPE
Greenland Sea
GREENLAND
(KALAALLIT NUNAAT)
Den.
ARCTIC CIRCLE
Chukchi Sea
Bering Sea
Bering Strait
Point Barrow
North Magnetic Pole
Queen Elizabeth Islands
Ellesmere Island
Parry Islands
Beaufort Sea
Banks Island
Victoria Island
Boothia Peninsula
Baffin Bay
Qeqertarsuaq
Davis Strait
Baffin Island
Nuuk (Godthab)
ALASKA
U.S.
Yukon
Gulf of Alaska
YUKON TERRITORY
Mackenzie
Great Bear Lake
NUNAVUT
NORTHWEST TERRITORIES
Great Slave Lake
Southampton Island
Labrador Sea
CANADA
Hudson Bay
BRITISH COLUMBIA
ALBERTA
Athabasca
SASKATCHEWAN
Churchill
MANITOBA
Severn
Lake Winnipeg
ONTARIO
QUEBEC
NEWFOUNDLAND AND LABRADOR
Gulf of St. Lawrence
St.-Pierre & Miquelon
Fr.
P.E.I.
N.B.
NOVA SCOTIA
Vancouver Island
ROCKY MOUNTAINS
PACIFIC OCEAN
WASHINGTON
OREGON
IDAHO
MONTANA
Missouri
NORTH DAKOTA
SOUTH DAKOTA
WYOMING
MINN.
Lake Superior
Ottawa
ME.
VT.
N.H.
MASS.
R.I.
CONN.
NEW YORK
L. Ontario
Lake Huron
MICHIGAN
WIS.
Lake Michigan
L. Erie
PA.
N.J.
DEL.
MD.
Great Salt Lake
NEVADA
UTAH
COLORADO
NEBRASKA
IOWA
ILL.
IND.
OHIO
W.VA.
VA.
Washington, D.C.
CALIFORNIA
UNITED STATES
KANSAS
MISSOURI
KENTUCKY
ATLANTIC OCEAN
ARIZONA
NEW MEXICO
OKLAHOMA
Arkansas
ARK.
TENNESSEE
N.C.
S.C.
Mississippi
MISS.
ALA.
GEORGIA
Bermuda Islands
U.K.
TEXAS
LA.
FLORIDA
Guadalupe I.
Mex.
Rio Grande
MEXICO
TROPIC OF CANCER
Gulf of Mexico
BAHAMAS
Nassau
Havana
CUBA
ANTIGUA AND BARBUDA
ST. KITTS AND NEVIS
BARBADOS
DOMINICAN REPUBLIC
Santo Domingo
HAITI
Port-au-Prince
PUERTO RICO
U.S.
DOMINICA
ST. LUCIA
ST. VINCENT AND THE GRENADINES
GRENADA
TRINIDAD AND TOBAGO
Cayman Is.
U.K.
JAMAICA
Kingston
Mexico City
BELIZE
Belmopan
Caribbean Sea
HONDURAS
Tegucigalpa
GUATEMALA
Guatemala
San Salvador
EL SALVADOR
NICARAGUA
Managua
COSTA RICA
San Jose
Panama Canal
Panama
PANAMA
Cocos I.
C.R.
SOUTH AMERICA
EQUATOR
180°
170°W
160°W
150°W
140°W
130°W
80°W
70°W
10°W
20°W
30°W
40°W
50°W
60°W
60°N
70°N
80°N
50°N
40°N
30°N
20°N
10°N
0°

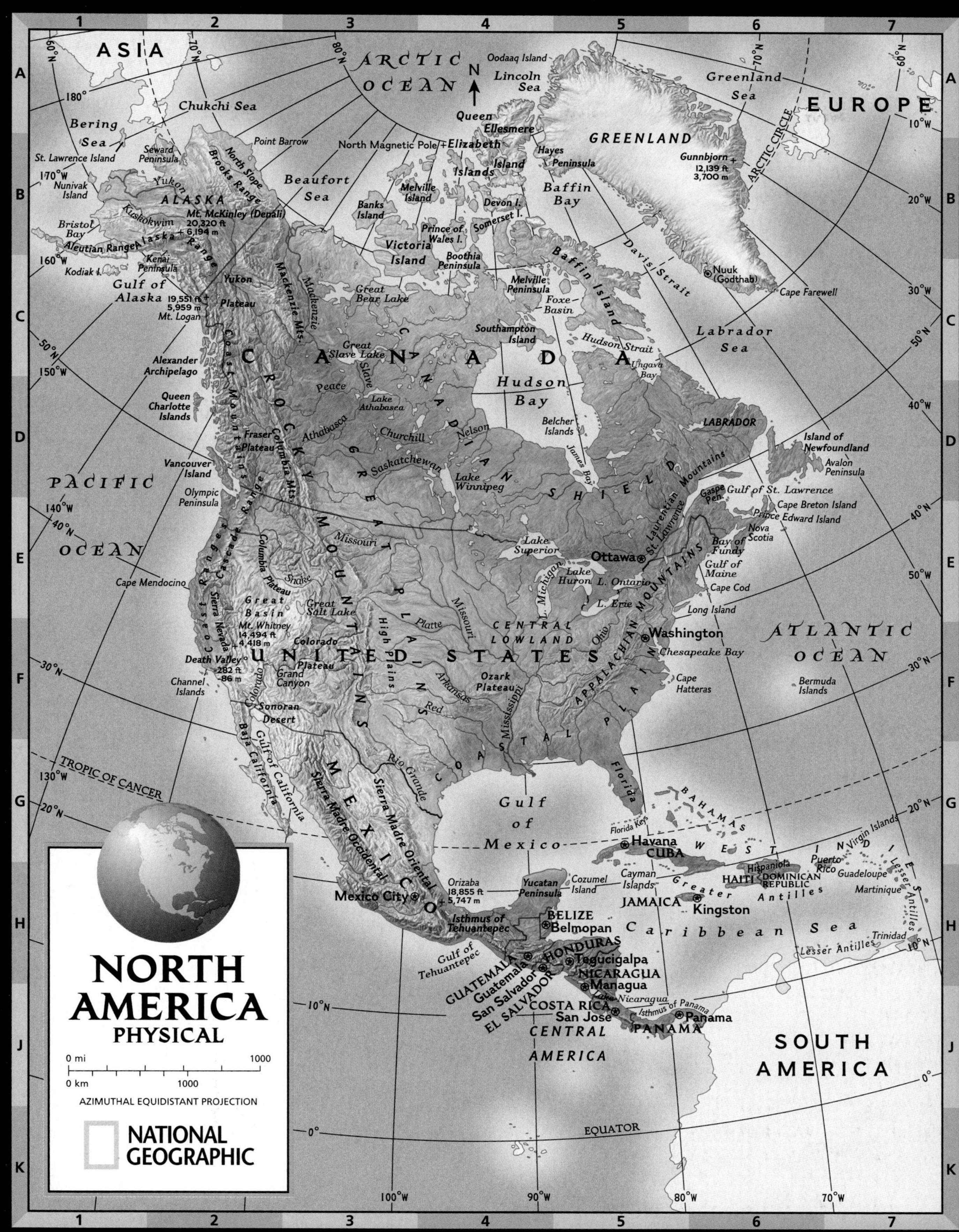
NORTH AMERICA
PHYSICAL
0 mi 1000
0 km 1000
AZIMUTHAL EQUIDISTANT PROJECTION
NATIONAL GEOGRAPHIC
ASIA
EUROPE
SOUTH AMERICA
ARCTIC OCEAN
PACIFIC OCEAN
ATLANTIC OCEAN
CANADA
UNITED STATES
MEXICO
GREENLAND
ALASKA
CENTRAL AMERICA
CANADIAN SHIELD
GREAT PLAINS
ROCKY MOUNTAINS
APPALACHIAN MOUNTAINS
COASTAL PLAIN
CENTRAL LOWLAND
WEST INDIES
Gulf of Mexico
Caribbean Sea
Hudson Bay
Baffin Bay
Labrador Sea
Beaufort Sea
Bering Sea
Chukchi Sea
Gulf of Alaska
Lincoln Sea
Greenland Sea
Mt. McKinley (Denali) 20,320 ft 6,194 m
Mt. Logan 19,551 ft 5,959 m
Mt. Whitney 14,494 ft 4,418 m
Death Valley -282 ft -86 m
Orizaba 18,855 ft 5,747 m
Gunnbjorn 12,139 ft 3,700 m
Ottawa
Washington
Mexico City
Havana
Kingston
Belmopan
Tegucigalpa
Managua
San Salvador
Guatemala
San Jose
Panama
Nuuk (Godthab)
TROPIC OF CANCER
ARCTIC CIRCLE
EQUATOR

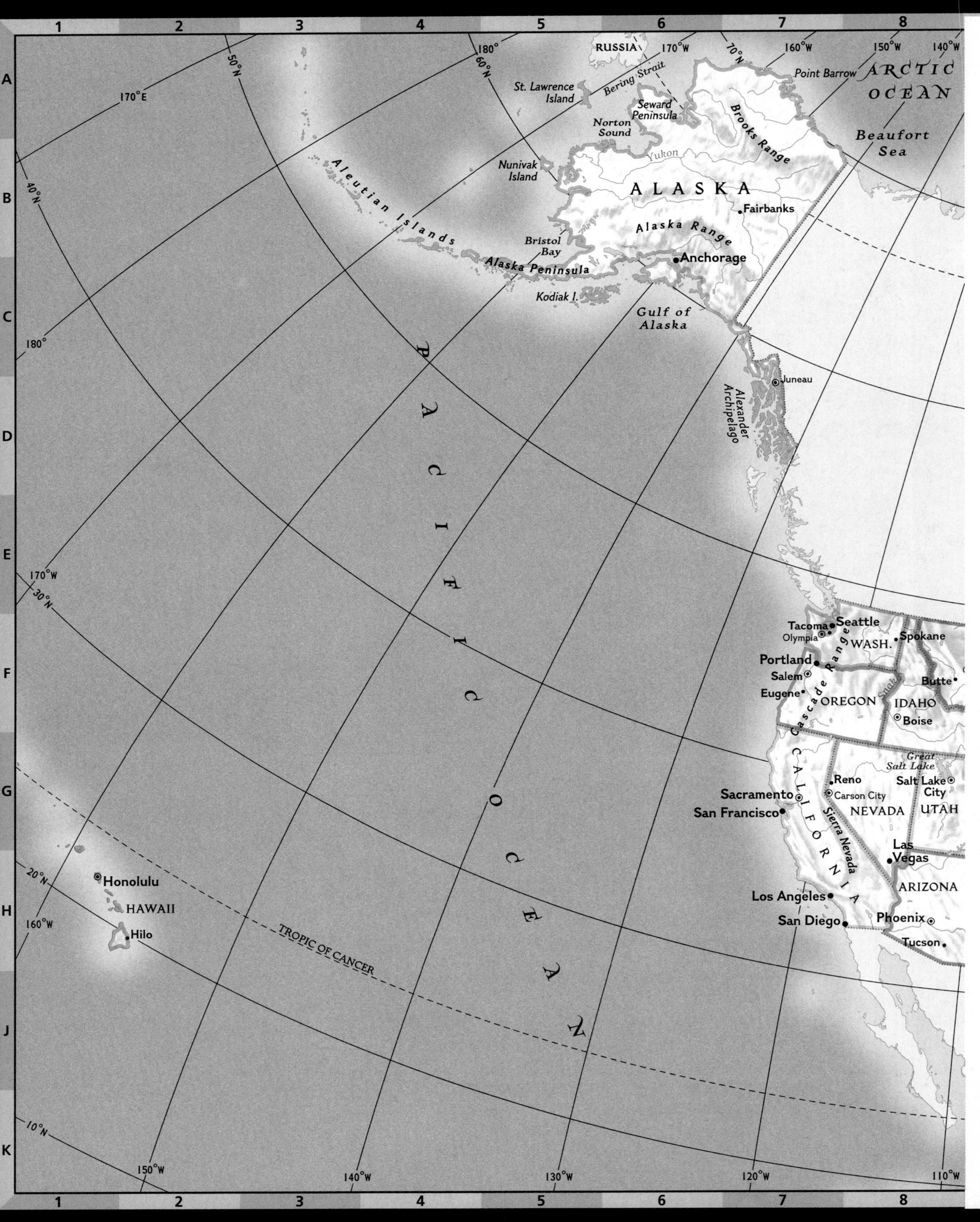
RUSSIA
St. Lawrence Island
Bering Strait
Seward Peninsula
Norton Sound
Nunivak Island
Brooks Range
Point Barrow
ARCTIC OCEAN
Beaufort Sea
Yukon
ALASKA
Fairbanks
Aleutian Islands
Alaska Range
Bristol Bay
Anchorage
Alaska Peninsula
Kodiak I.
Gulf of Alaska
Juneau
Alexander Archipelago
PACIFIC OCEAN
Tacoma
Seattle
Olympia
WASH.
Spokane
Portland
Salem
Eugene
Cascade Range
OREGON
Snake
IDAHO
Butte
Boise
Great Salt Lake
Salt Lake City
UTAH
CALIFORNIA
Reno
Carson City
NEVADA
Sacramento
San Francisco
Sierra Nevada
Las Vegas
ARIZONA
Los Angeles
San Diego
Phoenix
Tucson
Honolulu
HAWAII
Hilo
TROPIC OF CANCER
170°E
180°
170°W
160°W
150°W
140°W
130°W
120°W
110°W
160°W
150°W
140°W
170°W
70°N
60°N
50°N
40°N
30°N
20°N
10°N

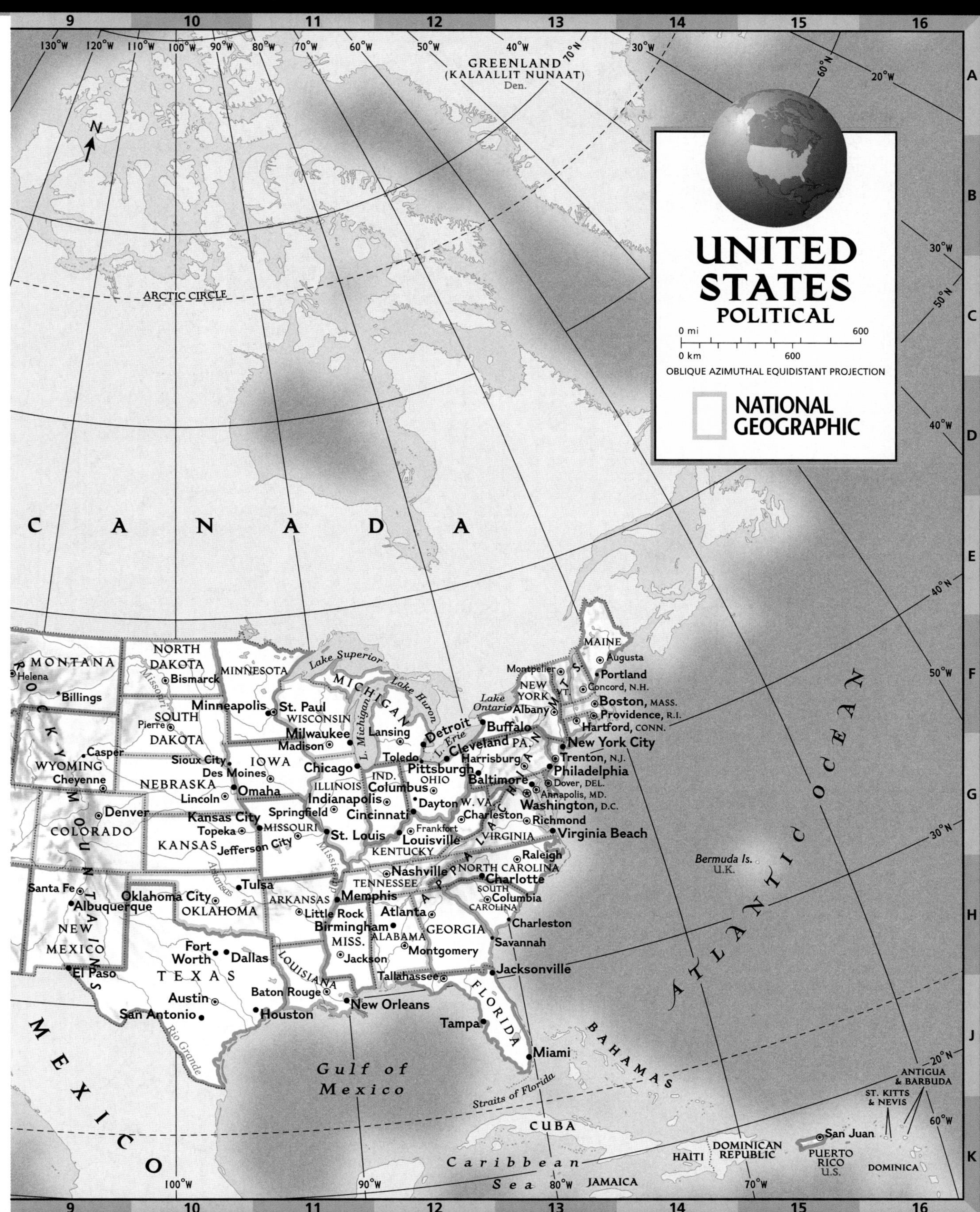
UNITED STATES
POLITICAL
0 mi 600
0 km 600
OBLIQUE AZIMUTHAL EQUIDISTANT PROJECTION
NATIONAL GEOGRAPHIC
GREENLAND (KALAALLIT NUNAAT) Den.
ARCTIC CIRCLE
CANADA
MONTANA
Helena
Billings
NORTH DAKOTA
Bismarck
MINNESOTA
SOUTH DAKOTA
Pierre
WYOMING
Casper
Cheyenne
NEBRASKA
Lincoln
Omaha
IOWA
Des Moines
Sioux City
Minneapolis
St. Paul
WISCONSIN
Milwaukee
Madison
MICHIGAN
Lansing
Detroit
ILLINOIS
Chicago
IND.
Indianapolis
OHIO
Columbus
Toledo
Cleveland
Dayton
Cincinnati
PA.
Pittsburgh
Harrisburg
Philadelphia
NEW YORK
Albany
Buffalo
New York City
Trenton, N.J.
MAINE
Augusta
Portland
Montpelier
VT.
Concord, N.H.
Boston, MASS.
Providence, R.I.
Hartford, CONN.
Dover, DEL.
Annapolis, MD.
Baltimore
Washington, D.C.
W. VA.
Charleston
VIRGINIA
Richmond
Virginia Beach
KENTUCKY
Frankfort
Louisville
NORTH CAROLINA
Raleigh
Charlotte
SOUTH CAROLINA
Columbia
Charleston
TENNESSEE
Nashville
Memphis
GEORGIA
Atlanta
Savannah
ALABAMA
Birmingham
Montgomery
MISS.
Jackson
FLORIDA
Tallahassee
Jacksonville
Tampa
Miami
LOUISIANA
Baton Rouge
New Orleans
ARKANSAS
Little Rock
MISSOURI
Jefferson City
St. Louis
Springfield
Kansas City
KANSAS
Topeka
OKLAHOMA
Oklahoma City
Tulsa
TEXAS
Fort Worth
Dallas
Austin
San Antonio
Houston
El Paso
NEW MEXICO
Santa Fe
Albuquerque
COLORADO
Denver
ROCKY MOUNTAINS
APPALACHIAN MTS.
Lake Superior
Lake Huron
L. Michigan
Lake Ontario
L. Erie
Missouri
Mississippi
Arkansas
Rio Grande
MEXICO
Gulf of Mexico
Straits of Florida
BAHAMAS
CUBA
HAITI
DOMINICAN REPUBLIC
JAMAICA
Caribbean Sea
San Juan
PUERTO RICO U.S.
ANTIGUA & BARBUDA
ST. KITTS & NEVIS
DOMINICA
Bermuda Is. U.K.
ATLANTIC OCEAN
N
130°W
120°W
110°W
100°W
90°W
80°W
70°W
60°W
50°W
40°W
30°W
20°W
70°N
60°N
50°N
40°N
30°N
20°N
9
10
11
12
13
14
15
16
A
B
C
D
E
F
G
H
J
K

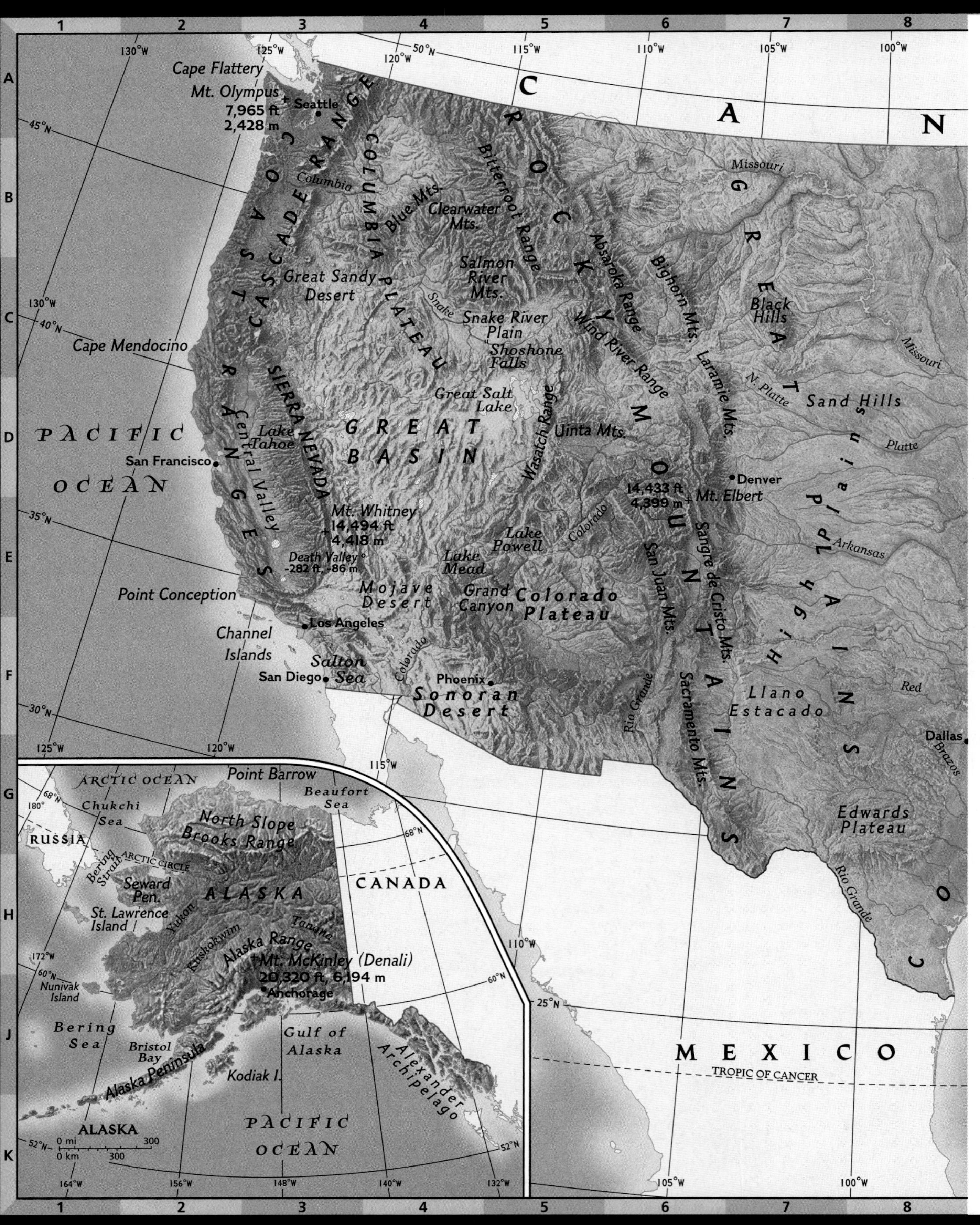

Cape Flattery
Mt. Olympus
7,965 ft
2,428 m
Seattle
CASCADE RANGE
COLUMBIA PLATEAU
ROCKY MOUNTAINS
CANADA
GREAT PLAINS
Columbia
Blue Mts.
Clearwater Mts.
Bitterroot Range
Missouri
COAST RANGES
Great Sandy Desert
Salmon River Mts.
Absaroka Range
Bighorn Mts.
Black Hills
Snake
Snake River Plain
Wind River Range
Cape Mendocino
Shoshone Falls
Laramie Mts.
N. Platte
Sand Hills
SIERRA NEVADA
Great Salt Lake
PACIFIC OCEAN
Lake Tahoe
GREAT BASIN
Wasatch Range
Uinta Mts.
Platte
San Francisco
Central Valley
Denver
14,433 ft
4,399 m
Mt. Elbert
Mt. Whitney
14,494 ft
4,418 m
Colorado
High Plains
Arkansas
Lake Powell
Death Valley
-282 ft, -86 m
Lake Mead
San Juan Mts.
Sangre de Cristo Mts.
Point Conception
Mojave Desert
Grand Canyon
Colorado Plateau
Los Angeles
Channel Islands
Salton Sea
San Diego
Phoenix
Sonoran Desert
Rio Grande
Sacramento Mts.
Llano Estacado
Red
Dallas
Brazos
Edwards Plateau
Rio Grande
MEXICO
TROPIC OF CANCER
ARCTIC OCEAN
Point Barrow
Beaufort Sea
Chukchi Sea
North Slope
Brooks Range
RUSSIA
Bering Strait
ARCTIC CIRCLE
Seward Pen.
ALASKA
CANADA
St. Lawrence Island
Yukon
Tanana
Kuskokwim
Alaska Range
Mt. McKinley (Denali)
20,320 ft, 6,194 m
Anchorage
Nunivak Island
Bering Sea
Bristol Bay
Gulf of Alaska
Alexander Archipelago
Alaska Peninsula
Kodiak I.
PACIFIC OCEAN
ALASKA
0 mi 300
0 km 300

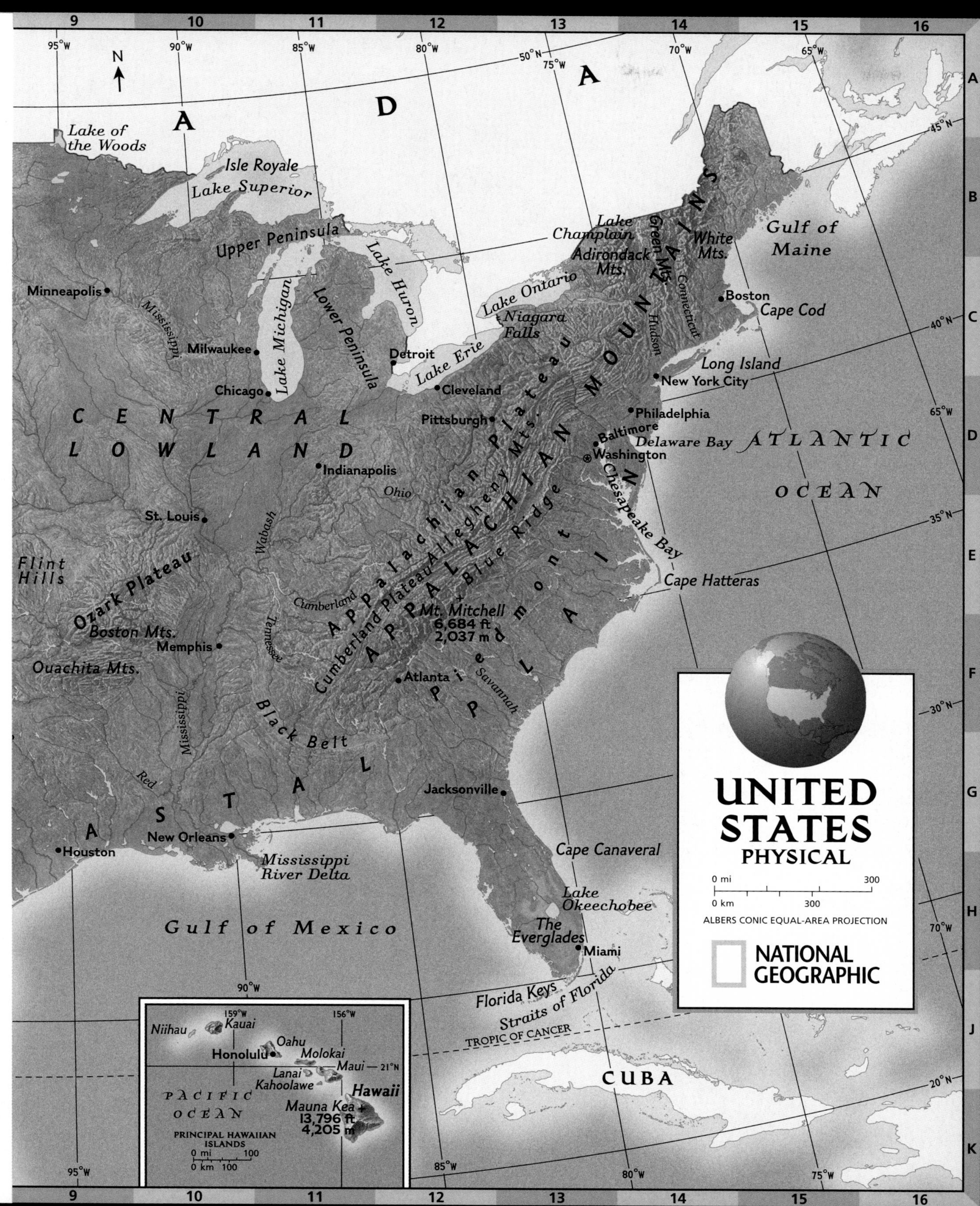

UNITED STATES
PHYSICAL
0 mi 300
0 km 300
ALBERS CONIC EQUAL-AREA PROJECTION
NATIONAL GEOGRAPHIC
CENTRAL LOWLAND
APPALACHIAN MOUNTAINS
Appalachian Plateau
Cumberland Plateau
Allegheny Mts.
Blue Ridge
Piedmont
Mt. Mitchell 6,684 ft 2,037 m
Ozark Plateau
Boston Mts.
Ouachita Mts.
Flint Hills
Black Belt
Lake of the Woods
Isle Royale
Lake Superior
Upper Peninsula
Lower Peninsula
Lake Michigan
Lake Huron
Lake Erie
Lake Ontario
Niagara Falls
Lake Champlain
Adirondack Mts.
Green Mts.
White Mts.
Gulf of Maine
Cape Cod
Long Island
Delaware Bay
Chesapeake Bay
Cape Hatteras
ATLANTIC OCEAN
Cape Canaveral
Lake Okeechobee
The Everglades
Florida Keys
Straits of Florida
TROPIC OF CANCER
CUBA
Gulf of Mexico
Mississippi River Delta
Minneapolis
Milwaukee
Chicago
Detroit
Cleveland
Pittsburgh
Indianapolis
St. Louis
Memphis
Atlanta
Jacksonville
New Orleans
Houston
Miami
Washington
Baltimore
Philadelphia
New York City
Boston
Mississippi
Ohio
Wabash
Cumberland
Tennessee
Savannah
Red
Hudson
Connecticut
Niihau
Kauai
Oahu
Honolulu
Molokai
Maui
Lanai
Kahoolawe
Hawaii
Mauna Kea 13,796 ft 4,205 m
PACIFIC OCEAN
PRINCIPAL HAWAIIAN ISLANDS

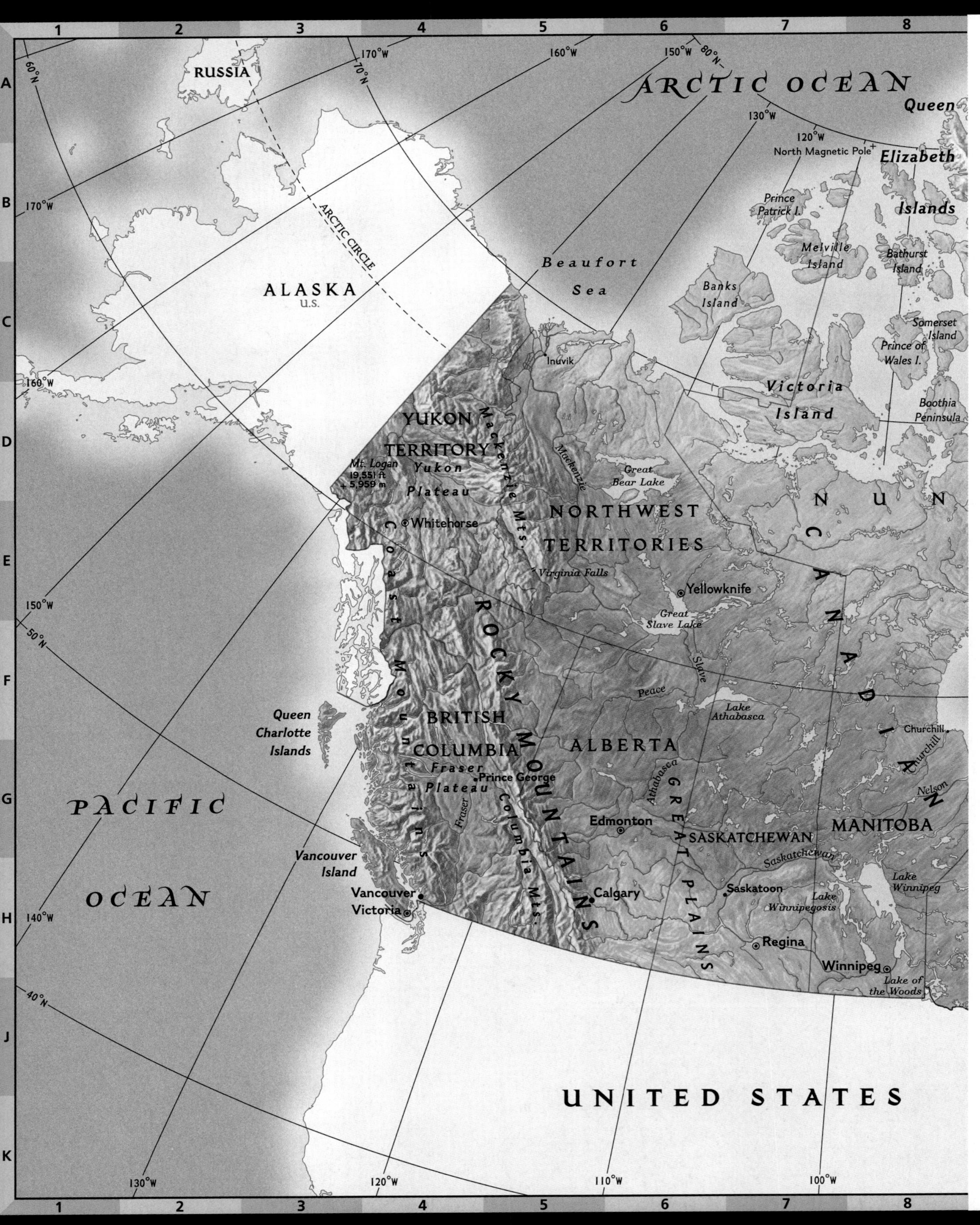
RUSSIA
ARCTIC OCEAN
Queen Elizabeth Islands
North Magnetic Pole
Prince Patrick I.
Melville Island
Bathurst Island
ARCTIC CIRCLE
Beaufort Sea
Banks Island
ALASKA
U.S.
Somerset Island
Prince of Wales I.
Inuvik
Victoria Island
Boothia Peninsula
YUKON TERRITORY
Mackenzie Mts.
Mt. Logan 19,551 ft 5,959 m
Yukon Plateau
Mackenzie
Great Bear Lake
NORTHWEST TERRITORIES
Whitehorse
Coast Mountains
Virginia Falls
Yellowknife
Great Slave Lake
ROCKY MOUNTAINS
Slave
Peace
Lake Athabasca
Queen Charlotte Islands
BRITISH COLUMBIA
ALBERTA
Churchill
Fraser Plateau
Prince George
Athabasca
Nelson
PACIFIC OCEAN
Fraser
Columbia Mts.
Edmonton
GREAT PLAINS
SASKATCHEWAN
MANITOBA
Vancouver Island
Saskatchewan
Lake Winnipeg
Vancouver
Victoria
Calgary
Saskatoon
Lake Winnipegosis
Regina
Winnipeg
Lake of the Woods
NUNAVUT
CANADIAN SHIELD
UNITED STATES

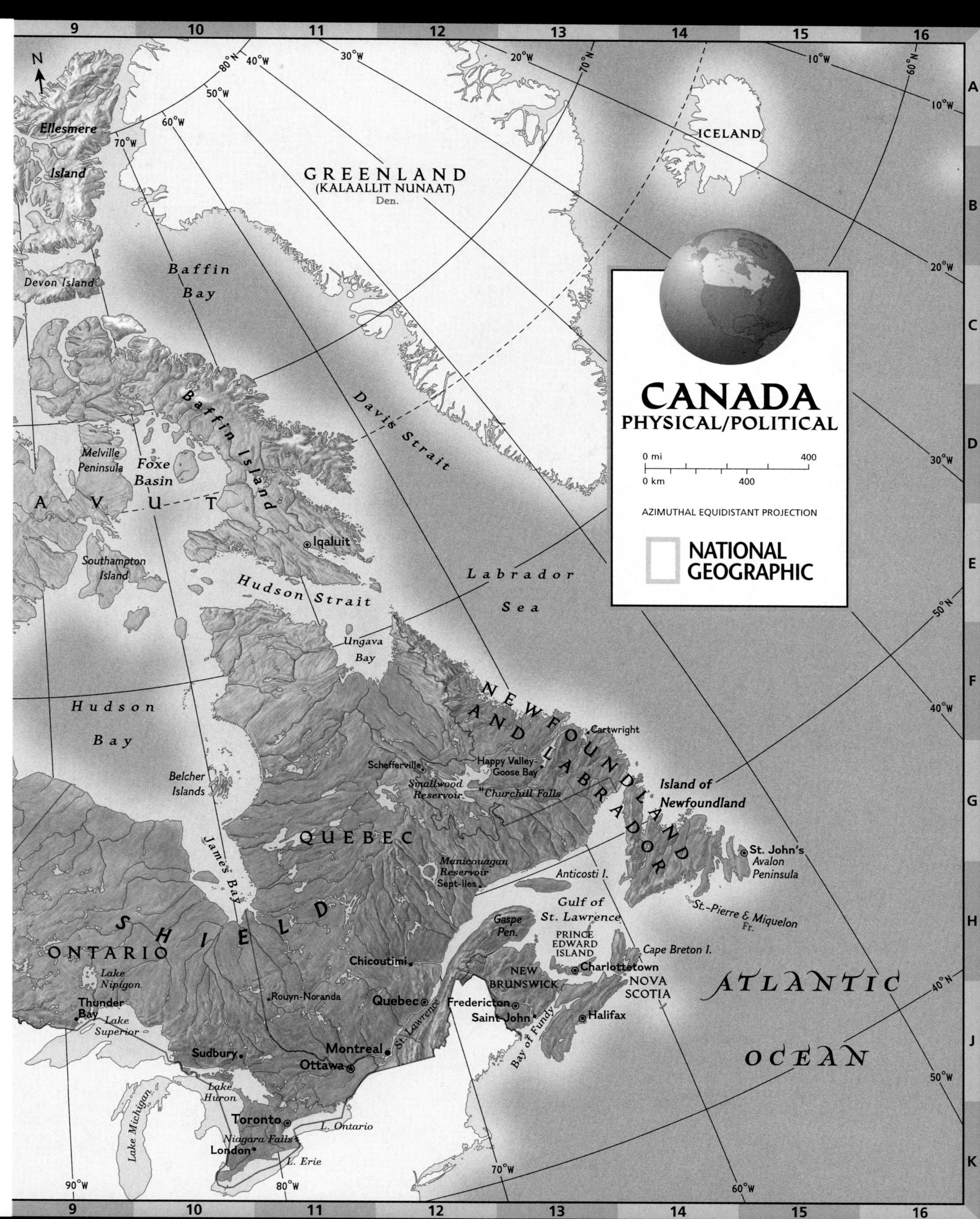
CANADA
PHYSICAL/POLITICAL
0 mi 400
0 km 400
AZIMUTHAL EQUIDISTANT PROJECTION
NATIONAL GEOGRAPHIC
GREENLAND
(KALAALLIT NUNAAT)
Den.
ICELAND
Ellesmere Island
Devon Island
Baffin Bay
Baffin Island
Davis Strait
Melville Peninsula
Foxe Basin
Southampton Island
Iqaluit
Hudson Strait
Labrador Sea
Ungava Bay
Hudson Bay
Belcher Islands
James Bay
NEWFOUNDLAND AND LABRADOR
Cartwright
Happy Valley-Goose Bay
Schefferville
Smallwood Reservoir
Churchill Falls
Island of Newfoundland
St. John's
Avalon Peninsula
QUEBEC
Manicouagan Reservoir
Sept-Iles
Anticosti I.
Gulf of St. Lawrence
St.-Pierre & Miquelon Fr.
Gaspe Pen.
PRINCE EDWARD ISLAND
Charlottetown
Cape Breton I.
NEW BRUNSWICK
NOVA SCOTIA
Fredericton
Saint John
Halifax
Bay of Fundy
ATLANTIC OCEAN
SHIELD
ONTARIO
Lake Nipigon
Thunder Bay
Lake Superior
Chicoutimi
Rouyn-Noranda
Quebec
St. Lawrence
Montreal
Ottawa
Sudbury
Lake Huron
Lake Michigan
Toronto
L. Ontario
Niagara Falls
London
L. Erie
AVUT
80°N 70°N 60°N 50°N 40°N
90°W 80°W 70°W 60°W 50°W 40°W 30°W 20°W 10°W
9 10 11 12 13 14 15 16
A B C D E F G H J K
N

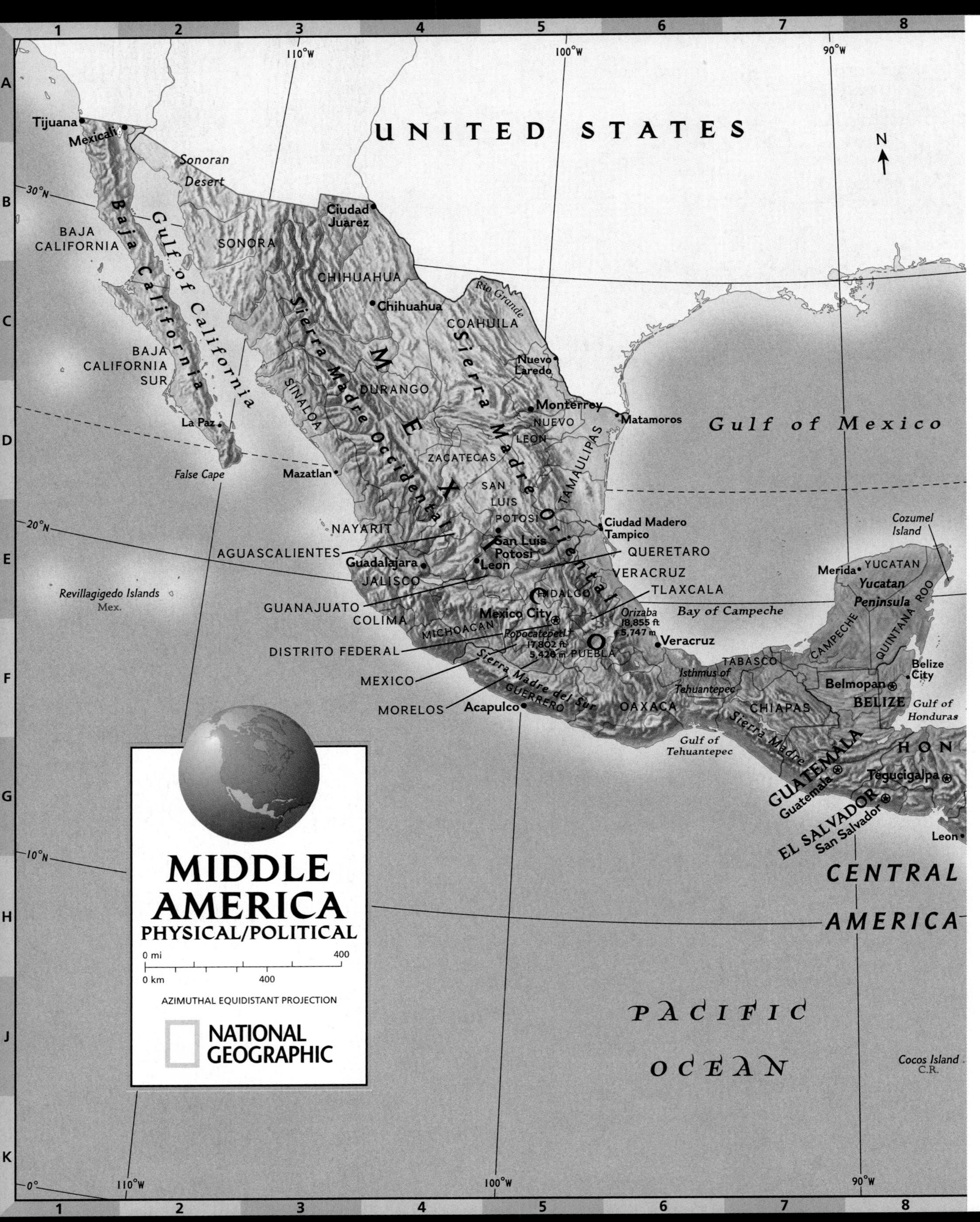
MIDDLE AMERICA
PHYSICAL/POLITICAL
0 mi
400
0 km
400
AZIMUTHAL EQUIDISTANT PROJECTION
NATIONAL GEOGRAPHIC
UNITED STATES
MEXICO
Gulf of Mexico
PACIFIC OCEAN
CENTRAL AMERICA
Tijuana
Mexicali
Sonoran Desert
Baja California
Gulf of California
BAJA CALIFORNIA
BAJA CALIFORNIA SUR
SONORA
CHIHUAHUA
Chihuahua
Ciudad Juarez
COAHUILA
Rio Grande
Sierra Madre Occidental
Sierra Madre Oriental
Nuevo Laredo
Monterrey
Matamoros
NUEVO LEON
TAMAULIPAS
DURANGO
SINALOA
La Paz
False Cape
Mazatlan
ZACATECAS
SAN LUIS POTOSI
San Luis Potosi
Ciudad Madero
Tampico
NAYARIT
AGUASCALIENTES
Guadalajara
Leon
JALISCO
QUERETARO
VERACRUZ
TLAXCALA
HIDALGO
GUANAJUATO
COLIMA
MICHOACAN
Mexico City
Popocatepetl
17,802 ft
5,426 m
Orizaba
18,855 ft
5,747 m
Veracruz
PUEBLA
DISTRITO FEDERAL
MEXICO
MORELOS
Acapulco
GUERRERO
Sierra Madre del Sur
OAXACA
Isthmus of Tehuantepec
Gulf of Tehuantepec
TABASCO
CHIAPAS
Bay of Campeche
CAMPECHE
Merida
YUCATAN
Yucatan Peninsula
QUINTANA ROO
Cozumel Island
Belize City
Belmopan
BELIZE
Gulf of Honduras
HON
Tegucigalpa
Sierra Madre
GUATEMALA
Guatemala
EL SALVADOR
San Salvador
Leon
Revillagigedo Islands
Mex.
Cocos Island
C.R.
N
110°W
100°W
90°W
30°N
20°N
10°N
0°

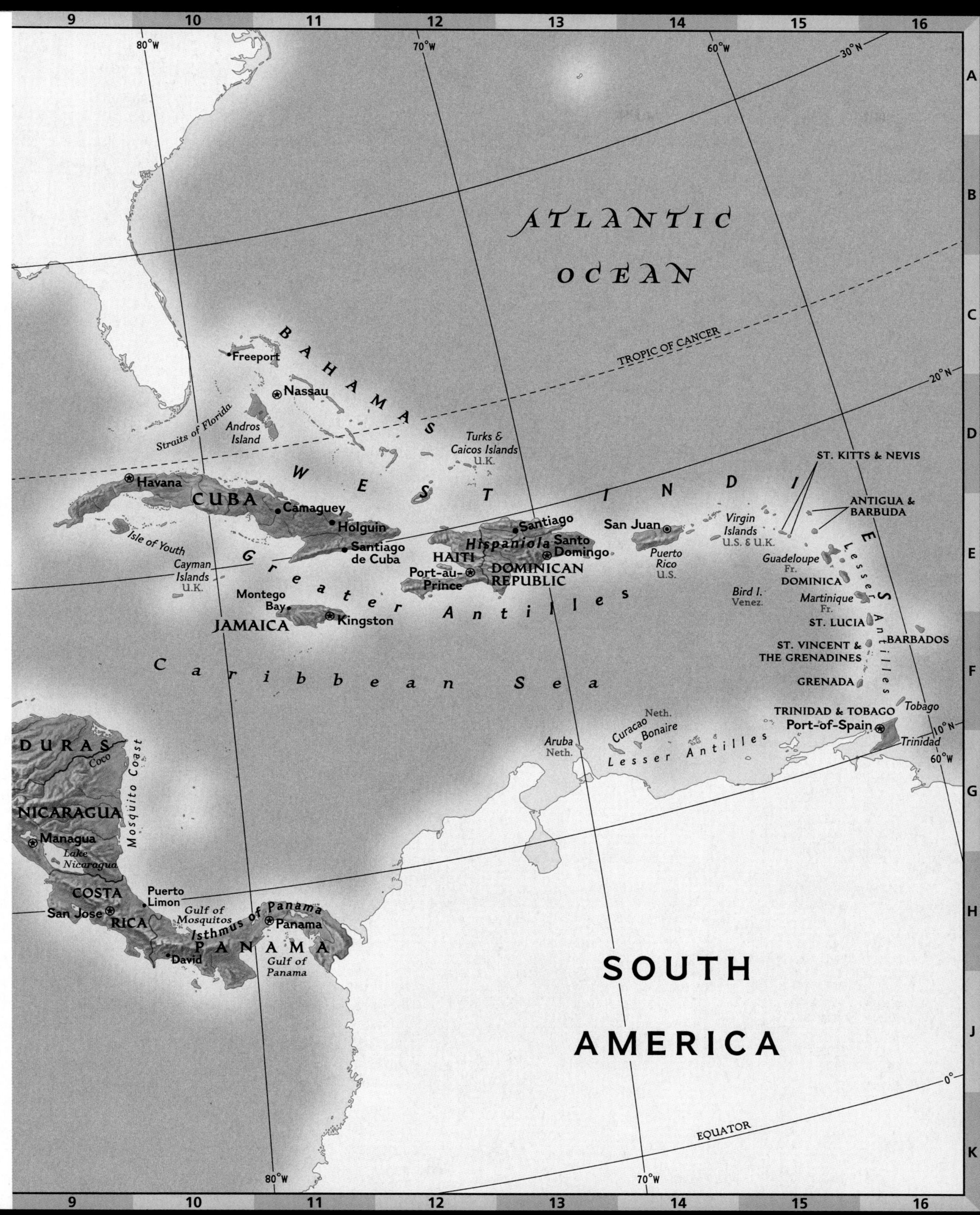

ATLANTIC OCEAN
BAHAMAS
Freeport
Nassau
Andros Island
Straits of Florida
TROPIC OF CANCER
Turks & Caicos Islands U.K.
WEST INDIES
Havana
CUBA
Camaguey
Holguin
Santiago de Cuba
Isle of Youth
Cayman Islands U.K.
Greater Antilles
HAITI
Port-au-Prince
Hispaniola
Santiago
Santo Domingo
DOMINICAN REPUBLIC
San Juan
Puerto Rico U.S.
Virgin Islands U.S. & U.K.
ST. KITTS & NEVIS
ANTIGUA & BARBUDA
Guadeloupe Fr.
DOMINICA
Martinique Fr.
ST. LUCIA
BARBADOS
ST. VINCENT & THE GRENADINES
GRENADA
TRINIDAD & TOBAGO
Tobago
Port-of-Spain
Trinidad
Lesser Antilles
Bird I. Venez.
Montego Bay
Kingston
JAMAICA
Caribbean Sea
Aruba Neth.
Curacao
Bonaire
Neth.
DURAS
Coco
Mosquito Coast
NICARAGUA
Managua
Lake Nicaragua
COSTA RICA
San Jose
Puerto Limon
Gulf of Mosquitos
Isthmus of Panama
Panama
PANAMA
David
Gulf of Panama
SOUTH AMERICA
EQUATOR
80°W
70°W
60°W
30°N
20°N
10°N
0°

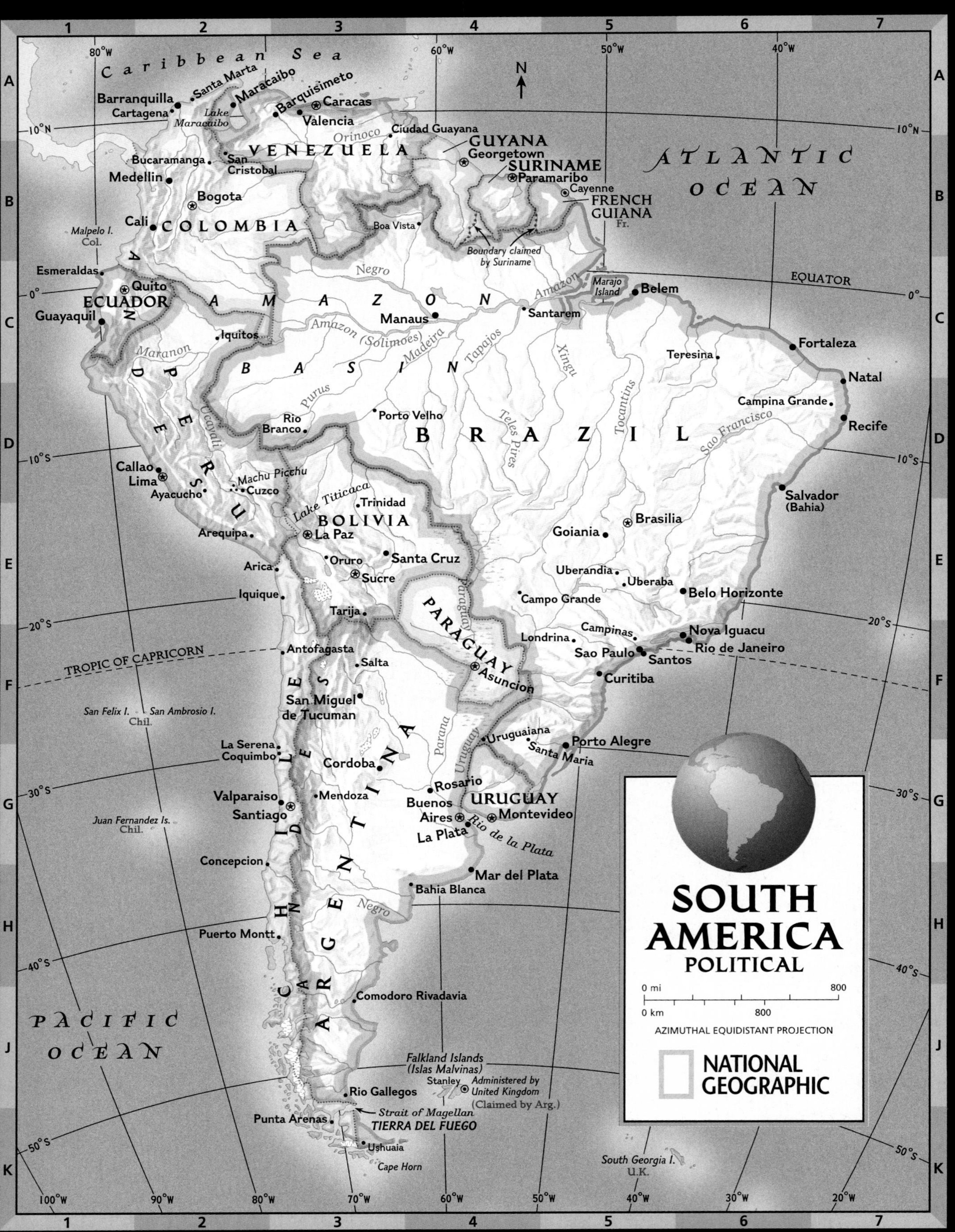
SOUTH AMERICA
POLITICAL
0 mi
800
0 km
800
AZIMUTHAL EQUIDISTANT PROJECTION
NATIONAL GEOGRAPHIC
N
Caribbean Sea
ATLANTIC OCEAN
PACIFIC OCEAN
Barranquilla
Santa Marta
Cartagena
Maracaibo
Lake Maracaibo
Barquisimeto
Caracas
Valencia
Ciudad Guayana
Orinoco
VENEZUELA
GUYANA
Georgetown
SURINAME
Paramaribo
Cayenne
FRENCH GUIANA
Fr.
Bucaramanga
San Cristobal
Medellin
Bogota
Cali
COLOMBIA
Malpelo I.
Col.
Boa Vista
Boundary claimed by Suriname
Esmeraldas
Quito
ECUADOR
Guayaquil
Negro
AMAZON BASIN
Amazon
Marajo Island
Belem
EQUATOR
Manaus
Santarem
Amazon (Solimoes)
Iquitos
Maranon
Madeira
Tapajos
Xingu
Purus
Fortaleza
Teresina
Natal
Campina Grande
Recife
Rio Branco
Porto Velho
Teles Pires
Tocantins
Sao Francisco
BRAZIL
ANDES
PERU
Ucayali
Callao
Lima
Machu Picchu
Cuzco
Ayacucho
Salvador (Bahia)
Lake Titicaca
Trinidad
BOLIVIA
La Paz
Brasilia
Goiania
Arequipa
Oruro
Santa Cruz
Sucre
Arica
Uberandia
Uberaba
Belo Horizonte
Iquique
Campo Grande
Paraguay
PARAGUAY
Tarija
Londrina
Campinas
Nova Iguacu
Rio de Janeiro
Sao Paulo
Santos
Antofagasta
TROPIC OF CAPRICORN
Salta
Asuncion
Curitiba
San Miguel de Tucuman
San Felix I.
San Ambrosio I.
Chil.
Parana
Uruguay
Uruguaiana
Porto Alegre
Santa Maria
La Serena
Coquimbo
Cordoba
ARGENTINA
Rosario
URUGUAY
Valparaiso
Santiago
Mendoza
Buenos Aires
Montevideo
La Plata
Rio de la Plata
Juan Fernandez Is.
Chil.
CHILE
Concepcion
Mar del Plata
Bahia Blanca
Negro
Puerto Montt
Comodoro Rivadavia
Falkland Islands (Islas Malvinas)
Stanley
Administered by United Kingdom
(Claimed by Arg.)
Rio Gallegos
Strait of Magellan
Punta Arenas
TIERRA DEL FUEGO
Ushuaia
Cape Horn
South Georgia I.
U.K.
10°N
0°
10°S
20°S
30°S
40°S
50°S
100°W
90°W
80°W
70°W
60°W
50°W
40°W
30°W
20°W
1
2
3
4
5
6
7
A
B
C
D
E
F
G
H
J
K

SOUTH AMERICA
PHYSICAL
Caribbean Sea
ATLANTIC OCEAN
PACIFIC OCEAN
Caracas
Lake Maracaibo
VENEZUELA
Orinoco
LLANOS
Angel Falls
Total drop 3,212 ft 979 m
GUYANA
Georgetown
SURINAME
Paramaribo
Cayenne
FRENCH GUIANA
GUIANA HIGHLANDS
Boundary claimed by Suriname
Bogota
COLOMBIA
Malpelo I.
Quito
ECUADOR
Negro
Amazon
Marajo Island
EQUATOR
AMAZON BASIN
Selvas
Madeira
Tapajos
Xingu
Purus
Ucayali
Teles Pires
Tocantins
Sao Francisco
BRAZIL
ANDES
PERU
Lima
Machu Picchu
Lake Titicaca
BOLIVIA
La Paz
Altiplano
Sucre
Salar de Uyuni
MATO GROSSO PLATEAU
Brasilia
BRAZILIAN HIGHLANDS
Paraguay
PARAGUAY
GRAN CHACO
Asuncion
Iguazu Falls
TROPIC OF CAPRICORN
San Felix I.
San Ambrosio I.
Parana
Uruguay
Aconcagua 22,834 ft 6,960 m
Santiago
CHILE
ARGENTINA
PAMPAS
Buenos Aires
URUGUAY
Montevideo
Rio de la Plata
Juan Fernandez Is.
Negro
PATAGONIA
-131 ft -40 m
Valdes Peninsula
Chiloe Island
Gulf of San Jorge
Taitao Peninsula
Wellington I.
Falkland Islands (Islas Malvinas)
Stanley
Strait of Magellan
Tierra del Fuego
Cape Horn
South Georgia I.
0 mi 800
0 km 800
AZIMUTHAL EQUIDISTANT PROJECTION
NATIONAL GEOGRAPHIC

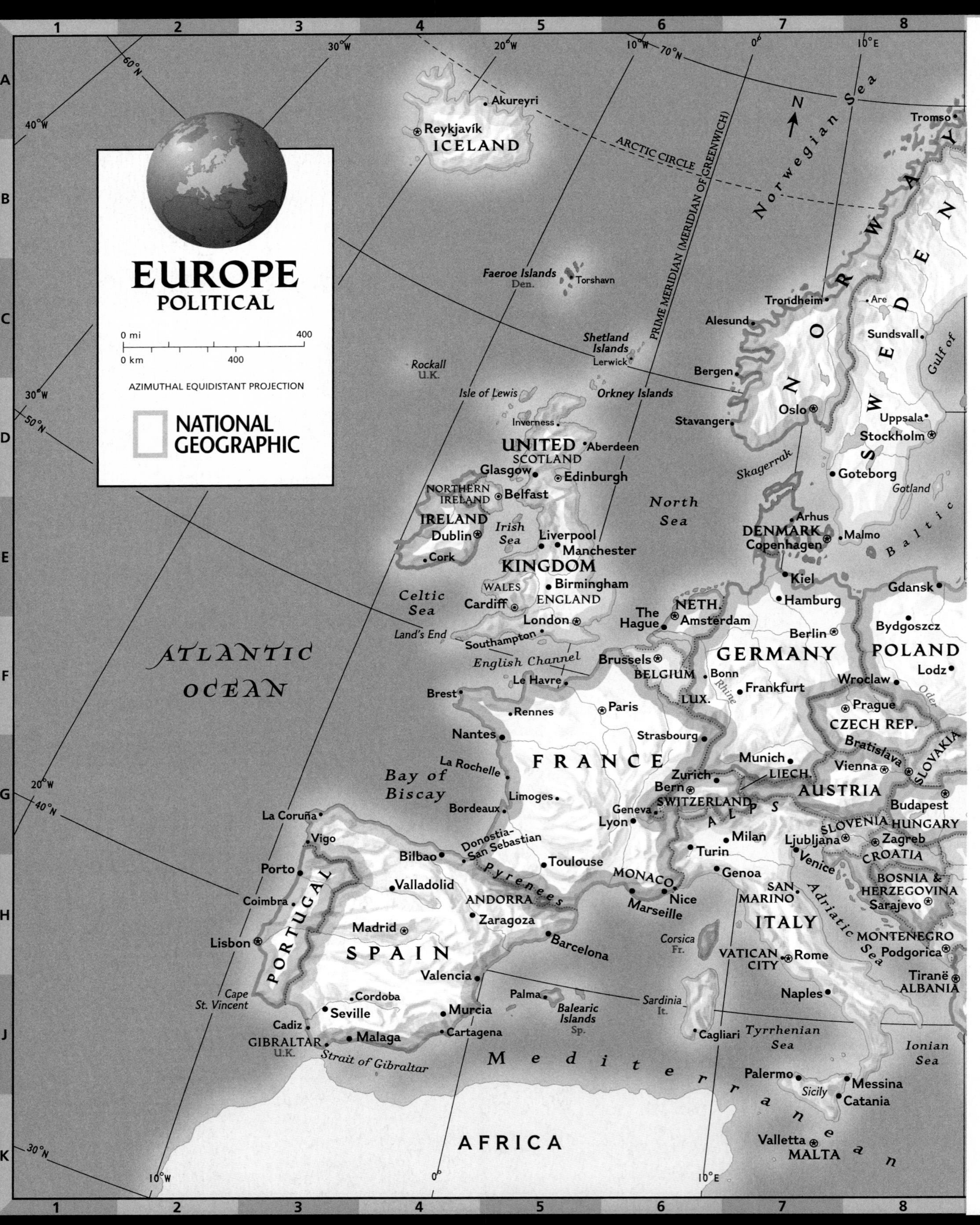
EUROPE
POLITICAL
0 mi 400
0 km 400
AZIMUTHAL EQUIDISTANT PROJECTION
NATIONAL GEOGRAPHIC
ATLANTIC OCEAN
ICELAND
Reykjavík
Akureyri
ARCTIC CIRCLE
PRIME MERIDIAN (MERIDIAN OF GREENWICH)
Norwegian Sea
Faeroe Islands
Den.
Torshavn
Shetland Islands
Lerwick
Orkney Islands
Rockall
U.K.
Isle of Lewis
Inverness
UNITED KINGDOM
SCOTLAND
Aberdeen
Glasgow
Edinburgh
NORTHERN IRELAND
Belfast
IRELAND
Dublin
Cork
Irish Sea
Liverpool
Manchester
WALES
Birmingham
ENGLAND
Cardiff
London
Celtic Sea
Land's End
Southampton
English Channel
North Sea
NORWAY
Tromso
Trondheim
Alesund
Bergen
Stavanger
Oslo
Skagerrak
SWEDEN
Are
Sundsvall
Gulf of
Uppsala
Stockholm
Goteborg
Gotland
Malmo
Baltic
DENMARK
Arhus
Copenhagen
Kiel
Hamburg
Gdansk
Bydgoszcz
POLAND
Lodz
Wroclaw
Oder
NETH.
The Hague
Amsterdam
Berlin
GERMANY
Brussels
BELGIUM
Bonn
Rhine
Frankfurt
LUX.
Prague
CZECH REP.
Bratislava
SLOVAKIA
Vienna
AUSTRIA
Munich
LIECH.
Zurich
Bern
SWITZERLAND
ALPS
Budapest
HUNGARY
SLOVENIA
Ljubljana
Zagreb
CROATIA
BOSNIA & HERZEGOVINA
Sarajevo
MONTENEGRO
Podgorica
Tiranë
ALBANIA
Le Havre
Brest
Rennes
Paris
Strasbourg
Nantes
FRANCE
La Rochelle
Bay of Biscay
Limoges
Bordeaux
Geneva
Lyon
Milan
Turin
Venice
Genoa
MONACO
Nice
Marseille
Toulouse
Donostia-San Sebastian
Bilbao
Pyrenees
ANDORRA
La Coruña
Vigo
Porto
Coimbra
PORTUGAL
Lisbon
Cape St. Vincent
Valladolid
Zaragoza
Madrid
SPAIN
Barcelona
Valencia
Cordoba
Seville
Cadiz
Malaga
Murcia
Cartagena
GIBRALTAR
U.K.
Strait of Gibraltar
Palma
Balearic Islands
Sp.
Corsica
Fr.
Sardinia
It.
Cagliari
SAN MARINO
Adriatic Sea
ITALY
VATICAN CITY
Rome
Naples
Tyrrhenian Sea
Ionian Sea
Palermo
Sicily
Messina
Catania
Valletta
MALTA
Mediterranean
AFRICA
60°N
50°N
40°N
30°N
70°N
40°W
30°W
20°W
10°W
0°
10°E
N

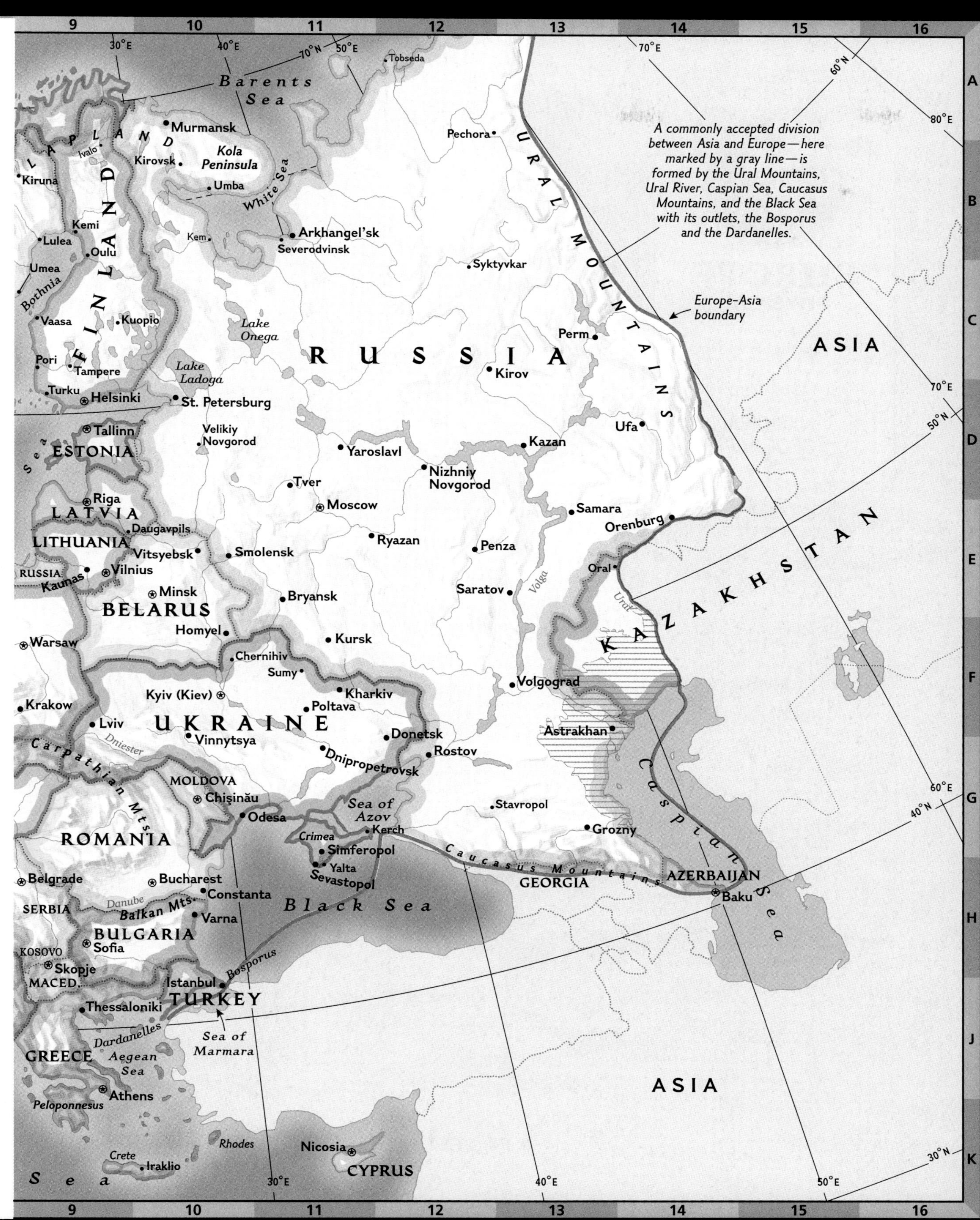
A commonly accepted division between Asia and Europe—here marked by a gray line—is formed by the Ural Mountains, Ural River, Caspian Sea, Caucasus Mountains, and the Black Sea with its outlets, the Bosporus and the Dardanelles.
Europe-Asia boundary
RUSSIA
ASIA
KAZAKHSTAN
URAL MOUNTAINS
Barents Sea
White Sea
Kola Peninsula
LAPLAND
FINLAND
ESTONIA
LATVIA
LITHUANIA
RUSSIA
BELARUS
UKRAINE
MOLDOVA
ROMANIA
SERBIA
BULGARIA
KOSOVO
MACED.
GREECE
TURKEY
GEORGIA
AZERBAIJAN
CYPRUS
Carpathian Mts.
Balkan Mts.
Caucasus Mountains
Black Sea
Sea of Azov
Caspian Sea
Aegean Sea
Sea of Marmara
Bosporus
Dardanelles
Lake Onega
Lake Ladoga
Murmansk
Kirovsk
Umba
Ivalo
Kiruna
Kemi
Lulea
Oulu
Umea
Bothnia
Vaasa
Kuopio
Pori
Tampere
Turku
Helsinki
St. Petersburg
Tallinn
Riga
Daugavpils
Vilnius
Kaunas
Minsk
Vitsyebsk
Smolensk
Velikiy Novgorod
Kem
Arkhangel'sk
Severodvinsk
Tobseda
Pechora
Syktyvkar
Perm
Kirov
Ufa
Kazan
Yaroslavl
Nizhniy Novgorod
Tver
Moscow
Ryazan
Samara
Orenburg
Penza
Oral
Saratov
Volga
Ural
Bryansk
Homyel
Kursk
Warsaw
Chernihiv
Sumy
Kharkiv
Kyiv (Kiev)
Poltava
Volgograd
Krakow
Lviv
Vinnytsya
Dniester
Donetsk
Rostov
Dnipropetrovsk
Astrakhan
Chişinău
Odesa
Crimea
Kerch
Stavropol
Grozny
Simferopol
Yalta
Sevastopol
Baku
Belgrade
Bucharest
Constanta
Danube
Varna
Sofia
Skopje
Istanbul
Thessaloniki
Athens
Peloponnesus
Crete
Iraklio
Rhodes
Nicosia
Sea
30°E
40°E
50°E
60°E
70°E
80°E
30°N
40°N
50°N
60°N
70°N
9 10 11 12 13 14 15 16
A B C D E F G H J K

EUROPE
PHYSICAL
0 mi 400
0 km 400
AZIMUTHEL EQUIDISTANT PROJECTION
NATIONAL GEOGRAPHIC
ARCTIC CIRCLE
PRIME MERIDIAN (MERIDIAN OF GREENWICH)
Reykjavík
ICELAND
Faeroe Islands
Shetland Islands
Orkney Islands
Norwegian Sea
SCANDINAVIA
NORWAY
SWEDEN
Gulf of
Oslo
Stockholm
Outer Hebrides
British Isles
Highlands
Edinburgh
Belfast
UNITED KINGDOM
IRELAND
Dublin
Irish Sea
Great Britain
Cardiff
London
North Sea
Jutland
DENMARK
Copenhagen
Zealand
Baltic
Amsterdam
NETH.
Berlin
NORT
POLAND
ATLANTIC OCEAN
English Channel
BELGIUM
Brussels
GERMANY
Rhine
Oder
LUX.
Seine
Paris
Elbe
Prague
CZECH REP.
Brittany
Loire
Danube
Bratislava
SLOVAKIA
FRANCE
LIECH.
Vienna
Bay of Biscay
Mont Blanc 15,771 ft 4,807 m
Bern
SWITZ.
AUSTRIA
Budapest
HUNGARY
ALPS
Massif Central
Rhone
SLOVENIA
Drava
Danube
Ljubljana
Zagreb
CROATIA
Sava
Po
Cantabrian Mountains
Pyrenees
MONACO
Douro
Riviera
SAN MARINO
Adriatic Sea
BOSNIA &
Sarajevo
HERZEGOVINA
IBERIAN PENINSULA
PORTUGAL
Madrid
SPAIN
Ebro
ANDORRA
Lisbon
Tagus
Corsica
Apennines
ITALY
VATICAN CITY
Rome
MONTENEGRO
Tiranë
ALBANIA
Sardinia
Tyrrhenian Sea
Balearic Islands
Baetic Mountains
GIBRALTAR
Strait of Gibraltar
Mediterranean
Ionian Sea
Sicily
Etna 10,902 ft 3,323 m
AFRICA
Valletta
MALTA
60°N
50°N
40°N
30°N
70°N
40°W
30°W
20°W
10°W
0°
10°E

Barents Sea
North Cape
Kola Peninsula
White Sea
Pechora
URAL MOUNTAINS
Europe-Asia boundary
ASIA
Bothnia
FINLAND
Lake Region
Lake Onega
Lake Ladoga
Northern Dvina
RUSSIA
EUROPEAN PLAIN
Helsinki
Gulf of Finland
Tallinn
ESTONIA
Kama
Ural
Volga
Riga
LATVIA
Moscow
LITHUANIA
Vilnius
RUSSIA
Oka
CENTRAL RUSSIAN UPLAND
Minsk
BELARUS
Dnieper
Don
Warsaw
KAZAKHSTAN
Caspian Depression
Vistula
Kyiv (Kiev)
UKRAINE
Carpathian Mountains
Dniester
MOLDOVA
Chişinău
Sea of Azov
Crimea
Elbrus 18,510 ft 5,642 m
Caucasus Mountains
ROMANIA
Tisza
Belgrade
Bucharest
Danube
BALKAN PENINSULA
SERBIA
BULGARIA
Balkan Mountains
Sofia
Skopje
MACED.
Black Sea
GEORGIA
AZERBAIJAN
Baku
Caspian Sea
Bosporus
TURKEY
Dardanelles
Sea of Marmara
GREECE
Aegean Sea
Athens
Peloponnesus
Rhodes
Crete
Nicosia
CYPRUS
ASIA
Sea
30°E
40°E
50°E
60°E
70°E
80°E
70°N
60°N
50°N
40°N
30°N

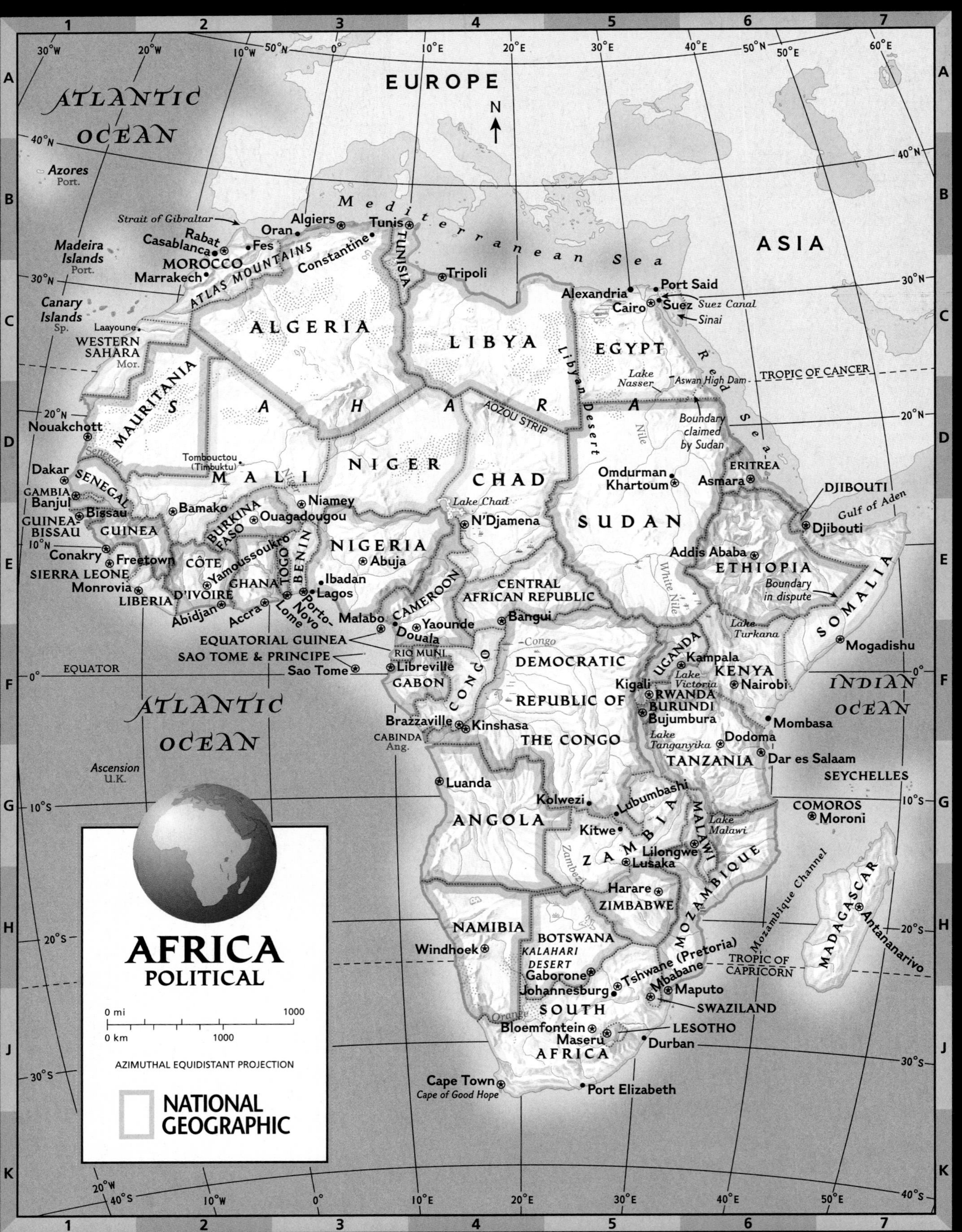
AFRICA
POLITICAL
AZIMUTHAL EQUIDISTANT PROJECTION
NATIONAL GEOGRAPHIC
EUROPE
ASIA
ATLANTIC OCEAN
INDIAN OCEAN
Mediterranean Sea
Red Sea
Gulf of Aden
Mozambique Channel
ALGERIA
LIBYA
EGYPT
MOROCCO
TUNISIA
WESTERN SAHARA
MAURITANIA
MALI
NIGER
CHAD
SUDAN
ERITREA
DJIBOUTI
ETHIOPIA
SOMALIA
SENEGAL
GAMBIA
GUINEA-BISSAU
GUINEA
SIERRA LEONE
LIBERIA
CÔTE D'IVOIRE
BURKINA FASO
GHANA
TOGO
BENIN
NIGERIA
CAMEROON
CENTRAL AFRICAN REPUBLIC
EQUATORIAL GUINEA
SAO TOME & PRINCIPE
GABON
CONGO
DEMOCRATIC REPUBLIC OF THE CONGO
UGANDA
KENYA
RWANDA
BURUNDI
TANZANIA
ANGOLA
ZAMBIA
MALAWI
MOZAMBIQUE
ZIMBABWE
NAMIBIA
BOTSWANA
SOUTH AFRICA
SWAZILAND
LESOTHO
MADAGASCAR
COMOROS
SEYCHELLES
Cairo
Tripoli
Tunis
Algiers
Rabat
Nouakchott
Dakar
Bamako
Niamey
N'Djamena
Khartoum
Asmara
Djibouti
Addis Ababa
Mogadishu
Abuja
Yaounde
Bangui
Kampala
Nairobi
Kinshasa
Brazzaville
Libreville
Luanda
Lusaka
Harare
Windhoek
Gaborone
Maputo
Cape Town
Antananarivo
Moroni
Dodoma
Lilongwe
Kigali
Bujumbura
Accra
Lome
Porto-Novo
Freetown
Conakry
Monrovia
Banjul
Bissau
Ouagadougou
Yamoussoukro
Malabo
Sao Tome
Tshwane (Pretoria)
Mbabane
Maseru
Bloemfontein
Johannesburg
Durban
Port Elizabeth
Casablanca
Marrakech
Fes
Oran
Constantine
Alexandria
Port Said
Suez
Suez Canal
Sinai
Omdurman
Lagos
Ibadan
Abidjan
Douala
Mombasa
Dar es Salaam
Kolwezi
Lubumbashi
Kitwe
Laayoune
Tombouctou (Timbuktu)
Strait of Gibraltar
ATLAS MOUNTAINS
SAHARA
Libyan Desert
AOZOU STRIP
Lake Nasser
Aswan High Dam
Boundary claimed by Sudan
Boundary in dispute
Lake Chad
Lake Turkana
Lake Victoria
Lake Tanganyika
Lake Malawi
Nile
White Nile
Niger
Congo
Zambezi
Orange
Senegal
KALAHARI DESERT
Cape of Good Hope
TROPIC OF CANCER
TROPIC OF CAPRICORN
EQUATOR
Azores Port.
Madeira Islands Port.
Canary Islands Sp.
Ascension U.K.
CABINDA Ang.
RIO MUNI

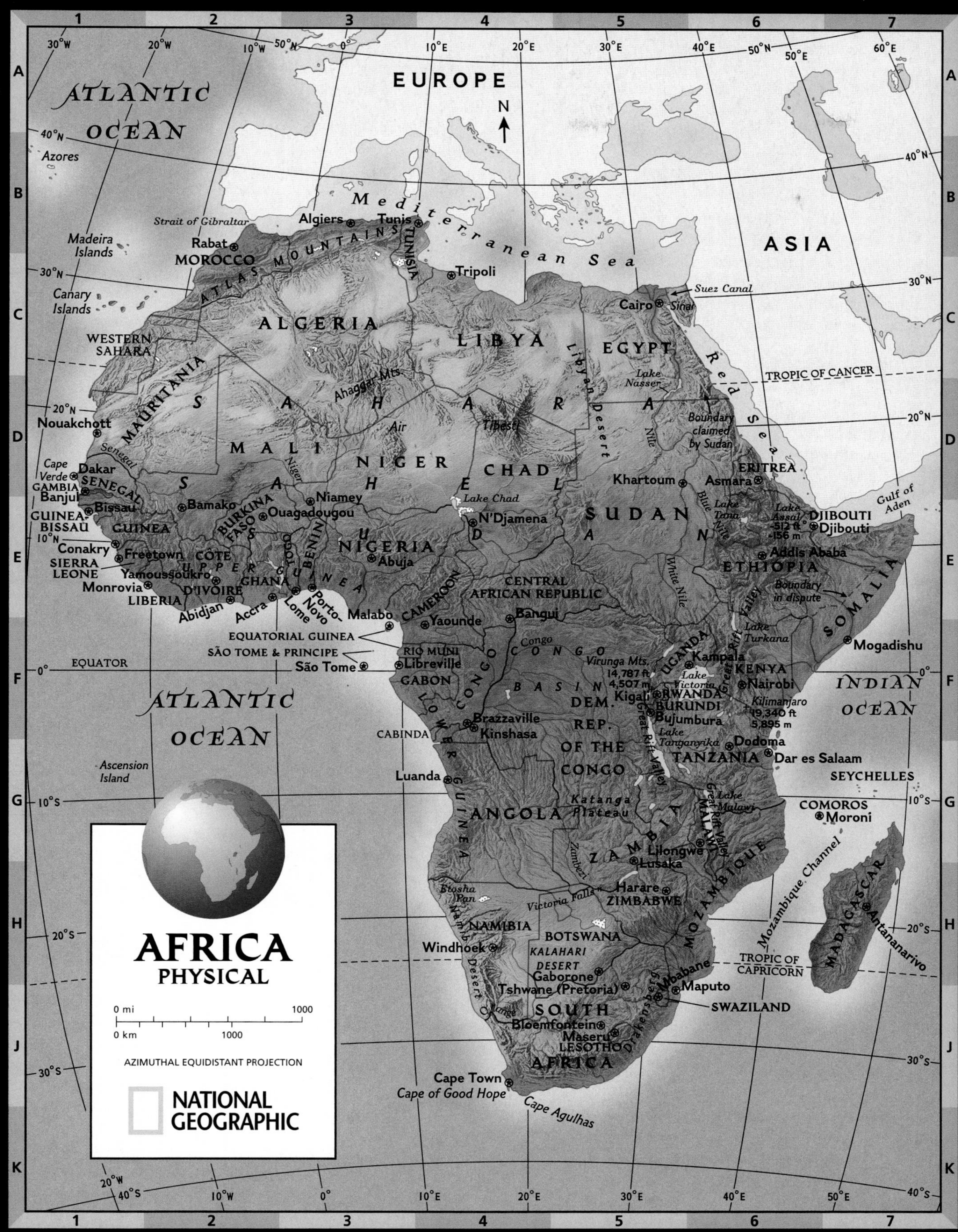

AFRICA
PHYSICAL
EUROPE
ASIA
ATLANTIC OCEAN
INDIAN OCEAN
Mediterranean Sea
Red Sea
ALGERIA
LIBYA
EGYPT
MOROCCO
TUNISIA
WESTERN SAHARA
MAURITANIA
MALI
NIGER
CHAD
SUDAN
NIGERIA
ETHIOPIA
SOMALIA
KENYA
TANZANIA
ANGOLA
ZAMBIA
NAMIBIA
BOTSWANA
ZIMBABWE
MOZAMBIQUE
SOUTH AFRICA
MADAGASCAR
DEM. REP. OF THE CONGO
CENTRAL AFRICAN REPUBLIC
CAMEROON
GABON
CONGO
SAHARA
SAHEL
Cairo
Tripoli
Algiers
Tunis
Rabat
Khartoum
Addis Ababa
Nairobi
Kinshasa
Luanda
Cape Town
Cape of Good Hope
Cape Agulhas
Lake Victoria
Lake Chad
Kilimanjaro 19,340 ft 5,895 m
0 mi 1000
0 km 1000
AZIMUTHAL EQUIDISTANT PROJECTION
NATIONAL GEOGRAPHIC

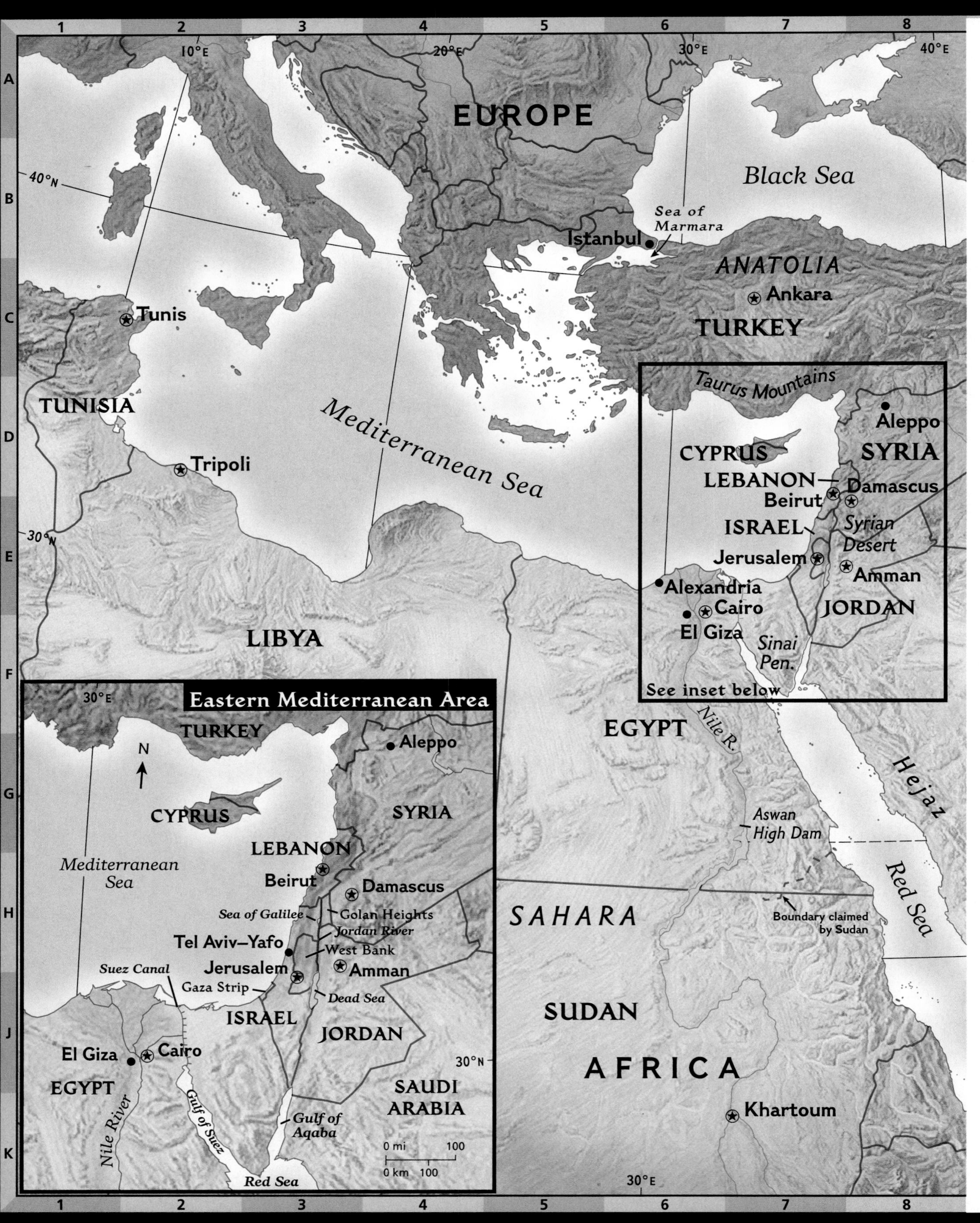
EUROPE
Black Sea
Sea of Marmara
Istanbul
ANATOLIA
Ankara
TURKEY
Tunis
TUNISIA
Tripoli
Mediterranean Sea
Taurus Mountains
Aleppo
CYPRUS
SYRIA
LEBANON
Beirut
Damascus
ISRAEL
Syrian Desert
Jerusalem
Amman
Alexandria
Cairo
El Giza
JORDAN
Sinai Pen.
See inset below
LIBYA
EGYPT
Nile R.
Hejaz
Aswan High Dam
Red Sea
SAHARA
Boundary claimed by Sudan
SUDAN
AFRICA
Khartoum
Eastern Mediterranean Area
TURKEY
Aleppo
CYPRUS
SYRIA
Mediterranean Sea
LEBANON
Beirut
Damascus
Sea of Galilee
Golan Heights
Jordan River
Tel Aviv–Yafo
West Bank
Jerusalem
Amman
Suez Canal
Gaza Strip
Dead Sea
ISRAEL
JORDAN
El Giza
Cairo
EGYPT
SAUDI ARABIA
Nile River
Gulf of Suez
Gulf of Aqaba
Red Sea
0 mi 100
0 km 100
10°E
20°E
30°E
40°E
40°N
30°N
1 2 3 4 5 6 7 8
A B C D E F G H J K

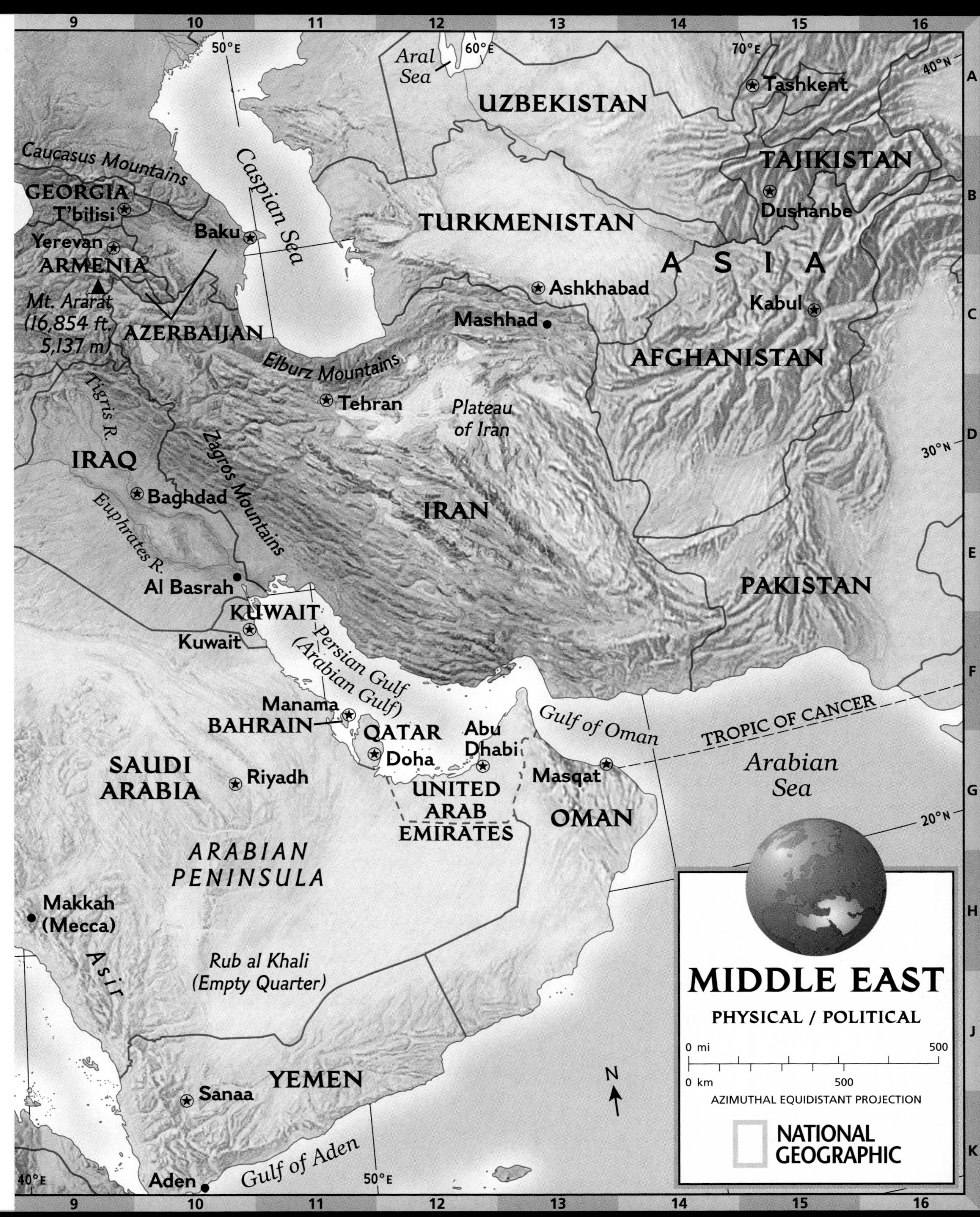
MIDDLE EAST
PHYSICAL / POLITICAL
0 mi 500
0 km 500
AZIMUTHAL EQUIDISTANT PROJECTION
NATIONAL GEOGRAPHIC
ASIA
UZBEKISTAN
TAJIKISTAN
TURKMENISTAN
AFGHANISTAN
PAKISTAN
IRAN
IRAQ
GEORGIA
ARMENIA
AZERBAIJAN
KUWAIT
BAHRAIN
QATAR
UNITED ARAB EMIRATES
OMAN
SAUDI ARABIA
YEMEN
Tashkent
Dushanbe
Kabul
Ashkhabad
Mashhad
Tehran
T'bilisi
Yerevan
Baku
Baghdad
Al Basrah
Kuwait
Manama
Doha
Abu Dhabi
Masqat
Riyadh
Makkah (Mecca)
Sanaa
Aden
Aral Sea
Caspian Sea
Caucasus Mountains
Mt. Ararat (16,854 ft. 5,137 m)
Elburz Mountains
Zagros Mountains
Plateau of Iran
Tigris R.
Euphrates R.
Persian Gulf (Arabian Gulf)
Gulf of Oman
TROPIC OF CANCER
Arabian Sea
ARABIAN PENINSULA
Rub al Khali (Empty Quarter)
Asir
Gulf of Aden
50°E
60°E
70°E
40°E
40°N
30°N
20°N
N

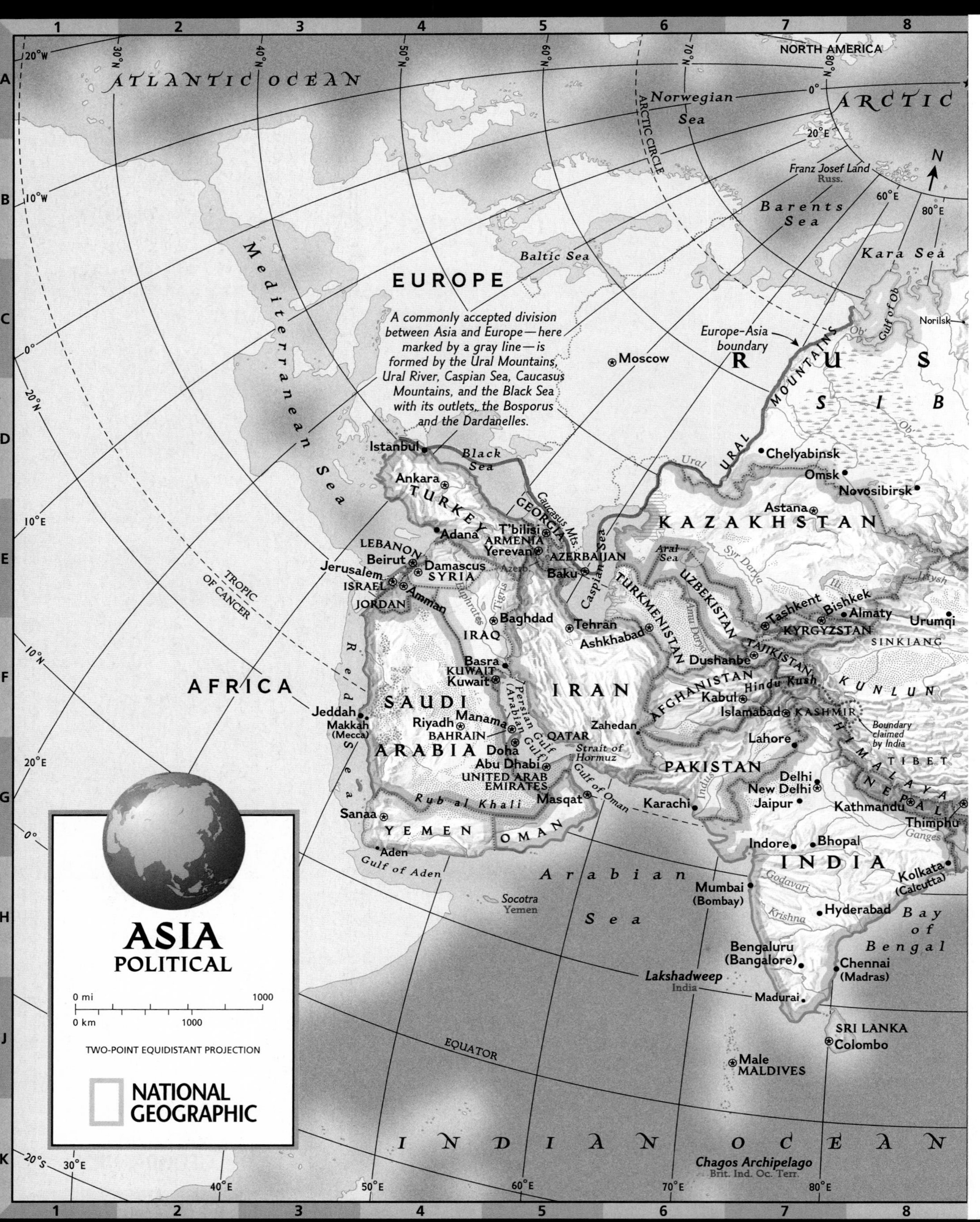

ASIA
POLITICAL
0 mi 1000
0 km 1000
TWO-POINT EQUIDISTANT PROJECTION
NATIONAL GEOGRAPHIC
A commonly accepted division between Asia and Europe—here marked by a gray line—is formed by the Ural Mountains, Ural River, Caspian Sea, Caucasus Mountains, and the Black Sea with its outlets, the Bosporus and the Dardanelles.
Europe-Asia boundary
ATLANTIC OCEAN
ARCTIC
NORTH AMERICA
Norwegian Sea
Barents Sea
Kara Sea
Franz Josef Land
Russ.
Baltic Sea
EUROPE
Mediterranean Sea
Black Sea
Caspian Sea
Aral Sea
Red Sea
Persian Gulf (Arabian Gulf)
Strait of Hormuz
Gulf of Oman
Gulf of Aden
Arabian Sea
Bay of Bengal
INDIAN OCEAN
AFRICA
RUSSIA
SIB
URAL MOUNTAINS
Caucasus Mts.
Hindu Kush
KUNLUN
HIMALAYA
Rub al Khali
Moscow
Chelyabinsk
Omsk
Novosibirsk
Norilsk
Astana
KAZAKHSTAN
Istanbul
Ankara
Adana
TURKEY
GEORGIA
T'bilisi
ARMENIA
Yerevan
AZERBAIJAN
Baku
Azerb.
LEBANON
Beirut
Damascus
SYRIA
Jerusalem
ISRAEL
Amman
JORDAN
Baghdad
IRAQ
Tehran
Ashkhabad
TURKMENISTAN
UZBEKISTAN
Tashkent
Bishkek
Almaty
KYRGYZSTAN
TAJIKISTAN
Dushanbe
Urumqi
SINKIANG
Basra
KUWAIT
Kuwait
IRAN
AFGHANISTAN
Kabul
Islamabad
KASHMIR
Boundary claimed by India
TIBET
Jeddah
Makkah (Mecca)
SAUDI ARABIA
Riyadh
Manama
BAHRAIN
QATAR
Doha
Abu Dhabi
UNITED ARAB EMIRATES
Masqat
OMAN
Sanaa
YEMEN
Aden
Zahedan
PAKISTAN
Lahore
Karachi
Delhi
New Delhi
Jaipur
NEPAL
Kathmandu
Thimphu
Indore
Bhopal
INDIA
Kolkata (Calcutta)
Mumbai (Bombay)
Hyderabad
Bengaluru (Bangalore)
Chennai (Madras)
Madurai
SRI LANKA
Colombo
Male
MALDIVES
Lakshadweep
India
Socotra
Yemen
Chagos Archipelago
Brit. Ind. Oc. Terr.
Ural
Ob'
Gulf of Ob
Syr Darya
Amu Darya
Euphrates
Tigris
Indus
Ganges
Godavari
Krishna
Irtysh
Ili
ARCTIC CIRCLE
TROPIC OF CANCER
EQUATOR

NORTH AMERICA
Bering Strait
Chukchi Sea
North Pole
OCEAN
Wrangel I.
Gulf of Anadyr
Anadyr
Bering Sea
East Siberian Sea
New Siberian Islands
North Land
Laptev Sea
Commander Is.
Kamchatka Peninsula
Cherskiy Range
Verkhoyanski Mountains
Kolyma Range
Magadan
Sea of Okhotsk
Lena
Aldan
Yakutsk
SIA
ERIA
Sakhalin
Kuril Islands
Yenisey
Lake Baikal
Irkutsk
Amur
MANCHURIA
Hokkaido
Sapporo
Sea of Japan (East Sea)
Vladivostok
Changchun
Ulaanbaatar
Herlen
MONGOLIA
ALTAY MTS.
GOBI
JAPAN
Tokyo
Honshu
Shenyang
NORTH KOREA
P'yŏngyang
Seoul
SOUTH KOREA
Kyoto
Osaka
Hiroshima
Kyushu
Beijing
Qingdao
Shijiazhuang
Yellow Sea
Huang He (Yellow R.)
Xuzhou
Lanzhou
Xian
SHAN
CHINA
Nanjing
Shanghai
East China Sea
Ryukyu Islands
Okinawa
Chang Jiang (Yangtze R.)
Nanchang
Chengdu
Fuzhou
Changsha
Taipei
TAIWAN
The People's Republic of China claims Taiwan as its 23rd province.
Boundary claimed by China
BHUTAN
BANGLADESH
Dhaka
Irrawaddy
Guiyang
Kunming
Guangzhou
Hong Kong
Macau
PACIFIC OCEAN
Marcus I. Jap.
TROPIC OF CANCER
Bonin Is. Jap.
Volcano Is. Jap.
Parece Vela Jap.
Philippine Sea
MYANMAR (BURMA)
Hanoi
Haiphong
LAOS
Vientiane
Yangon (Rangoon)
South China Sea
Hainan
Luzon
Quezon City
Manila
Samar
PHILIPPINES
Leyte
Mindoro
Panay
Negros
Palawan
Mindanao
Da Nang
THAILAND
Mekong
Bangkok
CAMBODIA
VIETNAM
Phnom Penh
Ho Chi Minh City
Andaman Islands India
Andaman Sea
Gulf of Thailand
EQUATOR
Biak
Jayapura
New Guinea
Morotai
Halmahera
Moluccas
Bandar Seri Begawan
BRUNEI
SABAH
SARAWAK
MALAYSIA
Nicobar Islands India
Kuala Lumpur
Medan
SINGAPORE
INDONESIA
Borneo
Celebes
Buru
Ceram
Aru Is.
Kepi
Merauke
Dolak
Tanimbar Is.
Sumatra
Jambi
GREATER SUNDA ISLANDS
Mentawai Islands
Java Sea
Jakarta
Java
Dili
EAST TIMOR (TIMOR-LESTE)
Timor Sea
Kupang
AUSTRALIA
80°N
70°N
60°N
50°N
40°N
30°N
20°N
10°N
0°
10°S
20°S
180°
160°E
120°E
100°E
160°W
170°W
170°E
110°E
130°E
140°E
150°E
9
10
11
12
13
14
15
16
A
B
C
D
E
F
G
H
J
K

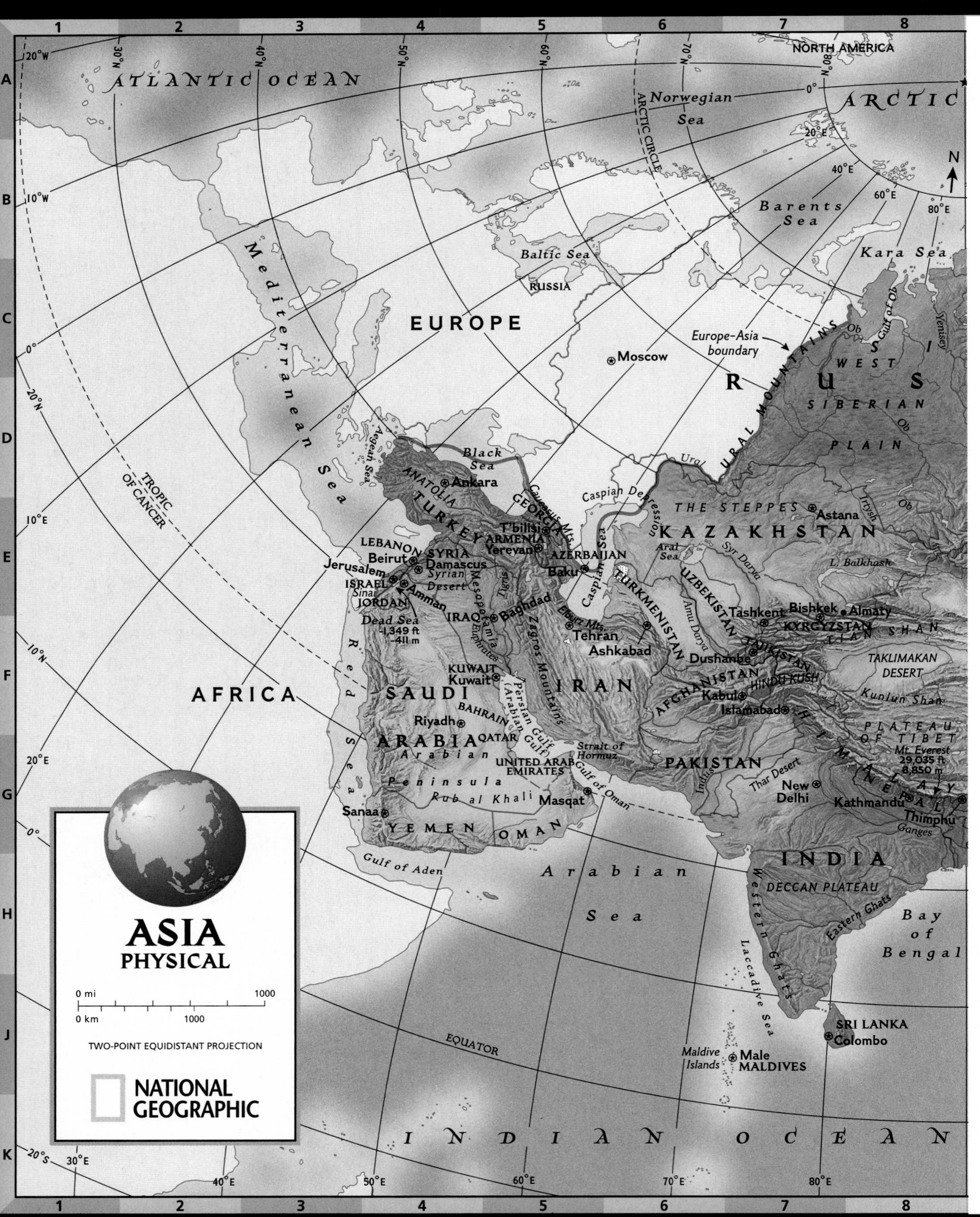
ASIA
PHYSICAL
0 mi 1000
0 km 1000
TWO-POINT EQUIDISTANT PROJECTION
NATIONAL GEOGRAPHIC
ATLANTIC OCEAN
ARCTIC
NORTH AMERICA
Norwegian Sea
ARCTIC CIRCLE
Barents Sea
Kara Sea
Baltic Sea
RUSSIA
EUROPE
Mediterranean Sea
Moscow
Europe-Asia boundary
URAL MOUNTAINS
RUSSIA
WEST SIBERIAN PLAIN
Ob
Gulf of Ob
Yenisey
Irtysh
Ural
Aegean Sea
Black Sea
Ankara
ANATOLIA
TURKEY
GEORGIA
Caucasus Mts.
T'bilisi
ARMENIA
Yerevan
AZERBAIJAN
Baku
Caspian Depression
Caspian Sea
THE STEPPES
Astana
KAZAKHSTAN
Aral Sea
Syr Darya
L. Balkhash
TROPIC OF CANCER
LEBANON
Beirut
SYRIA
Damascus
Jerusalem
ISRAEL
Sinai
JORDAN
Amman
Syrian Desert
Dead Sea
-1,349 ft
-411 m
IRAQ
Baghdad
Mesopotamia
Tigris
Euphrates
Zagros Mountains
Elburz Mts.
Tehran
Ashkabad
TURKMENISTAN
UZBEKISTAN
Amu Darya
Tashkent
Bishkek
Almaty
KYRGYZSTAN
TIAN SHAN
TAJIKISTAN
Dushanbe
TAKLIMAKAN DESERT
KUWAIT
Kuwait
AFRICA
Red Sea
SAUDI ARABIA
Riyadh
BAHRAIN
QATAR
Persian Gulf (Arabian Gulf)
IRAN
AFGHANISTAN
Kabul
HINDU KUSH
Islamabad
Kunlun Shan
PLATEAU OF TIBET
Mt. Everest
29,035 ft
8,850 m
HIMALAYA
Strait of Hormuz
UNITED ARAB EMIRATES
PAKISTAN
Indus
Thar Desert
New Delhi
NEPAL
Kathmandu
Thimphu
Ganges
Arabian Peninsula
Rub al Khali
Masqat
Gulf of Oman
Sanaa
YEMEN
OMAN
Gulf of Aden
Arabian Sea
INDIA
DECCAN PLATEAU
Western Ghats
Eastern Ghats
Bay of Bengal
Laccadive Sea
SRI LANKA
Colombo
EQUATOR
Maldive Islands
Male
MALDIVES
INDIAN OCEAN

NORTH AMERICA
Bering Strait
Chukchi Sea
Chukchi Peninsula
Gulf of Anadyr
North Pole
OCEAN
Wrangel Island
East Siberian Sea
Bering Sea
Aleutian Islands
North Land
New Siberian Islands
Laptev Sea
Taymyr Peninsula
Kolyma
Kolyma Range
Commander Islands
Cherskiy Range
Kamchatka Peninsula
Verkhoyanski Mountains
Lena
Aldan
CENTRAL
SIBERIAN
PLATEAU
SIBERIA
ASIA
Sea of Okhotsk
Sakhalin
Kuril Islands
Angara
Amur
Lake Baikal
Yablonovyy Range
Greater Khingan Range
Manchurian Plain
Sikhote Alin Range
Hokkaido
Yenisey
Ulaanbaatar
MONGOLIA
ALTAY MOUNTAINS
GOBI
Sea of Japan (East Sea)
JAPAN
Tokyo
Honshu
NORTH KOREA
P'yŏngyang
Seoul
SOUTH KOREA
Beijing
North China Plain
Shikoku
Kyushu
Nampo Shoto
TROPIC OF CANCER
PACIFIC OCEAN
Yellow Sea
Huang He (Yellow R.)
Qaidam Basin
East China Sea
Ryukyu Islands
CHINA
Yangtze
Mekong
Salween
Sichuan Basin
Chang Jiang (Yangtze R.)
Mariana Islands
Gongga Shan 24,790 ft 7,556 m
Taipei
TAIWAN
Philippine Sea
BHUTAN
Brahmaputra
BANGLADESH
Dhaka
MYANMAR (BURMA)
Hanoi
LAOS
Luzon
South China Sea
Hainan
PHILIPPINE ISLANDS
Caroline Islands
Yangon (Rangoon)
Vientiane
Manila
PHILIPPINES
THAILAND
Bangkok
CAMBODIA
VIETNAM
EQUATOR
Andaman Islands
Phnom Penh
Sulu Sea
Mindanao
Gulf of Thailand
Andaman Sea
Malay Peninsula
Bandar Seri Begawan
BRUNEI
Celebes Sea
New Guinea
Nicobar Islands
MALAYSIA
Moluccas
Kuala Lumpur
SINGAPORE
Borneo
Celebes
Sumatra
INDONESIA
Arafura Sea
GREATER SUNDA ISLANDS
EAST TIMOR (TIMOR-LESTE)
Dili
Timor Sea
Mentawai Islands
Java Sea
Java
Jakarta
AUSTRALIA
80°N
70°N
60°N
50°N
40°N
30°N
20°N
10°N
0°
10°S
20°S
180°
160°E
120°E
100°E
110°E
120°E
130°E
140°E
150°E
160°E
170°E
160°W
170°W
9
10
11
12
13
14
15
16
A
B
C
D
E
F
G
H
J
K

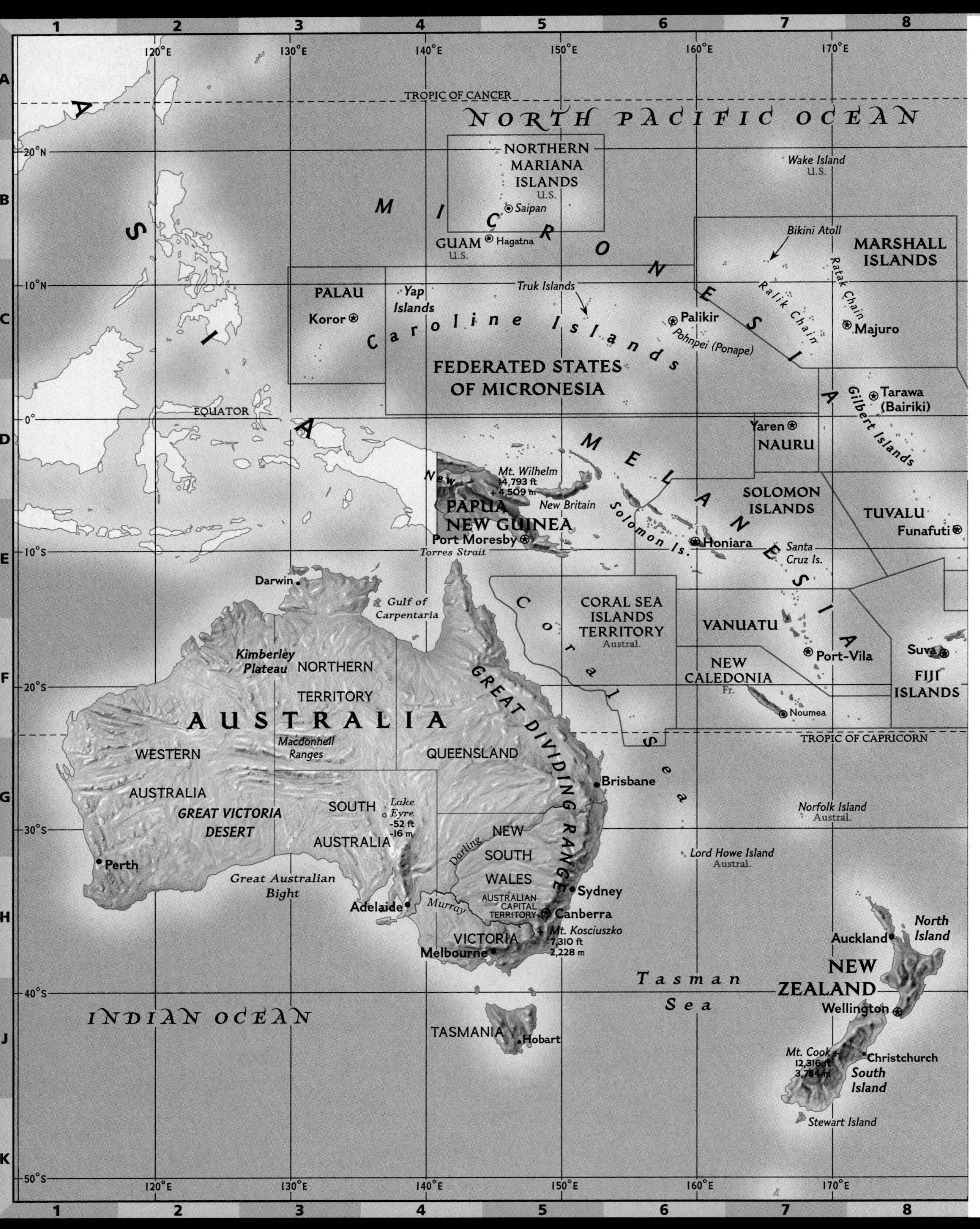

NORTH PACIFIC OCEAN
INDIAN OCEAN
TROPIC OF CANCER
TROPIC OF CAPRICORN
EQUATOR
ASIA
MICRONESIA
MELANESIA
NORTHERN MARIANA ISLANDS
U.S.
Saipan
GUAM
Hagatna
U.S.
Wake Island
U.S.
Bikini Atoll
MARSHALL ISLANDS
Ralik Chain
Ratak Chain
Majuro
PALAU
Koror
Yap Islands
Truk Islands
Caroline Islands
Palikir
Pohnpei (Ponape)
FEDERATED STATES OF MICRONESIA
Tarawa (Bairiki)
Gilbert Islands
Yaren
NAURU
Mt. Wilhelm
14,793 ft
4,509 m
New Guinea
PAPUA NEW GUINEA
New Britain
Port Moresby
Torres Strait
Solomon Is.
SOLOMON ISLANDS
Honiara
Santa Cruz Is.
TUVALU
Funafuti
Darwin
Gulf of Carpentaria
Coral Sea
CORAL SEA ISLANDS TERRITORY
Austral.
VANUATU
Port-Vila
NEW CALEDONIA
Fr.
Noumea
Suva
FIJI ISLANDS
Kimberley Plateau
NORTHERN TERRITORY
AUSTRALIA
GREAT DIVIDING RANGE
WESTERN AUSTRALIA
Macdonnell Ranges
QUEENSLAND
Brisbane
GREAT VICTORIA DESERT
SOUTH AUSTRALIA
Lake Eyre
-52 ft
-16 m
Darling
NEW SOUTH WALES
Norfolk Island
Austral.
Lord Howe Island
Austral.
Perth
Great Australian Bight
Sydney
Adelaide
Murray
AUSTRALIAN CAPITAL TERRITORY
Canberra
Mt. Kosciuszko
7,310 ft
2,228 m
VICTORIA
Melbourne
Tasman Sea
North Island
Auckland
NEW ZEALAND
Wellington
TASMANIA
Hobart
Mt. Cook
12,316 ft
3,754 m
Christchurch
South Island
Stewart Island
120°E
130°E
140°E
150°E
160°E
170°E
20°N
10°N
0°
10°S
20°S
30°S
40°S
50°S
1
2
3
4
5
6
7
8
A
B
C
D
E
F
G
H
J
K

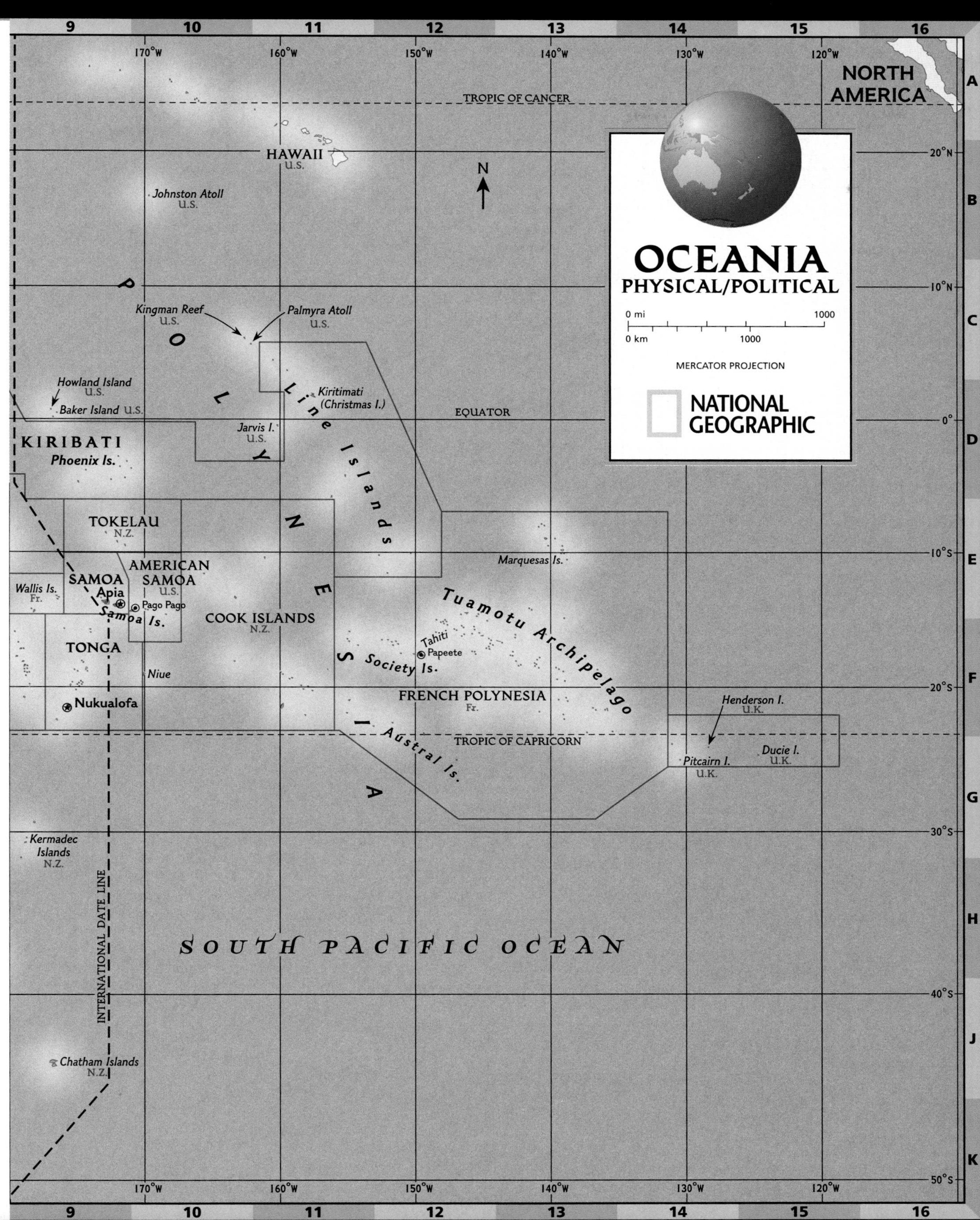
OCEANIA
PHYSICAL/POLITICAL
0 mi
1000
0 km
1000
MERCATOR PROJECTION
NATIONAL GEOGRAPHIC
NORTH AMERICA
TROPIC OF CANCER
HAWAII
U.S.
Johnston Atoll
U.S.
Kingman Reef
U.S.
Palmyra Atoll
U.S.
Howland Island
U.S.
Baker Island U.S.
Kiritimati (Christmas I.)
Jarvis I.
U.S.
EQUATOR
KIRIBATI
Phoenix Is.
POLYNESIA
Line Islands
TOKELAU
N.Z.
AMERICAN SAMOA
U.S.
SAMOA
Apia
Pago Pago
Samoa Is.
Wallis Is.
Fr.
COOK ISLANDS
N.Z.
TONGA
Niue
Nukualofa
Marquesas Is.
Tuamotu Archipelago
Tahiti
Papeete
Society Is.
FRENCH POLYNESIA
Fr.
Austral Is.
TROPIC OF CAPRICORN
Henderson I.
U.K.
Ducie I.
U.K.
Pitcairn I.
U.K.
Kermadec Islands
N.Z.
INTERNATIONAL DATE LINE
SOUTH PACIFIC OCEAN
Chatham Islands
N.Z.
170°W
160°W
150°W
140°W
130°W
120°W
20°N
10°N
0°
10°S
20°S
30°S
40°S
50°S

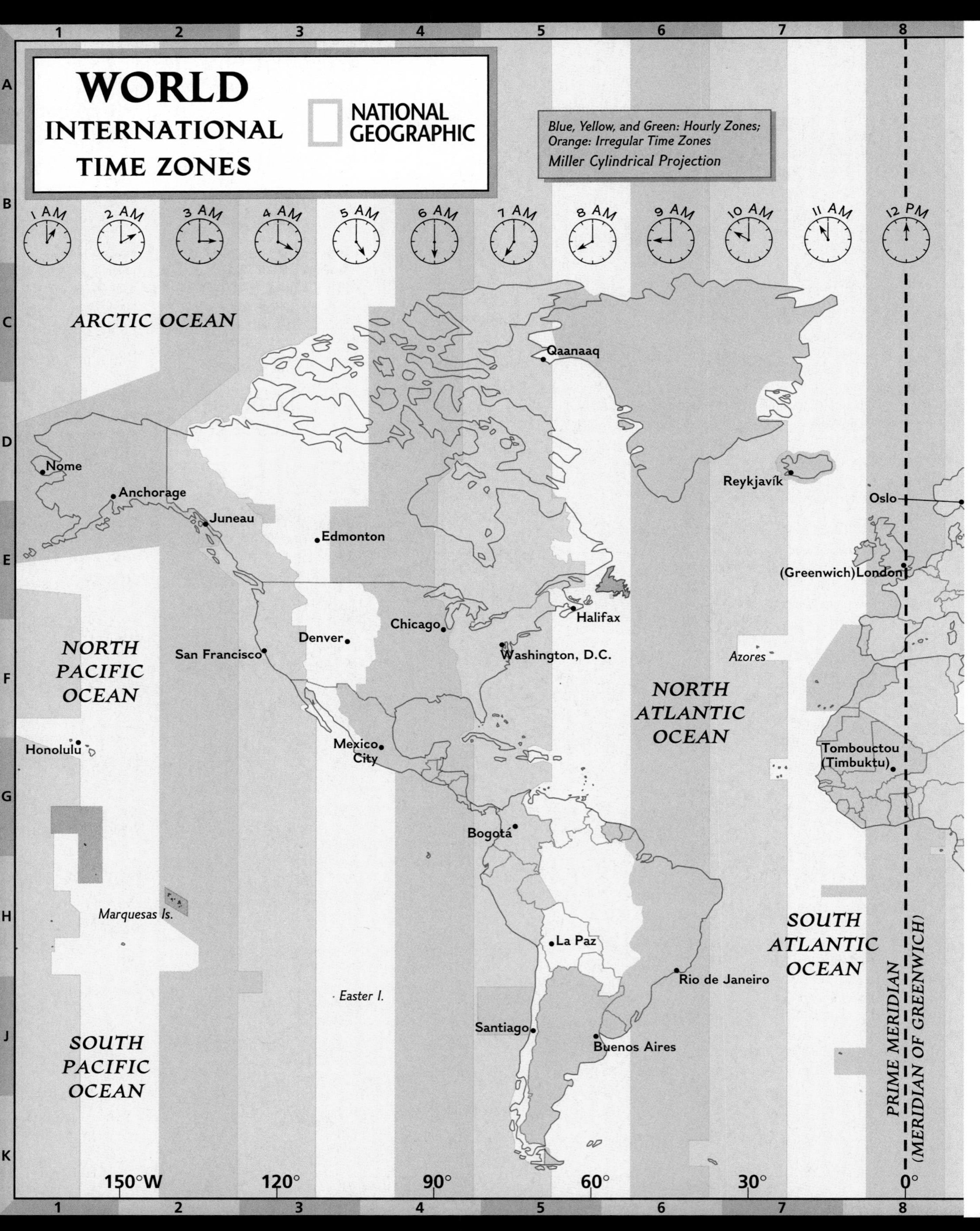

WORLD
INTERNATIONAL
TIME ZONES
NATIONAL GEOGRAPHIC
Blue, Yellow, and Green: Hourly Zones;
Orange: Irregular Time Zones
Miller Cylindrical Projection
1 AM
2 AM
3 AM
4 AM
5 AM
6 AM
7 AM
8 AM
9 AM
10 AM
11 AM
12 PM
ARCTIC OCEAN
Qaanaaq
Nome
Anchorage
Juneau
Edmonton
Reykjavík
Oslo
(Greenwich)London
Halifax
Chicago
Denver
San Francisco
Washington, D.C.
Azores
NORTH PACIFIC OCEAN
NORTH ATLANTIC OCEAN
Honolulu
Mexico City
Tombouctou (Timbuktu)
Bogotá
Marquesas Is.
SOUTH ATLANTIC OCEAN
La Paz
Rio de Janeiro
Easter I.
Santiago
Buenos Aires
SOUTH PACIFIC OCEAN
PRIME MERIDIAN (MERIDIAN OF GREENWICH)
150°W
120°
90°
60°
30°
0°

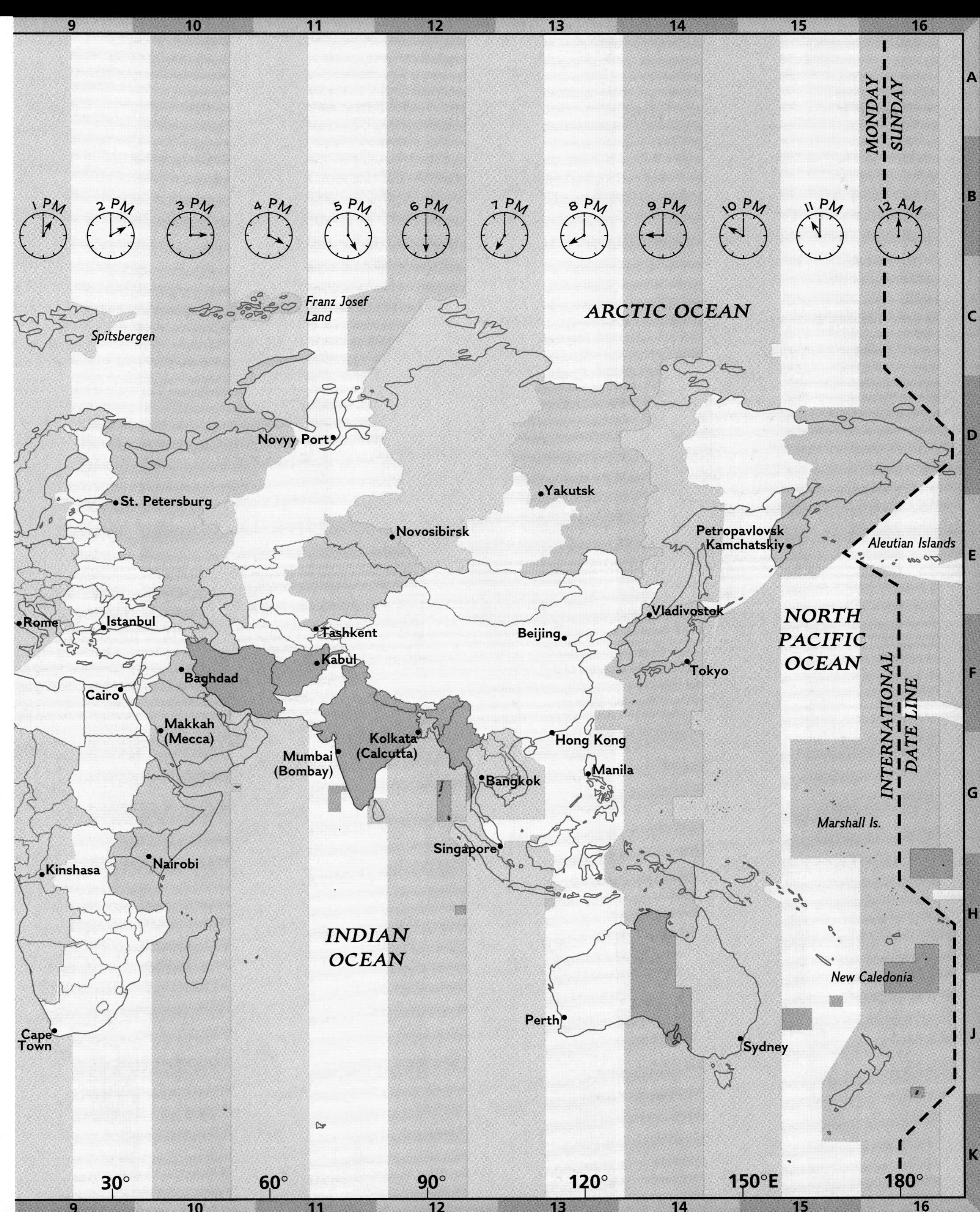

9
10
11
12
13
14
15
16
MONDAY
SUNDAY
1 PM
2 PM
3 PM
4 PM
5 PM
6 PM
7 PM
8 PM
9 PM
10 PM
11 PM
12 AM
Franz Josef Land
Spitsbergen
ARCTIC OCEAN
Novyy Port
St. Petersburg
Yakutsk
Novosibirsk
Petropavlovsk Kamchatskiy
Aleutian Islands
Rome
Istanbul
Tashkent
Vladivostok
NORTH PACIFIC OCEAN
Beijing
Kabul
Baghdad
Tokyo
Cairo
Makkah (Mecca)
Kolkata (Calcutta)
Hong Kong
Mumbai (Bombay)
Manila
Bangkok
INTERNATIONAL DATE LINE
Marshall Is.
Singapore
Nairobi
Kinshasa
INDIAN OCEAN
New Caledonia
Perth
Cape Town
Sydney
30°
60°
90°
120°
150°E
180°
A
B
C
D
E
F
G
H
I
J
K

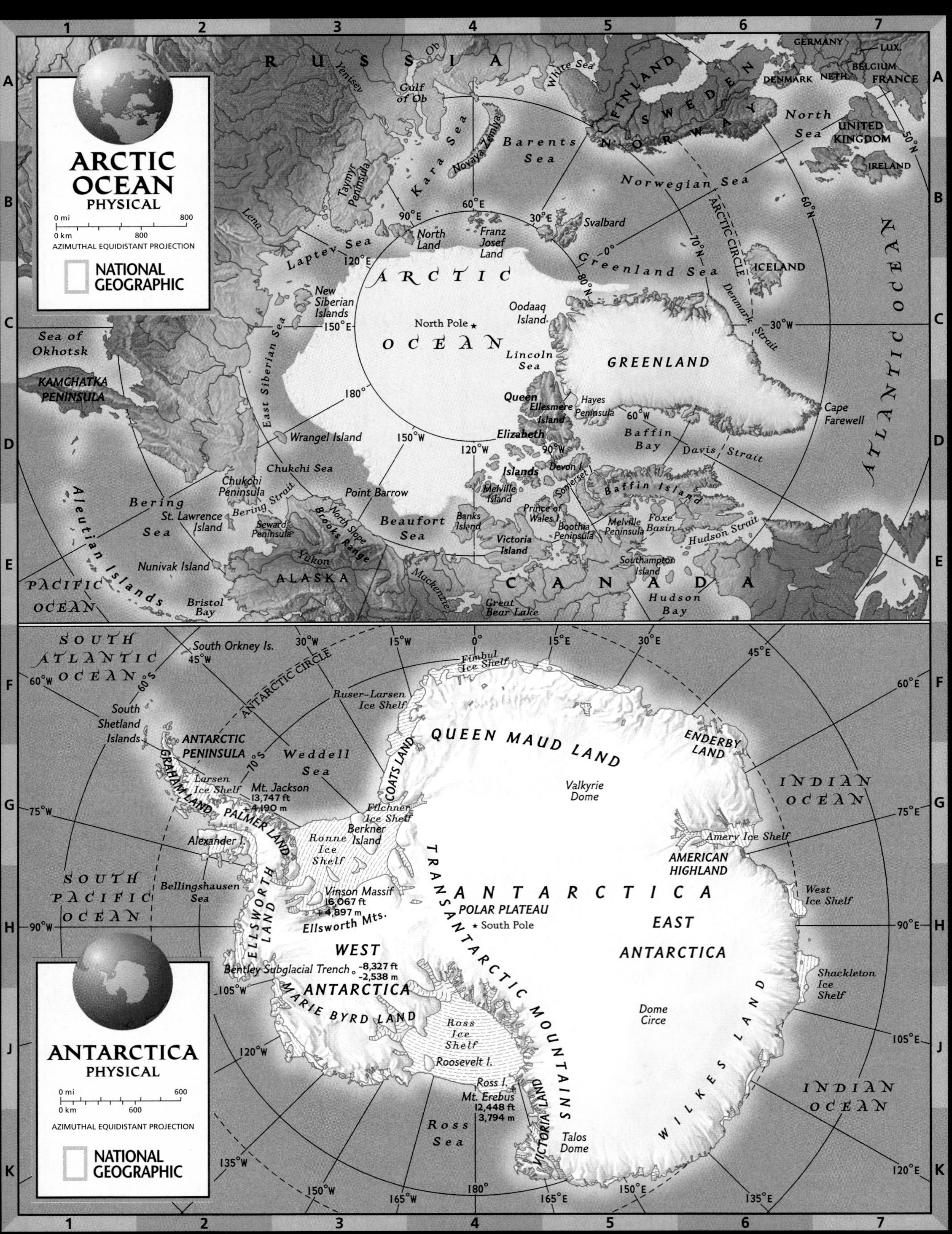

ARCTIC OCEAN
PHYSICAL
AZIMUTHAL EQUIDISTANT PROJECTION
NATIONAL GEOGRAPHIC
RUSSIA
Gulf of Ob
Kara Sea
Novaya Zemlya
Barents Sea
White Sea
FINLAND
SWEDEN
NORWAY
GERMANY
LUX.
BELGIUM
DENMARK
NETH.
FRANCE
North Sea
UNITED KINGDOM
IRELAND
Norwegian Sea
Taymyr Peninsula
North Land
Franz Josef Land
Svalbard
Laptev Sea
Greenland Sea
ARCTIC CIRCLE
ICELAND
New Siberian Islands
ARCTIC OCEAN
North Pole
Oodaaq Island
Denmark Strait
Sea of Okhotsk
East Siberian Sea
Lincoln Sea
GREENLAND
KAMCHATKA PENINSULA
Queen Elizabeth Islands
Ellesmere Island
Hayes Peninsula
Cape Farewell
Wrangel Island
Baffin Bay
Davis Strait
ATLANTIC OCEAN
Chukchi Sea
Devon I.
Chukchi Peninsula
Point Barrow
Melville Island
Somerset I.
Baffin Island
Bering Sea
Bering Strait
St. Lawrence Island
Seward Peninsula
North Slope
Brooks Range
Beaufort Sea
Banks Island
Prince of Wales I.
Boothia Peninsula
Melville Peninsula
Foxe Basin
Hudson Strait
Victoria Island
Aleutian Islands
Nunivak Island
Yukon
ALASKA
Mackenzie
Southampton Island
CANADA
PACIFIC OCEAN
Bristol Bay
Great Bear Lake
Hudson Bay
Lena
Yenisey
Ob
SOUTH ATLANTIC OCEAN
South Orkney Is.
ANTARCTIC CIRCLE
Fimbul Ice Shelf
Ruser-Larsen Ice Shelf
South Shetland Islands
QUEEN MAUD LAND
ENDERBY LAND
ANTARCTIC PENINSULA
Weddell Sea
COATS LAND
Larsen Ice Shelf
Mt. Jackson 13,747 ft 4,190 m
GRAHAM LAND
PALMER LAND
Valkyrie Dome
INDIAN OCEAN
Filchner Ice Shelf
Berkner Island
Amery Ice Shelf
Alexander I.
Ronne Ice Shelf
AMERICAN HIGHLAND
SOUTH PACIFIC OCEAN
Bellingshausen Sea
Vinson Massif 16,067 ft 4,897 m
ANTARCTICA
West Ice Shelf
POLAR PLATEAU
Ellsworth Mts.
South Pole
EAST ANTARCTICA
ELLSWORTH LAND
WEST ANTARCTICA
TRANSANTARCTIC MOUNTAINS
Bentley Subglacial Trench -8,327 ft -2,538 m
Shackleton Ice Shelf
MARIE BYRD LAND
Dome Circe
Ross Ice Shelf
WILKES LAND
ANTARCTICA
PHYSICAL
AZIMUTHAL EQUIDISTANT PROJECTION
NATIONAL GEOGRAPHIC
Roosevelt I.
Ross I.
Mt. Erebus 12,448 ft 3,794 m
VICTORIA LAND
INDIAN OCEAN
Ross Sea
Talos Dome

A WORLD OF EXTREMES

1 The largest continent is Asia with an area of 12,262,691 sq. miles (31,758,898 sq. km).

2 The smallest continent is Australia with an area of 2,988,888 sq. miles (7,741,184 sq. km).

3 The largest country is Russia with an area of 6,592,819 sq. miles (17,075,322 sq. km).

4 The smallest country is Vatican City with an area of 1 sq. mile (2.6 sq. km).

5 The longest river is the Nile River with a length of 4,160 miles (6,695 km).

6 The deepest freshwater lake is Lake Baikal with a maximum depth of 5,715 feet (1,742 m).

7 The highest waterfall is Angel Falls with a height of 3,212 feet (979 m).

8 The highest mountain is Mount Everest with a height of 29,028 feet (8,848 m) above sea level.

9 The largest desert is the Sahara with an area of 3,500,000 sq. miles (9,065,000 sq. km).

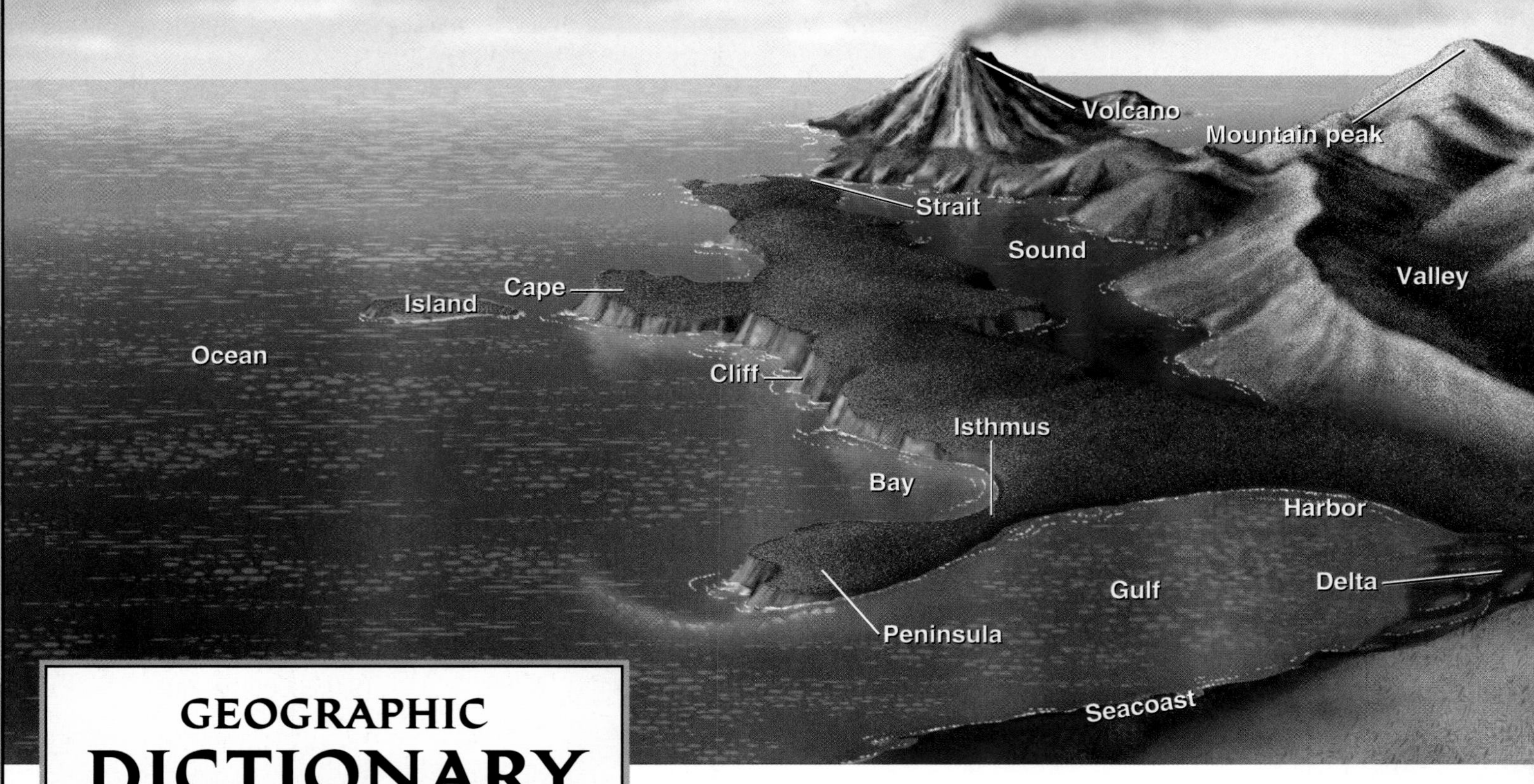

GEOGRAPHIC DICTIONARY

As you read about the world's geography, you will encounter the terms listed below. Many of the terms are pictured in the diagram.

absolute location exact location of a place on the Earth described by global coordinates

basin area of land drained by a given river and its branches; area of land surrounded by lands of higher elevations

bay part of a large body of water that extends into a shoreline, generally smaller than a gulf

canyon deep and narrow valley with steep walls

cape point of land that extends into a river, lake, or ocean

channel wide strait or waterway between two landmasses that lie close to each other; deep part of a river or other waterway

cliff steep, high wall of rock, Earth, or ice

continent one of the seven large landmasses on the Earth

delta flat, low-lying land built up from soil carried downstream by a river and deposited at its mouth

divide stretch of high land that separates river systems

downstream direction in which a river or stream flows from its source to its mouth

elevation height of land above sea level

Equator imaginary line that runs around the Earth halfway between the North and South Poles; used as the starting point to measure degrees of north and south latitude

glacier large, thick body of slowly moving ice

gulf part of a large body of water that extends into a shoreline, generally larger and more deeply indented than a bay

harbor a sheltered place along a shoreline where ships can anchor safely

highland elevated land area such as a hill, mountain, or plateau

hill elevated land with sloping sides and rounded summit; generally smaller than a mountain

island land area, smaller than a continent, completely surrounded by water

isthmus narrow stretch of land connecting two larger land areas

lake a sizable inland body of water

latitude distance north or south of the Equator, measured in degrees

longitude distance east or west of the Prime Meridian, measured in degrees

lowland land, usually level, at a low elevation

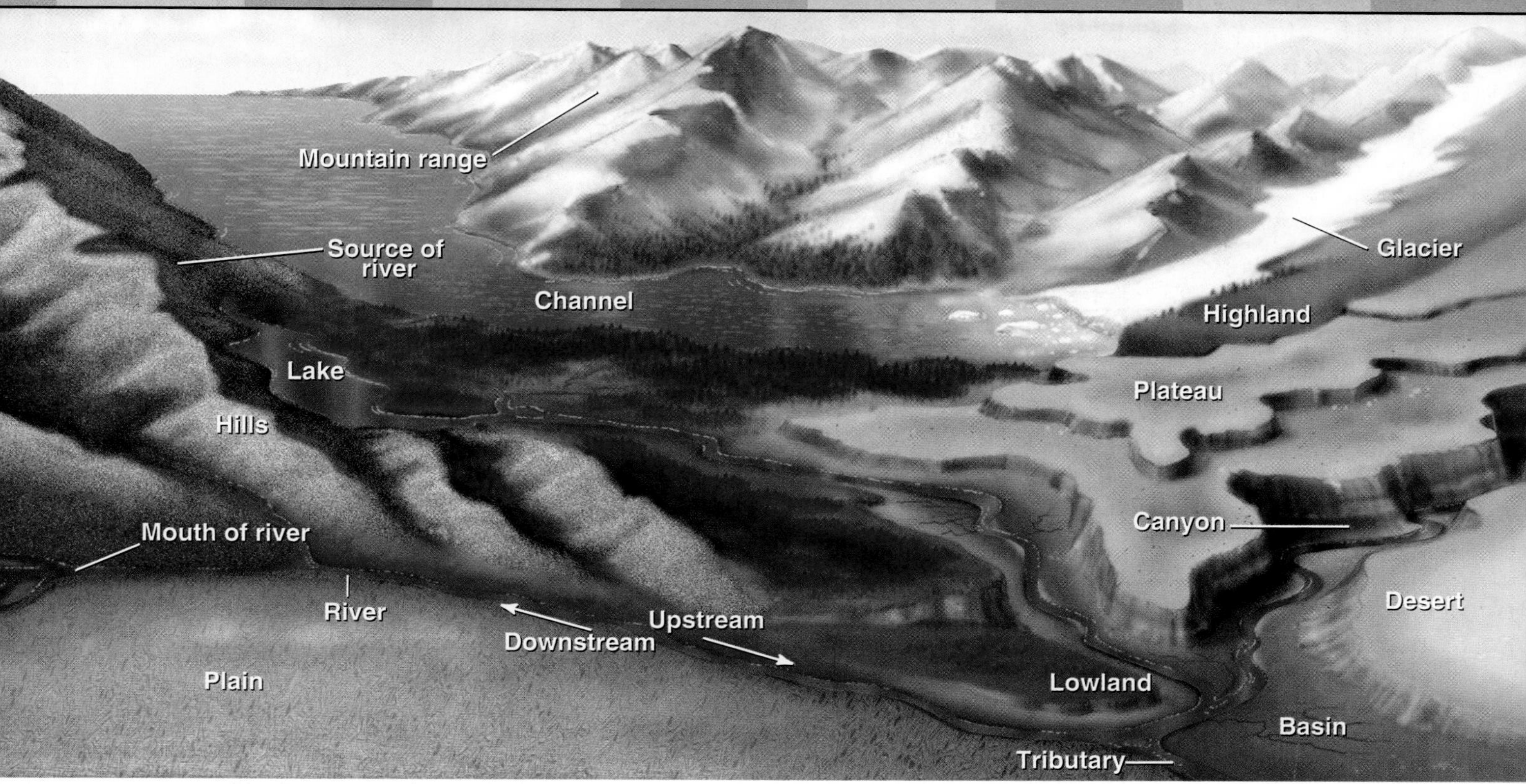

map drawing of the Earth shown on a flat surface

meridian one of many lines on the global grid running from the North Pole to the South Pole; used to measure degrees of longitude

mesa broad, flat-topped landform with steep sides; smaller than a plateau

mountain land with steep sides that rises sharply (1,000 feet or more) from surrounding land; generally larger and more rugged than a hill

mountain peak pointed top of a mountain

mountain range a series of connected mountains

mouth (of a river) place where a stream or river flows into a larger body of water

ocean one of the four major bodies of salt water that surround the continents

ocean current stream of either cold or warm water that moves in a definite direction through an ocean

parallel one of many lines on the global grid that circles the Earth north or south of the Equator; used to measure degrees of latitude

peninsula body of land jutting into a lake or ocean, surrounded on three sides by water

physical feature characteristic of a place occurring naturally, such as a landform, body of water, climate pattern, or resource

plain area of level land, usually at low elevation and often covered with grasses

plateau area of flat or rolling land at a high elevation, about 300 to 3,000 feet (90 to 900 m) high

Prime Meridian line of the global grid running from the North Pole to the South Pole at Greenwich, England; starting point for measuring degrees of east and west longitude

relief changes in elevation over a given area of land

river large natural stream of water that runs through the land

sea large body of water completely or partly surrounded by land

seacoast land lying next to a sea or an ocean

sound broad inland body of water, often between a coastline and one or more islands off the coast

source (of a river) place where a river or stream begins, often in highlands

strait narrow stretch of water joining two larger bodies of water

tributary small river or stream that flows into a large river or stream; a branch of the river

upstream direction opposite the flow of a river; toward the source of a river or stream

valley area of low land usually between hills or mountains

volcano mountain or hill created as liquid rock and ash erupt from inside the Earth

Unit 1 Planning Guide

UNIT PACING CHART				
Unit 1		Chapter 1	Chapter 2	Chapter 3
Day 1	Unit Opener	Chapter Opener	Chapter Opener	Chapter Opener
Day 2	Regional Atlas	Section 1	Section 1	Section 1
Day 3	Regional Atlas	Geography Handbook	Section 2	TIME Perspectives
Day 4	Reading Social Studies	Geography Handbook	World Literature Reading	TIME Perspectives
Day 5		Geography Handbook	Section 2	Section 2
Day 6		Geography Handbook	Section 3	Section 2
Day 7		Section 2	Section 3	You Decide
Day 8		Section 2	Section 3	Section 3
Day 9		Review	Geography & History	Review
Day 10		Chapter Assessment	Section 4	Chapter Assessment
Day 11			Review	TIME Journal
Day 12			Chapter Assessment	

Sharon Shelerud
Metcalf Junior High School
Eagan, Minnesota

Landform/Waterway Play Dough Test
Students will demonstrate their knowledge of landforms and waterways by creating replicas of them with play dough. Cover each desk with a paper grocery bag. Give each student a can of play dough. Write each landform or waterway that students will have to create on an index card and have the stack of cards lying face down on student desks. Students can easily do twenty cards in a 45-minute class period. When you say go, students flip over the stack and start making their landforms and waterways. Suggest that they look through the stack to do the ones they know first so they can earn maximum points. Take notes to keep track of each landform or waterway that each student completes. At the end of the class period, each student receives a number of points equal to the number of landforms and waterways for which you have given them credit.

Author Note

Dear Social Studies Teacher:

Unit 1 is crucial to you as a teacher. It explains all of the elements of geography—the people, places, and environments—and how geographers look at our world. The study of geography allows us to make sense out of varied physical environments, diverse cultural systems, why people live where they do, and how they earn a living. Unit 1 also addresses the new technologies that geographers use to map and understand where and how we live. You only need to watch automobile television ads to see how Geographic Positioning Systems (GPS) and Geographic Information Systems (GIS) are inching their way into our everyday lives.

Unit 1 introduces the student to the elegance of geography with superb pictures, maps, and explanatory text. The chapters also clearly send the message to the student that if you like geography and if you learn it well, exciting jobs and careers await you. You can be a geographer for life and pursue a subject that is both fun and interesting.

Richard G. Boehm
Senior Author

Unit Overview

The three chapters of this unit introduce students to the world. Important concepts covered in this unit include

- the five themes used by geographers to describe places and people
- the effects of the tilt of the Earth on climate and seasons
- the influence of landforms, water resources, and climate regions on where people live
- the negative impact of human activities on the environment
- the shared characteristics that define the culture of a group of people
- factors that lead to cultural change
- the four kinds of economic systems and growing interdependence among countries of the world

NATIONAL GEOGRAPHIC

www.nationalgeographic.com/education

NGS ONLINE This online resource provides lesson plans, atlas updates, cartographic activities with interactive maps, an online map store, and geographic links.

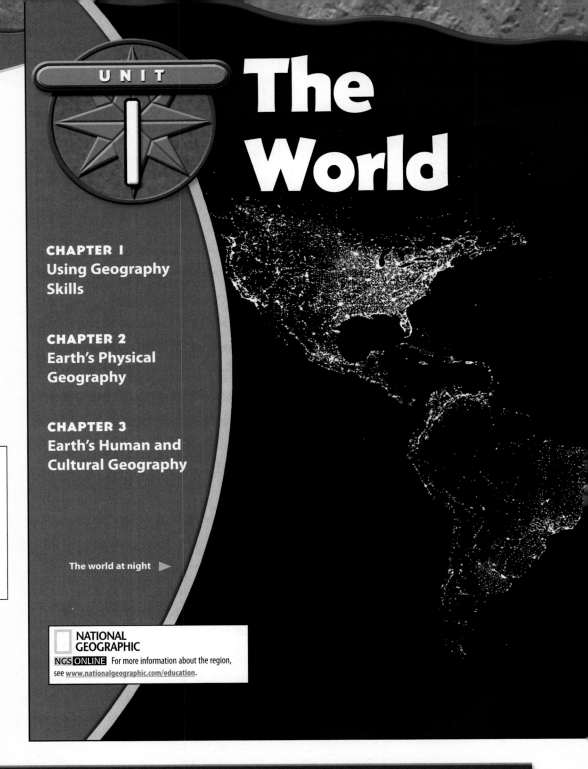

UNIT 1

The World

The world at night ▶

NATIONAL GEOGRAPHIC

NGS ONLINE For more information about the region, see www.nationalgeographic.com/education.

Activity: Launching the Unit

Why Study the World? Ask: In what way is your daily life influenced by global events and access to global goods? *(Students may mention positive influences, such as new forms of music or lower prices for some goods. Students may mention negative effects, such as higher prices for oil and gas when conflict arises in southwest Asia.)* Create a chart for students to see. Title the chart "Our Global Connections." Have students contribute specific ways their everyday life has been impacted by global connections. **Ask: What country produced your family's car? Where were your clothes manufactured? From which areas does the local supermarket get its fruit?** List student answers on the chart. Encourage students to continue to look for ways in which their lives are impacted by global connections. Add student contributions to the list as you study the unit. **OL**

Introducing Unit 1

Introduce the World

Analyzing Have students look at the population density map in the World Atlas. **Ask: What areas of the world are most densely populated?** *(South Asia, Southeast Asia, Europe, coastal West Africa, and the northeastern United States)* **What areas of the world are least densely populated?** *(Antarctica, North Africa, much of Russia, northern Canada)* Ask students to compare the world population density map to the satellite image of the world at night. **Ask: Given what you know about population density from examining the map in the World Atlas, where would you expect to see brightly lit areas in the image of the world at night?** *(in the areas that are most densely populated)* **Is there anything you find surprising about the image?** *(Answers may include that the lights in India are not as bright as the lights along the coast of the eastern United States.)* **What might explain this?** *(Developing countries, even when densely populated, may not have reliable power sources to generate lights. People may not be able to afford to light their homes and cities.)* OL

More About the Photo

Visual Literacy Remind students that the Earth is never all in the dark at the same time. This image of the world at night is actually a composite created from hundreds of photographs taken by satellites orbiting the Earth. Satellites are used for a variety of activities, including scientific research, collecting weather data, providing civilian and military communications, as part of the Global Positioning System, and mapping and photographing surface features. In this image of the world at night, human settlements with access to electricity are visible. Clusters of light indicate developed or densely populated areas of the Earth. The brightest lights are located in North America, Europe, and Japan, especially on the coasts. Dark areas, indicating low population densities or a lack of electric power, include the interiors of Africa, South America, Central Asia, and Australia.

World Atlas Activity

Comparing Have students compare climate and vegetation regions as shown on the maps in the World Atlas. **Ask: In what climate region are most of the world's tropical rain forests located?** *(tropical wet)* **In what climate region are most of the world's savannas located?** *(tropical dry)* **What types of vegetation does a humid continental climate support?** *(deciduous forest, coniferous forest, mixed forest, temperate grassland)* **What types of vegetation does a Mediterranean climate support?** *(Mediterranean scrub)* **OL**

Map Skills

Answers:

1. tundra and ice cap
2. mostly tropical wet

Skills Practice

Ask: Where are most Mediterranean climates located? *(near coastlines, above the Tropic of Cancer, below the Tropic of Capricorn)*

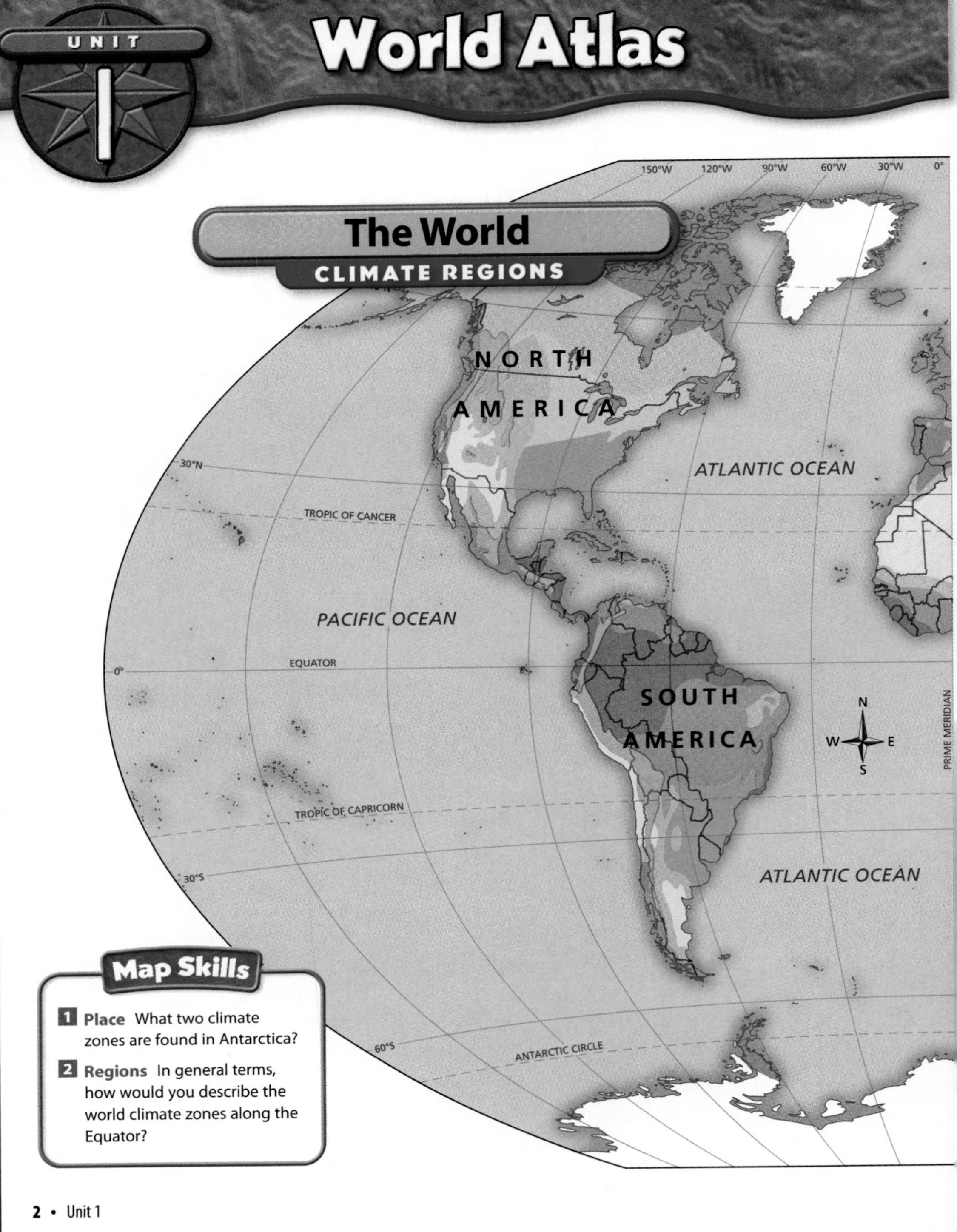

Activity: Using Maps

Categorizing Organize students into pairs. Ask each pair to select a continent. Direct students to the various political maps in the National Geographic Reference Atlas to find the names and locations of countries on their selected continent. Draw a chart on the board with the following headings: *Tropical Wet, Tropical Dry, Steppe, Desert, Mediterranean, Humid Subtropical, Marine West Coast, Humid Continental, Subarctic,* and *Tundra.* Have students copy this chart into their notebooks. Give students time to look through the political maps and list the countries on their continent that fit into each of the categories on the chart. **Ask: Are any of the climate regions not represented on your continent? Does most of your continent fit into one broad climate category (such as tropical, dry, mid-latitude, high-latitude)? Two categories? Which ones?** *(Answers will vary depending on the continent selected.)* **OL**

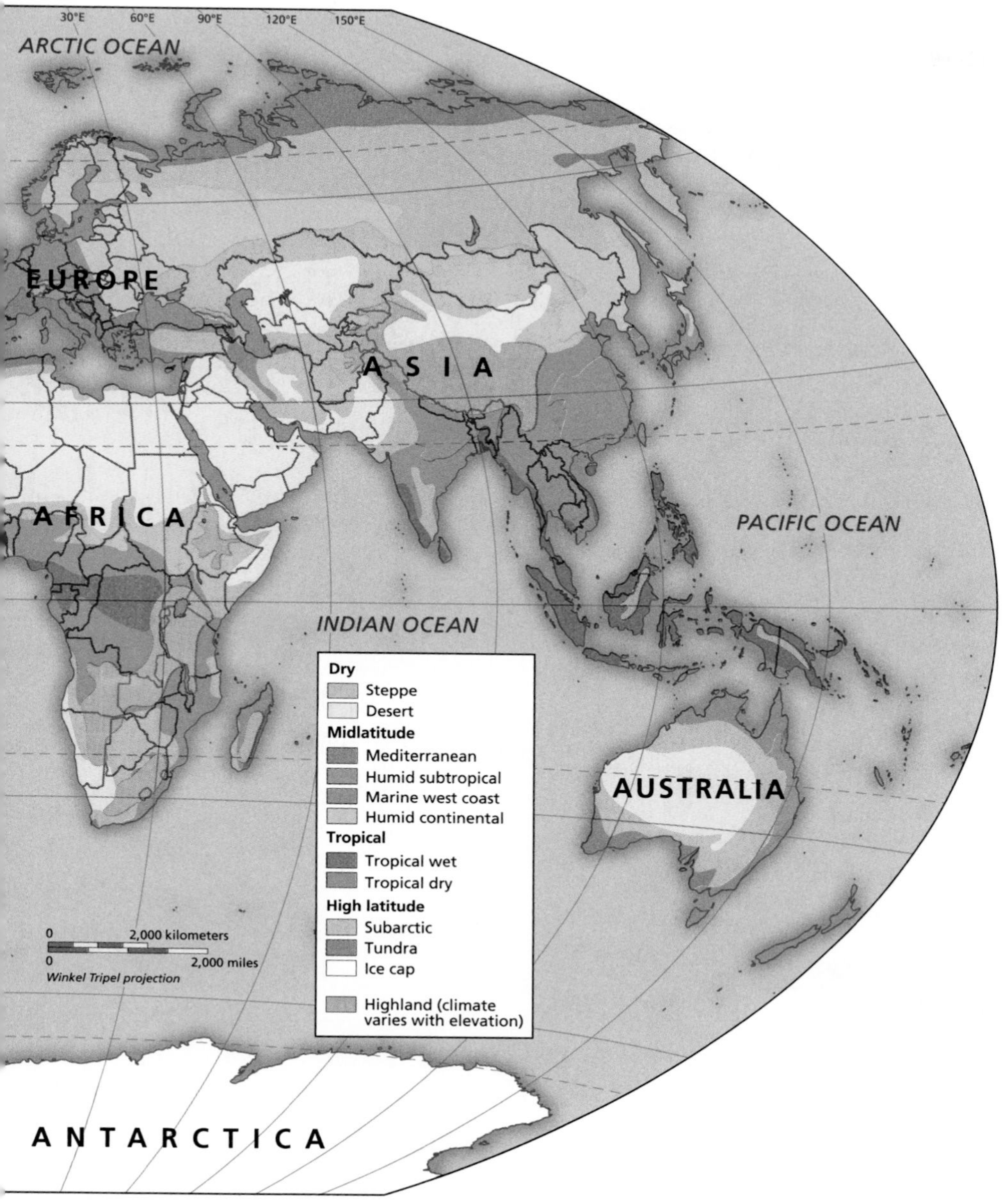

World Atlas Activity

Synthesizing Help students synthesize the information in the World Atlas maps by asking 20 questions. Ask students to review the maps in the World Atlas as well as the World: Political and World: Physical maps in the National Geographic Reference Atlas. Have each student select and write down a location. Ask for a student volunteer. Have other students take turns asking up to 20 "yes" or "no" questions to determine the location the student volunteer selected. *(Examples: Is it in a tropical climate? Do forests grow there? Is it in a place with more than 1,250 people per square mile? Is Hinduism the dominant religion in the location? Is the Nile River one of its geographic features?)*

Assign three points to each student who correctly guesses a location, assign three points to a student who stumps classmates, and deduct one point from any student who incorrectly guesses a location. The student with the highest score at the end of a class period wins. **OL**

Skills Practice

What climates are located along the Tropic of Capricorn? *(desert, subarctic, humid subtropical, steppe, tropical dry)*

FastFacts

- **Alaskan Fur Rush** In 1741 shipwrecked Russian sailors found the Alaskan coast teeming with sea otters. When survivors returned to Russia with sea otter pelts, they set off a fur rush similar to later gold rushes. Hundreds of thousands of otters were killed. For some Russians, one fur could be worth a year's pay. Within a century, sea otters on the Alaskan coast had been hunted almost to extinction.
- **Global Positioning System** The Global Positioning System is a space-based navigation system. It was originally developed by the U.S. Department of Defense and is operated by the Air Force. Using a system of 24 satellites that circle the Earth every 24 hours, an operator can calculate a user's longitude, latitude, and altitude. A less-accurate system is available free of charge for civilian use. GPS has a wide range of uses, ranging from its application for the space shuttle and the International Space Station to cell phones and family cars.

World Atlas Activity

Locating Information Assign each student one type of vegetation shown in the key of the vegetation map in the World Atlas. **Ask:** **What specific plants do you think belong in this category?** *(Answers will vary depending on the type of vegetation assigned.)* Have students research the plants that grow in their assigned vegetation areas. They may use encyclopedias, online resources, or other reference sources. After the students have finished their research, draw a chart on the board listing each vegetation type. Have student volunteers come to the board and fill in one specific plant that grows in an area with that vegetation type. Volunteers should continue until the chart includes all the information the students have found in their research. **OL**

Answers:

1. Southeast Asia is mostly made up of tropical rain forest.
2. coniferous forest

Skills Practice

Ask: **What types of vegetation are found on the island of Madagascar, the large island off the east coast of Africa?** *(deciduous forest along the coast, and temperate grassland in the interior)*

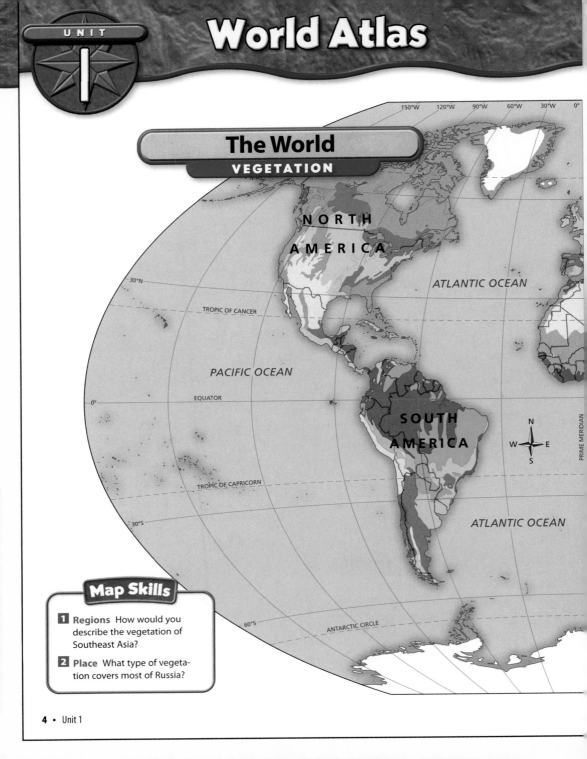

UNIT 1

World Atlas

The World

VEGETATION

NORTH AMERICA

SOUTH AMERICA

ATLANTIC OCEAN

PACIFIC OCEAN

TROPIC OF CANCER

EQUATOR

TROPIC OF CAPRICORN

ANTARCTIC CIRCLE

PRIME MERIDIAN

Map Skills

1. **Regions** How would you describe the vegetation of Southeast Asia?
2. **Place** What type of vegetation covers most of Russia?

4 • Unit 1

Activity: Geographic Theme

Human-Environment Interaction Review with the class how the climate of an area and the vegetation that grows there can influence population density. Ask students to think about how the climate of the area where they live may have influenced population density. Then have students review the maps showing climate regions and vegetation in the World Atlas. **Ask:** **Based on the climate regions and vegetation maps, where do you think most of the world's people live? Why?** *(Students may suggest that most people probably live in the mid-latitude climates, which are not too hot or too cold and which receive enough rainfall to support agriculture. Examples might be Southeast Asia, Europe, and eastern North America.)* **Ask:** **Which do you think has a greater impact on population density, climate or vegetation?** *(Students might answer climate, because harsher climates require more adaptation; or vegetation, because people settle where food is plentiful.)* Discuss with students what other factors might influence population density. *(Possible examples: access to water, annual rainfall, jobs, opportunities, manufacturing centers, trade)* **AL**

30°E 60°E 90°E 120°E 150°E

ARCTIC OCEAN

EUROPE

ASIA

AFRICA

PACIFIC OCEAN

INDIAN OCEAN

AUSTRALIA

ANTARCTICA

Tropical rain forest
Tropical grassland (savanna)
Desert scrub and desert waste
Temperate grassland
Mediterranean scrub
Deciduous forest
Coniferous forest
Mixed forest (deciduous and coniferous)
Tundra
Ice cap
Highland (vegetation varies with elevation)

0 2,000 kilometers
0 2,000 miles
Winkel Tripel projection

World Atlas Activity

Hypothesizing Have students use the political maps in the National Geographic Reference Atlas to help them locate Southwest Asia and North Africa on the vegetation map. **Ask: What type of vegetation covers most of Southwest Asia and North Africa?** *(desert scrub and desert waste)* **What is the exception?** *(a narrow band of tropical rain forest in North Africa)* **What could explain this?** List student hypotheses on the board. Then have students turn to the physical map of Africa in the National Geographic Reference Atlas. **Ask: What explains the band of tropical rain forest in the desert of North Africa?** *(The Nile River flows through the Sahara, providing the water needed for the vegetation in a tropical rain forest.)* **OL**

Skills Practice

Ask: What types of vegetation are found in Australia? *(tropical grassland along the northern coast, desert scrub and desert waste in the interior, and temperate grassland and tropical rain forests along the southern coast, as well as a swath of mixed forest in the west)*

FastFacts

- **The *Trieste*** In January 1960, Jacques Piccard and Donald Walsh used the bathyscaphe *Trieste*, a special submarine that can operate under great water pressure, to descend a record 35,810 feet to the bottom of the Mariana Trench. This is the deepest known point in the oceans. The *Trieste* pumped water into air tanks to descend. To ascend, Piccard and Walsh pumped the water out and released iron pellets carried onboard.
- **Igloos** The Inuit people inhabit Greenland, the northern coasts and islands of Canada, northern Alaska, and the north coast of Russia. They are known for one of their adaptations to the harsh arctic climate: they build round houses made of ice called igloos. These houses are primarily used as temporary shelters for fishers and hunters and are surprisingly warm and snug inside.

World Atlas Activity

Predicting Have students review the population density map and note cities with populations over 10,000,000. Explain that cities with over 10 million residents are known as megacities. **Ask: Can you guess which are the five largest cities today?** *(Tokyo, Mexico City, São Paulo, New York City, and Mumbai)* **Which cities do you think are expected to be the five largest in 2015?** *(Students' answers may vary, but the correct answer is Tokyo, Dhaka, Mumbai, São Paulo, and Delhi.)* Tell students that in 1995, there were 14 megacities. In 2015 there will be 21 megacities. By 2030, 60 percent of the world's people will be living in cities. **Ask: Using what you have learned about the location of the five largest cities in 2015, which continent do you predict will have the greatest population growth?** *(Asia)* **OL**

Map Skills

Answers:

1. East Asia, South Asia, Southeast Asia, Europe, and eastern North America, West Africa, and Central America
2. Like South America, most of Australia's population is concentrated in the coastal areas. The interior region of South America is thinly populated, whereas Australia's interior is virtually uninhabited.

Unit 1 World Atlas

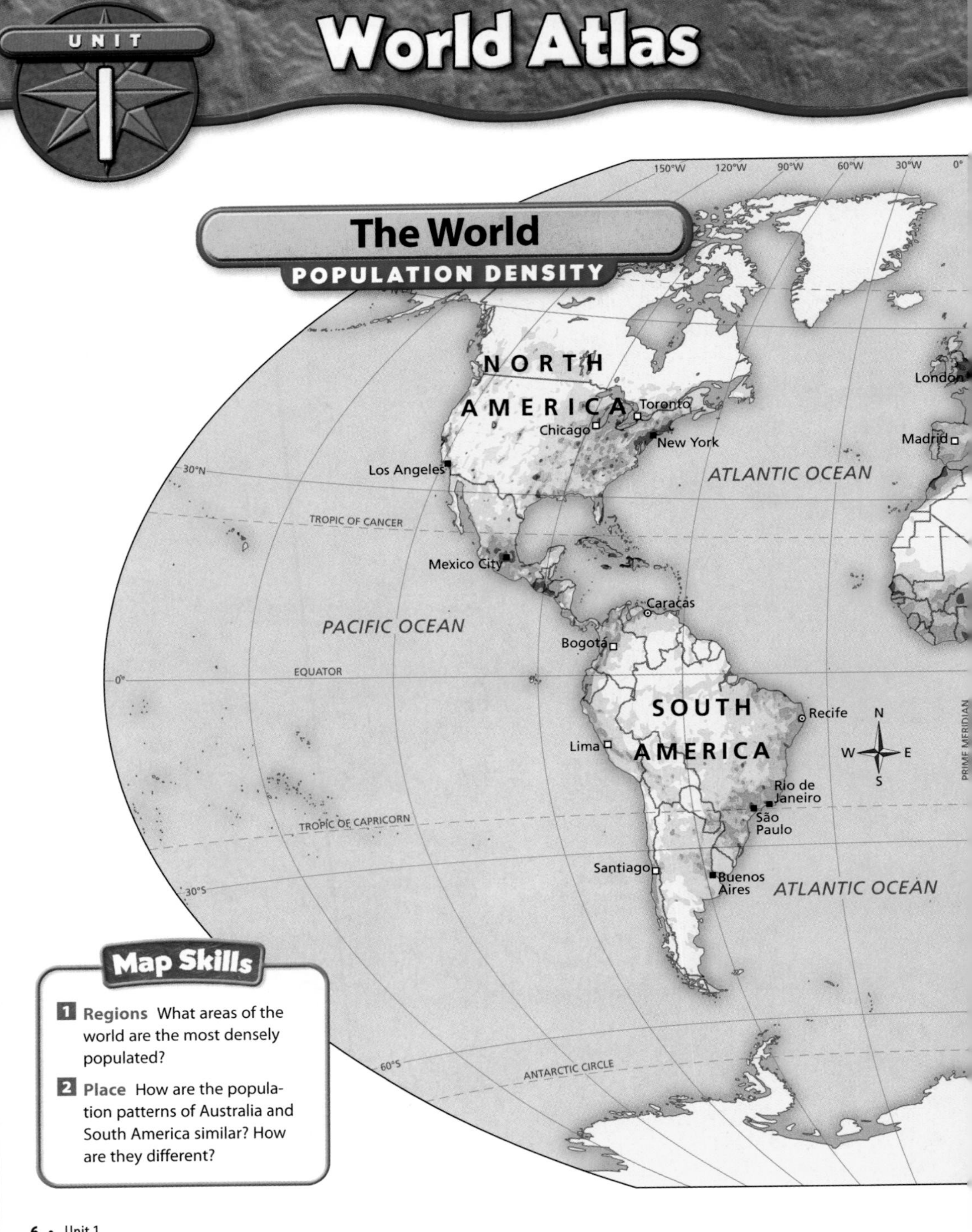

Map Skills

1 **Regions** What areas of the world are the most densely populated?

2 **Place** How are the population patterns of Australia and South America similar? How are they different?

Activity: Using Maps

Categorizing Ask each student to select a continent or region of the world. Have students create a three-column K-W-L chart. In the first column, have students list what they *Know* about their continent or region. This may be prior knowledge or information they have gained by reviewing the maps in the World Atlas. In the next column, have students list what they *Want* to learn about their continent or region. This list may include, but is not limited to, questions about language, ethnic groups, or culture. Tell students that the third column is for them to list what they *Learn* about the continent or region. Have students start filling in the *Learn* column by consulting the appropriate maps in the National Geographic Reference Atlas. Then have them find additional information, either in the text or in other sources, to complete the *Learn* column. **BL**

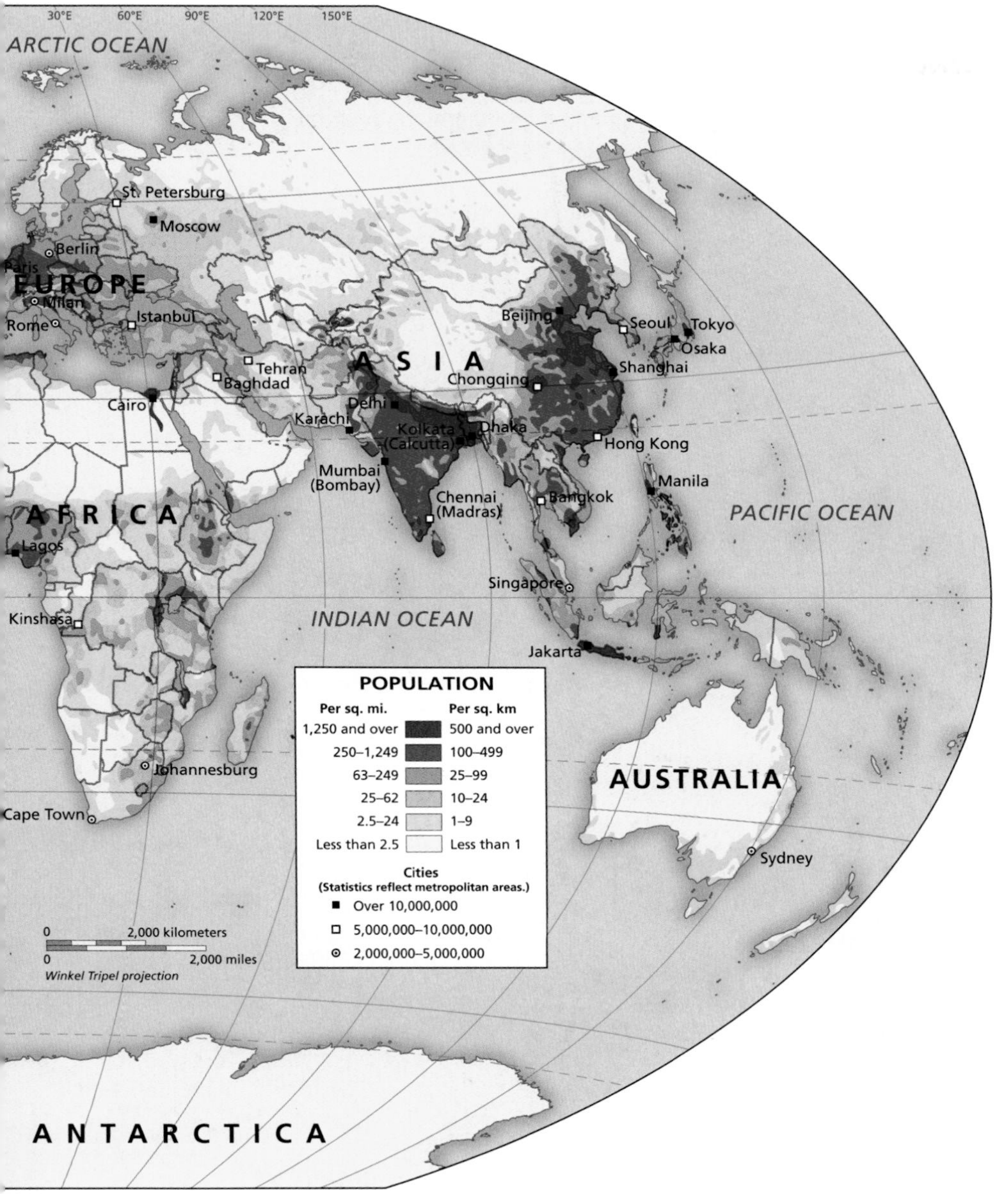

POPULATION		
Per sq. mi.		Per sq. km
1,250 and over		500 and over
250–1,249		100–499
63–249		25–99
25–62		10–24
2.5–24		1–9
Less than 2.5		Less than 1

Cities (Statistics reflect metropolitan areas.)
- ■ Over 10,000,000
- □ 5,000,000–10,000,000
- ⊙ 2,000,000–5,000,000

World Atlas Activity

Locating Cities Distribute one or two outline maps of various continents to each student. Explain that students will research additional cities in their continents and label them on their maps. Start by having students transfer the cities shown on the population density map to their outline map. Next, have them create a key that will represent the population of smaller cities, as well as those with populations over 2 million.

Have students use the political maps in the National Geographic Reference Atlas, as well as other world maps and atlases, to locate additional cities and research their populations. Students should record five to seven additional cities on each continent assigned to them. At the end of the class, have students who researched the same continents gather as a group and share their findings, adding cities to their own maps as appropriate. **AL**

Skills Practice

Ask: What do the locations of the world's most populated cities have in common? *(Most are near or on an ocean.)*

FastFacts

- **Greenpeace** The nonprofit organization Greenpeace was founded in 1971 in Canada to stop U.S. nuclear testing in the Aleutian Islands off the coast of Alaska. Since then, Greenpeace has embraced several environmental protection goals, including ending the practice of dumping toxic chemicals in the oceans and protecting endangered animals. Greenpeace has received media attention for its dramatic tactics, such as steering a small craft between a whaling ship and whales, or hanging banners from skyscrapers. Although dramatic and sometimes controversial, Greenpeace is committed to nonviolent protest.
- **Ancient Cultural Diffusion** The ancient trading route known as the Silk Road linked ancient China with people to the west. As luxury goods were traded on the route, ideas were exchanged between cultures. For example, Chinese techniques for making paper traveled west along the route. From India, Buddhism reached China.

World Atlas Activity

Drawing Conclusions Explain to students that an "indigenous religion" is usually specific to a particular place or ethnic group, and is not a major world religion. **Ask: Where are indigenous religions practiced in the world today?** *(the northern regions of North America and Asia; interior regions of Africa, Australia, and South America)* Have students compare this map to other maps in the World Atlas. **Ask: What conclusion can you draw about indigenous religions based on comparing the maps?** *(Answers may include that the major world religions replaced indigenous religions, or that more people practice indigenous religions than practice some world religions.)* **OL**

Map Skills

Answers:

1. South Asia, particularly India
2. North America is primarily Christian. In contrast, the African continent is more religiously diverse. Religions practiced there include forms of Islam, Christianity, and indigenous religions.

UNIT 1

World Atlas

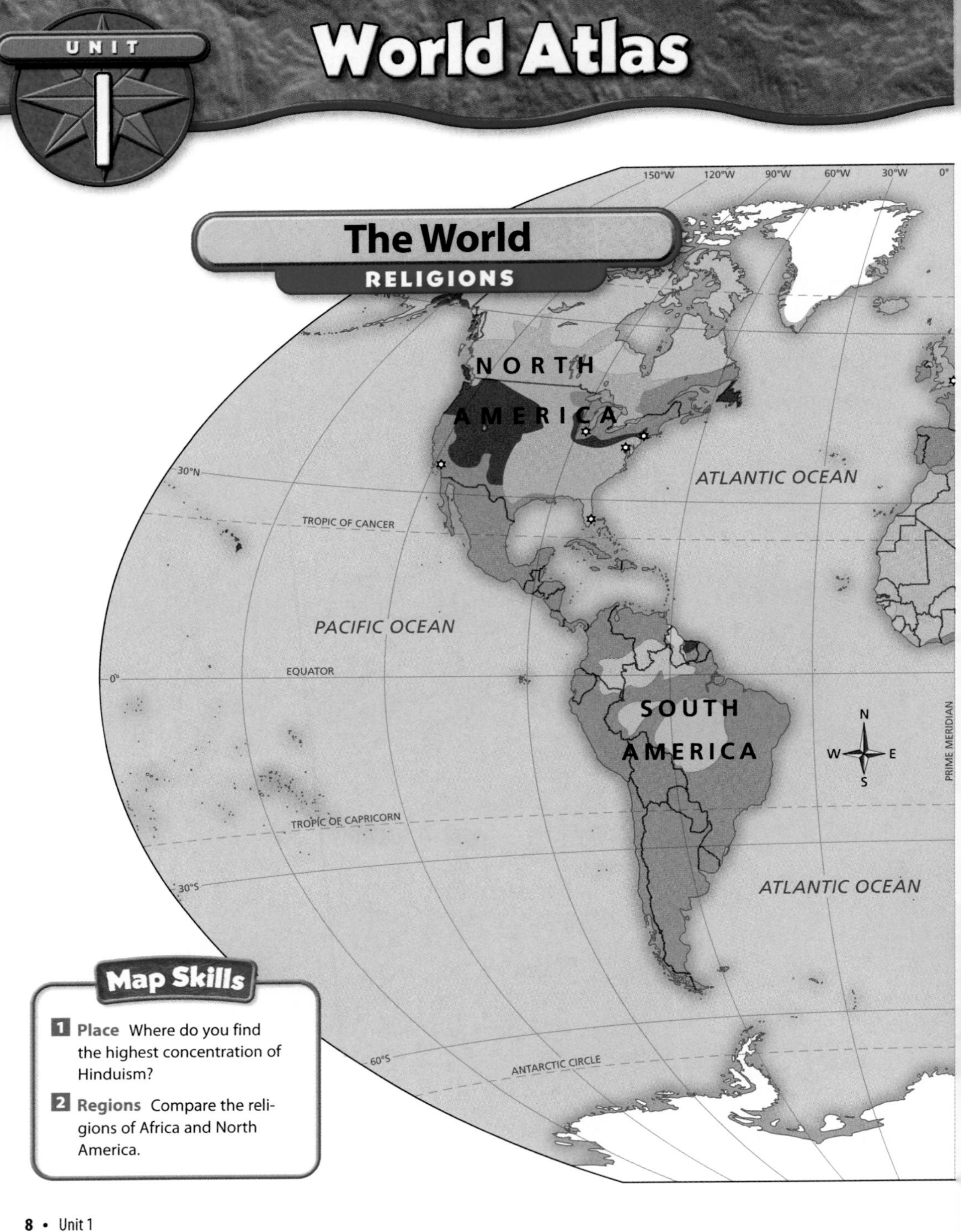

Map Skills

1. **Place** Where do you find the highest concentration of Hinduism?
2. **Regions** Compare the religions of Africa and North America.

8 • Unit 1

Activity: Using Maps

Locating Information Have students work alone or in pairs to research one of the religions shown on the map. **Ask: What questions do you have about this religion?** Have students make a list of six to eight questions based on the map and their interests. Questions might include when the religion began, where it began, when and how it spread to different areas of the world, and how its practice differs in different regions. Direct students to appropriate reference materials, including encyclopedias, world almanacs, atlases, and reliable online news and information sources to find the answers to their questions. Have students write their questions and the answers they locate on index cards. Group students according to the religion they researched. Have students share what they learned from their research with the group. Then have students quiz each other using the index cards. **AL**

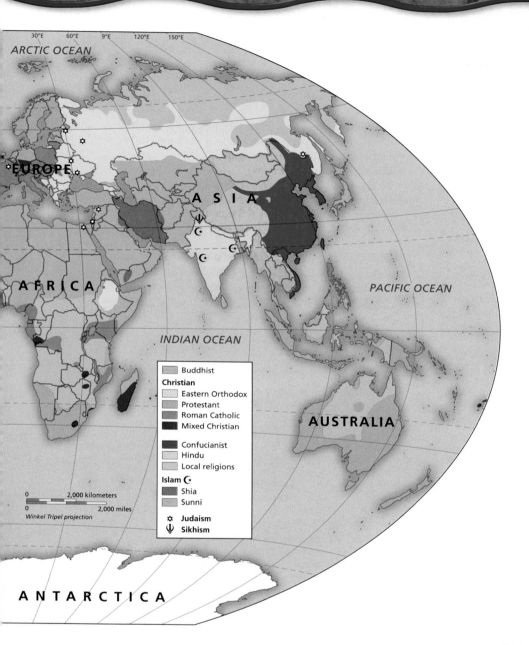

World Atlas Activity

Comparing and Contrasting Assign two continents to each student or group of students. Have students review climate regions, vegetation, population density, and religion as shown on the maps in the World Atlas. You may also refer students to the political and physical maps in the National Geographic Reference Atlas. Have students create a comparison frame that shows the similarities and differences between the two continents. Ask volunteers to share their results with the class. **OL**

Skills Practice

Ask: Where is Confucianism practiced? *(primarily in East Asia)* **In what areas of the world is Islam predominant?** *(Central Asia, Southwest Asia, and North Africa)*

FastFacts

- **Deadly Tropical Storms** The deadliest natural disaster in U.S. history was the hurricane that hit Galveston, Texas in 1900, killing 8,000 people. The deadliest tropical storm of the twentieth century was the 1970 cyclone that hit East Pakistan (now Bangladesh), killing an estimated 300,000 people. In both events, the storm surge accounted for most of the deaths.
- **Tuvalu** Tuvalu is a small country of nine islands in the western Pacific Ocean. None of the islands has an elevation of more than 16 feet (4.9 m) above sea level. As such, it is among the nations most threatened by rising oceans due to global warming. The United Nations has listed Tuvalu as a nation at risk of complete submersion.
- **Geocaching** Geocaching is an activity in which people go on treasure hunts looking for objects other people have concealed by using a GPS device and GPS coordinates that have been posted on a Web site. People can hide whatever they choose to hide.

Why Identifying the Main Idea Is Important

Locating the main idea of a reading passage is an essential skill for understanding many kinds of writing, from textbooks to essays to news articles. By identifying supporting details, students are better able to remember key information about the content. They also learn to distinguish the relative importance of different pieces of information. When students begin to analyze persuasive writing, identifying the main idea and supporting details is the first step in determining whether details an author provides are adequate to support the author's arguments.

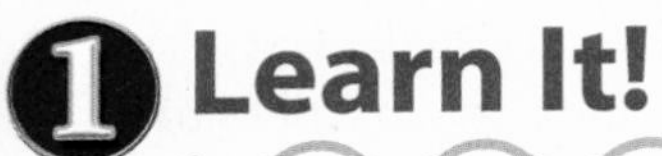

Write the following statement on the board: "The weather today is typical for this time of year." Have volunteers provide details that support the statement. Tell students that details can answer such questions as *why, when,* and *how*. Keep a list of details under the statement on the board. When done, have students discuss the difference between the original statement (the main idea) and the supporting details. **OL**

Reading Social Studies

Identifying the Main Idea

Reading Skill

1 Learn It!

Main ideas are the most important ideas in a paragraph, section, or chapter. The examples, reasons, and details that further explain the main idea are called *supporting details.*

- Read the paragraph below.
- Notice how the main idea is identified for you.
- Read the sentences that follow the main idea. These are supporting details that explain the main idea.

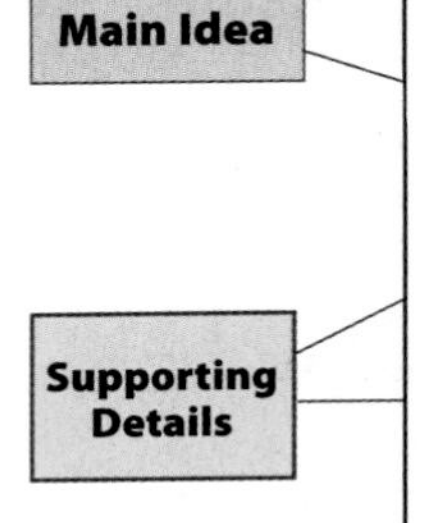

Main Idea

Supporting Details

Mountains are huge towers of rock and are the highest landforms. Some mountains may be only a few thousand feet high. Others can soar higher than 20,000 feet (6,096 m). The world's highest mountain is Mount Everest in South Asia's Himalaya ranges. It rises more than 29,028 feet (8,848 m), nearly five and a half miles high!

—from page 50

A web diagram like the one below can help you record the main idea and supporting details.

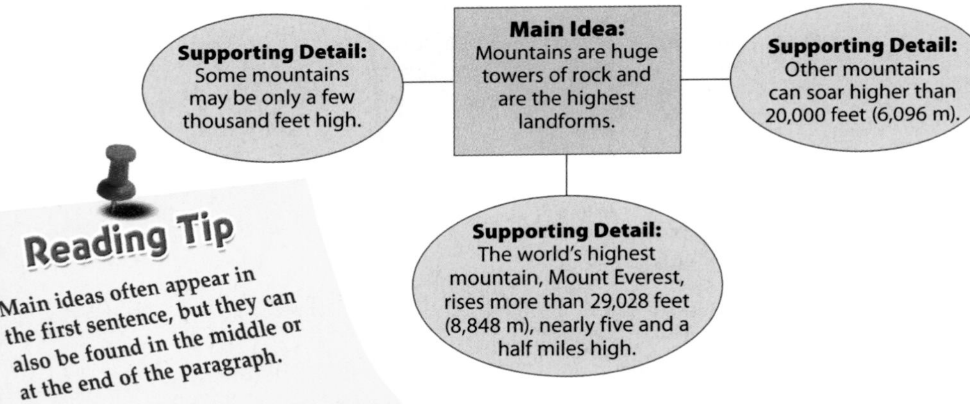

Main Idea:
Mountains are huge towers of rock and are the highest landforms.
Supporting Detail:
Some mountains may be only a few thousand feet high.
Supporting Detail:
Other mountains can soar higher than 20,000 feet (6,096 m).
Supporting Detail:
The world's highest mountain, Mount Everest, rises more than 29,028 feet (8,848 m), nearly five and a half miles high.
Reading Tip
Main ideas often appear in the first sentence, but they can also be found in the middle or at the end of the paragraph.

Reading Strategy — Organizing Information

Identifying the Main Idea Students can use clues in a written document to help them identify main ideas. Headings and subheadings often provide such clues by indicating a topic or theme that applies to the information grouped under that topic. Remind students that, as in the sample paragraph on this page, the first sentence of a paragraph often—though not always—states the main idea. At other times, the final sentence will state the main idea. Sometimes, the author does not directly state the main idea, but instead provides details that students must use as clues to identify the main idea. Ask students to choose a paragraph from one section in this unit and identify the main idea. **ELL**

2 Practice It!

Read the following paragraph from this unit.

- Draw a graphic organizer like the one shown below.
- Write the main idea for the paragraph in the center box.
- Write the supporting details in the ovals surrounding the box.

Remember that you do not need to include every word in the sentence when restating the main idea or supporting details.

Read to Write Activity

Read the main idea for Chapter 3, Section 2, and the paragraphs that follow. Using the main idea as a topic sentence, write a paragraph with supporting details. The supporting details should describe the elements that make up a culture.

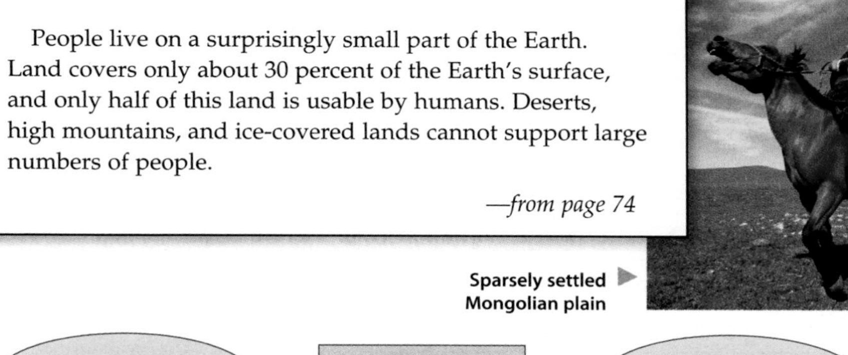

People live on a surprisingly small part of the Earth. Land covers only about 30 percent of the Earth's surface, and only half of this land is usable by humans. Deserts, high mountains, and ice-covered lands cannot support large numbers of people.

—*from page 74*

Sparsely settled Mongolian plain

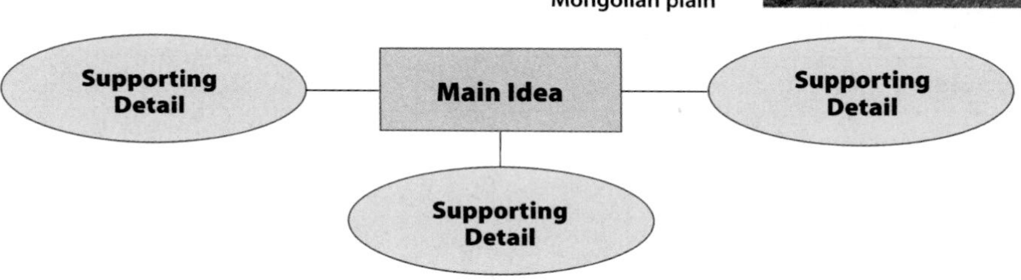

3 Apply It!

Create several web diagrams like the ones found on these pages. As you read Chapters 1, 2, and 3, write the main idea for each section in the center box of the diagram. Write supporting details in ovals surrounding the center box. Use your diagrams to help you study for the chapter assessments.

2 Practice It!

Main idea: People live on a surprisingly small part of the Earth.
Supporting details: Land covers only about 30% of the Earth's surface. Only half of the Earth's land is usable by humans. Deserts, high mountains, and ice-covered lands cannot support large numbers of people. **OL**

3 Apply It!

Bring to class a collection of news articles and opinion essays from magazines, newspapers, and news magazines. Organize the class into small groups, and have each group analyze a different piece of writing to identify the main idea and supporting details. After students have finished the work, have the class discuss the process. **OL**

Reading Strategy — Read to Write

Writing Summaries Have students choose a subsection from this unit. Tell them to stop and ask questions, such as *who, what, where, when, why,* and *how,* to identify the main ideas as they read. When students have finished reading, have them write a one-paragraph summary of the subsection, in their own words, stating the main idea and the most important supporting details. When done, have two or three student volunteers read their summaries aloud. Have students analyze each summary by checking it against the original text. For the summary to be successful, it should give students who have not yet read the text a clear and accurate overview of the subsection. **AL**

Planning Guide

Key to Ability Levels	
BL Below level	**AL** Above level
OL On level	**ELL** English Language Learners

Key to Teaching Resources	
Print Material	DVD
CD-ROM	Transparency

Levels				Resources	Chapter Opener	Section 1	Section 2	Chapter Assess
BL	OL	AL	ELL					
				FOCUS				
BL	OL	AL	ELL	**Daily Focus Skills Transparencies**		1-1	1-2	
				TEACH				
BL	OL		ELL	**Guided Reading Activity, URB***		p. 31	p. 32	
BL	OL	AL	ELL	**Content Vocabulary Activity, URB***		p. 33	p. 33	
BL	OL	AL	ELL	**Academic Vocabulary Activity, URB**		p. 35	p. 35	
BL	OL	AL	ELL	**Differentiated Instruction Activity, URB**		p. 37	p. 37	
BL	OL	AL	ELL	**Chart, Graph, and Map Skills Activity, URB**			p. 39	
	OL	AL		**Critical Thinking Activity, URB**		p. 41		
BL	OL	AL	ELL	**Speaking and Listening Skills Activity, URB**			p. 43	
BL	OL	AL	ELL	**Writing Skills Activity, URB**		p. 47		
BL	OL	AL	ELL	**School-to-Home Connection Activity, URB***		p. 51		
BL	OL	AL	ELL	**Regional Atlas Activities, URB**		pp. 1–7	pp. 1–7	
	OL	AL		**Geography and History Activity, URB**		p. 7		
BL	OL		ELL	**Time Line Activity, URB**		p. 13		
		AL		**Enrichment Activity, URB**		p. 15		
BL	OL		ELL	**Reading Skills Activity, URB**		p. 21		
BL	OL	AL	ELL	**Primary Source Readings, URB**			p. 23	
BL	OL		ELL	**Reading Essentials and Note-Taking Guide***		p. 1	p. 4	
	OL			**Interactive Geography Activity**	p. 1			
BL	OL	AL	ELL	**In-Text Map Overlay and Population Pyramid Transparencies**	1	1	1C	
	OL			**Foods Around the World**	pp. 2–5			
BL	OL	AL	ELL	**Outline Map Resource Book**	p. 59			
BL	OL	AL	ELL	**NGS World Atlas***	✓	✓	✓	
BL	OL	AL	ELL	**NGS World Desk Map**	✓	✓	✓	✓

Note: Please refer to the *Unit Resource Book: The World* for this chapter's URB materials.

* Also available in Spanish

- Interactive Lesson Planner
- Interactive Teacher Edition
- Fully editable blackline masters
- Section Spotlight Videos Launch
- Differentiated Lesson Plans
- Printable reports of daily assignments
- Standards Tracking System

Levels				Resources	Chapter Opener	Section 1	Section 2	Chapter Assess
BL	OL	AL	ELL					
				TEACH *(continued)*				
BL	OL	AL	ELL	World Literature Library	✓	✓	✓	✓
BL	OL	AL	ELL	Writer's Guidebook	✓	✓	✓	✓
BL	OL	AL	ELL	Vocabulary PuzzleMaker CD-ROM*	✓	✓	✓	✓
	OL	AL		Primary Sources CD-ROM	✓	✓	✓	✓
BL	OL	AL	ELL	StudentWorks™ Plus DVD	✓	✓	✓	✓
BL	OL	AL	ELL	Section Video Program Activities	✓	✓	✓	✓
BL	OL	AL	ELL	World Music: A Cultural Legacy	✓	✓	✓	✓
BL	OL	AL	ELL	Writing Process Transparencies	✓	✓	✓	✓
Teacher Resources				Building Academic Vocabulary	✓	✓	✓	✓
				Strategies for Success	✓	✓	✓	✓
				Teacher's Guide to Differentiated Instruction	✓	✓	✓	✓
				Presentation Plus! DVD	✓	✓	✓	✓
				ASSESS				
BL	OL	AL	ELL	Quizzes and Tests		p. 3	p. 4	p. 5
BL	OL	AL	ELL	Authentic Assessment With Rubrics		p. 1		p. 1
BL	OL	AL	ELL	Standardized Test Practice				p. 1
BL	OL	AL	ELL	*ExamView® Assessment Suite* CD-ROM*		1-1	1-2	Ch. 1
BL	OL	AL	ELL	Interactive Tutor Self-Assessment CD-ROM		1-1	1-2	
				CLOSE				
BL			ELL	Reteaching Activity, URB		p. 49	p. 49	p. 49
BL	OL		ELL	Reading and Study Skills Foldables™	p. 50	p. 50	p. 50	p. 50
BL	OL	AL	ELL	Graphic Organizer Transparencies and Strategies		✓	✓	
BL	OL	AL	ELL	*Exploring Our World* in Graphic Novel	p. 1			

Integrating Technology

Online Crossword Puzzles

Technology Product

Glencoe's Vocabulary PuzzleMaker™ 3.1 CD-ROM is an easy-to-use program that lets you create your own puzzles based on the glossary for classroom use. The PuzzleMaker allows you to

- create crossword puzzles based on content vocabulary and academic vocabulary that is specific to what is taught in the classroom;
- create online (LAN-based or local area network) or paper crossword puzzles.

Objectives

Completing the crossword puzzles helps students to

- recall vocabulary terms based on the clues provided for a puzzle;
- reinforce their understanding of the vocabulary.

Steps

- Run PuzzleMaker™ 3.1. On the main menu, click on **Create a New Puzzle.**
- From the list of *Puzzle Databases,* select the appropriate database for the vocabulary.
- The *PuzzleMaker Wizard* will take you through selecting a puzzle type and grid type.
- Then select one or more chapters from the list. Indicate whether you want the words selected randomly or manually.
- Select the language and words you wish to use within the maximum for the puzzle. Click **Finish.**
- Save your puzzle to a location that is easily accessible by your students with PuzzlePlayer™ 3.1, or print copies for your students to complete.
- Use PuzzlePlayer™ 3.1. to review the puzzles after your students have worked on and saved them.

Social Studies ONLINE

	Student	Teacher	Parent
Beyond the Textbook	●		●
Chapter Overviews	●		●
Concepts in Motion	●		●
ePuzzles and Games	●		●
Literature Connections		●	
Multi-Language Glossaries	●		●
Online Student Edition	●	●	●
Section Videos	●	●	●
Self-Check Quizzes	●		●
Student Web Activities	●		●
Study Central™	●		●
Teaching Today		●	
TIME Current Events	●		●
Vocabulary eFlashcards	●		●
Web Activity Lesson Plans		●	

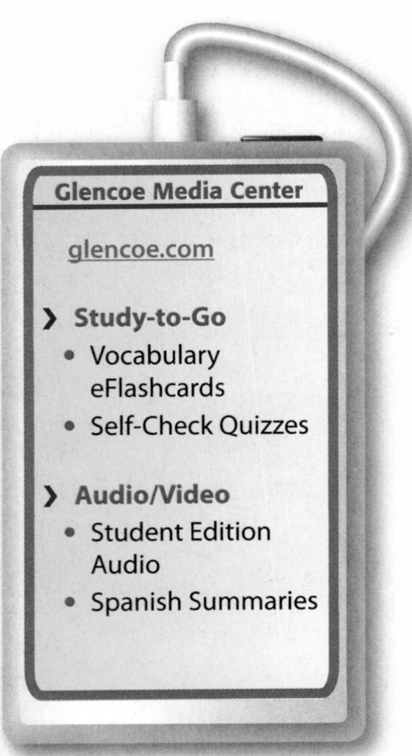

- **Timed Readings Plus in Social Studies** helps students increase their reading rate and fluency while maintaining comprehension. The 400-word passages are similar to those found on state and national assessments.
- **Reading in the Content Area: Social Studies** concentrates on six essential reading skills that help students better comprehend what they read. The book includes 75 high-interest nonfiction passages written at increasing levels of difficulty.
- **Reading Social Studies** includes strategic reading instruction and vocabulary support in Social Studies content for ELLs and native speakers of English.
- **Content Vocabulary Workout** (Grades 6–8) accelerates reading comprehension through focused vocabulary development. Social Studies content vocabulary comes from the glossaries of Glencoe's Middle School Social Studies texts. www.jamestowneducation.com

Index to National Geographic Magazine:

The following articles relate to this chapter:

- "Beautiful Stranger: Saturn's Mysteries Come to Light," by Bill Douthitt, December 2006.
- "Rocket for the Rest of Us," by Burt Rutan, April 2005.

National Geographic Society Products To order the following, call National Geographic at 1-800-368-2728:

- *National Geographic Atlas of the World* (Book).

Access National Geographic's new dynamic MapMachine Web site and other geography resources at:
www.nationalgeographic.com
www.nationalgeographic.com/maps

GLENCOE **BOOKLINK 3**

Use this database to search more than 30,000 titles to create a customized reading list for your students.

- Reading lists can be organized by students' reading level, author, genre, theme, or area of interest.
- The database provides Degrees of Reading Power™ (DRP) and Lexile™ readability scores for all selections.
- A brief summary of each selection is included.

Leveled reading suggestions for this chapter:

For students at a Grade 5 reading level:
- ***The Sun: Our Nearest Star,*** by Franklyn M. Branley
- ***Whatever the Weather,*** by Karen Wallace
- ***The Sun,*** by Patricia Whitehouse

For students at a Grade 6 reading level:
- ***The Planets in Our Solar System,*** by Franklyn M. Branley
- ***The Reason for Seasons,*** by Gail Gibbons
- ***Mercury,*** by Steven L. Kipp

For students at a Grade 7 reading level:
- ***The Sun,*** by Gregory Vogt
- ***A Tour of the Planets,*** by Melvin Berger
- ***Earth and the Solar System,*** by Darlene Lauw & Lim Cheng Puay

For students at a Grade 8 reading level:
- ***Mercury,*** by Seymour Simon
- ***Jupiter, the Fifth Planet,*** by Michael D. Cole
- ***Saturn: The Spectacular Planet,*** by Franklyn M. Branley

For students at a Grade 9 reading level:
- ***Earth Keepers,*** by Joan Anderson
- ***The Atlas of Space,*** by Jack Challoner
- ***What Shall We Do With the Land?*** by Laurence Pringle

Focus

The Essential Question

As students study the chapter, remind them to consider the chapter-based Essential Question. Answering this question will help them understand the important concepts in the chapter. In addition, the Hands-On Chapter Project relates the content from each section to the Essential Question. The steps in each section build on each other as students progress through the chapter. The Hands-On Chapter Project culminates in the Wrap Up activity on the Visual Summary page.

More About the Photo

Visual Literacy Lake Titicaca contains floating islands that were made by people with thick layers of reeds. The descendants of an ancient people, the Uru, live on these islands. The Uru replenish the top layer of reeds as the lower layer becomes saturated with water and loses its ability to float. This lower layer also rots. People who visit the area have to be mindful of the dark spots in the islands where water has soaked through the reeds, or they might accidentally sink through them!

The Uru travel among the islands in boats made of reeds known as *balsas*. *Balsas* are reeds bound together and are shaped like canoes. These boats will eventually rot after about a year of use because of the water they absorb.

CHAPTER 1

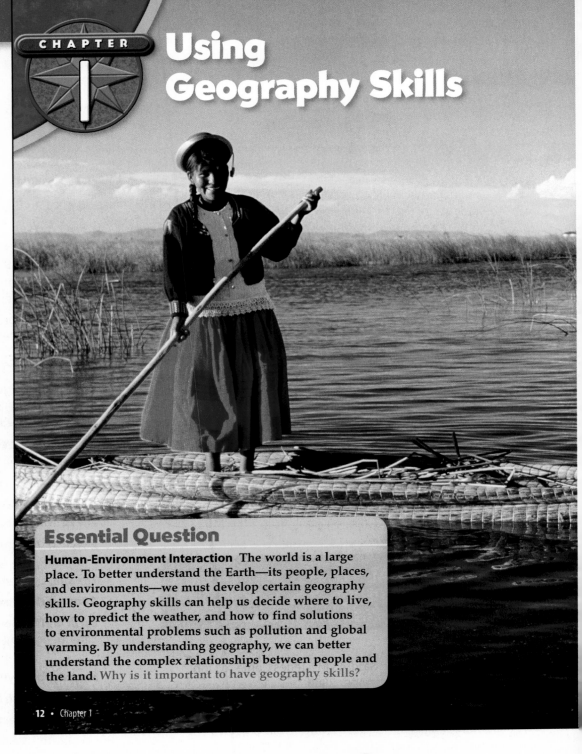

Using Geography Skills

Essential Question

Human-Environment Interaction The world is a large place. To better understand the Earth—its people, places, and environments—we must develop certain geography skills. Geography skills can help us decide where to live, how to predict the weather, and how to find solutions to environmental problems such as pollution and global warming. By understanding geography, we can better understand the complex relationships between people and the land. Why is it important to have geography skills?

12 • Chapter 1

Teach

The BIG Ideas *As you begin teaching each section, use these questions and activities to help students focus on the Big Ideas.*

Section 

Thinking Like a Geographer
Ask: **What are some decisions people might be able to make more effectively with a good understanding of geography?** *(Possible answers: where to locate cities, what kinds of fuels to use and where to find them, what activities are dangerous or harmful to the environment)* Point out to students that Section 1 discusses five important themes of geography: location, place, human-environment interaction, movement, and regions. Students also will learn about the types of geography and some of the tools geographers use to study our planet. **OL**

Section 

The Earth in Space **Ask:** **How is your life affected by the changing season?** *(Answers may include: choice of activities and clothing.)* Point out to students that the seasons, as well as night and day, are created by the continual

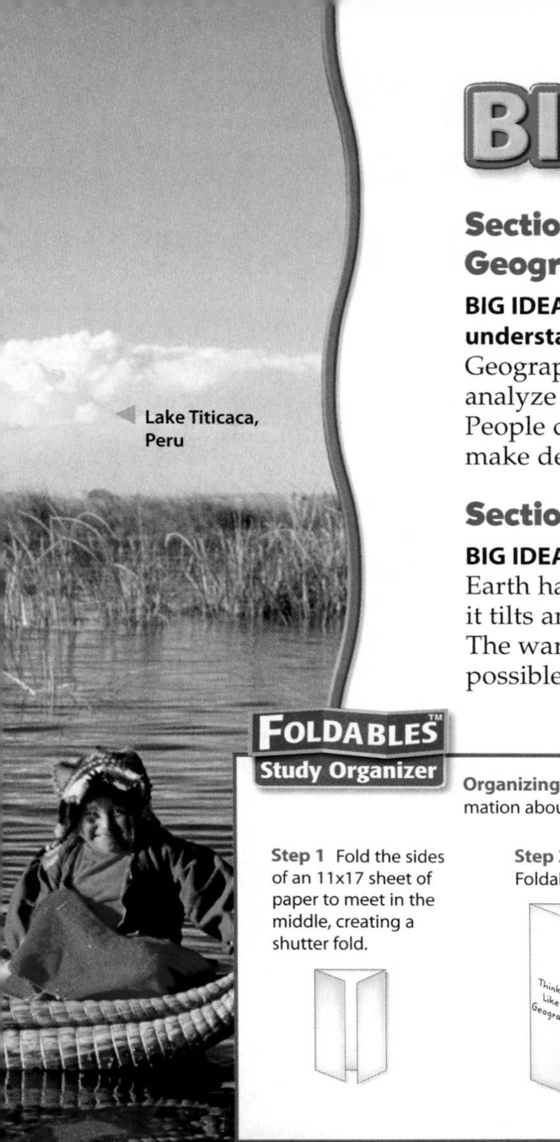

Lake Titicaca, Peru

BIG Ideas

Section 1: Thinking Like a Geographer

BIG IDEA Geography is used to interpret the past, understand the present, and plan for the future. Geography is the study of the Earth. It is used to analyze the Earth's physical and human features. People can use geographic information to plan, make decisions, and manage resources.

Section 2: The Earth in Space

BIG IDEA Physical processes shape Earth's surface. Earth has different seasons because of the way it tilts and the way it rotates around the sun. The warmth of the sun's rays makes life on Earth possible.

FOLDABLES™ Study Organizer

Organizing Information Make this Foldable to help you organize information about the uses of geography and about the Earth in space.

Step 1 Fold the sides of an 11x17 sheet of paper to meet in the middle, creating a shutter fold.

Step 2 Label your Foldable as shown.

Thinking Like a Geographer | The Earth in Space

Reading and Writing As you read the chapter, take notes under the appropriate flap of your Foldable. After you have completed your Foldable, use your notes to write a letter encouraging the study of geography by all students.

Social Studies ONLINE

To preview Chapter 1, go to glencoe.com.

Previewing the Region

If you have not already done so, engage students in the Regional Atlas and chart activities to help them become familiar with the general content of the region.

FOLDABLES™ Study Organizer **Dinah Zike's Foldables**

Purpose This Foldable helps students organize the information in the chapter about the uses of geography and Earth's place in the solar system. Students should note facts from their reading in the appropriate tabs on the Foldable. Then they can use the Foldable to help them compose their letter about why students should study geography and to prepare for assessment. **OL**

More Foldables activities for this chapter can be found in *Dinah Zike's Reading and Study Skills Foldables* ancillary.

Social Studies ONLINE

Introduce students to chapter content and key terms by having them access the Chapter Overview at glencoe.com.

movement of the Earth: its revolution around the sun, its tilt, and its rotation on its axis. In Section 2, students will learn about the Earth's place in the solar system and how the Earth's movements affect life on the planet. **OL**

Focus

Bellringer

Daily Focus Transparency 1-1

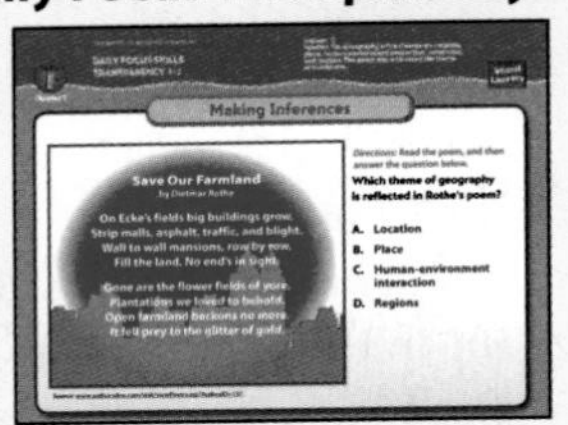

Guide to Reading

Answers to Graphic:

Answers may include:
Themes of Geography: location, place, human-environment interaction, movement, regions
Types of Geography: physical geography, human geography
Geographer's Tools: maps, GPS, GIS

Section Spotlight Video

To learn more about how to think like a geographer, have students watch the Section Spotlight Video.

Guide to Reading

BIG Idea

Geography is used to interpret the past, understand the present, and plan for the future.

Content Vocabulary

- geography *(p. 15)*
- absolute location *(p. 15)*
- relative location *(p. 15)*
- environment *(p. 15)*
- decade *(p. 16)*
- century *(p. 16)*
- millennium *(p. 16)*
- Global Positioning System (GPS) *(p. 17)*
- Geographic Information Systems (GIS) *(p. 17)*

Academic Vocabulary

- theme *(p. 15)*
- physical *(p. 15)*

Reading Strategy

Identifying Use a chart like the one below to identify two examples for each topic.

Themes of Geography
1.
2.
Types of Geography
1.
2.
Geographer's Tools
1.
2.

SECTION 1

Thinking Like a Geographer

Picture This The Italian Research Center, also known as the Pyramid, allows researchers from around the world to study everything from the effects of altitude on humans to the impact of global warming on the Earth. The Pyramid is located at the base of Mount Everest in Nepal. It is completely self-contained and can house up to 20 people. To get to the Pyramid, scientists have to trek through a national park and allow their bodies time to adjust to the extremely high altitude. To learn more about how geographers use information about the world to plan for the future, read Section 1.

▼ Research on Mount Everest

Resource Manager

R Reading Strategies	C Critical Thinking	D Differentiated Instruction	W Writing Support	S Skill Practice
Teacher Edition • Identifying, p. 15 • Questioning, p. 17 **Additional Resources** • Guid. Read., URB p. 31 • Cont. Vocab., URB p. 33 • Ac. Vocab., URB p. 35 • Read. Ess., p. 1	**Teacher Edition** • Making Comp., p. 15 **Additional Resources** • Crit. Think., URB p. 41 • Geo. & Hist., URB p. 7 • Authentic Assess., p. 1 • Quizzes and Tests, p. 3 • Time Line, URB p. 13	**Teacher Edition** • EL, p. 16 **Additional Resources** • Diff. Instr., URB p. 37 • Enrichment, URB p. 15 • Reteaching, URB p. 49	**Teacher Edition** • Descriptive Writing, p. 16 **Additional Resources** • Writing Skills, URB p. 47	**Teacher Edition** • Creating a Time Line, p. 16 **Additional Resources** • Read. Skills, URB p. 21 • Daily Focus Trans. 1-1 • Reg. Atlas, URB pp. 1–7

The Five Themes of Geography

Main Idea **Geographers use the Five Themes of Geography to help them study the Earth.**

Geography and You Suppose a teacher tells you to pick a topic for a research paper. How do you organize your ideas? Read to discover how geographers use themes to help them organize ideas about geography.

Geography is the study of the Earth and its people. People who study geography are geographers. Geographers use five **themes,** or topics, to describe places and people. These themes are location, place, human-environment interaction, movement, and regions.

Location

Location is the position of a place on the Earth's surface. Geographers describe location in two ways. **Absolute location** is the exact spot on Earth where a geographic feature, such as a city or mountain, is found. **Relative location** describes where that feature is in relation to the features around it.

Place

C

Place describes the characteristics of a location that make it unique, or different. A place can be defined by **physical** features, such as landforms, plants, animals, and weather patterns. Other characteristics of a place describe the people who live there—such as what languages they speak.

Human-Environment Interaction

Human-environment interaction describes how people affect their **environment,** or natural surroundings, and how their environment affects them. People affect the environment by using or changing it to

R

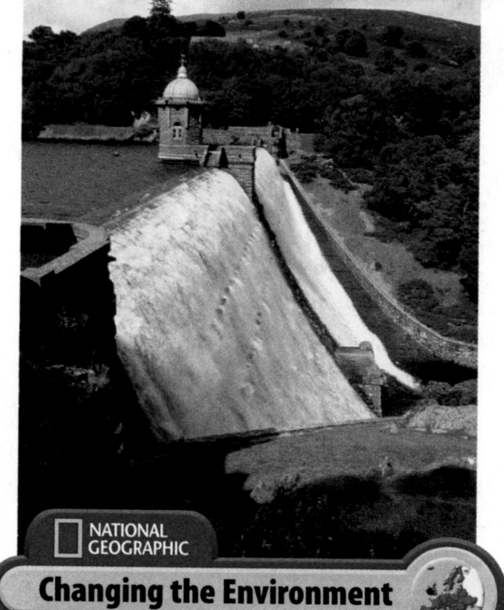

NATIONAL GEOGRAPHIC

Changing the Environment

Dams, like this one in Wales, can be built to control flooding, manage waterflow, and supply electricity. ***Human-Environment Interaction*** **How and why do people affect the environment?**

meet their needs. Environmental factors that people cannot control, such as temperature and natural disasters, influence how people live.

Movement

Movement explains how and why people, ideas, and goods move from place to place. For example, people might leave a country that is involved in a war. Such movements can lead to great cultural change.

Regions

Regions refers to areas of the Earth's surface that have several common characteristics, such as land, natural resources, or population. For example, the alpine region in Europe is a large area known for mining and supplying hydroelectric power.

Reading Check **Explaining** Explain the difference between *place* and *location.*

Teach

C Critical Thinking

Making Comparisons Ask: What is the relative location of our school? *(Students may pinpoint the street intersection nearest the building or may locate it relative to a landmark.)* **Now describe the place that is our school.** *(Students may note aspects that they feel makes your school special, such as its architecture, programs, classes, people, or activities.)* **OL**

For further practice on this skill (Making Comparisons), see the **Skills Handbook.**

R Reading Strategy

Identifying Ask: What are some ways that people can affect the environment? *(Possible answers: building dams to change rivers, cutting down forests, digging mines, and polluting air and water)* **BL**

Caption Answer:
They use it or change it to meet their needs.

Reading Check **Answer:** Location is the position of a place on Earth's surface; place describes the characteristics of a location that make it unique or special.

Hands-On Chapter Project Step 1

Designing a Building From Scratch

Step 1: Planning the Site Students will describe the sort of site necessary for placement of a specific facility or business.

Essential Question Why is it important to have geography skills?

Directions Organize students into groups of two or three. Assign each group a type of building or business, such as a hospital, police station, college, zoo, school, or grocery store. Tell students they will use geography to determine the best place to build their assigned facility. Students may wish to choose an actual physical location, such as a site in your town, or describe in general terms the type of site they would need for their facility. For example, students assigned to a college could describe a large parcel, preferably flat, with plenty of room for growth, without specifying the exact location. Remind students to think about the five themes of geography as they select their site. Explain to students that after they have chosen and described their site, they will make a picture or model of their facility in that site.

Describing Have a volunteer from each group describe their site, and the facility that will be placed there, to the rest of the class. **OL**

(Chapter Project continued in Section 2)

W Writing Support

Descriptive Writing Have students write a paragraph describing things in your community that a physical or human geographer might find interesting. *(Answers should demonstrate an understanding of the difference between physical and human geography.)* **OL**

D Differentiated Instruction

English Learners Have students look up *decade, century,* and *millennium* in a dictionary. Explain that these words have Latin roots. Help students find the Latin words for 10, 100, and 1,000. Discuss other words that contain these Latin roots. *(examples: decimal, centennial, millimeter)* **ELL**

S Skill Practice

Creating a Time Line Ask students to make a time line showing the four long periods of human history, as described in the text. **OL**

Caption Answer:
Possible answers: locate and manage natural resources; help determine where to build power plants, buildings, dams, or roads

A Geographer's Tools

Main Idea **Geographers use many different tools to help them study and analyze Earth's people and places.**

Geography and You Suppose a company wanted to build a new shopping center in your community. How would its managers know where to build it? Read to find out how geographers help make such decisions.

Geographers study the physical and human features of Earth. They rely on various tools to study people and places.

Types of Geography

When geographers study physical geography, they examine Earth's land areas, bodies of water, plant life, and other physical features. Physical geographers also study natural resources that are available in an area and the ways people use those resources. They help people make decisions about managing different types of resources such as water, forests, land, and **W** even the wind.

Other geographers study human geography, focusing on people and their activities. Human geographers look at people's religions, languages, and ways of life. They may examine a specific location, or they may study entire countries or continents. They also compare different places to see how they are similar and different. Human geographers help plan cities and aid in international business.

Places in Time

Geographers use knowledge from other subject areas. History, for example, helps them understand how places appeared in the past. Geographers learn about places by studying the changes that have occurred over time.

Using Geography

Surveyors, like this woman in Canada, use specialized equipment to measure land areas. ***Human-Environment Interaction*** **What tasks might geographers hired by the government carry out?**

History is divided into blocks of time known as periods. For example, a period **D** of 10 years is called a **decade.** A period of 100 years is known as a **century.** A period of 1,000 years is a **millennium.**

In Western societies, it is common to group history into four long periods. The first of these periods is called Prehistory. Prehistory refers to the time before people developed writing, about 5,500 years ago. **S** This time is followed by the period known as Ancient History, which lasted until about 1,500 years ago. The next thousand years is called the Middle Ages, or the medieval period. About 500 years ago, Modern History began and continues to the present.

Map Systems

Maps can provide geographers with different types of information about a place. Information for a map can be collected

Differentiated Instruction

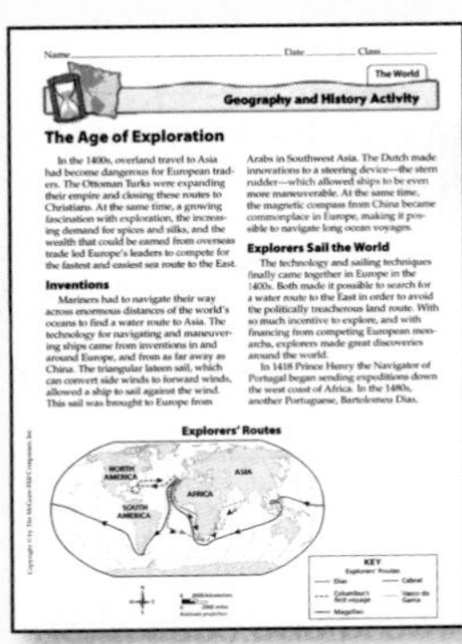
Geography and History Activity

The Age of Exploration

Explorers Sail the World

Explorers' Routes

Geography and History Activity, URB pp. 7–8

The Age of Exploration

Objective: To learn to apply geography skills to the study of history

Focus: Ask: What was the Age of Exploration?

Teach: Discuss with students what was learned about geography during the Age of Exploration.

Assess: Have students answer the questions that follow the article.

Close: Discuss how maps provide information about historical events.

Differentiated Instruction Strategies

BL Help students read the map to acquire the necessary information.

AL Have students research how the Age of Exploration changed the maps of the world.

ELL Ask students: How is the experience of moving to a new country similar to the experience of European explorers during the Age of Exploration?

by using modern technology, or tools and methods that help people perform tasks. Satellites circling the Earth provide detailed digital images and photographs to create maps. Satellites can also measure changing temperatures and the amount of pollution in the air or land. This information can then be added to maps.

Another group of satellites makes up the **Global Positioning System (GPS).** This system uses radio signals to determine the exact location of places on Earth. Hikers use GPS equipment to avoid getting lost. GPS is now built into some cars.

Geographic Information Systems (GIS) are computer hardware and software that gather, store, and analyze geographic information and then display it on a screen. It can display maps, but it also can show information that does not usually appear on maps, such as types of vegetation, types of soil, and even water quality.

R

Careers in Geography

Governments at all levels hire geographers for many kinds of tasks. Geographers help decide how land and resources might be used. For example, they analyze population trends, including why people live in certain areas and not in others.

In the business world, geographers often work as researchers and analysts. They can help companies decide where to locate new buildings. They also provide information about places and cultures where companies do business. Many geographers teach in high schools, colleges, and universities. As more schools recognize the importance of geography education, the demand for geography teachers is expected to grow.

Reading Check **Explaining** How does modern technology make maps more precise?

Section 1 Review

Social Studies ONLINE
Study Central™ To review this section, go to glencoe.com.

Vocabulary

1. **Explain** the significance of:
   - **a.** geography
   - **b.** absolute location
   - **c.** relative location
   - **d.** environment
   - **e.** decade
   - **f.** century
   - **g.** millennium
   - **h.** Global Positioning System (GPS)
   - **i.** Geographic Information Systems (GIS)

Main Ideas

2. **Explaining** Use a web diagram like the one below to summarize information about the Five Themes of Geography.

3. **Contrasting** How is physical geography different from human geography?

Critical Thinking

4. **Drawing Conclusions** Describe how helpful you think GIS would be in deciding where to build a gas station.
5. **BIG Idea** What factors might influence where a city would develop?
6. **Challenge** Give three examples of how someone might use geography to plan for the future.

Writing About Geography

7. **Using Your FOLDABLES** Use your Foldable to write a paragraph that describes the uses of geography.

R Reading Strategy

Questioning Have students write three questions and answers about map systems. Then have them exchange questions with a partner and answer them. OL

Reading Check **Answer:** Satellites make digital images, GPS uses radio signals to record the exact locations of places, and GIS uses computers to analyze and display information.

Assess

Social Studies ONLINE
Study Central™ provides summaries, interactive games, and online graphic organizers to help students review content.

Close

Categorizing Have students give examples of careers in geography. Then have them categorize those by physical or human geography. OL

Section 1 Review

Answers

1. Definitions for the vocabulary words are found in the section and the Glossary.
2. **Location:** position of a place on Earth; **Place:** characteristics of a location; **Human-Environment Interaction:** how people affect their environment and how the environment affects people; **Movement:** how and why people, ideas, and goods move from place to place; **Regions:** areas of Earth's surface that have common characteristics
3. Physical geography focuses on physical features of the Earth. Human geography focuses on people and their activities.
4. Answers should include an understanding that GIS uses up-to-date maps and detailed information.
5. Answers may include aspects of location, place, movement, human-environment interaction, and regions.
6. Answers will vary but should demonstrate an understanding that geography is useful for planning and decision making, especially where resources are concerned.
7. Paragraphs will vary but should use information in the student's Foldable to describe the uses of geography.

Geography Skills Activity

Understanding the 5 Themes of Geography In this activity, you will use what your students know about their school to make a connection with the five themes of geography. Have student volunteers read aloud each of the five themes of geography. As each theme is read aloud, write it on the board for students to see. **Ask:** **How could you describe the location of our school?** List student answers on the board. Then have students describe the physical and human characteristics that make the school unique. Continue until you have two or three student descriptions for each of the five themes of geography. **OL**

Using Geography Skills To help students better understand *Location*, have them turn in their textbooks to a chapter opener photo. Read to students the information from More About the Photo. Then have students create a two-column chart. In the left-hand column, have them list the location. In the right-hand column, have students include information from More About the Photo or information they have inferred from visual clues in the photo that describe the location. Repeat the exercise with two or three other chapters, then discuss what characteristics help define locations. **AL**

How Do I Study Geography?

Geographers have created these broad categories and standards as tools to help you understand the relationships among people, places, and environments.

- **5 Themes of Geography**
- **6 Essential Elements**
- **18 Geography Standards**

5 Themes of Geography

1 Location
Location describes where something is. Absolute location describes a place's exact position on the Earth's surface. Relative location expresses where a place is in relation to another place.

2 Place
Place describes the physical and human characteristics that make a location unique.

3 Regions
Regions are areas that share common characteristics.

4 Movement
Movement explains how and why people and things move and are connected.

5 Human-Environment Interaction
Human-Environment Interaction describes the relationship between people and their environment.

FastFacts

- **Origin of Geography** The first written document to use the word *geography* in the title was by Eratosthenes. He was a Greek scholar who lived ca. 276 B.C.–194 B.C. He was also the first to map the world using parallels and meridians.
- **American Geography** The first textbook on American geography was published in 1784. It was called *Geography Made Easy* and was written by Jedidiah Morse. The inventor of Morse Code, Samuel Morse, was Jedidiah's oldest son.
- **Astrogeology** With the advent of space travel, scientists have been able to study the geology of asteroids, planets, and moons. Rocks have been collected from the moon and brought back to the Earth for study. Unmanned spacecraft have analyzed soil samples from the planet Mars.

6 Essential Elements

18 Geography Standards

I. The World in Spatial Terms
Geographers look to see where a place is located. Location acts as a starting point to answer "Where Is It?" The location of a place helps you orient yourself as to where you are.

1 How to use maps and other tools
2 How to use mental maps to organize information
3 How to analyze the spatial organization of people, places, and environments

II. Places and Regions
Place describes physical characteristics such as landforms, climate, and plant or animal life. It might also describe human characteristics, including language and way of life. Places can also be organized into regions. **Regions** are places united by one or more characteristics.

4 The physical and human characteristics of places
5 How people create regions to interpret Earth's complexity
6 How culture and experience influence people's perceptions of places and regions

III. Physical Systems
Geographers study how physical systems, such as hurricanes, volcanoes, and glaciers, shape the surface of the Earth. They also look at how plants and animals depend upon one another and their surroundings for their survival.

7 The physical processes that shape Earth's surface
8 The distribution of ecosystems on Earth's surface

IV. Human Systems
People shape the world in which they live. They settle in certain places but not in others. An ongoing theme in geography is the movement of people, ideas, and goods.

9 The characteristics, distribution, and migration of human populations
10 The complexity of Earth's cultural mosaics
11 The patterns and networks of economic interdependence
12 The patterns of human settlement
13 The forces of cooperation and conflict

V. Environment and Society
How does the relationship between people and their natural surroundings influence the way people live? Geographers study how people use the environment and how their actions affect the environment.

14 How human actions modify the physical environment
15 How physical systems affect human systems
16 The meaning, use, and distribution of resources

VI. The Uses of Geography
Knowledge of geography helps us understand the relationships among people, places, and environments over time. Applying geographic skills helps you understand the past and prepare for the future.

17 How to apply geography to interpret the past
18 How to apply geography to interpret the present and plan for the future

Geography Skills Activity

Questioning Remind students that asking questions is an important learning tool. Point out to students that they can begin to understand how the first essential element, *The World in Spatial Terms,* applies to a geographic location by asking "Where is it?" **Ask: What questions will help us learn more about the second essential element, *Places and Regions*?** *(Possible answers: What is the climate of this area? What language is spoken here? How is the way of life of the people who live here similar across the region?)* **What questions will help us learn about the third essential element, *Physical Systems*?** *(Possible answers: What weather patterns are common in this area? Have landforms been affected by weather? Has the landscape been shaped by volcanoes or earthquakes? Was this region shaped by glaciers?)* Continue to have students develop questions for the remaining essential elements of geography. **OL**

Activity: Geographic Element

Human Systems Ask: What are some ways that human systems have influenced the region in which you live? Explain that the way people have shaped this region has changed over time. Organize students into groups and assign each group a point in time in the history of your area. You might choose to assign groups to the era before European contact, a point early in European colonization, and different periods up to and including the present. Have each group develop six to eight questions about its time period based on the six essential elements of geography. Questions might cover topics such as how people were employed, who moved in or out of the area, and how the natural surroundings affected the people who lived in the region. Direct students to appropriate reference materials, including local history sources, encyclopedias, almanacs, atlases, and reliable online information sources, to find answers to their questions. When finished, have each group prepare an oral report on its historical period. Reports can be given chronologically as a class presentation on the history of your region. **AL**

Geography Skills Activity

What's the Big Idea? Assign each student one of the bulleted Big Ideas on this page. Give each student an index card. Have students write their assigned Big Idea on one side of the card. On the same side, have students write the corresponding essential element. For example, a student may write the Big Idea "People's actions can change the physical environment" and the essential element "Environment and Society" on the index card. Then have students describe a specific idea, event, or fact that illustrates the Big Idea. For example, for the Big Idea given above, a student might write "The local college cut down a stand of trees to make room for a parking lot." Collect the cards. Read each description, and have students identify the essential element and the Big Idea that the description illustrates. **OL**

Understanding the BIG Ideas of Geography

The 15 Big Ideas will help you understand the information in *Exploring Our World: People, Places, and Cultures*. The Big Ideas are based on the Essential Elements and the Geography Standards. They help you organize important ideas, and they make it easier to understand patterns and relationships.

The World in Spatial Terms
- Geographers study how people and physical features are distributed on Earth's surface.

Places and Regions
- Places reflect the relationship between humans and the physical environment.
- Geographers organize the Earth into regions that share common characteristics.
- Culture influences people's perceptions about places and regions.

Physical Systems
- Physical processes shape Earth's surface.
- All living things are dependent upon one another and their surroundings for survival.

Human Systems
- The characteristics and movement of people impact physical and human systems.
- Culture groups shape human systems.
- Patterns of economic activities result in global interdependence.
- Geographic factors influence where people settle.
- Cooperation and conflict among people have an effect on the Earth's surface.

Environment and Society
- People's actions can change the physical environment.
- The physical environment affects how people live.
- Changes occur in the use and importance of natural resources.

The Uses of Geography
- Geography is used to interpret the past, understand the present, and plan for the future.

The World in Spatial Terms: Maps help you locate places on Earth's surface.

Physical Systems: Physical processes, such as hurricanes, shape the face of the Earth.

Human Systems: Technology impacts people and economies.

Environment and Society: Recycling is a choice people make to protect Earth's physical environment.

FastFacts

Careers in Geography Many students may assume that a career in geography is limited to mapmaking. Maps are extremely important, but becoming a cartographer is just one of many careers available to those who have studied geography. For example, geographers study environmental change and land use. They analyze population shifts and migration patterns, and they look for changing patterns of consumption, travel, and employment. They also analyze satellite images to gain strategic military information. Geographers also work as public transportation planners, airline route specialists, import/export and shipping logistics planners, and demographic analysts and marketers.

Using the BIG Ideas of Geography

You can find the Big Ideas throughout *Exploring Our World: People, Places, and Cultures.*

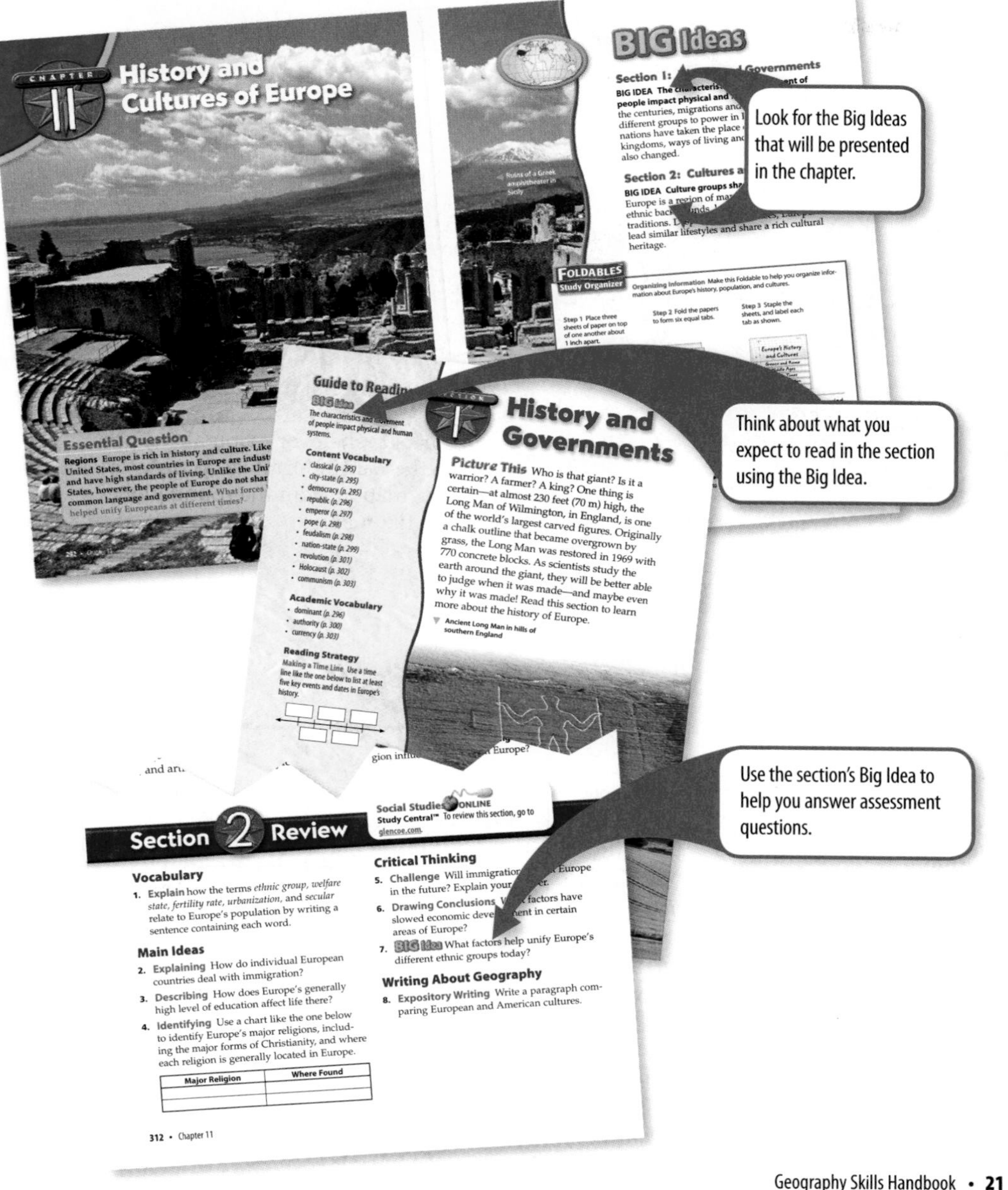

Geography Skills Activity

Identifying Review with students how studying the Big Ideas will help them understand the information in their textbook. Have students read the information on this page. **Ask: Why does the Big Idea appear at the beginning of each section?** *(to help students focus on and retain the main points of the section)* Have students look for the Big Ideas in this chapter. Have volunteers call out the page numbers where the Big Ideas appear. Ask students to hunt for details that support each Big Idea. **BL**

FastFacts

John Harrison In the early 1700s, the British government was concerned about disasters at sea. The government felt that better navigational tools might help avoid them. In 1714 an award was offered to the first man to develop a method of accurately finding a ship's longitude. John Harrison eventually won the prize. He submitted his first marine chronometer in 1735 and then spent most of his life perfecting it.

Activity: Defining Geographic Terms

Defining Have each student create a quiz that requires a fellow student to match the following terms with their definitions: place, region, physical systems, culture, human systems, geography, migration, latitude, longitude, globe, map, meridians, parallels. Write these terms on the board. Then have students list the terms on the left side of a sheet of paper and use information in their textbook to write a definition for each term. Tell students that the order of definitions should not match the order of terms. Remind students to create an answer key for their quiz. After students have completed their quizzes, have them trade quizzes, take the quiz, and then hand the quiz back to the first student to be checked for accuracy. **OL**

Geography Skills Activity

Comparing and Contrasting Discuss the difference between globes and maps with students, showing them examples of each. **Ask:** **Why might you use a globe?** *(to see a true representation of the Earth, to see the relative distances between continents, to get an accurate representation of the size and shape of landmasses)* **Why might you use a map?** *(to get driving directions, to see different types of information represented on special purpose maps, to see a small area in great detail)* Have students cover the chart on the page with their hand. Call out an advantage, or disadvantage, and have students determine if the statement refers to maps or globes. **OL**

Globes and Maps

What Is a Globe? ▶

A **globe** is a round model of the Earth that shows its shape, landforms, and directions as they truly relate to one another.

◀ What Is a Map?

A **map** is a flat drawing of all or part of the Earth's surface. Cartographers, or mapmakers, use mathematical formulas to transfer information from the round globe to a flat map.

Globes and Maps ▶

Globes and maps serve different purposes, and each has advantages and disadvantages.

	Advantages	Disadvantages
Globes	• Represent true land shape, distances, and directions	• Cannot show detailed information • Difficult to carry
Maps	• Show small areas in great detail • Display different types of information, such as population densities or natural resources • Transport easily	• **Distort,** or change, the accuracy of shapes and distances

Activity: Understanding Map Projections

Predicting Consequences Bring several oranges or grapefruits to class. Have small groups of students draw the continents on the fruit, so that the fruit looks as much like a globe as possible. **Ask:** **What do you think will happen if you try to turn this round representation into a flat representation?** Ask students to suggest ways to peel the fruit so that the peel will lay flat. Then have them carefully peel the fruit and lay it flat. **Ask:** **How has flattening the peel distorted the accuracy of the "globe"?** *(Distances are no longer accurate; there is extra space between landforms.)* **Ask:** **What have you learned about the difficulty of representing the round Earth on a flat map?** *(Students will recognize that it is difficult to represent a round object on a flat surface.)* **BL**

Map Projections

When the Earth's surface is flattened on a map, big gaps open up. Mapmakers stretch parts of the Earth to show either the correct shapes of places or their correct sizes. Mapmakers have developed different projections, or ways of showing the Earth on a flat piece of paper. Below are different map projections.

Goode's Interrupted Equal-Area Projection ▼

A map with this projection shows continents close to their true shapes and sizes. This projection is helpful to compare land area among continents.

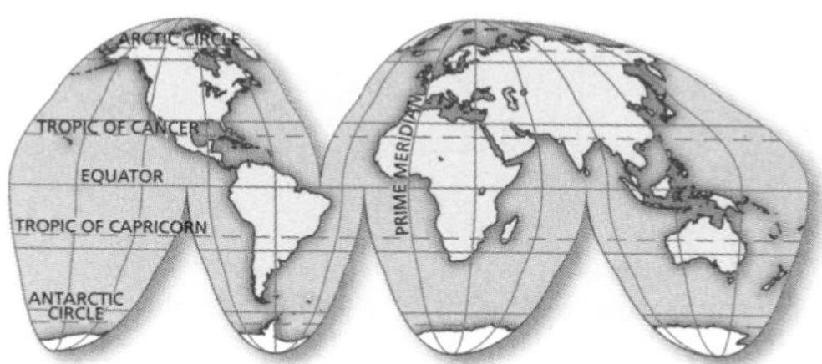

Robinson Projection ▼

The Robinson projection has minor distortions. Continents and oceans are close to their sizes and shapes, but the North and South Poles appear flattened.

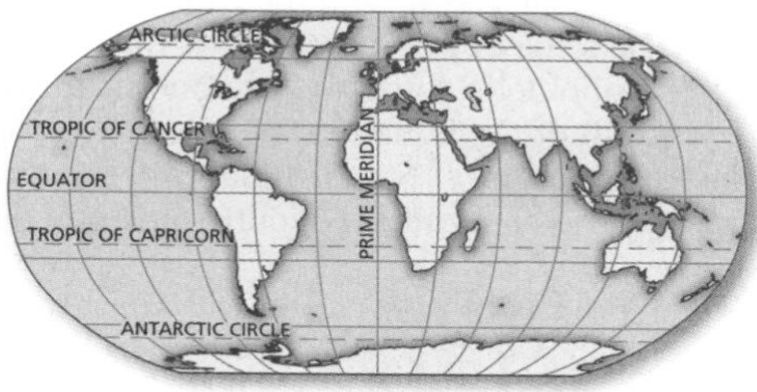

Mercator Projection ▼

The Mercator projection shows land shapes fairly accurately but not size or distance. Areas that are located far from the Equator are quite distorted. The Mercator projection shows true directions, however, making it useful for sea travel.

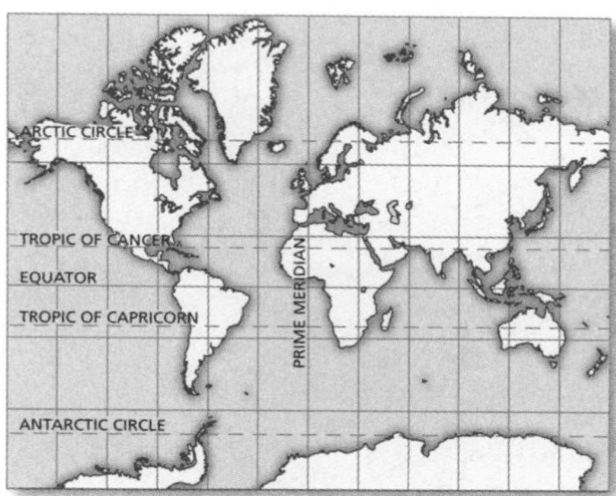

Winkel Tripel Projection ▼

This projection gives a good overall view of the continents' shapes and sizes. Land areas are not as distorted near the poles as they are in the Robinson projection.

Skills Practice

1. **Comparing and Contrasting** Explain similarities and differences between globes and maps.
2. **Describing** Why do map projections distort some parts of the Earth?

NATIONAL GEOGRAPHIC Geography Skills Handbook

Geography Skills Activity

Analyzing Information Have students review the information on this page. **Ask:** **What is a map projection?** *(a way of showing the Earth on a flat piece of paper)* Help students locate Greenland on each of the map projections on this page. **Ask:** **How does the depiction of Greenland change based on the map projection?** *(Goode's Interrupted Equal-Area Projection: appears on two different sections of the map; Robinson Projection and Winkel Tripel Projection: similar in shape and size, appears smaller than South America; Mercator Projection: very large, even larger than Africa)* **OL**

Skills Practice

Answers:

1. Both globes and maps represent the Earth's surface. A globe is more accurate than a map because it is a model of the Earth's shape, it depicts the true shape of lands, and it represents directions as they truly relate to one another. Maps are flat representations of the Earth that can show small areas in great detail.
2. A map projection distorts some parts of the Earth because when round Earth is depicted on a flat map, gaps develop. Mapmakers stretch parts of the Earth's surface to fill the gaps.

Activity: Exploring Map Projections

Summarizing Have students look through the textbook and note the various maps. Have them list any map projections that differ from those shown on this page. Create a list of the various projections on the board. Have students research the map projections that are new to them. Then have them write a summary for each map projection. Remind students to include the advantages and disadvantages of each type of projection. Tell them to refer to specific maps in their textbook by title and page number and explain why those map projections were used to represent those geographic areas. **AL**

Geography Skills Handbook

NATIONAL GEOGRAPHIC

Geography Skills Activity

Drawing Conclusions Remind students that lines of latitude and longitude form an imaginary global grid over the surface of the Earth. **Ask: Which lines run east to west?** *(latitude)* **Is the Equator a line of latitude or longitude?** *(latitude)* **What is 75°N called?** *(the Arctic Circle)* **Where is the Equator?** *(at 0° latitude)* **Where is the Prime Meridian?** *(0° longitude)* **Where is the International Date Line?** *(180° longitude)* **How can latitude and longitude be used to determine absolute location?** *(Identifying both the latitude and longitude of a place pinpoints it on a map.)* **How can latitude and longitude be used to determine relative location?** *(Relative location gives a place's location in relationship to another place. For example, you can say that Memphis, Tennessee is north of New Orleans, Louisiana.)* **OL**

Location

To locate places on Earth, geographers use a system of imaginary lines that crisscross the globe. These lines are called *latitude* and *longitude.*

Latitude ▶

- Lines of **latitude** are imaginary circles that run east to west around the globe. They are known as *parallels.* These parallels divide the globe into units called degrees.
- The **Equator** circles the middle of the Earth like a belt. It is located halfway between the North and South Poles. The Equator is 0° latitude.
- The letter *N* or *S* that follows the degree symbol tells you if the location is north or south of the Equator. The North Pole, for example, is 90°N (north) latitude, and the South Pole is at 90°S (south) latitude.

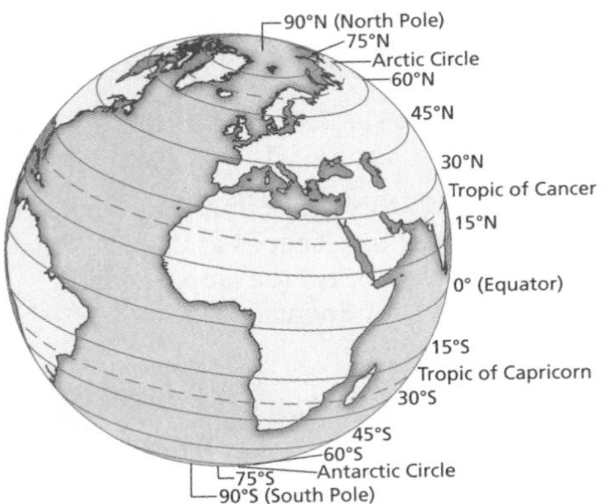

◀ Longitude

- Lines of **longitude,** also known as *meridians,* run from the North Pole to the South Pole. The **Prime Meridian** (also called the Meridian of Greenwich) is 0° longitude and runs through Greenwich, England.
- The letter *E* or *W* that follows the degree symbol tells you if the location is east or west of the Prime Meridian.
- On the opposite side of the Earth is the 180° meridian, also known as the International Date Line.

Absolute Location ▶

A place's exact location can be identified when you use both latitude and longitude. For example, Tokyo, Japan, is 36°N latitude and 140°E longitude.

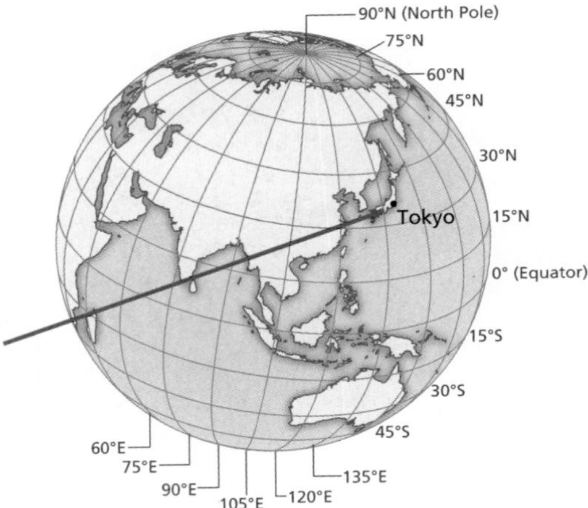

Activity: Using a Gazetteer

Identifying Absolute Location Organize the class into groups. Have students in each group study the World: Political map in the National Geographic Reference Atlas and identify 10 different cities on the map. **Ask: What is the absolute location of each of these cities?** Students may have to estimate the degrees for many of the cities. Have them record the location in degrees of latitude and longitude for each city. Remind students to include the cardinal directions. Refer students to the Gazetteer in their textbook. Explain that the Gazetteer is a geographic index or dictionary. Have students check their locations against the latitude and longitude listed in the Gazetteer. To extend the activity, ask groups to use the information in the Gazetteer to create a quiz. Have the groups use latitude and longitude to give either the absolute or relative location for a total of 10 cities and geographic features. Remind students to create an answer key. Then have groups exchange quizzes to test their knowledge of latitude and longitude. **OL**

Hemispheres

The Equator divides the Earth into Northern and Southern Hemispheres. Everything north of the Equator is in the Northern Hemisphere. Everything south of the Equator is in the Southern Hemisphere.

Northern Hemisphere

Southern Hemisphere

Equator

The Prime Meridian divides the Earth into Eastern and Western Hemispheres. Everything east of the Prime Meridian for 180 degrees is in the Eastern Hemisphere. Everything west of the Prime Meridian for 180 degrees is in the Western Hemisphere.

Eastern Hemisphere

Western Hemisphere

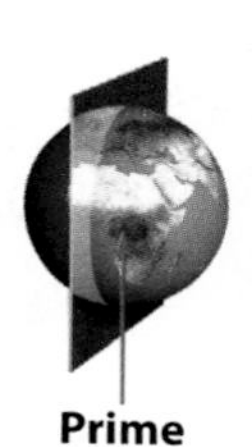

Prime Meridian

Skills Practice

1 **Identifying** What country is located at 30°S and 120°E?

2 **Analyzing Visuals** In which hemispheres is Europe located?

Geography Skills Activity

Locating Tell students that the word part *hemi* means "half." This will help them remember that a hemisphere is a half of the Earth. **Ask:** **What are the four hemispheres depicted on this page?** *(Northern, Southern, Eastern, Western)* Have students look at each hemisphere and state what geographic regions or continents are visible.

Test students' understanding of hemispheres by giving examples of places around the world and asking in which hemispheres those places are located. Examples: **Ask:** **In which hemispheres is New York City located?** *(the Northern and Western hemispheres)* **What continent is in both the Northern and Western Hemispheres?** *(North America)* **In which hemispheres is the Nile River located?** *(the Eastern and Northern Hemispheres)* **BL**

Skills Practice

Answers:

1. Australia
2. the Eastern and Northern hemispheres

FastFacts

- **The Compass** The primary device for finding direction is the compass. The magnetic compass probably was invented in the twelfth century at around the same time in China and in Europe. People discovered that magnetic ore, attached to a stick floating in water, aligned itself in a north-south direction.
- **Mapping in Other Cultures** It is not necessary to have a written language in order to create accurate maps. It has been reported that the Pawnee of North America painted star charts on elk skin. They used these maps to find their way across the Great Plains at night.

Geography Skills Activity

Reading a Map Review the parts of a map as indicated on this page. **Ask: What type of map is this? How do you know?** *(Political; you can tell from the title.)* **How can you determine if Paris or Lyon is the capital of France?** *(Use the map key and note the symbol for capitals.)* **Is Bulgaria east or west of Italy? How can you tell?** *(It is east. You can tell by using the compass rose.)* **BL**

Extending the Activity Have students turn to the first page of the National Geographic Reference Atlas. Direct students to the Atlas Key and the Symbol Key. Have students review the maps in the National Geographic Reference Atlas and note the parts of a map. Tell them to also look for features indicated by the Atlas Key and Symbol Key. You might want to point out that cartographers use different styles and sizes of fonts when labeling particular features. Have students compare how oceans, seas, rivers, and lakes are labeled on the maps. **OL**

Parts of a Map

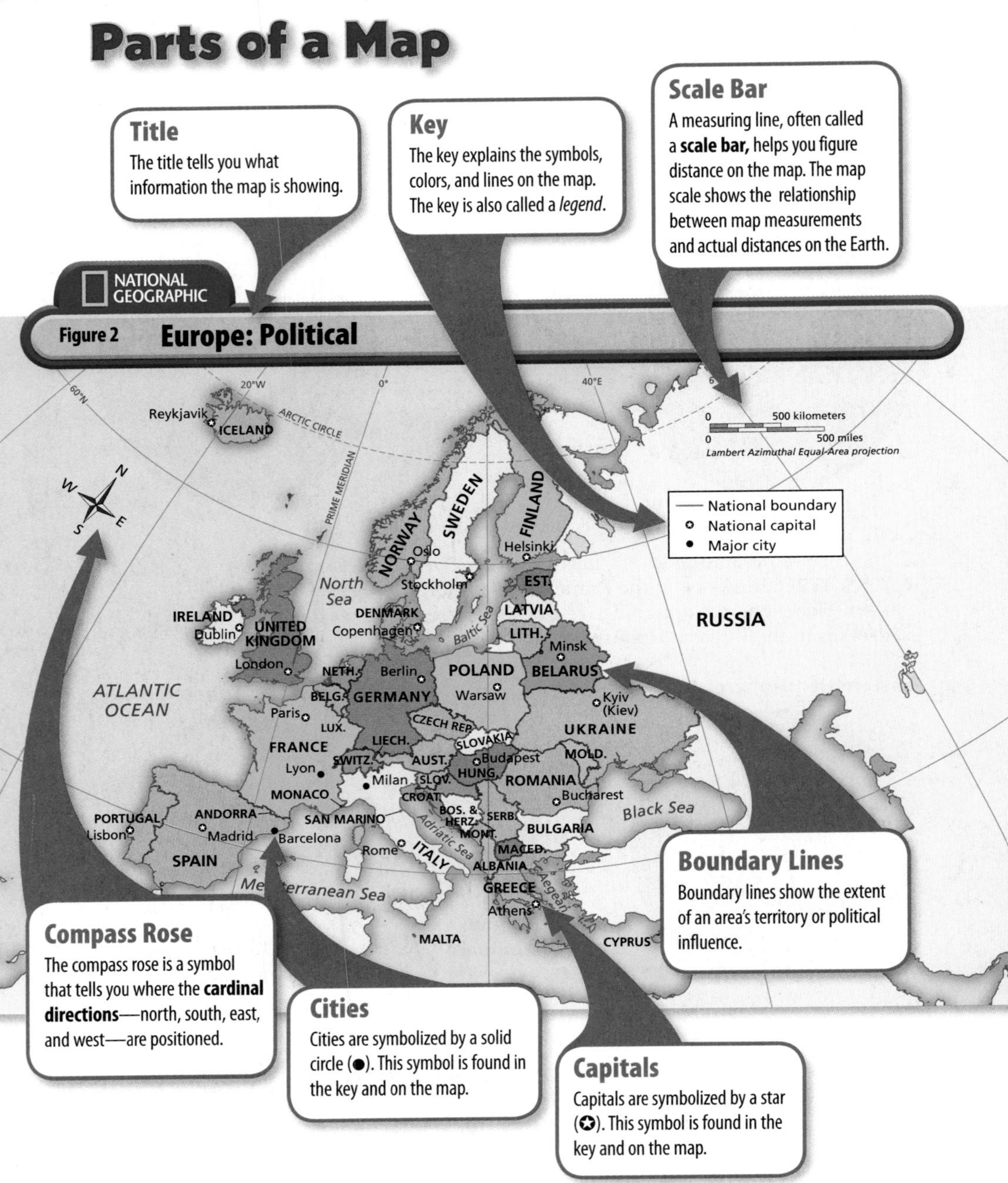

Activity: Creating a Map

Mapping a Continent Provide students with outline maps of different continents. Tell students they will practice identifying parts of a map by creating one of their own. **Ask: What features should you include on your maps?** *(Title, key, scale bar, boundary lines, capital cities, other cities, and a compass rose; students may choose to include physical features as well.)* Direct students to use the appropriate political and physical maps in the National Geographic Reference Atlas for their continents. Have them draw boundaries and cities on their maps, create a key, include a compass rose, and represent the map's scale. When finished, have students who have worked on the same continents work together to discuss their maps, revising them as needed. **OL**

Using Scale

All maps are drawn to a certain **scale.** The scale of a map is the size of the map compared to the size of the actual land surface. Thus, the scale of a map varies with the size of the area shown.

Small-Scale Maps ▼

A small-scale map, like this political map of Mexico, shows a large land area but little detail.

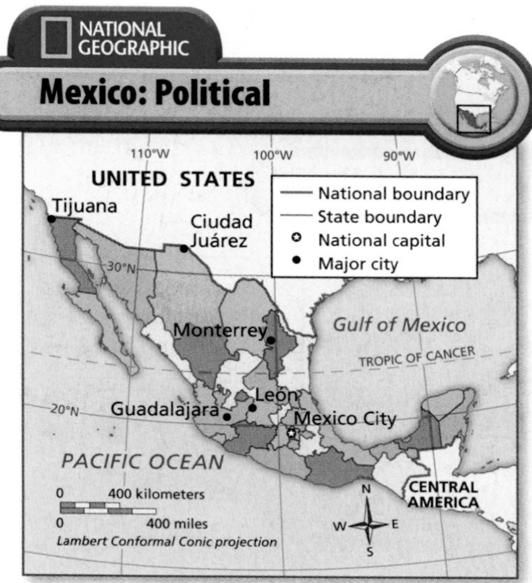

Large-Scale Maps ▼

A large-scale map, like this map of Mexico City, shows a small land area with a great amount of detail.

How Do I Use a Scale Bar?

Use the scale bar to find actual distances on a map. The scale bar tells you how many kilometers or miles are represented in that length. You can use a ruler, then, to calculate distances based on the scale bar's length.

0 300 kilometers
0 300 miles

About ½ of an inch equals 300 miles. A little more than ½ of a centimeter is equal to 300 kilometers.

Skills Practice

1. **Defining** What is scale?
2. **Contrasting** What is the difference between a small-scale map and a large-scale map?
3. **Identifying** What are the four cardinal directions?
4. **Describing** Would you use a small-scale or a large-scale map to plan a car trip across the United States? Why?

Geography Skills Activity

Comparing Maps of Different Scale Review with students the difference between a small-scale map and a large-scale map. **Ask:** **Would a map of your city or town be a small-scale map or a large-scale map? Why?** *(a large-scale map, because it would show a small land area with a lot of detail)* **Would a map of the United States be a small-scale map or a large-scale map? Why?** *(a small-scale map, because it would show a large land area with little detail)*

Direct students to examine the maps of Mexico and Mexico City. **Ask:** **What can you learn about Mexico City from the small-scale map that you cannot learn from the large-scale map?** *(Possible answer: where Mexico City is located within the country of Mexico)* **What can you learn from the large-scale map that you cannot learn from the small-scale map?** *(Possible answer: the names of streets in Mexico City and the location of particular buildings)* **BL**

Skills Practice

Answers:

1. The scale of a map is the size of the map compared to the size of the actual land surface.
2. A small-scale map shows a large land area but little detail, and a large-scale map shows a small land area with a great amount of detail.
3. north, south, east, west
4. a small-scale map in order to see the entire route at once

Activity: Determining Scale

Creating Maps to Scale In this activity, students will create a map of their classroom. Organize students into groups. Provide each group with a large piece of graph paper. Have students measure the classroom with a tape measure. **Ask:** **What scale makes sense to use to map this area on your graph paper?** *(Answers should take into account the size of the graph paper compared to the size of the classroom.)* Have students draw the outline of the classroom on the graph paper, according to the scale they have determined will work. The maps should include windows, doors, and major pieces of furniture. All features should be drawn to scale. Maps should include a key, labels, a title, a scale, and a compass rose. **OL**

Geography Skills Activity

Reading Maps **Ask:** **How does the physical map of South Asia differ from the political map of South Asia?** *(The physical map does not identify the different countries by color; more geographic features are shown; elevation is indicated by color.)*

Have students think about the uses of physical maps. **Ask:** **What important information is given on the physical map of South Asia?** *(the location of landforms such as mountains and plateaus; the location of deserts and rivers; the elevation of the highest mountain peaks)* **What physical features form natural boundaries between India and countries to the north?** *(mountain ranges and the Thar Desert)* **OL**

Types of Maps

General Purpose Maps

Maps are amazingly useful tools. You can use them to show information and to make connections between seemingly unrelated topics. Geographers use many different types of maps. Maps that show a wide range of information about an area are called **general purpose maps.** Two of the most common general purpose maps are physical maps and political maps.

Physical Maps ▼

Physical maps call out landforms and water features. The map key explains what each color and symbol stands for.

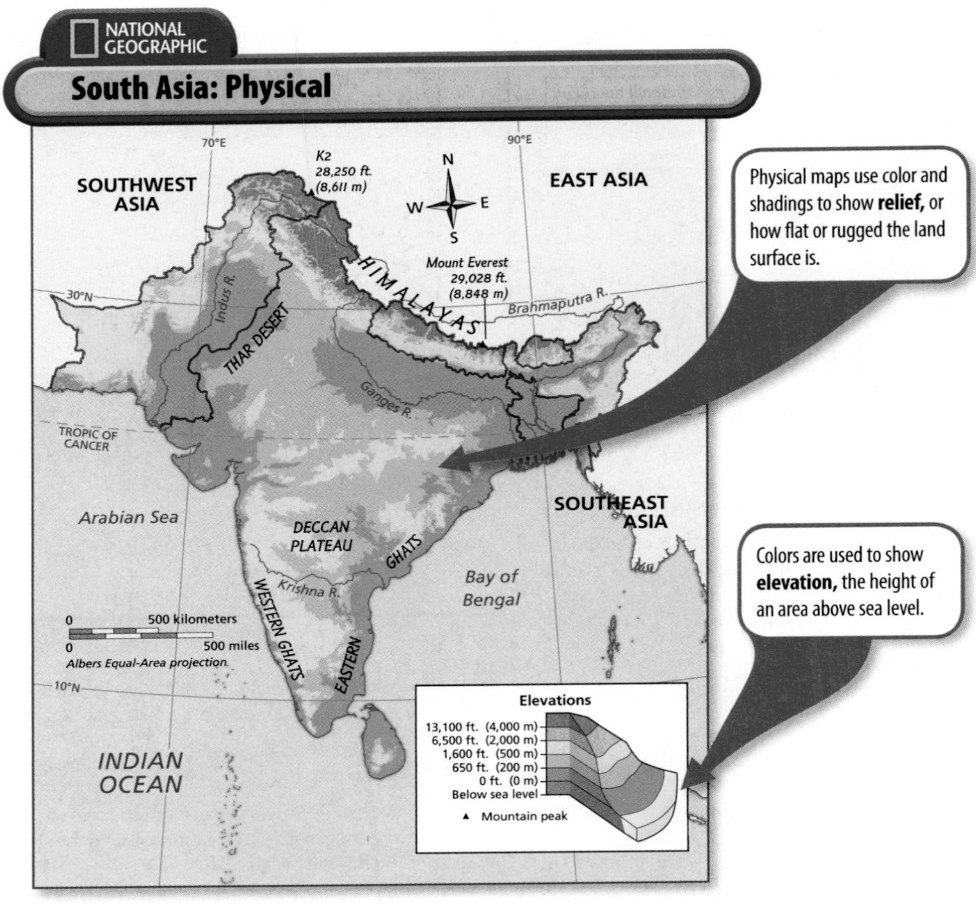

FastFacts

- **Amerigo Vespucci** Vespucci was an Italian navigator, explorer, and acquaintance of Christopher Columbus. Vespucci left a series of documents about his voyages. The humanist Martin Waldseemüller suggested in 1507 that the lands be named America in Vespucci's honor.
- **Marco Polo** Polo traveled from Europe to Asia in the late 1200s. His account of his time in Asia promoted interest in faraway places. This increased the sale and circulation of world maps. The geographic information he recorded was used by Columbus in his attempt to sail to Asia.

Political Maps ▼

Political maps show the names and political boundaries of countries, along with human-made features such as cities or transportation routes.

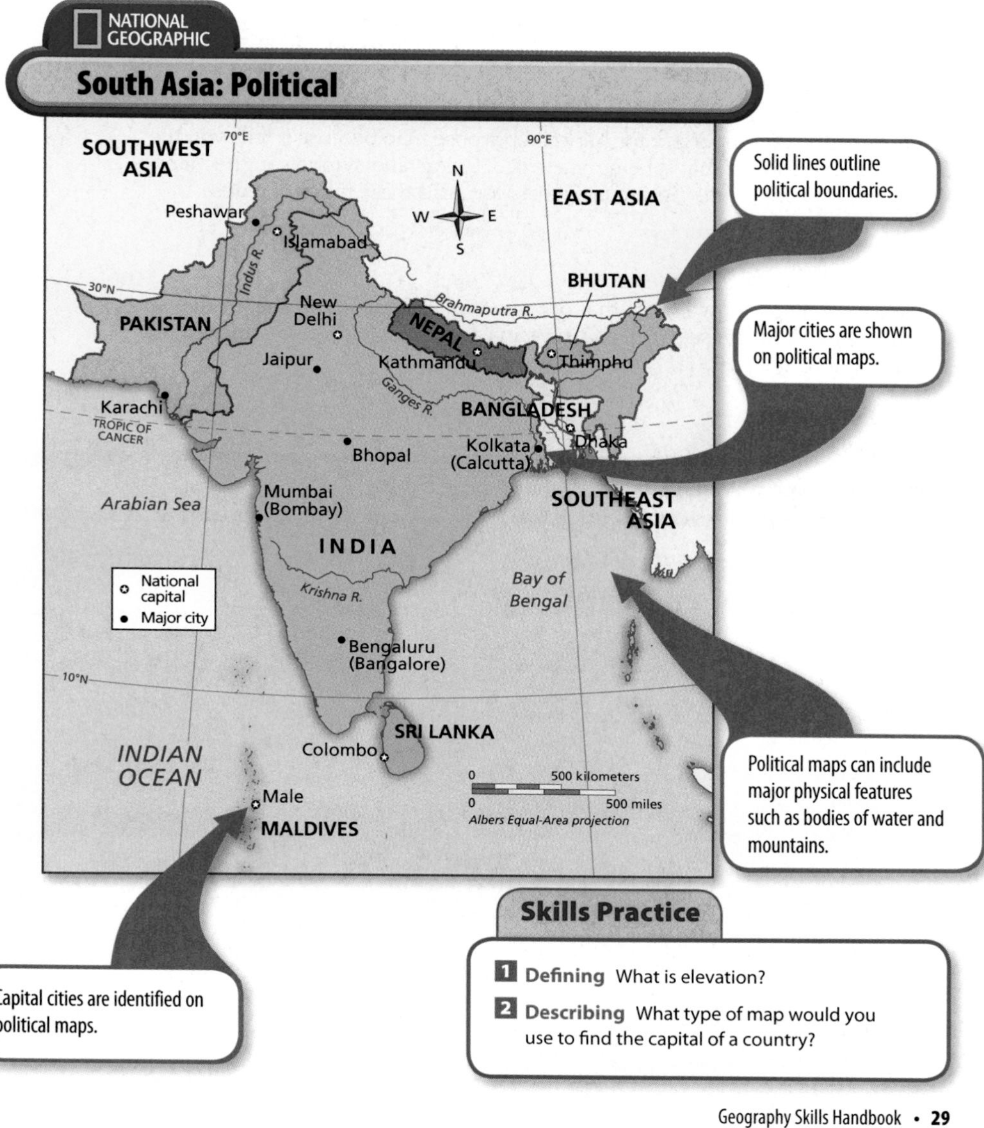

Skills Practice

1 Defining What is elevation?

2 Describing What type of map would you use to find the capital of a country?

Geography Skills Activity

Making Inferences Mapmakers often update maps. **Ask: What are some reasons that a political map would need to be revised?** *(because a national border changes, a capital city is relocated, or a new national highway is built)* Have students use encyclopedias to research the history of India, Pakistan, and Bangladesh. Have students create a chart listing the reasons a political map of South Asia would have changed over time. **OL**

Skills Practice

Answers:

1. Elevation is the height of an area above sea level.
2. A political map shows the capitals of countries.

Activity: Using a Political Map

Locating Information Have students use the World: Political map in the National Geographic Reference Atlas to identify a country they would like to visit. **Ask: What information can you gather about this country from the World: Political map?** *(Answers will vary depending on the country chosen.)* Have students begin to list information they have discovered from this map, including the capital of the country, its approximate size, and its relative location. Then have students turn to the World: Physical map and add to their lists. Continue to have students use additional maps in the National Geographic Reference Atlas to gather more detailed information about their selected country. Have students give a five-minute oral report on what they learned by studying the maps. **OL**

Geography Skills Activity

Categorizing Assign each student a unit of the textbook. **Ask: What types of maps are found in your unit?** Direct them to create a table in their notebooks with the following headings: Political Maps, Physical Maps, Special Purpose Maps. Then tell them to survey the unit, identifying the types of maps and listing their titles and page numbers in the appropriate place in their tables. **OL**

Analyzing Information Ask: What does the map of European settlement show? *(where European groups had settled in North America at a particular point in time and what lands were claimed by more than one country)* **How do you know?** *(The map title and the map key give us that information.)* **What other information does the map include?** *(major cities and bodies of water)* **What else might be useful information to include on this map?** *(Possible answer: the year or time span that this map refers to)* **OL**

Types of Maps

Special Purpose Maps

Some maps are made to present specific types of information. These are called **thematic** or **special purpose maps.** These maps usually show specific topics in detail. Special purpose maps may include information about:

- climate
- vegetation
- natural resources
- population density
- historical expansion

Look at some of the types of special purpose maps on these pages. The map's title is especially important for a special purpose map because it tells you the type of information that is being presented. Colors and symbols in the map key are also important tools to use when you read these types of maps.

Historical Maps ▼

Historical maps show events that occurred in a region over time. In the map below, you can see where Europeans settled in the North America continent in the past.

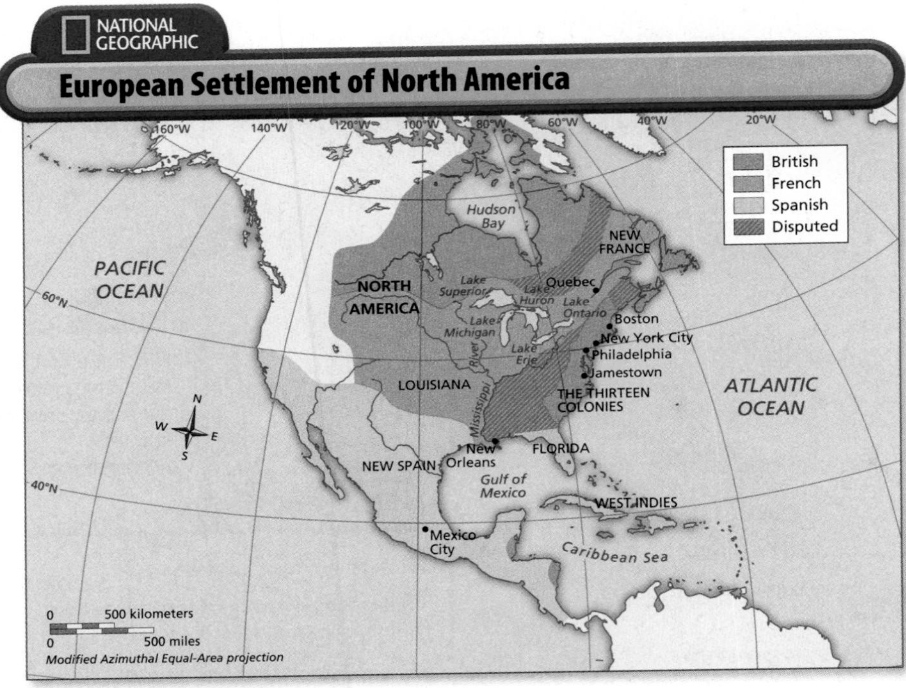

Activity: Using Special Purpose Maps

Building a Map Library Ask: What kinds of special purpose maps might exist for our region? *(Answers will vary but might include maps of bike trails, maps of parks, and so on.)* Direct students to appropriate reference materials, such as encyclopedias, world almanacs, and atlases, as a starting point to find some special purpose maps. Then help them brainstorm a list of places to contact to try to collect additional examples of special purpose maps. Students may contact the local chamber of commerce, local hiking or biking groups, historical societies, and other organizations. As students collect examples of local special purpose maps, create a classroom display titled Maps of Our Region. Have students create a caption for each map in the display that describes its intended purpose. **OL**

Contour Maps ▶

A contour map has **contour lines**—one line for each major level of elevation. All the land at the same elevation is connected by a line. These lines usually form circles or ovals—one inside the other. If contour lines are close together, the surface is steep. If the lines are spread apart, the land is flat or rises gradually.

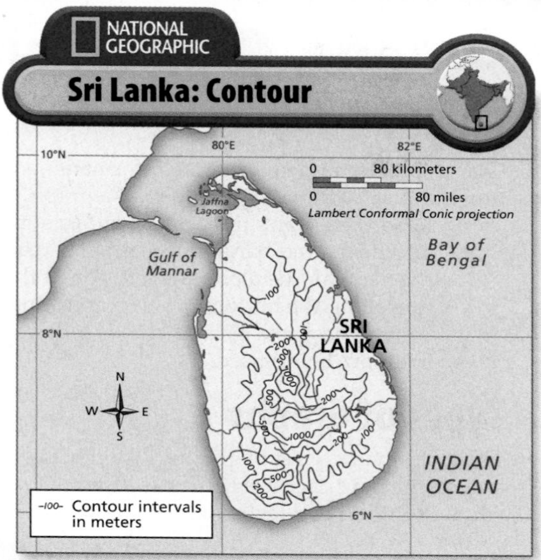

NATIONAL GEOGRAPHIC

Africa South of the Sahara: Vegetation

NORTH AFRICA · ATLANTIC OCEAN · INDIAN OCEAN · EQUATOR · Dakar · Abuja · Abidjan · Khartoum · Addis Ababa · Nairobi · Kinshasa · Luanda · Harare · Windhoek · Antananarivo · Cape Town

Tropical rain forest
Tropical grassland (savanna)
Desert scrub and desert waste
Temperate grassland
Mediterranean scrub
Deciduous forest

0 1,000 kilometers
0 1,000 miles
Lambert Azimuthal Equal-Area projection

◀ Vegetation Maps

Vegetation maps are special purpose maps that show the different types of plants that are found in a region.

Skills Practice

1. **Identifying** What type of special purpose map might show battles during World War II?
2. **Contrasting** What is the difference between a general purpose map and a special purpose map?

Geography Skills Activity

Synthesizing Have students create a fill-in-the-blank quiz on types of maps, map features, and geography terms discussed in the Geography Skills Handbook. Their fill-in-the-blank statements should follow this format: The _______________ of a map gives you important information about what the map is showing. *(title)* Ask students to write 10 fill-in-the-blank statements. Remind students to create an answer key on a separate sheet of paper. When students have finished the assignment, have them trade with a partner. After partners have completed their quizzes, have them hand the quizzes back to be scored. **ELL**

Skills Practice

Answers:

1. A historical map would show World War II battles.
2. A general purpose map shows a wide range of information about an area; a special purpose map shows specific topics about an area in detail.

Activity: Creating a Special Purpose Map

Illustrating Bring a map of your city or county to class. Post the map for students to see. Tell students that in this activity, the class will work together to create a special purpose map that depicts the recreational activities of your city or county. With the help of student volunteers, list on the board the various recreational activities. Have students discuss how to categorize and organize the information in a key. Encourage them to think of various ways to depict the activities on the map. For example, should they use an icon, a label, or a color to show the location of parks? How should they depict skating rinks and bowling alleys? Have student volunteers label and color the map to complete the activity. **OL**

Geography Skills Activity

Analyzing Information Bar graphs and circle graphs are used to compare information visually. **Ask: What could you learn from the circle graph if the percentages were not included?** *(You would not be able to learn exact percentages, but you could see by the breakdown the relative size of populations.)* **OL**

Synthesizing Have students select one of the visuals from these two pages and write a paragraph that explains the information in the visual. Follow up with a class discussion on the advantages and disadvantages of both methods of presenting information. **OL**

Graphs, Charts, and Diagrams

Graphs

Graphs present and summarize information visually. Each part of a graph provides useful information. To read a graph, follow these steps:

- Read the graph's title to find out its subject.
- To understand bar and line graphs, read the labels along the **axes**—the vertical line along the left side of the graph and the horizontal line along the bottom of the graph. One axis will tell you what is being measured. The other axis tells you what units of measurement are being used.

Types of Graphs

There are many types of graphs. Listed below and on the next page are the types of graphs you will find in this textbook.

Bar Graphs ►

Graphs that use bars or wide lines to compare data visually are called bar graphs.

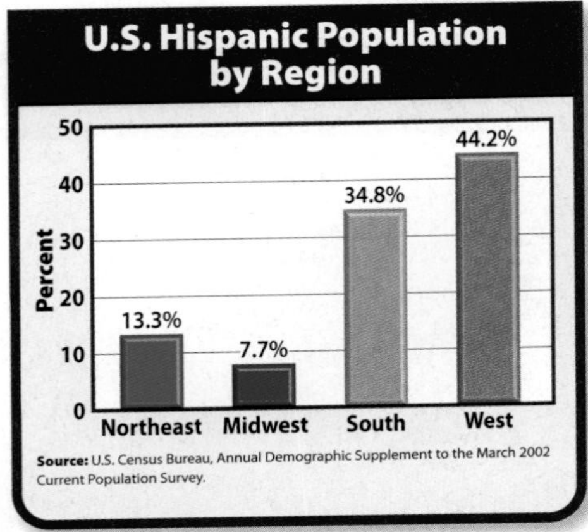

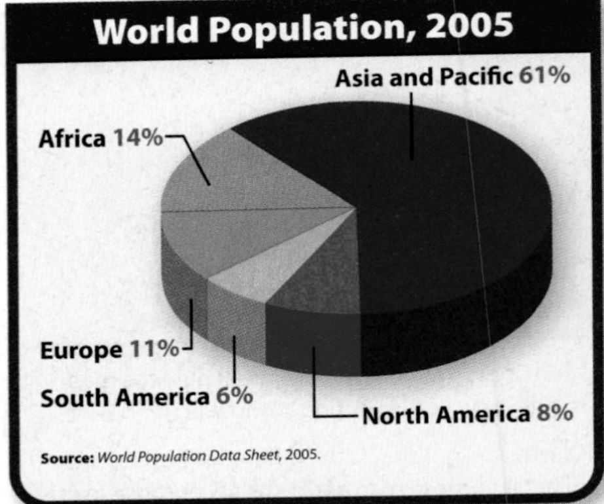

◄ Circle Graphs

You can use circle graphs when you want to show how the whole of something is divided into its parts. Because of their shape, circle graphs are often called *pie graphs.* Each slice represents a part or percentage of the whole pie. The whole graph generally totals 100 percent.

Activity: Using Graphs, Charts, and Diagrams

Speculating Ask: What types of graphs, charts, and diagrams do you think are most commonly used in geography? *(Answers will vary.)* Create a chart on the board with the following across the top: Bar Graph, Circle Graph, Line Graph, Chart, Diagram. Have students copy the chart into their notebooks. Assign each student a chapter of the textbook, and have them write the title of each chart, graph, or diagram they find in the chapter in the appropriate column. When students have finished, create a tally of the numbers of each type of graphic that they found, using the chart on the board. Discuss with students the types of information that tend to be presented in each type of graph and in charts and diagrams. Finally, have students suggest what type of graph would best present the information in your chart. **OL**

U.S. Farms, 1940–2005

Number of Farms (in millions): 0, 1, 2, 3, 4, 5, 6, 7

1940, 1950, 1960, 1970, 1980, 1990, 2000, 2005

Source: USDA, National Agricultural Statistics Service, www.nass.usda.gov

Line Graphs ▲

Line graphs help show changes over a period of time. The amounts being measured are plotted on the grid above each year and then are connected by a line.

Charts

Charts present related facts and numbers in an organized way. They arrange data, especially numbers, in rows and columns for easy reference.

Caribbean Island Populations

Aruba	71,891
Bermuda	65,773
British Virgin Islands	23,098
Jamaica	2,758,124

Source: *CIA World Factbook*, 2006.

NATIONAL GEOGRAPHIC

The Rain Shadow

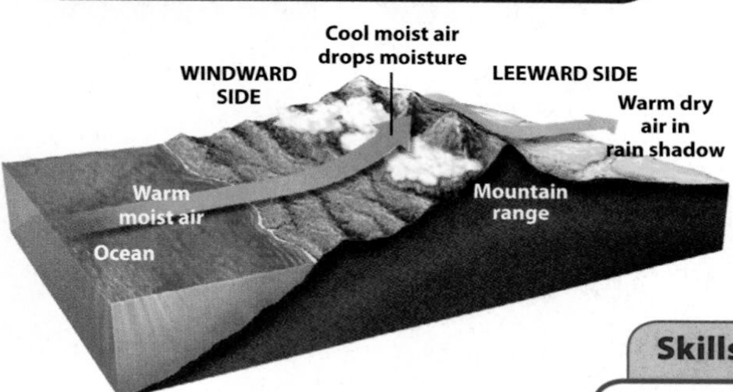

Diagrams

Diagrams are drawings that show steps in a process, point out the parts of an object, or explain how something works.

Skills Practice

1. **Identifying** What percentage does the whole circle in a circle graph represent?
2. **Analyzing Information** What type of graph would best show the number of Republicans and Democrats in the U.S. House of Representatives?

Geography Skills Activity

Graphing Information Ask each student to estimate the distance they travel to come to school. List the distances on the board. Have students discuss the best way to organize the information and depict it visually. Then organize students into groups. Provide graph paper. Have each group create a bar graph of the information. Allow groups to present their graphs to the class and explain the process they used to organize the information. **OL**

Skills Practice

Answers:

1. 100%
2. A bar graph could show the numbers of Democrats and Republicans.

Activity: Technology Connection

Displaying Have students determine another way to display the information in the Island Populations chart. Ask them to give reasons why their method is appropriate. Then have them use a software program to create a graph of the information. Many software programs, including word-processing and spreadsheet programs, can be used to make charts and then turn those charts into pie, line, or bar graphs. Have students present their graphs to the rest of the class. If students have used different types of graphs, have them discuss how each graph displays the information differently and which type of graph works best for displaying this type of information. **OL**

Focus

Bellringer

Daily Focus Transparency 1-2

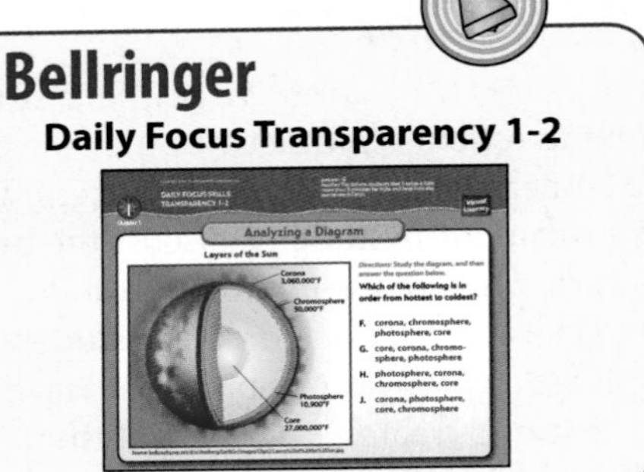

Guide to Reading

Answers to Graphic:

Answers may include:
Tropics: Temperatures are very warm.
High Latitudes: Temperatures are cool or cold.

Section Spotlight Video

To learn more about the Earth's place in the solar system, have students watch the Section Spotlight Video.

Resource Manager

R Reading Strategies	C Critical Thinking	D Differentiated Instruction	W Writing Support	S Skill Practice
Teacher Edition • Identifying, p. 35 • Summarizing, p. 36 **Additional Resources** • Guid. Read., URB p. 32 • Cont. Vocab., URB p. 33 • Ac. Vocab., URB p. 35 • Read. Ess., p. 4 • Pri. Source Read., URB p. 23	**Teacher Edition** • Analyzing Info., p. 35 • Making Generalizations, p. 38 **Additional Resources** • Quizzes and Tests, p. 4	**Teacher Edition** • Kinesthetic, p. 36 **Additional Resources** • Diff. Instr., URB p. 37 • Reteaching, URB p. 49	**Teacher Edition** • Personal Writing, p. 37	**Teacher Edition** • Visual Literacy, p. 37 **Additional Resources** • Speak./Listen. Skills, URB p. 43 • Daily Focus Trans. 1-2 • Reg. Atlas, URB pp. 1–7

Guide to Reading

BIG Idea

Physical processes shape Earth's surface.

Content Vocabulary

- solar system *(p. 35)*
- orbit *(p. 35)*
- revolution *(p. 36)*
- leap year *(p. 36)*
- rotate *(p. 36)*
- axis *(p. 36)*
- atmosphere *(p. 36)*
- summer solstice *(p. 37)*
- winter solstice *(p. 38)*
- equinox *(p. 38)*
- Tropics *(p. 38)*

Academic Vocabulary

- significant *(p. 37)*
- reverse *(p. 38)*
- identical *(p. 38)*

Reading Strategy

Determining Cause and Effect Use a diagram like the one below to show the effects of latitude on Earth's temperatures.

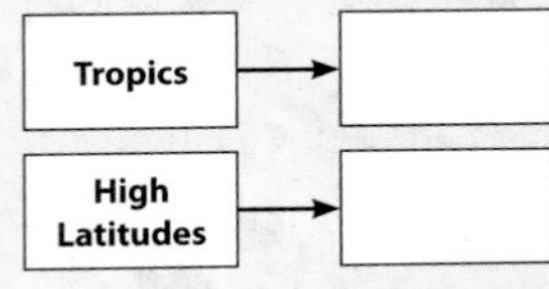

SECTION 2 The Earth in Space

Picture This From space, the Aral Sea in Central Asia can be easily seen. Once the fourth-largest lake in the world, the Aral Sea has shrunk significantly. Satellite photographs, taken over a period of years, help scientists measure the total area of water that has been lost. These images, in addition to other information, help scientists understand what has caused the sea to change size. Scientists also continue to explore space and how the Earth's location in the solar system affects our planet. Read the next section to learn how the Earth's rotation, orbit, tilt, and latitude affect life on Earth.

▼ The Aral Sea from space

The Solar System

Main Idea **The Earth is one of eight planets in the solar system. It rotates on its axis every 24 hours and takes a year to orbit the sun.**

Geography and You Have you watched a sunrise or sunset and wondered why the sun seems to move across the sky each day? Read to find out about the Earth and its place in our solar system.

The sun provides the heat necessary for life on our planet. Earth, seven other major planets, and thousands of smaller bodies all revolve around the sun. Together with the sun, these bodies form our **solar system**. R

Major Planets

The major planets differ from one another in size and makeup. Look at **Figure 1.** It shows that the inner planets—Mercury, Venus, Earth, and Mars—are relatively small and solid. The outer planets—Jupiter, Saturn, Uranus, and Neptune—are larger and composed mostly or entirely of gases. Pluto, once considered a major planet, is now called a minor planet.

Each planet follows its own path, or **orbit**, around the sun. The orbits vary from nearly circular to elliptical, or oval shaped.

Student Web Activity Visit glencoe.com and complete the Chapter 1 Web Activity about the solar system.

NATIONAL GEOGRAPHIC

Figure 1 **The Solar System**

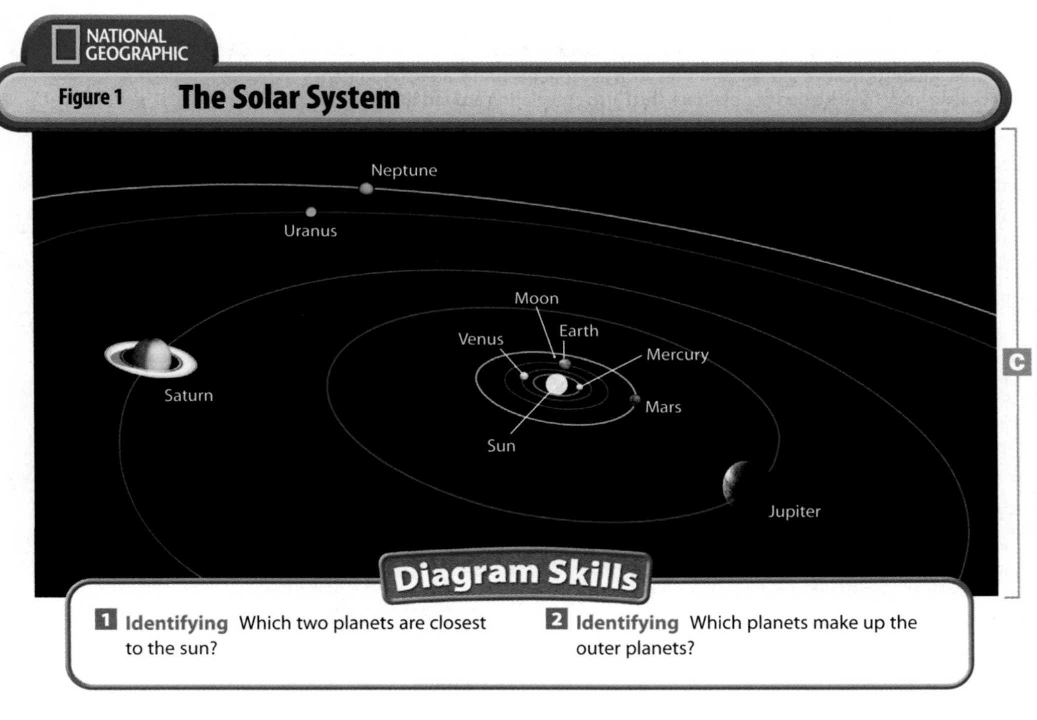

C

Diagram Skills

1. **Identifying** Which two planets are closest to the sun?
2. **Identifying** Which planets make up the outer planets?

Teach

R Reading Strategy

Identifying **Ask:** **What bodies make up our solar system?** *(the sun, eight major planets, and thousands of smaller bodies)* **OL**

C Critical Thinking

Analyzing Information Have students look at the diagram again.

Ask: **Why do you think it takes Neptune much longer to orbit the sun than Mercury?** *(It is much farther away from the sun, so it has a much longer distance to travel.)* **AL**

Diagram Skills

Answers:

1. Mercury and Venus
2. Jupiter, Saturn, Uranus, Neptune

Social Studies ONLINE

Objectives and answers to the Student Web Activity can be found at glencoe.com under the Web Activity Lesson Plan for this chapter.

Hands-On Chapter Project
Step 2

Designing a Building From Scratch

Step 2: Making the Model Students will make a drawing or model of the site they described in Step 1.

Directions After students have decided on the site for their facility, have them analyze what sort of infrastructure would be useful to have nearby. Does their facility need to be in a major city, near a highway, close to homes, or away from people? Have students use their site description and this analysis to create a drawing or model of their facility and its site. Encourage students to use photographs of similar facilities and sites to include as much detail as possible.

Putting It Together Have each group display their drawing or model and explain the special features of the site, including any nearby infrastructure. **OL**

(Chapter Project cont. on the Visual Summary page.)

R Reading Strategy

Summarizing Have students summarize why we have leap years. *(because the Earth's revolution around the sun takes 365¼ days the extra quarter days are added to every fourth year as February 29)* BL

D Differentiated Instruction

Kinesthetic Have students create a model of the Earth's rotation. Suggest that they use objects found easily in the classroom. OL

Caption Answer:
As it rotates, half of the Earth is in darkness and half is in light.

Reading Check Answer: Rotation is the Earth's spinning on its axis; revolution is the Earth's moving in a complete circuit around the sun.

Earth's Movements

Some scientists believe that ancient sites such as Stonehenge, located in southern England, may have helped people track the Earth's revolution around the sun and the change of the seasons. From space, astronauts can see the Earth (inset) in light and shadow at the same time. ***Movement*** **Why do different parts of the Earth experience sunlight or darkness?**

The time necessary to complete an orbit differs, too. Mercury needs only 88 days to circle the sun, but faraway Neptune takes 165 years.

Earth's Movement

R Earth takes almost 365¼ days to make one **revolution**, or a complete circuit, around the sun. This period is what we define as one year. Every four years, the extra fourths of a day are combined and added to the calendar as February 29th. A year that contains one of these extra days is called a **leap year.**

D As Earth orbits the sun, it **rotates**, or spins, on its axis. The **axis** is an imaginary line that passes through the center of Earth from the North Pole to the South Pole. Earth rotates in an easterly direction, making one complete rotation every 24 hours. As Earth turns, different parts of the planet are in sunlight or in darkness. The part facing the sun experiences daytime, and the part facing away has night.

Why do we not feel Earth moving as it rotates? The reason is that the **atmosphere,** the layer of oxygen and gases that surrounds Earth, moves with it.

Reading Check **Explaining** Describe Earth's two principal motions—revolution and rotation.

Differentiated Instruction

Name ______ Date ______ Class ______

The World

Primary Source Reading A

BEFORE YOU READ

Interpreting the Source
Seeing Earth from space for the first time made a strong impression on the astronauts who had this privilege. Some of them even compared Earth to a big blue marble. Although the astronauts and cosmonauts named below are from different countries, the descriptions of their experiences reveal a shared sense of mystery and awe as they viewed Earth from afar.

Reader's Dictionary
atoll: a coral island
spectacle: an eye-catching or dramatic display
relic: a valuable piece of the past
fragile: easily broken or destroyed
cherish: to care for deeply

Guided Reading
Read the first impressions of the astronauts and cosmonauts as they view Earth from their perspective in space. Then answer the questions that follow.

Astronauts' Views of Earth

My first view—a panorama of brilliant deep blue ocean, shot with shades of green and gray and white—was of atolls and clouds. Close to the window I could see that this Pacific scene in motion was rimmed by the great curved limb of the Earth. It has a thin halo of blue held close, and beyond, black space. I held my breath, but something was missing—I felt strangely unfulfilled. Here was a tremendous visual spectacle, but viewed in silence. There was no grand musical accompaniment; no triumphant, inspired sonata or symphony.
—*Charles Walker, U.S., crew member for three Space Shuttle missions*

The Earth was small, light blue, and so touchingly alone, our home that must be defended like a holy relic. The Earth was absolutely round. I believe that I never knew what the word *round* meant until I saw Earth from space.
—*Aleksei Leonov, USSR, Apollo-Soyuz flights and first man to walk in space*

For the first time in my life I saw the horizon as a curved line. It was accentuated by a thin seam of dark blue light—our atmosphere. Obviously this was not the ocean of air I had been told it was so many times in my life. I was terrified by its fragile appearance.
—*Ulf Merbold, Federal Republic of Germany, crew member for a Space Shuttle mission and the Russian Space Station Mir*

A Chinese tale tells of some men sent to harm a young girl who, upon seeing her beauty, became her protectors. . . . That's how I felt seeing the earth for the first time. I could not help but love and cherish her.
—*Taylor Wang, China/U.S., crew member on the Challenger*

Source: www.solarviews.com/eng/earthsp.htm

Primary Source Reading, URB pp. 23–24

An Astronaut's Eye View

Objective: To learn to analyze primary sources and learn about different viewpoints

Focus: Ask: What are primary sources?

Teach: Read the quotes and discuss how primary sources are different from secondary sources.

Assess: Have students answer the questions and then check their answers for accuracy.

Close: Discuss with students what historians can learn from primary sources.

Differentiated Instruction Strategies

- **BL** Have students think about how the primary sources reveal the authors' feelings as well as their observations.
- **AL** Have students write descriptive paragraphs explaining something they care deeply about.
- **ELL** Have students discuss the ways the quotes reflect the authors' backgrounds.

Sun and Seasons

Main Idea **The tilt of Earth and its revolution around the sun lead to changing seasons during the year.**

Geography and You Did you know that when it is winter in the United States, it is summer in Australia? Read to learn why seasons differ between the Northern and Southern Hemispheres.

Earth is tilted 23½ degrees on its axis. As a result, seasons change as Earth makes its year-long orbit around the sun. To see why this happens, look at **Figure 2.** Notice how sunlight falls directly on the northern or southern half of Earth at different times of the year. Direct rays from the sun bring more warmth than indirect, or slanted rays. When the people in a hemisphere receive direct rays, they enjoy the warmth of summer. When they receive only indirect rays, they experience the cold of winter.

Solstices and Equinoxes

Four days in the year are **significant,** or important, because of the position of the sun in relation to Earth. These days mark the beginnings of the four seasons. On or about June 21, the North Pole is tilted toward the sun. On noon of this day, the sun appears directly overhead at the Tropic of Cancer (23½°N latitude). In the Northern Hemisphere, this day is the **summer solstice**—the day with the most hours of sunlight. It is the beginning of summer—but only in the Northern Hemisphere. In the Southern Hemisphere, that same day is the day with the fewest hours of sunlight and marks the beginning of winter. **W**

NATIONAL GEOGRAPHIC **Maps In MOtion** See StudentWorks™ Plus or glencoe.com.

Figure 2 **The Sun and Earth's Seasons**

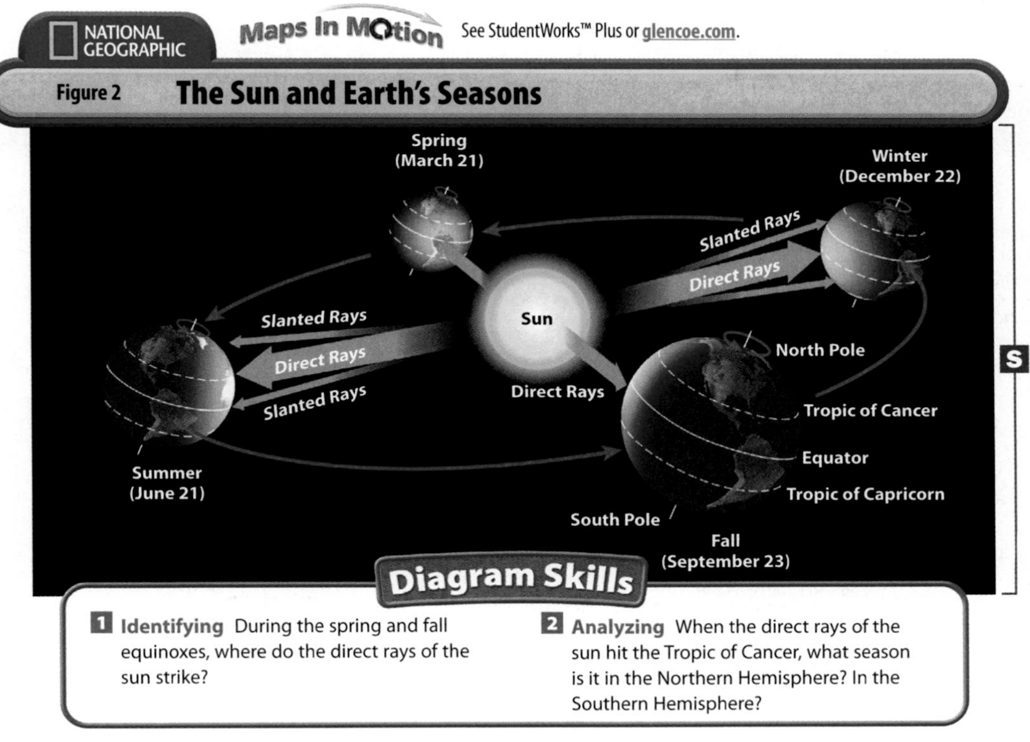

S

Diagram Skills

1 **Identifying** During the spring and fall equinoxes, where do the direct rays of the sun strike?

2 **Analyzing** When the direct rays of the sun hit the Tropic of Cancer, what season is it in the Northern Hemisphere? In the Southern Hemisphere?

W Writing Support

Personal Writing Discuss the seasons with students. Then have them write a short essay describing their favorite season of the year. Tell them to include details about what that season is like in the area in which they live. **BL**

S Skill Practice

Visual Literacy Tell students that scientists believe that Mars's tilt can vary between about 15 and 40 degrees. Have students look at the diagram. **Ask: Do you think Mars has seasons like Earth does? Why or why not?** *(Yes, the seasons are caused by the tilt, just like on Earth.)* Now tell students that Mars is farther away from the sun than the Earth. **Ask: How do you think this affects the length of Mars's seasons, compared to the Earth's?** *(They are longer.)* **AL**

Diagram Skills

Answers:

1. on the Equator
2. summer; winter

Leveled Activities

BL **Content Vocabulary Activity, URB p. 33**

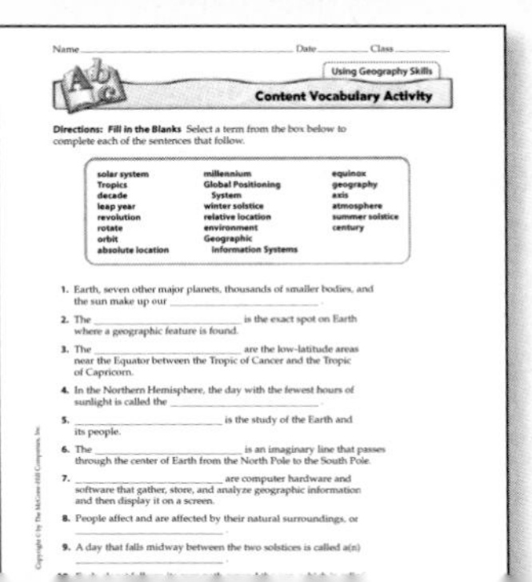

OL **Speaking and Listening Skills Activity, URB p. 43**

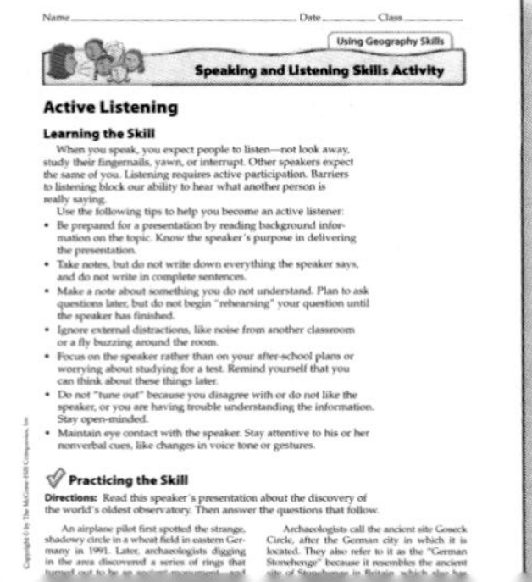

ELL **Academic Vocabulary Activity, URB p. 35**

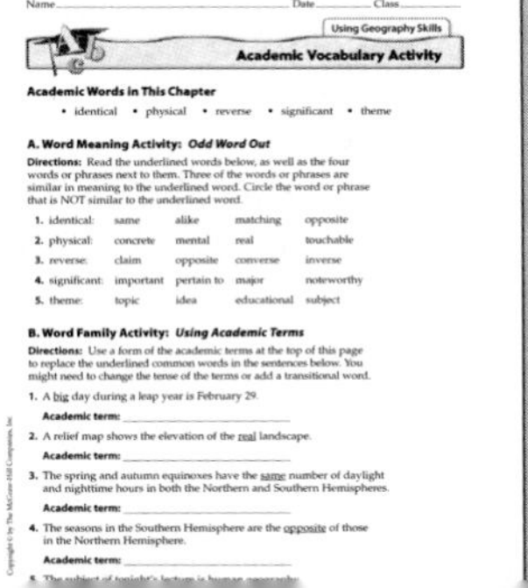

C Critical Thinking

Making Generalizations Ask: What do you think are some advantages to living in midlatitude regions of the Earth, compared to the tropics or the Poles? *(Possible answers: Different seasons in the midlatitudes allow for growing many different crops; warm and cold seasons allow for different animals to thrive; weather is not as extreme in midlatitude regions.)* **OL**

Reading Check **Answer:** The sun's rays hit these regions most directly.

Assess

Social Studies ONLINE
Study Central™ provides summaries, interactive games, and online graphic organizers to help students review content.

Close

Explaining Have each student answer this question: What is your favorite season, and what is the position of the Earth during that season? **OL**

Six months later—on or about December 22—the situation is **reversed,** or the opposite. The North Pole is tilted away from the sun. At noon, the sun's direct rays strike the Tropic of Capricorn. In the Northern Hemisphere, this day is the **winter solstice**—the day with the fewest hours of sunlight and the beginning of winter. This same day, however, marks the beginning of summer in the Southern Hemisphere.

Spring and autumn each begin on a day that falls midway between the two solstices. These two days are the **equinoxes,** when day and night are of **identical,** or equal, length in both hemispheres. On or about March 21, the spring equinox occurs. On or about September 23, the fall equinox occurs. On both days, the noon sun shines directly over the Equator.

Effects of Latitude

Earth's temperatures also are affected by the sun. Look again at **Figure 2.** The sun's rays directly hit places in the **Tropics,** the low-latitude areas near the Equator between the Tropic of Cancer and the Tropic of Capricorn. As a result, temperatures in the Tropics tend to be very warm.

At the high latitudes near the North and South Poles, the sun's rays hit indirectly. Temperatures in these regions are always cool or cold. In the midlatitudes—the areas between the Tropics of Cancer and Capricorn and the polar regions—temperatures, weather, and the seasons vary greatly. This is because air masses from both the high latitudes and the Tropics affect these areas.

Reading Check **Analyzing Information** Why are the Tropics the Earth's warmest regions?

Section 2 Review

Social Studies ONLINE
Study Central™ To review this section, go to glencoe.com.

Vocabulary

1. **Explain** the significance of:
   - a. solar system
   - b. orbit
   - c. revolution
   - d. leap year
   - e. rotate
   - f. axis
   - g. atmosphere
   - h. summer solstice
   - i. winter solstice
   - j. equinox
   - k. Tropics

Main Ideas

2. **Identifying** Name the inner and outer planets, and describe the differences between the two groups.
3. **Comparing** Use a diagram like the one below to compare the days that mark the beginnings of the seasons.

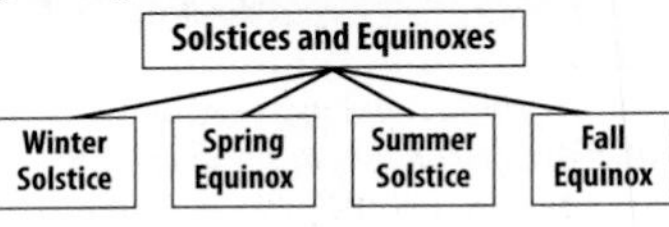

Critical Thinking

4. **Analyzing** Why do we not feel the Earth's movement as it rotates?
5. **BIG Idea** What causes different seasons on Earth?
6. **Challenge** How might latitude affect the population of a region?

Writing About Geography

7. **Expository Writing** Write a paragraph explaining why seasons in the Southern Hemisphere are the opposite of those in the Northern Hemisphere.

Section 2 Review

Answers

1. Definitions for the vocabulary words are found in the section and the Glossary.
2. The inner planets—Mercury, Venus, Earth, and Mars—are relatively small and solid. The outer planets—Jupiter, Saturn, Uranus, and Neptune—are larger and composed mostly or entirely of gases.
3. **winter solstice:** fewest hours of sunlight and first day of winter in Northern Hemisphere; **spring and fall equinox:** day and night of identical length in both hemispheres; **summer solstice:** most hours of sunlight and first day of summer in Northern Hemisphere
4. The atmosphere of the Earth moves with it.
5. The tilt of the Earth makes sunlight fall more directly either on the Northern or Southern Hemispheres at different times of the year.
6. Latitude affects how much sunlight reaches a region, which affects how many people the land can support.
7. Paragraphs will vary but should reflect an understanding that sunlight falls directly on the northern or southern half of the Earth at different times of year.

Visual Summary

Themes of Geography

- Geography is the study of the Earth and its people.
- In their study of people and places, geographers use five themes: location, place, human-environment interaction, movement, and regions.

Seven Sisters Waterfall, Norway

Kinds of Geography

- Physical geography examines physical aspects of the Earth, such as land areas, bodies of water, and plant life.
- Human geography focuses on people and their activities, including religions, languages, and ways of life.

Hiker using GPS

Geographers at Work

- To study the Earth, geographers use maps, globes, photographs, the Global Positioning System (GPS), and Geographic Information Systems (GIS).
- People can use information from geographers to plan, make decisions, and manage resources.

Solar System

- The sun, eight planets, and many smaller bodies form our solar system.
- Earth takes almost 365¼ days to make one revolution around the sun.
- Earth spins on its axis, causing day and night.

Sun and Seasons

- The Earth's tilt and its revolution around the sun cause the changes in seasons.
- Four days in the year mark the beginning points of the four seasons.

Luxembourg Palace, Paris, France

The Earth from space

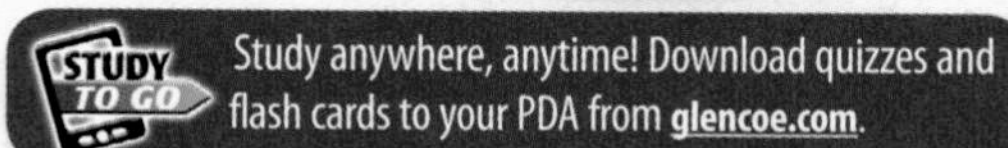

Study anywhere, anytime! Download quizzes and flash cards to your PDA from glencoe.com.

Visual Summary

Applying Have students review the summary information about the five themes of geography, the kinds of geography, and the work geographers do. Then ask them to contribute to a class list of how the use of geography has helped make your community what it is today.

To get the list started, you might point out that the theme of movement helps explain that your community was founded by people who moved here from other places. Ask students for examples of why people might have moved to the community. *(looking for better jobs, fleeing a place threatened by war or other violence, going to school)* Do the same with the other themes of geography. Students may also point out ways that physical geography has influenced what has been built in the community, ways that human geography is expressed through the diversity of your community, and specific examples of how geographers have contributed to planning and decision making. **OL**

Displaying Have students choose a subject from this chapter and create an exhibit, bulletin board, or other display about that subject. **OL**

Hands-On Chapter Project
Step 3: Wrap Up

Designing a Building From Scratch

Step 3: Learning From the Model Students will synthesize what they have learned in Steps 1 and 2.

Directions Write the Essential Question on the board. Compare and contrast the different sites that students chose for their facilities. Lead a discussion about how each group used geography to choose its site by using questions such as the following: Did students concentrate on the physical features of the site? The climate? The location? Did their site placement depend more on elements of physical geography or human geography? Which of the five themes of geography was most influential in their decision? Discuss with students how these same considerations affect people's personal choices of where to live and work and how world leaders make decisions about priorities for their nations. To conclude, have students use what they have learned to write several sentences in their journals answering the Essential Question. **OL**

Answers and Analyses

Reviewing Vocabulary

1. A A key to answering this question is the word *other* in the question stem. Help students realize that locating a geographic feature by referring to other features around it (those that *relate* to it), is called *relative location.* Choice B, *absolute location,* does not refer to other features. Choices C and D are not locations but rather technologies for locating geographic features.

2. C If students analyze the answer choices, they will see that each describes a specific length of time. Choice A, *years ago,* is far too short. *Decades*, choice B, equals only 50 years, also too short. Eliminating A and B leaves students a choice between 500 years (C) and 5,000 years (D). Students should recall that the modern period began around A.D. 1500, leaving C as the correct choice.

3. B Choice D can be eliminated first because *solar system* does not relate to the movement of the Earth; it is the group of objects closest to the Earth. Students may confuse the term *axis*, choice A, with the word *axle*, to which wheels are attached and spin. To understand the difference between B and C, students must realize that the motion of moving around the sun is called *revolution*, while the path a body takes as it makes its revolutions is its *orbit*, choice B.

4. B Students may be best able to answer this question by asking themselves, *During which season are days the shortest?* Knowing that days are shortest in the winter makes it clear that the choice with the word *winter*, B, is correct. Students may also be able to eliminate choices A and C because they contain the word *equinox*, which signals equal periods of light and dark.

STANDARDIZED TEST PRACTICE

TEST-TAKING TIP

Read every exam question twice to make certain you know exactly what it is asking.

Reviewing Vocabulary

Directions: Choose the word(s) that best completes the sentence.

1. _______ describes where a geographic feature is located by referring to other features around it.

A Relative location
B Absolute location
C The Global Positioning System
D A Geographic Positioning System

2. According to historians, the period known as Modern History began about five _______.

A years ago
B decades ago
C centuries ago
D millennia ago

3. The path each planet follows around the sun is called its _______.

A axis
B orbit
C revolution
D solar system

4. In the Northern Hemisphere, the day of the year with the fewest hours of sunlight is the _______.

A fall equinox
B winter solstice
C spring equinox
D summer solstice

Reviewing Main Ideas

Directions: Choose the best answer for each question.

Section 1 *(pp. 14–17)*

5. What geographic theme involves characteristics that make a location unique?

A place
B regions
C location
D movement

6. _______ provide(s) detailed photographs for creating maps.

A A globe
B A satellite
C A Global Positioning System
D Geographic Information Systems

Section 2 *(pp. 34–38)*

7. The Earth circles the sun every _______.

A 24 hours
B 365¼ days
C 88 years
D 165 years

8. Temperatures are always cool or cold near the North and South Poles because

A the Poles face the sun in daytime.
B the rays of the sun hit the Poles directly.
C the Poles turn away from the sun at night.
D the Poles receive only slanted rays from the sun.

GO ON

Reviewing Main Ideas

5. A Answer D can be eliminated because it does not name a place, but rather describes people moving around. Students may recall that the theme of *regions*, choice B, refers to areas that have common characteristics, such as mountains, plains, or jungles. *Location* refers to a place's position on the Earth's surface, while *place* refers to a place's unique or special features.

6. B Choice A can be eliminated because a *globe* does not provide photographs for maps; rather, it is a kind of three-dimensional map itself. Students may recognize that choice C, *Global Positioning System,* does not create maps but instead allows users to find their own location on the Earth's surface. Choice D, *Geographic Information System,* is an information system for storing geographic data. Eliminating these three choices leaves the correct one, B.

Critical Thinking

Directions: Base your answers to questions 9, 10, and 11 on the map below and your knowledge of Chapter 1. Choose the best answer for each question.

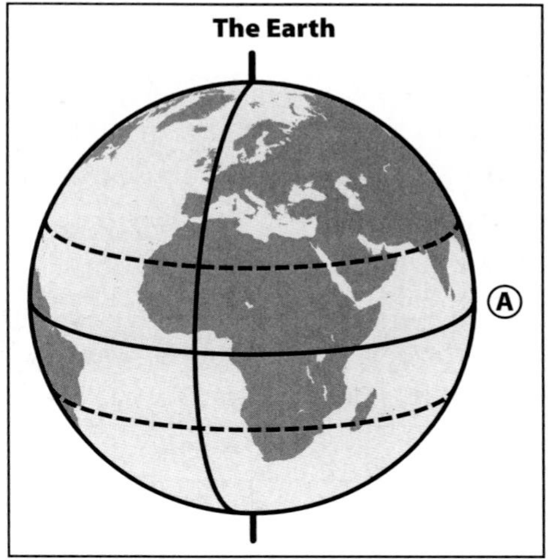

9. Label A is showing ______.
- **A** Earth's axis
- **B** the Equator
- **C** the Prime Meridian
- **D** the Tropic of Cancer

10. The Equator divides the Earth into
- **A** the North Pole and South Pole.
- **B** the Eastern and Western Hemispheres.
- **C** the Tropics of Cancer and Capricorn.
- **D** the Northern and Southern Hemispheres.

11. The sun's rays directly hit places in the ______.
- **A** midlatitudes
- **B** high latitudes
- **C** Tropics
- **D** spring equinox

Document-Based Questions

Directions: Analyze the following document and answer the short-answer questions that follow.

The following passage explains why scientists no longer consider Pluto a major planet.

> *Once known as the smallest, coldest, and most distant planet from the Sun, Pluto has a dual identity, not to mention being enshrouded in controversy since its discovery in 1930. On August 24, 2006, the International Astronomical Union (IAU) formally downgraded Pluto from an official planet to a dwarf planet. According to the new rules a planet meets three criteria: it must orbit the Sun, it must be big enough for gravity to squash it into a round ball, and it must have cleared other things out of the way in its orbital neighborhood. The latter measure knocks out Pluto and 2003UB313 (Eris), which orbit among the icy wrecks of the Kuiper Belt, and Ceres, which is in the asteroid belt.*
>
> —National Aeronautics and Space Administration, "Pluto"

12. In what two ways is Pluto like the major planets?

13. What other two bodies travel around the sun but are not considered planets?

Extended Response

14. Write a paragraph explaining how the concerns of physical geography and human geography often overlap.

Social Studies ONLINE
For additional test practice, use Self-Check Quizzes—Chapter 1 at glencoe.com.

Need Extra Help?

If you missed question...	1	2	3	4	5	6	7	8	9	10	11	12	13	14
Go to page...	15	16	35	38	15	17	36	38	25	25	25	35	35	16

Critical Thinking

9. B Students may be helped in choosing the right answer by analyzing the word *Equator*. It comes from the same root as the word *equal*; the line on the map divides the Earth into two equal halves.

10. D Helpful clues in this question are the word *Equator* and the prefix *hemi-* in answers B and D. The Equator divides the Earth into two *equal* halves. The prefix *hemi-* means "half." Knowing these meanings allows students to eliminate choices A and C. Choosing between choices B and D is made easier if students recall that the Equator runs around the "middle" of the Earth.

11. C To answer this question, students need to recall where the latitudes are on a map. *Mid latitudes* refers to the middle of the hemisphere, not the middle of the Earth. Also, if students remember that the tropics are hot, and that the sun's rays create this heat, they can choose *tropics*.

Document-Based Questions

12. It orbits the sun and is big enough for gravity to squash it into a round ball.

13. Eris and Ceres

Extended Response

14. Students' answers will vary but should give examples of how land, water, plant life, and other physical features affect people and their activities.

7. B For this question, students will need to think about how long a year is. A year represents the time it takes for a planet to make one revolution around the sun. A day is the time it takes a planet to make one complete rotation on its axis. Knowing these facts make choice B clearly correct. Choice A is one Earth day, or rotation on its axis. Choices C and D are not reasonable periods of time.

8. D Students may find this question difficult. Choices A and C may seem to be correct, but are misleading because the Poles are at the center of the axis and do not have the same result from Earth's rotation. Thsese choices are not the reasons why teperatures are low there. Choice B is incorrect because any place where the rays of the sun hit directly will be warmer, not colder.

Social Studies ONLINE
Have students visit the Web site at glencoe.com to review Chapter 1 and take the Self-Check Quiz.

Need Extra Help?
Have students refer to the pages listed if they miss any of the questions.

Planning Guide

Key to Ability Levels	
BL Below level	**AL** Above level
OL On level	**ELL** English Language Learners

Key to Teaching Resources	
Print Material	DVD
CD-ROM	Transparency

Levels				Resources	Chapter Opener	Section 1	Section 2	Section 3	Section 4	Chapter Assess
BL	OL	AL	ELL							
FOCUS										
BL	OL	AL	ELL	Daily Focus Skills Transparencies		2-1	2-2	2-3	2-4	
TEACH										
BL	OL		ELL	Guided Reading Activity, URB*		p. 55	p. 56	p. 57	p. 58	
BL	OL	AL	ELL	Content Vocabulary Activity, URB*		p. 59	p. 59	p. 59	p. 59	
BL	OL	AL	ELL	Academic Vocabulary Activity, URB		p. 61	p. 61	p. 61	p. 61	
BL	OL	AL	ELL	Differentiated Instruction Activity, URB			p. 63			
BL	OL	AL	ELL	Chart, Graph, and Map Skills Activity, URB		p. 65	p. 65			
	OL	AL		Critical Thinking Activity, URB				p. 67		
BL	OL	AL	ELL	Speaking and Listening Skills Activity, URB					p. 69	
BL	OL	AL	ELL	Writing Skills Activity, URB		p. 73	p. 73			
BL	OL	AL	ELL	School-to-Home Connection Activity, URB*				p. 77		
BL	OL	AL	ELL	Regional Atlas Activities, URB		pp. 1–7	pp. 1–7	pp. 1–7	pp. 1–7	
	OL	AL		Environmental Case Study, URB					p. 9	
BL	OL	AL	ELL	GeoLab Activity, URB			p. 19			
BL	OL		ELL	Reading Skills Activity, URB	p. 21					
BL	OL	AL	ELL	Primary Source Readings, URB					p. 23	
	OL	AL		World Literature Reading, URB					p. 27	
BL	OL		ELL	Reading Essentials and Note-Taking Guide*		p. 7	p. 10	p. 13	p. 16	
	OL			Interactive Geography Activity	p. 1					
BL	OL	AL	ELL	In-Text Map Overlay and Population Pyramid Transparencies	1	1	1	1C–E	1	
	OL			Foods Around the World	pp. 2–5					
BL	OL	AL	ELL	Outline Map Resource Book	p. 59					
BL	OL	AL	ELL	NGS World Atlas*	✓	✓	✓	✓	✓	
BL	OL	AL	ELL	NGS World Desk Map	✓	✓	✓	✓	✓	✓
BL	OL	AL	ELL	World Literature Library	✓	✓	✓	✓	✓	✓

Note: Please refer to the *Unit Resource Book: The World* for this chapter's URB materials.

* Also available in Spanish

- Interactive Lesson Planner
- Interactive Teacher Edition
- Fully editable blackline masters
- Section Spotlight Videos Launch
- Differentiated Lesson Plans
- Printable reports of daily assignments
- Standards Tracking System

Levels				Resources	Chapter Opener	Section 1	Section 2	Section 3	Section 4	Chapter Assess
BL	OL	AL	ELL							
				TEACH *(continued)*						
BL	OL	AL	ELL	Writer's Guidebook	✓	✓	✓	✓	✓	✓
BL	OL	AL	ELL	Vocabulary PuzzleMaker CD-ROM*	✓	✓	✓	✓	✓	✓
	OL	AL		Primary Sources CD-ROM	✓	✓	✓	✓	✓	✓
BL	OL	AL	ELL	StudentWorks™ Plus DVD	✓	✓	✓	✓	✓	✓
BL	OL	AL	ELL	Section Video Program Activities	✓	✓	✓	✓	✓	✓
BL	OL	AL	ELL	World Music: A Cultural Legacy	✓	✓	✓	✓	✓	✓
BL	OL	AL	ELL	Writing Process Transparencies	✓	✓	✓	✓	✓	✓
Teacher Resources				Building Academic Vocabulary	✓	✓	✓	✓	✓	✓
Teacher Resources				Strategies for Success	✓	✓	✓	✓	✓	✓
Teacher Resources				Teacher's Guide to Differentiated Instruction	✓	✓	✓	✓	✓	✓
Teacher Resources				Presentation Plus! DVD	✓	✓	✓	✓	✓	✓
				ASSESS						
BL	OL	AL	ELL	Quizzes and Tests		p. 13	p. 14	p. 15	p. 16	p. 17
BL	OL	AL	ELL	Authentic Assessment With Rubrics		p. 2				p. 2
BL	OL	AL	ELL	Standardized Test Practice						p. 5
BL	OL	AL	ELL	*ExamView® Assessment Suite* CD-ROM*		2-1	2-2	2-3	2-4	Ch. 2
BL	OL	AL	ELL	Interactive Tutor Self-Assessment CD-ROM		2-1	2-2	2-3	2-4	
				CLOSE						
BL			ELL	Reteaching Activity, URB		p. 75	p. 75	p. 75	p. 75	p. 75
BL	OL		ELL	Reading and Study Skills Foldables™	p. 52	p. 52	p. 52	p. 52	p. 52	p. 52
BL	OL	AL	ELL	Graphic Organizer Transparencies and Strategies		✓	✓	✓	✓	
BL	OL	AL	ELL	*Exploring Our World* in Graphic Novel	p. 1					

Integrating Technology

Using CyberScout

Research Using *Browse Famous People*

Technology Product

CyberScout is a convenient and dynamic search engine that provides several easy ways to locate information outside the McGraw-Hill Learning Network. CyberScout only searches Web sites that have been reviewed by teachers, so the information students find is always appropriate and accurate.

Objectives

After students learn to use CyberScout, they will be able to:

- research famous people in geography;
- exercise research and study skills;
- practice writing skills.

Steps

- From the McGraw-Hill Learning Network home page (www.mhln.com), click on **For Students.**
- Choose **CyberScout** below **Homework Help.**
- Click a **subject area link** to narrow the search.
- The CyberScout page will display a set of subcategories.
- Click the **Browse Famous People button** at the bottom of the page.
- The CyberScout page displays a set of names related to the subject area. Click a name.
- The CyberScout page displays a set of results.
- Click the link to a Web site of interest.
- Students will be redirected to the Web site in a new window.
- Students navigate through the chosen Web site to gain information on a topic and take notes.

Social Studies ONLINE

	Student	Teacher	Parent
Beyond the Textbook	●		●
Chapter Overviews	●		●
Concepts in Motion	●		●
ePuzzles and Games	●		●
Literature Connections		●	
Multi-Language Glossaries	●		●
Online Student Edition	●	●	●
Section Videos	●	●	●
Self-Check Quizzes	●		●
Student Web Activities	●		●
Study Central™	●		●
Teaching Today		●	
TIME Current Events	●		●
Vocabulary eFlashcards	●		●
Web Activity Lesson Plans		●	●

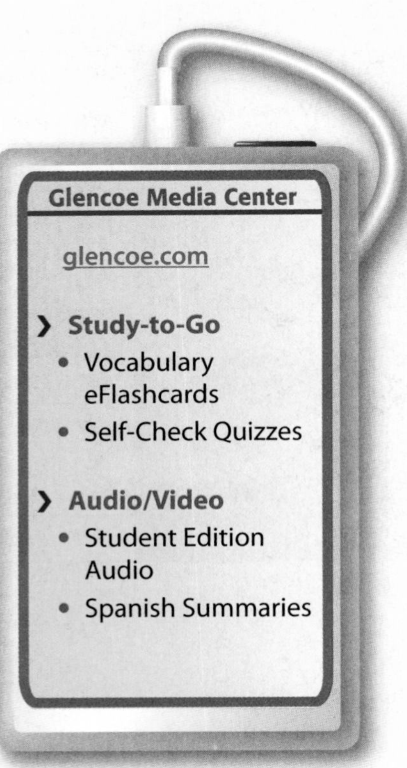

- **Timed Readings Plus in Social Studies** helps students increase their reading rate and fluency while maintaining comprehension. The 400-word passages are similar to those found on state and national assessments.
- **Reading in the Content Area: Social Studies** concentrates on six essential reading skills that help students better comprehend what they read. The book includes 75 high-interest nonfiction passages written at increasing levels of difficulty.
- **Reading Social Studies** includes strategic reading instruction and vocabulary support in Social Studies content for ELLs and native speakers of English.
- **Content Vocabulary Workout** (Grades 6–8) accelerates reading comprehension through focused vocabulary development. Social Studies content vocabulary comes from the glossaries of Glencoe's Middle School Social Studies texts.
  www.jamestowneducation.com

Index to National Geographic Magazine:

The following articles relate to this chapter:

- "The Next Big One," Joel Achenbach, April 2006.
- "Fire and Rain: Forecasting the Chaos of Weather," Tim Brooks, June 2005.

National Geographic Society Products To order the following, call National Geographic at 1-800-368-2728:

- *National Geographic Atlas of the World* (Book).

Access National Geographic's new dynamic MapMachine Web site and other geography resources at:
www.nationalgeographic.com
www.nationalgeographic.com/maps

GLENCOE **BOOKLINK 3**

Use this database to search more than 30,000 titles to create a customized reading list for your students.

- Reading lists can be organized by students' reading level, author, genre, theme, or area of interest.
- The database provides Degrees of Reading Power™ (DRP) and Lexile™ readability scores for all selections.
- A brief summary of each selection is included.

Leveled reading suggestions for this chapter:

For students at a Grade 5 reading level:

- ***Rain and Hail,*** by Franklyn M. Branley
- ***Rain,*** by Gail Saunders-Smith
- ***Where Do Puddles Go?*** by Fay Robinson

For students at a Grade 6 reading level:

- ***Weather,*** by Alice K. Flanagan
- ***Weather Patterns,*** by Monica Hughes
- ***Eruption!: The Story of Volcanoes,*** by Anita Ganeri

For students at a Grade 7 reading level:

- ***A Walk in the Tundra,*** by Rebecca L. Johnson
- ***A Walk in the Desert,*** by Rebecca L. Johnson
- ***Precipitation,*** by Terri Sievert

For students at a Grade 8 reading level:

- ***Mountains,*** by Philip Sauvain
- ***Erosion,*** by Cherie Winner
- ***Climates,*** by Theresa Jarosz Alberti

For students at a Grade 9 reading level:

- ***Temperate Forests,*** by Michael Allaby
- ***El Niño and La Niña: Deadly Weather,*** by Carmen Bredeson
- ***Wind,*** by Jennifer Fandel
- ***Ocean,*** by Edward R. Ricciuti

Focus

The Essential Question

As students study the chapter, remind them to consider the chapter-based Essential Question. Answering this question will help them understand the important concepts in the chapter. In addition, the Hands-On Chapter Project relates the content from each section to the Essential Question. The steps in each section build on each other as students progress through the chapter. The Hands-On Chapter Project culminates in the Wrap Up activity on the Visual Summary page.

More About the Photo

Visual Literacy Canyons, like this one in Arizona, are narrow crevices that formed as wind and water eroded sandstone. The result of thousands of years of erosion, slot canyons are twisting caverns of various hues of color. The southwestern Colorado Plateau (mostly northern Arizona and southern Utah) boasts more slot canyons than any other area in the world. In fact, few slot canyons exist elsewhere. National parks in the Colorado Plateau, such as Zion National Park in Utah, attract many adventuresome hikers who partake in the sport of canyoneering—climbing, and rappelling through canyons.

CHAPTER 2

Earth's Physical Geography

Essential Question

Place **Think about the characteristics of the area where you live. How does the land look? Is there a large body of water nearby? What is the climate like? Each place on the Earth is unique, with its own special characteristics.** What kinds of geographic characteristics define the region where you live?

Teach

The BIG Ideas *As you begin teaching each section, use these questions and activities to help students focus on the Big Ideas.*

Section 

Forces Shaping the Earth **Ask: How might wind, water, and ice affect people?** *(People's homes might be flooded, or be damaged by earthquakes, high winds, tornadoes, or hurricanes. Oceans also play an important role. Pounding waves continually erode coastal cliffs and move sand on beaches to other coastal areas. Violent storms speed up this process that affects people living along ocean coastlines.)* Point out to students that Section 1 describes the makeup of the Earth and the forces that change it. **OL**

Section 

Landforms and Water Resources

Ask: How do landforms and water resources affect the economy of a region? *(Regions near large bodies of water might rely on fishing for economic prosperity; mountains might create remote regions that affect transportation costs; plains regions might have an agricultural economy.)* Point out to students that in Section 2, they will learn about the different landforms, types of water, and the water cycle. **OL**

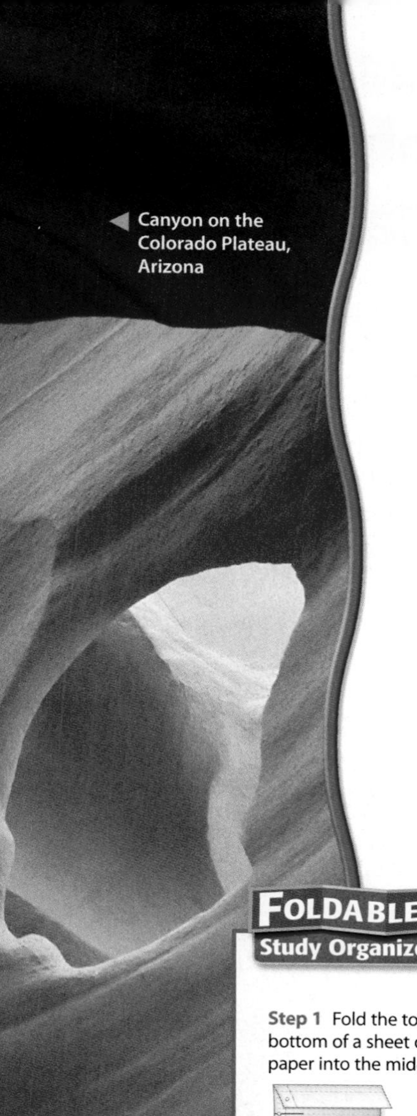

◀ Canyon on the Colorado Plateau, Arizona

BIG Ideas

Section 1: Forces Shaping the Earth

BIG IDEA Physical processes shape the Earth's surface. Forces from within and the actions of wind, water, and ice have shaped Earth's surface.

Section 2: Landforms and Water Resources

BIG IDEA Geographic factors influence where people settle. Physical features determine where people live.

Section 3: Climate Regions

BIG IDEA Geographers organize the Earth into regions that share common characteristics. Geographers use climate to define world regions.

Section 4: Human-Environment Interaction

BIG IDEA All living things are dependent upon one another and their surroundings for survival. Human actions greatly affect the natural world.

FOLDABLES™ Study Organizer

Organizing Information Use this four-tab Foldable to help you record what you learn about the Earth's physical geography.

Step 1 Fold the top and bottom of a sheet of paper into the middle.

Step 2 Cut each flap at the midpoint to form 4 tabs.

Step 3 Label the tabs as shown.

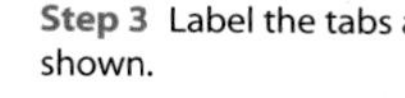

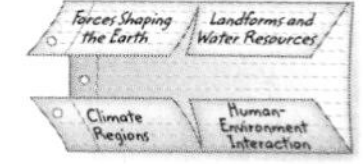

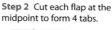

Reading and Writing As you read the chapter, take notes about each section under the appropriate head. Use your Foldable to help you write a summary for each section.

Social Studies ONLINE

To preview Chapter 2, go to glencoe.com.

Previewing the Region

If you have not already done so, engage students in the Regional Atlas and chart activities to help them become familiar with the general content of the region.

FOLDABLES™ Study Organizer **Dinah Zike's Foldables**

Purpose This Foldable helps students organize information contained in the chapter, under the thematic titles of each section. The tabs of the Foldable should be labeled with the section headings. Students' notes will help them write their summaries and prepare for assessment **OL**

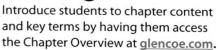

More Foldables activities for this chapter can be found in *Dinah Zike's Reading and Study Skills Foldables* ancillary.

Social Studies ONLINE

Introduce students to chapter content and key terms by having them access the Chapter Overview at glencoe.com.

Section 3

Climate Regions Ask: What factors affect the weather? *(sun, wind, water, landforms)* Point out to students that in Section 3, they will learn how various factors affect the climate of a region. They will also read about the different climate zones. **OL**

Section 

Human-Environment Interaction
Ask: In what ways do humans affect the environment? *(Humans can change the environment, when they pollute the air, water, and ground, or cut down trees.)* Point out to students that Section 4 explains how humans affect the Earth and describes actions people can take to protect the environment. **OL**

Focus

Bellringer
Daily Focus Transparency 2-1

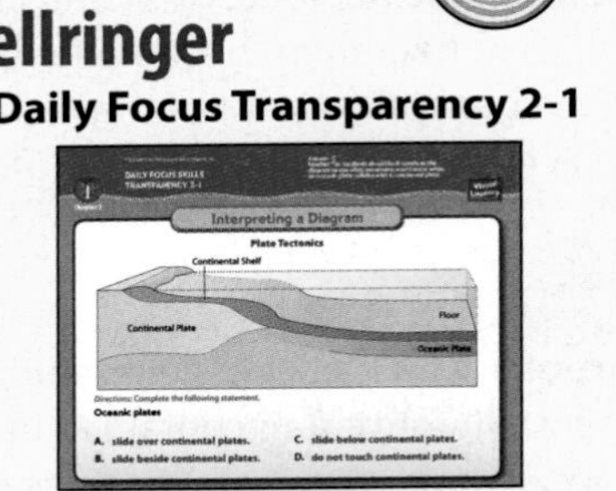

Guide to Reading
Answers to Graphic:

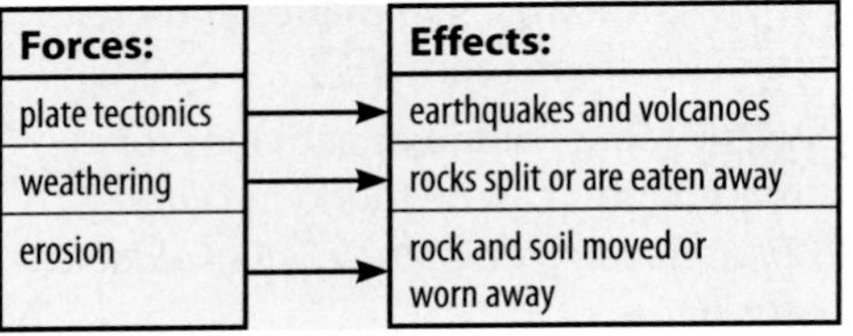

Forces:	Effects:
plate tectonics	earthquakes and volcanoes
weathering	rocks split or are eaten away
erosion	rock and soil moved or worn away

Section Spotlight Video

To learn more about forces shaping the Earth, have students watch the Section Spotlight Video.

Resource Manager

Guide to Reading

BIG Idea

Physical processes shape the Earth's surface.

Content Vocabulary

- core *(p. 45)*
- mantle *(p. 45)*
- magma *(p. 45)*
- crust *(p. 45)*
- continent *(p. 45)*
- plate tectonics *(p. 46)*
- earthquake *(p. 47)*
- fault *(p. 47)*
- weathering *(p. 47)*
- erosion *(p. 48)*

Academic Vocabulary

- release *(p. 45)*
- constant *(p. 47)*
- accumulate *(p. 48)*

Reading Strategy

Determining Cause and Effect
As you read, use a diagram like the one below to list the forces shaping the Earth and the effects of each.

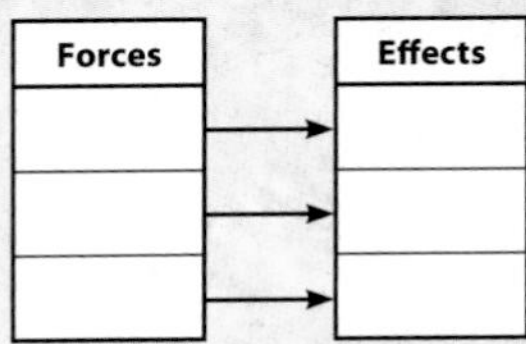

Forces	Effects

SECTION 1

Forces Shaping the Earth

Picture This This spectacular gash is California's San Andreas Fault. The San Andreas Fault is about 800 miles long and extends 10 miles beneath the Earth's surface. It is the source of the deadly earthquakes that occurred in California in 1906 and 1989. Read this section to learn more about processes that have shaped the surface of the Earth.

▼ The San Andreas Fault, located 100 miles north of Los Angeles, California

R Reading Strategies	C Critical Thinking	D Differentiated Instruction	W Writing Support	S Skill Practice
Teacher Edition • Academic Vocab., p. 46 • Inferring, p. 46 • Questioning, p. 46 **Additional Resources** • Guid. Read., URB p. 55 • Cont. Vocab., URB p. 59 • Ac. Vocab., URB p. 61 • Read. Ess., p. 7	**Teacher Edition** • Det. Cause/Effect, p. 48 **Additional Resources** • Authentic Assess., p. 2 • Quizzes and Tests, p. 13	**Teacher Edition** • Kinesthetic, pp. 45, 47 **Additional Resources** • Reteach., URB p. 75	**Teacher Edition** • Expository Writing, p. 45 **Additional Resources** • Writing Skills, URB p. 73	**Teacher Edition** • Using Geo. Skills, p. 47 **Additional Resources** • Chart, Graph, and Map Skills, URB p. 65 • Daily Focus Trans. 2-1 • Reg. Atlas, URB pp. 1–7

Inside the Earth

Main Idea **The Earth is made up of several layers that have different characteristics.** W

Geography and You What do you see when you cut a melon in half? Like a melon, the Earth has distinct sections or layers.

NATIONAL GEOGRAPHIC

Figure 1 **Earth's Layers**

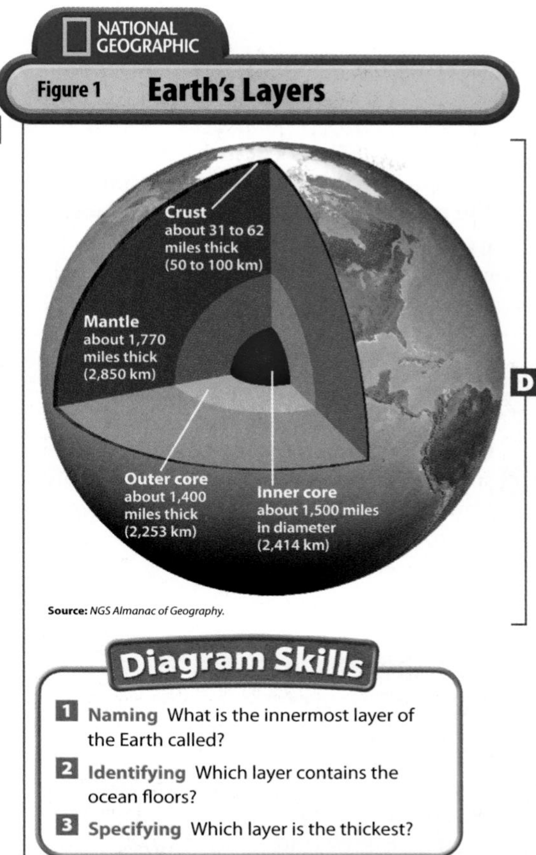

Source: *NGS Almanac of Geography.* D

Diagram Skills

1. **Naming** What is the innermost layer of the Earth called?
2. **Identifying** Which layer contains the ocean floors?
3. **Specifying** Which layer is the thickest?

The ground feels solid when you walk on it and downright hard if you should happen to fall. Yet Earth is not a large rock, solid through the middle. Beneath our planet's solid shell lies a center that is partly liquid. As **Figure 1** shows, the Earth has different layers, much like a melon or a baseball.

At the center of the Earth is a dense solid **core** of hot iron mixed with other metals and rock. The inner core lies about 3,200 miles (5,150 km) below the surface. Scientists think it is made up of iron and nickel. They also believe the inner core is under tremendous pressure. The next layer, the outer core, is so hot that the metal has melted into a liquid. The temperature in the outer core can reach an incredible 8,500°F (about 4,700°C).

Surrounding the core is the **mantle,** a layer of hot, dense rock about 1,770 miles (2,850 km) thick. Like the core, the mantle has two parts. The section nearest the core is solid. The rock in the outer mantle, however, can be moved, shaped, and even melted. If you have seen photographs of an active volcano, then you have seen this melted rock called **magma.** It flows to the surface during a volcanic eruption. Once it reaches the surface, magma is called lava. This movement of the matter in the mantle **releases** much of the energy generated in the Earth's interior.

Earth's upper layer is the **crust,** a thin rocky shell that forms the surface. It reaches only 31 to 62 miles (50 to 100 km) deep. The crust includes ocean floors and seven large land areas known as **continents.** The continents are North America, South America, Europe, Asia, Africa, Australia, and Antarctica. The crust is just a few miles thick on the ocean floor, but is much thicker below the continents.

Reading Check **Explaining** What is magma, and where does it originate?

Teach

W Writing Support

Expository Writing Have students write an entry titled "Earth's Layers" for a children's encyclopedia. Instruct students to use facts from the text, making them easy for children to understand. **OL**

D Differentiated Instruction

Kinesthetic Have students use construction paper to create a pop-up display of the Earth's layers. Have students label each layer and present their finished products to the class. **OL**

Diagram Skills

Answers:
1. inner core
2. crust
3. mantle

Reading Check **Answer:** melted rock that flows to the surface during a volcanic eruption

Hands-On Chapter Project
Step 1

Capturing Your Region on Postcards

Step 1: Identifying the Region and Its Characteristics Pairs of students will create a series of four postcards that illustrate geographic characteristics that distinguish the region in which they live from other regions.

Essential Question What kinds of geographic characteristics define the region where you live?

Directions Direct student pairs to use the maps and diagrams in this chapter, the Regional Atlas, and outside resources as needed to identify the distinctive geographic characteristics of the region where you live. Urge students to focus on characteristics that set their region apart. Tell students that they will create a series of postcards to illustrate important characteristics. They may illustrate these characteristics with photos, their own drawings, maps, or diagrams. Have students begin by locating their region and identifying its geographic characteristics.

Summarizing Ask student pairs to share the characteristics they have identified. List the characteristics they name on the board under the categories Land, Water, Climate, People, and the Environment. **OL**

(Chapter Project continued in Section 2)

R1 Reading Strategy

Academic Vocabulary **Ask:** **What other word could be used instead of "constant?"** *(continual, on-going)* What does it mean that the Earth's surface has been in constant motion? **OL**

R2 Reading Strategy

Inferring **Ask:** **What might happen as a result of continental drift?** *(Earthquakes might occur, and volcanoes may form when plates collide.)* **AL**

R3 Reading Strategy

Questioning Have students turn the heading "When Plates Meet" into a question, asking, "What happens when plates meet?" Then, have them read the section to find the answer to their question. **BL**

Caption Answer:
Eathquakes are common in areas where the collision of ocean and continental plates makes the Earth's crust unstable.

Shaping the Earth's Surface

Main Idea **Forces acting both inside and outside the Earth work to change the appearance of the Earth's surface.**

Geography and You Have you been in an earthquake? Or, do you know anyone who has? Read on to discover what causes earthquakes.

The Earth's crust is not a fixed layer. It changes over time as new landforms are created and existing ones change forms. For hundreds of millions of years, the Earth's **R1** surface has been in constant motion, slowly transforming. Old mountains are worn down, while new mountains grow taller. Even the continents move.

Earthquake in Japan

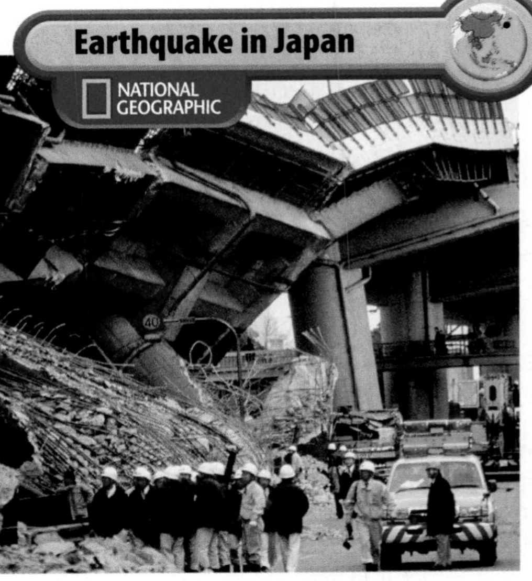

▲ City officials look over damage to an expressway that fell on one side during the 1995 earthquake in Kobe, Japan. ***Location*** **Where in the world are earthquakes common?**

Plate Movements

The theory of **plate tectonics** explains how the continents were formed and why they move. As **Figure 2** shows, each continent **R2** sits on one or more large bases called plates. As these plates move, the continents on top of them move. This movement is called continental drift.

The rate of movement varies from just under 1 inch (2.3 cm) to 7 inches (17 cm) per year. This movement is too slow for people to notice, but over millions of years, it can have dramatic effects.

Look at a map of the world. If you think of the eastern coast of South America as a giant puzzle piece, you will see that it seems to fit into the western coast of Africa. This is because these two continents were once joined together in a gigantic landmass that scientists call Pangaea. About 200 million years ago, however, the continents began to break and move apart because of tectonic activity.

When Plates Meet R3

The movements of Earth's plates have actually shaped the surface of the Earth. Sometimes the plates pull away from each other. Plates usually pull apart in ocean areas, but this kind of plate activity also occurs in land areas, such as Iceland and East Africa.

Plates can also collide. When two continental plates collide, they push against each other with tremendous force. This causes the land along the line where the plates meet to rise and form mountains. The Himalaya mountain ranges of Asia, the highest on Earth, were formed from such a collision.

Collisions of continental and oceanic plates produce a different result. The thinner ocean plate slides underneath the thicker continental plate. The downward

Differentiated Instruction

Leveled Activities

BL **Reteaching Activity, URB p. 75**

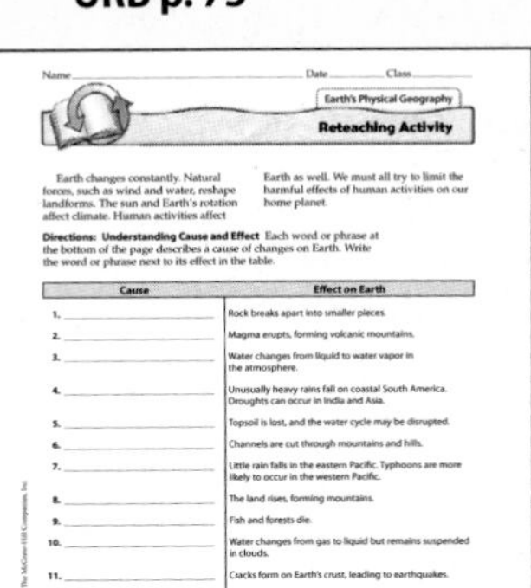

AL **Authentic Assessment, p. 2**

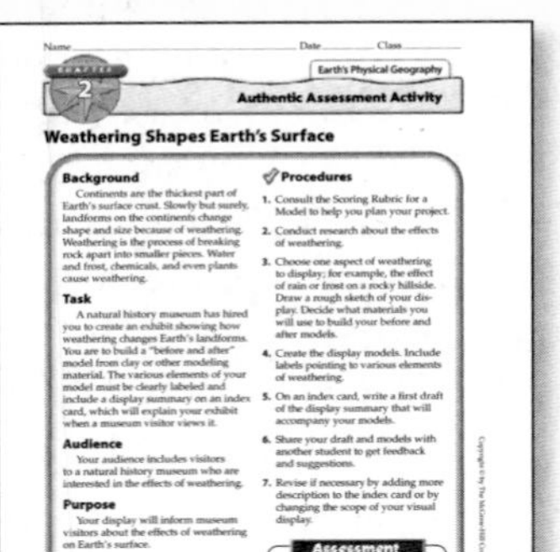

ELL **Academic Vocabulary Activity, URB p. 61**

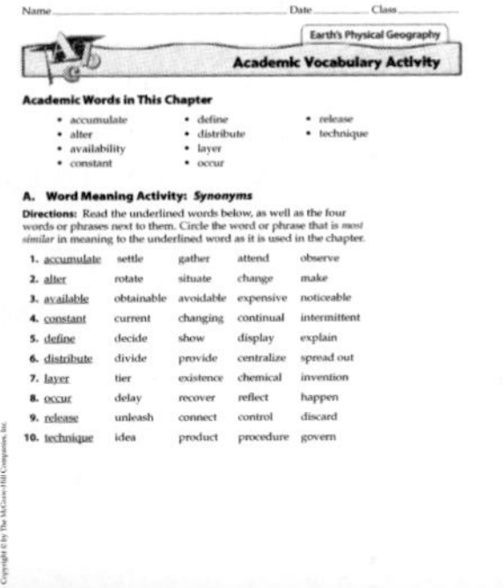

NATIONAL GEOGRAPHIC

Figure 2 **Tectonic Plate Boundaries**

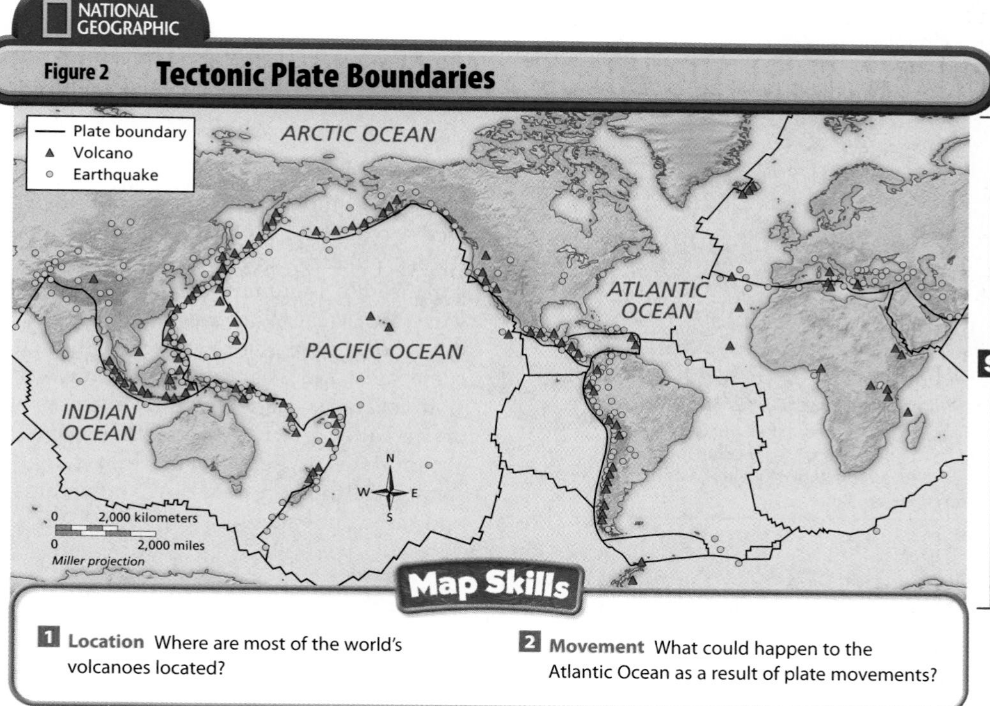

Map Skills

1 Location Where are most of the world's volcanoes located?

2 Movement What could happen to the Atlantic Ocean as a result of plate movements?

force of the lower plate causes magma to build up. Then the magma erupts and slowly hardens, forming volcanic mountains. This is how the Andes of South America were created.

Earthquakes are sudden and violent movements of the Earth's crust. They are common in areas where the collision of ocean and continental plates makes the Earth's crust unstable. For example, so many earthquakes and volcanoes occur around the edge of the Pacific Ocean that people call this region the Ring of Fire.

Sometimes two plates do not meet head-on but move alongside each other. This movement makes cracks in the Earth's crust called **faults.** Movements along faults do not take place **constantly,** but occur in sudden bursts that cause earthquakes. One of the most well-known faults in the United States is California's San Andreas Fault. A number of very destructive earthquakes have occurred in the region, and the threat of more still exists.

Weathering

The movement of tectonic plates causes volcanoes and earthquakes to change the Earth's landforms. Once created, however, these landforms will continue to change because of other forces that work on the Earth's surface.

One of these forces is called weathering. **Weathering** is when water and ice, chemicals, and even plants break rocks apart into smaller pieces. For example, water can run into cracks of rocks, freeze, and then expand. D

Social Studies ONLINE

Student Web Activity Visit glencoe.com and complete the Chapter 2 Web Activity about plate tectonics.

S Skill Practice

Using Geography Skills Ask: What do you notice about the location of the volcanoes on the map? *(Many form along plate boundaries.)* **OL**

D Differentiated Instruction

Kinesthetic Have students investigate weathering that occurs in your region. Then have them simulate weathering by using materials found in nature, such as pouring water over a pile of sand. **AL**

Map Skills

Answers:

1. around the Pacific Ocean
2. Possible answer: Volcanoes might form in the Atlantic Ocean and create islands, or the ocean might grow larger as the plates pull the land masses away from each other.

Social Studies ONLINE

Objectives and answers to the Student Web Activity can be found at glencoe.com under the Web Activity Lesson Plan for this chapter.

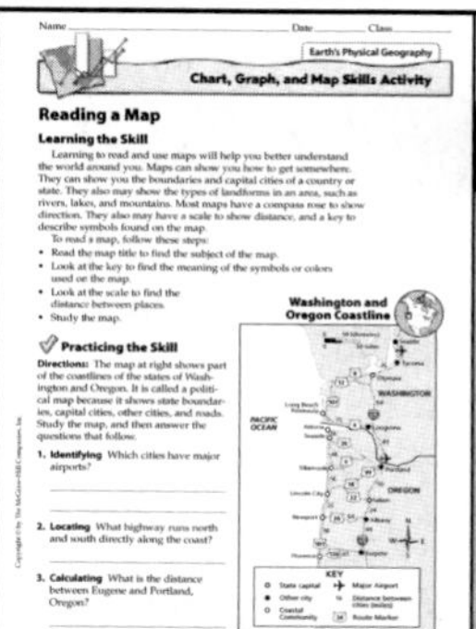
Earth's Physical Geography

Chart, Graph, and Map Skills Activity

Reading a Map

Learning the Skill

Practicing the Skill

Washington and Oregon Coastline

Chart, Graph, and Map Skills, URB pp. 65–66

Reading A Map

Objective:	To use map parts to read a political map
Focus:	Review map parts (title, key, scale, compass rose) and the purpose of each.
Teach:	Explain what a political map shows. Discuss symbols used on a political map.
Assess:	Have students answer questions about places, location, and distance on a political map.
Close:	Have students use map parts to read a map in Section 1.

Differentiated Instruction Strategies

BL Have students locate symbols on other maps and explain their meaning.

AL Have students make a map of the city where you live that includes a key, scale, and compass rose.

ELL Have students use the compass rose to describe to the class the relative location of places on a political map.

C Critical Thinking

Determining Cause and Effect
Ask: What other effects might result from erosion? *(Answers may include soil near rivers can be carried away, canyons can form, and dunes may form on sandy soil.)* OL

Caption Answer: wind and ice

Reading Check Answer: Plates collide along plate boundaries, which creates earthquakes.

Assess

Social Studies ONLINE
Study Central™ provides summaries, interactive games, and online graphic organizers to help students review content.

Close

Summarizing Have students summarize the forces affecting the Earth. OL

NATIONAL GEOGRAPHIC
Erosion in Bangladesh

Heavy seasonal rains, called monsoons, lead to flooding and increased erosion in South Asia. ***Movement*** **Besides water, what other forces can cause erosion?**

These actions can split the rock. Chemicals, too, cause weathering when acids in air pollution mix with rain and fall back to Earth. The chemicals eat away rock and stone surfaces.

Erosion

C Water, wind, and ice can move away weathered rock in a process called **erosion.** Rivers, streams, and even rainwater can cut through mountains and hills. Ocean waves can wear away coastal rocks. Wind can scatter loose bits of rock, which often rub against and wear down larger rocks.

In cold areas, giant, slow-moving masses of ice called glaciers form where water **accumulates.** When glaciers move, they carry rocks that can wear down mountains and carve out valleys.

Reading Check **Synthesizing** Why are earthquakes common where plates meet?

Section 1 Review

Social Studies ONLINE
Study Central™ To review this section, go to glencoe.com.

Vocabulary

1. **Illustrate** the meaning of *core, mantle, magma, crust, continent, plate tectonics, earthquake, fault, weathering,* and *erosion* by drawing and labeling one or more diagrams.

Main Ideas

2. **Summarizing** Which layers of the Earth are solid? Which layers are liquid?
3. **Describing** Use a chart like the one below to list and describe the different results when plates meet.

Type of Plate Meeting	Results
1.	1.
2.	2.
3.	3.

Critical Thinking

4. **Drawing Conclusions** Where do you think an earthquake is more likely to occur—along North America's Pacific coast or along North America's Atlantic coast? Why?
5. **BIG Idea** How was the formation of the Himalaya and the Andes similar and different?
6. **Challenge** How do the shapes of South America and Africa support the theory of plate tectonics? Find another example of land areas that once might have been joined together but separated as plates moved apart.

Writing About Geography

7. **Using Your FOLDABLES** Use your Foldable to write a paragraph explaining how forces both beneath and on the surface help shape the surface of the Earth.

Answers

1. Definitions for the vocabulary words are found in the section and the Glossary.
2. center: solid; inner core: solid; outer core: liquid; inner mantle: solid rock; outer mantle: meltable rock; crust: rocky shell
3. (1) collision of continental plates: land rises and forms mountains; (2) collision of continental and oceanic plates: magma hardens into volcanic mountains; earthquakes; (3) plates move alongside each other: makes faults; also earthquakes
4. along North America's Pacific coast because plate boundaries are located along the coast and are more likely to collide there
5. Both resulted from collision of plates, but the Himalaya were a result of the collision of continental plates, and the Andes were a result of the collision of continental and oceanic plates.
6. The shapes of the eastern coast of South America and the western coast of Africa suggest that they may once have been joined together. Students may observe that the shapes of the eastern coast of Australia and the western coast of South America suggest that they were once joined.
7. Students' paragraphs should describe and provide examples of plate movements, weathering, and erosion.

Guide to Reading

BIG Idea

Geographic factors influence where people settle.

Content Vocabulary

- continental shelf *(p. 50)*
- trench *(p. 50)*
- groundwater *(p. 52)*
- aquifer *(p. 52)*
- water cycle *(p. 53)*
- evaporation *(p. 53)*
- condensation *(p. 54)*
- precipitation *(p. 54)*
- collection *(p. 54)*

Academic Vocabulary

- occur *(p. 50)*
- define *(p. 50)*
- availability *(p. 52)*

Reading Strategy

Identifying Use a diagram like the one below to identify the various bodies of water that can be found on the Earth's surface.

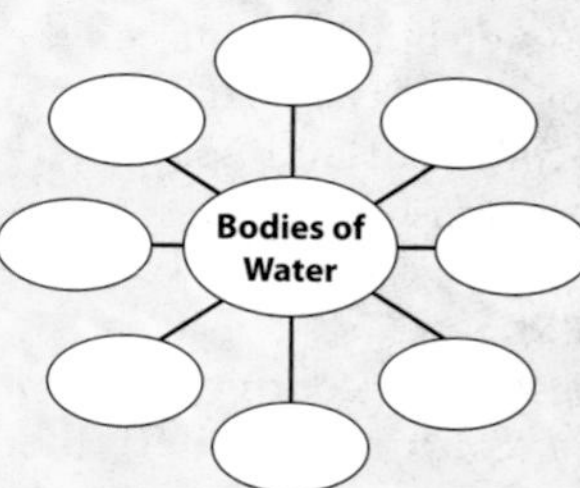

Landforms and Water Resources

Picture This This fisherman in Indonesia uses a hand dredge to catch fish. He lowers the dredge into the water and drags it along the bottom of the shallow, sandy ocean floor. There it scoops up fish, scallops, and oysters. Read this section to learn how landforms and water influence human activities.

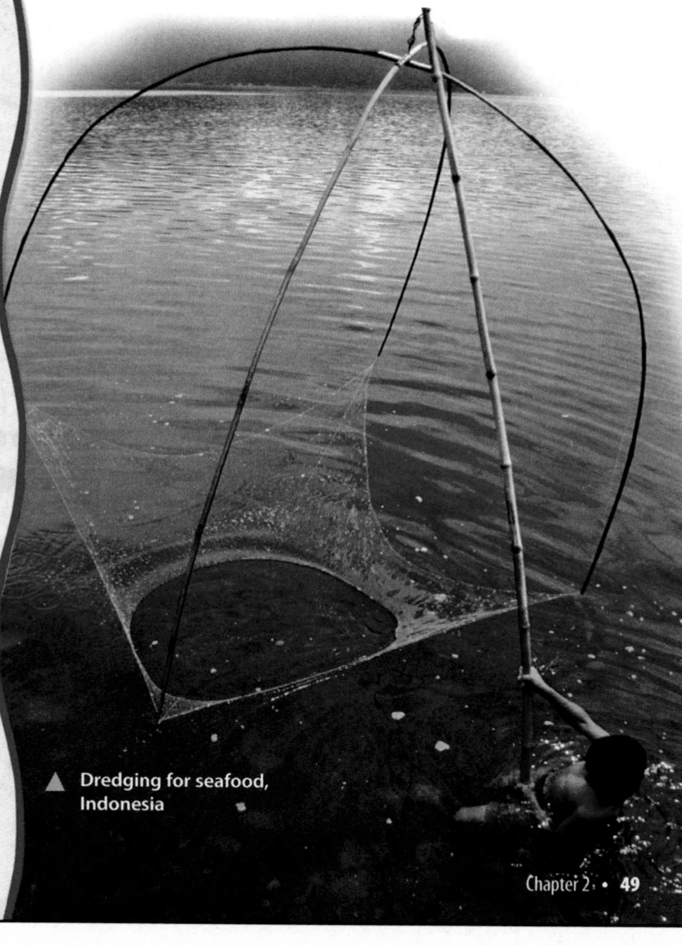

▲ Dredging for seafood, Indonesia

Focus

Bellringer

Daily Focus Transparency 2-2

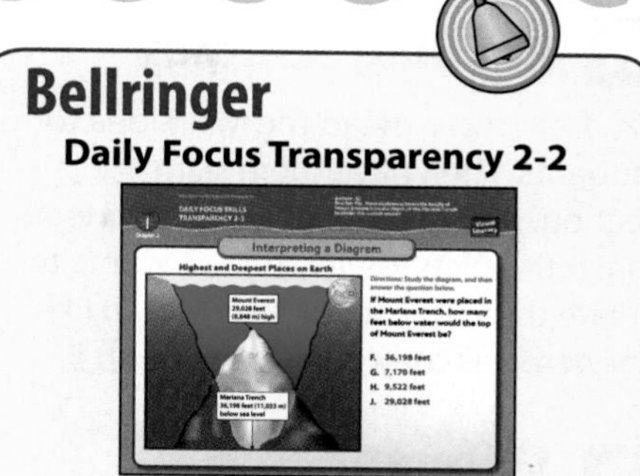

Guide to Reading

Answers to Graphic:

Bodies of water: streams, rivers, lakes, seas, oceans, glaciers, ice sheets, groundwater such as aquifers

Section Spotlight Video

To learn more about landforms and water resources, have students watch the Section Spotlight Video.

Resource Manager

R Reading Strategies	C Critical Thinking	D Differentiated Instruction	W Writing Support	S Skill Practice
Teacher Edition • Questioning, p. 50 • Identifying, p. 52 **Additional Resources** • Guid. Read., URB p. 56 • Cont. Vocab., URB p. 59 • Ac. Vocab., URB p. 61 • Read. Ess., p. 10	**Teacher Edition** • Pred. Consequences, p. 52 • Making Generalizations, p. 53 • Making Inferences, p. 54 **Additional Resources** • GeoLab, URB p. 19 • Quizzes and Tests, p. 14	**Teacher Edition** • Kinesthetic, p. 50 **Additional Resources** • Diff. Instr., URB p. 63 • Reteach., URB p. 75	**Teacher Edition** • Narrative Writing, p. 53 **Additional Resources** • Writing Skills, URB p. 73	**Teacher Edition** • Visual Literacy, p. 50 **Additional Resources** • Chart, Graph, and Map Skills, URB p. 65 • Daily Focus Trans. 2-2 • Reg. Atlas, URB pp. 1–7

Teach

R Reading Strategy

Questioning Read the Main Idea to students. Then have them skim the section, reading the headings and looking at the pictures. Instruct students to create three questions they would like answered as they read the text. **BL**

D Differentiated Instruction

Kinesthetic Have students use art materials to create three-dimensional models of the landforms discussed in the text. Instruct students to make sure their models are to scale and to label each landform. When finished, invite students to share their models with the class. **OL**

S Skill Practice

Visual Literacy Ask: What landform is shown in the photo? *(mountain)* **What generalization can you make about living conditions on high mountain ranges based on this photo?** *(Answers may include that living conditions would be difficult because of the cold climate; also difficult to build homes there)* **OL**

Caption Answer:
South Asia in the Himalaya

Differentiated Instruction

Types of Landforms

Main Idea **Earth has a variety of landforms, and many of the landforms can be found both on the continents and the ocean floors.** R

Geography and You Do you know that there are mountains underwater? If the area where you live was underwater, what would it look like?

The Earth has a great variety of landforms—from mountains that soar miles high to lowlands that barely peek above the sea. These landforms appear not only on continents but also under the oceans.

On Land

D Mountains are huge towers of rock and are the highest landforms. Some mountains may be only a few thousand feet high. Others can soar higher than 20,000 feet (6,096 m). The world's highest mountain is Mount Everest in South Asia's Himalaya ranges. It rises more than 29,028 feet (8,848 m), nearly five and a half miles high!

Hills are lower and more rounded than mountains. Between mountains and hills lie valleys. A valley is a long stretch of land that is lower than the land on either side. Flatlands **occur** in one of two forms, depending on their height above sea level. Plains are flat lowlands, typically found along coasts and lowland river valleys. Plateaus are flatlands at higher elevations.

D Geographers **define** some landforms by their relationship to other landforms or to bodies of water. Look back at the geographic dictionary in the Reference Atlas to see examples of the following landforms.

An isthmus is a narrow strip of land that connects two larger landmasses and has water on two sides. An example is Central America, which connects North and South America. A peninsula, such as Florida, is a piece of land that is connected to a larger landmass on one side but has water on the other three sides. A body of land that is smaller than a continent and completely surrounded by water is an island.

Karakoram Range, South Asia

NATIONAL GEOGRAPHIC

S The Karakoram Range in South Asia is home to more than 60 peaks above 23,000 feet (7,000 m).
Location **Where is Mount Everest, the world's tallest peak, located?**

Under the Oceans

Off each coast of a continent lies a plateau called a **continental shelf** that stretches for several miles underwater. At the edge of the shelf, the land drops down sharply to the ocean floor.

On the ocean floor, tall mountains thousands of miles wide line the edges of ocean plates that are pulling apart. Tectonic activity also makes deep cuts in the ocean floor called **trenches**. The Mariana Trench in the western Pacific Ocean is the deepest. It plunges 36,198 feet (11,033 m) below sea level.

Leveled Activities

BL Guided Reading Activity, URB p. 56

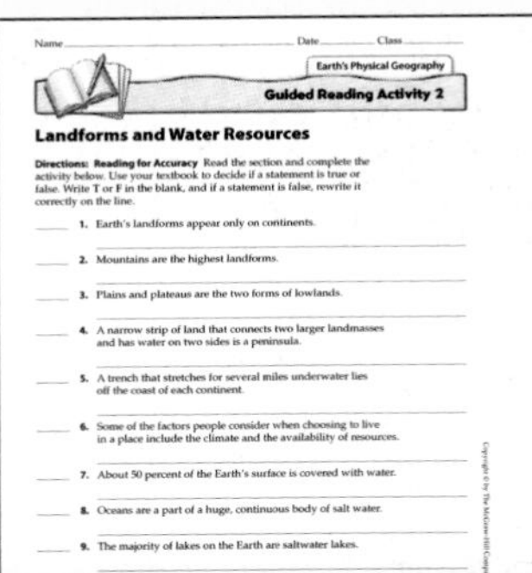

Name ______ Date ______ Class ______

Earth's Physical Geography

Guided Reading Activity 2

Landforms and Water Resources

Directions: Reading for Accuracy Read the section and complete the activity below. Use your textbook to decide if a statement is true or false. Write T or F in the blank, and if a statement is false, rewrite it correctly on the line.

____ 1. Earth's landforms appear only on continents.

____ 2. Mountains are the highest landforms.

____ 3. Plains and plateaus are the two forms of lowlands.

____ 4. A narrow strip of land that connects two larger landmasses and has water on two sides is a peninsula.

____ 5. A trench that stretches for several miles underwater lies off the coast of each continent.

____ 6. Some of the factors people consider when choosing to live in a place include the climate and the availability of resources.

____ 7. About 50 percent of the Earth's surface is covered with water.

____ 8. Oceans are a part of a huge, continuous body of salt water.

____ 9. The majority of lakes on the Earth are saltwater lakes.

OL Writing Skills Activity, URB p. 73

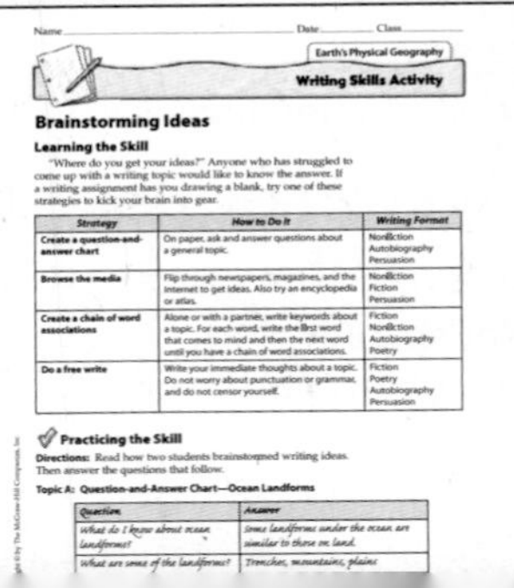

Name ______ Date ______ Class ______

Earth's Physical Geography

Writing Skills Activity

Brainstorming Ideas

Learning the Skill

"Where do you get your ideas?" Anyone who has struggled to come up with a writing topic would like to know the answer. If a writing assignment has you drawing a blank, try one of these strategies to kick your brain into gear.

Strategy	How to Do It	Writing Format
Create a question-and-answer chart	On paper, ask and answer questions about a general topic.	Nonfiction Autobiography Persuasion
Browse the media	Flip through newspapers, magazines, and the Internet to get ideas. Also try an encyclopedia or atlas.	Nonfiction Fiction Persuasion
Create a chain of word associations	Alone or with a partner, write keywords about a topic. For each word, write the first word that comes to mind and then the next word until you have a chain of word associations.	Fiction Nonfiction Autobiography Poetry
Do a free write	Write your immediate thoughts about a topic. Do not worry about punctuation or grammar, and do not censor yourself.	Fiction Poetry Autobiography Persuasion

Practicing the Skill

Directions: Read how two students brainstormed writing ideas. Then answer the questions that follow.

Topic A: Question-and-Answer Chart—Ocean Landforms

Question	Answer
What do I know about ocean landforms?	*Some landforms under the ocean are similar to those on land.*
What are some of the landforms?	*Trenches, mountains, plains*

ELL Differentiated Instruction, URB p. 63

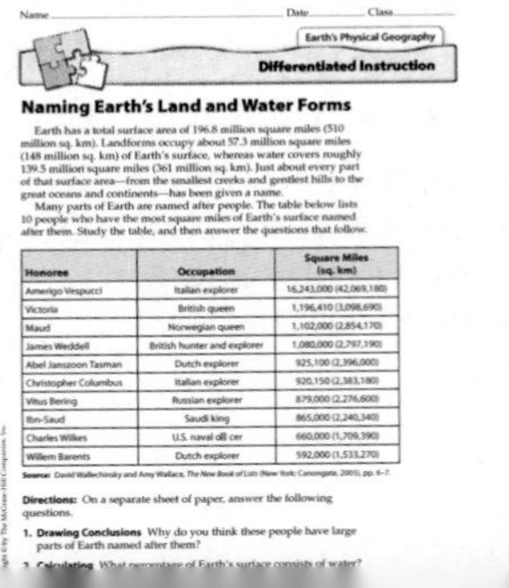

Name ______ Date ______ Class ______

Earth's Physical Geography

Differentiated Instruction

Naming Earth's Land and Water Forms

Earth has a total surface area of 196.8 million square miles (510 million sq. km). Landforms occupy about 57.3 million square miles (148 million sq. km) of Earth's surface, whereas water covers roughly 139.5 million square miles (361 million sq. km). Just about every part of that surface area—from the smallest creeks and gentlest hills to the great oceans and continents—has been given a name.

Many parts of Earth are named after people. The table below lists 10 people who have the most square miles of Earth's surface named after them. Study the table, and then answer the questions that follow.

Honoree	Occupation	Square Miles (sq. km)
Amerigo Vespucci	Italian explorer	16,243,000 (42,069,180)
Victoria	British queen	1,196,410 (3,098,690)
Maud	Norwegian queen	1,102,000 (2,854,170)
James Weddell	British hunter and explorer	1,080,000 (2,797,190)
Abel Janszoon Tasman	Dutch explorer	925,100 (2,396,000)
Christopher Columbus	Italian explorer	920,150 (2,383,180)
Vitus Bering	Russian explorer	879,000 (2,276,600)
Ibn-Saud	Saudi king	865,000 (2,240,340)
Charles Wilkes	U.S. naval officer	660,000 (1,709,390)
Willem Barents	Dutch explorer	592,000 (1,533,270)

Source: *David Wallechinsky and Amy Wallace, The New Book of Lists (New York: Canongate, 2005), pp. 6–7.*

Directions: On a separate sheet of paper, answer the following questions.

1. **Drawing Conclusions** Why do you think these people have large parts of Earth named after them?

Roughing It

By Mark Twain

We jumped into the **stage,** the driver cracked his whip, and we bowled away. . . . It was a superb summer morning, and all the landscape was brilliant with sunshine. There was a freshness and breeziness, too, and an **exhilarating** sense of **emancipation** from all sorts of cares and responsibilities, that almost made us feel that the years we had spent in the close, hot city, toiling and slaving, had been wasted and thrown away. We were spinning along through Kansas, and in the course of an hour and a half we were fairly abroad on the great Plains. Just here the land was rolling—a grand sweep of regular elevations and depressions as far as the eye could reach—like the stately heave and swell of the **ocean's bosom** after a storm. And everywhere were cornfields, **accenting** with squares of deeper green this limitless expanse of grassy land. But presently this sea upon dry ground was to lose its "rolling" character and stretch away for seven hundred miles as level as a floor! . . .

There is not a tree of any kind in the deserts, for hundreds of miles—there is no vegetation at all . . . except the sage-brush and its cousin the "greasewood," which is so much like the sage-brush that the difference amounts to little. Camp-fires and hot suppers in the deserts would be impossible but for the friendly sage-brush.

From *Roughing It,* Mark Twain. New York: Harper & Brothers Publishers, 1899.

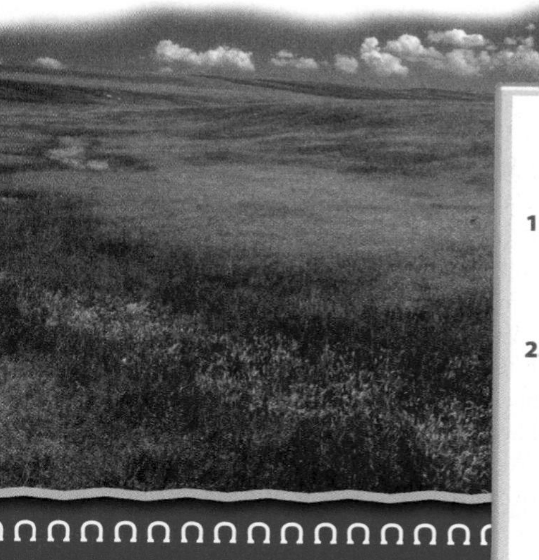

Analyzing Literature

1. **Making Inferences** What landform is Twain describing? What details make that clear?
2. **Read to Write** Think about the landforms in the area where you live. Write a letter describing what it would be like to travel over those landforms by foot or on a bicycle.

Mark Twain
(1835–1910)

Samuel Langhorne Clemens, who used the pen name "Mark Twain," was born in a Missouri river town along the banks of the Mississippi River. He held many jobs, including working as the pilot of a riverboat, before becoming a writer and humorist. He was one of the most popular American authors of the late 1800s.

Background Information

In *Roughing It,* Twain describes his experiences living and traveling in Nevada, California, and Hawaii in the 1860s. In this excerpt, he describes his trip from Missouri to Nevada. Twain traveled by stagecoach, a horse-drawn vehicle for carrying passengers.

Reader's Dictionary

stage: horse-drawn stagecoach

exhilarating: exciting

emancipation: freedom

ocean's bosom: ocean's surface

accenting: standing out

World Literature

Teach

Reading Strategy

Identifying Main Ideas Remind students that identifying the main idea requires them to distinguish supporting details from the most important idea of a passage. **Ask: What did Mark Twain describe in this passage?** *(the countryside, especially the Great Plains)* **What are three descriptive phrases Twain uses to convey his feelings?** *(Examples: "all the landscape was brilliant with sunshine," "exhilarating sense of emancipation," "friendly sagebrush")* Explain to students that they can use these details to find the main idea. **Ask: What is the main idea of this passage?** *(After his hard life working in the city, Twain found the Plains to be beautiful, exciting, and exhilarating.)* **OL**

Analyzing Literature

Answers:

1. the Great Plains, with rolling hills and grassy lands
2. Answers will vary but should reflect the geography of the place where students live.

Additional Reading

Review suggested books before assigning them.

Biography: ***Women Explorers of the Oceans*** by Margo McLoone describes the accomplishments of five women ocean explorers: Ann Davison, Eugenie Clark, Sylvia Earle, Naomi James, and Tania Aebi.

Nonfiction: ***Fur, Feathers, and Flippers: How Animals Live Where They Do*** by Patricia Lauber describes animals that have adapted to special environments around the world.

Fiction: ***The Voyage Begun*** by Nancy Bond is a story set in the future when the world's energy supply is depleted. Sixteen-year-old Paul lives in a world that is dealing with the long-term effects of climate changes and pollution.

For further reading, see BookLink 3

C Critical Thinking

Predicting Consequences
Ask: **What might happen in areas where resources are used up?** *(People might move to other areas, or ship resources in from other areas.)* OL

R Reading Strategy

Identifying the Main Idea **Ask:** **Which sentence in this paragraph states the main idea?** *(The first sentence: "All of the oceans on Earth are part of a huge, continuous body of salt water.")* OL

This Reading Skill (Identifying the Main Idea) was introduced in this unit.

Reading Check **Answer:** tectonic activity

Caption Answer:
Deltas are formed when rivers break off and form many different streams.

Humans and Landforms

Humans settle on all types of landforms. People choose a place to live based on a number of factors. Climate—the average temperature and rainfall of a region—is one factor that people must consider. The **availability** of resources is another factor. People settle where they can C get freshwater and where they can grow food, catch fish, or raise animals.

Reading Check **Explaining** What forces form ocean trenches?

▲ The Black River forms a delta as it flows into the Mississippi River in Wisconsin. River deltas are often rich in wildlife, including birds and mammals.
Place **How are deltas formed?**

The Water Planet

Main Idea **Water covers much of the planet, but only some of this water is usable.**

Geography and You Have you ever watched steam rise from a boiling pot of water? Read to learn how water changes from a solid, to a liquid, to a gas on Earth.

Earth is sometimes called the "water planet" because so much of it—about 70 percent of the surface—is covered with water. Water exists in many different forms. Streams, rivers, lakes, seas, and oceans contain water in liquid form. The atmosphere holds water vapor, or water in the form of gas. Glaciers and ice sheets are masses of water that have been frozen solid.

Salt Water

All of the oceans on Earth are part of a huge, continuous body of salt water. Almost 97 percent of the planet's water is salt water. Oceans have smaller arms or areas that are called seas, bays, or gulfs. These larger bodies of salt water can be linked to oceans by the more narrow bodies called straits or channels. R

Freshwater

Only 3 percent of the water on Earth is freshwater. Much of this freshwater is frozen in ice that covers polar regions and parts of mountains. Some is **groundwater,** which filters through the soil into the ground. Groundwater often gathers in **aquifers** (A·kwuh·fuhrz). These are underground layers of rock through which water flows. People can pump the freshwater from aquifers. Only a tiny amount of all

Hands-On Chapter Project
Step 2

Many types of landforms are found on the Earth's surface. These include mountains.

Capturing Your Region on Postcards

Step 2: Focusing on Landforms and Water Features Student pairs will select a landform and a water feature in the region and design a postcard for each.

Directions Have student pairs select a specific landform and water feature of their region to feature in a picture postcard. Tell students to research the land and water features they have chosen. Direct them to locate a visual of each feature (photo, map, or diagram) and note key facts about it. Then have students design and create one postcard for each feature with an illustration on one side and a short description on the other side.

Summarizing Confer with each pair briefly. Ask them what features they have chosen for their postcards, how they plan to illustrate them, and what key information they will provide about each. OL

(Chapter Project continued in Section 3)

NATIONAL GEOGRAPHIC

Figure 3 **The Water Cycle**

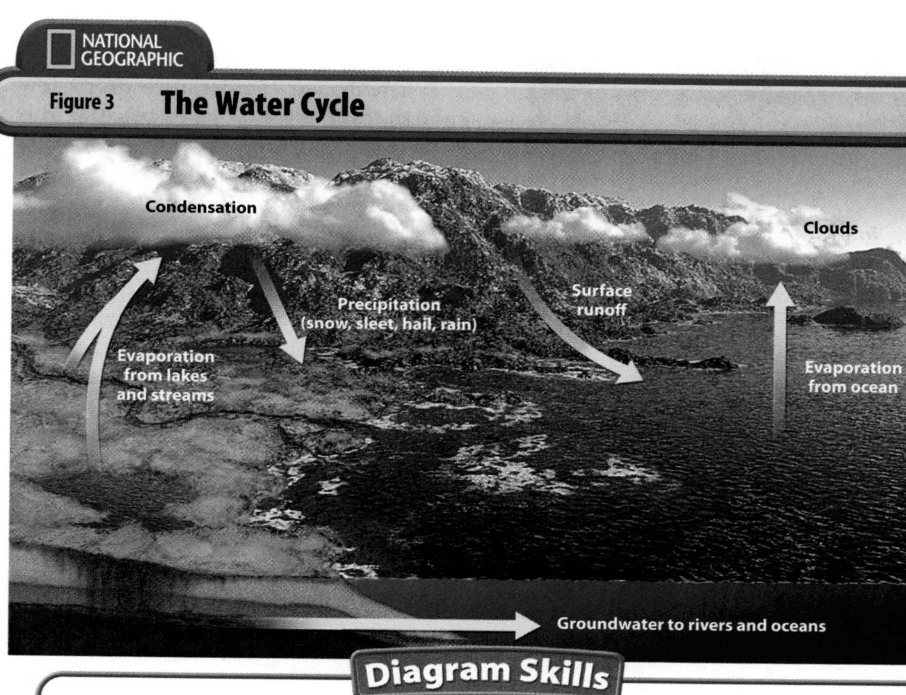

Diagram Skills

1 **Identifying** In which step of the water cycle does water vapor form clouds?

2 **Explaining** How does the sun's heat drive the water cycle?

the water in the world is found in lakes and rivers. This water is often not safe to drink until it has been purified.

Large inland bodies of water are called lakes. Most lakes are freshwater lakes. Long, flowing bodies of water are called rivers. They begin at a source and end at a mouth. The mouth is the place where a river empties into another body of water, such as an ocean or a lake.

The largest rivers often have many tributaries, which are separate streams or rivers that feed into them. Many rivers form deltas at their mouths. A delta is an area where a river breaks into many different streams flowing toward the sea. Rivers often carry rich soil to their deltas and deposit it, building up the land. C

The Water Cycle

The total amount of water on Earth does not change. It does not stay in one place, either. Instead the water moves constantly. In a process called the **water cycle**, the water goes from the oceans, to the air, to the ground, and finally back to the oceans.

Look at **Figure 3** to see how the water cycle works. The sun's heat drives the water cycle because it evaporates the water W on the Earth's surface. This **evaporation** changes water from liquid to a gas, called water vapor. Water vapor rises from the Earth's oceans and other bodies of water, and then circulates in the atmosphere. The air's temperature determines how much water the air holds. Warm air holds more water vapor than cool air.

C Critical Thinking

Making Generalizations **Ask:** **What settlement patterns might be found near deltas? Why?** *(Answers may include that people move to areas surrounding deltas because the soil is rich for farming and water is plentiful.)* **OL**

W Writing Support

Narrative Writing Have students write stories from the point of view of a drop of water. Instruct students to use facts from the text to explain the water cycle and include a beginning, a middle, and an end to their story. When finished, students may illustrate their stories and share them with the class. **OL**

Diagram Skills

Answers:

1. the evaporation stage
2. It evaporates the water.

Differentiated Instruction

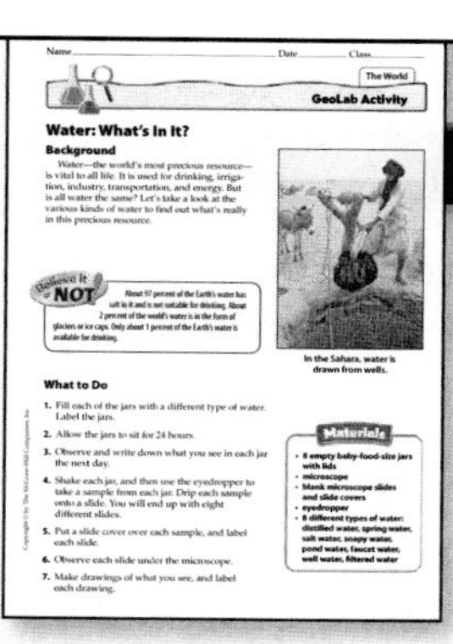

GeoLab Activity, URB pp. 19–20

Water: What's In It?

Objective: To determine whether all water is the same

Focus: Examine what percentage of the Earth's water is available for drinking.

Teach: Have students observe water samples in jars. Then have them observe and make drawings of samples under a microscope.

Assess: Have students answer questions and draw conclusions about the best drinking water.

Close: Have students create a World Water Day poster.

Differentiated Instruction Strategies

BL Have students work with partners, with one person observing and the other making notes.

AL Have students research the methods being used worldwide to increase the availability of drinking water.

ELL Have students read lab reports to a small group and respond to questions about the activity.

C Critical Thinking

Making Inferences Ask: How might precipitation be affected by air pollution? *(Answers may note that pollution in the air comes back to the Earth when it rains or snows, polluting the soil and vegetation.)* **OL**

Caption Answer:
Air temperature determines the type of precipitation the water vapor takes—either rain, snow, sleet, or hail.

Reading Check Answer: It is frozen in glaciers or on mountaintops.

Assess

Social Studies ONLINE
Study Central™ provides summaries, interactive games, and online graphic organizers to help students review content.

Close

Comparing and Contrasting Have students write several sentences comparing and contrasting saltwater and freshwater sources. **OL**

NATIONAL GEOGRAPHIC
Monroe Lake, Quebec

Fog is a low-lying cloud that can form when moist air blows over a cool surface. ***Place***
How does air temperature affect water vapor in the air?

When the air temperature drops low enough, **condensation** takes place. In this process, water changes from gas back to a liquid. Tiny droplets of water form in the air, although they are suspended in clouds.

C When conditions in the atmosphere are right, these water droplets fall to the ground as some form of **precipitation**. This can be rain, snow, sleet, or hail. The form of precipitation depends on the temperature of the surrounding air.

Completing the cycle is the process called **collection.** The water collects on the ground and in rivers, lakes, and oceans. There it evaporates to begin the cycle again.

Reading Check **Making Inferences** Why is very little of the Earth's freshwater usable?

Section 2 Review

Social Studies ONLINE
Study Central™ To review this section, go to glencoe.com.

Vocabulary

1. **Explain** the meaning of the following terms by using each one in a sentence.
   - **a.** continental shelf
   - **b.** trench
   - **c.** groundwater
   - **d.** aquifer
   - **e.** water cycle
   - **f.** evaporation
   - **g.** condensation
   - **h.** precipitation
   - **i.** collection

Main Ideas

2. **Contrasting** How do an isthmus, a peninsula, and an island differ?
3. **Summarizing** Use a diagram like the one below to summarize the water cycle.

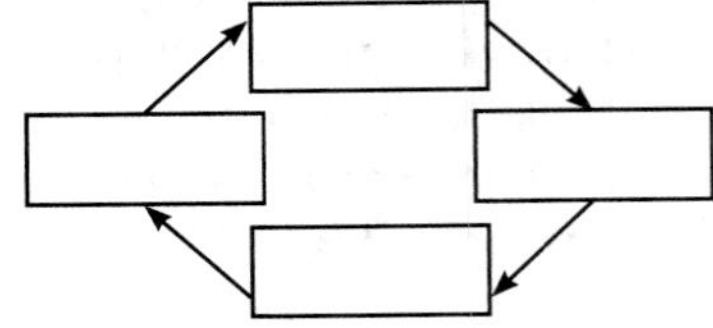

Critical Thinking

4. **Comparing and Contrasting** How are plains and plateaus similar and different?
5. **BIG Idea** Describe several factors that people consider when choosing a place to settle.
6. **Challenge** Which landforms do you think attracted people to settle in the area where you live? Which landforms, if any, may have kept people away?

Writing About Geography

7. **Expository Writing** Write a paragraph describing the major landforms found in the state where you live.

Answers

1. Sentences should use vocabulary words according to their definitions in the section and Glossary.
2. An isthmus is a narrow strip of land that connects two larger landmasses and has water on two sides; a peninsula is a piece of land that is connected to a larger landmass on one side but has water on the other three sides; an island is a body of land that is completely surrounded by water.
3. Students' diagrams should show these steps in the water cycle: evaporation, condensation, precipitation, and collection.
4. Plains and plateaus are flat, but plains are lowlands, and plateaus have higher elevations.
5. When choosing a place to settle, people consider climate and availability of resources, including water for drinking and in which they can fish, and land on which they can grow food or raise animals.
6. Answers will vary depending on where students live; students may respond that plains attracted farmers, or mountains or deserts have kept people away.
7. Students' paragraphs should describe major landforms in their state, such as mountains, hills, valleys, plains, and plateaus.

Guide to Reading

BIG Idea

Geographers organize the Earth into regions that share common characteristics.

Content Vocabulary

- weather *(p. 56)*
- climate *(p. 56)*
- prevailing wind *(p. 57)*
- current *(p. 57)*
- El Niño *(p. 58)*
- La Niña *(p. 58)*
- local wind *(p. 59)*
- rain shadow *(p. 59)*
- climate zone *(p. 59)*
- biome *(p. 60)*
- urban climate *(p. 61)*

Academic Vocabulary

- distribute *(p. 56)*
- alter *(p. 57)*

Reading Strategy

Identifying Central Issues Use a diagram like the one below to identify the effects of both El Niño and La Niña.

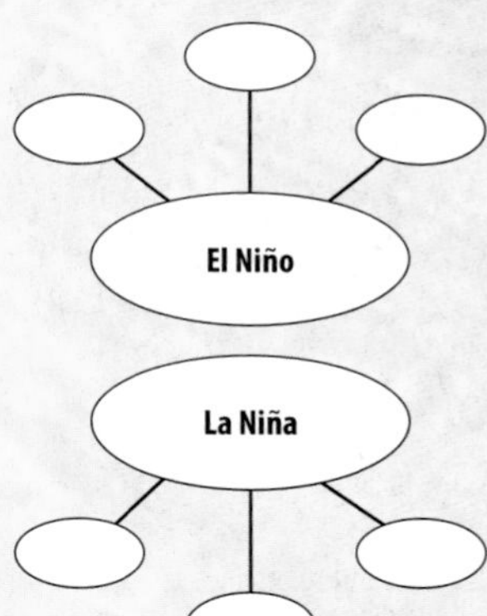

Climate Regions

Picture This Residents rush to escape the swirling winds and pelting rain during the annual typhoon season in China. Typhoons are hurricanes that can topple buildings, snap power lines, and uproot trees. These violent thunderstorms draw their power from warm ocean waters and are common in the Tropics of southeast China. Read this section to learn about the variety of climates that are found on Earth.

Fleeing Typhoon Haitang, July 2005

Focus

Bellringer

Daily Focus Transparency 2-3

Guide to Reading

Answers to Graphic:

El Niño:
warm waters reach South America; heavy rains in South America; little rain in Australia and Africa; severe storms in North America

La Niña:
cool waters; little rainfall in the eastern Pacific; heavy rains in the western Pacific

Section Spotlight Video

To learn more about climate regions, have students watch the Section Spotlight Video.

Resource Manager

R Reading Strategies	C Critical Thinking	D Differentiated Instruction	W Writing Support	S Skill Practice
Teacher Edition • Act. Prior Know., p. 56 • Predicting, p. 58 • Reading Charts, p. 60 • Visualizing, p. 61 **Additional Resources** • Guid. Read., URB p. 57 • Cont. Vocab., URB p. 59 • Ac. Vocab., URB p. 61 • Read. Ess., p. 13	**Teacher Edition** • Making Inferences, p. 59 **Additional Resources** • Quizzes and Tests, p. 15	**Teacher Edition** • Logical/Math., p. 57 • Kinesthetic, p. 58 • Visual/Spatial, p. 60 **Additional Resources** • Reteach., URB p. 75 • School-to-Home Conn., URB p. 77	**Teacher Edition** • Expository Writing, p. 59 **Additional Resources** • Crit. Think., URB p. 67	**Teacher Edition** • Using Geo. Skills, p. 56 **Additional Resources** • Daily Focus Trans. 2-3 • Reg. Atlas, URB pp. 1–7

Teach

R Reading Strategy

Activating Prior Knowledge Read the Main Idea aloud to students. **Ask:** **How would you explain the concept of "climate" to someone who has never used the word before?** *(Answers may explain that climate is the weather pattern of a place over a period of years.)* Ask students to describe the climate where they live. **OL**

S Skill Practice

Using Geography Skills Have students use a globe to investigate the movement of winds. Divide students into pairs. Direct one student to place a finger on North America and the partner to rotate the globe to the left so that the partner's finger crosses the globe like a westerly wind. Discuss with students the effects of winds. **BL**

Map Skills

Answers:

1. from southwest to southeast
2. areas on the Equator, where the doldrums are, and areas on the horse latitudes at 30°N or 30°S.

Effects on Climate

Main Idea **Sun, wind, and water influence Earth's climate.**

Geography and You What is the weather today in your area? Is it typical of the particular season you are in, or is it unusual? Read to find out about the difference between weather and climate.

When you turn on the television to find out the day's high and low temperatures, you are checking the local weather. **Weather** refers to the changes in temperature, wind direction and speed, and air moisture that take place over a short period of time. When geographers look at the usual, predictable patterns of weather in an area over many years, they are studying **climate**.

The Sun

Earth's climate is linked directly to the sun. As you recall from Chapter 1, the Earth does not heat evenly. The Tropics receive more of the sun's heat energy and the Poles receive less. The movement of air and water over the Earth helps to **distribute** the sun's heat more evenly around the globe.

NATIONAL GEOGRAPHIC Maps In MOtion See StudentWorks™ Plus or glencoe.com.

Figure 4 **Prevailing Wind Patterns**

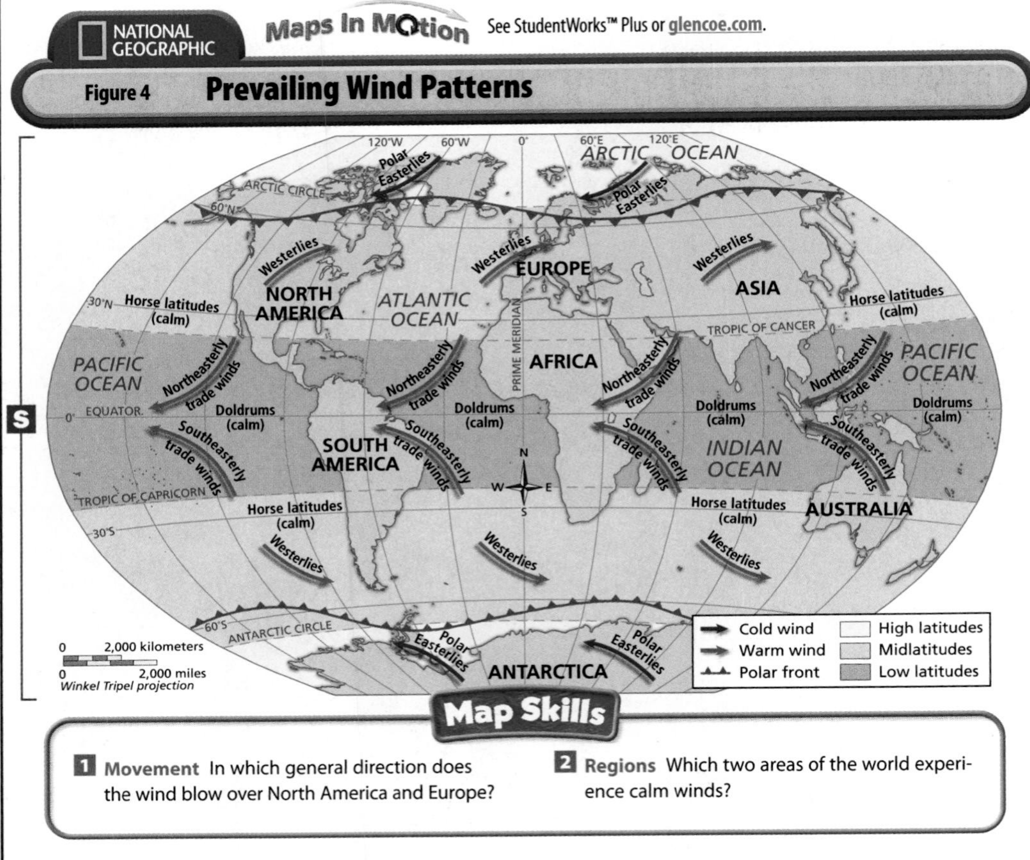

Map Skills

1. **Movement** In which general direction does the wind blow over North America and Europe?
2. **Regions** Which two areas of the world experience calm winds?

Hands-On Chapter Project Step 3

Capturing Your Region on Postcards

Step 3: Capturing Climate Student pairs will choose an aspect of their region's climate to illustrate on a postcard.

Directions Have student pairs examine the information they have gathered about their region's climate and discuss which aspect of the climate is most interesting and would lend itself best to illustration on a postcard. After they have decided on a characteristic, direct students to discuss the best way to present it visually. Then tell students to sketch the visual on one side of the postcard and write a short description for the other side.

Summarizing Continue to circulate and confer with student pairs. Ask student partners to summarize what their postcard will show and tell about the region's climate. **OL**

(Chapter Project continued in Section 4)

Winds

Air in the Tropics, which is warmed by the sun, moves north and south toward the Poles of the Earth. Colder air from the Poles moves toward the Equator. These movements of air are winds. Major wind systems follow patterns that are similar over time. These patterns, shown in **Figure 4,** are called **prevailing winds.**

Because the planet rotates, winds curve across Earth's surface. The winds that blow from east to west between the Tropics and the Equator are called the trade winds. Long ago sailing ships used these winds to carry out trade. The westerlies, which blow over North America, move from west to east in the area between the Tropics and about 60° north latitude.

Storms

When moist, warm air rises suddenly and meets dry, cold air, major storms can develop. In the summer, these storms can include thunder and lightning, heavy rain, and, sometimes, tornadoes. Tornadoes are violent, funnel-shaped windstorms with wind speeds up to 450 miles (724 km) per hour. **D** In the winter, storms can become blizzards that bring much snow.

Other types of destructive storms are hurricanes and typhoons. Hurricanes occur in the western Atlantic and eastern Pacific Oceans. Typhoons occur in the western Pacific Ocean. These storms arise in the warm ocean waters of the Tropics and can reach great size and power. Some are as much as 300 miles (483 km) across and create strong winds and heavy rains.

Ocean Currents

The steadily flowing streams of water in the world's seas are called **currents.** Like winds, they follow patterns, which are shown in **Figure 5,** on the next page.

NATIONAL GEOGRAPHIC

Effects of El Niño

South America can experience dramatic changes in weather due to El Niño and La Niña. Forest fires, like this one in Brazil, occur during periods of drought. ***Place*** **How do El Niño and La Niña differ?**

Currents that carry warm water to higher latitudes can affect the climates in those latitudes. For example, the North Atlantic Current carries warm water from the Tropics to western Europe. Winds blowing over the warm water bring warmth and moisture to western Europe, which enjoys an unexpectedly mild climate.

El Niño and La Niña

Every few years, changes in normal wind and water patterns in the Pacific Ocean cause unusual weather in some places. In one of these events, weakened winds allow warmer waters to reach South America's coast. This change **alters** weather there and beyond.

D Differentiated Instruction

Logical/Mathematical Provide students with the following statistics:

U.S. Spring/Summer Tornado Statistics		
	2003	2005
March	43	62
April	157	132
May	543	123
June	292	316
July	167	138
August	44	123

Ask: Which two months have the greatest number of tornadoes? *(May and June)* **What conclusions can you draw from this data?** *(Students may answer that tornadoes are occurring more frequently in late spring/early summer.)* Instruct students to find additional data about the number of tornadoes in recent years to see if there are any other patterns over time. **AL**

Caption Answer:
In an El Niño, weakened winds allow warm water to reach South America's coast, causing heavy rains. In a La Niña, the opposite happens, causing heavy rains in the western Pacific.

Differentiated Instruction

Critical Thinking Skills Activity

Distinguishing Relevant from Irrelevant Information

Critical Thinking Skills Activity, URB pp. 67–68

Distinguishing Relevant from Irrelevant Information

Objective: To analyze information by distinguishing relevant from irrelevant information

Focus: Explain that relevant information supports the main topic. Review bulleted steps.

Teach: Have students create a two-column chart to categorize a passage's information as relevant or irrelevant.

Assess: Have students identify the main topic and relevant information in a second passage.

Close: Students should compare analyses.

Differentiated Instruction Strategies

BL Have students circle the main topic and underline relevant information.

AL Have students include relevant and irrelevant information in a paragraph and then trade paragraphs with a partner and analyze.

ELL Have students use a graphic organizer to show the main topic and relevant information in each passage.

D Differentiated Instruction

Kinesthetic Provide students with red and blue string or yarn and outline maps of the Earth. Have them label the continents and use the yarn or string to re-create the motion of ocean currents. Instruct students to demonstrate the movement of the currents to a partner before gluing the yarn or string onto their map. **BL**

R Reading Strategy

Predicting Read the paragraph aloud to students. Ask students to name some of Earth's landforms. Have them predict ways that landforms might affect the climate. Instruct students to keep their predictions in mind as they read the chapter. **OL**

Reading Check Answer: Winds are formed as warm air from the Tropics moves towards the Poles or cold air from the Poles moves towards the Equator.

Map Skills

Answers:
1. a warmer climate
2. eastern South America

Additional Support

These conditions are called **El Niño,** Spanish for "the boy."

In an El Niño, very heavy rains fall on western South America, causing floods. Meanwhile, little rain falls on Australia, southern Asia, and Africa. Also, North America may see severe storms.

In some years the opposite occurs, producing conditions called **La Niña,** Spanish for "the girl." La Niña causes unusually cool waters and low rainfall in the eastern Pacific. In the western Pacific, rains are heavy and typhoons can occur.

Reading Check **Explaining** How are winds formed?

Landforms and Climate

Main Idea **Landforms, especially mountains, can affect winds, temperature, and rainfall.**

Geography and You Have you ever felt a cooling sea breeze on a hot summer's day? Read on to learn how the sea can affect climate.

R Sun, wind, and water affect climate, but the shape of the land has an effect on climate as well. The distance between landforms as well as their nearness to water influence climate.

NATIONAL GEOGRAPHIC

Figure 5 **World Ocean Currents**

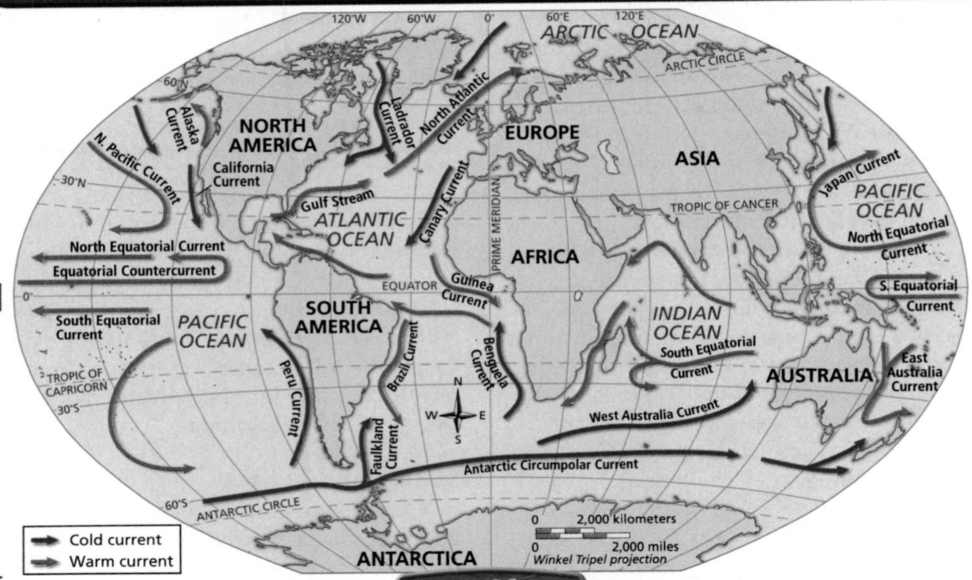

D

Map Skills

1. **Movement** What kind of climate is the North Atlantic Current likely to bring to Europe?
2. **Regions** Which area generally has warmer waters, western South America or eastern South America?

Activity: Technology Connection

Analyzing **Ask:** **Does El Niño affect weather in the United States?** *(yes)* Have students work individually to investigate El Niño's impact on weather in the United States. Direct students to conduct research online to identify instances of unusual weather in the United States caused by El Niño in the last 10 years. Tell students to locate news articles and photographs that describe weather events in at least two different regions of the country. When students have completed their research, have them prepare a weather documentary on El Niño to present to the class. Suggest that students structure their documentary as follows: introduction to the El Niño phenomenon, chronology and analysis of events caused by El Niño in the United States, conclusion. **AL**

Landforms and Local Winds

Some landforms cause **local winds**, or wind patterns that are typical only in a small area. Some local winds occur because land warms and cools more quickly than water does. As a result, cool sea breezes keep coastal areas cool during the day. After the sun sets, the opposite occurs. The air over the land cools more quickly than the air over the water. At night, then, a cool breeze blows from the land out to sea.

Local winds also occur near tall mountains. When the air along a mountain slope is warmer than the air in the valley below, it rises and a cool valley breeze moves up the mountain.

Mountains, Temperature, and Rainfall

The slopes of a mountain facing the sun can heat more quickly than nearby land. Higher up in the mountains, however, the air is thin and cannot hold the heat very well. As a result, mountain peaks are cold. This explains why some mountains in the Tropics are covered with snow.

Mountains have an effect on rainfall called a **rain shadow** that blocks rain from
W reaching interior regions. As warm, moist ocean air moves up the mountain slopes, it cools and releases its moisture. As a result, the side of mountains facing the wind, called the windward side, receives large amounts of rainfall.

As the air passes over the mountain peaks to the other side, called the leeward side, it becomes cool and dry. As a result, the land on the leeward side of the mountains is often very dry. Deserts can develop on the leeward side of mountain ranges.

Reading Check **Determining Cause and Effect** How do mountains cause the rain shadow effect?

Climate Zones

Main Idea **The effects of wind, water, latitude, and landforms combine to create different climate zones.**

Geography and You Suppose you visited two islands that were thousands of miles apart. Read to find out how similar their climates might be.

As you have read, the effects of wind, water, latitude, and landforms combine to shape the climate of an area. Scientists have found that many parts of the world, even though they are very distant from one another, have similar climates. Southern California, for instance, has a warm, dry climate similar to that around the Mediterranean Sea in Europe. These areas have the same **climate zone**, or similar patterns of temperature and precipitation. These regions would also have similar vegetation. C

NATIONAL GEOGRAPHIC

Figure 6 The Rain Shadow

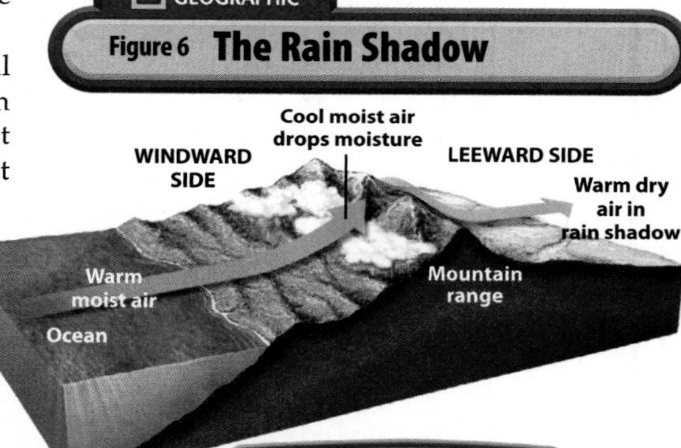

Diagram Skills

1. **Identifying** What type of air blows from the ocean toward the mountain?
2. **Explaining** Why is the land on the leeward side of the mountain dry?

W Writing Support

Expository Writing Instruct students to write a summary of the climate in mountain regions. Have students include a verbal summary of the rain shadow diagram. **OL**

C Critical Thinking

Making Inferences **Ask:** **Why do you think different parts of the world have similar climates?** *(They have similar latitudes, landforms, and wind and water effects.)* **OL**

Reading Check **Answer:** As warm, moist ocean air rises up the mountain slopes, it cools and releases its moisture. The side of the mountains facing the wind receives large amounts of rainfall. The air passing to the other side of the mountain is cool and dry.

Diagram Skills

Answers:

1. warm, moist air
2. The air loses its precipitation on the windward side of the mountain, so the air on the leeward side is dry.

Differentiated Instruction

Leveled Activities

BL Reading Essentials and Note-Taking Guide, p. 13

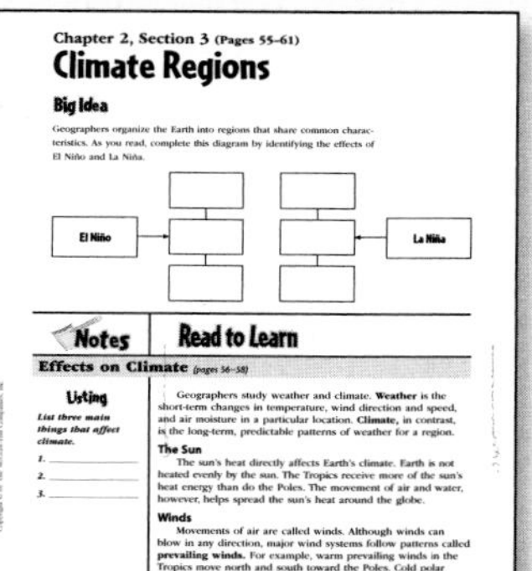
Chapter 2, Section 3 (Pages 55–61)

Climate Regions

Big Idea

Notes | Read to Learn

Effects on Climate

OL Content Vocabulary Activity, URB p. 59

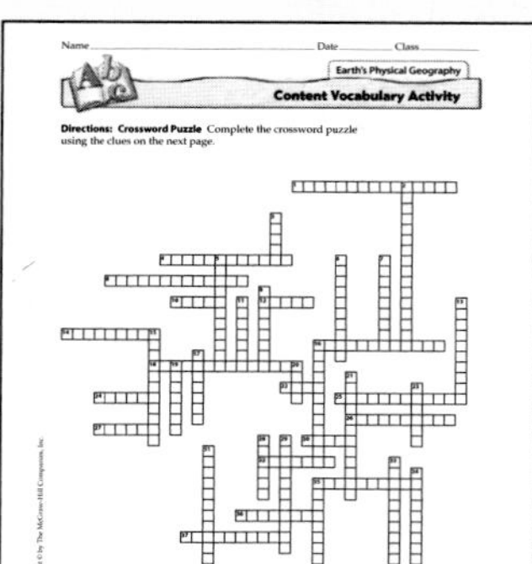
Content Vocabulary Activity

ELL School-to-Home Connection, URB p. 77

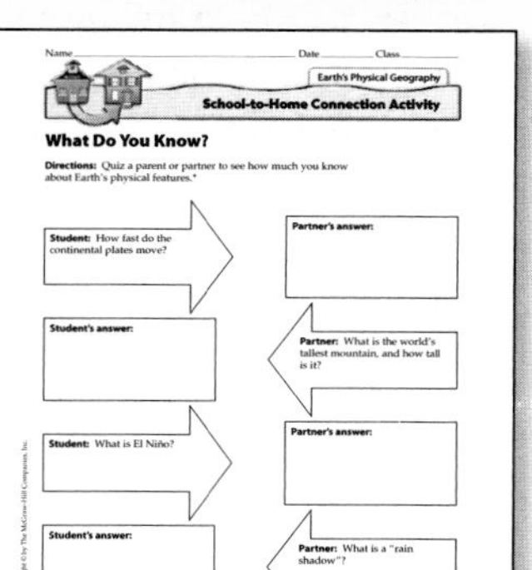
School-to-Home Connection Activity

What Do You Know?

D Differentiated Instruction

Visual/Spatial Have students use outline maps to depict the information about world climate zones. Instruct students to use colored pencils to color the different climate zones, using one color for each zone. **OL**

R Reading Strategy

Reading Charts Have students study the information in the chart. **Ask: What type of climate does the United States have?** *(midlatitude)* **What subcategories are in the midlatitude climate?** *(marine west coast, Mediterranean, humid subtropical, and humid continental)* Have students identify the climate of their state. Next, **ask: What subcategories of climate are the Amazon basin and Congo basin examples of?** *(tropical rain forest)* **eastern China?** *(humid subtropical)* **western Russia?** *(humid continental and subarctic)* **OL**

Climate zones include **biomes,** or areas such as rain forest, desert, grassland, and tundra in which particular kinds of plants and animals have adapted to particular climates.

Major Climates

Scientists have identified five major climate zones, which are described in the chart below. Four of these zones have several subcategories. For example, the dry climate zone is subdivided into steppe and desert subcategories. These generally dry climates differ slightly in rainfall and temperature. **D** Locations in the highland zone show great variation. In these areas, altitude, the position of a place toward or away from the sun, and other factors can make large differences in climate even though two locations may be near each other.

R

World Climate Zones

Category	Subcategory	Characteristics	Vegetation	Example
Tropical	Tropical rain forest	Warm temperatures; heavy rainfall throughout year	Dense rain forests	Amazon basin (South America); Congo basin (Africa)
	Tropical savanna	Warm temperatures throughout year; dry winter	Grasslands dotted by scattered trees	Southern half of Brazil; eastern Africa
Dry	Steppe	Temperatures can be warm or mild; rainfall low and unreliable	Grasses, shrubs	Western Great Plains (United States); Sahel region south of the Sahara (Africa)
	Desert	Temperatures can be warm or mild; rainfall very low and very unreliable	Drought-resistant shrubs and bushes	Sonoran Desert (southwestern United States, Mexico); Sahara (Africa)
Midlatitude	Marine west coast	Cool summers, mild winters; ample rainfall	Deciduous or evergreen forests	Northwestern United States; northwestern Europe
	Mediterranean	Warm, dry summers; mild, wet winters	Shrubs, low trees, drought-resistant plants	Southern California; Mediterranean region (Europe)
	Humid subtropical	Hot, wet summers; mild, wet winters	Mixed forests	Southeastern United States; eastern China
	Humid continental	Hot, wet summers; cold, somewhat wet winters	Deciduous forests	Northeastern United States; eastern Europe; western Russia
High Latitude	Subarctic	Short, mild summers; long, cold winters; light precipitation	Coniferous forests	Most of Alaska, Canada; western Russia
	Tundra	Short, cool summers; long, cold winters; precipitation varies	Low-lying grasses, mosses, shrubs	Extreme north of North America; Europe
	Ice cap	Cold all year long	None to very little	Greenland; Antarctica
Highland		Varies depending on local conditions	Changes with altitude	Northern Rocky Mountains (United States); the Himalaya (Asia)

Additional Support

Activity: Collaborative Learning

Illustrating Pair students and assign each pair a climate zone subcategory from the chart of world climate zones. Have pairs create a mural that illustrates seasonal weather, vegetation, and housing that might be found in one of the locations listed for their subcategory. Tell students to use library resources, such as encyclopedias and almanacs, to gather information about their location to illustrate in their murals. Have students label their murals with the name of the subcategory. Display the murals in the classroom, and allow time for students to view each other's work. Then use the following question as a springboard to class discussion of world climate zones. **Ask: How is life in other climate zones different from life in the zone in which you live?** *(Answers will vary; students should use what they have learned from their group's research and that of other groups to compare and contrast conditions in different climate zones.)* **OL**

Urban Climates

Large cities show significant climate differences from surrounding areas in their climate zone. These **urban climates** are marked by higher temperatures and other differences. Paved streets and stone buildings soak up and then release more of the sun's heat energy than areas covered by plants. This absorption leads to higher temperatures—as much as 10° to 20°F (6° to 11°C) higher—than in the nearby countryside. These different heat patterns cause winds to blow into cities from several directions instead of the prevailing direction experienced in rural areas. Some scientists believe cities also have more precipitation than rural areas. R

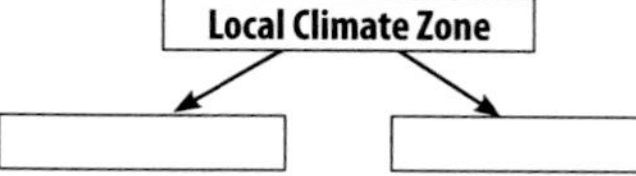
Drawing Conclusions How do large cities affect climate?

NATIONAL GEOGRAPHIC

Shanghai, China: City Heat

City temperatures can soar in the summer. Buildings and pavement absorb the sun's heat, raising temperatures within the city. ***Location*** **How does urban heat affect winds in the urban area?**

Section 3 Review

Social Studies ONLINE
Study Central™ To review this section, go to glencoe.com.

Vocabulary

1. **Explain** the meaning of the following terms by writing three paragraphs that include all of the terms: *weather, climate, prevailing wind, current, El Niño, La Niña, local wind, rain shadow, climate zone, biome,* and *urban climate.*

Main Ideas

2. **Explaining** How do wind and water affect the Earth's climates?
3. **Reviewing** Describe two types of local winds and why they form.
4. **Identifying** Use a diagram like the one below to identify the main characteristics of the climate zone in which you live.

Local Climate Zone → [ ] [ ]

Critical Thinking

5. **BIG Idea** Choose two climate zones, and compare and contrast their characteristics.
6. **Challenge** How might El Niño affect weather conditions in the central United States?

Writing About Geography

7. **Expository Writing** Choose a place in the world you would like to visit because of its climate. Write a paragraph describing the climate of that area.

R Reading Strategy

Visualizing Remind students that good readers create pictures in their minds as they read. Have students read the paragraph and draw a diagram depicting an urban climate. OL

Reading Check **Answer:** Paved streets and stone buildings in large cities soak up the sun's heat and increase the air temperature. This can change local wind and rain patterns.

Caption Answer:
The urban heat causes winds to blow into cities from different directions.

Assess

Social Studies ONLINE
Study Central™ provides summaries, interactive games, and online graphic organizers to help students review content.

Close

Naming Have students identify the factors that affect the climate of a region. OL

Section 3 Review

Answers

1. Sentences should use vocabulary words according to their definitions in the section and Glossary.
2. Wind and water help distribute the sun's heat more evenly across the Earth.
3. During the day, cool sea breezes blow inland because air over water warms more slowly than air over land; breezes along mountain slopes become warm air along slopes rises.
4. Students should include details about temperature and precipitation in their diagrams.
5. Answers will vary depending on the climate zones students choose; sample response: The tropical rain forest and desert zones are similar in that they have warm temperatures, but different in the amount of precipitation they receive. The desert receives little to no rain and the rain forest receives heavy rain.
6. El Niño may cause severe storms and flooding in the central United States.
7. Students' paragraphs should reflect accurate information about the climate zone in which the place is located.

R1 Reading Strategy

Predicting Ask students to predict how plants and animals might cause harm if they are moved into an environment that is not their own. **Ask: How do you think people affect where plants and animals live?** *(Answers may note that people bring plants and animals to other places with them when they travel or settle in an area.)* **OL**

R2 Reading Strategy

Reading Maps Ask: What general trend do you see in the map? *(The number of zebra mussels is increasing as time goes on, and they are branching out along rivers and waterways in all directions from their original location.)* **OL**

Think About It

Answers:

1. They "invade" areas and crowd out local plants and animals.
2. World trade is increasing and making invasive species more common.

Additional Support

NATIONAL GEOGRAPHIC **Geography & History**

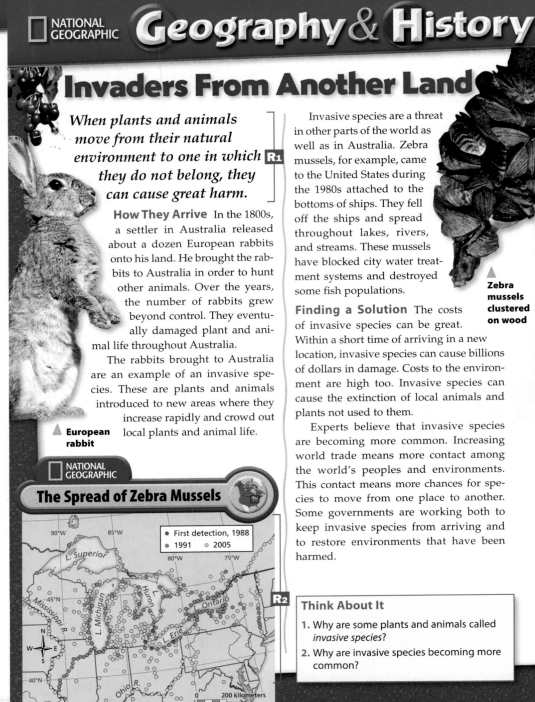

Invaders From Another Land

European rabbit

When plants and animals move from their natural environment to one in which they do not belong, they can cause great harm. R1

How They Arrive In the 1800s, a settler in Australia released about a dozen European rabbits onto his land. He brought the rabbits to Australia in order to hunt other animals. Over the years, the number of rabbits grew beyond control. They eventually damaged plant and animal life throughout Australia.

The rabbits brought to Australia are an example of an invasive species. These are plants and animals introduced to new areas where they increase rapidly and crowd out local plants and animal life.

Invasive species are a threat in other parts of the world as well as in Australia. Zebra mussels, for example, came to the United States during the 1980s attached to the bottoms of ships. They fell off the ships and spread throughout lakes, rivers, and streams. These mussels have blocked city water treatment systems and destroyed some fish populations.

Zebra mussels clustered on wood

Finding a Solution The costs of invasive species can be great. Within a short time of arriving in a new location, invasive species can cause billions of dollars in damage. Costs to the environment are high too. Invasive species can cause the extinction of local animals and plants not used to them.

Experts believe that invasive species are becoming more common. Increasing world trade means more contact among the world's peoples and environments. This contact means more chances for species to move from one place to another. Some governments are working both to keep invasive species from arriving and to restore environments that have been harmed.

R2

Think About It

1. Why are some plants and animals called *invasive species*?
2. Why are invasive species becoming more common?

Activity: Collaborative Learning

Evaluating Have students work in three groups to investigate the economic effects of invasive species in the United States. Have one group examine the national impact of invasive species, the second group the impact at the state level, and the third group local effects. Direct students to conduct their research online, using the U.S. Department of Agriculture's National Invasive Species Information Center and links provided there as a starting point. Suggest that each group narrow their research to a particular species and the measures being taken to offset its economic impact at the level the group has been assigned. Tell students to compile their findings in a fact sheet to use as a reference during class discussion. **Ask: What effect do invasive species have on national, state, and local economies?** *(Students should discuss the economic impact of invasive species using information they have gathered as a group.)* **OL**

Guide to Reading

BIG Idea

All living things are dependent upon one another and their surroundings for survival.

Content Vocabulary

- smog *(p. 64)*
- acid rain *(p. 64)*
- greenhouse effect *(p. 64)*
- crop rotation *(p. 65)*
- deforestation *(p. 65)*
- conservation *(p. 66)*
- irrigation *(p. 66)*
- pesticide *(p. 66)*
- ecosystem *(p. 66)*
- biodiversity *(p. 66)*

Academic Vocabulary

- layer *(p. 64)*
- technique *(p. 65)*

Reading Strategy

Solving Problems Use a chart like the one below to identify environmental problems and what people are doing to solve them.

Problem	Solution
1.	1.
2.	2.
3.	3.

SECTION 4 Human-Environment Interaction

Picture This Imagine guiding hundreds of logs through rough waters in a tugboat. In Deception Pass State Park in Washington, boats move newly-cut logs along the waters of the park to reach the highway. The logs are loaded on trucks and taken to lumber yards. Read this section to learn about the effects of human activities on the Earth.

▼ Logs moving through Deception Pass State Park in Washington

Focus

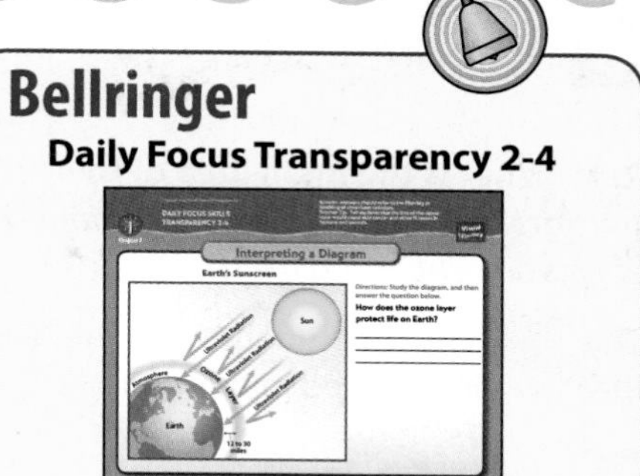

Bellringer

Daily Focus Transparency 2-4

Guide to Reading

Answers to Graphic:

Answers may include:

Problem	Solution
1. Air pollution	1. Nations are limiting their release of CFCs.
2. Global warming	2. Nations are trying to use energy more efficiently.
3. Erosion due to farming	3. Some farmers are using contour plowing, or crop rotation.

Section Spotlight Video

To learn more about human-environment interaction, have students watch the Section Spotlight Video.

Resource Manager

R Reading Strategies	C Critical Thinking	D Differentiated Instruction	W Writing Support	S Skill Practice
Teacher Edition • Identifying the Main Idea, p. 64 **Additional Resources** • Guid. Read., URB p. 58 • Cont. Vocab., URB p. 59 • Ac. Vocab., URB p. 61 • Pri. Source, URB p. 23 • Read. Ess., p. 16	**Teacher Edition** • Analyzing Info., p. 65 **Additional Resources** • Env. Case Studies, URB p. 9 • Quizzes and Tests, p. 16	**Teacher Edition** • Verbal/Linguistic, p. 65 • Naturalist, p. 66 **Additional Resources** • Reteach., URB p. 75	**Teacher Edition** • Persuasive Writing, p. 64 **Additional Resources** • World Lit., URB p. 27	**Teacher Edition** • Visual Literacy, p. 65 **Additional Resources** • Speak./Listen. Skills, URB p. 69 • Daily Focus Trans. 2-4 • Reg. Atlas, URB pp. 1–7

Teach

R Reading Strategy

Identifying the Main Idea

Ask: What is the main idea of this paragraph? *(Air pollution has serious effects on people and the planet.)* **OL**

This **Reading Skill** (Identifying the Main Idea) was introduced in this unit.

W Writing Support

Persuasive Writing Have students choose a stand on global warming either affirming or disaffirming the phenomenon. Then instruct students to conduct further research on global warming and write a persuasive essay convincing readers that it is either a serious problem or nothing to worry about. Direct students to include facts from their research to support their stance. **OL**

Caption Answer:
burning of coal, oil, and natural gas

Reading Check Answer: Some scientists argue that computer models showing global warming are unrealistic.

The Atmosphere

Main Idea **Human activity can have a negative impact on the air.**

Geography and You Have you ever seen a blanket of dirty air hanging over a large city? Read to find out how human actions affect the atmosphere.

Throughout the world, people burn oil, coal, or gas to make electricity, to power factories, or to move cars. These actions often cause air pollution.

Air Pollution

Air pollution has serious effects on people and the planet. Some polluting chemicals combine with ozone, a form of oxygen, to create **smog.** This is a thick haze of smoke and chemicals. Thick smog above cities can lead to serious breathing problems.

Chemicals in air pollution can also combine with precipitation to form **acid rain.** Acid rain kills fish, eats away at the surfaces of buildings, and destroys trees and entire forests. Because the chemicals that form acid rain come from the burning of coal and oil, solving this problem has proved difficult.

Some human-made chemicals, particularly chlorofluorocarbons (CFCs), destroy the ozone **layer.** Ozone forms a shield high in the atmosphere against damaging rays from the sun that can cause skin cancer. Nations today are working to limit the release of CFCs.

The Greenhouse Effect

Like the glass in a greenhouse, gases in the atmosphere trap the sun's warmth. Without this **greenhouse effect,** the Earth would be too cold for most living things. **Figure 7** shows the greenhouse effect.

NATIONAL GEOGRAPHIC

Global Warming

Scientists are concerned that global warming might be harming wildlife, such as this polar bear. ***Human-Environment Interaction*** **What human activities might contribute to global warming?**

Some scientists, however, say that pollution is strengthening the greenhouse effect. They claim that the increased burning of coal, oil, and natural gas has released more gases into the atmosphere. These greenhouse gases have trapped more of the sun's heat near the Earth's surface, raising temperatures around the planet. Such warming could cause climate changes and melt polar ice. Ocean levels could rise and flood low-lying coastal areas.

The issue of global warming is debated. Critics argue that computer models showing global warming are unrealistic. Many nations, however, are addressing the problem. They are trying to use energy more efficiently, burn coal more cleanly, and adopt nonpolluting forms of energy such as wind and solar power.

Reading Check **Explaining** Why do some scientists debate the issue of global warming?

Differentiated Instruction

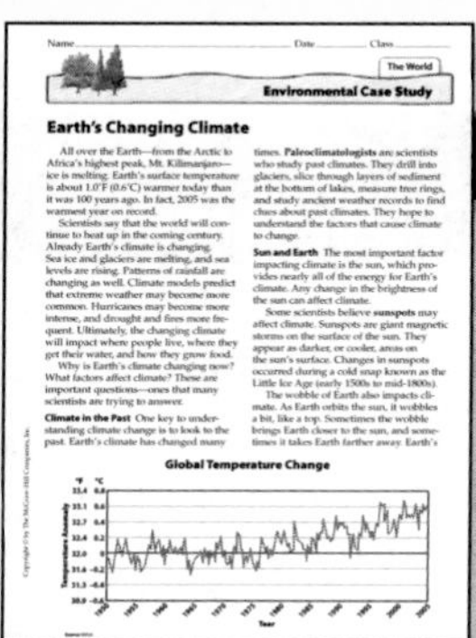

Name ______ Date ______ Class ______

The World

Environmental Case Study

Earth's Changing Climate

All over the Earth—from the Arctic to Africa's highest peak, Mt. Kilimanjaro—ice is melting. Earth's surface temperature is about 1.0°F (0.6°C) warmer today than it was 100 years ago. In fact, 2005 was the warmest year on record.

Scientists say that the world will continue to heat up in the coming century. Already Earth's climate is changing. Sea ice and glaciers are melting, and sea levels are rising. Patterns of rainfall are changing as well. Climate models predict that extreme weather may become more common. Hurricanes may become more intense, and drought and fires more frequent. Ultimately, the changing climate will impact where people live, where they get their water, and how they grow food.

Why is Earth's climate changing now? What factors affect climate? These are important questions—ones that many scientists are trying to answer.

Climate in the Past One key to understanding climate change is to look to the past. Earth's climate has changed many times. **Paleoclimatologists** are scientists who study past climates. They drill into glaciers, slice through layers of sediment at the bottom of lakes, measure tree rings, and study ancient weather records to find clues about past climates. They hope to understand the factors that cause climate to change.

Sun and Earth The most important factor impacting climate is the sun, which provides nearly all of the energy for Earth's climate. Any change in the brightness of the sun can affect climate.

Some scientists believe **sunspots** may affect climate. Sunspots are giant magnetic storms on the surface of the sun. They appear as darker, or cooler, areas on the sun's surface. Changes in sunspots occurred during a cold snap known as the Little Ice Age (early 1500s to mid-1800s).

The wobble of Earth also impacts climate. As Earth orbits the sun, it wobbles a bit, like a top. Sometimes the wobble brings Earth closer to the sun, and sometimes it takes Earth farther away. Earth's

Environmental Case Study, URB pp. 9–12

Earth's Changing Climate

Objective: To consider the possible causes and effects of climate change

Focus: Have students discuss signs of climate change.

Teach: Examine a graph showing climate change and identify factors that influence climate.

Assess: Have students create a greenhouse in a jar and answer questions about climate change.

Close: Ask students to propose strategies to limit global warming.

Differentiated Instruction Strategies

BL Have students make a list of the factors affecting climate and their effects.

AL Have students create a model that illustrates the greenhouse effect.

ELL Have students compile a glossary of boldface key terms and other new vocabulary from the text.

The Lithosphere

Main Idea **Some human activity damages our environment.**

Geography and You How might your community have looked 200 years ago? Read to discover how human actions have affected the land.

The lithosphere is another name for the Earth's crust. It includes all the land above and below the oceans. Human activities, such as farming, logging, and mining can have negative effects on the lithosphere. C

Rich topsoil is a vital part of the lithosphere that, if not carefully managed, can be carried away by wind or water. Some farmers use contour plowing to limit the loss of topsoil. With this **technique,** farmers plow along the curves of the land rather than in straight lines, preventing the soil from washing away. **Crop rotation**, or changing what is planted from year to year, also protects topsoil. Planting grasses in fields without crops holds the soil in place.

Deforestation, or cutting down forests without replanting, is another way in which topsoil is lost. When the tree roots are no longer there to hold the soil, wind and water can carry the soil away. Many rain forests, such as the Amazon rain forest, are being cut down at high rates. This has raised concerns because the forests support the water cycle and help replace the oxygen in the atmosphere. Forests also are home to many kinds of plants and animals. D

Reading Check **Identifying Central Issues** Why is deforestation a problem?

NATIONAL GEOGRAPHIC

Figure 7 **The Greenhouse Effect**

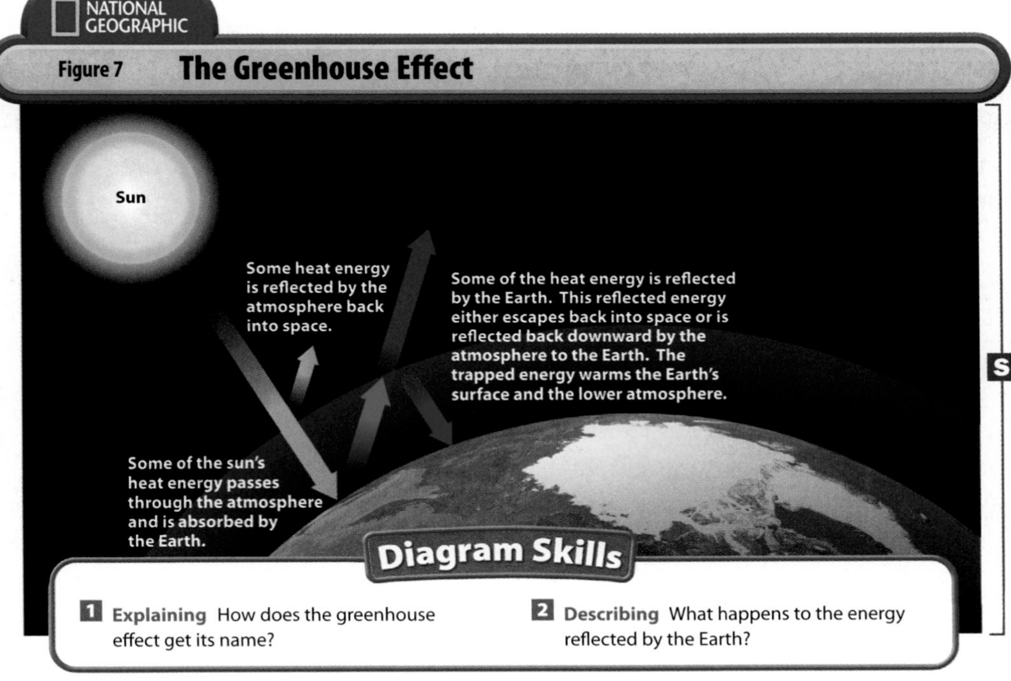

Sun
Some heat energy is reflected by the atmosphere back into space.
Some of the heat energy is reflected by the Earth. This reflected energy either escapes back into space or is reflected back downward by the atmosphere to the Earth. The trapped energy warms the Earth's surface and the lower atmosphere.
Some of the sun's heat energy passes through the atmosphere and is absorbed by the Earth.

S

Diagram Skills

1. **Explaining** How does the greenhouse effect get its name?
2. **Describing** What happens to the energy reflected by the Earth?

C Critical Thinking

Analyzing Information **Ask:** **Where is the lithosphere located?** *(It is the top layer of the Earth.)* **OL**

D Differentiated Instruction

Verbal/Linguistic Have students read stories about deforestation in South America, such as *The Great Kapok Tree* by Lynne Cherry. Then have them write a poem about the loss of the rain forest. **OL**

S Skill Practice

Visual Literacy **Ask:** **What do you think would happen to the Earth's temperature without the greenhouse effect?** *(the Earth's temperature would be much colder)* **AL**

Reading Check **Answer:** Tree roots no longer hold soil, so wind and water can carry it away; forests support the water cycle and help replace oxygen.

Diagram Skills

Answers:

1. The atmosphere reflects the sun's energy like a greenhouse.
2. It escapes into space or is reflected back down by the atmosphere.

Hands-On Chapter Project Step 4

Capturing Your Region on Postcards

Step 4: Depicting Human-Environment Interaction Student pairs will design a fourth postcard showing an example of how people affect the environment in the region. Then students will finish their series of postcards.

Directions Have partners scan Section 4 and discuss how human activities affect the environment in the region in which they live. Tell students to identify an environmental problem caused by people in their region and its possible solution(s) to present on their fourth postcard. Suggest that students design a postcard that either illustrates the problem and solution(s) on the front with a short description on the back or shows only the problem on the front and describes possible solutions in a short paragraph on the back. When students have completed their final design, direct them to finish their cards.

Putting It Together Invite student partners to present their postcard series to the rest of the class. Ask students to explain why they chose these subjects to represent the geographic characteristics of the region. **OL**

(Chapter Project cont. on the Visual Summary page)

D Differentiated Instruction

Naturalist Have students study the biosphere of their neighborhood by observing the plants and animals outdoors and using library resources. Then have them interview someone who has lived in the area for a long time to find out what changes the resident has seen over the years. Ask students to describe how their neighborhood has changed and identify any threatened plants or animals in their region. **OL**

Reading Check Answer: because the supply of freshwater is limited

Assess

Social Studies ONLINE
Study Central™ provides summaries, interactive games, and online graphic organizers to help students review content.

Close

Categorizing Have students identify one environmental problem and paraphrase the information given about it in the text. **OL**

The Hydrosphere and Biosphere

Main Idea Water pollution poses a threat to a vital and limited resource.

Geography and You How much water do you use each day? How much of that water is wasted? Read to find out how people use water resources.

The hydrosphere refers to the Earth's surface water and groundwater. Water is vital to human life. Because the amount of freshwater is limited, people should practice **conservation**, the careful use of a resource, to avoid wasting water.

Throughout the world, farmers use **irrigation**, a process in which water is collected and distributed to crops. Irrigation is often wasteful, however, as much of the water evaporates or soaks into the ground before it reaches the crops. Pollution also threatens water supplies. Chemicals from industrial processes sometimes spill into waterways. **Pesticides**, or powerful chemicals that farmers use to kill crop-destroying insects, can also be harmful.

The biosphere is the collection of plants and animals of all types that live on Earth. The entire biosphere is divided into many **ecosystems.** An ecosystem is a place shared by plants and animals that depend on one another for survival. **D**

Shrinking **biodiversity**, or the variety of plants and animals living on the planet, is also a concern. Changes to the environment can lead to decreasing populations of plants and animals in an ecosystem.

Reading Check **Explaining** Why is the conservation of water important?

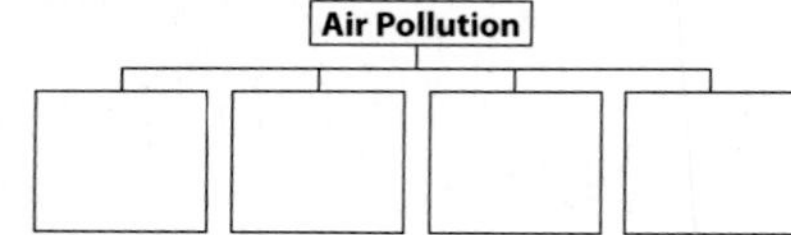

Social Studies ONLINE
Study Central™ To review this section, go to glencoe.com.

Vocabulary

1. **Explain** the significance of
   a. smog
   b. acid rain
   c. greenhouse effect
   d. crop rotation
   e. deforestation
   f. conservation
   g. irrigation
   h. pesticide
   i. ecosystem
   j. biodiversity

Main Ideas

2. **Organizing** Use a diagram like the one below to identify problems related to air pollution.

Air Pollution
[ ] [ ] [ ] [ ]

3. **Explaining** How do contour plowing and crop rotation preserve topsoil?
4. **Identifying** What is the biosphere?

Critical Thinking

5. **BIG Idea** What might happen to the animals of the rain forest if large areas of trees are cut down? Why?
6. **Challenge** Do you think countries should cooperate to solve problems like air and water pollution? Why?

Writing About Geography

7. **Persuasive Writing** Write a brief essay identifying the environmental issue you think is most important and what people can do about it.

Answers

1. Sentences should use vocabulary words according to their definitions in the section and Glossary.
2. Students' diagrams might include the following problems: breathing problems, destruction of forests and buildings, killing of fish, skin cancer.
3. Contour plowing keeps topsoil from washing away by moving along the curve of the land instead of in straight lines; crop rotation preserves topsoil by changing what is planted from year to year.
4. the collection of plants and animals of all types that live on Earth
5. The animals of the rain forest might become extinct. The animals will no longer have a habitat, or place to live.
6. Possible response: Yes; both have a global impact and are difficult to solve without international cooperation.
7. Students' essays should identify a current environmental issue, explain its importance, and propose solutions.

Visual Summary

Inside the Earth

- Earth has four layers: the inner and outer cores, the mantle, and the crust.
- The continents are on large plates that move.
- Plates colliding or pulling apart reshape the land.

Shaping Landforms

- Water, chemicals, and plants break rock apart into smaller pieces.
- Water, wind, and ice can cause erosion.

Windstorm in West Africa

Types of Landforms

- Mountains, plateaus, valleys, and other landforms are found on land and under oceans.
- Climate and availability of resources affect where humans settle.

The Water Planet

- About 70 percent of the Earth's surface is water.
- In a process called the water cycle, water travels from the oceans to the air to the ground and back to the oceans.

Boaters on Inle Lake, South Asia

Climate

- Climate is the usual pattern of weather over a long period of time.
- Sun, winds, ocean currents, landforms, and latitude affect climate.
- Geographers divide the world into different climate zones.

AREA
BEYOND
THIS
SIGN
CLOSED
All public entry prohibited
By Foot, Bike, Or Vehicle
Violations Punishable

Hawk in protected area, United States

Humans and the Environment

- A delicate balance exists among the Earth's atmosphere, lithosphere, hydrosphere, and biosphere.
- Human actions, such as burning fuels and clearing rain forests, affect the environment.

Hills in Italy

Study anywhere, anytime! Download quizzes and flash cards to your PDA from glencoe.com.

Visual Summary

Analyzing Ask student volunteers to read aloud the last two bulleted points in the Visual Summary. Create a chart on the board with atmosphere, lithosphere, hydrosphere, and biosphere as headings. Ask students to define each of these terms.

Lead a class discussion about how human actions can affect the environment. As students name each human action, have them indicate which part of the environment (atmosphere, lithosphere, hydrosphere, or biosphere) would be affected. Write their responses under the correct heading in the chart.

Conclude the discussion by asking students to think of ways that they themselves affect the environment and what steps they can take to help protect the environment. **OL**

Identifying the Main Idea Instruct students to use the headings in the Visual Summary to write main idea sentences that fit the chapter content. Model the process by changing "Inside the Earth" to "Earth has many layers and plates that move." **OL**

This **Reading Skill** (Identifying the Main Idea) was introduced in this unit.

Hands-On Chapter Project

Step 5: Wrap Up

Capturing Your Region on Postcards

Step 5: Learning From the Project Students will synthesize what they have learned in Steps 1–4.

Directions Write the Essential Question on the board. Underline the phrase *define the region* in the question. Then challenge student pairs to offer a "definition" of the geography of the region based on what they learned while creating their postcards. Tell students that their geographic definition of the region should name and describe its defining, or major, landforms and water features, summarize its climate, and provide at least one example of human-environment interaction. Allow time for each student pair to share its definition with the rest of the class. Then tell students to respond to the Essential Question individually in their journals. **OL**

Answers and Analyses

Reviewing Vocabulary

1. C All of the answer choices have to do with the Earth's makeup, but only *plate tectonics* explains how the continents formed and were distributed. Plate tectonics, or shifting plates, are the cause of the breakup of the continents from their original form, Pangaea.

2. B All of the answer choices begin with word *continental*, which might confuse students. If students focus on the next term in each choice, they will see that two answer choices are obviously wrong. Answer choice A contains the term *aquifer*, which is water under the ground. Answer choice C contains the phrase *water cycle*, which would not make sense as part of an ocean. The last choice may seem reasonable to some students, but remind them that a trench occurs where plates meet, not off the coast of continents.

3. A This question may prove challenging to some because more than one answer choice seems to fit the question. However, careful analysis of the answer choices shows that only answer choice A can be correct. A *biome* is part of a climate zone and includes plants and animals, and although *El Niño* is a weather pattern, it is not a permanent pattern.

4. D The greenhouse effect occurs regardless of air pollution. The ozone layer already exists, and chlorofluorocarbons are the chemicals, not the combination of chemicals and precipitation.

Reviewing Main Ideas

5. A A visual may help students recall the answer to this question. If necessary, students can sketch and label the layers of the Earth. In doing so, they may recall that the crust surrounds the mantle, and the mantle surrounds the core.

CHAPTER 2

STANDARDIZED TEST PRACTICE

TEST-TAKING TIP

As you read the first part of a multiple-choice question, try to anticipate the answer before you look at the choices. If your answer is one of the choices, it is probably correct.

Reviewing Vocabulary

Directions: Choose the word(s) that best completes the sentence.

1. The theory of _______ explains how continents were formed and why they move.

A magma formation
B erosion
C plate tectonics
D mantle disbursement

2. A plateau called a _______ lies off the coast of each continent and stretches for several miles underwater.

A continental aquifer
B continental shelf
C continental water cycle
D continental trench

3. Areas that have similar patterns of temperature and precipitation are known as _______.

A climate zones
B biomes
C El Niño
D currents

4. Chemicals in air pollution can combine with precipitation to form _______.

A chlorofluorocarbons
B the ozone layer
C the greenhouse effect
D acid rain

Reviewing Main Ideas

Directions: Choose the best answer for each question.

Section 1 *(pp. 44–48)*

5. Surrounding Earth's core is a layer of hot, dense rock called the _______.

A mantle
B crust
C magma
D core

Section 2 *(pp. 49–54)*

6. Almost 97 percent of the planet's water is _______.

A groundwater
B freshwater
C salt water
D frozen in glaciers and ice sheets

Section 3 *(pp. 55–61)*

7. The usual, predictable patterns of weather in an area over many years are called _______.

A climate
B current
C El Niño
D biome

Section 4 *(pp. 63–66)*

8. The careful use of resources to avoid wasting them is called _______.

A deforestation
B biodiversity
C irrigation
D conservation

GO ON

6. C Students might recall from their reading that freshwater is vital and not as available as salt water. If students do not recall the reading, they can draw on prior knowledge of oceans. Students might know that ocean water is salty. In picturing a globe, they can see that oceans cover much of the Earth.

7. A Process of elimination will help students answer this question. The only answer left is answer A, *climate*. El Niño is an unusual phenomenon. Biomes and currents do not refer to weather patterns.

Critical Thinking

Directions: Base your answers to questions 9 and 10 on the map below and your knowledge of Chapter 2. Choose the best answer for each question.

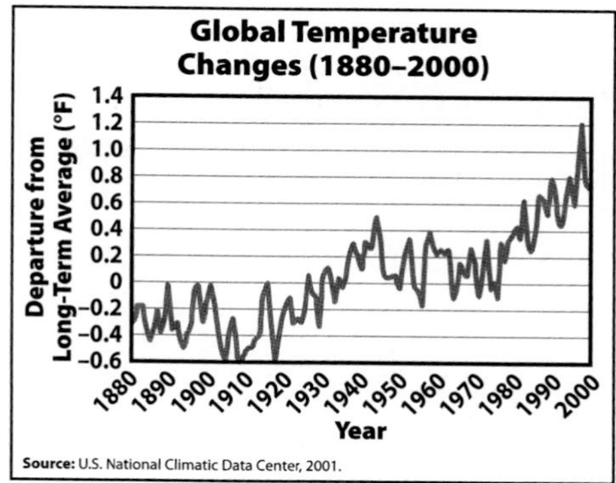

Source: U.S. National Climatic Data Center, 2001.

9. What is the overall trend of global temperature change in the twentieth century?

A There has been a stable or flat trend throughout the century.

B There has been an overall upward trend.

C There has been an overall downward trend.

D There was an upward trend early in the century followed by a downward trend.

10. During what twenty-year period of time did the sharpest rise in global temperatures take place?

A 1880–1900

B 1910–1930

C 1950–1970

D 1980–2000

Document-Based Questions

Directions: Analyze the document and answer the short-answer questions that follow.

> *Under the Kyoto Protocol, industrialized countries are to reduce their combined emissions of six major greenhouse gases during the five-year period 2008–2012 to below 1990 levels. The European Union, for example, is to cut its combined emissions by eight percent, while Japan should reduce emissions by six percent. For many countries, achieving the Kyoto targets will be a major challenge that will require new policies and new approaches. . . .*
>
> *Developing countries, including Brazil, China, India and Indonesia, are also Parties to the Protocol but do not have emission reduction targets. Many developing countries have already demonstrated success in addressing climate change.*
>
> *—UNEP, "Kyoto Protocol to Enter into Force 16 February 2005"*

11. According to this press release, what is the purpose of the Kyoto Protocol?

12. Compare how industrialized and developing countries would be affected by the Kyoto Protocol.

Extended Response

13. Which part of Earth's environment—the atmosphere, lithosphere, hydrosphere, or biosphere—do you feel is most threatened by human activity? In several paragraphs, define the part that you chose, explain why you think it is threatened, and describe what actions may help decrease the threat to that area.

Social Studies ONLINE
For additional test practice, use Self-Check Quizzes—Chapter 2 at glencoe.com.

Need Extra Help?

If you missed question. . .	1	2	3	4	5	6	7	8	9	10	11	12	13
Go to page. . .	46	50	59	64	45	52	56	66	64	64	64	64	64

10. B Students will need to look for the highest and lowest points in each group to determine the answer. The answer is not looking for a single spike, but the change from beginning to end.

Document-Based Questions

11. The purpose is to reduce collective emissions of greenhouse gases from six countries.

12. Industrialized countries are to reduce emissions to pre-1990 levels. Developing countries do not have emission reduction targets, and have already demonstrated success at addressing climate charge.

Extended Response

13. Answers will vary, but students' responses should reflect an understanding of how human activity threatens a specific part of the Earth's environment, as well as suggestions for changing that trend.

8. B The key words in the question are *avoid wasting*. In looking at the answer choices, students will see that one answer choice is negative: A, *deforestation*. If they still struggle, have them break words down to their roots. *Conserve* means "to keep safe."

Critical Thinking

9. B To answer this question correctly, students need to clue in to the overall, or complete, trend. Suggest that they follow the mid point of each high and low with their finger in a gently sloping line. This should help them see that the trend moves upward over time.

Social Studies ONLINE
Have students visit the Web site at glencoe.com to review Chapter 2 and take the Self-Check Quiz.

Need Extra Help?
Have students refer to the pages listed if they miss any of the questions.

Planning Guide

Key to Ability Levels

- **BL** Below level
- **OL** On level
- **AL** Above level
- **ELL** English Language Learners

Key to Teaching Resources

- Print Material
- DVD
- CD-ROM
- Transparency

Levels				Resources	Chapter Opener	Section 1	Section 2	Section 3	Chapter Assess
BL	OL	AL	ELL						
FOCUS									
BL	OL	AL	ELL	Daily Focus Skills Transparencies		3-1	3-2	3-3	
TEACH									
BL	OL		ELL	Guided Reading Activity, URB*		p. 81	p. 82	p. 83	
BL	OL	AL	ELL	Content Vocabulary Activity, URB*		p. 85	p. 85	p. 85	
BL	OL	AL	ELL	Academic Vocabulary Activity, URB		p. 87	p. 87	p. 87	
BL	OL	AL	ELL	Differentiated Instruction Activity, URB			p. 89		
BL	OL	AL	ELL	Chart, Graph, and Map Skills Activity, URB		p. 91		p. 91	
	OL	AL		Critical Thinking Activity, URB		p. 93		p. 93	
BL	OL	AL	ELL	Speaking and Listening Skills Activity, URB		p. 95			
BL	OL	AL	ELL	Writing Skills Activity, URB				p. 99	
BL	OL	AL	ELL	School-to-Home Connection Activity, URB*		p. 103	p. 103	p. 103	
BL	OL	AL	ELL	Regional Atlas Activities, URB		pp. 1–7	pp. 1–7	pp. 1–7	
		AL		Geography and Economics Activity, URB				p. 5	
	OL	AL		Geography and History Activity, URB			p. 7		
BL	OL		ELL	Time Line Activity, URB	p. 13				
		AL		Enrichment Activity, URB			p. 15		
	OL	AL		World Literature Reading, URB			p. 27		
BL	OL		ELL	Reading Essentials and Note-Taking Guide*		p. 19	p. 22	p. 25	
	OL	AL		TIME Perspectives: Exploring World Issues		p. 1			
	OL			Interactive Geography Activity	p. 1		p. 1		
BL	OL	AL	ELL	In-Text Map Overlay and Population Pyramid Transparencies	1	1A	1B, 1F		
	OL			Foods Around the World			pp. 2–5	p. 2	
BL	OL	AL	ELL	Outline Map Resource Book	p. 59				
BL	OL	AL	ELL	NGS World Atlas*	✓	✓	✓	✓	
BL	OL	AL	ELL	NGS World Desk Map	✓	✓	✓	✓	✓

Note: Please refer to the *Unit Resource Book: The World* for this chapter's URB materials.

* Also available in Spanish

- Interactive Lesson Planner
- Interactive Teacher Edition
- Fully editable blackline masters
- Section Spotlight Videos Launch
- Differentiated Lesson Plans
- Printable reports of daily assignments
- Standards Tracking System

Levels				Resources	Chapter Opener	Section 1	Section 2	Section 3	Chapter Assess
BL	OL	AL	ELL						
TEACH *(continued)*									
BL	OL	AL	ELL	World Literature Library	✓	✓	✓	✓	✓
BL	OL	AL	ELL	Writer's Guidebook	✓	✓	✓	✓	✓
BL	OL	AL	ELL	Vocabulary PuzzleMaker CD-ROM*	✓	✓	✓	✓	✓
	OL	AL		Primary Sources CD-ROM	✓	✓	✓	✓	✓
BL	OL	AL	ELL	StudentWorks™ Plus DVD	✓	✓	✓	✓	✓
BL	OL	AL	ELL	Section Video Program Activities	✓	✓	✓	✓	✓
BL	OL	AL	ELL	World Music: A Cultural Legacy	✓	✓	✓	✓	✓
BL	OL	AL	ELL	Writing Process Transparencies	✓	✓	✓	✓	✓
Teacher Resources				Building Academic Vocabulary	✓	✓	✓	✓	✓
				Strategies for Success	✓	✓	✓	✓	✓
				Teacher's Guide to Differentiated Instruction	✓	✓	✓	✓	✓
				Presentation Plus! DVD	✓	✓	✓	✓	✓
ASSESS									
BL	OL	AL	ELL	Quizzes and Tests		p. 25	p. 26	p. 27	p. 29
BL	OL	AL	ELL	Authentic Assessment With Rubrics				p. 3	p. 3
BL	OL	AL	ELL	Standardized Test Practice					p. 9
BL	OL	AL	ELL	*ExamView® Assessment Suite* CD-ROM*		3-1	3-2	3-3	Ch. 3
BL	OL	AL	ELL	Interactive Tutor Self-Assessment CD-ROM		3-1	3-2	3-3	
CLOSE									
BL			ELL	Reteaching Activity, URB		p. 101	p. 101	p. 101	p. 101
BL	OL		ELL	Reading and Study Skills Foldables™	p. 54	p. 54	p. 54	p. 54	p. 54
BL	OL	AL	ELL	Graphic Organizer Transparencies and Strategies		✓	✓	✓	
BL	OL	AL	ELL	*Exploring Our World* in Graphic Novel					p. 1

Integrating Technology

Using ExamView® Assessment Suite

Quick Test

Technology Product

Glencoe's *ExamView® Assessment Suite* CD-ROM includes powerful assessment tools and enables you to quickly create, adapt, and assess tests for your students.

ExamView® allows you to

- develop online testing materials that focus on the specific skills and competencies of what has been taught in the classroom;
- create several versions of these test materials that are adjusted to meet the different ability levels of your students;
- provide a variety of test formats, including Multiple Choice, True/False, Yes/No, Matching, Completion (Fill-in-the-Blank), and Numeric Response.

Steps

- Open the *ExamView®* Test Generator.
- Select **Create a new test using the QuickTest Wizard** and click **OK.**
- Name the test you are creating.
- From the list, select the *Chapter Banks* you would like to use. Click **Next.**
- Indicate the number of questions you want per question type. Click **Next.**
- Enter the number of matching groups. Click **Next.**
- Verify summary of selections and Click **Finish.**
- The *QuickTest Wizard* will build your test. Print the test or save it for students to take the test on a computer using the Internet.

Social Studies ONLINE

	Student	Teacher	Parent
Beyond the Textbook	●		●
Chapter Overviews	●		●
Concepts in Motion	●		●
ePuzzles and Games	●		●
Literature Connections		●	
Multi-Language Glossaries	●		●
Online Student Edition	●	●	●
Section Videos	●	●	●
Self-Check Quizzes	●		●
Student Web Activities	●		●
Study Central™	●		●
Teaching Today		●	
TIME Current Events	●		●
Vocabulary eFlashcards	●		●
Web Activity Lesson Plans		●	

- **Timed Readings Plus in Social Studies** helps students increase their reading rate and fluency while maintaining comprehension. The 400-word passages are similar to those found on state and national assessments.
- **Reading in the Content Area: Social Studies** concentrates on six essential reading skills that help students better comprehend what they read. The book includes 75 high-interest nonfiction passages written at increasing levels of difficulty.
- **Reading Social Studies** includes strategic reading instruction and vocabulary support in Social Studies content for ELLs and native speakers of English.
- **Content Vocabulary Workout** (Grades 6–8) accelerates reading comprehension through focused vocabulary development. Social Studies content vocabulary comes from the glossaries of Glencoe's Middle School Social Studies texts.
  www.jamestowneducation.com

Index to National Geographic Magazine:

The following articles relate to this chapter:

- "The Greatest Journey," by James Shreeve, March 2006.
- "Future Power: Where Will the World Get Its Next Fix?" by Michael Parfit, August 2005.

National Geographic Society Products To order the following, call National Geographic at 1-800-368-2728:

- *National Geographic Atlas of the World* (Book).

Access National Geographic's new dynamic MapMachine Web site and other geography resources at:
www.nationalgeographic.com
www.nationalgeographic.com/maps

GLENCOE **BOOKLINK 3**

Use this database to search more than 30,000 titles to create a customized reading list for your students.

- Reading lists can be organized by students' reading level, author, genre, theme, or area of interest.
- The database provides Degrees of Reading Power™ (DRP) and Lexile™ readability scores for all selections.
- A brief summary of each selection is included.

Leveled reading suggestions for this chapter:

For students at a Grade 5 reading level:

- ***It's My Earth, Too: How I Can Help the Earth Stay Alive?*** by Kathleen Krull
- ***Journey of the Red-Eyed Tree Frog,*** by Tanis Jordan

For students at a Grade 6 reading level:

- ***Rachel Carson,*** by William Accorsi
- ***Recycle Every Day!,*** by Nancy Elizabeth Wallace
- ***Protecting Rivers and Seas,*** by Kamini Khanduri

For students at a Grade 7 reading level:

- ***Let's Look After Our World,*** by Diana Noonan & Keith Olsen
- ***Air Pollution,*** by Darlene R. Stille
- ***Rain Forest Secrets,*** by Arthur Dorros

For students at a Grade 8 reading level:

- ***Will We Miss Them?: Endangered Species,*** by Alexandra Wright
- ***Pollution,*** by Janine Amos
- ***Coal,*** by John Cranfield & David Buckman

For students at a Grade 9 reading level:

- ***The Dangers of Noise,*** by Lucy Kavaler
- ***Future Sources of Energy,*** by Mark Lambert
- ***Vanishing Forests,*** by Lim Cheng Puay

Focus

The Essential Question

As students study the chapter, remind them to consider the chapter-based Essential Question. Answering this question will help them understand the important concepts in the chapter. In addition, the Hands-On Chapter Project relates the content from each section to the Essential Question. The steps in each section build on each other as students progress through the chapter. The Hands-On Chapter Project culminates in the Wrap Up activity on the Visual Summary page.

More About the Photo

Visual Literacy The Damnoen Saduak Floating Market is a popular tourist attraction in Thailand. The market is about 2 hours from Bangkok. The fertile soils along its canals provide rich farmland for the people who live in surrounding rural areas. The canals serve as a marketplace for the foods grown in local gardens and orchards. Tourists use boats to navigate the waterways and buy produce from boat vendors, or they stroll the walkways along the canals.

CHAPTER 3

Earth's Human and Cultural Geography

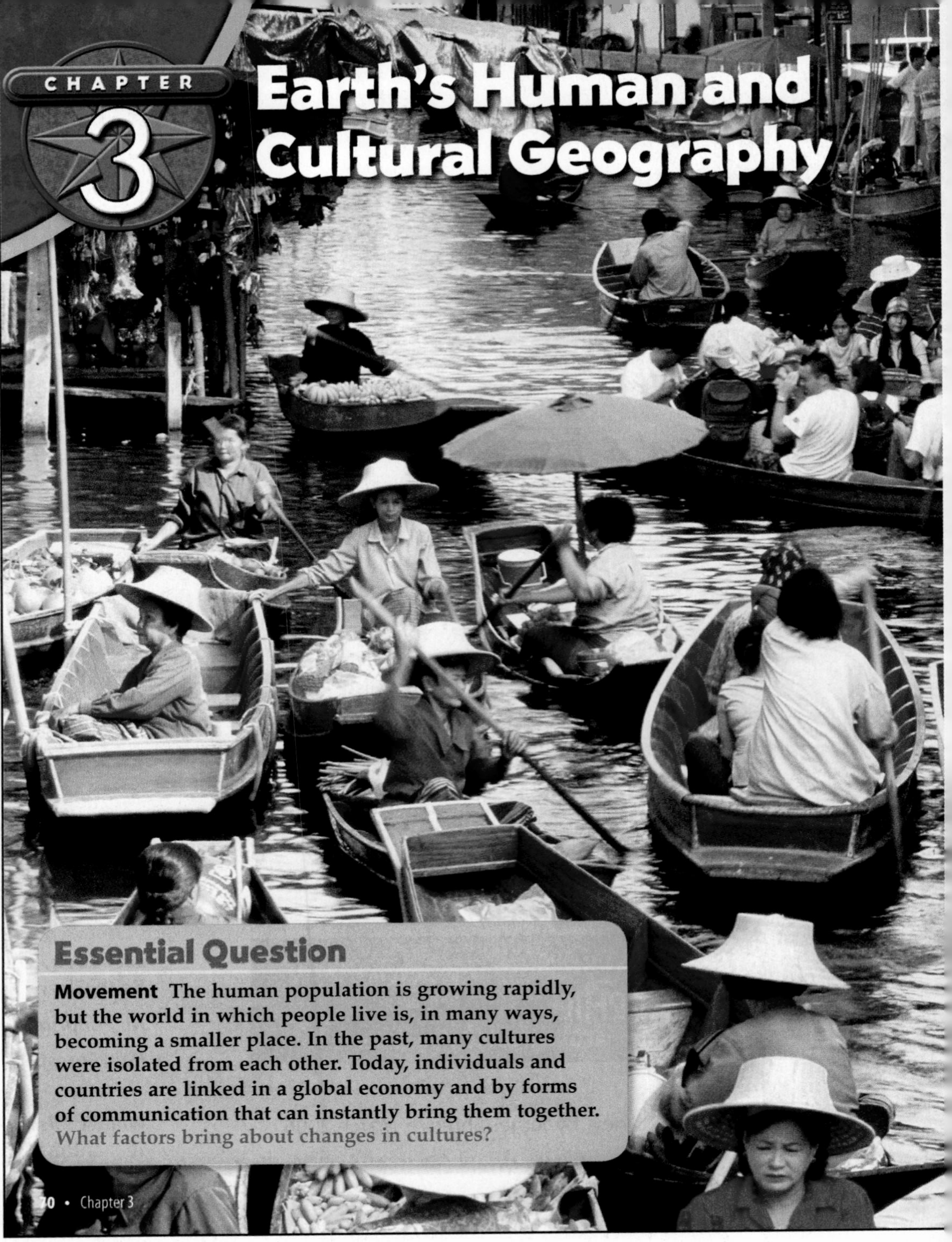

Essential Question

Movement The human population is growing rapidly, but the world in which people live is, in many ways, becoming a smaller place. In the past, many cultures were isolated from each other. Today, individuals and countries are linked in a global economy and by forms of communication that can instantly bring them together. What factors bring about changes in cultures?

70 • Chapter 3

Teach

The BIG Ideas *As you begin teaching each section, use these questions and activities to help students focus on the Big Ideas.*

Section 

World Population Ask: How can you tell that an area's population is growing? *(Possible answers: new construction, increased traffic, more students in school)* **What might be some effects of an increase in world population?** *(Answers may include bigger cities; growth of residential areas, schools, and workplaces; increased need for food, and increased pollution and environmental issues.)* Point out to students that Section 1 explains the world population growth rates, the distribution of people in the world, and the migration patterns of people. It also explains the effects of migration and world population growth. **OL**

Section 

Global Cultures Ask: What factors do you think influence cultures in different parts of the world? *(Answers may include education, government, social roles, location, history, climate, and technology.)* Tell students that Section 2 details cultural regions around the world. It also explains the elements of culture and how cultures influence each other and contribute to globalization. **OL**

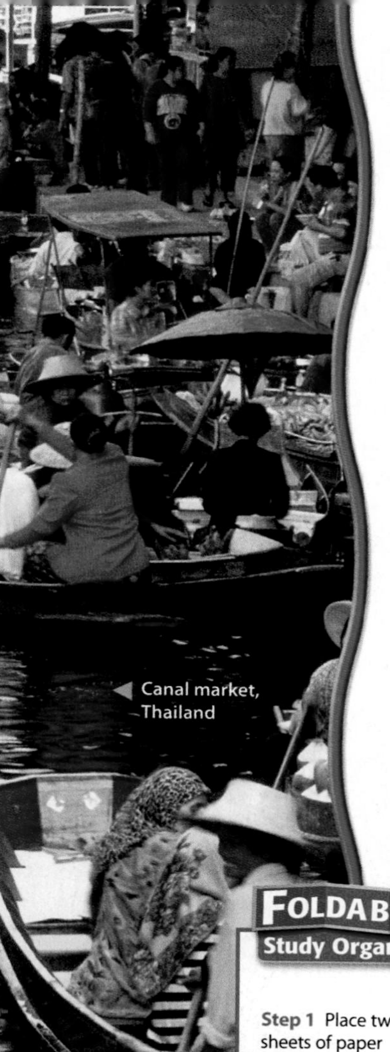

Canal market, Thailand

BIG Ideas

Section 1: World Population

BIG IDEA Geographers study how people and physical features are distributed on Earth's surface. Although the world's population is increasing, people still live on only a small part of the Earth's surface.

Section 2: Global Cultures

BIG IDEA Culture influences people's perceptions about places and regions. The world's population is made up of different cultures, each of which is based on common beliefs, customs, and traits.

Section 3: Resources, Technology, and World Trade

BIG IDEA Patterns of economic activities result in global interdependence. Because resources are unevenly distributed, the nations of the world must trade with each other. New technologies make the economies of nations more dependent on one another.

FOLDABLES™ Study Organizer

Categorizing Information Make this Foldable to organize information about Earth's population; cultures; and resources, technology, and trade.

Step 1 Place two sheets of paper about 1 inch apart.

Step 2 Fold the paper to form four equal tabs.

Step 3 Staple the sheets, and label each tab as shown.

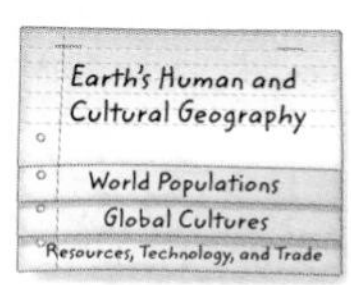

Reading and Writing As you read the chapter, take notes under the appropriate tab. Write a main idea for each section using your Foldable.

Social Studies ONLINE

To preview Chapter 3, go to glencoe.com.

Previewing the Region

If you have not already done so, engage students in the Regional Atlas and chart activities to help them become familiar with the general content of the region.

FOLDABLES Study Organizer **Dinah Zike's Foldables**

Purpose This Foldable helps students categorize facts about Earth's population, cultures, and resources, technology, and trade. Students should note facts from each section under the appropriate tab. Then they should use their notes to write a main idea for each section. Completed Foldables can be used to prepare for assessment. **OL**

More Foldables activities for this chapter can be found in *Dinah Zike's Reading and Study Skills Foldables* ancillary.

Social Studies ONLINE

Introduce students to chapter content and key terms by having them access the Chapter Overview at glencoe.com.

Section 3

Resources, Technology, and World Trade Ask: What might be some advantages and disadvantages of international trade? *(Possible answers: advantages—a variety of products, access to important resources, low prices because of competition; disadvantages—interdependence of countries, job insecurities, loss of individual customs and traditions, smaller companies put out of business)* Point out to students that in Section 3, they will learn about trade among countries and its effects, including increased globalization. The section also discusses factors that affect trade, such as global resources, technology, national legislation, and economic systems. **OL**

Focus

Bellringer

Daily Focus Transparency 3-1

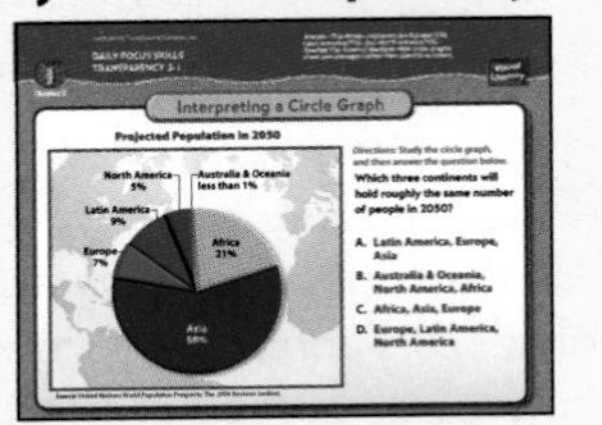

Guide to Reading

Answers to Graphic:

Answers may include:
Causes: shortage of farmland, few jobs in homeland
Effects: population decrease in homeland, population increase in new land, division of families, negative economic effects, violence among ethnic groups, increased diversity in new land

Section Spotlight Video

To learn more about the world's population, have students watch the Section Spotlight Video.

Guide to Reading

BIG Idea

Geographers study how people and physical features are distributed on Earth's surface.

Content Vocabulary

- death rate *(p. 73)*
- birthrate *(p. 73)*
- famine *(p. 73)*
- population density *(p. 74)*
- urbanization *(p. 75)*
- emigrate *(p. 75)*
- refugee *(p. 76)*

Academic Vocabulary

- technology *(p. 73)*
- internal *(p. 75)*

Reading Strategy

Determining Cause and Effect Use a diagram like the one below to show the causes and effects of global migration.

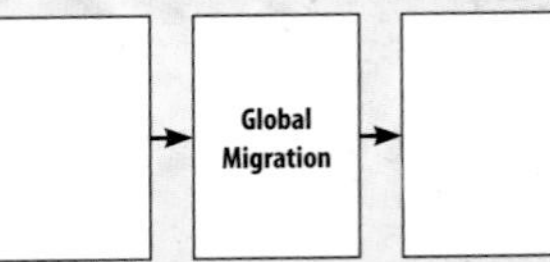

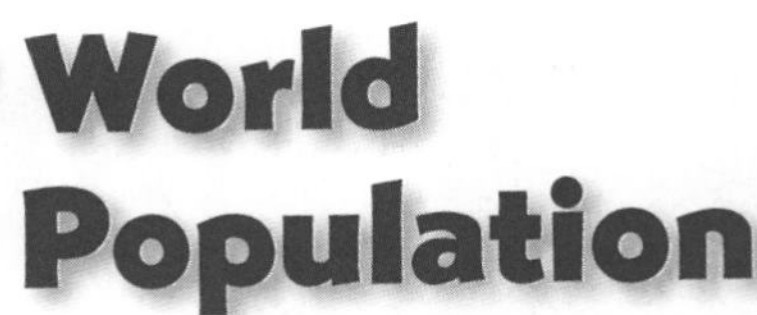

SECTION 1 World Population

Picture This Forty years ago, for every car in China, there were 250 bicycles, earning the country the nickname "Bicycle Kingdom." Today, however, China, which is the world's most populous country, has a new love—the automobile. People are earning more money, and the number of people who own cars is increasing. Because of this, it is feared that China's cities will become more polluted and congested with traffic. Read this section to learn about the world's population and the effects it has on the Earth.

▼ Residents of Shanghai, China

Resource Manager

R Reading Strategies	C Critical Thinking	D Differentiated Instruction	W Writing Support	S Skill Practice
Teacher Edition • Questioning, p. 75 • Identifying, p. 76 **Additional Resources** • Guid. Read., URB p. 81 • Cont. Vocab., URB p. 85 • Ac. Vocab., URB p. 87 • Read. Ess., p. 19	**Teacher Edition** • Predicting, p. 73 **Additional Resources** • Crit. Think., URB p. 93 • Quizzes and Tests, p. 25	**Teacher Edition** • Visual/Spatial, p. 74 • EL, p. 75 **Additional Resources** • Reteach., URB p. 101 • School-to-Home Conn., URB p. 103	**Teacher Edition** • Narrative Writing, p. 75 • Personal Writing, p. 76	**Teacher Edition** • Visual Literacy, p. 73 • Using Geo. Skills, p. 74 **Additional Resources** • Speak./Listen. Skills, URB p. 95 • Chart, Graph, and Map Skills, URB p. 91 • Daily Focus Trans. 3-1 • Reg. Atlas, URB pp. 1–7

Population Growth

Main Idea **The world's population has increased rapidly in the past two centuries, creating many new challenges.**

Geography and You Has the population in your community increased or decreased in recent years? Are new schools being built, for example? Read to find out why the world's population has grown so fast.

In the past 200 years, the world's population has increased rapidly. Around 1800, a billion people lived on Earth. Today the population is more than 6 billion.

Reasons for Population Growth

One reason the population has grown so fast in the last 200 years is that the death rate has gone down. The **death rate** is the number of deaths per year for every 1,000 people. Better health care and living conditions, as well as more plentiful food supplies, have decreased the death rate.

Another reason why the population has grown is high birthrates in Asia, Africa, and Latin America. The **birthrate** is the number of children born each year for every 1,000 people. High numbers of healthy births combined with lower death rates have increased the population growth, especially in these areas of the world.

Challenges of Population Growth

More food is needed for a growing population. Advances in **technology,** such as improved irrigation systems and the creation of hardier plants, will continue to increase food production. On the other hand, warfare and crop failures can lead to **famine,** or a severe lack of food. Some countries may also face shortages of water and housing. Additionally, growing populations require more services, like those provided by hospitals and schools. C

Reading Check **Identifying** What has caused population growth in the last 200 years?

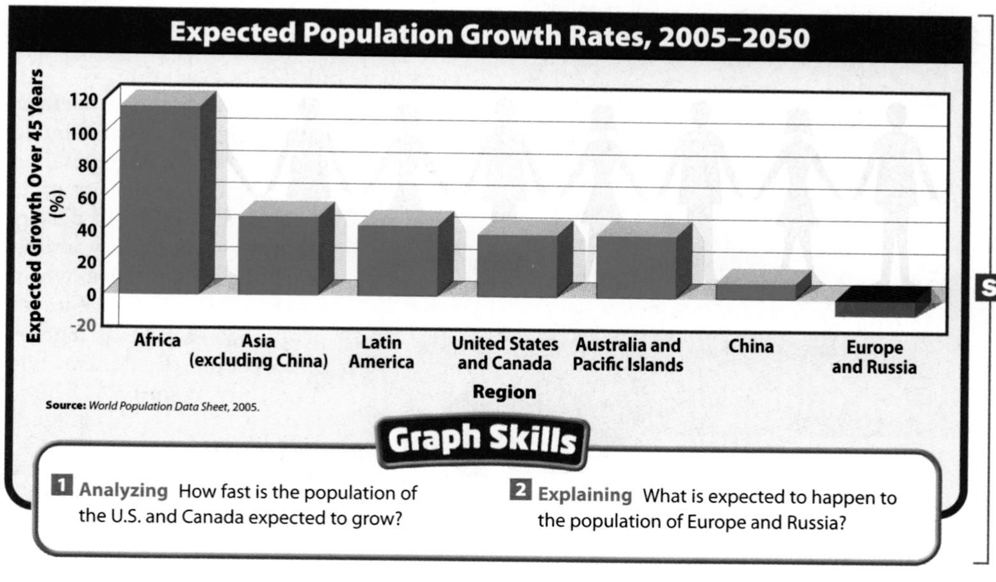

Source: *World Population Data Sheet, 2005.*

Graph Skills

1. **Analyzing** How fast is the population of the U.S. and Canada expected to grow?
2. **Explaining** What is expected to happen to the population of Europe and Russia?

S

Teach

C Critical Thinking

Predicting Ask: How might population growth affect the environment? *(Possible answer: More resources and land will be needed to support more people.)* **OL**

For further practice on this skill (Predicting), see the **Skills Handbook.**

S Skill Practice

Visual Literacy Ask: Which region is expected to have the greatest population growth? *(Africa)* **If China and Asia's population growth are combined, how much increase might there be?** *(about 60%)* **OL**

Reading Check Answer: the decreased death rate worldwide and the increased birthrate in Asia, Africa, and Latin America

Graph Skills

Answers:

1. 40%
2. It is expected to decrease.

Differentiated Instruction

Leveled Activities

BL Reteaching Activity, URB p. 101

AL Critical Thinking Activity, URB p. 93

ELL Guided Reading Activity, URB p. 81

S Skill Practice

Using Geography Skills Have students use a world atlas to find the world's most populated regions. **Ask: What resources in the regions might attract people and industry?** *(Possible answers: rivers, oil)* Then have students look at the areas where few people live. Discuss how the resources there might contribute to low population rates. OL

D Differentiated Instruction

Visual/Spatial Have students use graph paper to find the population density of an imaginary town. Tell students to outline a shape that will be their town, making each square 1 mile. Then have them draw dots in the shape to represent people. Help them use the formula on this page to calculate the population density. OL

Caption Answer:
East Asia, South Asia, Southeast Asia, Europe, and eastern North America

Reading Check Answer: because they live where land is usable and only a very small portion of Earth's land meets this requirement

Where People Live

Main Idea **The Earth's population is not evenly distributed.**

Geography and You Do you live in a city, a suburb, a small town, or a rural area? What are the advantages and disadvantages of your location? Read to find out where the world's people choose to live.

People live on a surprisingly small part of the Earth. Land covers only about 30 percent of the Earth's surface, and only half of this land is usable by humans. Deserts, high mountains, and ice-covered lands cannot support large numbers of people.

Population Distribution

On the usable land, population is not distributed, or spread, evenly. People naturally prefer to live in places that have fertile soil, mild climates, natural resources, and water resources, such as rivers and coastlines. S Two-thirds of the world's people are clustered into five regions with these resources—East Asia, South Asia, Southeast Asia, Europe, and eastern North America. In most regions, more people live in cities than in rural areas because of the jobs and resources found there.

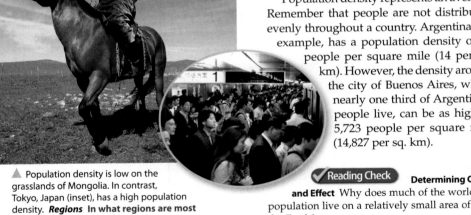

Population Density

NATIONAL GEOGRAPHIC

▲ Population density is low on the grasslands of Mongolia. In contrast, Tokyo, Japan (inset), has a high population density. ***Regions*** **In what regions are most of the world's people clustered?**

Population Density

D Geographers have a way to figure out how crowded a country or region is. They measure **population density**—the average number of people living in a square mile or square kilometer. To arrive at this figure, the total population is divided by the total land area.

As you have just read, the world's population is not evenly distributed. Malaysia and Norway, for example, have about the same total land area, around 130,000 square miles (336,697 sq. km). Norway's population density is about 40 people per square mile (15 per sq. km). Malaysia, on the other hand, has a density of 205 people per square mile (79 per sq. km).

Population density represents an average. Remember that people are not distributed evenly throughout a country. Argentina, for example, has a population density of 36 people per square mile (14 per sq. km). However, the density around the city of Buenos Aires, where nearly one third of Argentina's people live, can be as high as 5,723 people per square mile (14,827 per sq. km).

Reading Check **Determining Cause and Effect** Why does much of the world's population live on a relatively small area of the Earth?

Hands-On Chapter Project Step 1

Creating a Time Line for Your State

Step 1: Researching Your State's History Students will research the history of human settlement in their state in order to create a class time line about their state.

Essential Question What factors bring about changes in cultures?

Directions Ask: Do you know what Native American groups lived in your state? Do you know where the first European settlers to our state came from and when they arrived? Organize students into three or four groups. Assign each group a time period in your state's history. For example, one group could study Native American settlement, another could study the first European settlers, a third could study more recent migration to the area, and the fourth group could study current population trends. Ask each group to learn about the dates of settlement, as well as about the cultural impact of migration to the state. Tell them that they will use this information to create a time line in Step 2.

Summarizing Have each group briefly summarize the important events and cultural elements during their assigned period. OL

(Chapter Project continued in Section 2)

Population Movement

Main Idea **Large numbers of people migrate from one place to another.**

Geography and You Have you and your family ever moved? Read to learn some of the reasons why people all over the world move from one place to another.

Throughout history, millions of people have moved from one place to another. People continue to move today, sometimes as individuals, sometimes in large groups.

Types of Migration

Moving from place to place in the same country is known as **internal** migration. One kind of internal migration is the movement of people from farms and villages to cities. Such migrants are often in search of jobs. This type of movement results in **urbanization**, or the growth of cities. Urbanization has occurred rapidly in Asia, Africa, and Latin America.

Movement between countries is called international migration. Some people **emigrate**, or leave the country where they were born and move to another. They are emigrants in their homeland and immigrants in their new country. **Figure 1** shows the immigrant populations in regions of the world. Immigration has increased greatly in the past 200 years, partly due to better transportation.

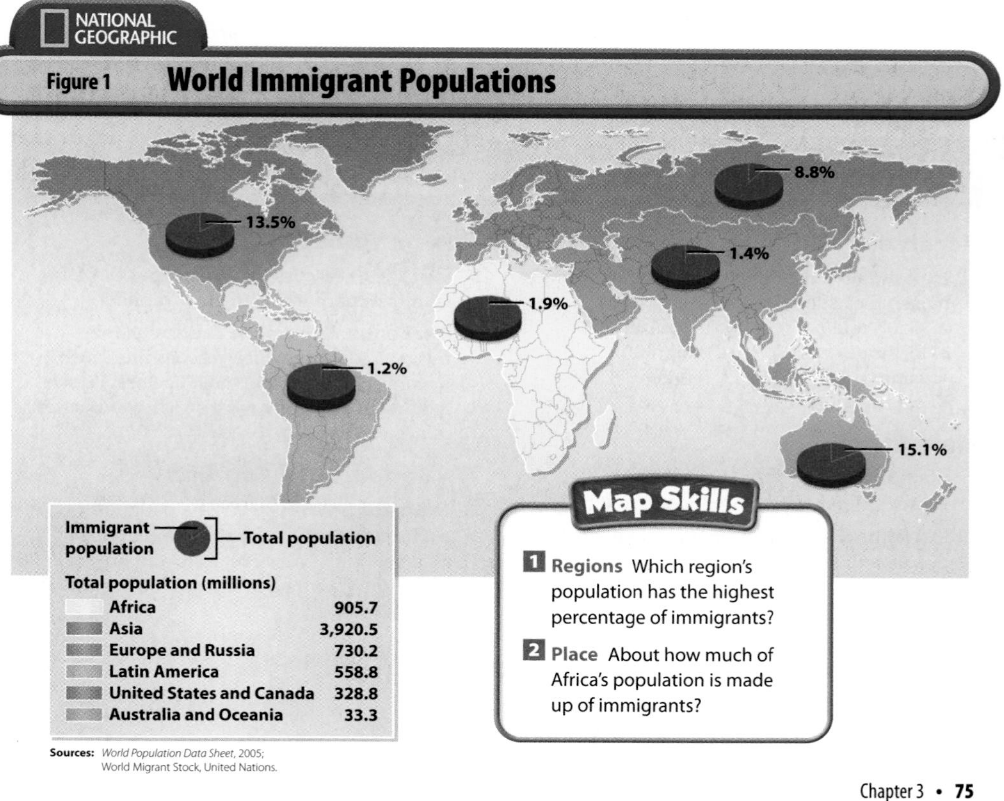

Sources: *World Population Data Sheet*, 2005; World Migrant Stock, United Nations.

R Reading Strategy

Questioning Have students turn the Main Idea into a question, such as "Why do large numbers of people migrate from one place to another?" Have pairs of students take turns reading aloud the subsection to find the answer. BL

W Writing Support

Narrative Writing Have each student write a children's story about moving. The story can be based on students' experiences, or it can be purely fictional. Tell students to include concerns a child might have about life in a new city, state, or country, as well as what might be exciting or interesting about a new place. AL

D Differentiated Instruction

English Learners Students may confuse the terms *emigrant* and *immigrant*. Explain that the term *immigrant* begins with the same letter as the term *into*, and immigrants come "into" a country. Ask students to say a sentence using each term correctly. ELL

Map Skills

Answers:

1. Australia, Oceania, and Antarctica
2. 1.9%

Differentiated Instruction

Conducting an Interview

Speaking and Listening Skills, URB pp. 95–98

Objective: To learn to conduct interviews

Focus: Define and describe an interview for students.

Teach: Have students read the activity and conduct an interview with a partner.

Assess: Assess using the assessment checklist.

Close: Discuss with students how interviews are different from other learning tools.

Differentiated Instruction Strategies

- BL Help students develop questions to ask in an interview.
- AL Ask students what questions they would change in the activity interview and why.
- ELL Have students use a dictionary to define *clarify* and *body language*.

W Writing Support

Personal Writing Have students read current news articles about refugees in a particular part of the world. Then have them write journal entries describing their thoughts about the situation. OL

R Reading Strategy

Identifying the Main Idea **Ask:** Which sentence tells the main idea of this paragraph? *(the first sentence)* OL

This Reading Skill (Identifying the Main Idea) was introduced in this unit.

Reading Check **Answer:** They moved in search of jobs.

Assess

Social Studies ONLINE
Study Central™ provides summaries, interactive games, and online graphic organizers to help students review content.

Close

Summarizing Have students summarize the types of migration. OL

Reasons People Move

People migrate for a variety of reasons. Historians say that "push" factors convince people to leave their homes and "pull" factors attract them to another place. A shortage of farmland or few jobs in a region or country may "push" residents to emigrate. The lure of jobs has worked as a "pull" factor, attracting many immigrants to the United States.

W People who are forced to flee to another country to escape wars, persecution, or natural disasters are called **refugees.** For example, 2 million refugees fled mass killings in Rwanda during the late 1990s.

Impact of Migration

Mass migrations of people have major impacts—both on the region they leave and on the region where they settle. When emigrants leave a country, its population decreases or does not increase as quickly. This can ease overcrowding. However, if skilled or educated workers leave, emigration may hurt the country's economy. Emigration can also divide families.

R Migration also affects the country to which people move. Immigrants bring with them new forms of music, art, foods, and language. Some native-born citizens, however, fear or resent immigrants and the changes that they bring. This has led to violence and unjust treatment toward newcomers in some instances.

Reading Check **Making Generalizations** Why have so many rural citizens moved to cities in Asia, Africa, and Latin America?

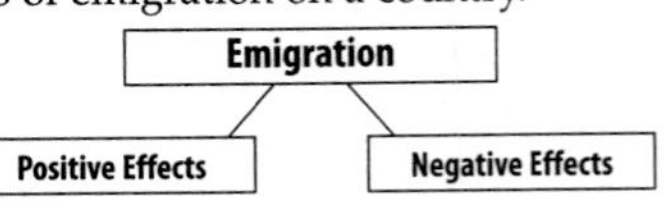

Social Studies ONLINE
Study Central™ To review this section, go to glencoe.com.

Vocabulary

1. **Explain** the meaning of the following terms by using each one in a sentence.
 a. death rate
 b. birthrate
 c. famine
 d. population density
 g. urbanization
 h. emigrate
 i. refugee

Main Ideas

2. **Making Connections** How might the availability of food affect population growth?
3. **Explaining** What geographic factors lead people to live in certain areas of the world?
4. **Summarizing** Use a diagram like the one below to summarize the positive and negative effects of emigration on a country.

Emigration	
Positive Effects	Negative Effects

Critical Thinking

5. **BIG Idea** Discuss the factors that can cause a country's population to grow rapidly.
6. **Challenge** Explain the reasons people migrate. Identify which reasons are "push" factors and which are "pull" factors. Which factors do you think most strongly influence migrants? Explain.

Writing About Geography

7. **Expository Writing** Write a paragraph explaining how the Earth's population has changed in the past 200 years and how you think it will change in the next 50 years.

Answers

1. Sentences should use vocabulary words according to their definitions in the section and Glossary.
2. Availability of food can increase birthrates and decrease death rates, which leads to population growth. Famine can increase death rates, which leads to population decline.
3. High mountains, deserts, and frozen landscapes cannot support large populations. People need to live on usable land.
4. Possible answer: **Positive Effects**—can ease overcrowding; **Negative Effects**—can divide families, can hurt the country's economy.
5. Better health care and living conditions can decrease the death rate and increase the birthrate. Better technologies can improve agriculture and lead to longer lives and population growth. Refugees leaving one country can increase the population of neighboring countries.
6. Possible answer: push factors— war, persecution, natural disaster, limited farmland or jobs; pull factors—job opportunities, better standard of living
7. Answers will vary. Students should include that the population has increased from 1 billion to more than 6 billion.

TIME PERSPECTIVES
EXPLORING WORLD ISSUES

THE WORLD GOES GLOBAL

Technology and new methods of trade are affecting how the world interacts.

A local Inuit uses a laptop in the Canadian Arctic.

Around the world, technological advances are changing the way we live and work. Every day, new technologies make it possible for billions of e-mails and trillions of dollars to crisscross national borders. Communication between people and businesses and the movement of goods and money is done more quickly than ever before because of the Internet.

As technology continues to change, what might the world look like ten years from now? Inventions that create faster ways to communicate might make the world seem even smaller than it does today. And as globalization connects the world's economies as never before, people everywhere will learn about other nations and cultures.

Focus

Introducing TIME Perspectives

Ask: What device is the man using in the photo? *(a laptop computer)* **How might using technology like this affect people who live in isolated regions?** *(Possible answer: Access to the Internet and technology allows people in isolated regions to communicate more easily with people around the world.)* **OL**

FYI

Read the *Technology Briefing Paper,* a summary of technology's advances and its effects on people around the world, at www.un.org, the United Nations Web site.

Use the **TIME Perspectives: Focus on World Issues Teacher Guide and Student Activities,** pp. 1–4, to reinforce and extend the concepts in "The World Goes Global."

Additional Support

Background

Who Invented the Web? The Internet was developed in the 1960s, but it was a lot different from the Internet we know today. The Internet was first developed mainly as a way to transfer files and share information. At that time, there was no such thing as a Web page, only commands from one computer to another. In the 1980s, people started to use domain names for computers, rather than numbers, as an easier way to track where files were being sent. A programmer at Apple Computer created a way to put graphics and text together on "filing cards" in the late 1980s. Finally, in 1990, Tim Berners-Lee pulled it all together and created the World Wide Web. Berners-Lee developed a way to link one part of a document to another part or to another document. He also created the naming convention www.name.suffix that is still used today. The first Web browser, which he called *WorldWideWeb* (the name was later changed to Nexus), was both a way to make and view Web pages. The World Wide Web caught on quickly; by 1993, there were several Web browsers available. Berners-Lee never charged for his invention and continues to fight for open Web access for everyone.

Teach

W Writing Support

Expository Writing Have students research the effect of globalization on U.S. workers, including changes in job trends due to globalization. Then have them report their findings in a newspaper article that explains the following elements of the issue: *who, what, when, where, why,* and *how.* AL

C Critical Thinking

Determining Cause and Effect
Ask: What effect has globalization had on software engineers in India? *(They have been hired to work for foreign companies.)* OL

R Reading Strategy

Identifying Ask: What is this paragraph mainly about? *(the history of the Internet)* OL

INTERPRETING CHARTS
Answer:
Canada and Mexico are adjacent to the United States.

TIME PERSPECTIVES

EXPLORING WORLD ISSUES

Workers at a call center in India answer questions from American customers.

A GLOBAL MARKETPLACE

Venugopla Rao Moram is a highly sought after worker. Recently, the computer software engineer who lives in Bangalore, India, was offered five jobs during a two-week period. All of the offers were from companies whose headquarters are located thousands of miles from India.

Luckily, Moram will not have to travel that far to get to work. Computer companies from around the world are opening offices in Bangalore in order to hire Indian workers. Many Indians speak English and are well educated. This makes them valuable to foreign companies that are establishing workplaces in countries where labor is inexpensive. This type of labor helps manufacturers keep their production costs low.

As a result of **globalization**, a trend that is linking the world's nations through trade, thousands of Indians are working for foreign companies. In Moram's case, a business in California hired him to create software that makes the characters in video games jump and run. The software Moram produces becomes part of a product that is assembled in other countries and sold all over the world. All types of products, from toys to clothes to TVs, are being made and traded this way. As a result, economies are becoming much more connected—or global.

The United States and the Global Economy

The United States trades with countries all over the world. It sells, or exports, some products, and buys, or imports, others. Here are the countries the U.S. did the most business with in 2005.

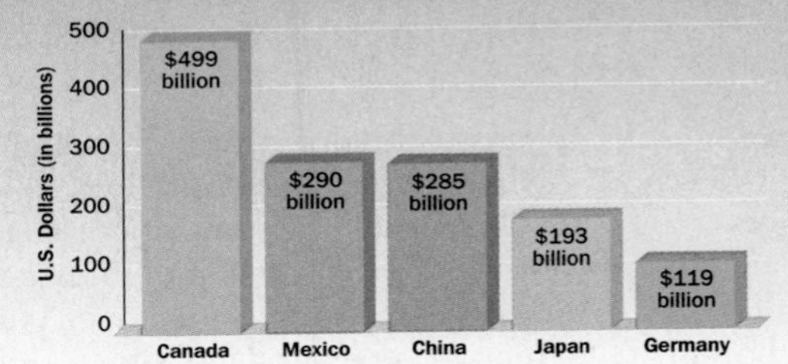

Source: U.S. Census Bureau, Foreign Trade Statistics Division.

INTERPRETING CHARTS

Making Inferences Why might Canada and Mexico be the United States's top trading partners?

The Internet

The Internet has fueled globalization. The Internet is a giant electronic network that links computers all over the world. It was developed in the late 1960s when the U.S. military worked to connect its computers with those of college researchers so that they could share their ideas more easily. Over time, the Internet became available to everyone, and the way the world interacts changed forever.

Additional Support

Teacher Tip

One method for making connections is to pick a single category or fact that each thing being considered has in common. All of these countries have populations that can be measured. Have students consider the impact of the vast differences in populations for these countries.

Activity: Connecting With the United States

Making Connections Ask students to look at the chart on this page. **Ask: What trading partner mentioned in this chapter is not on the chart?** *(India)* Explain that although Canada and Mexico are currently the United States' largest trading partners, some economists believe that in coming years, India and China will take their places. The economies of China and India are growing rapidly, and the United States trades many products and services with both countries. Have students write two to three paragraphs explaining whether they believe China and India will overtake Canada and Mexico as the United States's biggest trading partners and why. OL

An anti-globalization demonstrator protests in Japan.

People all over the world can trade stocks on the New York Stock Exchange.

A Thai woman uses a bank machine.

The Internet also changed how people and companies buy goods. Today, just like you can shop online for games or CDs, so can businesses. For example, a business in need of computer software can use the Internet to research the products of computer companies from all over the world. With the click of a mouse, the buyer can research and compare prices for software products on a computer company's Web site or at an online store. Then, in seconds, the buyer can purchase the product. **R**

Before the days of the Internet, a company in need of software could not have learned about suppliers and products as easily. As a result, business tended to be conducted more locally and at a slower pace. Today, a buyer can shop and trade online in minutes without leaving his or her desk. Companies can conduct business in less time and from anywhere in the world.

Sharing Globalization's Gains

The impact of globalization has been amazing, but its benefits have not been shared equally. **Developed countries**, or countries in which a great deal of manufacturing is carried out, have more goods to trade than **developing countries** that are still trying to industrialize. Also many companies prefer to build factories in wealthier countries rather than in poor ones, where support systems like roads and airports are often unavailable. As a result, some of the poorer nations in Asia and Africa have had a hard time creating any new jobs.

What steps can be taken to spread the benefits of globalization? International businesses and wealthy nations can be part of the solution. By 2002, businesses and countries had spent more than $3 trillion to help poorer countries build factories and transportation systems. Investing in such support systems could help businesses trade more effectively and grow. There is still much work to be done. Finding ways to help every nation share the gains of globalization is one of biggest challenges the world faces. **C**

Lumber is processed at a Canadian mill for shipment to the United States.

EXPLORING THE ISSUE

1. **Making Inferences** Why do you think companies are concerned about how much money it costs to make a product?
2. **Analyzing Information** How might investing in transportation systems help developing countries?

TIME PERSPECTIVES

R Reading Strategy

Analyzing Text Structure Have students read aloud the paragraphs with a partner. **Ask:** **How is the text ordered?** *(It first talks about the Internet today, and then it discusses the days before the Internet.)* **How do you know that the text has switched to discussing the past?** *(The verbs are in past tense, and the phrase "before the days of the Internet" is a clue.)* **OL**

C Critical Thinking

Draw Conclusions **Ask:** **Why might it benefit developed countries to help poorer countries?** *(Possible answers: Developed countries might benefit through trade. Labor and startup costs are often cheaper in developing countries.)* **OL**

EXPLORING THE ISSUE

Answers:

1. The costs to make a product take away from a company's profits.
2. If countries had adequate transportation systems, they would attract more business from developed countries. This would improve their economies.

Differentiated Instruction

TIME Perspectives: Exploring World Issues Workbook, p. 2

Following a Sequence

Objective: To learn how to read a flow chart

Focus: Discuss with students the kind of information a flow chart shows.

Teach: Read the introductory paragraph and compare the three stages to the five steps shown in the flow chart.

Assess: Have students use the flow chart to answer the questions.

Close: Ask students how they might use a flow chart to organize other information.

Differentiated Instruction Strategies

BL Have students locate the places mentioned in the flow chart on a map and connect them with arrows.

AL Ask students to create a flow chart for another process.

ELL Have students define the terms *manufacturing, distribution,* and *globalization.*

D Differentiated Instruction

Auditory/Musical Have students listen to the music of various international artists available on the Internet. Ask students to identify cultural elements in the music, either in the lyrics or the instrumentation. **ELL**

FastFacts

Wyclef Jean's influence has moved beyond music and into politics. The Haitian-born musician was recently appointed roving ambassador for Haiti. The Haitian president asked Jean to represent the country in hopes of improving its image in the international community.

EXPLORING THE ISSUE

Answers:

1. Listeners can go online and listen to or download music from different genres.
2. Possible answer: People do not need transportation to buy music online, more music is available online than in stores, and people can listen to snippets of music online before they commit to buying it.

Additional Support

TIME PERSPECTIVES

MUSIC GOES GLOBAL

It has been said that music is the universal language. This has never been more true than in the Internet age. Today, music lovers can listen to music from all over the world. Online music stores and portable music players make it easy to listen to what you want, when you want.

In the past, listeners had much less control over the music they heard. Record producers and companies recorded the music of homegrown musicians, and radio stations played their songs. Artists and songs from different regions of the world were rarely played.

D In the Internet age, however, music lovers are being exposed to sounds from around the world. West African drumming or Latin American dance music, for example, is available to anyone online. Listeners can just search for a **genre**, or style of music, and download a song for a small fee.

With such easy access to global sounds, it is not uncommon for a portable player to include a list of songs and artists from several countries. As a result, musicians are working to please the public by blending "international" material and elements into their acts. The American pop singer Christina Aguilera sings in English, but she has also recorded a CD completely in Spanish. Hip-hop artist Wyclef Jean mixes **Creole**, the language of Haiti, into his songs. Madonna has worn traditional costumes from Japan and Scotland during her tours.

In the twenty-first century, musicians and music lovers are no longer tied to the sounds of one nation. In fact, cross-cultural appeal in the music industry is becoming a key to success.

Wyclef Jean uses Haitian elements in his music.

REUTERS/GARY HERSHORN

EXPLORING THE ISSUE

1. **Determining Cause and Effect** How does the Internet help people learn about the music styles of performers from other countries?
2. **Making Inferences** List three reasons why it may be easier to buy music online than in a store that sells CDs.

80

Activity: Connecting With the United States

Analyzing Tell students that many U.S. companies hire people in other countries, but foreign companies also build factories and other facilities in the United States. **Ask:** **Why would foreign companies set up factories in the United States?** *(Possible answer: It might be more beneficial to pay higher U.S. wages and avoid shipping costs and import taxes.)* Tell students that Toyota has eight facilities in the United States that produce cars and parts, each of which employs more than 20,000 Americans. Have each student look in his or her backpack for three items made by different companies (for example, school supplies or personal items such as radios, cell phones, or MP3 players). Have students research where the items were made and where the companies that manufactured these items are based. As a class, mark students' findings on a map. Discuss how students' lives are connected with the rest of the world in ways they may never have considered. Have each student write a paragraph describing his or her findings and what they show about the ways countries are interconnected. **OL**

REVIEW AND ASSESS

UNDERSTANDING THE ISSUE

1 **Making Connections** How has globalization affected the way some products are produced?

2 **Writing to Inform** Write a short article about how the Internet has changed the way that businesses shop for and buy goods.

3 **Writing to Persuade** Do you think that American musicians who combine music from other countries and cultures can become stars in the United States? Defend your answer in a letter to the president of a record company.

INTERNET RESEARCH ACTIVITIES

4 Go online to research the history of the Internet. Write an essay explaining why the Internet was created. Develop a time line that notes important developments.

5 With your teacher's help, use the Internet to research how many homes have access to the Internet in developed and developing nations. Compare the information and create a bar graph showing the top three countries in both categories.

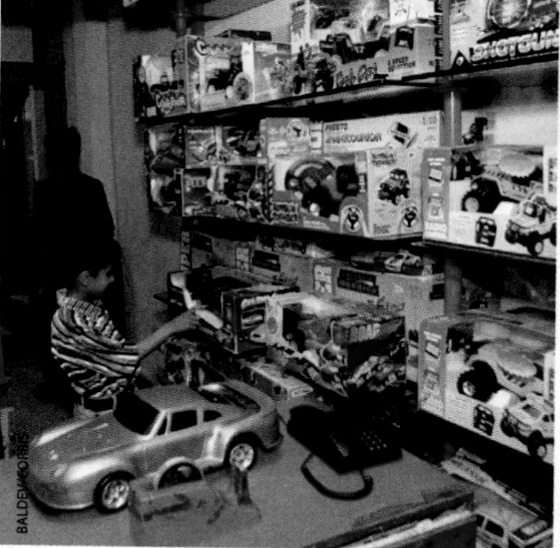

Many toys made in China are sold in other countries.

BEYOND THE CLASSROOM

6 **Organize the class into three teams.** One group should represent developed nations, and another should represent developing nations. Debate this resolution: "Globalization is good for everyone." The third group of students will decide which team has the most convincing arguments.

7 **Take an inventory of your home.** Look for products that were made in other countries. Count the items that were imported from different countries. Make a chart to show how many countries are represented in your home.

The Universal Language

The Internet is changing the way people listen to music. In the Internet age, music lovers around the world are shopping online. Here is a look at the number of people visiting music sites.

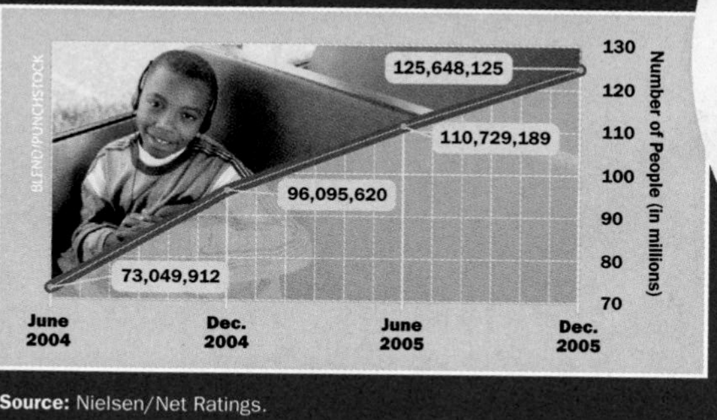

Source: Nielsen/Net Ratings.

Building Graph Reading Skills

1. **Comparing** How many more people visited music Web sites in December 2005 than in December 2004?
2. **Making Inferences** How might the increase of shopping online for music affect traditional music stores?

TIME PERSPECTIVES

Review and Assess

Questions from **Understanding the Issue, Internet Research Activities,** and **Beyond the Classroom** may have more than one correct answer. Pick and choose the two or three activities that work best for your class.

Building Graph Reading Skills

Answers:

1. 29,552,505 people
2. Possible answer: Traditional music stores may lose money or go out of business if more people buy music online.

Close

Debating the Issue Organize students into two teams, and have them debate the benefits and challenges of globalization. OL

Activity: Why It Matters

Evaluating Explain that the Internet has given people access to a world of new music, but it has also made it easier for people to pirate recordings. **Ask:** **What is music piracy?** *(copying musical recordings without permission)* Tell students that because computers and the Internet have made it easy to copy and share music, people routinely copy CDs rather than buy them in stores. This matters because when someone makes an illegal copy of a musician's work, the musician does not get paid for it. In China, illegal copying of CDs is rampant. Even legitimate stores sell pirated CDs. However, artists have found other ways to make money off their music, such as playing concerts and endorsing products. American record companies are fighting piracy in the United States and abroad, but some people think they are fighting a losing battle. Lead a class discussion about whether piracy should be made legal. Ask students whether they think the U.S. music industry is right to try to stop music copying or whether the industry should try to find other ways to take advantage of technology to make a profit. Then have students write a paragraph supporting or opposing music piracy. OL

Focus

Bellringer
Daily Focus Transparency 3-2

Guide to Reading
Answers to Graphic:

Answers may include:
social groups; language; religion; history; daily life; arts; government; economy

Section Spotlight Video

To learn more about global cultures, have students watch the Section Spotlight Video.

Resource Manager

R Reading Strategies	C Critical Thinking	D Differentiated Instruction	W Writing Support	S Skill Practice
Teacher Edition • Skimming, p. 83 • Sequencing Info., p. 86 • Identifying, p. 87 • Act. Prior Know., p. 88 **Additional Resources** • Guid. Read., URB p. 82 • Cont. Vocab., URB p. 85 • Ac. Vocab., URB p. 87 • Read. Ess., p. 22	**Teacher Edition** • Compare/Contrast, p. 83 • Predicting, p. 84 • Det. Cause/Effect, p. 86 **Additional Resources** • Quizzes and Tests, p. 26	**Teacher Edition** • Intrapersonal, p. 84 • Auditory/Musical, p. 85 • Verbal/Linguistic, p. 87 **Additional Resources** • Diff. Instr., URB p. 89 • Reteach., URB p. 101 • School-to-Home Conn., URB p. 103	**Teacher Edition** • Expository Writing, pp. 85, 88 • Narrative Writing, p. 89 **Additional Resources** • Interactive Geography, p. 1	**Teacher Edition** • Visual Literacy, p. 86 • Using Geo. Skills, p. 88 **Additional Resources** • Daily Focus Trans. 3-2 • Reg. Atlas, URB pp. 1–7

Guide to Reading

BIG Idea

Culture influences people's perceptions about places and regions.

Content Vocabulary
- culture *(p. 83)*
- ethnic group *(p. 84)*
- dialect *(p. 84)*
- democracy *(p. 85)*
- dictatorship *(p. 86)*
- monarchy *(p. 86)*
- civilization *(p. 86)*
- cultural diffusion *(p. 87)*
- culture region *(p. 88)*
- globalization *(p. 89)*

Academic Vocabulary
- widespread *(p. 86)*
- unique *(p. 89)*

Reading Strategy

Identifying Use a diagram like the one below to identify the elements of culture.

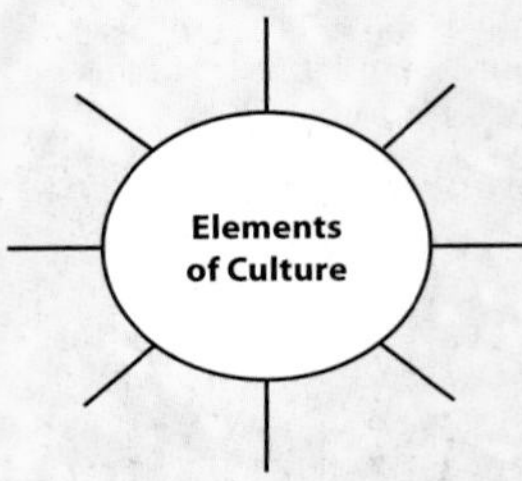

Global Cultures

Picture This The eagles that soar through the skies of the American southwest have long been sacred to the native peoples of the area. Many Native Americans believe that eagles have special qualities such as wisdom and courage. Eagle feathers are treated with respect and are often given as rewards for great deeds. Native American groups, such as the Tewa of New Mexico, perform dances to honor this beautiful bird. To learn more about how traditions reflect a culture's beliefs, read Section 2.

▼ Honoring the eagle

What Is Culture?

Main Idea **Culture refers to the many shared characteristics that define a group of people.**

Geography and You Think about the clothes you wear, the music you listen to, and the foods you eat. Read to learn about the many things that make up culture.

Culture is the way of life of a group of people who share similar beliefs and customs. A particular culture can be understood by looking at various elements: what languages the people speak, what religions they follow, and what smaller groups are part of their society. The study of culture also includes examining people's daily lives, the history they share, and the art forms they have created.

Geographers, anthropologists, and archaeologists all study culture. For example, geographers look at physical objects, such as food and housing. They also study elements such as religion, social groups, types of government, and economies. Anthropologists analyze cultures today to learn how different elements of culture are related. Archaeologists use the physical and historical objects of a culture, such as pottery and tools, to try to understand how people lived in the past. The work of all of these experts helps us better understand the world we live in.

NATIONAL GEOGRAPHIC

Figure 2 **World Language Families**

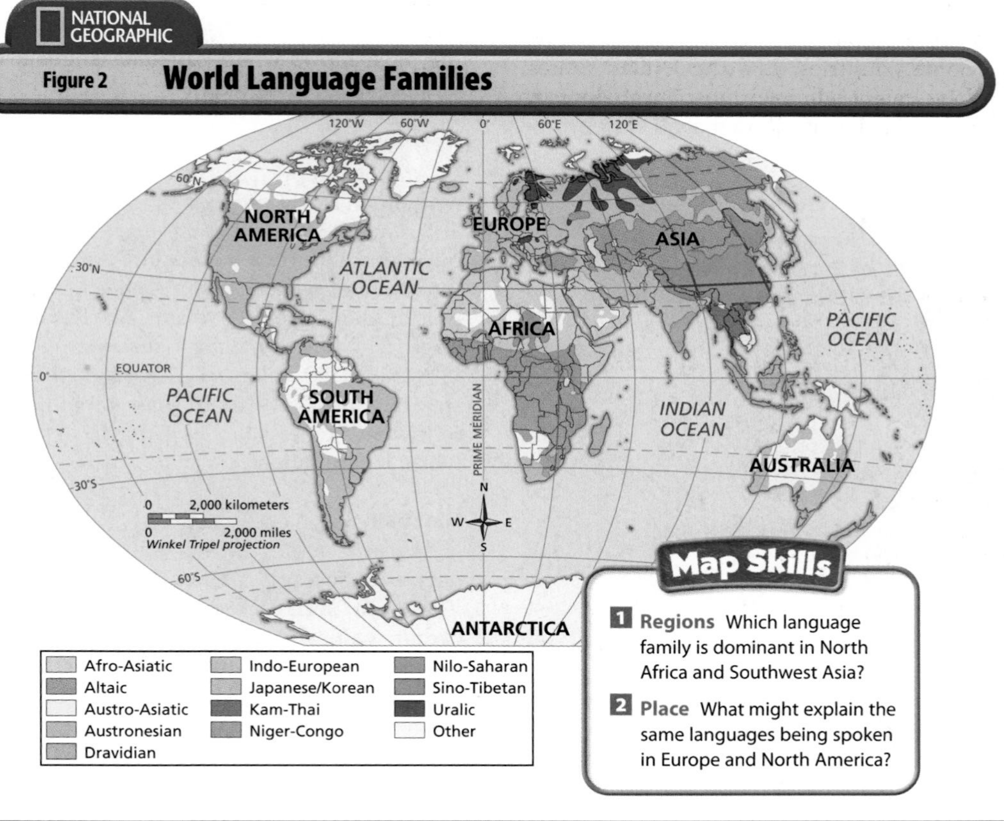

Map Skills

1. **Regions** Which language family is dominant in North Africa and Southwest Asia?
2. **Place** What might explain the same languages being spoken in Europe and North America?

Teach

R Reading Strategy

Skimming Read the Main Idea to students. Then have them skim the section, reading the headings and boldface terms and looking at the maps and pictures. Ask students to predict what they might read about in the section. BL

C Critical Thinking

Comparing and Contrasting

Ask: How are geographers, anthropologists, and archaeologists similar? *(They are interested in culture.)* **How do anthropologists differ from archaeologists?** *(Anthropologists study cultures as they are today, whereas archaeologists focus on past cultures.)* OL

For further practice on this skill (Comparing and Contrasting), see the **Skills Handbook**.

Map Skills

Answers:

1. Afro-Asiatic
2. Europeans settled and gained control over North America, spreading their language as they went.

Hands-On Chapter Project
Step 2

Creating a Time Line for Your State

Step 2: Building Group Time Lines Students will work in groups to create and present their part of the time line.

Directions Distribute large sheets of butcher paper to each group. Have students use their research from Step 1 to create a time line that illustrates the cultural elements of that period in their state's history. Time lines should include a horizontal line with vertical lines marked by important dates and also should include pictures, drawings, illustrations, and captions.

Explaining Have students present their section of the time line to the class and explain the illustrations and captions. Allow time for students to ask questions. OL

(Chapter Project continued in Section 3.)

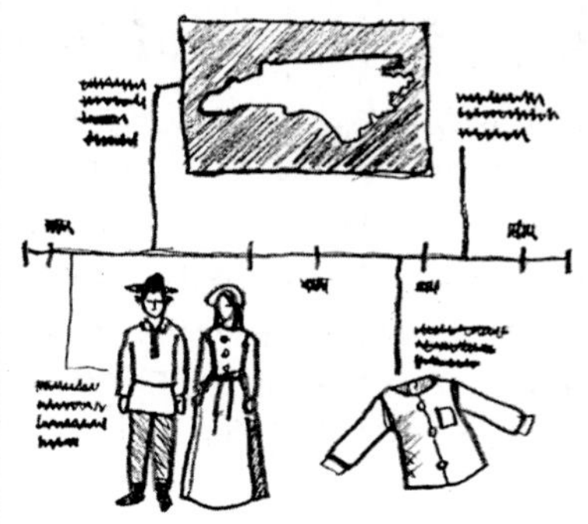

D **Differentiated Instruction**

Intrapersonal Have each student create a "social group tree," which shows the student's place in a social group. Students' trees should include their place in their family, their ethnic group, their language group, and their city, state, and country of residence. **OL**

C **Critical Thinking**

Predicting Ask: How might today's migration patterns affect ethnocentrism? *(Possible answer: Continued migration may increase ethnocentrism in areas with many immigrant groups.)* **OL**

For further practice on this skill (Predicting), see the **Skills Handbook**.

Caption Answer:
daily life, social groups, eating habits

Social Groups

One way scientists study culture is by looking at different groups of people in a society. Each of us belongs to many social groups. For example, are you old or young? Male or female? A student, a worker, or both? Most social groups have rules of behavior that group members learn. The process by which people adjust their behavior to meet these rules is called socialization. Within society, each person has a certain status. Status refers to a person's importance or rank. **D** In all cultures, the family is the most important social group. Although family structures vary from culture to culture, most of us first learn how to behave from our families.

People also belong to an **ethnic group.** This is a group that shares a language, history, religion, and some physical traits. Some countries, like the United States, have many ethnic groups. Such countries have a national culture that all their people share, as well as ethnic cultures.

Culture and Family Life

▲ Households in Japan can include several generations. ***Place*** **What elements of culture are found in this family gathering?**

C In some cases, people come to believe that their own culture is superior to, or better than, other cultures. This attitude is called ethnocentrism. If carried to extremes, ethnocentrism may cause hatred and persecution of other groups.

Language

Sharing a language is one of the strongest unifying forces for a culture. A language, however, may have different variations called dialects. A **dialect** is a local form of a language that may have a distinct vocabulary and pronunciation. Despite different dialects, speakers of the same language can usually understand one another.

More than 2,000 languages are spoken around the world today. Most can be grouped with related languages into a specific language family. **Figure 2** on the preceding page shows where different language families are spoken today.

Religion

Another important cultural element is religion. In many cultures, religious beliefs and practices help people answer basic questions about life's meaning. Although hundreds of religions are practiced in the world, there are five major world religions. The following chart describes each of these major religions. Together, these five religions have more than 4.5 billion followers—more than two-thirds of the world's population.

History

History shapes how a culture views itself and the world. Stories about the challenges and successes of a culture support certain values and help people develop cultural pride and unity. Cultural holidays mark important events and enable people to celebrate their heritage.

Additional Support

Activity: Collaborative Learning

Comparing and Contrasting Tell students that the United States and England have been called two countries separated by a common language. **Ask: What do you think "separated by a common language" means?** *(Possible answer: The Americans and the English think they speak the same language, but their forms of English are quite different and can lead to misunderstandings.)* The same could be said of the United States, England, and Australia, or New Zealand. These English-speaking countries all speak the language differently, with different pronunciations, spellings, and meanings of words. Americans spell *color*; the English spell *colour*. Americans say "I'll call my lawyer"; the English say, "I'll phone my solicitor." **OL**

Major World Religions

Religion	Major Leader	Followers	Beliefs
Buddhism	Siddhartha Gautama, the Buddha	378.8 million	Buddhism is based on the teachings of Siddhartha Gautama, known as the Buddha. The Buddha taught that the goal of life is to escape the cycle of birth and death by achieving a state of spiritual understanding called nirvana. Buddhists believe that they must follow an eight-step path to achieve nirvana.
Christianity	Jesus Christ	2.1 billion	Christianity is based on the belief in one God and the teachings and life of Jesus as described in the New Testament of the Bible. Christians believe that Jesus was the Son of God and was sent to Earth to save people from their sins.
Hinduism	Unknown	860.1 million	Hinduism is based on the belief in a supreme spiritual force known as Brahman as recorded in sacred texts, including the Upanishads. Hindus believe that to unite with Brahman, they must first pass through many lives, being reborn into new forms. To move closer to Brahman they must make improvements in each of their lives.
Islam	Muhammad	1.3 billion	Islam is based on the belief in one God, Allah, as revealed through the prophet Muhammad. The Muslim sacred text is the Quran. Muslims follow five major acts of worship known as the Five Pillars of Islam.
Judaism	Abraham	15.1 million	Judaism is based on the belief in one God and the spiritual and ethical principles handed down by God. These principles, including the Ten Commandments, are presented in Jewish sacred texts collected in the Hebrew Bible.

Source: *Encyclopædia Britannica*, 2005.

Chart Skills

1. **Identifying** Which two religions include the belief that people are reborn into new forms?
2. **Explaining** What help do these religions give to their followers?

Daily Life

Food, clothing, and shelter are basic human needs. The type of food you eat and how you eat it reflect your culture. Do you use chopsticks, a fork, or bread to scoop up your food? The home you live in and the clothing that you wear reflect your culture and your physical surroundings. For example, the clothing people wear in the high, chilly Andes of South America differs greatly from the clothing people wear on the warm savannas of Africa. **W**

Arts

Through music, painting, sculpture, dance, and literature, people express what they think is beautiful and meaningful. The arts can also tell stories about important figures and events in the culture. **D**

Government

People need rules in order to live together without conflict. Governments fulfill this need. They can be either limited or unlimited. A limited government restricts the powers of its leaders. For example, in a **democracy**, power is held by the people.

Social Studies ONLINE

Student Web Activity Visit glencoe.com to learn more about forms of government around the world.

W Writing Support

Expository Writing Have students imagine that they are writing to a peer in another country with a different culture, such as China. Tell them to write a letter to the peer, describing their daily life, including their clothing, food, and daytime routine. **OL**

D Differentiated Instruction

Auditory/Musical Bring to class recordings of music from different cultures. As you play each song, have students draw a response to the music. Encourage them to focus on what the music makes them think of and how it makes them feel. **BL**

Chart Skills

Answers:
1. Buddhism and Hinduism
2. They offer teachings that provide meaning to life and offer guidance for daily living.

Social Studies ONLINE

Objectives and answers to the Student Web Activity can be found at glencoe.com under the Web Activity Lesson Plan for this chapter.

Differentiated Instruction

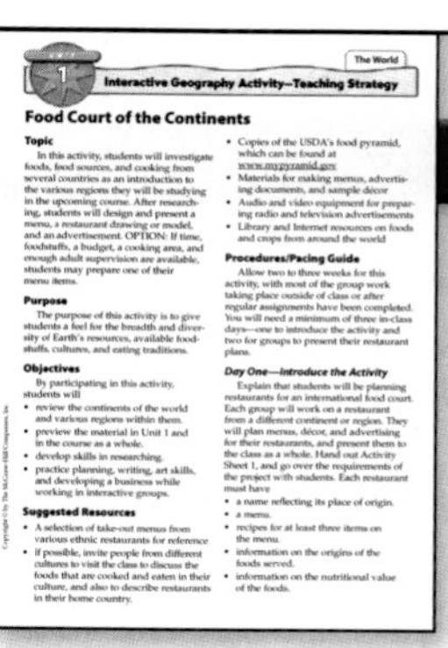

Interactive Geography Activity, pp. 1–8

Food Court of the Continents

Objective: To learn about the world by using food

Focus: Discuss how an area's food and eating traditions reflect its culture.

Teach: Have students follow the steps to design a restaurant that serves regional food.

Assess: Have students complete the self-assessment.

Close: Discuss with students which restaurants they found most appealing and why.

Differentiated Instruction Strategies

- **BL** Use menus from restaurants in your area to guide students.
- **AL** Have students interview a local chef to learn about food traditions and create their own recipe for that culture.
- **ELL** Invite students to bring in recipes or food from their ancestral cultures.

R Reading Strategy

Sequencing Information Have students list the three forms of government, in order of most freedoms to fewest freedoms. *(democracy, monarchy, dictatorship)* OL

S Skill Practice

Visual Literacy Ask: How has U.S. culture changed compared to this image? *(Possible answer: Women's clothing has changed, and factories today rely more on technology.)* **How is it the same?** *(Possible answer: Women can work outside the home, and factories are needed to make cloth.)* OL

C Critical Thinking

Determining Cause and Effect
Ask: What were the effects of farming? *(larger populations and civilizations, a more reliable source of food, the ability to live in one place)* OL

Reading Check Answer: Students should list three of the following: social groups, language, religion, history, daily life, arts, government, economy.

Caption Answer:
use of computers, advances in communications, new medical technology

Additional Support

Most democracies today are called representative democracies because the people choose leaders to represent them and make decisions. In unlimited governments, leaders are all-powerful. In a **dictatorship**, for instance, the leader, or dictator, rules by force. Dictators often limit citizens' freedoms. R

A **monarchy** is a government led by a king or queen who inherits power by being born into the ruling family. For much of history, monarchies had unlimited power. Today, most monarchies are constitutional monarchies in which elected legislatures hold most of the power.

Economy

People in every culture must earn a living. Geographers study economic activities to see how a culture uses its resources and trades with other places. An economy's success can be seen in people's quality of life—how well they eat and live and what kind of health care they receive.

Reading Check **Describing** Describe three elements that help unify a culture.

The Growth of Industry

NATIONAL GEOGRAPHIC

S

Some of the earliest factories, like this one in Lowell, Massachusetts, used machines to make cloth. ***Movement*** **What recent technological advancements have led to cultural changes?**

Cultural Change

Main Idea Cultures are constantly changing and influencing each other.

Geography and You What influences from other cultures can you see in your community? Read on to see how cultures relate to each other and change.

Over time, all cultures experience change. Sometimes that change results from inventions and innovations, or technological improvements that bring about new ways of life. Sometimes change results from the influence of other cultures.

Inventions and Technology

Thousands of years ago, humans were hunters and gatherers who lived and traveled in small groups. After 8000 B.C., people learned to farm. Planting crops led to more reliable food supplies and larger populations. It also allowed people to settle in one place. Historians call this change the Agricultural Revolution. It had a huge impact C on human culture because it led people to create **civilizations**, or highly developed cultures, in river valleys found in present-day Iraq, Egypt, India, and China. The people of these civilizations made a number of important advancements including building cities, forming governments, founding religions, and developing writing systems.

The world remained largely agricultural through the A.D. 1700s. Around that time, some countries began to industrialize, or use machines to make goods. The **widespread** use of machines made economies more productive. Industrial nations produced more food, goods, and wealth, which caused sweeping cultural changes.

The world has changed greatly in the past three decades. Computers have

Activity: Interdisciplinary Connection

Art Review with students the information on the previous page about the arts. **Ask: How does art reflect the culture of a group of people?** *(Possible answers: Art shows what is important to people or what people consider beautiful. Art reveals a culture's history.)* Ask each student to search online or at the library for an example of art that represents the culture of a foreign country or an ancient civilization. Discuss with students how art can relay information to people who are unable to read and write. Have each student describe what the artwork they chose shows about the people who created it. Encourage students to think about how the images on the artwork, the materials used in the artwork, and the way the artwork was displayed reveal clues about the culture of the people who created it. Then ask students to draw their own conclusions about the culture based on the artwork. OL

transformed businesses and households. Advances in communications allow people throughout the world to send and receive information almost instantly. Medical technology has dramatically increased human life expectancy. Each of these developments has sparked cultural changes.

Cultural Diffusion

The other major cause of cultural change is influence from other cultures. The process of spreading ideas, languages, or customs from one culture to another is called **cultural diffusion**. In the past, diffusion has taken place through trade, migration, and conquest. In recent years, new methods of communication have also led to cultural diffusion.

Historically, trade began with the exchange of goods, often over great distances. Soon trade also brought new ideas and practices to an area. Buddhist merchants brought their religion to China along trade routes, and Muslim traders shared their religious beliefs with people in West Africa. Trade continues to be a major means of cultural diffusion.

The movement of people from one place to another also leads to cultural diffusion. When Europeans arrived in North America, they brought horses, which were new **R** to the continent. Native Americans living on the Great Plains quickly adopted the horse because it made hunting easier.

The conquest of one group by another is a third way culture can spread. Conquerors bring their culture to conquered areas. For example, the Romance languages, such as Italian, French, Spanish, **D** and Portuguese, reflect the influence of the Roman Empire. These languages are based on Latin, the language of ancient Rome. In turn, conquered peoples can influence the culture of the conquerors. Christianity arose among the Jews, a people conquered by the Roman Empire. In time, Christianity became a major religion in the empire.

Today television, movies, and the Internet contribute to cultural diffusion. For example, movies made in the United States, Mexico, Brazil, and India are seen around the world, introducing people to different ways of life. The Internet allows people to have contact with and be influenced by people from other cultures.

NATIONAL GEOGRAPHIC

Cultural Influences

Children around the world, such as these students in China, anticipate each new Harry Potter book and movie. The books have been translated into 47 languages. ***Movement*** **What is cultural diffusion?**

Reading Check **Analyzing Information**
Describe one way that cultural diffusion takes place.

R Reading Strategy

Identifying **Ask:** **What is the main idea of this paragraph?** *(Migration can lead to cultural diffusion.)* **OL**

D Differentiated Instruction

Verbal/Linguistic Have students research the Romance languages to find answers to the following questions: How did the Romance languages begin and spread? What characteristics do they share? About how many people speak them today? **OL**

Caption Answer:
the process of spreading ideas, languages, or customs from one culture to another

Reading Check **Answer:** Students should describe one of the following: trade, migration, conquest, communication.

Activity: Collaborative Learning

Making Connections Tell students that the Internet has increased the rate of cultural diffusion around the world. **Ask:** **What aspects of culture are easily shared through the Internet?** *(Answers may include art, music, writing, religion, and political ideas.)* Explain to students that some leaders do not want their people to have access to information from other cultures. For example, in North Korea, which is ruled by an absolute dictator, only a few thousand privileged people are allowed access to the Internet. Have student groups research which nations have suppressed or censored Internet access and content. Also, have students research how companies providing services in those countries have cooperated with or fought against the government. Ask each group to prepare an oral presentation describing what they have learned. Encourage students to think about how their lives would be different if they did not have access to the Internet. **OL**

R Reading Strategy

Activating Prior Knowledge Ask students to name other cultures they know about. **Ask:** **What similarities do you see between other cultures and your own?** *(Answers may include the culture's food, customs, and language.)* **OL**

S Skill Practice

Using Geography Skills **Ask:** **Which culture region lies northeast of the United States?** *(Europe)* **OL**

W Writing Support

Expository Writing Tell students to choose two countries, such as the United States and Canada, from the same culture region. Have them research and write about similarities between the countries. Suggest that students group similarities into categories, such as religion and history. **OL**

Map Skills

Answers:

1. Russia
2. Their culture regions are generally the same as those on nearby continents.

Regional and Global Cultures

Main Idea **As countries and regions share cultural traits, a global culture is emerging.** R

Geography and You What do you have in common with a student who lives across town or across the country? Read to learn how similarities help to define cultural regions.

As you recall, geographers use the term *regions* for areas that share common physical characteristics. Likewise, geographers divide the world into several culture regions, as shown in **Figure 3.** A **culture region** is an area that includes different countries that share similar cultural traits.

Culture Regions

The countries in each culture region generally have similar social groups, governments, economic systems, religions, languages, ethnic groups, and histories. One example of a culture region is North Africa, Southwest Asia, and Central Asia. In that area, Islam is the dominant religion. W Another culture region is Canada and the United States. These countries have similar languages, histories, and ethnic groups.

As you study the world, you will begin to recognize the characteristics shared by the

NATIONAL GEOGRAPHIC

Figure 3 **World Culture Regions**

S

120°W 60°W 0° 60°E 120°E
ARCTIC CIRCLE
60°N
30°N
TROPIC OF CANCER
ATLANTIC OCEAN
PACIFIC OCEAN
EQUATOR
0°
PACIFIC OCEAN
INDIAN OCEAN
PRIME MERIDIAN
TROPIC OF CAPRICORN
30°S
0 2,000 kilometers
0 2,000 miles
Winkel Tripel projection
N W E S
60°S
ANTARCTIC CIRCLE

- United States and Canada
- Latin America
- Europe
- Russia
- North Africa, Southwest Asia, and Central Asia
- Africa south of the Sahara
- South Asia
- East Asia and Southeast Asia
- Australia, Oceania, and Antarctica

Map Skills

1. **Regions** Which culture region is one country?
2. **Place** What generalization can you make about islands and their cultural regions?

Differentiated Instruction

Leveled Activities

BL **School-to-Home Connection, URB p. 103**

School-to-Home Connection Activity
What Do You Know?

OL **Content Vocabulary Activity, URB p. 85**

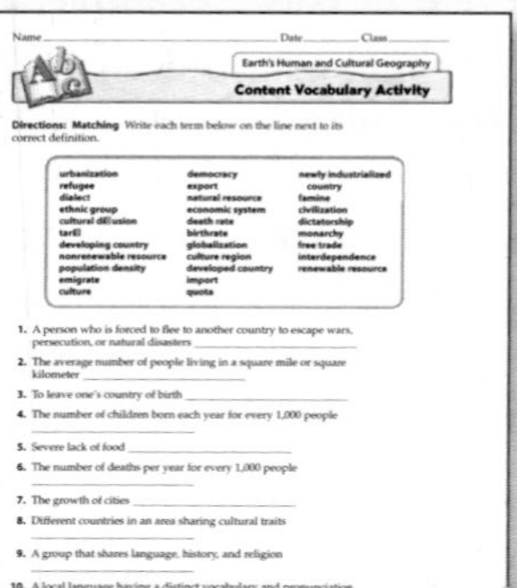
Earth's Human and Cultural Geography
Content Vocabulary Activity

ELL **Differentiated Instruction, URB p. 89**

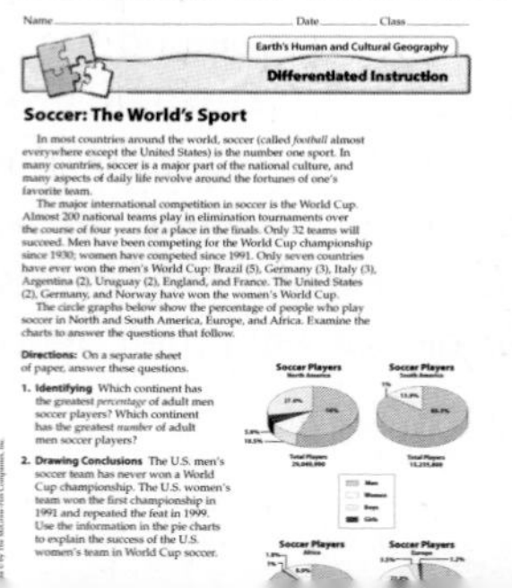
Earth's Human and Cultural Geography
Differentiated Instruction
Soccer: The World's Sport

countries in each culture region. Although these countries are similar, they also have **unique** traits that set them apart.

Global Culture

Recent advances in communications and technology have helped break down barriers between culture regions. The result is **globalization**, or the development of a worldwide culture with an interdependent economy.

With globalization, individual economies rely greatly upon one another for resources and markets. Some people believe that as the global culture grows, local cultures will become less important. They point out that globalization might even erase the traditions and customs of smaller groups. W

✔ Reading Check **Defining** What are culture regions?

NATIONAL GEOGRAPHIC **Global Communications**

The Internet and other forms of communications have helped link people around the world, such as these boys in rural India. ***Movement*** **What might happen as the global culture grows?**

W Writing Support

Narrative Writing Have students write a short story about a culture threatened by globalization. For example, they might write about a family in conflict over losing their culture's traditions. **AL**

✔ Reading Check **Answer:** areas that include different countries that share similar cultural traits

Caption Answer:
Economies will rely greatly on one another, and local cultures will become less important.

Section 2 Review

Social Studies ONLINE
Study Central™ To review this section, go to glencoe.com.

Vocabulary

1. **Explain** the meaning of *culture, ethnic group, dialect, democracy, dictatorship, monarchy, civilization, cultural diffusion, culture region,* and *globalization* by writing three to four paragraphs that use all of the terms.

Main Ideas

2. **Explaining** What is an ethnic group, and how do ethnic groups relate to a region's culture?
3. **Summarizing** Use a diagram like the one below to identify the advancements made by the world's earliest civilizations.

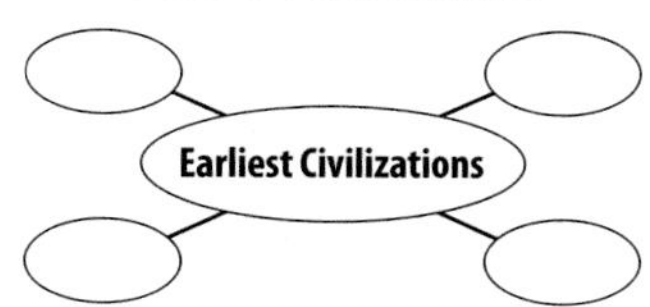

4. **Explaining** Why is globalization occurring?

Critical Thinking

5. **BIG Idea** Explain the different ways that cultural change can occur.
6. **Challenge** How do local and national differences affect culture on a regional or global level?

Writing About Geography

7. **Personal Writing** Write a journal entry describing examples of globalization that you have witnessed. Then add your predictions about how globalization might affect your community in the future.

Assess

Social Studies ONLINE
Study Central™ provides summaries, interactive games, and online graphic organizers to help students review content.

Close

Explaining Have students explain the causes and effects of globalization. **OL**

Section 2 Review

Answers

1. Sentences should use vocabulary words according to their definitions in the section and Glossary.
2. An ethnic group shares a language, history, religion, and some physical traits. Its characteristics reflect and influence a region's culture.
3. Answers may include agriculture, civilizations, cities, governments, religions, and writing systems.
4. Advances in communications and technology have broken down barriers between culture regions.
5. Answers should include inventions and innovations, technological improvements, or the influence of other cultures through diffusion or conquest.
6. The movement of people to neighboring areas changes the culture of those areas.
7. Students should give examples of globalization, such as exposure to foreign foods and movies. They might predict that globalization will cause their community to have more large businesses and fewer independent stores, or they might predict job growth.

Focus

R Reading Strategy

Activating Prior Knowledge

Ask: What products do you use that might come from other countries? *(Answers may include fruits and vegetables, clothing, or a family car.)* How does foreign trade affect local culture? *(Possible answer: It affects the foods people eat, the music they listen to, and the language people use.)* Do you think these effects are positive or negative? Why? *(Possible answer: positive; because they add diversity and make a local culture more interesting)* OL

Teach

Have students create a T-chart with the headings "For Globalization" and "Against Globalization." As they read the feature, have them note important details for and against globalization. OL

Additional Support

YOU Decide: Is Globalization Good for Everyone?

R Globalization is sometimes defined as the linking together of the world's nations through trade. This trade among nations allows people from different cultures to interact with each other. As a result, cultures begin sharing traits with others. People disagree about the effects of globalization on economies and cultures. Some people think that globalization helps countries by providing them with jobs and new technologies. However, others believe that globalization destroys the cultural traditions and customs of smaller groups.

For Globalization

One of the main restraints on liberty has always been "the tyranny [unjust use of power] of place." At its crudest, this has meant restrictions, both political and economic, on where people can live, but it also includes restrictions on where people can go, what they can buy, where they can invest, and what they can read, hear, or see. Globalization by its nature brings down these barriers, and it helps hand the power to choose to the individual.

—John Micklethwait and Adrian Wooldridge
A Future Perfect: The Essentials of Globalization

FastFacts

Globalization Through the Ages The history of globalization can be traced as far back as 1295, when Italian explorer Marco Polo brought Chinese silk and jewels to Europe. Protectionism also has a long history. Around 1500 the emperor of China closed the nation to the outside world and ordered all large ships destroyed. For several hundred years, China greatly limited trade with the outside world, allowing foreign traders into only one port. In the mid-1800s, Europeans forced China to open its ports to trade. Globalization grew in the rest of the world over the centuries. In 1914, British economist John Maynard Keynes wrote that a person in England could order anything by phone from home and have it delivered to his or her doorstep. However, globalization ebbed after World War I, when nations blamed a buildup of military alliances for the war. After World War II, globalization grew again, but a backlash has been gaining ground. In recent years, globalization critics have protested at the annual meeting of the World Trade Organization.

Against Globalization

For millions of people globalization has not worked. Many have been actually made worse off, as they have seen their jobs destroyed and their lives become more insecure. They have felt increasingly powerless against forces beyond their control. They have seen their democracies undermined, their cultures eroded. **C**

If globalization continues to be conducted in the way that is has been in the past, if we continue to fail to learn from our mistakes, globalization will not only not succeed in promoting development but will continue to create poverty and instability.

—Joseph Stiglitz
Globalization and Its Discontents

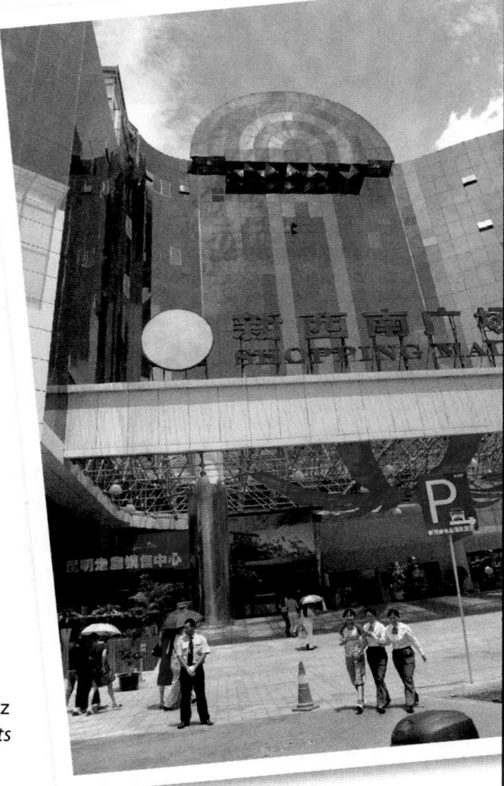

You Be the Geographer

1. **Identifying** Choose a sentence from each opinion that best summarizes the authors' views about globalization.
2. **Critical Thinking** What does Stiglitz mean when he writes "... globalization ... will continue to create poverty and instability"? Use the definition of *globalization* to explain your answer.
3. **Read to Write** Write one paragraph that identifies how globalization might benefit a nation. Then write a paragraph that describes how globalization might harm a nation.

YOU Decide

C Critical Thinking

Determining Cause and Effect Ask: What effect does the author say globalization will have on people's work life? *(The author says people will lose their jobs, which will make their lives less secure.)* **OL**

Assess/Close

Read the second paragraph of the argument against globalization on this page. Divide students into small groups. Ask them to brainstorm ways that globalization could be conducted differently. Encourage them to consider international trade, business conducted in foreign countries, and advanced technologies. Have students discuss how their methods would help preserve local cultures. **OL**

You Be the Geographer

Answers:

1. Possible answer: For—Globalization by its nature brings down these barriers, and it helps hand the power to choose to the individual. Against—For millions of people, globalization has not worked.
2. Possible answer: The development of an interdependent worldwide culture will cost people jobs, which then creates poverty and instability.
3. Answers will vary but should show a balance of facts from the text.

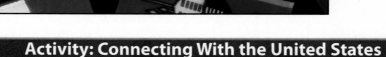

Activity: Connecting With the United States

Describing Remind students that globalization includes the creation of free trade zones among nations. **Ask: What is a free trade zone?** *(a region that is free of barriers to trade, such as tariffs and quotas, and in which investment is freely allowed)* Remind students that in 1994, the United States signed the North American Free Trade Agreement (NAFTA) with Canada and Mexico. The agreement was designed to eliminate barriers to trade, promote fair competition, increase investment, protect intellectual property rights, and establish a framework for cooperation. The three nations created the NAFTA Secretariat to administer the agreement and to resolve disputes among the three nations. Ask students to research the NAFTA Secretariat, its purpose, and recent accomplishments. Have students write their findings in their journals. Advanced learners might also research and write about how NAFTA has affected American businesses. **OL**

Focus

Bellringer

Daily Focus Transparency 3-3

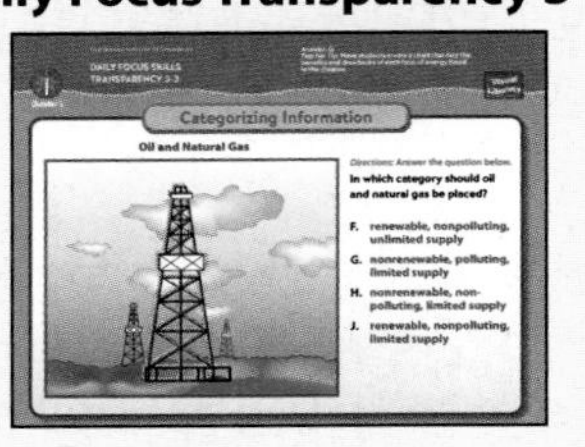

Guide to Reading

Answers to Graphic:

Answers may include:

Renewable Resources:	Nonrenewable Resources:
1. sun	minerals
2. soil	oil
3. rivers	coal
4. trees	fossil fuels
5. wind	

Section Spotlight Video

To learn more about resources, technology, and world trade, have students watch the Section Spotlight Video.

Guide to Reading

BIG Idea

Patterns of economic activities result in global interdependence.

Content Vocabulary

- natural resource *(p. 93)*
- renewable resource *(p. 93)*
- nonrenewable resource *(p. 93)*
- economic system *(p. 94)*
- developed country *(p. 94)*
- developing country *(p. 94)*
- newly industrialized country *(p. 94)*
- export *(p. 95)*
- import *(p. 95)*
- tariff *(p. 95)*
- quota *(p. 95)*
- free trade *(p. 96)*
- interdependence *(p. 96)*

Academic Vocabulary

- finite *(p. 93)*
- finance *(p. 95)*

Reading Strategy

Categorizing Information Use a diagram like the one below to list three specific examples of each type of natural resource.

Renewable Resources	Nonrenewable Resources
1.	
2.	
3.	

SECTION 3

Resources, Technology, and World Trade

Picture This It might not have temperature controls, but this solar stove is one of the most important household appliances in Chinese homes. China is a world leader in the use of solar energy. As China's economy has grown, the demand for fuel has driven energy costs up, increasing the desire to use alternative energy sources. Read this section to learn more about other resources and how the world's people use them.

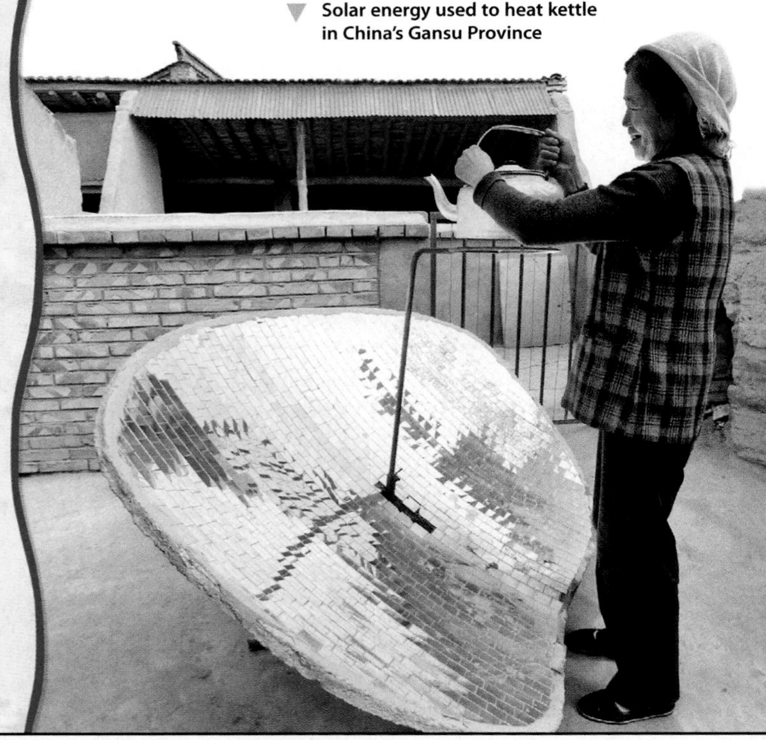

▼ Solar energy used to heat kettle in China's Gansu Province

Resource Manager

R Reading Strategies	C Critical Thinking	D Differentiated Instruction	W Writing Support	S Skill Practice
Teacher Edition • Reading Maps, p. 93 • Det. Importance, p. 94 • Summarizing, p. 95 **Additional Resources** • Guid. Read., URB p. 83 • Cont. Vocab., URB p. 85 • Ac. Vocab., URB p. 87 • Read. Ess., p. 25	**Teacher Edition** • Compare/Contrast, p. 94 **Additional Resources** • Crit. Think., URB p. 93 • Geo. & Econ., URB p. 5 • Authentic Assess., p. 3 • Quizzes and Tests, p. 27	**Teacher Edition** • Kinesthetic, p. 93 • Logical/Math., p. 94 **Additional Resources** • School-to-Home Conn., URB p. 103	**Teacher Edition** • Persuasive Writing, p. 95 **Additional Resources** • Writing Skills, URB p. 99	**Teacher Edition** • Using Geo. Skills, p. 96 **Additional Resources** • Chart, Graph, and Map Skills, URB p. 91 • Daily Focus Trans. 3-3 • Reg. Atlas, URB pp. 1–7

Natural Resources

Main Idea **Earth's resources are not evenly distributed, nor do they all exist in endless supply.**

Geography and You What natural resources can you name? Read to learn about two kinds of natural resources.

Natural resources are materials from the Earth that people use to meet their needs. Soil, trees, wind, and oil are examples of natural resources. Such resources can provide food, shelter, goods, and energy.

Renewable resources are natural resources that cannot be used up or that can be replaced. For example, the sun, the wind, and water cannot be used up, and forests can replace themselves. Some renewable resources, such as rivers, the wind, and the sun, can produce electricity and are important sources of energy.

Most natural resources are **finite,** or limited in supply. They are called **nonrenewable resources.** Once humans use up these resources, they are gone. Minerals like iron ore and gold are nonrenewable, as are oil, coal, and other fossil fuels. Fossil fuels heat homes, run cars, and generate electricity. D

Reading Check **Identifying** Which energy resources are renewable? Nonrenewable?

NATIONAL GEOGRAPHIC **Maps In MOtion** See StudentWorks™ Plus or glencoe.com.

Figure 4 **World Energy Production and Consumption**

Energy production (quadrillion Btus)
Energy consumption (quadrillion Btus)

111.8
88.5
92.9
60.3
72.7
27.4
101.0
70.6
49.2
29.1
10.2
14.0
36.0
28.7
19.6
11.0
10.3
5.1

Europe
Latin America
Russia
South Asia
Africa south of the Sahara
Australia, Oceania, and Antarctica
East Asia and Southeast Asia
North Africa, Southwest Asia, and Central Asia
United States and Canada

Map Skills

1. **Regions** Which region of the world consumes the least energy?
2. **Movement** Where do regions obtain the extra energy they need?

Source: Energy Information Administration, 2004.

R

Teach

D Differentiated Instruction

Kinesthetic Ask students to find photos of renewable and nonrenewable resources in magazines. Have them cut out the photos and glue them onto large sheets of paper under the headings "Renewable" and "Nonrenewable." **ELL**

R Reading Strategy

Reading Maps **Ask: What does the map show?** *(the amounts of energy produced and used in regions of the world)* **What unit of measurement is used?** *(Btus)* Explain that *Btu* is an abbreviation for "British thermal unit," which is a standard way of measuring energy. **OL**

Reading Check **Answer:** Renewable: sun, soil, rivers, trees, wind; Nonrenewable: minerals, fossil fuels

Map Skills

Answers:

1. Australia, Oceania, and Antarctica
2. Possible answer: They purchase through trade with other regions.

Differentiated Instruction

Leveled Activities

BL **Writing Skills Activity, URB p. 99**

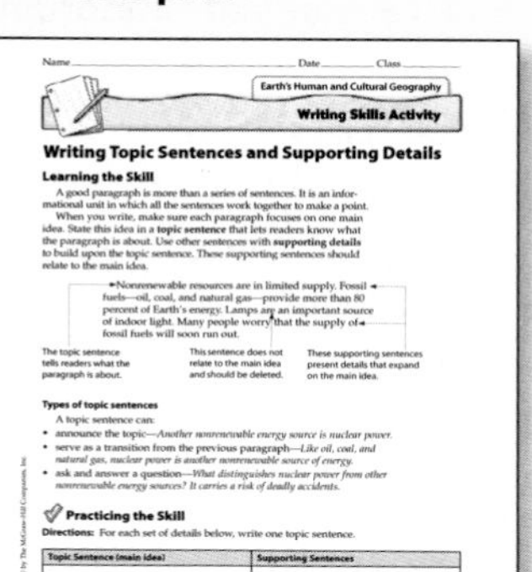

OL **Chart, Graph, and Map Skills Activity, URB p. 91**

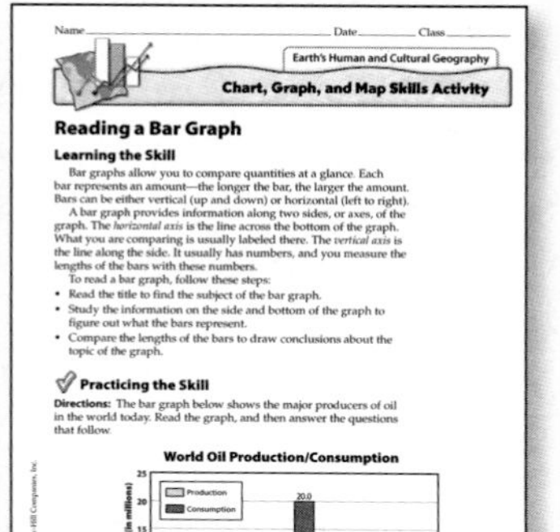

ELL **Academic Vocabulary Activity, URB p. 87**

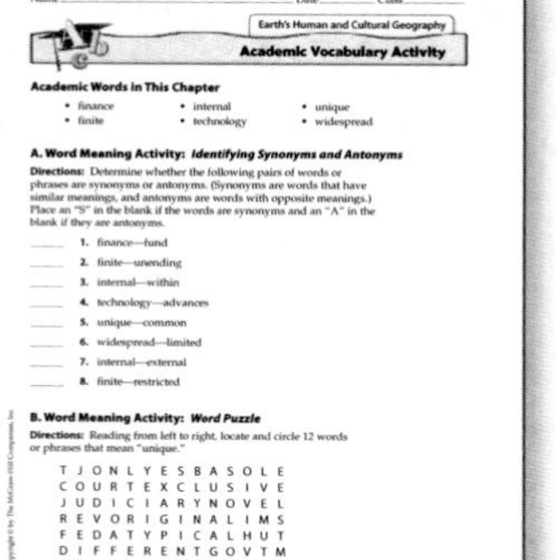

R Reading Strategy

Determining Importance After students read the text on economic systems, have them work in pairs to write a sentence that tells the main idea of the section. Tell them that they must use the words from the heading in their sentence. **OL**

C Critical Thinking

Comparing and Contrasting

Ask: How are developed countries different from developing countries? *(Developed countries have less agriculture and more technology, and their workers have higher incomes.)* **OL**

For further practice on this skill (Comparing and Contrasting), see the **Skills Handbook**.

D Differentiated Instruction

Logical/Mathematical Ask: Which country has about equal amounts of industry and services? *(Thailand)* **How much greater is the service sector in the United States than in Sierra Leone?** *(57.7%)* **OL**

Economies and Trade

Main Idea An economy is the way people use and manage resources.

Geography and You What kinds of goods and services do the people in your community produce? Read to find out about how economic decisions are made.

Economic Systems

To help make economic decisions, societies develop economic systems. An **economic system** is the method used to answer three key questions: what goods and services to produce, how to produce them, and who will receive them.

There are four kinds of economic systems. In a traditional economy, individuals decide what to produce and how to produce it. These choices are based on custom or habit. In these economies, people often do the same work as their parents and grandparents. Technology is often limited.

R In a command economy, the government makes the key economic decisions about resources. It decides the costs of products and the wages workers earn, and individuals have little economic freedom.

In a market economy, individuals make their own economic decisions. People have the right to own property or businesses. Businesses make what they think customers want (supply). Consumers have choices about which goods and services to buy (demand). Prices are determined by supply and demand. People will buy less of an item as it gets more expensive. On the other hand, if the price is low, people will tend to buy more of an item.

Most nations have mixed economies, which is the fourth type of economic system. China, for example, has mostly a command economy, but the government allows some features of a market economy. The United States has mainly a market economy with some government involvement.

Developed and Developing Countries

Geographers look at economies in another way—how developed they are. A **developed country** has a mix of agriculture, a great deal of manufacturing, and service industries. Service industries, such as banking and health care, provide services rather than making products. Developed economies tend to rely on new technologies, C and workers have relatively high incomes. Examples of developed countries include the United States, France, and Japan.

Countries with economies that are not as advanced are called **developing countries.** These countries have little industry. Agriculture remains important, and incomes per person are generally low. Developing countries include Sierra Leone, Cambodia, and Guatemala.

Still other countries are becoming more industrial. Geographers call these countries **newly industrialized countries.** South Korea, Thailand, and Singapore are all moving toward economies like those in developed countries. The chart below shows divisions in the economies of a developed, a developing, and a newly industrialized country.

D

Economic Divisions

Country	Agriculture	Industry	Services
United States	1%	20.4%	78.7%
Sierra Leone	49%	31%	21%
Thailand	9.9%	44.1%	46%

Source: *World Factbook*, 2006.

Hands-On Chapter Project Step 3

Creating a Time Line for Your State

Step 3: Compiling a Class Time Line Students will work as a class to make a single time line for their state.

Directions Tape all of the groups' time lines together to create a large class time line that depicts the history of settlement in your state. Write on the board the characteristics that define a group's culture: social groups, language, religion, history, daily life, arts, government, and economy. Have students work together to decide on a title for the time line that captures an important characteristic of the state.

Putting It Together Have students study the completed time line and look for trends and patterns. Encourage students to use vocabulary words from the chapter as they draw conclusions from the time line. **OL**

(Chapter Project cont. on the Visual Summary page.)

World Trade

Resources, like people, are not distributed evenly around the world. Because most countries have more than they need of some resources and not enough of others, trade is important.

Trade allows nations to **export**, or sell to other countries, the resources they have in abundance or the products made from those resources. They also **import**, or buy from other countries, the resources they do not have or the products they cannot make themselves. R

Trade is important for both developed and developing nations. For example, the countries of Europe import what they need—food, energy resources, and minerals—to maintain their successful economies. The developing nations, in turn, rely on the sale of their products and resources to **finance**, or pay for, efforts to further industrialize and build their economies.

Barriers to Trade

Nations try to manage trade in order to boost their own economies. Some nations use **tariffs**, or taxes, to increase the price of imported goods. By making imported items more expensive, tariffs encourage consumers to buy less expensive items that are manufactured in their own country. W

Quotas are another barrier to trade. A **quota** is a limit on how many items of a particular product can be imported from a certain nation.

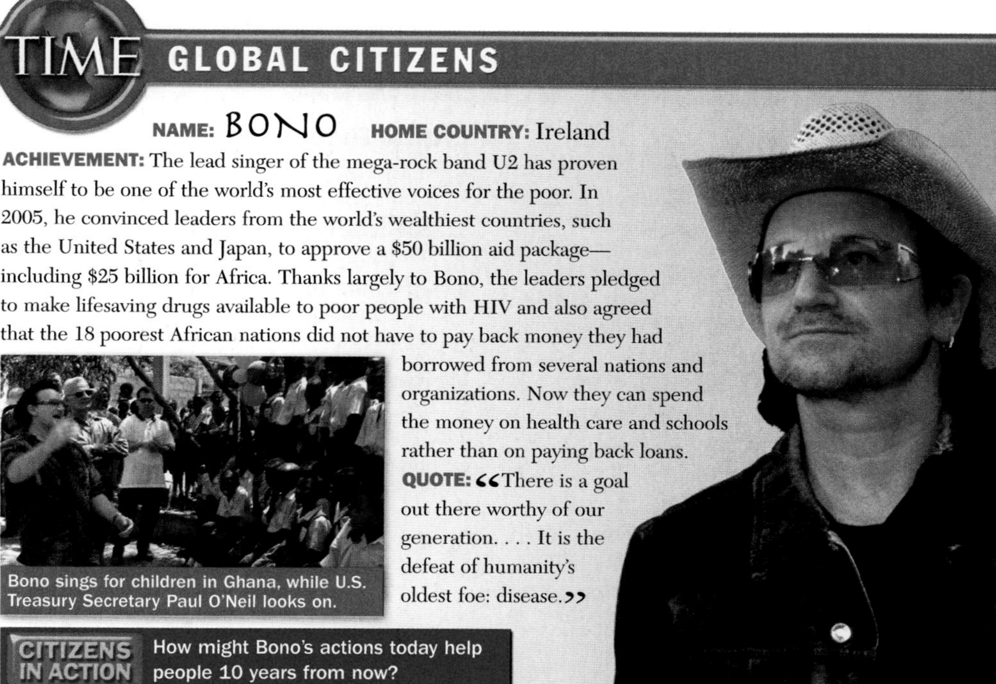

TIME GLOBAL CITIZENS

NAME: BONO **HOME COUNTRY:** Ireland

ACHIEVEMENT: The lead singer of the mega-rock band U2 has proven himself to be one of the world's most effective voices for the poor. In 2005, he convinced leaders from the world's wealthiest countries, such as the United States and Japan, to approve a $50 billion aid package—including $25 billion for Africa. Thanks largely to Bono, the leaders pledged to make lifesaving drugs available to poor people with HIV and also agreed that the 18 poorest African nations did not have to pay back money they had borrowed from several nations and organizations. Now they can spend the money on health care and schools rather than on paying back loans.

QUOTE: "There is a goal out there worthy of our generation. . . . It is the defeat of humanity's oldest foe: disease."

Bono sings for children in Ghana, while U.S. Treasury Secretary Paul O'Neil looks on.

GEORGE PIMENTEL/WIREIMAGE.COM; (INSET) AP WIDE WORLD

CITIZENS IN ACTION How might Bono's actions today help people 10 years from now?

R Reading Strategy

Summarizing Have students work in pairs to summarize the text under "World Trade." Students should include in their summaries the vocabulary words *export*, *import*, and *finance*. OL

W Writing Support

Persuasive Writing Read and discuss the text under "Barriers to Trade." Discuss with students possible advantages and disadvantages of tariffs and quotas. Then have them choose a side, either for or against tariffs and quotas, and write a persuasive paragraph to support their position. Ask volunteers to share their writings with the class. OL

CITIZENS IN ACTION

Possible Answer:
People who might have died will live, become educated, and lead healthier lives.

Differentiated Instruction

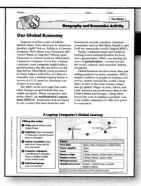

Geography and Economics Activity, URB pp. 5–6

Our Global Economy

Objective: To help students understand globalization and relate it to their own lives

Focus: Have students explain their understanding of globalization.

Teach: Review the map and table, and discuss what they show about globalization.

Assess: Have students answer the questions using the information in the map and table.

Close: Discuss with students how globalization affects young people.

Differentiated Instruction Strategies

- BL Help students find on a map the nations discussed in the activity.
- AL Have students research which nations export the most goods to the United States.
- ELL Ask students to describe how globalization affects their native country.

S Skill Practice

Using Geography Skills Have students work in pairs to research several goods produced in the United States and sold to other countries. Then have them find several products produced by those countries and sold to other countries. After students complete their list, have them use a world atlas to map their findings. As a class, discuss the interdependence of the countries that students studied. **AL**

Reading Check Possible Answers: Trade barriers exist so that nations can boost their own economies. Tariffs are taxes, and quotas are limits on the number of items a country can import.

Assess

Social Studies ONLINE
Study Central™ provides summaries, interactive games, and online graphic organizers to help students review content.

Close

Defining Have students define the four types of economic systems: traditional, command, market, and mixed. **OL**

Free Trade

In recent years, many countries have agreed to get rid of trade barriers. The removal of trade limits so that goods flow freely among countries is called **free trade.** Often countries sign formal treaties agreeing to free trade. For example, in 1992 Canada, the United States, and Mexico signed the North American Free Trade Agreement (NAFTA). This pact removed most trade barriers between the three nations.

Interdependence and Technology

S Growing trade among the world's countries has resulted in the globalization of the world's economies. As a result, the world's people and economies have become more interdependent. **Interdependence** means that countries rely on each other for ideas, goods, services, and markets, or places to sell their goods. When economies are linked together, a drought or a war in one region can cause price increases or shortages in another region far away.

Interdependence has come about in part because of new technologies. During the past 200 years, the invention of new technologies has occurred much faster than at any other time in history. Advances in transportation, such as trains and airplanes, and in communication, such as telephones and the Internet, have contributed greatly to globalization.

Reading Check **Explaining** Explain why trade barriers exist, and describe two types of trade barriers.

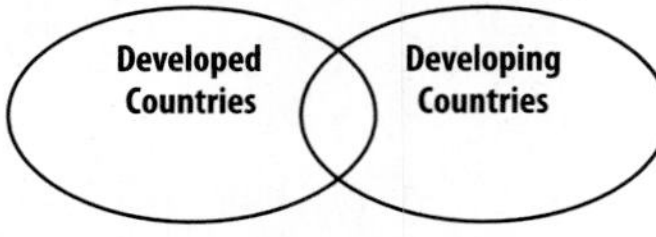

Social Studies ONLINE
Study Central™ To review this section, go to glencoe.com.

Vocabulary

1. **Explain** the significance of:
   a. natural resource
   b. renewable resource
   c. nonrenewable resource
   d. economic system
   e. developed country
   f. developing country
   g. newly industrialized country
   h. export
   i. import
   j. tariff
   k. quota
   l. free trade
   m. interdependence

Main Ideas

2. **Explaining** Why do people need natural resources?
3. **Comparing and Contrasting** Use a Venn diagram like the one below to compare and contrast developed and developing countries.

Developed Countries		Developing Countries

Critical Thinking

4. **Analyzing** Why has the world become more interdependent in recent years?
5. **BIG Idea** Explain how the distribution of natural resources relates to world trade.
6. **Challenge** In what ways might interdependence influence a place's cultural identity? Explain in two paragraphs.

Writing About Geography

7. **Using Your FOLDABLES** Use your Foldable to write a paragraph that predicts how population patterns might affect world resources in the future.

96 • Chapter 3

Answers

1. Definitions for the vocabulary words are found in the section and the Glossary.
2. to meet their needs for food, shelter, goods, and energy
3. Possible answer: Developed Countries—rely on new technologies, workers tend to have high incomes; Developing Countries—little industry, incomes for most people tend to be low; Both—mix of agriculture, manufacturing, and service industries
4. Global trade has led countries to depend on each other for ideas, goods, services, and markets.
5. Nations with many natural resources export those goods to nations with few natural resources.
6. Answers should include details from the text and should show an understanding of the relationship between economic interdependence and culture.
7. Paragraphs should include facts and details from the text about the relationship between population and resources.

Visual Summary

World Population

- Low death rates and high birthrates have led to rapid population growth.
- Some areas of the world are more densely populated than others.
- Nearly half of the world's population lives in cities.

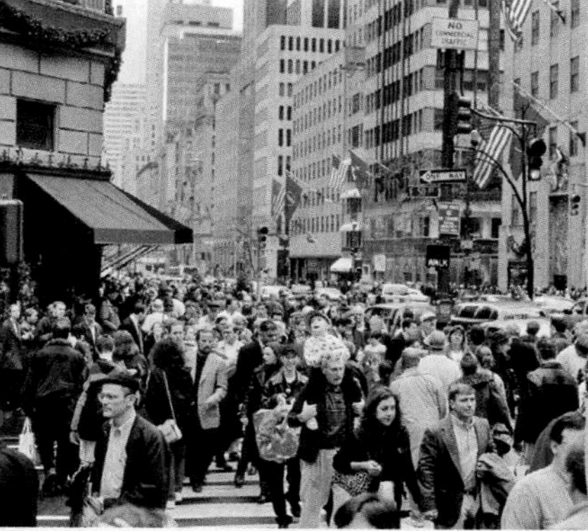

Commuters, New York City

Culture

- Culture is the way of life of a group of people who share similar beliefs and customs.
- Cultures change over time and influence one another.
- Modern technology has broken down barriers and helped create a global culture.

Oil worker, Iraq

Natural Resources

- Renewable resources either cannot be used up or can be replaced.
- Some resources—such as fossil fuels and minerals—are nonrenewable.

World Economies

- The four kinds of economic systems are traditional, command, market, and mixed.
- Developed countries use advanced technology and are highly productive.
- Developing countries have less advanced technology and are generally less productive.

World Trade

- In recent years, many countries have agreed to eliminate trade barriers.
- Growing trade among countries has made the world's people more interdependent.

Mexican president Vicente Fox (left), Canadian prime minister Jean Chrétien (center), and U.S. president George W. Bush (right) celebrate a trade agreement.

Grocery store in Yogakarta, Indonesia

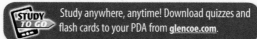

STUDY TO GO Study anywhere, anytime! Download quizzes and flash cards to your PDA from glencoe.com.

Visual Summary

Explaining Tell students that the bulleted items under each heading are main ideas about the chapter content. Explain that each bulleted item could be expanded into a paragraph by adding details from the chapter.

Organize students into pairs, and assign each pair a bulleted item. Tell them to find the text in the chapter that relates to each bulleted item and then add several details to the bulleted item to create a paragraph.

When students finish writing, have them share their paragraphs with other pairs who wrote on the same topic. Then have them organize their paragraphs according to the order in the Visual Summary and bind the papers together to make a book. Ask the class to create a title for the book, and keep it in class to use as a reference. **OL**

Analyzing Visuals Direct students' attention to the photograph of commuters in New York City. **Ask: What characteristics of a developed country do you see in the photo?** *(Possible answer: Workers live in an urban environment and not on farms, and the buildings likely contain businesses that produce goods or provide services.)* **OL**

Hands-On Chapter Project
Step 4: Wrap Up

Creating a Time Line for Your State

Step 4: Learning From the Time Line Students will synthesize what they have learned in Steps 1, 2, and 3.

Directions Write the Essential Question on the board. Ask students how creating the time line helped them understand the cultures in their state. Draw a two-column chart on the board. In one column, write each major group of settlers. In the other column, write one or two important cultural features that each group brought to the state. Ask students what, if any, cultural characteristics from each group are evident in the state. Discuss with students how the state has changed or may change in the future because of population movement, changes in population density, and changes in population distribution. Have students write a paragraph in their journal describing what they learned from making the time line and another paragraph answering the Essential Question. **OL**

Answers and Analyses

Reviewing Vocabulary

1. B If students understand the concept of density, they will have a better chance of answering the question correctly. Density relates to the number of people or items in a given amount of space. The denser an area is, the more crowded it is. Thus, it is logical that geographers use a measure of population density to determine how crowded a region is.

2. C Students can analyze word parts to help them answer this question. The term *refugee* contains the term *refuge*, or "safe haven." People who are refugees are seeking safety, or refuge, from a situation in their home country.

3. D Students' prior knowledge might lead them to the term *social* because they likely share many characteristics with their own social groups. They also might be tempted to choose the term *global* because it means "all-encompassing" and relates to geography. Remind them that ethnic groups are groups that share traits.

4. A Students might struggle to remember the difference between a developing country and a developed country. Tell them that developed countries have already developed industries and services and thus rely less on agriculture. Developing countries do not yet have much industry.

STANDARDIZED TEST PRACTICE

TEST-TAKING TIP

Think of answers in your head before looking at the possible answers so that the choices on the test will not throw you off or trick you.

Reviewing Vocabulary

Directions: Choose the word(s) that best completes the sentence.

1. Geographers measure ______ to determine how crowded a country or region is.

A refugees
B population density
C death rates
D birthrates

2. ______ are people who are forced to flee to another country to escape wars, persecution, or natural disasters.

A Immigrants
B Free traders
C Refugees
D Importers

3. A(n) ______ group shares a language, history, religion, and some physical traits.

A democratic
B global
C social
D ethnic

4. Countries with a mix of agriculture and a great deal of manufacturing and service industries are called ______ countries.

A developed
B underdeveloped
C overdeveloped
D developing

Reviewing Main Ideas

Directions: Choose the best answer for each question.

Section 1 *(pp. 72–76)*

5. One reason for the rapid increase in world population over the last two centuries is ______.

A increased migration
B increased population density
C improved health care
D urbanization

6. An example of a "push factor" for migration is ______ in the homeland.

A a shortage of jobs
B an abundance of jobs
C low population density
D an abundance of farmland

Section 2 *(pp. 82–89)*

7. In recent years more and more countries and regions are sharing cultural traits resulting in a(n) ______ culture.

A isolated
B global
C refugee
D ethnic

Section 3 *(pp. 92–96)*

8. To answer the questions of what goods and services to produce, how to produce them, and who will receive them, societies develop ______.

A quota systems
B trading systems
C manufacturing systems
D economic systems

GO ON

Reviewing Main Ideas

5. C If students read the question carefully, they will see that it is asking about the world population, not the population of a region or country; thus, *increased migration* is not a valid choice. *Increased population density* would not necessarily increase the world population, as people could simply be moving to a more crowded place. *Urbanization* involves people moving to cities, which would not increase the world population. Hence, answer choice C, *improved health care,* is the correct answer.

6. A It might help students to recall that a "push factor" is something that pushes people from their home country to another country. In analyzing the answer choices, students will note that answer choice A, *a shortage of jobs,* is the best choice.

Critical Thinking

Directions: Choose the best answer for each question.

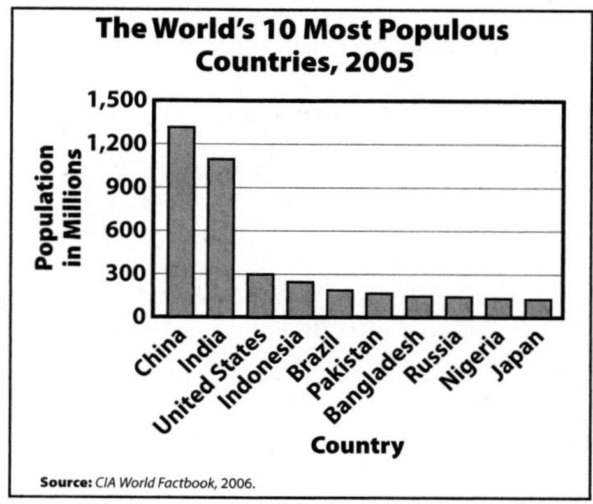

9. Based on the graph, what continent would likely be the most densely populated?

A North America

B South America

C Asia

D Africa

10. In which two countries would you expect to see the highest birthrates?

A United States and Russia

B India and China

C Pakistan and Bangladesh

D Brazil and Nigeria

Document-Based Questions

Directions: Analyze the document and answer the short-answer questions that follow.

[I]magine . . . that the world really is a 'global village.' . . . Say this village has 1,000 individuals, with all the characteristics of today's human race distributed in exactly the same proportions. . . .

Some 150 of the inhabitants live in [a wealthy] area of the village, about 780 in poorer districts. Another 70 or so live in a neighborhood that is [changing]. The average income per person is $6,000 a year. . . . But just 200 people [own] 86 percent of all the wealth, while nearly half of the villagers are eking out an existence on less than $2 per day. . . .

Life expectancy in the affluent district is nearly 78 years, in the poorer areas 64 years—and in the very poorest neighborhoods a mere 52 years. . . . Why do the poorest lag so far behind? Because in their neighborhoods there is a far higher incidence of infectious diseases and malnutrition, combined with an [serious] lack of access to safe water, sanitation, health care, adequate housing, education, and work.

—*Kofi Annan,* Millennium Report, *2000*

11. Describe the differences in income in the village.

12. According to the writer, where is life expectancy higher and why is this so?

Extended Response

13. Write a letter to a government leader in which you try to persuade him or her to invest taxpayer money into research on how to better use our energy resources. Explain why you think either renewable or nonrenewable resources deserve more funds for research.

Social Studies ONLINE
For additional test practice, use Self-Check Quizzes—Chapter 3 at glencoe.com.

Need Extra Help?

If you missed question. . .	1	2	3	4	5	6	7	8	9	10	11	12	13
Go to page. . .	74	76	84	94	73	76	89	94	73	73	94	94	93

Critical Thinking

9. C Students should conclude that the countries with the highest populations would likely be the most densely populated. Because the top two countries are in Asia, and because the area of land in each continent is not shown, answer choice C is the best choice.

10. B Students can assume that the countries with the greatest number of people would have the greatest number of births. Hence, B is the correct answer choice.

Document-Based Questions

11. According to the writer, 800, or 80%, of the people sharing just 14% of the world's wealth, thereby resulting in poverty and its accompanying problems.

12. According to the writer, just 200 of the 1000 people in the global village own 86% of the wealth. Life expectancy is higher in the affluent district of the global village because the area has less infectious diseases and malnutrition, plus better sanitation, health care, housing, education, and employment.

Extended Response

13. Answers will vary but might include an argument in favor of renewable energy sources because they will not run out in the future. The paragraph should demonstrate an understanding of the difference between renewable and nonrenewable resources.

7. B In reading the chapter, students should understand that people around the world are becoming more interconnected through technology and trade and that this interconnectedness is resulting in a shared culture around the world. This worldwide culture is known as a *global culture.*

8. D Students can use a process of elimination to answer the question. Answer choice A involves limits to trade and does not involve manufacturing, so it is incorrect. Not all countries manufacture items, so answer choice C is incorrect. The broad concept of a trading system does not include the manufacturing of goods, so answer choice B is incorrect. Hence, answer choice D is the correct answer.

Social Studies ONLINE
Have students visit the Web site at glencoe.com to review Chapter 3 and take the Self-Check Quiz.

Need Extra Help?
Have students refer to the pages listed if they miss any of the questions.

Teach

Using Geography Skills Have students use a time zone map to identify the locations of the different time zones around the world. Then have them write five quiz questions, such as "What time is it in New York City if it is 1 P.M. in London?" Assign students to a partner, and have them answer each other's questions. **OL**

Logical/Mathematical Have students use the text to answer the following questions: **What is the time difference between Los Angeles and Rio de Janeiro?** *(4 hours)* **If it is 3 P.M. in Washington, D.C., what time is it in Paris, France?** *(9 P.M.)* **Which country listed on this page will see daybreak on Tuesday before France?** *(Egypt)* **OL**

TIME JOURNAL

It may be the middle of the night where you live, but in many parts of the world, people are well into their day. It's all because of the 24 time zones that divide up Earth. So while one part of the world sleeps, somewhere, kids are at school, workers are at their jobs, and some folks are having dinner. Take a look at what is happening on Earth at exactly the same moment during one day in April.

Monday, 7 a.m. LOS ANGELES, CALIFORNIA Some people are just waking up. Others are sitting down to breakfast. Early birds are headed to their jobs hoping to avoid traffic jams on the state's freeways.

Monday, 10 a.m. WASHINGTON, D.C. Workers are at their desks. And at the White House, the wheels of government have been turning since 7 a.m. or even earlier, where 12-hour workdays are routine.

Monday, 11 a.m. RIO DE JANEIRO, BRAZIL Almost every day is a beach day in Rio. While beachgoers are enjoying sun and sand, traffic jams clog the city's streets, students are at their desks, and Rio's stores are filled with shoppers.

Monday, 2 p.m. DAKAR, SENEGAL Outdoor markets are packed in this west African nation. School is winding down for the day, and fishers are returning home with their day's catch from the Atlantic Ocean.

Monday, 5 p.m. CAIRO, EGYPT This capital city is filled with the sounds of people being called to prayer, vendors selling their goods at outdoor bazaars, and the blare of car and bus horns on traffic-clogged streets. Tourists and residents alike can marvel at the Pyramids of Giza built almost 5,000 years ago.

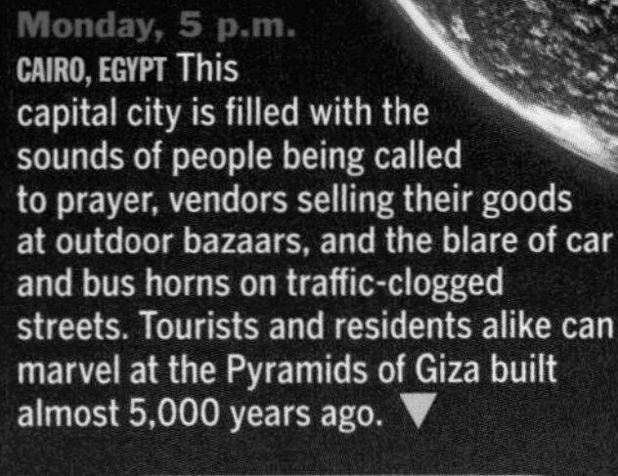

Monday, 4 p.m. PARIS, FRANCE School is out and some kids are playing soccer, a favorite pastime. Other students are studying for exams to get into special high schools. Some tourists are having their pictures taken in front of the Eiffel Tower while others are visiting the city's famous museums, perhaps catching a glimpse of the *Mona Lisa*.

TOP TO BOTTOM: CREATAS/SUPERSTOCK; AP PHOTO; JIM ZUCKERMAN/CORBIS; KURT SCHOLZ/SUPERSTOCK; LISA ENGLEBRECHT/DANITADELIMONT.COM; GARY COOK/ALAMY; GLOBE: NASA

Additional Support

Additional Statistics You can find data like this and much more in the *CIA World Factbook*. Go to www.cia.gov and click on the link to the *World Factbook*. From there you can click on the countries you wish to learn more about.

Time Zones	
Number of time zones in Australia	3
Number of time zones in Brazil	4
Number of time zones in Canada	6
Number of time zones in China	1
Number of time zones in India	1
Number of time zones in Mexico	4
Number of time zones in Russia	11
Number of time zones in the United States (including Alaska and Hawaii)	6

Source: *CIA World Factbook*, 2006.

A DAY IN THE LIFE OF THE WORLD'S PEOPLE

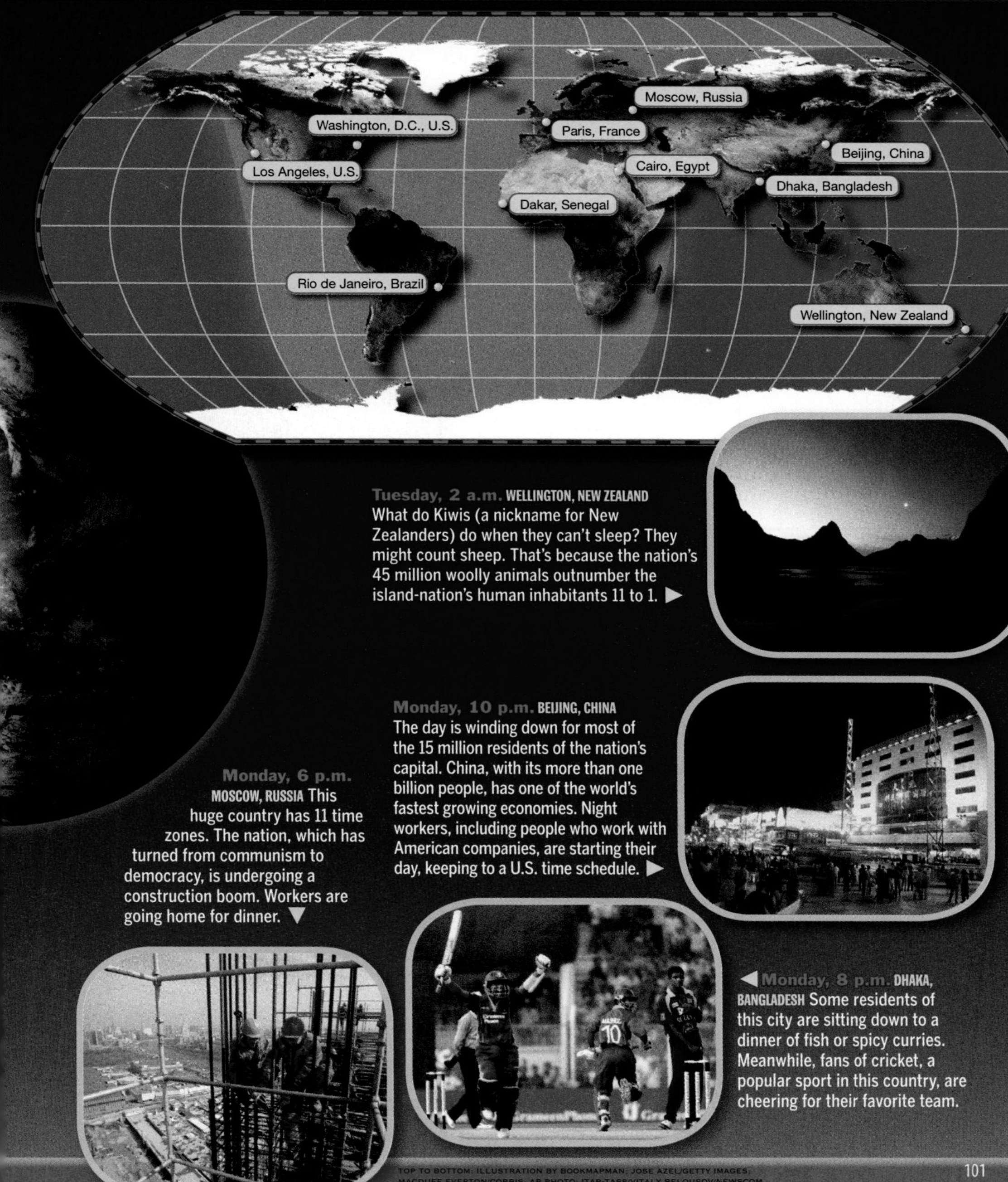

Tuesday, 2 a.m. WELLINGTON, NEW ZEALAND What do Kiwis (a nickname for New Zealanders) do when they can't sleep? They might count sheep. That's because the nation's 45 million woolly animals outnumber the island-nation's human inhabitants 11 to 1. ▶

Monday, 10 p.m. BEIJING, CHINA The day is winding down for most of the 15 million residents of the nation's capital. China, with its more than one billion people, has one of the world's fastest growing economies. Night workers, including people who work with American companies, are starting their day, keeping to a U.S. time schedule. ▶

Monday, 6 p.m. MOSCOW, RUSSIA This huge country has 11 time zones. The nation, which has turned from communism to democracy, is undergoing a construction boom. Workers are going home for dinner. ▼

◀ **Monday, 8 p.m.** DHAKA, BANGLADESH Some residents of this city are sitting down to a dinner of fish or spicy curries. Meanwhile, fans of cricket, a popular sport in this country, are cheering for their favorite team.

TOP TO BOTTOM: ILLUSTRATION BY BOOKMAPMAN; JOSE AZEL/GETTY IMAGES; MACDUFF EVERTON/CORBIS; AP PHOTO; ITAR-TASS/VITALY BELOUSOV/NEWSCOM

101

TIME JOURNAL

What's Popular Around the World

Soccer First played in England in the mid-1800s, soccer has become one of the most popular sports in the world. Soccer, which is called football in most countries of the world, is a simple game in which a ball is manipulated primarily by players' feet. Soccer spread from England to other western European countries in the 1870s, and then to South America and Southwest Asia and the rest of Asia. Soccer in the United States has slowly increased in popularity. Today millions of U.S. school-age children play youth soccer.

Say It in English

English Dialects Many people across the United States and in other countries of the world speak a common language—English. But the dialects, or variations, of English differ by country and region. Some experts state that the number of dialects in the United States ranges from 3 to 24. Others say it's impossible to determine an exact number because thousands of cities and groups have their own dialects. Some U.S. dialects include Californian, African American English, and Spanglish.

Activity: Persuasive Writing

Evaluating Explain to students that the original agreement on time zones established Greenwich, England, as the "prime" meridian, or the start of measurement for both time zones and longitude. With 360 degrees of longitude around the Earth and the need for 24 time zones to reflect 24 hours in a day, the standard time zones were each 15 degrees longitude wide. Actual time zone boundaries vary widely because governments have established them according to local preference and national boundaries. In fact, China stretches across 60 degrees longitude, but it is all in the same time zone. This would be the same as having the entire continental United States in the same time zone.

Ask students to research and write a persuasive essay arguing for keeping the continental United States in four different time zones or for making one time zone stretch across the entire country. Remind students to use specific facts and details to support their arguments. **OL**

Unit 2 Planning Guide

UNIT PACING CHART				
	Unit 2	Chapter 4	Chapter 5	Chapter 6
Day 1	Unit Opener	Chapter Opener	Chapter Opener	Chapter Opener
Day 2	Regional Atlas	Section 1	Section 1	Section 1
Day 3	Regional Atlas	Section 1	Section 1	TIME Perspectives
Day 4	Reading Social Studies	Geography & History	You Decide	TIME Perspectives
Day 5		Section 2	Section 2	Section 2
Day 6		Section 2	World Literature Reading	Review
Day 7		Review	Section 2	Chapter Assessment
Day 8		Chapter Assessment	Review	
Day 9			Chapter Assessment	
Day 10			TIME Journal	

Kevin Copes
Southwestern Middle School
Deland, Florida

Geography Through People Write the names of all 50 states on separate slips of paper and put them into a container. Have students draw a state randomly from the box. The state they choose becomes their assigned state. Next, students have to select a person who they think represents their assigned state in some way. The person can be living or a historical figure. Students will conduct research in order to present their selected person to the class. Presentations may be in whatever format students desire, so encourage creativity. For example, some students may use a simple poster board; others might make an elaborate multimedia presentation; still others might create an artifact they feel represents the person. To prepare for presentations, students can dress in costume or reenact a moment in history.

Author Note

Dear Social Studies Teacher:

The story of the United States and Canada is one of democracy and capitalism fueled by individual initiative. Having said that, it is useful for students to understand the diversity that has existed in both of these countries from their beginnings to the present day. For example in Quebec province, French culture and language are so strong that many people think the province should seek independence from Canada, which is largely English-speaking. For now, unity has been preserved. However, you will have much more fun traveling to Quebec if you are able to answer "oui" for yes and say "bonjour" for good-day!

In the United States, diversity is common. For example, there are Native American groups that have their own lands. All of the great American cities have ethnic neighborhoods populated by Italians, Germans, Greeks, Czechs, Irish, Poles, Bosnians, or others. Chinatowns often stand out with vivid displays of language and culture. In Louisiana, Cajun country is defined by language, culture, and even a flag.

The history of forced migration of African Americans to this country evokes pain, suffering, and abuse, but their descendants have carved out an important cultural piece of our historical "pie." Several states have witnessed massive migrations of Latinos. Latino culture is playing an increasingly important role in states such as Florida, Texas, Arizona, New Mexico, New York, and California. Of course, in California, we must emphasize the increasing role of immigrants from Asia.

Thus, we have a unity based on diversity, which requires respect, equal opportunity, improvement with hard work, and a chance to participate in the American dream.

Richard G. Boehm
Senior Author

Introducing Unit 2

What Makes the United States and Canada a Region?

The three chapters of this unit introduce students to the cultural region of the United States and Canada. The countries in this region share the following characteristics:

- a vast territory that includes a variety of landforms and climate regions
- a wealth of natural resources
- a colonial past
- diverse ethnic and religious groups and traditions
- free market economies that are closely tied to each other
- environmental challenges, including air pollution, diminishing water resources, and urban sprawl

NATIONAL GEOGRAPHIC

www.nationalgeographic.com/education

NGS ONLINE This online resource provides lesson plans, atlas updates, cartographic activities with interactive maps, an online map store, and geographic links.

UNIT 2

The United States and Canada

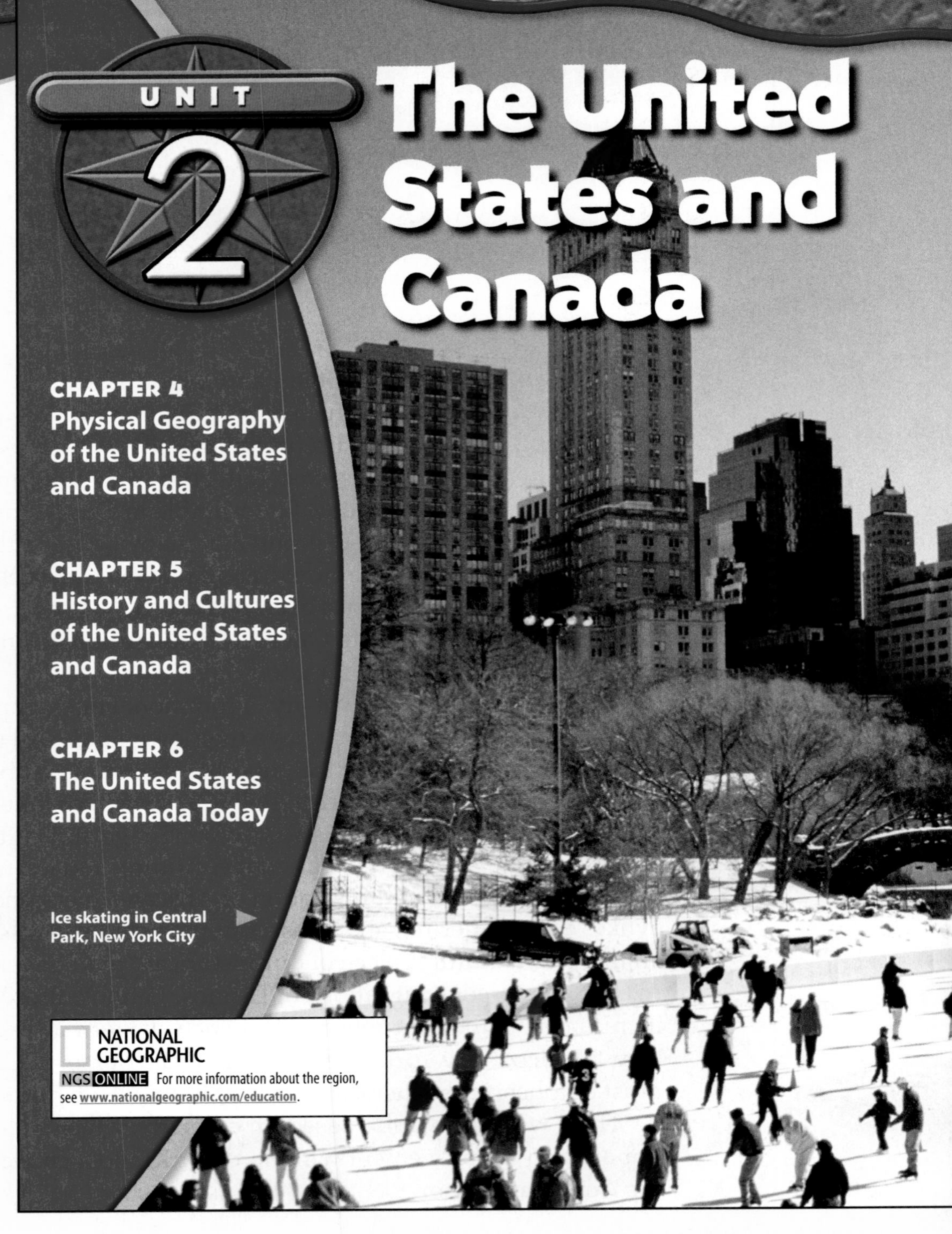

Ice skating in Central Park, New York City

NATIONAL GEOGRAPHIC

NGS ONLINE For more information about the region, see www.nationalgeographic.com/education.

Activity: Launching the Unit

Why Study the United States and Canada? Ask: What do you think are the biggest problems the United States faces today? *(Students might answer environmental problems, including global warming; dependence on foreign oil; terrorism; the rising cost of health care; poverty; and so on.)* Have students list in their notebooks the three problems they think are most serious. As students read through the chapters, ask them to take notes as they learn more about the causes and potential solutions for these problems. At the end of the unit, have each student write an essay about the one problem that concerns him or her most. The essay should explain what the problem is, what is already being done to address the problem, and what the student believes should be done to solve the problem, or how current efforts might be done differently. **OL**

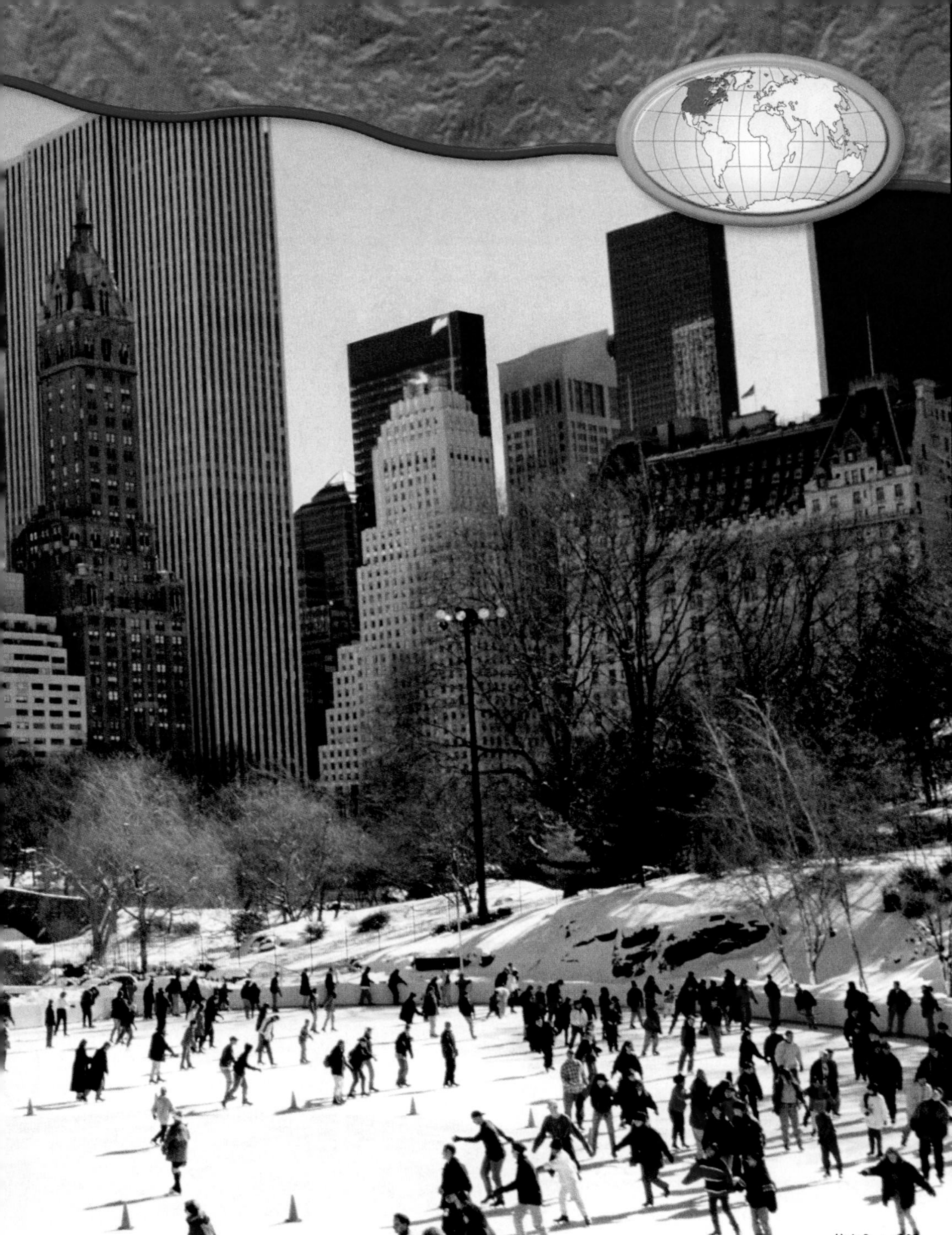

Introducing Unit 2

Introduce the Region

Mental Mapping Distribute outline maps of the United States and Canada that include boundaries of the states, provinces, and territories. **Ask:** **How many states in the United States and provinces and territories in Canada can you identify?** Have students write the names of all the states, provinces, and territories they can identify on their maps. When they have identified as many as they can remember, have them fill in the rest of the information using the Political map in the Regional Atlas. Then have them use the chart pages in the Regional Atlas to find the capital of each state, province, and territory and place the capitals on their maps.

Test the students' recall by distributing another blank outline map to each student and setting a timer for three minutes. Tell students to record as many state, province, territory, and capital names on the map as they can in the time allowed. **OL**

More About the Photo

Visual Literacy Central Park in Manhattan occupies an area of 840 acres between 59th and 110th Streets and Fifth and Eighth Avenues. Development of the park began in 1857, using landscape architecture techniques—one of the first American parks to do so. Architects Frederick Law Olmsted and Calvert Vaux won a competition with their plan for the park. Construction involved shifting millions of cartloads of dirt to build the rolling terrain, planting more than 270,000 trees and shrubs, laying a water-supply system, and constructing bridges, arches, and roads. Central Park officially opened in 1876 and is still considered a great achievement of artificial landscaping because of its highly varied terrain, interesting vistas, and wide variety of vegetation. Today, the park includes the ice-skating rink shown in the photo (in the winter), as well as Central Park Zoo, three small lakes, a theater and bandstand, athletic playing fields, playgrounds, and many rolling footpaths and bicycle paths.

Regional Atlas Activity

Where Is It?

Using a Compass Rose Ask: **What direction would you travel when flying from New York City to Edmonton?** *(northwest)* **What direction would you travel when flying from New York City to Los Angeles?** *(southwest)* **BL**

How Big Is It?

Estimating Ask: **If the land area of the region of the United States and Canada is about 7.7 million square miles, about how big do you think Canada's land area is? Why?** *(Answers may vary somewhat, but students may suggest from the outlines of the United States and Canada that Canada has slightly more than half of the total land area.)* **OL**

Comparing Population

Ask: **About how much larger is the population of the United States than the population of Canada?** *(nearly 10 times as large)* **Why do you think Canada's population might be so much smaller than that of the United States?** *(Because Canada is farther north, it has a colder and harsher climate than the United States.)* **OL**

Regional Atlas

The United States and Canada

Where Is It?

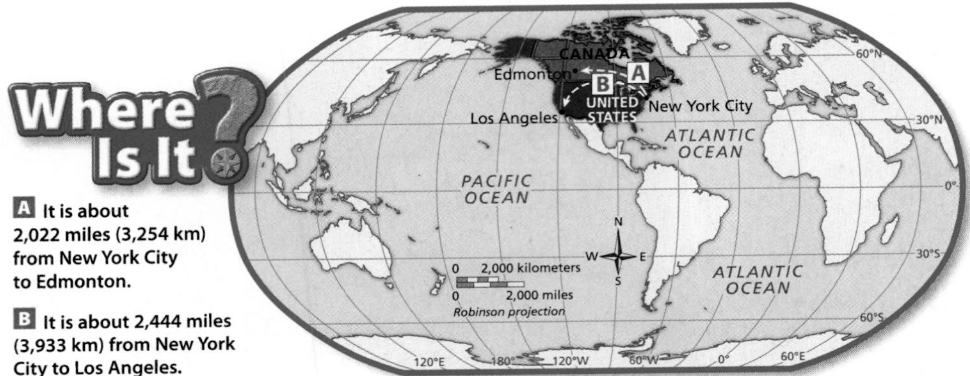

A It is about 2,022 miles (3,254 km) from New York City to Edmonton.

B It is about 2,444 miles (3,933 km) from New York City to Los Angeles.

How Big Is It?

The land area of the region of the United States and Canada is about 7.7 million square miles (19.9 million sq. km). In area, Canada is the second-largest country in the world, and the United States is the third largest. The United States has many more people than Canada, however, and is the third-most-populous country in the world, after China and India.

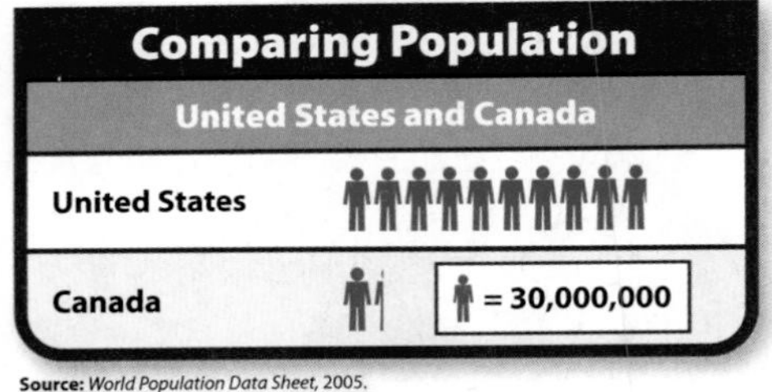

Comparing Population

United States and Canada	
United States	10 figures
Canada	1 figure (1 figure = 30,000,000)

Source: *World Population Data Sheet, 2005.*

Activity: Geographic Theme

Movement Ask: **Where did Europeans first settle in this region?** *(Europeans first settled in Florida, along the East Coast, and along the St. Lawrence River in Canada.)* Have students compare their answer with the Population Density map in the Regional Atlas. **Ask:** **Where do most people in the region live today?** *(Students should note that the areas along the east coast have high population densities and that areas east of the Mississippi River tend to be more heavily populated than areas west of it.)* **What can you tell about the movement of European settlers across the continent by looking at the Population Density map?** *(People moved westward from their original settlements on the East Coast, particularly in the United States; the Central Plains were settled relatively sparsely, but many people moved to the West Coast.)* **AL**

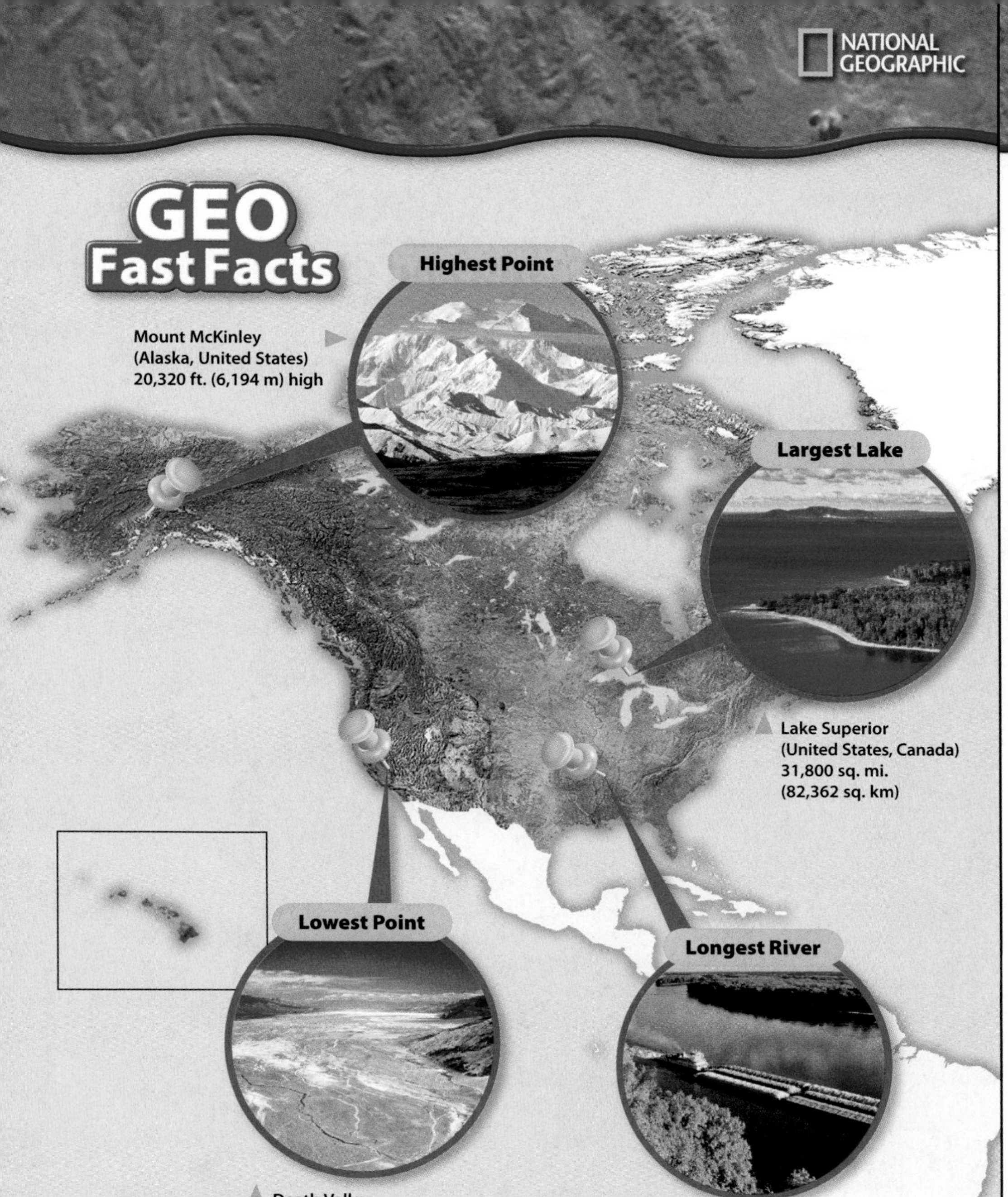

Geo Fast Facts

Researching Information Ask: What kinds of physical features are shown on this map? *(largest lake, longest river, lowest point, and highest point)*

Have each student choose a state in the United States or a province or territory in Canada. Explain that each student will be creating a Geo FastFacts poster for the state, province, or territory he or she has chosen. Direct students to appropriate reference sources—including world atlases, encyclopedias, and reliable online sources to find information on their chosen area. Have them collect appropriate facts on index cards. Then have them create a poster that includes an outline map of their state, province, or territory and at least five Geo FastFacts. Encourage students to add pictures of the features if they can find them. **OL**

FastFacts

- **The Great White Hurricane** The legendary blizzard that paralyzed the East Coast of the United States in March 1888 lasted for 36 hours and dumped an estimated 50 inches of snow in Connecticut and Massachusetts and 40 inches of snow in New York and New Jersey, while winds blew up to 48 miles per hour, creating snowdrifts up to 50 feet high.
- **St. Augustine** The oldest continually settled city in the United States is St. Augustine, in northeastern Florida. It was founded in 1565 by Spanish explorer Pedro Menendez de Aviles and was the main northern outpost of the Spanish colonial empire for most of the next 250 years, until it was acquired by the United States in 1821.
- **Klondike Gold Rush** One of the last great North American gold rushes occurred in bitterly cold northern Canada along the Klondike River. The rush began in 1896 and was over by 1899. Some of the most memorable novels and short stories of Jack London were set during the Klondike Gold Rush.

Regional Atlas Activity

Locating Before class, trace the latitude and longitude lines from the western half of a Winkel Tripel Projection map and label the lines appropriately. Make a copy for each student. Tell students to use the Physical map in the Regional Atlas to draw an outline of the North American continent on their latitude and longitude grid. Have them draw the approximate boundaries between Canada and the United States, including Alaska, and between the United States and Mexico. Then have them locate New York City at approximately 41°N, 73°W and Los Angeles at approximately 34°N, 118°W.

Remind students that New York City and Los Angeles are about 2,500 miles apart. **Ask:** **What is the approximate scale of your map?** *(Answers will vary, depending on the size of the maps; students should use the distance between New York and Los Angeles to determine the scale.)* **AL**

Answers:

1. Hudson Bay
2. The highest point in the region, Mt. McKinley, is in south-central Alaska.

The United States and Canada

PHYSICAL

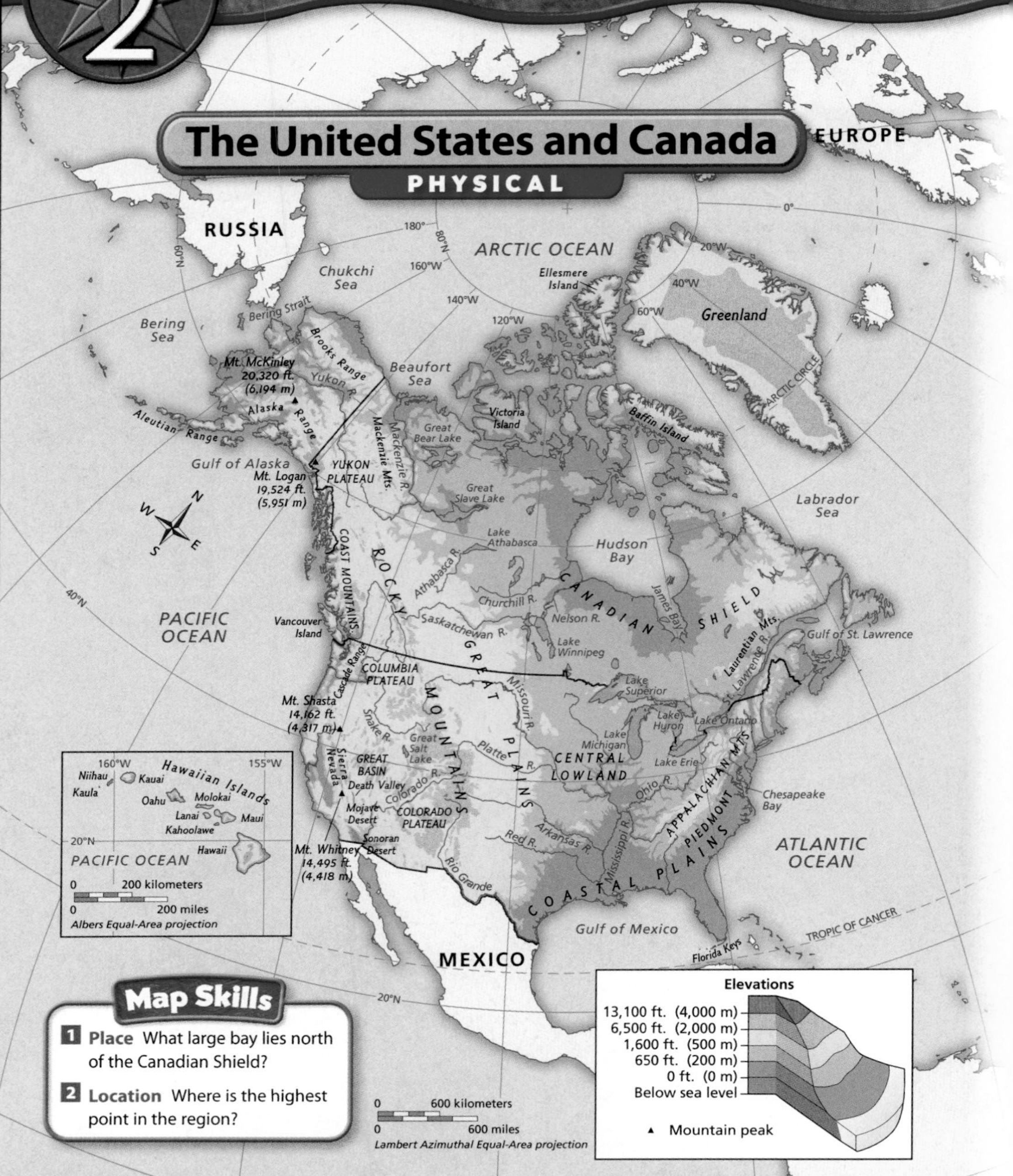

Map Skills

1 Place What large bay lies north of the Canadian Shield?

2 Location Where is the highest point in the region?

Elevations

13,100 ft. (4,000 m)
6,500 ft. (2,000 m)
1,600 ft. (500 m)
650 ft. (200 m)
0 ft. (0 m)
Below sea level

▲ Mountain peak

0 600 kilometers
0 600 miles
Lambert Azimuthal Equal-Area projection

0 200 kilometers
0 200 miles
Albers Equal-Area projection

Background: Land and Climate

Two Vast Nations The United States and Canada cover most of the North American continent; Canada, the world's second-largest country, lies in the northern part of the continent, and the United States, the world's third-largest country, is to the south. The climate ranges from cold Arctic tundra in the far north to warm, tropical areas in the south.

A broad coastal plain along the Atlantic coast and the Gulf of Mexico includes areas of fertile farmland as well as excellent harbors where several huge urban centers are located. To the west and north of these coastal plains lie the Appalachians, a mountain range that runs from eastern Canada to the southeastern United States. Vast interior lowlands to the west of the Appalachians have important mineral resources and energy reserves, navigable waterways, and areas of fertile farmland. Farther west lies a series of mountain ranges created by collisions between tectonic plates millions of years ago. The Rocky Mountains, which begin in Alaska and run south to Mexico, are the tallest of these mountain ranges.

NATIONAL GEOGRAPHIC

The United States and Canada

POLITICAL

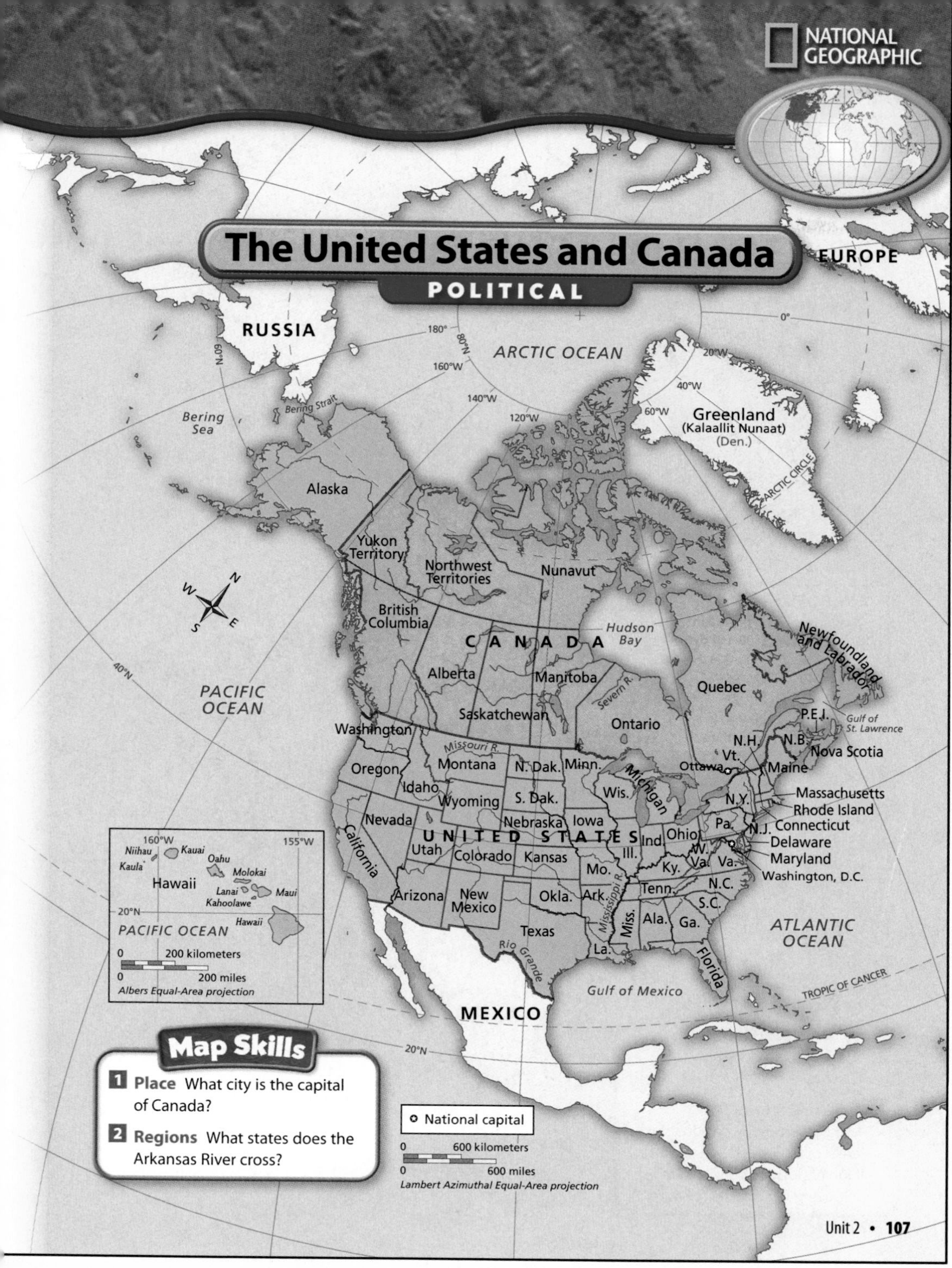

Map Skills

1. **Place** What city is the capital of Canada?
2. **Regions** What states does the Arkansas River cross?

National capital

Unit 2 Regional Atlas

Regional Atlas Activity

Synthesizing Tell each student to choose five states, provinces, or territories. Instruct them to use the maps in the Regional Atlas to come up with at least five clues to describe each state, province, or territory. Explain that the clues must uniquely identify each one.

Next, organize students into pairs. Set a timer for one minute. Have one member of each pair read his or her clues aloud while the other student guesses the state, province, or territory. The goal is to guess all five areas correctly within one minute. When the first student has read all of his or her clues, have students reverse roles. **OL**

Map Skills

Answers:

1. Ottawa
2. Colorado, Kansas, Oklahoma, and Arkansas

Skills Practice

Ask: **In which state is the mouth of the Mississippi River located?** *(Louisiana)* **Which river forms the border between Texas and Mexico?** *(Rio Grande)*

Background: Current Issues

Fossil Fuels and the Environment Both the United States and Canada are highly dependent on fossil fuels for their energy needs. This includes fueling automobiles, furnaces to heat homes, and machinery used in huge manufacturing plants. Burning fossil fuels pollutes the air. The pollution mixes with water vapor and makes acid rain. Acid rain has damaged plants as well as rivers and lakes, especially in the eastern part of North America. The pollutants released by burning fossil fuels contribute to global warming. If global warming continues, the region may be affected by changing weather patterns and rising sea levels that will threaten low-lying coastal areas.

Canada and the United States have begun to address these environmental issues. Canada has responded by passing legislation designed to limit the burning of fossil fuels. The United States funds research into alternative energy sources that will do less damage to the environment.

Regional Atlas Activity

Making Connections **Ask: If you were born in the United States, in what state were you born? If you were born in another country, in what state did you first live when you came to the United States?** *(Answers will vary.)* Write student responses on the board. Have students study the Population Density and Political maps in the Regional Atlas to determine the approximate population density of the states where they were born or in which they first lived. Create a chart on the board that lists the different states students mentioned and their corresponding population densities. Then have students work in small groups to design a graph showing the population densities for these states. **OL**

Map Skills

Answers:

1. Most Canadians live in southern Canada near the U.S. border, particularly in the east.
2. Rivers, oceans, and lakes provide an easy way to transport people and goods, as well as water for drinking and irrigation.

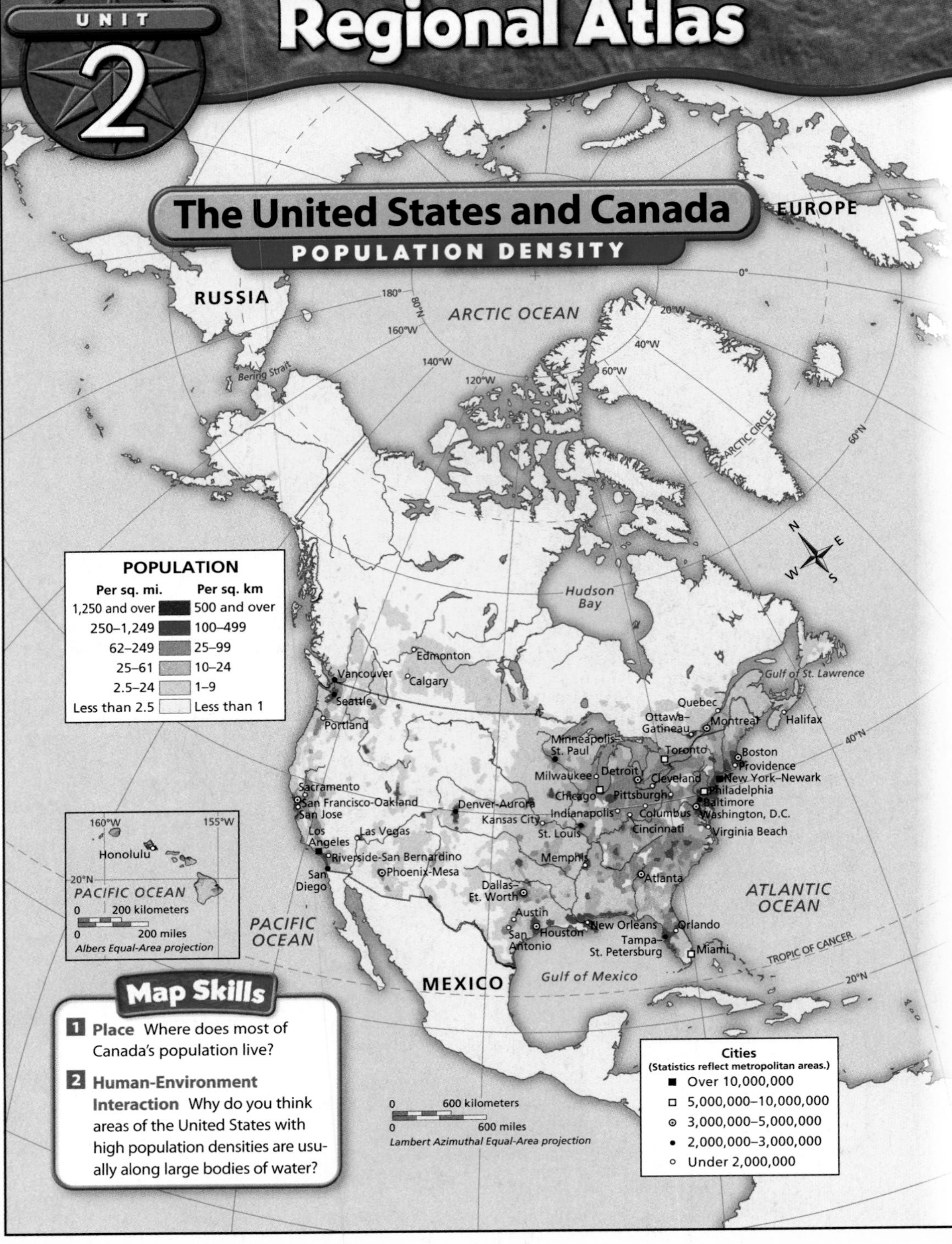

Background: People and Culture

Nations of Immigrants Both the United States and Canada were settled largely by immigrants from around the world. As a result, their populations are very diverse. The United States continues to attract immigrants from around the globe. Throughout the nation's history, large numbers of immigrants have come from Europe, Africa, Asia, and Latin America. Current immigration trends continue to alter the composition of the population. While people of European descent make up about two-thirds of the population, Latinos are the fastest-growing ethnic group. Despite their ethnic and religious diversity, Americans of all backgrounds have a strong national identity.

Canada is also a nation of immigrants, but because of its vast size and isolated cultural regions, it has had difficulty achieving a strong national identity. About 25% of Canadians are of French ancestry; most of them live in Quebec. Another 25% are of British ancestry, and 15% are from other European backgrounds. Canada is also home to people of Asian, African, and Latin American descent, as well as a sizable native population.

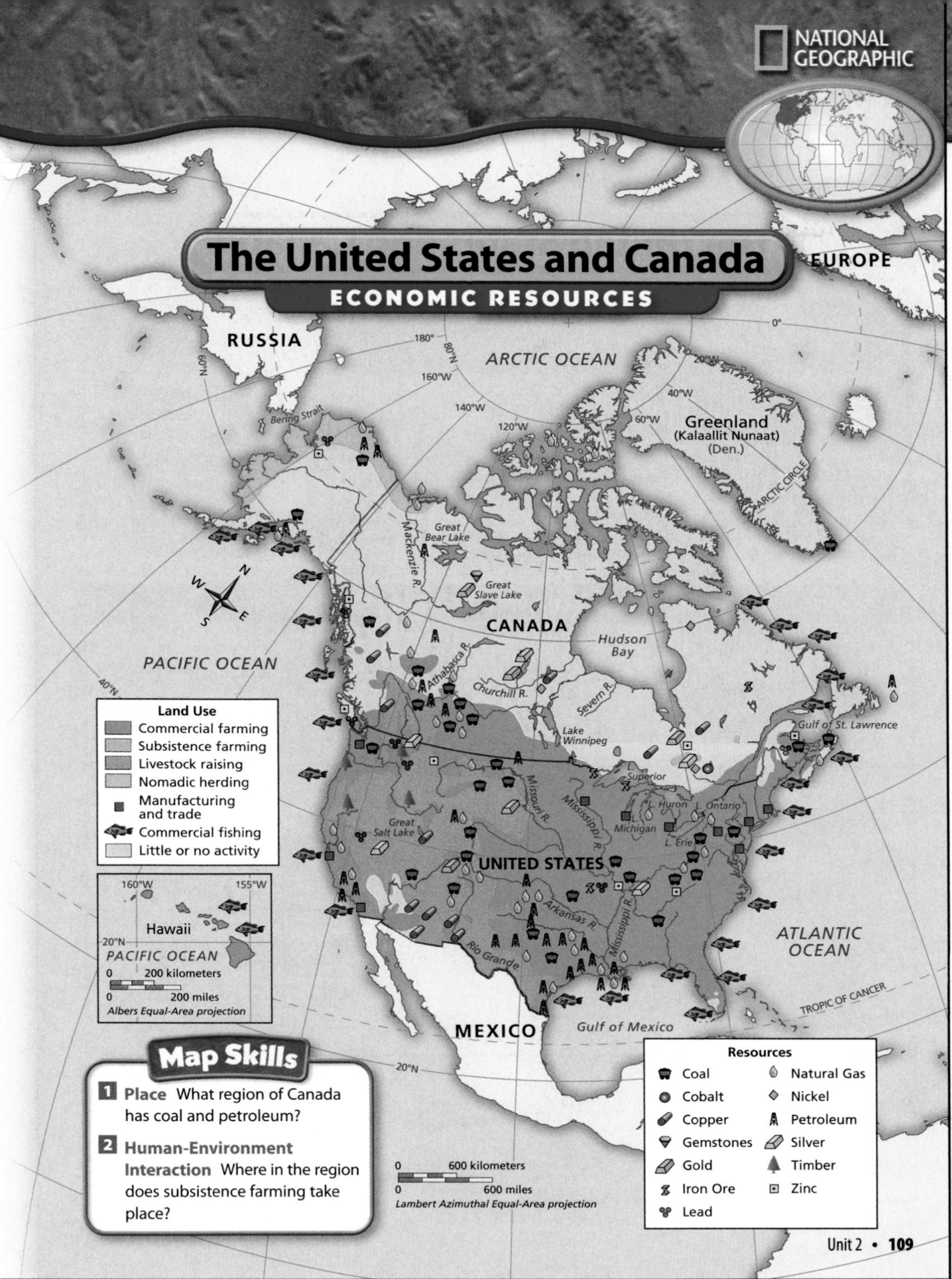

Unit 2
Regional Atlas

Regional Atlas Activity

Comparing and Contrasting Draw a Venn diagram on the board. Label one circle the United States and one circle Canada. **Ask: What economic resources are found in Canada?** *(all of the resources shown in the key except timber)* As students list each one, ask if that resource is also found in the United States. Then list the resources in the appropriate place on the diagram. **Ask: What resources found in Canada are not found in the United States?** *(nickel and cobalt)* Finally, ask students to concentrate on the land use colors and symbols. **Ask: What are the primary differences in land use between the two countries?** *(Much of Canada has little or no land use activity, but in the United States, only Alaska has substantial areas of little or no land use activity. Canada also lacks major manufacturing and trade centers.)* **OL**

Map Skills

Answers:

1. western Canada
2. small areas in Canada

Skills Practice

Ask: Where is commercial fishing a major economic activity? *(along the Atlantic and Pacific coasts of both countries)*

Background: The Economy

Economic Regions In the free market economies of the United States and Canada, the resources available in different regions help determine the economic activities of the area. The northeastern United States has many excellent harbors and specializes in business and trade. The Midwest and South have rich, fertile farmland, and the South also has tourism and manufacturing industries. The main economic activities of the Interior West are mining, ranching, and lumbering, although tourism and service industries are growing in importance. The fertile soils along the Pacific produce fruits and vegetables, and many high-tech industries also thrive there.

In the Atlantic Provinces of Canada, fishing, manufacturing, mining, and tourism are important industries. The Central and Eastern Region has some manufacturing industries, including paper and hydroelectric power production, and the region's cities are centers of business and trade. In the West, farming and ranching are major economic activities in the North, the economy depends on mineral resources, including gold and diamonds.

Regional Atlas Activity

Hypothesizing Ask: What is the GDP per capita of the United States? *($40,100)* **What is the GDP per capita of Canada?** *($31,500)* Have students look again at the Economic Resources map in the Regional Atlas. **Ask: What might explain the lower GDP per capita in Canada?** *(Students might mention that less of the land in Canada is suitable for farming and that Canada lacks major manufacturing and trade centers.)* **OL**

Categorizing Assign small groups of students five states, territories, or provinces shown in the chart. Send them to reliable information sources to find the populations of the capitals of those areas. When finished, discuss what categories to use to represent cities similar in size. For example, students may decide to group all cities with populations over 5 million together, all cities with populations of 3 million to 5 million together, and so on. Create a chart with these categories on the board and have students list their cities in the appropriate categories. **OL**

Regional Atlas

The United States and Canada

Country and Capital	Literacy Rate	Population and Density	Land Area	Life Expectancy (Years)	GDP* Per Capita (U.S. dollars)	Television Sets (per 1,000 people)	Flag and Language
UNITED STATES Washington, D.C.	97%	296,500,000 80 per sq. mi. 31 per sq. km	3,717,796 sq. mi. 9,629,047 sq. km	78	$40,100	844	English
CANADA Ottawa	97%	32,000,000 8 per sq. mi. 3 per sq. km	3,849,670 sq. mi. 9,970,599 sq. km	80	$31,500	709	English, French

Sources: *CIA World Factbook*, 2005; Population Reference Bureau, *World Population Data Sheet*, 2005.

*Gross Domestic Product

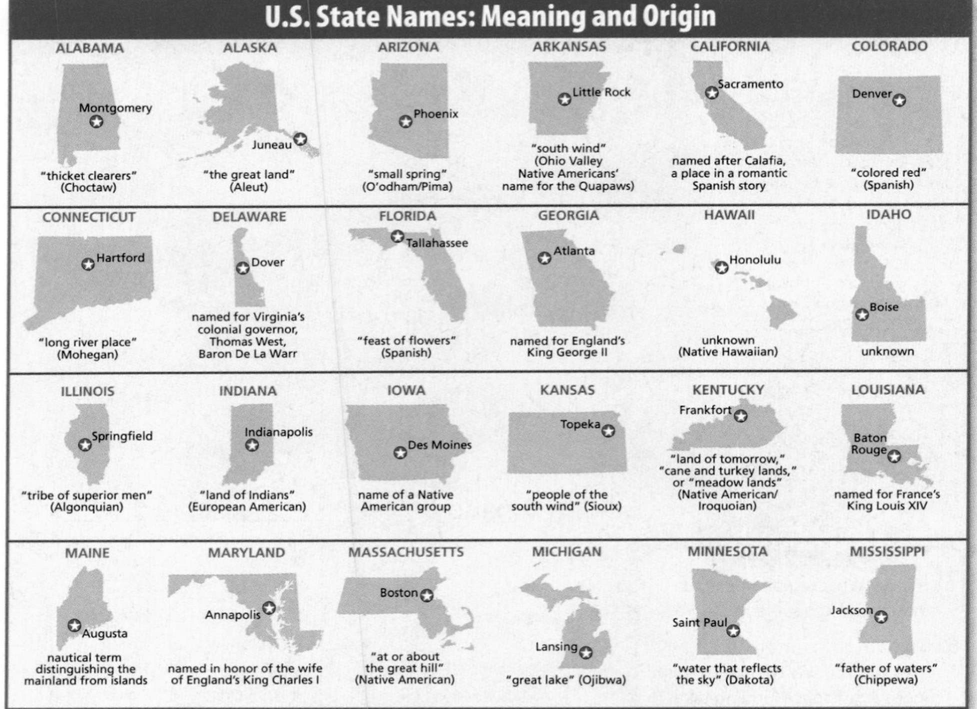

Land areas and flags not drawn to scale

Activity: Using the Chart

Locating Information Ask: Which state in the United States or province or territory in Canada are you most interested in visiting? Have each student choose a different state, province, or territory. Tell students that they are going to create a travel brochure for this state, province, or territory. Tell students to begin by using atlases, encyclopedias, and reliable online news and information sources to find out interesting facts about this area. Encourage them to e-mail the tourism office for this area to request additional information. After students have gathered the information they need, have them create a brochure using desktop publishing software or by folding an $8\frac{1}{2} \times 11$ piece of paper into thirds and then gluing pictures, text, and clip art to make the brochure. Tell students to include some of the information provided in the Regional Atlas chart in their brochures. At the end of the project, ask each student to present his or her travel brochure to the rest of the class, or create a "tourist center" in your classroom where the brochures can be displayed. **AL**

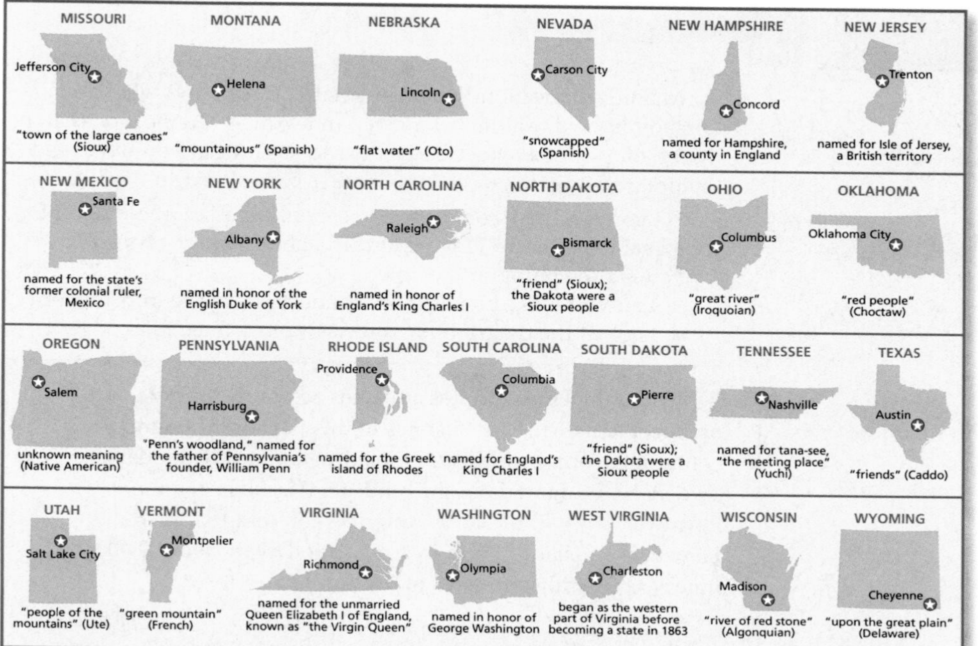

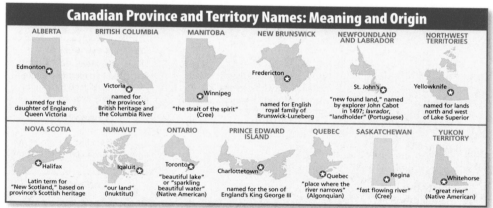

Canadian Province and Territory Names: Meaning and Origin

Province/Territory	Capital	Meaning and Origin
ALBERTA	Edmonton	named for the daughter of England's Queen Victoria
BRITISH COLUMBIA	Victoria	named for the province's British heritage and the Columbia River
MANITOBA	Winnipeg	"the strait of the spirit" (Cree)
NEW BRUNSWICK	Fredericton	named for English royal family of Brunswick-Luneberg
NEWFOUNDLAND AND LABRADOR	St. John's	"new found land," named by explorer John Cabot in 1497; *lavrador,* "landholder" (Portuguese)
NORTHWEST TERRITORIES	Yellowknife	named for lands north and west of Lake Superior
NOVA SCOTIA	Halifax	Latin term for "New Scotland," based on province's Scottish heritage
NUNAVUT	Iqaluit	"our land" (Inuktitut)
ONTARIO	Toronto	"beautiful lake" or "sparkling beautiful water" (Native American)
PRINCE EDWARD ISLAND	Charlottetown	named for the son of England's King George III
QUEBEC	Quebec	"place where the river narrows" (Algonquian)
SASKATCHEWAN	Regina	"fast flowing river" (Cree)
YUKON TERRITORY	Whitehorse	"great river" (Native American)

For more country facts, go to the **Nations of the World Databank** at glencoe.com.

Activity: Using the Chart

Comparing Ask: What other statistics about Canada and the United States would you like to compare? *(Answers will vary; examples might include number of years children are required to attend school, percent of population in minority group, percent of national budget spent on defense, and so on.)* Have each student choose three additional statistical categories to research. Direct them to appropriate reference materials, including world atlases, encyclopedias, almanacs, and reliable online information sources. After students have collected the statistics about the United States and Canada, have each student present a brief report on how the United States and Canada compare in the categories they researched. **OL**

Regional Atlas Activity

Drawing Conclusions Have students study the meanings and origins of the names of the states, provinces, and territories, as shown in the chart. **Ask: If you knew nothing else about the history of the United States and Canada, what conclusions could you draw about the history of this region from these place names alone?** *(Possible answers: Various Native American groups originally settled this region; European countries that explored or settled the region included Spain, England, France, and Portugal; William Penn and George Washington were important figures in the history of the United States.)* **OL**

Comparing and Contrasting Ask: Based on the chart alone, how are the United States and Canada similar? *(Students should answer that the two countries have similar land areas, equivalent literacy rates, and similar life expectancies.)* **How are the United States and Canada different?** *(The GDP per capita is more than 20% lower in Canada; the population density is significantly lower in Canada; Canadians own fewer television sets per 1,000 people; and Canada has two official languages instead of one.)* **OL**

Reading Social Studies

Making Connections

Why Making Connections Is Important

Students who are constantly looking for ways to make connections between what they read and what they already know stay actively engaged in the text as they read. This helps students better remember the text. Students also can use what they already know to better comprehend difficult material.

Learn It!

Bring a newspaper to class. Choose a headline, and write it on the board. **Ask:** **What do you know about this subject?** As students volunteer what they know, write brief descriptive phrases on the board. **Ask:** **How do you know that information?** Ask whether they know the information through personal experience (a text-to-self connection), through other reading they have done (a text-to-text connection), or through their knowledge of the wider world (a text-to-world connection). Repeat this exercise with other headlines, pointing out text-to-self connections, text-to-text connections, and text-to-world connections. **OL**

Reading Skill

Learn It!

Making connections between what you read and what you already know is an important step in learning. Connections can be based on personal experiences (text-to-self), what you have read before (text-to-text), or events in other places (text-to-world).

As you read, ask connecting questions. Are you reminded of a personal experience? Have you read about the topic before?

- Read the paragraph below.
- Can you make one or more connections to the information?
- Look at the diagram for some sample connections.

> Most of the United States stretches across the middle part of North America. The 48 states in this part of the country are contiguous, or joined together inside a common boundary. Two states lie apart from the other 48. Alaska lies in the northwestern part of North America, adjacent to Canada. Hawaii is an island group in the Pacific Ocean, about 2,400 miles (3,862 km) southwest of California.
>
> *—from page 117*

Most of the United States extends across the middle section of North America.
Topic

I know someone who is from Alaska.
Connection

I have seen maps of the United States, and I remember where Alaska, Hawaii, and the other 48 states are located.
Connection

I watched a television program about Hawaiian beaches and the Pacific Ocean.
Connection

Reading Tip

Make connections that relate to memorable times in your life. The stronger the connection is, the more likely it is that you will remember the information.

Reading Strategy: Questioning

Making Connections Drawing text-to-self, text-to-text, and text-to-world connections can help students make sense of confusing or unfamiliar material as they read. Encourage students to stop regularly to ask themselves questions that will help them connect the materials to things they already know. Have each student read a section in this unit. Direct them to stop after every paragraph and ask themselves questions, such as: "Does this remind me of a personal experience?" "Have I read anything about this topic before?" "What else do I know about this topic?" Ask them to jot down at least one connection they have made after each paragraph. When they have finished, discuss with students how pausing often to ask connection questions helped deepen their understanding of the text. **BL**

② Practice It!

Read the following paragraph from this unit.

- Draw a graphic organizer like the one below.
- List the topic of the reading along with connections to the information.
- Share your connections with a partner.
- Compare your list with your partner's, and discuss their similarities and differences.

> Canadians are enthusiastic about hockey—a sport that began in Canada—as well as lacrosse, which began as a Native American game. Many Canadians also enjoy hunting and fishing.
>
> —*from page 150*

Read to Write Activity

As you read Chapters 4, 5, and 6, choose five words or phrases from each chapter that make a connection to something you already know.

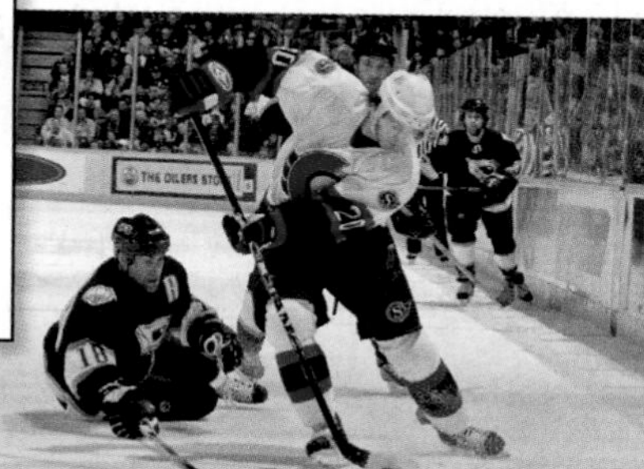

▲ Ice hockey in Canada

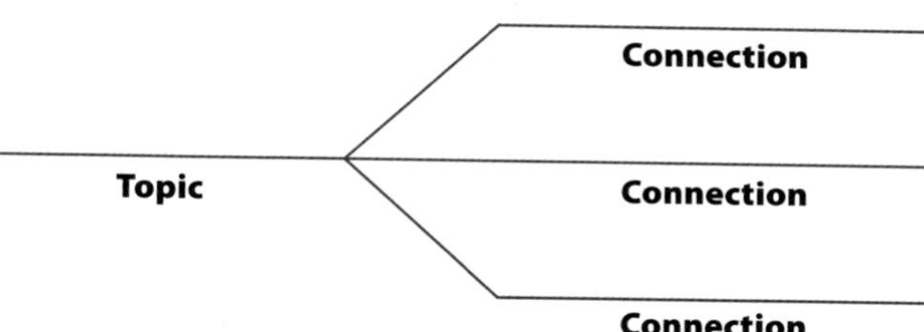

③ Apply It!

As you read the chapters in the unit, try to identify one concept that makes the following connections.

Chapter	Connection
4	**Text-to-self:**
5	**Text-to-text:**
6	**Text-to-world:**

② Practice It!

Students may write "Sports" on the line to the left of the diagram. On the lines to the right, students may describe the types of sports they participate in or that they like to watch on television. Students might describe a hockey game or other sporting event that they have seen on TV that included Canadian teams. **OL**

③ Apply It!

Have students skim through a chapter in this unit and choose a passage with which they can easily make a connection. Have them draw, write, or describe orally the connection they made to this passage. **OL**

Reading Strategy — Read to Write

Writing Summaries Summaries require students to put the main idea of a reading passage into their own words. Making connections between the text and what they already know will help students better understand the passage and be able to summarize the main idea. Ask students to read a subsection in this unit. Tell them to note the topic of the subsection as they read the first paragraph. Then have them write down the connections they make as they read the rest of the passage. When finished, ask them to write a two- or three-sentence summary of the main idea of the subsection. Have volunteers read their summaries aloud and describe how making connections to what they already knew helped them better understand the main idea. **OL**

Planning Guide

Key to Ability Levels

- **BL** Below level
- **OL** On level
- **AL** Above level
- **ELL** English Language Learners

Key to Teaching Resources

- Print Material
- DVD
- CD-ROM
- Transparency

BL	OL	AL	ELL		Resources	Chapter Opener	Section 1	Section 2	Chapter Assess
					FOCUS				
BL	OL	AL	ELL	Transparency	**Daily Focus Skills Transparencies**		4-1	4-2	
					TEACH				
BL	OL		ELL	Print Material	**Guided Reading Activity, URB***		p. 37	p. 38	
BL	OL	AL	ELL	Print Material	**Content Vocabulary Activity, URB***		p. 39	p. 39	
BL	OL	AL	ELL	Print Material	**Academic Vocabulary Activity, URB**		p. 41	p. 41	
BL	OL	AL	ELL	Print Material	**Differentiated Instruction Activity, URB**			p. 43	
BL	OL	AL	ELL	Print Material	**Chart, Graph, and Map Skills Activity, URB**		p. 45		
	OL	AL		Print Material	**Critical Thinking Activity, URB**		p. 47	p. 47	
BL	OL	AL	ELL	Print Material	**Speaking and Listening Skills Activity, URB**		p. 49		
BL	OL	AL	ELL	Print Material	**Writing Skills Activity, URB**		p. 53		
BL	OL	AL	ELL	Print Material	**School-to-Home Connection Activity, URB***		p. 57		
BL	OL	AL	ELL	Print Material	**Regional Atlas Activities, URB**		pp. 1–7	pp. 1–7	
	OL	AL		Print Material	**Environmental Case Study, URB**			p. 13	
BL	OL	AL	ELL	Print Material	**GeoLab Activity, URB**			p. 23	
BL	OL		ELL	Print Material	**Reading Skills Activity, URB**			p. 25	
BL	OL	AL	ELL	Print Material	**Primary Source Readings, URB**			p. 29	
BL	OL		ELL	Print Material	**Reading Essentials and Note-Taking Guide***		p. 28	p. 31	
	OL			Print Material	**Interactive Geography Activity**		p. 9		
BL	OL	AL	ELL	Transparency	**In-Text Map Overlay and Population Pyramid Transparencies**	2A	2B, 2D	2E, 2F	
BL	OL	AL	ELL	Print Material	**Outline Map Resource Book**	pp. 5–24	p. 7		
BL	OL	AL	ELL	Print Material	**NGS World Atlas***	✓	✓	✓	
BL	OL	AL	ELL	Print Material	**NGS World Desk Map**	✓	✓	✓	✓
BL	OL	AL	ELL	Print Material	**World Literature Library**	✓	✓	✓	✓
BL	OL	AL	ELL	Print Material	**Writer's Guidebook**	✓	✓	✓	✓

Note: Please refer to the *Unit Resource Book: The United States and Canada* for this chapter's URB materials.

* Also available in Spanish

- Interactive Lesson Planner
- Interactive Teacher Edition
- Fully editable blackline masters
- Section Spotlight Videos Launch
- Differentiated Lesson Plans
- Printable reports of daily assignments
- Standards Tracking System

Levels				Resources	Chapter Opener	Section 1	Section 2	Chapter Assess
BL	OL	AL	ELL					
TEACH *(continued)*								
BL	OL	AL	ELL	Vocabulary PuzzleMaker CD-ROM*	✓	✓	✓	✓
	OL	AL		Primary Sources CD-ROM	✓	✓	✓	✓
BL	OL	AL	ELL	StudentWorks™ Plus DVD	✓	✓	✓	✓
BL	OL	AL	ELL	Section Video Program Activities	✓	✓	✓	✓
BL	OL	AL	ELL	World Music: A Cultural Legacy	✓	✓	✓	✓
BL	OL	AL	ELL	Writing Process Transparencies	✓	✓	✓	✓
Teacher Resources				Building Academic Vocabulary	✓	✓	✓	✓
Teacher Resources				Strategies for Success	✓	✓	✓	✓
Teacher Resources				Teacher's Guide to Differentiated Instruction	✓	✓	✓	✓
Teacher Resources				Presentation Plus! DVD	✓	✓	✓	✓
ASSESS								
BL	OL	AL	ELL	Quizzes and Tests		p. 41	p. 42	p. 43
BL	OL	AL	ELL	Authentic Assessment With Rubrics			p. 4	p. 4
BL	OL	AL	ELL	Standardized Test Practice				p. 13
BL	OL	AL	ELL	*ExamView® Assessment Suite* CD-ROM*		4-1	4-2	Ch. 4
BL	OL	AL	ELL	Interactive Tutor Self-Assessment CD-ROM		4-1	4-2	
CLOSE								
BL			ELL	Reteaching Activity, URB*		p. 55	p. 55	
BL	OL		ELL	Reading and Study Skills Foldables™	p. 56	p. 56	p. 56	p. 56
BL	OL	AL	ELL	Graphic Organizer Transparencies and Strategies		✓	✓	
BL	OL	AL	ELL	*Exploring Our World* in Graphic Novel			p. 17	

Integrating Technology

Using Interactive Tutor Self Assessment

Electronic Quiz

Technology Product

Glencoe's Interactive Tutor Self-Assessment CD-ROM software allows students to assess their mastery of chapter content, taking as much time as they need to review each section of a chapter. The Interactive Tutor Self Assessment

- contains quizzes for individual section of chapters, with section overviews covering important concepts and keywords;
- allows students to read overviews based on sections, chapters, or units, before starting quizzes;
- lets students check their answers, receive feedback and hints, and identify content areas for review;
- permits student to move back and forth among the questions during a quiz;
- generates performance reports and graphs to monitor student progress section by section.

Objective

Using the Interactive Tutor Self Assessment allows students to

- assess their mastery of chapter content;
- identify chapter content they need to review.

Steps

- Install Interactive Tutor Self-Assessment CD-ROM.
- Register yourself and create classes.
- Register new students/users in the database, organized by classes. Assign individual passwords to students.
- Save student records to a location easily accessible to students.
- Assign section quizzes to students.
- Generate performance reports and graphs for individual students and classes.

Social Studies ONLINE

	Student	Teacher	Parent
Beyond the Textbook	●		●
Chapter Overviews	●		●
Concepts in Motion	●		●
ePuzzles and Games	●		●
Literature Connections		●	
Multi-Language Glossaries	●		●
Online Student Edition	●	●	●
Section Videos	●	●	●
Self-Check Quizzes	●		●
Student Web Activities	●		●
Study Central™	●		●
Teaching Today		●	
TIME Current Events	●		●
Vocabulary eFlashcards	●		●
Web Activity Lesson Plans		●	

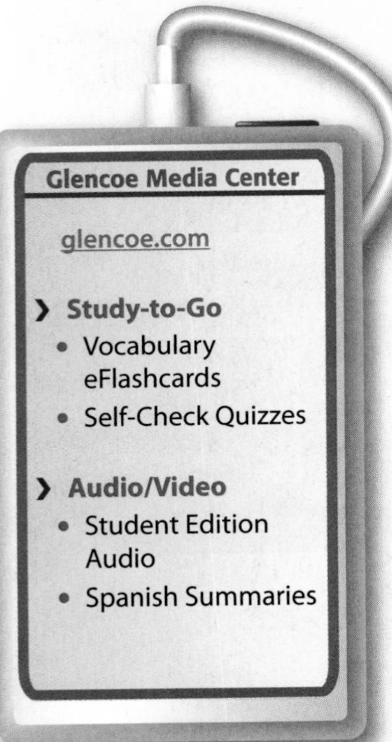

- **Timed Readings Plus in Social Studies** helps students increase their reading rate and fluency while maintaining comprehension. The 400-word passages are similar to those found on state and national assessments.
- **Reading in the Content Area: Social Studies** concentrates on six essential reading skills that help students better comprehend what they read. The book includes 75 high-interest nonfiction passages written at increasing levels of difficulty.
- **Reading Social Studies** includes strategic reading instruction and vocabulary support in Social Studies content for ELLs and native speakers of English.
- **Content Vocabulary Workout** (Grades 6–8) accelerates reading comprehension through focused vocabulary development. Social Studies content vocabulary comes from the glossaries of Glencoe's Middle School Social Studies texts.
www.jamestowneducation.com

Index to National Geographic Magazine:

The following articles relate to this chapter:

- "Seasons of Smoke," Adam Goodheart, August 2006.
- "When Currents Collide," Paul Nicklen, August 2006.

National Geographic Society Products To order the following, call National Geographic at 1-800-368-2728:

- *National Geographic Atlas of the World* (Book).

Access National Geographic's new dynamic MapMachine Web site and other geography resources at:
www.nationalgeographic.com
www.nationalgeographic.com/maps

Biography  

The following videotape programs are available from Glencoe as supplements to Chapter 4:

- The Mighty Mississippi (ISBN 0-76-701090-6)
- The Erie Canal (ISBN 0-76-703154-7)

To order, call Glencoe at 1-800-334-7344. To find classroom resources to accompany many of these videos, check the following home pages:

A&E Television: www.aetv.com
The History Channel: www.historychannel.com

GLENCOE BOOKLINK 3

Use this database to search more than 30,000 titles to create a customized reading list for your students.

- Reading lists can be organized by students' reading level, author, genre, theme, or area of interest.
- The database provides Degrees of Reading Power™ (DRP) and Lexile™ readability scores for all selections.
- A brief summary of each selection is included.

Leveled reading suggestions for this chapter:

For students at a Grade 5 reading level:
- ***Death Valley: A Day in the Desert,*** by Nancy Smiler Levinson

For students at a Grade 6 reading level:
- ***Go Home, River,*** by James Magdanz

For students at a Grade 7 reading level:
- ***Eye of the Storm: Chasing Storms with Warren Faidley,*** by Stephen Kramer.

For students at a Grade 8 reading level:
- ***Destination: Rocky Mountains,*** by Jonathan Grupper

For students at a Grade 9 reading level:
- ***Exploring the Arctic,*** by Rose Blue and Corinne J. Naden

Focus

The Essential Question

As students study the chapter, remind them to consider the chapter-based Essential Question. Answering this question will help them understand the important concepts in the chapter. In addition, the Hands-On Chapter Project relates the content from each section to the Essential Question. The steps in each section build on each other as students progress through the chapter. The Hands-On Chapter Project culminates in the Wrap Up activity on the Visual Summary page.

More About the Photo

Visual Literacy Wheat is a major food and one of the first grains to be grown by people. It was cultivated by the early Egyptians, and it became the primary food of Europeans and West Asians. Wheat was introduced to the Western Hemisphere by the Spanish around 1520. Today the leading producers of wheat are the United States, Russia, and China. Wheat also is grown in Canada, Australia, Argentina, and Western Europe. The flat, central regions of North America are especially well suited to growing wheat on a vast scale. About half of all wheat grown in the United States is exported.

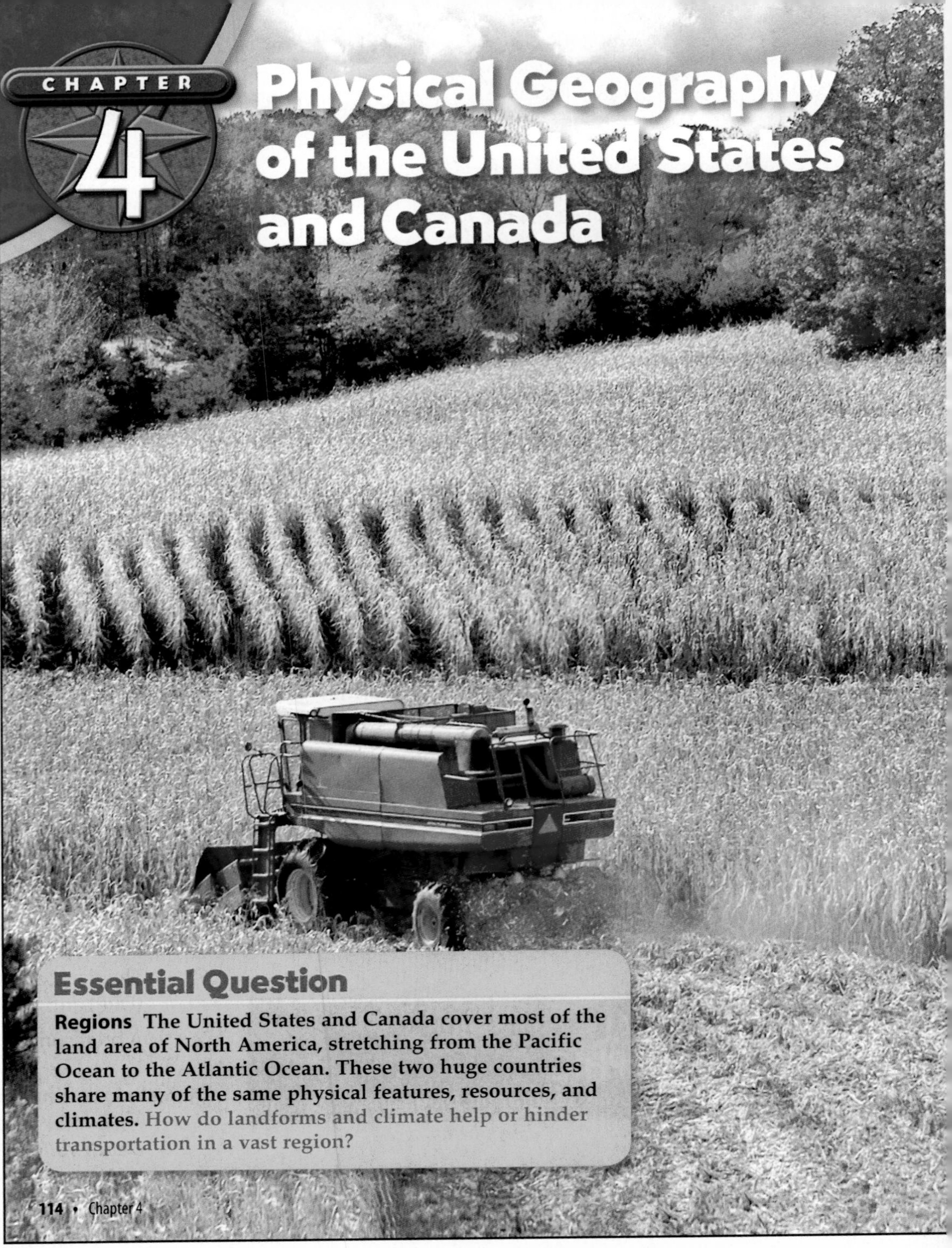

CHAPTER 4

Physical Geography of the United States and Canada

Essential Question

Regions **The United States and Canada cover most of the land area of North America, stretching from the Pacific Ocean to the Atlantic Ocean. These two huge countries share many of the same physical features, resources, and climates.** How do landforms and climate help or hinder transportation in a vast region?

Teach

The BIG Ideas *As you begin teaching each section, use these questions and activities to help students focus on the Big Ideas.*

Section 

Physical Features Ask: What are some ways the physical geography of United States and Canada is alike? What are some ways they are different? *(Possible answers: Alike: both are large countries with many different physical features, they share a long border and the Great Lakes; Different: the United States has hot, dry areas in the south with swamps and deserts, Canada extends to the far North with many islands)* Tell students that Section 1 describes the characteristics that the United States and Canada have in common. **OL**

Section 

Climate Regions Ask: How might the lives of people who live in a warm climate differ from the lives of people who live in a cold climate? *(Possible answers: the type of clothing worn in each climate, the*

BIG Ideas

Section 1: Physical Features

BIG IDEA Geographers organize the Earth into regions that share common characteristics. The United States and Canada share a long border and many landforms. Their economies are closely linked by trade. Their governments have also worked together on major projects that have changed the land and benefited both countries.

◀ Wheat harvest, Michigan

Section 2: Climate Regions

BIG IDEA The physical environment affects how people live. A diversity of climates in the United States and Canada leads to different ways of life. Some parts of this region experience natural hazards that can threaten people's safety.

FOLDABLES™ Study Organizer

Organizing Information Make this Foldable to help you organize information about the physical features and climates of the United States and Canada.

Step 1 Fold a sheet of paper in half, leaving a ½-inch tab along one edge.

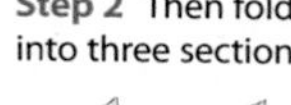

Step 2 Then fold into three sections.

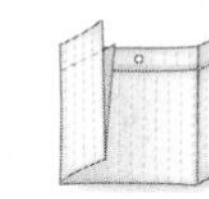

Step 3 Draw a Venn diagram like the one below and then cut along the folds to create three tabs.

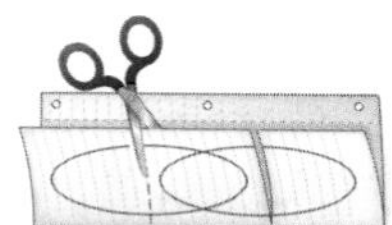

Step 4 Label your Foldable as shown.

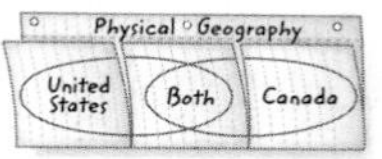

Reading and Writing Using the notes in your Foldable, write several short journal entries from an imaginary trip through Canada and the United States. In your entries, describe the landforms and climates you encounter.

Social Studies ONLINE

To preview Chapter 4, go to glencoe.com.

Previewing the Region

If you have not already done so, engage students in the Regional Atlas and chart activities to help them become familiar with the general content of the region.

FOLDABLES Study Organizer Dinah Zike's Foldables

Purpose This Foldable helps students organize information about the physical features and climates of the United States and Canada. Remind students that the information can be found in the text, illustrations, charts, and headings in the chapter. As they read, students should keep in mind the kinds of facts that would make good journal entries about their imaginary trip. Completed Foldables can be used to write journal entries and prepare for assessment. **OL**

More Foldables activities for this chapter can be found in *Dinah Zike's Reading and Study Skills Foldables* ancillary.

Social Studies ONLINE

Introduce students to chapter content and key terms by having them access the Chapter Overview at glencoe.com.

styles of houses built in each climate, and the recreational activities available in each climate) Tell students that in Section 2, they will learn about how climate affects the lives of their fellow North Americans. **OL**

Focus

Bellringer

Daily Focus Transparency 4-1

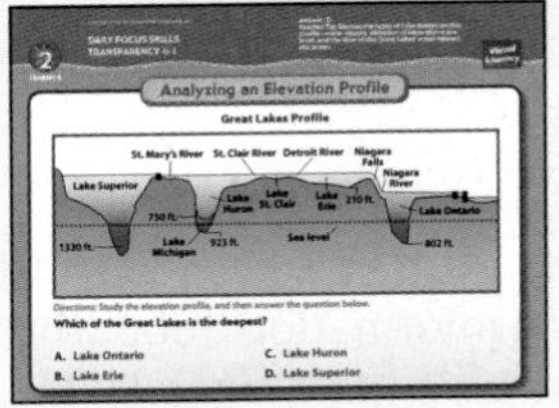

Guide to Reading

Answers to Graphic:

Encourage students to consider shared features. Unique features include:
Eastern: large cities on coastal plains, excellent harbors, some highland areas, large coal deposits
Western: a cordillera, high mountains, a high plateau and dry basin
Interior: Canadian Shield and Central Lowlands; flat, fertile areas; mineral resources; Great Plains have good grazing

Section Spotlight Video

To learn more about the physical features and climates of the United States and Canada, have students watch the Section Spotlight Video.

Guide to Reading

BIG Idea

Geographers organize the Earth into regions that share common characteristics.

Content Vocabulary

- contiguous *(p. 117)*
- megalopolis *(p. 117)*
- prairie *(p. 118)*
- cordillera *(p. 118)*
- canyon *(p. 119)*
- navigable *(p. 119)*
- glacier *(p. 119)*
- divide *(p. 120)*

Academic Vocabulary

- constrain *(p. 117)*
- route *(p. 119)*

Reading Strategy

Analyzing Information Use a Venn diagram like the one below to compare landforms in the eastern, western, and interior parts of the United States and Canada.

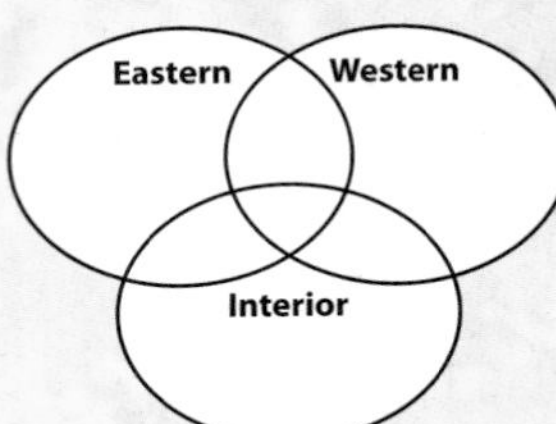

Physical Features

Picture This Standing at the Grand Canyon's edge, you can see for miles. Its sheer size—277 miles (445 km) long, with walls rising up to 6,000 feet (1,829 m)—is almost mind-boggling. The Grand Canyon was formed by the Colorado River over a period of 6 million years. To learn more about the physical features of the United States and Canada, read Section 1.

Grand Canyon

Resource Manager

R Reading Strategies	C Critical Thinking	D Differentiated Instruction	W Writing Support	S Skill Practice
Teacher Edition • Identifying, pp. 118, 120 • Using Word Parts, p. 117 • Det. Importance, p. 121 • Organizing, p. 122 **Additional Resources** • Guid. Read., URB p. 37 • Cont. Vocab., URB p. 39 • Ac. Vocab., URB p. 41 • Read. Ess., p. 28	**Teacher Edition** • Drawing Con., pp. 117, 121 • Analyzing, p. 118 • Det. Cause/Effect, pp. 118, 121 **Additional Resources** • Quizzes and Tests, p. 41 • Critical Think., URB p. 47	**Teacher Edition** • Visual/Spatial, p. 119 **Additional Resources** • Reteach., URB p. 55 • School-to-Home Conn., URB p. 57	**Teacher Edition** • Expository Writing, p. 119 **Additional Resources** • Writing Skills, URB p. 53	**Teacher Edition** • Using Geo. Skills, p. 120 **Additional Resources** • Chart, Graph, and Map Skills, URB p. 45 • Speak./Listen. Skills, URB p. 49 • Daily Focus Trans. 4-1 • Reg. Atlas, URB pp. 1–7

Major Landforms

Main Idea **The region rises in elevation from east to west.**

Geography and You Do you live in an area that is flat, hilly, or mountainous? Read to find out about the major landforms of the United States and Canada.

The United States and Canada form a region that covers most of North America. This region is bordered by the cold Arctic Ocean in the north, the Atlantic Ocean to the east, and the warm waters of the Gulf of Mexico in the southeast. The Pacific Ocean borders the western coast.

Canada occupies most of the northern part of North America. Canada's vast size makes it the second-largest country in the world, after Russia. The United States is the third-largest country. Most of the United States stretches across the middle part of North America. The 48 states in this part of the country are **contiguous,** or joined together inside a common boundary. Two states lie apart from the other 48. Alaska lies in the northwestern part of North America, adjacent to Canada. Hawaii is an island group in the Pacific Ocean, about 2,400 miles (3,862 km) southwest of California.

Eastern Lowlands and Highlands

The United States and Canada have a variety of landforms. A broad lowland runs along the Atlantic and the Gulf of Mexico coasts. In northeastern areas, the thin and rocky soil **constrains,** or limits, farming. A fertile, hilly area called the Piedmont, however, stretches inland from the coastal plain. Excellent harbors along the Atlantic coast have led to the growth of shipping ports.

The cities of Halifax, Boston, New York City, Philadelphia, and Washington, D.C., all lie along or near the Atlantic coast. In the United States, Atlantic coastal cities and their suburbs form an almost continuous line of settlement. Geographers call this connected area of urban communities a **megalopolis.** The Atlantic megalopolis has long been an important economic, cultural, and political center of the United States. R

The coastal plain along the Gulf of Mexico is wider than the Atlantic plain. Soils in this region are better than those along the Atlantic coast. Large cities here include Houston and New Orleans.

West and north of the Atlantic coastal plain spread a number of highland areas.

NATIONAL GEOGRAPHIC

New York City

New York City is one of several huge cities that developed along the Atlantic coastal plain.
Location **Where is the area called the Piedmont located?** C

Student Web Activity Visit glencoe.com and complete the Chapter 4 Web Activity about the Piedmont.

Teach

C Critical Thinking

Drawing Conclusions Ask: Why do you think so many large cities are located on coastal plains? *(Possible answers: A coastal location provides access to trade and fishing; boat transportation was key to growth in earlier times; flatter areas are easier to build in than mountainous areas.)* **AL**

R Reading Strategy

Using Word Parts Ask: Figure out the meaning of the word *megalopolis*. Do you recognize any word parts? *(Students may recognize the prefix* mega-, *which means "large," and the word part* polis, *which means "city.")* **OL**

Caption Answer:
It stretches inland from the coastal plain.

Objectives and answers to the Student Web Activity can be found at glencoe.com under the Web Activity Lesson Plan for this chapter.

Differentiated Instruction

Leveled Activities

BL Reteaching Activity, URB p. 55

OL Writing Skills Activity, URB p. 53

ELL School-to-Home Connection, URB p. 57

R Reading Strategy

Identifying **Ask:** What physical process has created the rounded peaks of the Appalachian Mountains? *(erosion)* BL

C1 Critical Thinking

Analyzing **Ask:** Why is the climate of the Canadian Shield colder than that of the Central Lowlands? *(It is farther north.)* OL

C2 Critical Thinking

Determining Cause and Effect
Ask: Why do you think large cities like Toronto, Detroit, and Chicago developed in the Central Lowlands? *(Students should point out that cities usually develop on waterways which are important for trade.)* AL

Caption Answer:
The Appalachians are much older and have been eroded over time.

The Rocky and Appalachian Mountains

NATIONAL GEOGRAPHIC

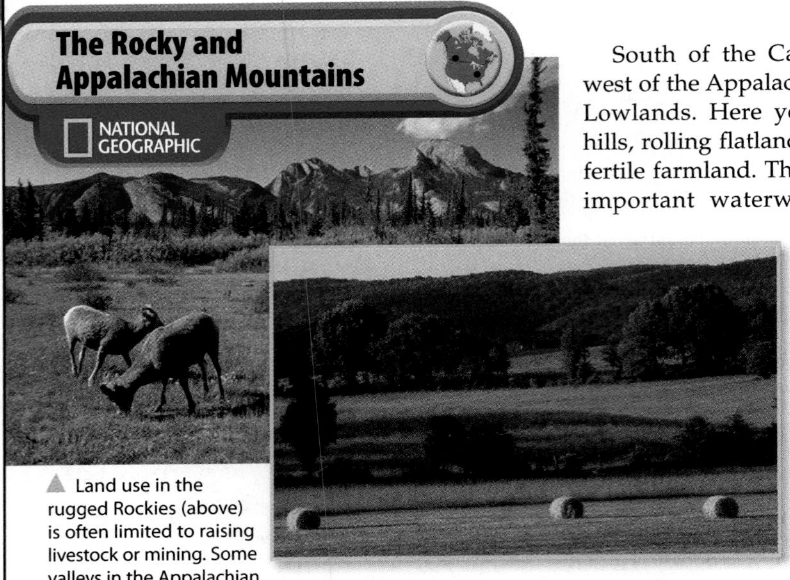

▲ Land use in the rugged Rockies (above) is often limited to raising livestock or mining. Some valleys in the Appalachian Mountains, like this one in Tennessee (right), have fertile soil and are good for farming. ***Place*** **Why do the Appalachian and Rocky Mountains appear physically different?**

These include the Appalachian Mountains, which run from eastern Canada to Alabama. R The Appalachians are the oldest mountains in North America. Their rounded peaks show their age. Erosion has worn them down over time. The highest peak, Mount Mitchell in North Carolina, reaches 6,684 feet (2,037 m). Rich coal deposits in the Appalachians fueled industrial growth in the late 1800s and early 1900s.

Interior Lowlands

West of the eastern highlands are vast interior lowlands. In the north lies the Canadian Shield. This horseshoe-shaped area of rocky hills, lakes, and evergreen forests C1 wraps around the Hudson Bay. With poor soil and a cold climate, the Canadian Shield is not farmable. It does, however, contain many mineral deposits, such as iron ore, copper, and nickel.

South of the Canadian Shield and west of the Appalachians lie the Central Lowlands. Here you will find grassy hills, rolling flatlands, thick forests, and fertile farmland. This area also contains important waterways, including the Great Lakes and the Mississippi River. Large cities, C2 such as Chicago, Detroit, Cleveland, and Toronto, are located in the Central Lowlands.

The Great Plains stretch west of the Mississippi River, gradually rising in elevation from east to west. Much of this vast region is a **prairie,** or rolling inland grasslands with fertile soil. The Great Plains once provided food for millions of buffalo and the Native Americans who lived there. Today farmers grow grains, and ranchers raise cattle on the land. The Great Plains also have reserves of coal, oil, and natural gas.

Western Mountains and Plateaus

West of the Great Plains is a **cordillera,** which is a group of mountain ranges that run side by side. Millions of years ago, collisions between tectonic plates created these towering mountains. At the eastern edge of the cordillera, the Rocky Mountains begin in Alaska and run south to New Mexico. Although they are younger and higher than the Appalachians, the Rockies have not been a barrier to travel. The Rockies contain passes, or low areas in the mountains, that allow people to cross them.

Hands-On Chapter Project Step 1

How Did They Build That?

Step 1: Conducting Research Groups of students will research the construction of some of North America's major transportation systems.

Essential Question How do landforms and climate help or hinder transportation in a vast region?

Directions Organize students into four groups. Assign each group one of the following transportation systems: the Erie Canal, the transcontinental railroad, the St. Lawrence Seaway, or the Interstate Highway System. Write the Essential Question on the board, and tell students that they will be answering the question by learning about their assigned transportation system. Tell them to find out how landforms and climate hindered the construction of the system, as well as any ways that landforms and climate may have facilitated it.

Describing After students have researched their transportation systems, have each group describe its system to the rest of the class and trace the route of the system on a large wall map. OL

(Chapter Project continued in Section 2)

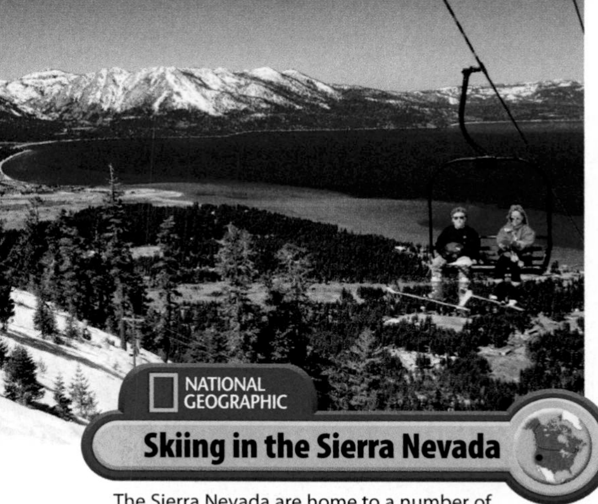

NATIONAL GEOGRAPHIC

Skiing in the Sierra Nevada

The Sierra Nevada are home to a number of popular ski resorts, including those around Lake Tahoe on the California-Nevada border. ***Place*** **What other mountain chains are found near the Pacific coast of North America?**

Near the Pacific coast is a series of mountain chains that make up the western part of the cordillera. They are the Sierra Nevada, the Cascade Range, the Coast Ranges, and the Alaska Range. Mount McKinley in the Alaska Range rises to 20,320 feet (6,194 m) and is the highest point in North America. **D**

Between these Pacific ranges and the Rocky Mountains is a stretch of dry basins and high plateaus. In the southern part of this area, rivers have worn through rock to create magnificent **canyons,** or deep valleys with steep sides. The most famous of these is the Grand Canyon of the Colorado River.

In the Pacific Ocean, eight large islands and 124 smaller islands make up the American state of Hawaii. The islands of Hawaii extend over a distance of about 1,500 miles (2,400 km). Volcanoes on the ocean floor erupted and formed these islands.

Reading Check **Making Generalizations** Describe the areas that make up the interior lowlands.

Bodies of Water

Main Idea **The region's waterways provide transportation and electric power.**

Geography and You Do you live near a river, lake, or ocean? What are the advantages and disadvantages of living by a body of water? Read to find out about the importance of waterways in the United States and Canada.

The United States and Canada have numerous freshwater lakes and rivers. Many of the region's rivers are **navigable,** or wide and deep enough to allow the passage of ships.

The Great Lakes

The Great Lakes—the world's largest group of freshwater lakes—lie in the central part of the region. Thousands of years ago, **glaciers,** or giant sheets of ice, formed Lake Superior, Lake Michigan, Lake Huron, Lake Erie, and Lake Ontario. The waters of these connected lakes flow into the St. Lawrence River, which empties into the Atlantic Ocean.

The St. Lawrence River is one of Canada's most important rivers. It flows for 750 miles (1,207 km) from Lake Ontario to the Gulf of St. Lawrence in the Atlantic Ocean. The Canadian cities of Quebec, Montreal, and Ottawa developed along the St. Lawrence River and its tributaries. They depend on the St. Lawrence as an important transportation link.

For many years, rapids, waterfalls, and other obstructions kept ships from navigating the entire **route,** or journey, from the Great Lakes to the Atlantic Ocean. Then, in the mid-1900s, the United States and Canada built the St. Lawrence Seaway. As shown in **Figure 1,** the Seaway links the Great Lakes and the Atlantic Ocean. **W**

D Differentiated Instruction

Visual/Spatial Ask students to create a graphic representation, using either pen and paper or computer software, of the relative heights of the tallest peaks in the Appalachian Mountains and the Alaska Range. *(Students' work should show that Mount Mitchell is 6,684 feet high and that Mount McKinley in 20,320 feet high.)* **OL**

W Writing Support

Expository Writing Have students write a paragraph explaining why the St. Lawrence Seaway was built. *(Paragraphs should make clear that obstructions prevented ships from navigating inland from the Atlantic Ocean along the entire length of the river, and raw materials and manufactured goods needed to be shipped.)* **OL**

Caption Answer: the Cascade Range, the Coast Range, and the Alaska Range

Reading Check **Answer:** The Canadian Shield has poor soil and a cold climate, but does have mineral resources; the Central Lowlands have grassy hills, thick forests, fertile farmland, and important waterways.

Differentiated Instruction

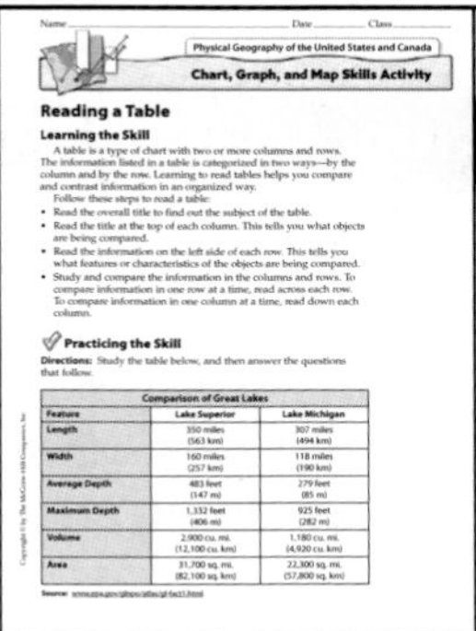

Name ______ Date ______ Class ______

Physical Geography of the United States and Canada

Chart, Graph, and Map Skills Activity

Reading a Table

Learning the Skill

A table is a type of chart with two or more columns and rows. The information listed in a table is categorized in two ways—by the column and by the row. Learning to read tables helps you compare and contrast information in an organized way.

Follow these steps to read a table:

- Read the overall title to find out the subject of the table.
- Read the title at the top of each column. This tells you what objects are being compared.
- Read the information on the left side of each row. This tells you what features or characteristics of the objects are being compared.
- Study and compare the information in the columns and rows. To compare information in one row at a time, read across each row. To compare information in one column at a time, read down each column.

Practicing the Skill

Directions: Study the table below, and then answer the questions that follow.

Comparison of Great Lakes

Feature	Lake Superior	Lake Michigan
Length	350 miles (563 km)	307 miles (494 km)
Width	160 miles (257 km)	118 miles (190 km)
Average Depth	483 feet (147 m)	279 feet (85 m)
Maximum Depth	1,332 feet (406 m)	925 feet (282 m)
Volume	2,900 cu. mi. (12,100 cu. km)	1,180 cu. mi. (4,920 cu. km)
Area	31,700 sq. mi. (82,100 sq. km)	22,300 sq. mi. (57,800 sq. km)

Source: [illegible]

Chart, Graph, and Map Skills Activity, URB pp. 45–46

Reading a Table

Objective: To compare information using a table

Focus: Discuss with students the elements of a table and how it organizes information.

Teach: Have students study the table comparing two of the Great Lakes, then answer the questions.

Assess: Review correct answers with the class.

Close: Discuss with students how tables can be used as a learning tool.

Differentiated Instruction Strategies

- **BL** Have students work with a partner to locate information to fill in the table.
- **AL** Ask students to create a table comparing items of their choice.
- **ELL** Use either table in the activity to ask and answer questions orally.

S Skill Practice

Using Geography Skills Have students look at the map and diagram of the St. Lawrence Seaway. **Ask: Which is the deepest of the Great Lakes shown? Which is the shallowest? How do you know?** *(Lake Superior; Lake Erie; the map shows the relative depths of each lake.)* **Which Great Lake is not a part of the St. Lawrence Seaway system?** *(Lake Michigan)* **OL**

R Reading Strategy

Identifying Ask: What is a divide? Where is the Continental Divide located? *(It is the high point that determines which way rivers flow; it is the highest ridge of the Rocky Mountains.)* **OL**

Map Skills

Answers:

1. Lake Superior and Lake Huron
2. 325 feet (99 m), from Lake Erie to Lake Ontario

Reading Check Answer: St. Louis, Memphis

Additional Support

NATIONAL GEOGRAPHIC

Figure 1 St. Lawrence Seaway and Locks

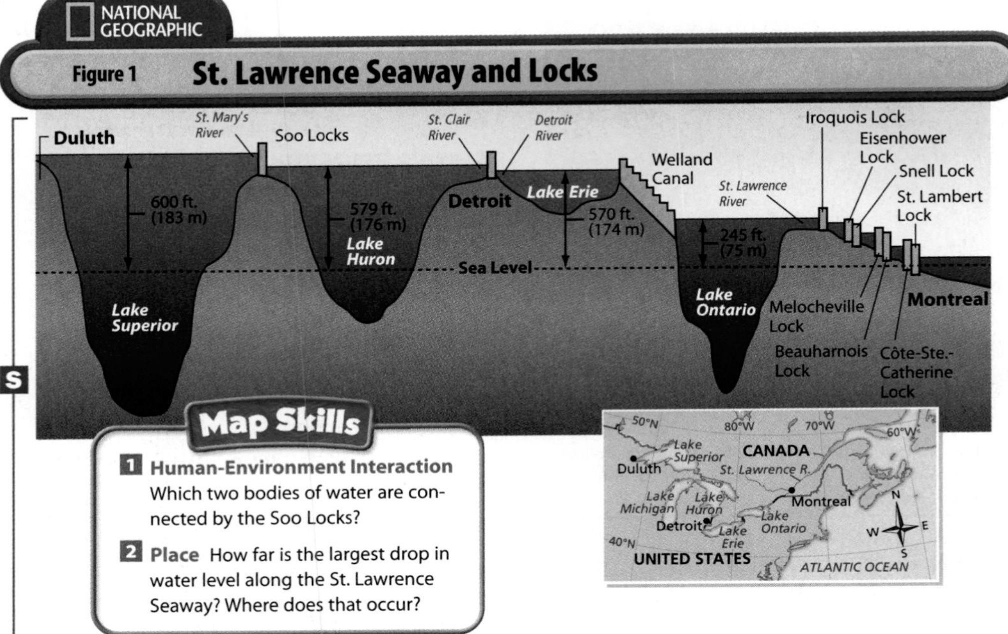

Map Skills

1. **Human-Environment Interaction** Which two bodies of water are connected by the Soo Locks?
2. **Place** How far is the largest drop in water level along the St. Lawrence Seaway? Where does that occur?

Today, ships carry raw materials and manufactured goods from Great Lakes cities, such as Chicago, Detroit, Cleveland, and Toronto, to the rest of the world.

The Mississippi River

The Mississippi River is North America's longest river. It flows 2,350 miles (3,782 km), beginning as a stream in Minnesota and enlarging to a width of 1.5 miles (2.4 km) before emptying into the Gulf of Mexico. Ships can travel on the Mississippi and some of its tributaries for great distances. Products from inland port cities, such as St. Louis and Memphis, are shipped down the river and on to foreign ports.

The Mississippi River system is the major waterway for the central part of the region. It drains about 1.2 million square miles (3.1 million sq. km) of land. This area includes all or part of 31 American states and much of central Canada.

The Continental Divide

Many rivers, such as the Colorado and Rio Grande, flow from the Rocky Mountains. A number of smaller rivers and streams connect with one of these rivers. The high ridge of the Rockies is called the Continental Divide. A **divide** is a high point that determines the direction that rivers flow. East of the Continental Divide, rivers flow toward the Arctic Ocean, the Atlantic Ocean, and the Mississippi River system into the Gulf of Mexico. To the west of the divide, rivers flow toward the Pacific Ocean.

Northeast of the Rockies, the Mackenzie River flows from the Great Slave Lake to the Arctic Ocean. It drains much of northern Canada's interior.

Reading Check **Identifying** What are some inland ports along the Mississippi River?

Activity: Interdisciplinary Connection

Literature Tell students that the Mississippi River is centrally located and has been the centerpiece of the lives of many people in the region as well as the setting and inspiration of important works of American literature. Assign students excerpts from Mark Twain's *Adventures of Huckleberry Finn* and *Life on the Mississippi* that describe life along the Mississippi. Have them discuss the selections in small groups, focusing on Twain's portrayal of river life. Then have students share their ideas in a class discussion. **Ask: What role has the Mississippi River played in the lives of people in the region?** *(Answers will vary.)* **OL**

Natural Resources

Main Idea **The region has many energy, mineral, and other natural resources.**

Geography and You Think about if you like to eat canned, frozen, or fresh vegetables. Where were these foods grown and processed? Read to learn about the natural resources that provide products for the United States and Canada.

In addition to major river systems, the United States and Canada have a great variety of other natural resources. Energy sources and raw materials have made it possible for both countries to develop strong industrial economies.

Energy and Mineral Resources

The United States and Canada have major energy resources, such as oil and natural gas. Texas ranks first in oil and natural gas reserves in the United States. Alaska also has major oil reserves. The United States, however, uses nearly three times the amount of oil that it produces. So, even though the United States has a large reserve of oil, it must import more to meet the nation's needs.

Canada exports both oil and natural gas. Much of Canada's energy exports go to the United States. Most of Canada's oil and natural gas reserves lie in or near the province of Alberta. This province has the world's largest reserves of oil in the form of oil mixed with sands. Obtaining oil from these sands is more costly than working with liquid crude oil.

C1 The United States and Canada also have significant amounts of coal. Coal is mined in the Appalachian Mountains, Wyoming, and British Columbia. The region has enough coal to supply energy for about 400 years, but using this energy source adds to air pollution.

R In eastern areas, highlands drop to the lower Atlantic plain. Along this fall line, rivers break into waterfalls that provide hydroelectric power. Niagara Falls is a major source of hydroelectric power for both Canada and the United States. The falls lie on the Niagara River, which flows north from Lake Erie to Lake Ontario. The falls also form part of the border between Ontario, Canada, and the state of New York.

C2 Mineral resources are also plentiful in the United States and Canada. Parts of eastern Canada and the northern United States have large iron ore deposits. The Rocky Mountains yield gold, silver, and copper. Deep within the Canadian Shield are iron ore, copper, nickel, gold, and uranium. Minerals from the shield helped create a manufacturing region in southern Ontario and Quebec.

NATIONAL GEOGRAPHIC

Mining for Gold in Canada

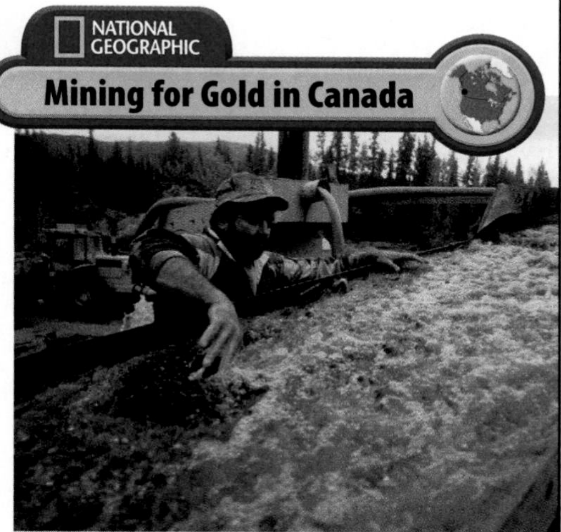

▲ Gold is still mined in British Columbia. Here, a stream of rushing water is used to wash away mud and rocks to help find gold nuggets. ***Place*** **What minerals are found in the Canadian Shield?**

C1 Critical Thinking

Drawing Conclusions Point out to students that the United States has large reserves of coal. **Ask:** **Should the United States use more coal in order to lessen its dependence on imported oil? Why or why not?** *(Answers will vary, but students should be aware of the potential pollution of increased reliance on coal.)* **AL**

R Reading Strategy

Determining Importance **Ask:** **How does this fall line support hydroelectric power?** *(The river breaks into waterfalls that provide hydroelectric power.)* **OL**

C2 Critical Thinking

Determining Cause and Effect
Ask: **What was a cause of the creation of a manufacturing region in southern Ontario and Quebec?** *(the presence of important minerals in the nearby Canadian Shield)* **BL**

Caption Answer:
iron ore, nickel, copper, gold, and uranium

Activity: Economics Connection

Analyzing Visuals **Ask:** **How does oil production in the United States compare with oil consumption?** *(The United States produces less oil than it consumes.)* Have students work in a group or with a partner to research oil production and consumption in the United States over several decades to the present decade. Suggest that students use a world almanac to research U.S. oil production and consumption figures. Tell students to display their findings in a double bar graph, with pairs of bars showing production and consumption at five- or ten-year intervals. Then ask students to share their graphs with the rest of the class. Have them use their graphs to make observations and predictions about oil production and consumption in the United States. **AL**

R Reading Strategy

Organizing Have students work with a partner to make a table listing the different geographic areas of the United States and Canada, the agricultural products raised in each area and why the climate is appropriate. *(Chart information should reflect the text discussion.)* **OL**

Reading Check Answer: It has the world's largest deposits of oil mixed with sands.

Assess

Social Studies ONLINE
Study Central™ provides summaries, interactive games, and online graphic organizers to help students review content.

Close

Evaluating Ask: What do you think contributes to the wealth and prosperity of the United States and Canada? *(Answers will vary.)* **OL**

Soil, Timber, and Fish

Rich soil in parts of the United States and Canada is excellent for farming. Crops vary throughout the region, depending on the local climate. Farmers grow corn in the Central Lowlands, which receive plentiful rainfall, and wheat on the drier Great Plains. The wet, mild climate of western Washington and Oregon supports dairy farming and the growing of fruits and vegetables. Irrigation is used in the drier eastern areas of these two states to grow grain. The warm, wet valleys of central California yield more than 200 different crops. In the south central part of British Columbia, fruits and vegetables are grown on irrigated land.

Timber is another important resource in the region. Forests once covered much of the United States and Canada. Today, however, forests cover less than 50 percent of Canada and about one-third of the United States. Still, lumber and wood products, such as paper, are major Canadian exports. The timber industry is also strong in the states of Oregon and Washington.

Coastal waters are important to the region's economies. Large fishing industries depend on the fish and shellfish in these waters. In recent years, however, the region's Atlantic fishing grounds have suffered from overfishing. The Grand Banks, located off Canada's southeast coast, was once one of the world's richest fishing grounds. Overfishing has harmed the area, and the Canadian government has banned fishing here for some species.

Reading Check **Explaining** What is unique about oil deposits in Alberta, Canada?

Section Review

Social Studies ONLINE
Study Central™ To review this section, go to glencoe.com.

Vocabulary

1. **Explain** the significance of:
   a. contiguous
   b. megalopolis
   c. prairie
   d. cordillera
   e. canyon
   f. navigable
   g. glacier
   h. divide

Main Ideas

2. **Describing** Describe the Canadian Shield and its resources.
3. **Summarizing** Use a diagram like the one below to summarize important facts about the Mississippi River.

4. **Comparing and Contrasting** Compare and contrast the agricultural conditions and crops grown in various parts of the region.

Critical Thinking

5. **BIG Idea** How did building the St. Lawrence Seaway change the land? How have the United States and Canada benefited from the St. Lawrence Seaway?
6. **Challenge** What conditions led to the formation of a megalopolis along the United States's Atlantic coast?

Writing About Geography

7. **Using Your FOLDABLES** Use your Foldable to make and write captions for a map of the region that describes the impact of landforms and waterways on people's lives.

Answers

1. Definitions for vocabulary words are found in the section and the Glossary.
2. It has rocky hills, lakes, evergreen forests, poor soil, a cold climate, iron ore, copper, and nickel.
3. longest river in North America, begins in Minnesota, empties into Gulf of Mexico, ports include St. Louis and Memphis, drains 31 American states and much of central Canada, is a major waterway for central part of region
4. Corn is grown in the Central Lowlands, which has plentiful rainfall. Wheat is grown in the drier Great Plains. The wet, mild climate in Oregon and Washington supports dairy farming, fruits, and vegetables. In drier parts of these states, irrigation is used to grow wheat. More than 200 different crops are grown in the warm, wet valleys of California. Irrigation is used to grow fruits and vegetables in south central British Columbia.
5. Obstructions between Great Lakes and Atlantic Ocean were overcome; shipping of manufactured goods for United States and Canada was improved.
6. The economic growth of shipping ports led to increased settlement, turning them into large cities with expanding suburbs.
7. Students' captions should identify major landforms and waterways and describe their impact on people's lives.

Geography & History

Danger Zone

In August of 2005, a massive hurricane struck the southern United States. The damage it caused was overwhelming.

The Storm and the Damage Hurricane Katrina struck the Gulf coast of the United States on August 29, 2005. Katrina reached land as a category 4 hurricane, the second-strongest category of storm. The hurricane blasted the region with winds of more than 140 miles per hour (225 km/hr). It caused a storm surge—rising seas—of more than 30 feet (9 m) and brought as many as 16 inches (41 cm) of rainfall in a short time.

Storm conditions raged along the coasts of Louisiana, Mississippi, and Alabama. More than 1,800 people died, more than 500,000 were left homeless, and property damage exceeded $30 billion. Katrina was one of the worst natural disasters in American history. **R**

▲ **Flooding from Hurricane Katrina, New Orleans**

Katrina and New Orleans The city of New Orleans suffered extensive damage from Katrina. The strength of the storm and the geography of the city helped lead to disaster. New Orleans lies below sea level, and the city is almost surrounded by water. Lake Pontchartrain lies to the north. The Mississippi flows to the west and south of town. Many years ago, a complex system of high walls, called levees, was built along the lake and river to protect the city from flooding.

The power of Katrina overwhelmed the levees, some of which had weakened with age. Water rushed through breaks in the barriers. Floodwaters rose as high as 20 feet (6 m) in parts of the city. Fortunately, most of New Orleans's 450,000 residents were evacuated before the storm hit. Many months after Katrina, fewer than half of the city's people had returned to their homes. **C**

NATIONAL GEOGRAPHIC

Path of Hurricane Katrina

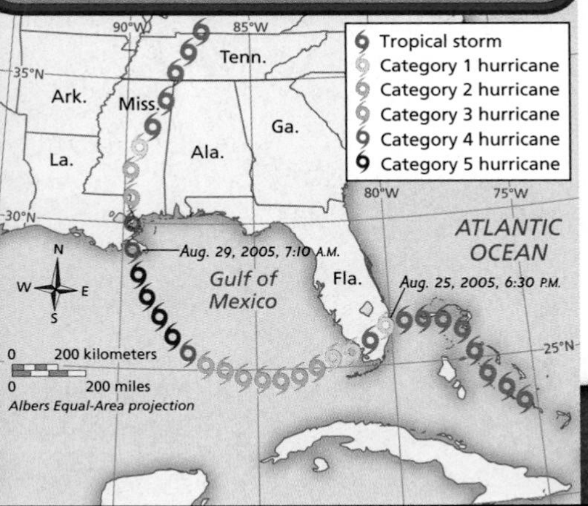

Think About It

1. **Regions** Where did Katrina strike? How much damage did it cause?
2. **Place** Why was the threat of flooding especially dangerous for New Orleans?

R Reading Strategy

Making Connections Ask students to think about images they have seen and reports they have read of the people of New Orleans and Mississippi struggling to recover from the effects of Hurricane Katrina. **Ask: If a disaster like Katrina hit this community, what factors would encourage people to stay and rebuild?** *(Answers will vary. Encourage discussions.)* **OL**

This **Reading Skill** (Making Connections) was introduced in this unit.

C Critical Thinking

Determining Cause and Effect
Ask: Why did New Orleans's levees fail to protect the city? *(Katrina was too powerful, and some of the levees had been weakened with age.)* **OL**

Think About It

Answers:

1. The Gulf Coast of the United States; it caused more than $30 billion in damage.
2. It lies below sea level and is almost completely surrounded by water.

Additional Support

Activity: Technology Connection

Analyzing Primary Sources Ask: What challenges do people living in areas hit by Hurricane Katrina face today? *(Answers will vary but may include that people are struggling to rebuild or reclaim their homes and businesses and are trying to lead normal lives once again.)* Have students search online news sources for firsthand accounts of life today in New Orleans and other places that were hit by Hurricane Katrina. Direct students to look for quotations from people who live in the area that tell about conditions there, problems they face, and their thoughts and feelings about the storm and the damage it caused. Tell students to select two quotations to read aloud to the class and explain what each taught them about the hurricane and its aftermath. **OL**

Focus

Bellringer

Daily Focus Transparency 4-2

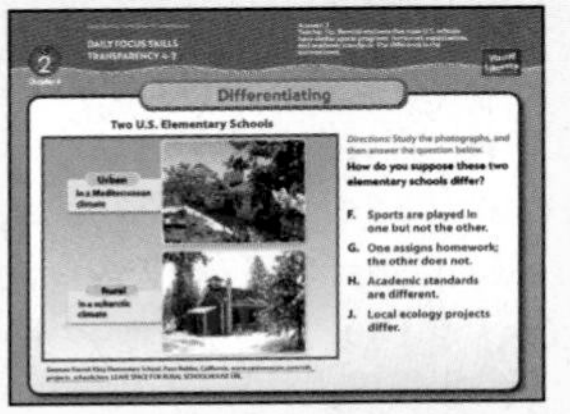

Guide to Reading

Answers to Graphic:

Answers may include:

1. tundra; far north; extremely cold, little vegetation
2. Mediterranean; southern California; warm, dry summers and mild, wet winters
3. tropical wet; southern Florida and Hawaii; hot summers, warm winters, abundant rainfall

Section Spotlight Video

To learn more about the climate regions of the United States and Canada, have students watch the Section Spotlight Video.

Guide to Reading

BIG Idea

The physical environment affects how people live.

Content Vocabulary

- drought *(p. 126)*
- tornado *(p. 127)*
- hurricane *(p. 127)*
- blizzard *(p. 128)*

Academic Vocabulary

- diverse *(p. 125)*
- adapt *(p. 125)*
- restore *(p. 126)*

Reading Strategy

Organizing Information Use a chart like the one below to organize key facts about at least three different climate zones in the region.

Climate Zones	Location	Description
1.		
2.		
3.		

Section 2 Climate Regions

Picture This This sea of red is actually a sea of cranberries. The small, red fruit—also known as bounce berries, crane berries, and rubies of the pines—grows on ground-hugging vines in wetlands and bogs. To harvest the cranberries, farmers flood the bogs. Small air pockets in the cranberries cause them to rise to the surface, where they can be gathered by harvesting machines. Read this section to learn more about the climates of the United States and Canada and how they influence farming and other human activities.

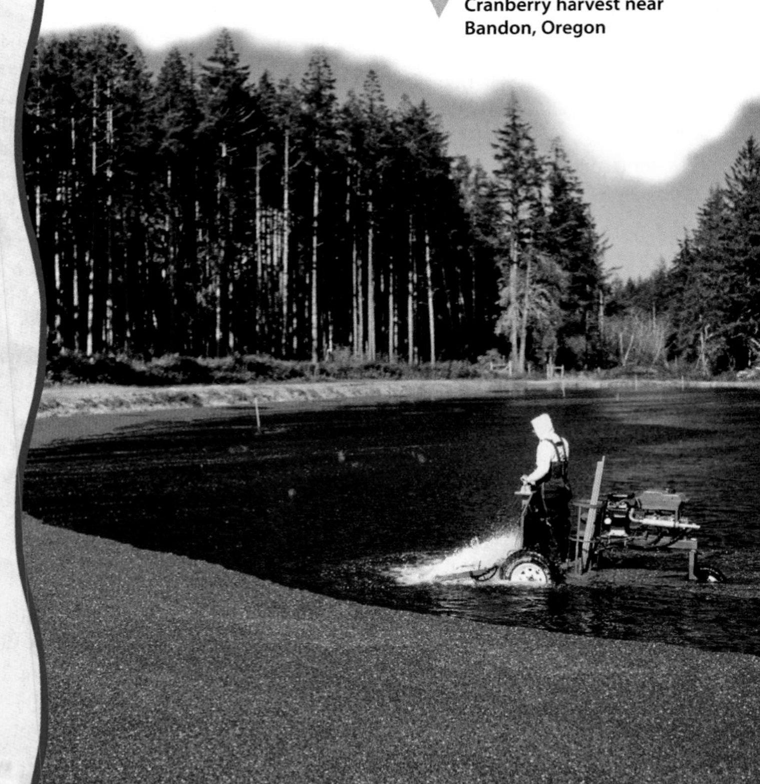

▼ Cranberry harvest near Bandon, Oregon

Resource Manager

R Reading Strategies	C Critical Thinking	D Differentiated Instruction	W Writing Support	S Skill Practice
Teacher Edition • Making Con., p. 125 • Identifying, p. 126 **Additional Resources** • Guid. Read., URB p. 38 • Cont. Vocab., URB p. 39 • Ac. Vocab., URB p. 41 • Read. Ess., p. 31 • Pri. Source Read., URB p. 29	**Teacher Edition** • Drawing Con., p. 125 • Making Inferences, p. 126 **Additional Resources** • Crit. Think., URB p. 47 • GeoLab, URB p. 23 • Authentic Assess., p. 4 • Quizzes and Tests, p. 42 • En. Case Study, URB p. 13	**Teacher Edition** • Kinesthetic, p. 126 **Additional Resources** • Diff. Instr., URB p. 43	**Teacher Edition** • Descriptive Writing, p. 127	**Teacher Edition** • Visual Literacy, p. 127 **Additional Resources** • Read. Skills, URB p. 25 • Daily Focus Trans. 4-2 • Reg. Atlas, URB pp. 1–7

A Varied Region

Main Idea **Most people in the United States and Canada live in temperate climate regions.**

Geography and You What is the climate like in your area? Read to learn about the different climate regions of the United States and Canada.

The region of the United States and Canada stretches from cold Arctic wastelands in the far north to warm, sunny vacation areas near the Tropic of Cancer. This vast territory is **diverse** in both climate and vegetation. Most people in the United States and Canada, however, avoid the extremes of tropical and Arctic climates. They live in the middle latitudes where climates are more moderate. **Figure 2** shows all of the region's climates. C

The Far North

Tundra and subarctic climates are found in the northern parts of Alaska and Canada. Winters are long and cold, while summers are brief and cool. As a result, few people live in this harsh environment.

Along the Arctic Ocean's coastline, the extremely cold tundra prevents the growth of trees and most plants. In the subarctic region farther south, dense forests of evergreen trees are specially **adapted,** or adjusted, to the climate. The waxy coating of evergreen needles keeps in moisture during the bitterly cold winters. R

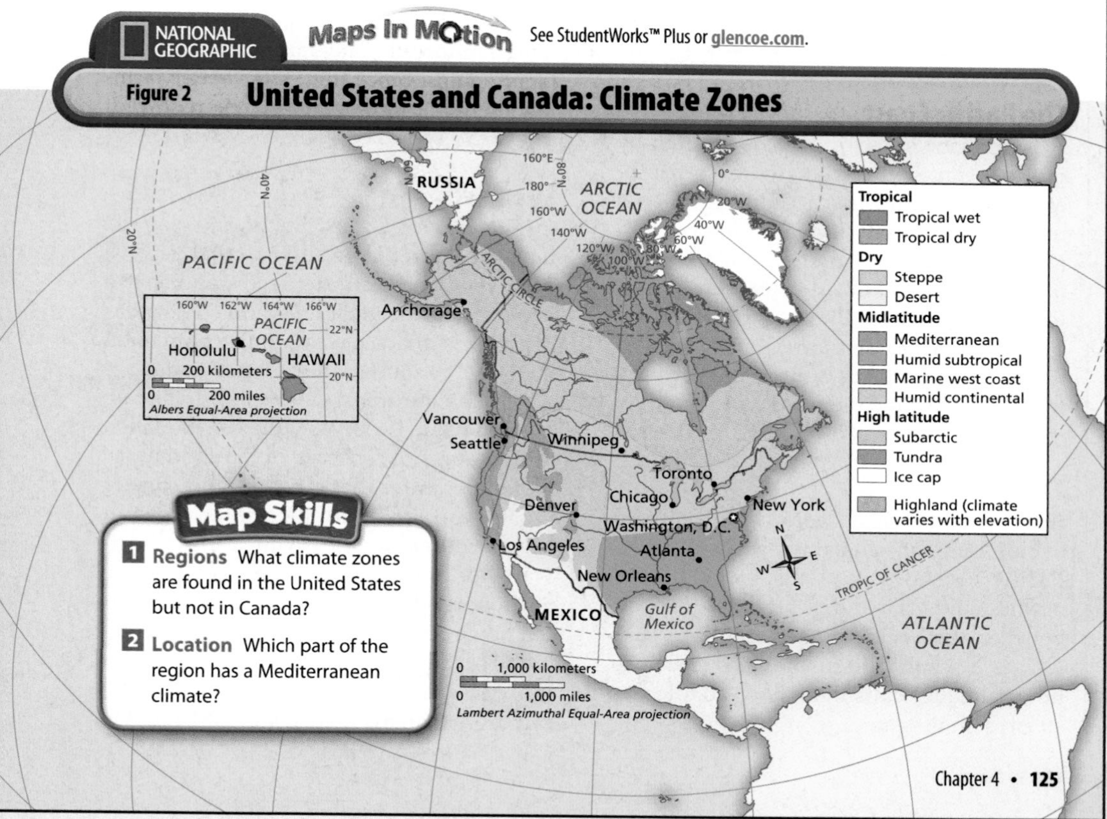

Figure 2 **United States and Canada: Climate Zones**

Map Skills

1 Regions What climate zones are found in the United States but not in Canada?

2 Location Which part of the region has a Mediterranean climate?

Teach

C Critical Thinking

Drawing Conclusions **Ask:** **Why do you think most people in the United States and Canada live in the middle latitudes?** *(Possible answers: climates are relatively mild and the fact that most cities, and therefore most jobs, are located in the middle latitudes)* **OL**

R Reading Strategy

Making Connections Ask students to find the example in the text of how a living thing adapts to a harsh environment. *(the waxy coating on evergreen needles)* **Ask:** **What are some other examples of living things that have adapted to harsh climates?** *(Possible examples include polar bears hibernating and cactus plants storing water.)* **OL**

This **Reading Skill** (Making Connections) was introduced in this unit.

Map Skills

Answers:

1. humid subtropical, desert, Mediterranean, tropical wet
2. the southern west coast of the United States

Hands-On Chapter Project Step 2

How Did They Build That?

Step 2: Illustrating the Project Groups will illustrate the transportation systems they researched in Step 1.

Directions Have each group locate specific places on the route of their transportation system where the construction would have especially difficult. Have them create a map indicating these places along the route. Then have them use the Internet to identify pictures that illustrate the difficulties involved, such as getting through a mountain or around river rapids. If research proves difficult, students may create their own images.

Putting It Together Have each group create a collage linking the images to the corresponding places on their map. **OL**

(Chapter Project cont. on the Visual Summary page)

D Differentiated Instruction

Kinesthetic Ask students to create a mural, case display, or other exhibit about the climate regions of the Pacific Coast. Display the artwork as you study the region. **AL**

R Reading Strategy

Identifying Ask: **What is the reason the inland West receives little rainfall?** *(Coastal mountains block humid ocean winds and trap hot dry air between the Pacific ranges and the Rockies.)* **OL**

C Critical Thinking

Making Inferences Ask: **In what way did the disaster of the Dust Bowl bring about improvements?** *(Better farming methods have restored the area's soils.)* **Ask:** **Can you think of any positive effects that might have resulted from recent natural disasters?** *(Possible answers include better flood control, levee construction, and building plans after Hurricane Katrina, or stronger buildings, bridges, and roads after the 1989 San Francisco earthquake.)* **AL**

Caption Answer:
Crops or animals may die from lack of water.

NATIONAL GEOGRAPHIC

Snow Day

Heavy snowfall is common during the winter in Iowa, as well as in other states across the Great Plains. ***Human-Environment Interaction*** **How might a drought affect a farmer or rancher?**

The Pacific Coast

The region's Pacific coast is affected by moist ocean winds. The area from southern Alaska to northern California has a marine west coast climate of year-round mild temperatures and abundant rainfall. It is common to see evergreen forests, ferns, and mosses. By contrast, southern California has a Mediterranean climate of warm, dry summers and mild, wet winters. There is much less rainfall here than in northern areas.

The West

The inland West has a desert climate of hot summers and mild winters. Here, Pacific coastal mountains block humid ocean winds. Hot, dry air gets trapped between the Pacific ranges and the Rockies. As a result, the inland West receives little rainfall. Plants there have adapted to survive on little rain.

Areas on the eastern side of the Rockies have a partly dry steppe climate. **Droughts,** or long periods without rainfall, are a serious challenge, especially to farmers and ranchers who can lose crops and animals. In some areas, a growing population also strains water resources.

The Great Plains

The Great Plains area benefits from moisture-bearing winds from the Gulf of Mexico and from the Arctic. As a result, much of this area has a humid continental climate with cold, snowy winters and hot, humid summers. Enough precipitation falls to support prairie grasses and grains. Dry weather, however, sometimes affects the area. In the 1930s, winds eroded loose topsoil and turned the area into a wasteland called the Dust Bowl. Economic hardship forced many farmers to leave the Great Plains. Since the 1930s, better farming methods have **restored,** or renewed, this area's soil.

The East

The eastern United States and Canada have humid climate regions that receive plenty of year-round precipitation. The northeastern United States and some areas of eastern Canada have a humid continental climate. The southeastern United States has a humid subtropical climate. Both climate areas have a variety of forests. Wetlands and swamps cover some of the southeast.

Temperatures in the two humid climate regions are similar in the summer but can be very different in the winter. In summer, warm air from the south blocks cold Arctic air from reaching the eastern areas. In winter, however, the northeast receives strong blasts of icy Arctic air. For example, in Boston, Massachusetts, January temperatures can drop to an average low of 22°F (–6 °C).

Leveled Activities

BL Guided Reading Activity, URB p. 38

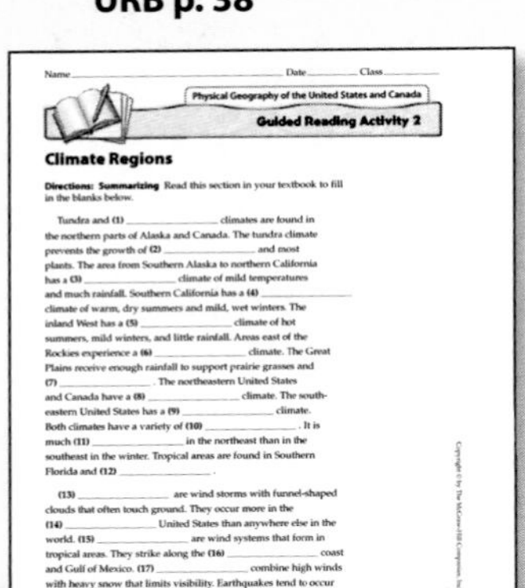

Physical Geography of the United States and Canada
Guided Reading Activity 2
Climate Regions

OL Content Vocabulary Activity, URB p. 39

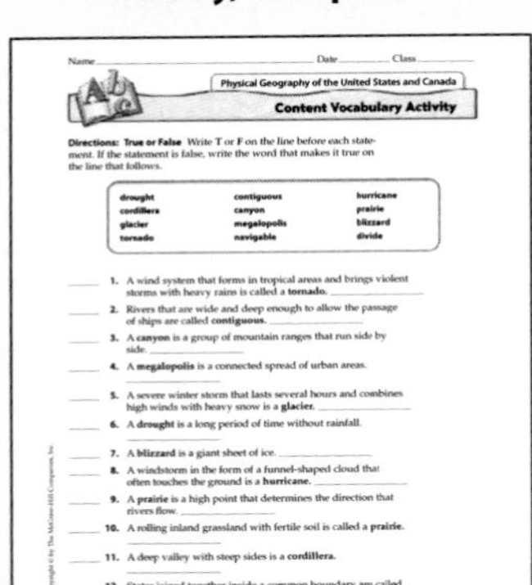

Physical Geography of the United States and Canada
Content Vocabulary Activity

AL Critical Thinking Activity, URB p. 47

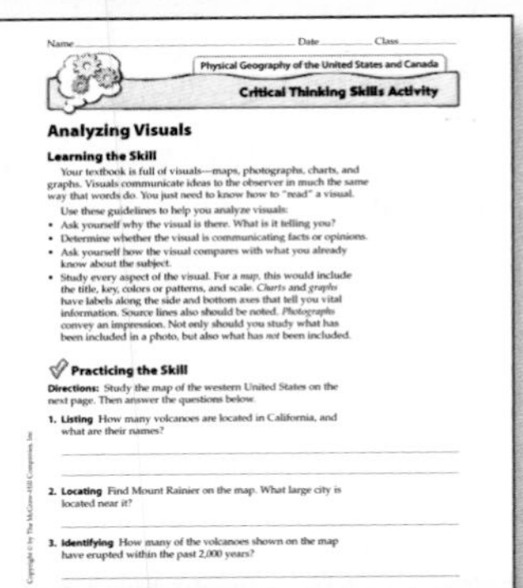

Physical Geography of the United States and Canada
Critical Thinking Skills Activity
Analyzing Visuals

ELL Academic Vocabulary Activity, URB p. 41

Areas in the southeast still receive some warmth from the south. As a result, the average January temperature in Atlanta, Georgia, is 41°F (5°C).

Tropical Areas

Tropical climates are found in two areas of the United States. Southern Florida has a tropical savanna climate. Temperatures are hot in summer and warm in winter. Rainfall occurs mainly during the summer. Hawaii, the other tropical area, has year-round temperatures that average above 70°F (21°C). The mild climate draws many visitors throughout the year. Rainfall, which varies throughout the state, supports tropical rain forests.

Reading Check **Explaining** What factors affect climate in the Great Plains?

Kayaking in Florida

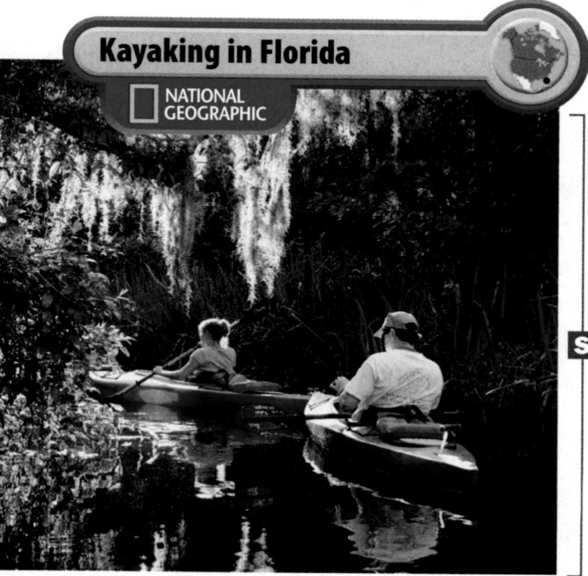

▲ In the large wetlands area known as the Everglades, south Florida's tropical climate produces lush vegetation. ***Location*** **Besides Florida, what other state has a tropical climate?**

Natural Hazards

Main Idea **Hurricanes, tornadoes, and earthquakes can threaten parts of the region.**

Geography and You Does the area where you live experience severe storms? Read to learn about the environmental challenges that affect the United States and Canada.

The landforms and climate of this region provide people with many benefits. They also pose challenges in the form of severe storms and other natural hazards.

Severe Weather

One hazard related to severe weather is a tornado. A **tornado** is a windstorm in the form of a funnel-shaped cloud that often touches the ground. The high winds of a tornado, which can reach more than 300 miles per hour (482 km per hour), can level houses, knock down trees, and hurl cars from one place to another. These storms can occur anywhere in the region and at any time of the year. The central United States sees more tornadoes each year than any other place in the world. As a result, this area has been nicknamed "Tornado Alley." **W**

S Another severe storm is a hurricane. **Hurricanes** are wind systems that form over the ocean in tropical areas and bring violent storms with heavy rains. As with tornadoes, high winds can do serious damage. In addition, hurricanes can create a storm surge, or high levels of seawater. The high waters can flood low-lying coastal areas. Hurricanes generally develop from June to September. They most often strike along the southeastern Atlantic coast and the Gulf of Mexico. However, northeastern states can also be affected by hurricanes.

S Skill Practice

Visual Literacy **Ask:** **What evidence of a tropical climate can you see in the photograph?** *(the lush vegetation, the lightweight clothing)* **BL**

W Writing Support

Descriptive Writing Have students write a description of what it would be like if a tornado hit a nearby city. Encourage them to use vivid words to describe the experience. Have volunteers share their writing with the class. **OL**

Reading Check **Answer:** moisture-bearing winds from the Gulf of Mexico and the Arctic

Caption Answer: Hawaii

Differentiated Instruction

Authentic Assessment Activity, p. 4

Hurricane Warnings

Objective: To give an oral presentation about a major hurricane and its impact

Focus: Discuss with students the research and planning required for an oral presentation.

Teach: Have students complete the seven procedures in the activity.

Assess: Use the scoring rubric to evaluate the presentation.

Close: Discuss the value of oral presentations.

Differentiated Instruction Strategies

- **BL** Use a K-W-L chart to list questions for research and to take notes for answers.
- **AL** Include eyewitness accounts of the hurricane in the presentation.
- **ELL** Copy an outline on note cards. Practice using cards only as reminders of main points.

Reading Check **Answer:** A hurricane's high winds and heavy rains can cause flooding, destroy buildings, knock down power lines, and create storm surges.

Assess

Social Studies ONLINE

Study Central™ provides summaries, interactive games, and online graphic organizers to help students review content.

Close

Discussing Ask: What types of natural hazards does our community need to be prepared for? *(Answers will vary.)* OL

One of the most damaging hurricanes in history, Hurricane Katrina, struck the coast of the Gulf of Mexico in August of 2005. It damaged a wide area from Mobile, Alabama, to New Orleans, Louisiana. More than 1,800 people died, and hundreds of thousands lost their homes. Most of New Orleans and many nearby towns were completely flooded. In Mississippi, entire towns were destroyed.

Winter weather can also be hazardous. **Blizzards** are severe winter storms that last several hours and combine high winds with heavy snow. The blowing snow limits how far people can see. "White-out" conditions, or snow that falls so heavily that a person cannot see very far, make driving dangerous. Also, the wind and snow can knock down electric power lines and trees and create icy road conditions. Blizzards can halt activity in a busy city for days as city workers attempt to clear the streets.

Earthquakes and Volcanoes

While earthquakes can occur anywhere in the region, most take place along the Pacific coast. This area lies along various fault lines, or areas of weakness in the Earth where two tectonic plates meet. A 1906 earthquake heavily damaged buildings in San Francisco. Many of the buildings that remained standing were destroyed by fires triggered by broken natural gas lines. Today, buildings in the region are often built using special techniques to protect them from damage.

The area where tectonic plates meet can also be the site of volcanoes. Volcanoes are found in the Pacific coast mountains, southern Alaska, and Hawaii. Most are now dormant, or unlikely to erupt soon. Several of Hawaii's volcanoes are still active.

Reading Check **Describing** Describe the types of damage that hurricanes can cause.

Section 2 Review

Social Studies ONLINE
Study Central™ To review this section, go to glencoe.com.

Vocabulary

1. **Describe** each of these weather conditions and where they are likely to occur: *drought, tornado, hurricane,* and *blizzard.*

Main Ideas

2. **Summarizing** Use a diagram like the one below to summarize information about one of the region's climate zones. Write the name of a climate zone in the large oval and details about it in the small ovals.

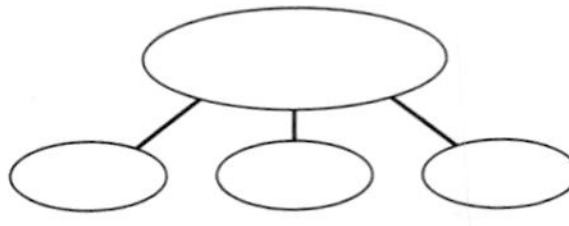

3. **Comparing and Contrasting** Compare and contrast tornadoes and hurricanes.

Critical Thinking

4. **Determining Cause and Effect** How do mountains in the region influence climate?
5. **BIG Idea** What were some of the effects of Hurricane Katrina?
6. **Challenge** Based on climate and the occurrence of natural hazards, which areas of the region do you think are most populated? Explain your answer.

Writing About Geography

7. **Personal Writing** Write a paragraph identifying which of the climates described in this section you think sounds most enjoyable to live in, and explain why.

Section 2 Review

Answers

1. Students' descriptions should demonstrate an understanding of each word as defined in the section and Glossary.
2. Sample answer: Large oval: dry steppe climate; Small ovals: eastern side of Rockies, droughts, strained water resources
3. Both generate windstorms that can do serious damage. Tornadoes form as funnel-shaped clouds. They can occur anywhere in the region but most often in the central United States. Hurricanes form over the ocean in tropical areas, occur most often along the southeastern Atlantic coast and Gulf of Mexico, and develop mostly from June to September.
4. Pacific coastal mountains block humid ocean winds from reaching inland West; hot, dry air trapped between Pacific ranges and Rockies creates a desert climate; little rain falls on the eastern side of Rockies, producing a dry steppe climate.
5. flooding, loss of lives, homes and businesses and entire towns destroyed
6. Possible answers: northeast and northwest coasts, since climate is milder and fewer natural hazards exist than in other parts of the region
7. Students' paragraphs should demonstrate an understanding of the climates of the region.

Visual Summary

Major Landforms

- The East has low coastal plains and heavily eroded highlands.
- Lowland areas with minerals and rich soil make up the region's interior.
- The West has several parallel mountain ranges. Plateaus, basins, and valleys lie between the mountains.

Lowland marsh, Virginia

Major Bodies of Water

- The Great Lakes and the St. Lawrence Seaway support trade between the region's interior areas and other parts of the world.
- The Mississippi River is the most important waterway in the central part of the United States.

Riverboat, Mississippi River

Farming in Manitoba, Canada

Natural Resources

- The region's energy resources include oil, natural gas, and coal.
- Abundant mineral resources are found in the eastern highlands, the Canadian Shield, and the western mountains.
- Rich soils support farming in the Central Lowlands, the Great Plains, and western valleys.

Climate Regions

- Most Americans and Canadians live in moderate, middle-latitude climate areas.
- The inland West has dry and semidry climates because mountains block moist air.
- Pacific coastal areas generally have mild, wet climates.

Natural Hazards

- Tornadoes occur primarily in the central area of the region.
- Hurricanes can bring heavy winds and rain to the Atlantic and Gulf coasts.
- Earthquakes are a destructive threat along coastal fault lines in the West.
- Volcanoes are found in western coastal areas, Alaska, and Hawaii. Most are dormant.

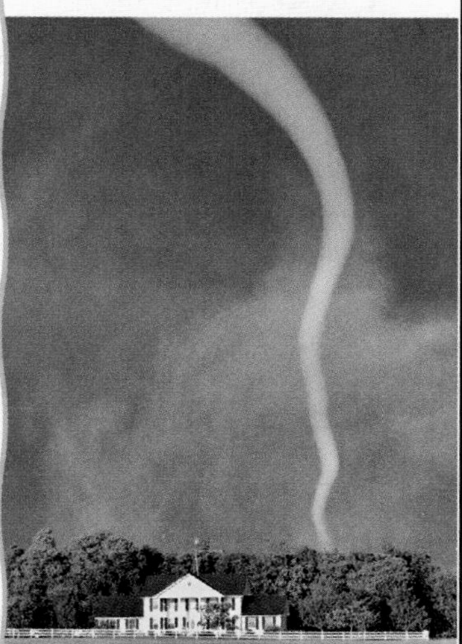

Tornado, Kansas

STUDY TO GO Study anywhere, anytime! Download quizzes and flash cards to your PDA from glencoe.com.

Visual Summary

Making Generalizations Have students study the bulleted items. Ask them to identify those items that have contributed to the economic prosperity of the United States and Canada.

Using the bulleted items they selected, have students make a list of generalizations about how a region's geographic features can contribute to its prosperity. *(One possible example is "Regions with abundant natural resources can be prosperous.")* Have students take turns sharing their generalizations with the rest of the class. **OL**

Understanding Question-Answer Relationships Have students work in pairs to write questions based on the Visual Summary. Have each pair write eight questions on index cards, one per card. Then have the pair write the answers, one per index card. For example, an answer might be "in moderate, middle-latitude climate areas." The question is "Where do most Americans and Canadians live?" Ask pairs to exchange answers with another pair, identify the matching questions, and discuss the answers and questions. **OL**

Hands-On Chapter Project
Step 3: Wrap Up

How Did They Build That?

Step 3: Learning from the Project Students will synthesize what they have learned in Steps 1 and 2.

Directions Refer again to the Essential Question on the board. Ask students to respond to the question based on what they learned from researching their transportation systems. Have students name landforms and climates that helped or hindered the construction of each system. List these on the board. **Ask:** **Where and how do landforms, waterways, or climate in the United States and Canada promote easy travel? What obstacles to transportation exist? How have they been overcome?** After discussion, have students write a paragraph in their journals about how landforms and climate affect transportation in their local area. **OL**

Answers and Analyses

Reviewing Vocabulary

1. B The key to finding the correct answer in this question is to know the meaning of the word parts of *megalopolis*. If students remember that *mega-* means "large" and *polis* means "city," they will have no trouble with this one. The other choices are all geographic features, not human features.

2. A Choices B and C can be eliminated because *canyon* and *glacier* should be relatively familiar terms for most students. Choice D may prove more difficult. Remind students that a *cordillera* is a chain of mountains running in the same direction.

3. A The clue is the word *dry* in the stem. Students should associate dryness with *drought*, or a long period without rain. Although the other choices are natural hazards, they are unlikely to be major causes of crop and animal loss.

4. C Many students may associate *hurricanes* with Katrina and recall that New Orleans and the Mississippi coast lie along the Gulf of Mexico. Students should associate *droughts* and *tornadoes* with the Midwestern plains. They also might associate *earthquakes* with California and Pacific coastal regions.

STANDARDIZED TEST PRACTICE

TEST-TAKING TIP

Do not wait until the last minute to study for an exam. Beginning about one week before the test, set aside some time each day for review.

Reviewing Vocabulary

Directions: Choose the word(s) that best completes the sentence.

1. Atlantic coastal cities and their suburbs form an almost continuous line of settlement called a ________.

A Piedmont
B megalopolis
C coastal plain
D coastal lowland

2. Much of the Great Plains is a ________, or rolling grassland.

A prairie
B canyon
C glacier
D cordillera

3. Ranchers in the dry steppe region east of the Rockies sometimes lose crops and animals due to ________.

A droughts
B blizzards
C hurricanes
D earthquakes

4. ________ most often strike along the southeastern Atlantic coast and the Gulf of Mexico.

A Droughts
B Tornadoes
C Hurricanes
D Earthquakes

Reviewing Main Ideas

Directions: Choose the best answer for each question.

Section 1 *(pp. 116–122)*

5. Which of the following areas of the United States has the highest elevation?

A Gulf coastal plain
B eastern Great Plains
C western Great Plains
D Atlantic coastal plain

6. ________ depend on the Mississippi River for shipping products on their way to foreign ports.

A Chicago and Detroit
B Quebec and Montreal
C Toronto and Cleveland
D St. Louis and Memphis

Section 2 *(pp. 124–128)*

7. The area from southern Alaska to northern California has a ________ climate with year-round mild temperatures and abundant rainfall.

A subtropical
B Mediterranean
C marine west coast
D humid continental

8. ________ has more tornadoes each year than any other place in the world.

A Eastern Canada
B Northern Canada
C The northeastern United States
D The central United States

GO ON

Reviewing Main Ideas

5. C Students should eliminate choices A and D first because they understand that coastal plains are closer to sea level than those inland. In choosing between B and C, remind students to think about where the Rocky Mountains are.

6. D A general grasp of North American geography will help students choose correctly on this question. *Chicago and Detroit,* as well as *Toronto and Cleveland,* are in the Great Lakes region. They would be unlikely to benefit directly from the Mississippi River. *Quebec and Montreal* are eastern Canadian cities and depend on the St. Lawrence Seaway.

Critical Thinking

Directions: Choose the best answers to the following questions. Base your answers to questions 9 and 10 on the map below and your knowledge of Chapter 4.

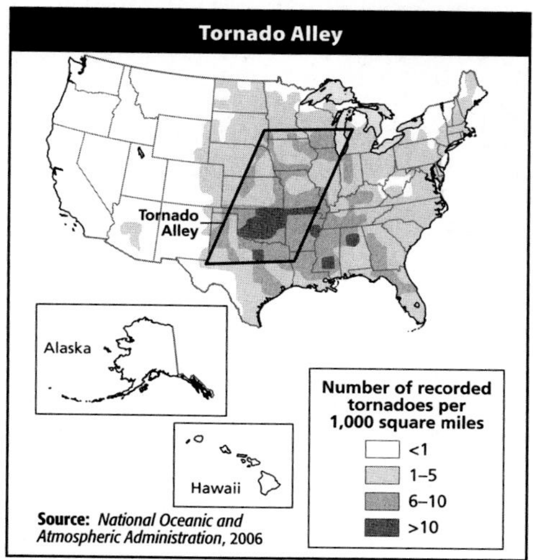

9. According to the map, which states have the most tornado activity?

A Texas and Oklahoma

B Texas and Louisiana

C Oklahoma and Kansas

D Missouri and Arkansas

10. According to the information in the map, which generalization is most accurate?

A The western United States never experiences tornadoes.

B Most tornadoes occur in the southeastern United States.

C "Tornado Alley" is an area of moderate tornado activity.

D The central United States has more tornadoes than the rest of the country.

Document-Based Questions

Directions: Analyze the following document and answer the short-answer questions that follow.

The news story below sums up findings in a 2005 study on recent hurricanes:

> *The number of Category 4 and 5 hurricanes worldwide has nearly doubled over the past 35 years, even though the total number of hurricanes has dropped since the 1990s. . . . The shift occurred as global sea surface temperatures have increased over the same period. . . .*
>
> *"What we found was rather astonishing," said [Peter Webster, professor at Georgia Tech's School of Earth and Atmospheric Sciences]. "In the 1970s, there was an average of about 10 Category 4 and 5 hurricanes per year globally. Since 1990, the number of Category 4 and 5 hurricanes has almost doubled, averaging 18 per year globally."*
>
> *Category 4 hurricanes have sustained winds from 131 to 155 miles per hour; Category 5 systems, such as Hurricane Katrina at its peak over the Gulf of Mexico, feature winds of 156 mph or more.*
>
> —The National Center for Atmospheric Research, 2005

11. How have hurricanes changed in the past 35 years?

12. What might be causing this hurricane intensity?

Extended Response

13. Suppose you are a foreign visitor to North America. Describe one region of the United States or Canada and write a letter to a friend, persuading him or her to visit.

STOP

For additional test practice, use Self-Check Quizzes—Chapter 4 at glencoe.com.

Need Extra Help?

If you missed question. . .	1	2	3	4	5	6	7	8	9	10	11	12	13
Go to page. . .	117	118	126	127	118	120	126	127	26	26	127	127	116–128

Critical Thinking

9. A The trick in this question is to look at both states in the answers. The states listed with the largest areas of high tornado events are Texas and Oklahoma.

10. D Answer A is incorrect because the map does not indicate that there were no tornadoes in the west, only that there were not many. Although many tornadoes occur in the Southeast, there are more in "Tornado Alley." As for answer C, the map deals only with numbers, not degree of intensity. Besides this, "Tornado Alley" has the highest number of tornadoes—that is not usually considered "moderate."

Document-Based Questions

11. The number of Category 4 and 5 hurricanes has nearly doubled.

12. Sea surface temperatures have risen around the world.

Extended Response

13. Letters will vary, but they should be well written and show understanding of the characteristics of the different climate regions discussed in the chapter.

7. C If students cannot remember the correct answer, have them think about the geographic location of Alaska and California relative to the rest of the region. This should help them pick up on "West Coast."

8. D While tornadoes can occur anywhere, remind students to recall the phrase *tornado alley* and its geographic location. If they still struggle, tell them that Oklahoma is in tornado alley.

Social Studies ONLINE

Have students visit the Web site at glencoe.com to review Chapter 4 and take the Self-Check Quiz.

Need Extra Help?

Have students refer to the pages listed if they miss any of the questions.

Planning Guide

Key to Ability Levels

BL Below level
OL On level
AL Above level
ELL English Language Learners

Key to Teaching Resources

Print Material
DVD
CD-ROM
Transparency

Levels					Resources	Chapter Opener	Section 1	Section 2	Chapter Assess
BL	OL	AL	ELL						
FOCUS									
BL	OL	AL	ELL	Transparency	Daily Focus Skills Transparencies		5-1	5-2	
TEACH									
BL	OL		ELL	Print Material	Guided Reading Activity, URB*		p. 61	p. 62	
BL	OL	AL	ELL	Print Material	Content Vocabulary Activity, URB*		p. 63	p. 63	
BL	OL	AL	ELL	Print Material	Academic Vocabulary Activity, URB		p. 65	p. 65	
BL	OL	AL	ELL	Print Material	Differentiated Instruction Activity, URB		p. 67		
BL	OL	AL	ELL	Print Material	Chart, Graph, and Map Skills Activity, URB		p. 69	p. 69	
	OL	AL		Print Material	Critical Thinking Activity, URB		p. 71		
BL	OL	AL	ELL	Print Material	Speaking and Listening Skills Activity, URB		p. 73	p. 73	
BL	OL	AL	ELL	Print Material	Writing Skills Activity, URB		p. 77		
BL	OL	AL	ELL	Print Material	School-to-Home Connection Activity, URB*		p. 81		
BL	OL	AL	ELL	Print Material	Regional Atlas Activities, URB		pp. 1–7	pp. 1–7	
	OL	AL		Print Material	Geography and History Activity, URB		p. 11		
BL	OL		ELL	Print Material	Time Line Activity, URB		p. 17		
		AL		Print Material	Enrichment Activity, URB		p. 19		
BL	OL		ELL	Print Material	Reading Skills Activity, URB		p. 25		
BL	OL	AL	ELL	Print Material	Primary Source Readings, URB		p. 27		
	OL	AL		Print Material	World Literature Readings, URB		p. 33	p. 31	
BL	OL		ELL	Print Material	Reading Essentials and Note-Taking Guide*		p. 34	p. 37	
BL	OL	AL	ELL	Transparency	In-Text Map Overlay and Population Pyramid Transparencies	2A	2A	2C	
	OL			Print Material	Foods Around the World			pp. 6, 8	
BL	OL	AL	ELL	Print Material	Outline Map Resource Book	p. 6	pp. 9, 25	pp. 6, 22	
BL	OL	AL	ELL	Print Material	NGS World Atlas*	✓	✓	✓	
BL	OL	AL	ELL	Print Material	NGS World Desk Map	✓	✓	✓	✓
BL	OL	AL	ELL	Print Material	World Literature Library	✓	✓	✓	✓
BL	OL	AL	ELL	Print Material	Writer's Guidebook	✓	✓	✓	✓

Note: Please refer to the *Unit Resource Book: The United States and Canada* for this chapter's URB materials.

* Also available in Spanish

- Interactive Lesson Planner
- Interactive Teacher Edition
- Fully editable blackline masters
- Section Spotlight Videos Launch
- Differentiated Lesson Plans
- Printable reports of daily assignments
- Standards Tracking System

Levels				Resources	Chapter Opener	Section 1	Section 2	Chapter Assess
BL	OL	AL	ELL					
				TEACH *(continued)*				
BL	OL	AL	ELL	NGS World Desk Map	✓	✓	✓	✓
BL	OL	AL	ELL	World Literature Library	✓	✓	✓	✓
BL	OL	AL	ELL	Writer's Guidebook	✓	✓	✓	✓
BL	OL	AL	ELL	Vocabulary PuzzleMaker CD-ROM*	✓	✓	✓	✓
	OL	AL		Primary Sources CD-ROM	✓	✓	✓	✓
BL	OL	AL	ELL	StudentWorks™ Plus DVD	✓	✓	✓	✓
BL	OL	AL	ELL	Section Video Program Activities	✓	✓	✓	✓
BL	OL	AL	ELL	World Music: A Cultural Legacy	✓	✓	✓	✓
BL	OL	AL	ELL	Writing Process Transparencies	✓	✓	✓	✓
Teacher Resources				Building Academic Vocabulary	✓	✓	✓	✓
				Strategies for Success	✓	✓	✓	✓
				Teacher's Guide to Differentiated Instruction	✓	✓	✓	✓
				Presentation Plus! DVD	✓	✓	✓	✓
				ASSESS				
BL	OL	AL	ELL	Quizzes and Tests		p. 51	p. 52	p. 53
BL	OL	AL	ELL	Authentic Assessment With Rubrics				p. 5
BL	OL	AL	ELL	Standardized Test Practice				p. 17
BL	OL	AL	ELL	*ExamView® Assessment Suite* CD-ROM*		5-1	5-2	Ch. 5
BL	OL	AL	ELL	Interactive Tutor Self-Assessment CD-ROM		5-1	5-2	
				CLOSE				
BL			ELL	Reteaching Activity, URB*		p. 79	p. 79	p. 79
BL	OL		ELL	Reading and Study Skills Foldables™	p. 58	p. 58	p. 58	p. 58
BL	OL	AL	ELL	Graphic Organizer Transparencies and Strategies		✓	✓	
BL	OL	AL	ELL	*Exploring Our World* in Graphic Novel			p. 17	

Integrating Technology

Searching by Chronology

Technology Product

Glencoe's *American History Primary Source Document Library CD-ROMs* includes more than 200 primary source documents. The documents provide new sources of knowledge that encourage students to think critically about history and historical concepts. The *American History Primary Source Document Library* allows you to

- select chronological periods from Prehistory through Modern America;
- choose from selected documents within each time period to read and/or listen to;
- utilize **Teaching Strategies, Questions/Answers,** and **Blackline Masters** resources in conjunction with the primary source document to maximize student learning.

Steps

- After launching **Primary Source Document Library CD-ROM,** choose the **Chronology** button.
- Select a topic.
- Select from the list of documents available on the chosen topic. An **audio clip** icon in the margin indicates documents that include audio.
- Review the **Document Overview** and **Guided Reading Questions** at the top of each document.
- Click on the **User's Guide and Teaching Strategies** link in at the bottom of the bookmarks listed on the left. Select **To the Teacher** and **Teaching Strategies** for teaching suggestions and procedures using the primary source documents.
- Select **Questions/Activities** and **Blackline Masters** for worksheets and organizers created for use with the primary source documents.

Social Studies ONLINE

	Student	Teacher	Parent
Beyond the Textbook	●		●
Chapter Overviews	●		●
Concepts in Motion	●		●
ePuzzles and Games	●		●
Literature Connections		●	
Multi-Language Glossaries	●		●
Online Student Edition	●	●	●
Section Videos	●	●	●
Self-Check Quizzes	●		●
Student Web Activities	●		●
Study Central™	●		●
Teaching Today		●	
TIME Current Events	●		●
Vocabulary eFlashcards	●		●
Web Activity Lesson Plans		●	

Reading Support From JAMESTOWN EDUCATION

- **Timed Readings Plus in Social Studies** helps students increase their reading rate and fluency while maintaining comprehension. The 400-word passages are similar to those found on state and national assessments.
- **Reading in the Content Area: Social Studies** concentrates on six essential reading skills that help students better comprehend what they read. The book includes 75 high-interest nonfiction passages written at increasing levels of difficulty.
- **Reading Social Studies** includes strategic reading instruction and vocabulary support in Social Studies content for ELLs and native speakers of English.
- **Content Vocabulary Workout** (Grades 6–8) accelerates reading comprehension through focused vocabulary development. Social Studies content vocabulary comes from the glossaries of Glencoe's Middle School Social Studies texts. www.jamestowneducation.com

NATIONAL GEOGRAPHIC
Index to National Geographic Magazine:

The following articles relate to this chapter:

- "Iron v. Oak: The Day the Wooden Navy Died," Joel K. Bourne, Jr., March 2006.
- "Shall We Dance?" Cathy Newman, July 2006.

National Geographic Society Products To order the following, call National Geographic at 1-800-368-2728:

- *National Geographic Atlas of the World* (Book).

Access National Geographic's new dynamic MapMachine Web site and other geography resources at:
www.nationalgeographic.com
www.nationalgeographic.com/maps

Biography

The following videotape programs are available from Glencoe as supplements to Chapter 5:

- George Washington: Founding Father (ISBN 1-56-501377-8)
- The Vikings in North America (ISBN 1-56-501663-7)

To order, call Glencoe at 1-800-334-7344. To find classroom resources to accompany many of these videos, check the following home pages:

A&E Television: www.aetv.com
The History Channel: www.historychannel.com

GLENCOE BOOKLINK 3

Use this database to search more than 30,000 titles to create a customized reading list for your students.

- Reading lists can be organized by students' reading level, author, genre, theme, or area of interest.
- The database provides Degrees of Reading Power™ (DRP) and Lexile™ readability scores for all selections.
- A brief summary of each selection is included.

Leveled reading suggestions for this chapter:

For students at a Grade 5 reading level:

- ***If You Lived in Colonial Times,*** by Ann McGovern

For students at a Grade 6 reading level:

- ***Janey G. Blue: Pearl Harbor, 1941,*** by Kathleen Duey

For students at a Grade 7 reading level:

- ***Inuit Indians,*** by Caryn Yacowitz

For students at a Grade 8 reading level:

- ***Across Five Aprils,*** by Irene Hunt

For students at a Grade 9 reading level:

- ***Exploring the Pacific Northwest,*** by Rose Blue and Corinne J. Naden

Focus

The Essential Question

As students study the chapter, remind them to consider the chapter-based Essential Question. Answering this question will help them understand the important concepts in the chapter. In addition, the Hands-On Chapter Project relates the content from each section to the Essential Question. The steps in each section build on each other as students progress through the chapter. The Hands-On Chapter Project culminates in the Wrap Up activity on the Visual Summary page.

More About the Photo

Visual Literacy Fort McLeod was established in 1874 as the first permanent fort in the foothills of the Canadian Rockies for the North-West Mounted Police. Since 1920, this police force has been known as the Royal Canadian Mounted Police, or the Mounties. Now numbering more than 20,000, the Mounties serve as Canada's provincial police. They operate crime labs, police airports, guard important visitors, fight illegal drugs, and go on peacekeeping missions around the world. The red-coated Mounties have also served as a symbol of Canada for more than a century.

CHAPTER 5

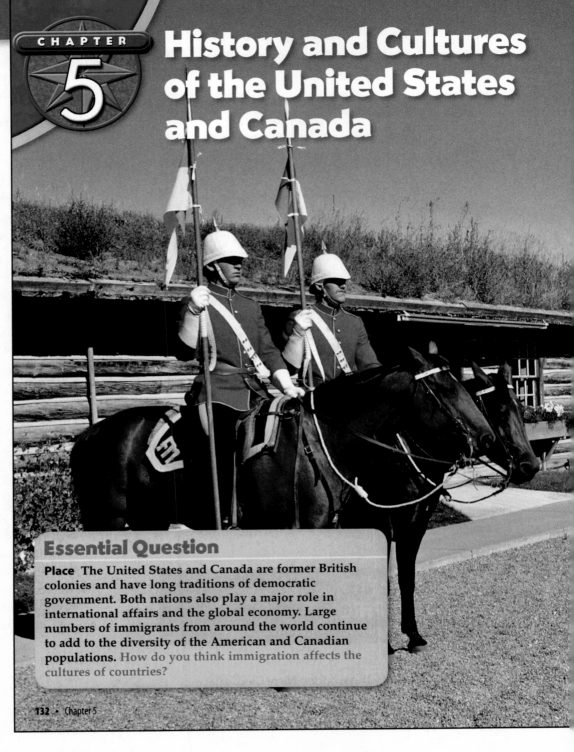

History and Cultures of the United States and Canada

Essential Question

Place The United States and Canada are former British colonies and have long traditions of democratic government. Both nations also play a major role in international affairs and the global economy. Large numbers of immigrants from around the world continue to add to the diversity of the American and Canadian populations. How do you think immigration affects the cultures of countries?

Teach

The BIG Ideas *As you begin teaching each section, use these questions and activities to help students focus on the Big Ideas.*

Section 

History and Governments Ask: How many of you know someone who was born in another country? Why did that person come to the United States? *(Answers will vary; some of your students may be foreign-born.)* Discuss reasons why immigrants come to the United States or other developed countries. Encourage students to look for information about immigrants and why they come to the United States and Canada as they read the section. **OL**

Section 

Cultures and Lifestyles Ask: What are some things that you have experienced today that reflect the influence of different ethnic groups? *(Answers may include listening to music, eating foods, playing a*

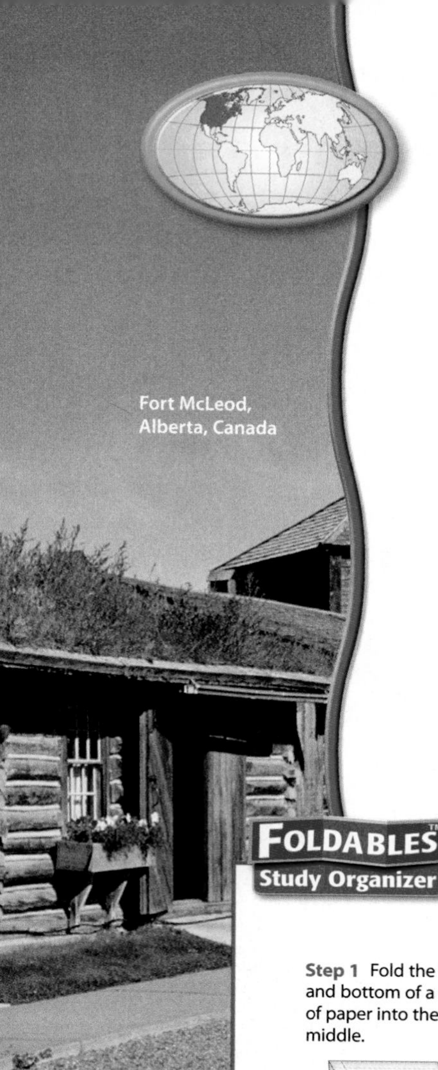
Fort McLeod, Alberta, Canada

BIG Ideas

Section 1: History and Governments

BIG IDEA The characteristics and movement of people impact physical and human systems. England established several colonies in North America during the 1600s and 1700s. These colonies later formed two large, independent democracies: the United States and Canada. Today they have become home to millions of people from around the world who moved to these lands to start new lives.

Section 2: Cultures and Lifestyles

BIG IDEA Culture influences people's perceptions about places and regions. The cultures of the United States and Canada reflect the influence of many different ethnic groups. These groups range from the Native Americans who first lived in the area to the most recent arrivals from all parts of the world.

FOLDABLES™ Study Organizer

Categorizing Information Make this four-tab Foldable to help you learn about the history, governments, and cultures of the United States and Canada.

Step 1 Fold the top and bottom of a piece of paper into the middle.

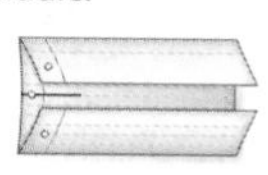

Step 2 Cut each flap at the midpoint to form 4 tabs.

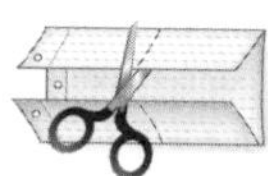

Step 3 Label the tabs as shown.

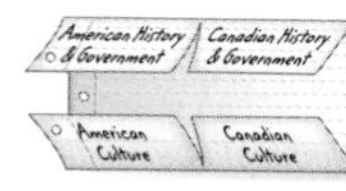

Reading and Writing As you read the chapter, take notes about each section under the appropriate head. Use your Foldable to help you write a summary for each section.

To preview Chapter 5, go to glencoe.com.

Previewing the Region

If you have not already done so, engage students in the Regional Atlas and chart activities to help them become familiar with the general content of the region.

FOLDABLES Study Organizer **Dinah Zike's Foldables**

Purpose This Foldable helps students organize information about the history, governments, and cultures of the United States and Canada. Remind students that summaries are concentrated accounts of factual information that include only the main ideas and do not include unimportant and irrelevant details. Completed Foldables can be used to write summaries and prepare for assessment. **OL**

More Foldables activities for this chapter can be found in *Dinah Zike's Reading and Study Skills Foldables* ancillary.

Social Studies ONLINE

Introduce students to chapter content and key terms by having them access the Chapter Overview at glencoe.com.

game or sport, or reading a book associated with different ethnic groups or their members.) Have students discuss how life in their community would be different without the contributions of different immigrant groups. **OL**

Focus

Bellringer

Daily Focus Transparency 5-1

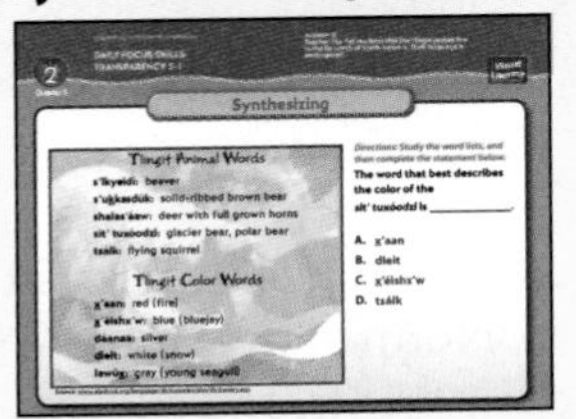

Guide to Reading

Answers to Graphic:

Answers may include:
United States: 1620: Pilgrims land at Plymouth; **1776:** Colonists declare independence; **1991:** Cold War ends; **2001:** Terrorists attack New York and Washington, D.C.;
Canada: 1500s and 1600s: England and France claim Canada;
1867: Canada becomes a dominion;
1982: Canada gains right to change constitution

Section Spotlight Video

To learn more about the history and governments of the United States and Canada, have students watch the Section Spotlight Video.

Resource Manager

R Reading Strategies	**C** Critical Thinking	**D** Differentiated Instruction	**W** Writing Support	**S** Skill Practice
Teacher Edition • Det. Importance, p. 136 • Taking Notes, p. 137 • Sequencing Ev., p. 138 • Setting a Purpose, p. 140 **Additional Resources** • Guid. Read., URB p. 61 • Cont. Vocab., URB p. 63 • Ac. Vocab., URB p. 65 • Read. Ess., p. 34	**Teacher Edition** • An. Pri. Sources, p. 135 • Ident. Cent. Issues, pp. 136, 140 • Pred. Con., p. 137 • Making Comp., p. 139 **Additional Resources** • Crit. Think., URB p. 71 • Geo. & Hist., URB p. 11 • Authentic Assess., p. 5 • Enrichment, URB p. 19	**Teacher Edition** • Intrapersonal, p. 141 **Additional Resources** • Diff. Instr., URB p. 67 • School-to-Home Conn., URB p. 81 • Reteach., URB p. 79	**Teacher Edition** • Persuasive Writing, p. 140 **Additional Resources** • Writing Skills, URB p. 77	**Teacher Edition** • Using Geo. Skills, p. 135 • Reading a Time Line, p. 136 **Additional Resources** • Chart, Graph, and Map Skills, URB p. 69 • Daily Focus Trans. 5-1 • Reg. Atlas, URB pp. 1–7

Guide to Reading

BIG Idea

The characteristics and movement of people impact physical and human systems.

Content Vocabulary
- colony *(p. 136)*
- annex *(p. 136)*
- terrorism *(p. 137)*
- dominion *(p. 139)*
- representative democracy *(p. 140)*
- federalism *(p. 140)*
- amendment *(p. 141)*
- parliamentary democracy *(p. 141)*

Academic Vocabulary
- economy *(p. 136)*
- regime *(p. 137)*
- principle *(p. 140)*
- core *(p. 141)*

Reading Strategy

Making a Time Line Use a diagram like the one below to list and compare key events and dates in the history of the United States and Canada.

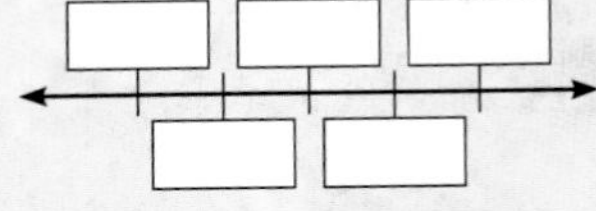

SECTION 1

History and Governments

Picture This This is not just any rock. It is the famous Plymouth Rock. Plymouth Rock, in the American state of Massachusetts, is believed to have been at the site where the Pilgrims first landed in 1620. The 10-ton rock is only about one-third of its original size. This is because, over the years, many souvenir hunters have broken off pieces to take home. To learn how people can affect the development of a nation, read Section 1.

Plymouth Rock, Massachusetts

History of the United States

Main Idea **The United States emerged as a world power in the 1900s.**

Geography and You Do you like to make your own decisions without someone else telling you what to do? Read to find out why the Americans wanted to make their own decisions without British interference.

For thousands of years, people have been living in what is now the United States. They have come from many different parts of the world to settle a vast territory that stretches across much of North America. In the past few hundred years, Americans have made their country the most powerful nation in the world. C

The First Americans

About 15,000 years ago, hunters in Asia followed herds of animals across a land bridge between eastern Siberia and Alaska. They are believed to be among the first people to settle the Americas. Eventually groups of people spread across the entire landmass. Their descendants today are called Native Americans. Over many centuries, Native American groups developed different ways of life using local resources.

The Colonial Era

Europeans were not aware of the Americas until 1492. That year, explorer Christopher Columbus sailed west from Europe in hopes of reaching Asia. Instead, he reached islands in the Caribbean Sea. His tales of these new lands excited many Europeans.

NATIONAL GEOGRAPHIC Maps In MOtion See StudentWorks™ Plus or glencoe.com.

Figure 1 **United States Expansion**

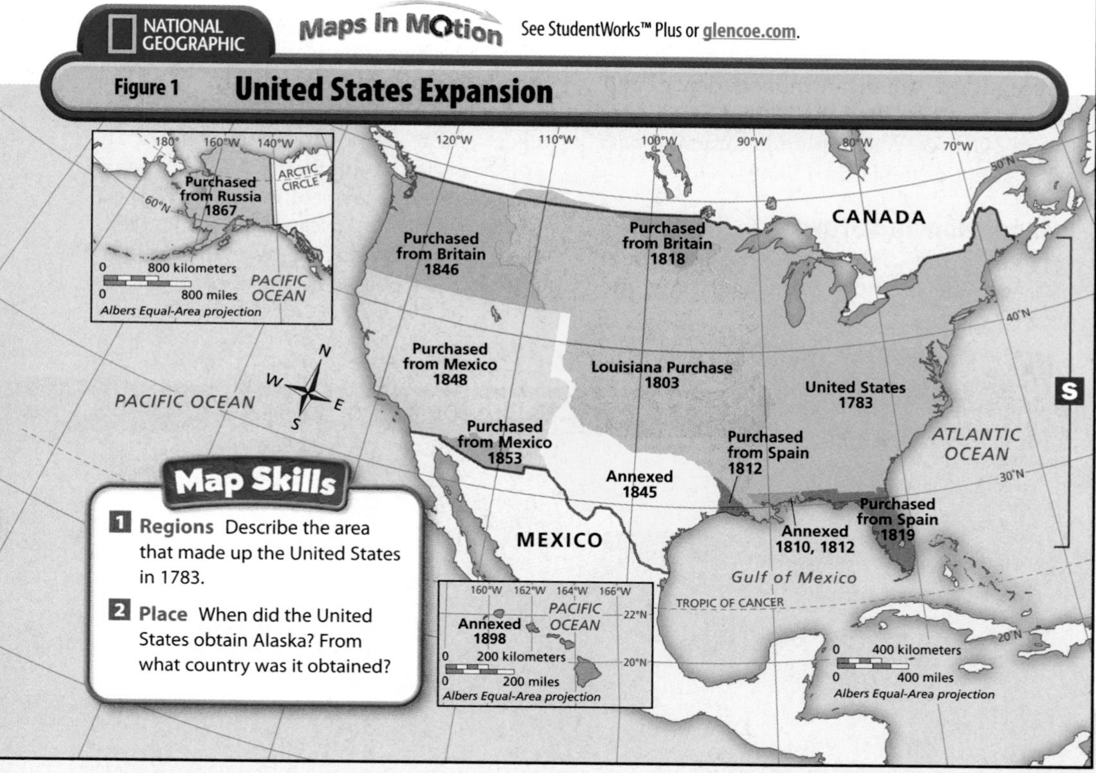

Map Skills

1. **Regions** Describe the area that made up the United States in 1783.
2. **Place** When did the United States obtain Alaska? From what country was it obtained?

Teach

C Critical Thinking

Analyzing Primary Sources Have students use online or library sources to locate historical maps of the United States. Tell students to choose one historical map and compare it to a current map of the United States. Have students present their findings to the class. **AL**

For additional practice on this activity (Analyzing Primary Sources), see the **Skills Handbook**.

S Skill Practice

Using Geography Skills **Ask: Which single acquisition doubled the size of the country? When did it take place?** *(the Louisiana Purchase in 1803)* **OL**

Map Skills

Answers:

1. the area east of the Mississippi River, except for Florida
2. from Russia in 1867

Hands-On Chapter Project Step 1

Creating a Historical Calendar

Step 1: Gathering Information Students will search for images that represent the history and culture of the United States and Canada to create a 12-month calendar.

Essential Question How do you think immigration affects the cultures of countries?

Directions Show students several examples of visually strong calendars. Then have students search online or library sources for images of the people, places, and events that have impacted the history and culture of the region, paying particular attention to immigration. Ask students to select twelve images, or twelve groups of images, one for each month in the year. Students should also gather information that explains the importance of each image. Some images should reflect the effects of immigration.

Summarizing Ask students to discuss the significance of the images they found. **OL**

(Chapter Project continued in Section 2)

S Skill Practice

Reading a Time Line **Ask:** When was the U.S. Constitution written? *(1787)* OL

C Critical Thinking

Identifying Central Issues **Ask:** What are three reasons for the rapid growth of the U.S. population in the 1800s? *(a high birthrate, advances in public health, and the arrival of immigrants)* How have these factors changed today? *(Possible answer: Public health is still improving, but the birthrate is lower.)* OL

R Reading Strategy

Determining Importance Have students scan the bracketed paragraph to identify significant facts about economic growth in the United States during the 1800s. **Ask:** What factors helped the U.S. economy change and grow? *(new agricultural machines, the development of the factory system, better transportation)* OL

Quickly, many other people began making their own trips. Spain soon set up **colonies,** which are overseas settlements tied to a parent country. The Spanish gained great wealth from gold and silver mines in Mexico and South America. They also had colonies in what is now the southern United States, but they focused primarily on the lands farther south.

France and Great Britain also established colonies in North America. The French controlled eastern Canada, the Great Lakes area, and the Mississippi River valley. The British settled along the Atlantic coast. In 1763 Great Britain defeated France in a war and won France's North American colonies.

Soon after, the people in Great Britain's 13 coastal colonies grew resentful of British taxes and trade policies. Discontent boiled over, and fighting broke out between the colonists and British forces. In 1776 the colonists declared their independence. In 1783, after several years of fighting, Britain recognized American independence, and a new nation called the United States was born. George Washington became the first president of the United States.

Expansion and Growth

When the United States won independence, the country controlled only the eastern coast from Maine to Georgia. During the 1800s, however, it expanded all the way to the Pacific Ocean, as seen in **Figure 1** on the previous page. Some of this growth came through treaties with other countries. Some came when the United States **annexed** lands, or declared ownership of a particular area. This expansion brought suffering, however, including loss of land, culture, and often life, to Native Americans who had lived in the region for centuries.

C Throughout the 1800s, the United States grew in population as well. High birthrates, advances in public health, and the arrival of millions of European immigrants helped the population grow.

R The American **economy,** or way of producing goods, also changed. New machines made planting and harvesting crops faster and easier. Manufacturers developed the factory system to produce many goods. Roads, canals, steamboats, and railroads allowed manufacturers to move their goods to markets more quickly.

Social and economic differences, however, came to deeply divide the country. The southern states built their economy on agriculture and the labor of hundreds of thousands of enslaved Africans. By the mid-1800s, the practice of slavery was increasingly criticized by people in the northern states.

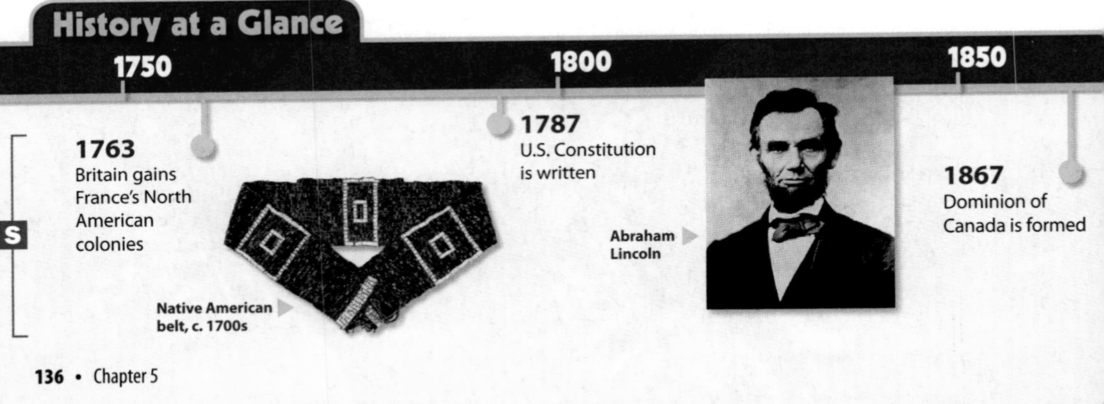

Native American belt, c. 1700s

Abraham Lincoln

Differentiated Instruction

Leveled Activities

BL School-to-Home Connection, URB p. 81

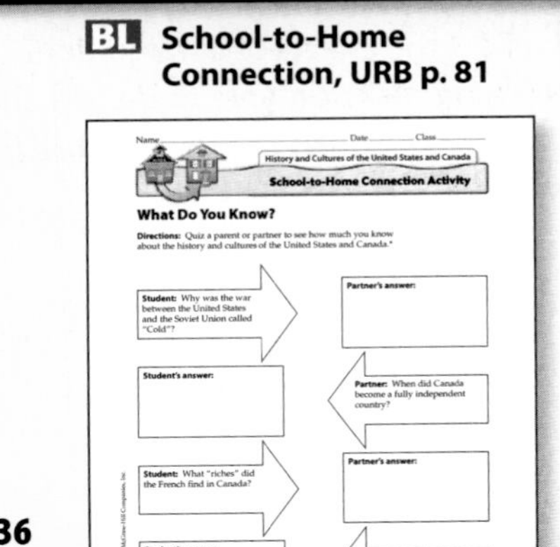
History and Cultures of the United States and Canada

School-to-Home Connection Activity

What Do You Know?

OL Writing Skills Activity, URB p. 77

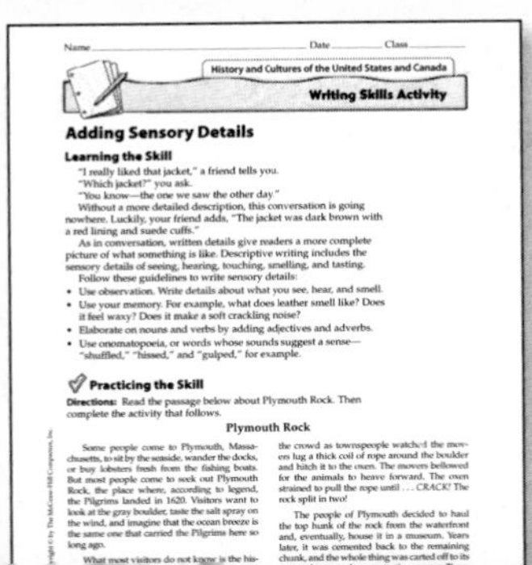
History and Cultures of the United States and Canada

Writing Skills Activity

Adding Sensory Details

AL Geography and History Activity, URB p. 11

The United States and Canada

Geography and History Activity

Transcontinental Railroads: Settling the West

ELL Differentiated Instruction, URB p. 67

History and Cultures of the United States and Canada

Differentiated Instruction

The 100 Most Influential Americans

Southerners worried that northerners would attempt to end slavery. In 1860 Abraham Lincoln, an opponent of slavery, was elected president. By early 1861, several southern states had withdrawn from the United States to set up a new country. This action led to a civil war. After four years of fighting, northern forces won. The country was reunited, and slavery ended. Racial tensions, however, continued.

The late 1800s saw the spread of industry in the United States. Waves of new immigrants provided workers for the growing economy. By 1900, the United States was one of the world's major industrial powers. C

A World Leader

During the 1900s, the United States became a world leader. Its armies fought in World War I and World War II. During these conflicts, United States leaders urged the world's people to fight for freedom against oppressive **regimes,** or governments. American factories produced tanks and airplanes, while American soldiers helped win the wars.

After World War II, the United States and the Soviet Union became the world's two major powers. They competed for world leadership in a rivalry known as the Cold War. This rivalry was called the Cold War because the conflict never became "hot," with actual combat between the two powers. Nevertheless, tensions remained high as the countries competed politically and economically. The Cold War ended with the breakup of the Soviet Union in 1991.

During this period, African Americans, Latino Americans, Native Americans, and women became more active in seeking equal rights in the United States. Leaders such as Martin Luther King, Jr.; Rosa Parks; and César Chávez used peaceful methods that led to social changes for these groups.

Since 2000, the United States has faced challenges from the growth of terrorism R both at home and throughout the world. **Terrorism** refers to the use of violence against civilians, by individuals or groups, to reach political goals. On September 11, 2001, terrorists seized four passenger planes. Two planes were crashed into the World Trade Center in New York City. A third aircraft damaged the Pentagon, the headquarters of the U.S. military, in Washington, D.C. A fourth plane crashed in rural Pennsylvania after what is believed to have been a passenger uprising against the terrorists. About 3,000 people died in the attacks.

Soon after, the United States sent troops to the southwest Asian country of Afghanistan.

1900 | 1950 | 2000

c. 1900
Immigration and industry transform the United States and Canada

1941
U.S. and Canada become allies in World War II

2001
Terrorists attack the United States

COME AND DO YOUR BIT
JOIN NOW

World War I poster

U.S. DEPARTMENT OF HOMELAND SECURITY

Seal, Department of Homeland Security

C Critical Thinking

Predicting Consequences Remind students that by 1900, the United States was one of the world's leading industrial powers. **Ask: How do you think the end of the Civil War affected the industrial development of the United States?** *(Possible answer: The country could put more resources into industrial development and scientific advances to spur industry.)* AL

R Reading Strategy

Taking Notes To help students comprehend the series of events from the end of World War II through 2001, instruct them to take notes on the material. Tell students that their notes should include brief phrases and key words to help them understand the time period at a glance. OL

Additional Support

Activity: Collaborative Learning

Diagramming Tell students that the movement that sought equal rights for African Americans inspired other groups to seek equal rights as well. **Ask: What other groups might have worked for social changes during the 1960s and 1970s?** *(Native Americans, Latinos, and women)* Organize students into groups of three or four. Ask each group to research the life of someone who fought for equal rights, such as Martin Luther King, Jr., Rosa Parks, César Chávez, Malcolm X, or Betty Friedan. Ask each group to learn about the person's philosophy and the techniques he or she used to work for change. Have groups write a short skit that conveys the influence their person has had on society. For example, scenes might be set during a rally on a college campus in the 1960s or in a modern-day corporate environment. Once students have had enough time to write and rehearse their skits, have them perform their skits for the rest of the class. OL

R Reading Strategy

Sequencing Events Have students list the sequence of events in the early settlement of Canada. *(Lists should include: Native American groups; Vikings from Scandinavia; the English; the French)* **OL**

For additional practice on this activity (Sequencing Events), see the **Skills Handbook**.

Reading Check **Answer:** It became a world leader fighting in wars, competing in the Cold War, and leading the battle against terrorism.

Caption Answer:
The rulers of Afghanistan had protected the Muslim terrorist group al-Qaeda, which carried out the September 11, 2001, attacks.

Afghanistan's rulers, the Taliban, had protected the Muslim terrorist group al-Qaeda, which carried out the September 11 attacks. The Taliban were overthrown, although many terrorists escaped.

In 2003 U.S. troops overthrew Iraq's dictator, Saddam Hussein, who was accused of hiding illegal weapons and helping terrorists. In the years that followed, the United States worked with Afghanistan and Iraq to set up democratic governments. Continued fighting within both countries, though, made these efforts difficult.

Reading Check **Explaining** What role did the United States play in global affairs after 1900?

Women in Uniform

NATIONAL GEOGRAPHIC

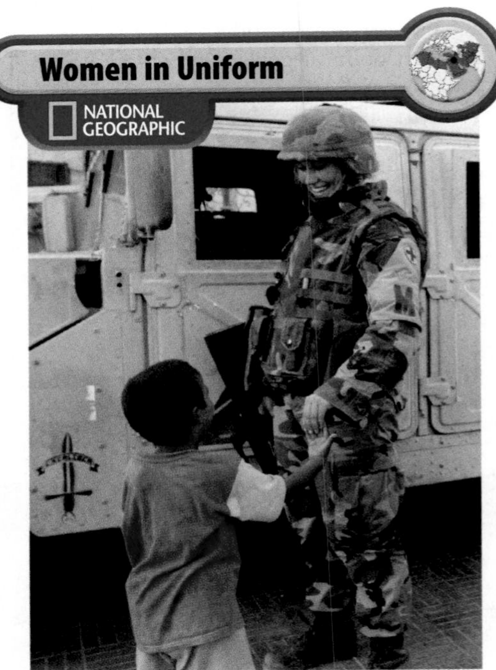

▲ Women make up about 20 percent of the U.S. military and are actively involved in operations around the world. ***Place*** **Why did the United States send troops into Afghanistan?**

History of Canada

Main Idea **Canada gradually won independence from British rule during the late 1800s and early 1900s.**

Geography and You What similarities do you share with your neighbors? In what ways are you different? Read to find out how Canada's history is similar to and different from that of the United States.

Canada and the United States share similar backgrounds. Nonetheless, the two countries traveled different paths to becoming nations.

Early Settlement

Like the United States, Canada was originally settled by Native American groups. The first Europeans to arrive in the area that is today Canada were Viking explorers from Scandinavia. They landed in about A.D. 1000. The Vikings briefly lived on the Newfoundland coast, but they did not stay in their settlements very long. Eventually they left the Americas.

In the 1500s and 1600s, both England and France claimed areas of Canada. French explorers, settlers, and missionaries founded several cities. The most important were Quebec and Montreal. For almost 230 years, France ruled the area around the St. Lawrence River and the Great Lakes. This region was called New France.

The French knew that the Spanish had gained riches in South America from gold and silver mines. They hoped to become wealthy in the same way in Canada. They did find riches, but not in gold and silver mines. Instead, the French traded with Native Americans for beaver furs, which were then sent back to Europe and sold.

During the 1600s and 1700s, the English and French fought each other for terri-

Additional Support

Teacher Tip

Encourage students Interdisciplinary Connections activities require students to consider disciplines outside of geography. In this case, students ought to consider social aspects of how people live.

Activity: Interdisciplinary Connection

Daily Life Tell students that during the 1500s and 1600s, beaver hunting was a common part of daily life in Canada. Hunters caught the animals for their pelts and also traded with Native Americans for beaver furs. These furs were then sent to Europe. **Ask: What were beaver furs used for in Europe?** *(making hats)* Beaver fur was highly prized because it is very thick and soft. For many years, beaver-fur hats were the height of fashion in Europe. Ask students to research the effect hunting had on the beaver population in Canada. Students' research should answer the following questions: What eventually led to the decline of beaver hunting? How stable is the beaver population in Canada now? Is the population increasing or declining? Have each student write a brief history of the beaver's role in Canada's history and culture. **OL**

tory around the globe. In 1707 England and Scotland united to form Great Britain. This union laid the foundation for the British Empire. By the 1760s, the British had won control of most of France's Canadian colony.

Beginning in the late 1700s, British and American settlers began moving to Canada in greater numbers. They set up farms along the Atlantic coast and in what is now Ontario. French-speaking Canadians lived mostly in present-day Quebec. Tragically, European warfare and diseases had nearly destroyed many Native American cultures by this time.

An Independent Nation

For the next 75 years, Great Britain held various colonies in eastern Canada. These colonies constantly quarreled with one another over colonial government policies. Fears of a United States takeover, however, forced them together. In 1867 most of the colonies became one nation known as the Dominion of Canada. As a **dominion**, Canada had its own central government to run local affairs. Great Britain, though, still controlled Canada's relations with other countries. C

Under Canada's central government, the colonies became provinces, much like states in the United States. At first, there were four provinces—Quebec, Ontario, Nova Scotia, and New Brunswick. Neighboring British-ruled areas—Manitoba, British Columbia, Saskatchewan (suh·SKA·chuh·wuhn), and Alberta in the west and Prince Edward Island and Newfoundland along the Atlantic coast—became provinces of Canada during the next 100 years. Today Canada is made up of 10 provinces and 3 additional territories—the Yukon Territory, the Northwest Territories, and Nunavut (NOO·nah·voot).

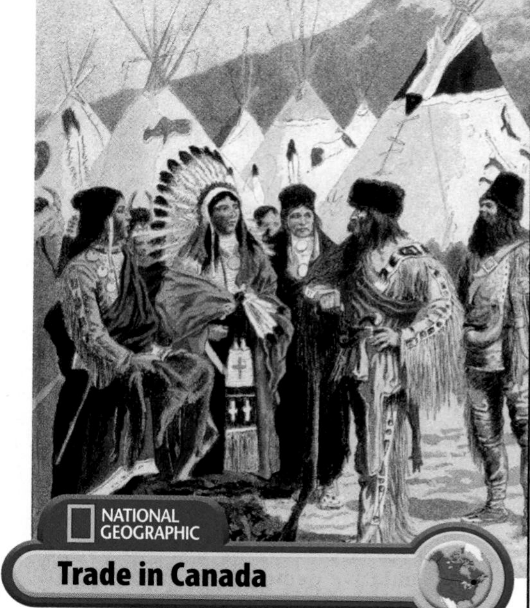

NATIONAL GEOGRAPHIC

Trade in Canada

As Europeans explored Canada, they made treaties and traded with the Native Americans who lived there. ***Place*** **What two European nations colonized Canada?**

At Canada's founding, the government promised to protect the French language and culture in Quebec. However, the English-speaking minority there was far wealthier and ran the economy. This led to tensions between the two groups. French speakers claimed that they were treated unfairly because of their heritage.

During the early 1900s, many immigrants arrived, and Canada's population and economy grew. Meanwhile, Canadians fought alongside the British and Americans in the two World Wars. Canada's support in these wars led to its full independence. In 1982 Canadians won the right to change their constitution without British approval. Today Canada still faces the possibility that Quebec will separate and become independent.

Reading Check **Summarizing** How did Canada's government change over time?

C Critical Thinking

Making Comparisons Ask: How does a dominion differ from a fully independent country? *(In a dominion, a country has control over local affairs, but another country controls international relations.)* **BL**

For additional practice on this activity (Making Comparisons), see the **Skills Handbook**.

Caption Answer:
France and Great Britain

Reading Check Answer: It was originally a set of separate British colonies; most colonies united in 1867 to form a dominion; today it is fully independent and made up of 10 provinces and 3 territories.

Activity: Connecting With the United States

Problem Solving In both the United States and the Dominion of Canada, groups that disagreed about many issues banded together. **Ask: Why did the colonies in each country unite?** *(Canadian colonies united because they feared the United States. American colonies united to gain independence from British rule.)* To help students understand this dynamic, separate the class into five or six groups. Tell each group to draw up a list of rules for behavior in the classroom and related punishments. Next, have all the groups work together to make a single list for the entire class. Tell students that if they cannot agree on a list, you will impose strict rules and punishments of your own. Give students about 20 minutes to negotiate, and then ask students whether the threat from the teacher helped them negotiate. Discuss with students how their situation was similar to that of colonists in North America. *(They decided to work together because of a common threat.)* **OL**

R Reading Strategy

Setting a Purpose Have students read the heading and main idea of this section. Then ask them to write a one-sentence purpose for reading. *(Sample sentence: I want to learn how the governments of the United States and Canada are similar.)* **BL**

C Critical Thinking

Identifying Central Issues Ask: What two ideas were the writers of the United States Constitution trying to balance? *(They wanted a strong government to guide the country, but with limited powers so people's rights would be protected.)* **AL**

W Writing Support

Persuasive Writing Have students write a letter to the editor of a local newspaper either supporting or opposing this statement: Our system of checks and balances should be eliminated because it creates a weak government. Remind students to support their position with valid reasons. **OL**

Caption Answer:
to prevent the government from taking away people's freedoms

Governments of the United States and Canada

R

Main Idea **The United States and Canada are democracies, but their governments are organized differently.**

Geography and You Do you think democracy is a good government system? Why? Read to discover the similarities and differences between the democracies of the United States and Canada.

The United States and Canada are both **representative democracies**, in which voters choose leaders who make and enforce the laws. However, the two government systems have some important differences.

U.S. Democracy

C

The United States Constitution is the basic plan that explains how our national or central government is set up and how it works. The document was written in the late 1780s by leaders who wanted to create a government strong enough to guide the country. Those leaders also wanted a government with limited powers so that people's rights would be protected from government interference.

W

To achieve these goals, the writers of the Constitution applied the **principle,** or rule, of separation of powers. This means they divided the power of the national government among three branches: executive, legislative, and judicial. In addition, they gave each branch unique powers as a way to prevent the other branches from abusing their power. This idea is called checks and balances. With it, the Founders aimed to prevent one branch from becoming too powerful.

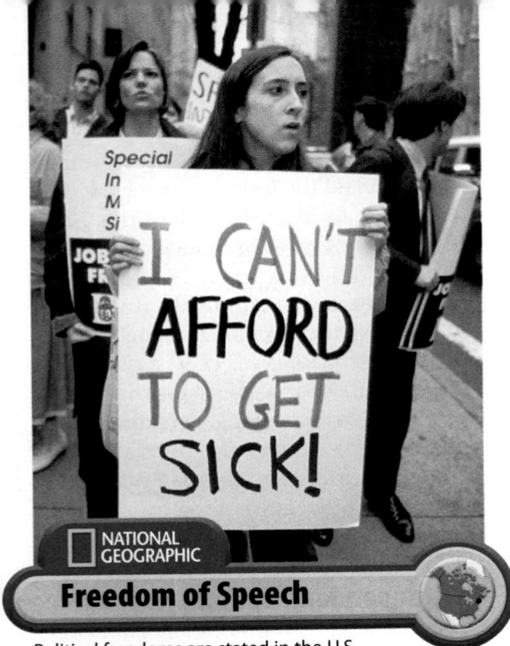

NATIONAL GEOGRAPHIC

Freedom of Speech

Political freedoms are stated in the U.S. Constitution. The First Amendment allows citizens to disagree with the U.S. government. ***Place*** **What is the purpose of the Bill of Rights?**

The U.S. Constitution created a strong central government, but state governments were given certain responsibilities. This structure reflects the idea called federalism. In **federalism,** power is divided between the federal, or national, government and state governments. The national government makes treaties with other countries, coins money, and has the power to make laws about trade between states. State governments handle such issues as the health and education of their citizens.

In the U.S. federal system, people are citizens of both the nation and their state. As a result, citizens have the right to vote for both national and state leaders. The U.S. Constitution and state constitutions provide for that right. Citizens have the duty to make informed decisions when they vote. Citizens also have the responsibility to obey national and state laws.

Differentiated Instruction

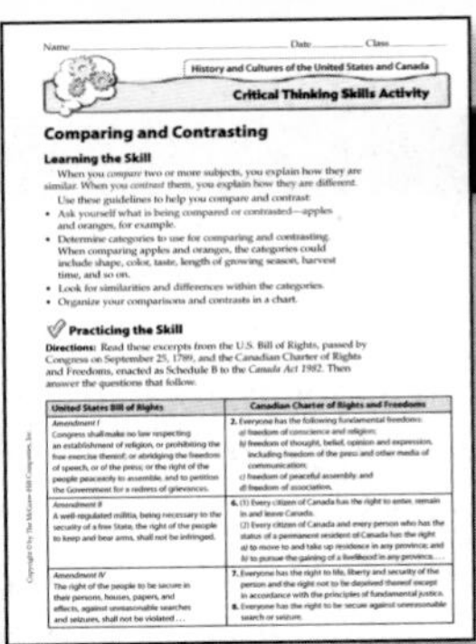

Name ______ Date ______ Class ______

History and Cultures of the United States and Canada

Critical Thinking Skills Activity

Comparing and Contrasting

Learning the Skill

When you *compare* two or more subjects, you explain how they are similar. When you *contrast* them, you explain how they are different.

Use these guidelines to help you compare and contrast:

- Ask yourself what is being compared or contrasted—apples and oranges, for example.
- Determine categories to use for comparing and contrasting. When comparing apples and oranges, the categories could include shape, color, taste, length of growing season, harvest time, and so on.
- Look for similarities and differences within the categories.
- Organize your comparisons and contrasts in a chart.

Practicing the Skill

Directions: Read these excerpts from the U.S. Bill of Rights, passed by Congress on September 25, 1789, and the Canadian Charter of Rights and Freedoms, enacted as Schedule B to the *Canada Act 1982*. Then answer the questions that follow.

United States Bill of Rights	Canadian Charter of Rights and Freedoms
Amendment I Congress shall make no law respecting an establishment of religion, or prohibiting the free exercise thereof; or abridging the freedom of speech, or of the press; or the right of the people peaceably to assemble, and to petition the Government for a redress of grievances.	**2.** Everyone has the following fundamental freedoms: *a)* freedom of conscience and religion; *b)* freedom of thought, belief, opinion and expression, including freedom of the press and other media of communication; *c)* freedom of peaceful assembly; and *d)* freedom of association.
Amendment II A well-regulated militia, being necessary to the security of a free State, the right of the people to keep and bear arms, shall not be infringed.	**6.** (1) Every citizen of Canada has the right to enter, remain in and leave Canada. (2) Every citizen of Canada and every person who has the status of a permanent resident of Canada has the right *a)* to move to and take up residence in any province; and *b)* to pursue the gaining of a livelihood in any province. . . .
Amendment IV The right of the people to be secure in their persons, houses, papers, and effects, against unreasonable searches and seizures, shall not be violated . . .	**7.** Everyone has the right to life, liberty and security of the person and the right not to be deprived thereof except in accordance with the principles of fundamental justice. **8.** Everyone has the right to be secure against unreasonable search or seizure.

Critical Thinking Skills Activity, URB pp. 71–72

Comparing and Contrasting

Objective: To analyze similarities and differences

Focus: Have students explain when they should compare and contrast different items.

Teach: Tell students to read the excerpts, answer the questions, and complete the table.

Assess: Have students check their charts to be sure content is placed correctly.

Close: Ask students how comparing and contrasting helps them learn about a subject.

Differentiated Instruction Strategies

BL Tell students to list all the similarities before listing the differences.

AL Have students write a paragraph explaining why they think freedom of speech and religion are included in both excerpts.

ELL Have students write a paragraph describing the rights guaranteed in their home country.

In 1791 ten **amendments,** or additions, known as the Bill of Rights were added to the U.S. Constitution. Their purpose was to prevent the government from taking away people's freedoms. For example, the Bill of Rights ensures that the government cannot limit Americans' freedom of speech or religion. D

Throughout its history, the Constitution has had other amendments added to it. Individual freedom is a **core,** or basic, value of the United States. Another is equality. The Constitution's Fourteenth Amendment requires the states to provide equal protection under the law to all persons within their boundaries.

Still, all Americans have not always enjoyed equal rights. Some groups suffered unfair treatment. For several decades after independence, only white males could vote. African American males gained the right to vote only when the Constitution was changed in 1870. All women were given the right to vote in 1920.

Canadian Democracy

Canada has a **parliamentary democracy** in which voters elect representatives to a lawmaking body called Parliament. These representatives then choose an official called the prime minister to head the government. The British monarch serves as king or queen of Canada.

Like the United States, Canada has a federal system. Power is divided between the central government and the provinces and territories. Canada's Charter of Rights and Freedoms is similar to the U.S. Bill of Rights. It protects the liberties of Canadian citizens.

Reading Check **Identifying** What powers do U.S. national and state governments have?

Section 1 Review

Social Studies ONLINE
Study Central™ To review this section, go to glencoe.com.

Vocabulary

1. **Explain** the significance of:
   - **a.** colony
   - **b.** annex
   - **c.** terrorism
   - **d.** dominion
   - **e.** representative democracy
   - **f.** federalism
   - **g.** amendment
   - **h.** parliamentary democracy

Main Ideas

2. **Describing** What was the Cold War, and what brought it to an end?
3. **Categorizing** Use a chart like the one below to list five major events in American and Canadian history. Categorize each event as social, economic, or political, and explain why each is significant.

Event	Category	Significance

4. **Comparing and Contrasting** How are the governments of the United States and Canada similar? How are they different?

Critical Thinking

5. **BIG Idea** How did the French and British colonies in Canada differ from the Spanish colonies in Mexico and South America?
6. **Challenge** Why do you think it is important in a democracy for people to make informed decisions?

Writing About Geography

7. **Using Your FOLDABLES** Use your Foldable to write a paragraph explaining how the core American values of freedom and equality are evident in America's government and laws.

D Differentiated Instruction

Intrapersonal Ask students to imagine what living in the United States would be like without the Bill of Rights. Have students write a journal entry describing everyday life. OL

Reading Check **Answer:** The national government makes international treaties, coins money, and regulates interstate trade; the states handle such issues as health and education.

Assess

Social Studies ONLINE
Study Central™ provides summaries, interactive games, and online graphic organizers to help students review content.

Close

Synthesizing Have students write a paragraph explaining ways that the current governments of the United States and Canada have been influenced by the countries' past experiences. OL

Answers

1. Definitions for the vocabulary words are found in the section and the Glossary.
2. It was a competition for world leadership between the United States and the Soviet Union that ended with the breakup of the Soviet Union in 1991.
3. Charts should determine category and significance for each of the five events that students list.
4. **Similarities:** democratic government, federal style of government, Canada's Charter of Rights similar to U.S. Bill of Rights; **Differences:** Canada: monarch, government led by prime minister; United States: chief executive is president
5. French—founded cities in Canada, ruled around St. Lawrence River and Great Lakes, gained wealth from fur trade with Native Americans; British—claimed areas on Atlantic coast; Spanish—gained wealth from gold and silver in colonies
6. Answers will vary. Students may recognize that people need to be informed in order to choose the best leaders.
7. Paragraphs should display an understanding of the role of the federal government and the Bill of Rights in preserving individual freedoms.

Focus

R Reading Strategy

Understanding Question-Answer Relationships Ask: Do you think that the candidate who receives the most votes in an election should always be the winner? Why or why not? *(Many students will say yes, citing basic fairness, the rule of the majority, and other ideas.)* OL

Teach

Have students create a graphic organizer to list the basic points of each argument about the Electoral College. OL

For change	Against change
The Electoral College gives extra weight to votes from small states.	*The Electoral College has worked well in practice.*
People who disagree with their state's vote are not represented.	*The system usually produces a decisive vote.*
The Electoral College allows the election of a president who does not get the most votes.	*The Electoral College prevents candidates from ignoring small states.*
Abolishing the Electoral College might lead to increased voting.	*The Electoral College reinforces a two-party system.*

Additional Support

YOU Decide The Electoral College: Should It Be Changed?

R **When people vote for the president and vice president of the United States, they are really voting for electors who will vote for these people. These electors make up the Electoral College. The number of electors each state has is based on the total number of its U.S. senators and representatives. Electors cast votes for the candidate who wins the popular vote in their state. In every state except Maine and Nebraska, the winner of the popular vote will get all of that state's electoral votes.**

For Change

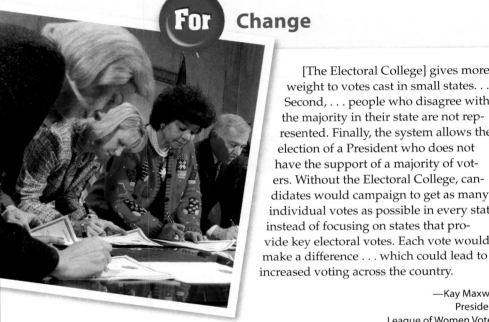

[The Electoral College] gives more weight to votes cast in small states. . . . Second, . . . people who disagree with the majority in their state are not represented. Finally, the system allows the election of a President who does not have the support of a majority of voters. Without the Electoral College, candidates would campaign to get as many individual votes as possible in every state, instead of focusing on states that provide key electoral votes. Each vote would make a difference . . . which could lead to increased voting across the country.

—Kay Maxwell
President,
League of Women Voters

FastFacts

Electoral College The framers of the U.S. Constitution created the Electoral College as part of the system of shared power between the states and the federal government. The Electoral College not only ensured states' power, but also guaranteed that no single region could control the presidential election. Each state gets a number of electoral votes equal to the sum of that state's members of the House of Representatives and Senate. Electors are generally selected by the political parties in each state. When voters cast their vote for president and vice president, they are actually choosing which party's electors will cast the final vote. The electors then vote for the president and vice president. Forty-eight states and the District of Columbia have "winner-take-all" systems in which the candidate that wins the popular vote gets all the electoral votes for that state. In Maine and Nebraska, one vote is given to the candidate who wins the popular vote in each congressional district and two electoral votes go to the candidate who wins the popular vote statewide.

Change

[The Electoral College] has worked well in practice. . . . This system usually produces a decisive result, even when the popular vote is very close. Second, if America were to vote for President by direct popular vote, the campaigns might ignore smaller states and rural areas and concentrate only on the big metropolitan areas. Third, the Electoral College reinforces our two-party system. Because candidates are required to win elections in states in different parts of the country, the candidates' parties must have a broad base, not a regional one. C

—John Fortier
American Enterprise Institute

You Be the Geographer

1. **Analyzing** How might presidential candidates change their campaign plans if the Electoral College were done away with?
2. **Critical Thinking** Do you think that candidates would change where they campaign if elections were based on the popular vote? Why or why not?
3. **Read to Write** Write a paragraph that explains whether you think the current process of electing a president and vice president is effective. You might want to give examples from what you know about American history and government.

C Critical Thinking

Predicting Consequences After students have read the article on this page, have them review the article on the previous page. Then, have them predict what would happen if the Electoral College were abolished and popular voting were introduced. Remind them to support their prediction. **OL**

Assess/Close

Have students participate in a panel discussion on whether the Electoral College should be changed. **OL**

You Be the Geographer

Answers:

1. Candidates might spend most of their time in places that have many voters, such as large cities and their suburbs.
2. Probably yes, because campaigning in highly populated areas would be the most cost-effective.
3. Answers will vary. Those supporting the current system may agree with points raised by John Fortier; others will agree with the arguments cited by Kay Maxwell.

Activity: Connecting With You

Simulating To help students understand how the Electoral College works, hold a mock election in your classroom. **Ask:** **Who actually chooses the president and vice president of the United States?** *(electors)* Ask for candidates who wish to run for president and vice president of the class. Ask candidates to make speeches and campaign for classmates' support. Organize the class into five to seven groups, and tell groups they represent an electoral district. Have candidates choose a student in each group to be their elector. Each candidate will have as many electors as there are groups. Hold a confidential vote, keeping the votes for each group separate from other groups' votes. Tally the votes for each group, then call forward the elector for the winning candidate in each group. Finally, have electors cast their votes for the president and vice president. Compare the actual popular vote to the electors' vote, and lead a discussion about how the electoral process reflects the actual vote. Keep the focus of the discussion on the election process, not on the winning candidates. **OL**

Focus

Bellringer

Daily Focus Transparency 5-2

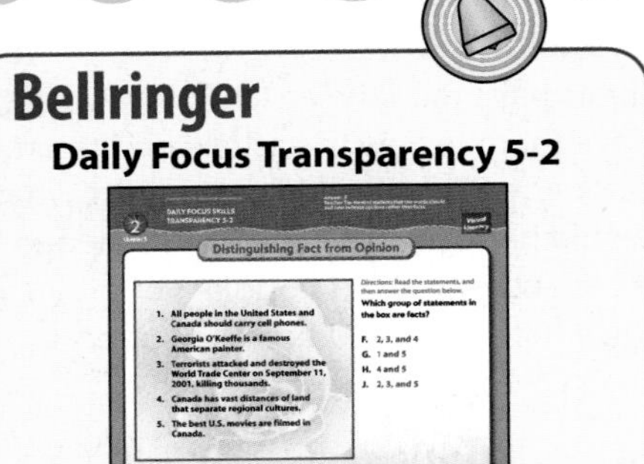

Guide to Reading

Answers to Graphic:

Answers may include:

	Key Facts
Language	U.S.: English primary language, Spanish and other languages spoken; Canada: English and French are official languages
Art and Literature	Common themes: beauty of landscape, movies, pop and rock music
Daily Life	people are mobile, enthusiastic about sports, honor diversity

Section Spotlight Video

To learn more about the cultures and lifestyles of the United States and Canada, have students watch the Section Spotlight Video.

Resource Manager

R Reading Strategies	C Critical Thinking	D Differentiated Instruction	W Writing Support	S Skill Practice
Teacher Edition • Act. Prior Know., p. 146 • Predicting, p. 149 **Additional Resources** • Guid. Read., URB p. 62 • Cont. Vocab., URB p. 63 • Ac. Vocab., URB p. 65 • Read. Ess., p. 37 • World Lit. Read., URB p. 31	**Teacher Edition** • An. Pri. Sources, p. 145 • Drawing Con., p. 147 • Making In., p. 150 **Additional Resources** • Quizzes and Tests, p. 52	**Teacher Edition** • Logical/Math., p. 146 • EL, p. 149 **Additional Resources** • Reteach., URB p. 79	**Teacher Edition** • Descriptive Writing, p. 146 • Persuasive Writing, p. 147 **Additional Resources** • Enrichment, URB p. 19	**Teacher Edition** • Using Geo. Skills, p. 149 **Additional Resources** • Chart, Graph, and Map Skills, URB p. 69 • Speak./Listen. Skills, URB p. 73 • Daily Focus Trans. 5-2 • Reg. Atlas, URB pp. 1–7

Guide to Reading

BIG Idea

Culture influences people's perceptions about places and regions.

Content Vocabulary

- ban *(p. 145)*
- suburb *(p. 147)*
- indigenous *(p. 149)*
- bilingual *(p. 149)*

Academic Vocabulary

- evolve *(p. 147)*
- generate *(p. 147)*
- participate *(p. 147)*

Reading Strategy

Organizing Information Use a chart like the one below to organize key facts about the languages, cultures, and lifestyles of the United States and Canada.

	Key Facts
Language	
Art and Literature	
Daily Life	

SECTION 2

Cultures and Lifestyles

Picture This Cadillacs, instead of cattle, populate this dusty wheat field near Amarillo, Texas. In 1974 a Texas millionaire had this unusual display of cars created to honor the Cadillac. Layers of graffiti have been added to the Cadillacs over the years, and new guests are invited to add their own messages. Read Section 2 to learn more about the unique cultures in the United States and Canada.

Cadillac Ranch near Amarillo, Texas

Cultures and Lifestyles of the United States

Main Idea **The culture of the United States has been shaped by immigrants from around the world.**

Geography and You Have you ever decorated a Christmas tree or seen one at a store? This tradition actually comes from Germany. Read on to discover how immigration has transformed culture in the United States.

About 300 million people live in the United States, making it the third-most-populous country. The population of the United States includes people of many different ethnic backgrounds. You can see this diversity in many aspects of American culture.

NATIONAL GEOGRAPHIC

Becoming U.S. Citizens

Many immigrants eventually decide to become U.S. citizens. Once they meet the requirements and pass the citizenship test, they are officially sworn in as citizens and recite the Pledge of Allegiance. ***Movement*** **How have immigration trends changed since the late 1900s?**

Diverse Traditions

The United States has been called "a nation of immigrants." Throughout its history, the United States has attracted vast numbers of immigrants from around the globe. Yet the pattern of immigration has changed over time. During the late 1700s and early 1800s, the largest number of immigrants came from Great Britain, Ireland, western and central Africa, and the Caribbean. From the late 1800s to the 1920s, most immigrants came from southern, central, and eastern Europe. Large numbers of Chinese, Japanese, Mexican, and Canadian immigrants also arrived during this period.

C

The diverse backgrounds of so many late-1800s immigrants caused some Americans to become concerned about cultural change. As a result, they passed laws limiting immigration. In 1882 Congress passed a law that **banned**, or legally blocked, almost all immigration from China. In 1924 another law limited the numbers of immigrants from many countries. Over the next 40 years, immigration to the United States slowed.

By the 1960s, opinions in the country had changed, in part due to growing support for civil rights. As a result, the country changed its immigration laws. A new law passed in 1965 based entry into the United States on a person's work skills and links to relatives already living in the United States. Changes in U.S. laws and in economic and political conditions worldwide led to a rise in the number of immigrants to the United States during the late 1900s. By 2000, nearly half of all the country's immigrants came from Latin America and Canada, and another third came from Asia. Less than 15 percent came from Europe.

Teach

C Critical Thinking

Analyzing Primary Sources Have students conduct research to locate a primary source written by an immigrant to the United States, such as a letter or diary entry. Have students write a summary of their chosen source, describing what life was like for that immigrant and some of the challenges he or she faced upon arriving in America. **OL**

Caption Answer:
Many more immigrants come from Latin America, Canada, and Asia and far fewer from Europe.

Social Studies ONLINE
Objectives and answers to the Student Web Activity can be found at glencoe.com under the Web Activity Lesson Plan for this chapter.

Differentiated Instruction

Chart, Graph, and Map Skills Activity, URB pp. 69–70

Reading a Line Graph

Objective: To learn to interpret a line graph

Focus: Ask students to describe a line graph.

Teach: Tell students to read the introduction and study the graph, and then complete the graph that follows.

Assess: Students should double-check their data points against the table.

Close: Have students list different types of information that are appropriate for display in a line graph.

Differentiated Instruction Strategies

BL As students examine the graph, have them say aloud the information noted by each dot.

AL Have students conduct a survey of their classmates' birthdates. Then have them display the results on a line graph.

ELL Have students write a sentence explaining what each graph shows.

D Differentiated Instruction

Logical/Mathematical Ask students to create a graph of their choice, using pen and paper or graphing software, to show the breakdown by percentages of the five different ethnic groups discussed in the text. Have students share their graphs with the class. **OL**

W Writing Support

Descriptive Writing Have students locate a work of art created by an American artist. Tell students that many museums feature their collections online. Have students write a paragraph describing the work of art and what makes it distinctly American. **OL**

R Reading Strategy

Activating Prior Knowledge Ask students to think of a favorite novel, story, or poem by an American author that illustrates the theme of diversity. Have volunteers describe the work and how it reflects the theme. **AL**

Caption Answer:
the diversity of the American people and the landscape and history of particular regions

Current immigration trends are changing the makeup of the American population. People of European descent still make up about two-thirds of the population, but the percentage of people from other areas is growing. Latinos, or Hispanics—who trace their heritages to the countries of Latin America and Spain—make up 15 percent of Americans. They are the fastest-growing ethnic group. African Americans, at 12 percent, are the next-largest ethnic group. Asian Americans make up 4 percent of the population, and Native Americans make up 1 percent.

The languages spoken in the United States reflect the diversity of its people. English is the primary language, but for one person in six, English is not their most familiar language. Spanish is the most widely spoken language after English. More than 1 million people speak one or more of the following: Chinese, French, Vietnamese, Tagalog, German, and Italian.

Diversity also extends to religion, which has long been an important factor in American life. Most Americans follow some form of Christianity. The largest number of Christians in the United States belongs to one of the many Protestant churches. These groups vary widely in their beliefs and practices. Roman Catholics make up the next-largest group of American Christians, followed by members of Eastern Orthodox churches. Judaism and Islam each have about 5 million followers in the United States. About 2 to 3 million Americans practice Buddhism, and another 2.5 million are followers of Hinduism.

Literature and the Arts

American artists, writers, and musicians have developed distinctly American styles. The earliest American artists used materials from their environments to create works of art. For centuries, Native Americans have carved wooden masks or created beautiful designs on pottery made from clay found in their areas. Later artists were attracted to the beauty of the landscape. For example, Winslow Homer painted the stormy waters of the North Atlantic. Georgia O'Keeffe painted the colorful deserts of the Southwest. In contrast, Thomas Eakins and John Sloan often painted the gritty, or rough, side of city life.

Two themes are common in American literature. One theme focuses on the rich diversity of the people in the United States. The poetry of Langston Hughes and the novels of Toni Morrison portray the triumphs and sorrows of African Americans. The novels of Amy Tan examine the lives of Chinese Americans. Oscar Hijuelos and Sandra Cisneros write about the country's Latinos.

Georgia O'Keeffe

NATIONAL GEOGRAPHIC

▲ Originally from Wisconsin, O'Keeffe began her career as an art teacher. She moved to New Mexico in 1946, and lived and worked there until her death at the age of 98. ***Regions*** **What themes or subjects have attracted American artists?**

Hands-On Chapter Project
Step 2

Creating a Historical Calendar

Step 2: Creating the Calendar Students will use the images they collected in Step 1 to create a calendar of American and Canadian history and culture.

Directions Show students your calendar again for design ideas. Then have students make their own calendars using the images they collected. Ask students to include a description of each image and its importance. Finally, have students research the government and religious holidays celebrated in each country and include them on the appropriate dates on their calendar.

Putting It Together Have students display their calendars and explain why they chose their images. **OL**

(Chapter Project cont. on the Visual Summary page)

A second theme in American literature focuses on the landscape and history of particular regions. Mark Twain's books tell about life along the Mississippi River in the mid-1800s. Nathaniel Hawthorne wrote about the people of New England. Willa Cather and Laura Ingalls Wilder portrayed the struggles people faced in settling the Great Plains. William Faulkner wrote about life in the South.

Americans have created several new musical styles. Country music grew out of folk music from the rural South in the 1920s. The style gained many fans as it **evolved,** or developed, over the following decades. In the early 1900s, African Americans developed blues and jazz. Blues later inspired rock and roll in the 1950s. More recently, rap and hip-hop have gained popularity. **W**

In the early 1900s, movies started attracting large audiences. Today, the movie industry **generates,** or makes, enormous profits and continues to entertain audiences around the world. In addition to movies, after 1950, television became an important part of American culture.

Life in the United States

At one time, most Americans lived in rural areas. Today the United States is a land of urban dwellers. Many people, however, have moved from cities to **suburbs,** or smaller communities surrounding a larger city. They also have moved from one region to another. **C** Since the 1970s, the fastest-growing regions have been the South and Southwest, often called the Sunbelt because of their sunny, mild climates.

Lifestyles vary across the United States. Americans live in different types of homes, from one-story houses in the suburbs to high-rise apartments in cities. About two-thirds of American families own their own homes. This is one of the highest home ownership rates in the world. Because of their economic well-being, Americans also lead the world in the ownership of cars and personal computers and in Internet use.

Many Americans watch movies and television, but they also exercise and play sports. Millions of young Americans **participate** in sports leagues devoted to games such as baseball and soccer. Important U.S. holidays include Thanksgiving, the Fourth of July, and other celebrations based on religious and ethnic traditions.

Reading Check **Summarizing** How has the United States controlled immigration?

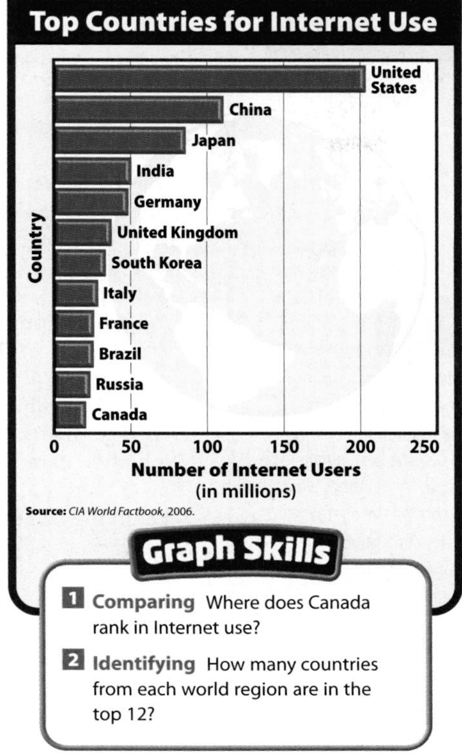

Source: *CIA World Factbook*, 2006.

Graph Skills

1. **Comparing** Where does Canada rank in Internet use?
2. **Identifying** How many countries from each world region are in the top 12?

W Writing Support

Persuasive Writing Have students write a paragraph that answers this question: Which popular art form (music, movies, or television) do you think has had the greatest impact on American life? Remind students to include reasons to support their answers. **OL**

C Critical Thinking

Drawing Conclusions **Ask: Why do you think so many people have moved from cities to suburbs?** *(Answers may include the desire for bigger homes, more green space, less congestion, and the desire to be closer to family and friends.)* **OL**

Graph Skills

Answers:

1. 12th
2. North America: 2; Europe: 5; Asia: 4; South America: 1

Reading Check **Answer:** It has blocked the immigration of people from certain countries, and it has changed its policy so that work skills and links to relatives are now most important.

Differentiated Instruction

Leveled Activities

BL Content Vocabulary Activity, URB p. 63

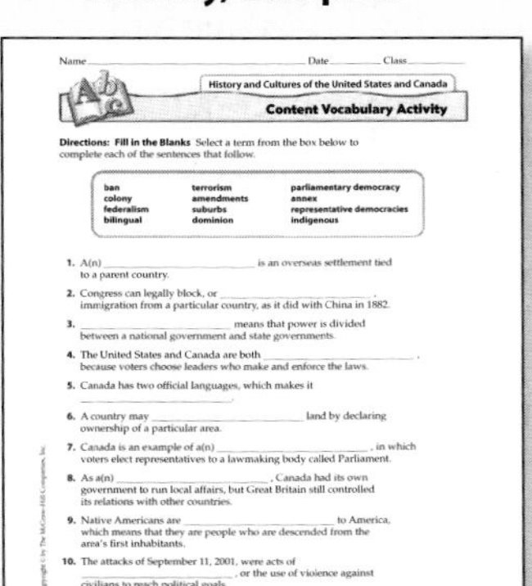

OL World Literature Reading, URB p. 31

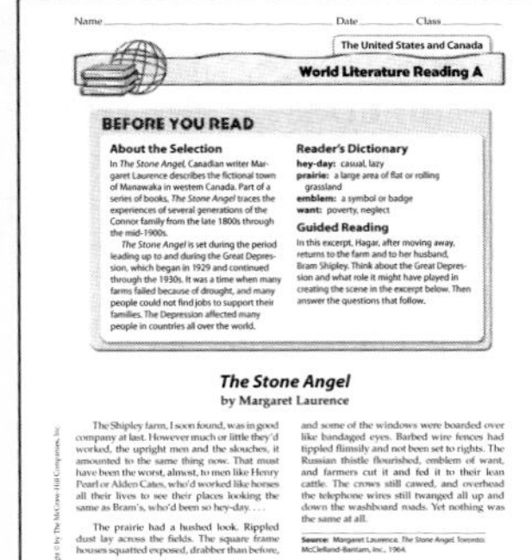

AL Enrichment Activity, URB p. 19

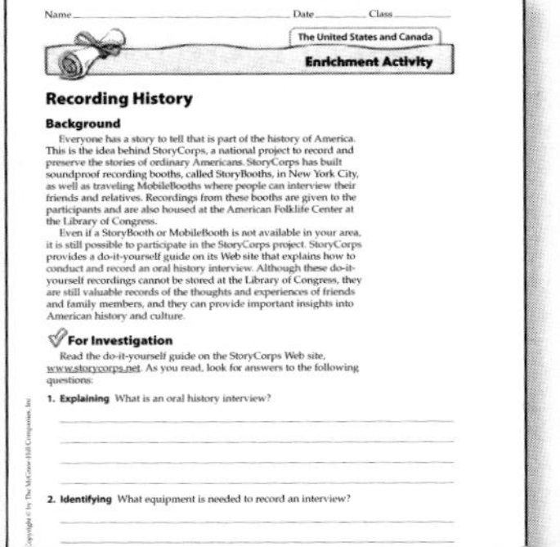

ELL Academic Vocabulary Activity, URB p. 65

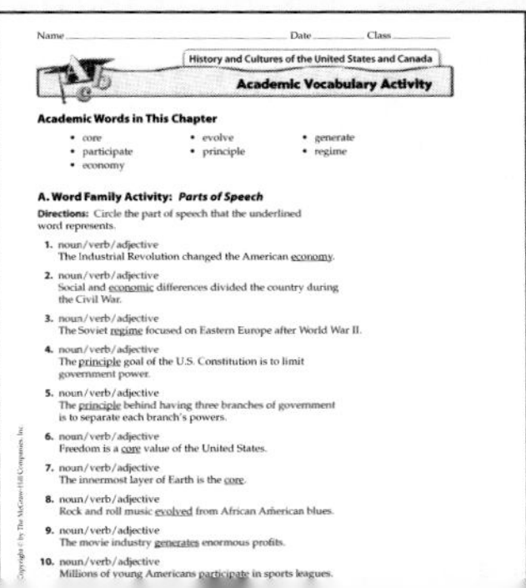

World Literature

Teach

Reading Strategy

Making Connections Remind students that they should make connections between what they are reading and what they have read before, as well as events in other parts of the world and their own personal experiences. **Ask: What do you know about the civil rights movement in the United States?** *(Answers will vary, but students may mention key figures such as Martin Luther King, Jr.)* **Do you think Hughes would have supported the civil rights movement? Why or why not?** *(Probably yes, because he was proud to be an African American and believed a time would come—"tomorrow"—when discrimination would end)* **OL**

Analyzing Literature

Answers:

1. He believes that African Americans are treated unjustly because of the color of their skin.
2. Answers will vary but should reflect Hughes's feeling of pride about being an African American.

Langston Hughes (1902–1967)

Langston Hughes was one of the first African Americans to earn a living as a writer. He wrote plays, novels, essays, and children's stories, but he became best known for his poetry. Hughes's works celebrated the energy of life in New York City's Harlem, a largely African American neighborhood.

Background Information

Hughes was active in the Harlem Renaissance, an African American artistic movement of the 1920s. Inspired by jazz and blues, Hughes wove the rhythms of these forms of music into his poems. He urged African Americans to take pride in their culture and to stand up for their rights.

Reader's Dictionary

company: guests

ashamed: feel sorry or guilty for having done something wrong

I, Too

By Langston Hughes

I, too, sing America.

I am the darker brother.
They send me to eat in the kitchen
When company comes,
But I laugh,
And eat well,
And grow strong.

Tomorrow,
I'll be at the table
When **company** comes.
Nobody'll dare
Say to me,
"Eat in the kitchen,"
Then.

Besides,
They'll see how beautiful I am
And be **ashamed**—

I, too, am America.

Analyzing Literature

1. **Making Inferences** How does Hughes view the role of African Americans in society at the time he wrote this poem?
2. **Read to Write** Write a poem or paragraph that responds to Hughes's feelings in "I, Too."

Additional Reading

Review suggested books before assigning them.

Biography: *Madam C.J. Walker* by Jim Haskins is the story of Sarah Breedlove, the daughter of two freed slaves, who created a million-dollar business selling hair balm in the years after the Civil War.

Nonfiction: *Magnetic North: Trek Across Canada* by David Halsey and Diana Landau tells the story of Halsey's travels by foot, dogsled, and canoe from coast to coast across Canada's wilderness.

Fiction: *White Fang* by Jack London relates the story of White Fang, part dog, part wolf, who after years of abuse finally is tamed by the affection of one man.

For further reading, see BOOKLINK 3

Cultures and Lifestyles of Canada

Main Idea **Canadians of many different backgrounds live in towns and cities close to the U.S. border.**

Geography and You Have you played hockey or seen a hockey game? Hockey is a Canadian sport. Read to find out how Canadians have developed unique cultures.

Like the United States, Canada is a nation formed by immigrants with many different cultures. Unlike the United States, Canada has had difficulty achieving a strong sense of national identity. Canada's vast distances and separate cultures cause some Canadians to feel more closely attached to their own region than to Canada as a country. R

A Mix of Cultures

About one-fourth of Canadians are of French ancestry. Most of these people live in Quebec, where they make up 80 percent of that province's population. People of British ancestry form another fourth of Canada's population, and they live mainly in Ontario, the Atlantic Provinces, and British Columbia. People of other European backgrounds form about 15 percent of Canada's population. S

Canada also is home to people of Asian, African, and Latin American backgrounds. Indigenous Canadians, similar to Native Americans, number more than a million. **Indigenous** refers to people who are descended from an area's first inhabitants. Many people in Canada call these indigenous groups the "First Nations."

Canada is a **bilingual** country, which means it has two official languages. In Canada, the languages are English and French. D

Quebec's French Culture

The French-speaking city of Quebec, founded in 1608, is one of Canada's oldest settlements.
Regions **What percentage of Canadians are of French ancestry?**

Despite promises of protection, many French speakers in Quebec do not believe that their language and culture can survive in largely English-speaking Canada. They would like Quebec to separate from Canada and become independent. So far, they have been defeated in two important votes on this issue. Canada's future as a united country, however, is still uncertain.

One cultural issue the country has been able to solve concerns the Inuit (IH·nu·wuht). The Inuit are a northern indigenous people who have wanted self-rule while remaining part of Canada. In 1999 the Canadian government created the territory of Nunavut for them. The name means "Our Land" in the Inuit language. There, the Inuit govern themselves, although they still rely on the national government for some services.

R Reading Strategy

Predicting Ask students to list several possible reasons for Canada's lack of national identity. Write student responses on the board as you read this section. Then have students rate the accuracy of each reason based on information in the text. **OL**

S Skill Practice

Using Geography Skills Have students locate on a map of Canada the following places noted in the text: Quebec, Ontario, the Atlantic Provinces, and British Columbia. **Ask: What generalization can you make about where most French-speaking Canadians live?** *(Most French speakers live in eastern Canada.)* **BL**

D Differentiated Instruction

English Learners Point out that the term *bilingual* contains a common prefix, *bi-*, which means "two." **Ask: How is the idea of "two" contained in the word *bilingual*?** *(A bilingual person speaks two languages.)* **ELL**

Caption Answer: about 25%

Additional Support

Activity: Economics Connection

Predicting Tell students that in recent years, lower costs and tax breaks in Canada have attracted American movie and television production companies from the United States. In Canada, these companies find a variety of landscapes and cityscapes, as well as an educated workforce, so some movies and television shows that once would have been filmed in the United States are now filmed in Canada. **Ask: How do you think this movement of productions affects American film workers?** *(They may be losing jobs, working less, or moving to Canada.)* Have students find the Bureau of Labor Statistic's *Career Guide to Industries* at www.bls.gov and search for "Motion Picture and Video Industries." Have students review the "Outlook" section for the industry and write a paragraph describing how this industry will be affected if more production moves offshore. Students may wish to search the *Occupational Outlook Handbook* for a specific job related to the movie or television industry and review that job's outlook. **OL**

C Critical Thinking

Making Inferences Ask: Why do you think that many immigrant groups prefer foods that reflect their ethnic traditions? *(Possible answers: Those foods are familiar; they remind them of their heritage; they reinforce a cultural heritage for children; immigrants may not have learned to cook other kinds of foods.)* **OL**

Reading Check Answer: The Inuit wanted self-rule.

Assess

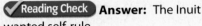

Social Studies ONLINE

Study Central™ provides summaries, interactive games, and online graphic organizers to help students review content.

Close

Summarizing Ask students to summarize in a few sentences how immigrants have contributed to American and Canadian culture. **OL**

Art and Literature

The first Canadian artists were indigenous peoples who carved figures from stone and wood, made pottery, or were weavers. Today, Canadian art reflects both European and indigenous influences. The beauty of Canada's landscape has long been a favorite subject for many artists. Nature and history have been popular subjects for Canadian writers.

Centuries ago, indigenous peoples used song and dance as part of their religious rituals. European music, such as Irish and Scottish ballads, gained popularity after the 1700s. In recent decades, pop and rock have become as popular in Canada as in the United States.

Movies are also a major part of Canadian culture. The nation's film industry earns $5 billion each year. Theater is popular in Canada as well. Ontario's Stratford Festival is world famous for its productions of William Shakespeare's plays. The festival runs for a number of months each year and attracts over half a million fans.

Life in Canada

Like Americans, Canadians are a mobile people. Millions of them use cars to commute to work every day.

C Certain foods are regional favorites. Seafood dishes are popular in the Atlantic Provinces, while French cuisine is preferred in Quebec. Ontario features Italian or Eastern European foods, reflecting the immigrant traditions there. British Columbia is known for salmon and Asian foods.

Canadians are enthusiastic about hockey—a sport that began in Canada—as well as lacrosse, which began as a Native American game. Many Canadians also enjoy hunting and fishing.

Canadians celebrate the founding of their country on July 1 and the fall Thanksgiving holiday in October. As in the United States, different ethnic groups celebrate their heritage at different times of the year.

Reading Check **Explaining** Why was the territory of Nunavut created?

Section 2 Review

Social Studies ONLINE
Study Central™ To review this section, go to glencoe.com.

Vocabulary

1. **Explain** the meaning of *ban, suburb, indigenous,* and *bilingual* by using each word in a sentence.

Main Ideas

2. **Identifying** Which styles of music did Americans invent?
3. **Summarizing** Use a diagram like the one below to show three ways immigration has shaped Canada.

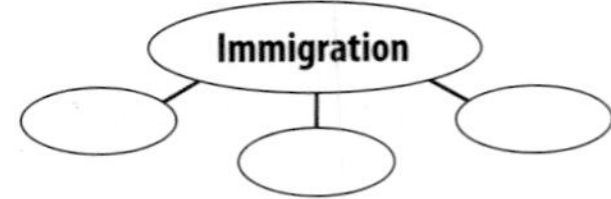

Critical Thinking

4. **Analyzing Information** How are immigration trends changing in the United States?
5. **BIG Idea** Explain why many people in Quebec have wanted to form a separate nation.
6. **Challenge** Why do you think the lifestyles of Americans and Canadians are similar?

Writing About Geography

7. **Expository Writing** Write a paragraph summarizing the styles of American art and literature.

Section 2 Review

Answers

1. Sentences should use vocabulary words according to their definitions in the section and the Glossary.
2. country, blues, jazz, rock and roll, rap, and hip-hop
3. Answers may include three of the following: different languages, varied styles of art and music, different foods, ethnic heritage celebrations, people attached to regions but not whole country.
4. Immigration laws base entry on work skills and relatives already living in the United States. By 2000, nearly half of U.S. immigrants came from Latin America and Canada, and another third came from Asia.
5. Many people in Quebec are of French ancestry and do not believe their language and culture can survive in largely English-speaking Canada.
6. Answers may include common ancestry and language, and similar histories.
7. Summaries will vary but should mention that American artists and writers have developed a distinctly American style, such as paintings of landscapes and gritty city life. Literature focused on the rich diversity of people, and the landscape and history of different regions. Americans have also created distinct musical styles.

Visual Summary

American History

- Native Americans, or indigenous peoples, are North America's earliest inhabitants.
- The 13 British colonies declared independence in 1776.
- During the 1800s, the United States grew in population and had a prosperous economy.
- The United States became a global power during the 1900s.

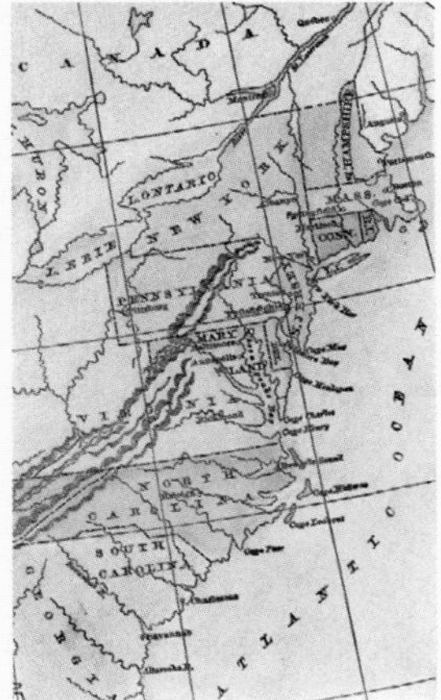

Map of original 13 colonies

Canadian History

- France and then Britain acquired control of the area that today is Canada.
- In 1867 the Dominion of Canada was founded.
- Canada grew through immigration and developed a modern economy.

American and Canadian Governments

- The United States and Canada are democracies based on federal systems.
- The U.S. government has three branches, each with special powers to check the power of the others.
- Canada has a parliamentary system. Legislative members choose a prime minister to head the government.

American Culture

- Immigration has created a diversity of groups, languages, and religions.
- American art and literature have focused on nature and freedom. American music includes country and jazz.
- American lifestyles reflect the economic well-being of the people.

Elvis Presley

Toronto, Canada

Canadian Culture

- Canadian culture reflects the diversity of the many peoples who settled the country.
- Canadian art and literature draw on nature and the history of the country.
- Foods and pastimes in Canada reflect regional life and the contributions of immigrants.

Hockey, Canada

STUDY TO GO Study anywhere, anytime! Download quizzes and flash cards to your PDA from glencoe.com.

Comparing and Contrasting Have students review the Visual Summary text and illustrations and create a Venn diagram that compares and contrasts the governments of the United States and Canada. Tell students to add descriptive statements about each government based on the summary, chapter text, and their own previous knowledge. Remind them that the overlapping part of the diagram should include characteristics that the governments share. *(Sample answers: U.S.: government has three branches; executive branch headed by the president; Canada: parliamentary system; prime minister elected by parliament; Both: democracies, have federal systems with powers assigned to national and state/provincial governments)*

Have students contribute to a Venn diagram on the board. If time permits, make similar diagrams for culture and history of the two nations. **OL**

Making Connections Have students discuss this question: **How have the diverse populations of Canada and the United States affected each country's culture?** *(Possible answer: The varied languages and ethnic backgrounds of the populations in each country have led to a diverse culture. This is evident in each country's artwork, music, and regional cuisine.)* **OL**

Hands-On Chapter Project
Step 3: Wrap Up

Creating a Historical Calendar

Step 3: Learning From the Calendars Students will synthesize what they have learned in Steps 1 and 2.

Directions Ask students if the process of making a calendar has changed their understanding of American and Canadian history and culture. Write on the board the dates of different waves of immigration to the United States and Canada. **Ask: How do American and Canadian art and literature reflect the changes brought by immigration? How has music been affected by new groups of immigrants? What historical events have led to major waves of immigration?** Write the Essential Question on the board, and ask students to write a few sentences in their journals answering the question. Ask for volunteers to share their answers with the class. **OL**

Answers and Analyses

Reviewing Vocabulary

1. B Help students recall the common phrase "thirteen colonies." Point out that the original American colonies were overseas settlements tied by social, cultural, political, and economic connections to a parent country, Great Britain.

2. C Students should look for an answer that describes *both* the United States and Canada. Choices A and B can be eliminated because students should recall that the United States is neither a monarchy nor a colony of another country. If students get confused by D, remind them that the British have a Parliament. This should help them remember that the United States does not.

3. A Knowing the term *urban*, which comes from the Latin word for "city," will help students select the correct answer. Urban areas, then, are city areas. *Sub* means "close to" or "under". A suburb is a settlement that is close to a city.

4. B Students can eliminate choices A and C immediately because they have nothing to do with early settlement of an area. *Federalist* describes a relationship between national and local governments. Point out that the correct choice, *indigenous*, is a synonym for the word *native*.

STANDARDIZED TEST PRACTICE

TEST-TAKING TIP

Outline information from your textbook to study for an exam. Use bold type, questions, and summary paragraphs for headings and details in your outline.

Reviewing Vocabulary

Directions: Choose the word(s) that best completes the sentence.

1. Overseas settlements tied to a parent country are called ________.

A suburbs
B colonies
C dominions
D provinces

2. Both the United States and Canada have ________.

A monarchs
B colonial governments
C representative democracies
D parliamentary democracies

3. Smaller communities surrounding a larger city are known as ________.

A suburbs
B colonies
C dominions
D provinces

4. The term ________ is used to describe people who are descended from an area's first inhabitants.

A terrorist
B indigenous
C bilingual
D federalist

Reviewing Main Ideas

Directions: Choose the best answer for each question.

Section 1 *(pp. 134–141)*

5. How did the United States become a world leader during the 1900s?

A by developing the factory system
B by building an economy based on agriculture
C by enslaving hundreds of thousands of Africans
D by helping to win World War I and World War II

6. What accomplishment marked Canada's full independence?

A Canada's colonies became provinces.
B Canada established its own central government.
C Canadians fought in World War I and World War II.
D Canadians won the right to change their constitution.

Section 2 *(pp. 144–150)*

7. By 2000 where did most immigrants in the United States come from?

A Latin America, Canada, and Asia
B Ireland and Great Britain
C western and central Africa
D southern and eastern Europe

8. What percentage of Canadians has a European background?

A 15 percent
B 25 percent
C 50 percent
D 65 percent

GO ON

Reviewing Main Ideas

5. D Becoming a world leader requires actions on the world stage. Answer D most clearly refers to this type of accomplishment. The other answers can be distractors for students who think themselves into a corner. Ask them to think about which answer involves the whole world.

6. D Students need to keep in mind that *full independence* means not subject to another power and implies unity. Answer choice A supports the idea that Canada would still be under foreign control. Answer C is tricky: although it led to independence later, it was not the immediate cause or marker of independence. Gaining the right to change their constitution was the legal action that marked true independence.

Critical Thinking

Directions: Base your answers to questions 9 and 10 on the circle graph below and your knowledge of Chapter 5. Choose the best answer for each question.

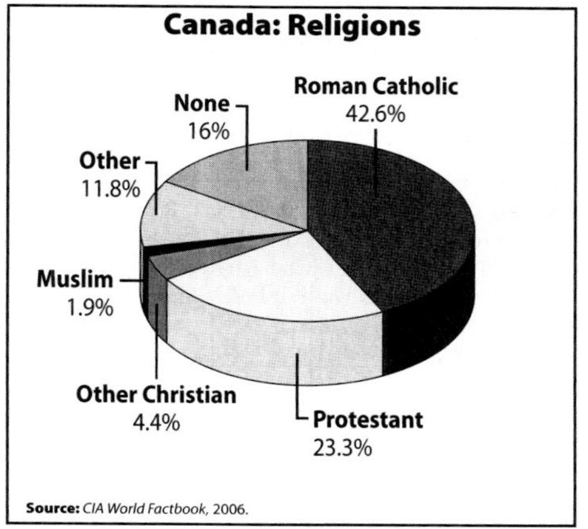

9. Which of the following generalizations is based on the circle graph?

A No Buddhists live in Canada.

B All Canadians are deeply religious.

C A majority of Canadians are Christian.

D Canadians are very tolerant of religious differences.

10. According to the graph, which of the following statements is correct?

A More Protestants than Catholics live in Canada.

B Muslims and other Christians (not including Catholics) outnumber Protestants.

C Islam has almost as many followers as Christianity.

D There are more Protestants than people who claim no religion.

Document-Based Questions

Directions: Analyze the following document and answer the short-answer questions that follow.

The following passage is from the *Canadian Charter of Rights and Freedoms* enacted in 1982.

> Guarantee of Rights and Freedoms
>
> *1. The* Canadian Charter of Rights and Freedoms *guarantees the rights and freedoms set out in it subject only to such reasonable limits prescribed by law as can be demonstrably justified in a free and democratic society.*
>
> Fundamental Freedoms
>
> *2. Everyone has the following fundamental freedoms:*
> *a) freedom of conscience and religion;*
> *b) freedom of thought, belief, opinion and expression, including freedom of the press and other media of communication;*
> *c) freedom of peaceful assembly; and*
> *d) freedom of association.*
>
> Democratic Rights
>
> *3. Every citizen of Canada has the right to vote in an election of members of the House of Commons or of a legislative assembly and to be qualified for membership therein.*

11. Do only Canadian citizens enjoy freedom of expression in Canada? Explain.

12. What qualification for membership in the Canadian House of Commons is mentioned?

Extended Response

13. Explain why Canada's future as a united country is uncertain.

Social Studies ONLINE

For additional test practice, use Self-Check Quizzes—Chapter 5 at glencoe.com.

Need Extra Help?

If you missed question...	1	2	3	4	5	6	7	8	9	10	11	12	13
Go to page...	136	140	147	149	137	139	145	149	149	149	141	141	149

Critical Thinking

9. C The graph shows that the total of Christian Canadians is comprised of Roman Catholics, Protestants, and Other Christians, which add up to almost 70% of all Canadians. The graph does not say anything about whether any Canadians are Buddhists, about the depth of Canadians' religious beliefs, or about their degree of tolerance for other faiths.

10. D This question requires students to compare data. By comparing the numbers in each response, they will see that answers A, B, and C are false.

Document-Based Questions

11. No; the charter explicitly states that "everyone" has the right to freedom of expression.

12. A Members must be Canadian citizens.

Extended Response

13. Most answers will explain that the cultural and linguistic minority in French-speaking Quebec may at some time decide to break away and form a separate nation.

7. A Students should understand the change over the years in the composition of immigrants, resulting from changes in policy. Choices B and C reflect the sources of immigration for the years around 1800. Choice D reflects the sources of immigration for the years around 1900.

8. D The correct answer is found by adding the percentage of people of French descent (25%), of British descent (25%), and of other European descent (15%), for a total of 65%.

Social Studies ONLINE

Have students visit the Web site at glencoe.com to review Chapter 5 and take the Self-Check Quiz.

Need Extra Help?

Have students refer to the pages listed if they miss any of the questions.

Teach

C1 Critical Thinking

Comparing and Contrasting **Ask:** How is Taylor's morning routine like yours? How is it different? *(Answers will vary.)* How many of the differences that you identified are because Taylor lives in Canada, and how many are because Taylor lives on a ranch? *(Answers will vary. Most differences will probably result from the difference in rural and urban/suburban lifestyles.)* What generalization can you make about daily lifestyles in Canada and the United States? *(Possible answer: They are fairly similar.)* **OL**

C2 Critical Thinking

Predicting Consequences Point out to students that Taylor is studying French, an official language of her country.
Ask: What advantages could Canada gain if every English-speaking Canadian studied French? *(It might increase a sense of national identity; it would bring the different language groups closer together; it might make French-speaking Canadians feel less isolated.)* **OL**

TIME JOURNAL

"Hello! My name is Taylor.

I'm 13 years old and live in Ashcroft, British Columbia. British Columbia is one of Canada's 10 provinces. My family runs a horse ranch and lodge there. Here's how I spend my day."

7:15 a.m. I wake up to the sound of my alarm clock. I shower and put on jeans, a T-shirt, and my tan cowboy boots. Then I head to the kitchen and say good morning to my parents and older brother, Daniel.

7:45 a.m. My mom has made pancakes and bacon for breakfast, and it smells great. I dig in. A hot breakfast is a nice treat. On most days, I just have cereal and toast.

C1 **8:25 a.m.** Everyone goes their separate ways. My dad leaves for work in town. My brother goes off to high school, and my mom gets ready to work in the ranch office. I walk down our rural road and wait for the school bus.

9:00 a.m. My school day begins with math class. It's okay, but I am happy when the bell rings because I have English next. I love reading and writing and would like to become an author.

10:30 a.m. I stop at my locker, then go to French class. French is the official language in Quebec, **C2** Canada's biggest province. We speak English throughout the rest of Canada, but many kids study French as a second language.

11:40 a.m. It's time for lunch. Sometimes I walk to my friend's house for lunch (she lives near the school). Today, I stay at school and buy a grilled cheese sandwich and an apple.

12:20 p.m. In physical education class, we play basketball. In Canada, kids take "phys. ed." until tenth grade. We learn everything from softball to gymnastics.

1:20 p.m. I head to the school wood shop for woodworking class. I put on my safety goggles and use a power tool to carve a wooden sign. In a few weeks, woodworking will be over and I will start a new class—health.

3:00 p.m. I take the bus back home. There, I feed the horses and tackle some other ranch chores. In the summer, when the ranch is full of guests, I will be much busier! Then I will have to set up for meals and wash dishes.

4:45 p.m. I have some free time before dinner, so I grab my helmet, get my horse from the stable, and go riding.

6:15 p.m. Tonight, my grandfather and two uncles join us for dinner. They live in a separate house here on the ranch, so we see them all the time. We eat thick steaks and salad.

7:30 p.m. I help clear the table then do my homework. For one assignment, I have to use the family computer to log on to the Internet.

10:00 p.m. I read in my room for a while then get ready for bed. I'm tired!

ILLUSTRATIONS BY BOOKMAPMAN

SCHOOL TIME Taylor and her classmates share a laugh. Each semester Taylor studies four or five subjects. She gets three minutes between classes to get to her next lesson.

HORSING AROUND Ranching and tourism are big business in Taylor's village. Taylor's family owns a guest ranch. One of Taylor's chores is to feed the horses.

GREAT OUTDOORS Hiking is a popular pastime around Ashcroft. Here, Taylor and her dog take a break at a scenic spot overlooking the Thompson River.

Additional Support

Additional Statistics You can find data like this and much more in the *CIA World Factbook*. Go to www.cia.gov and click on the link to the *World Factbook*. From there you can click on the countries you wish to learn more about.

Comparing Canada and the United States

	Canada	United States
Lowest point	Atlantic Ocean 0 ft. (0m)	Death Valley 282 ft. (86m) below sea level
Highest point	Mount Logan 19,551 ft. (5,959 m)	Mount McKinley 20,320 ft. (6,194 m) high
Arable Land	4.57%	18.01%
GDP per capita	$35,200 (2006 estimate)	$43,500 (2006 estimate)
National Holiday	Canada Day, July 1	Independence Day, July 4

Source: *CIA World Factbook*, 2006.

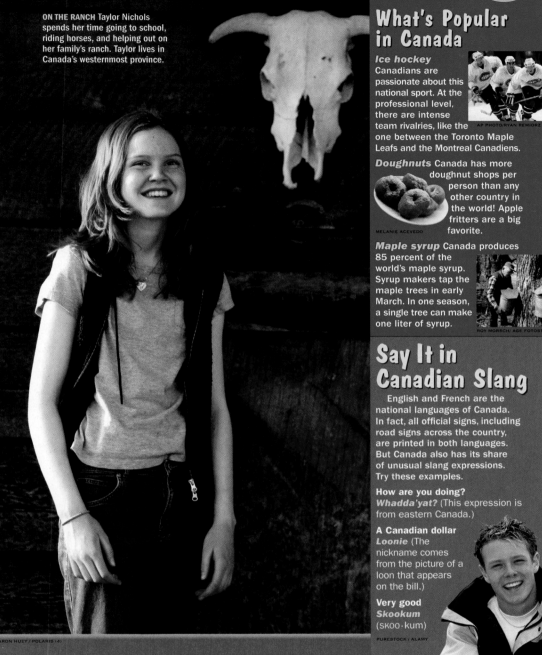

ON THE RANCH Taylor Nichols spends her time going to school, riding horses, and helping out on her family's ranch. Taylor lives in Canada's westernmost province.

AARON HUEY / POLARIS (4)

What's Popular in Canada

Ice hockey Canadians are passionate about this national sport. At the professional level, there are intense team rivalries, like the one between the Toronto Maple Leafs and the Montreal Canadiens.

AP PHOTO/RYAN REMIORZ

Doughnuts Canada has more doughnut shops per person than any other country in the world! Apple fritters are a big favorite.

MELANIE ACEVEDO

Maple syrup Canada produces 85 percent of the world's maple syrup. Syrup makers tap the maple trees in early March. In one season, a single tree can make one liter of syrup.

ROY MORSCH/ AGE FOTOSTOCK

Say It in Canadian Slang

English and French are the national languages of Canada. In fact, all official signs, including road signs across the country, are printed in both languages. But Canada also has its share of unusual slang expressions. Try these examples.

How are you doing?
Whadda'yat? (This expression is from eastern Canada.)

A Canadian dollar
Loonie (The nickname comes from the picture of a loon that appears on the bill.)

Very good
Skookum (SKOO·kum)

PURESTOCK / ALAMY

What's Popular in Canada

Maple Syrup Maple syrup is produced only in North America. It is made from the sap of maple trees, primarily the sugar maple and the black maple. The sap is drawn by cutting a hole, called a taphole, into the tree.

Canadians enjoy not only maple syrup but also candy made with maple sugar. The maple leaf is the national symbol of Canada and appears on its flag.

Say It in Canadian

Scots Gaelic Most Canadians speak English, but French is the native language of a large minority of citizens. A small number of Canadians speak Scots Gaelic, a Celtic language of the Scottish Highlands and Western Isles. About 3,000 Scots Gaelic speakers live in Nova Scotia (or Alba Nuadh in Scots Gaelic). The language was brought to Nova Scotia during the 1800s by thousands of immigrants from Scotland.

Activity: Personal Writing

Writing a Biography This journal gives students a glimpse into what life is like for a girl living on a ranch in British Columbia. Ask students to review Taylor's journal, then write a similar description of their typical day. Have students include as many details as possible about their lifestyle, such as what kind of clothes they wear, what classes they take, how they get to school, what activities they do outside of school, what family members they live with, whether they have pets, and whether they live in a city or a rural area. Encourage students to include details about their community, such as what activities are popular among teens and what slang terms their friends might use. **OL**

Planning Guide

Key to Ability Levels	
BL Below level	AL Above level
OL On level	ELL English Language Learners

Key to Teaching Resources	
Print Material	DVD
CD-ROM	Transparency

BL	OL	AL	ELL	Resources		Chapter Opener	Section 1	Section 2	Chapter Assess
FOCUS									
BL	OL	AL	ELL	Transparency	**Daily Focus Skills Transparencies**		6-1	6-2	
TEACH									
BL	OL		ELL	Print Material	**Guided Reading Activity, URB***		p. 85	p. 86	
BL	OL	AL	ELL	Print Material	**Content Vocabulary Activity, URB***		p. 87	p. 87	
BL	OL	AL	ELL	Print Material	**Academic Vocabulary Activity, URB**		p. 89	p. 89	
BL	OL	AL	ELL	Print Material	**Differentiated Instruction Activity, URB**		p. 91		
BL	OL	AL	ELL	Print Material	**Chart, Graph, and Map Skills Activity, URB**		p. 93	p. 93	
	OL	AL		Print Material	**Critical Thinking Activity, URB**			p. 95	
BL	OL	AL	ELL	Print Material	**Speaking and Listening Skills Activity, URB**		p. 97		
BL	OL	AL	ELL	Print Material	**Writing Skills Activity, URB**		p. 101	p. 101	
BL	OL	AL	ELL	Print Material	**School-to-Home Connection Activity, URB***		p. 105		
BL	OL	AL	ELL	Print Material	**Regional Atlas Activities, URB**		pp. 1–7	pp. 1–7	
		AL		Print Material	**Geography and Economics Activity, URB**			p. 9	
	OL	AL		Print Material	**Environmental Case Study, URB**			p. 13	
BL	OL	AL	ELL	Print Material	**GeoLab Activity, URB**			p. 23	
BL	OL		ELL	Print Material	**Reading Skills Activity, URB**		p. 25		
BL	OL	AL	ELL	Print Material	**Primary Source Readings, URB**			p. 29	
BL	OL		ELL	Print Material	**Reading Essentials and Note-Taking Guide**		p. 40	p. 43	
	OL	AL		Print Material	**TIME Perspectives: Exploring World Issues**		p. 5		
	OL			Print Material	**Interactive Geography Activity**		p. 9		
BL	OL	AL	ELL	Transparency	**In-Text Map Overlay and Population Pyramid Transparencies**	2	2A, 2D	2A	
	OL			Print Material	**Foods Around the World**		p. 6	p. 6	
BL	OL	AL	ELL	Print Material	**Outline Map Resource Book**		p. 8	p. 22	
BL	OL	AL	ELL	Print Material	**NGS World Atlas***	✓	✓	✓	
BL	OL	AL	ELL	Print Material	**NGS World Desk Map**	✓	✓	✓	✓
BL	OL	AL	ELL	Print Material	**World Literature Library**	✓	✓	✓	✓
BL	OL	AL	ELL	Print Material	**Writer's Guidebook**	✓	✓	✓	✓

Note: Please refer to the *Unit Resource Book: The United States and Canada* for this chapter's URB materials.

* Also available in Spanish

- Interactive Lesson Planner
- Interactive Teacher Edition
- Fully editable blackline masters
- Section Spotlight Videos Launch
- Differentiated Lesson Plans
- Printable reports of daily assignments
- Standards Tracking System

Levels					Resources	Chapter Opener	Section 1	Section 2	Chapter Assess
BL	OL	AL	ELL						
TEACH *(continued)*									
BL	OL	AL	ELL		Vocabulary PuzzleMaker CD-ROM*	✓	✓	✓	✓
	OL	AL			Primary Sources CD-ROM	✓	✓	✓	✓
BL	OL	AL	ELL		StudentWorks™ Plus DVD	✓	✓	✓	✓
BL	OL	AL	ELL		Section Video Program Activities	✓	✓	✓	✓
BL	OL	AL	ELL		World Music: A Cultural Legacy	✓	✓	✓	✓
BL	OL	AL	ELL		Writing Process Transparencies	✓	✓	✓	✓
Teacher Resources					Building Academic Vocabulary	✓	✓	✓	✓
					Strategies for Success	✓	✓	✓	✓
					Teacher's Guide to Differentiated Instruction	✓	✓	✓	✓
					Presentation Plus! DVD	✓	✓	✓	✓
ASSESS									
BL	OL	AL	ELL		Quizzes and Tests		p. 61	p. 62	p. 63
BL	OL	AL	ELL		Authentic Assessment With Rubrics		p. 6		p. 6
BL	OL	AL	ELL		Standardized Test Practice				p. 21
BL	OL	AL	ELL		*ExamView® Assessment Suite* CD-ROM*		6-1	6-2	Ch. 6
BL	OL	AL	ELL		Interactive Tutor Self-Assessment CD-ROM		6-1	6-2	
CLOSE									
BL			ELL		Reteaching Activity, URB*		p. 103	p. 103	p. 103
BL	OL		ELL		Reading and Study Skills Foldables™	p. 60	p. 60	p. 60	p. 60
BL	OL	AL	ELL		Graphic Organizer Transparencies and Strategies		✓	✓	
BL	OL	AL	ELL		*Exploring Our World* in Graphic Novel		p. 9		

Integrating Technology

Using TechConnect: Using a Web Browser

Objective
- Students will find credible information online and incorporate it into projects.

Technology
- Glencoe TechCONNECT (For more information or to get a free 30-day trial of Glencoe TechCONNECT for your classroom, visit techconnect.glencoe.com and click the **Free Trial** button.)
- Web browser

Focus/Teach
- To see activities correlated to this textbook, log on to TechCONNECT and click the **Find your textbook** link. You can also search for activities. After you log on, click **Activity Search.** Choose **Social Studies, Web Browsers,** and your grade level.
- Have students log on and enter the letters AC and the three-digit activity number. For example, to access activity #68, Becoming a Concerned Citizen, enter AC068.
- Have students read each page of the activity and follow the on-screen instructions.

Assess
- Have students complete the activity's self-assessment rubric.
- Students may also complete the activity's TechCheck, a five-question multiple-choice quiz. Enter the letters TC and the three-digit activity number, such as TC068.

Close
- Review this activity with the class.

Social Studies ONLINE

	Student	Teacher	Parent
Beyond the Textbook	●		●
Chapter Overviews	●		●
Concepts in Motion	●		●
ePuzzles and Games	●		●
Literature Connections		●	
Multi-Language Glossaries	●		●
Online Student Edition	●	●	●
Section Videos	●	●	●
Self-Check Quizzes	●		●
Student Web Activities	●		●
Study Central™	●		●
Teaching Today		●	
TIME Current Events	●		●
Vocabulary eFlashcards	●		●
Web Activity Lesson Plans		●	

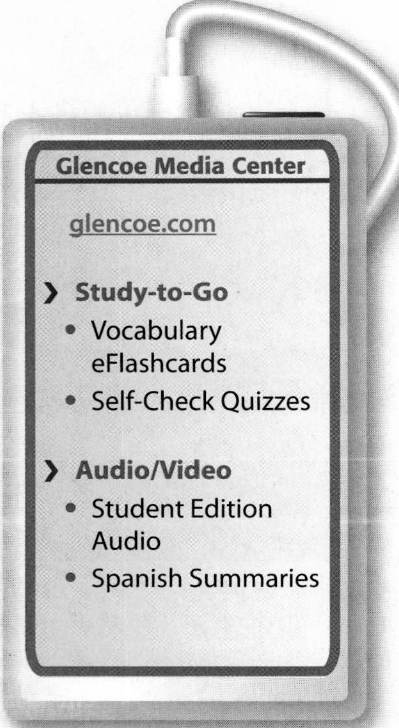

Additional Resources

- **Timed Readings Plus in Social Studies** helps students increase their reading rate and fluency while maintaining comprehension. The 400-word passages are similar to those found on state and national assessments.
- **Reading in the Content Area: Social Studies** concentrates on six essential reading skills that help students better comprehend what they read. The book includes 75 high-interest nonfiction passages written at increasing levels of difficulty.
- **Reading Social Studies** includes strategic reading instruction and vocabulary support in Social Studies content for ELLs and native speakers of English.
- **Content Vocabulary Workout** (Grades 6–8) accelerates reading comprehension through focused vocabulary development. Social Studies content vocabulary comes from the glossaries of Glencoe's Middle School Social Studies texts. www.jamestowneducation.com

Index to National Geographic Magazine:

The following articles relate to this chapter:

- "When Mountains Move," John G. Mitchell, March 2006.
- "Refuge in White: Winter in a Canadian National Park," John L. Eliot, December 2005.

National Geographic Society Products To order the following, call National Geographic at 1-800-368-2728:

- *National Geographic Atlas of the World* (Book).

Access National Geographic's new dynamic MapMachine Web site and other geography resources at:
www.nationalgeographic.com
www.nationalgeographic.com/maps

Biography 

The following videotape programs are available from Glencoe as supplements to Chapter 6:

- Ellis Island (ISBN 0-76-704451-7)
- Drive for the American Dream (ISBN 1-56-501221-6)

To order, call Glencoe at 1-800-334-7344. To find classroom resources to accompany many of these videos, check the following home pages:

A&E Television: www.aetv.com
The History Channel: www.historychannel.com

GLENCOE BOOKLINK 3

Use this database to search more than 30,000 titles to create a customized reading list for your students.

- Reading lists can be organized by students' reading level, author, genre, theme, or area of interest.
- The database provides Degrees of Reading Power™ (DRP) and Lexile™ readability scores for all selections.
- A brief summary of each selection is included.

Leveled reading suggestions for this chapter:

For students at a Grade 5 reading level:
- ***It's My Earth, Too: How I can Help the Earth Stay Alive?*** by Kathleen Krull

For students at a Grade 6 reading level:
- ***Oil Spill!*** by Melvin Berger

For students at a Grade 7 reading level:
- ***A Safe Home for Manatees,*** by Priscilla Belz Jenkins

For students at a Grade 8 reading level:
- ***America the Not-So-Beautiful,*** by Andrew A. Rooney

For students at a Grade 9 reading level:
- ***Earth Keepers,*** by Joan Anderson

Focus

The Essential Question

As students study the chapter, remind them to consider the chapter-based Essential Question. Answering this question will help them understand the important concepts in the chapter. In addition, the Hands-On Chapter Project relates the content from each section to the Essential Question. The steps in each section build on each other as students progress through the chapter. The Hands-On Chapter Project culminates in the Wrap Up activity on the Visual Summary page.

More About the Photo

Visual Literacy Known by many as the Painted Ladies, the colorful Victorian-era wood houses in the foreground are found on Alamo Square in San Francisco, California. Their image appears on countless postcards and tourist guidebooks of the city. Built between 1850 and 1900, many Painted Ladies were destroyed in the fire that followed the earthquake in 1906. Fortunately, the westward spread of the fire stopped short of this neighborhood, sparing these and other relics of a past time.

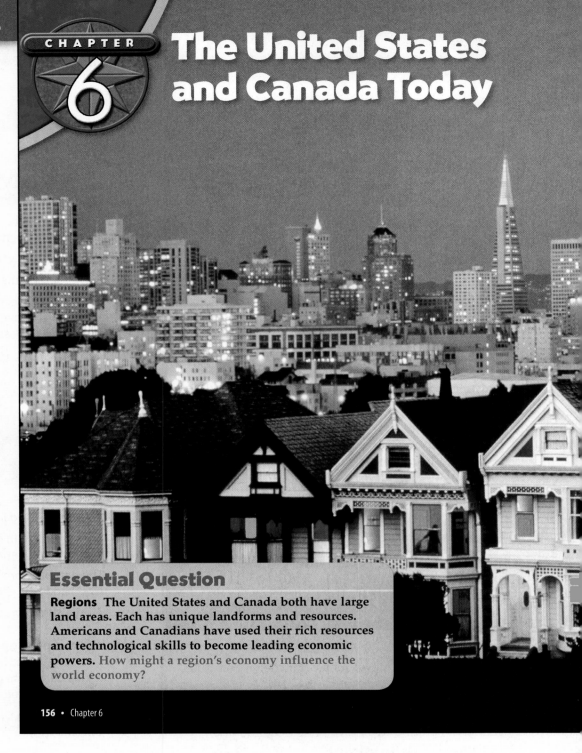

CHAPTER 6

The United States and Canada Today

Essential Question

Regions The United States and Canada both have large land areas. Each has unique landforms and resources. Americans and Canadians have used their rich resources and technological skills to become leading economic powers. How might a region's economy influence the world economy?

Teach

The BIG Ideas *As you begin teaching each section, use these questions and activities to help students focus on the Big Ideas.*

Section 

Living in the United States and Canada Today Ask: What region of the country do we live in? How would you describe it to someone from another place? *(Answers will vary; students may describe climate, culture, geographic features, or economic elements.)* Tell students that in Section 1, they are going to learn about the different economic regions of the United States and Canada and what makes each country distinctive. **OL**

Section 

Issues and Challenges Ask: What are some examples of actions Americans take that affect our neighbors? What are some actions our neighbors take that have an effect on us? *(Answers may include*

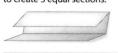

San Francisco, California

Section 1: Living in the United States and Canada Today

BIG IDEA Places reflect the relationship between humans and the physical environment. Both the United States and Canada are often divided into economic regions. These regions are based on similar resources and climates. People in each region have developed distinctive ways of life based on the different physical characteristics of their area.

Section 2: Issues and Challenges

BIG IDEA Cooperation and conflict among people have an effect on the Earth's surface. The United States and Canada are peaceful neighbors, sharing the longest undefended border in the world. Landforms and weather patterns do not stop at the border, however, and environmental actions by one country can affect the other.

FOLDABLES™ Study Organizer

Organizing Information Make this Foldable to help you organize information about the economic regions and issues related to the United States and Canada.

Step 1 Fold an 11x17 piece of paper lengthwise to create 3 equal sections.

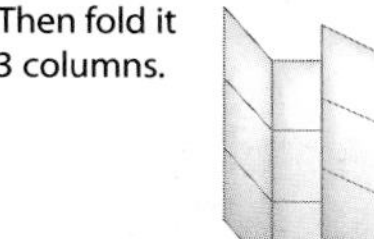

Step 2 Then fold it to form 3 columns.

Step 3 Label your Foldable as shown.

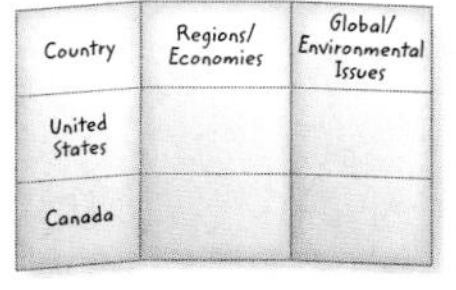

Country
Regions/ Economies
Global/ Environmental Issues
United States
Canada

Reading and Writing As you read the chapter, take notes in the correct area of your Foldable. Use your notes to write the script of a short newscast describing the economies of the United States and Canada today.

To preview Chapter 6, go to glencoe.com.

Previewing the Region

If you have not already done so, engage students in the Regional Atlas and chart activities to help them become familiar with the general content of the region.

Dinah Zike's Foldables

Purpose This Foldable helps students organize information about economic regions and issues in the United States and Canada. Students should record information from their reading in the appropriate column. Completed Foldables can be used to create a newscast about the economies of the United States and Canada, as well as prepare for assessment. OL

More Foldables activities for this chapter can be found in *Dinah Zike's Reading and Study Skills Foldables* ancillary.

Social Studies ONLINE

Introduce students to chapter content and key terms by having them access the Chapter Overview at glencoe.com.

actions that Americans take in economic, environmental, legal, social, and political spheres.) Tell students that in Section 2, they will learn how the United States and Canada trade with countries around the world. Students also will read about the environmental challenges facing the region. OL

Focus

Bellringer

Daily Focus Transparency 6-1

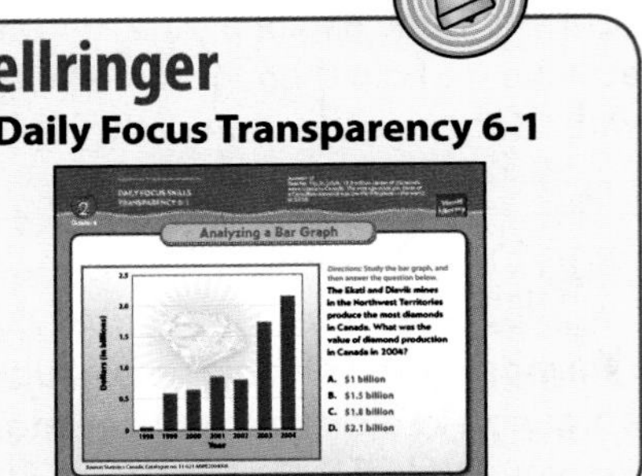

Guide to Reading

Answers to Graphic:

Answers may include:
Northeast: few mineral resources and poor soil; focuses on business
Midwest: rich soil for farming; manufacturing grew up in 1800s, but has since fallen off
South: formerly relied on agriculture; now manufacturing and oil are strong
Interior West: mining, ranching, lumber have been strong; information technology growing
Pacific: rich in natural resources; home to many industries

Section Spotlight Video

To learn more about living in the United States and Canada today, have students watch the Section Spotlight Video.

Resource Manager

Guide to Reading

BIG Idea

Places reflect the relationship between humans and the physical environment.

Content Vocabulary

- free market *(p. 159)*
- profit *(p. 159)*
- stock *(p. 159)*
- biotechnology *(p. 159)*
- newsprint *(p. 162)*

Academic Vocabulary

- guarantee *(p. 159)*
- media *(p. 159)*
- reluctant *(p. 162)*

Reading Strategy

Categorizing Information Use a diagram like the one below to list the economic regions in the United States and provide several key facts about each.

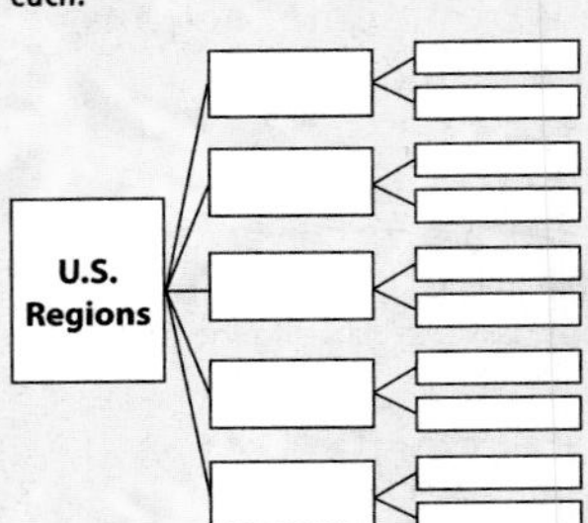

SECTION 1

Living in the United States and Canada Today

Picture This "The doctor will see you now." Well, almost. This doctor of the future is actually a robot. It allows doctors who may be miles away to talk to patients, inspect wounds, and read charts through the use of a video camera and screen. A computer and a joystick allow the doctor to move through the hospital and visit patients. The robots have been developed for hospitals that are looking for ways to reduce expenses. Read Section 1 to find out more about other industries that shape the United States and Canada.

▼ A new type of doctor

R Reading Strategies	C Critical Thinking	D Differentiated Instruction	W Writing Support	S Skill Practice
Teacher Edition • Academic Vocab., p. 159 • Monitoring, p. 162 **Additional Resources** • Guid. Read., URB p. 85 • Cont. Vocab., URB p. 87 • Ac. Vocab., URB p. 89 • Read. Ess., p. 40	**Teacher Edition** • Analyzing Info., p. 160 **Additional Resources** • Authentic Assess., p. 6 • Quizzes and Tests, p. 61	**Teacher Edition** • Verbal/Linguistic, p. 159 • Adv. Learners, p. 161 **Additional Resources** • Diff. Instr., URB p. 91 • Reteach., URB p. 103 • School-to-Home Conn., URB p. 105 • Interactive Geography, p. 9	**Teacher Edition** • Personal Writing, p. 161 **Additional Resources** • Writing Skills, URB p. 101	**Teacher Edition** • Using Geo. Skills, p. 161 **Additional Resources** • Read. Skills, URB p. 25 • Chart, Graph, and Map Skills, URB p. 93 • Speak./Listen. Skills, URB p. 97 • Daily Focus Trans. 6-1 • Regional Atlas, URB pp. 1–7

Economic Regions

Main Idea **The United States can be organized into economic regions.**

Geography and You Do you live in an area with many office buildings, factories, or farms? Read to discover why economic regions have developed.

Geographers group states together into five economic regions. These regions, and those of Canada, are shown in **Figure 1** on the next page. All of these regions are linked by the country's free market economy.

The Free Market Economy

In a **free market** economy, people are free to buy, sell, and produce whatever they want, with limited government involvement. They also can work wherever they want. A free market economy has two key groups: business owners and consumers. Business owners produce the products they think will make the most **profits,** or the most money after business expenses are paid. Consumers shop for the best products at the lowest prices.

People also take part in a free market economy by investing in businesses. People can buy **stock,** which represents part ownership in a company. When a company succeeds, it often pays some of its profits to the people who own its stock. Investing in stock involves risk, however. If the business fails, the stock becomes worthless. R Consumers can also save their money in a bank, which is safer than buying stock. Because of government **guarantees,** or promises, savers have some of their money protected should a bank fail or go out of business. Although savings accounts are better protected, stocks provide a greater chance for high financial payoff.

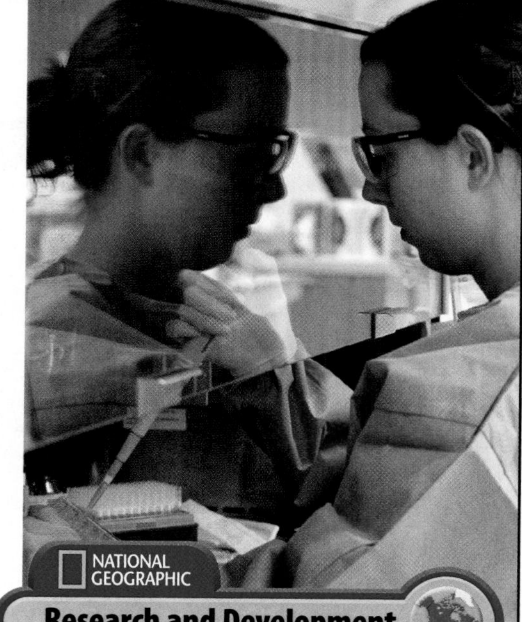

Research and Development

In Boston, biotechnology scientists study cells and how they respond to treatment. ***Regions*** **Why has the Northeast focused on business?**

A free market economy allows people to produce what they want. Resources are needed to produce a good or service, but some resources in a region are more available than others. As a result, economic regions have developed that specialize in producing products using their available resources.

The Northeast

The Northeast is made up of several large urban areas. Among them are New York City, the country's most populous city, and Boston, Massachusetts. With few mineral resources and poor soil for farming in many areas, the economic focus of the Northeast has been on business and trade. New York City has many financial and **media,** or communications, companies. Boston is an important center for **biotechnology** research. D Biotechnology is the study of cells to find ways of improving health.

Teach

R Reading Strategy

Academic Vocabulary **Ask:** **In what way does owning stock in a company represent a possible financial benefit or a possible financial loss?** *(If the company does well, stock owners will benefit by getting a share of the profits; if the business fails, the stock will be worthless and the owners will lose money.)* **AL**

D Differentiated Instruction

Verbal/Linguistic Ask students to identify the prefix at the beginning of the term *biotechnology*. *(bio-)* **Ask:** **What does *bio-* mean?** *(life)* **How does this word contain the idea of "life"?** *(Biotechnology is the science of studying the smallest unit of life—cells.)* **What other words contain this prefix?** *(Possible answers: biology, biography, bionic, autobiography, biopsy, biofeedback, biosphere)* Have students explain how each word incorporates the idea of "life." **OL**

Caption Answer:
It has few mineral resources and poor soil for farming.

Hands-On Chapter Project
Step 1

Creating Cartoons About the Global Economy

Step 1: Choosing a Topic Pairs of students will consider how the economy of the United States or Canada influences the world economy and then create a cartoon that expresses their ideas on the subject.

Essential Question How might a region's economy influence the world economy?

Directions Pair students and have them read the chapter and conduct research to identify ways that the economies of the United States and Canada influence the global economy. Tell students that they will be using their research to create a cartoon about the influence of the United States and Canada on the world economy. When students have finished their research, have them review their notes and choose an example of the region's impact on the global economy to represent visually.

Summarizing Have student pairs write one or two sentences that summarize the main idea or purpose of their cartoon. Review students' cartoon ideas, and help them narrow or fine-tune them as needed. **OL**

(Chapter Project continued in Section 2)

C Critical Thinking

Analyzing Information Ask: Based on information in the text and on the map, how would you grade each region of the United States (A–F), based on its economic future? *(Grades will vary, but students may rate the Midwest lower than the other regions.)* Have students discuss the reasons for their ratings. **AL**

Map Skills

Answers:

1. Alaska, Hawaii, Washington, Oregon, and California
2. the Atlantic Provinces

NATIONAL GEOGRAPHIC Maps In MOtion See StudentWorks™ Plus or glencoe.com.

Figure 1 United States and Canada: Regions

Canada: Atlantic Provinces; Central and Eastern; West; North

United States: Northeast; South; Midwest; Interior West; Pacific

0 600 kilometers / 0 600 miles — Azimuthal Equal-Area projection

PACIFIC OCEAN — ATLANTIC OCEAN — ARCTIC CIRCLE

Inset: PACIFIC OCEAN, 160°W, 155°W, 20°N; 0 200 kilometers / 0 200 miles — Azimuthal Equal-Area projection

C

Map Skills

1. **Regions** Which states make up the Pacific region?
2. **Regions** Which of Canada's regions includes the least territory?

The Midwest

The Midwest's rich soil enables farmers to grow crops such as corn, wheat, and soybeans. Mineral resources found here include iron ore, coal, lead, and zinc. Beginning in the 1800s, manufacturing developed in the Midwest. Towns like Cleveland and Detroit made steel and automobiles. Over time, however, the area's factories grew outdated. Many closed down, and thousands lost their jobs.

The South

With its rich soils, the South relied on agriculture. In recent decades the South has changed rapidly. The area now has expanding cities, growing industries, and diverse populations. Workers in cities such as Houston, Dallas, and Atlanta make textiles, electrical equipment, computers, and airplane parts. Texas, Louisiana, and Alabama produce oil and related products. In Florida, tourism and trade are major activities.

The Interior West

The Interior West has magnificent scenery and outdoor recreation that attracts many people. Although the region is dry, irrigation allows for some agriculture. For many decades, mining, ranching, and lumbering were the Interior West's main economic activities. In recent years, other parts of the economy have grown rapidly. The cities of Denver and Salt Lake City have growing information technology industries. Tourism and service industries are important to Albuquerque and Phoenix.

Differentiated Instruction

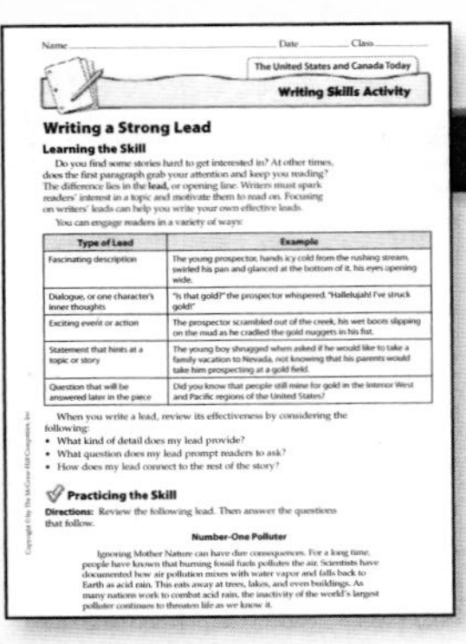
The United States and Canada Today — Writing Skills Activity

Writing a Strong Lead

Learning the Skill

Practicing the Skill

Number-One Polluter

Writing Skills Activity, URB pp. 101–102

Writing a Strong Lead

Objective: To understand the importance of writing a strong lead in engaging readers

Focus: Define and discuss with students the purpose of a lead.

Teach: Work with students to identify types of leads and examine effective examples.

Assess: Have students write two interesting leads for the same article.

Close: Ask students to critique each other's leads.

Differentiated Instruction Strategies

BL Have students work with a partner to write a "question" lead for each passage in the activity.

AL Ask students to share examples of weak leads from print media and to replace them with more effective leads.

ELL Have pairs find examples of strong leads and read them aloud to the class.

The Pacific

Fruits and vegetables are important crops in the fertile valleys of California, Oregon, and Washington. Sugarcane, pineapples, and coffee grow in the rich volcanic soil of Hawaii. Fish, timber, and mineral resources are important in the Pacific area as well. California has gold, lead, and copper, and Alaska has vast reserves of oil.

Many industries thrive in the Pacific area. Workers in California and Washington build airplanes and develop computer software. The city of Los Angeles is the world center of the movie industry. The area's booming economy draws many newcomers. California, the nation's most populous state, has wide ethnic diversity. Nearly half of its people are Latino or Asian American.

Reading Check **Summarizing** How has the south's economy changed?

▲ This parade in Los Angeles, California, celebrates the participants' Latino heritage. ***Movement*** **Why are people drawn to the Pacific region?**

Regions of Canada

Main Idea **With a few exceptions, Canada's economic regions are similar to those in the United States.**

Geography and You Have you worked hard to build or make something? Did you feel a sense of accomplishment when you finished? Read to learn how Canadians have worked to build their economy despite geographic obstacles.

Like the United States, Canada consists of different economic regions. It also has a free market economy with limited government involvement. Canada's government, however, plays a more direct role in providing services. Unlike the United States, Canada's national and provincial governments provide health care for citizens. The government also regulates broadcasting, transport, and power companies.

Atlantic Provinces

Fishing was for many years a major industry in the Atlantic Provinces of Newfoundland and Labrador, Nova Scotia, Prince Edward Island, and New Brunswick. Overfishing, however, has weakened the industry. Today most people in the area hold jobs in manufacturing, mining, and tourism. The city of Halifax, in Nova Scotia, is a major shipping center in the region.

Central and Eastern Region

Canada's Central and Eastern Region includes the large provinces of Quebec and Ontario. The paper industry is important in Quebec, as is the creation of hydroelectric power. Montreal, on the St. Lawrence River, is a major port and leading financial and industrial center. Many in Quebec's largely French-speaking population would like the province to separate from Canada.

W Writing Support

Personal Writing Have students write a paragraph responding to these questions: If you were starting a business, in which region of the United States would you choose to start it? Why? **OL**

S Skill Practice

Using Geography Skills **Ask:** **Why do you think that many people of Latino heritage live in California?** *(Answers may highlight the shared border or the state's strong economy.)* **OL**

D Differentiated Instruction

Advanced Learners **Ask:** **Do you think the United States should create a national health care system? Why?** *(Answers will vary.)* **AL**

Reading Check **Answer:** It relies less on agriculture and now has expanding cities, growing industries, and diverse populations.

Caption Answer:
the region's booming economy

Leveled Activities

BL **Reteaching Activity, URB p. 103**

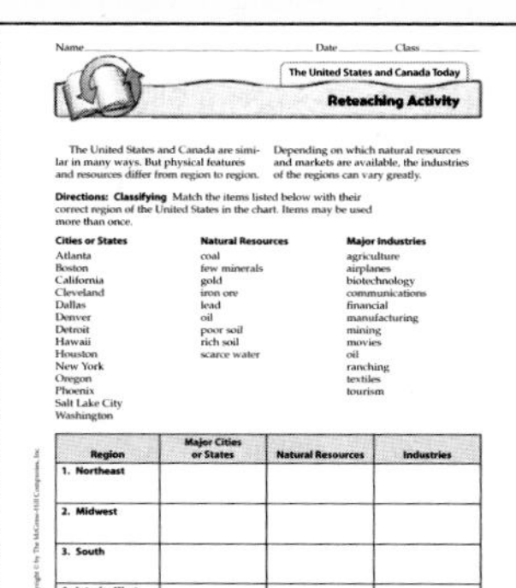
The United States and Canada Today
Reteaching Activity

OL **Interactive Geography Activity, p. 9**

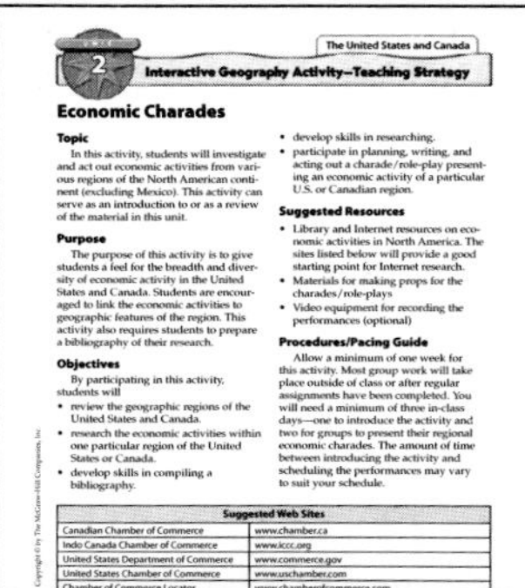
Interactive Geography Activity—Teaching Strategy
Economic Charades

AL **Chart, Graph, and Map Skills Activity, URB p. 93**

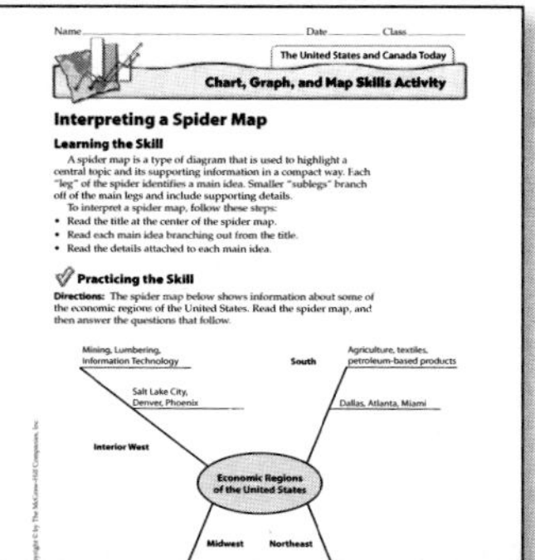
Chart, Graph, and Map Skills Activity
Interpreting a Spider Map

ELL **School-to-Home Connection, URB p. 105**

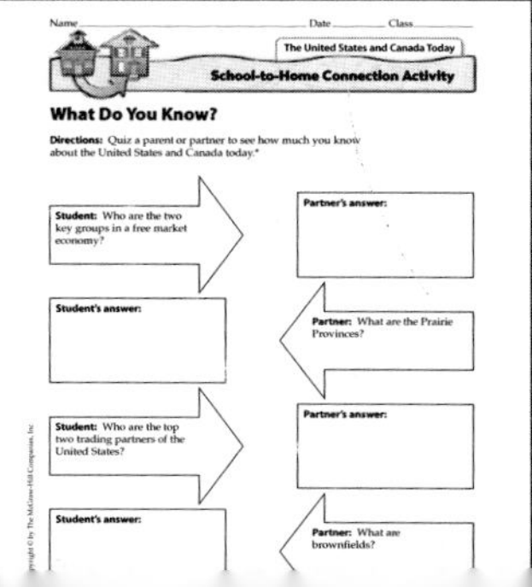
School-to-Home Connection Activity
What Do You Know?

R Reading Strategy

Monitoring After students finish reading the section, have them monitor their comprehension by writing one fact about each of Canada's economic regions. Then have them exchange facts with a partner and identify the region that each fact describes. OL

Reading Check **Answer:** It has made businesses reluctant to invest in Quebec.

Assess

Social Studies ONLINE
Study Central™ provides summaries, interactive games, and online graphic organizers to help students review content.

Close

Synthesizing Have students list ways that the economies of different U.S. and Canadian regions reflect geographic factors. OL

Because of the political and economic uncertainty this creates, many outside businesses have been **reluctant,** or hesitant, to invest in Quebec's economy.

Ontario has the largest population and greatest wealth of Canada's provinces. It is a major agricultural, manufacturing, forestry, and mining center. Ontario's capital, Toronto, is Canada's largest city and a major center of finance and business. Because of recent immigration, Toronto is now home to people from about 170 countries.

The West

Farming and ranching are major economic activities in the provinces of Manitoba, Saskatchewan, and Alberta. This area produces large amounts of wheat for export and contains some of the world's largest reserves of oil and natural gas.

The province of British Columbia has extensive forests. The forests help make Canada the world's largest producer of **newsprint,** the type of paper used for printing newspapers. Mining, fishing, and tourism also support British Columbia's economy. The city of Vancouver, its capital, is Canada's main Pacific port.

The North

R Canada's vast north covers about one-third of the country. This area includes the Yukon Territory, the Northwest Territories, and Nunavut. Many of the 25,000 people in this area are indigenous (ihn·DIH·juh·nuhs) peoples. The main resources in the North are minerals such as gold and diamonds.

Reading Check **Explaining** How has political uncertainty affected Quebec's economy?

Section Review

Social Studies ONLINE
Study Central™ To review this section, go to glencoe.com.

Vocabulary

1. **Explain** the significance of:
   a. free market
   b. profit
   c. stock
   d. biotechnology
   e. newsprint

Main Ideas

2. **Analyzing** Describe the basic principles of a free market economy.
3. **Summarizing** Use a chart like the one below to list important facts about the economies of three regions of Canada, and identify a physical characteristic of the region that relates to that fact.

Economic Fact	Physical Characteristic
1.	1.
2.	2.
3.	3.

Critical Thinking

4. **BIG Idea** What economic activities in the Interior West of the United States are related to the area's natural resources?
5. **Comparing and Contrasting** Compare and contrast the Northeast region of the United States and the Atlantic Provinces of Canada.
6. **Challenge** Which region of the United States do you think has undergone the greatest economic change? Why?

Writing About Geography

7. **Descriptive Writing** Create a map that shows the economic regions of either the United States or Canada. Write a paragraph for each region describing the economy and people of that region.

Answers

1. Definitions for the vocabulary words are found in the section and the Glossary.
2. People are free to buy, sell, and produce whatever they want, with limited government involvement; people also can work wherever they want.
3. Possible answers: **Economic Fact:** (1) fishing once important (2) hydroelectric power (3) largest producer of newsprint; **Physical Characteristic:** (1) Atlantic Provinces on Atlantic Ocean (2) Central and Eastern region includes St. Lawrence River (3) large forests in West
4. mining, ranching, lumbering, tourism
5. The Northeast region of the United States and the Atlantic Provinces of Canada are located next to each other on the Atlantic Ocean. Trade is important in both regions. However, the Northeast has several large urban areas, where the economic focus is on business, including financial and media companies; the Atlantic Provinces have smaller cities, and manufacturing, mining, and tourism are important economic activities.
6. Possible answers: the Midwest, because manufacturing was once strong, but many factories have now closed; the South, because it has changed from a largely agricultural to an industrial area
7. Students' maps should include all of the economic regions of the United States or Canada; students' paragraphs should include key information about the economy and people of each region.

TIME PERSPECTIVES

EXPLORING WORLD ISSUES

PROTECTING AMERICA FROM DISASTER

From terrorist attacks to hurricanes, the United States has faced a variety of deadly disasters. Will it be ready for the next crisis?

A victim of Hurricane Katrina is evacuated by helicopter.

Four years after the terrorist attacks of September 11, 2001, the United States was struck by three powerful hurricanes—Katrina, Rita, and Wilma. The massive storms brought a flood of despair as they tore through the U.S. Gulf Coast region. The hurricanes' strong winds and storm surges left death, destruction, and economic ruin in their paths.

As the government struggled to respond, thousands of survivors were left stranded. Many Americans wondered if the country had been too focused on preventing terrorist attacks and questioned whether officials had failed to plan for other types of disasters. People were also worried that the U.S. would be unprepared when the next catastrophe struck.

AP PHOTO

TIME PERSPECTIVES

Focus

Introducing TIME Perspectives

Ask students to share some of their recollections of national disasters, such as September 11, 2001, and Hurricane Katrina. **Ask:**

- **Where were you when you first heard about these events?**
- **What were your first reactions?**
- **How did pictures and T.V. coverage of the events affect your impressions?**
- **Did your impressions of the events change over time?** **OL**

FYI

The Web site of the U.S. Department of Homeland Security describes the department's programs. Students can find the site at www.dhs.gov/index.shtm.

Use the **TIME Perspectives: Exploring World Issues Teacher Guide and Student Activities,** pages 5–8, to reinforce and extend the concepts in "Protecting America From Disaster."

Additional Support

Background

Protecting the Nation President George W. Bush announced the creation of a Department of Homeland Security on September 20, 2001, following the September 11 terrorist attacks on the United States. The idea for such a department was not new. Discussion and examination of how best to protect the nation from terrorism had already been going on for several years. In fact, in February 2001, a federal commission established by the Department of Defense in 1998 to study national security needs had recommended creating a National Homeland Security Agency that would bring together such government agencies as the U.S. Border Patrol, the Coast Guard, the U.S. Customs Service, and the Federal Emergency Management Agency, or FEMA. FEMA itself represents an earlier effort to centralize emergency response. It was created in 1979 by the executive order of President Jimmy Carter to bring together various federal emergency agencies.

C1 Critical Thinking

Drawing Conclusions Ask: Why do you think that 9/11 and the aftermath of Katrina stunned the country? *(**9/11:** Many students will cite the unexpectedness of 9/11, the sheer scale of the destruction, and the knowledge that the United States was so despised by some people of the world. **Katrina:** Students may point out that the poor of New Orleans had been invisible until Katrina, that New Orleans was a beloved city, and that the government response was ineffective.)* OL

C2 Critical Thinking

Determining Cause and Effect Ask: Why did Hurricane Katrina get stronger after it hit southern Florida? *(It gained strength from the warm waters of the Gulf of Mexico.)* OL

INTERPRETING DIAGRAMS

Answer:

Because so much of the city is below sea level, keeping the levees in good working order is critical.

Additional Support

TIME PERSPECTIVES EXPLORING WORLD ISSUES

BETH DIXSON

Smoke poured from the World Trade Center's two towers after terrorists flew airplanes into them.

DISASTER STRIKES AMERICA

In recent years, the United States has been deeply affected by both human-made and natural disasters. On September 11, 2001, or "**9/11**," as the terrible events of that day are called, terrorists hijacked a jet airliner and crashed it into the north tower of the World Trade Center in New York City at 8:46 A.M. A second hijacked plane hit the south tower at 9:03 A.M. About an hour later, the south tower collapsed, crumbling to the ground.

At 9:43 A.M. outside Washington, D.C., a third hijacked plane crashed into the Pentagon, the headquarters of the U.S. military. About 20 minutes later, a fourth airliner went down in a field near Shanksville, Pennsylvania. Its target, which it never reached, might have been the White House or the U.S. Capitol. Back in New York City, the north tower of the World Trade Center collapsed at 10:28 A.M. In less than two hours, 19 terrorists had murdered thousands of people.

Crisis Along the Coast

C1 The 9/11 attacks stunned the country. Nearly four years later, a series of monster hurricanes would do the same. On August 29, 2005, Hurricane Katrina slammed into the Gulf Coast. The storm packed 145-mile-per-hour winds that pushed powerful storm surges, or walls of water, inland from the Gulf of Mexico.

C2 Katrina hit southern Florida first. Then, after strengthening while over the warm waters of the Gulf of Mexico, the hurricane struck Biloxi and Gulfport in Mississippi with deadly force. Homes, businesses, and entire towns were destroyed. The strong winds knocked down electrical lines. Power was lost across the Southeast, leaving millions without electricity.

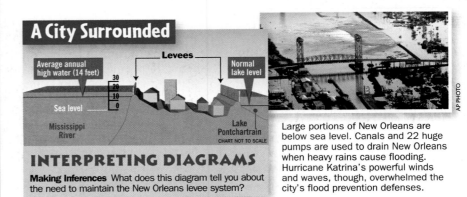

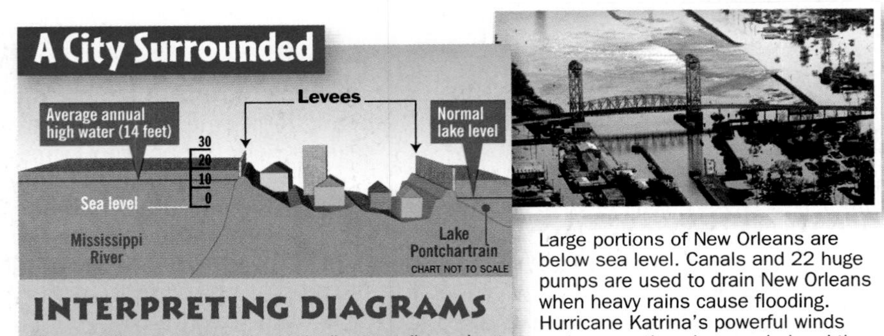

INTERPRETING DIAGRAMS

Making Inferences What does this diagram tell you about the need to maintain the New Orleans levee system?

Large portions of New Orleans are below sea level. Canals and 22 huge pumps are used to drain New Orleans when heavy rains cause flooding. Hurricane Katrina's powerful winds and waves, though, overwhelmed the city's flood prevention defenses.

Activity: Interdisciplinary Connection

Science Ask: Are levees an effective method of flood control? *(Students may note that levees can help control flooding but also can be overwhelmed by floodwaters in certain circumstances.)* Have interested students research levee systems and present their findings in an oral presentation. Tell students to look for answers to these questions during their research: *What is a natural levee? Why do people build levees? Where are levees used in the United States? Where else in the world are levees used? How do levees help control flooding? When are they ineffective?* Encourage students to create visuals or a model to illustrate how a levee works and how it can fail. OL

Survivors of Hurricane Katrina climbed to rooftops waiting to be rescued.

Young and old survivors of Hurricane Katrina hoped relief would come.

A roof was thrown onto the sidewalk by Hurricane Wilma's powerful winds.

TIME PERSPECTIVES

Turmoil in New Orleans

Although New Orleans avoided a direct hit from Katrina, the storm punched four holes into the **levees**, or flood walls, that protect New Orleans from the sea. Soon, 80 percent of the city was under water.

Chaos followed. Officials called for all residents to leave the city. Across the city, thousands waited to be taken to safety. More than 20,000 people took shelter from the storm in New Orleans's Superdome. Conditions inside the stadium, however, had become unbearable as supplies of food and water ran out. People soon had to be evacuated. **R**

The government was slow to respond with help. Evacuation plans were confusing, and coordination between local and national officials was poor. New Orleans would be a disaster area for months.

Soon after Katrina struck, another powerful storm, Hurricane Rita, ripped along the Gulf Coast with winds that reached 120 miles (193 km) per hour. More than 3 million people evacuated their homes. Then, in late October, Hurricane Wilma slammed into southwest Florida, leaving 6 million people without electricity.

A Stormy Economy

The devastation created by these deadly hurricanes affected Americans everywhere. Much of the country's oil and natural gas comes from the Gulf Coast. Oil platforms, refineries, and pipelines were damaged or shut down by Katrina. President George W. Bush authorized the release of oil from the nation's emergency reserve to help meet the country's energy demand.

Exports, or products sold outside the country, were affected too. Hundreds of barges that carried crops and products through the port of New Orleans to other countries sat backed up on the Mississippi River. Restoring the region would be costly. Experts estimated that the total price tag to rebuild the Gulf Coast would reach $200 billion. **D**

Planning for the Future

Many Americans thought all levels of government—city, state, and federal—were unprepared to protect Gulf Coast residents. President Bush said, "Americans have every right to expect a more effective response in a time of emergency." Determining how to keep citizens safe will take time and hard work, but it is vital to the country's well-being.

EXPLORING THE ISSUE

1. **Understanding Cause and Effect** How did the 2005 hurricane season affect the broader U.S. economy?
2. **Interpreting Points of View** Do Americans have a right to expect the government to provide an "effective response" to emergencies? Why or why not?

R Reading Strategy

Making Connections **Ask:** **What challenges might your community face if it were evacuated because of a disaster like Katrina?** *(Answers will vary; students should be aware that not all residents would find it easy to leave.)* **OL**

This **Reading Skill** (Making Connections) was introduced in this unit.

D Differentiated Instruction

Interpersonal Organize students into small groups to discuss the following question: *Should the city of New Orleans be rebuilt just as it was before Katrina? Why or why not?* Have groups present their thoughts in a class discussion. **OL**

EXPLORING THE ISSUE

Answers:

1. Oil and gas production were curtailed because of storm damage, and important river freight traffic slowed.
2. Answers will vary; many students may argue that only the government is big enough to address disasters on the scale of 9/11 or Katrina.

Differentiated Instruction

Interpreting Bar Graphs

TIME Perspectives: Exploring World Issues Workbook, p. 7

Interpreting Bar Graphs

Objective: To interpret bar graphs showing survey results related to Hurricane Katrina

Focus: Invite students to discuss what they know about Hurricane Katrina.

Teach: Discuss with students the subject and parts of each graph.

Assess: Have students answer the questions by analyzing the graphs.

Close: Help students make generalizations based on the data.

Differentiated Instruction Strategies

BL Have students use the graph data to write three sentences beginning *The survey shows that* ______.

AL Ask each student to write a short essay based on the graph data.

ELL Have small groups survey the class using the same questions and responses and then present the results orally.

C Critical Thinking

Identifying Central Issues Ask: Do you think that the federal or local government should be more responsible for addressing a disaster like Hurricane Katrina? Why? *(Answers will vary; some students may claim that the responsibility should be shared equally.)* **OL**

D Differentiated Instruction

Auditory/Musical Have students research and prepare a sampling of some of the musicians who performed in benefit concerts for the rebuilding of New Orleans. **OL**

EXPLORING THE ISSUE

Answers:

1. Students may point out that combating terrorism requires a wide-scale, broad approach, while single natural disasters such as Katrina must be addressed on an individual basis.
2. Answers will vary but should show awareness of the complexity of the problems.

Additional Support

TIME PERSPECTIVES

AMERICA REACTS TO CATASTROPHES

The 2001 terrorist attacks and the 2005 hurricane season shocked many Americans. The tragic events also forced government leaders to take action. Finding new ways to protect the United States became a top priority.

Following 9/11, President George W. Bush signed a bill that created the **Department of Homeland Security**. The new department combined the duties and responsibilities of 22 different agencies. This included the Coast Guard and the **Federal Emergency Management Agency** (FEMA), the agency that responds to the nation's emergencies.

Lawmakers hoped the reorganization would improve communication between government agencies and help prevent future attacks. While some people thought the government changes were an effective response to terrorism, they were not useful for dealing with other types of disasters.

A Massive Cleanup

C The aftermath of Hurricane Katrina made it clear that better coordination between local and national officials was required for disaster relief. The government was harshly criticized for its slow first response to Hurricane Katrina.

Congress approved $62 billion for relief work. These funds were used to find housing and provide health care for survivors. In the months after the hurricanes struck, local leaders and federal agencies began to reconstruct the Gulf Coast. By December 2005, the president pledged another $3.1 billion to repair New Orleans's levee system.

D The task of rebuilding New Orleans and other areas of the Gulf Coast will take many years. As the government examines the results of these catastrophes, it hopes to make America safe from future disasters.

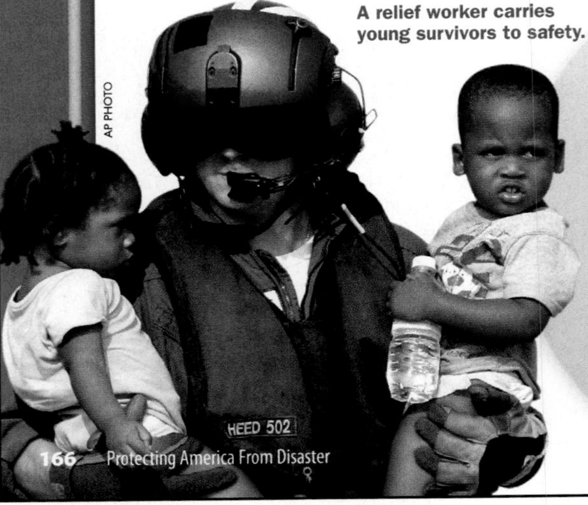

AP PHOTO

A relief worker carries young survivors to safety.

EXPLORING THE ISSUE

1. **Making Inferences** How might the Department of Homeland Security help officials fight terrorism? In what ways might the large department be ineffective in fighting natural disasters?

2. **Problem Solving** What steps do you think the government should take to fight terrorism and other types of catastrophes?

Activity: Connecting With the United States

Identifying Ask: Do you know what agencies are included in the Department of Homeland Security? Divide the class into groups, and have each group research the structure of the Department of Homeland Security and the agencies it now includes. Tell the groups to use their findings to create an organizational chart that shows the following directorates of the department: Border and Transportation Security, Emergency Preparedness and Response, Science and Technology, Information Analysis and Infrastructure Protection; describes the general responsibilities of each; and lists the agencies under the umbrella of each. Students' charts also should include agencies in the department that are not part of a directorate. Then ask each student to select an agency and find out how it contributes to the protection of the United States. Have students share what they discover in a class discussion. **AL**

REVIEW AND ASSESS

UNDERSTANDING THE ISSUE

1 **Making Connections** How did Hurricane Katrina affect the country's oil supply?

2 **Writing to Inform** In a brief essay, explain how the nation is preparing for natural and human-made disasters.

3 **Writing to Persuade** Write a letter to the editor of a newspaper expressing your views about the government's response to Hurricane Katrina and its readiness for future disasters.

INTERNET RESEARCH ACTIVITIES

4 With your teacher's help, go to www.ready.gov. Explore one of the three main items on the Web site's home page. Write a short essay that explains what you learned about preparing for a terrorist attack.

5 Navigate to www.fema.gov/kids. Click through some of the Web site's links to learn more about FEMA, how it is organized, and what its responsibilities are. Summarize your findings in a short written report.

AP PHOTO

A survivor carries her belongings as she wades through water in New Orleans.

BEYOND THE CLASSROOM

6 **Research the impact of terrorism on nations such as Sri Lanka and Ireland.** How have these nations tried to prevent terrorist attacks? Describe these ways, and discuss as a class whether they would be effective in preventing terrorist attacks in the United States.

7 **Work in Groups.** Create and display posters that explain how to prepare for any disaster, including hurricanes and terrorist attacks.

After Hurricane Katrina, the Costly Recovery Plan

Congress approved $62.3 billion in Gulf Coast aid for FEMA (though the final relief tab could well top $200 billion). Here is how FEMA distributed some of the funds.

- **$23 billion** for temporary housing, health care, clothing, household costs
- **$8 billion** for search and rescue missions, roads and bridge safety, and adequate water
- **$3 billion** to the Defense Department for emergency repairs and evacuation
- **$5 billion** for FEMA to set up support and recovery work
- **$15 billion** for the Department of Homeland Security to monitor how relief aid was spent and distributed

Building Chart-Reading Skills

1. **Analyzing Data** How much money did FEMA give to search and rescue work and to keeping roads and bridges safe?
2. **Explaining** Why do you think most of the government relief funds were used to help Katrina survivors find housing, clothing, and health care?

TIME PERSPECTIVES

Review and Assess

Questions from **Understanding the Issue, Internet Research Activities,** and **Beyond the Classroom** may have more than one correct answer. Pick and choose the two or three activities that work best for your class.

Building Chart-Reading Skills

Answers:

1. $8 billion
2. There were many, many people who were homeless and had lost everything in the flooding; many displaced people were old and sick and in need of health care.

Close

Have small groups of students discuss this question: Do you think events like 9/11 and Katrina bring Americans closer together or drive them further apart? OL

Activity: Why It Matters

Evaluating Ask: How do the government's efforts to protect the nation affect you? *(Answers will vary depending on students' personal experiences and where they live.)* Use the question to elicit ideas and anecdotes from students about ways that they have been affected by measures taken by the government to protect Americans from different kinds of disasters. Ask students what natural disasters have happened or might happen where they live and what they would expect the government to do to help before, during, or after a catastrophic event. Close the activity by discussing the impact of natural disasters such as Hurricane Katrina and terrorist attacks, and why such events matter to everyone in the country. OL

Focus

Bellringer

Daily Focus Transparency 6-2

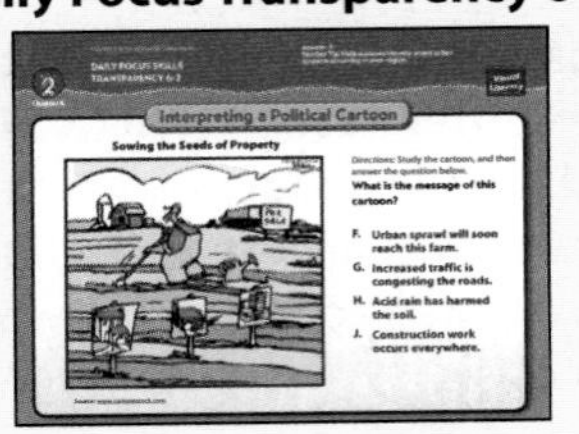

Guide to Reading

Answers to Graphic:

Answers may include:

I. The Region and the World
   A. Economic ties based on free market system
   B. U.S. and Canada work together to fight terrorism
II. Environmental Issues
   A. U.S. and Canada cooperate to end acid rain, fight global warming
   B. Other concerns include Great Lakes, brownfields, urban sprawl

Section Spotlight Video

To learn more about the issues and challenges facing the United States and Canada today, have students watch the Section Spotlight Video.

Resource Manager

R Reading Strategies	C Critical Thinking	D Differentiated Instruction	W Writing Support	S Skill Practice
Teacher Edition • Making Connections, p. 170 **Additional Resources** • Guid. Read., URB p. 86 • Cont. Vocab., URB p. 87 • Ac. Vocab., URB p. 89 • Read. Ess., p. 43	**Teacher Edition** • Pred. Consequences, p. 169 • Compare/Contrast, p. 170 • Det. Cause/Effect, p. 172 **Additional Resources** • Crit. Think., URB p. 95 • Geo. & Econ., URB p. 9 • Quizzes and Tests, p. 62	**Teacher Edition** • Special Ed., p. 169 **Additional Resources** • Env. Case Studies, URB p. 13	**Teacher Edition** • Personal Writing, p. 170 • Narrative Writing, p. 171 **Additional Resources** • Writing Skills, URB p. 101	**Teacher Edition** • Visual Literacy, p. 171 **Additional Resources** • Daily Focus Trans. 6-2 • Regional Atlas, URB pp. 1–7

Guide to Reading

BIG Idea

Cooperation and conflict among people have an effect on the Earth's surface.

Content Vocabulary
- trade deficit *(p. 169)*
- tariff *(p. 170)*
- trade surplus *(p. 170)*
- acid rain *(p. 171)*
- brownfield *(p. 172)*
- urban sprawl *(p. 172)*

Academic Vocabulary
- restrict *(p. 169)*
- community *(p. 172)*

Reading Strategy

Outlining Use a format like the one below to make an outline of the section. Write each main heading on a line with a Roman numeral, and list important facts below it.

I. First Main Heading
   A. Key Fact 1
   B. Key Fact 2
II. Second Main Heading
   A. Key Fact 1
   B. Key Fact 2

Section 2: Issues and Challenges

Picture This Long ago, ice canoeing was a way to deliver supplies across the icy Saint Lawrence River during winter. Ice canoes were small enough to dodge floating ice and light enough to carry over solid ice. Traveling between the river's islands was dangerous, difficult work, but it was necessary to carry vital items such as medicine and mail. Today, ice canoes are used for sport. Many Canadian teams compete in ice races at winter festivals. Learn more about Canada today in Section 2.

Ice canoe racing in Toronto, Canada

The Region and the World

Main Idea **The United States and Canada trade with countries throughout the world.**

Geography and You Think about all the trucks or trains you have seen carrying products to stores or to ports. Read to learn about our region's economic ties to the world.

Because of their large economies, the United States and Canada trade with many countries. In addition, the United States is one of the world's leading political and military powers.

Economic Ties

The free market system has helped the United States and Canada build productive economies. In fact, the United States has the world's largest economy and is a leader in world trade. The United States exports chemicals, farm products, and manufactured goods, as well as raw materials such as metals and cotton fiber. Canada sends many of the same goods overseas, as well as large amounts of seafood and timber products. Both countries also import many items from all around the world. **D**

In recent years, the United States and Canada have supported free trade. This means the removal of trade **restrictions,** or barriers, so that goods flow freely among countries. In 1994 the United States, Canada, and Mexico joined together in the North American Free Trade Agreement (NAFTA). They promised to take away most barriers to trade among the three countries. Canada now sends more than 80 percent of its exports to the United States and buys nearly 60 percent of its imports from it. Canada is the largest trading partner of the United States, and Mexico is the second largest. **C**

The United States depends on trade to supply most of its energy resources. As you may recall, the country uses nearly three times the amount of oil it produces. The United States must import additional oil from major suppliers such as Canada, Mexico, Venezuela, Saudi Arabia, Nigeria, and Angola.

Americans buy many additional products from other countries. In fact, the United States spends hundreds of billions of dollars more on imports than it earns from exports. The result is a massive **trade deficit.**

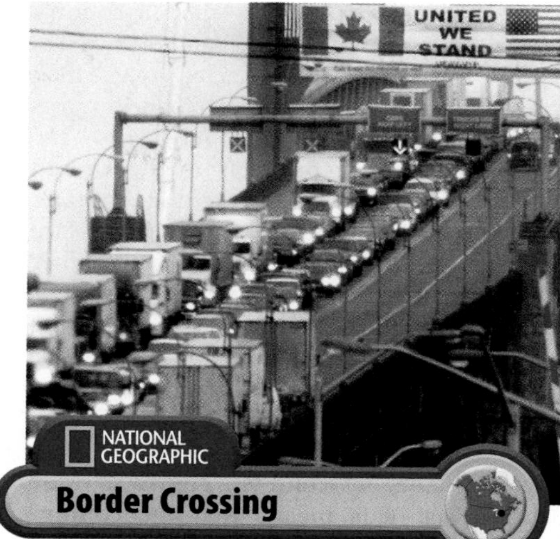

NATIONAL GEOGRAPHIC

Border Crossing

The Ambassador Bridge is the busiest international border crossing in North America. More than 10,000 trucks cross the bridge daily between Detroit, Michigan, and Windsor, Canada.
Regions **What did NAFTA establish?**

Student Web Activity Visit glencoe.com and complete the Chapter 6 Web Activity about U.S. trade.

Teach

D Differentiated Instruction

Special Education Have pairs of students make a two-column chart with the headings "U.S. Exports" and "Canadian Exports." Then have students draw or cut out an image to represent each type of export. **BL**

C Critical Thinking

Predicting Consequences **Ask:** **Do you think that trade among the United States, Canada, and Mexico will continue to be strong? Why or why not?** *(Students may predict that North American trade will continue to be strong because of NAFTA, the proximity of the three countries, and unrest in other parts of the world.)* **OL**

For additional practice on this activity (Predicting), see the **Skills Handbook**.

Caption Answer:
no trade barriers among the United States, Canada, and Mexico

Social Studies ONLINE
Objectives and answers to the Student Web Activity can be found at glencoe.com under the Web Activity Lesson Plan for this chapter.

Differentiated Instruction

Leveled Activities

BL **Guided Reading Activity, URB p. 86**

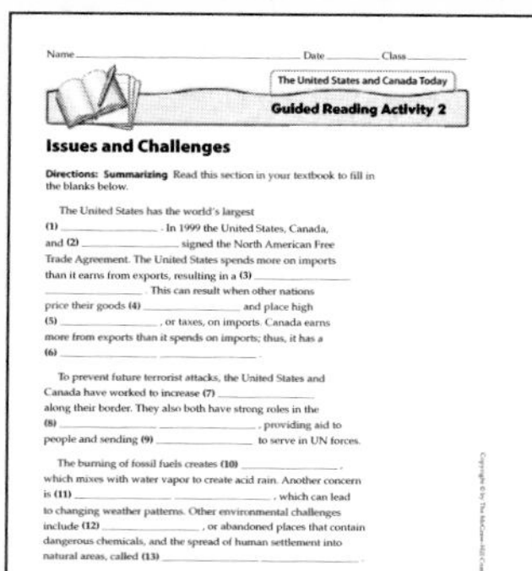

OL **Academic Vocabulary Activity, URB p. 89**

AL **Geography and Economics, URB p. 9**

ELL **Reading Essentials and Note-Taking Guide, p. 43**

R Reading Strategy

Making Connections Ask: Have you ever bought a foreign-made product that was cheaper than an American-made product? Why do you think that the foreign product was cheaper? *(Possible answers: cheaper labor, production, or material costs in the foreign country)* **OL**

C Critical Thinking

Comparing and Contrasting
Ask: What is the difference between a trade surplus and a trade deficit? *(A trade surplus occurs when a country earns more from exports than it spends on imports. A trade deficit is the opposite.)* **BL**

W Writing Support

Personal Writing Ask students to write about what they would do to improve world conditions if they could establish a similiar foundation. **OL**

CITIZENS IN ACTION

Possible Answer:
people living in developing countries; yes, as poor people lack resources and political power to improve their lives

A trade deficit occurs when a country spends more on imports than it earns from exports. A trade deficit that lasts over a long period can cause serious economic troubles for a country.

To sell their products in the United States, some nations set the prices of their goods very low. Also, some countries place high **tariffs,** or taxes, on imports in order to protect their own industries from foreign competition. These tariffs then raise the price of U.S. products and thus reduce the sale of the products abroad. Such practices hurt American companies and cost American workers their jobs.

Canada, by contrast, enjoys a **trade surplus**. This means that the country earns more from exports than it spends for imports. Canada's smaller population makes its energy needs less costly. Also, Canada's export earnings have been growing.

Global Terrorism

Since the beginning of the 2000s, the United States and Canada have joined other nations to deal with increasing terrorism and violence around the world. As you may recall, the world changed dramatically on September 11, 2001, when terrorists attacked sites in New York City and Washington, D.C. To prevent further terrorist attacks, the United States and Canada have worked to increase security along their long border. They have also participated in international efforts to stop terrorism.

TIME GLOBAL CITIZENS

NAMES: BILL AND MELINDA GATES

HOME COUNTRY: United States

ACHIEVEMENT: In 2005 the Bill and Melinda Gates Foundation gave more money away faster than anyone ever has. Bill Gates, the head of Microsoft, and his wife, Melinda, created the foundation that is now the world's largest charitable organization. About 60 percent of the foundation's grants go toward global efforts—such as fighting disease—in more than 100 countries. The rest is dedicated to improving people's lives in the U.S. The foundation is committed to giving away more than $9 billion, including more than $1 billion to U.S. high schools and libraries. Another $1 billion is used for college scholarships for African Americans.

Melinda and Bill Gates visit a health research center in Mozambique.

QUOTE: "I felt I had a role to give some voice to the voiceless."—Melinda Gates, referring to grants to developing countries

CHRIS CORDER/UPI PHOTO SERVICE/NEWSCOM; (INSET) COURTESY THE BILL AND MELINDA GATES FOUNDATION

CITIZENS IN ACTION Who are the "voiceless" that Melinda Gates refers to? Do they need champions such as the Gateses? Why or why not?

Hands-On Chapter Project Step 2

Creating Cartoons About the Global Economy

Step 2: Creating the Cartoon Student pairs will draw a cartoon that conveys a message about the influence of the United States or Canada on the world economy.

Directions Provide examples of editorial cartoons and discuss the point or message of each, noting how cartoons convey information. Direct student partners to discuss how they will represent their main idea in a cartoon. Then have pairs sketch an illustration that conveys their idea through figures, symbols, and captions.

Putting It Together Post the cartoons on a bulletin board, and allow time for students to view and interpret them. Then discuss each cartoon, with students offering interpretations and each pair answering questions about the elements and message of its cartoon. **OL**

(Chapter Project cont. on the Visual Summary page)

Guarding Against Terrorism

Since the 2001 terrorist attacks against New York City and Washington, D.C., new safeguards are in place to protect Americans. ***Place*** **How did the U.S. and Canada disagree over Iraq policy?**

Despite their generally close relations, the United States and Canada sometimes differ in their policies. In 2003 Canada opposed the U.S. decision to invade Iraq. Instead, it wanted the American government to continue seeking a peaceful solution through the United Nations (UN). The United Nations is the world organization that promotes cooperation among nations in settling disputes.

The United States and Canada both have strong roles in the United Nations. They provide much of the money that funds the organization. They also take part in UN agencies that provide aid to people in areas affected by war or natural disasters. The United States and especially Canada have sent soldiers to serve in UN forces that act as peacekeepers in troubled areas of the world.

Reading Check **Explaining** Why does the United States have a large trade deficit?

Environmental Issues

Main Idea **The United States and Canada face similar environmental issues.**

S

Geography and You Have you witnessed instances of air or water pollution in your area? Read to learn about challenges for the region's environment.

The United States and Canada face several environmental challenges. Because they are neighbors, some concerns are shared. Both countries have made progress in cleaning up their air and water. Still, pollution remains a problem.

Acid Rain and Climate Change

Americans and Canadians burn coal, oil, and natural gas to power their factories and run their cars. Burning these fossil fuels pollutes the air. The pollution also mixes with water vapor in the air to make **acid rain,** or rain containing high amounts of chemical pollutants. Acid rain damages trees and harms rivers, lakes, and the stone used in buildings. The United States and Canada have acted to reduce the amount of chemicals that are released into the air. They are particularly concerned about damage to some areas in the eastern parts of the region.

Many people in the United States and Canada also worry about global warming. Some scientists believe that global warming will lead to changing weather patterns. For example, a warmer climate could lead to drought conditions in some areas, or W it could melt the polar ice caps. Melting would raise sea levels, which would be a problem for low-lying areas like Florida.

To address the issue of global warming, Canada has passed laws to reduce the amount of fossil fuels that are burned.

S Skill Practice

Visual Literacy **Ask:** **What building is this man guarding? How do you know?** *(the U.S. Capitol in Washington; the dome and flags)* **Why do you think this building might have been chosen as one of the 9/11 targets?** *(Possible answer: Destroying it could have severely hurt the U.S. government.)* **OL**

W Writing Support

Narrative Writing Have students write a short story set 30 years in the future, describing the effects of global warming on a community, a family, or an individual. Before writing, have students map out the story's setting, characters, conflict, climax, and resolution. **AL**

Caption Answer:
Canada wanted the U.S. government to continue seeking a peaceful solution.

Reading Check **Answer:** It spends more on imports than it earns on exports.

Differentiated Instruction

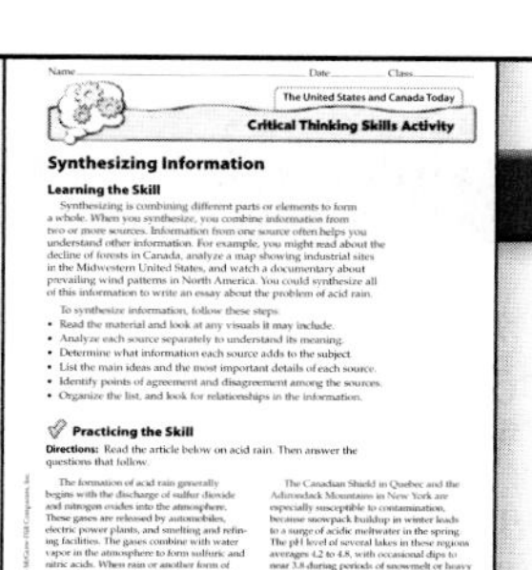
The United States and Canada Today
Critical Thinking Skills Activity
Synthesizing Information
Learning the Skill
Practicing the Skill

Critical Thinking Activity, URB pp. 95–96

Synthesizing Information

Objective: To combine information from different sources to reach a new understanding

Focus: Tell students that synthesizing is combining different parts or elements to form a whole.

Teach: Explain to students the steps involved in synthesizing.

Assess: Check that students have synthesized information from the article and diagram.

Close: Describe real-life situations in which synthesizing information is a useful skill.

Differentiated Instruction Strategies

- **BL** Explain to students how to read the pH scale step-by-step.
- **AL** Add a third source of information about acid rain, and have students synthesize information from all three sources.
- **ELL** Have students use a graphic organizer to illustrate the process of synthesizing information.

C Critical Thinking

Determining Cause and Effect Have student pairs create a chart showing the effects of urban sprawl. Encourage them to add effects that are not discussed in the text. *(loss of farmland and wilderness, greater traffic, more pollution, strain on water and other resources, loss of traditional farm lifestyles, tensions between farmers and new residents, higher prices for agricultural products, family farms giving way to housing developments)* OL

Reading Check **Answer:** Canada has passed laws to reduce fossil fuel use; the United States has funded research to find new energy sources.

Assess

Social Studies ONLINE
Study Central™ provides summaries, interactive games, and online graphic organizers to help students review content.

Close

Assessing Ask students if they think the United States and Canada are good neighbors. Have them provide support for their answers. OL

The United States has funded research to find new energy sources that are less harmful to the environment.

Pollution Issues

Changing climatic conditions and a rising demand for water have lowered water levels of the Great Lakes. Loss of water can cause a variety of problems. Lower lake levels decrease the amount of goods that can be shipped. Ships cannot carry extremely heavy loads into river channels or they might run aground. In addition, lower lake levels can harm fish populations. Tourism is also affected as water pulls back from the area's beaches. Government leaders of both countries have urged people to conserve water.

Brownfields are another challenge. **Brownfields** are places, such as old factories and gas stations, that have been abandoned and contain dangerous chemicals. These chemicals hinder any new development. Governments in the United States and Canada have given money to **communities,** or neighborhoods, for cleanup.

C **Urban sprawl,** or the spread of human settlement into natural areas, also has created difficulties. Urban growth leads to the loss of farmland and wilderness areas. The building of homes and roadways can also produce traffic jams and increase air pollution. Growing populations put strains on water and other resources as well. People in some areas that are growing rapidly want to slow the rate of growth. They fear that having too many people will destroy the wide-open spaces and magnificent scenery that attracted them.

Reading Check **Explaining** How have the United States and Canada dealt with the issue of global warming?

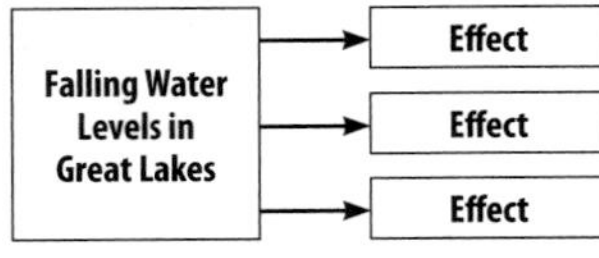

Section 2 Review

Social Studies ONLINE
Study Central™ To review this section, go to glencoe.com.

Vocabulary

1. **Explain** the significance of:
   a. trade deficit
   b. tariff
   c. trade surplus
   d. acid rain
   e. brownfield
   f. urban sprawl

Main Ideas

2. **Describing** Describe the trade relationship between the United States and Canada.
3. **Determining Cause and Effect** Use a diagram like the one below to list the effects of falling water levels in the Great Lakes.

Falling Water Levels in Great Lakes	Effect
	Effect
	Effect

Critical Thinking

4. **Making Generalizations** Why is the U.S. economy important to the rest of the world?
5. **BIG Idea** Should the United States and Canada cooperate to try to reduce the problem of acid rain? Explain.
6. **Challenge** How would you describe overall relations between the United States and Canada? Why?

Writing About Geography

7. **Using Your FOLDABLES** Use the notes in your Foldable to write a letter to a member of Congress explaining what you think should be done about the U.S. trade deficit.

Answers

1. Definitions for the vocabulary words are found in the section and the Glossary.
2. Canada is the largest trading partner of the United States.
3. Students' diagrams might include the following effects: decrease in amount of goods shipped on lakes; damage to fish populations; decrease in tourism.
4. The United States imports many items from around the world, spending more on imports than it earns from exports.
5. Possible answer: Yes, because both are causing acid rain, and it is affecting not just one country but the region as a whole.
6. Possible answer: Excellent; both have strong free market economies, are major trading partners of each other, and cooperate to solve problems affecting the region.
7. Students' letters should demonstrate an understanding of the U.S. trade deficit and offer a solution to the trade deficits based on logical reasoning.

Visual Summary

Free Market Economies

- The United States and Canada have free market economies that allow people to own businesses and earn profits.
- Producers and consumers decide what to produce, how much to produce, and for whom to produce.
- Governments play a limited role in free market economies.

Small business owner, Los Angeles, California

U.S. Regions

- The five economic regions of the United States are the Northeast, the Midwest, the South, the Interior West, and the Pacific.
- The South and the Interior West are growing rapidly in population and economic strength.
- The Northeast focuses on business. The Midwest is rebuilding its industries.
- The Pacific area has diverse economies and populations.

Canadian wheelchair athlete

Canadian Regions

- Canada's main economic regions are the Atlantic Provinces, the Central and Eastern Region, the West, and the North.
- The Atlantic Provinces suffer from the decline of the fishing industry.
- Many people in French-speaking Quebec want their province to be independent.
- Ontario is Canada's most populous and economically prosperous province.
- The West includes the grain-producing areas and the Pacific coastal province of British Columbia.

Port at Seattle, Washington

Global Ties

- The United States and Canada have joined Mexico in promoting free trade among their countries.
- The United States is a major global trading power. Its trade deficits, however, could cause future economic problems.
- The United States and other countries are working to prevent terrorist attacks.

The Environment

- The United States and Canada are reducing the amount of chemicals released into the air to reduce acid rain.
- Declining water levels and rising demand for water are affecting the Great Lakes.
- The United States and Canada face the loss of farmland and wilderness areas as urban sprawl increases.

New home construction, Florida

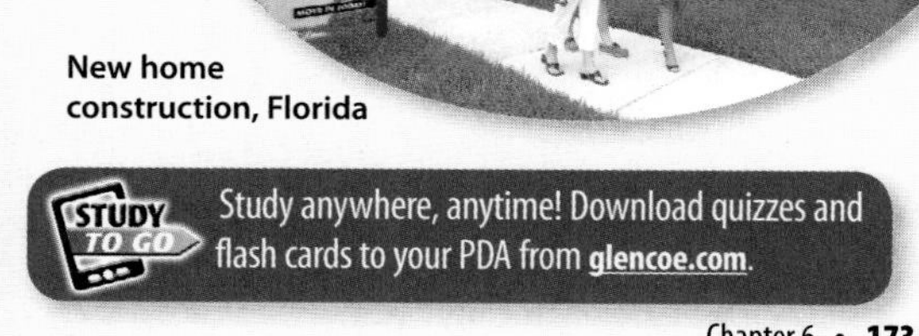

Study anywhere, anytime! Download quizzes and flash cards to your PDA from glencoe.com.

Visual Summary

Problem Solving Have students review the Visual Summary text about global ties and the environment. Then organize the class into four groups, and have each group create a list of ways that the United States and Canada could work together to address a problem discussed in this chapter. Write these choices on the board:

- fighting terrorism
- reducing acid rain
- conserving water and preventing pollution in the Great Lakes
- reducing urban sprawl and preserving valuable farmland

Assign each group a topic, and have the groups come up with five specific steps that the United States and Canada could take together to address the problem. Have each group report to the class and lead a discussion about its topic. **OL**

Speculating Have students speculate about the future of the United States and Canada. **Ask:** **Do you think the relationship between the two countries will get better, stay about the same, or get worse? Why?** *(Answers will vary, but students should provide facts from the text to support their answers.)* **OL**

Hands-On Chapter Project
Step 3: Wrap Up

Creating Cartoons About the Global Economy

Step 3: Learning From the Project Students will synthesize what they have learned in Steps 1 and 2.

Directions Write the Essential Question on the board. Ask students to respond to the question by summarizing the main ideas of the cartoons they created for the chapter project. List these ideas on the board and lead students in making generalizations based on the ideas. **Ask:** **Would you describe this region's economic influence on the world economy as positive? Why or why not? What negative effects do you observe? What impact do the economies of other regions have on the world economy? On the economies of the United States and Canada?** To close, have students write two or three sentences in their journals in response to the Essential Question. **OL**

Answers and Analyses

Reviewing Vocabulary

1. D If students ask themselves why people start businesses, the answer to this question will be clear. Business owners are in business not necessarily to make beautiful, affordable, or useful products, but profitable ones.

2. B Students should understand that of the four choices, only one is a product: newsprint, which is made from wood pulp. Stocks represent ownership in a company, biotechnology is an area of scientific study, and acid rain is an environmental problem.

3. A All four choices are economic terms that relate to international trade, but students need to recognize that only two, A and D, describe the balance of trade. Tell students to focus on the key words "spends more…than it earns." This situation creates a deficit, or a loss of money. A surplus, on the other hand, is a gain of money. Students might remember this by focusing on the word part *plus*.

4. B Students can eliminate C first because free markets are those without artificial protections. Students may recognize the meaning of choices A and D from the previous question. If not, you may help them reason that a country cannot place a trade deficit or surplus; these terms represent conditions that exist based on a country's actions. This leaves choice B, *tariffs*.

STANDARDIZED TEST PRACTICE

TEST-TAKING TIP

During an exam, answer the questions you know first. Then go back to those that need more thought.

Reviewing Vocabulary

Directions: Choose the word(s) that best completes the sentence.

1. Business owners produce products they think will be most ______.

A beautiful
B affordable
C useful
D profitable

2. British Columbia's forests help make Canada the world's largest producer of ______.

A stocks
B newsprint
C acid rain
D biotechnology

3. A ______ occurs when a country spends more on its imports than it earns from its exports.

A trade deficit
B import tariff
C free market
D trade surplus

4. A country sometimes places ______ on imports to protect industries from foreign competition.

A trade deficits
B tariffs
C free markets
D trade surpluses

Reviewing Main Ideas

Directions: Choose the best answer for each question.

Section 1 *(pp. 158–162)*

5. Because it has abundant oil, the ______ economic region of the United States produces petroleum-based products.

A South
B Pacific
C Midwest
D Interior West

6. Most people in Canada's Atlantic provinces make a living through the ______ industries.

A fishing, farming, and forestry
B oil, natural gas, and exporting
C manufacturing, mining, and tourism
D finance, hydroelectricity, and ranching

Section 2 *(pp. 168–172)*

7. The largest trading partner of the United States is ______.

A Mexico
B Canada
C Nigeria
D Venezuela

8. To address the issue of ______, Canada passed laws to lower the amount of fossil fuels that are burned.

A low water levels
B urban sprawl
C global warming
D brownfields

GO ON

Reviewing Main Ideas

5. A Most students will likely associate Texas with oil wealth; they need only place Texas in the correct economic region to find the right answer. If necessary, have students refer to the map of economic regions in Section 1.

6. C Students may be tempted to choose A, associating the Atlantic Provinces with fishing. Remind them, however, that this industry has declined. Choice D can be eliminated because there is not enough land for large-scale ranching. The region does not possess significant energy reserves, eliminating choice B. Use this question to show students that eliminating just one part of a possible answer can help them identify the right one.

Critical Thinking

Directions: Base your answers to questions 9 and 10 on the graph below and your knowledge of Chapter 6.

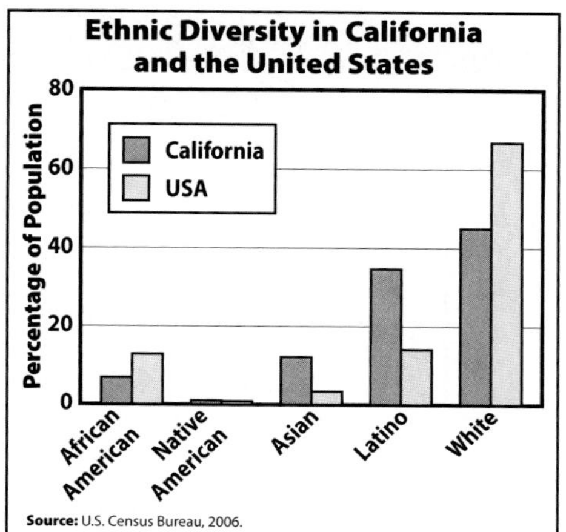

9. What conclusion can you make from the data?

A More Latinos live in California than in the rest of the United States.

B California's population is about one-tenth of the nation's total population.

C California has a larger percentage of Japanese Americans than the country has as a whole.

D The U.S. population has a larger percentage of African Americans than does California's.

10. Which of these generalizations is accurate?

A Latinos are the fastest growing U.S. group.

B African Americans outnumber Asians 3 to 1 in California.

C Latinos and whites make up most of the nation's population.

D Whites outnumber the combined members of all other ethnic groups in the state.

Document-Based Questions

Directions: Analyze the following document and answer the short-answer questions that follow.

The following news story was broadcast in Canada on October 30, 2005.

> *Quebec Premier Jean Charest called federalism the "best choice for the future of Quebec" as provincial separatists vowed to continue to seek independence on Sunday—the 10th anniversary of the province's second referendum on sovereignty.*
>
> *On Oct. 30, 1995, more than 93 per cent of the province's 5.1 million registered voters cast a ballot. A razor-thin majority kept the province from heading towards independence, with 50.58 per cent voting No to 49.42 per cent voting Yes.*
>
> *Charest, in a closing speech to about 800 Liberals at the provincial party's general meeting on Sunday, said . . . he hoped the province would one day sign the Constitution.*
>
> *"Recognizing Quebec as being different, recognizing our history, recognizing our identity, has never meant a weakening of Quebec and has never been a threat to national unity," Charest said.*
>
> —Debate still rages on 10th anniversary of Quebec's sovereignty referendum, *CBC News*.

11. What statement indicates that Charest believes Quebec should remain part of Canada?

12. Did most Quebecois in 1995 have strong feelings about Quebec's independence? How do you know?

Extended Response

13. If you lived in Quebec, would you like to see it become independent or remain part of Canada? Explain your answer.

STOP

Social Studies ONLINE

For additional test practice, use Self-Check Quizzes—Chapter 6 at glencoe.com.

Need Extra Help?

If you missed question...	1	2	3	4	5	6	7	8	9	10	11	12	13
Go to page...	159	162	169	170	160	161	169	172	161	161	161	161	161–162

Critical Thinking

9. D Students need to read the labels correctly and identify the bars for California and the nation as a whole. Choices A and B are incorrect because the graph indicates the *percentage* of the population in California and the United States, not the actual numbers of people. C is incorrect because the graph shows Asian Americans, not Japanese Americans.

10. C Students need to carefully observe chart data and make calculations as necessary. A is incorrect because the chart does not reference grow rate. B is incorrect because there are more Asians than African Americans in California. D is incorrect because whites are less than 50%.

Document-Based Questions

11. He believes that federalism is the best choice for the future of Quebec.

12. Yes; more than 93 percent of them went to the polls to express their opinion.

Extended Response

13. Answers will vary but should reflect an understanding of the text, including the challenges an independent Quebec would face.

7. B Students may benefit from thinking about Canada's size, proximity, and similarity to the United States to recognize that it is our leading trading partner. Explain that common barriers to trade, such as language, different cultures and governments, distance, and conflicts, do not exist to hamper U.S.–Canadian trade.

8. C If students understand the possible causes of global warming—the burning of fossil fuels such as coal, oil, and natural gas—they will recognize choice C as the correct one. None of the other answer choices are problems caused by fossil fuels. Sometimes looking for similarities in word meanings will help. In this case, global *warming* and the *burning* of fossil fuels.

Social Studies ONLINE

Have students visit the Web site at glencoe.com to review Chapter 6 and take the Self-Check Quiz.

Need Extra Help?

Have students refer to the pages listed if they miss any of the questions.

Unit 3 Planning Guide

UNIT PACING CHART				
Unit 3		Chapter 7	Chapter 8	Chapter 9
Day 1	Unit Opener	Chapter Opener	Chapter Opener	Chapter Opener
Day 2	Regional Atlas	Section 1	Section 1	Section 1
Day 3	Regional Atlas	Geography & History	Section 1	Section 2
Day 4	Reading Social Studies	Section 2	You Decide	TIME Perspectives
Day 5		Review	Section 2	TIME Perspectives
Day 6		Chapter Assessment	World Literature Reading	Section 3
Day 7			Section 2	Section 3
Day 8			Review	Review
Day 9			Chapter Assessment	Chapter Assessment
Day 10			TIME Journal	

Clifford Neeley
Clanton Middle School
Clanton, Alabama

Creating a Multimedia Presentation With the right kind of direction, theme, and technology, students can really get into a topic. Write up a list of questions about the region that cover all the main ideas from each section in each chapter of the unit. Organize students into groups of three or four people, and assign each group one section. As students read the section, have them answer the questions, then begin designing a multimedia presentation to present their main ideas to the class. Provide students opportunities to do additional research online or in library books to find artwork or photos to include. Encourage them to create charts, maps, or graphs as well. Suggest students look at historical sites, physical or climatic extremes, or cultural comparisons to the United States to give their presentations added variety. When you finish the unit, have a "movie night" in which each group presents their multimedia presentations to the class as though they were at a movie screening. Bringing treats can add a little extra flavor.

Author Note

Dear Social Studies Teacher:

Latin America's colonial history is apparent in the human characteristics of places and regions. Most apparent are the languages—Spanish is spoken throughout most of Latin America, Portuguese is spoken in Brazil, and English and French are spoken in places like Belize and Haiti. The dominance of the Roman Catholic faith is a further link to the region's colonial past. Native American populations were decimated by European diseases and wars throughout much of Latin America.

A dominant theme in Latin America's colonial history has been monoculture, or the production of one or a very few products or resources for export to the former mother country. Monoculture was an integral part of mercantilism 200 years ago. Colonies were encouraged to produce food and raw materials that could be traded for European manufactured goods. This system still shapes the economy and basic infrastructure of many Latin American countries. This presents a danger for these countries, however. When something affects the main crop or principal export, such as volatile prices or climatic catastrophes, the whole economy of a country can falter. In addition, transport and commerce are concentrated on the coasts. This has resulted in the rise of large port cities and the unequal distribution of population.

The colonial era left a lasting imprint on rural areas as well. Large estates controlled by wealthy land owners still dominate the rural landscape. A vast number of these estates are only marginally productive. Land reform has redistributed millions of acres, but there is still unused or poorly used land throughout the region.

Richard G. Boehm

Senior Author

Introducing Unit 3

What Makes Latin America a Region?

The three chapters of this unit introduce students to the cultural region of Latin America. The countries in this region share the following characteristics:

- a colonial past that is reflected in the official languages of each country
- cultures with Native American, African, and European influences
- a daily life centered on family and religion, primarily Roman Catholicism
- a location in the Western Hemisphere, with much of the region within the Tropics
- many mountains and highland areas that create a variety of climates
- a wealth of natural resources in much of the region

NATIONAL GEOGRAPHIC

www.nationalgeographic.com/education

NGS ONLINE This online resource provides lesson plans, atlas updates, cartographic activities with interactive maps, an online map store, and geographic links.

UNIT 3 Latin America

Rio de Janeiro, Brazil ▶

NATIONAL GEOGRAPHIC

NGS ONLINE For more information about the region, see www.nationalgeographic.com/education.

Activity: Launching the Unit

Why Study Latin America? Tell students that Latin America includes Mexico, Central America, the Caribbean, and South America. **Ask: Why should events in Latin America be of special interest to Americans?** *(Students might mention that the United States, Canada, and Latin America make up the Western Hemisphere; that the United States shares a border with Mexico; that some of the Caribbean islands are close to Florida; or that many people migrate from Latin American countries to the United States.)* **Ask: What conditions in Latin America might motivate people to come to the United States?** *(better economic conditions, political stability)* Tell students that many Latin American immigrants come to this country to work and send money back to their relatives in their home countries. Many plan to return to their home country someday. As students read through the unit, encourage them to look for additional connections between the United States and Latin America. **OL**

Introducing Unit 3

Introduce the Region

Using Maps Have students compare the Political, Population Density, and Economic Resources maps in the Regional Atlas. **Ask:** **Where is most of South America's population concentrated?** *(along the coasts)* **Where are most of the economic resources in South America located?** *(along the coasts as well)* **Where do most people in Mexico live?** *(in the central and southern parts of the country)* **Where are most of the natural resources of Mexico located?** *(in the central and northern parts of the country, although petroleum is found in the southern part of the country)* **What natural resources does Cuba possess?** *(petroleum, cobalt, nickel)* **What is the primary land use in that country?** *(commercial farming)* **OL**

More About the Photo

Visual Literacy Rio de Janeiro is an important port city in Brazil. The city was founded by Portuguese explorers who first arrived at the port in 1502 and laid the foundations of the town in 1565. From 1822 to 1960, Rio de Janeiro was the capital of Brazil. Although the capital was moved to Brasília in 1960, Rio de Janeiro remains an important economic center. International trade, banking, research, education, and tourism are some of the economic activities that take place there.

Rio de Janeiro is also known for its beautiful beaches and the magnificent peaks, ridges, and hills that surround it. The city has a well-deserved reputation as a center for leisure and recreation, perhaps best displayed during the annual pre-Lenten Carnival. During this celebration, the city comes alive with music, dances, and parades day and night.

The giant statue of Jesus shown here overlooks the city. The statue, with its open arms, has come to represent both Christianity and the warmth of the Brazilian people.

Regional Atlas Activity

Where Is It?

Using the Map Scale **Ask:** **About how far is it from the northernmost point to the southern tip of South America?** *(about 4,500 miles or about 7,250 km)* **OL**

How Big Is It?

Math Question Tell students that the land area of the world is about 57.5 million square miles (148.94 million square km). **Ask:** **Approximately what percentage of the world's land area is in Latin America?** *(about 14%)* **OL**

Comparing Population

Ask: **Which country in Latin America has a population that is about one-third of the population of the United States?** *(Mexico)* **How does Peru's population compare to the population of the United States?** *(It is about one-tenth as large.)* **OL**

Regional Atlas

Latin America

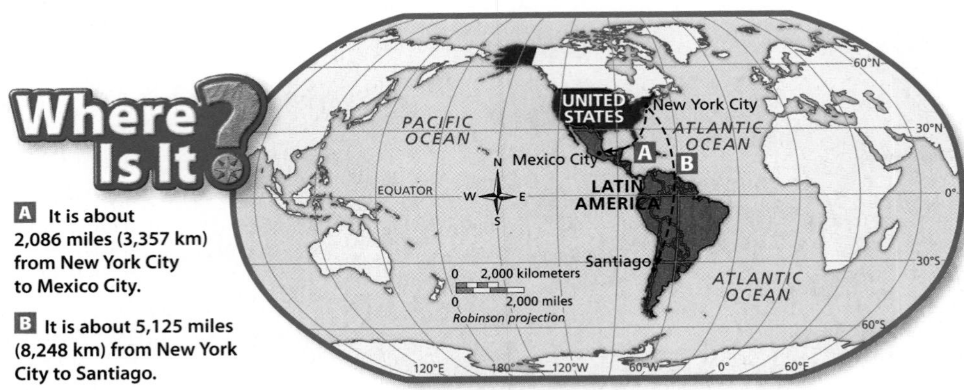

A It is about 2,086 miles (3,357 km) from New York City to Mexico City.

B It is about 5,125 miles (8,248 km) from New York City to Santiago.

The region of Latin America is about two-and-a-half times the size of the continental United States. Its land area is about 7.9 million square miles (20.5 million sq. km). Latin America has about 558 million people, almost twice as many as the United States.

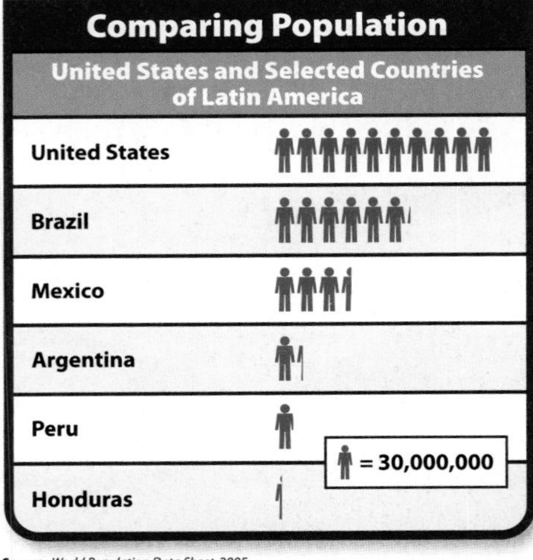

Source: *World Population Data Sheet, 2005.*

Activity: Geographic Theme

Human/Environment Interaction Have students consider the Population Density map in the Regional Atlas. **Ask:** **What factors influence why people live in some areas and not others?** *(climate, availability of water and other resources, fertility of farmland, or ease of transportation.)* **Ask:** **In what parts of Latin America do most people live?** *(along the coasts of South America, on the Caribbean islands, and in parts of Central America and southern Mexico)* Have students look at the Physical map. **Ask:** **What factors might prevent people from living in other areas?** *(Fewer people live in the most mountainous regions and in the desert areas.)* **AL**

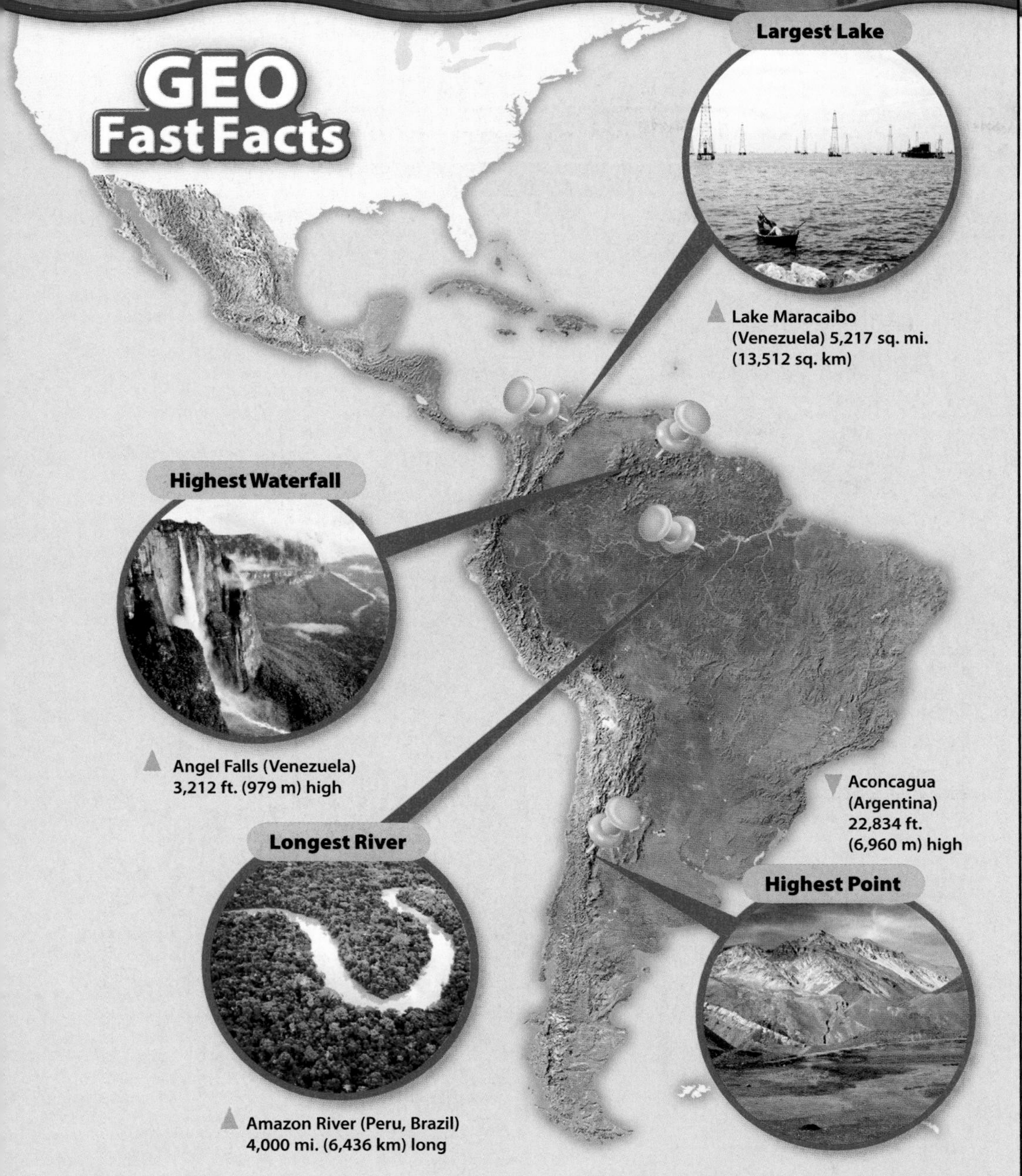

NATIONAL GEOGRAPHIC

GEO Fast Facts

Largest Lake

Lake Maracaibo (Venezuela) 5,217 sq. mi. (13,512 sq. km)

Highest Waterfall

Angel Falls (Venezuela) 3,212 ft. (979 m) high

Longest River

Amazon River (Peru, Brazil) 4,000 mi. (6,436 km) long

Highest Point

Aconcagua (Argentina) 22,834 ft. (6,960 m) high

Geo Fast Facts

Locating Information **Ask:** **What features of Latin America are shown on this map?** *(the highest waterfall, the largest lake, the longest river, the highest point)*

Tell students that Angel Falls is both the highest waterfall in Latin America, as well as the highest waterfall in the world. Have them conduct research to learn what other geographic "extremes" are located in Latin America. Tell them to find pictures of these features and then create a poster-size version of the Geo FastFacts that includes the FastFacts on this page and the other extremes that they have identified. *(Students' research may identify the Andes as the world's longest system of high mountain ranges, and the Amazon rain forest as the world's largest rain forest)* **OL**

FastFacts

- **Jaguars** Cockscomb Basin Wildlife Sanctuary in Belize covers 395 square miles (1,024 square km) and has the most concentrated jaguar population in the world.
- **Baseball** Each February, winners of the professional baseball leagues in the Dominican Republic, Mexico, Puerto Rico, and Venezuela meet in the Caribbean World Series. Summer leagues in the Dominican Republic, Venezuela, and Mexico are affiliated with Minor League baseball in the United States.
- **War of the Pacific** Between 1879 and 1883, Chile, Bolivia, and Peru fought a war to control the part of the Atacama Desert that contained valuable mineral resources. When the fighting was over, Chile was victorious, and Bolivia lost its entire Pacific coastline. Until World War I, most of Chile's wealth came from mining the area's resources.

Regional Atlas Activity

Categorizing Create a chart on the board with the headings "Greater Antilles" and "Lesser Antilles." Have students compare the Physical map and the Political map in the Regional Atlas. Ask them to name the countries that are part of the Greater Antilles and those that are part of the Lesser Antilles. If students are uncertain, explain that the Greater Antilles are the four largest islands in the Caribbean—Cuba, Jamaica, Hispaniola, and Puerto Rico. **Ask: Which two countries share the island of Hispaniola?** *(Haiti and the Dominican Republic)* **OL**

Answers:

1. the Andes
2. Panama is the narrowest part of Central America. Building a canal there allows ships to move between the Atlantic and Pacific Oceans without traveling thousands of miles around the southern tip of South America.

Skills Practice

Ask: What is the name of the archipelago, or group of islands, that is separated from the South American mainland by the Strait of Magellan? *(Tierra del Fuego)* **What is the name of the southernmost point on this archipelago?** *(Cape Horn)*

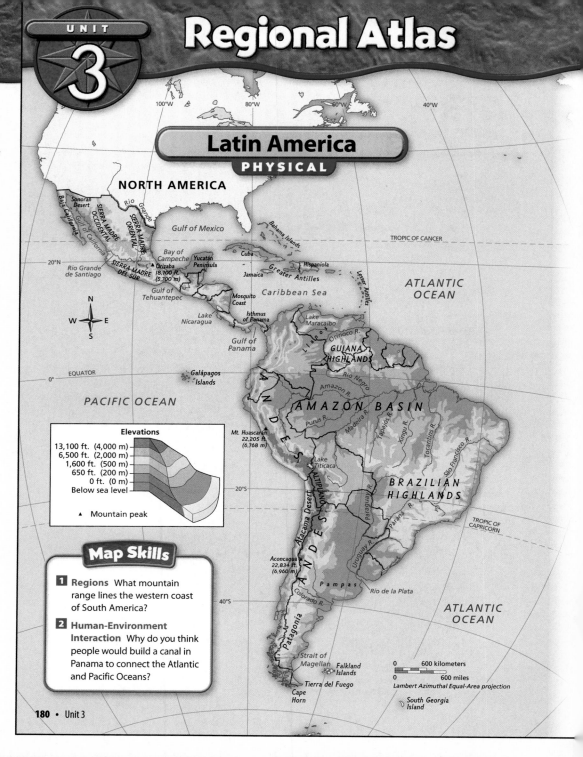

UNIT 3 **Regional Atlas**

Latin America

PHYSICAL

NORTH AMERICA
Sonoran Desert
Baja California
Gulf of California
SIERRA MADRE OCCIDENTAL
SIERRA MADRE ORIENTAL
Rio Grande
Gulf of Mexico
Bay of Campeche
Yucatán Peninsula
Rio Grande de Santiago
SIERRA MADRE DEL SUR
Orizaba 18,700 ft. (5,700 m)
Gulf of Tehuantepec
Bahama Islands
Cuba
Jamaica
Hispaniola
Greater Antilles
Lesser Antilles
Caribbean Sea
Mosquito Coast
Lake Nicaragua
Isthmus of Panama
Gulf of Panama
TROPIC OF CANCER
ATLANTIC OCEAN
Lake Maracaibo
Llanos
Orinoco R.
GUIANA HIGHLANDS
Rio Negro
Amazon R.
Galápagos Islands
EQUATOR
PACIFIC OCEAN
AMAZON BASIN
Purus R.
Madeira R.
Tapajós R.
Xingu R.
Tocantins R.
São Francisco R.
ANDES
Mt. Huascarán 22,205 ft. (6,768 m)
Lake Titicaca
ALTIPLANO
BRAZILIAN HIGHLANDS
Paraguay R.
Atacama Desert
Paraná R.
TROPIC OF CAPRICORN
Uruguay R.
Aconcagua 22,834 ft. (6,960 m)
Pampas
Río de la Plata
Colorado R.
Patagonia
ATLANTIC OCEAN
Strait of Magellan
Falkland Islands
Tierra del Fuego
Cape Horn
South Georgia Island
0 600 kilometers
0 600 miles
Lambert Azimuthal Equal-Area projection
100°W 80°W 60°W 40°W 20°N 0° 20°S 40°S

Elevations

13,100 ft. (4,000 m)
6,500 ft. (2,000 m)
1,600 ft. (500 m)
650 ft. (200 m)
0 ft. (0 m)
Below sea level
▲ Mountain peak

Map Skills

1. **Regions** What mountain range lines the western coast of South America?
2. **Human-Environment Interaction** Why do you think people would build a canal in Panama to connect the Atlantic and Pacific Oceans?

180 • Unit 3

Background: Land and Climate

Regional Differences Most of Latin America lies within the Tropics and has generally warm temperatures. Mexico and Central America lie on a narrow strip of land connecting North America and South America. Four tectonic plates meet in this region, resulting in frequent earthquakes and many active volcanoes. Mexico and Central America are mountainous. The thick forests and coastal marshes of Central America make transportation there especially difficult.

The islands in the Caribbean Sea, including the islands of the Greater Antilles, the Lesser Antilles, and the Bahamas, make up the Caribbean region. Most of these islands are small. Many have been formed by volcanoes and have fertile volcanic soil.

South America has two major landforms: the Andes mountain ranges in the west, and the vast Amazon Basin, which is home to the world's largest rain forest. The rivers of South America provide an important means of transportation. In the Andes and other mountainous areas, the climate varies greatly by elevation.

NATIONAL GEOGRAPHIC

Latin America

POLITICAL

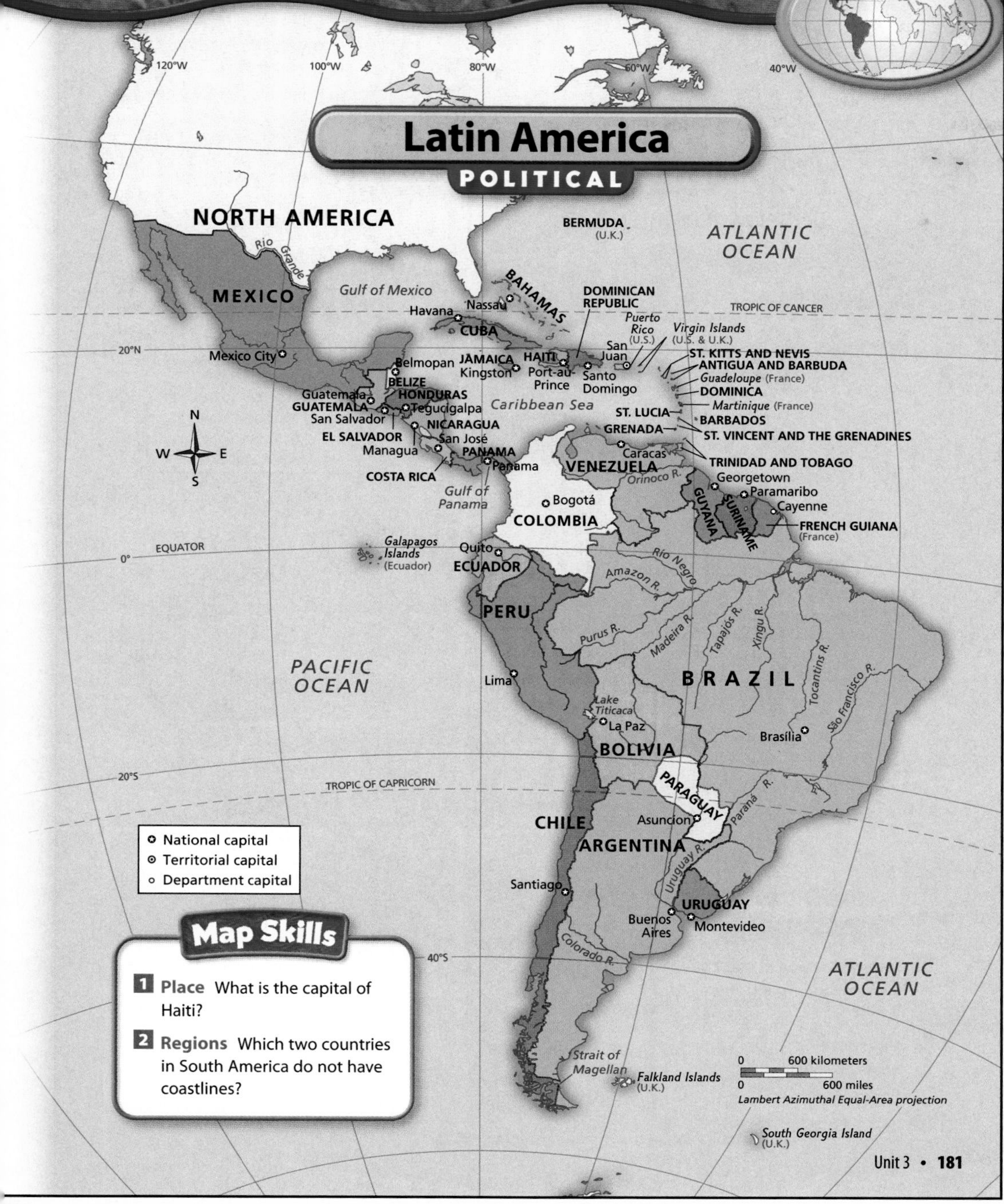

Map Skills

1 Place What is the capital of Haiti?

2 Regions Which two countries in South America do not have coastlines?

Regional Atlas Activity

Drawing Conclusions Have students study the location of capital cities in Latin America. **Ask: Why do you think capital cities developed in these locations?** *(Possible answer: Many capital cities are located on the ocean or on rivers and are accessible by ship, and have water for drinking and irrigation.)*

Randomly assign a different capital city to pairs of students. Send them to encyclopedias, online resources, or other reference sources to research the founding and history of their city. When students have finished, have them create an index card detailing when and why their city was founded and any factors that explain its location. Create a large display titled *The Founding of Latin America's Capitals.* Include a map of Latin America in the center of the display and post the cards around the periphery, connecting them by string to each city's location on the map. **OL**

Map Skills

Answers:

1. Port-au-Prince
2. Bolivia and Paraguay

Skills Practice

Ask: What islands in the Caribbean are U.S. territories? *(Puerto Rico and the Virgin Islands)* **Which two Latin American capitals are closest to the United States?** *(Nassau and Havana)*

Background: Current Issues

Urbanization More and more Latin Americans are moving out of the rural countryside and into rapidly growing urban areas, a process called urbanization. Some of the biggest cities in the world are in Latin America, including Mexico City, Mexico; Rio de Janeiro, Brazil; and Buenos Aires, Argentina. Most Latin Americans who leave rural areas move to cities to try to find better jobs and improve the conditions of their lives. However, as the number of people looking for work in cities has grown, jobs and housing have become scarce, and schools and health care centers have been unable to keep pace with the swelling population. Many people who have moved in search of a better life do not find good jobs and have been forced to live in substandard housing in crowded, unsafe, and dirty neighborhoods.

Regional Atlas Activity

Making Maps Have each student pick one country in Latin America in order to make a detailed map of the country. Explain to students to begin by tracing the outline of their country in the Political map in the Regional Atlas and then use a photocopy machine to enlarge this outline. Make sure that students keep track of the map scale when they do this step. Next, tell students to consult an atlas to identify major cities in their country and locate them on their map. Students should use a key similar to the one on the Population Density map to show the population of the cities noted on their maps. Finally, tell students to transfer physical features onto their maps. They might begin by using the Physical map in the Regional Atlas but should consult other reference sources to get more detailed information about their country. Students may choose to include other features on their maps as well, such as elevation, parks, or major roadways. **AL**

Map Skills

Answers:

1. Mexico City and the area around it
2. Mexico City, Buenos Aires, Rio de Janeiro, and São Paulo

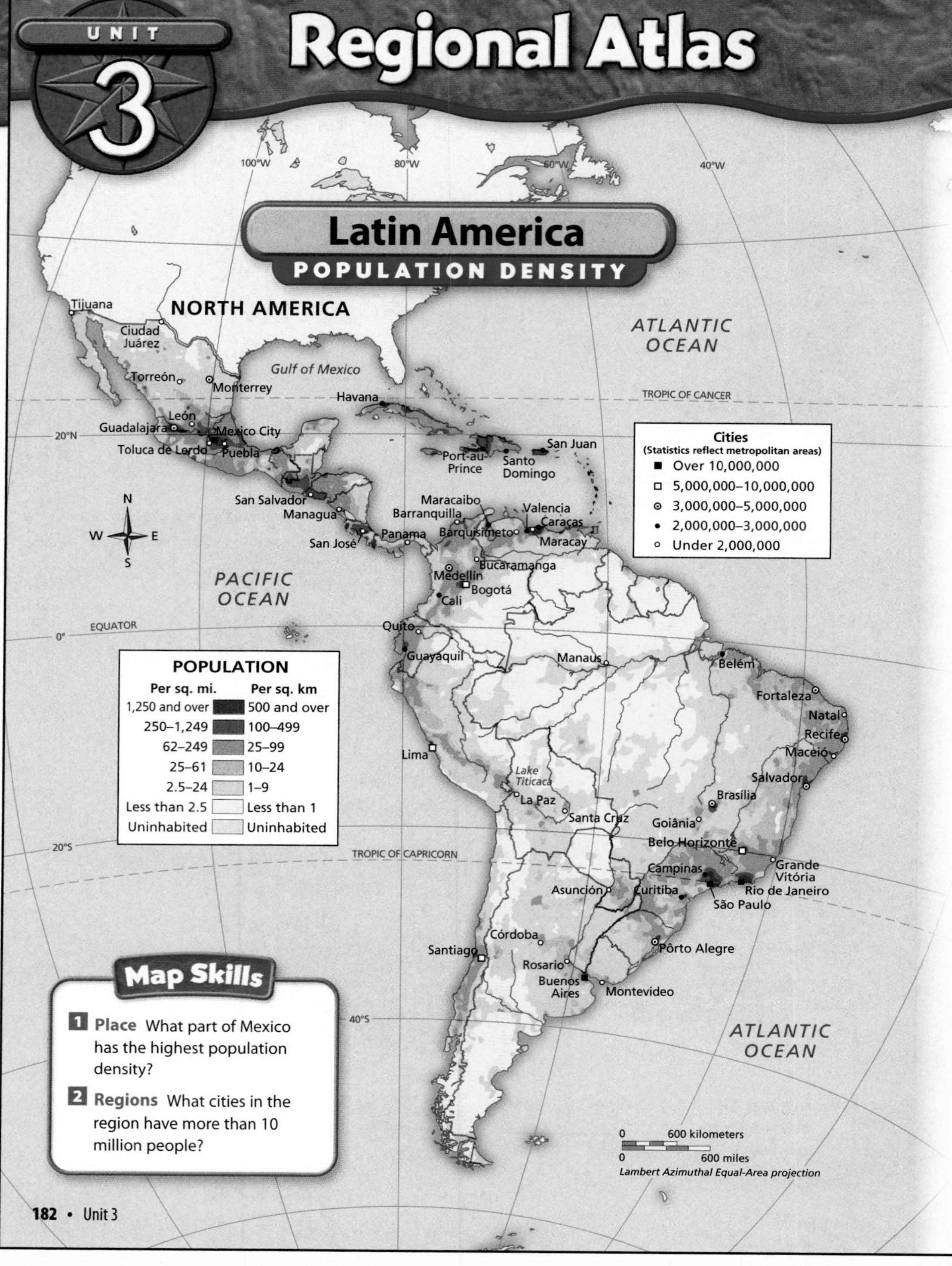

Background: People and Culture

Religion and Family Since the colonial period, religion has been central to the lives of Latin Americans. Roman Catholic holidays are celebrated throughout the region. Carnival is a huge festival in the region and is held each spring on the last day before the Christian holy period of Lent. In recent years, Protestant forms of Christianity also have been on the rise. Immigrants have also brought other religions to the area, including Islam, Hinduism, Buddhism, and Judaism. Traditional Native American and African religions continue to thrive in the region as well, often mixed with elements of Christianity and other faiths.

Daily life centers on the family, and extended families often live together. Adults are expected to care for their elderly parents. Adult siblings often live close together and their children often form close relationships with one another. Traditionally, most Latin American families have been patriarchal, with the father as the main decision maker. However, in some parts of the Caribbean, families are matriarchal, and the mother is the leader of the family.

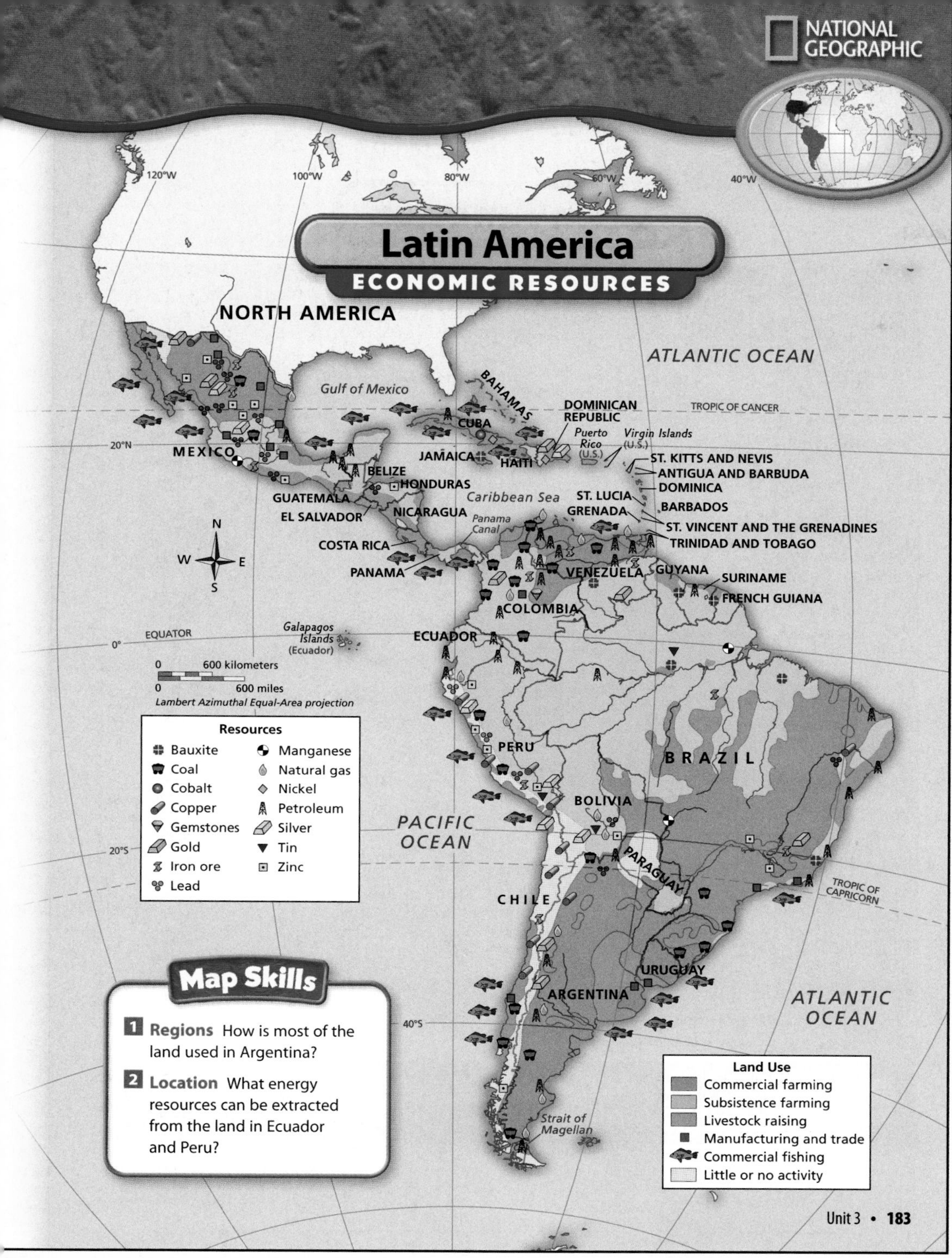

NATIONAL GEOGRAPHIC

Latin America

ECONOMIC RESOURCES

Resources

Bauxite	Manganese
Coal	Natural gas
Cobalt	Nickel
Copper	Petroleum
Gemstones	Silver
Gold	Tin
Iron ore	Zinc
Lead	

Land Use

- Commercial farming
- Subsistence farming
- Livestock raising
- Manufacturing and trade
- Commercial fishing
- Little or no activity

0 600 kilometers
0 600 miles
Lambert Azimuthal Equal-Area projection

Map Skills

1. **Regions** How is most of the land used in Argentina?
2. **Location** What energy resources can be extracted from the land in Ecuador and Peru?

Unit 3 Regional Atlas

Regional Atlas Activity

Drawing Conclusions Have students examine the Economic Resources and Political maps in the Regional Atlas. **Ask: In what parts of Latin America is there little or no economic activity?** *(along much of the coast of Chile and Peru, in a large part of Paraguay, and in the northern part of Mexico)* Have students turn to the Physical map in the Regional Atlas. **Ask: What physical features might explain why little or no economic activity takes place in these areas?** *(The Andes mountains in Chile and Peru, the Atacama Desert in Chile, and the Sonoran Desert in northern Mexico explain the lack of economic activity in those areas. However, nothing on the Physical map itself explains the lack of economic activity in Paraguay.)* **OL**

Map Skills

Answers:

1. livestock raising
2. petroleum, coal, and natural gas

Skills Practice

Ask: What natural resources does Brazil possess? *(coal, petroleum, gold, iron ore, zinc, copper, lead, manganese, tin, bauxite)*

Background: The Economy

Mexico's Economic Regions Mexico has many natural resources and workers, and its economy is growing. In 1994, the North American Free Trade Agreement (NAFTA) among the United States, Canada, and Mexico ended most trade barriers among the three countries. The agreement helped Mexico's manufacturing and service industries grow. Mexico's geography and climate give the country three distinct economic regions. In the North, farmland must be irrigated, and grasslands support cattle ranches. This region also has rich deposits of natural resources, such as copper, zinc, iron, lead, and silver. Central Mexico has mild year-round temperatures and fertile soil, allowing for productive farming. This area has several large industrial cities that make cars, clothing, household items, and electronics. Major oil and gas deposits are tapped offshore. The South is the poorest economic region. Because of poor soil in the mountains, farmers can grow only enough food to feed their families. Along the coast, wealthy plantation owners raise cash crops for sale, and beautiful beaches attract tourists from around the world.

Regional Atlas Activity

Drawing Conclusions Have students study the chart and then guess which European nation colonized each country in Latin America. **Ask: How do you know?** *(Students should understand that the official language of each country reflects which European nation once colonized it. For example, countries with Spanish as an official language were once colonies of Spain.)* Explain to students that this region is called "Latin" America because many countries in the region have a strong Spanish and Portuguese heritage, and have Spanish or Portuguese as their official language. These two languages are based on Latin. **OL**

FastFacts

Brasília The capital of Brazil was moved to Brasília in the country's interior in 1960. Brasília was a completely planned city and was built very quickly. Thousands of miles of highways were constructed to connect Brasília to other cities. By the end of the twentieth century, the results of the city's rapid construction were beginning to show, including cracks in concrete plazas and deteriorating housing.

Regional Atlas

Latin America

Country and Capital	Literacy Rate	Population and Density	Land Area	Life Expectancy (Years)	GDP* Per Capita (U.S. dollars)	Television Sets (per 1,000 people)	Flag and Language
ANTIGUA AND BARBUDA St. John's	89%	100,000 588 per sq. mi. 227 per sq. km	170 sq. mi. 440 sq. km	71	$11,000	493	English
ARGENTINA Buenos Aires	97.1%	38,600,000 36 per sq. mi. 14 per sq. km	1,073,514 sq. mi. 2,780,388 sq. km	74	$12,400	293	Spanish
BAHAMAS Nassau	95.6%	300,000 60 per sq. mi. 22 per sq. km	5,359 sq. mi. 13,880 sq. km	70	$17,700	243	English
BARBADOS Bridgetown	97.4%	300,000 1,807 per sq. mi. 698 per sq. km	166 sq. mi. 430 sq. km	72	$16,400	290	English
BELIZE Belmopan	94.1%	300,000 34 per sq. mi. 13 per sq. km	8,865 sq. mi. 22,960 sq. km	70	$6,500	183	English
BOLIVIA La Paz Sucre	87.2%	8,900,000 21 per sq. mi. 8 per sq. km	424,162 sq. mi. 1,098,574 sq. km	64	$2,600	118	Spanish, Quechua, Aymara
BRAZIL Brasília	86.4%	184,200,000 56 per sq. mi. 22 per sq. km	3,300,154 sq. mi. 8,547,359 sq. km	71	$8,100	333	Portuguese
CHILE Santiago	96.2%	16,100,000 55 per sq. mi. 21 per sq. km	292,135 sq. mi. 756,626 sq. km	76	$10,700	240	Spanish
COLOMBIA Bogotá	92.5%	46,000,000 105 per sq. mi. 40 per sq. km	439,734 sq. mi. 1,138,906 sq. km	72	$6,600	279	Spanish
UNITED STATES Washington, D.C.	97%	296,500,000 80 per sq. mi. 31 per sq. km	3,717,796 sq. mi. 9,629,047 sq. km	78	$40,100	844	English

*Gross Domestic Product

Countries and flags not drawn to scale

184 • Unit 3

Activity: Using the Chart

Locating Information Give students a few minutes to study the Flag and Language column on the chart. **Ask: Which countries have official languages that are not European languages?** *(Bolivia, Haiti, Paraguay, and Peru)* Explain that all of these languages, except for Creole, are the languages of Native American groups. Ask each student to choose one of these languages and conduct research to learn more about that language and the people who speak it. As part of their research, have students learn how many people speak the language and where these people live, as well as some common greetings in the language. Then have students share what they have learned with the class. **AL**

Unit 3 Regional Atlas

Latin America

Country and Capital	Literacy Rate	Population and Density	Land Area	Life Expectancy (Years)	GDP* Per Capita (U.S. dollars)	Television Sets (per 1,000 people)	Flag and Language
COSTA RICA San José	96%	4,300,000 218 per sq. mi. 84 per sq. km	19,730 sq. mi. 51,100 sq. km	79	$9,600	229	Spanish
CUBA Havana	97%	11,300,000 264 per sq. mi. 102 per sq. km	42,803 sq. mi. 110,859 sq. km	77	$3,000	248	Spanish
DOMINICA Roseau	94%	100,000 345 per sq. mi. 133 per sq. km	290 sq. mi. 751 sq. km	74	$5,500	232	English
DOMINICAN REPUBLIC Santo Domingo	84%	8,900,000 471 per sq. mi. 168 per sq. km	18,815 sq. mi. 48,731 sq. km	68	$6,300	96	Spanish
ECUADOR Quito	92.5%	13,000,000 119 per sq. mi. 46 per sq. km	109,483 sq. mi. 283,560 sq. km	74	$3,700	213	Spanish
EL SALVADOR San Salvador	80.2%	6,900,000 849 per sq. mi. 328 per sq. km	8,124 sq. mi. 21,041 sq. km	70	$4,900	191	Spanish
FRENCH GUIANA Cayenne	83%	200,000 6 per sq. mi. 2 per sq. km	34,749 sq. mi. 89,999 sq. km	75	$8,300	information not available	French
GRENADA St. George's	98%	100,000 769 per sq. mi. 295 per sq. km	131 sq. mi. 339 sq. km	71	$5,000	376	English
GUATEMALA Guatemala	70.6%	12,700,000 302 per sq. mi. 117 per sq. km	42,042 sq. mi. 108,888 sq. km	66	$4,200	61	Spanish
UNITED STATES Washington, D.C.	97%	296,500,000 80 per sq. mi. 31 per sq. km	3,717,796 sq. mi. 9,629,047 sq. km	78	$40,100	844	English

Sources: *CIA World Factbook*, 2005; Population Reference Bureau, *World Population Data Sheet*, 2005.

For more country facts, go to the **Nations of the World Databank** at glencoe.com.

Regional Atlas Activity

Synthesizing Conduct a tournament to help students remember information about Latin America from the chart and the maps in the Regional Atlas. Organize students into pairs. Have pairs work together to create a set of flashcards listing country names on one side and capital names on the other. Set a timer for one minute, and have one member of each pair test the other member and keep track of how many capitals he or she answers correctly in one minute. Set the timer for one minute again and have students switch roles.

The member of the pair with the most correct responses moves to the next round of the tournament. For this round, have students who lost in the first round create another set of cards, this time testing student knowledge of official languages. For example, "What is the official language of Nicaragua?" Have the students who created the cards use them to test the students who are still in the tournament. Students who answer at least 10 questions correctly advance to the next round.

For the final round, have students who were eliminated in the previous rounds write questions based on the maps. For example, "Through which countries does the Amazon River flow?" or "Bolivia is southwest of what country?" The student who answers the most questions correctly in this round is the tournament winner. **OL**

Activity: Using the Chart

Comparing and Contrasting Have students compare the seven countries of Central America by creating bar graphs. Tell them to use the graphs to compare literacy rate, life expectancy, and GDP per capita. Remind students that they can use spreadsheet software to make charts and then turn those charts into bar graphs. **Ask: Which country has the highest literacy rate?** *(Guyana)* **The highest life expectancy?** *(Costa Rica and the Virgin Islands)* **The highest GDP per capita?** *(Costa Rica)* Tell students that they will learn more about the countries of Central America as they read this unit. Encourage them to look for factors that might explain the differences in the statistics for these countries. **AL**

Regional Atlas Activity

Hypothesizing Ask: Which country in Latin America has the lowest life expectancy? *(Haiti has a life expectancy of only 52.)* **Which country has the lowest GDP per capita?** *(also Haiti; its GDP per capita is only $1,500.)* **Ask: What might be the relationship between the low GDP per capita and the low life expectancy?** *(Possible answer: The low GDP per capita means that Haiti's people are very poor, and poor people often suffer from malnutrition and a lack of health care.)*

Have students locate Haiti on the Political map in the Regional Atlas. **Ask: What other country shares the same island as Haiti?** *(the Dominican Republic)* Have students compare Haiti's life expectancy and GDP per capita with that of the Dominican Republic. **Ask: What difference do you see?** *(The GDP per capita and life expectancy are much higher in the Dominican Republic than in Haiti.)*

Have interested students study the history of Haiti and the Dominican Republic to learn more about the differences between the two countries. **OL**

Regional Atlas

Latin America

Country and Capital	Literacy Rate	Population and Density	Land Area	Life Expectancy (Years)	GDP* Per Capita (U.S. dollars)	Television Sets (per 1,000 people)	Flag and Language
GUYANA, Georgetown	98.8%	800,000 10 per sq. mi. 4 per sq. km	83,000 sq. mi. 214,969 sq. km	63	$3,800	70	English
HAITI, Port-au-Prince	52.9%	8,300,000 775 per sq. mi. 299 per sq. km	10,714 sq. mi. 27,749 sq. km	52	$1,500	5	French, Creole
HONDURAS, Tegucigalpa	76.2%	7,200,000 166 per sq. mi. 64 per sq. km	43,278 sq. mi. 112,090 sq. km	71	$2,800	95	Spanish
JAMAICA, Kingston	87.9%	2,700,000 636 per sq. mi. 246 per sq. km	4,243 sq. mi. 10,989 sq. km	73	$4,100	191	English
MEXICO, Mexico City	92.2%	107,000,000 142 per sq. mi. 55 per sq. km	756,082 sq. mi. 1,958,243 sq. km	75	$9,600	272	Spanish
NICARAGUA, Managua	67.5%	5,800,000 116 per sq. mi. 45 per sq. km	50,193 sq. mi. 129,999 sq. km	69	$2,300	69	Spanish
PANAMA, Panama	92.6%	3,200,000 110 per sq. mi. 42 per sq. km	29,158 sq. mi. 75,519 sq. km	75	$6,900	192	Spanish
PARAGUAY, Asunción	94%	6,200,000 39 per sq. mi. 15 per sq. km	157,046 sq. mi. 406,747 sq. km	71	$4,800	205	Spanish, Guarani
PERU, Lima	0.9%	27,900,000 56 per sq. mi. 22 per sq. km	496,224 sq. mi. 1,285,214 sq. km	70	$5,600	147	Spanish, Quechua
UNITED STATES, Washington, D.C.	97%	296,500,000 80 per sq. mi. 31 per sq. km	3,717,796 sq. mi. 9,629,047 sq. km	78	$40,100	844	English

*Gross Domestic Product

Countries and flags not drawn to scale

Activity: Using the Chart

Visual Literacy Have students study the flags in the chart. **Ask: What similarities do you see?** *(Students may note the frequent use of stars and stripes or that many flags have a symbol in the center.)* Organize students into pairs. Have each pair choose a flag and conduct research to learn about the flag's history and the meaning of the colors, shapes, and symbols on the flag. Then have each pair create an enlarged picture of their flag and present a brief oral report, explaining the flag's symbolism and how the flag reflects the history and culture of that country. **OL**

Latin America

Country and Capital	Literacy Rate	Population and Density	Land Area	Life Expectancy (Years)	GDP* Per Capita (U.S. dollars)	Television Sets (per 1,000 people)	Flag and Language
PUERTO RICO, San Juan	94.1%	3,900,000 1,128 per sq. mi. 436 per sq. km	3,456 sq. mi. 8,951 sq. km	77	$17,700	information not available	Spanish
ST. KITTS-NEVIS, Basseterre	97%	50,000 360 per sq. mi. 139 per sq. km	139 sq. mi. 360 sq. km	70	$8,800	256	English
ST. LUCIA, Castries	67%	200,000 837 per sq. mi. 323 per sq. km	239 sq. mi. 619 sq. km	74	$5,400	368	English
ST. VINCENT AND THE GRENADINES, Kingstown	96%	100,000 737 per sq. mi. 256 per sq. km	151 sq. mi. 391 sq. km	72	$2,900	230	English
SURINAME, Paramaribo	93%	438,000 7 per sq. mi. 3 per sq. km	62,344 sq. mi. 161,470 sq. km	69	$4,300	241	Dutch
TRINIDAD AND TOBAGO, Port-of-Spain	98.6%	1,300,000 656 per sq. mi. 253 per sq. km	1,981 sq. mi. 5,131 sq. km	71	$10,500	337	English
URUGUAY, Montevideo	98%	3,400,000 50 per sq. mi. 19 per sq. km	68,498 sq. mi. 177,409 sq. km	75	$14,500	531	Spanish
VENEZUELA, Caracas	93.4%	26,700,000 76 per sq. mi. 29 per sq. km	352,143 sq. mi. 912,046 sq. km	73	$5,800	185	Spanish
VIRGIN ISLANDS (U.S.), Charlotte Amalie	information not available	108,708 799 per sq. mi. 309 per sq. km	136 sq. mi. 352 sq. km	79	$17,200	information not available	English
UNITED STATES, Washington, D.C.	97%	296,500,000 80 per sq. mi. 31 per sq. km	3,717,796 sq. mi. 9,629,047 sq. km	78	$40,100	844	English

Sources: *CIA World Factbook*, 2005; Population Reference Bureau, *World Population Data Sheet*, 2005.

For more country facts, go to the **Nations of the World Databank** at glencoe.com.

Unit 3 Regional Atlas

Regional Atlas Activity

Analyzing Ask: Which three countries in Latin America have the highest GDP per capita? *(Bahamas, Puerto Rico, and the Virgin Islands)* Have students locate these three countries on the Political map in the Regional Atlas. **Ask: What do these three countries have in common?** *(They are located in the Caribbean.)* **What do Puerto Rico and the Virgin Islands have in common?** *(There are both territories of the United States.)* **OL**

FastFacts

Virgin Islands The Virgin Islands consist of about 90 small islands, islets, and cays in the eastern Caribbean. They are divided into two groups, the British Virgin Islands, which is a territory of the United Kingdom, and the Virgin Islands of the United States. The warm waters and beaches of the Virgin Islands attract many visitors. As a result, tourism is the main economic activity in the islands.

Activity: Using the Chart

Synthesizing Ask: What countries in Latin America would you like to visit? *(Answers will vary.)* Tell students to plan a trip through Latin America starting in Mexico and ending at the tip of South America. Have them use information from the chart and maps in the Regional Atlas to plan the trip. Tell them that they will travel by land and should include at least 12 different countries in their itinerary. As part of their itinerary, have them indicate what cities they will visit and what languages they will need to be able to speak in each country. Encourage them to consult other sources to learn more about the countries on their itinerary and the places that they would like to visit in each country. Have students share their itineraries with the rest of the class by tracing the route on a large map of the region and explaining what places they plan to visit and why. **OL**

Why Summarizing Information Is Important

Summarizing information requires students to recognize the main idea of a passage and its most important supporting details. Restating the main idea in their own words helps students better understand and remember what they have read.

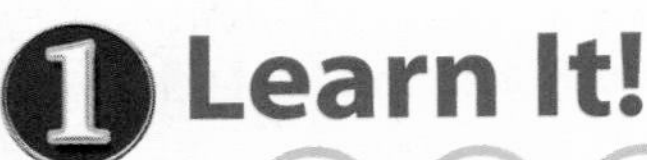

Read any paragraph from the unit aloud. Ask: What is this paragraph about? *(Students should volunteer the paragraph's topic.)* **What is the author trying to tell us about the topic?** *(Students should volunteer the main idea.)* **What are the most important details that the author provides?** *(Students should volunteer any important details.)* Write all student responses on the board. Then have students write a one- or two-sentence summary of the paragraph in their own words, using the information collected on the board. OL

Reading Social Studies

Summarizing Information

Reading Skill

1 Learn It!

Summarizing helps you focus on main ideas. By restating the important facts in a short summary, you can reduce the amount of information to remember. A summary can be a short paragraph that includes the main ideas.

Use these steps to help you summarize:
- Be brief—do not include many supporting details.
- Restate the text in a way that makes sense to you.

Read the text below. Then review the graphic organizer to see how you could summarize the information.

> A people called the Maya lived in Mexico's Yucatán Peninsula and surrounding areas between A.D. 300 and A.D. 900. The Maya built huge stone temples in the shape of pyramids with steps. They were skilled at astronomy and used their knowledge of the stars, moon, and planets to develop a calendar. They also had a number system based on 20. Using hieroglyphics, which is a form of writing that uses signs and symbols, the Maya recorded the history of their kings.
>
> —*from page 209*

Reading Tip

As you read and summarize in your own words, try not to change the author's original meanings or ideas.

Fact: The Maya used their knowledge of the stars, moon, and planets to develop a calendar.	**Fact:** The Maya had a number system based on 20.	**Fact:** The Maya recorded the history of their kings using hieroglyphics.

Summary:
The Maya developed a calendar, created a number system, and recorded their history using hieroglyphics.

Reading Strategy — Analyzing Text Structure

Summarizing Emphasize to students that in order to summarize a passage, they must first identify the topic and the main idea. Explain that passages are often structured in a way that makes finding the main idea fairly easy. The main idea of a section can often be found in the headings and subheadings of that section or in the first paragraph. The main idea of a paragraph is often, but not always, found in the first sentence. Tell students that once they identify the main idea, they should read further to discover the most important supporting details. Have students use these steps to analyze a passage in this unit and then summarize the main idea and any important supporting details in their own words. ELL

2 Practice It!

Read the following paragraph from this unit.

- Draw an organizer like the one shown below.
- Write the main facts from the paragraph in the top boxes.
- Write a summary of the paragraph in the bottom box.

Read to Write Activity

After you read each chapter in this unit, summarize its information. Then, use the chapter's Visual Summary to check to see if you identified the main ideas.

> Family life is important in Latin America. Often several generations live together, and adults are expected to care for their aged parents. Adult brothers and sisters often live near each other, and their children—who are cousins—can form close relationships. Traditionally, the father is the family leader and the chief decision maker. In some parts of the Caribbean, however, the mother is the leader of the family.
>
> *—from page 223*

Latin American teenagers

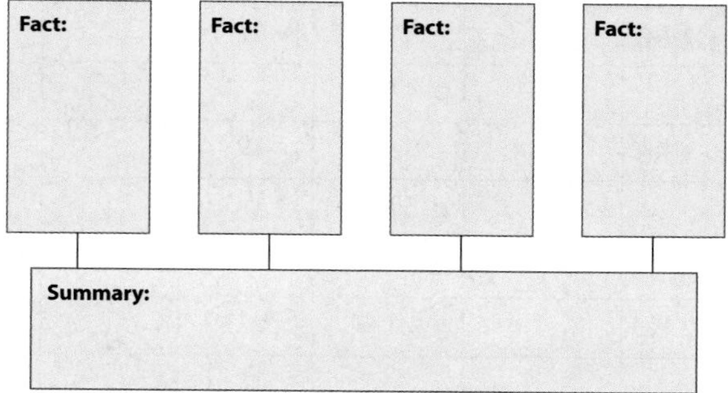

3 Apply It!

With a partner, choose a section to summarize. After each of you summarizes the section on your own, exchange your papers and check to see if the summaries are complete. Note whether any important ideas are missing. Return your summaries to each other and make the changes. Use your summaries to help you study for assessment.

2 Practice It!

Fact: Several generations of Latin American families often live together.
Fact: Adult children are expected to care for their parents.
Fact: Brothers and sisters often live near each other, and their children can form close relationships.
Fact: In much of Latin America, the father is the leader of the family, but in parts of the Caribbean, the mother is.
Summary:
Several generations of Latin American families often live together or near each other and take care of older parents. In much of the region, the father is the head of the family, but in other areas, the mother is the leader. **OL**

3 Apply It!

Have students read a newspaper or short magazine article. Ask them to identify the sentence that best expresses the main idea of the article. Then have them summarize the article in one or two sentences. **OL**

Reading Strategy — Read to Write

Writing Summaries From Notes Have students read a section from the unit and take notes as they read to answer questions and prepare to write a summary. As students read, tell them to ask themselves questions, such as: *What is the topic of this section? What events or ideas are being emphasized? What caused the events? What resulted from the events?* When students are finished reading the section, tell them to use their notes to write a summary. Emphasize to students that they should be careful to put the summary into their own words while not changing the author's meaning. **OL**

Planning Guide

Key to Ability Levels

BL Below level
OL On level
AL Above level
ELL English Language Learners

Key to Teaching Resources

Print Material
DVD
CD-ROM
Transparency

BL	OL	AL	ELL		Resources	Chapter Opener	Section 1	Section 2	Chapter Assess
					FOCUS				
BL	OL	AL	ELL	Transparency	**Daily Focus Skills Transparencies**		7-1	7-2	
					TEACH				
BL	OL		ELL	Print Material	**Guided Reading Activity, URB***		p. 37	p. 38	
BL	OL	AL	ELL	Print Material	**Content Vocabulary Activity, URB***		p. 39	p. 39	
BL	OL	AL	ELL	Print Material	**Academic Vocabulary Activity, URB**		p. 41	p. 41	
BL	OL	AL	ELL	Print Material	**Differentiated Instruction Activity, URB**		p. 43		
BL	OL	AL	ELL	Print Material	**Chart, Graph, and Map Skills Activity, URB**			p. 45	
	OL	AL		Print Material	**Critical Thinking Activity, URB**		p. 47		
BL	OL	AL	ELL	Print Material	**Speaking and Listening Skills Activity, URB**			p. 49	
BL	OL	AL	ELL	Print Material	**Writing Skills Activity, URB**		p. 53		
BL	OL	AL	ELL	Print Material	**School-to-Home Connection Activity, URB***		p. 57		
BL	OL	AL	ELL	Print Material	**Regional Atlas Activities, URB**		pp. 1–7	pp. 1–7	
	OL	AL		Print Material	**Environmental Case Study, URB**			p. 13	
		AL		Print Material	**Enrichment Activity, URB**			p. 19	
BL	OL	AL	ELL	Print Material	**GeoLab Activity, URB**		p. 23		
BL	OL		ELL	Print Material	**Reading Essentials and Note-Taking Guide***		p. 46	p. 49	
	OL			Print Material	**Interactive Geography Activity**	p. 17			
BL	OL	AL	ELL	Transparency	**In-Text Map Overlay and Population Pyramid Transparencies**	3	3B, 3D	3E, 3F	
	OL			Print Material	**Foods Around the World**	p. 10			
BL	OL	AL	ELL	Print Material	**Outline Map Resource Book**	pp. 28, 30			
BL	OL	AL	ELL	Print Material	**NGS World Atlas***	✓	✓	✓	
BL	OL	AL	ELL	Print Material	**NGS World Desk Map**	✓	✓	✓	✓
BL	OL	AL	ELL	Print Material	**World Literature Library**	✓	✓	✓	✓
BL	OL	AL	ELL	Print Material	**Writer's Guidebook**	✓	✓	✓	✓

Note: Please refer to the *Unit Resource Book: Latin America* for this chapter's URB materials.

* Also available in Spanish

- Interactive Lesson Planner
- Interactive Teacher Edition
- Fully editable blackline masters
- Section Spotlight Videos Launch
- Differentiated Lesson Plans
- Printable reports of daily assignments
- Standards Tracking System

Levels				Resources	Chapter Opener	Section 1	Section 2	Chapter Assess
BL	OL	AL	ELL					
TEACH *(continued)*								
BL	OL	AL	ELL	Vocabulary PuzzleMaker CD-ROM*	✓	✓	✓	✓
	OL	AL		Primary Sources CD-ROM	✓	✓	✓	✓
BL	OL	AL	ELL	StudentWorks™ Plus DVD	✓	✓	✓	✓
BL	OL	AL	ELL	Section Video Program Activities	✓	✓	✓	✓
BL	OL	AL	ELL	World Music: A Cultural Legacy	✓	✓	✓	✓
BL	OL	AL	ELL	Writing Process Transparencies	✓	✓	✓	✓
Teacher Resources				Building Academic Vocabulary	✓	✓	✓	✓
				Strategies for Success	✓	✓	✓	✓
				Teacher's Guide to Differentiated Instruction	✓	✓	✓	✓
				Presentation Plus! DVD	✓	✓	✓	✓
ASSESS								
BL	OL	AL	ELL	Quizzes and Tests		p. 75	p. 76	p. 77
BL	OL	AL	ELL	Authentic Assessment With Rubrics		p. 7		p. 7
BL	OL	AL	ELL	Standardized Test Practice				p. 25
BL	OL	AL	ELL	*ExamView® Assessment Suite* CD-ROM*		7-1	7-2	Ch. 7
BL	OL	AL	ELL	Interactive Tutor Self-Assessment CD-ROM		7-1	7-2	
CLOSE								
BL			ELL	Reteaching Activity, URB*		p. 55	p. 55	p. 55
BL	OL		ELL	Reading and Study Skills Foldables™	p. 62	p. 62	p. 62	p. 62
BL	OL	AL	ELL	Graphic Organizer Transparencies and Strategies		✓	✓	
BL	OL	AL	ELL	*Exploring Our World* in Graphic Novel	p. 33			

CHAPTER 7

Integrating Technology

Using Skillbuilder Interactive Workbook CD-ROM

Comparing and Contrasting

Technology Product

Glencoe's *Skillbuilder Interactive Workbook CD-ROM* provides self-paced instruction, practice, and assessment of key skills your students need in social studies, including comparing and contrasting. The *Skillbuilder Interactive Workbook*

- lets students learn, practice, and assess their knowledge of social studies skills.
- lists key terms and a glossary where appropriate.
- includes a **Management System** to create class rosters and monitor student progress.

Objective

The *Skillbuilder Interactive Workbook* helps students

- learn and practice comparing and contrasting;
- identify areas for reinforcement.

Steps

Provide students with the following information:

- Select **Comparing and Contrasting** from the Main Menu page. Then select one of the options.
- The **Instruction** option on the Activities page provides a step-by-step tutorial to learn the skill being taught, along with an audio component.
- The **Guided Practice** section presents comprehension questions to review the material covered in the Instruction section. Question types include multiple choice, true/false, fill-in-the-blank, and drag-and-drop.
- The **Assessment** section includes 10 questions that test student mastery of skill.

Have students complete the activity and use the Management System to monitor their progress.

Social Studies ONLINE

	Student	Teacher	Parent
Beyond the Textbook	●		●
Chapter Overviews	●		●
Concepts in Motion	●		●
ePuzzles and Games	●		●
Literature Connections		●	
Multi-Language Glossaries	●		●
Online Student Edition	●	●	●
Section Videos	●	●	●
Self-Check Quizzes	●		●
Student Web Activities	●		●
Study Central™	●		●
Teaching Today		●	
TIME Current Events	●		●
Vocabulary eFlashcards	●		●
Web Activity Lesson Plans		●	

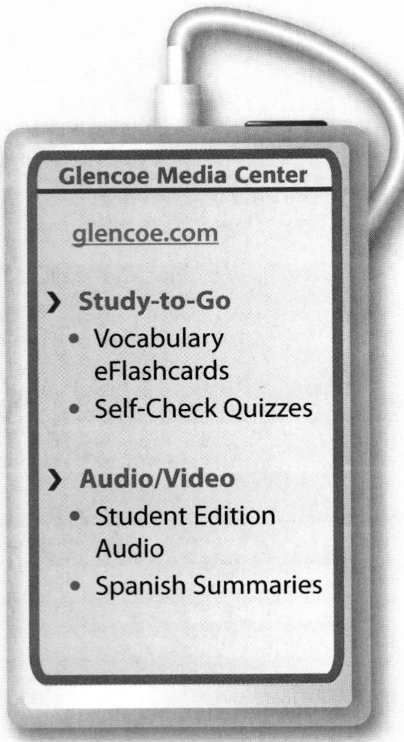

- **Timed Readings Plus in Social Studies** helps students increase their reading rate and fluency while maintaining comprehension. The 400-word passages are similar to those found on state and national assessments.
- **Reading in the Content Area: Social Studies** concentrates on six essential reading skills that help students better comprehend what they read. The book includes 75 high-interest nonfiction passages written at increasing levels of difficulty.
- **Reading Social Studies** includes strategic reading instruction and vocabulary support in Social Studies content for ELLs and native speakers of English.
- **Content Vocabulary Workout** (Grades 6–8) accelerates reading comprehension through focused vocabulary development. Social Studies content vocabulary comes from the glossaries of Glencoe's Middle School Social Studies texts. www.jamestowneducation.com

NATIONAL GEOGRAPHIC

Index to National Geographic Magazine:

The following articles relate to this chapter:

- "The Rain Forest in Rio's Backyard," Virginia Morrell, March 2004.
- "Big Ice in Patagonia," Børge Ousland, August 2004.

National Geographic Society Products To order the following, call National Geographic at 1-800-368-2728:

- *National Geographic Atlas of the World* (Book).

Access National Geographic's new dynamic MapMachine Web site and other geography resources at:
www.nationalgeographic.com
www.nationalgeographic.com/maps

Biography  

The following videotape programs are available from Glencoe as supplements to Chapter 7:

- The Panama Canal (ISBN 1-56-501243-7)
- Mexico: A Story of Courage and Conquest (ISBN 0-76-701622-X)

To order, call Glencoe at 1-800-334-7344. To find classroom resources to accompany many of these videos, check the following home pages:

A&E Television: www.aetv.com
The History Channel: www.historychannel.com

GLENCOE BOOKLINK 3

Use this database to search more than 30,000 titles to create a customized reading list for your students.

- Reading lists can be organized by students' reading level, author, genre, theme, or area of interest.
- The database provides Degrees of Reading Power™ (DRP) and Lexile™ readability scores for all selections.
- A brief summary of each selection is included.

Leveled reading suggestions for this chapter:

For students at a Grade 5 reading level:
- ***Amazon River Rescue,*** by Amanda Lumry and Laura Hurwitz

For students at a Grade 6 reading level:
- ***Mexico,*** by Michael Dahl

For students at a Grade 7 reading level:
- ***South America,*** by Mike Graf

For students at a Grade 8 reading level:
- ***El Salvador: A Question and Answer Book,*** by Kathleen W. Deady

For students at a Grade 9 reading level:
- ***Argentina: The Land,*** by Greg Nickles

Focus

The Essential Question

As students study the chapter, remind them to consider the chapter-based Essential Question. Answering this question will help them understand the important concepts in the chapter. In addition, the Hands-On Chapter Project relates the content from each section to the Essential Question. The steps in each section build on each other as students progress through the chapter. The Hands-On Chapter Project culminates in the Wrap Up activity on the Visual Summary page.

More About the Photo

Visual Literacy Llamas, native to Peru, were as important to the Incas in 1500 as they are to Peruvians today. These gentle animals are surefooted and hardy. Llamas can withstand the variety of highland climates as they carry packs up and down remote trails in the Andes. They require only 10% to 20% of the feed a horse needs, and they produce valuable wool which can be dyed in a variety of colors.

CHAPTER 7

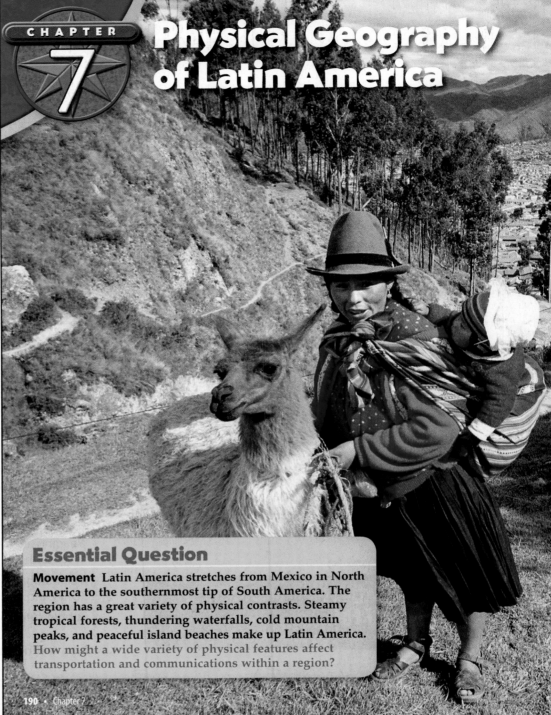

Physical Geography of Latin America

Essential Question

Movement Latin America stretches from Mexico in North America to the southernmost tip of South America. The region has a great variety of physical contrasts. Steamy tropical forests, thundering waterfalls, cold mountain peaks, and peaceful island beaches make up Latin America. How might a wide variety of physical features affect transportation and communications within a region?

190 • Chapter 7

Teach

The BIG Ideas *As you begin teaching each section, use these questions and activities to help students focus on the Big Ideas.*

Section 

Physical Features Ask: What geographic factors influence where people live? *(Possible answers: Some people might want to live near water or mountains because of job or cultural opportunities. Some people might want to live on an island for its isolation and closeness to the ocean.)* Point out to students that in Section 1, they will learn how Latin America's vast river systems, mountains, and forests have affected transportation and trade in region. They also will learn about the area's natural resources. **OL**

Section 

Climate Regions Ask: How does climate affect how people live? *(Possible answers: It affects what people wear and what food is grown in the region. It affects what industries succeed in the area.)* Tell students that in

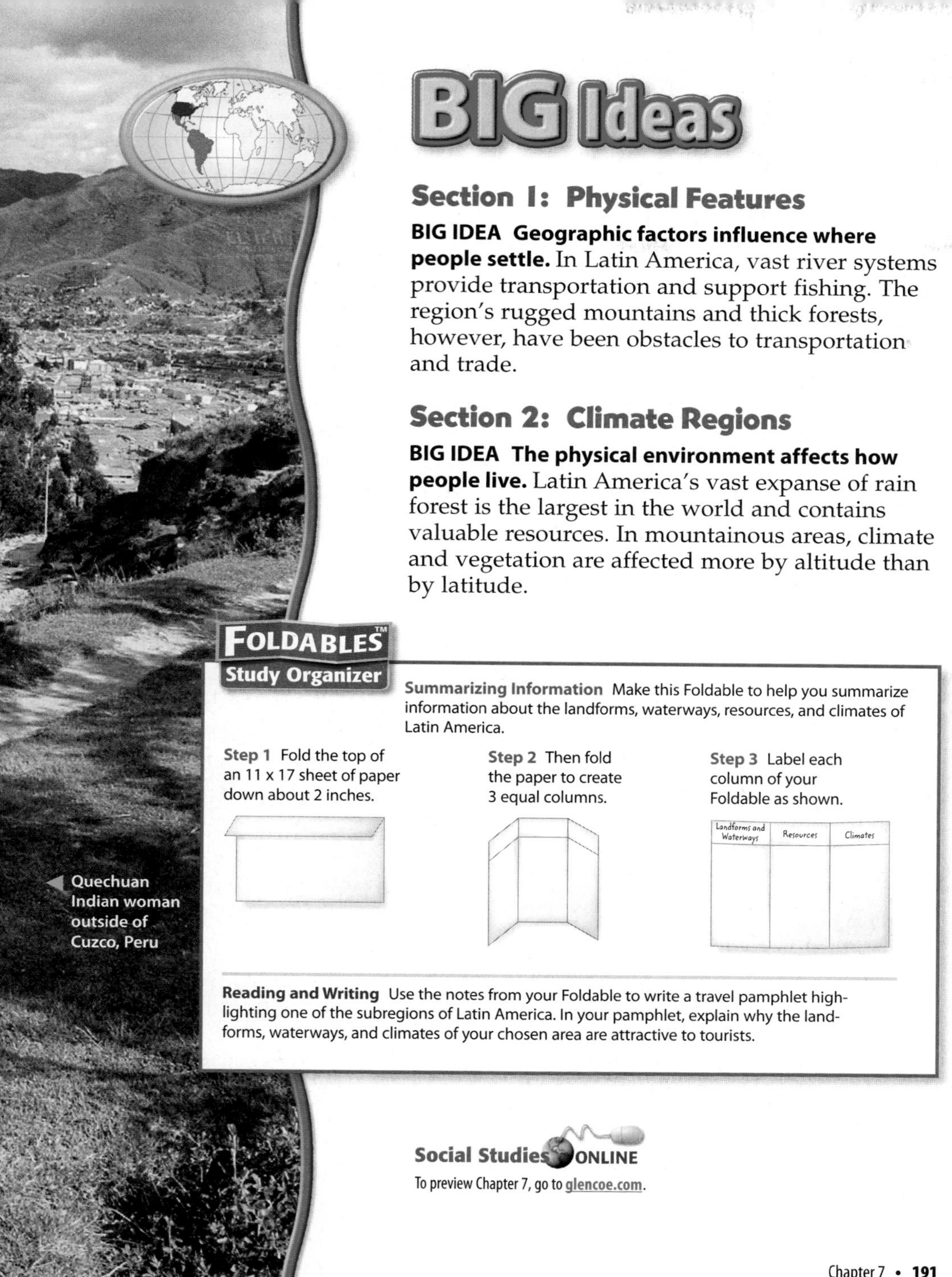

BIG Ideas

Section 1: Physical Features

BIG IDEA Geographic factors influence where people settle. In Latin America, vast river systems provide transportation and support fishing. The region's rugged mountains and thick forests, however, have been obstacles to transportation and trade.

Section 2: Climate Regions

BIG IDEA The physical environment affects how people live. Latin America's vast expanse of rain forest is the largest in the world and contains valuable resources. In mountainous areas, climate and vegetation are affected more by altitude than by latitude.

FOLDABLES™ Study Organizer

Summarizing Information Make this Foldable to help you summarize information about the landforms, waterways, resources, and climates of Latin America.

Step 1 Fold the top of an 11 x 17 sheet of paper down about 2 inches.

Step 2 Then fold the paper to create 3 equal columns.

Step 3 Label each column of your Foldable as shown.

Reading and Writing Use the notes from your Foldable to write a travel pamphlet highlighting one of the subregions of Latin America. In your pamphlet, explain why the landforms, waterways, and climates of your chosen area are attractive to tourists.

◀ Quechuan Indian woman outside of Cuzco, Peru

Social Studies ONLINE
To preview Chapter 7, go to glencoe.com.

Previewing the Region

If you have not already done so, engage students in the Regional Atlas and chart activities to help them become familiar with the general content of the region.

FOLDABLES™ Study Organizer **Dinah Zike's Foldables**

Purpose This Foldable helps students summarize landforms, waterways, resources, and climates of Latin America. Students should note facts from their reading in the appropriate columns on the Foldable. Completed Foldables can be used to write a travel pamphlet highlighting one of the subregions of Latin America, as well as prepare for assessment.

More Foldables activities for this chapter can be found in *Dinah Zike's Reading and Study Skills Foldables* ancillary.

Social Studies ONLINE

Introduce students to chapter content and key terms by having them access the Chapter Overview at glencoe.com.

Section 2, they will learn about the variety of climate zones found in Latin America. They also will learn the important role altitude plays in determining the region's climate and vegetation. **OL**

Focus

Bellringer

Daily Focus Transparency 7-1

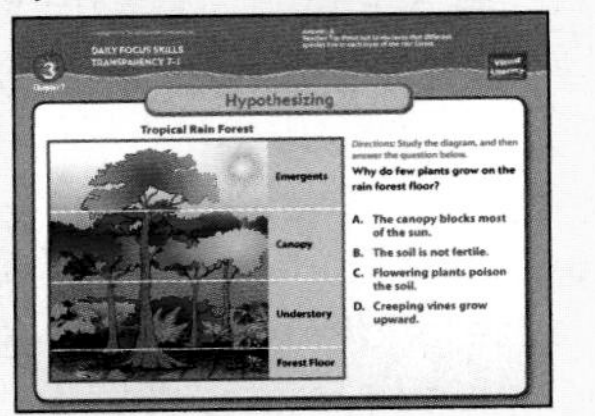

Guide to Reading

Answers to Graphic:

Answers may include:

isthmus: a narrow piece of land that links two larger areas of land

archipelago: a group of islands

The Andes: a cordillera, or a long mountain chain

plateau: flat expanse of land

escarpment: a series of sharp cliffs that drop down to a plain

Llanos: tropical grasslands

Pampas: plain important for cattle grazing

Section Spotlight Video

To learn more about the physical features of Latin America, have students watch the Section Spotlight Video.

Guide to Reading

BIG Idea

Geographic factors influence where people settle.

Content Vocabulary

- subregion *(p. 193)*
- isthmus *(p. 193)*
- archipelago *(p. 193)*
- escarpment *(p. 194)*
- Llanos *(p. 194)*
- Pampas *(p. 194)*
- tributary *(p. 194)*
- estuary *(p. 194)*
- gasohol *(p. 195)*

Academic Vocabulary

- transport *(p. 193)*
- reside *(p. 194)*

Reading Strategy

Identifying Central Issues Use a diagram like the one below to identify and briefly describe six key landforms in the region.

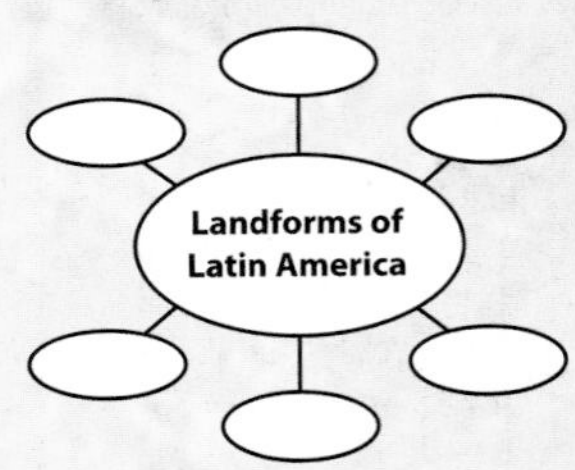

SECTION 1

Physical Features

Picture This How do you farm when there is no flat land? The Inca, an advanced civilization that existed hundreds of years ago in Peru, used a method called terracing. They carved layered fields, like wide steps, into the mountainsides. Today, descendants of the Inca still use this method to raise crops at high altitudes. To learn how the physical landscape has affected other human activities, read Section 1.

A terraced hillside near Pisac, Peru

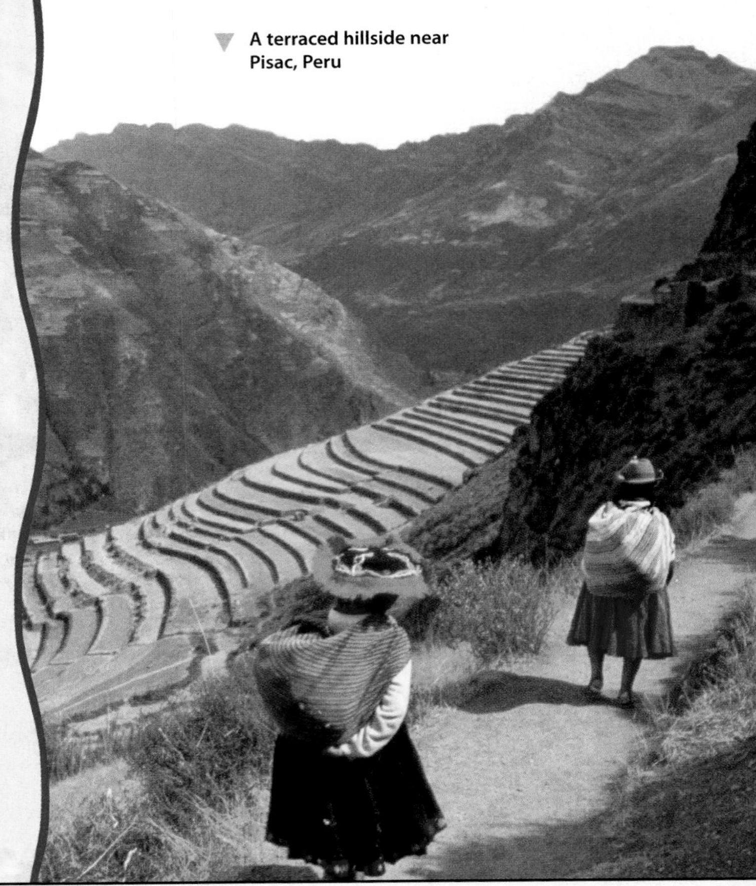

Resource Manager

R Reading Strategies	C Critical Thinking	D Differentiated Instruction	W Writing Support	S Skill Practice
Teacher Edition • Identifying, p. 193 **Additional Resources** • Guid. Read., URB p. 37 • Cont. Vocab., URB p. 39 • Ac. Vocab., URB p. 41 • Read. Ess., p. 46	**Teacher Edition** • Analyzing Info., p. 193 • Compare/Contrast, p. 196 **Additional Resources** • Crit. Think., URB p. 47 • GeoLab, URB p. 23 • Authentic Assess., p. 7 • Quizzes and Tests, p. 75	**Teacher Edition** • Special Ed., p. 193 • EL, p. 195 **Additional Resources** • Diff. Instr., URB p. 43 • Reteach., URB p. 55 • School-to-Home Conn., URB p. 57	**Teacher Edition** • Persuasive Writing, p. 195 **Additional Resources** • Writing Skills, URB p. 53	**Teacher Edition** • Using Geo. Skills, p. 194 • Visual Literacy, p. 195 **Additional Resources** • Daily Focus Trans. 7-1 • Regional Atlas, URB pp. 1–7

Landforms D

Main Idea **Mountains are prominent features in many parts of Latin America.**

Geography and You If you traveled across your state, what geographic features would you see? Read on to learn about the landforms that Latin Americans would encounter if they crossed their region.

Geographers divide the region of Latin America into three **subregions,** or smaller areas. These subregions are Middle America, the Caribbean, and South America.

Middle America

Middle America is made up of Mexico and Central America. Central America is an **isthmus** (IHS·muhs), or a narrow piece of land that links two larger areas of land—North America and South America. Middle America lies where four tectonic plates meet. As a result, it has active volcanoes and frequent earthquakes. Deposits of ash and lava make the soil fertile.

Mexico has mountain ranges along its eastern and western coasts with a high plateau between. Farther south, mountains rise like a backbone through Central America. Lowlands along the coasts are often narrow. Thick forests, rugged mountains, and coastal marshes make it difficult R to **transport** goods in Central America.

The Caribbean

The islands of the Caribbean Sea, also known as the West Indies, can be divided into three groups: the Greater Antilles, the Lesser Antilles, and the Bahamas. The Greater Antilles include the largest islands—Cuba, Hispaniola, Puerto Rico, and Jamaica. The Lesser Antilles is an **archipelago** (AHR·kuh·PEH·luh·GOH), or group of islands. It curves from the Virgin Islands to Trinidad. The third group is the Bahamas, another archipelago.

Andean Village

In the Andes, most people live in valleys and work fields that have been cut into the hillsides.
Regions **Besides the Andes, what is South America's other major landform?**

Except for the largest islands, most Caribbean islands are small. Cuba alone has about half of the Caribbean's land area. Some islands are very low-lying. Others, formed by volcanoes, have rugged mountains. Some of the volcanoes are still active and can cause great damage. Farmers use C the fertile volcanic soil here to grow crops such as sugarcane and tobacco.

South America

The Andes mountain ranges and the vast Amazon Basin are South America's major landforms. The Andes, the world's longest mountain system, are a cordillera (KAWR·duhl·YEHR·uh). They stretch along the Pacific coast of South America for about 5,500 miles (8,851 km). The high Andes ranges have many peaks that soar over 20,000 feet (6,096 m). Between the mountain chains lie plateaus and valleys.

Teach

D Differentiated Instruction

Special Education Before students read the section on landforms, make up an outline for them. As students read, have them refer to the outline to make sure that they are focusing on the most important points and are not getting sidetracked by details. **BL**

R Reading Strategy

Identifying **Ask:** **What physical features make transportation in Middle America difficult?** *(thick forests, rugged mountains, and coastal marshes)* **AL**

C Critical Thinking

Analyzing Information **Ask:** **How have volcanoes helped and hurt islands in the Caribbean?** *(They have formed the islands and provided fertile soil for farming, but also have caused damage.)* **OL**

Caption Answer:
the Amazon Basin

Hands-On Chapter Project
Step 1

Creating a Board Game About Latin America

Step 1: Planning the Game Student groups will design board games that explore the physical landscapes and climates of Latin America.

Essential Question How might a wide variety of physical features affect transportation and communications in a region?

Directions Organize students into small groups. Tell the groups that they will be creating board games that explore the physical landscapes of Latin America and how those landscapes might affect transportation and communications. Explain that they should start with a map of Latin America and create a game board that requires players to travel across many parts of Latin America. In addition to the board itself, groups may include cards with questions or clues and game pieces or cards that represent forms of transportation.

Designing Allow time in class for groups to plan their board games. Tell them that their game should require knowledge of the terrain and climates in the region to be played successfully and should make players use appropriate forms of transportation to travel throughout the region. **OL**

(Chapter Project continued in Section 2)

S Skill Practice

Using Geography Skills Display a large map of South America that shows landforms. **Ask: What clues from the text help you locate the Llanos and Pampas?** *(The text says that the Llanos "stretch through eastern Colombia and Venezuela" and that the Pampas "covers much of Argentina and Uruguay.")* Invite students to locate the two regions on the map. **OL**

Reading Check Answer: Mexico and Central America

Caption Answer:
tropical grasslands that stretch through eastern Colombia and Venezuela

Social Studies ONLINE
Objectives and answers to the Student Web Activity can be found at glencoe.com under the Web Activity Lesson Plan for this chapter.

That is where most people **reside,** or live, and the land can be farmed.

East of the Andes is the huge Amazon Basin. This low area contains the Amazon River and covers 2.7 million square miles (7.0 million sq. km). Highlands to the north and south border the basin. The Brazilian Highlands are so vast that they cross several climate zones. They end in an **escarpment,** a series of steep cliffs that drop down to the Atlantic coastal plain.

S Other lowland plains are found north and south of the Amazon Basin. Tropical grasslands known as the **Llanos** (LAH·nohs) stretch through eastern Colombia and Venezuela. Another well-known plain, the **Pampas,** covers much of Argentina and Uruguay. Like North America's Great Plains, the Pampas is used for cattle herding and grain farming.

Reading Check **Identifying** What areas make up Middle America?

The Pampas

NATIONAL GEOGRAPHIC

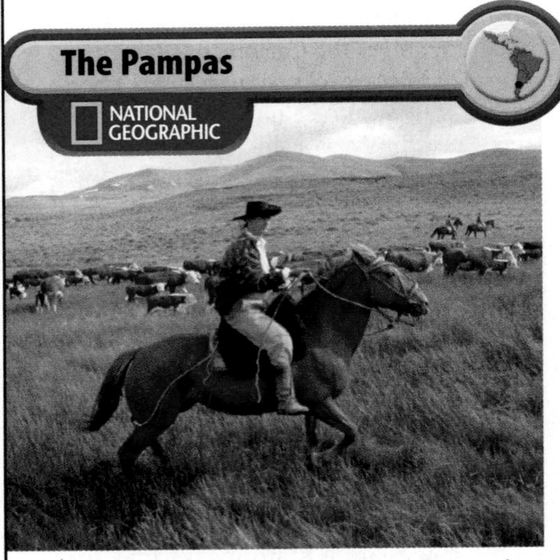

▲ Herding cattle is a major economic activity on the Pampas of Argentina and Uruguay. ***Place*** **What are the Llanos?**

Waterways

Main Idea Latin America's waterways provide important transportation routes.

Geography and You What major rivers flow through your part of the country? How are they important to your area? Read on to find out about the amazing Amazon, one of the world's longest rivers.

Latin America has many natural rivers and lakes, most of which are in South America. The people of the region have used these waterways for transportation and water resources for ages.

Rivers

Latin America's longest river is the Amazon, which starts in the Andes and flows east about 4,000 miles (6,437 km) to the Atlantic Ocean. Heavy rains and many tributaries feed the Amazon. A **tributary** is a small river that flows into a larger river. Some ships can follow the Amazon as far west as Peru, more than 2,500 miles (4,023 km) inland. People also rely on the river for its fish.

Three rivers—the Paraná (PAH·rah·NAH), Paraguay (PAH·rah·GWY), and Uruguay (OO·roo·GWY)—form Latin America's second-largest river system. Together, they drain the rainy eastern half of South America. After winding through inland areas, the three rivers flow into a broad estuary. An **estuary** is an area where river currents and ocean tides meet. This estuary, the Río de la Plata, or "River of Silver," meets the Atlantic Ocean.

Social Studies ONLINE
Student Web Activity Visit glencoe.com and complete the Chapter 7 Web Activity about the Amazon River.

Differentiated Instruction

Leveled Activities

BL School-to-Home Connection, URB p. 57

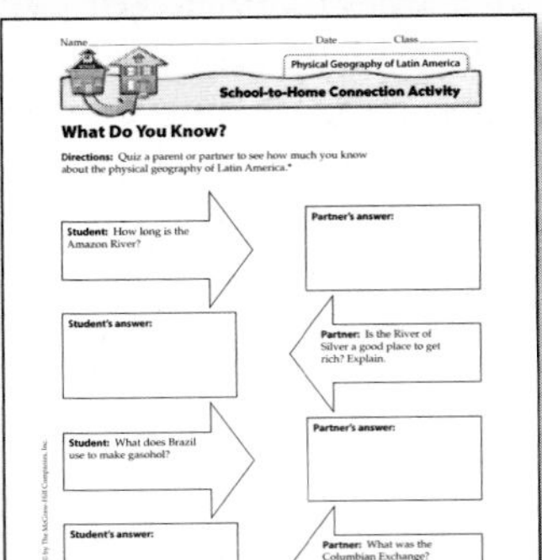

OL Content Vocabulary Activity, URB p. 39

AL Critical Thinking Activity, URB p. 47

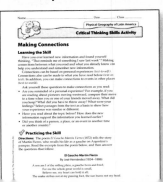

ELL Differentiated Instruction, URB p. 43

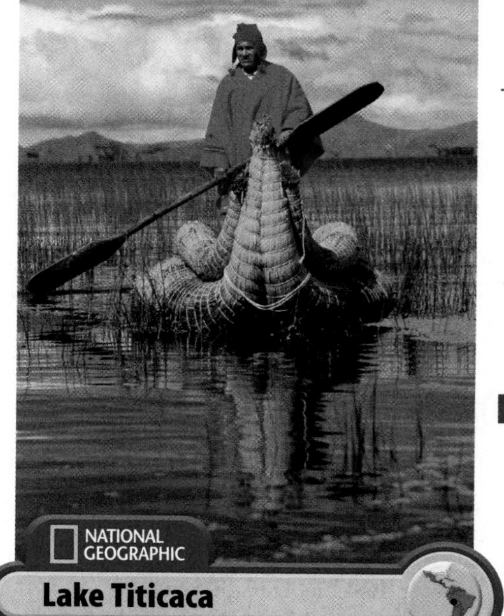

Lake Titicaca

For hundreds of years, the native peoples around Lake Titicaca have traveled its waters using boats made from reeds. ***Place*** **What is unique about Lake Titicaca?**

The Orinoco is another important river. It flows through Venezuela to the Caribbean Sea. This river carries fertile soil into the Llanos region.

Other Waterways

Latin America has few large lakes. Lake Maracaibo, in Venezuela, is South America's largest lake. It contains some of Venezuela's oil fields. Lake Titicaca lies between Bolivia and Peru. About 12,500 feet (3,810 m) above sea level, it is the world's highest lake that can be used by large ships. The Panama Canal, a human-made waterway, stretches across the narrow Isthmus of Panama. Ships use the canal to shorten travel time between the Atlantic and Pacific Oceans.

Reading Check **Identifying** Why is Lake Maracaibo important to Venezuela?

A Wealth of Natural Resources

D

Main Idea **Latin America has vast natural resources, but political and economic troubles have kept some countries from fully using them.**

S

Geography and You Do you use aluminum foil to wrap dinner leftovers? Bauxite, a mineral used to make aluminum, is an important resource on the Caribbean island of Jamaica. Read to find out about the kinds of mineral wealth in Latin America.

W

Latin America has many natural resources. These include minerals, forests, farmland, and water. Not all of Latin America's countries, however, share equally in this wealth. Remote locations, lack of money for development, and the wide gap between rich and poor have kept many of the region's natural resources from being fully developed.

Brazil's Abundant Resources

Brazil, the largest country in Latin America, possesses a great wealth of natural resources. More than 55 percent of Brazil is covered in forests, including a large area of tropical rain forests. The rain forests provide timber and a range of products such as rubber, palm oil, and Brazil nuts.

Brazil also has great mineral wealth. It has large amounts of bauxite, gold, and tin. Its deposits of iron ore and manganese help support one of the world's largest iron and steel industries. Brazil's oil and natural gas reserves, however, are limited. They provide only some of the energy this huge country needs. To reduce its dependence on oil imports, Brazil uses alcohol produced from sugarcane and gasoline to produce a fuel for cars called **gasohol.**

S Skill Practice

Visual Literacy **Ask: What conclusion can you draw about the availabilty of reeds from the image and caption?** *(Possible answer: Reeds must be abundant in the area because boats have been made of them for hundreds of years.)* **OL**

D Differentiated Instruction

English Learners Organize students into groups of three, and assign each student a subsection about natural resources: Brazil's Abundant Resources, Energy Resources, and Other Resources. Tell students to learn the content of their assigned subsection and then teach it orally to the rest of their group. **ELL**

W Writing Support

Persuasive Writing Have students research the benefits and challenges of tapping natural resources in Latin America. Then have them write a persuasive essay supporting one side of the issue. **OL**

Caption Answer:
It is the world's highest lake that can be used by large ships.

Reading Check **Answer:** It contains some of Venezuela's oil fields.

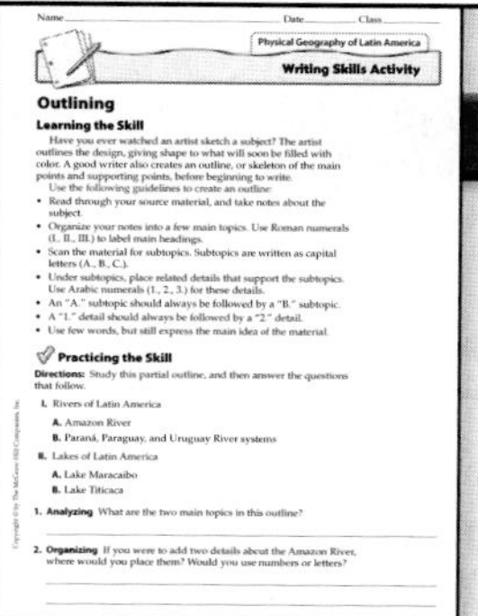

Name______ Date______ Class______

Physical Geography of Latin America

Writing Skills Activity

Outlining

Learning the Skill

Have you ever watched an artist sketch a subject? The artist outlines the design, giving shape to what will soon be filled with color. A good writer also creates an outline, or skeleton of the main points and supporting points, before beginning to write.

Use the following guidelines to create an outline:

- Read through your source material, and take notes about the subject.
- Organize your notes into a few main topics. Use Roman numerals (I., II., III.) to label main headings.
- Scan the material for subtopics. Subtopics are written as capital letters (A., B., C.).
- Under subtopics, place related details that support the subtopics. Use Arabic numerals (1., 2., 3.) for these details.
- An "A." subtopic should always be followed by a "B." subtopic.
- A "1." detail should always be followed by a "2." detail.
- Use few words, but still express the main idea of the material.

Practicing the Skill

Directions: Study this partial outline, and then answer the questions that follow.

I. Rivers of Latin America
  A. Amazon River
  B. Paraná, Paraguay, and Uruguay River systems
II. Lakes of Latin America
  A. Lake Maracaibo
  B. Lake Titicaca

1. **Analyzing** What are the two main topics in this outline?

2. **Organizing** If you were to add two details about the Amazon River, where would you place them? Would you use numbers or letters?

Writing Skills Activity, URB p. 53–54

Outlining

Objective: To learn how to make an outline

Focus: Discuss with students how outlining can improve their writing.

Teach: Have students read the guidelines and study the partial outline.

Assess: Tell students to answer the questions and then write their own outlines.

Close: Ask students to explain why outlining is a helpful study skill.

Differentiated Instruction Strategies

BL After students take notes, have them color code the main topics, subtopics, and supporting points.

AL Have students write a paragraph comparing an artist's sketch to a writer's outline.

ELL Have students find the definition of each of these terms: *subtopic, numeral, guideline.*

C Critical Thinking

Comparing and Contrasting Ask: How does Jamaica's mineral wealth compare to that of other Caribbean islands? *(Jamaica has large deposits of bauxite, but the rest of the Caribbean islands have relatively few mineral resources.)* **OL**

Reading Check Answer: remote locations, lack of money for development, wide gap between rich and poor, foreign control of resources

Assess

Social Studies ONLINE
Study Central™ provides summaries, interactive games, and online graphic organizers to help students review content.

Close

Listing Have students list the major landforms, waterways, and natural resources found in Latin America. **OL**

Energy Resources

In addition to Brazil, other countries of Latin America have energy resources. Venezuela has the region's largest oil and natural gas reserves. Mexico has large amounts of oil and natural gas along the coast of the Gulf of Mexico. Both Mexico and Venezuela use the supplies for their own energy needs as well as for exports.

Bolivia and Ecuador also have valuable oil and natural gas deposits. In Bolivia, however, foreign companies have attempted to control the country's energy resources. Bolivia's government has struggled to prevent this. As a result, production has slowed, and Bolivia has not been able to fully benefit from exports.

Other Resources

Other mineral resources found in Latin America include silver mined in Mexico and Peru. Venezuela has rich iron ore deposits and is a major exporter of the mineral. Colombian mines produce the world's finest emeralds. Chile is the world's largest exporter of copper.

C By contrast, the Caribbean islands have relatively few mineral resources, with a few important exceptions. Jamaica has large deposits of bauxite, a mineral used to make aluminum. In addition, Cuba mines nickel, and the Dominican Republic mines gold and silver.

Certain Central American countries, such as Nicaragua and Guatemala, have rich gold deposits. However, political conflicts and transportation difficulties make mining these deposits difficult.

Reading Check **Analyzing** Why are some Latin American countries unable to make full use of their natural resources?

Section 1 Review

Social Studies ONLINE
Study Central™ To review this section, go to glencoe.com.

Vocabulary

1. **Explain** the significance of:
   a. subregion
   b. isthmus
   c. archipelago
   d. escarpment
   e. Llanos
   f. Pampas
   g. tributary
   h. estuary
   i. gasohol

Main Ideas

2. **Describing** Describe the various mountains found throughout Middle America, the Caribbean, and South America.
3. **Explaining** Use a chart like the one below to note the significance of the listed waterways.

Waterway	Significance
Amazon River	
Paraguay, Paraná, Uruguay system	
Orinoco River	

4. **Identifying** Which Latin American country has the greatest resources? What are they?

Critical Thinking

5. **BIG Idea** What effects can volcanoes have on the peoples and economies of a region?
6. **Challenge** Based on Latin America's natural resources and physical geography, do you think the region will become more important economically in the future? Explain your answer.

Writing About Geography

7. **Using Your FOLDABLES** Use your Foldable to write a paragraph giving examples of how physical geography has affected the lives of people in the region.

Section 1 Review

Answers

1. Definitions for the vocabulary words are found in the section and the Glossary.
2. Mountains run like a backbone through Central America. In the Caribbean, some islands have mountains formed by volcanoes. The Andes stretch along the Pacific coast of South America for about 5,500 miles and have many peaks over 20,000 feet.
3. **Amazon River:** Latin America's longest river, important for transportation, and fish; **Paraguay, Paraná, Uruguay system:** drains the eastern half of South America; **Orinoco River:** carries fertile soil into the Llanos of western Venezuela
4. Brazil; timber, rubber, palm oil, Brazil nuts, bauxite, gold, tin, iron ore, manganese, oil, and natural gas.
5. Volcanoes create frequent earthquakes, and eruptions can cause great damage. Ash and lava from eruptions create fertile soil.
6. Answers will vary. Students may mention Latin America's resources, such as forests, minerals, and energy resources, and Latin America's close proximity to the United States. Students also may mention the importance of the Panama Canal as a transit point.
7. Paragraphs should include examples of how people in Latin America have adapted to living in thick rain forests, steep mountains, and remote areas.

The Columbian Exchange

What do corn, beans, and potatoes have in common? All of these foods were first grown in the Americas.

Separate Worlds For thousands of years, people living in the Eastern Hemisphere had no contact with those living in the Western Hemisphere. This changed in 1492 when European explorer Christopher Columbus arrived in the Americas. Columbus's voyages began what became known as "the Columbian Exchange"—a transfer of people, animals, plants, and even diseases between the two hemispheres. W

For Better and for Worse The Europeans brought many new things to the Americas. They brought horses, which helped the Native Americans with labor, hunting, and transportation. European farm animals, such as sheep, pigs, and cattle, created new sources of income for people in the Americas. Europeans also brought crops—oats, wheat, rye, and barley. The sugarcane brought by Europeans grew well on plantations in the tropical Americas.

▲ Tomato sauce on Italian pasta

Some parts of the Exchange were disastrous, however. Europeans brought diseases that killed millions of Native Americans. Plantation owners put enslaved Africans to work in their fields.

From the Americas, explorers returned home with a wide variety of plants. Spanish sailors carried potatoes to Europe. Nutritious and easy to grow, the potato became one of Europe's most important foods. Corn from the Americas fed European cattle and pigs. Peanuts, tomatoes, hot peppers, and chocolate changed the diets of people in Europe, Asia, and Africa.

▼ Mexican Indian making chocolate

Think About It

1. **Place** What foods were unknown in Europe before 1492?
2. **Human-Environment Interaction** Why were some foods adopted from the Americas so important in other parts of the world?

W Writing Support

Narrative Writing Have students write a story about a South American family whose lives have been changed by the Columbian Exchange. Students might choose to build their stories around a positive or negative aspect (for example, the introduction of rice or the spread of disease). Invite volunteers to explain the plot of their story to the class. **AL**

Think About It

Answers:

1. potatoes, corn, peanuts, tomatoes, hot peppers, and chocolate
2. Some of the foods had high nutritional value and were easy to grow.

Additional Support

Activity: Interdisciplinary Connection

Daily Life Tell students that foods introduced as part of the Columbian Exchange remain important in daily life today. In fact, some regions are best known for foods that were brought there as part of the Columbian Exchange. It's hard to imagine Italian food without tomatoes or Ireland without potatoes. **Ask:** **Think of your favorite food. Was its development in any way related to the Columbian Exchange?** *(Answers will vary.)* Ask students to choose one food that was part of the Columbian Exchange and to find a recipe that shows the food's use in the country to which it was introduced. For example, students could find an Italian recipe using tomatoes or a Mexican recipe using wheat. Have students make a chart showing the recipe and the place of origin of each of its ingredients. If possible, have students work with their caregivers to prepare the recipe. Then hold a food fair in the classroom, showing how the Columbian Exchange changed food tastes around the world. **OL**

Focus

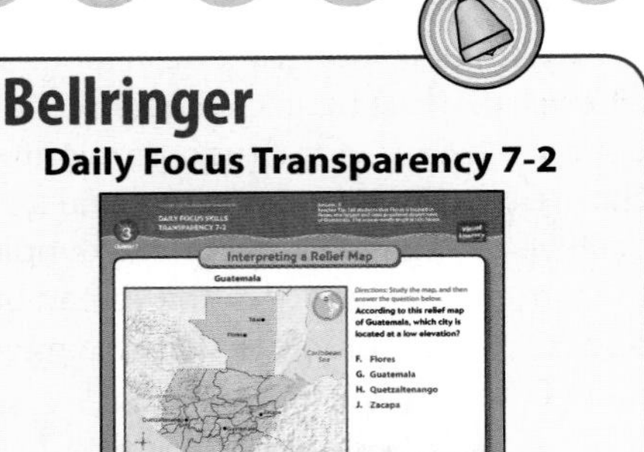

Bellringer
Daily Focus Transparency 7-2

Guide to Reading
Answers to Graphic:

Answers may include:
Rain Forest: is found in much of Central and South America; a dense stand of trees and other plants
Savanna: has a long dry season; is found in parts of Middle America, north central South America, and in most Caribbean islands; attracts tourism
Both: have year-round warm temperatures and heavy rainfall

Section Spotlight Video

To learn more about the climate regions of Latin America, have students watch the Section Spotlight Video.

Guide to Reading

BIG Idea
The physical environment affects how people live.

Content Vocabulary
- Tropics *(p. 199)*
- rain forest *(p. 199)*
- canopy *(p. 200)*
- altitude *(p. 201)*

Academic Vocabulary
- facilitate *(p. 199)*
- considerable *(p. 200)*

Reading Strategy
Comparing and Contrasting Use a Venn diagram like the one below to compare and contrast the tropical rain forest and tropical savanna climate zones.

Climate Regions

Picture This These huge, 6-foot-wide water lilies are found deep in Brazilian rain forests near the mighty Amazon River. They are so strong that an average-sized adult could rest his or her full weight on them! The warm temperatures and heavy rains of the rain forest create an ideal growing environment for many exotic plants. To learn more about how climate affects the people, vegetation, and wildlife of Latin America, read Section 2.

▼ Rain forest water lilies

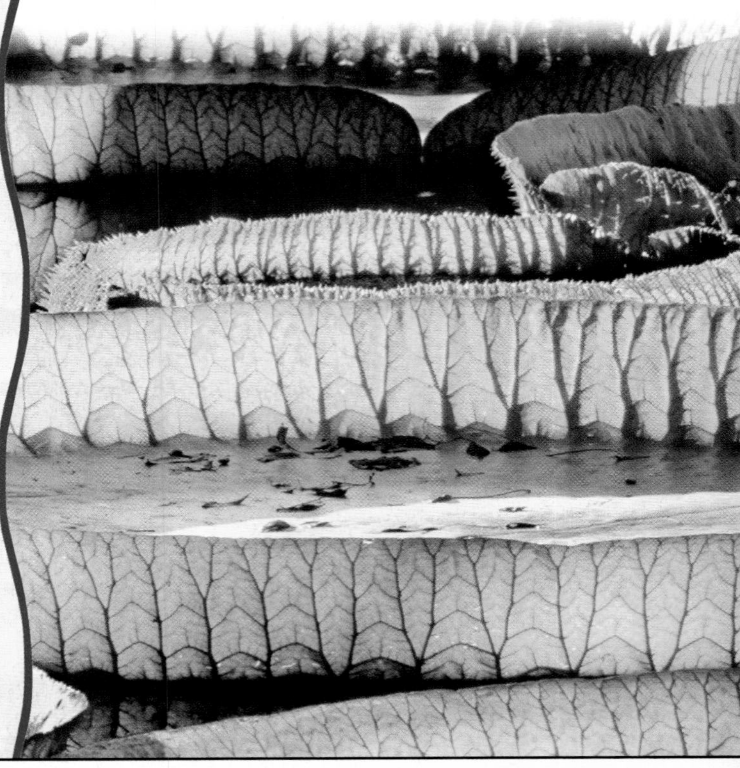

Resource Manager

R Reading Strategies	C Critical Thinking	D Differentiated Instruction	W Writing Support	S Skill Practice
Teacher Edition • Und. Q/A Relationships, p. 199 • Analyzing Text Structure, p. 201 • Summarizing, p. 200 **Additional Resources** • Guid. Read., URB p. 38 • Cont. Vocab., URB p. 39 • Ac. Vocab., URB p. 41 • Read. Ess., p. 49	**Teacher Edition** • Drawing Con., p. 200 • Compare/Contrast, p. 202 **Additional Resources** • Quizzes and Tests, p. 76	**Teacher Edition** • Kinesthetic, p. 201 **Additional Resources** • Enrichment, URB p. 19	**Teacher Edition** • Descriptive Writing, p. 200 **Additional Resources** • Env. Case Studies, URB p. 13	**Teacher Edition** • Using Geo. Skills, p. 199 • Visual Literacy, p. 201 **Additional Resources** • Chart, Graph, and Map Skills, URB p. 45 • Speak./Listen. Skills, URB p. 49 • Daily Focus Trans. 7-2 • Regional Atlas, URB pp. 1–7

Hot to Mild Climates

Main Idea Much of Latin America is located in the Tropics and has year-round high temperatures and heavy rainfall.

Geography and You What might the view be like at the top of a rain forest tree 130 feet up? Read to find out why rain forests thrive in Latin America's tropical areas.

Most of Latin America lies within the **Tropics**—the area between the Tropic of Cancer and the Tropic of Capricorn. This area has generally warm temperatures because it receives the direct rays of the sun for much of the year. Yet even within the Tropics, mountain ranges and wind patterns create a variety of climates in the region. **Figure 1** shows Latin America's different climate zones. R

Tropical Climates

A tropical wet climate is found in some Caribbean islands and much of Central America and South America. This climate is marked by year-round hot temperatures and heavy rainfall. Vast areas of rain forest cover much of this climate zone. A **rain forest** is a dense stand of trees and other plants that receive high amounts of precipitation. Warm temperatures and heavy rains **facilitate,** or make possible, the growth of rain forests.

South America's Amazon Basin is home to the world's largest rain forest.

NATIONAL GEOGRAPHIC Maps In MOtion See StudentWorks™ Plus or glencoe.com.

Figure 1 Latin America: Climate Zones

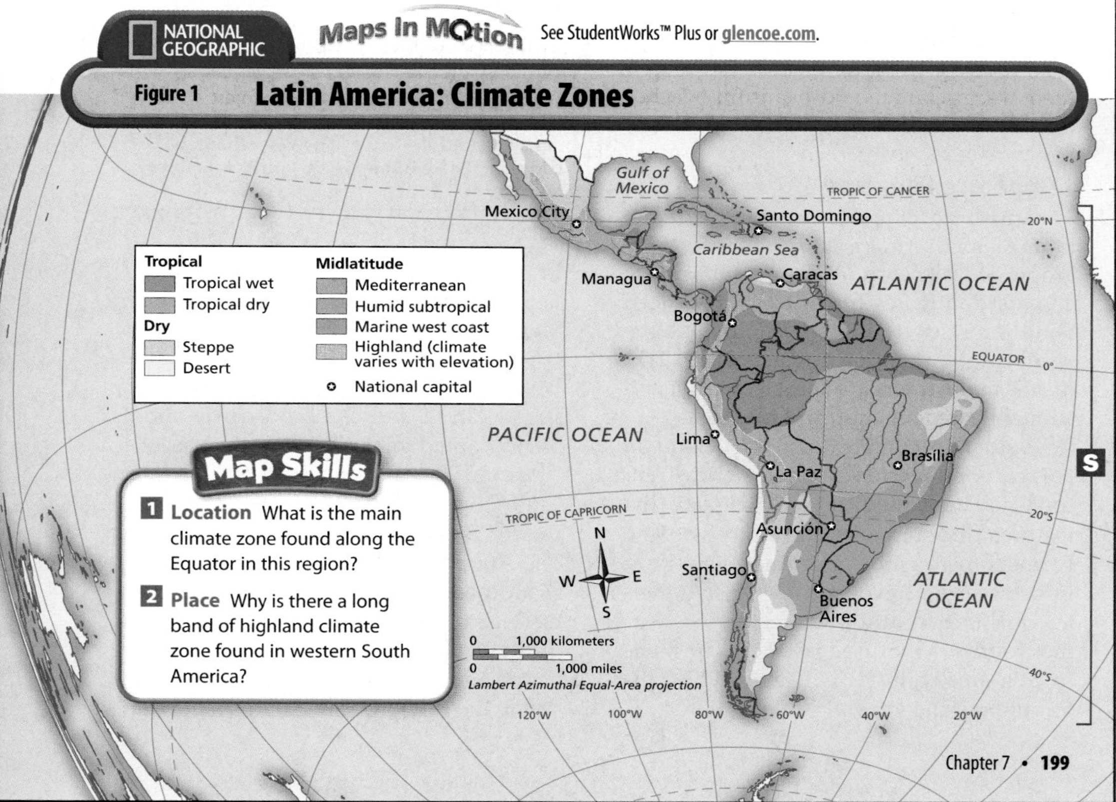

S

Teach

R Reading Strategy

Understanding Question-Answer Relationships Explain to students that some questions can be answered with wording that appears in the question. Have students identify the part of the following question that needs to be found to supply the answer. **Ask: What two factors create a variety of climates in tropical Latin America?** *(What two factors)* Have students construct a response sentence replacing the three words with the answer from the text. *(Mountain ranges and wind patterns create a variety of climates in tropical Latin America.)* **BL**

S Skill Practice

Using Geography Skills Ask: In which climate zones do the following cities lie: Mexico City, Lima, La Paz, and Buenos Aires? *(Mexico City—highland; Lima—desert; La Paz—highland; Buenos Aires—humid subtropical)* **OL**

Map Skills

Answers:

1. tropical wet
2. The band follows the Andes, which provide the varied elevations.

Differentiated Instruction

Leveled Activities

BL Academic Vocabulary Activity, URB p. 41

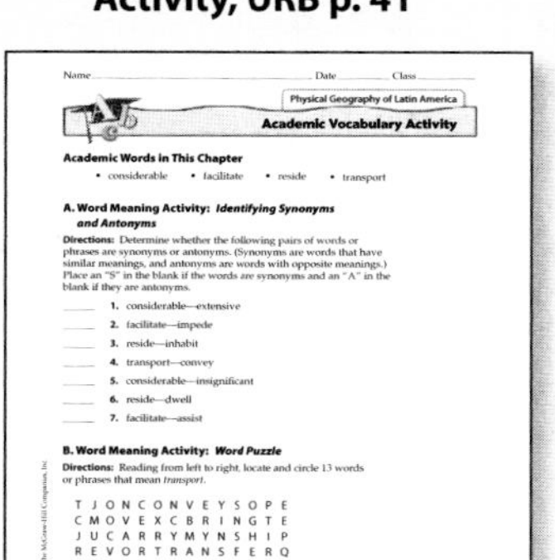
Physical Geography of Latin America
Academic Vocabulary Activity

OL Environmental Case Study, URB p. 13

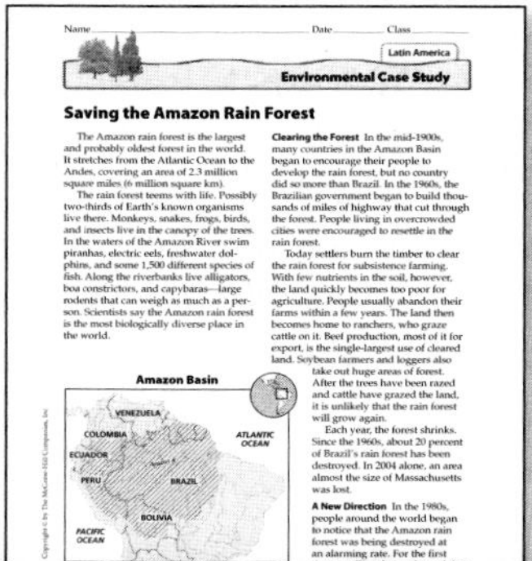
Latin America
Environmental Case Study
Saving the Amazon Rain Forest

AL Enrichment Activity, URB p. 19

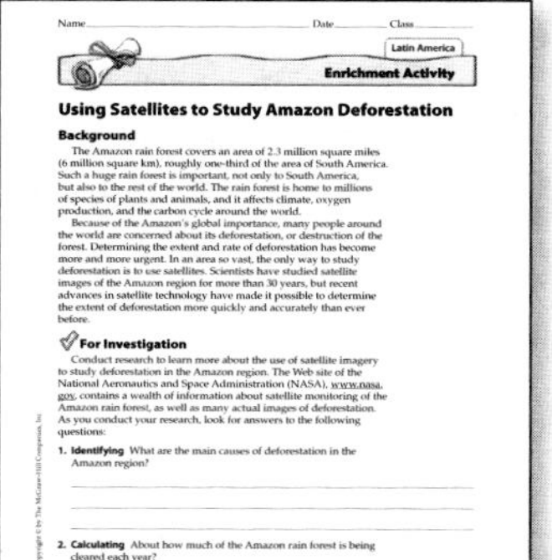
Latin America
Enrichment Activity
Using Satellites to Study Amazon Deforestation

ELL Chart, Graph, and Map Skills, URB p. 45

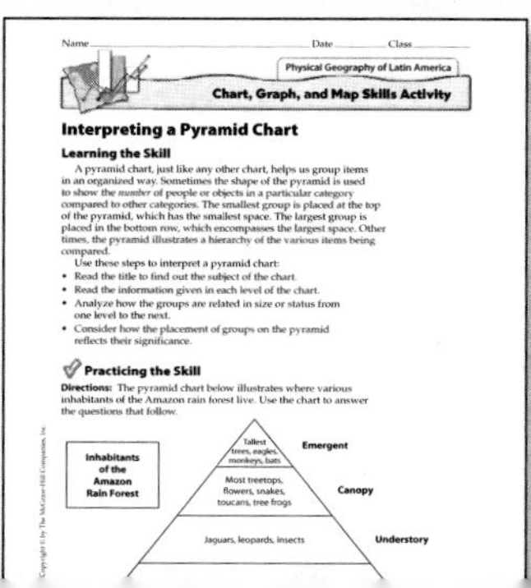
Physical Geography of Latin America
Chart, Graph, and Map Skills Activity
Interpreting a Pyramid Chart

C Critical Thinking

Drawing Conclusions **Ask:** **What kind of plants do you think grow on the rain forest floor? Explain.** *(Plants that grow in the shade; the canopy does not allow much sunlight to filter through to the floor.)* OL

R Reading Strategy

Summarizing Ask students to write an essay explaining how Americans are able to enjoy a variety of vegetables and fruits year-round. OL

W Writing Support

Descriptive Writing Review with students the difference between similes and metaphors: both compare two different things; a simile uses the words *like* or *as*, while a metaphor does not. Have each student write one simile and one metaphor inspired by the images. Give students the following examples: metaphor—The tree was a sentinel standing guard over the creatures of the forest; simile—The parrots flew through the trees like living, breathing rainbows. OL

Caption Answer:
South America's Amazon Basin

It shelters more species of plants and animals per square mile than anywhere else on Earth. Trees there grow so close together that their tops form a dense **canopy,** an umbrella-like covering of leaves. The canopy may soar to 130 feet (40 m) above the ground. It is so dense that sunlight seldom reaches the forest floor. C

A tropical dry climate zone extends over parts of Middle America, most Caribbean islands, and north central South America. This savanna area has hot temperatures and abundant rainfall but also experiences a long dry season.

From June to November, powerful hurricanes often strike the Caribbean islands. The heavy winds and rain of these storms can cause **considerable,** or much, damage. Still, many Caribbean islands have used their warm climate and beautiful beaches to build a strong tourist industry.

NATIONAL GEOGRAPHIC

Rain Forests

W Vegetation can be dense on the rain forest floor. Many species of birds, including colorful macaws (inset), live in the rain forest canopy.
Location **Where is the world's largest rain forest found?**

Temperate Climates

Temperate climates are found in the parts of South America that lie south of the Tropic of Capricorn. A humid subtropical climate dominates much of southeastern South America from southern Brazil to the Pampas of Argentina and Uruguay. This means that winters are short and mild, and summers are long, hot, and humid.

R Temperate climates also are found in parts of southwestern South America. Central Chile has a Mediterranean climate that features dry summers and rainy winters. Farmers there grow large amounts of fruit in summer and export it to North America during that area's winter season. Farther south is a marine coastal climate zone. In this area, rainfall is heavier and falls throughout the year.

Dry Climates

Some parts of Latin America—northern Mexico, coastal Peru and Chile, northeastern Brazil, and southeastern Argentina—have dry climates. Grasses cover partly dry steppe lands, and cacti and hardy shrubs have adapted to harsher desert areas.

Along the Pacific coast of northern Chile lies the Atacama (AH·tah·KAH·mah) Desert. It is one of driest places on Earth. The Atacama Desert is located in the rain shadow of the Andes. Winds from the Atlantic Ocean bring rainfall to the regions east of the Andes, but they carry no moisture past them. In addition, the cold Peru Current in the Pacific Ocean does not evaporate

Hands-On Chapter Project
Step 2

Creating a Board Game About Latin America

Step 2: Creating the Game Students will create the board game they planned in Step 1.

Directions Provide groups with art supplies, including poster board or some other kind of board material. Have them create the game board for the game they planned in Step 1, as well as any cards or game pieces that will be needed to play the game. Encourage students to incorporate various forms of transportation as they create the different parts of the game. Make sure each group writes instructions explaining how its game is to be played.

Putting It Together Have the groups take turns playing each other's games. Then have them evaluate the games, based on creativity and how well each game helps answer the Essential Question. OL

(Chapter Project cont. on the Visual Summary page)

as much moisture as a warm current does. As a result, only dry air hits the coast.

El Niño

As you may recall, weather in South America is strongly influenced by the El Niño effect. This is a set of changes in air pressure, temperature, and rainfall that begins in the Pacific Ocean.

When El Niño takes place, the Pacific waters off Peru's coast are unusually warm. As a result, winds blowing toward land carry heavy rains that lead to severe flooding along Peru's coast. El Niño can also bring a long dry season to northeastern Brazil, causing crop failures. **D**

Reading Check **Summarizing** Why do the Tropics tend to have warm temperatures?

Elevation and Climate

Main Idea **In tropical Latin America, altitude causes great changes in climate and vegetation.**

Geography and You Have you ever traveled in the mountains and felt it getting cooler as you went higher? Read to find out how mountains affect climate in tropical areas of Latin America.

As you have read, mountains and highlands cover much of Latin America. **Altitude**, a place's height above sea level, affects climate in these rugged areas. **R** The higher the altitude is, the cooler the temperatures are—even within the warm areas of the Tropics. The Andes, for example, have four altitude zones of climate.

NATIONAL GEOGRAPHIC

Figure 2 **Altitude Climate Zones**

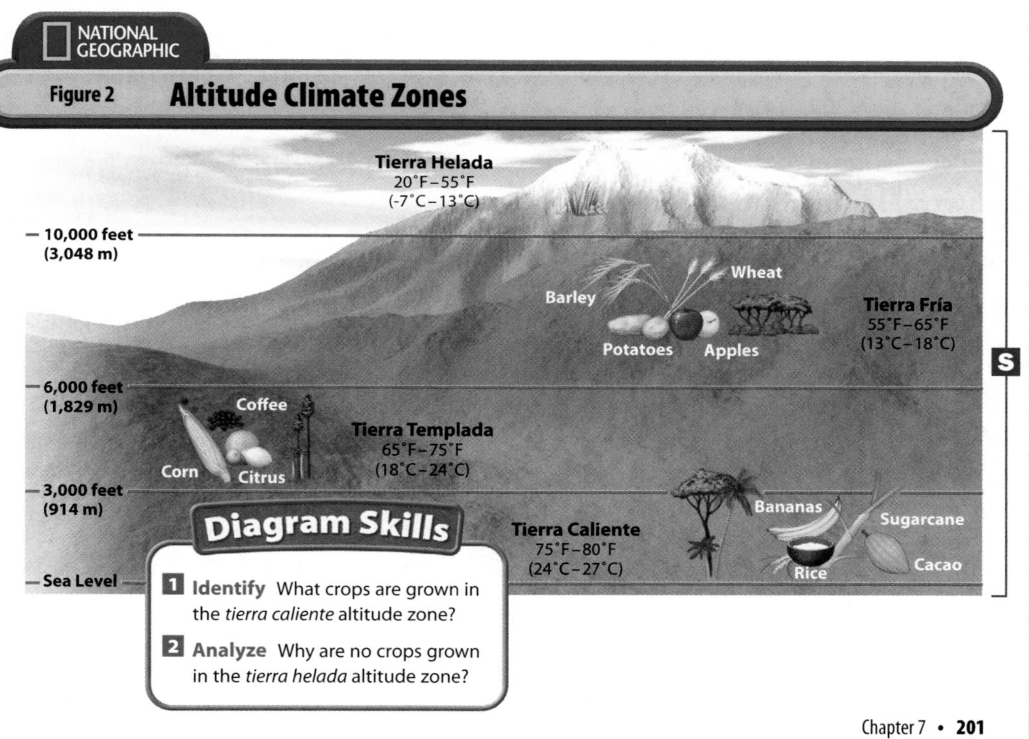

S

Diagram Skills

1. **Identify** What crops are grown in the *tierra caliente* altitude zone?
2. **Analyze** Why are no crops grown in the *tierra helada* altitude zone?

D Differentiated Instruction

Kinesthetic Organize students in small groups. Ask each group to create a short presentation that physically dramatizes the El Niño effect. **AL**

R Reading Strategy

Analyzing Text Structure Tell students that definitions of key terms are often set apart by commas after the key term. **Ask:** **What is the definition of *altitude?*** *(a place's height above sea level)* Tell students to look for this structure throughout the text. **BL**

S Skill Practice

Visual Literacy Ask students to describe three facts based on the diagram. *(Tropical foods grow in the* tierra caliente. *The* tierra caliente *is the warmest altitude climate zone. It is warm in the* tierra caliente.*)* **OL**

Reading Check **Answer:** They receive the direct rays of the sun for much of the year.

Diagram Skills

Answers:
1. bananas, sugarcane, rice, and cacao
2. It is below freezing there.

Differentiated Instruction

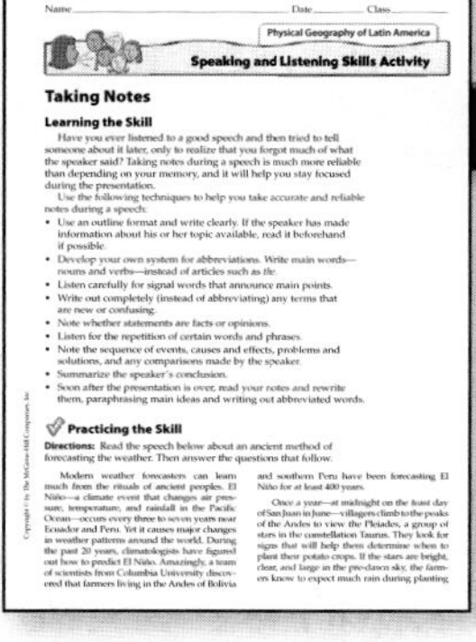

Speaking and Listening Skills, URB pp. 49–52

Taking Notes

Objective: To learn to take notes effectively
Focus: Discuss ways in which students can stay focused in class.
Teach: Have students read and take notes on the speech.
Assess: Compare students' outlines to the checklist.
Close: Discuss with students how the skills of outlining and note taking are similar.

Differentiated Instruction Strategies

BL Guide students in highlighting important words and concepts in the speech.
AL Have students share their notes with the class and explain how they organized them.
ELL Have students take notes on the speech as you read it aloud.

C Critical Thinking

Comparing and Contrasting Ask: How are the *tierra caliente* and *tierra fría* alike and different? Tierra caliente: *average temperature between 75°F and 80°F, conditions remain about the same year-round, farmers grow tropical crops there;* Tierra fría: *average temperature between 55°F and 65°F, has forested and grassy areas, farmers grow crops that must be able to live in difficult conditions; Both: in the Andes, land allows for some farming.)* OL

Reading Check **Answer:** The altitudes have different climates, and different crops grow at each type.

Assess

Social Studies ONLINE
Study Central™ provides summaries, interactive games, and online graphic organizers to help students review content.

Close

Explaining Have students explain the relationship between elevation and climate. OL

As **Figure 2** on the previous page shows, terms in the Spanish language are used to label the different zones.

The *tierra caliente,* or "hot land," refers to the hot and humid elevations near sea level. The average temperature range is between 75°F to 80°F (24°C to 27°C). There is little change from one month to another. In the *tierra caliente,* farmers grow a number of different tropical crops, including bananas, sugarcane, and rice.

Higher up the mountains—from 3,000 feet to 6,000 feet (914 m to 1,829 m), the air becomes cooler. Abundant rainfall encourages the growth of forests. This zone of moist, pleasant climates is called the *tierra templada,* or "temperate land." The mild temperatures—between 65°F and 75°F (18°C and 24°C)—make the *tierra templada* the most densely populated of the climate zones. Here, people grow corn and citrus fruits. Coffee, an important export crop in the region, is grown at this level.

The next zone is the *tierra fría,* or "cold land." It begins at 6,000 feet (1,829 m) and stretches up to 10,000 feet (3,048 m). Average yearly temperatures here can be as low as 55°F (13°C). The *tierra fría* has forested and grassy areas. Farming can take place in this zone in the warmer summers. The crops, however, are those that thrive in cooler, more difficult conditions. Potatoes, barley, and wheat are some of the major crops in this zone.

The *tierra helada,* or "frozen land," is the zone of highest elevation. It lies above 10,000 to 12,000 feet (3,048 m to 3,658 m). Conditions here can be harsh. The climate is cold, and the temperature can be as low as 20°F (–7°C). Vegetation throughout this zone is sparse. Relatively few people live at these heights.

Reading Check **Making Generalizations**
Why do people grow different crops at different altitudes?

Section 2 Review

Social Studies ONLINE
Study Central™ To review this section, go to glencoe.com.

Vocabulary

1. **Explain** the significance of *Tropics, rain forest, canopy,* and *altitude* by using each word in a sentence.

Main Ideas

2. **Identifying** Use a diagram like the one below to list the effects of El Niño.

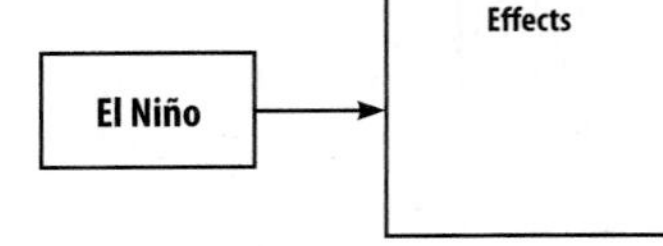

3. **Explaining** Why is the *tierra templada* the most populated altitude zone in the Latin American highlands?

Critical Thinking

4. BIG Idea How do some Caribbean countries benefit economically from their environment?
5. **Determining Cause and Effect** Why is the Pacific coast of northern Chile one of the driest places on Earth?
6. **Challenge** Why do parts of Latin America have mild temperatures even though they are located in the Tropics?

Writing About Geography

7. **Expository Writing** Create a chart that lists the climate zones of Latin America, explains where each zone is located, and describes the conditions and vegetation found in each zone.

Answers

1. Sentences should use vocabulary words according to their definitions in the section and Glossary.
2. El Niño warms the Pacific waters off Peru's coast, causing warm winds blowing toward land to carry heavy rains, which leads to severe flooding along Peru's coast. El Niño can also bring a long dry season to northeastern Brazil, causing crop failures.
3. The *tierra templada* is the temperate zone. It has mild temperatures and can support a variety of crops, so many people choose to live there.
4. Many Caribbean islands have used their warm climate and beautiful beaches to build a tourist industry.
5. It is located in the rain shadow of the Andes. In addition, the cold Peru Current in the Pacific Ocean brings only dry air to the coast.
6. Areas in the Tropics that are at high altitudes will be cooler and will have mild temperatures.
7. Charts should include and describe the tropical climate of some Caribbean Islands and much of Central and South America; the dry savanna of Middle America, most Caribbean islands, and north central South America; the temperate climates of South America south of the Tropic of Capricorn; and the dry climate of northern Mexico, coastal Peru and Chile, northeastern Brazil, and southeastern Argentina.

Visual Summary

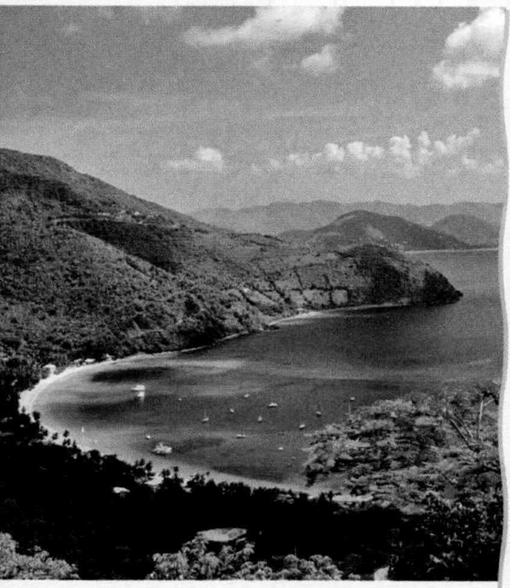

Tortola, British Virgin Islands

Landforms

- Geographers divide Latin America into three subregions—Middle America, the Caribbean, and South America.
- Middle America, which joins North America and South America, has central mountains and narrow coastal plains.
- Caribbean islands can be low-lying or mountainous. Many have volcanoes.
- The towering Andes and the vast Amazon Basin are South America's major landforms.
- Highlands border the Amazon Basin. Lowland plains cross parts of Colombia, Venezuela, Uruguay, and Argentina.

Waterways

- Latin America's waterways provide food and transportation.
- The Panama Canal, a human-made waterway, links the Atlantic and Pacific Oceans.
- Large reserves of oil are found near Venezuela's Lake Maracaibo.

Fishing on the Amazon River

An emerald from Colombia

Resources of Latin America

- Venezuela, Mexico, and Bolivia export oil and natural gas.
- Mineral resources from Latin America include iron ore, copper, tin, silver, and emeralds.
- Political conflicts and transportation difficulties keep some countries from fully using their resources.

Climate Regions

- Latin America's tropical rain forest and savanna climates have warm temperatures.
- Rain forests, such as those in the Amazon Basin, have a great variety of plant and animal life.
- The El Niño effect brings heavy rain or drought to parts of South America.
- Climates tend to be drier and cooler at higher elevations, even within the Tropics.

Andes, Argentina

Study anywhere, anytime! Download quizzes and flash cards to your PDA from glencoe.com.

Visual Summary

Identifying Central Issues Organize students into six small groups. Assign each group one of the following subjects: Landforms, Waterways, Resources, the Columbian Exchange, Climate Regions, and Elevation and Climate.

Have each group create an interesting display that includes information from the Visual Summary as well as the text. Suggest the use of photographs, drawings, and actual objects. For example, students may use magazine photos or plastic fruits and vegetables to illustrate climate zones.

When groups have finished preparing their displays, invite groups to present their work to the class. Have students take notes during each presentation. **OL**

Taking Notes Have students take notes from each section of the Visual Summary. Offer the following example for Landforms: *The varied landforms of Latin America include volcanic islands, low islands, the towering Andes, the vast Amazon Basin, highlands, lowland plains, and narrow coastal plains.* **OL**

Hands-On Chapter Project
Step 3: Wrap Up

Creating a Board Game About Latin America

Step 3: Learning From the Games Students will synthesize what they have learned in Steps 1 and 2.

Directions Write the Essential Question on the board. Discuss the ways that different games explored the landscapes and climates of Latin America. **Ask:** **How did players of each game interact with the different landscapes in the region? What forms of transportation did you need to use in different areas?** Ask students how they might deal with a lack of communication options while traveling in a remote area. Discuss the ways that people who live in these areas have dealt with the same issues. Then have students write several sentences in their journals answering the Essential Question. **OL**

Answers and Analyses

Reviewing Vocabulary

1. B Students will likely eliminate answer choice D because it is a generic term for a smaller area found within a larger area. To choose from the three remaining answer choices, students must remember the definition for each term. An *isthmus* is a narrow piece of land that links two larger areas of land. The *Pampas* is a plain that covers most of Argentina and Uruguay. Suggest that students remember the definition of an *archipelago* by visualizing a group of islands curving, or arching, across the sea.

2. D Point out the key words *steep cliff* in the question. Students can eliminate answer choices B and C because they involve water rather than land. Answer choice A, *Llanos,* is a tropical grassland in eastern Colombia and Venezuela. To remember the meaning of *escarpment,* students might find it helpful to rhyme the word part *scarp* with *sharp*; an escarpment is a series of steep cliffs that drop sharply from one land level to the next.

3. B Encourage students to visualize each answer choice. Savannas have rainfall but are interrupted by a long dry season. Grassy steppe lands are dry. Mountains have cooler temperatures because they are at high altitudes. Only lush, hot rain forests have both high temperatures and heavy, year-round rainfall.

4. C The higher the altitude is, the cooler the temperatures are; students can remember this by picturing a snowcapped mountaintop. Explain that although wind can cool temperatures, it is not constant. The Tropics are known for year-round heat, and canopies are the umbrella formed by treetops in the rain forest.

CHAPTER 7

STANDARDIZED TEST PRACTICE

TEST-TAKING TIP

Look for words such as *usually, never, most,* and other qualifying words in exam questions. They indicate under what circumstances an answer is correct.

Reviewing Vocabulary

Directions: Choose the word(s) that best completes the sentence.

1. A group of islands is called a(n) ______.

A isthmus
B archipelago
C Pampas
D subregion

2. The Brazilian Highlands end with a(n) ______, or a steep cliff that drops down to the Atlantic coastal plain.

A Llanos
B estuary
C tributary
D escarpment

3. South American ______ have high temperatures and heavy rainfall year round.

A savannas
B rain forests
C steppes
D mountains

4. Cooler temperatures are found at higher ______.

A winds
B Tropics
C altitudes
D canopies

Reviewing Main Ideas

Directions: Choose the best answer for each question.

Section 1 *(pp. 192–196)*

5. The dominant landform along the Pacific coast of South America is ______.

A the Andes
B coastal marshes
C the Amazon Basin
D the Brazilian Highlands

6. ______, in South America, is the world's largest exporter of copper.

A Chile
B Brazil
C Bolivia
D Venezuela

Section 2 *(pp. 198–202)*

7. The Tropics have generally warm temperatures because

A hurricanes often strike the Tropics.
B the Tropics have a long dry season.
C they receive the direct rays of the sun.
D more plants grow there than anywhere else.

8. Vegetation is sparse in the ______ climate zone.

A *tierra fría*
B *tierra helada*
C *tierra caliente*
D *tierra templada*

GO ON

Reviewing the Main Ideas

5. A Show students a map of South America so that they can see how the Andes stretch the full length of the Pacific coast. The coastal marshes, Amazon Basin, and Brazilian Highlands are located to the east of the Andes.

6. A Students may guess Brazil, as it has the greatest wealth of natural resources in South America. However, it is Chile that is known for exporting copper. Bolivia and Venezuela are known for their energy resources.

Critical Thinking

Directions: Base your answers to questions 9 and 10 on the chart below and your knowledge of Chapter 7.

Average Monthly Rainfall in Latin America		
	Manaus, Brazil	Lima, Peru
January	9.8 in. (24.9 cm)	0.1 in. (0.3 cm)
February	9.0 in. (23.1 cm)	0.0 in. (0.0 cm)
March	10.3 in. (26.2 cm)	0.0 in. (0.0 cm)
April	8.7 in. (22.1 cm)	0.0 in. (0.0 cm)
May	6.7 in. (17.0 cm)	0.2 in. (0.5 cm)
June	3.3 in. (8.4 cm)	0.2 in. (0.5 cm)
July	2.3 in. (5.8 cm)	0.3 in. (0.8 cm)
August	1.5 in. (3.8 cm)	0.3 in. (0.8 cm)
September	1.8 in. (4.6 cm)	0.3 in. (0.8 cm)
October	4.2 in. (10.7 cm)	0.1 in. (0.3 cm)
November	5.6 in. (14.2 cm)	0.1 in. (0.3 cm)
December	8.0 in. (20.3 cm)	0.0 in. (0.0 cm)

Source: BBC Weather Center, 2006.

9. In which month does the average rainfall differ the least in Manaus and Lima?

A January
B May
C August
D December

10. Based on the chart, which of the following statements is accurate?

A Lima has a much dryer climate than Manaus.
B March is in the rainy season in both cities.
C During Lima's rainy season, it gets more rainfall than Manaus.
D Over the year, rainfall averages for both cities are about equal.

Document-Based Questions

Directions: Analyze the following document and answer the short-answer questions that follow.

The following passage is from an analysis by the Council on Foreign Relations of the struggle over control of Bolivia's natural gas.

> *[Bolivian President] Morales, a former coca farmer and union leader, won a resounding victory in the December 2005 elections. As the Movement to Socialism (MAS) candidate, he campaigned in favor of nationalizing, among other sectors of the economy, the gas and oil industries with the cooperation of foreign investors. Experts say that, given such promises, the nationalization was no surprise. But Peter DeShazo, director of the Center for Strategic and International Studies' Americas Program, says the move to occupy the gas fields with military forces lent a dramatic effect. "The confrontational nature of his move was certainly intended to get people's attention," he says, adding that Morales may be looking to garner [gain] votes in July elections for a[n] . . . assembly that will redraft Bolivia's constitution.*
>
> —Carin Zissis, "Bolivia's Nationalization of Oil and Gas"

11. What does it mean to "nationalize" the gas and oil industries?

12. What ideas expressed in the passage indicate that nationalization is popular among Bolivians?

Extended Response

13. Explain how El Niño affects the weather in South America.

Social Studies ONLINE

For additional test practice, use Self-Check Quizzes—Chapter 7 at glencoe.com.

Need Extra Help?

If you missed question. . .	1	2	3	4	5	6	7	8	9	10	11	12	13
Go to page. . .	193	194	199	201	194	196	199	201	199	199	196	196	201

Critical Thinking

9. C By horizontally scanning both rainfall data columns and subtracting one from the other, students eventually will discover that August is the correct response. They can save time by looking at the entries only for the months listed in the question. Selecting only one unit of measure before calculation, either inches or centimeters, also will save time.

10. A Lima, located in the desert, is far drier than Manaus, which is in the Amazon River Basin. Students can scan the data vertically to compare the numbers. As long as students use only one unit of measure, either inches or centimeters, the difference is so great that it is not necessary to perform any calculations.

Document-Based Questions

11. The government takes control of the industries from private business.

12. President Morales won "a resounding victory in the December 2005 elections" after "he campaigned in favor of nationalizing . . . the gas and oil industries," and Morales took control of the industries so dramatically because he "may be looking to garner votes in July elections."

Extended Response

13. Students should explain El Niño's effects on Peru's coast and on northeastern Brazil.

7. C Point out to students that they can eliminate answer choices A, B, and D because the question is looking for a *cause* of warm temperatures, not an *effect*; hurricanes, a long dry season, and plant growth might be effects of warm temperatures, but they would not cause it on their own. However, direct rays of the sun *would* cause warmer temperatures, and the Tropics' location near the Equator makes this possible.

8. B Most Spanish-speaking students will easily choose *tierra helada* because *helada* means "frozen," and an extremely cold climate cannot support much vegetation. Students who do not know Spanish must memorize the meanings of the terms *tierra* (land), *fría* (cold), *caliente* (hot), and *templada* (temperate).

Social Studies ONLINE

Have students visit the Web site at glencoe.com to review Chapter 7 and take the Self-Check Quiz.

Need Extra Help?

Have students refer to the pages listed if they miss any of the questions.

Planning Guide

Key to Ability Levels	
BL Below level	AL Above level
OL On level	ELL English Language Learners

Key to Teaching Resources	
Print Material	DVD
CD-ROM	Transparency

BL	OL	AL	ELL		Resources	Chapter Opener	Section 1	Section 2	Chapter Assess
					FOCUS				
BL	OL	AL	ELL	Transparency	**Daily Focus Skills Transparencies**		8-1	8-2	
					TEACH				
BL	OL		ELL	Print	**Guided Reading Activity, URB***		p. 61	p. 62	
BL	OL	AL	ELL	Print	**Content Vocabulary Activity, URB***		p. 63	p. 63	
BL	OL	AL	ELL	Print	**Academic Vocabulary Activity, URB**		p. 65	p. 65	
BL	OL	AL	ELL	Print	**Differentiated Instruction Activity, URB**			p. 67	
BL	OL	AL	ELL	Print	**Chart, Graph, and Map Skills Activity, URB**		p. 69		
	OL	AL		Print	**Critical Thinking Activity, URB**		p. 71		
BL	OL	AL	ELL	Print	**Speaking and Listening Skills Activity, URB**			p. 73	
BL	OL	AL	ELL	Print	**Writing Skills Activity, URB**		p. 77		
BL	OL	AL	ELL	Print	**School-to-Home Connection Activity, URB***		p. 81		
BL	OL	AL	ELL	Print	**Regional Atlas Activities, URB**		pp. 1–7	pp. 1–7	
	OL	AL		Print	**Geography and History Activity, URB**		p. 11		
BL	OL		ELL	Print	**Time Line Activity, URB**		p. 17		
BL	OL		ELL	Print	**Reading Skills Activity, URB**		p. 25		
BL	OL	AL	ELL	Print	**Primary Source Readings, URB**		p. 27		
	OL	AL		Print	**World Literature Readings, URB**		p. 31	p. 33	
BL	OL		ELL	Print	**Reading Essentials and Note-Taking Guide***		p. 52	p. 55	
	OL			Print	**Interactive Geography Activity**	p. 17			
BL	OL	AL	ELL	Transparency	**In-Text Map Overlay and Population Pyramid Transparencies**	3	3B	3C	
	OL			Print	**Foods Around the World**			pp. 10, 12	
BL	OL	AL	ELL	Print	**Outline Map Resource Book**	p. 28	p. 29		
BL	OL	AL	ELL	Print	**NGS World Atlas***	✓	✓	✓	
BL	OL	AL	ELL	Print	**NGS World Desk Map**	✓	✓	✓	✓
BL	OL	AL	ELL	Print	**World Literature Library**	✓	✓	✓	✓
BL	OL	AL	ELL	Print	**Writer's Guidebook**	✓	✓	✓	✓

Note: Please refer to the *Unit Resource Book: Latin America* for this chapter's URB materials.

* Also available in Spanish

- Interactive Lesson Planner
- Interactive Teacher Edition
- Fully editable blackline masters
- Section Spotlight Videos Launch
- Differentiated Lesson Plans
- Printable reports of daily assignments
- Standardized Tracking System

Levels				Resources	Chapter Opener	Section 1	Section 2	Chapter Assess
BL	OL	AL	ELL					
				TEACH *(continued)*				
BL	OL	AL	ELL	**Vocabulary PuzzleMaker CD-ROM***	✓	✓	✓	✓
	OL	AL		**Primary Sources CD-ROM**	✓	✓	✓	✓
BL	OL	AL	ELL	**StudentWorks™ Plus DVD**	✓	✓	✓	✓
BL	OL	AL	ELL	**Section Video Program Activities**	✓	✓	✓	✓
BL	OL	AL	ELL	**World Music: A Cultural Legacy**	✓	✓	✓	✓
BL	OL	AL	ELL	**Writing Process Transparencies**	✓	✓	✓	✓
Teacher Resources				**Building Academic Vocabulary**	✓	✓	✓	✓
				Strategies for Success	✓	✓	✓	✓
				Teacher's Guide to Differentiated Instruction	✓	✓	✓	✓
				Presentation Plus! DVD	✓	✓	✓	✓
				ASSESS				
BL	OL	AL	ELL	**Quizzes and Tests**		p. 85	p. 86	p. 87
BL	OL	AL	ELL	**Authentic Assessment With Rubrics**				p. 8
BL	OL	AL	ELL	**Standardized Test Practice**				p. 29
BL	OL	AL	ELL	***ExamView® Assessment Suite* CD-ROM***		8-1	8-2	Ch. 8
BL	OL	AL	ELL	**Interactive Tutor Self-Assessment CD-ROM**		8-1	8-2	
				CLOSE				
BL			ELL	**Reteaching Activity, URB***		p. 79	p. 79	p. 79
BL	OL		ELL	**Reading and Study Skills Foldables™**	p. 64	p. 64	p. 64	p. 64
BL	OL	AL	ELL	**Graphic Organizer Transparencies and Strategies**		✓	✓	
BL	OL	AL	ELL	***Exploring Our World* in Graphic Novel**	p. 33	p. 25		

Integrating Technology

Using Study Central: Build Vocabulary

Technology Product

The **Build Vocabulary** tab on the Study Central Web site allows you to reinforce the content vocabulary and academic vocabulary in each section of a chapter. Build Vocabulary

- provides a definition, an example of its correct usage, and a textbook page reference for each glossary term;
- allows students to test their understanding of the content vocabulary in each section through Flying Answers, an interactive vocabulary activity.

Objective

Build Vocabulary helps students

- build vocabulary skills;
- reinforce their understanding of the content and academic vocabulary in each section.

Steps

- Locate the Web page for the textbook being studied on the Glencoe Web site glencoe.com.
- Click on **Study Central** under *Textbook Resources.*
- On the Study Central Web site (a new window will have opened), select a chapter and section using the drop-down arrows and click **Enter.**
- Click on the **Main Ideas** tab and then on the **Build Vocabulary** tab.
- Under the **Content Vocabulary** tab and the **Academic Vocabulary** tab, click on each term and discuss its definition, proper usage, and location in the textbook.
- On the Key Vocabulary tab, then click on **Flying Answers** to engage students in the interactive game.

Social Studies ONLINE

	Student	Teacher	Parent
Beyond the Textbook	●		●
Chapter Overviews	●		●
Concepts in Motion	●		●
ePuzzles and Games	●		●
Literature Connections		●	
Multi-Language Glossaries	●		●
Online Student Edition	●	●	●
Section Videos	●	●	●
Self-Check Quizzes	●		●
Student Web Activities	●		●
Study Central ™	●		●
Teaching Today		●	
TIME Current Events	●		●
Vocabulary eFlashcards	●		●
Web Activity Lesson Plans		●	

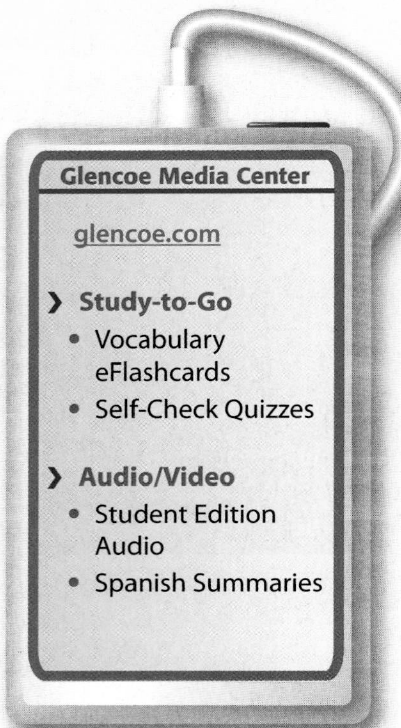

- **Timed Readings Plus in Social Studies** helps students increase their reading rate and fluency while maintaining comprehension. The 400-word passages are similar to those found on state and national assessments.
- **Reading in the Content Area: Social Studies** concentrates on six essential reading skills that help students better comprehend what they read. The book includes 75 high-interest nonfiction passages written at increasing levels of difficulty.
- **Reading Social Studies** includes strategic reading instruction and vocabulary support in Social Studies content for ELLs and native speakers of English.
- **Content Vocabulary Workout** (Grades 6–8) accelerates reading comprehension through focused vocabulary development. Social Studies content vocabulary comes from the glossaries of Glencoe's Middle School Social Studies texts.
  www.jamestowneducation.com

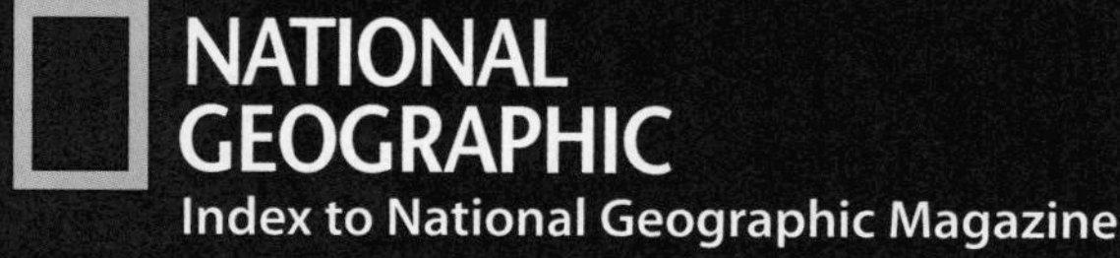

Index to National Geographic Magazine:

The following articles relate to this chapter:

- "Mystery of the Tattooed Mummy," A. R. Williams, June 2006.
- "Medellin: Stories from an Urban War," Eliza Griswold, March 2005.

National Geographic Society Products To order the following, call National Geographic at 1-800-368-2728:

- *National Geographic Atlas of the World* (Book).

Access National Geographic's new dynamic MapMachine Web site and other geography resources at:
www.nationalgeographic.com
www.nationalgeographic.com/maps

The following videotape programs are available from Glencoe as supplements to Chapter 8:

- The Maya (ISBN 0-76-700697-6)
- Carmen Miranda: The South American (ISBN 0-76-700097-8)

To order, call Glencoe at 1-800-334-7344. To find classroom resources to accompany many of these videos, check the following home pages:

A&E Television: www.aetv.com
The History Channel: www.historychannel.com

Reading List Generator CD-ROM

Use this database to search more than 30,000 titles to create a customized reading list for your students.

- Reading lists can be organized by students' reading level, author, genre, theme, or area of interest.
- The database provides Degrees of Reading Power™ (DRP) and Lexile™ readability scores for all selections.
- A brief summary of each selection is included.

Leveled reading suggestions for this chapter:

For students at a Grade 5 reading level:
- ***World Myths and Legends II: Central America,*** by Martha Schmitt

For students at a Grade 6 reading level:
- ***A Visit to Colombia,*** by Mary Virginia Fox

For students at a Grade 7 reading level:
- ***The Aztecs,*** by Anita Ganeri

For students at a Grade 8 reading level:
- ***The Yanomami of South America,*** by Raya Tahan

For students at a Grade 9 reading level:
- ***Cuba: The Culture,*** by April Fast & Susan Hughes

Focus

The Essential Question

As students study the chapter, remind them to consider the chapter-based Essential Question. Answering this question will help them understand the important concepts in the chapter. In addition, the Hands-On Chapter Project relates the content from each section to the Essential Question. The steps in each section build on each other as students progress through the chapter. The Hands-On Chapter Project culminates in the Wrap Up activity on the Visual Summary page.

More About the Photo

Visual Literacy Artist Diego Rivera, (1886–1957) expressed his love of the beauty of his native Mexico, its history, and culture through his work. He is perhaps best known for his monumental murals, such as the *Carnival of Mexican Life,* shown here in Mexico City's Palace of Fine Arts. Through these, he brought fresco painting into the modern world. Rivera liked the fact that his murals could be seen by people from all walks of life. During the Great Depression in the United States, he was commissioned to create several works, in which he showed people of the working class as they struggled with war and industrial technology.

CHAPTER 8

History and Cultures of Latin America

Essential Question

Regions **Common threads of language and religion unite Latin America. Once claimed as European colonies, Latin American countries today are primarily Roman Catholic, and most still use either Spanish or Portuguese as the official language. These two languages are based on Latin, which is how the region gets its name.** In what ways can language and religion both unite and divide a region?

206 • Chapter 8

Teach

The BIG Ideas *As you begin teaching each section, use these questions and activities to help students focus on the Big Ideas.*

Section 

History and Governments **Ask: In what ways do people depend on one another and their surroundings for survival?** *(People get resources from their environment and through trade.)* Tell students that in Section 1, they will learn how ancient peoples in Latin America used local resources and traded what they produced. They also will read about European contact and trade with the region. Finally, they will learn about the formation of independent nations and their political and economic struggles. **OL**

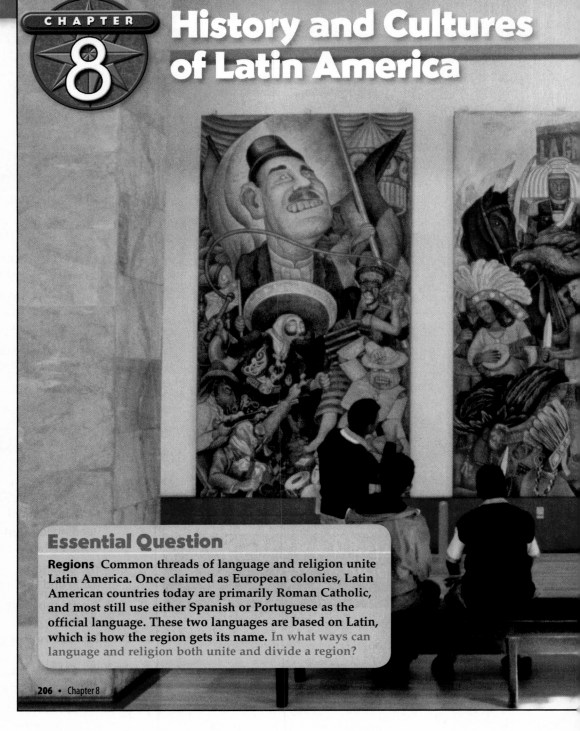

Section 

Cultures and Lifestyles **Ask: How are physical and human systems affected by the characteristics and movements of people?** *(Varied cultures and climates influence parts of daily life such as food, art, and religion.)* Point out to students that in Section 2, they will learn about the differ-

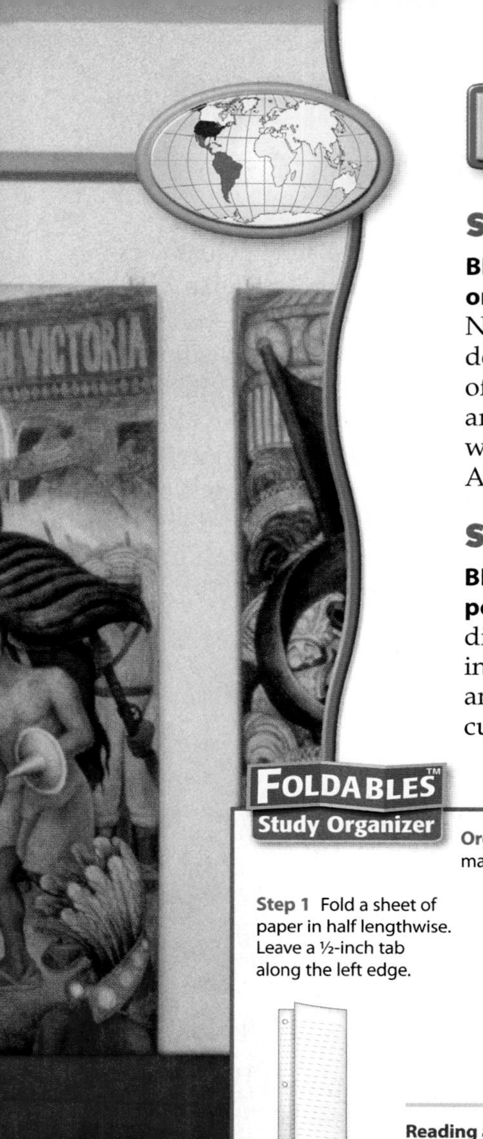

BIG Ideas

Section 1: History and Governments

BIG IDEA All living things are dependent upon one another and their surroundings for survival. Native American civilizations of Latin America developed ways of living that used the resources of their environment. People who lived in different areas depended on trade to obtain the goods they wanted. In colonial times, the people of Latin America exchanged goods with Europeans.

Section 2: Cultures and Lifestyles

BIG IDEA The characteristics and movement of people impact physical and human systems. The different groups who have settled Latin America include Native Americans, Europeans, Africans, and Asians. These groups have influenced the cultures and lifestyles of the region.

FOLDABLES™ Study Organizer

Organizing Information Make this Foldable to help you organize information about the history, peoples, cultures, and daily life of Latin America.

Step 1 Fold a sheet of paper in half lengthwise. Leave a ½-inch tab along the left edge.

Step 2 Cut the top layer only to make four equal tabs.

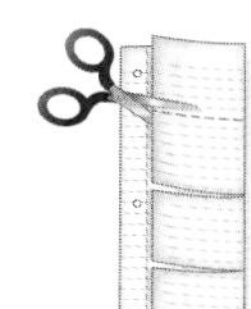

Step 3 Label the tabs as shown.

Reading and Writing Use the notes in your Foldable to write a short essay that describes the development of the countries and peoples of Latin America.

◀ Murals by Diego Rivera, Mexico City, Mexico

To preview Chapter 8, go to glencoe.com.

Previewing the Region

If you have not already done so, engage students in the Regional Atlas and chart activities to help them become familiar with the general content of the region.

Dinah Zike's Foldables

Purpose Students will practice organizing information as they add notes to their Foldables. The Foldables will provide them with an opportunity to focus on the main ideas presented as they read about the history, cultures, and lifestyles of Latin America. The completed Foldables can be used to write essays about the development of the countries and people of Latin America, as well as prepare for assessment.

More Foldables activities for this chapter can be found in *Dinah Zike's Reading and Study Skills Foldables* ancillary.

Social Studies ONLINE

Introduce students to chapter content and key terms by having them access the Chapter Overview at glencoe.com.

ent ethnic groups, languages, and religions of Latin America. They also will learn about the influence of African, European, and Asian cultures, and about the strain on resources resulting from the area's growing population. **OL**

Focus

Bellringer

Daily Focus Transparency 8-1

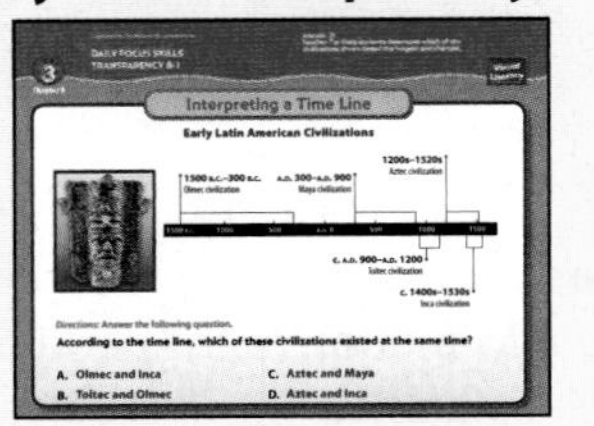

Guide to Reading

Answers to Graphic:

Answer suggestions provided for Olmec, Maya, and Toltec. Students should provide similar answers for the Aztec and Inca.

	Key Facts
Olmec	lived in southern Mexico from 1500 B.C. to 300 B.C., grew corn, controlled mineral resources, built temples
Maya	lived in the Yucatán Peninsula from A.D. 300 to A.D. 900, built temples, skilled in astronomy, developed calendar, hieroglyphics
Toltec	conquered areas from northern Mexico to Yucatán Peninsula from around A.D. 900 to A.D. 1200, control of obsidian trade resulted in advantage in weaponry

Section Spotlight Video

To learn more about the history and governments of Latin America, have students watch the Section Spotlight Video.

Guide to Reading

BIG Idea

All living things are dependent upon one another and their surroundings for survival.

Content Vocabulary

- maize *(p. 209)*
- jade *(p. 209)*
- obsidian *(p. 209)*
- hieroglyphics *(p. 209)*
- empire *(p. 210)*
- cash crop *(p. 211)*
- caudillo *(p. 213)*
- communist state *(p. 215)*

Academic Vocabulary

- complex *(p. 210)*
- transform *(p. 211)*
- stable *(p. 213)*
- revolution *(p. 215)*

Reading Strategy

Identifying Central Issues Use a chart like the one below to organize key facts about the Native American civilizations of the region.

	Key Facts
Olmec	
Maya	
Toltec	
Aztec	
Inca	

History and Governments

Picture This A Mayan village in Guatemala remembers its dead in a spectacular way. For their Day of the Dead celebration—when people remember relatives and friends who have died—villagers create enormous kites of tissue paper, bamboo, and wire. Finished kites can reach 40 feet across! Sailing above local cemeteries, the kites create a symbolic link between the living and the dead. Read this section to learn more about the historical traditions that have shaped Latin America.

▼ Ready to fly in Guatemala

Resource Manager

R Reading Strategies	C Critical Thinking	D Differentiated Instruction	W Writing Support	S Skill Practice
Teacher Edition • Identifying, p. 211 • Setting a Purpose, p. 212 • Summarizing, p. 213 • Academic Vocab., p. 215 **Additional Resources** • Guid. Read., URB p. 61 • Cont. Vocab., URB p. 63 • Read. Ess., p. 52 • Pri. Source, URB p. 27 • World Lit., URB p. 31	**Teacher Edition** • Det. Cause/Effect, pp. 209, 212 • Making Inferences, p. 211 **Additional Resources** • Crit. Think., URB p. 71 • Geo. & Hist., URB p. 11 • Authentic Assess., p. 8 • Quizzes and Tests, p. 85	**Teacher Edition** • Visual/Spatial, p. 210 • Adv. Learners, p. 214 **Additional Resources** • Reteach., URB p. 79 • School-to-Home Conn., URB p. 81	**Teacher Edition** • Persuasive Writing, pp. 209, 214 **Additional Resources** • Writing Skills, URB p. 77	**Teacher Edition** • Read. a Time Line, pp. 212, 213 **Additional Resources** • Read. Skills, URB p. 25 • Chart, Graph, and Map Skills, URB p. 69 • Time Line, URB p. 17 • Daily Focus Trans. 8-1 • Reg. Atlas, URB pp. 1–7

Early History

Main Idea **Some Native Americans developed advanced civilizations in the region. Europeans later conquered much of the region and set up colonies.**

Geography and You What sorts of things do you like to read? History books, novels, comics? Read to find out what kinds of things the Maya wrote down.

The first people to arrive in Latin America were the ancestors of today's Native Americans. They came many thousands of years ago. Some settled and farmed. Eventually, some groups developed advanced civilizations. **Figure 1** on the next page shows these Native American civilizations.

Early Native American Civilizations

The Olmec of southern Mexico built Latin America's first civilization, which lasted from 1500 B.C. to 300 B.C. Each Olmec city focused on a certain activity, and they all depended on one another. Some cities were located near farming areas that grew **maize**, or corn, as well as squash and beans. Others controlled important mineral resources such as **jade**, a shiny green semiprecious stone; and **obsidian**, a hard, black, volcanic glass useful in making weapons. Some cities were religious centers with pyramid-shaped stone temples.

A people called the Maya lived in Mexico's Yucatán Peninsula and surrounding areas between A.D. 300 and A.D. 900. The Maya built huge stone temples in the shape of pyramids with steps. They were skilled at astronomy and used their knowledge of the stars, moon, and planets to develop a calendar. They also had a number system based on 20. Using **hieroglyphics** (HY·ruh·GLIH·fihks), which is a form of writing that uses signs and symbols, the

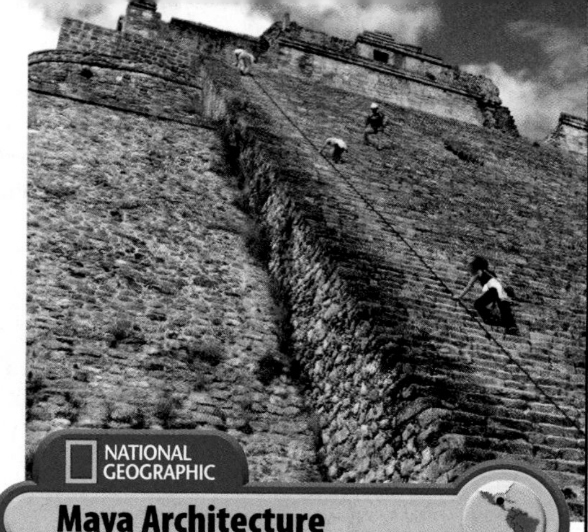

Maya Architecture

A steep stairway leads to a temple at the top of the Pyramid of the Magician. The Maya built the pyramid about A.D. 800. ***Place*** **How did the Maya record their history?**

Maya recorded the history of their kings. About A.D. 900, the Maya civilization mysteriously collapsed. Despite intensive research, historians have not yet been able to determine what happened to the Maya.

Toltec, Aztec, and Inca

As the Maya civilization declined, a people called the Toltec seized what is now northern Mexico. These warriors built the city of Tula, northwest of present-day Mexico City. From Tula, they conquered lands all the way to the Yucatán (YOO·kah·TAHN) Peninsula.

Toltec rulers tightly controlled trade. They held a monopoly (muh·NAH·puh·lee), or sole right, to the trade in obsidian. As a result, the Toltec had the most powerful weapons in the surrounding areas. For many years this weaponry gave them the advantage they needed to maintain their rule.

Around A.D. 1200, the Aztec people from the north moved into central Mexico and captured Tula. They adopted Toltec culture, conquered neighboring peoples, and took control of the region's trade.

Teach

W Writing Support

Persuasive Writing Tell students that several theories exist about why the Maya civilization collapsed. Have students use reliable online sources to conduct research about some of these theories. Tell students to choose one theory, or come up with their own, and write a persuasive essay with logical reasoning in support of that theory. **AL**

C Critical Thinking

Determining Cause and Effect

Ask: What effect did the Toltec monopoly on the obsidian trade have on the region? *(The Toltec had the most powerful weapons in the area, which gave them the advantage they needed to maintain their rule.)* **OL**

Caption Answer:
They used a form of writing called hieroglyphics.

Differentiated Instruction

Leveled Activities

BL Reteaching Activity, URB p. 79

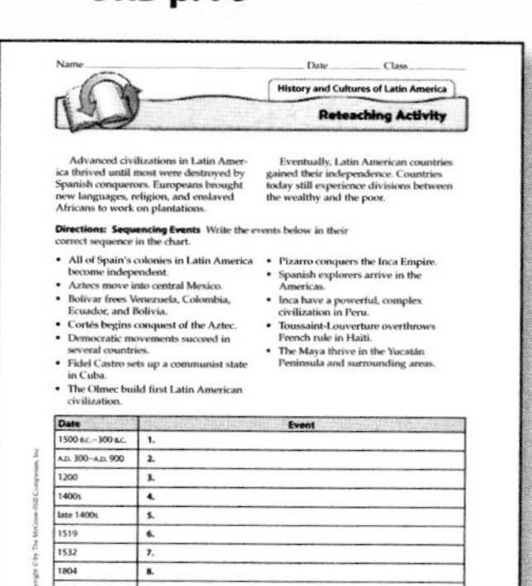
History and Cultures of Latin America
Reteaching Activity

OL Reading Skills Activity, URB p. 25

Latin America
Reading Skills Activity
Summarizing

AL Critical Thinking Activity, URB p. 71

History and Cultures of Latin America
Critical Thinking Skills Activity
Evaluating New Information

ELL Chart, Graph, and Map Skills, URB p. 69

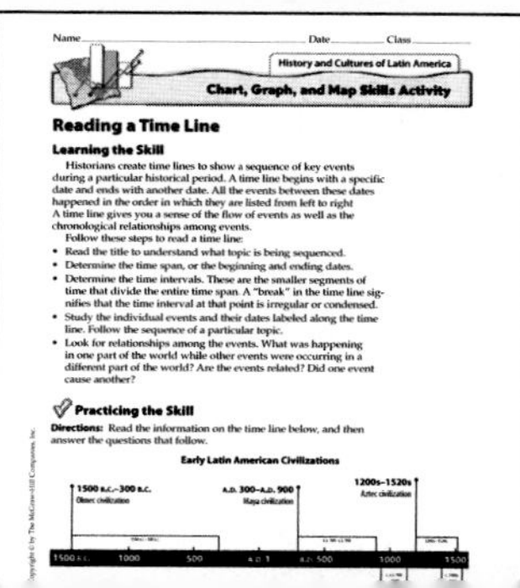
History and Cultures of Latin America
Chart, Graph, and Map Skills Activity
Reading a Time Line

D Differentiated Instruction

Visual/Spatial Have students imagine what Tenochtitlán might have looked like. Remind them of the mural by Diego Rivera, shown on this chapter's opening pages. Have students use information in the text to design a reduced-size mural depicting a scene in busy Tenochtitlán 500 years ago. **OL**

Map Skills

Answers:
1. Maya
2. Aztec and Maya

Skills Practice

Ask: **What sort of borders do the gray lines on the map depict?** *(borders between present-day countries)* **What modern-day countries encompass territory controlled by the Inca?** *(Ecuador, Peru, Bolivia, Chile, Argentina)*

NATIONAL GEOGRAPHIC Maps In MOtion See StudentWorks™ Plus or glencoe.com.

Figure 1 Native American Civilizations

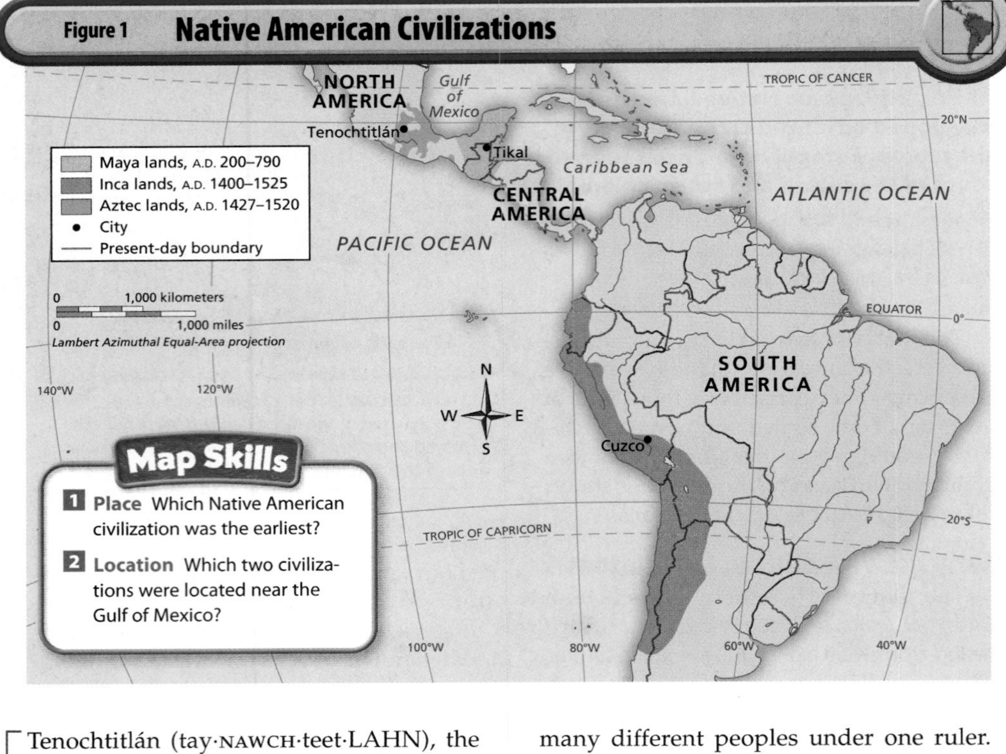

Map Skills

1 Place Which Native American civilization was the earliest?

2 Location Which two civilizations were located near the Gulf of Mexico?

Tenochtitlán (tay·NAWCH·teet·LAHN), the Aztec capital, was a beautiful city built on an island in a lake. It held about 250,000 people, which was a large population at that time. Tenochtitlán had huge temples, including one that was more than 100 feet (30 m) tall. Roads and bridges joined the city to the mainland, allowing the Aztec to bring food and other goods to their busy markets. Aztec farmers grew their crops on "floating gardens," or rafts filled with mud. The rafts eventually sank to the lake bottom and piled up. Over time, many of these rafts formed fertile islands.

During the 1400s, the Inca had a powerful civilization in South America in what is now Peru. Their empire stretched more than 2,500 miles (4,023 km) along the Andes. An **empire** is a large territory with many different peoples under one ruler. The Inca ruler founded military posts and put in place a **complex,** or highly developed, system of record keeping. Work crews built irrigation systems, roads, and suspension bridges that linked regions of the empire to Cuzco, the capital. You can still see the remains of magnificent fortresses and buildings erected centuries ago by the skilled Inca builders.

European Conquests

In the late 1400s and early 1500s, Spanish explorers arrived in the Americas. They were greatly impressed by the magnificent cities and the great riches of the Native Americans.

In 1519 a Spanish army led by Hernán Cortés landed on Mexico's Gulf coast.

Differentiated Instruction

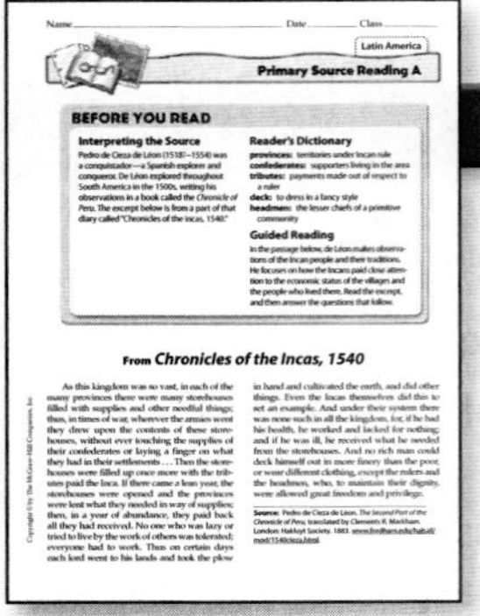

Primary Source Readings, URB pp. 27–28

Chronicles of the Incas, 1540

Objective: To interpret primary sources about the Inca and Mexico

Focus: Explain the significance of primary sources as they relate to the study of history.

Teach: Guide a group discussion about each excerpt's perspective on its topic.

Assess: Have students answer the questions that follow each excerpt.

Close: Ask students to summarize what they learned from analyzing each excerpt.

Differentiated Instruction Strategies

BL Have students outline each excerpt's main ideas and supporting details.

AL Ask students to write scripts for interviews with each author and present them to the class.

ELL Pair students and have each partner take turns paraphrasing sentences in the excerpts.

He and about 600 soldiers marched to Tenochtitlán, which they had heard was filled with gold. Some Native Americans who opposed the harsh rule of the Aztec joined forces with the Spanish. The Aztec's simple weapons were no match for the guns, cannons, and horses of the Spanish. The Spanish also had the help of unknown allies—germs that carried diseases, such as measles and smallpox. These diseases killed more Aztec than did the Spanish weapons. Within two years, Cortés's conquest of the Aztec was complete.

Another Spanish explorer named Francisco Pizarro desired the Inca's gold and silver. In 1532 Pizarro took a small group of Spanish soldiers to South America. The Spanish attacked the Inca with cannons and swords. Pizarro captured the Inca ruler and had him killed. The Inca had already been weakened by smallpox and other European diseases. After the death of their ruler, the Inca soldiers collapsed into disorder. Pizarro then quickly conquered the Inca Empire.

Colonial Latin America

The Aztec and Inca conquests provided Spain with enormous wealth and control over vast territories. Spain then built an empire that included much of South America, the Caribbean, Middle America, and parts of the present-day United States. Other European countries wanted the same power and influence that Spain had achieved. So, these countries seized different parts of the Americas. Portugal became the colonial ruler of what is today Brazil. France, Britain, and the Netherlands took control of some Caribbean areas and parts of North America. C

European rule **transformed,** or greatly changed, the populations of these lands. Europeans settled the land, set up colonial governments, and spread Christianity among the Native Americans. They also used Native Americans as workers to grow **cash crops**, or farm products grown for export.

When hardship and disease greatly reduced the numbers of Native Americans, Europeans brought enslaved Africans to meet the labor shortage. R A busy trade eventually resulted. Ships carried enslaved people from Africa and manufactured goods from Europe to the Americas. On the return trip, products including sugar, cotton, tobacco, gold, and silver went from the Americas to Europe. Despite European control, many Native American and African ways survived, leading to a blending of cultures.

Reading Check **Explaining** Why did the Spanish conquer Native American empires?

Preparing for Battle

NATIONAL GEOGRAPHIC

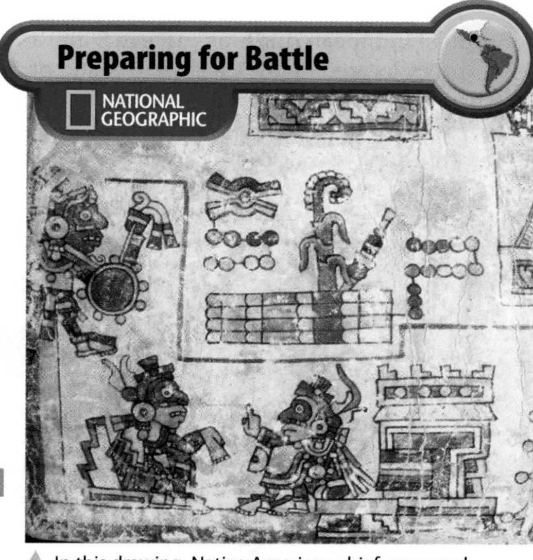

In this drawing, Native American chiefs opposed to the Aztec discuss whether to join with Cortés's forces. ***Regions*** **Why did some Native Americans support the Spanish?**

C Critical Thinking

Making Inferences Ask: Why is Portuguese spoken in Brazil today? *(It was once a colony ruled by the Portuguese.)* OL

R Reading Strategy

Identifying Ask: For what reason were enslaved Africans brought to South America? *(European landowners needed more workers to grow cash crops because hardship and disease had reduced the number of Native American workers.)* OL

Reading Check Answer: They wanted wealth and control of vast territories to build a new empire.

Caption Answer:
They opposed the harsh rule of the Aztec.

Hands-On Chapter Project Step 1

Presenting a Latin American Cultural Fair

Step 1: Conducting Research Groups of students will research a Latin American country's history and culture for a booth at a class cultural fair.

Essential Question In what ways can language and religion unite both and divide a region?

Directions Organize students into small groups, and assign each group one of the Latin American countries mentioned in the text. Explain that each group will create a booth about its assigned country for a Latin American cultural fair. Have students read this section and the next and take notes on the history, languages, and religious traditions of their assigned country. Then have students research these topics in greater detail using library and online sources. Tell students to take notes on what they want to include in their booth as they conduct their research.

Summarizing After students have had adequate time to research their countries, meet with each group. Ask students to summarize what they have discovered about the history, languages, and religious traditions of their assigned country. OL

(Chapter Project continued in Section 2)

R Reading Strategy

Setting a Purpose Have students create a time line that shows the important people and events in this subsection, including those in the History at a Glance time line. In addition, have students include the significance of each person or event. OL

C Critical Thinking

Determining Cause and Effect
Ask: **What events inspired Native Americans and enslaved Africans to fight for freedom?** *(revolutions in North America and France)* OL

S Skill Practice

Reading a Time Line **Ask:** **About how long did the Aztec civilization flourish?** *(about 300 years)* OL

R Forming New Nations

Main Idea **Most of Latin America gained independence in the 1800s, but hardships followed for many of the new nations.**

Geography and You Suppose you have just been elected class president. What challenges would you face? Read to find out what challenges faced new governments in Latin America.

C In the late 1700s, revolutions in North America and France stirred the people of Latin America to action. Colonists tried to take charge of their own affairs. While European colonists called for self-rule, Native Americans and enslaved Africans wanted freedom from mistreatment and slavery.

Independence

Latin America's first successful revolt against European rule took place in Haiti, a territory located on the Caribbean island of Hispaniola. There, enslaved Africans under François-Dominique Toussaint-Louverture began a revolt that threw off French rule in 1804. Haiti, which was established as a republic, became the only nation ever created as a result of a successful revolt by enslaved people.

In Spanish and Portuguese Latin America, the fight for freedom increased in the next decade. In Mexico, two Catholic priests, Miguel Hidalgo and José María Morelos, urged poorer Mexicans to fight for freedom from Spanish rule. Both men were defeated and executed.

Despite many battles, Mexicans did not gain their independence until 1821. After a short period of rule under an emperor, Mexico became a republic in 1823. That same year, the countries of Central America won their freedom from Spain.

In northern South America, a wealthy military leader named Simón Bolívar (see·MOHN buh·LEE·VAHR) led the fight for independence. In 1819 Bolívar defeated the Spanish and won freedom for the present-day countries of Venezuela, Colombia, Ecuador, and Bolivia.

While Bolívar fought for self-rule in the north, a soldier named José de San Martín (hoh·SAY day SAN MAHR·TEEN) was fighting for freedom in the south. In 1817 San Martín led his army from Argentina across the Andes Mountains and into Chile. Although the crossing was difficult, San Martín was able to take Spanish forces by surprise, and

History at a Glance
1250
1400
1550
c. 1200
Aztec settle in central Mexico
c. 1400
Inca Empire expands in South America
1521
Cortés conquers the Aztec
S
c. 1400s, Aztec mask

Atahuallpa, last Inca ruler

Activity: Technology Connection

Categorizing **Ask:** **When did the nations of Latin America become independent?** *(Mexico, 1821; Venezuela, Colombia, Ecuador, and Bolivia, 1819; all of Spain's colonies, by 1824; Brazil, 1820s)* Have students work in pairs to gather and categorize facts about how five Latin American nations gained their independence. Direct students to use a variety of online sources, such as reputable encyclopedias and the countries' government Web sites, to find facts related to the independence of each country, including important dates and the people involved. When pairs have completed their research, tell them to use a word-processing program to create a chart of the information, with the country names as row labels and appropriate categories as column headings. OL

Additional Support

Teacher Tip

Recognizing Bias Remind students to be careful when choosing Web sites to use for their research. Tell them to keep the following questions in mind when conducting research online: Is the information on the Web site from a reputable source? How might the creator of the Web site be biased?

he began winning battles. A few years later, the armies of San Martín and Bolívar jointly defeated Spanish forces in Peru.

Political and Economic Challenges

By the end of 1824, all of Spain's colonies in Latin America had won their independence. The 1820s also saw Brazil break away from Portugal without bloodshed. Brazil was the only independent monarchy in Latin America before becoming a republic in 1889.

After winning independence, many of the new Latin American countries passed laws that ended slavery. Some people of African descent made economic and political gains. However, they generally did not have the advantages of Latin Americans of European background. On the other hand, African Latin Americans were better off than Native Americans, most of whom lived in poverty.

Although independent, many Latin American nations hoped their countries would become **stable,** or secure, democracies with prosperous economies. Because of a variety of problems, these goals proved hard to reach.

One major problem was frequent political conflict. Latin Americans quarreled over the role of religion in their society. Individual countries fought over boundary lines, and tensions developed between the rich and poor.

Meanwhile, strong leaders made it difficult for democracy and prosperity to develop. These leaders were known as caudillos (kow·THEE·yohs). **Caudillos** were usually high-ranking military officers or rich men supported by the upper class. **R** They often ruled as dictators. Some built roads, schools, and new cities.

Many caudillos, however, favored the wealthy over the poor. Wealthy Latin Americans owned almost all of the land. The caudillos did nothing to help workers in the countryside. The workers remained landless and struggled to make a living.

Exporting Products

During the late 1800s, Latin America's economy depended on agriculture and mining. At this time, the United States and other industrial countries in Europe began to demand more of Latin America's food products and mineral resources. Businesspeople from these outside countries set up companies throughout Latin America. The companies exported Latin American products such as bananas, sugar, coffee, copper, and oil.

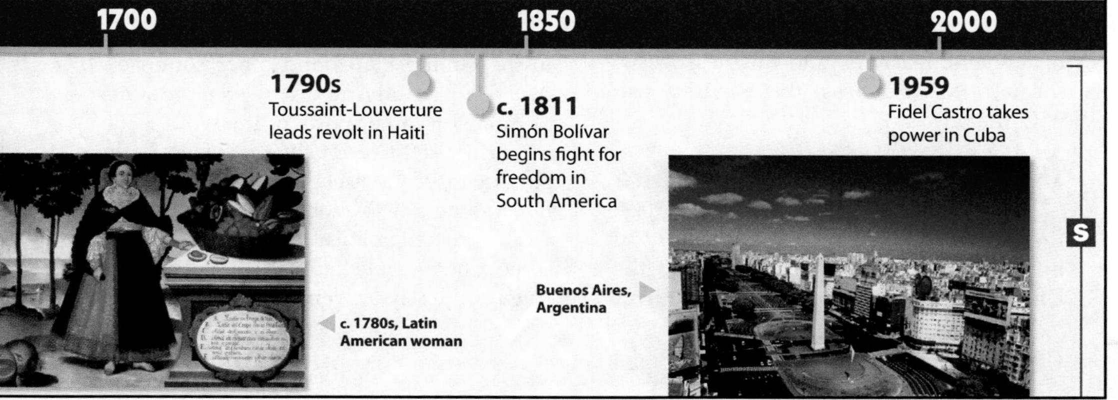
1700
1850
2000
1790s
Toussaint-Louverture leads revolt in Haiti
c. 1811
Simón Bolívar begins fight for freedom in South America
1959
Fidel Castro takes power in Cuba
S

c. 1780s, Latin American woman

Buenos Aires, Argentina

R Reading Strategy

Summarizing Ask: As newly independent countries developed, what problems created frequent political conflict? *(the role of religion in their society, boundary lines, tensions between rich and poor)* What economic problem was made worse under the rule of caudillos? *(Caudillos favored the wealthy, so workers could not afford to own land and struggled to make a living.)* Why do you think it would be difficult for a democracy to develop under this type of leadership? *(Possible answer: Caudillos were often dictators who did not value equality and fair wages for all people.)* **OL**

This Reading Skill (Summarzing) was introduced in this unit.

S Skill Practice

Reading a Time Line Ask: What event took place in 1959? *(Fidel Castro took power in Cuba.)* **BL**

Additional Support

Activity: Economics Connection

Analyzing Information Ask: Why were Latin American countries unable to develop strong economies after becoming independent? *(Leaders of many of the new nations in the region favored the wealthy over the poor, and the wealthy continued to own almost all of the land, leaving workers landless and struggling to make a living.)* Write students' responses on one side of the board. **Ask:** How might the countries in Latin America have avoided or solved these problems? Write students' responses on the board and lead a class discussion analyzing the viability of each option. **OL**

D Differentiated Instruction

Advanced Learners **Ask:** **What economic advantage might the Panama Canal offer to shippers?** *(Possible answer: Because cargo ships no longer have to travel all the way around the tip of South America, shippers can deliver more shiploads in less time.)* **What economic advantage might the Panama Canal offer to consumers?** *(Possible answer: Shorter shipping times result in lower shipping costs, so goods should cost less.)* AL

W Writing Support

Persuasive Writing Have students write a letter to the editor of a Latin American newspaper published in the 1920s. Letters are to discuss reasons why Latin Americans either should or should not distrust the United States. OL

Caption Answer:
It allowed for increased political and economic influence, sometimes protected by U.S. military force.

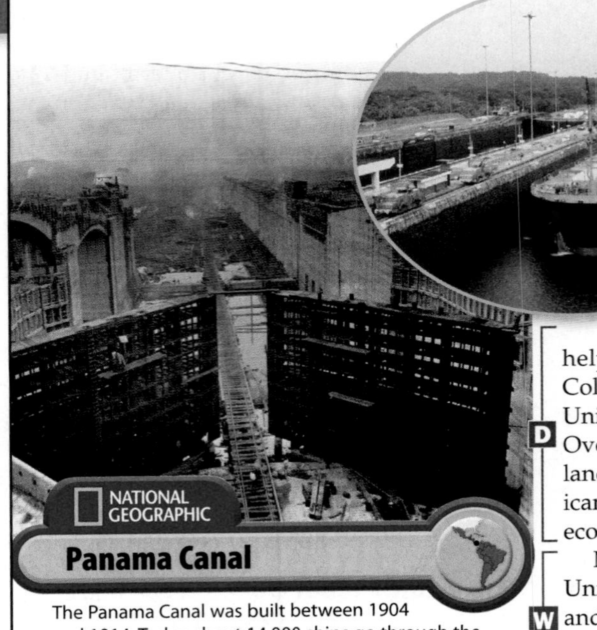

NATIONAL GEOGRAPHIC

Panama Canal

The Panama Canal was built between 1904 and 1914. Today about 14,000 ships go through the canal each year (inset). ***Place*** **How did the Panama Canal affect the U.S. role in Latin America?**

As the number of exports rose, some Latin American countries chose to grow only one or two key products. Prices and profits increased as a result, but a decline in demand had serious effects. Prices dropped, and people lost income and jobs.

Despite the problems it caused, Latin America's dependence on exports also brought benefits. Foreign investors built ports, roads, and railroads. Cities grew in size and population, and a middle class of lawyers, teachers, and businesspeople formed. Nevertheless, the wealthy still held the power.

The United States and Latin America

During the late 1800s and early 1900s, the United States increased its political influence in Latin America. In 1898 the United States and Spain fought a war over Spanish-ruled Cuba. Spain was defeated, and Cuba became a republic under U.S. protection. The United States also gained control of the Caribbean island of Puerto Rico.

D In 1903 the United States helped Panama win its freedom from Colombia. In return, Panama allowed the United States to build the Panama Canal. Over the next 25 years, American troops landed in Haiti, Nicaragua, and the Dominican Republic to protect U.S. political and economic interests.

W Many Latin Americans distrusted the United States because of its great wealth and power. They thought the United States might try to control them as their former rulers had. To improve relations, the United States announced the Good Neighbor Policy toward Latin America in the 1930s. Under this policy, the United States promised not to send military forces to Latin America. It also pledged a greater respect for the rights of Latin American countries.

Modern Times

In the mid-1900s, agriculture was still important in Latin America, but many industries had developed there as well. To encourage economic growth, Latin American leaders borrowed heavily from banks in the United States and other countries. As a result, Latin America owed large sums of money to other parts of the world. The increasing debt seriously weakened Latin American economies. Prices rose, wages fell, and people lost jobs.

Dissatisfied political and social groups in some countries rebelled against leaders who ruled ruthlessly or were in power too long.

Additional Support

Activity: Collaborative Learning

Identifying Central Issues **Ask:** **What is the history of the United States' relations with Latin America?** *(increased U.S. political influence; Cuba under U.S. protection; U.S. control of Puerto Rico; Panama Canal built; U.S. troops in Haiti, Nicaragua, and Dominican Republic; distrust of United States leads to Good Neighbor Policy)* Have students work in groups to investigate and report on the Monroe Doctrine, a principle regarding U.S. relations with Latin America that developed from a policy statement made to Congress by President James Monroe in 1823. **Ask:** **Why was President Monroe concerned about Latin America in 1823? What was his message to Congress? How did other U.S. presidents apply the Monroe Doctrine?** Have students share their findings with the class in a panel discussion. Moderate the panel discussion to make sure students address each question. Then open up the discussion to the rest of the class. Ask students to identify positive and negative effects of the Monroe Doctrine and how people in the United States and Latin America might feel about the use of the Monroe Doctrine. AL

For example, in 1959 a young lawyer named Fidel Castro carried out a **revolution,** or a sudden, violent change of government, in Cuba. Instead of favoring democracy, Castro set up a **communist state,** in which the government controlled the economy and society. R

At the same time, other countries were divided by civil wars among political, ethnic, or social groups. In El Salvador, fighters supported by Castro battled government troops armed by the United States. Thousands of people died before a settlement ended the fighting.

Difficult economic and political reforms made during the 1980s helped strengthen many Latin American countries. These changes were often very harsh, which turned many Latin Americans against dictators. During the 1990s, democratic movements succeeded in several countries.

Today's Latin American governments face many challenges. Population is growing rapidly, but resources are limited. Growing trade in illegal drugs has increased crime and corruption. Differences between rich and poor still create social tensions. In the early 2000s, angry voters in Venezuela, Bolivia, Peru, Mexico, and Chile elected new leaders. These leaders promised significant changes that would weaken the power of the wealthy and benefit the poor.

✓ Reading Check **Analyzing Information** Why were economies in Latin America hurt by focusing on one or two products?

Section 1 Review

Social Studies ONLINE
Study Central™ To review this section, go to glencoe.com.

Vocabulary

1. **Explain** the significance of:
   - **a.** maize
   - **b.** jade
   - **c.** obsidian
   - **d.** hieroglyphics
   - **e.** empire
   - **f.** cash crop
   - **g.** caudillo
   - **h.** communist state

Main Ideas

2. **Comparing and Contrasting** Use a Venn diagram like the one below to show similarities and differences between the Aztec and Inca civilizations.

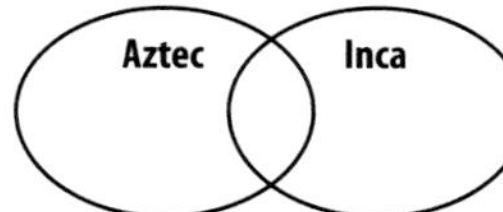

3. **Explaining** What was the social status of African Americans and Native Americans in the newly independent countries of Latin America?

Critical Thinking

4. **Drawing Conclusions** How did European colonial rule change the populations of the region?
5. **BIG Idea** How were the economies of Latin American colonies and European countries connected by trade?
6. **Challenge** Write a paragraph explaining whether you think U.S. involvement in Latin America has helped or hurt the region.

Writing About Geography

7. **Using Your FOLDABLES** Use your Foldable to write a paragraph that explains how political unrest in much of Latin America can be tied to social and economic challenges in the region.

R Reading Strategy

Academic Vocabulary Ask: How was Castro's 1959 revolution in Cuba different from Brazil's break from Portugal 140 years earlier? *(Brazil broke away without bloodshed, but Castro's revolution was a violent change of government.)* **OL**

✓ Reading Check **Answer:** A decline in demand resulted in a drop in prices, which caused severe losses in income and jobs.

Assess

Social Studies ONLINE
Study Central™ provides summaries, interactive games, and online graphic organizers to help students review content.

Close

Summarizing Have students list as many significant dates and events from the section as they can in one minute. **OL**

Answers

1. Definitions for the vocabulary words are found in the section and the Glossary.
2. **Aztec:** Middle America in 1200s, huge temples, busy markets, floating gardens, adopted Toltec culture; **Inca**–South America in 1400s, vast empire, military posts, record-keeping system, irrigation, fortresses; **Both**–conquered others, built roads and bridges, capital cities, farming important
3. After most countries abolished slavery, some people of African American descent made economic and political gains. They did not have the advantages of Latin Americans of European background, but African Americans were better off than Native Americans, most of whom lived in poverty.
4. Europeans spread Christianity to Native Americans and brought enslaved Africans to the region; cultures eventually blended. European settlers brought hardship and disease to Latin America. This greatly reduced the number of Native Americans.
5. enslaved Africans, manufactured goods brought from Europe to Americas; sugar, cotton, tobacco, gold, and silver brought from Americas to Europe
6. Paragraphs should include details from the text about U.S. economic and military influence in Latin America from the late 1800s to the early 1900s.
7. Paragraphs should show an understanding of social and economic challenges and make a logical connection to political unrest in Latin America.

Focus

R Reading Strategy

Inferring Remind students that people's jobs sometimes provide clues about how they might feel about an issue. **Ask: What is the occupation of the author quoted on this page?** *(president of the Republic of Colombia)* **Why might you expect him to support building in the Darien Gap?** *(He would encourage economic growth to benefit his country.)* **OL**

Teach

As they read the feature, have students fill in a chart like the one below. **OL**

For Construction	Against Construction
• The road will help the region's economy. *• It is easier to watch over the ecology by opening up avenues.* *• The park could be destroyed without anyone noticing.*	*• The Darien National Park is a unique environment and should be preserved.* *• Ecotourism can help the economy.* *• A road will increase access and speed up deforestation.*

Additional Support

The Darien Gap: Should a Highway Be Built?

The Pan-American Highway extends from Alaska to the tip of South America. The road stops short in Panama, at Darien National Park. In Colombia, the road starts again, where it continues for the length of South America. Roads have not been built through the Darien Gap because of its unique environment. Supporters of a road believe that it will help the region's economy and that the rain forest can still be preserved. Others, however, think that the forest could be lost forever.

For Construction

I cannot understand why, having [come] to the end of the twentieth century and beginning of the twenty-first, we still have no Pan-American Highway. . . . We are behind in identifying the point in the Darien where the highways should interconnect. And they must first be built. The ecological issue must be confronted realistically. It is easier to safeguard our ecology by opening up the avenues so that we can watch over it than to keep that ecology hidden, just to wake up and suddenly find that it has been destroyed.

—Álvaro Uribe Vélez
President of the
Republic of Colombia

FastFacts

The Pan-American Highway The first Pan-American Highway Congress met in Buenos Aires, Argentina, in 1925 to discuss construction of a highway running from the northern reaches of North America to the southernmost tip of South America. By 2001, all but 54 miles of the almost 16,000-mile route had been completed. The uncompleted segment at the border of Colombia and Panama is called the Darien Gap after Darien Province in Panama. It cuts through a 3-million-acre rain forest that is recognized as an area of intense biodiversity. The break in the route is an inconvenience for travelers on the highway who must veer off course to ports on the Caribbean to be ferried to the other side of the gap by boat.

Construction

C

I get very angry, seeing how the Panamanian economy . . . places value on felled trees and does not recognize the terrible damage to an area suffering constant deforestation. . . . One of the most comforting and encouraging sights that you can see today in the Darien is the presence of eco-tourists. . . . The worst enemy of a rain forest is the road. . . .

We should look at the Darien rain forest as a highly productive mine of eco-dollars. That is really the value of it. . . . If the Darien were to be lost, Panama would lose its soul, because nature is the base of everything.

—Hernan Arauz
Panamanian naturalist guide

You Be the Geographer

1. **Analyzing** What argument does Vélez make for building the highway?
2. **Critical Thinking** What does Arauz claim is an encouraging sight in the Darien Gap? Why do you think he feels that way?
3. **Read to Write** Write a paragraph describing how a road might benefit trade between North America and South America.

YOU Decide

C Critical Thinking

Predicting Consequences Ask: What do you think could happen to Colombia if no road is built? *(Possible answer: Its economy might suffer.)* **What could happen to the rain forest in the Darien Gap if the highway is built?** *(As logging and traffic increase, animal life could be disrupted, and the remainder of the forest could be destroyed.)* **OL**

Assess/Close

Have students review the arguments that they wrote in their charts. **Ask: Which argument do you feel most compelling? Why?** *(Answers will vary.)* **OL**

You Be the Geographer

Answers:

1. Opening up avenues to watch over the ecology can better safeguard it.
2. the presence of ecotourists; because ecotourists boost the economy and support preservation efforts
3. Paragraphs should use details from the text to explain the benefits.

Activity: Connecting With the United States

Identifying Points of View Ask: How important might the completion of the Pan-American Highway be to the United States? *(Answers should mention that the Pan-American Highway extends from Alaska and its construction could affect the U.S. economy.)* Tell students that the idea for a Pan-American Highway developed from a plan for a Pan-American Railway that was introduced in Congress in 1884. Once construction of the highway was underway, the United States financed a large part of it, not only within the United States but also through Central America. Organize students into four groups, such as U.S. government officials, taxpayers, conservationists, and ecotourists to debate this topic. **OL**

Focus

Bellringer

Daily Focus Transparency 8-2

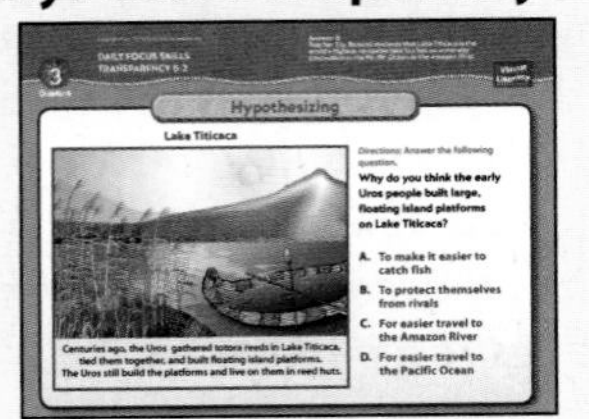

Guide to Reading

Answers to Graphic:

Sample Answers:
Language: Spanish, Portuguese, Quechua, Creole
Religion: Most Latin Americans are Christian
Daily Life: family life important, generations live together; elders cared for by their children
Recreation: soccer, baseball, and cricket; carnivals, feasting
Arts: Rivera's murals reflect Maya and Aztec traditions; writers comment on social and political conflicts

Section Spotlight Video

To learn more about the cultures and lifestyles of Latin America, have students watch the Section Spotlight Video.

Resource Manager

R Reading Strategies	C Critical Thinking	D Differentiated Instruction	W Writing Support	S Skill Practice
Teacher Edition • Sequencing, p. 220 • Und. Q/A Relationships, p. 223 **Additional Resources** • Guid. Read., URB p. 62 • Cont. Vocab., URB p. 63 • Ac. Vocab., URB p. 65 • Read. Ess., p. 55 • World Lit., URB p. 33	**Teacher Edition** • Ident. Cent. Issues, p. 219 • Predicting, p. 221 **Additional Resources** • Quizzes and Tests, p. 86	**Teacher Edition** • Interpersonal, p. 219 • EL, p. 220 • Auditory/Musical, p. 224 **Additional Resources** • Diff. Instr., URB p. 67	**Teacher Edition** • Persuasive Writing, p. 220 **Additional Resources** • Speak./Listen. Skills, URB p. 73	**Teacher Edition** • Using Geo. Skills, p. 221 • Visual Literacy, p. 223 **Additional Resources** • Daily Focus Trans. 8-2 • Regional Atlas, URB pp. 1–7

Guide to Reading

BIG Idea

The characteristics and movement of people impact physical and human systems.

Content Vocabulary

- migration *(p. 219)*
- mestizo *(p. 221)*
- pidgin language *(p. 221)*
- carnival *(p. 224)*
- mural *(p. 224)*

Academic Vocabulary

- element *(p. 219)*
- comment *(p. 224)*
- style *(p. 224)*

Reading Strategy

Summarizing Use a diagram like the one below to summarize the cultures of Latin America by adding one or more facts to each of the outer boxes.

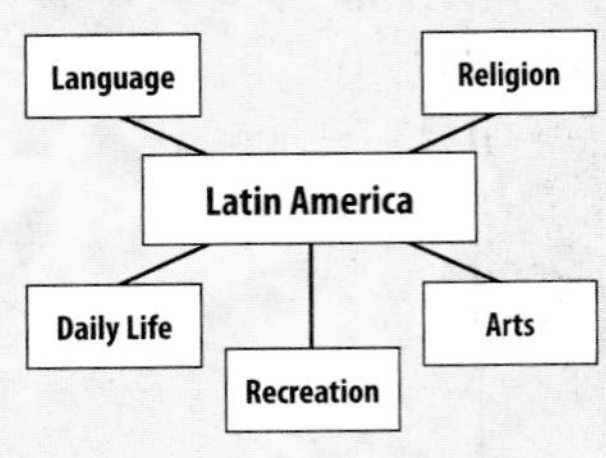

SECTION 2 Cultures and Lifestyles

Picture This Teenage girls celebrate their African heritage during Trinidad's Children's Carnival Competition. Carnival is celebrated in the days before Lent begins. Lent is a time of prayer and fasting in the Roman Catholic Church. During Carnival, both young people and adults dress in costumes. Costumes include characters from nursery rhymes and movie superheroes. As you read this section, you will learn about the different cultures of the people of Latin America.

Celebration in Port-of-Spain, Trinidad

The People

Main Idea **Latin Americans come from a variety of cultures, but many share common characteristics.**

Geography and You Does anyone in your neighborhood speak a foreign language? Read to discover the mix of languages and cultures in Latin America.

Latin Americans come from many different backgrounds. Native Americans, Europeans, Africans, and others all have left their mark. Most Latin Americans today practice the Roman Catholic faith and speak either Spanish or Portuguese.

Population Patterns

Latin America has a high population growth rate. The region's highest birthrates are in Central America, except for Costa Rica, whose birthrate is relatively low. As a result, the Central American countries are growing most quickly in population. In fact, Guatemala and Honduras are expected to double in population by 2050.

Latin America's varied climates and landscapes affect where people live. Temperature extremes, rain forests, deserts, and mountains are common in many parts of Latin America. In these areas, harsh living conditions and poor soil limit where people live. As a result, most Latin Americans live in more favorable climates along the coasts of South America or in an area reaching from Mexico into Central America. These areas provide fertile land and easy access to transportation.

Migration

Migration, or the movement of people, has greatly shaped Latin America's population. In the past, Europeans, Africans, and Asians came to Latin America in large numbers, either willingly or by force. Today, people from places as far away as Korea and Syria come to Latin America looking for jobs or personal freedom.

In addition to people immigrating into the region, some leave Latin America for other parts of the world. Many Latin Americans move north to the United States to escape political unrest or to find a better way of life. Some go through the process of legally entering the United States, while others enter illegally. All of these new arrivals bring **elements,** or parts, of their culture with them. Most stay in close contact with family and friends in their home countries. Many also plan to return when economic conditions in their home countries improve.

A Young Population

About 30 percent of people in Latin America are age 15 and younger. In the United States, 21 percent are 15 and younger. ***Regions*** **Which area of Latin America has the highest birthrate?**

Student Web Activity Visit glencoe.com and complete the Chapter 8 Web Activity about Latin American populations.

Teach

C Critical Thinking

Identifying Central Issues **Ask: What two environment-related factors limit the number of people who live in certain areas of Latin America?** *(harsh living conditions and poor soil)* **Can you name three types of areas with such problems?** *(rain forests, deserts, and mountains)* **OL**

D Differentiated Instruction

Interpersonal Organize students into groups of five or six. Have each group brainstorm to come up with a list of challenges that immigrants might face when leaving their country. **Ask: What might immigrants miss about their home country?** *(relatives, language, food, cultural and religious traditions)* **AL**

Caption Answer:
Central America

Social Studies ONLINE

Objectives and answers to the Student Web Activity can be found at glencoe.com under the Web Activity Lesson Plan for this chapter.

Differentiated Instruction

Leveled Activities

BL **Guided Reading Activity, URB p. 62**

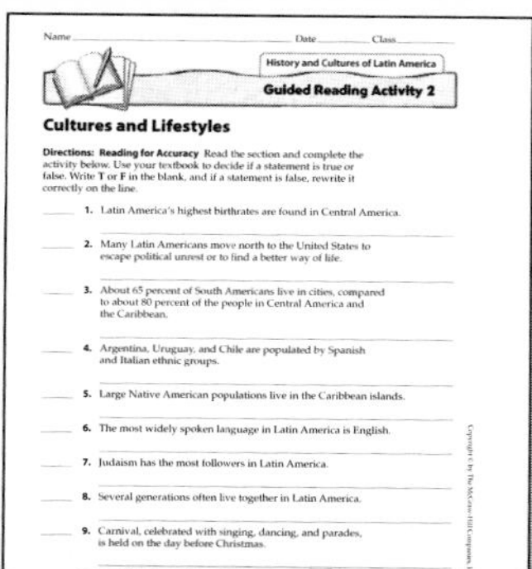

Name ______ Date ______ Class ______

History and Cultures of Latin America

Guided Reading Activity 2

Cultures and Lifestyles

Directions: Reading for Accuracy Read the section and complete the activity below. Use your textbook to decide if a statement is true or false. Write **T** or **F** in the blank, and if a statement is false, rewrite it correctly on the line.

____ 1. Latin America's highest birthrates are found in Central America.

____ 2. Many Latin Americans move north to the United States to escape political unrest or to find a better way of life.

____ 3. About 65 percent of South Americans live in cities, compared to about 80 percent of the people in Central America and the Caribbean.

____ 4. Argentina, Uruguay, and Chile are populated by Spanish and Italian ethnic groups.

____ 5. Large Native American populations live in the Caribbean islands.

____ 6. The most widely spoken language in Latin America is English.

____ 7. Judaism has the most followers in Latin America.

____ 8. Several generations often live together in Latin America.

____ 9. Carnival, celebrated with singing, dancing, and parades, is held on the day before Christmas.

OL **Academic Vocabulary Activity, URB p. 63**

Name ______ Date ______ Class ______

History and Cultures of Latin America

Academic Vocabulary Activity

Academic Words in This Chapter

- comment
- stable
- complex
- element
- style
- revolution
- transform

A. Word Meaning Activity: *Odd Word Out*

Directions: Read the underlined words below, as well as the four words next to them. Three of the words are similar in meaning to the underlined word. Circle the word that is NOT similar to the underlined word.

1. comment	remark	observation	speech	statement
2. complex	simple	complicated	difficult	involved
3. element	part	component	factor	outlook
4. revolution	rebellion	civil	revolt	uprising
5. stable	secure	established	wavering	steady
6. style	topic	method	manner	form
7. transform	charge	change	alter	convert

B. Word Usage Activity: *Understanding Words with Multiple Meanings*

Word Usage Note: The word *element* has several meanings:
a. (n.) a necessary part of something
b. (n.) a smaller group of people that is usually not approved of within a larger group
c. (n.) any of about 100 substances in chemistry
d. (n.) part of electrical equipment that makes heat
e. (n.-pl.) the weather, especially bad weather

The word *element* also is used in the following expressions: to be in or out of one's *element* / an *element* of danger or truth or risk.

AL **Content Vocabulary Activity, URB p. 65**

Name ______ Date ______ Class ______

History and Cultures of Latin America

Content Vocabulary Activity

Directions: Definitions Select a term that matches each definition below. Write the correct term in the space provided.

pidgin language	caudillo	empire
carnival	communist state	mural
migration	obsidian	hieroglyphics
mestizo	cash crop	maize
jade		

1. *Definition:* a shiny green stone
Term: ______
2. *Definition:* a form of writing that uses signs and symbols
Term: ______
3. *Definition:* a large festival held on the last day before the Christian holy period called Lent, which is marked by singing, dancing, and parades
Term: ______
4. *Definition:* a farm product grown for export
Term: ______
5. *Definition:* a person of mixed Native American and European descent
Term: ______
6. *Definition:* a large artwork painted directly on a wall
Term: ______
7. *Definition:* a language that is made by combining parts of different languages
Term: ______
8. *Definition:* another term for corn

ELL **Reading Essentials and Note-Taking Guide, p. 55**

Chapter 8, Section 2 (Pages 218–224)

Cultures and Lifestyles

Big Idea

The characteristics and movement of people impact physical and human systems. As you read, complete the diagram below. Add one or more facts to each of the outer boxes.

Language | Latin America | Religion | Daily Life | Recreation | Arts

Notes | **Read to Learn**

The People (pages 219–221)

Summarizing

Summarize three types of migration that occur in Latin America.

1. ______
2. ______
3. ______

Latin America has a high population growth rate. Central America has the fastest growing populations. Guatemala and Honduras are expected to double their populations by the year 2050.

The region's climates and landscapes affect where people live. Areas with extreme temperatures, rain forests, deserts, and mountains are sparsely populated. Most people live in moderate climates along the coasts of South America or in an area stretching from Mexico into Central America. These areas have fertile soil and allow for easy movement of people and goods.

Latin America's population has been affected by **migration,** or the movement of people. People immigrate into the region in search of jobs or personal freedom. At the same time, some Latin Americans leave the region to escape political unrest or to find a better way of life. Many legally and illegally enter the United

R Reading Strategy

Sequencing Write the following on the board:

a. Smaller farms cannot always support large families.
b. People seek work in cities.
c. Rural population increases.
d. Less land is available for each family.

Have students place in order the events that have led to urbanization in Latin America. *(c, d, a, b)* OL

W Writing Support

Persuasive Writing Have students write a letter to persuade the leader of a Latin American country to help solve the problems of the urban poor. Letters should follow a business format, include specific problems from the text, and offer possible solutions. OL

D Differentiated Instruction

English Learners Have small groups of students conduct research about the cultural traditions in Ecuador, Peru, and Bolivia. Have groups create a map that depicts the cultural elements of each country. ELL

Caption Answer:
80 percent

Latin Americans also move within their country or the region. As in many parts of the world, Latin America's rural areas have increased greatly in population. In certain areas, this growth has resulted in a shortage of fertile land. **R** Smaller farms cannot always support large families. People often leave to find jobs elsewhere, usually in cities. The result is urbanization, or the movement of people from the countryside to the cities.

Growth of Cities

In the past, most Latin Americans lived in the countryside and worked the land. Today most of them live in rapidly growing cities. Some of the largest urban areas in the world are in Latin America, including Mexico City, Mexico; São Paulo (sow POW·loo) and Rio de Janeiro (REE·oo dee zhah·NAY·roo) in Brazil; and Buenos Aires, Argentina.

The number of urban dwellers, however, varies throughout the region. In South America, about 80 percent of people live in cities—about the same as in the United States. In Central America and the Caribbean, only about 65 percent of people are urban dwellers.

Most Latin Americans leave villages for the cities to find better jobs, schools, housing, and health care. In many cases, people do not find what they seek. As city populations grow, jobs and housing become scarce. At the same time, rural dwellers often lack the education and skills to find good jobs. There have been too few schools and health care centers to serve the growing **W** number of city dwellers. Unable to return to the countryside, many people have been forced by poverty to live in crowded neighborhoods with poor housing, lack of sanitation, and rising crime.

Rio de Janeiro

NATIONAL GEOGRAPHIC

Once the capital city of Brazil, Rio de Janeiro remains an important center for trade and industry. ***Place*** **What percentage of South Americans live in cities?**

Ethnic Groups and Languages

Latin America's people include Native Americans, Europeans, Africans, Asians, and mixtures of these groups. The blend of ethnic groups varies from area to area.

Most of Latin America's Native Americans live in Mexico, Central America, and the Andes countries of Ecuador, Peru, and Bolivia. Great Native American empires **D** thrived in these places before Europeans arrived there. Today, Native Americans work to keep their languages and traditions alive while adopting features of other cultures.

Since the 1400s, millions of Europeans have settled in Latin America. Most settlers have been Spanish or Portuguese. Over the

Hands-On Chapter Project
Step 2

Presenting a Latin American Cultural Fair

Step 2: Preparing the Booths Groups of students will prepare booths that portray the cultural and religious traditions of Latin American countries.

Directions Have groups use the research they completed in Step 1 to plan their booths. For each booth, have students design a decorative banner that reflects their country's cultural traditions. Each booth also should include a brief summary of the country's history, religion, and politics. Encourage students to include examples of music, art, and food from their assigned country.

Putting It Together Have groups assemble and present their booths to the rest of the class. Then invite students from other classes to attend the fair. OL

(Chapter Project cont. on the Visual Summary page)

years, other Europeans—Italians, British, French, and Germans—have come as well. In the 1800s, many Spanish and Italian immigrants settled in Argentina, Uruguay, and Chile. As a result, these three nations today are mainly populated by people of European descent.

African Latin Americans form a high percentage of the populations in the Caribbean islands and northeastern Brazil. They are descended from enslaved Africans whom Europeans brought as laborers during colonial days. Over the years, Africans have added their rich cultural influences to the food, music, and arts of Latin America.

Large Asian populations live in the Caribbean islands and some countries of South America. Most Asians came during the 1800s to work as temporary laborers. They remained and formed ethnic communities. In Guyana about one-half of the population is of South Asian or Southeast Asian ancestry. Many people of Chinese descent make their homes in Peru, Mexico, and Cuba. About 1 million people of Japanese descent live in Brazil, making Brazil home to the largest number of Japanese in one place outside of Japan. S

Over the centuries, there has been a blending of the different ethnic groups throughout Latin America. In countries such as Mexico, Honduras, El Salvador, and Colombia, **mestizos,** or people of mixed Native American and European descent, make up the largest part of the population. In Cuba, the Dominican Republic, and Brazil, people of mixed African and European descent form a large percentage of the population.

Because Spain once ruled most of Latin America, Spanish is the most widely spoken language in the region. In Brazil, which was once a colony of Portugal, most people speak Portuguese. Native American languages are still spoken in many countries. For example, Quechua (KEH·chuh·wuh), spoken centuries ago by the Inca, is an official language of Peru and Bolivia. C In the Caribbean, where the British and French once ruled many islands, English and French are widely spoken. In some countries, people have developed a **pidgin language** by combining parts of different languages. An example is Creole, spoken in Haiti. Most Creole words are from French, but sentence structure, or organization, reflects African languages.

NATIONAL GEOGRAPHIC

Ethnic Diversity

São Paulo, Brazil, has a large Japanese community. Drummers in Barbados (inset) celebrate their African heritage. ***Place*** **What Latin American nations have populations that are mainly of European background?**

Reading Check **Analyzing** What challenges do Latin America's growing cities face?

S Skill Practice

Using Geography Skills Display a world map. Have students locate Guyana and Southeast Asia. **Ask: Why might the climate of Guyana have seemed familiar to its Southeast Asian immigrants?** *(Both areas are near the Equator, and the sea influences climates in both areas.)* **OL**

C Critical Thinking

Predicting Ask: What can you predict about the long-term consequences of Peru and Bolivia maintaining Quechua as their official language? *(Possible answer: By making Quechua their official language, these countries will preserve the language spoken by the Inca centuries ago. This might help preserve their cultural heritage as well.)* **OL**

For further practice on this skill (Predicting), see the **Skills Handbook**.

Caption Answer:
Argentina, Uruguay, and Chile

Reading Check Answer: scarce jobs, few schools and health care centers, poor housing, poverty, crowding, lack of sanitation, and rising crime

Additional Support

Activity: Interdisciplinary Connection

World Languages Ask: What languages do Latin Americans speak? *(Spanish, Portuguese, English, French, Quechua, Creole, and others)* Have students work in pairs to research and create a glossary of useful and interesting phrases in a Latin American language of their choice. When students have completed their glossaries, allow time for each pair to give their classmates a language lesson, teaching them the words and phrases they have discovered, their meanings, and their pronunciations. You might want to invite a language teacher to share words and phrases from Latin American languages with your class. **OL**

World Literature

Teach

Reading Strategy

Summarizing Information Remind students that summarizing involves restating the main ideas of a passage in fewer words. **Ask: What did the old couple do?** *(They visited their son, hoping for some food.)* **What did the son do?** *(He hid his food and refused to feed his parents.)* **What happened after the old couple left their son's home?** *(The son found that all of his food had spoiled, and a snake strangled him when he tried to eat candy.)* **How would you summarize this folktale?** *(A son who refuses to care for his elderly parents will be punished.)* **OL**

This **Reading Skill** (Summarizing Information) was introduced in this unit.

Analyzing Literature

Answers:

1. Children should be respectful and generous to their parents, taking care of them when they are old.
2. Stories will vary, but might describe someone's bad behavior, ending with the punishment that person receives.

Mexican Folktale

Folktales are stories that have no known author. They are the literature of the common people of a country or region. They express the views these people have about life, what is important to society, and how individuals are expected to behave.

Background Information

The folktales of Mexico reflect Mexican society. Like that society, they include a mix of Spanish and Native American cultures. Some tales point out the tensions between different social and ethnic groups. This folktale reflects basic Mexican values, including the respect that children owe to their parents.

Reader's Dictionary

crystal: expensive, high-quality glass

weevil: a kind of beetle

The Hard-Hearted Son

Mexican Folktale

There was an old couple who had a married son. They were very poor, and one day they went to visit their son to see if he would give them some corn and ask them to dinner. His corn bins were full, and his table was laid out with many good things. For dessert there was candy in a large dish made of **crystal.**

When he saw his parents coming, he told his wife, "There come those old people! Put the cover on the candy dish and hide the food, so we won't have to ask them to dinner."

The wife did so, and when his parents came in and saw it all, they asked their son for a few handfuls of corn. But he told them he didn't have anything, that he hadn't harvested his crop yet. "It's all right," his parents said. "God bless you and give you more." And they left.

When [the son and his wife] sat down to dinner, they found the food had spoiled. The man went to his corn bins and found it all eaten by **weevils.** He came back, and when he was going to eat the candy, a serpent came out and wound itself about his neck and strangled him.

It [wasn't] his parents' curse; rather, [it was] a punishment for his greed and hard-heartedness.

From: *Folktales of Mexico*, ed. and trans. by Américo Paredes. Chicago: The University of Chicago Press, 1970.

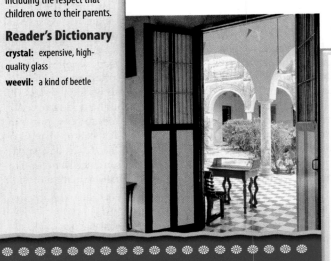

Analyzing Literature

1. **Making Inferences** What message does this tale give about how children should behave?
2. **Read to Write** Think about a kind of behavior or attitude that you think is important for people to have. Write a brief story like this one to illustrate why people should behave that way or have that attitude.

Additional Reading

Review suggested books before assigning them.

Biography: *Ponce De Leon: Juan Ponce de Leon Searches for the Fountain of Youth* by Ann Heinrichs tells the story of the explorer who became the governor of Puerto Rico and traveled to Florida to search for the fabled Fountain of Youth.

Nonfiction: *Out of War* by Sara Cameron tells the story of The Children's Movement for Peace, a coalition of courageous young people who work together to end more than four decades of civil war in Colombia.

Fiction: *The Tree Is Older than You Are* by Naomi Shihab Nye is an illustrated collection of poems and stories from Mexico.

For further reading, see  BOOKLINK 3

Daily Life

Main Idea **Many aspects of daily life in Latin America reflect the region's blend of cultures.**

Geography and You Do you enjoy eating tomatoes, potatoes, and chocolate? These foods were first eaten in Latin America. Read to find out about other features of Latin American daily life.

Religion and family play an important role in Latin American life. The region's history and politics are reflected in celebrations and art.

Religion

Religion has long played an important role in Latin American cultures. During colonial times, most Latin Americans became Christians, and Christianity still has the most followers. Roman Catholics form the largest Christian group. In recent years, however, Protestant missionaries have encouraged many people to convert, or to change their beliefs, to Protestant forms of Christianity.

Other faiths are also practiced in the region. For example, many traditional Native American and African religions thrive, often mixed with Christianity and other faiths. Islam, Hinduism, and Buddhism, brought by Asian immigrants, are practiced in the Caribbean region and coastal areas of South America. Judaism has followers in the largest Latin American cities.

Family

Family life is important in Latin America. Often several generations live together, and adults are expected to care for their aged parents. Adult brothers and sisters often live near each other, and their children—who are cousins—can form close relationships. Traditionally, the father is the family leader and the chief decision maker. In some parts of the Caribbean, however, the mother is the leader of the family.

S

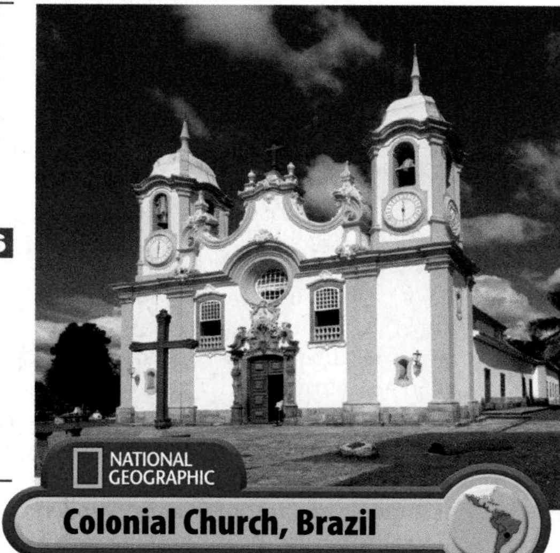

NATIONAL GEOGRAPHIC

Colonial Church, Brazil

In Brazil, many churches—such as this one in the town of Tiradentes—were built during the 1700s under Portuguese rule. ***Regions*** **How is Christianity changing in Latin America?**

R

Recreation and Celebrations

Most Latin Americans are devoted sports fans. Soccer is popular throughout the region, and Brazil and Argentina have produced outstanding players and world championship teams. Cuba was the second country in the world—after the United States—to play baseball. This sport has taken hold throughout the Caribbean, Central America, and northern South America. Several countries have their own leagues, and many skilled players have gone to play in the United States. In Caribbean countries that were once ruled by the British, cricket is a favorite sport.

S Skill Practice

Visual Literacy **Ask:** **Does this church resemble the temples of early civilizations in Latin America? Explain your answer.** *(Possible answer: No, early temples were shaped like pyramids. This church was built under the direction of Portuguese rulers who must have wanted it to look like the churches of their native land.)* **AL**

R Reading Strategy

Understanding Question-Answer Relationships Tell students that to ask or answer a question about differences, people often use words or phrases such as *but, however,* or *in contrast to.* Tell students to use one of these words or phrases in response to the following question: What aspect of family life in the Caribbean is *different* from the rest of Latin America? *(In most of Latin America, the father is the family leader, but in the Caribbean, the mother fills that role.)* **OL**

Caption Answer:
Roman Catholics form the largest Christian group, but missionaries have encouraged many people to convert to Protestant forms of Christianity.

Differentiated Instruction

Speaking and Listening Skills Activity, URB p. 73

Delivering a Narrative Presentation

Objective: To develop engaging storytelling techniques

Focus: Tell students to recall a good story.

Teach: Ask students to model verbal and nonverbal narrative techniques.

Assess: Have students use the checklist to assess their storytelling techniques.

Close: Create a class story by having one student start the story and every student in the class add one more sentence to the story.

Differentiated Instruction Strategies

BL Tell students to use a chart to organize events in their narrative.

AL Have students select a narrative poem and use narrative techniques as they read it to the class.

ELL Ask students to share a favorite story or personal experience, using the storytelling techniques they have learned.

D Differentiated Instruction

Auditory/Musical Bring in samples of Cuban and Brazilian music and a sample of American jazz music. Play portions of songs from each type of music, and tell students to listen for the similarities in each style. **OL**

Reading Check **Answer:** soccer, baseball, and cricket

Assess

Social Studies ONLINE
Study Central™ provides summaries, interactive games, and online graphic organizers to help students review content.

Close

Paraphrasing Have students recall the effects of population patterns, migration, and urbanization on Latin America. Then have students paraphrase the information given about it in the text. **OL**

Religious and patriotic holidays are celebrated throughout Latin America. Each spring, many countries hold a large festival called **carnival** on the last day before the Christian holy period called Lent. The celebration is marked by singing, dancing, and parades. The Carnival held in Rio de Janeiro, Brazil, is famous for its color and excitement. On the Mexican holiday known as the Day of the Dead, people honor family members who have died.

Feasting is an important part of Latin American celebrations. The foods of Latin America blend the traditions of the region's many peoples. Corn and beans—crops grown by Native Americans since ancient times—are important in Mexico and Central America. Beans and rice are a standard meal in the islands of the Caribbean and in Brazil. Fresh fish from the sea is also popular in those areas. Beef is the national dish in Argentina, Uruguay, and Chile.

The Arts

Culture in Latin America shows the influence of its ethnic mix. Cuban music is famous for its use of African rhythms. During the 1930s, Mexican artists, such as Diego Rivera, painted **murals,** or large paintings on walls, that recall the artistic traditions of the ancient Maya and Aztec. In Latin America, many writers have used their work to **comment** on, or talk about, social and political conflicts.

D Latin American artists have influenced those in other countries. The music of Cuba and Brazil has shaped American jazz. Latin American writers of the late 1900s invented a **style,** or form, of writing called magic realism that combined fantastic events with the ordinary. This style was adopted by European and Asian writers.

Reading Check **Identifying** What sports are popular in Latin America?

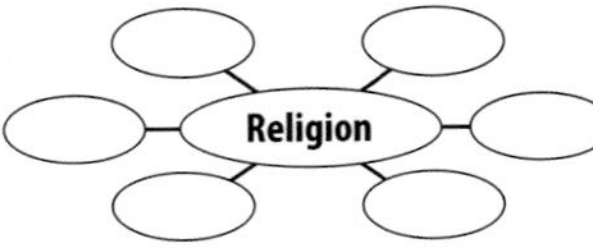

Social Studies ONLINE
Study Central™ To review this section, go to glencoe.com.

Vocabulary

1. **Explain** the significance of:
   a. migration
   b. mestizo
   c. pidgin language
   d. carnival
   e. mural

Main Ideas

2. **Describing** Describe patterns of migration in Latin America in the past and today.
3. **Summarizing** Use a diagram like the one below to summarize key facts about religion in Latin America.

Religion

Critical Thinking

4. **BIG Idea** How do pidgin languages show the blending of different cultures in Latin America?
5. **Identifying Central Issues** In what parts of the region do most Latin Americans live? Why?
6. **Challenge** How has the region been influenced by other regions of the world?

Writing About Geography

7. **Expository Writing** Make a map of Latin America. Add labels that highlight facts about the population patterns, religions, and cultures of different countries and areas within the region. Then write a short paragraph describing the patterns you see.

Answers

1. Definitions for the vocabulary words are found in the section and the Glossary.
2. In the past, Europeans, Africans, and Asians came to Latin America willingly or by force; today immigrants come to Latin America for jobs or personal freedom, and many Latin Americans move to the United States and other parts of the world to escape political unrest or to find a better way of life.
3. Diagrams may include the following: mostly Christian; Roman Catholics largest Christian group; more Protestants in recent years; traditional Native American and African religions; Islam, Hinduism, Buddhism in Caribbean and coastal areas; Judaism in largest cities.
4. Pidgin languages combine parts of different languages; many Creole words, for example, come from French, but Creole sentence structure is African.
5. Most live along coasts of South America or in areas from Mexico into Central America. The population in rural areas has grown, resulting in a shortage of fertile land. Smaller farms cannot always support large families, so people move to cities.
6. The region's ethnic groups, languages, religions, and ways of life reflect the influence of Europeans, Africans, and Asians who came to the region.
7. Maps and paragraphs should demonstrate an understanding of the population patterns, religions, and cultures of the region.

Visual Summary

Native American Civilizations

- The Olmec built the first civilization in Latin America.
- The Maya created a calendar and a complex number system.
- The Aztec set up a large empire in central Mexico.
- The Inca developed a network of roads to unite their territories.

Aztec stone calendar

Colonial Rule

- Spanish explorers conquered the Aztec and Inca Empires.
- Spain and Portugal ruled most of Latin America from the 1500s to the early 1800s.
- Colonial rule brought a mixing of different cultures.

Hernán Cortés

Forming New Nations

- Most Latin American countries achieved independence during the 1800s.
- Dictators, the military, or wealthy groups ruled Latin American countries, while most people remained poor and powerless.
- Many Latin American countries developed more democratic systems in the 1900s.

People

- About 80 percent of South Americans live in urban areas.
- Most people in Latin America are of European, Native American, or African background.
- Most Latin Americans speak Spanish or Portuguese, and most practice the Roman Catholic faith.

Culture

- Family life is important to most Latin Americans.
- Soccer and baseball are major sports in Latin America.
- Food, arts, and music reflect the diverse ethnic mixture of the region.
- Religious and patriotic holidays are important throughout Latin America.

Baseball players, Dominican Republic

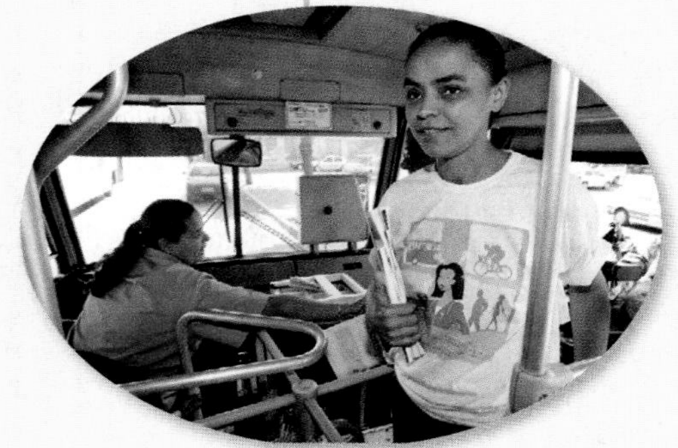

Bus rider in Brasília, Brazil

Study anywhere, anytime! Download quizzes and flash cards to your PDA from glencoe.com.

Visual Summary

Visual/Spatial Explain that the illustrations in the Visual Summary were chosen to help the reader recall the main ideas from the chapter.

Have students study each illustration in the Visual Summary. Then have them read the information that accompanies the illustration. Point out to students that the heading "Forming New Nations" does not have an accompanying illustration. Ask students to draw an illustration to serve as a visual summary for that heading. Tell students that the information they convey is more important than their artistry. Ask volunteers to share their work with the class. **OL**

Using Geography Skills Display a large map of Latin America. Have each student write down a question from this chapter that can be answered by pointing to an area on the map. Example: Which country was the second in the world to play baseball? *(Cuba)*

Organize the class into two or more teams. Give each team a sticky note. When you ask a question, the first competitor to place a sticky note on the correct location will earn a team point. **OL**

Hands-On Chapter Project

Step 3: Wrap Up

Presenting a Latin American Cultural Fair

Step 3: Learning From the Booths Students will synthesize what they have learned in Steps 1–2.

Directions Write the Essential Question on the board. Use students' booths as a springboard for discussion of the question. Have students name the languages and religions of each country and list them on the board. Then have students identify which languages and religions are predominant in Latin America. Put an asterisk next to these on the board. Underline the word *unite* in the Essential Question, and ask students to describe ways language and religion have united people in Latin America. Then underline the word *divide,* and discuss how language, religion, and cultural differences have divided or caused conflict among the region's people. Ask students to think about how language and religion have united or divided people in other regions of the world. Then have them respond to the Essential Question by writing a few sentences in their journals. **OL**

Answers and Analyses

Reviewing Vocabulary

1. B Maize, a food similar to corn, and jade, a semi-precious stone, were both resources used by the Olmec. Copper is not associated with the early peoples of Latin America.

2. A Students might recall that the Inca took control of a large territory in the Andes. There they developed a vast empire. The terms *caudillo, communist state,* and *Good Neighbor Policy* all relate to the recent history of Latin America.

3. D Creole is a pidgin language, which is made up of mostly French vocabulary and African structure. A mestizo is a person of mixed heritage. A cash crop is a product grown only for trade. A hieroglyphic is part of a written system of language.

4. C The words *artists* and *paintings* in the question stem should help students determine the correct answer, *murals,* which are a type of painting created by artists. The other terms may prove challenging for students who have not memorized them yet, especially *mestizos* and *caudillos,* which are Spanish terms. Sometimes memorization is the best strategy for learning terms that will appear in questions with few clues.

STANDARDIZED TEST PRACTICE

TEST-TAKING TIP

On answer sheets for standardized tests, neatly print information, such as your name, and carefully fill in ovals.

Reviewing Vocabulary

Directions: Choose the word(s) that best completes the sentence.

1. The Olmec made weapons with a volcanic glass called ______.

A jade
B obsidian
C maize
D copper

2. The Inca of Peru established a(n) ______ in the Andes.

A empire
B caudillo
C communist state
D Good Neighbor Policy

3. Creole is an example of a ______.

A mestizo
B cash crop
C hieroglyphic
D pidgin language

4. In Mexico, some artists painted ______, or large paintings on walls, recalling the artistic traditions of the Maya and Aztec.

A mestizos
B carnivals
C murals
D caudillos

Reviewing Main Ideas

Directions: Choose the best answer for each question.

Section 1 *(pp. 208–215)*

5. The Maya built their civilization in an area that is known today as ______.

A Brazil
B the Caribbean
C central Mexico
D the Yucatán Peninsula

6. What happened because Latin American leaders borrowed heavily from United States banks in the mid-1900s?

A Wages fell and people lost jobs.
B Prices in their countries dropped.
C Latin economies became stronger.
D American troops landed in Nicaragua.

Section 2 *(pp. 218–224)*

7. ______ is populated mainly by people of European descent.

A Bolivia
B Ecuador
C Guatemala
D Argentina

8. In ______, Quechua is an official language.

A Peru
B Brazil
C Honduras
D El Salvador

GO ON

Reviewing the Main Ideas

5. D The Maya lived in the Yucatán Peninsula. The only other location mentioned that had an early Native American population is central Mexico, where the Aztec lived.

6. A The huge debts of Latin American countries in the mid-1900s weakened their economies, so wages fell and people lost jobs. Prices dropped during the late 1800s, when just a few products were produced in certain countries and demand fell. Though cities were improved by foreign investment, their economies remained vulnerable to outside influences. American involvement in Nicaragua resulted in distrust because of U.S. wealth and power.

Critical Thinking

Directions: Base your answers to questions 9 and 10 on the table below and your knowledge of Chapter 8. Choose the best answer for each question.

Internet and Cell Phone Users in Central America

	Population	Internet Users	Cell Phone Users
Belize	287,730	35,000	93,100
Honduras	7,326,496	223,000	1,282,000
Guatemala	12,293,545	756,000	3,168,300
Costa Rica	4,075,261	1,000,000	1,101,000

Source: *CIA World Factbook.*

9. Divide the population by the number of cell phone users to find out the number of people per cell phone in each country. Which country has the fewest cell phones in proportion to its population?

A Belize

B Honduras

C Guatemala

D Costa Rica

10. Divide the number of Internet users by the population. Which country has the most Internet users in proportion to its population?

A Belize

B Honduras

C Guatemala

D Costa Rica

Document-Based Questions

Directions: Analyze the following document and answer the short-answer questions that follow.

The following passage is by a Catholic priest who came to the Yucatán Peninsula in the 1560s.

> *Before the Spaniards subdued [overcame] the country the Indians lived together in well ordered communities; they kept the ground in excellent condition, free from noxious [harmful] vegetation and planted with fine trees. The habitation was as follows: in the center of the town were the temples, with beautiful plazas, and around the temples stood the houses of the chiefs and the priests, and next those of the leading men. Closest to these came the houses of those who were wealthiest and most [respected], and at the borders of the town were the houses of the common people. The wells, where they were few, were near the houses of the chiefs; their plantations were set out in the trees for making wine, and sown with cotton, pepper and maize. They lived in these communities for fear of their enemies, lest [for fear that] they be taken in captivity; but after the wars with the Spaniards they dispersed [scattered] through the forests.*
>
> —Friar Diego de Landa,
> *Yucatán Before and After the Conquest*

11. How did the friar feel about the Indian communities? Explain your answer.

12. How did conquest by the Spaniards affect communities in the Yucatán Peninsula?

Extended Response

13. Describe challenges and successes for Latin Americans in the 1990s and 2000s.

STOP

Social Studies ONLINE

For additional test practice, use Self-Check Quizzes—Chapter 8 at glencoe.com.

Need Extra Help?

If you missed question...	1	2	3	4	5	6	7	8	9	10	11	12	13
Go to page...	209	210	221	224	209	214	221	221	219	219	210	210	213–224

Critical Thinking

9. B Students do not have to perform each division problem, but can round off and estimate. For example, they can round off the population of Belize to 300,000 and its cell phone users to 100,000. By eliminating the zeros, students can assume that Belize has approximately three people per cell phone. *Honduras,* choice B, has 5.71 people per cell phone, the fewest cell phones per person.

10. D To answer this question, students may round off and divide. Students should not simply scan the number of Internet users, because the population numbers are in such a wide range. Costa Rica, choice D, has a far greater proportion of Internet users than that of the others listed.

Document-Based Questions

11. Friar Diego seems to have liked or admired the communities. Evidence lies in his favorable descriptions, such as "well ordered communities," "kept the ground in excellent condition," and "beautiful plazas."

12. After the wars with the Spaniards, the Indians dispersed through the forests, leaving behind their well-ordered communities.

Extended Response

13. Students' descriptions will vary but should mention the success of democratic movements in the 1990s and 2000s as well as the increase in crime and corruption.

7. D Argentina, Uruguay, and Chile were settled by Spanish and Italian immigrants. As a result, these countries today are populated mainly by people of European descent. Bolivia, Ecuador, and Peru are mostly populated by Native Americans. Middle America is mainly populated by mestizos.

8. A People in Brazil speak mostly Portuguese. The text does not specify languages for Honduras and El Salvador. However, in both Peru and Bolivia the official language is Quechua.

Social Studies ONLINE

Have students visit the Web site at glencoe.com to review Chapter 8 and take the Self-Check Quiz.

Need Extra Help?

Have students refer to the pages listed if they miss any of the questions.

Teach

D Differentiated Instruction

Intrapersonal Read Miguel's 7:45 A.M. entry to students. **Ask:** **Has something similar happened to you?** *(Answers may include examples of assemblies about crime prevention and antidrug programs that took the place of a class.)* Point out that communities in Latin America are concerned with many of the same issues that concern communities in the United States. **BL**

C Critical Thinking

Analyzing Primary Sources **Ask:** **What evidence can you find to show that Miguel is a responsible person?** *(Miguel is working for a good grade in history and Spanish, his elective class involves volunteer work, and he takes care of his dogs and his uncle's roosters, helps in the kitchen, helps at the family store, and does his homework.)* **OL**

TIME JOURNAL

"Hello! My name is Miguel.

I'm 14 years old and I live in San Cristóbal Ecatepec, a town near Mexico City, the capital of Mexico. I live in a small house with my mother, sister, and grandmother. Read about my day."

6:15 a.m. I wake up and get dressed then have breakfast with my family. This morning, my two young cousins come over to eat with us. We have quesadillas, which are corn tortillas with melted cheese. My grandmother also puts out a plate of bananas and papayas.

6:45 a.m. I comb my hair, brush my teeth, and put my books in my backpack. It's time to leave for school, even though it's still pretty dark outside. I walk to school with my sister, Areli (ah•ray•LEE).

7:00 a.m. The sun is starting to come up as we arrive at José María Morelos y Pavón Middle School. The school is named for a famous leader in Mexico's struggle for independence from Spain. (We have learned about him in history class!)

7:10 a.m. English is my first class of the day. Our teacher, Mr. Aranda, encourages us to speak mostly English during class.

D **7:45 a.m.** It is time for my least favorite class—math. Today, though, I get a break. The local police visit our school to lead an assembly on crime prevention. They talk to us about staying safe and drug-free.

8:45 a.m. In physical education class, we play *fútbol*, or soccer. Then I move on to music, where I practice my skills on the recorder. I am learning to play a song from a musical.

10:30 a.m. During a short recess, I sit outside and talk with my friends Alejandra, Ismael, and José.

10:45 a.m. I go to history class, then to Spanish. I am working hard for a good grade in both classes. In Mexico, we are graded on a 10-point scale. A passing grade is a 6 or higher. C

12:45 p.m. It is time for my elective class—family values. It's about respecting family and friends, and doing community volunteer work.

1:00 p.m. The school day is over. While I walk home, I chat with my dad on my cell phone. He and my mother are separated, so he does not live with us. I see him often though.

1:10 p.m. I change clothes and feed my dogs. Then I help my grandmother with lunch. I squeeze oranges for juice while she makes chicken and rice. My mom comes home for lunch from her job as a secretary.

2:30 p.m. I ride my bike to the hardware store that my family owns. My grandmother and uncles work there. In the back of the store, my Uncle Ricardo raises roosters. I help my uncle by feeding the birds and cleaning their cages.

4:30 p.m. I go back home and play soccer outside with my cousins. Then I start my homework.

6:30 p.m. For dinner, we have *pollo con mole*. It is chicken in a delicious black sauce made with chocolate and spices. Later, I watch some TV (I like to watch reality shows).

10:00 p.m. I am tired, so I go to bed.

ILLUSTRATIONS BY BOOKMAPMAN

WHAT'S THE WORD? Miguel works on a team project in Spanish class.

MAKING MUSIC Miguel plays the recorder in music class. He also knows how to play the flute.

AT HOME Miguel, his sister, cousins, and grandmother spend time together.

228

Additional Support

Additional Statistics You can find data like this and much more in the *CIA World Factbook*. Go to www.cia.gov and click on the link to the *World Factbook*. From there you can click on the countries you wish to learn more about.

The People of Mexico	
Age of population	
0–14 years	30.6%
15–64 years	63.6%
65 years and over	5.8%
Life expectancy at birth	75.41 years
People age 15 and over who can read and write	92.2%

Source: *CIA World Factbook*, 2006.

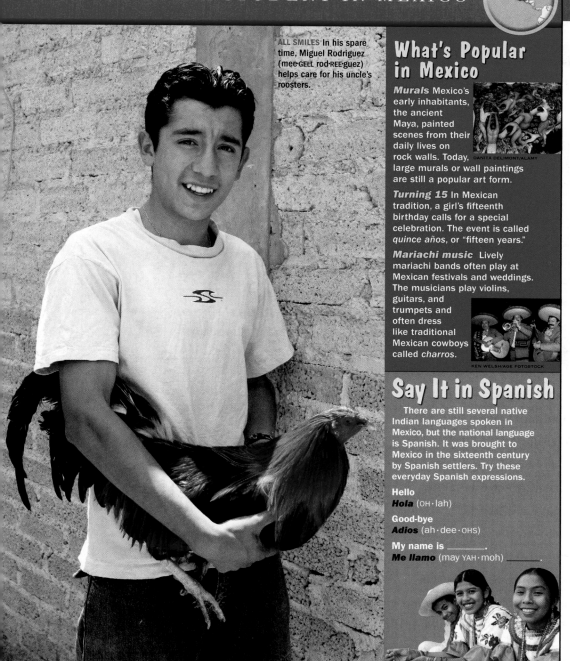

ALL SMILES In his spare time, Miguel Rodriguez (mee·GELL rod·REE·guez) helps care for his uncle's roosters.

What's Popular in Mexico

Murals Mexico's early inhabitants, the ancient Maya, painted scenes from their daily lives on rock walls. Today, large murals or wall paintings are still a popular art form.

DANITA DELIMONT/ALAMY

Turning 15 In Mexican tradition, a girl's fifteenth birthday calls for a special celebration. The event is called *quince años*, or "fifteen years."

Mariachi music Lively mariachi bands often play at Mexican festivals and weddings. The musicians play violins, guitars, and trumpets and often dress like traditional Mexican cowboys called *charros*.

KEN WELSH/AGE FOTOSTOCK

Say It in Spanish

There are still several native Indian languages spoken in Mexico, but the national language is Spanish. It was brought to Mexico in the sixteenth century by Spanish settlers. Try these everyday Spanish expressions.

Hello
Hola (OH·lah)

Good-bye
Adios (ah·dee·OHS)

My name is _____.
Me llamo (may YAH·moh) _____.

ADRIANA ZEHBRAUSKAS / POLARIS (4)

LUC NOVOVITCH/ALAMY

229

What's Popular in Mexico

Mariachi Before the Spanish conquest, musicians in Mexico used drums, flutes, rattles, and conch-shell horns. Music was already an important part of religious celebrations. Europeans introduced their own instruments and music. Native American musicians learned to play stringed instruments, brass horns, and woodwinds from Europe, and they began making their own versions of them.

Say It in Spanish

Spanish Spanish has become an important second language in many parts of the United States. Some Americans go to Latin America to attend language schools. They may choose to live with a family, take a university course, or even take specialized courses for a career. One such course helps health professionals learn medical terms. Here are some health words that might come in handy on a trip to Latin America:

headache: *el dolor de cabeza*
upset stomach: *estómago disgustado*
earache: *dolor de oídos*
prescription: *la prescripción*
allergy: *alergia*

Activity: Descriptive Writing

Describing Show students a selection of murals by Diego Rivera and other Latin American artists, and ask them to choose one to describe in a paragraph. Direct students to choose lively, colorful words to describe the scene shown and the artist's techniques and style. Encourage students to tell about the details in the scene in a logical order and to use spatial order words, such as *behind, in front of, next to,* and *to the left of.* Display photos of the murals in the classroom, and have students read their descriptive paragraphs aloud to the class without identifying the mural they are describing. Challenge the rest of the class to try to identify the mural each student has written about from his or her description. **OL**

Planning Guide

Key to Ability Levels

BL Below level
OL On level
AL Above level
ELL English Language Learners

Key to Teaching Resources

Print Material
DVD
CD-ROM
Transparency

Levels BL	OL	AL	ELL	Resources	Chapter Opener	Section 1	Section 2	Section 3	Chapter Assess
FOCUS									
BL	OL	AL	ELL	Daily Focus Skills Transparencies		9-1	9-2	9-3	
TEACH									
BL	OL		ELL	Guided Reading Activity, URB*		p. 85	p. 86	p. 87	
BL	OL	AL	ELL	Content Vocabulary Activity, URB*		p. 89	p. 89	p. 89	
BL	OL	AL	ELL	Academic Vocabulary Activity, URB		p. 91	p. 91	p. 91	
BL	OL	AL	ELL	Differentiated Instruction Activity, URB		p. 93			
BL	OL	AL	ELL	Chart, Graph, and Map Skills Activity, URB			p. 95		
	OL	AL		Critical Thinking Activity, URB		p. 97			
BL	OL	AL	ELL	Speaking and Listening Skills Activity, URB			p. 99		
BL	OL	AL	ELL	Writing Skills Activity, URB				p. 103	
BL	OL	AL	ELL	School-to-Home Connection Activity, URB*		p. 107	p. 107	p. 107	
BL	OL	AL	ELL	Regional Atlas Activities, URB		pp. 1–7	pp. 1–7	pp. 1–7	
		AL		Geography and Economics Activity, URB		p. 9			
	OL	AL		Environmental Case Study, URB				p. 13	
		AL		Enrichment Activity, URB				p. 19	
	OL	AL		World Literature Readings, URB				p. 31	
BL	OL		ELL	Reading Essentials and Note-Taking Guide*		p. 58	p. 61	p. 64	
	OL	AL		TIME Perspectives: Exploring World Issues			p. 9		
	OL			Interactive Geography Activity	p. 17				
BL	OL	AL	ELL	In-Text Map Overlay and Population Pyramid Transparencies	3	3A, 3D	3A, 3D	3A, 3D	
	OL			Foods Around the World		p. 10	p. 12		
BL	OL	AL	ELL	Outline Map Resource Book	p. 28	p. 32	p. 30	p. 27	
BL	OL	AL	ELL	NGS World Atlas*	✓	✓	✓	✓	
BL	OL	AL	ELL	NGS World Desk Map	✓	✓	✓	✓	✓
BL	OL	AL	ELL	World Literature Library	✓	✓	✓	✓	✓
BL	OL	AL	ELL	Writer's Guidebook	✓	✓	✓	✓	✓

Note: Please refer to the *Unit Resource Book: Latin America* for this chapter's URB materials.

* Also available in Spanish

- Interactive Lesson Planner
- Interactive Teacher Edition
- Fully editable blackline masters
- Section Spotlight Videos Launch
- Differentiated Lesson Plans
- Printable reports of daily assignments
- Standards Tracking System

Levels				Resources	Chapter Opener	Section 1	Section 2	Section 3	Chapter Assess
BL	OL	AL	ELL						
TEACH *(continued)*									
BL	OL	AL	ELL	**Vocabulary PuzzleMaker CD-ROM***	✓	✓	✓	✓	✓
	OL	AL		**Primary Sources CD-ROM**	✓	✓	✓	✓	✓
BL	OL	AL	ELL	**StudentWorks™ Plus DVD**	✓	✓	✓	✓	✓
BL	OL	AL	ELL	**Section Video Program Activities**	✓	✓	✓	✓	✓
BL	OL	AL	ELL	**World Music: A Cultural Legacy**	✓	✓	✓	✓	✓
BL	OL	AL	ELL	**Writing Process Transparencies**	✓	✓	✓	✓	✓
Teacher Resources				**Building Academic Vocabulary**	✓	✓	✓	✓	✓
				Strategies for Success	✓	✓	✓	✓	✓
				Teacher's Guide to Differentiated Instruction	✓	✓	✓	✓	✓
				Presentation Plus! DVD	✓	✓	✓	✓	✓
ASSESS									
BL	OL	AL	ELL	**Quizzes and Tests**		p. 95	p. 96	p. 97	p. 99
BL	OL	AL	ELL	**Authentic Assessment With Rubrics**					p. 9
BL	OL	AL	ELL	**Standardized Test Practice**					p. 33
BL	OL	AL	ELL	***ExamView® Assessment Suite* CD-ROM***		9-1	9-2	9-3	Ch. 9
BL	OL	AL	ELL	**Interactive Tutor Self-Assessment CD-ROM**		9-1	9-2	9-3	
CLOSE									
BL			ELL	**Reteaching Activity, URB***		p. 105	p. 105	p. 105	p. 105
BL	OL		ELL	**Reading and Study Skills Foldables™**	p. 66	p. 66	p. 66	p. 66	p. 66
BL	OL	AL	ELL	**Graphic Organizer Transparencies and Strategies**		✓	✓	✓	
BL	OL	AL	ELL	***Exploring Our World* in Graphic Novel**	pp. 25, 33				

Integrating Technology

Daily Assignments and Grade Log

Technology Product

Glencoe's *StudentWorks™ Plus* CD-ROM contains everything your students need, including the complete Student Edition and access to all student workbooks. *StudentWorks™ Plus* also includes a Daily Assignment and Activity Log that allows students to

- record and track progress on their daily assignments and responsibilities;
- log results achieved, including their grades;
- sort assignments alphabetically or by category;
- view and print the assignment and grade log in a table or calendar format.

Objective

Using *StudentWorks™ Plus* will help your students

- take responsibility for their individual tasks;
- improve independent study skills.

Steps

Provide students with the following information:

- Launch *StudentWorks™ Plus.*
- Select the **Daily Assignments and Grade Log** button at the bottom of the launch screen.
- Create a new file or open an existing one. The log is organized as a table, with a row of information for each assignment.
- Add information for each assignment, including the date of the assignment, the name, additional comments, the due date, and the grade.
- Edit rows as assignment information is provided or changed. Add a new row to the log for each new assignment.

Social Studies ONLINE

	Student	Teacher	Parent
Beyond the Textbook	●		●
Chapter Overviews	●		●
Concepts in Motion	●		●
ePuzzles and Games	●		●
Literature Connections		●	
Multi-Language Glossaries	●		●
Online Student Edition	●	●	●
Section Videos	●	●	●
Self-Check Quizzes	●		●
Student Web Activities	●		●
Study Central™	●		●
Teaching Today		●	
TIME Current Events	●		●
Vocabulary eFlashcards	●		●
Web Activity Lesson Plans		●	

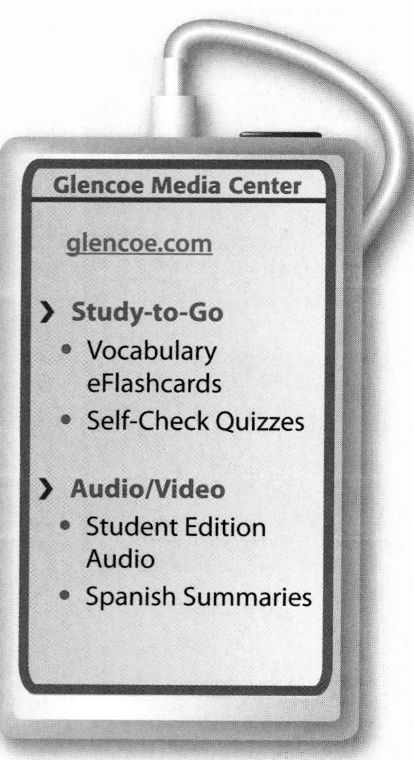

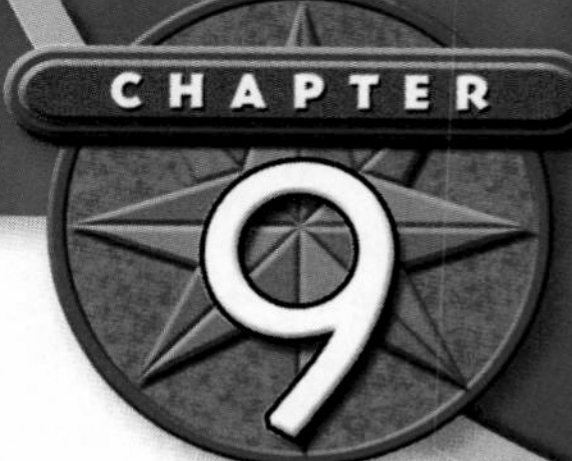

- **Timed Readings Plus in Social Studies** helps students increase their reading rate and fluency while maintaining comprehension. The 400-word passages are similar to those found on state and national assessments.
- **Reading in the Content Area: Social Studies** concentrates on six essential reading skills that help students better comprehend what they read. The book includes 75 high-interest nonfiction passages written at increasing levels of difficulty.
- **Reading Social Studies** includes strategic reading instruction and vocabulary support in Social Studies content for ELLs and native speakers of English.
- **Content Vocabulary Workout** (Grades 6–8) accelerates reading comprehension through focused vocabulary development. Social Studies content vocabulary comes from the glossaries of Glencoe's Middle School Social Studies texts.
www.jamestowneducation.com

NATIONAL GEOGRAPHIC

Index to National Geographic Magazine:

The following articles relate to this chapter:

- "Last of the Amazon," Scott Wallace, January 2007.
- "Venezuela According to Chavez," Alma Guillermoprieto, April 2006.

National Geographic Society Products To order the following, call National Geographic at 1-800-368-2728:

- *National Geographic Atlas of the World* (Book).

Access National Geographic's new dynamic MapMachine Web site and other geography resources at:
www.nationalgeographic.com
www.nationalgeographic.com/maps

The following videotape programs are available from Glencoe as supplements to Chapter 9:

- Cuba and Castro (ISBN 0-76-701426-X)
- Evita: The Woman Behind the Myth (ISBN 0-76-700029-3)

To order, call Glencoe at 1-800-334-7344. To find classroom resources to accompany many of these videos, check the following home pages:

A&E Television: www.aetv.com
The History Channel: www.historychannel.com

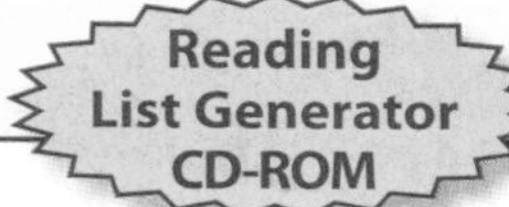

GLENCOE BOOKLINK 3

Use this database to search more than 30,000 titles to create a customized reading list for your students.

- Reading lists can be organized by students' reading level, author, genre, theme, or area of interest.
- The database provides Degrees of Reading Power™ (DRP) and Lexile™ readability scores for all selections.
- A brief summary of each selection is included.

Leveled reading suggestions for this chapter:

For students at a Grade 5 reading level:
- ***My Home in Mexico,*** by Donna Bailey

For students at a Grade 6 reading level:
- ***The Streets Are Free,*** by Kurusa

For students at a Grade 7 reading level:
- ***On the Pampas,*** by Maria Cristina Brusca

For students at a Grade 8 reading level:
- ***Mexico: The People,*** by Bobbie Kalman

For students at a Grade 9 reading level:
- ***Brazil: A Study of an Economically Developing Country,*** by Anna Lewington and Edward Parker

Focus

The Essential Question

As students study the chapter, remind them to consider the chapter-based Essential Question. Answering this question will help them understand the important concepts in the chapter. In addition, the Hands-On Chapter Project relates the content from each section to the Essential Question. The steps in each section build on each other as students progress through the chapter. The Hands-On Chapter Project culminates in the Wrap Up activity on the Visual Summary page.

More About the Photo

Visual Literacy Buenos Aires is a cultural center that includes museums, theater, and art enjoyed by a diverse population of citizens and tourists. In the center of the city lies the Plaza de Mayo, a square where some of the city's most important buildings are located, including the office of the Argentine president and a national museum. Buenos Aires is known for tango, a rhythm that combines European and African music. The words used in tango lyrics come from *lunfardo*, the slang of the residents of Buenos Aires. The music is accompanied by the tango dance, a colorful dance composed of eight basic steps.

CHAPTER 9

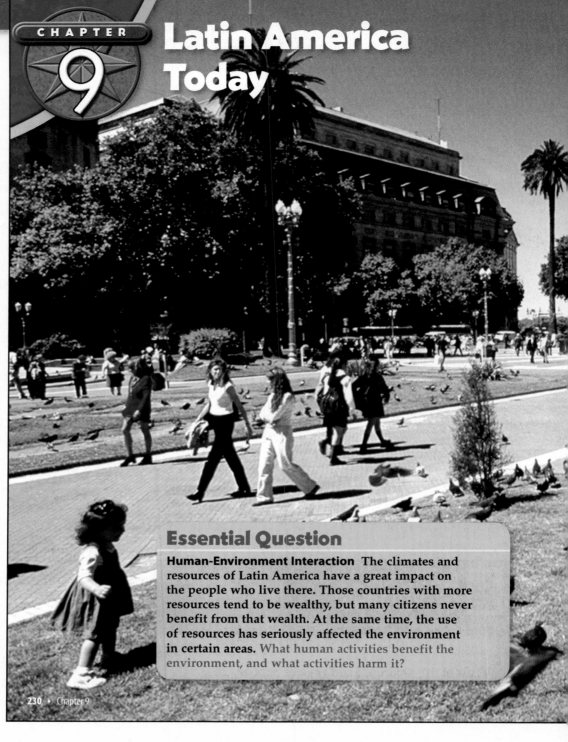

Latin America Today

Essential Question

Human-Environment Interaction The climates and resources of Latin America have a great impact on the people who live there. Those countries with more resources tend to be wealthy, but many citizens never benefit from that wealth. At the same time, the use of resources has seriously affected the environment in certain areas. What human activities benefit the environment, and what activities harm it?

Teach

The BIG Ideas *As you begin teaching each section, use these questions and activities to help students focus on the Big Ideas.*

Section 

Mexico Ask: **How might a country's economy be connected to other regions of the world?** *(Possible answers: It might rely on other regions to buy its products. It might make parts that form a product sold in other regions. Workers from other regions might move to the country.)* Tell students that Section 1 describes Mexico's government, people, culture, and economy, as well as the challenges facing the country as it makes important social and economic changes. **OL**

Section 

Central America and the Caribbean
Ask: **How might waterways affect a country's economy?** *(Possible answer: Waterways allow ships to travel, thus increasing trade and tourism.)* Point out to students that Section 2 describes the government and economies of countries in Central America and the Caribbean, including the role of waterways in the region. **OL**

BIG Ideas

Section 1: Mexico

BIG IDEA Patterns of economic activities result in global interdependence. Many Mexicans now depend on factory jobs. Those who cannot find work at home migrate to the United States in search of work.

Section 2: Central America and the Caribbean

BIG IDEA The physical environment affects how people live. Many Caribbean islands have limited resources. Their warm climate and beautiful beaches, however, make tourism an important industry.

Section 3: South America

BIG IDEA People's actions can change the physical environment. The Amazon basin holds the world's largest rain forest. People are now using the rain forest's resources to boost economic growth. Their actions greatly affect the Amazon basin's fragile environment.

FOLDABLES™ Study Organizer

Organizing Information Make this Foldable to help you organize information about the countries of Latin America today.

Step 1 Place two 11x17 pieces of paper together.

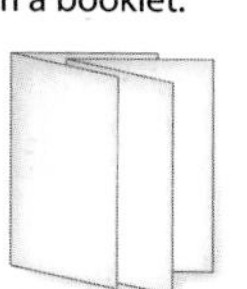

Step 2 Fold the papers in half to form a booklet.

Step 3 Label your booklet as shown.

Reading and Writing As you read the chapter, take notes about each Latin American country. Use your notes to write five quiz questions for each section of the chapter.

Plaza de Mayo, Buenos Aires, Argentina

Social Studies ONLINE

To preview Chapter 9, go to glencoe.com.

Previewing the Region

If you have not already done so, engage students in the Regional Atlas and chart activities to help them become familiar with the general content of the region.

FOLDABLES™ Study Organizer — Dinah Zike's Foldables

Purpose This Foldable helps students organize information about the countries of Latin America today. As students read the chapter, they should note facts from each section on the pages of the Foldable. Students will use the Foldable to write quiz questions for each section of the chapter—Mexico, Central America and the Caribbean, and South America. In addition, completed Foldables can be used to prepare for assessment. **OL**

More Foldables activities for this chapter can be found in *Dinah Zike's Reading and Study Skills Foldables* ancillary.

Social Studies ONLINE

Introduce students to chapter content and key terms by having them access the Chapter Overview at glencoe.com.

Section 3

South America Ask: How can people hurt or help the environment? *(Possible answers: hurt—waste water and energy, pollute, drive when it isn't necessary; help—conserve resources, recycle, walk or bike instead of drive, buy from environmentally friendly companies, replant trees)* Tell students that Section 3 describes the governments, economies, and people of countries in South America, as well as challenges facing the region. Students also will learn about the causes and effects of deforestation. **OL**

Focus

Bellringer

Daily Focus Transparency 9-1

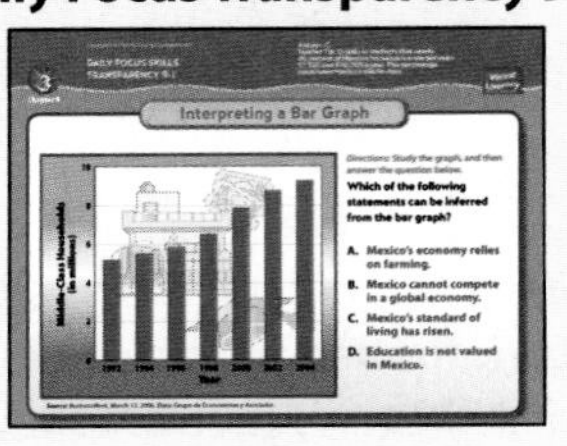

Guide to Reading

Answers to Graphic:

Answers may include:

Region	Key Facts
North	farmers use canals to grow crops; ranchers raise cattle; rich natural resources
Central	holds more than half of country's population; productive farming; manufacturing area
South	poorest economic region; subsistence farming; wealthy plantations; coastal tourism

Section Spotlight Video

To learn more about Mexico, have students watch the Section Spotlight Video.

Guide to Reading

Mexico

BIG Idea

Patterns of economic activities result in global interdependence.

Content Vocabulary

- plaza *(p. 233)*
- vaquero *(p. 234)*
- maquiladora *(p. 235)*
- subsistence farm *(p. 235)*
- plantation *(p. 235)*
- migrant worker *(p. 236)*

Academic Vocabulary

- reveal *(p. 234)*
- assemble *(p. 235)*

Reading Strategy

Summarizing Use a chart like the one below to organize key facts about Mexico's economic regions.

Region	Key Facts
North	
Central	
South	

Picture This They may not look like soccer balls, but these piles of plastic panels will be stitched together by workers in San Miguelito, Mexico, to create thousands of balls for the popular sport. The soccer balls are then sold to large companies that export them. Read this section to learn about Mexico's economy today and how it is connected to other regions of the world.

Soccer ball beginnings in San Miguelito, Mexico

Resource Manager

R Reading Strategies

Teacher Edition
- Taking Notes, p. 233
- Read. Pri. Sources, p. 235

Additional Resources
- Guid. Read., URB p. 85
- Cont. Vocab., URB p. 89
- Ac. Vocab., URB p. 91
- Read. Ess., p. 58

C Critical Thinking

Teacher Edition
- Making Inferences, p. 233
- Analyzing Info., p. 236

Additional Resources
- Crit. Think., URB p. 97
- Interactive Geography, p. 17
- Authentic Assess., p. 9
- Quizzes and Tests, p. 95

D Differentiated Instruction

Teacher Edition
- Auditory/Musical, p. 234
- Intrapersonal, p. 236

Additional Resources
- Diff. Instr., URB p. 93
- Reteach., URB p. 105
- School-to-Home Conn., URB p. 107

W Writing Support

Teacher Edition
- Descriptive Writing, p. 233
- Personal Writing, p. 234

Additional Resources
- Geo. & Econ., URB p. 9

S Skill Practice

Teacher Edition
- Visual Literacy, p. 234
- Using Geo. Skills, p. 235

Additional Resources
- Daily Focus Trans. 9-1
- Regional Atlas, URB pp. 1–7

Mexico's People, Government, and Culture

R

Main Idea **Mexico's culture reflects its Native American and Spanish past as well as modern influences.**

Geography and You Do you like tacos or enchiladas? These are tasty Mexican dishes. Read to learn about Mexico's people and culture.

Mexico is the United States's nearest southern neighbor. It is the third-largest country in area in Latin America, after Brazil and Argentina. Mexico also ranks second in population.

Mexico's People

Mexico's people reflect the blending of Spanish and Native American populations over the centuries. About two-thirds of Mexicans are mestizos. A quarter of Mexico's people are mostly or completely Native American.

In Mexico, rural traditions remain strong, but about 75 percent of Mexicans now live in cities. The largest city by far is Mexico City, the country's capital. With nearly 22 million people, Mexico City is one of the world's largest and most crowded urban areas.

W Mexican cities show the influence of Spanish culture. Many of them are organized around large **plazas**, or public squares. City plazas serve as centers of public life. The main government buildings and the largest church are located alongside each city's plaza. Newer sections of the cities have glass office buildings and modern houses. In poorer sections, homes are built of boards, sheet metal, or even cardboard.

Plaza in Mexico City

The plazas of Mexican cities are popular places to gather. The church on this plaza in Mexico City was built in 1536. ***Place*** **About what percentage of Mexico's people live in cities today?**

Mexico's Government

Mexico, like the United States, is a federal republic, where power is divided between national and state governments. A strong president leads the national government. He or she can serve only one six-year term but has more power than the legislative and judicial branches.

C After a revolution in the early 1900s, one political party ruled Mexico for many decades. Then, in the 1990s, economic troubles and the people's lack of political power led to calls for change. In 2000 Mexican voters elected a president from a different political party for the first time in more than 70 years. In the next presidential election six years later, the vote count was too close to call. An election court finally ruled Felipe Calderón president of Mexico, despite bitter protests from supporters of the opposing candidate.

Teach

R Reading Strategy

Taking Notes Ask pairs of students to create a three-column chart labeled "Mexico's People," "Mexico's Government," and "Mexican Culture." Tell students that they will use the chart to take notes as they read the subsection. Remind them to write important words or phrases rather than complete sentences directly from the text. **BL**

W Writing Support

Descriptive Writing Ask students to write a paragraph describing what they might expect to hear and see in a Mexican city plaza. Students also can use the image on this page for inspiration. Discuss students' descriptions and how they compare to town squares or city centers found in the United States. **OL**

C Critical Thinking

Making Inferences **Ask:** **Who did the people of Mexico blame for their troubles?** *(the president or his political party)* **Why do you think so?** *(They elected a president from a different political party.)* **OL**

Caption Answer:
about 75 percent

Hands-On Chapter Project Step 1

Creating an Environmental Mobile

Step 1: Conducting Research Students will find images that show human activities common in Latin America and the effects of those activities on the environment.

Essential Question What human activities benefit the environment, and what activities harm it?

Directions Discuss with students the ways in which humans can improve their environment, such as by preserving open spaces and planting trees, and the ways humans can harm the environment, such as by clear-cutting forests and polluting. Ask students to name various activities and explain whether they benefit or harm the environment. Then have students research activities common in Mexico and their effects on the environment. Tell students that as part of their research, they will need to find images that show the activities and their impact on the environment. Explain that they will be using the images to create a mobile.

Visualizing Bring examples or pictures of mobiles to class to help students begin to visualize their final project. **OL**

(Chapter Project continued in Section 2)

W Writing Support

Personal Writing Show students a work of art by Diego Rivera or Frida Kahlo, such as one of his murals or one of her self-portraits. Instruct students to study the work's subject, colors, and style. Then have them write a journal entry describing their reactions to the art and impressions of the artist. **OL**

D Differentiated Instruction

Auditory/Musical Play for students a recording of a type of Mexican music, such as mariachi or norteño. Ask students to try to identify various instruments in the music. Discuss whether students think the music might be appropriate to play at a fiesta. **OL**

S Skill Practice

Visual Literacy **Ask:** How can you tell that the fiesta pictured is a celebration? *(dancing, special clothing, crowd)* **EL**

Reading Check Answer: European and Native American influences

Caption Answer: parades, fireworks, music, food

Mexican Culture

Mexican culture **reveals** both European and Native American influences. Folk arts, such as wood carving, are deeply rooted in Native American traditions. Favorite sports, such as soccer, were brought from Europe. Carved and painted religious statues display the mixing of the two cultures.

W Mexican artists and writers have created many national treasures. In the early 1900s, Diego Rivera and his wife, Frida Kahlo, became well-known for their paintings. Carlos Fuentes and Octavio Paz have written works about the values of Mexico's people.

D Mexicans enjoy celebrations called fiestas (fee·EHS·tuhs) that include parades, fireworks, music, and dancing. Food is an important part of Mexican fiestas. Tacos and enchiladas are now as popular in the United States as they are in Mexico.

Reading Check **Identifying** What are the sources of Mexico's culture?

Mexican Fiesta

NATIONAL GEOGRAPHIC

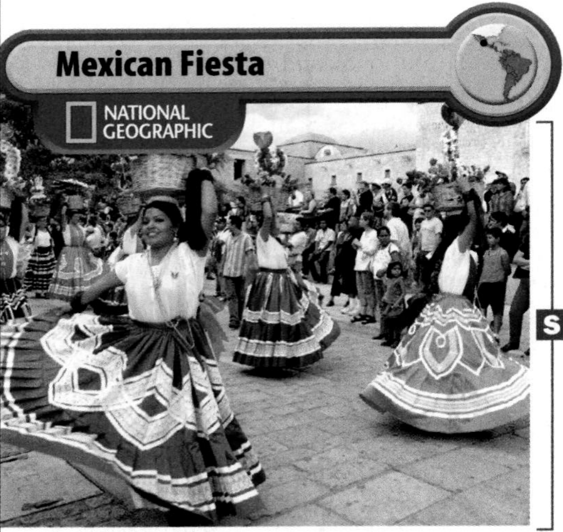

S

Women wearing traditional clothes dance in a parade at a fiesta in Oaxaca, Mexico. ***Place*** **In what other ways do Mexicans celebrate at a fiesta?**

Mexico's Economy and Society

Main Idea **While Mexico's economy is improving, the country still faces significant challenges from poverty, overcrowded cities, and environmental issues.**

Geography and You Have you seen the brown haze of smog? Read to find out how economic growth in Mexico City has contributed to the increase of smog there.

With many resources and workers, Mexico has a growing economy. Mexico has tried to use its resources to improve the lives of its people. Although these efforts have brought some gains for Mexicans, they have also created some challenges for the future.

Economic Regions

Mexico's physical geography and climate together give the country three distinct economic regions. These regions are the North, Central Mexico, and the South.

Mexico's North has large stretches of land that are too dry and rocky to farm without irrigation. So farmers have built canals to carry water to their fields. As a result, they are able to grow cotton, grains, fruits, and vegetables for export. Areas in the North have grasslands that support cattle ranches. Mexican cowhands called **vaqueros** (vah·KEHR·ohs) developed tools and methods for raising cattle during Spanish colonial times. Their skills were later passed on to American cowhands. Vaqueros still carry on this work today.

In addition to farming and ranching, the North profits from rich deposits of copper, zinc, iron, lead, and silver. Manufacturing is located in cities near

Differentiated Instruction

Critical Thinking Activity, URB pp. 97–98

Finding the Main Idea

Objective: To learn how to find the most important idea in a text

Focus: Discuss with students the difference between main ideas and details.

Teach: Review the steps for finding main ideas and apply the steps to the first two paragraphs.

Assess: Have students read the passage and answer the questions that follow.

Close: Ask students how finding the main idea can help them better understand a text.

Differentiated Instruction Strategies

BL Show students the main idea and supporting details in the first paragraph.

AL Ask students to find examples of a main idea that is stated and a main idea that is implied.

ELL Have students underline the sentence that contains the main idea in each paragraph.

or along the Mexico–United States border. These cities include Monterrey, Tijuana (tee·HWAH·nah), and Ciudad Juárez (syoo·THAHTH HWAHR·EHS). In the North, many companies from the United States and elsewhere have built **maquiladoras** (muh·KEE·luh·DOHR·uhs). These are factories in which workers **assemble** parts made in other countries. The finished products are then exported to the United States and other countries. S

Central Mexico holds more than half of Mexico's people. Although it is situated in the Tropics, this area has a high elevation that keeps it from being hot and humid. Temperatures are mild, and the climate is pleasant year-round. Fertile soil created by volcanic eruptions over the centuries allows for productive farming.

Large industrial cities, such as Mexico City and Guadalajara (GWAH·thuh·lah·HAH·rah), prosper in central Mexico. Workers in these cities make cars, clothing, household items, and electronic goods. The coastal area along the Gulf of Mexico is a center of Mexico's energy industry. This is because of the major oil and gas deposits that lie offshore.

Mexico's South is the poorest economic region. The mountains towering in the center of this region have poor soil. **Subsistence farms**, or small plots where farmers grow only enough food to feed their families, are common here. In contrast, coastal lowlands have good soil and abundant rain. Wealthy farmers grow sugarcane or bananas on **plantations**, large farms that raise a single crop for sale. Both coasts in the South have beautiful beaches and a warm climate. Tourists from all over the world flock to resort cities, such as Acapulco on the Pacific coast and Cancun on the Caribbean coast's Yucatán (YOO·kah·TAHN) Peninsula. R

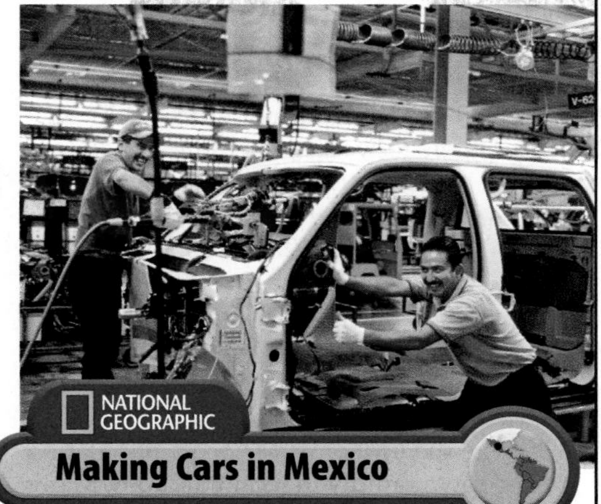

NATIONAL GEOGRAPHIC

Making Cars in Mexico

Workers build a new car at an assembly plant in central Mexico. American and Japanese companies have located hundreds of plants in Mexico. ***Regions*** **What agreement has helped Mexico's economy?**

Economic and Social Changes

For years Mexico's economy relied on agriculture. Today, Mexico still exports food products, but it relies less on farming and more on manufacturing. Much of the change has come about because of Mexico's closer ties with its northern neighbors: the United States and Canada. As you recall, Mexico, the United States, and Canada entered into the North American Free Trade Agreement (NAFTA) in 1994. Under NAFTA, the three countries decided to end barriers to trade among themselves.

Mexico's growing industries now provide a wide range of goods, such as steel, cars, and consumer goods. Many service industries, such as banking and tourism, also contribute to Mexico's economy.

Social Studies ONLINE

Student Web Activity Visit glencoe.com and complete the Chapter 9 Web Activity about economic changes in Mexico.

S Skill Practice

Using Geography Skills Have students locate on a map the cities in northern Mexico. **Ask: What geographical factors might make the north appealing to U.S. businesses?** *(Possible answers: proximity to the United States; access to cities with large populations of workers.)* EL

R Reading Strategy

Reading Primary Sources Read aloud a personal essay about traveling in Mexico from a travel magazine or Web site. Discuss with students how a personal essay presents a different point of view from what might be conveyed in a textbook or an encyclopedia. OL

Caption Answer:
NAFTA

Social Studies ONLINE

Objectives and answers to the Student Web Activity can be found at glencoe.com under the Web Activity Lesson Plan for this chapter.

Differentiated Instruction

Leveled Activities

BL Reteaching Activity, URB p. 105

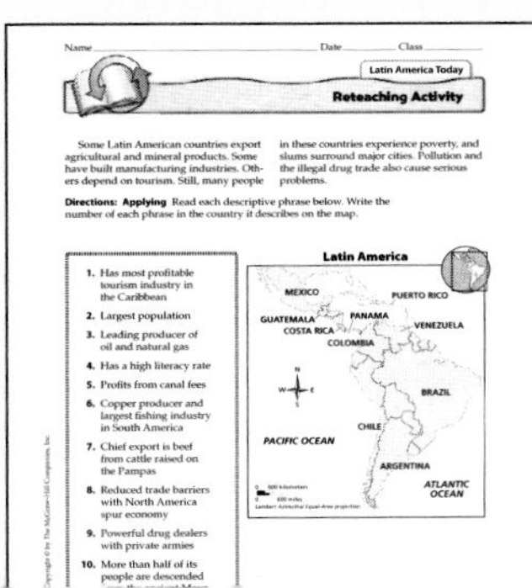

Reteaching Activity

OL Content Vocabulary Activity, URB p. 89

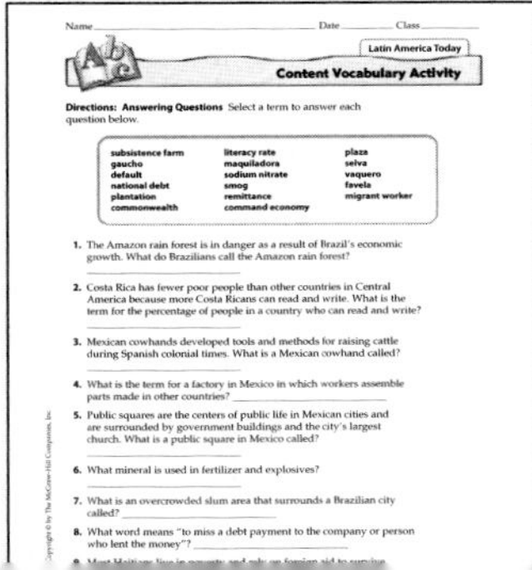

Content Vocabulary Activity

AL Geography and Economics, URB p. 9

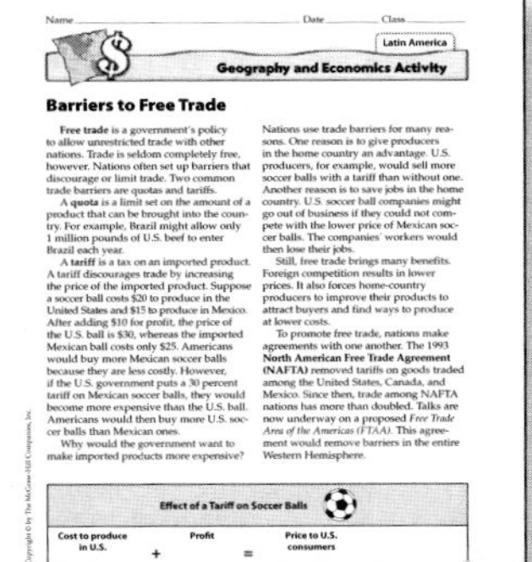

Geography and Economics Activity

Barriers to Free Trade

ELL Guided Reading Activity, URB p. 85

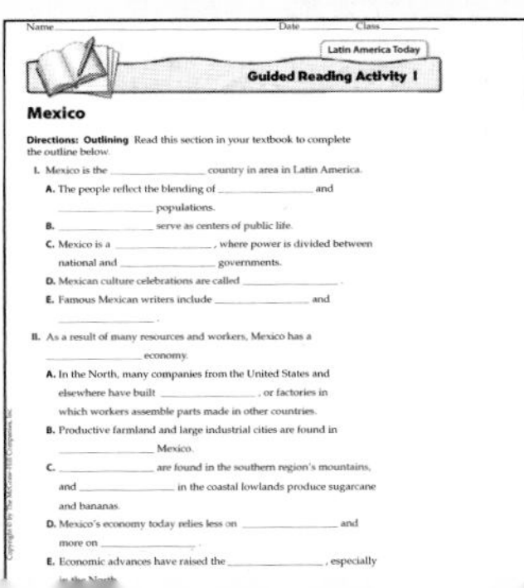

Guided Reading Activity 1

Mexico

C Critical Thinking

Analyzing Information Ask: **How might Mexico City reduce the amount of smog covering the city?** *(encourage people to drive less, regulate factory emissions, use solar energy)* **OL**

D Differentiated Instruction

Intrapersonal Ask students to write a journal entry about immigration to the United States. Then have them read a work of fiction on the topic. As students read, have them note in their journals how their thoughts and feelings on immigration change or stay the same. **OL**

Reading Check **Answer:** to find work

Assess

Social Studies ONLINE
Study Central™ provides summaries, interactive games, and online graphic organizers to help students review content.

Close

Listing Have students list three facts about modern-day Mexico. **OL**

Economic advances have raised the standard of living, especially in the North. The speed of growth also has brought concerns about damage to the environment, as well as dangers to workers' health and safety.

C As Mexico's economy has grown, pollution has increased. For example, the mountains that surround Mexico City trap car fumes and factory smoke. As a result, the city is often covered by unhealthy smog, a thick haze of fog and chemicals.

Population and Ethnic Challenges

Like the economy, Mexico's population has grown rapidly in recent decades. Many people have moved to the cities to find jobs. Because many jobs pay low wages, people have had to live crowded together in slums, or poor sections of the cities.

Many Mexicans who cannot find work become **migrant workers.** These are people who travel to find work when extra help is needed to plant or harvest crops. They legally and sometimes illegally cross Mexico's long border to work in the United States. Despite low pay, migrant workers can earn more in the United States than in D Mexico. To reduce illegal immigration, the United States has tightened controls along the border. This has increased tensions with Mexico. Poorer Mexicans depend on money sent from relatives in the United States.

Many of Mexico's Native Americans are poor and live in rural areas. In the 1990s, Native Americans in southern Mexico rose up against the Mexican government. They demanded changes that would improve their lives. By the early 2000s, the struggle between Native Americans and the government had not been resolved.

Reading Check **Determining Cause and Effect** Why have many Mexicans migrated to the United States?

Social Studies ONLINE
Study Central™ To review this section, go to glencoe.com.

Vocabulary

1. **Explain** the significance of:
   - a. plaza
   - b. vaquero
   - c. maquiladora
   - d. subsistence farm
   - e. plantation
   - f. migrant worker

Main Ideas

2. **Describing** Describe Mexico's form of government and recent events concerning the government.
3. **Identifying** Use a diagram like the one below to explain the challenges facing Mexico.

Mexico's Challenges

Critical Thinking

4. **Determining Cause and Effect** Why is irrigation needed to farm parts of the northern region?
5. **BIG Idea** Compare Mexico's three economic regions.
6. **Challenge** What problems might people in northern Mexico face if maquiladoras are closed, even if they do not work in the maquiladoras?

Writing About Geography

7. **Persuasive Writing** Choose one of the challenges facing Mexico. Write a newspaper editorial in which you suggest steps Mexico's government could take to improve the situation.

Answers

1. Definitions for the vocabulary words are found in the section and the Glossary.
2. federal republic; strong president serves a six-year term; decades of one-party rule ended in 2000; close 2006 election decided by an election court
3. population growth, growing slums in cities, tensions with the United States over illegal border crossings, low-paying jobs, demands for changes by Native Americans
4. Mexico's north has large stretches of land that are too dry and rocky to farm without irrigation.
5. Possible answer: The north grows crops because of irrigation; has grasslands that support cattle ranches; is rich in deposits of copper, zinc, iron, lead, and silver; and has maquiladoras. Central Mexico has fertile soil that supports farming, prosperous industrial cities, and oil and gas deposits on the coast. The south is poor economically, has poor soil for farming in the mountains, supports plantations, and has a thriving tourism industry.
6. Maquiladoras provide many jobs, and money from those jobs supports other businesses. Those businesses would suffer if maquiladoras closed.
7. Students might describe steps for improving Mexico's pollution, poverty, slums, or ethnic challenges.

Guide to Reading

BIG Idea

The physical environment affects how people live.

Content Vocabulary

- literacy rate *(p. 239)*
- command economy *(p. 240)*
- remittance *(p. 240)*
- commonwealth *(p. 240)*

Academic Vocabulary

- shift *(p. 239)*
- fee *(p. 239)*

Reading Strategy

Comparing and Contrasting Use a Venn diagram like the one below to compare and contrast Guatemala and Costa Rica.

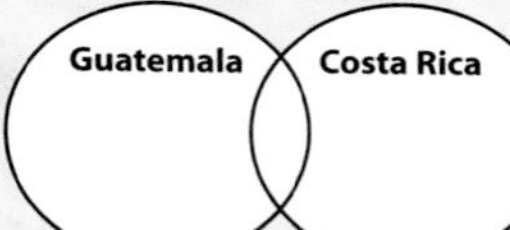

Central America and the Caribbean

Picture This What is it like to glide along a cable 230 feet (70 m) above a lagoon? Tourists can use this method to enjoy the spectacular views of Tiscapa Lagoon and the surrounding forest in Nicaragua. Opportunities like this show why ecotourism is fast replacing coffee, meat, and seafood as Nicaragua's primary source of income. Read this section to learn more about Central America and the Caribbean today.

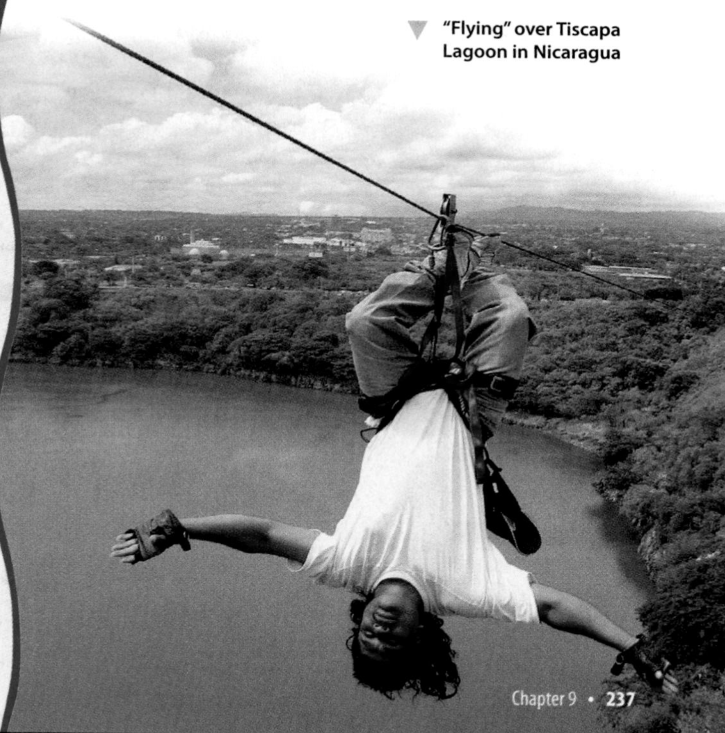

"Flying" over Tiscapa Lagoon in Nicaragua

Focus

Bellringer

Daily Focus Transparency 9-2

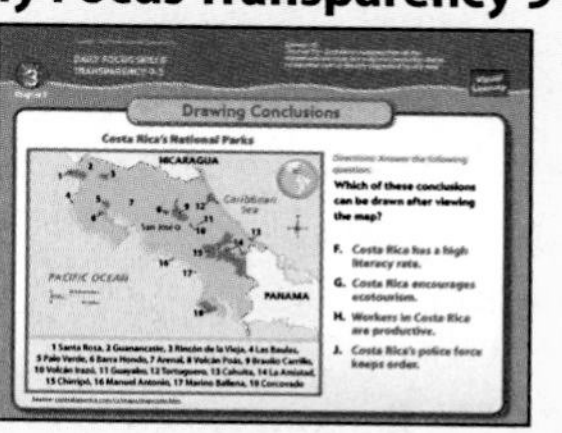

Guide to Reading

Answers to Graphic:

Answers may include:
Guatemala: agricultural economy; few hold wealth and power
Costa Rica: a stable, democratic government; high literacy rate and few poor people
Both: located in Central America

Section Spotlight Video

To learn more about Central America and the Caribbean, have students watch the Section Spotlight Video.

Resource Manager

R Reading Strategies	C Critical Thinking	D Differentiated Instruction	W Writing Support	S Skill Practice
Teacher Edition • Previewing, p. 238 • Using Context Clues, p. 239 **Additional Resources** • Guid. Read., URB p. 86 • Cont. Vocab., URB p. 89 • Ac. Vocab., URB p. 91 • Read. Ess., p. 61	**Teacher Edition** • Making Inferences, p. 239 **Additional Resources** • Authentic Assess., p. 9 • Interactive Geography, p. 17 • Quizzes and Tests, p. 96	**Teacher Edition** • Interpersonal, p. 240 **Additional Resources** • Reteach., URB p. 105 • School-to-Home Conn., URB p. 107	**Teacher Edition** • Expository Writing, p. 240 **Additional Resources** • Speak./Listen. Skills, URB p. 99	**Teacher Edition** • Using Geo. Skills, p. 238 **Additional Resources** • Chart, Graph, and Map Skills, URB p. 95 • Daily Focus Trans. 9-2 • Regional Atlas, URB pp. 1–7

Teach

R Reading Strategy

Previewing Set a timer for two minutes, and have students preview the section. Remind them to skim the main ideas, headings, and images. After they finish, have them complete this sentence: In this section, I will learn about ____. **BL**

S Skill Practice

Using Geography Skills Give students an outline map of the western hemisphere, and have them color in the countries of Central America. Point out the nearness of Mexico, South America, and the United States. Ask students to think about how location affects economic systems as they read the chapter. **OL**

CITIZENS IN ACTION

Possible Answer:
Humans could learn about nature and work and live in nature without harming the environment.

R Countries of Central America

Main Idea **Farming is the main way of life in Central America, where many people are poor.**

Geography and You Do you enjoy eating bananas at breakfast? They might have come from Central America. Read to find out about other ways in which Central Americans use their land and resources.

S Central America is made up of seven countries: Belize, Guatemala, El Salvador, Honduras, Nicaragua, Costa Rica, and Panama. Most people in Central America depend on farming. For many decades, they have produced crops, such as bananas, sugarcane, and coffee, for export. In some Central American countries, conflict between ethnic or political groups has held back their economies.

Guatemala

Guatemala is a country of rugged mountains, thick forests, and blue lakes. About half of its people are descended from the ancient Maya. Many Guatemalans are also of mixed Maya and Spanish origin. Maya languages and Spanish are spoken.

Guatemala has fertile volcanic soil. Most of the land is owned by a small group of people who hold most of the wealth and power. During the late 1990s, rebel groups fought the government for control of the land.

GLOBAL CITIZENS

NAME: MARIE CLAIRE PAIZ **HOME COUNTRY:** Guatemala

ACHIEVEMENT: Biologist Marie Claire Paiz directs a major preservation project for The Nature Conservancy in the Maya Forest, one of the world's largest rain forests. Here, for more than 1,000 years, ancient Maya flourished on both sides of the Usumacinta River, which divides Guatemala and Mexico. Maya ruins and writings that date back to 2300 B.C. attract tourists and scientists. Today, however, the forest is being destroyed by farmers clearing the land. And the possible construction of a hydroelectric dam threatens to flood the area. Paiz works to educate Latin Americans about the importance of the site's cultural heritage and what they can do to protect it.

QUOTE: "I hope that through conservation work, the wonders shared by Guatemala and Mexico can endure."

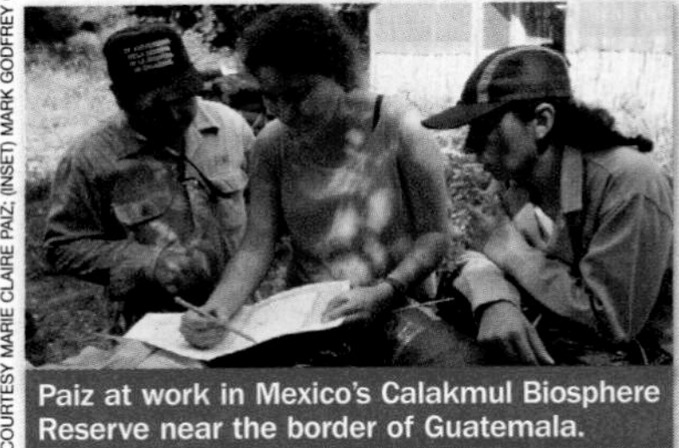

Paiz at work in Mexico's Calakmul Biosphere Reserve near the border of Guatemala.

CITIZENS IN ACTION Paiz believes that it is important for human-made structures and nature to exist in harmony. How would that benefit both nature and humans?

Hands-On Chapter Project Step 2

Creating an Environmental Mobile

Step 2: Designing the Mobile Students will collect images and plan their mobiles.

Directions Have students continue to research activities that affect the environment in Central America. Next, have them print or copy the images they found so far in their research. Make sure students have pictures of both the activities and their effects. Also encourage students to consider a variety of activities in their mobiles, and to think creatively when they search for images. For example, students wanting to show the effects of deforestation could use a picture of a bare patch of forest or a satellite photo of deforestation. Ask students to put together pairs of pictures, with one picture showing an activity and another picture showing its impact.

Designing Once students have an idea of the images they want to include, have them draw a sketch of their mobile before they begin to build it. **OL**

(Chapter Project continued in Section 3)

When the conflict ended, more than 200,000 people had been killed or were missing.

Guatemala has shown recent signs of economic change. In the past, many farmers produced only bananas and coffee. Today they are **shifting** production to other crops that have higher values, such as fruits, flowers, and spices. In the early 2000s, Guatemala and its Central American neighbors agreed to free trade with the United States. This will remove trade barriers among these countries. Central Americans hope they can then sell more of their goods to the United States. C

Costa Rica

Costa Rica has long stood out from its war-torn neighbors. A stable democracy is in place, and no wars have been fought within or outside the country since the 1800s. As a result, Costa Rica has no army—only a police force to keep law and order.

Costa Rica also has fewer poor people than other Central American countries. One reason is that Costa Rica has a higher literacy rate. **Literacy rate** is the percentage of people who can read and write. Workers with reading skills can be more productive and earn higher incomes.

Panama

Panama lies on the narrowest part of Central America. It is best known for the Panama Canal. The canal shortens distance and travel time between the Atlantic and Pacific Oceans. In 1999 the United States gave Panama control of the canal. Today, Panama profits from **fees,** or set charges, that ships pay to use the canal. Because of the commerce brought by the canal, Panama is an important banking center.

✓ Reading Check **Determining Cause and Effect** How does literacy rate affect income?

Countries of the Caribbean

Main Idea **Although most Caribbean island countries are poor, several are turning to tourism to help their economies grow.**

Geography and You Do many tourists visit the community where you live? Read to find out how several countries in the Caribbean are turning to tourism to boost their economies.

Many of the island countries of the Caribbean face political and economic challenges. For example, the people of Cuba and Haiti endure great poverty. Puerto Rico, which has connections to the United States, is more stable economically. R

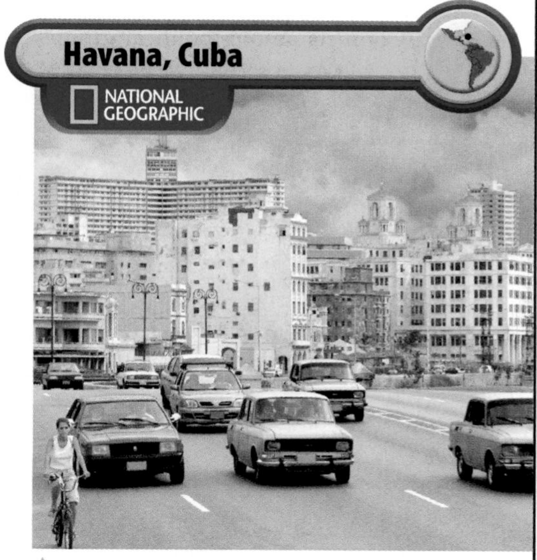

▲ Cars zoom down the Malecón, a famous avenue that runs along the coastline in Havana. ***Regions*** **What major economic challenge do Cuba and other Caribbean nations face?**

C Critical Thinking

Making Inferences **Ask:** **What can you infer about economic policies in Guatemala?** *(Possible answer: Policies are becoming more open to industry changes and foreign trade.)* **OL**

R Reading Strategy

Using Context Clues **What might Cuba and Haiti do to improve their economic situation?** *(improve ties with the United States)* **Do you think that would be easy to do?** *(probably not, given the troubled histories of Cuba and Haiti)* **OL**

✓ Reading Check **Answer:** Workers with reading skills can be more productive and earn higher incomes.

Caption Answer: poverty

Differentiated Instruction

Chart, Graph, and Map Skills Activity, URB pp. 95–96

Reading a Bar Graph

Objective:	To learn to read and interpret a bar graph
Focus:	Ask students about bar graphs that they have seen in their reading or research.
Teach:	Review the parts of a bar graph and explain how to tell what each bar represents.
Assess:	Have students analyze the bar graphs and answer the questions.
Close:	Compare bar graphs to other kinds of graphs.

Differentiated Instruction Strategies

BL Ask students to identify the countries being compared in the first graph and the areas of comparison.

AL Have students create their own bar graphs comparing three other Latin American countries.

ELL Ask students to convert the data in the first graph into a chart with figures.

W Writing Support

Expository Writing Have students write a report on an aspect of U.S.–Cuba relations, such as U.S. embargos, historical conflicts, or Cuban immigration to the United States. AL

D Differentiated Instruction

Interpersonal Have small groups discuss how Puerto Rico might be different if it were not a U.S. territory. Ask groups to share their thoughts with the class. OL

Reading Check **Answer:** not very, because many Cubans have not prospered and new economic efforts have not succeeded

Assess

Social Studies ONLINE

Study Central™ provides summaries, interactive games, and online graphic organizers to help students review content.

Close

Discussing Have small groups discuss the characteristics of Central American and Caribbean countries. OL

Cuba

Cuba lies about 90 miles (145 km) south of Florida. It has a **command economy**, in which the communist government decides how resources are used and what goods and services are produced. Many Cubans have not prospered under this system.

For years Cuba relied on selling its chief crop, sugar. To end that dependence, Cuba's government is developing tourism and other industries. These efforts, however, have not yet succeeded. Meanwhile, Cuba's longtime dictator, Fidel Castro, tightly controls society. People who criticize the government are often arrested and jailed. The United States condemns Cuba's government for these actions. Because Fidel Castro is aging, Cuba's future is uncertain. W

Haiti

Located on the western half of the island of Hispaniola, Haiti has had a troubled history. Conflicts among political groups have made for an unstable government. In addition, most of Haiti's people are poor. A major source of income is **remittances**, or money sent back home by Haitians who work in other countries.

Puerto Rico

Since 1952, Puerto Rico has been a **commonwealth**, or a self-governing territory, of the United States. Puerto Ricans are American citizens. They can come and go as they wish between Puerto Rico and the United States mainland.

D Puerto Rico has a high standard of living compared to most other Caribbean islands. It has industries that produce medicines, machinery, and clothes. Farmers there grow sugarcane and coffee. Puerto Rico makes more money from tourism than any other Caribbean island.

Reading Check **Drawing Conclusions** Is Cuba's command economy effective?

Section 2 Review

Social Studies ONLINE **Study Central™** To review this section, go to glencoe.com.

Vocabulary

1. **Explain** the meaning of *literacy rate, command economy, remittance,* and *commonwealth* by using each term in a sentence.

Main Ideas

2. **Analyzing** How is Costa Rica different from its Central American neighbors?
3. **Comparing** Use a chart like the one below to examine the economies of Cuba, Haiti, and Puerto Rico.

Country	Economy
Cuba	
Haiti	
Puerto Rico	

Critical Thinking

4. **Contrasting** How does Cuba's government contrast with Costa Rica's?
5. **BIG Idea** Why are many people on the Caribbean islands poor?
6. **Challenge** Do you think farmers in Guatemala will earn more money by growing different crops? Why?

Writing About Geography

7. **Expository Writing** Write a paragraph explaining how specific countries in this region have achieved some economic success and how they have done it.

Answers

1. Sentences should use vocabulary words according to their definitions in the section and Glossary.
2. stable democracy, no wars have been fought within or outside the country, no army, fewer poor people, higher literacy rate
3. **Cuba:** command economy, reliance on selling sugar, trying to develop tourism; **Haiti:** most people are poor; remittances are a major source of income; **Puerto Rico:** high standard of living, varied industries, sugarcane and coffee crops, strong tourism industry
4. In Cuba, the communist government rules the economy, which has not allowed many Cubans to prosper. Costa Rica, on the other hand, has a stable democracy and fewer poor people in the country.
5. In Cuba, the government's control of the economy has stifled growth. In Haiti, political instability has created an unstable government and economy.
6. Probably, because the new crops have higher values and they are varied, so if one crop is damaged, it won't have such a strong impact on the economy.
7. Paragraphs should include facts from the text about specific countries' economic successes, such as Puerto Rico's thriving tourism industry, varied industries, and farming of sugarcane and coffee.

TIME PERSPECTIVES

EXPLORING WORLD ISSUES

PROTECTING NATURAL RESOURCES

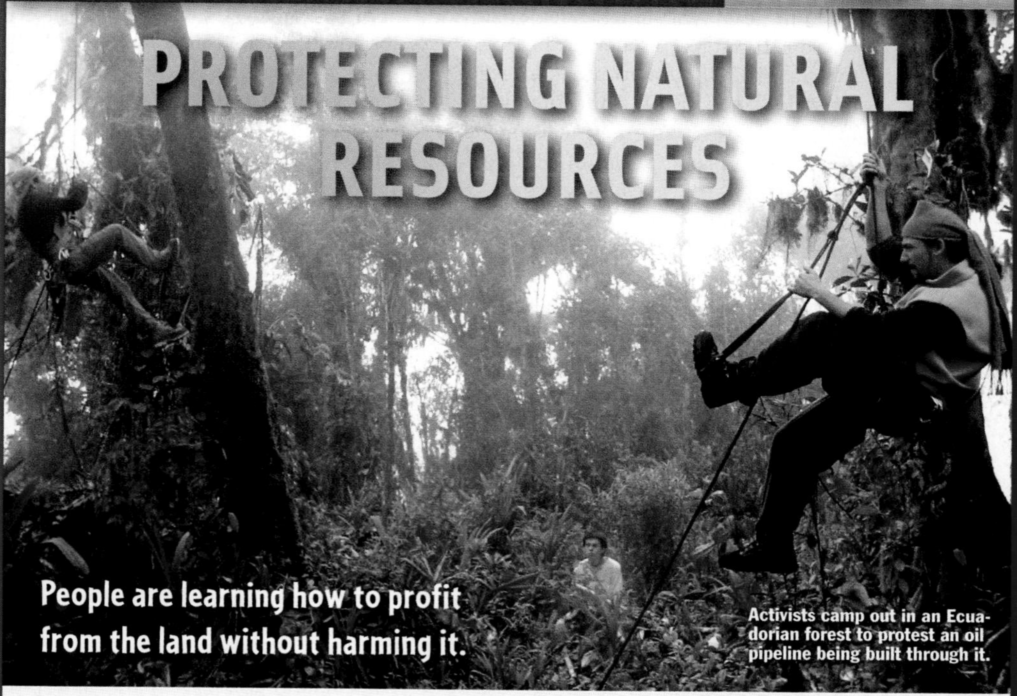

People are learning how to profit from the land without harming it.

Activists camp out in an Ecuadorian forest to protest an oil pipeline being built through it.

For decades many natural environments and wildlife species have been damaged by human activity. Farmers and loggers in Brazil and Ecuador have cut down or set fire to countless trees in order to acquire the land for farming and other economic activities. Miners in Bolivia have also cleared land in search of minerals. As a result, thousands of miles of forests have disappeared and wildlife populations have suffered. Human activities have also hurt other environments. In Chile, fish farms that raise salmon in large tanks have harmed marine ecosystems.

In recent years, however, people have been working to protect but still profit from natural resources. Governments and citizens are working to limit the damage to forests and wildlife. Industries are developing alternative energy sources that are less harmful to natural environments. But is it too late?

AP PHOTO/DOLORES OCHOA

Focus

Introducing TIME Perspectives

Ask: What natural resource is shown in the photo? *(the rain forest)* Read aloud the caption. **Ask: How might the building of an oil pipeline damage the rain forest?** *(Possible answers: The pipe could break and spill oil; land would have to be cleared for it; animal habitats would be disrupted.)* **OL**

FYI

Read to find out how the Amazon rain forest affects the atmosphere at http://earthobservatory.nasa.gov/, the Web site of the Earth Sciences Division of NASA.

Use the **TIME Perspectives: Exploring on World Issues Teacher Guide and Student Activities,** pp. 9–12, to reinforce and extend the concepts in "Protecting Natural Resources."

Additional Support

Background

Keeping an Eye on Deforestation How do scientists know how much of the rain forest is being destroyed? Scientists use satellite imagery to track changes in rain forest density from year to year. Some information comes from NASA satellite images, which have shown that the rate of deforestation in tropical Africa, Southeast Asia, and South America has remained steady or increased over recent years. The images also show bare patches where people have clear-cut forests, as well as fires burning, sometimes out of control, in the Amazon. Deforestation affects far more than just the areas where the trees have been removed. Because clear-cutting separates groups of wildlife and lets too much light into bordering areas of forest, deforestation affects more than twice the area actually cut. Even so, 80 percent of the Amazon remains standing, and scientists are devising ways to help the people in the Amazon and surrounding areas use the forest in a sustainable way.

TIME PERSPECTIVES

Teach

C Critical Thinking

Determining Cause and Effect
Ask: What are the negative effects of deforestation? *(destruction of ecosystems and wildlife habitats, increased global warming)* **OL**

D Differentiated Instruction

Logical/Mathematical Point out that the deforestation rate between 2002 and 2004 has been about 10,000 square miles (25,900 square km) per year. Ask students to calculate the total deforestation in 2008 and 2016 if the rate remains at 10,000 square miles (25,900 square km) per year. *(2008: 244,000 square miles (631,957 square km); 2016: 324,000 square miles (839,156 square km))* **OL**

INTERPRETING GRAPHS

Answer:
1994 and 1995; about 11,500 square miles (29,785 square km)

TIME PERSPECTIVES

EXPLORING WORLD ISSUES

Colorful macaws live in the Amazon rain forest.

ENVIRONMENT-FRIENDLY SOLUTIONS

South America has some of the world's largest and most beautiful forests. From the Amazon rain forest to the woodlands of the Andes mountain ranges, the region's green lush forests are home to many species of wildlife.

In recent decades, however, this fragile environment has changed. Since the 1960s, loggers, miners, and farmers have been clearing the trees from this region's forests. Some people cut down trees to produce wood and paper. Others burn the trees to clear land for mining, farming, and industry. The process of clearing an area of forest is called **deforestation**.

Deforestation is a major challenge for South America and the world. Developing countries in this region need the land for industries that will help their economies grow. But deforestation destroys ecosystems and wildlife habitats. **C** Deforestation also contributes to global warming. The burning of wooded areas sends large amounts of carbon dioxide into the atmosphere and speeds up the rate of global warming.

There is much work to be done to protect these lush forests. After years of neglect, the region's governments and citizens are beginning to realize how much is at stake. In recent years, people have been working to reverse decades of damage.

The Destruction of the Amazon Rain Forest

By 2004, nearly 204,000 square miles (528,358 square km) of the Amazon rain forest had been cleared. Here is a look at the amount of deforestation in recent years.

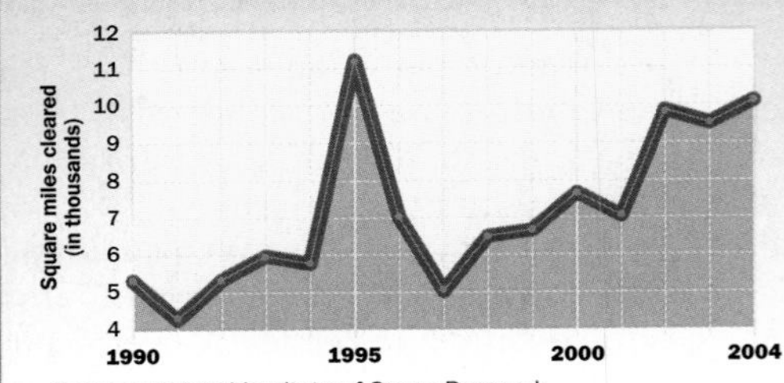

Source: National Institute of Space Research.

INTERPRETING GRAPHS

Analyzing Information During which two years did the largest amount of deforestation occur? About how many total square miles were cleared during those two years?

Amazon Alert!

The Amazon rain forest covers about 2.7 million square miles (7 million sq. km) of land in South America—mostly in Brazil. Parrots, jaguars, and piranhas are just some of the thousands of animals that make their home in the Amazon and the many rivers that run through it.

For decades, this tropical environment has been shrinking. In addition to farmers, cattle ranchers, and others clearing the land, the rain forest **D** has also been cut down to make way for roads and highways that crisscross through the center of it. By 2004, nearly 204,000 square miles (528,358 sq. km) of the rain forest had been destroyed.

Differentiated Instruction

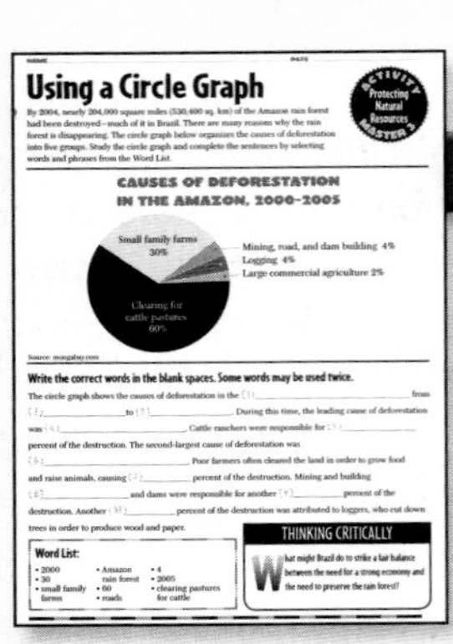

TIME Perspectives: Exploring World Issues Workbook, p. 12

Using a Circle Graph

Objective: To learn how to read and interpret information on a circle graph

Focus: Draw a circle graph on the board and explain that all sections must total 100%.

Teach: Have students name the causes of deforestation, along with their percentages.

Assess: Have students use the graph in the activity to complete the blanks that follow.

Close: Ask students what sort of information would be best presented in a circle graph.

Differentiated Instruction Strategies

BL Guide students by pointing them to relevant parts of the graph for each answer.

AL Have students display a different set of data in a circle graph.

ELL Have students list the causes of deforestation from greatest to least.

At a Brazilian ranch, cattle graze on cleared land.

This land was deforested by Brazilian farmers in order to grow soybeans.

The beauty and ecological diversity of the rain forest are at risk.

Stopping the Damage

Brazil's government has been working to preserve the Amazon rain forest. In order to slow the rate of deforestation, Brazil is studying ways to make land that has been cleared more productive. If deforested land can grow more crops or feed more cattle, it will lessen the need for more deforestation.

Legal limits on the amount of land that can be cleared have also been created. However, these laws have not always been enforced. In recent years, though, Brazilian officials are doing a better job at imposing and enforcing laws that protect the Amazon rain forest. Now companies and individuals who ignore the limits are punished with large fines. **W**

Saving Wildlife Populations

Citizens throughout South America are also taking action to protect wildlife. In Chile, fish are often raised on fish farms in giant tanks, called cages. Breeding fish in captivity raises production. Chile is one of the world's biggest exporters of cage-bred salmon. In 2004 the country exported 782 million pounds of fish (355 million kg).

But success has created its share of problems. Fish raised in crowded cages pollute the ocean floor and are prone to illness. Critics of the farms say that the fish are given large amounts of antibiotics and other chemicals to keep them from getting sick. When people eat the fish, the drugs may be passed on to them, which can be unhealthy. **C**

A Chilean worker observes tanks full of farmed salmon.

Juan Carlos Cárdenas is the director of Centro Ecocéanos, an organization that works to protect marine life. For years, the center has been working to improve the production methods of Chile's fishing industry. The center teaches local fisheries how to catch more fish using traditional methods. It also conducts research and educates the public about how fish farms affect ecosystems.

Cárdenas says there is still much work to do. He is encouraged that consumers are learning about the health risks associated with eating cage-bred fish. Cárdenas hopes that if people buy fewer farmed fish, the lower sales will force the fish industry to make changes in how it operates.

EXPLORING THE ISSUE

1. **Identifying Cause and Effect** How does deforestation speed up the process of global warming?
2. **Finding Solutions** Human activity can threaten the environment. What can you do in your community to help protect your natural environment?

W Writing Support

Persuasive Writing Invite interested students to write a persuasive essay about the importance of preserving the Amazon rain forest. Encourage students to begin their essays with an attention-grabbing quotation from a public figure or person involved in the field. Remind students that they need to persuade readers with facts rather than their opinions alone. Have students use information in outside resources to support their opinions. **OL**

C Critical Thinking

Predicting Consequences **Ask:** **What do you think might happen if fish farms continue to be run this way?** *(Possible answers: People's health will suffer from eating contaminated or medicated fish; the pollution in the ocean will kill other marine life.)* **OL**

EXPLORING THE ISSUE

Answers:

1. The burning of forested areas releases large amounts of carbon dioxide into the atmosphere.
2. Answers may include recycle waste, conserve water, and avoid littering.

Additional Support

Activity: Economics Connection

Problem Solving Tell students that in Brazil, the rain forest is an important economic resource for individual farmers, commercial farms, loggers, and the government. Peasant farmers clear a few acres of land and then burn the trees to create arable land. Commercial farms and ranches clear miles at a time, using the same slash-and-burn techniques. The government sells concessions, or permission to cut areas of forest, to logging companies. This provides money for the government, and loggers are able to sell the rain forest's valuable woods. **Ask:** **What nations create demand for beef, vegetables, fruits, wood pulp, and hardwoods from the rain forest?** *(Much of the demand comes from developed nations such as the United States.)* Have students work in groups to come up with at least three ways that they can change their lifestyles to reduce demand for products that rely on deforestation for their production. Then have each group present its list to the class and explain how the changes they listed would reduce deforestation. **OL**

TIME PERSPECTIVES

R Reading Strategy

Predicting Instruct students to read the title and subheading and look at the photo on the page. Then remind them that the overall topic of the feature is environmental issues. **Ask:** **What do you think you will learn about from reading the text on this page?** *(an environmentally friendly car)* **OL**

D Differentiated Instruction

Logical/Mathematical Have students use the text and outside research to make a two-column chart listing the pros and cons of ethanol versus gasoline. Then invite students to share their opinions on whether the United States is wise to develop more ethanol. **AL**

C Critical Thinking

Making Inferences **Ask:** **What kind of opportunity is the president of Brazil's carmaker's association talking about?** *(an economic opportunity)* **BL**

EXPLORING THE ISSUE

Answers:

1. because oil costs skyrocketed
2. It might increase their confidence in using alternative fuels.

Additional Support

R A SWEET RIDE IN BRAZIL

Brazil's "Flex car" has a sweet tooth. *Flex* is short for "flexible," which describes the kinds of fuel the car uses. The Flex car looks and works like a regular vehicle, but it can run on gasoline or ethanol. Many Brazilians are filling up their gas tanks with ethanol—a fuel that is produced from sugarcane. The alternative fuel is pressed from sugarcane and then blended with gasoline. This "gasohol" mixture could eventually take the place of fossil fuels to keep cars running.

Ethanol-powered cars are not new in Brazil. The country developed them—and the fuel they operate on—in the 1980s, when the cost of buying oil from foreign nations began to soar. Over time, ethanol-powered cars zoomed onto the fast track. By 1988, more than 88 percent of cars sold each year in Brazil were running on a combination of ethanol and gasoline. Throughout Brazil there are now about 29,000 ethanol stations.

Today, Brazil is the world's largest producer of ethanol, and Flex cars are seen everywhere. In 2006 sales of Flex vehicles were higher than sales of cars that ran only on gasoline. Flex car technology is also spreading to other Brazilian industries. Small planes, such as crop dusters, are using ethanol because it is more widely available than conventional aviation fuel.

Added Mileage

Flex cars are also good for the environment and the economy. The ethanol they run on is cleaner than gasoline, so Flex cars create less air pollution. And ethanol is less expensive. Its price is almost half that of gasoline. **D**

As gasoline prices continue to skyrocket, the nations of the world are expected to follow Brazil's example. In 2006 President George W. Bush called for the United States to develop more ethanol. "There is an enormous demand from abroad to know more," said the president of Brazil's carmakers' association. "This is an opportunity for Brazil." **C** Perhaps it will be an opportunity for the rest of the world to have a sweet ride, too.

REUTERS/JAMIL BITTAR

A Flex car

EXPLORING THE ISSUE

1. **Explaining** Why did Brazil develop ethanol as an alternative fuel?
2. **Identifying Cause and Effect** How might Brazil's success with ethanol inspire other nations to develop and use alternative fuels?

Activity: Connecting With the United States

Analyzing Tell students that ethanol can be made from a number of different plant products, including corn, sugar beets, wood, sugarcane, soybeans, and sunflowers. **Ask:** **What plant is most often used to make ethanol in the United States?** *(corn)* One recent study found that current technologies use 29 percent more energy to make ethanol from corn than was produced. However, other plants are more efficient at producing ethanol, including sugar beets, which are used in France, and the sugarcane used in Brazil. Using one unit of energy to process sugar beets produces two units of energy. Sugarcane produces eight times as much energy as is used to make it. Have students research where corn, sugarcane, and sugar beets can be grown in the United States. Ask students to consider this information and then state whether they believe the United States should switch from corn to sugarcane or sugar beets for its ethanol needs. Have students write several sentences explaining their position. **OL**

This ethanol distillery produces fuel from sugarcane.

REVIEW AND ASSESS

UNDERSTANDING THE ISSUE

1 **Making Connections** How does deforestation affect wildlife?

2 **Writing to Inform** In a short article, explain some of the ways governments are working to preserve the natural environments in their countries.

3 **Writing to Persuade** In a letter to an editor of a newspaper, discuss your beliefs about driving vehicles that use alternative fuels.

INTERNET RESEARCH ACTIVITIES

4 Go to www.savethehighseas.org, the Web site of the Deep Sea Conservation Coalition. Click the "About Us" link and scroll down to the "Coalition Steering Group Members." Read about some of the organizations and how they work to protect marine ecosytems. Write a short essay describing one of these activities.

5 With your teacher's help, do an online search on alternative fuel sources, such as ethanol or solar power. Read about how the nations of the world are developing these energy sources. Write a brief article that explains your findings.

BEYOND THE CLASSROOM

6 **Work in groups** to create and display an ecological mural on paper that illustrates how people can protect natural environments in your community.

7 **At your school or local library,** research what other countries are doing to decrease their dependency on foreign oil imports. Do you think their strategies will succeed? Why or why not?

Major Producers of Ethanol

Ethanol can be made from sugarcane and corn. As oil prices soar, the nations of the world are expected to produce more ethanol. Here is a look at major producers in 2006.

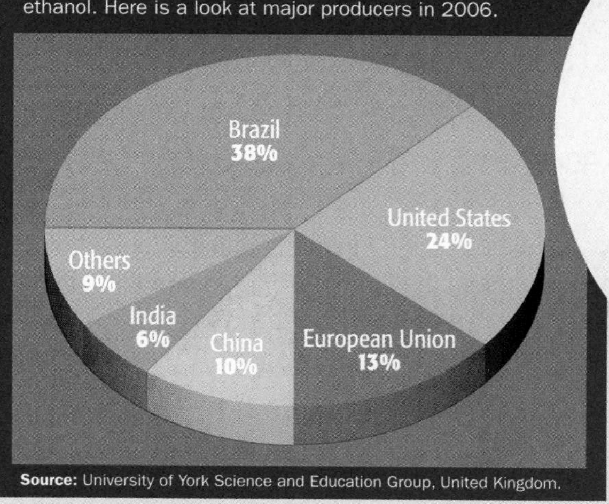

Source: University of York Science and Education Group, United Kingdom.

Building Graph Reading Skills

1. **Analyzing Data** What percentage of the world's ethanol is produced by the United States and the European Union?
2. **Identifying Cause and Effect** Brazil is the world's largest producer of ethanol. As the world searches for less expensive energy sources, how might Brazil's top ranking help its economy grow?

TIME PERSPECTIVES

Review and Assess

Questions from **Understanding the Issue, Internet Research Activities,** and **Beyond the Classroom** may have more than one correct answer. Pick and choose the two or three activities that work best for your class.

Building Graph Reading Skills

Answers:

1. 37%
2. Other countries might purchase ethanol from Brazil.

Close

Summarizing Have students explain the process of deforestation and how it affects the environment. OL

Activity: Why It Matters

Making Connections Tell students that researchers working in the Panamanian forests have found chemicals in plants that may be effective against malaria. Scientists hope to find similarly useful chemicals in the Amazon rain forest. **Ask: What would happen if a useful medicine were found in a rain forest plant, but the rain forest had almost been completely destroyed?** *(The world probably would not be able to benefit from that drug.)* Today, drug companies sometimes gather plants in the rain forest but perform research and development in other countries. For example, two researchers from Utah have asked U.S. drug companies to do some of their research and development in the countries where rain forests grow. They believe this would give developing countries an economic reason to protect the rain forests. They have started working in Panama, which has helped that country's economy. Ask students to write a letter to an American drug company urging it to invest in research and development that will help preserve rain forests and build up developing nations. OL

Focus

Bellringer

Daily Focus Transparency 9-3

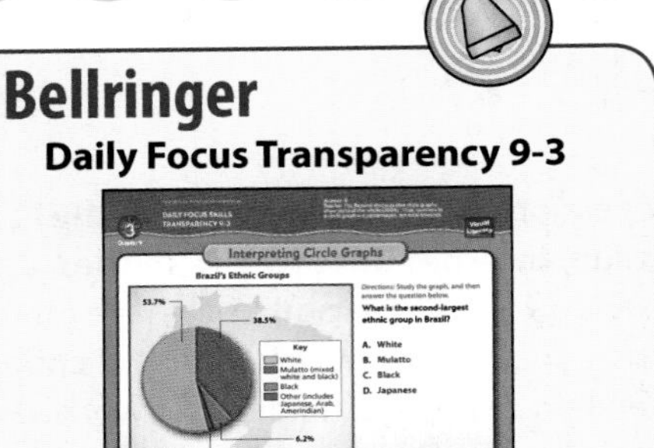

Guide to Reading

Answers to Graphic:

Answers may include:

Main Idea: Brazil's industries include farming, natural resources, and manufacturing.

Detail: Brazil grows more coffee, oranges, and cassava than any other country.

Detail: Brazil has iron ore, bauxite, tin, manganese, gold, silver, diamonds, oil and sugarcane.

Detail: Brazil produces airplanes, machinery, and cars.

Section Spotlight Video

To learn more about South America, have students watch the Section Spotlight Video.

Resource Manager

R Reading Strategies	C Critical Thinking	D Differentiated Instruction	W Writing Support	S Skill Practice
Teacher Edition • Act. Prior Know., p. 247 • Sequencing Info., p. 250 • Monitoring, p. 251 **Additional Resources** • Guid. Read., URB p. 87 • Cont. Vocab., URB p. 89 • Ac. Vocab., URB p. 91 • Read. Ess., p. 64 • World Lit., URB p. 31	**Teacher Edition** • Making Gen. p. 247 • Analyzing Info., p. 248 • Det. Cause/Effect, p. 250 **Additional Resources** • Env. Case Study, URB p. 13 • Interactive Geo., p. 17 • Authentic Assess., p. 9 • Quizzes and Tests, p. 97	**Teacher Edition** • Special Ed., p. 249 • Adv. Learners, p. 252 **Additional Resources** • Enrichment, URB p. 19 • Reteach., URB p. 105 • School-to-Home Conn., URB p. 107	**Teacher Edition** • Expository Writing, p. 249 • Descriptive Writing, p. 251 **Additional Resources** • Writing Skills, URB p. 103	**Teacher Edition** • Using Geo. Skills, pp. 248, 251 **Additional Resources** • Daily Focus Trans. 9-3 • Regional Atlas, URB pp. 1–7

Guide to Reading

South America

BIG Idea

People's actions can change the physical environment.

Content Vocabulary

- selva *(p. 247)*
- favela *(p. 247)*
- gaucho *(p. 249)*
- national debt *(p. 250)*
- default *(p. 250)*
- sodium nitrate *(p. 252)*

Academic Vocabulary

- maintain *(p. 248)*
- issue *(p. 248)*

Reading Strategy

Identifying Central Issues Use a diagram like the one below to describe Brazil's economy. Write the main idea on the line to the left and supporting details on the lines to the right. You can add as many additional lines as you have details.

Picture This This giant dish is like an "eye" studying the universe. The Swedish ESO (European Southern Observatory) Sub-millimeter Telescope, or SEST, is not like some telescopes that use light from stars or planets to "see" them. SEST is able to study distant objects by gathering radio waves that radiate from them. The telescope is located in the southern Atacama Desert in Chile, where the clear sky conditions are ideal for this type of research. To learn more about South America today, read Section 3.

▼ Learning about the universe in Chile

Brazil

Main Idea **Brazil is a leading economic power, but concerns have grown about its use of the Amazon rain forest.** R

Geography and You Did you know that some of the best farmland in the United States was once forestland? The forests were cleared by farmers. Read to find out how Brazil's forests are being cut down for mining, logging, and farming.

Brazil is the fifth-largest country in the world and the largest in South America. The country is known for its Amazon rain forest, which Brazilians call the **selva.** This resource is threatened by Brazil's economic growth.

Brazil's People

With 187 million people, Brazil has the largest population of all Latin American countries. Brazil's culture is largely Portuguese because they were the first and largest European group to settle Brazil. Today Brazilians are of European, African, Native American, Asian, or mixed ancestry. Almost all of them speak a Brazilian form of Portuguese, which includes many words from Native American and African languages.

Most of Brazil's people live in cities along the Atlantic coast. São Paulo and Rio de Janeiro are among the largest cities in the world. In recent years, millions of Brazilians have moved from rural areas to coastal cities to find better jobs. Many of these migrants have settled in favelas. **Favelas** are overcrowded slum areas that surround many Brazilian cities. To reduce city crowding, the government now encourages people to move back to less-populated, inland areas. In 1960 Brazil moved its capital from Rio de Janeiro to the newly built city of Brasília 600 miles (966 km) inland. With more than 2 million people, Brasília is a modern and rapidly growing city. C

NATIONAL GEOGRAPHIC
Harvesting Sugarcane

A truck is loaded with sugarcane at a farm in southeastern Brazil. ***Human-Environment Interaction*** **In what unique way does Brazil make use of its sugarcane?**

Brazil's Economy

Brazil is one of the world's leading producers of food crops. It grows more coffee, oranges, and cassava than any other country. Brazil's agricultural output has grown greatly in recent years. This is partly because Brazilian farmers have cleared more land in rain forest areas to grow crops. They also now use machinery to perform many tasks. Finally, farmers have planted crops that have been scientifically changed to produce more and to prevent disease.

In addition to productive farms, Brazil has valuable mineral resources, such as iron ore, bauxite, tin, manganese, gold, silver, and diamonds. Offshore deposits of oil, as well as hydroelectric power from rivers, supply the country with energy. Brazil also uses sugarcane to produce a substitute for gasoline.

Teach

R Reading Strategy

Activating Prior Knowledge Read aloud the Main Idea. **Ask: What do you know about the Amazon rain forest and Brazil?** *(Possible answers: The rain forest is threatened. Coffee is grown in Brazil.)* Write students' comments on the board. As students read, have them add new facts to the list on the board. Then discuss the facts that students noted. **BL**

C Critical Thinking

Making Generalizations Ask each student to make a generalization about Brazil's people based on the text. Then have them exchange statements with a partner and mark whether the generalization is true or false, and then discuss their responses. **OL**

Caption Answer:
to make a substitute for gasoline

Differentiated Instruction

Writing Skills Activity, URB pp. 103–104

Types of Sentences

Objective: To add variety to writing by using different types of sentences

Focus: Read a paragraph that has only one type of sentence and then a similar paragraph that has different types of sentences.

Teach: Review the types of sentences and give examples of each.

Assess: Have students write their own paragraphs using different types of sentences.

Close: Discuss the importance of variety in writing.

Differentiated Instruction Strategies

- **BL** Have students color-code each type of sentence in the passage.
- **AL** Challenge students to rewrite one of the paragraphs in the passage using just one type of sentence. **Ask: Which paragraph is better?**
- **ELL** Have students write an example of each type of sentence in the chart.

S Skill Practice

Using Geography Skills Have students look at your state on a U.S. map. Then have them compare the state with the rain forest area of Brazil on a world map. Discuss the size of the area of deforestation. Then discuss the rate of deforestation and the long-term prognosis of the rain forest if the deforestation rate continues. **OL**

C Critical Thinking

Analyzing Information Ask: What are the positive effects of the rain forest and the negative effects of deforestation? *(Positive effects: keep up the Earth's climate patterns, provide shelter to wildlife, provide home to Native Americans; Negative effects: increased soil erosion, destruction of ecosystem and biodiversity, destruction of Native American cultures)* **OL**

Map Skills

Answers:

1. in the east and southeast area
2. Generally, deforestation occurs along or near roads.

NATIONAL GEOGRAPHIC Maps In MOtion See StudentWorks™ Plus or glencoe.com.

Figure 1 Deforestation in Brazil

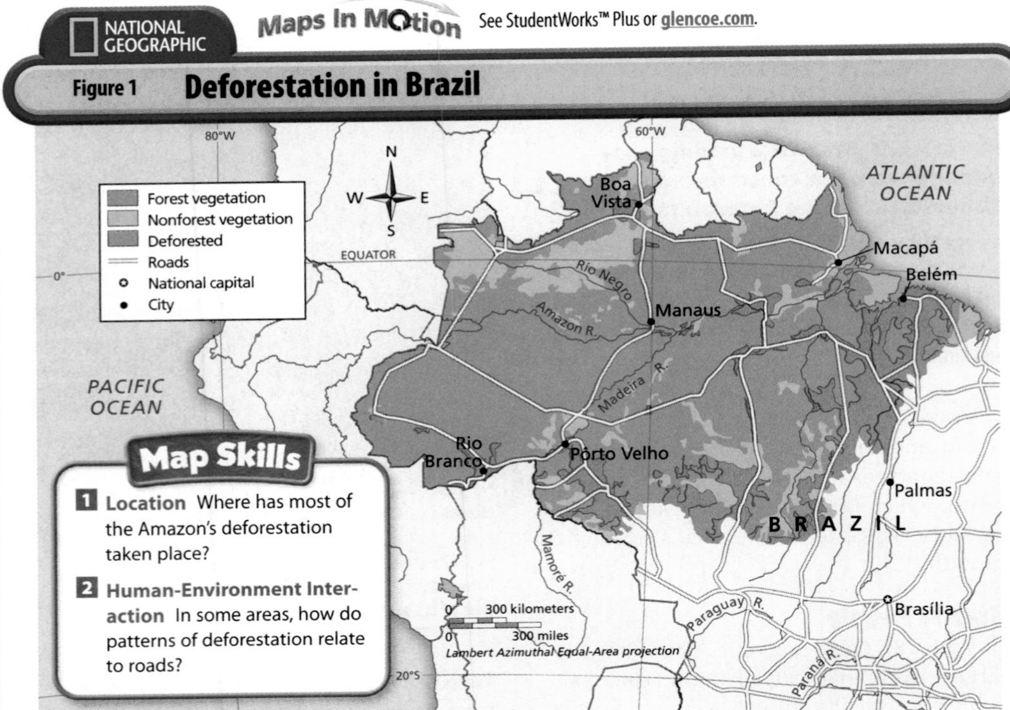

Map Skills

1. **Location** Where has most of the Amazon's deforestation taken place?
2. **Human-Environment Interaction** In some areas, how do patterns of deforestation relate to roads?

Brazil has successful industries too. Most manufacturing takes place in São Paulo and other southeastern cities. Factory workers produce heavy industrial goods, such as machinery, airplanes, and cars. They also make food products, medicines, paper, and clothing.

The Rain Forest

Brazil's greatest natural resource is the Amazon rain forest. It is the world's largest rain forest area, yet it also has the highest rate of deforestation. Each year, the land deforested in the Amazon rain forest is equal in size to Ohio. **Figure 1** shows how much of the rain forest has been lost.

Why is the rain forest shrinking? To increase jobs and make products for export, Brazil's government has encouraged mining, logging, and farming in the rain forest. These activities lead to soil erosion and harm the rain forest's ecosystem and biodiversity.

As deforestation takes place, roads are built, bringing companies, farmers, and change. Native Americans who live in the rain forest find it difficult to follow their traditional cultures as this occurs.

In addition, tropical forests give off huge amounts of oxygen and play a role in **maintaining,** or keeping up, the Earth's climate patterns. They also provide shelter to many wildlife species that may not survive if deforestation continues. Thus, although the rain forest belongs to Brazil, the effects of deforestation are felt worldwide. Because deforestation is a global **issue,** or problem, other nations have convinced Brazil to protect at least part of the rain forest from economic development.

Differentiated Instruction

Leveled Activities

BL School-to-Home Connection, URB p. 107

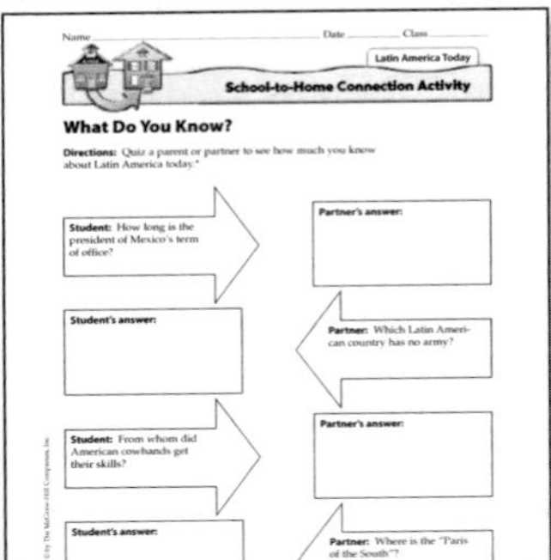
School-to-Home Connection Activity

What Do You Know?

OL Environmental Case Study, URB p. 13

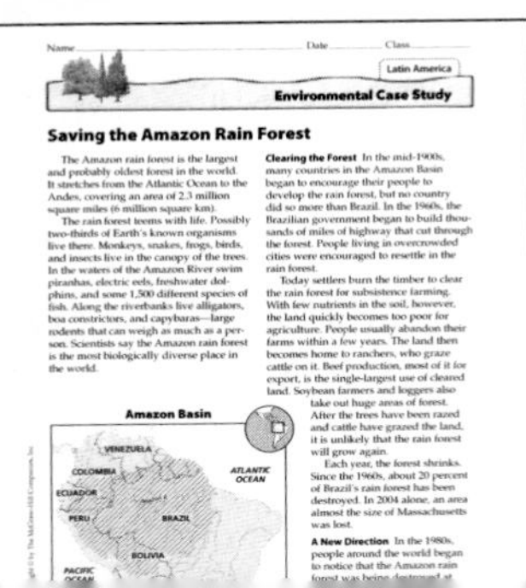
Environmental Case Study

Saving the Amazon Rain Forest

AL Enrichment Activity, URB p. 19

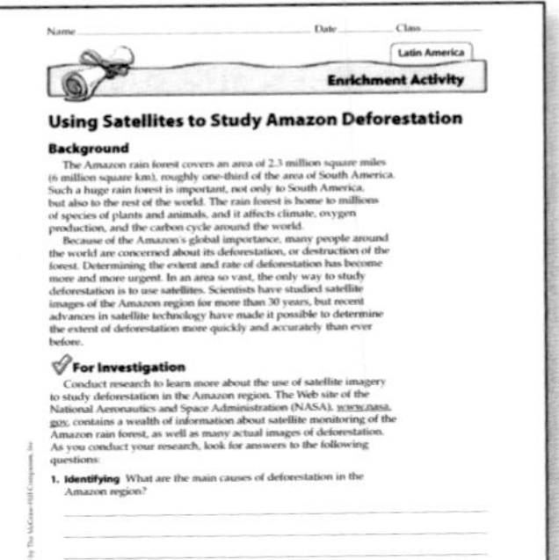
Enrichment Activity

Using Satellites to Study Amazon Deforestation

ELL Academic Vocabulary Activity, URB p. 91

Academic Vocabulary Activity

Brazil's Government

Brazil declared independence from Portugal in 1822. During most of the 1800s, emperors ruled the country. Today Brazil is a democratic federal republic, in which people elect a president and other leaders. Brazil has many political parties, not just two main ones, as does the United States.

The national government of Brazil is much stronger than its 26 state governments. Like the United States, Brazil's national government has three branches. The president heads the executive branch, which carries out the laws. The National Congress, which is similar to the U.S. Congress, makes the laws. A Supreme Federal Tribunal, or court, heads a judicial system that interprets the laws.

Reading Check **Analyzing Information** Why has Brazil's agricultural output greatly increased?

NATIONAL GEOGRAPHIC

Brazil's Government

▲ Brazil's President Luiz Inacio Lula da Silva (left) talks with Governor Rosinha Garotinho of the state of Rio de Janeiro. ***Place*** **How is Brazil's government like that of the United States?**

Argentina

Main Idea **Argentina has experienced harsh military rule but now has a democratic government.**

Geography and You How would you feel if the government seized a member of your family and you never saw him or her again? Read to find out how Argentina went through a period of violent rule in recent decades.

Argentina is South America's second-largest country after Brazil. It is about the size of the United States east of the Mississippi River. The Andes tower over western Argentina. South and east of the Andes lies a dry, windswept plateau called Patagonia. The center of Argentina has vast treeless plains known as the Pampas. More than two-thirds of Argentina's people live in this central area.

Argentina's People

About 85 percent of Argentina's people are of European ancestry, especially Spanish and Italian. European cultural traditions are stronger in Argentina than in most other Latin American countries.

The majority of people in Argentina are city dwellers. In fact, more than one-third of the country's population lives in the capital, Buenos Aires. This bustling city is a seat of government, a busy port, and a center of culture. Buenos Aires resembles a European city with its parks, beautiful buildings, wide streets, and cafés. It has been nicknamed "the Paris of the South." **W**

Argentina's Economy

Argentina's economy depends heavily on farming and ranching. Huge ranches cover the pampas. There, **gauchos** **D** (GOW·chohs), or cowhands, raise livestock. Gauchos are Argentina's national symbol.

W Writing Support

Expository Writing Have students work with a partner to find out more about the history and culture of Buenos Aires. Then have them write a magazine article about the city for an audience of first-time visitors. Encourage students to write an engaging headline and illustrate their article with images of popular tourist attractions. **OL**

D Differentiated Instruction

Special Education Show students a picture of a gaucho working with livestock. **Ask:** **What do gauchos remind you of?** *(Students will likely say cowboys.)* Discuss similar characteristics between the two. *(work with livestock, independent spirit, skilled at riding horses)* **BL**

Reading Check **Possible Answers:** Farmers have cleared more land for farming, they use machinery for many tasks, and they have planted crops that have been scientifically changed to produce more and to prevent disease.

Caption Answer: They have an elected president and state governments, a lawmaking body, and a court system.

Additional Support

Activity: Interdisciplinary Connection

Civics In Brazil, people in a certain age range who are allowed to vote are required to vote. In the United States, every citizen over the age of 18 has the right to vote, but no one is required to vote. As a result, voter turnout in the United States can sometimes be very low. **Ask:** **Do you believe that voting should be required by law?** *(Answers will vary.)* Ask students to give their ideas on why people in the United States might not vote. Have them take a poll of voting-age citizens in your community, asking each person whether he or she voted in the most recent election and why or why not. (Make sure students do not record the person's name with the response.) Have students tabulate the responses and present the information in a graph or table. Lead a discussion about the sorts of responses students received. Then ask students whether they believe it is important for people to vote. **OL**

C Critical Thinking

Determining Cause and Effect Have students fill out a cause-and-effect chain that explains the events leading up to Argentina's economic slowdown. *(Argentina borrowed money from foreign banks. → This increased their national debt. → Argentina didn't make payments on its debts. → Other countries stopped investing money in Argentina's businesses. → Argentina's economy slowed down severely.)* **OL**

R Reading Strategy

Sequencing Information Write the following events on the board:

- A revolt drives Juan Perón from power.
- Argentina loses a war with the United Kingdom.
- Juan Perón becomes dictator of Argentina.
- Civil war ends and a strong national government emerges in Argentina.

Tell students to read the section under "Argentina's Government" and write the dates beside each item. *(1955, 1982, late 1940s, mid-1850s)* **OL**

Caption Answer:
on the pampas

Reading Check Possible Answers:
because the economy depends on farming and ranching

NATIONAL GEOGRAPHIC

Beef Cattle in Argentina

Beef plays an important role in Argentina's foreign trade. Earnings from exports of animal products were about 1.9 billion dollars a year in the early 2000s. ***Location*** **Where are most of Argentina's livestock raised?**

They are admired for their independence and horse-riding skills. The livestock that the gauchos herd and tend are a vital part of the economy. Beef and beef products are Argentina's chief exports.

Argentina is one of the most industrialized countries in South America. Most factories are in or near Buenos Aires. They produce food products, cars, chemicals, and textiles. Zinc, iron ore, and copper are mined in the Andes. Oil fields also lie in the Andes as well as in Patagonia.

C Despite these resources, Argentina's economy has struggled. To help its economy grow, Argentina borrowed money from foreign banks during the late 1900s. However, this led to a high **national debt,** or money owed by the government. A few years ago, Argentina had to default on its debts to the foreign banks. To **default** is to miss a debt payment to the company or person who lent the money. People in other countries stopped investing money in Argentina's businesses. This caused a severe economic slowdown in Argentina. Recently the economy has recovered, and the government has paid off part of the debt.

Argentina's Government

After independence in the early 1800s, Argentina was torn apart by civil war. By the mid-1850s, a strong national government had emerged, and Argentina prospered. During the early 1900s, though, the economy suffered, and the military took over. One of the military leaders, Juan Perón, became a dictator in the late 1940s. Perón tried to improve the economy and to help the workers. At the same time, he restricted freedom of speech and the press. These actions made people unhappy. In 1955 a revolt drove Perón from power and restored democracy.

Military officers again took control of Argentina in the 1970s. They ruled harshly and secretly seized and killed thousands R of people they believed opposed their policies. The families of these people did not know what had happened to them. It was a time of fear.

In 1982 Argentina suffered defeat in a war with the United Kingdom over control of the Falkland Islands. The Falklands, known to Argentinians as the Malvinas, lie in the Atlantic Ocean. After this loss, military leaders gave up power, and elected leaders gained control of the government.

Today, Argentina is a democratic federal republic. It consists of a national government and 23 provincial, or state, governments. The nation is led by a powerful president who is elected every four years. A legislature with two houses makes the laws. A Supreme Court heads a system of judges.

Reading Check **Explaining** Why are food products among the leading manufactured items in Argentina?

Hands-On Chapter Project Step 3

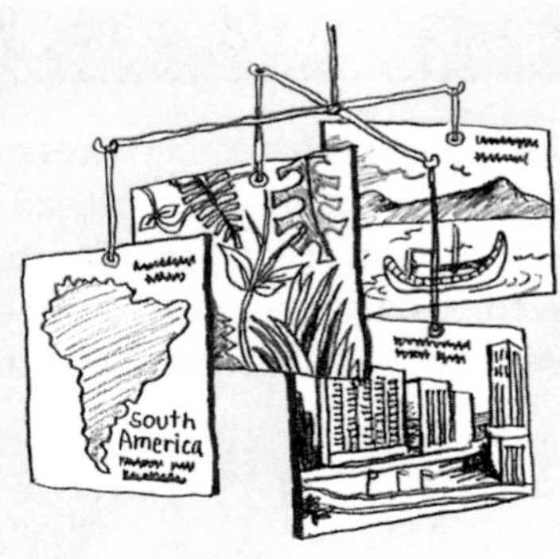

Creating an Environmental Mobile

Step 3: Making the Mobile Students will complete the mobiles they planned in Steps 1 and 2.

Directions Have students complete their research by looking at South American issues. Then allow students time to build their mobiles. The images they found in Steps 1 and 2 should be glued or taped back-to-back, with a human activity on one side and its effect on the other. Then students can use string or ribbon to hang the images from a hanger, a piece of PVC pipe, or from two pieces of wood or cardboard joined in an "x" shape.

Putting It Together Display students' mobiles in the classroom. Ask students to describe what the images show and why they are significant. **OL**

(Chapter Project cont. on the Visual Summary page)

Other Countries of South America

Main Idea **Economic growth for other countries of South America has been hindered by political and social troubles.**

Geography and You Can you recall hard times and good times in your life? Read on to learn which nations in South America are experiencing hard times and which are experiencing good times.

Many countries in South America face the same challenges as Brazil and Argentina. Some, such as Venezuela, Colombia, and Chile, have relatively strong economies. Others, however, face more difficult economic hardships.

Venezuela

Venezuela lies along the Caribbean Sea in northern South America. It is one of the world's leading producers of oil and natural gas. Although it relies mainly on oil production, Venezuela also benefits from mining bauxite, gold, diamonds, and emeralds. The country's factories make steel, chemicals, and food products. Farmers grow sugarcane and bananas or raise cattle. Most Venezuelans are poor, and some live in slums that sprawl over the hills around the capital, Caracas. R

In 1998 Venezuelans elected a former military leader, Hugo Chávez, as president. Chávez promised to use oil money to better the lives of Venezuela's poor. His strong rule, however, split the country into opposing groups. Chávez also tried to spread his influence overseas. He became friendly with Cuba's leader, Fidel Castro, and frequently criticized the United States.

Colombia

Venezuela's neighbor, Colombia, has coasts on both the Caribbean Sea and the Pacific Ocean. The Andes rise in the western part of Colombia. Nearly 80 percent of Colombia's people live in the valleys and highland plateaus of the Andes. Bogotá (BOH·goh·TAH), the capital and largest city, lies on one of these plateaus. S

Colombia has many natural resources, such as coal, oil, and copper. It is the world's leading supplier of emeralds. Colombian coffee, a major export, is famous for its rich flavor. Colombia also exports bananas, sugarcane, rice, and cotton.

Despite these economic strengths, Colombia has much political unrest. Wealth remains in the hands of a few, and many people are poor. Since the 1970s, rebel forces have fought the government and now control parts of the country.

Medical Technology

NATIONAL GEOGRAPHIC

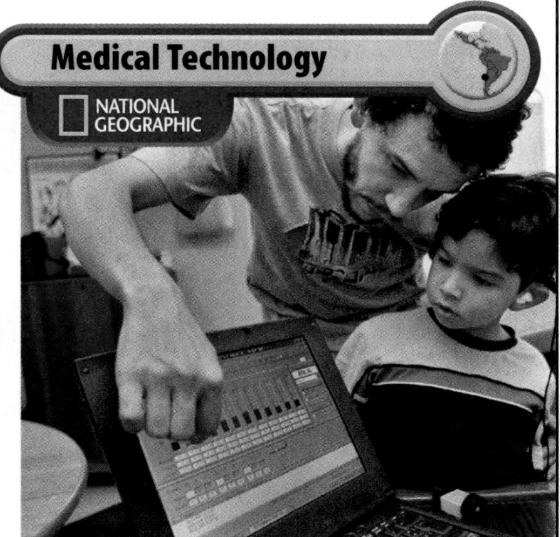

▲ A six-year-old boy hears for the first time as a result of new medical equipment provided by Chile's government. ***Regions*** **In addition to Chile, what other South American countries have relatively strong economies?** W

R Reading Strategy

Monitoring As students read the passage, have them make up test questions on a sheet of paper. Then instruct them to close the book and answer the questions that they have written. If they cannot recall the answers, have them reread the passage. **BL**

S Skill Practice

Using Geography Skills Have students locate the Caribbean Sea, the Pacific Ocean, the Andes, and Bogotá on a map. **Ask:** **Why do you think so many people live in the valleys and highland plateaus of the Andes?** *(Possible answer: The terrain is easier to farm and build houses on.)* **OL**

W Writing Support

Descriptive Writing Have students imagine what the boy in the photo is experiencing as he hears for the first time. Tell them to write a paragraph imagining the details of the experience, including what sounds the boy might be hearing. **OL**

Caption Answer:
Venezuela and Colombia

Additional Support

Activity: Connecting With the United States

Making Connections Tell students that Venezuela is the fourth-largest supplier of oil to the United States. However, relations between the countries have not always been cordial. In 2006 Venezuelan president Hugo Chavez made a speech at the United Nations in which he criticized U.S. president George W. Bush. **Ask:** **Do you think that the United States should buy oil from countries whose leaders spread anti-Americanism?** *(Answers will vary.)* Have students write a paragraph responding to the question. Then explain that although Chavez spoke angrily against the United States, Venezuela and the United States need each other economically. The United States needs oil. Chavez uses money from oil sales to support health care, education, and housing and social projects aimed at improving life for his country's poor. Discuss with students what might happen to both countries if their relationship dissolved. **AL**

D Differentiated Instruction

Advanced Learners Have students research the conflict between the government and drug dealers in Colombia. Instruct students to look at the issue from multiple perspectives—social, economic, and political—and also to study the problem from the U.S. point of view. Have students offer an opinion about how involved they think the United States should be in Colombia's drug problem. Ask students to share their findings with the class. AL

Reading Check Possible Answer: oil

Assess

Social Studies ONLINE
Study Central™ provides summaries, interactive games, and online graphic organizers to help students review content.

Close

Labeling Have students label an outline map with the names of the South American countries discussed in the text. Then have them write one fact about each country. OL

D Drug dealers are a major problem in Colombia. The dealers pay farmers to grow coca leaves, which are used to make the illegal drug cocaine. Much of the cocaine is smuggled into the United States and Europe. Drug dealers have used their profits to build private armies. The United States has lent Colombia support in an effort to break the power of the drug dealers.

Chile

Chile lies along the southern Pacific coast of South America. It has an unusual ribbonlike shape that is 2,652 miles long (4,268 km) and an average of 110 miles (177 km) wide. Chile's landscapes range from extremely dry desert in the north to ice formations in the south.

In recent years, Chile has had strong economic growth. Mining forms the backbone of Chile's economy. Chile is a major world producer of copper. It also mines and exports gold, silver, iron ore, and **sodium nitrate,** a mineral used in fertilizer and explosives.

Agriculture is also a major economic activity. Farmers produce wheat, corn, beans, sugarcane, and potatoes. The grapes and apples you eat in winter may come from Chile's summer harvest. Many people also raise cattle, sheep, and other livestock. Northern Chile's fishing industry is the largest in South America.

Like Argentina, Chile has emerged from a long period of military rule. During that time, the government treated its opponents harshly. Today, Chile is a democracy. In 2006 Michelle Bachelet was elected the country's first woman president.

Reading Check **Identifying** What resource is especially important to Venezuela?

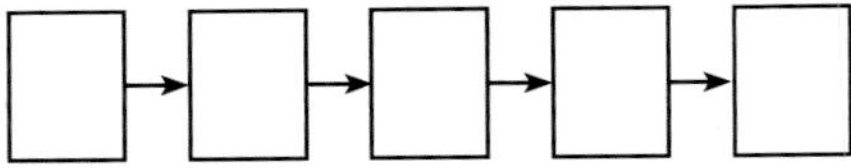

Social Studies ONLINE
Study Central™ To review this section, go to glencoe.com.

Vocabulary

1. **Explain** the significance of:
   a. selva c. gaucho e. default
   b. favela d. national debt f. sodium nitrate

Main Ideas

2. **Explaining** In what ways has Brazil improved its economy?
3. **Sequencing** Use a diagram like the one below to show changes in Argentina's government following independence.

→	→	→	→	

4. **Describing** Describe the problem of illegal drugs in Colombia.

Critical Thinking

5. **BIG Idea** How are Brazilians changing the rain forest, and why does that matter to people in other areas of the world?
6. **Challenge** Do you think Venezuela is likely to suffer from focusing on one major product? Why or why not?

Writing About Geography

7. **Using Your FOLDABLES** Use your Foldable to write a paragraph comparing the roles that two governments of South America play in economic affairs. Be sure to analyze how effective you think their governments are.

Answers

1. Definitions for vocabulary words can be found in the section and Glossary.
2. Brazil has increased its agricultural output by clearing more land for crops, using machinery to perform many tasks, and planting crops that have been scientifically changed to produce more and prevent disease. Brazil also has valuable mineral resources and successful industries.
3. civil war, strong national government, military dictatorship, democratic government, military takes power, democratic federal republic
4. Drug dealers pay farmers to grow products used to make cocaine, which they smuggle into other countries. They also have built private armies.
5. The rain forest is being destroyed by deforestation. Others should care because rain forests help maintain Earth's climate patterns and biodiversity.
6. Yes, because changes in world prices affect the country, and oil will eventually run out.
7. Paragraphs will vary but should include analysis.

Visual Summary

Mexico

- Mexico City is one of the world's largest cities.
- Mexico's culture reflects both European and Native American influences.
- Industry and farming dominate Mexico's North; agriculture leads in the South.
- Many Mexicans have migrated to cities and to the United States to find jobs.

Subsistence farming, Mexico

Central America and the Caribbean

- Civil wars have held back economic growth in parts of Central America.
- Costa Rica's citizens have a high literacy rate and enjoy a stable government.
- The Panama Canal enables ships to pass between the Atlantic and Pacific Oceans.
- Many Caribbean islands' economies rely on tourism.

Logs from Amazon forest, Brazil

Brazil

- Brazil is the biggest and most populous country in South America.
- Brazil's people, who speak Portuguese, are a mix of many different ethnic backgrounds.
- Brazil has many resources and a productive economy.
- Economic development threatens the Amazon rain forest.

Cruise ship docked in the British Virgin Islands

Argentina

- A large grassland called the pampas covers much of Argentina.
- Argentina's economy depends on farming and ranching.
- More than a third of Argentina's people live in the capital, Buenos Aires.
- After years of military rule, Argentina is today a democracy.

Oil rig in Venezuela

Other Countries of South America

- Venezuela has relied on oil wealth to build a stronger economy.
- Colombia has been weakened by political unrest and illegal drug trade.
- Chile's economy depends on the export of copper and agricultural products.

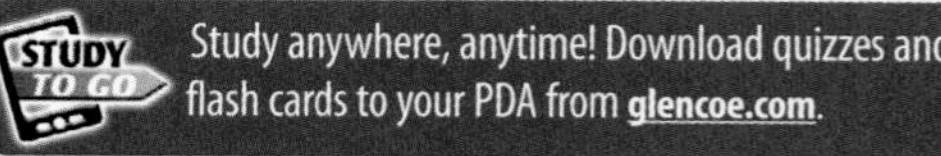

Study anywhere, anytime! Download quizzes and flash cards to your PDA from glencoe.com.

Visual Summary

Summarizing Information Have students read the bulleted items on the page with a partner. Ask students how they think the writers of the text created the summary sentences in the bulleted items. Remind students that summaries contain the main ideas of a passage.

Assign pairs of students a Latin American country. Tell students to return to the text and analyze the information to find what is most important in order to add three additional bullet items to their country. Remind students that their items should not repeat the information that is already on the page. When students finish their items, have them trade with another pair and analyze the items to see whether they summarize the main ideas. **OL**

This **Reading Skill** (Summarizing Information) was introduced in this unit.

Identifying Central Issues After students read the Visual Summary, ask them to choose the area that they feel is most important to the well-being of the people of Latin America: environment, economy, or government. Have students explain their opinions. **OL**

Hands-On Chapter Project
Step 4: Wrap Up

Creating an Environmental Mobile

Step 4: Learning From the Mobiles Students will synthesize what they have learned in Steps 1–3.

Directions Write the Essential Question on the board. Next to the Essential Question, draw a chart with two columns, one for beneficial activities and one for harmful activities. Based on what they have learned from making their mobiles and viewing others' work, ask students to name activities that belong in the "beneficial" column and activities that belong in the "harmful" column. Ask students to give their ideas on how beneficial activities might be encouraged and harmful activities might be discouraged in a country. Discuss with students how governments shape people's behavior, either through laws or through economic rewards or fees. Have students write several sentences in their journals stating which human activity they believe to be the most harmful in Latin America and why. **OL**

Answers and Analyses

Reviewing Vocabulary

1. A Only two answers refer to architectural features in cities—*plazas* and *favelas.* Favelas are overcrowded slum areas in Brazilian cities that are inhabited by many migrants. Plazas, on the other hand, are public squares in Mexico. Government buildings would logically be located in public squares because they house public offices.

2. D Understanding the meaning of the term *subsistence* will help students answer this question. *Subsistence* means "the minimum amount necessary to survive." *Subsistence* farming, then, is producing just enough food for a family to survive but not enough to sell for profit.

3. C Students can use a process of elimination to answer the question if they do not understand the meaning of the word *remittance*. Answer choice A, *canal-use fees,* does not make sense because Haiti does not have a major canal. Answer choices B and D can be eliminated because Haiti's literacy rate and economy type are not things that in and of themselves generate income.

4. A Students will likely struggle to choose between *vaqueros* and *gauchos* because both terms refer to people who work with livestock. The difference between the two is location—gauchos are in Argentina, and vaqueros are in Mexico.

STANDARDIZED TEST PRACTICE

TEST-TAKING TIP

Before answering essay questions, jot down a list of things you want to discuss.

Reviewing Vocabulary

Directions: Choose the word(s) that best completes the sentence.

1. Main government buildings in Mexican cities are located around central squares called ______.

A plazas
B murals
C selvas
D favelas

2. ______ are small plots where farmers grow only enough food for their families.

A Plantations
B Maquiladoras
C Commonwealths
D Subsistence farms

3. An important source of income in Haiti is ______.

A canal-use fees
B the literacy rate
C remittances
D the command economy

4. ______ take care of the livestock on ranches in Argentina.

A Gauchos
B Vaqueros
C Farmers
D Migrant workers

Reviewing Main Ideas

Directions: Choose the best answer for each question.

Section 1 *(pp. 232–236)*

5. Which expression of Mexican culture is rooted in Native American traditions?

A soccer
B bullfighting
C wood carving
D public squares

6. What helped change the Mexican economy in recent years?

A farmers' small plots
B foreign-built factories
C large sugarcane farms
D resort cities along the coast

Section 2 *(pp. 237–240)*

7. What country makes more money in tourism than any other country in the Caribbean?

A Cuba
B Haiti
C Puerto Rico
D El Salvador

Section 3 *(pp. 246–252)*

8. Why is deforestation in Brazil felt worldwide?

A Farmers grow crops in the rain forest.
B Native Americans live in the rain forest.
C The rain forest has large deposits of oil.
D The rain forest helps maintain climate patterns.

GO ON

Reviewing Main Ideas

5. C Students may recognize all of the answer choices as having to do with Mexico, so they will need to analyze further to make the correct choice. For this question, students should focus on the key words *Native American traditions*. Soccer, bullfighting, and public squares are Spanish traditions. Students may remember that folk art is a Native American tradition, one of which is wood carving.

6. B Two answer choices can be eliminated easily. Answer choice A does not make sense because small plots of farmland do not generally make a big impact on an economy. Answer choice D also is illogical because resort cities have been on the coasts of Mexico for years. Of the two remaining choices, Mexico is not known for sugarcane production, which leaves choice B.

Critical Thinking

Directions: Base your answers to questions 9 and 10 on the graph below and your knowledge of Chapter 9. Choose the best answer for each question.

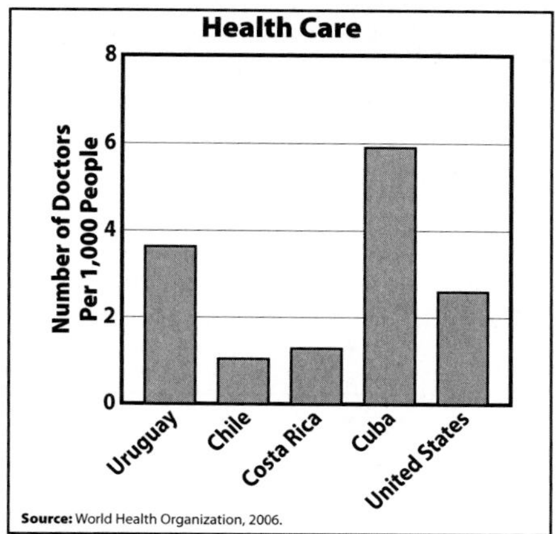

9. Which of the following countries has the fewest doctors per thousand population?

A Cuba

B Chile

C Uruguay

D Costa Rica

10. Which of the following generalizations does the graph support?

A Chile has more disease than the other countries.

B Chile is healthier than the other countries.

C Cuba has more doctors per 1,000 people than either the United States or Uruguay.

D The United States has more doctors per 1,000 people than all Latin American countries.

Document-Based Questions

Directions: Analyze the following document and answer the short-answer questions that follow.

The following passage discusses a movement that has helped strengthen Argentina's economy.

> *Since 1972 the Mil Hojas pasta factory [in Argentina] has churned out delicacies like ravioli and Italian desserts. But Mil Hojas' fortunes—along with those of the national economy—began to decline with the late 1990s as deep recession set in.*
>
> *The factory owners decided to abandon it amid a national epidemic of bankruptcies. Mil Hojas, like many other factories in Argentina, was to permanently close its doors.*
>
> *That was when its workers decided to act. They took back, or "recovered" Mil Hojas, transforming it into what today is a thriving cooperative, as Argentina emerges from one of the worst economic crises in its history.*
>
> *Today, thousands of workers are reactivating previously closed factories on their own terms and . . . breathing life into the national economy.*
>
> —Eduardo Stanley, "Argentina's Recovered Factories: A Story of Economic Success"

11. What happened to factories during economic hard times in Argentina?

12. Were the workers' actions consistent with a command economy or with free enterprise? Explain.

Extended Response

13. Compare and contrast the political systems of Brazil and the United States.

For additional test practice, use Self-Check Quizzes—Chapter 9 at glencoe.com.

Need Extra Help?

If you missed question. . .	1	2	3	4	5	6	7	8	9	10	11	12	13
Go to page. . .	233	235	240	249	234	235	240	248	239	239	249	249	249

Critical Thinking

9. B To find the correct answer, students can check each answer against the chart to determine its accuracy. In doing so, students will find that Chile has the lowest bar on the graph, which means that it has the lowest number of doctors per thousand people.

10. C Students might struggle with this question because several answers seem plausible until thoroughly analyzed. Generalization about specific diseases can't be made based on this chart because the incidence of diseases does not relate to the number of doctors a country has. Therefore, answer choice A is incorrect. The same logic applies to answer choice B. By comparing the bars, students will see that D is incorrect because the United States' number is lower than Cuba's.

Document-Based Questions

11. Many factories closed.

12. Free enterprise; the workers, not the government, decided to recover the factories.

Extended Response

13. Students' answers will vary but should point out that people in both countries elect officials. However, Brazil, unlike the United States, has dozens of political parties and requires its citizens to vote.

7. C To answer this question correctly, students will need to analyze the political and social situations in each answer choice. Cuba does not have a thriving tourist industry because of its command economy and dictatorship. Haiti is plagued by political strife and is not a welcoming tourist destination. El Salvador was not discussed in the text. Puerto Rico is the logical choice because it is a stable country.

8. D Students must take a worldview when considering the answer choices. Answer choices A and B are contained in the Brazilian rain forest, so the worldwide effects of deforestation would not be felt by either choice. Oil is not the major resource of the rain forest—the forest is. The logical choice is D because climate patterns can be felt all over the world.

Social Studies ONLINE

Have students visit the Web site at glencoe.com to review Chapter 9 and take the Self-Check Quiz.

Need Extra Help?

Have students refer to the pages listed if they miss any of the questions.

Unit 4 Planning Guide

UNIT PACING CHART				
	Unit 4	**Chapter 10**	**Chapter 11**	**Chapter 12**
Day 1	Unit Opener	Chapter Opener	Chapter Opener	Chapter Opener
Day 2	Regional Atlas	Section 1	Section 1	Section 1
Day 3	Regional Atlas	Section 1	Section 1	World LIterature Reading
Day 4	Reading Social Studies	Geography & History	Section 1	Section 1
Day 5		Section 2	You Decide	Section 2
Day 6		Section 2	Section 2	Section 2
Day 7		Review	Section 2	Section 3
Day 8		Chapter Assessment	Review	Section 3
Day 9			Chapter Assessment	TIME Perspectives
Day 10			Chapter TIME Journal	TIME Perspectives
Day 11				Section 4
Day 12				Section 4
Day 13				Section 4
Day 14				Review
Day 15				Chapter Assessment

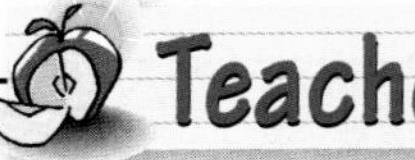

Eric Dauberman
Whitehall-Coplay Middle School
Whitehall, PA

My Euro Have students research images of the euro on the Internet. As a class, discuss why a particular country chose to use the image on their euro. Students will then pick a European country from Unit 4 and create a new euro for that country. The new image should be associated with information and facts acquired about that country in Unit 4. Students may construct a euro out of a small round piece of oak, approximately 5 inches (13 cm) in diameter. Students can draw, trace or use magazine or computer images to fashion their new euro. On the reverse side of the euro, students should write a brief description describing why they used the image they did to represent the country they chose.

Author Note

Dear Social Studies Teacher:

Much of the world has been influenced by Europe in culture, language, religion, clothing, and law. There once was a telling statement: "The sun never sets on the British Empire." This phrase underscores a long period of British colonialism and is inaccurate only to the extent that other European countries were not included. The great colonial powers of the seventeenth, eighteenth, and nineteenth centuries were Spain, Portugal, The Netherlands, France, Italy, and Germany, in addition to the United Kingdom.

Today, former colonies are free and independent countries, and European nations face a world in which their influence is declining, their populations are getting older, and their businesses and industries require a greater labor force than their slow population growth can provide. To address this problem, most European countries have opened their borders to citizens of former colonies. They also have initiated "guest worker" strategies to bring foreign workers into their countries. These workers have contributed to the rise of richly diverse multicultural populations in many areas of Europe.

Meanwhile, countries throughout Europe have been slowly giving up the symbols of sovereignty—national currency, national tariffs, and closed borders—in order to create the European Union. The European Union is a cooperative economic, political, and social organization that now boasts a membership of more than 20 countries, with others waiting to join. Through the European Union, member-nations can share resources, markets, and agricultural and industrial products. This cooperative relationship encourages trade and economic growth within the Union. Today, the European Union has become an economic superpower on par with the United States and is well prepared to compete in the twenty-first century.

Richard G. Boehm
Senior Author

Introducing Unit 4

What Makes Europe a Region?

The three chapters of this unit introduce students to the region of Europe. This region has the following characteristics:

- a long coastline bordering the Atlantic Ocean and several seas
- one of the densest populations on Earth
- a mild climate and fertile agricultural plains
- highly industrialized economies and high standards of living
- a variety of peoples with diverse ethnic and religious backgrounds
- a rich cultural heritage

NATIONAL GEOGRAPHIC

www.nationalgeographic.com/education

NGS ONLINE This online resource provides lesson plans, atlas updates, cartographic activities with interactive maps, an online map store, and geographic links.

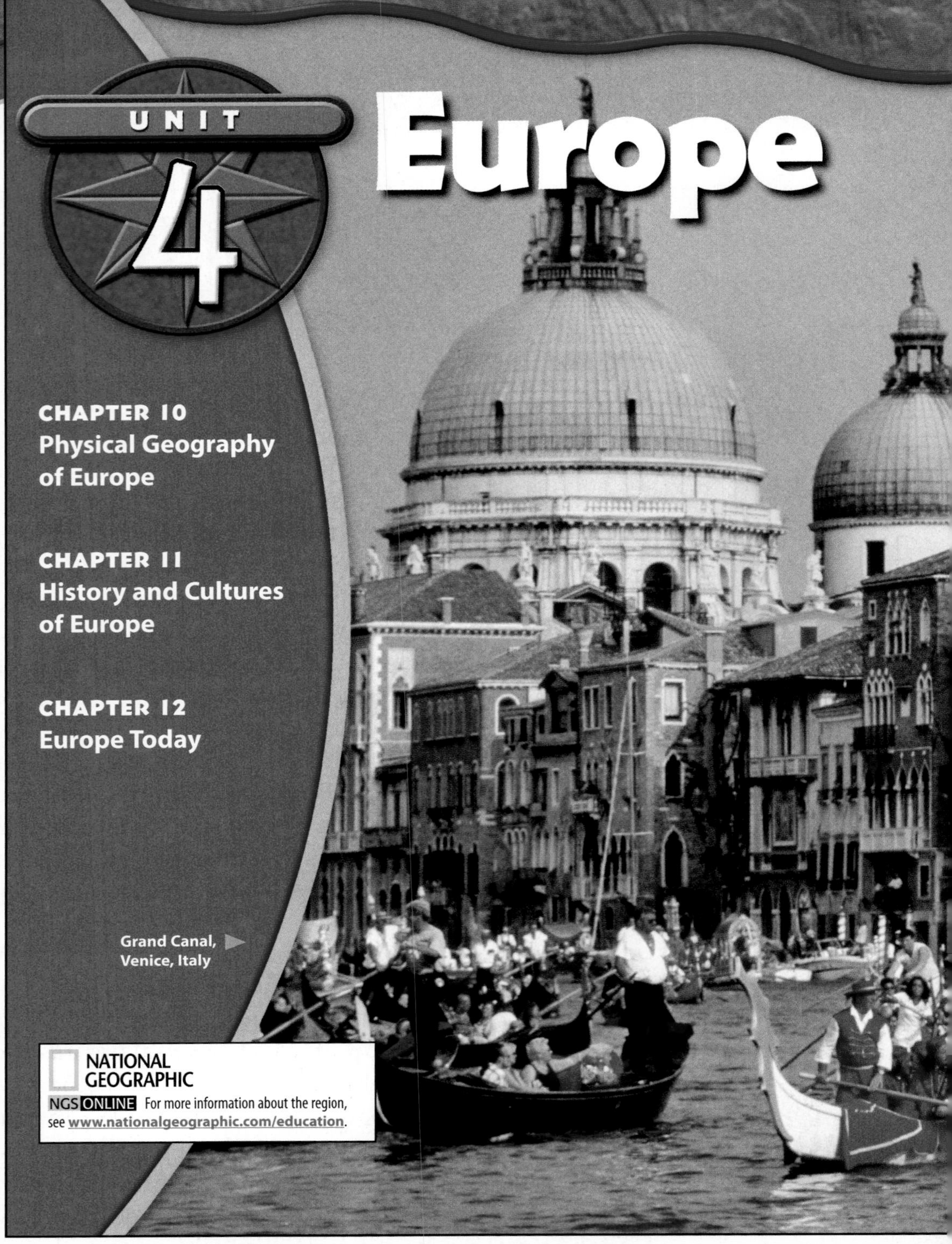

UNIT 4 Europe

Grand Canal, Venice, Italy

NATIONAL GEOGRAPHIC

NGS ONLINE For more information about the region, see www.nationalgeographic.com/education.

Activity: Launching the Unit

Why Study Europe? Ask: What European countries can you name? *(Answers might include: United Kingdom, France, Germany, Italy, Spain, etc.)* Explain that Europe is changing politically. In 1989 communist governments in many eastern European countries were forced from power. A year later, the Berlin Wall was torn down. In 1990 East Germany and West Germany united to become one democratic state. Then, in 1991 the Soviet Union itself broke apart, and communism collapsed. Many formerly communist countries in eastern Europe have introduced free market reforms and have joined the European Union. **OL**

Introducing Unit 4

Introduce the Region

Using Maps Have students look at the maps of physical features and political boundaries of Europe in the Regional Atlas. Point out that Europe includes more than 40 countries. **Ask: What physical region of Europe extends north of the Arctic Circle?** *(Scandinavia)* **What specific countries extend north of the Arctic Circle?** *(Norway, Sweden, and Finland)* Tell students that most areas of Europe lie within 300 miles (483 km) of an ocean or a sea. **Ask: Which ocean borders much of Europe?** *(Atlantic Ocean)* **Which seas border the countries of Europe?** *(Norwegian Sea, North Sea, Baltic Sea, Celtic Sea, Irish Sea, Mediterranean Sea, Tyrrhenian Sea, Adriatic Sea, Aegean Sea, Black Sea, Sea of Azov)* **What European countries are located on islands?** *(Iceland, United Kingdom, Ireland, Malta, Cyprus)* **OL**

Unit 4 • 257

More About the Photo

Visual Literacy The city of Venice, in northeastern Italy, is located on more than 100 islands. These islands are connected by a system of more than 150 canals and about 400 pedestrian bridges. The Grand Canal is Venice's main thoroughfare. It is about 2 miles (3.2 km) long and follows an S-shaped course from northwest to southeast. For centuries, the main means of transportation in Venice was by gondola, a flat-bottomed boat rowed with one oar. Today, most Venetians use motor-boats for transportation. However, tourists visiting the Grand Canal can hire a gondola to view the nearly 200 palaces, built between the A.D. 1100s and 1700s, that line its banks.

Regional Atlas Activity

Where Is It?

Remembering Latitude and Longitude Remind students that lines of latitude circle the earth parallel to the Equator and that lines of longitude circle the earth from pole to pole. **Ask:** **How can you remember which is latitude and which is longitude?** *(You might offer this as a suggestion: Lines of longitude are all equally long; lines of latitude vary in length, with 0° the longest and 89°, near each pole, the shortest.)* **BL**

How Big Is It?

Math Question Tell students that the total land area of Ukraine, the largest country in Europe, is 233,089 square miles (603,698 sq. km). **Ask:** **About what percentage of Europe's land is in Ukraine?** *(about 10 percent)* **OL**

Comparing Population

Ask: **About how many people live in France?** *(60 million)* **What other European countries have about the same population as France?** *(the United Kingdom and Italy)* **BL**

Regional Atlas

Europe

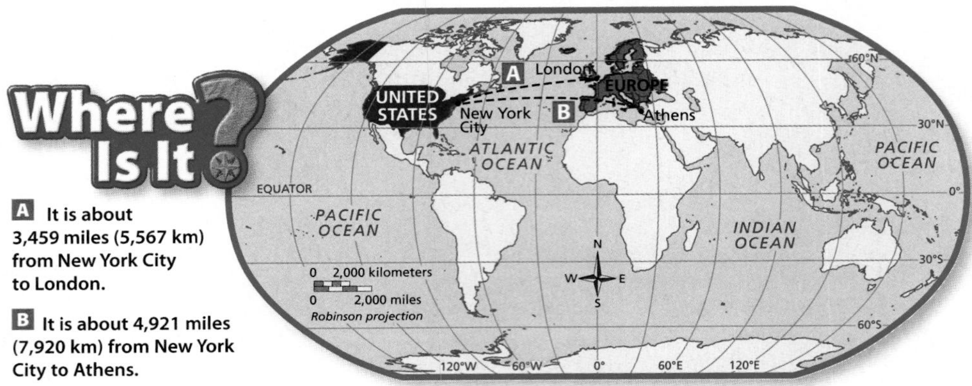

A It is about 3,459 miles (5,567 km) from New York City to London.

B It is about 4,921 miles (7,920 km) from New York City to Athens.

At about 2.3 million square miles (5.9 million sq. km), Europe is about three-fourths the size of the United States. More than 580 million people—almost twice the population of the United States—live in this area, which is one of the most densely populated regions on Earth.

Comparing Population

United States and Selected Countries of Europe

United States	
Germany	
France	
United Kingdom	
Italy	
Ukraine	
Czech Republic	

= 30,000,000

Source: *World Population Data Sheet, 2005.*

Activity: Geographic Theme

Movement Tell students that Europe's closeness to the Atlantic Ocean and to several seas, as well as its long, navigable rivers, has allowed people throughout history to move easily within Europe and between Europe and other continents. Have them look at the map showing the physical features of Europe in the Regional Atlas. **Ask:** **How might people have traveled by ship from the Balkan Peninsula to Russia?** *(through the Black Sea)* **Ask:** **How might people have traveled by ship from Scandinavia to Iceland?** *(by sailing through the Norwegian Sea to the Atlantic Ocean and then on to Iceland, or through the North Sea to the Atlantic Ocean to Iceland, or through the Baltic Sea to the North Sea to the Atlantic Ocean to Iceland)* **Ask:** **How might people have traveled by ship from the Alps region to the British Isles?** (by sailing down the Rhine River to the North Sea and then on to the British Isles) **OL**

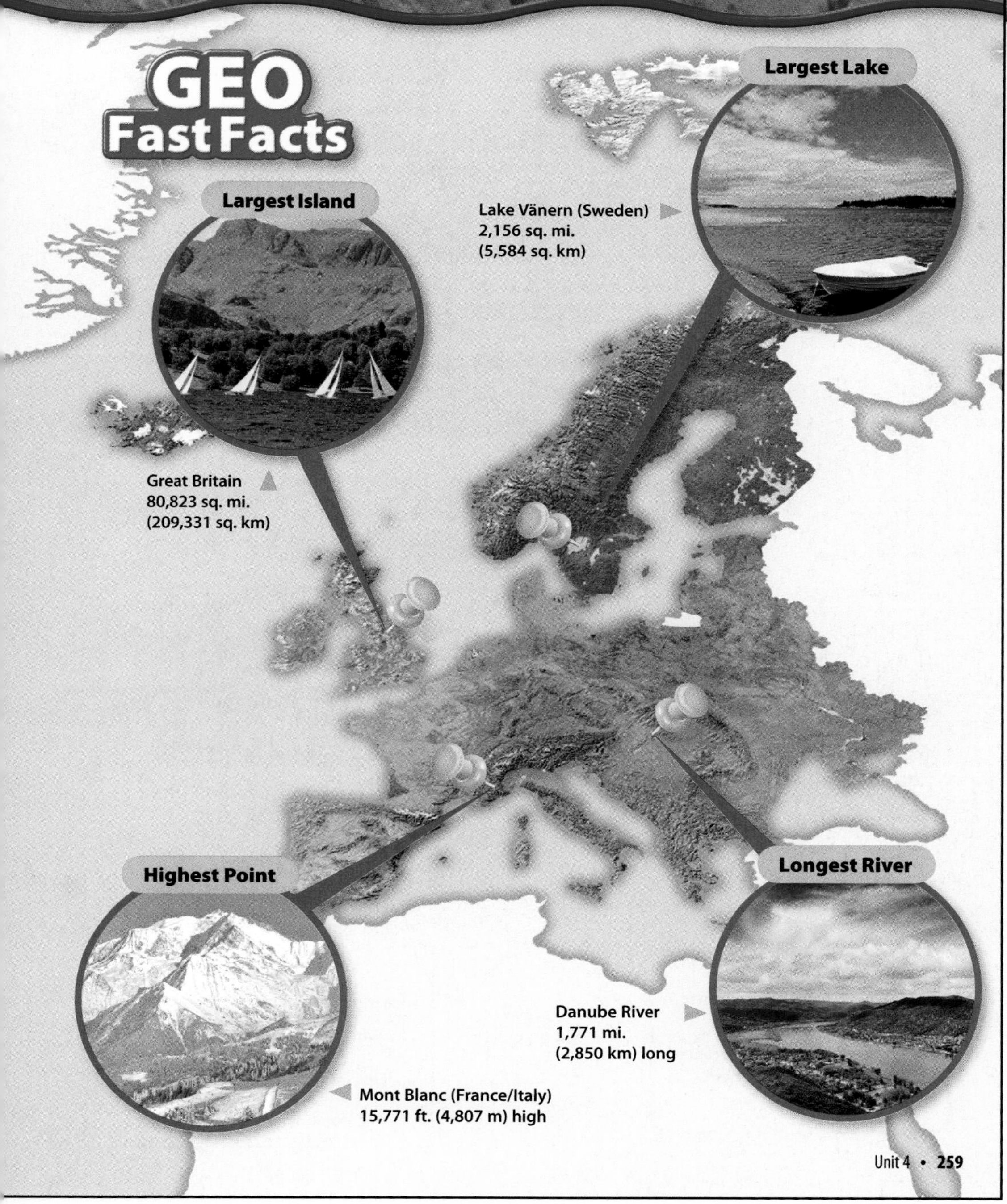

GEO Fast Facts

Largest Island

Great Britain
80,823 sq. mi.
(209,331 sq. km)

Largest Lake

Lake Vänern (Sweden)
2,156 sq. mi.
(5,584 sq. km)

Highest Point

Mont Blanc (France/Italy)
15,771 ft. (4,807 m) high

Longest River

Danube River
1,771 mi.
(2,850 km) long

Geo Fast Facts

Listing Physical Features **Ask: What four features of Europe are highlighted on this map?** *(the largest island, largest lake, highest point, and longest river)* **What countries do the largest island, largest lake, and highest point lie within?** *(The largest island is Great Britain, which is part of the United Kingdom; Lake Vänern is in Sweden; and Mont Blanc is on the border of France and Italy.)*

Have students use the map of political boundaries to choose three countries of Europe they would like to know more about. Ask them to begin making lists of the physical features found in each country, using the physical features map in the Regional Atlas. You may choose to allow class time for students to use other sources to research their countries.

Tell students to keep their lists and to update them with additional facts about their chosen countries as they read the chapters in this unit. At the end of the unit, ask pairs of students who have chosen the same country to compare their lists, making each list as complete as possible. Repeat until students have had the opportunity to compare and complete each of their lists. **BL**

FastFacts

- **The Olympic Games** The Olympic Games began in ancient Greece in 776 B.C. Every fourth summer, the Greek city-states sent athletes to compete in the sanctuary of the god Zeus at Olympia. Events included footraces, boxing, wrestling, horse racing, discus throwing, javelin hurling, and long jumping. The modern Olympic Games began in 1896 as a way to promote a more peaceful world; the first modern games were held in Athens as a tribute to their ancient Greek origins.
- **The Land of the Midnight Sun** Norway is among the world's most northern countries. A third of Norway's land area lies north of the Arctic Circle, where there is almost continuous daylight during early summer. For this reason, Norway is sometimes called the Land of the Midnight Sun.
- **Poland** Unlike other European countries, Poland is not ethnically diverse. Almost all Poles are Slavs, are Roman Catholics, and speak Polish. The importance of agriculture in Poland is reflected in the name of the people of the first Polish kingdom—*Polani*—meaning "people of the fields."

Regional Atlas Activity

Identifying Tell students that Europe has many rivers that are wide and deep enough for navigation. Have them work in pairs and select three rivers in the region. **Ask: Into what body of water does each river empty?** Then instruct students to use appropriate reference materials to find out more about their rivers. Suggest questions they may want to answer, including: *Is the population more dense near the river? In what country does each river originate? Through what countries does each river flow? How does the river contribute to national economies? Is the river navigable?* When students have finished their research, ask each student pair to present a brief report on one of the rivers they have researched to the rest of the class. **AL**

Answers:

1. Iberian Peninsula, Balkan Peninsula
2. Much of northern Europe lies on the Northern European Plain—a lowlands area that extends from western France into Russia—while southern Europe is more mountainous.

Skills Practice

Ask: What mountain range includes the highest mountain in Europe? *(the Alps)* **What area of Europe contains numerous lakes?** *(Scandinavia)*

Unit 4 Regional Atlas

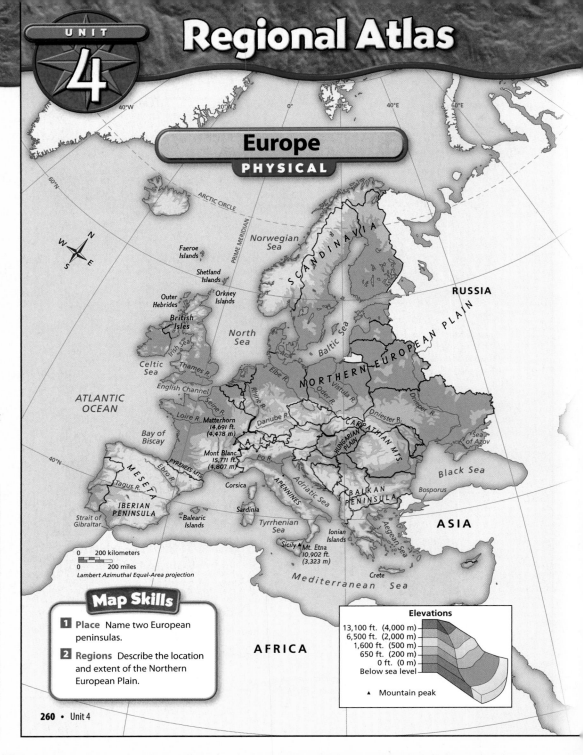

Europe
PHYSICAL

Map Skills

1 Place Name two European peninsulas.

2 Regions Describe the location and extent of the Northern European Plain.

260 • Unit 4

Background: Land and Climate

The Importance of Water Europe has been shaped by its proximity to water. Most of the land in Europe lies within 300 miles (483 km) of an ocean or a sea. The continent has a long, jagged coastline along the Atlantic Ocean and several seas, including the Baltic, North, Mediterranean, Norwegian, and Black Seas. Only a few countries have no coastline on the ocean or a sea. Even within these landlocked nations, navigable rivers flow from inland highlands and mountains toward the sea, giving residents access to water. Canals that link rivers and inland ports are also used to transport goods.

Because of this nearness to the sea, Europeans became expert sailors and fishers. Trade flourished along the region's waterways. Nearness to water also encouraged the movement of peoples and the spread of ideas between areas within Europe and between Europe and other continents.

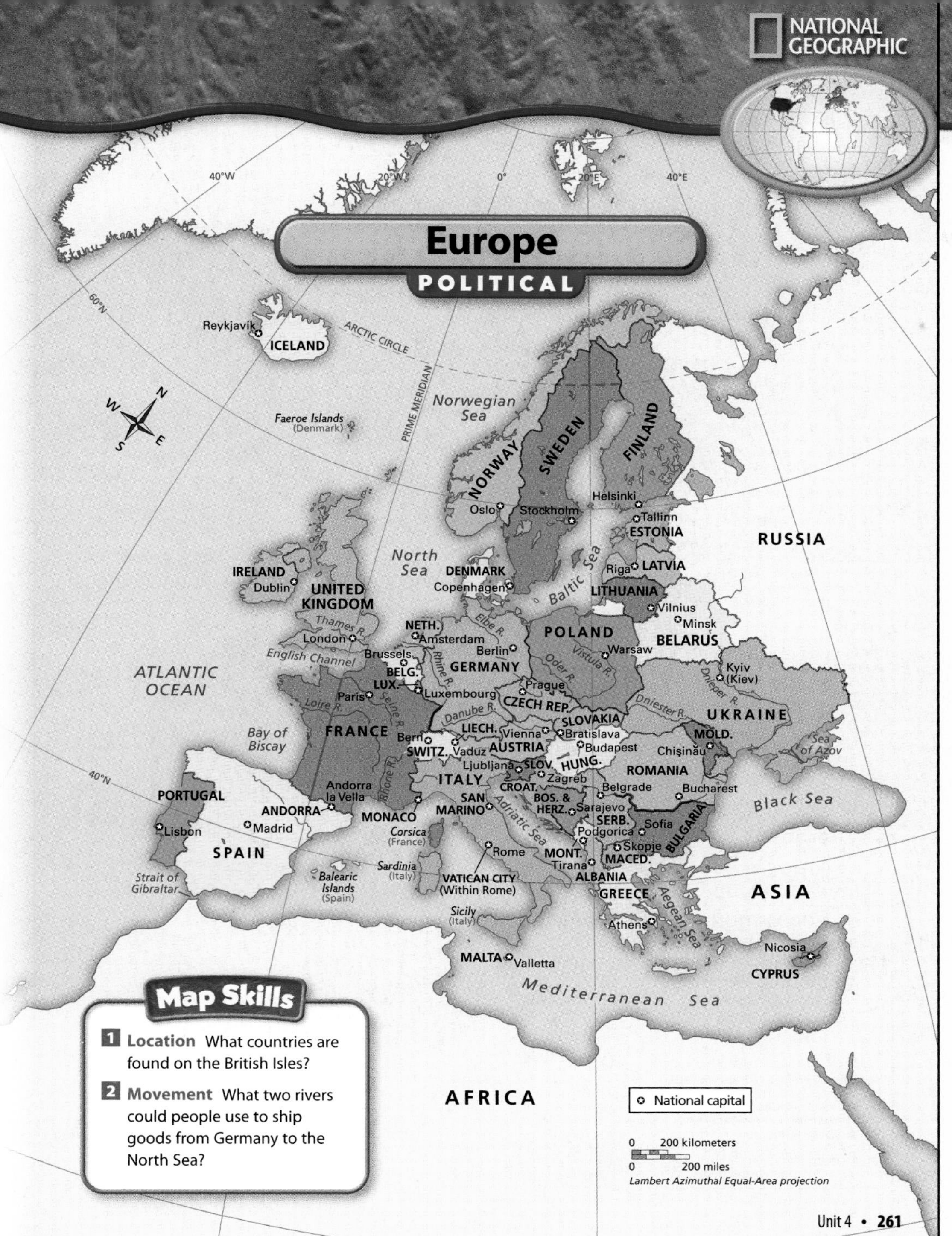

Regional Atlas Activity

Identifying Countries and Subregions Distribute outline maps of Europe. Tell students that Europe can be divided into four subregions or smaller regions: northern Europe, western Europe (Europe's heartland), southern Europe, and eastern Europe. Have students work in pairs or small groups and use the chapters in this unit to identify the countries in each subregion. Have them color code each subregion and then label each country within each subregion. **BL**

Comparing and Contrasting After students have completed the activity above, assign each pair or group two subregions of Europe. Have students compare their color-coded map of Europe with the physical features map in the Regional Atlas and create a Venn diagram that lists the similarities and differences of the physical features in the two subregions. **OL**

Map Skills

Answers:

1. the United Kingdom and Ireland
2. the Rhine and Elbe rivers

Background: Current Issues

A Changing Population Europe is home to many different ethnic groups, or people with shared customs and language. Recent immigration to many European countries is contributing to the ethnic diversity. The region has become home to many people from Asia, Africa, and Latin America. In addition, many people from eastern Europe are moving to western Europe in search of better economic opportunities.

Although immigration is on the rise, the population of Europe is declining, because Europeans are having fewer children. Europe is expected to have 10 percent fewer people by 2050. In addition, a greater share of the population will be older people, as people are living longer due to better health care. Many Europeans are concerned about these trends because there will be fewer Europeans of working age to keep Europe's economy growing.

Regional Atlas Activity

Organizing Information Explain to students that they will organize the cities shown on the population density map from most populous to least populous. **Ask: What is the first step?** *(Group cities into three categories: over 5,000,000, 2,000,000–5,000,000, and 1,250,000–2,000,000.)* Tell students to list the cities that belong in each category. **Ask: What do you think is the next step?** Direct groups of four students to online or other reference sources to find the exact populations of each city. Each student in a group should research 10 or 11 of the 41 cities. Once the research has been completed, have student volunteers take turns coming to the board to list the cities from most populous to least populous. **OL**

Map Skills

Answers:

1. the central part of Europe, from The Netherlands to Italy, and the United Kingdom
2. because of its cold climate and rugged terrain

Skills Practice

Ask: Which southern European country is the least densely populated? *(Spain)* **Which city in eastern Europe has the largest population?** *(Kyiv)*

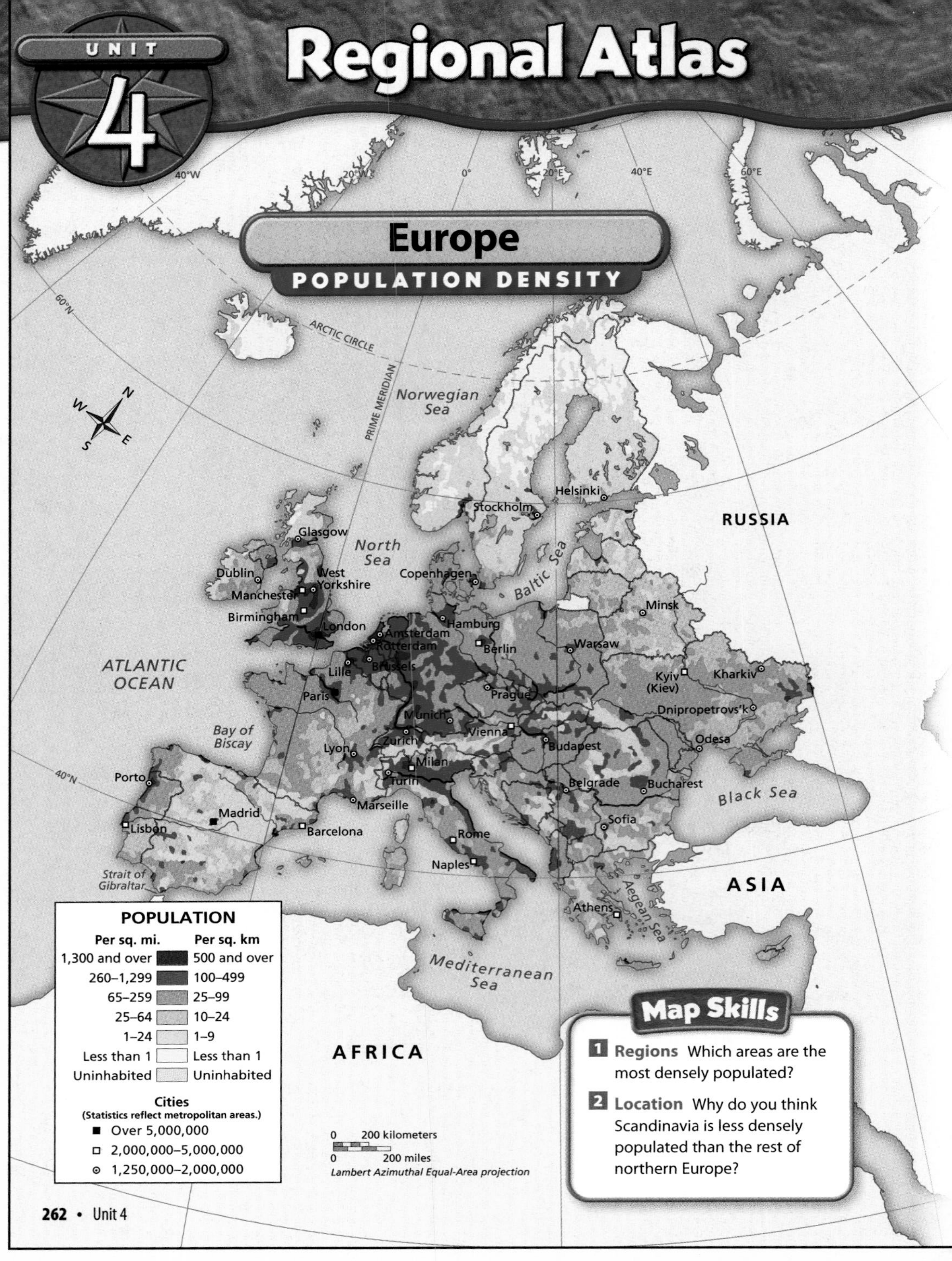

Background: People and Culture

Unity Amid Diversity National borders in Europe have changed many times over the centuries, often with little regard for the ethnic groups affected by the borders. As a result, many Europeans identify more strongly with their ethnic group than with their nation. These ethnic loyalties have often led to conflict in the region. Recently, however, Europeans have begun to share a growing sense of regional unity despite their differences. Many Europeans realize that cooperation, rather than deepening divisions, will help bring peace and prosperity to the region. Most Europeans value democracy and human rights and believe that the government should help those who cannot support themselves. These shared values transcend ethnic and national divisions.

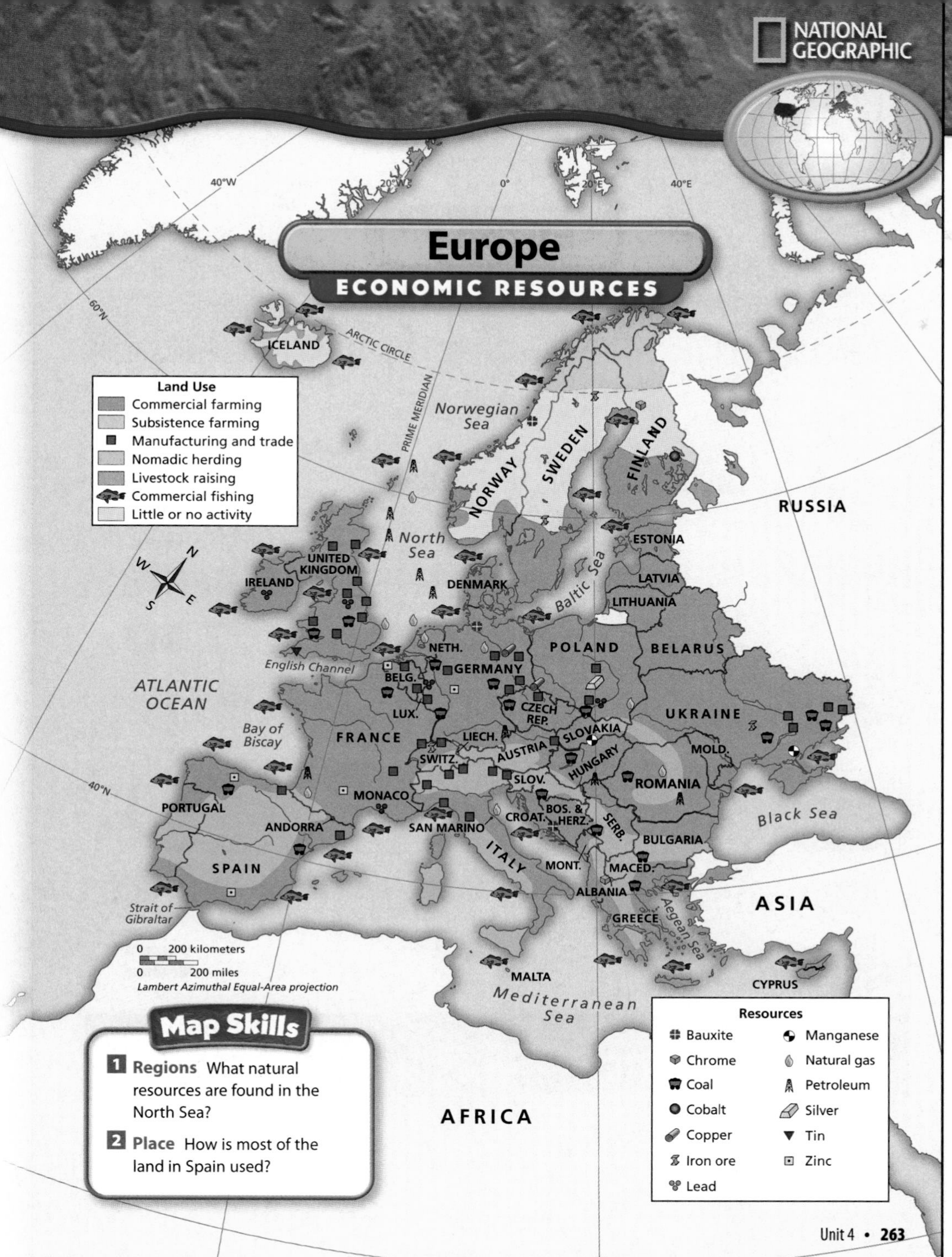

Map Skills

1. **Regions** What natural resources are found in the North Sea?
2. **Place** How is most of the land in Spain used?

Unit 4 • **263**

Unit 4 Regional Atlas

Regional Atlas Activity

Drawing Conclusions Help students understand the relationship between land use and population patterns by comparing the Economic Resources and Population Density maps in the Regional Atlas. **Ask:** **Where is land used primarily for subsistence farming?** *(much of Spain and Portugal; the west coast of Italy; a large area stretching from Switzerland and northern Italy to Bulgaria and Greece; and an arc from Slovakia through Ukraine and into Romania)* **What do you notice about population density in those areas?** *(It tends to be lower than in other areas.)* **Where is land put to little or no use?** *(Norway, Sweden, FInland, and Iceland)* **What do you notice about population densities in those areas?** *(It is low.)* **How is land used throughout most of the rest of Europe?** *(for commercial farming)* **What do you notice about population density in those areas?** *(It is higher than in other areas.)* Ask students to state a conclusion about the relationship between land use and population density in a complete sentence and share their conclusions. **OL**

Map Skills

Answers:

1. petroleum, natural gas, and fish
2. for subsistence farming

Background: The Economy

Economic Differences Many nations in Europe have strong economies, although the differences between eastern Europe and the rest of the region are profound. Northern Europe is a major industrial and trading region, although service industries are also strong. Agriculture is still important in certain countries, such as Ireland. Europe's heartland relies on both agriculture and manufacturing. France, for example, has many high-tech industries, but also produces wine and cheese and has a thriving tourism industry. Southern Europe depends on agriculture, tourism, and manufacturing.

In contrast, eastern Europe is struggling after decades of Communist rule. While some countries, like Belarus, still have command economies, others have moved toward free market economies. These changes initially created hardships for many people, but most economies in eastern Europe have improved in recent years. Countries that are still highly agricultural, however, have had slow economic growth.

Regional Atlas Activity

Locating Play the following game to help students remember national capitals. Organize students into teams of four or five. Give clues about national capitals, such as: "This is the capital of Bulgaria." Call on the first student who raises a hand. Instruct students to phrase their answer in the form of a question, such as: "What is Sofia?" Allow teams to use the Regional Atlas, if necessary, to find answers. Give teams five points for each correct answer; subtract three points for each incorrect answer. The team with the most points wins. **BL**

Identifying **Ask:** **What countries in Europe have more than one official language?** *(Belgium, Finland, Ireland, Luxembourg, Malta, Montenegro, Switzerland, and Vatican City)* **Why might a country need to have more than one official language?** *(Possible answer: because ethnic groups in the country speak different languages)* **OL**

UNIT 4

Regional Atlas

Europe

Country and Capital	Literacy Rate	Population and Density	Land Area	Life Expectancy (Years)	GDP* Per Capita (U.S. dollars)	Television Sets (per 1,000 people)	Flag and Language
Tiranë, ALBANIA	86.5%	3,200,000 286 per sq. mi. 111 per sq. km	11,100 sq. mi. 28,749 sq. km	74	$4,900	146	Albanian
ANDORRA, Andorra la Vella	100%	100,000 426 per sq. mi. 222 per sq. km	174 sq. mi. 451 sq. km	—	$26,800	440	Catalan
Vienna, AUSTRIA	98%	8,200,000 252 per sq. mi. 98 per sq. km	32,378 sq. mi. 83,859 sq. km	79	$31,300	526	German
Minsk, BELARUS	99.6%	9,800,000 122 per sq. mi. 47 per sq. km	80,154 sq. mi. 207,598 sq. km	69	$6,800	331	Belarusian
Brussels, BELGIUM	98%	10,500,000 887 per sq. mi. 344 per sq. km	11,787 sq. mi. 30,528 sq. km	79	$30,600	532	Dutch, French, German
BOSNIA AND HERZEGOVINA, Sarajevo	—	3,800,000 195 per sq. mi. 74 per sq. km	19,741 sq. mi. 51,129 sq. km	74	$6,500	112	Bosnian
BULGARIA, Sofia	98.6%	7,700,000 181 per sq. mi. 69 per sq. km	42,822 sq. mi. 110,908 sq. km	72	$8,200	429	Bulgarian
Zagreb, CROATIA	98.5%	4,400,000 203 per sq. mi. 78 per sq. km	21,830 sq. mi. 56,539 sq. km	75	$11,200	286	Croatian
UNITED STATES, Washington, D.C.	97%	296,500,000 80 per sq. mi. 31 per sq. km	3,717,796 sq. mi. 9,629,047 sq. km	78	$40,100	844	English

*Gross Domestic Product

Countries and flags not drawn to scale

Activity: Using the Chart

Evaluating Have students examine the country profile data and choose three countries where they think they might like to live. Have them write a statement about each country in this form: "I would like to live in Austria because…" **Ask:** **What more would you like to know about these countries in order to decide which country you would most like to live in?** Tell students to make a list of questions and direct them to appropriate reference materials—including encyclopedias, world almanacs, atlases, and reliable online news and information sources—to find answers to their questions. Have students write their notes on index cards. When they have finished their research, students should write a one-page composition about one European country and why they think they would like to live there. **OL**

Europe

Country and Capital	Literacy Rate	Population and Density	Land Area	Life Expectancy (Years)	GDP* Per Capita (U.S. dollars)	Television Sets (per 1,000 people)	Flag and Language
CYPRUS, Nicosia	97.6%	1,000,000 270 per sq. mi. 108 per sq. km	3,571 sq. mi. 9,249 sq. km	77	$20,300	154	Greek
CZECH REPUBLIC, Prague	99.9%	10,200,000 335 per sq. mi. 129 per sq. km	30,448 sq. mi. 78,860 sq. km	75	$16,800	487	Czech
DENMARK, Copenhagen	100%	5,400,000 326 per sq. mi. 125 per sq. km	16,637 sq. mi. 43,090 sq. km	77	$32,200	776	Danish
ESTONIA, Tallinn	99.8%	1,300,000 77 per sq. mi. 29 per sq. km	17,413 sq. mi. 45,099 sq. km	72	$14,300	567	Estonian
FINLAND, Helsinki	100%	5,200,000 40 per sq. mi. 15 per sq. km	130,560 sq. mi. 338,149 sq. km	79	$29,000	643	Finnish, Swedish
FRANCE, Paris	99%	60,700,000 285 per sq. mi. 110 per sq. km	212,934 sq. mi. 551,497 sq. km	80	$28,700	620	French
GERMANY, Berlin	99%	82,500,000 598 per sq. mi. 231 per sq. km	137,830 sq. mi. 356,978 sq. km	79	$28,700	581	German
GREECE, Athens	97.5%	11,100,000 218 per sq. mi. 84 per sq. km	50,950 sq. mi. 131,960 sq. km	76	$21,300	480	Greek
UNITED STATES, Washington, D.C.	97%	296,500,000 80 per sq. mi. 31 per sq. km	3,717,796 sq. mi. 9,629,047 sq. km	78	$40,100	844	English

Sources: *CIA World Factbook*, 2005; Population Reference Bureau, *World Population Data Sheet*, 2005.

For more country facts, go to the **Nations of the World Databank** at glencoe.com.

Regional Atlas Activity

Synthesizing Information Write the names of the countries in Europe on slips of paper, and put them in a hat. Randomly assign each student three countries by having them pick three slips of paper from the hat. Then have them study the Regional Atlas maps, as well as the information given in the charts, to find facts about their countries.

After students have studied the maps and charts, have them write six "I" statements for each of their countries. (Examples: "I have a population density that is among the highest in Europe" and "My literacy rate is higher than that of the United States.") Students should base at least two statements on Regional Atlas maps and at least two statements on chart information. Call on students to share the statements they wrote about each country, one at a time, until another student correctly identifies the country. **ELL**

FastFacts

Traveling in France France has one of the most efficient, on time, speedy, and comfortable train systems in the world. The TGV (high speed train) travels at a speed of more than 200 miles (322 km) per hour.

Activity: Using the Chart

Comparing and Contrasting Assign each student a country in Europe, randomly or based on student interest. **Ask: What information do you need in order to compare your country to the United States?** *(Students might mention comparing information given on the chart or information given in the Regional Atlas.)* Instruct students to create a Venn diagram that compares their country to the United States. **Ask: What other information might you use to compare and contrast European countries with the United States?** Have students make a list of at least five factors, not shown on the charts, that they might consider. *(Examples: percentage of young people who attend college, miles of railroad track, percentage of people who live in cities, etc.)* Then direct students to appropriate reference sources—including atlases, encyclopedias, and reliable online news and information services—to research the factors they have identified. Tell them to add information to their Venn diagrams as appropriate. Have students post their diagrams around a map of the region and use string to connect their diagrams to the country that is the subject of the diagram. **AL**

Regional Atlas Activity

Evaluating Ask: What three countries have the highest GDP per capita? *(Luxembourg, Norway, San Marino)* **What three countries have the lowest GDP per capita?** *(Moldova, Montenegro, Serbia)*

Have students turn to the Economic Resources map in the Regional Atlas. **Ask: Based on this map, what economic activities take place in Norway, San Marino, and Luxembourg?** *(Norway: petroleum in the North Sea; San Marino: commercial agriculture; Luxembourg: commercial agriculture)* **What economic activities take place in Moldova, Montenegro, and Serbia?** *(Moldova: commercial agriculture; Montenegro: commercial agriculture; Serbia: subsistence and commercial agriculture)*

Ask: Is the information on the Economic Resources map enough to explain the differences between the GDP per capita in these nations? *(probably not)* Remind students that *per capita* means *per person,* so the population of a country may also be a factor. Then organize students into six groups, and assign each group one of these countries. Direct them to appropriate research materials to find more information about the economies and recent histories of these nations. Have each group prepare a two-to-three minute summary of the information from their research that might explain the low or high GDP per capita in their country. **OL**

Regional Atlas

Europe

Country and Capital	Literacy Rate	Population and Density	Land Area	Life Expectancy (Years)	GDP* Per Capita (U.S. dollars)	Television Sets (per 1,000 people)	Flag and Language
HUNGARY Budapest	99.4%	10,100,000 281 per sq. mi. 109 per sq. km	35,919 sq. mi. 93,030 sq. km	68	$14,900	447	Hungarian
ICELAND Reykjavík	99.9%	300,000 8 per sq. mi. 3 per sq. km	39,768 sq. mi. 102,999 sq. km	81	$31,900	505	Icelandic
IRELAND Dublin	98%	4,100,000 151 per sq. mi. 58 per sq. km	27,135 sq. mi. 70,279 sq. km	78	$31,900	406	English, Irish
ITALY Rome	98.6%	58,700,000 505 per sq. mi. 195 per sq. km	116,320 sq. mi. 301,267 sq. km	77	$27,700	492	Italian
LATVIA Riga	99.8%	2,300,000 92 per sq. mi. 36 per sq. km	24,942 sq. mi. 64,599 sq. km	72	$11,500	757	Latvian
LIECHTENSTEIN Vaduz	100%	40,000 645 per sq. mi. 248 per sq. km	62 sq. mi. 161 sq. km	80	$25,000	469	German
LITHUANIA Vilnius	99.6%	3,400,000 135 per sq. mi. 52 per sq. km	25,174 sq. mi. 65,200 sq. km	72	$12,500	422	Lithuanian
LUXEMBOURG Luxembourg	100%	500,000 501 per sq. mi. 193 per sq. km	999 sq. mi. 2,587 sq. km	78	$58,900	599	Luxembourgish, German, French
UNITED STATES Washington, D.C.	97%	296,500,000 80 per sq. mi. 31 per sq. km	3,717,796 sq. mi. 9,629,047 sq. km	78	$40,100	844	English

*Gross Domestic Product

Countries and flags not drawn to scale

Activity: Using the Chart

Assessing Geographic Patterns Explain that the chart gives information about each country, but that it is difficult to tell if there are any geographic patterns in the information. Give each student an outline map of Europe. **Ask: How might we use these outline maps to find out if there are any geographic patterns in GDP per capita?** After discussing this question, ask students to first categorize GDP per capita. *(for example, $0–$10,000, $10,000–$20,000, etc.—but let students decide what categories to use)* Then have them create a color-coded legend to distinguish the GDP per capita categories. Tell students to color each country on the map appropriately, based on the map legend and the information in the chart. When students have completed their maps, ask them to make a conclusion about geographic patterns in GDP per capita based on their maps. Then, have them write the conclusion at the bottom of the map. Ask volunteers to share their maps and conclusions with the class. **AL**

Europe

Country and Capital	Literacy Rate	Population and Density	Land Area	Life Expectancy (Years)	GDP* Per Capita (U.S. dollars)	Television Sets (per 1,000 people)	Flag and Language
Skopje MACEDONIA	—	2,000,000 201 per sq. mi. 78 per sq. km	9,927 sq. mi. 25,711 sq. km	71	$7,100	273	Macedonian
MALTA Valletta	92.8%	400,000 3,278 per sq. mi. 1,246 per sq. km	124 sq. mi. 321 sq. km	79	$18,200	549	Maltese, English
MOLDOVA Chişinău	99.1%	4,200,000 323 per sq. mi. 125 per sq. km	13,012 sq. mi. 33,701 sq. km	65	$1,900	297	Moldovan
MONACO Monaco	99%	30,000 30,000 per sq. mi. 11,538 per sq. km	1 sq. mi. 2.6 sq. km	—	$27,000	758	French
MONTENEGRO Podgorica	97%	650,000 122 per sq. mi. 47 per sq. km	5,333 sq. mi. 13,812 sq. km	73	$2,200	277	Montenegrin, Serbian, Albanian
Amsterdam NETHERLANDS	99%	16,400,000 1,023 per sq. mi. 395 per sq. km	13,082 sq. mi. 33,883 sq. km	79	$29,500	540	Dutch
NORWAY Oslo	100%	4,600,000 37 per sq. mi. 14 per sq. km	125,050 sq. mi. 323,878 sq. km	80	$40,000	653	Norwegian
Warsaw POLAND	99.8%	38,200,000 306 per sq. mi. 118 per sq. km	124,807 sq. mi. 323,249 sq. km	71	$12,000	387	Polish
UNITED STATES Washington, D.C.	97%	296,500,000 80 per sq. mi. 31 per sq. km	3,717,796 sq. mi. 9,629,047 sq. km	78	$40,100	844	English

Sources: *CIA World Factbook*, 2005; Population Reference Bureau, *World Population Data Sheet*, 2005.

For more country facts, go to the **Nations of the World Databank** at glencoe.com.

Regional Atlas Activity

Comparing Have students compare the population, population density, and land area of Norway and Poland as shown on the chart on page 268. **Ask: What is the land area of each country?** *(Norway: 125,050 sq. mi.; Poland: 124,807 sq. mi.)* **What is the population of each country?** *(Norway: 4.6 million; Poland: 38.2 million)* **Which country has a higher population density?** *(Poland—306 per sq. mi. (118 per sq. km) vs. Norway—37 per sq. mi. (14 per sq. km))*

Next, have students compare the population, population density, and land area of Sweden and Spain. **Ask: What is the land area of each country?** *(Sweden: 173,730 sq. mi. (449,959 sq. km); Spain: 193,363 sq. mi. (500,808 sq. km))* **What is the population of each country?** *(Sweden: 9 million; Spain: 43.5 million)* **Which country has a higher population density?** *(Spain—225 per sq. mi. (87 per sq. km) vs. Sweden—52 per sq. mi. (20 per sq. km))*

Have students turn to the population density map in the Regional Atlas. **Ask: What additional information about population density in these four countries does the map provide?** *(Possible answer: Spain has large areas of land where the population density is comparable to the low population density in the Scandinavian countries, even though its overall population density is greater than that of the Scandinavian countries.)* **OL**

Activity: Using the Chart

Researching Information Have students examine the country profile data. **Ask: What other kinds of information would you like to see included in the chart?** After a class discussion, have pairs of students choose one piece of information to research further. Examples might include fertility rate, annual immigration statistics, percentage of homes with Internet access, etc. Direct students to appropriate reference materials—including encyclopedias, world almanacs, atlases, and reliable online news and information sources—to find the additional information about each European country. Have students work together to create a chart for a bulletin board display that includes the new information that all of the pairs have gathered. **OL**

Regional Atlas Activity

Drawing Conclusions Organize students into small groups. Instruct them to look over the charts and discuss the standard of living in the countries of the region. Ask them to consider the following questions: *Which country has the highest standard of living? Which country has the lowest standard of living?* Tell the groups to discuss these questions, come to a consensus, and be prepared to explain their answers to the class. When groups have finished their discussions, call on one group to explain which country they think has the highest standard of living and which categories from the chart they used to make their decision. Ask other groups if they agree or disagree and to explain their positions. Try to discuss the question until the class has come to a consensus. Use the same format to discuss which country probably has the lowest standard of living.

If the class cannot come to a consensus, brainstorm what other information they might need to consider in order to assess standard of living and assign a research task to each group. When groups have completed their research, discuss the groups' findings as a class. **OL**

Regional Atlas

Europe

Country and Capital	Literacy Rate	Population and Density	Land Area	Life Expectancy (Years)	GDP* Per Capita (U.S. dollars)	Television Sets (per 1,000 people)	Flag and Language
PORTUGAL Lisbon	93%	10,600,000 298 per sq. mi. 115 per sq. km	35,502 sq. mi. 91,951 sq. km	78	$17,900	567	Portuguese
ROMANIA Bucharest	98.4%	21,600,000 235 per sq. mi. 91 per sq. km	92,042 sq. mi. 238,388 sq. km	68	$7,700	312	Romanian
SAN MARINO San Marino	96%	30,000 1,304 per sq. mi. 500 per sq. km	23 sq. mi. 60 sq. km	81	$34,600	875	Italian
SERBIA Belgrade	96%	10,100,000 272 per sq. mi. 114 per sq. km	34,107 sq. mi. 88,337 sq. km	74	$2,200	277	Serbian
SLOVAKIA Bratislava	—	5,400,000 285 per sq. mi. 110 per sq. km	18,923 sq. mi. 49,010 sq. km	70	$14,500	418	Slovak
SLOVENIA Ljubljana	99.7%	2,000,000 256 per sq. mi. 99 per sq. km	7,819 sq. mi. 20,251 sq. km	77	$19,600	362	Slovenian
SPAIN Madrid	97.9%	43,500,000 225 per sq. mi. 87 per sq. km	193,363 sq. mi. 500,808 sq. km	80	$23,300	555	Spanish
SWEDEN Stockholm	99%	9,000,000 52 per sq. mi. 20 per sq. km	173,730 sq. mi. 449,959 sq. km	81	$28,400	551	Swedish
UNITED STATES Washington, D.C.	97%	296,500,000 80 per sq. mi. 31 per sq. km	3,717,796 sq. mi. 9,629,047 sq. km	78	$40,100	844	English

*Gross Domestic Product

Countries and flags not drawn to scale

Activity: Using the Chart

Theorizing Ask: Do you think literacy rate is related to any of the other factors given on the chart? Which ones? *(Students may answer that literacy rate may be affected by GDP per capita or that it may affect life expectancy.)* Instruct students, either individually or in small groups, to choose five countries from the chart. Have them use a spreadsheet program to create double-bar graphs that show the literacy rate and another factor from the chart, side by side, for each country. **Ask: Do you see any relationship between literacy rate and the other factor?** If students see a relationship, have them theorize what the cause of the relationship might be. *(For example, a higher literacy rate and a higher life expectancy might be related; perhaps the higher literacy rate causes people to be better informed about health and health care, leading to a higher life expectancy.)* **AL**

Europe

Country and Capital	Literacy Rate	Population and Density	Land Area	Life Expectancy (Years)	GDP* Per Capita (U.S. dollars)	Television Sets (per 1,000 people)	Flag and Language
Bern SWITZERLAND	96%	7,400,000 464 per sq. mi. 179 per sq. km	15,942 sq. mi. 41,290 sq. km	80	$33,800	457	German, French, Italian
Kyiv (Kiev) UKRAINE	93%	47,100,000 202 per sq. mi. 70 per sq. km	233,089 sq. mi. 603,698 sq. km	63	$6,300	433	Ukrainian
UNITED KINGDOM London	—	60,100,000 636 per sq. mi. 245 per sq. km	94,548 sq. mi. 244,878 sq. km	78	$29,600	661	English
VATICAN CITY	99.7%	1,000 1,000 per sq. mi. 385 per sq. km	1 sq. mi. 2.6 sq. km	—	—	—	Italian, Latin
UNITED STATES Washington, D.C.	97%	296,500,000 80 per sq. mi. 31 per sq. km	3,717,796 sq. mi. 9,629,047 sq. km	78	$40,100	844	English

Sources: *CIA World Factbook*, 2005; Population Reference Bureau, *World Population Data Sheet*, 2005.

For more country facts, go to the **Nations of the World Databank** at glencoe.com.

L'Arc de Triomphe, Paris, France

More About the Photo

Visual Literacy L'Arc de Triomphe (Triumphal Arch) was commissioned by Napoleon I in 1806. It is the national war memorial of France. The arch commemorates the military victories of Napoleon and subsequent military victories and treaties. France's Tomb of the Unknown Soldier lies beneath it. Four sculptures at the base of the arch's four pillars commemorate the Triumph of 1810, Resistance, Peace, and the Departure of the Volunteers. At the top of the arch, the names of major victories during the Revolutionary and Napoleonic periods are engraved. The names of less important victories are engraved on the inside walls. Visitors who venture to the top of the Arc de Triomphe are treated to spectacular views of Paris, some 164 feet (50 m) high.

Regional Atlas Activity

Analyzing Ask: What country in Europe has the largest land area? *(Ukraine)* **The smallest land area?** *(Vatican City and Monaco)* **Why are Vatican City and Monaco such small countries?** *(Both countries consist of a single city.)* **OL**

FastFacts

Swiss Environmentalism

Switzerland is a small, landlocked country with few natural resources but a breathtaking natural beauty that draws many tourists. For this reason, the Swiss are committed to protecting the environment, and the country is among the "greenest" in the industrialized world. The Swiss, for example, recycle half of their household waste, and their annual garbage production per person is half that of Americans.

Reading Social Studies

Making Inferences

Why Making Inferences Is Important

Making inferences means interpreting information to find ideas that the author has not stated directly. This skill requires students to read to find both statements of fact and the author's ideas. Then students must put those facts and ideas together to decide what else must be true. This is sometimes referred to as "reading between the lines." Making inferences requires students to understand what they read and to think about it critically.

1 Learn It!

Use the following activity to teach students about making inferences. Write "Jane is crying" on the board. **Ask:** **What can you infer from this statement?** *(Students may answer that Jane has been hurt or is upset.)* After discussing this question, write this statement on the board: "Jane only cries when she cuts onions." **Ask:** **What inference can you make now?** *(Jane is cutting onions.)* Explain that students could not make a valid inference from the first statement without more information. With the second piece of information, they can make a valid inference. **OL**

Reading Skill

1 Learn It!

It is impossible for authors to write every detail about a topic in a textbook. Because of this, good readers must make inferences to help them understand what they are reading. To infer means to evaluate information and form a conclusion.

- Read the paragraph below.
- Think about what you already know about the topic.
- Then, look for clues that might explain what is happening in the passage even though it might not be stated.
- What inference can you make about Napoleon's skill as a military leader?

Clues

> A brilliant military leader named Napoleon Bonaparte gained power and made himself emperor. Napoleon was a small man with big ambitions. His armies conquered much of Europe, until several countries united to defeat him in 1815.
>
> —*from page 301*

Use the diagram below to help you make an inference about Napoleon's skill as a military leader.

What you already know:
What traits must brilliant military leaders have?

Clues in the text:
- Napoleon was able to gain power and lead armies to conquer much of Europe.
- The word *several* hints that it took many European countries to defeat him.

Inference:
Napoleon must have been a skillful military leader.

Reading Tip

Making inferences is an everyday part of life. For example, if you look at the sky and see dark clouds, you may infer that it is going to rain. As you read, use the facts in the text to make inferences by thinking beyond the words on the page.

Reading Strategy: Organizing Information

Making Inferences Explain to students that one way to make inferences is to pull statements from a text and think about what else they can conclude from each of these statements. Have students create a chart with three columns and three rows. Ask them to read one section of the text. In the first row of the chart, have them list three statements of fact from that section one statement in each column. In the second row, have them list something they already know that is related to each of the statements in the row above. Finally, have them draw one inference from each of these statements and write these inferences in the third row. When the chart is done, tell students to examine all three inferences and draw a conclusion about the entire section of text. **OL**

2 Practice It!

Read the following paragraph from this unit.

- Draw a diagram like the one shown below.
- Write what you know about the United Kingdom's constitutional monarchy, along with facts from the text.
- Make an inference about the power of the king or queen in the United Kingdom.

> The government of the United Kingdom is a constitutional monarchy. A king or queen serves as head of state and takes part in ceremonies, but elected officials actively run the government.
>
> *—from page 322*

What you already know:

Clues in the text:

Inference:

Read to Write Activity

In Chapter 11, Section 1, read the paragraphs titled "Industry and Conflict." Then take notes about the Industrial Revolution. Write a statement in which you make an inference about what life was like for a teenager during the Industrial Revolution.

Queen Elizabeth II of the United Kingdom and members of the royal family

3 Apply It!

For each chapter in this unit choose a topic, and create a diagram like the one above. Write related information that you already know, along with facts from the text, in the diagrams. Make inferences using this information. Read your facts to a partner, and ask your partner to make inferences from them. Are your inferences the same?

2 Practice It!

Students may place the following facts in the Clues in the text box:

- The government of the United Kingdom is a constitutional monarchy; a constitution restricts the power of the monarchy.
- The king or queen serves as head of state and takes part in ceremonies.
- Elected officials actively run the government.

Students may make an inference that elected officials have more power in a constitutional monarchy than kings or queens. **OL**

3 Apply It!

Students' inferences will vary, depending upon the topics and text students choose. Example: Students may choose to read a paragraph that discusses the islands of Europe. Facts from the text may include: *Europe includes thousands of islands. Some of the major islands are in the Atlantic Ocean. Other islands are in the Mediterranean Sea.* From these facts, students may make a statement inferring that many people who live in Europe live near water, or they may infer that Europeans travel over bridges or by air to get to a neighboring country. **OL**

Reading Strategy — Read to Write

Organizing a Paragraph When making inferences in a paper or an essay, students should restate the facts, opinions, and outside knowledge that led to that inference. Ask students to use the chart they developed in the Reading Strategy activity on the previous page. Tell them to use their conclusion sentence as the thesis sentence for a paragraph. Then have them summarize the statements of fact, in their own words, in two or three sentences. Next, have them restate the inferences they drew from these facts. Have them write a final sentence that ties the facts and inferences to their conclusion. **AL**

Planning Guide

Key to Ability Levels

BL Below level
OL On level
AL Above level
ELL English Language Learners

Key to Teaching Resources

Print Material
DVD
CD-ROM
Transparency

Levels				Resources	Chapter Opener	Section 1	Section 2	Chapter Assess
BL	OL	AL	ELL					
				FOCUS				
BL	OL	AL	ELL	Daily Focus Skills Transparencies		10-1	10-2	
				TEACH				
BL	OL		ELL	Guided Reading Activity, URB*		p. 37	p. 38	
BL	OL	AL	ELL	Content Vocabulary Activity, URB*		p. 39	p. 39	
BL	OL	AL	ELL	Academic Vocabulary Activity, URB		p. 41	p. 41	
BL	OL	AL	ELL	Differentiated Instruction Activity, URB		p. 43		
BL	OL	AL	ELL	Chart, Graph, and Map Skills Activity, URB			p. 45	
	OL	AL		Critical Thinking Activity, URB		p. 47		
BL	OL	AL	ELL	Speaking and Listening Skills Activity, URB			p. 49	
BL	OL	AL	ELL	Writing Skills Activity, URB			p. 53	
BL	OL	AL	ELL	School-to-Home Connection Activity, URB*		p. 57	p. 57	
BL	OL	AL	ELL	Regional Atlas Activities, URB		pp. 1–7	pp. 1–7	
BL	OL	AL	ELL	GeoLab Activity, URB		p. 23		
BL	OL		ELL	Reading Skills Activity, URB		p. 25	p. 25	
BL	OL	AL	ELL	Primary Source Readings, URB				
	OL	AL		World Literature Readings, URB			p. 31	
BL	OL		ELL	Reading Essentials and Note-Taking Guide*		p. 67	p. 70	
	OL			Interactive Geography Activity		p. 25		
BL	OL	AL	ELL	In-Text Map Overlay and Population Pyramid Transparencies	4	4B, 4D	4C–4F	
BL	OL	AL	ELL	Outline Map Resource Book	p. 36	p. 36		
BL	OL	AL	ELL	NGS World Atlas*	✓	✓	✓	
BL	OL	AL	ELL	NGS World Desk Map	✓	✓	✓	✓
BL	OL	AL	ELL	World Literature Library	✓	✓	✓	✓
BL	OL	AL	ELL	Writer's Guidebook	✓	✓	✓	✓
BL	OL	AL	ELL	Vocabulary PuzzleMaker CD-ROM*	✓	✓	✓	✓

Note: Please refer to the *Unit Resource Book: Europe* for this chapter's URB materials.

* Also available in Spanish

- Interactive Lesson Planner
- Interactive Teacher Edition
- Fully editable blackline masters
- Section Spotlight Videos Launch
- Differentiated Lesson Plans
- Printable reports of daily assignments
- Standards Tracking System

Levels BL	OL	AL	ELL	Resources	Chapter Opener	Section 1	Section 2	Chapter Assess
				TEACH *(continued)*				
	OL	AL		Primary Sources CD-ROM	✓	✓	✓	✓
BL	OL	AL	ELL	StudentWorks™ Plus DVD	✓	✓	✓	✓
BL	OL	AL	ELL	Section Video Program Activities	✓	✓	✓	✓
BL	OL	AL	ELL	World Music: A Cultural Legacy	✓	✓	✓	✓
BL	OL	AL	ELL	Writing Process Transparencies	✓	✓	✓	✓
Teacher Resources				Building Academic Vocabulary	✓	✓	✓	✓
				Strategies for Success	✓	✓	✓	✓
				Teacher's Guide to Differentiated Instruction	✓	✓	✓	✓
				Presentation Plus! DVD	✓	✓	✓	✓
				ASSESS				
BL	OL	AL	ELL	Quizzes and Tests		p. 111	p. 112	p. 113
BL	OL	AL	ELL	Authentic Assessment With Rubrics		p. 10		p. 10
BL	OL	AL	ELL	Standardized Test Practice				p. 37
BL	OL	AL	ELL	*ExamView® Assessment Suite* CD-ROM*		10-1	10-2	Ch. 10
BL	OL	AL	ELL	Interactive Tutor Self-Assessment CD-ROM		10-1	10-2	
				CLOSE				
BL			ELL	Reteaching Activity, URB*		p. 55	p. 55	p. 55
BL	OL		ELL	Reading and Study Skills Foldables™	p. 68	p. 68	p. 68	p. 68
BL	OL	AL	ELL	Graphic Organizer Transparencies and Strategies		✓	✓	
BL	OL	AL	ELL	*Exploring Our World* in Graphic Novel				pp. 41, 49

Integrating Technology

Research Using *Famous Person*

Technology Product

CyberScout is a convenient and dynamic search engine that provides several easy ways to locate information outside the McGraw-Hill Learning Network. CyberScout only searches Web sites that have been reviewed by teachers, so the information students find is always appropriate and accurate.

Objectives

After students learn to use CyberScout, they will be able to

- research famous people in geography;
- exercise research and study skills;
- practice writing skills.

Steps

- From the McGraw-Hill Learning Network home page (www.mhln.com), click on **For Student.**
- Choose **CyberScout** below **Homework Help.**
- Enter a name (last, or first and last) in the **Famous Person** field and click **Go.**
- The CyberScout page will display a set of results.
- Select the Famous Person's name from the results.
- Click the link to a Web site of interest.
- Students will be redirected to the Web site in a new window.
- Students navigate through the chosen Web site to gain information on their topic and take notes.

Social Studies ONLINE

	Student	Teacher	Parent
Beyond the Textbook	●		●
Chapter Overviews	●		●
Concepts in Motion	●		●
ePuzzles and Games	●		●
Literature Connections		●	
Multi-Language Glossaries	●		●
Online Student Edition	●	●	●
Section Videos	●	●	●
Self-Check Quizzes	●		●
Student Web Activities	●		●
Study Central™	●		●
TIME Current Events	●		●
Teaching Today		●	
Vocabulary eFlashcards	●		●
Web Activity Lesson Plans		●	

- **Timed Readings Plus in Social Studies** helps students increase their reading rate and fluency while maintaining comprehension. The 400-word passages are similar to those found on state and national assessments.
- **Reading in the Content Area: Social Studies** concentrates on six essential reading skills that help students better comprehend what they read. The book includes 75 high-interest nonfiction passages written at increasing levels of difficulty.
- **Reading Social Studies** includes strategic reading instruction and vocabulary support in Social Studies content for ELLs and native speakers of English.
- **Content Vocabulary Workout** (Grades 6–8) accelerates reading comprehension through focused vocabulary development. Social Studies content vocabulary comes from the glossaries of Glencoe's Middle School Social Studies texts. www.jamestowneducation.com

Index to National Geographic Magazine:

The following articles relate to this chapter:

- "The Alps From End to End," by Alex Crevar, September 2006.
- "Running the Marathon," by Lisa Moore LaRoe, August 2004.

National Geographic Society Products To order the following, call National Geographic at 1-800-368-2728:

- *National Geographic Atlas of the World* (Book).

Access National Geographic's new dynamic MapMachine Web site and other geography resources at:
www.nationalgeographic.com
www.nationalgeographic.com/maps

Biography  

The following videotape programs are available from Glencoe as supplements to Chapter 10:

- Pompeii (ISBN 0-76-700537-6)
- Lost City of Atlantis (ISBN 0-76-700627-5)

To order, call Glencoe at 1-800-334-7344. To find classroom resources to accompany many of these videos, check the following home pages:

A&E Television: www.aetv.com
The History Channel: www.historychannel.com

GLENCOE BOOKLINK 3

Use this database to search more than 30,000 titles to create a customized reading list for your students.

- Reading lists can be organized by students' reading level, author, genre, theme, or area of interest.
- The database provides Degrees of Reading Power™ (DRP) and Lexile™ readability scores for all selections.
- A brief summary of each selection is included.

Leveled reading suggestions for this chapter:

For students at a Grade 5 reading level:
- ***France,*** by Ted Park

For students at a Grade 6 reading level:
- ***Ireland,*** by Ryan Patrick

For students at a Grade 7 reading level:
- ***Italy: The Land,*** by Greg Nickles

For students at a Grade 8 reading level:
- ***Germany: The Land,*** by Kathryn Lane

For students at a Grade 9 reading level:
- ***England: The Land,*** by Erinn Banting

Focus

The Essential Question

As students study the chapter, remind them to consider the chapter-based Essential Question. Answering this question will help them understand the important concepts in the chapter. In addition, the Hands-On Chapter Project relates the content from each section to the Essential Question. The steps in each section build on each other as students progress through the chapter. The Hands-On Chapter Project culminates in the Wrap Up activity on the Visual Summary page.

More About the Photo

Visual Literacy The bridges over the Vltava River, which flows through the city of Prague in the Czech Republic, include the Manes, Charles, Legii, and Jirasek. The Charles Bridge, built in the fourteenth century, is lined with statues and sculptures. Floods of the Vltava River have destroyed bridges in the past, but the Charles Bridge, which was reconstructed in 1970, remains intact. Each year, thousands of tourists cross the Charles Bridge during their visit to Prague's historic city center.

CHAPTER 10

Physical Geography of Europe

Essential Question

Regions Europe's landforms include high, snowcapped mountains and broad, fertile plains that are good for farming. Europe might be most influenced, however, by its nearness to water. A number of oceans and seas border Europe's countries. Europe also has many important rivers. How do people use waterways?

272 • Chapter 10

Teach

The BIG Ideas *As you begin teaching each section, use these questions and activities to help students focus on the Big Ideas.*

Section 

Physical Features Ask: What physical features might draw people to a region? Why? *(People might be drawn to plains for farming, to mountains for logging or mining, to seaside regions for fishing, or to mountains and beaches for recreational purposes.)* Point out to students that Section 1 describes the physical features of Europe, which include peninsulas, islands, plains, mountains, and highlands, as well as rivers, lakes, seas, and other waterways. This section also describes the rich natural resources that have helped make Europe an economic powerhouse and the environmental effects that industrial growth has had on the region. **OL**

Section 

Climate Regions Ask: How might climate affect the way people live? *(Warm climates make it possible for people to farm more of the year and allow for warm-weather activities, such as swimming and boating; cold climates may create challenges for agriculture but allow for cold-weather activities, such as skiing and sledding; climate also*

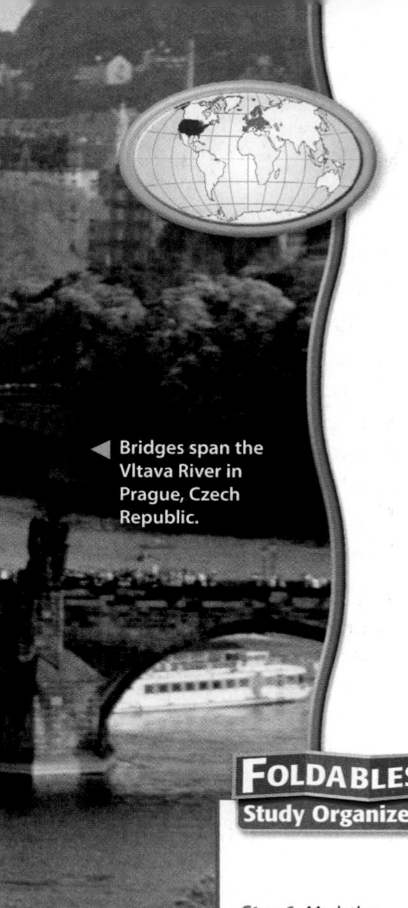

Bridges span the Vltava River in Prague, Czech Republic.

BIG Ideas

Section 1: Physical Features

BIG IDEA Geographic factors influence where people settle. Europe has a variety of landforms and plentiful natural resources that have attracted a large population. Most people live on Europe's plains, where industry and agriculture flourish. Such successes, however, have contributed to environmental problems in the region.

Section 2: Climate Regions

BIG IDEA The physical environment affects how people live. Although Europe is located relatively far north, much of the region has a mild climate that is ideal for farming and development. However, many Europeans are concerned that the climate is warming, which may have dangerous consequences.

FOLDABLES™ Study Organizer

Summarizing Information Make this Foldable to help you gather notes and summarize information about Europe's physical features, climate, and environmental issues.

Step 1 Mark the midpoint of the side edge of a sheet of paper.

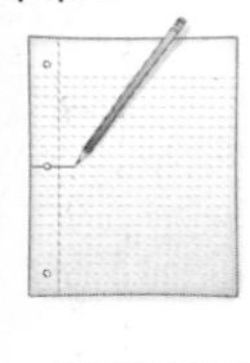

Step 2 Fold the top and bottom of the paper into the middle to make a shutter fold.

Step 3 Fold the paper in half from side to side.

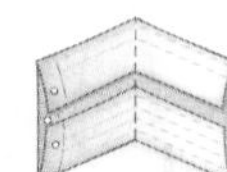

Step 4 Open and cut along the inside fold lines to form four tabs.

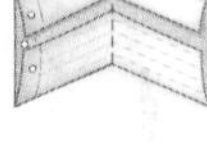

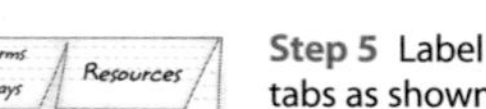

Step 5 Label the tabs as shown.

Reading and Writing As you read the chapter, fill in the Foldable. When you have finished the chapter, use your Foldable to write a list of the 10 most important facts about Europe's physical geography.

Social Studies ONLINE

To preview Chapter 10, go to glencoe.com.

Previewing the Region

If you have not already done so, engage students in the Regional Atlas and chart activities to help them become familiar with the general content of the region.

Dinah Zike's Foldables

Purpose This Foldable helps students understand the physical features and climate region of Europe. The four main categories help students organize specific details thematically. The completed Foldable will help them identify important facts about Europe's geography as well as prepare for assessment.

More Foldables activities for this chapter can be found in *Dinah Zike's Reading and Study Skills Foldables* ancillary.

Social Studies ONLINE

Introduce students to chapter content and key terms by having them access the Chapter Overview at glencoe.com.

affects people's clothing and transportation choices.) Explain that in Section 2 students will learn about the climate regions of Europe and the effect of wind and water on Europe's climate. They will also learn about the vegetation and other features of each climate region. In addition, they will learn about the debate concerning global warming, which is the gradual increase in the temperature of the Earth's lower atmosphere. **OL**

Focus

Bellringer

Daily Focus Transparency 10-1

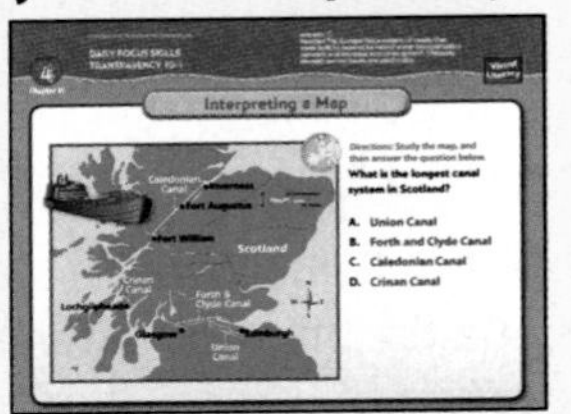

Guide to Reading

Answers to Graphic:

Islands and Peninsulas: Europe is a huge peninsula with many smaller peninsulas. There are also many large and small islands; **Plains:** The Northern European Plain has rich soil, energy and mineral resources, and is densely populated; **Mountains and Highlands:** Mountains have isolated certain countries, while highland areas support livestock and mining.

Section Spotlight Video

To learn more about the physical features of Europe, have students watch the Section Spotlight Video.

Guide to Reading

BIG Idea

Geographic factors influence where people settle.

Content Vocabulary

- landlocked *(p. 275)*
- pass *(p. 277)*
- navigable *(p. 277)*

Academic Vocabulary

- access *(p. 275)*
- affect *(p. 275)*
- impact *(p. 279)*

Reading Strategy

Organizing Information Use a diagram like the one below to organize key facts about each of Europe's major landforms (Islands and Peninsulas, Plains, Mountains and Highlands).

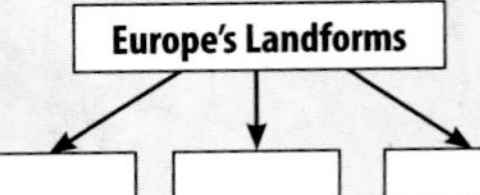

SECTION 1 Physical Features

Picture This Snowdrifts? No, these snow-like mounds were formed about 1,500 years ago during a volcanic eruption on the island of Lipari, off the coast of Sicily, in Italy. The mounds are made of pumice, a stone formed from the cooling of lava, which rained down on the island during the eruption. Today the volcano is quiet, but Lipari hums with the sounds of open-pit pumice mines. Pumice is used to polish smooth surfaces. The stone is often used to give "stonewashed" jeans their worn look. In Section 1, you will learn about the different European landforms and the effect they have had on people living in the region.

▼ Walking on the island of Lipari

Resource Manager

R Reading Strategies	C Critical Thinking	D Differentiated Instruction	W Writing Support	S Skill Practice
Teacher Edition • Setting a Purpose, p. 275 • Academic Vocab., p. 277 • Outlining, p. 278 • Using Context Clues, p. 279 **Additional Resources** • Guid. Read., URB p. 37 • Cont. Vocab., URB p. 39 • Ac. Vocab., URB p. 41 • Read. Ess., p. 67	**Teacher Edition** • Det. Cause/Effect, p. 275 • Pred. Consequences, p. 278 • Drawing Conclusions, p. 279 **Additional Resources** • Crit. Think., URB p. 47 • GeoLab, URB p. 23 • Authentic Assess., p. 10 • Quizzes and Tests, p. 111	**Teacher Edition** • Kinesthetic, p. 276 • Visual/Spatial, p. 276 • Adv. Learners, p. 277 • Naturalist, p. 278 **Additional Resources** • Diff. Instr., URB p. 43 • Reteach., URB p. 55 • School-to-Home Conn., URB p. 57	**Teacher Edition** • Descriptive Writing, p. 276 • Narrative Writing, p. 280	**Teacher Edition** • Visual Literacy, p. 279 **Additional Resources** • Read. Skills, URB p. 25 • Daily Focus Trans. 10-1 • Reg. Atlas, URB pp. 1–7

Landforms and Waterways

Main Idea **Europe's landforms and waterways have greatly influenced where and how Europeans live.**

Geography and You What landforms can you find near your community? In Europe you would find impressive mountains, shimmering seas, and rolling farmland. Read to learn more about the variety of landscapes on this small continent.

When you look at a map of Europe, one of the first things you notice is that the continent is not a separate landmass. Instead, Europe and Asia share a common landmass called Eurasia. Europe extends to the west, from Asia to the Atlantic Ocean.

Europe's long coastline is framed by the Atlantic and by several seas. These include the Baltic, North, Mediterranean, and Black Seas. Most land in Europe lies within 300 miles (483 km) of a coast. Only a few countries are **landlocked,** meaning they do not border an ocean or a sea. Relatively long rivers, however, do give these inland countries **access** to coastal ports.

C This nearness to water has shaped the lives and history of Europe's people. Europeans developed skills in sailing and fishing, which encouraged trade and helped Europe's economy grow. The closeness to the sea also allowed people to move easily between Europe and other continents. As a result, European culture has both influenced and been influenced by the cultures of Asia, Africa, and the Americas.

Peninsulas and Islands

Look at the physical map in this unit's Regional Atlas. You can see that Europe is a huge peninsula, with many smaller peninsulas branching out from it. Europe also includes many islands. Some of the major islands are Great Britain, Ireland, and Iceland in the Atlantic Ocean. Other large islands, such as Sicily, Crete, and Cyprus, are located in the Mediterranean Sea.

R The large number of peninsulas and islands has **affected** Europe's history. Groups of people were separated by Europe's many seas, rivers, and mountains. As a result, many different cultures developed. Today, Europe is home to more than 40 independent countries. That is a remarkable number of neighbors squeezed together on a relatively small continent.

Plains

Europe's major landform is the Northern European Plain. This large lowland area stretches like a rumpled blanket across the northern half of mainland Europe.

The Northern European Plain

NATIONAL GEOGRAPHIC

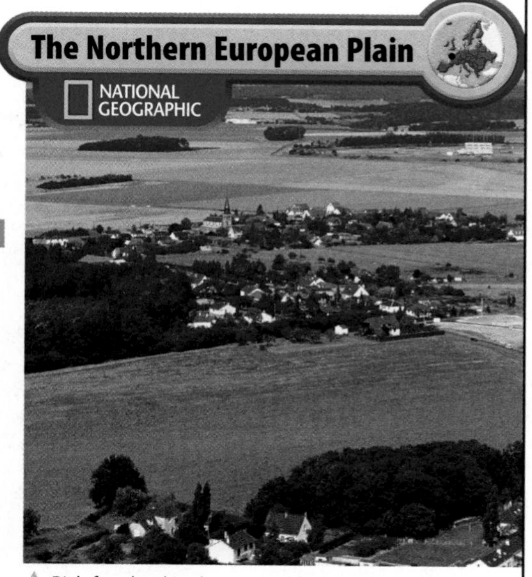

Rich farmland in the region of Normandy in France is part of the Northern European Plain. ***Regions*** **Describe the Northern European Plain.**

Teach

R Reading Strategy

Setting a Purpose Have students create a K-W-L chart. They can write what they know about Europe's landforms and waterways in the K column and what they want to know about them in the W column. Tell students that their purpose is to read to find out what they want to know. After they read the section, have students complete the L column with what they learned. OL

C Critical Thinking

Determining Cause and Effect
Write the following sentence on the board: "This nearness to water has shaped the lives and history of Europe's people." Have students list the effects of living near water. *(Europeans developed skills in sailing and fishing, which helped them trade, and it also helped the economy grow. Nearness to water also allowed people to move among continents, which encouraged the sharing of cultures.)* OL

Caption Answer:
The plain is a large lowland area containing rich farmland.

Additional Support

Activity: Economics Connection

Making Connections Explain to students that until recently, most of the countries in Europe had their own currencies. **Ask: Would using different currencies aid or hinder trade? Why?** *(In general, using different currencies can make trade more difficult because currencies must be converted in order for trade among countries to take place.)* Tell students that many of the countries in Europe have addressed this problem by switching to a single currency, called the euro. Explain that they will learn more about the euro in this unit. OL

Teacher Tip

Economics Connection This activity requires students to understand economic terms. Before beginning, define and discuss the terms *trade* and *currency*.

D1 Differentiated Instruction

Kinesthetic Have students create three-dimensional models of plains, mountains, and highlands. Encourage students to use art materials such as clay and paint to make their models as realistic as possible. Refer students to the photos in the text and, if necessary, have them locate more photos of these landforms in library resources. **OL**

W Writing Support

Descriptive Writing Have students imagine they are using the photographs on this page to create a travel blog for a ski resort they visited in Switzerland. Have them write a descriptive paragraph based on these photographs that would entice friends to visit the area. **OL**

D2 Differentiated Instruction

Visual/Spatial To help students follow the text's description of these mountains, have students locate the mountains on a map or globe as they read. **BL**

Caption Answer:
The Alps of south-central Europe, the Pyrenees, and the Carpathians

It has rolling land with isolated hills. The Northern European Plain reaches from Belarus and Ukraine westward to France and also extends to the British Isles.

The plain's rich soil makes its farms highly productive. Farmers grow a great variety of grains, fruits, and vegetables. Some farmers raise dairy cattle to produce milk used in making cheese and other dairy products.

The Northern European Plain also has important energy and mineral resources. Deposits of coal, iron ore, and other minerals lie underground. These resources aided Europe's industrial growth.

Because the plain is so rich agriculturally and industrially, it is densely populated. Today, most of Europe's people live in this area. The landscape is dotted with villages, towns, and cities, including the busy capital cities of Warsaw, Berlin, Paris, and London.

Europe has other lowlands in addition to the Northern European Plain. For example, narrow plains rim the coasts of southern Europe. Two larger lowlands in the east—the Hungarian Plain, east of the Alps, and the Ukrainian Steppe, a broad, grassy plain north of the Black Sea—have rich soil that supports farming.

Mountains and Highlands

Highlands mark the northern border of the Northern European Plain. Steeper mountains lie south of the plain. Europe's highest mountain ranges form the Alpine Mountain System, which stretches from Spain to the Balkan Peninsula. The system takes its name from the Alps of south-central Europe. It also includes the Pyrenees, which lie between France and Spain, and the Carpathians, in east-central Europe.

The region's highest peak is Mont Blanc in the Alps of France. It rises to 15,771 feet (4,807 m). Most of Europe's mountains, however, are not very tall compared to those of Asia.

NATIONAL GEOGRAPHIC

The Alps

▲ Rugged beauty and good skiing conditions make the Alps a popular tourist destination. ***Place*** **What mountain ranges form the Alpine Mountain System?**

Differentiated Instruction

Interactive Geography Activity, pp. 25–32

Europe Travel Expo

Objective: To increase students' familiarity with Europe's physical, political, and cultural features

Focus: Ask students to tell what they know about the countries of Europe.

Teach: Explain that students will be learning more about Europe by creating booths for a Travel Expo.

Assess: Have students design a booth that focuses on a particular country or region.

Close: Conduct the expo and give students opportunities to visit other booths.

Differentiated Instruction Strategies

BL Make a list of facts about the country or region that is the focus of the booth.

AL Conduct research for the booth's brochure, including sites to see, transportation, food, costs, and other information a traveler would want to know.

ELL Design posters and maps to decorate the booth, and provide visual information about the country or region.

Like some of Europe's other landforms, mountains have helped isolate certain countries and peoples. Switzerland, for example, is located high in the Alps. While European wars have raged around it, the country has remained free from conflict and invasion for many centuries. Europe's mountains have never completely blocked movement though. **Passes,** or low areas between mountains, allow the movement of people and goods. R

Less dramatic than Europe's mountains are three older highland areas that have eroded over time. Uplands in the northwest extend from Sweden through northern Great Britain to Iceland. Stripped of soil by glaciers, the land here is poor for farming, so many people raise sheep. A second highland area, the Central Uplands, contains much of Europe's coal. The area reaches from southern Poland to France. The third highland, the Meseta in Spain, is a plateau on which people grow grains and raise livestock.

Waterways

In addition to plains and mountains, Europe has an abundance of rivers, lakes, and other waterways. Europe's major rivers flow from inland highlands and mountains into the oceans and seas surrounding the region.

Many European rivers are **navigable,** or wide and deep enough for ships to use. People and goods can sail easily from inland areas to the open sea and, from there, around the world. The Danube and the Rhine, two of Europe's longest rivers, are important for transporting goods. D Canals link these rivers, further improving Europe's water transportation network.

Rivers carry rich soil downstream, creating productive farmland along their banks

Hydroelectric Power

This hydroelectric power plant is located on the Danube River between Austria and Germany. ***Human-Environment Interaction*** **How do Europeans use their rivers?**

and at their mouths. For this reason, river valleys have long been home to large numbers of people. Today, fast-flowing rivers are also used to generate electricity to support these large populations.

Lakes cover only a small fraction of Europe. They are valuable for recreation, though, and for tourism. Most lakes are located on the Northern European Plain and in Scandinavia. The highland lakes in northern Great Britain and the Alps, however, are among the most beautiful and frequently visited. People flock to these lakes to boat, fish, swim, and appreciate nature.

Reading Check **Explaining** How have Europeans improved their water transportation network?

Social Studies ONLINE
Student Web Activity Visit glencoe.com and complete the Chapter 10 Web Activity about the Northern European Plain.

R Reading Strategy

Academic Vocabulary Ask: What does the word "isolate" mean? *(to separate from others)* **What other physical features can isolate a country?** *(Answers may include oceans and deserts.)* **OL**

D Differentiated Instruction

Advanced Learners Have students choose either the Danube or the Rhine River and research the importance of the river throughout history. Have students present their findings in an oral report that includes visual aids. **AL**

Caption Answer:
for transportation and to generate electricity

Reading Check Answer: Europeans have created canals to improve their water transportation network.

Social Studies ONLINE
Objectives and answers to the Student Web Activity can be found at glencoe.com under the Web Activity Lesson Plan for this chapter.

Hands-On Chapter Project Step 1

Promoting Europe's Waterways

Step 1: Planning the Brochure Pairs of students will plan an advertising brochure to promote Europe's waterways for the tourism industry.

Essential Question How do people use waterways?

Directions Tell pairs of students to use the physical map of Europe in the Regional Atlas to locate and identify the region's major waterways. Ask pairs to choose one specific lake, river, or other waterway to promote in an advertising brochure for tourists. Then have pairs use information in this section and additional research to take notes about the waterway. Details should include the waterway's location and physical environment, interesting facts about the waterway, activities enjoyed by people on the waterway, and surrounding geographic features.

Summarizing Ask students why recreation and tourism are among the many ways people use Europe's waterways. Pairs may also explain why they selected specific waterways for their brochure. **OL**

(Chapter Project continued in Section 2)

R Reading Strategy

Outlining To help students understand the text under the heading "Energy Resources," have them complete an outline with the headings "Coal," "Petroleum and Natural Gas," and "Clean Energy Sources." **BL**

D Differentiated Instruction

Naturalist Have students find examples of products at home or at school that are made from natural resources. Have students identify the natural resource that makes up each product. Have students present their findings to the class. **BL**

C Critical Thinking

Predicting Consequences Ask: What negative effects might result from the clearing of forests? *(Answers may include the loss of wildlife that depend on the forests and the loss of soil due to erosion.)* **OL**

Caption Answer:
because wind power does not create pollution

Additional Support

Europe's Resources

Main Idea Europe has valuable resources that strengthen its economy.

Geography and You Think of the products that you use every day. What are these products made of? As you read, think about how Europe's natural resources benefit people around the world.

Europe is a leader in the world economy. Part of this success comes from Europe's rich supply of natural resources.

Energy Resources

R Coal has been a major energy source in Europe for many decades. By burning coal, Europeans fueled the development of modern industry in the 1800s. Today, almost half of the world's coal comes from Europe. Coal mining provides jobs for people from the United Kingdom in the west to Ukraine, Poland, and the Czech Republic in the east.

Petroleum and natural gas are other important energy resources found in Europe. The region's most productive oil fields lie beneath the North Sea, in areas controlled by the United Kingdom and Norway. To discourage dependence on oil, though, European governments tax gasoline heavily. Drivers in Europe pay some of the highest gasoline prices in the world.

Europe also relies on several "clean" energy sources that cause less pollution than burning coal or oil. In the highlands and mountains, swift-flowing rivers are used to create hydroelectric power. Europeans also make use of the wind's power. Germany, Spain, and Denmark are leaders in building wind farms, which use large turbines to create electricity from the wind.

Wind Farm in Spain

NATIONAL GEOGRAPHIC

▲ Europe produces more electricity from wind turbines than any other world region. ***Human-Environment Interaction*** **Why is wind power considered a "clean" energy source?**

Other Natural Resources

Besides energy resources, Europe has many other important natural resources. European mines produce about one-third of the world's iron ore, which is used in making steel. Ukraine has deposits of manganese, another important ingredient of steel. **D** The United Kingdom exports a special clay used to make fine china dishes. Marble from Italy and granite from Norway and Sweden provide fine building materials. Of course, stone has always been used for building. Many European towns have narrow cobblestone streets and quaint stone houses that are centuries old.

C Forests once covered a large part of Europe. Long ago, however, people cleared the land for farms and used much of the wood for building and for fuel. Today, only small pockets of forest remain. Sweden and Finland have the most forestland and produce the most lumber.

Activity: Interdisciplinary Connection

Categorizing Invite a science teacher to discuss renewable versus nonrenewable resources with the class. After this presentation, **Ask: What is a renewable resource? What is a nonrenewable resource?** *(renewable: a natural resource that cannot be used up or can be replaced; nonrenewable: a natural resource that is limited in supply and cannot be replaced)* Have students help you create a list on the board that categorizes Europe's energy and natural resources as renewable or nonrenewable. Fossil fuels, such as coal, petroleum, and natural gas, are considered nonrenewable resources, as are minerals and other mined materials. Soil, water, forests, plants, animals, and oxygen are examples of renewable resources. Solar energy and wind energy are also based on renewable resources. Then ask students to think about what Europeans might do to conserve their nonrenewable resources. Have students discuss possible solutions in small groups. Ask volunteers from each group to share their solutions with the class. **OL**

Air Pollution

Air pollution from industrial plants, such as this one in Wales, can destroy forests in Poland (inset). ***Human-Environment Interaction*** **What is acid rain, and why is it harmful?**

Environmental Issues

Main Idea **Europe's plentiful resources have helped its economy, but environmental problems are a growing concern.**

Geography and You Do you recycle at home and try to use energy wisely? As you read, see how Europeans are taking similar steps to protect their resources.

By taking advantage of its natural resources, Europe has become an economic powerhouse. The **impact** on the environment, however, has sometimes been harmful. For instance, in deforested areas of Southern Europe, tree roots no longer hold the soil in place. Valuable topsoil can be washed away.

Fertile soil is another valuable resource, providing Europe with some of the best farmland on the planet. European farmers grow large amounts of grains, including nearly all of the world's rye, most of its oats, and nearly half of its wheat. Europe also produces more potatoes than any other region in the world.

The waters around Europe contain yet another resource—fish. From the Mediterranean Sea to the North Atlantic, Europeans catch salmon, cod, and other varieties of fish. Fishing is important to the economy, but many Europeans also eat a lot of fish and value its health benefits.

Reading Check **Describing** Where are Europe's most productive oil fields?

Air Pollution and Acid Rain

Industrial growth in Europe has also hurt the environment—and created health risks. For example, car exhaust and smoke from burning oil and coal create air pollution. This pollution causes breathing problems, eye irritation, and lung disease.

Air pollution has another serious effect. When pollutant particles mix with precipitation, acid rain falls to Earth. Acid rain can make trees vulnerable to attack from insects and disease. Forests in eastern Europe are especially threatened. In that region, lignite coal is a major fuel source because it is cheap. It burns poorly, however, and pollutes heavily. The resulting acid rain has destroyed many forest areas in Hungary, Poland, the Czech Republic, and Slovakia.

Acid rain falls on Europe's waterways as well as its forests. As acids build up in lakes, rivers, and streams, fish and other wildlife are poisoned and die.

S Skill Practice

Visual Literacy **Ask:** **What cause and effect is shown in the photograph?** *(cause: air pollution; effect: acid rain)* **OL**

C Critical Thinking

Drawing Conclusions Have students discuss among themselves the ways natural resources can affect people's lives. Ask them to consider food, clothing, shelter, and transportation, as well as economic effects. **OL**

R Reading Strategy

Using Context Clues **Ask:** **What does "powerhouse" mean in this sentence?** *(a powerful force)* **ELL**

Caption Answer:
Acid rain is pollutant particles mixed with precipitation. Acid rain can destroy forests, kill fish in waterways, and damage buildings.

Reading Check **Answer:** The most productive oil fields lie beneath the North Sea in areas controlled by the United Kingdom and Norway.

Differentiated Instruction

Leveled Activities

BL **Academic Vocabulary Activity, URB p. 41**

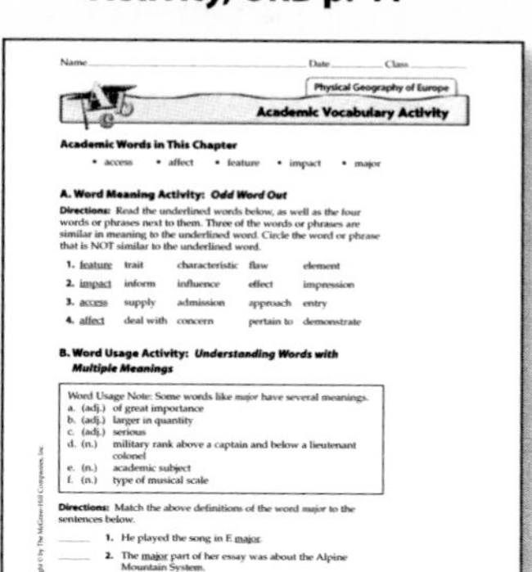

Name ______ Date ______ Class ______

Physical Geography of Europe

Academic Vocabulary Activity

Academic Words in This Chapter

- access • affect • feature • impact • major

A. Word Meaning Activity: *Odd Word Out*

Directions: Read the underlined words below, as well as the four words or phrases next to them. Three of the words or phrases are similar in meaning to the underlined word. Circle the word or phrase that is NOT similar to the underlined word.

1. feature	trait	characteristic	flaw	element
2. impact	inform	influence	effect	impression
3. access	supply	admission	approach	entry
4. affect	deal with	concern	pertain to	demonstrate

B. Word Usage Activity: *Understanding Words with Multiple Meanings*

Word Usage Note: Some words like *major* have several meanings.
a. (adj.) of great importance
b. (adj.) larger in quantity
c. (adj.) serious
d. (n.) military rank above a captain and below a lieutenant colonel
e. (n.) academic subject
f. (n.) type of musical scale

Directions: Match the above definitions of the word *major* to the sentences below.

____ 1. He played the song in E major.

____ 2. The major part of her essay was about the Alpine Mountain System.

____ 3. When I attend a university, I want to be a geography major.

OL **Critical Thinking Skills Activity, URB p. 47**

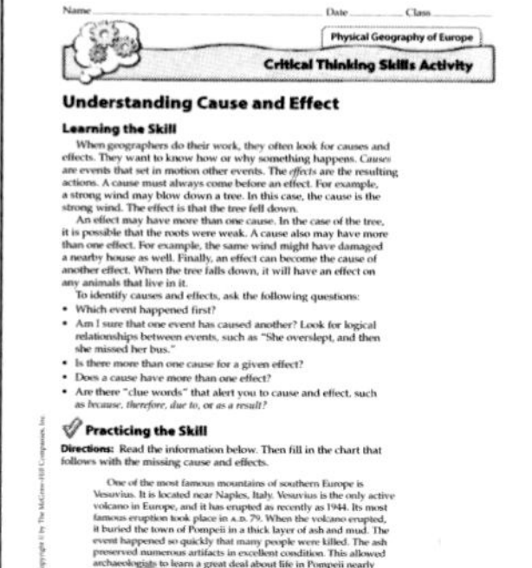

Name ______ Date ______ Class ______

Physical Geography of Europe

Critical Thinking Skills Activity

Understanding Cause and Effect

Learning the Skill

When geographers do their work, they often look for causes and effects. They want to know how or why something happens. *Causes* are events that set in motion other events. The *effects* are the resulting actions. A cause must always come before an effect. For example, a strong wind may blow down a tree. In this case, the cause is the strong wind. The effect is that the tree fell down.

An effect may have more than one cause. In the case of the tree, it is possible that the roots were weak. A cause also may have more than one effect. For example, the same wind might have damaged a nearby house as well. Finally, an effect can become the cause of another effect. When the tree falls down, it will have an effect on any animals that live in it.

To identify causes and effects, ask the following questions:

- Which event happened first?
- Am I sure that one event has caused another? Look for logical relationships between events, such as "She overslept, and then she missed her bus."
- Is there more than one cause for a given effect?
- Does a cause have more than one effect?
- Are there "clue words" that alert you to cause and effect, such as *because, therefore, due to,* or *as a result?*

Practicing the Skill

Directions: Read the information below. Then fill in the chart that follows with the missing cause and effects.

One of the most famous mountains of southern Europe is Vesuvius. It is located near Naples, Italy. Vesuvius is the only active volcano in Europe, and it has erupted as recently as 1944. Its most famous eruption took place in A.D. 79. When the volcano erupted, it buried the town of Pompeii in a thick layer of ash and mud. The event happened so quickly that many people were killed. The ash preserved numerous artifacts in excellent condition. This allowed archaeologists to learn a great deal about life in Pompeii nearly

AL **GeoLab Activity, URB p. 23**

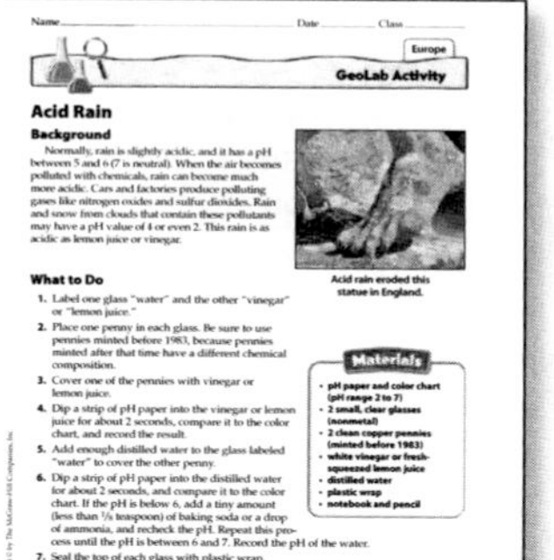

Name ______ Date ______ Class ______

Europe

GeoLab Activity

Acid Rain

Background

Normally, rain is slightly acidic, and it has a pH between 5 and 6 (7 is neutral). When the air becomes polluted with chemicals, rain can become much more acidic. Cars and factories produce polluting gases like nitrogen oxides and sulfur dioxides. Rain and snow from clouds that contain these pollutants may have a pH value of 4 or even 2. This rain is as acidic as lemon juice or vinegar.

Acid rain eroded this statue in England.

What to Do

1. Label one glass "water" and the other "vinegar" or "lemon juice."
2. Place one penny in each glass. Be sure to use pennies minted before 1983, because pennies minted after that time have a different chemical composition.
3. Cover one of the pennies with vinegar or lemon juice.
4. Dip a strip of pH paper into the vinegar or lemon juice for about 2 seconds, compare it to the color chart, and record the result.
5. Add enough distilled water to the glass labeled "water" to cover the other penny.
6. Dip a strip of pH paper into the distilled water for about 2 seconds, and compare it to the color chart. If the pH is below 6, add a tiny amount (less than ⅛ teaspoon) of baking soda or a drop of ammonia, and recheck the pH. Repeat this process until the pH is between 6 and 7. Record the pH of the water.
7. Seal the top of each glass with plastic wrap.
8. Place in a safe, dry place for about 5 days.

Materials

- pH paper and color chart (pH range 2 to 7)
- 2 small, clear glasses (nonmetal)
- 2 clean copper pennies (minted before 1983)
- white vinegar or fresh-squeezed lemon juice
- distilled water
- plastic wrap
- notebook and pencil

ELL **Differentiated Inst. Activity, URB p. 43**

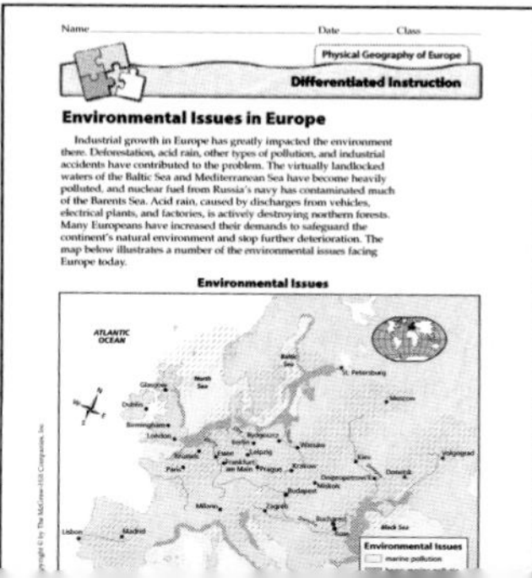

Name ______ Date ______ Class ______

Physical Geography of Europe

Differentiated Instruction

Environmental Issues in Europe

Industrial growth in Europe has greatly impacted the environment there. Deforestation, acid rain, other types of pollution, and industrial accidents have contributed to the problem. The virtually landlocked waters of the Baltic Sea and Mediterranean Sea have become heavily polluted, and nuclear fuel from Russia's navy has contaminated much of the Barents Sea. Acid rain, caused by discharges from vehicles, electrical plants, and factories, is actively destroying northern forests. Many Europeans have increased their demands to safeguard the continent's natural environment and stop further deterioration. The map below illustrates a number of the environmental issues facing Europe today.

Environmental Issues

W Writing Support

Narrative Writing Have students write a children's fable that includes a lesson about air pollution and acid rain and how leaders can solve these problems. Encourage them to illustrate their story. Then arrange to have students read their stories to a class of younger students. OL

Reading Check Answer: Chemicals run off into rivers and cause algae growth, which results in the death of fish.

Assess

Social Studies ONLINE
Study Central™ provides summaries, interactive games, and online graphic organizers to help students review content.

Close

Identifying Have students name as many of the landforms, waterways, and resources of Europe as they can, without referring to their text. OL

Section Review

Acid rain is also a problem for Europe's historic buildings. The famous Tower of London, Germany's Cologne Cathedral, and ancient buildings and monuments dating from Greek and Roman times all show damage from acid deposits.

Water Pollution

Water pollution is another challenge for Europe. Sewage, garbage, and industrial waste have all been dumped into the region's seas, lakes, and rivers. As populations and tourism have increased, the problem has worsened.

Runoff from farms is also a problem for Europe's waters. Runoff is precipitation that flows over the ground, often picking up pesticides and fertilizers along the way. When chemicals from runoff enter a river, they encourage the growth of algae. Algae rob the river of so much oxygen that fish cannot survive. Runoff spilling into the Danube River, for example, has killed much of its marine life.

Finding Solutions

W European leaders are trying to solve environmental problems in a number of ways. Many are working to prevent air pollution and acid rain by limiting the amount of chemicals that factories and cars can release into the air. Norway and Sweden are adding lime to their lakes. This substance stops the damage caused by acid rain and allows fish to multiply again.

Europeans are also making their lakes and rivers cleaner by treating waste and sewage. In addition, some countries encourage farmers to use less fertilizer to reduce damaging runoff.

Recycling is another strategy for protecting the environment. Europeans now recycle more paper, plastics, and glass than in the past. This saves energy that would otherwise be needed to produce these goods and cuts down on wastes.

Reading Check **Explaining** How does runoff contribute to water pollution?

Section Review

Social Studies ONLINE
Study Central™ To review this section, go to glencoe.com.

Vocabulary

1. **Explain** the significance of:
   a. landlocked
   b. pass
   c. navigable

Main Ideas

2. **Organizing Information** Use a diagram like the one below to explain the importance of rivers in Europe.

3. **Analyzing** Why are Europe's clean energy sources important to the region?

4. **Explaining** Why and where is acid rain especially a problem?

Critical Thinking

5. **BIG Idea** Which resources helped industry and farming develop in Europe?
6. **Challenge** Describe how Europe's landforms and bodies of water influenced where people settled.

Writing About Geography

7. **Expository Writing** Write a paragraph explaining which physical feature you think has most helped Europe's economy to prosper.

Answers

1. Definitions for the vocabulary words are found in the section and the Glossary.
2. Europe's major landform is the Northern European Plain. Its rich soil makes farms highly productive, and its energy and mineral resources aid Europe's industrial growth. These agricultural and industrial riches keep this area densely populated.
3. Europe's Rivers: provide transportation, create productive farmland, generate electricity, support recreation and tourism
4. The northern highlands were stripped of soil by glaciers. These older highland areas have eroded over time, making them lower than the younger mountains of southern Europe.
5. coal, petroleum, natural gas, iron ore, manganese, clay, marble, granite and other stone, forests, rivers, and fertile soil
6. Because Europe is bordered on many sides by seas and oceans, people were able to easily reach and settle many areas. The rich soil in river valleys led many people to settle in them. Today, however, most of Europe's people live on the plains, where rich soil and other natural resources support agriculture and industry.
7. Answers may vary but should identify a physical feature and explain how this feature has helped Europe's economy prosper.

NATIONAL GEOGRAPHIC **Geography & History**

Disaster at Chernobyl

▲ **Abandoned amusement park, Pripyat', Russia**

In the modern world, we depend on technology to survive. What happens when technology goes wrong? C

The Accident On April 26, 1986, the world saw its worst nuclear disaster. That day, a reactor at the Chernobyl nuclear power plant in Ukraine exploded. Dangerous radioactive material shot into the sky. The explosion also caused a fire that raged for 10 days, pouring out more radioactive dust and ash. During that time, radioactive material—called fallout—fell to the Earth over large parts of Ukraine and Belarus, as well as other parts of Europe.

The Impact Fewer than a hundred people died from the high levels of radiation that resulted from the explosion and fire. About 4,000 more, however, are expected to die from cancers caused by the accident. Fortunately, these numbers are far below what had originally been feared.

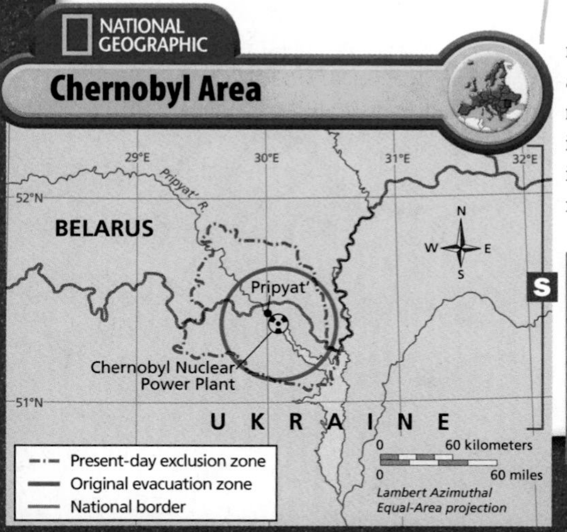

S

Nevertheless, more than 20 years after the accident, its effects are ongoing. Around the area contaminated by fallout, officials created an exclusion zone of about 1,545 square miles (4,002 sq. km). People are prohibited from living within this zone. More than 350,000 people were forced to leave their homes following the accident. The disaster scarred the land as well. More than 1.8 million acres (728,435 hectares) of farmland and 1.7 million acres (687,966 hectares) of forest were abandoned because of contamination from fallout.

Meanwhile, a threat remains at Chernobyl. A protective concrete shell, built around the reactor to contain the contamination, could collapse. Also, rainwater leaks into the shell. When the water seeps back into the ground, it carries radioactive material with it, further poisoning the land. R

Think About It

1. **Movement** How many people were forced to leave the contaminated area?
2. **Human-Environment Interaction** What effect did the accident have on the environment?

C Critical Thinking

Drawing Conclusions Ask: Why might leaders of countries around the world be concerned about nuclear technology? *(Nuclear weapons are very dangerous. If the wrong people get them, a disaster could happen. In addition, nuclear power plants must be carefully monitored because nuclear disasters can be deadly.)* **OL**

S Skill Practice

Using Geography Skills Ask: Which countries have area included in the exclusion zone? *(Belarus and Ukraine)* **OL**

R Reading Strategy

Summarizing Have students use a tape recorder to dictate a brief summary of the article. Then have students listen to a partner's recording and provide feedback on the completeness of the summary. **BL**

Think About It

Answers:

1. more than 350,000 people
2. Millions of acres of farmland and forest were abandoned because of contamination. Today when rainwater leaks into the shell around the reactor and then seeps into the ground, it poisons the land with radioactive material.

Additional Support

Activity: Connecting With the United States

Comparing and Contrasting Ask: What were some of the effects of the Chernobyl disaster? *(Some people died from acute radiation exposure, and many more died from related cancers; contamination from the fallout caused forests and farmland to be abandoned; more than 350,000 people have been forced to move.)* Explain that in March 1979, the most serious nuclear power plant accident in the United States took place at Three Mile Island in Middletown, Pennsylvania. Organize the class into two groups, one to learn more about the Chernobyl disaster and the other to research the Three Mile Island accident. Direct the groups to consult at least three library or Internet resources. Each group should look for answers to the following questions: What caused this accident? What were the long-term health effects? What changes have been made since the accident? After their research is completed, have the groups present their findings to the class. Compare and contrast the two events, focusing on the research questions. **AL**

Focus

Bellringer

Daily Focus Transparency 10-2

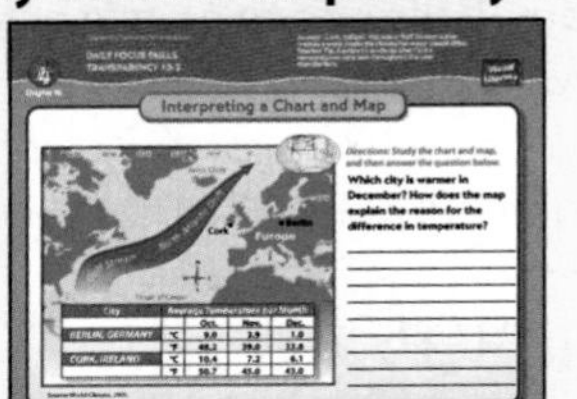

Guide to Reading

Answers to Graphic:

marine west coast: mild temperature, abundant precipitation; humid continental: cooler summers, colder winters, and less rain and snow than marine west coast zone; Mediterranean: hot, dry summers with little rain and mild and wet winters; subarctic: extreme cold; tundra: extreme cold; highland: cool to cold, temperatures and precipitation vary; steppe: dry, treeless grasslands; humid subtropical: hot, wet summers, and mild, wet winters

Section Spotlight Video

To learn more about the climate regions of Europe, have students watch the Section Spotlight Video.

Guide to Reading

BIG Idea

The physical environment affects how people live.

Content Vocabulary

- deciduous *(p. 285)*
- coniferous *(p. 285)*
- mistral *(p. 287)*
- sirocco *(p. 287)*

Academic Vocabulary

- major *(p. 283)*
- feature *(p. 284)*

Reading Strategy

Categorizing Information Use a chart like the one below to describe Europe's climate zones.

Climate Zone	Characteristics
1.	1.
2.	2.
3.	3.
4.	4.

Climate Regions

Picture This These carefully balanced baskets will carry grapes that are handpicked in the Côte d'Or ("Golden Hill") region of Burgundy, France. The region has been producing wine since A.D. 900, and the grape harvest is vital to the local economy. Because of this, and because grapes are highly sensitive to the climate, big changes in temperature are always cause for concern. Read this section to find out about climate conditions in Europe and the concern over the warming trend.

Carrying grape baskets in Burgundy, France

Resource Manager

R Reading Strategies	C Critical Thinking	D Differentiated Instruction	W Writing Support	S Skill Practice
Teacher Edition • Inferring, p. 285 • Identifying, p. 286 • Monitoring, p. 287 **Additional Resources** • Guid. Read., URB p. 38 • Cont. Vocab., URB p. 39 • Ac. Vocab., URB p. 41 • Read. Ess., p. 70 • World Lit., URB p. 31	**Teacher Edition** • Making Inferences, p. 283 • Compare/Contrast, p. 287 **Additional Resources** • Quizzes and Tests, p. 112	**Teacher Edition** • Kinesthetic, p. 283 • Logical/Math., p. 286 • Adv. Learners, p. 288 **Additional Resources** • School-to-Home Conn., URB p. 57	**Teacher Edition** • Expository Writing, p. 286 **Additional Resources** • Writing Skills, URB p. 53	**Teacher Edition** • Using Geo. Skills, pp. 284, 285 **Additional Resources** • Chart, Graph, and Map Skills, p. 45 • Speak./Listen. Skills, URB p. 49 • Daily Focus Trans. 10-2 • Reg. Atlas, URB pp. 1–7

Wind and Water

Main Idea **Wind patterns and water currents shape Europe's climate.**

Geography and You Doesn't a cool breeze feel great on a hot day? Read to learn how winds are helpful to Europe too.

Look at the physical map of the world in the Reference Atlas. Because Europe is farther north than the United States, you might expect Europe's climate to be colder than ours. In fact, much of Europe enjoys a milder climate. Why?

As **Figure 1** shows, the North Atlantic Current carries warm waters from the Gulf of Mexico toward Europe. Winds from the west pass over this water and carry more warmth to Europe. These prevailing winds, known as westerlies, are a **major** influence on warming the European climate. C

Other wind patterns also affect the climate in parts of Europe. For example, warm winds from Africa contribute to the high temperatures in southern Europe. Blustery winter winds from Asia lower temperatures throughout much of eastern Europe.

The water surrounding Europe also affects the region's climate. Winds blowing off the water cool the hot land in the summer and warm the cold land in the winter. For this reason, coastal areas tend to have a more moderate climate than inland areas. D

Reading Check **Explaining** Why does northwestern Europe have a mild climate?

NATIONAL GEOGRAPHIC **Maps In Motion** See StudentWorks™ Plus or glencoe.com.

Figure 1 **Europe: Currents and Wind Patterns**

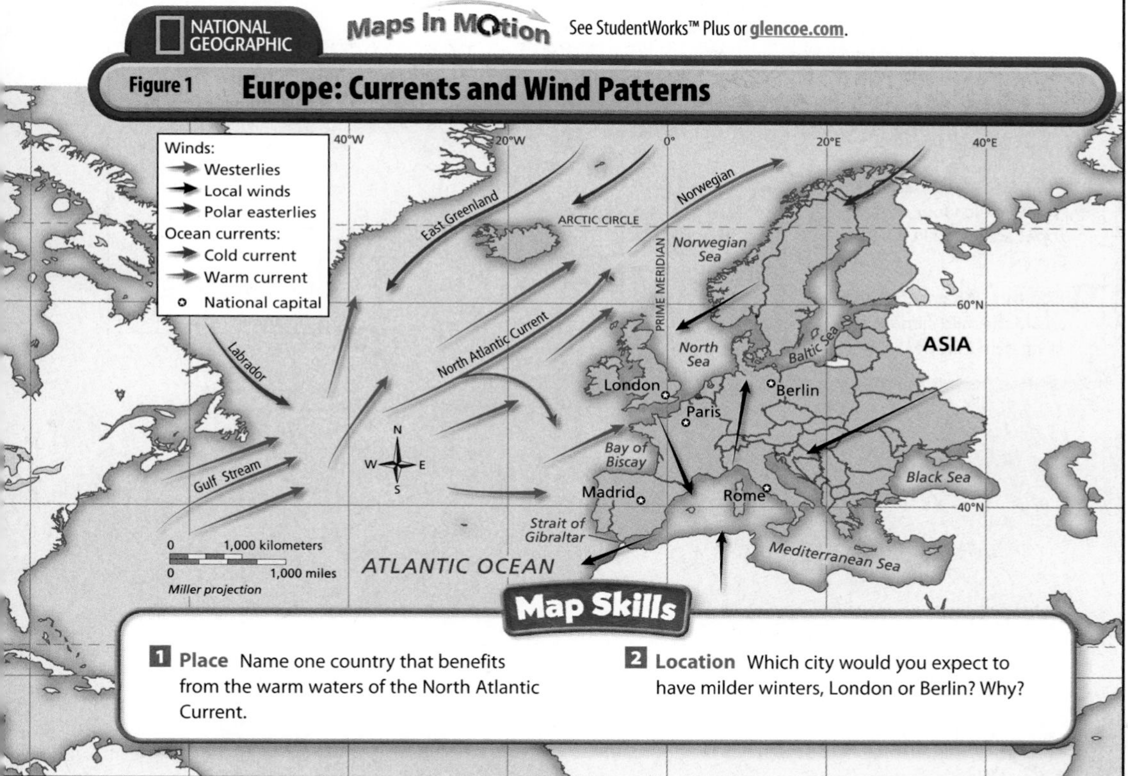

Map Skills

1. **Place** Name one country that benefits from the warm waters of the North Atlantic Current.
2. **Location** Which city would you expect to have milder winters, London or Berlin? Why?

Teach

C Critical Thinking

Making Inferences **Ask: What sort of air temperature would you expect in regions that lie along the Gulf of Mexico?** *(warm)* OL

D Differentiated Instruction

Kinesthetic To help students understand the concept discussed in the passage, use a small fan to blow air across a tray of ice cubes. Have students feel the air just after it comes across the tray. Then remove the tray and have them feel the air again. BL

Map Skills

Answers:

1. Answers may include England, France, and Iceland.
2. London, because it lies nearer to the North Atlantic Current

Reading Check **Answer:** Winds pass over the warm waters of the North Atlantic Current and warm the northwestern part of Europe.

Additional Support

Activity: Collaborative Learning

Applying **Ask: How do westerlies affect the European climate?** *(Winds from the west pass over the North Atlantic Current and carry warm air to Europe.)* Point out that different prevailing winds are present at different latitudes. Organize the class into three groups to research global wind patterns—specifically westerlies, polar easterlies, and trade winds. Have groups investigate the latitudes where the wind patterns are located, the direction of the wind flow, and the effects of this type of wind pattern on the climate in those areas. Students will need to gather information and visuals to make a display for each type of wind pattern. After their work is completed, have groups present their displays to the class. OL

S Skill Practice

Using Geography Skills **Ask:** What is the climate of the southernmost part of Europe? *(Mediterranean)* **OL**

D Differentiated Instruction

English Learners Point out the term *window* in the sentence. Ask students to define the word or point to a window. **Tell students:** The word *window* has more than one meaning. Here the word means "a length of time". **ELL**

Map Skills

Answers:

1. tundra, subarctic, humid continental, marine west coast
2. The North Atlantic Current brings warm winds, the mountains of southern Europe block northern winds, and hot, dry winds blow in from Africa.

Climate Zones

Main Idea **Europe has eight climate zones, each with different vegetation.**

Geography and You What is your ideal climate? Chances are, you can find it in Europe! Read to learn how Europe's climate varies from area to area.

Most of Europe falls into three main climate zones—marine west coast, humid continental, and Mediterranean. **Figure 2** also shows five other climate zones that appear in smaller areas—subarctic, tundra, highland, steppe, and humid subtropical.

Marine West Coast

Much of northwestern and central Europe has a marine west coast climate. This climate has two **features,** one of which is mild temperatures. The North Atlantic Current carries so much warmth that southern Iceland has mild temperatures, even though it is near the Arctic Circle. Because of the mild temperatures, this climate zone has surprisingly long growing seasons. In the United Kingdom, for example, farmers have a window of 250 or more days for planting and harvesting—nearly 60 more days than in eastern Canada—which is located at the same latitude. **D**

NATIONAL GEOGRAPHIC

Figure 2 **Europe: Climate Zones**

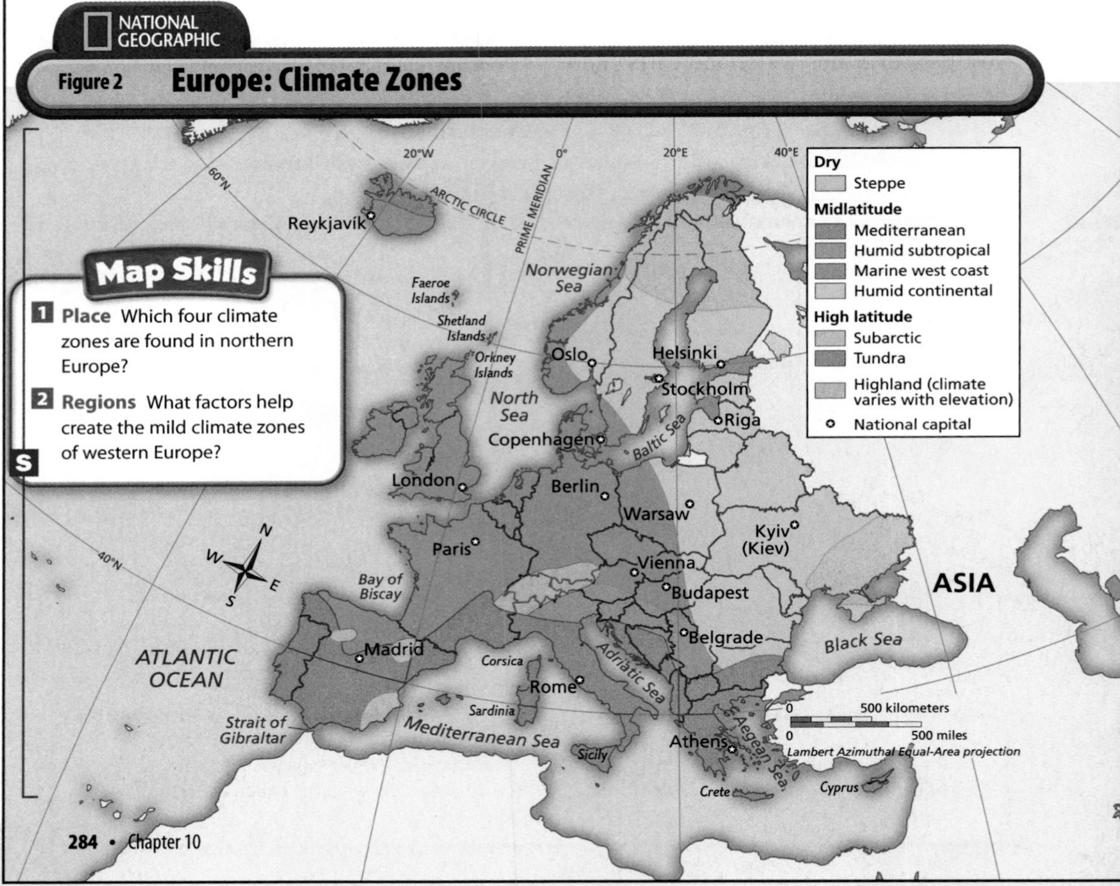

Map Skills

1. **Place** Which four climate zones are found in northern Europe?
2. **Regions** What factors help create the mild climate zones of western Europe? **S**

Hands-On Chapter Project Step 2

Promoting Europe's Waterways

Step 2: Making the Brochure Pairs of students will make the brochure they planned in Section 1.

Directions Ask pairs to take notes from the text about the climate zone in which their selected waterway is located. Then have pairs make their brochure. Pairs should include at least one picture or sketch from their research. Encourage pairs to give their brochure an interesting title and to make their brochures as descriptive as possible in order to persuade tourists to visit the waterway.

Putting It Together Ask volunteers to present their brochures and discuss what parts of the region they would like to visit. **OL**

(Chapter Project cont. on the Visual Summary page.)

Although temperatures stay mild, differences do exist across the region. In the north, summers are shorter and cooler. Also, the farther away you get from water, the wider the range of temperatures will be. For example, in the coastal city of Brest, France, a December day might be only 20 degrees cooler than a July day. However, in Strasbourg, France, which is more than 400 miles (644 km) from the Atlantic Ocean, the temperature can differ by 40 degrees between summer and winter. **R1**

The second feature of the marine west coast climate, besides mild temperatures, is abundant precipitation. This typically falls in autumn and early winter. Although the zone as a whole gets plenty of rain, certain mountainous areas stay dry because of the rain shadow effect. For example, the coastal area of Norway, on the western edge of highlands, receives a yearly average of 90 inches (229 cm) of precipitation. The eastern slopes of those same highlands receive only one-third that amount.

Forests thrive in much of Europe's marine west coast climate zone. Some forests consist of **deciduous** trees, which lose their leaves in the fall. **Coniferous** trees, also called evergreens, grow in cooler areas of the marine west coast climate zone. **R2**

NATIONAL GEOGRAPHIC

Figure 3 **Europe: Natural Vegetation**

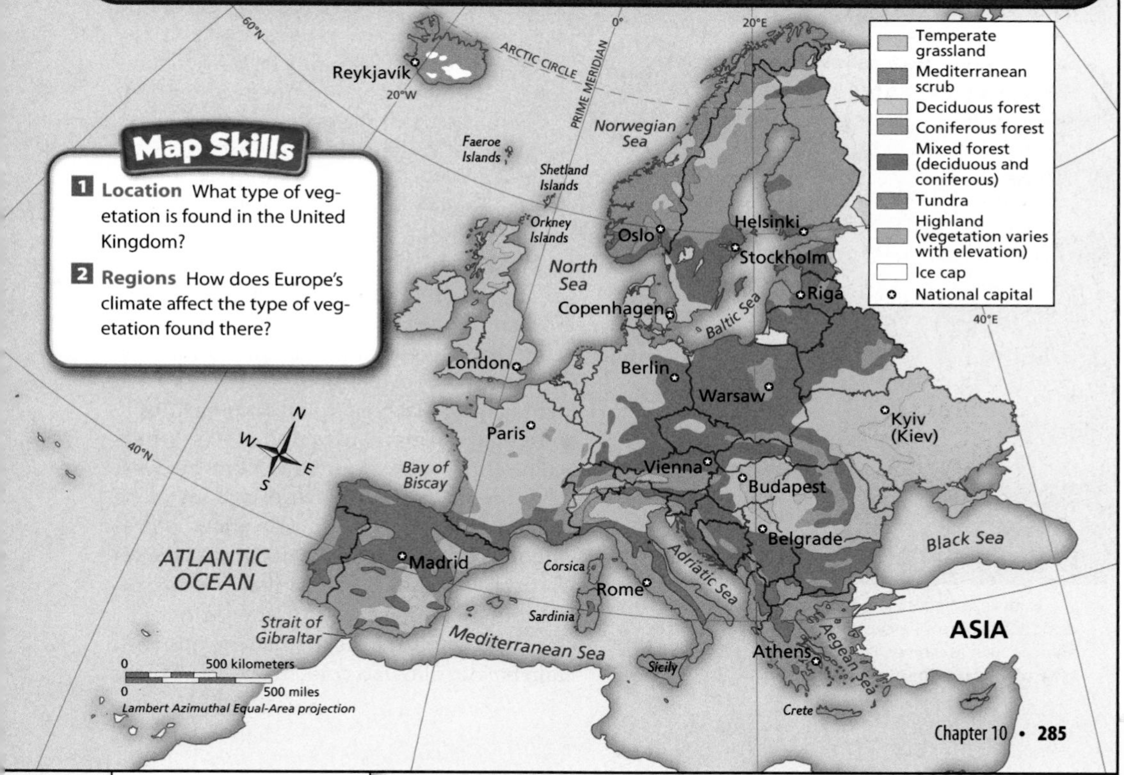

Map Skills

1. **Location** What type of vegetation is found in the United Kingdom?
2. **Regions** How does Europe's climate affect the type of vegetation found there?

Chapter 10 • 285

R1 Reading Strategy

Inferring Ask: How might latitude affect farming? *(The farther north one goes, the shorter the summer, or growing season is.)* **Why do Brest and Strasbourg not have similar climates even though they are at roughly the same latitude?** *(Brest is warmed by the North Atlantic Current, and Strasbourg is far enough inland not to receive warmth from the current.)* **AL**

R2 Reading Strategy

Monitoring Ask: What is the difference between deciduous and coniferous trees? *(Deciduous trees lose their leaves in the fall and thrive in the marine west coast climate zone. Coniferous trees are evergreens that grow in cooler areas of the marine west coast climate zone.)*

Map Skills

Answers:

1. mixed forest and deciduous forest
2. The vegetation depends on the temperature and level of precipitation. In areas with milder temperatures and abundant rains, forests and crops thrive. In colder temperatures, only evergreens grow. Hot climate zones have low-lying shrubs but no forests.

Differentiated Instruction

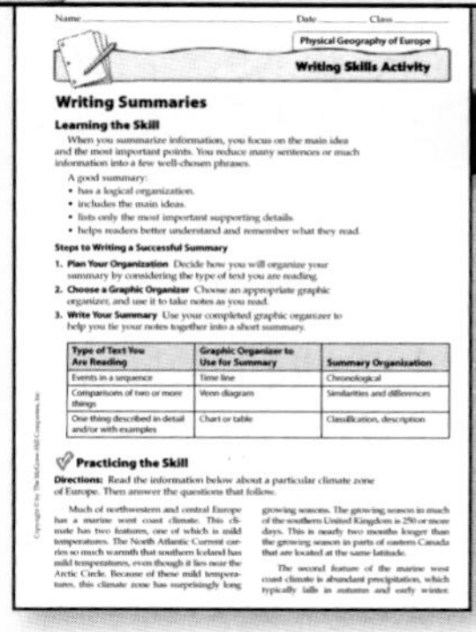

Writing Skills Activity, URB 4 pp. 53–54

Writing Summaries

Objective: To summarize the main climate zones of Europe

Focus: Have students examine what makes a good summary. Refer to the bulleted list while reading.

Teach: Read the passage and underline key words and phrases. Determine whether the underlined sentences express the main points.

Assess: Use the graphic organizer to write a summary of the article.

Close: Summarize a subsection in this section.

Differentiated Instruction Strategies

BL List the three most important ideas in the article and use them to write the summary.

AL Find a different text on the same subject. Then write a summary based on the new text.

ELL Write a short phrase listing one characteristic per climate zone.

R Reading Strategy

Identifying Have students rewrite the sentence using a synonym for the word "blanket." *(Sentences should include the word "cover" or something similar.)* **ELL**

D Differentiated Instruction

Logical/Mathematical Have students research the average temperatures in their community. Then have them compare their temperatures to those in Minsk. Have students formulate a hypothesis to explain why they are similar or different. **AL**

W Writing Support

Expository Writing Have students write an illustrated encyclopedia entry about the Mediterranean climate zone. Tell students to write their entry for an audience of young students. Discuss how the tone and vocabulary of their writing should be adapted to the age and knowledge level of their audience. **OL**

Caption Answer:
marine west coast and humid continental

Additional Support

They dominate the landscape in southern Norway, Sweden, and parts of eastern Europe.

R Although forests no longer blanket the continent, many people still earn their living from forest-related industries. They cut timber and produce a huge array of products, from lumber and paper to charcoal and turpentine.

Humid Continental

Eastern Europe and some areas of northern Europe have a humid continental climate. Cool, dry winds from the Arctic and Asia give this zone cooler summers and colder winters than the marine west coast zone. D The city of Minsk in Belarus does not get much warmer than 70°F (21°C) in July. By January, however, you would definitely need a warm jacket—the high temperature averages only 22°F (–6°C)!

Poland's Forests

NATIONAL GEOGRAPHIC

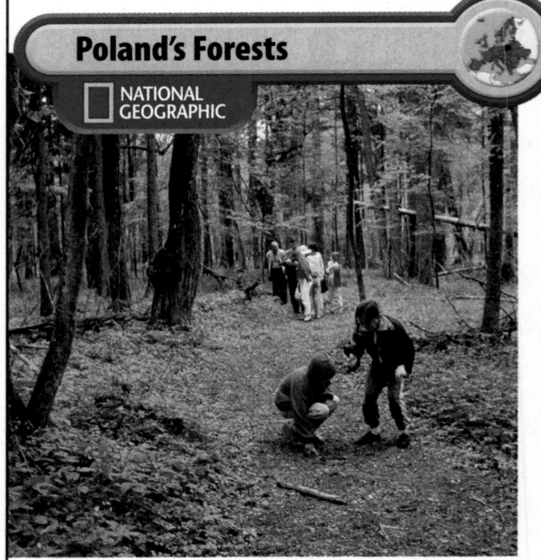

▲ Bialowieza National Park in eastern Poland contains deciduous and coniferous trees. The park is home to animals such as wolves, lynx, and bison. ***Place*** **What type of climate does Poland have?**

Because of drier winds, the humid continental zone gets less rain and snow than the marine west coast zone. Nonetheless, some low-lying areas are wet and marshy. This is because the precipitation that does fall can be slow to evaporate in the cool climate. The humid continental zone supports mixed forests of deciduous and evergreen trees. However, only evergreens grow farther north and in higher elevations.

Mediterranean

W Europe's third major climate zone, the Mediterranean zone, includes much of southern Europe. With average high temperatures in July ranging from 83°F to 98°F (28°C to 37°C), Mediterranean summers are hot. They are also very dry. Many Mediterranean areas receive just a trace of rainfall during the summer.

Because of the heat, the pace of life seems to slow down in the summer. Many people take August vacations. Others take long midday lunches and relax at outdoor cafes for hours in the evening.

Winters in the Mediterranean zone are mild and wet. With temperatures in the 50s Fahrenheit (low teens Celsius), nobody worries about snow. Rainfall, however, averages 3 to 4 inches (7.6 to 10.2 cm) per month, so an umbrella comes in handy.

The mountains of southern Europe affect the Mediterranean climate zone. The Pyrenees and Alps block chilly northern winds from reaching Spain and Italy. Some mountains also create rain shadows. Winds coming over the mountains from the west bring more rain to the western slopes. The eastern side stays drier. The effect is dramatic in Spain, where the northwest region is cool, wet, and green. Inland Spain, on the other hand, is hot, dry, and brown.

In southern France, the lack of a mountain barrier allows a cold, dry wind to blow

Activity: Collaborative Learning

Formulating Questions Ask: What are Europe's eight climate zones? *(marine west coast, humid continental, Mediterranean, subarctic, tundra, highland, steppe, and humid subtropical)* To help differentiate the eight zones, ask students to create questions for a class game. Organize the class into small groups. Assign each group to a different climate zone. Groups will research and create questions about their zone. Questions could include the countries located in this zone, types of vegetation, temperatures, lengths of seasons, amounts of precipitation, and so on. Encourage students to write an array of questions with different levels of difficulty. Caution against questions that are too detailed and those that could pertain to several different zones. Decide as a class the point value that will be assigned to each level of difficulty and the number of questions to write per level or point value. After groups have finished their work, gather the questions and organize them by point value. Play the game in teams so all students are included. **OL**

Herding goats and sheep is a common economic activity in areas with a Mediterranean climate. ***Regions*** **What types of vegetation grow in Europe's Mediterranean climate zone?**

in from the north. This wind, the **mistral** (MIHS·truhl), occurs in winter and spring. It also creates waves, making southern France a popular site for windsurfing.

Countries in the Mediterranean climate zone are also affected by hot, dry winds from Africa to the south. In Italy, these winds are called **siroccos** (suh·RAH·kohs). They pick up moisture as they cross the Mediterranean, bringing uncomfortably humid conditions to southern Europe.

Because of the Mediterranean zone's low rainfall, plants that grow there must be drought resistant. Vegetation includes low-lying shrubs and grasses, as well as the olive trees and grapevines that the region is known for. Forests are rare, and stands of trees appear only on rainy mountainsides or along rivers.

Subarctic and Tundra

Farther north, Europe has two zones of extreme cold. The subarctic zone covers parts of Norway, Sweden, and Finland. Evergreens grow in this region at low altitudes. The tundra zone is found in the northern reaches of these countries and in Iceland. The tundra is an area of vast treeless plains near the North Pole. With cool summers that reach only about 40°F (4°C) and frigid winter temperatures that plunge as low as –25°F (–32°C), only low shrubs and mosses can grow in this region.

Because of Earth's tilt, the sun shines on the far north for up to 20 hours per day in late spring and early summer. As a result, the nights are extremely short. In the deep of winter, however, conditions are reversed. The days are short, and nights can last as long as 20 hours. Some people are so affected by the scarce light in winter that they lose energy and feel depressed.

Highland

The highland zone is found in the higher altitudes of the Alps and Carpathians where the climate is generally cool to cold. However, temperatures and precipitation vary greatly from place to place, depending on three factors—wind direction, orientation to the sun, and altitude. As an example, consider two peaks in the Swiss Alps—Säntis and Saint Gall. Säntis receives more than twice the precipitation of Saint Gall even though the two mountains are only 12 miles (19 km) apart. The difference is due to altitude—Säntis is about three times higher than Saint Gall.

Sturdy trees add color to the highland zone, but they grow only so far up the mountainsides. The point at which they stop growing is called the timberline. Above the timberline, where the sun barely warms the ground, only scrubby bushes and low-lying plants can survive.

Other Climate Zones

Europe's last two climate zones cover a relatively small part of the region. The steppe zone includes the southern part of Ukraine.

R Reading Strategy

Monitoring Remind students to check their comprehension of the text. Students should be asking questions such as "What is a sirocco?" and "Why must plants in the Mediterranean be drought resistant?" **BL**

C Critical Thinking

Comparing and Contrasting Ask: How is the vegetation in the highland climate zone different from that in the steppe climate zone? *(The highlands have sturdy trees up to the timberline, then scrubby bushes and low-lying plants. Steppes are dry, treeless grasslands.)* **OL**

Caption Answer:
low-lying shrubs and grasses, olive trees, grapevines, and forests

Leveled Activities

BL School-to-Home Con. Act., URB, p. 57

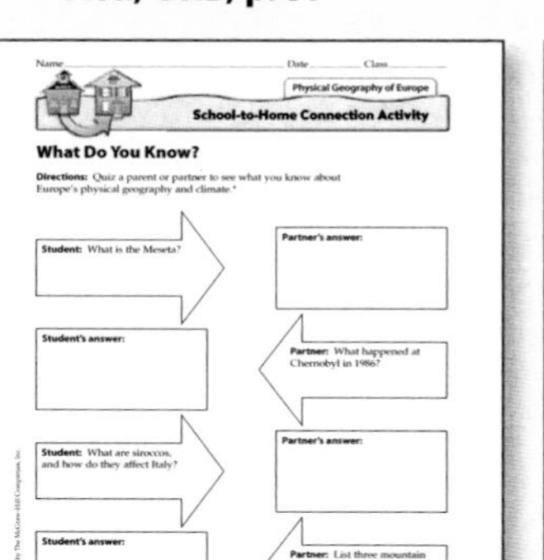

OL Chart, Graph, and Map Skills Act., URB p. 45

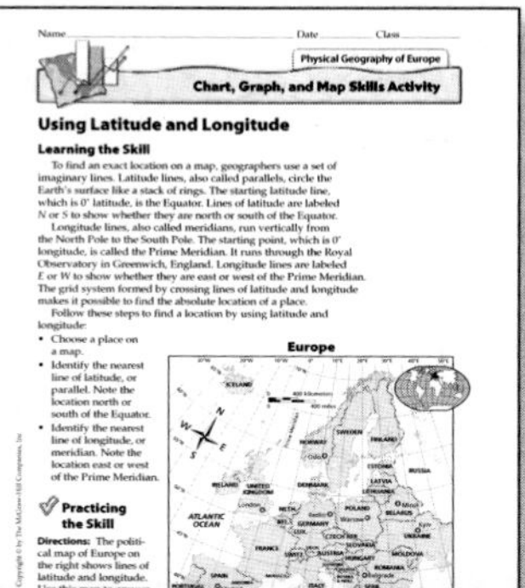

ELL Content Vocabulary Act., URB p. 39

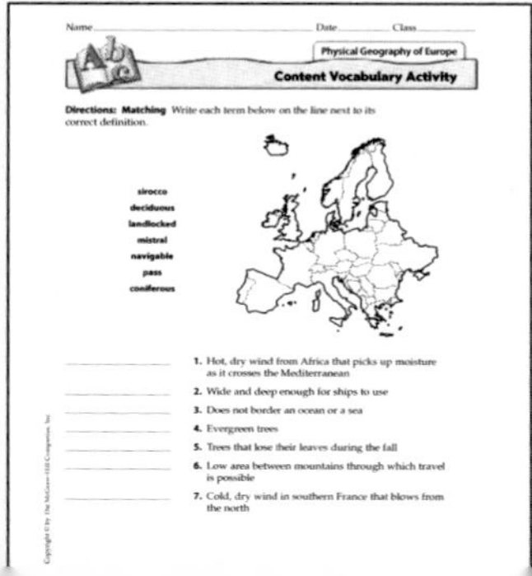

D Differentiated Instruction

Advanced Learners Have students research global warming in order to determine steps people can take to help prevent it. Then have them create a presentation of global warming for the class and distribute pamphlets with prevention tips for students to share with their families. **AL**

Reading Check Answer: Mountains block chilly northern winds from reaching Spain and Italy. Mountains also create rain shadows, such as those in Spain.

Assess

Social Studies ONLINE
Study Central™ provides summaries, interactive games, and online graphic organizers to help students review content.

Close

Summarizing Have students describe one main characteristic for each climate zone. **OL**

Steppes are dry, treeless grasslands, much like prairies but with shorter grass. Here the climate is not dry enough to be classified as desert, but not wet enough for forests to flourish.

A small sliver of land north of the Adriatic Sea falls into the humid subtropical zone. This zone has hot, wet summers and mild, wet winters.

Climate Change

Most scientists agree that the world's climate is growing warmer. Average temperatures have been inching upward for several decades. Measurements and photos show that glaciers are steadily eroding. In 2003 western Europe suffered its worst heat wave since the Middle Ages.

People debate whether this global warming is just part of nature's cycle or is instead related to human activities. Many scientists, though, believe that burning fossil fuels, such as coal and oil, contributes to the greenhouse effect. Gases build up in the atmosphere and trap large amounts of warm air near Earth's surface.

People also debate what this warming means for the planet. Many European leaders are worried. They fear that melting glaciers will produce higher ocean levels that will flood low-lying areas, such as the Netherlands and coastal cities like Venice, Italy. Such flooding would affect millions of people.

D As a result, European officials are taking action. They are trying to slow global warming by encouraging changes in energy use. Most European governments have signed the Kyoto Treaty. This is an international agreement to limit the output of greenhouse gases, but its terms are not yet fully in effect.

Reading Check **Explaining** How do mountains affect southern Europe's Mediterranean climate zone?

Section 2 Review

Social Studies ONLINE
Study Central™ To review this section, go to glencoe.com.

Vocabulary

1. **Explain** the meaning of *deciduous, coniferous, mistral,* and *sirocco* by using each term in a sentence.

Main Ideas

2. **Identifying** What factors affect Europe's climates?
3. **Summarizing** Using a diagram like the one below, identify each of Europe's climate zones and the vegetation found in each zone.

Critical Thinking

4. **Comparing and Contrasting** How are Norway and Spain similar in climate? How are they different?
5. **BIG Idea** How does the North Atlantic Current affect farming in the marine west coast climate zone?
6. **Challenge** Describe how latitude and altitude affect climate and vegetation in Europe.

Writing About Geography

7. **Using Your FOLDABLES** Use your Foldable to write a paragraph comparing and contrasting two of Europe's climate zones.

Answers

1. Sentences should use vocabulary words according to their definitions in the section and Glossary.
2. wind patterns, water currents, and landforms such as mountains
3. **marine west coast:** deciduous and coniferous trees; **humid continental:** deciduous and evergreen trees; **Mediterranean:** low-lying shrubs and grasses, olive trees and grapevines; **subarctic:** evergreen trees; **tundra:** low shrubs and mosses; **highland:** sturdy trees up to the timberline and scrubby bushes and low-lying plants above that; **steppe:** treeless grasslands; **humid subtropical:** mixed forest
4. Both: areas of marine west coast climate with mild temperatures and abundant rainfall. Norway: areas of humid continental climate with less precipitation and cool, dry winds, as well as a subarctic region of extreme cold. Spain: a Mediterranean climate with hot temperatures and low precipitation, as well as areas with the dry steppe climate
5. The North Atlantic Current's warm air lengthens the growing season
6. The farther north, the shorter and cooler the summer is. The farther away from water, the wider the range of temperatures is. Higher altitudes yield colder climates and less vegetation.
7. Students should identify two of Europe's climate zones and compare and contrast specific details about those zones.

Visual Summary

Landforms

- The Northern European Plain is a rich farming region and has a high population density.
- Mountains separate much of northern and southern Europe.
- Uplands regions are found in northwest and central Europe and in Spain.

Berlin, Germany, on the Northern European Plain

Waterways

- Waterways have had a major impact on Europe's population and ways of life.
- Rivers provide transportation, good soil for farming, and hydroelectric power.

European Resources

- Europe's energy resources include coal, petroleum, natural gas, and hydroelectric and wind power.
- In some areas, good soil promotes farming and dairy farming.
- Fishing is important to coastal Europe.

Tulip harvest in the Netherlands

Fishers in Spain

Environmental Issues

- The European environment has been damaged by deforestation, pollution, and acid rain.
- Europeans are working to protect and improve their environment through recycling and limiting forms of chemical pollution.

Climate Regions

- Europe's nearness to water and its wind patterns greatly affect its climates.
- Europe has eight main climate zones: marine west coast, humid continental, Mediterranean, subarctic, tundra, highland, steppe, and humid subtropical.
- Europeans are concerned about the negative effects of global warming.

Reindeer on Norwegian tundra

Study anywhere, anytime! Download quizzes and flash cards to your PDA from glencoe.com.

Visual Summary

Organizing Have students create a graphic organizer with the headings listed on the page. Then have them review the chapter and list three facts under each heading that are not mentioned on this page. **Ask: How does a graphic organizer help you understand the information in the chapter?** *(Possible answer: The diagrams keep the information in categories.)* Have students discuss their diagrams in small groups and add or delete information as appropriate. **BL**

Identifying Central Issues Have students use the text and library or Internet resources to find out about current issues related to Europe's resources. Have students analyze their findings for the pros and cons, then present their findings to the class. **AL**

Formulating Questions Have students write three questions that they still have about Europe's physical geography after reading this chapter. Then have them use the library or the Internet to find answers to their questions. Have them write the answers to their questions in a brief paragraph. **OL**

Hands-On Chapter Project

Step 3: Wrap Up

Promoting Europe's Waterways

Step 3: Learning from the Brochure Students will synthesize what they have learned in Steps 1 and 2.

Directions Write the Essential Question from the chapter opening page on the board. Encourage students to answer this question by using what they learned while planning and making their advertising brochures about European waterways. Begin by asking students to review Europe's bodies of water. Build into a discussion of how people in Europe use waterways. Ask questions such as: **Why are these waterways important? How have Europe's waterways influenced where people settle and how they live? How do the waterways affect Europe's transportation systems and economy?** List students' responses on the board. Then have each student write several sentences in his or her journal that answers the Essential Question. **OL**

Answers and Analyses

Reviewing Vocabulary

1. C Students may easily be able to eliminate answer choices A and D, since neither of these deals with the ability of ships to travel through water. Students may have a difficult time choosing between the remaining options, *passable* and *navigable*. If students cannot remember the correct answer from their reading, they may be able to draw on their prior knowledge of ship travel terminology and note that *navigation* and *navigable* are related words.

2. D Most students will have no difficulty eliminating choice A. Even if they are not certain of the meaning of choices B and C, they should be able to determine that choice D, *passes*, is correct, because the term itself implies that people can "pass" or move between mountains.

3. A The two answer choices dealing with wind are answer choice A, *siroccos*, and answer choice B, *the mistral*. Students must distinguish between the two: *the mistral* is a cold, dry wind from the north, whereas *siroccos* are hot winds from the south. To help students remember the difference, tell them that *siroccos* starts with an "s" as does the term *south*, which is where the winds come from.

4. B This question might challenge students because all of the answer choices are types of classifying or describing trees. However, *deciduous* and *coniferous* are classes of trees, whereas *palm* and *banyan* are specific types of trees. Students then must distinguish between trees that keep their leaves all year—evergreens—and those that don't. To help students remember, tell them that pine trees are green all year, and they have pine *cones*, which is where the term *coniferous* comes from.

STANDARDIZED TEST PRACTICE

TEST-TAKING TIP

Eliminate answers that you know for certain are incorrect. Then choose the most likely answer from those remaining.

Reviewing Vocabulary

Directions: Choose the word(s) that best completes the sentence.

1. Europe has many ________ rivers—rivers that are deep and wide enough for ships to travel.

A polluted
B passable
C navigable
D deciduous

2. In Europe, ________, or low areas between mountains, have allowed the movement of people and goods.

A ports
B siroccos
C runoffs
D passes

3. Hot, dry winds that pick up moisture as they cross the Mediterranean Sea and bring uncomfortable humidity to southern Europe are called ________.

A siroccos
B the mistral
C currents
D El Niño

4. Evergreens, or ________ trees, grow in cooler areas of Europe's marine west coast climate zone.

A palm
B coniferous
C deciduous
D banyan

Reviewing Main Ideas

Directions: Choose the best answer for each question.

Section 1 *(pp. 274–280)*

5. Europeans developed skills in fishing, sailing, and trading because

A much of Europe is landlocked.
B most Europeans live close to a coast or a navigable river.
C Europeans were more adventurous than other people.
D Europeans did not like farming or manufacturing.

6. One of Europe's most important resources has been ________, which helped modern industry grow there in the 1800s.

A clay
B granite
C soil
D coal

Section 2 *(pp. 282–288)*

7. The ________ has a major warming effect on Europe's climate.

A North Atlantic Current
B Asian landmass
C polar easterly
D region's position on the Equator

8. Much of northwest and central Europe has a(n) ________ climate.

A tundra
B highland
C marine west coast
D equatorial

GO ON

Reviewing Main Ideas

5. B Logic will help students determine that if people live near water, they are more likely to develop water-related skills. Therefore, answer choice A is incorrect. Answer choices C and D are not logical because it is highly unlikely that entire populations would not be adventurous or dislike manufacturing and farming.

6. D Although all of the answer choices are resources, the only energy resource listed is *coal*, and an energy resource was necessary to help modern industry grow.

Critical Thinking

Directions: Choose the best answer for each question.

Base your answers to questions 9 and 10 on the bar graph below and your knowledge of Chapter 10.

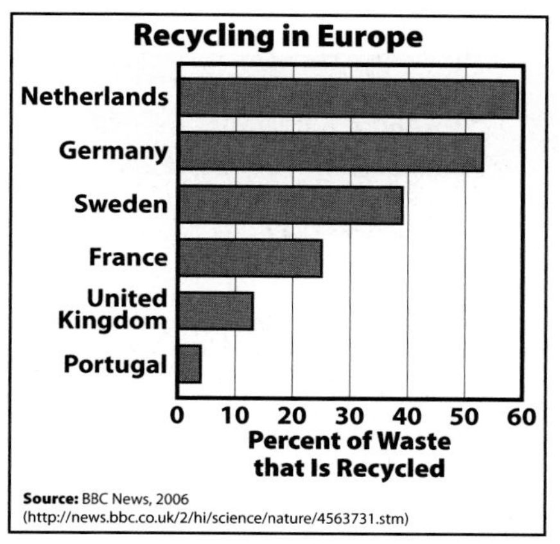

9. Which two European countries recycle more than 50 percent of their waste?

A Sweden and Portugal
B Netherlands and Germany
C Sweden and the United Kingdom
D France and Germany

10. Based on the graph, which of the following statements is accurate?

A Most European countries recycle more than half their waste.
B The seven countries represented in the graph pollute more than any other European nations.
C The Netherlands relies more on recycling to handle waste than does France.
D The Netherlands produces more waste than the other six countries represented on the graph.

Document-Based Questions

Directions: Analyze the document and answer the short-answer questions that follow.

Eyewitness Account of Natalia Ivanovna Ivanova, Deputy Director, Vesnova Orphanage, Mogilev Oblast, Belarus:

> *It was terrible having to knock on the door or window in the middle of the night to tell the parents that their children should be evacuated the next morning. We said it was because of the radioactivity, which could have bad consequences for all of them. We arranged a place for everyone to gather to be put on buses. It was a dreadful sight.*
>
> —Natalia Ivanovna Ivanova, "Return to Chernobyl: 20 Years 20 Lives"

11. What did Natalia Ivanova have to do following the accident?

12. Describe Ivanova's reaction to the Chernobyl accident. How did she feel about the situation?

Extended Response

13. Write a short essay describing how Europe's successful use of its many resources has led to environmental problems in the region. Also describe what is being done to solve those problems.

For additional test practice, use Self-Check Quizzes—Chapter 10 at glencoe.com.

Need Extra Help?

If you missed question...	1	2	3	4	5	6	7	8	9	10	11	12	13
Go to page...	277	277	287	285	275	278	283	284	280	280	281	281	279

Critical Thinking

9. B To answer this question, students must focus on the top of the graph, which shows percentages. Since the question asks for the countries that recycle more than 50% of their waste, students need only look at the 50 mark. The Netherlands and Germany are the only two countries with bars beyond that mark.

10. C The question calls for students to make a generalization from the data in the graph. Students must first study the graph and then find the statement that best fits the data in the graph. Answer choice C makes sense because the Netherlands recycles nearly 60 percent of its waste, while France recycles less than 30 percent. The other choices cannot be determined from this data.

Document-Based Questions

11. Ivanova warned parents that they had to evacuate children after the accident because of the danger of radioactivity.

12. She thought the situation was "terrible" and that the evacuation was a "dreadful sight."

Extended Response

13. Answers should correctly describe environmental problems facing Europe, such as deforestation and air and water pollution. Answers should also describe solutions now being used to fix those problems, including stricter pollution controls and reliance on cleaner forms of energy.

7. A Students' recollection of the text and the geography surrounding Europe will help them answer this question. The North Atlantic Current blows from the southwest across the Atlantic Ocean and brings with it warm winds, which warm Europe. Choice C, *polar easterly,* is not a logical answer because a polar easterly would come from the poles and would be cold. The remaining choices, *Asian landmass* and the *Equator,* are not factors in Europe.

8. C If students picture Europe on a map, they will note that the northwest and central area lies on or near the Atlantic Ocean. This proximity to the ocean affects the climate of the continent. The answer choice with words related to the ocean is answer choice C, *marine west coast.*

Social Studies ONLINE

Have students visit the Web site at glencoe.com to review Chapter 10 and take the Self-Check Quiz.

Need Extra Help?

Have students refer to the pages listed if they miss any of the questions.

Planning Guide

Key to Ability Levels

BL Below level
OL On level
AL Above level
ELL English Language Learners

Key to Teaching Resources

Print Material
DVD
CD-ROM
Transparency

Levels: BL	OL	AL	ELL		Resources	Chapter Opener	Section 1	Section 2	Chapter Assess
					FOCUS				
BL	OL	AL	ELL	Transparency	**Daily Focus Skills Transparencies**		11-1	11-2	
					TEACH				
BL	OL		ELL	Print Material	**Guided Reading Activity, URB***		p. 61	p. 62	
BL	OL	AL	ELL	Print Material	**Content Vocabulary Activity, URB***		p. 63	p. 63	
BL	OL	AL	ELL	Print Material	**Academic Vocabulary Activity, URB**		p. 65	p. 65	
BL	OL	AL	ELL	Print Material	**Differentiated Instruction Activity, URB**		p. 67		
BL	OL	AL	ELL	Print Material	**Chart, Graph, and Map Skills Activity, URB**			p. 69	
	OL	AL		Print Material	**Critical Thinking Activity, URB**		p. 71	p. 71	
BL	OL	AL	ELL	Print Material	**Speaking and Listening Skills Activity, URB**			p. 73	
BL	OL	AL	ELL	Print Material	**Writing Skills Activity, URB**		p. 77	p. 77	
BL	OL	AL	ELL	Print Material	**School-to-Home Connection Activity, URB***		p. 81		
BL	OL	AL	ELL	Print Material	**Regional Atlas Activities, URB**		pp. 1–7	pp. 1–7	
		AL		Print Material	**Geography and Economics Activity, URB**			p. 9	
	OL	AL		Print Material	**Geography and History Activity, URB**		p. 11		
	OL	AL		Print Material	**Environmental Case Study, URB**			p. 13	
BL	OL		ELL	Print Material	**Time Line Activity, URB**		p. 17		
		AL		Print Material	**Enrichment Activity, URB**		p. 19		
BL	OL	AL	ELL	Print Material	**GeoLab Activity, URB**			p. 23	
BL	OL		ELL	Print Material	**Reading Skills Activity, URB**		p. 25		
BL	OL	AL	ELL	Print Material	**Primary Source Readings, URB**		p. 27		
	OL	AL		Print Material	**World Literature Readings, URB**		p. 31		
BL	OL		ELL	Print Material	**Reading Essentials and Note-Taking Guide***		p. 73	p. 76	
	OL			Print Material	**Interactive Geography Activity**			p. 25	
BL	OL	AL	ELL	Transparency	**In-Text Map Overlay and Population Pyramid Transparencies**	4	4A	4C	
	OL			Print Material	**Foods Around the World**			p. 14	
BL	OL	AL	ELL	Print Material	**Outline Map Resource Book**	p. 36	pp. 37–41		

Note: Please refer to the *Unit Resource Book: Europe* for this chapter's URB materials.

* Also available in Spanish

- Interactive Lesson Planner
- Interactive Teacher Edition
- Fully editable blackline masters
- Section Spotlight Videos Launch
- Differentiated Lesson Plans
- Printable reports of daily assignments
- Standards Tracking System

Levels				Resources	Chapter Opener	Section 1	Section 2	Chapter Assess
BL	OL	AL	ELL					
BL	OL	AL	ELL	NGS World Atlas*				
TEACH *(continued)*								
BL	OL	AL	ELL	NGS World Desk Map	✓	✓	✓	✓
BL	OL	AL	ELL	World Literature Library	✓	✓	✓	✓
BL	OL	AL	ELL	Writer's Guidebook	✓	✓	✓	✓
BL	OL	AL	ELL	Vocabulary PuzzleMaker CD-ROM*	✓	✓	✓	✓
	OL	AL		Primary Sources CD-ROM	✓	✓	✓	✓
BL	OL	AL	ELL	StudentWorks™ Plus DVD	✓	✓	✓	✓
BL	OL	AL	ELL	Section Video Program Activities	✓	✓	✓	✓
BL	OL	AL	ELL	World Music: A Cultural Legacy	✓	✓	✓	✓
BL	OL	AL	ELL	Writing Process Transparencies	✓	✓	✓	✓
Teacher Resources				Building Academic Vocabulary	✓	✓	✓	✓
				Strategies for Success	✓	✓	✓	✓
				Teacher's Guide to Differentiated Instruction	✓	✓	✓	✓
				Presentation Plus! DVD	✓	✓	✓	✓
ASSESS								
BL	OL	AL	ELL	Quizzes and Tests		p. 121	p. 122	p. 123
BL	OL	AL	ELL	Authentic Assessment With Rubrics		p. 11		p. 11
BL	OL	AL	ELL	Standardized Test Practice		p. 41		p. 41
BL	OL	AL	ELL	*ExamView® Assessment Suite* CD-ROM*		11-1	11-2	Ch. 11
BL	OL	AL	ELL	Interactive Tutor Self-Assessment CD-ROM		11-1	11-2	
CLOSE								
BL			ELL	Reteaching Activity, URB*		p. 79	p. 79	p. 79
BL	OL		ELL	Reading and Study Skills Foldables™	p. 70	p. 70	p. 70	p. 70
BL	OL	AL	ELL	Graphic Organizer Transparencies and Strategies		✓	✓	
BL	OL	AL	ELL	*Exploring Our World* in Graphic Novel		pp. 41, 49		

Integrating Technology

Using an E-mail Application

Objective
Students will learn the basics of responsible e-mailing.

Technology
- Glencoe TechCONNECT (For more information or to get a free 30-day trial of Glencoe TechCONNECT for your classroom, visit techconnect.glencoe.com and click the **Free Trial** button.)
- E-mail application software

Focus/Teach
- To see activities correlated to this textbook, log on to TechCONNECT and click the **Find your textbook** link. You can also search for activities. After you log on, click **Activity Search.** Choose **E-Mail** and your grade level.
- Have students log on and enter the letters AC and the three-digit activity number. For example, to access activity #107, Our Changing Ecosystems, enter AC107.
- Have students read each page of the activity and follow the on-screen instructions.

Assess
- Have students complete the activity's self-assessment rubric.
- Students may also complete the activity's TechCheck, a five-question multiple-choice quiz. Enter the letters TC and the three-digit activity number, such as TC107.

Close
- Review this activity with the class.

Social Studies ONLINE

	Student	Teacher	Parent
Beyond the Textbook	●		●
Chapter Overviews	●		●
Concepts in Motion	●		●
ePuzzles and Games	●		●
Literature Connections		●	
Multi-Language Glossaries	●		●
Online Student Edition	●	●	●
Section Videos	●	●	●
Self-Check Quizzes	●		●
Student Web Activities	●		●
Study Central™	●		●
Teaching Today		●	
TIME Current Events	●		●
Vocabulary eFlashcards	●		●
Web Activity Lesson Plans		●	

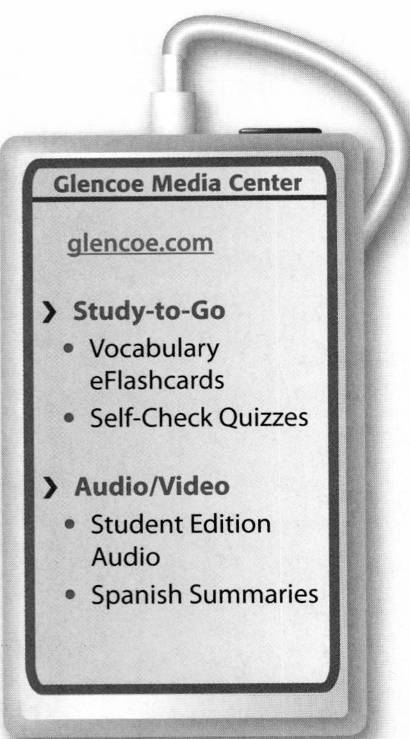

- **Timed Readings Plus in Social Studies** helps students increase their reading rate and fluency while maintaining comprehension. The 400-word passages are similar to those found on state and national assessments.
- **Reading in the Content Area: Social Studies** concentrates on six essential reading skills that help students better comprehend what they read. The book includes 75 high-interest nonfiction passages written at increasing levels of difficulty.
- **Reading Social Studies** includes strategic reading instruction and vocabulary support in Social Studies content for ELLs and native speakers of English.
- **Content Vocabulary Workout** (Grades 6–8) accelerates reading comprehension through focused vocabulary development. Social Studies content vocabulary comes from the glossaries of Glencoe's Middle School Social Studies texts. www.jamestowneducation.com

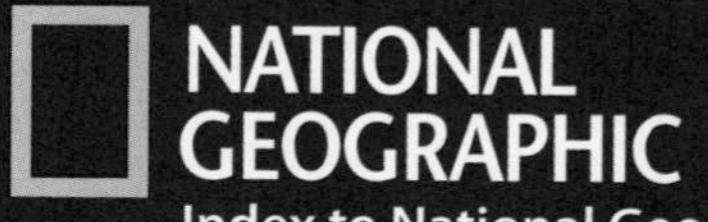

Index to National Geographic Magazine:

The following articles relate to this chapter:

- "Italy Before the Romans," Erla Zwingle, January 2005.
- "Admiral Lord Nelson's Fatal Victory," October 2005.

National Geographic Society Products To order the following, call National Geographic at 1-800-368-2728:

- *National Geographic Atlas of the World* (Book).

Access National Geographic's new dynamic MapMachine Web site and other geography resources at:
www.nationalgeographic.com
www.nationalgeographic.com/maps

Biography  

The following videotape programs are available from Glencoe as supplements to Chapter 11:

- Augustus: First of the Emperors (ISBN 0-76-700573-2)
- The Holocaust Untold Story (ISBN 0-76-703992-0)

To order, call Glencoe at 1-800-334-7344. To find classroom resources to accompany many of these videos, check the following home pages:

A&E Television: www.aetv.com
The History Channel: www.historychannel.com

GLENCOE BOOKLINK 3

Use this database to search more than 30,000 titles to create a customized reading list for your students.

- Reading lists can be organized by students' reading level, author, genre, theme, or area of interest.
- The database provides Degrees of Reading Power™ (DRP) and Lexile™ readability scores for all selections.
- A brief summary of each selection is included.

Leveled reading suggestions for this chapter:

For students at a Grade 5 reading level:

- ***A Child's War: World War II Through the Eyes of Children,*** by Kati David

For students at a Grade 6 reading level:

- ***The Ancient Romans,*** by Jane Shuter

For students at a Grade 7 reading level:

- ***You Are in Ancient Greece,*** by Ivan Minnis

For students at a Grade 8 reading level:

- ***Anne Frank: The Diary of a Young Girl,*** by Anne Frank

For students at a Grade 9 reading level:

- ***The Ancient Roman World,*** by Ronald Mellor and Marni McGee

Focus

The Essential Question

As students study the chapter, remind them to consider the chapter-based Essential Question. Answering this question will help them understand the important concepts in the chapter. In addition, the Hands-On Chapter Project relates the content from each section to the Essential Question. The steps in each section activity build on each other as students progress through the chapter. The Hands-On Chapter Project culminates in the Wrap Up activity on the Visual Summary page.

More About the Photo

Visual Literacy The Teatro Greco di Taormina, or Greek Theater of Taormina, Sicily, attracts hundreds of visitors each year. The theater, which was built by the Greeks in the third century B.C., lies within sight of Mount Etna, a volcano nicknamed "the friendly giant" because of its slow-moving lava. The ancient theater still hosts live performances and film festivals each year.

CHAPTER 11

History and Cultures of Europe

Essential Question

Regions Europe is rich in history and culture. Like the United States, most countries in Europe are industrialized and have high standards of living. Unlike the United States, however, the people of Europe do not share a common language and government. What forces have helped unify Europeans at different times?

Teach

The BIG Ideas *As you begin teaching each section, use these questions and activities to help students focus on the Big Ideas.*

Section 

History and Governments Ask: What factors do you think affect the type of government people have? *(Answers may include: religion, culture and customs, values and ideals, education, outcomes of war, and other events in a country's history.)* Explain that countries in Europe have had many different forms of government over the centuries, including monarchies, democracies, and dictatorships. Tell students that Section 1 discusses the history and governments of Europe from ancient to modern times. Religious developments are highlighted. The chapter concludes with a brief description of the political changes in Europe during the late twentieth century. **OL**

Section 

Cultures and Lifestyles Ask: How might ethnic diversity have a positive influence on a society? *(Answers may include: It provides an opportunity to learn other languages and understand different traditions and cultures; it exposes people to different ways of living and thinking and can lead to greater tolerance; it allows people to enjoy foods and arts from other cultures.)* Explain

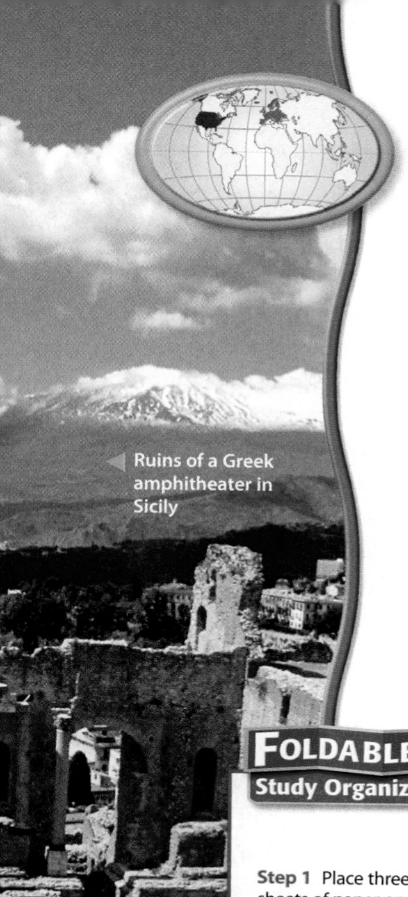

Ruins of a Greek amphitheater in Sicily

BIG Ideas

Section 1: History and Governments

BIG IDEA The characteristics and movement of people impact physical and human systems. Over the centuries, migrations and wars have brought different groups to power in Europe. As modern nations have taken the place of empires and kingdoms, ways of living and thinking have also changed.

Section 2: Cultures and Lifestyles

BIG IDEA Culture groups shape human systems. Europe is a region of many peoples with different ethnic backgrounds, languages, religions, and traditions. Despite their differences, Europeans lead similar lifestyles and share a rich cultural heritage.

FOLDABLES™ Study Organizer

Organizing Information Make this Foldable to help you organize information about Europe's history, population, and cultures.

Step 1 Place three sheets of paper on top of one another about 1 inch apart.

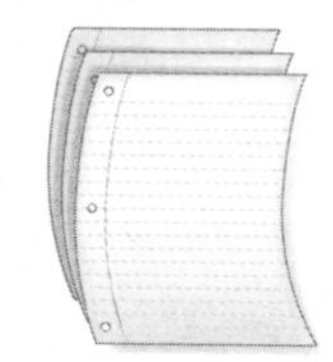

Step 2 Fold the papers to form six equal tabs.

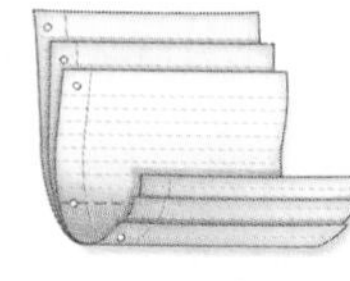

Step 3 Staple the sheets, and label each tab as shown.

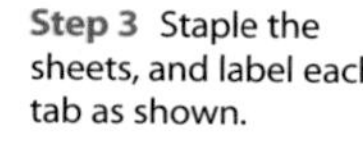

Reading and Writing As you read, use your Foldable to write down facts related to each period of European history, Europe's population, and European cultures. Then use the facts to write brief summaries for each of the tabs on the Foldable.

Social Studies ONLINE

To preview Chapter 11, go to glencoe.com.

Previewing the Region

If you have not already done so, engage students in the Regional Atlas and chart activities to help them become familiar with the general content of the region.

Dinah Zike's Foldables

Purpose This Foldable helps students organize information about Europe's history, population, and cultures. After students read the chapter and complete their Foldables, they can use the Foldables to write summaries and prepare for assessment. **OL**

More Foldables activities for this chapter can be found in the *Dinah Zike's Reading and Study Skills Foldables* ancillary.

Social Studies ONLINE

Introduce students to chapter content and key terms by having them access the Chapter Overview at glencoe.com.

that in Section 2 students will learn about the population changes that have taken place in Europe and the effect of these changes on European society. The section also describes the lifestyles of Europeans as well as changes in religion and the arts throughout Europe's history. **OL**

Focus

Bellringer

Daily Focus Transparency 11-1

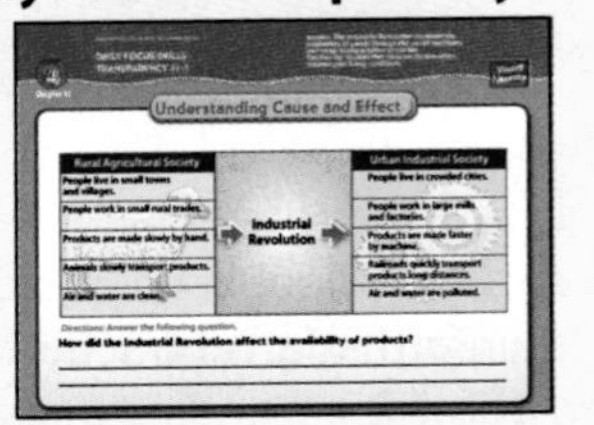

Guide to Reading

Answers to Graphic:

Time lines should include at least five key events and dates in Europe's history, such as:

- Rome becomes a republic, 509 B.C.
- Augustus becomes 1st Roman emperor, 27 B.C.
- Christianity becomes Rome's official religion, A.D. 392
- Charlemagne unites western Europe, c. A.D. 800
- European Union forms, A.D. 1993

Section Spotlight Video

To learn more about the history and governments of Europe, have students watch the Section Spotlight Video.

Guide to Reading

BIG Idea

The characteristics and movement of people impact physical and human systems.

Content Vocabulary

- classical *(p. 295)*
- city-state *(p. 295)*
- democracy *(p. 295)*
- republic *(p. 296)*
- emperor *(p. 297)*
- pope *(p. 298)*
- feudalism *(p. 298)*
- nation-state *(p. 299)*
- revolution *(p. 301)*
- Holocaust *(p. 302)*
- communism *(p. 303)*

Academic Vocabulary

- dominant *(p. 296)*
- authority *(p. 300)*
- currency *(p. 303)*

Reading Strategy

Making a Time Line Use a time line like the one below to list at least five key events and dates in Europe's history.

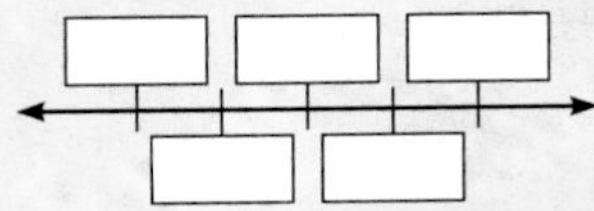

History and Governments

Picture This Who is that giant? Is it a warrior? A farmer? A king? One thing is certain—at almost 230 feet (70 m) high, the Long Man of Wilmington, in England, is one of the world's largest carved figures. Originally a chalk outline that became overgrown by grass, the Long Man was restored in 1969 with 770 concrete blocks. As scientists study the earth around the giant, they will be better able to judge when it was made—and maybe even why it was made! Read this section to learn more about the history of Europe.

▼ Ancient Long Man in hills of southern England

Resource Manager

R Reading Strategies	C Critical Thinking	D Differentiated Instruction	W Writing Support	S Skill Practice
Teacher Edition • Questioning, p. 295 • Visualizing, p. 295 • An. Text, p. 297 • Outlining, p. 298 • Previewing, p. 301 • Using Con. Clues, p. 301 • Summarizing, p. 302 **Additional Resources** • Primary Source, URB p. 27 • World Lit., URB p. 31	**Teacher Edition** • Draw Con., pp. 295, 302 • Det. Cause/Effect, pp. 299, 300 • Mak. Inferences, p. 299 • An. Pri. Sources, p. 301 **Additional Resources** • Geo. & Hist., URB p. 11 • Authentic Assess., p. 11 • Crit. Think., URB p. 71	**Teacher Edition** • Visual/Spatial, pp. 296, 298 • Adv. Learners, p. 297 • English Learners, p. 303 **Additional Resources** • Diff. Instr., URB p. 67 • Enrichment, URB p. 19 • School-to-Home Conn., URB p. 81	**Teacher Edition** • Narrative Writing, p. 300 **Additional Resources** • Writing Skills, URB p. 77	**Teacher Edition** • Using Geo. Skills, p. 296 • Visual Literacy, p. 298 **Additional Resources** • Daily Focus Trans. 11-1 • Reg. Atlas, URB pp. 1–7 • Read. Skills, URB p. 25 • Stand. Test Skills Prac., p. 41

Ancient Europe

Main Idea **Ancient Greece and Rome laid the foundations of European civilization.**

Geography and You Do you get to vote on family decisions or elect leaders to your student government? Read to find out how voting rights arose with the ancient Greeks and Romans.

The story of European civilization begins with the ancient Greeks and Romans. More than 2,500 years ago, these peoples settled near the Mediterranean Sea. Eventually their cultures spread throughout Europe and beyond. Even today, the influence of the **classical** world—meaning ancient Greece and Rome—lingers. R1

Ancient Greece

Physical geography naturally shaped the development of ancient Greece. The people felt deep ties to the land, which is ruggedly beautiful. At the same time, Greece's many mountains, islands, and the surrounding seas isolated early communities and kept them fiercely independent.

The earliest Greek civilizations began among farming and fishing peoples who lived near the Aegean Sea. These civilizations became wealthy through trade. After warfare led to their decline, independent territories called **city-states** developed throughout Greece. Each city-state was made up of a city and its surrounding area. Although separated by geography, the Greek city-states shared the same language and culture. R2

One of the most prosperous and powerful city-states was Athens. The people of Athens introduced the world's first **democracy**, a political system in which all citizens share in running the government. Although women and enslaved persons could not vote because they were not citizens, Athenian democracy set an example for later civilizations. Learning and the arts also thrived in Athens. Among the city-state's great thinkers were Socrates, Plato, and Aristotle. Their ideas about the world and humankind had a major influence on Europe. C

NATIONAL GEOGRAPHIC

Socrates and Plato

Socrates, on the left, taught by asking students pointed questions. His most famous student was Plato, another great Greek thinker.
Place **In which Greek city-state did democracy develop?**

During the mid-300s B.C., warfare weakened the Greek city-states. Soon an invader from the north, Philip II of Macedonia, conquered Greece. Philip's son earned the name Alexander the Great by making even more conquests. As shown in **Figure 1** on the next page, his empire included Egypt and Persia and stretched eastward into India. Trade boomed, Greek culture mixed with Egyptian and Persian cultures, and scientific advances spread. Alexander died young, however, and his empire quickly broke into several smaller kingdoms. By about 130 B.C., the Romans had conquered most of the Greek kingdoms.

Teach

R1 Reading Strategy

Questioning Ask students to think of a question about the Greeks and Romans that they would like to have answered. Students might want to use one of the words *who, what, why, where, when,* or *how* to help them focus on a specific topic. Then have them read the section to see if their question is answered there. **OL**

R2 Reading Strategy

Visualizing **Ask:** **Based on this description, were city-states large territories?** *(No; they included only a city and its surrounding area.)* **OL**

C Critical Thinking

Drawing Conclusions **Ask:** **How might a democracy promote the spread of learning, the arts, and new ideas?** *(In a democracy, people are able to participate in government and express their ideas freely.)* **OL**

Caption Answer:
Athens

Additional Support

Activity: Collaborative Learning

Creating Displays Show students a picture of the Parthenon. **Ask:** **What is this monument?** *(the Parthenon, a temple on the Acropolis in Athens, Greece)* Tell students that Greece has many ancient monuments and that these monuments are some of the most recognized structures in the world. Organize the class into small groups and have each group research one of Greece's landmarks, monuments, or historic sites. Groups should gather information and visuals to make a display. Facts about the landmark or site should reflect its importance in Greek history. Groups should document the sources for the facts and images used in their displays. After they complete their research, have groups present their displays to the class. **OL**

S Skill Practice

Using Geography Skills **Ask:** **Which bodies of water would have had the most impact on Roman development? Why?** *(the Black Sea, the Mediterranean Sea, and the Atlantic Ocean, because these bodies of water allowed Romans to get from one end of their empire to the other)* **OL**

D Differentiated Instruction

Visual/Spatial To help students understand the vast scope of the Roman Empire, have them compare this map to the political map of Europe in the Regional Atlas. Ask them to describe the countries that currently make up the area controlled by Rome. **BL**

Map Skills

Answers:
1. Answers may include Egypt and Greece.
2. The Roman Empire surrounded the Mediterranean Sea.

Social Studies ONLINE
Objectives and answers to the Student Web Activity can be found at glencoe.com under the Web Activity Lesson Plan for this chapter.

NATIONAL GEOGRAPHIC **Maps In MOtion** See StudentWorks™ Plus or glencoe.com.

Figure 1 Ancient Greek and Roman Empires

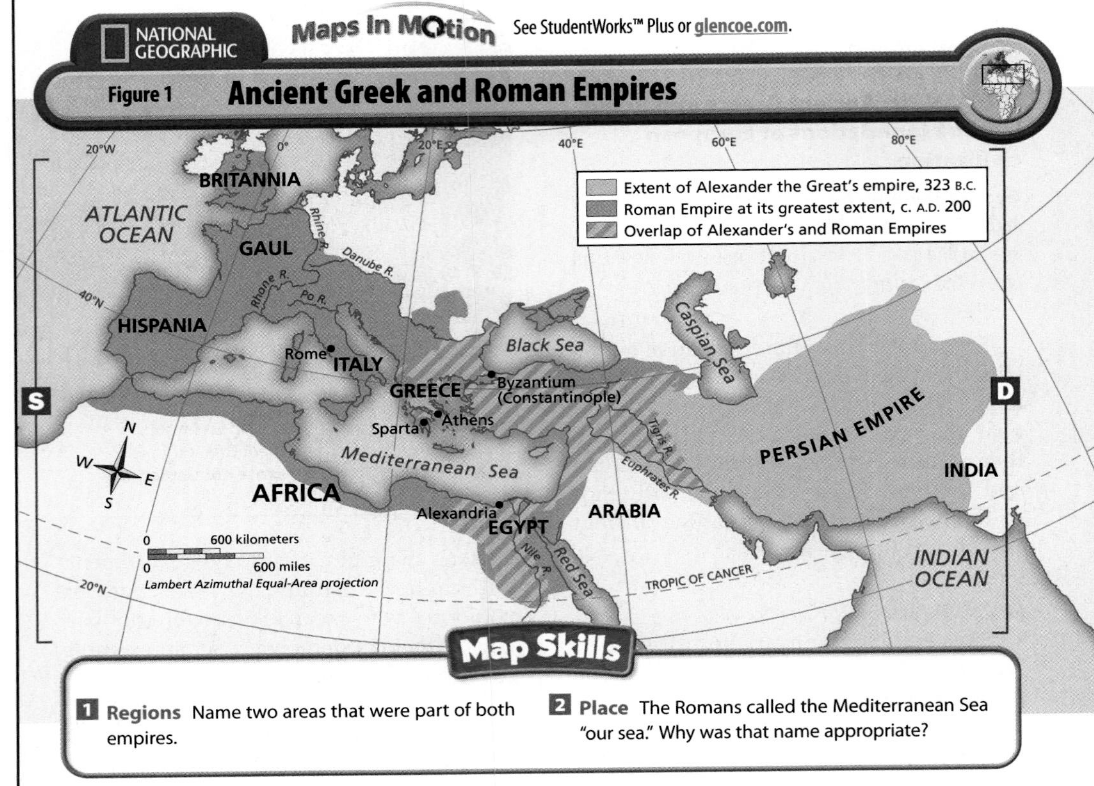

Map Skills

1 Regions Name two areas that were part of both empires.

2 Place The Romans called the Mediterranean Sea "our sea." Why was that name appropriate?

The Roman Empire

While Greece ruled the eastern Mediterranean, Rome became a **dominant** power on the Italian Peninsula. Rome began as a monarchy but changed to a republic in 509 B.C. In a **republic**, people choose their leaders. Rome was led by two consuls who were elected by the citizens. The consuls reported to and were advised by the Senate, an assembly of rich landowners who served for life. One of the government's great achievements was the development of a code of laws. Written on bronze tablets known as the Twelve Tables, the laws stated that all free citizens had the right to be treated equally. Roman law led to standards of justice still used today. For example, a person was regarded as innocent until proven guilty. Also, judges were expected to examine evidence in a case.

About 200 B.C., Roman armies began seizing territory throughout the Mediterranean region. Instead of ruling only by force, though, the Romans allowed many of the people they conquered to become Roman citizens. By granting people citizenship, the Romans were able to build a strong state with loyal members.

Social Studies ONLINE
Student Web Activity Visit glencoe.com and complete the Chapter 11 Web Activity on ancient Rome.

Differentiated Instruction

Leveled Activities

BL Reteaching Activity, URB p. 79

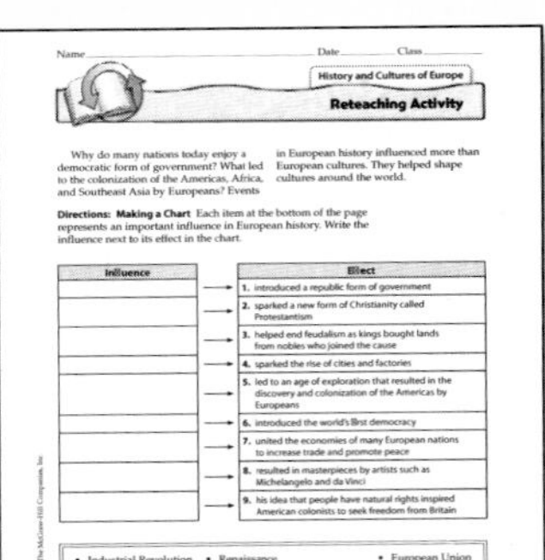

OL Writing Skills Activity, URB p. 77

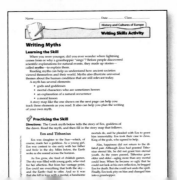

AL Primary Source Readings, URB p. 27

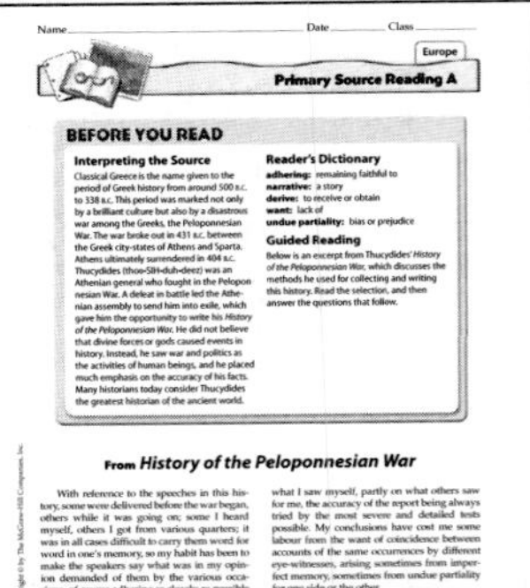

ELL School-to-Home Con. Act., URB p. 81

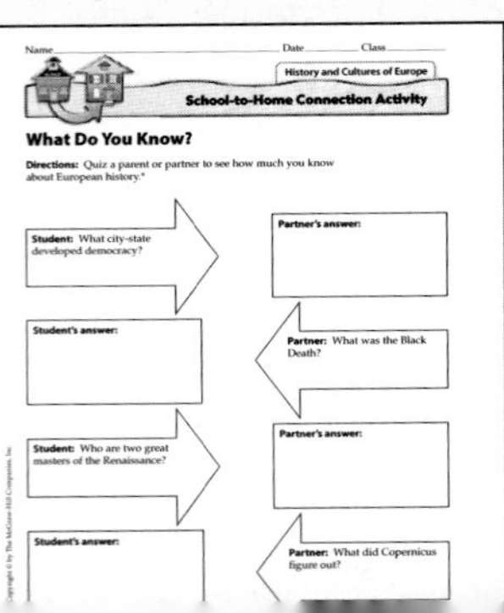

As the Roman Republic expanded, it evolved into the massive Roman Empire. The first **emperor**, or all-powerful ruler, was Augustus, who gained that position in 27 B.C. His rule brought order to Rome's vast lands. This period, called the *Pax Romana*, was a time of peace, artistic growth, and expanding trade that lasted about 200 years.

Christianity

During the *Pax Romana*, Christianity was developing in Palestine in the eastern part of the Roman Empire. There, a Jewish teacher, Jesus of Nazareth, preached a message of love and forgiveness. Jesus soon attracted followers as well as enemies. Fearing public unrest, the Roman authorities had Jesus executed. Yet within days, Jesus' followers, known as Christians, reported that he had risen from the dead. They took this as proof that Jesus was the son of God.

Eager to spread Jesus' teachings, two early Christian leaders, Peter and Paul, established the Christian Church in Rome. Roman officials at first persecuted, or mistreated, Christians. Despite this abuse, the new religion grew in popularity. In A.D. 392, Christianity became Rome's official religion.

Rome's Decline

By the late A.D. 300s, the Roman Empire was in decline. Rivals struggled to become emperor, and Germanic groups attacked from the north. About A.D. 395, the empire was divided into eastern and western parts. The eastern part remained strong and prosperous. Known as the Byzantine Empire, it lasted another thousand years. The western part was occupied by Germanic groups. In A.D. 476, Germanic leaders overthrew the last emperor in Rome and brought the Western Roman Empire to an end.

Despite its fall, Rome had great influence on Europe and the West. It helped spread classical culture and Christianity. Roman law shaped the legal systems in many countries. The Roman idea of a republic later influenced the founders of the United States. The Latin language of Rome became the basis for many modern European languages known as the Romance languages, such as Italian, French, and Spanish. Ancient Rome also influenced architectural styles in the Western world. For example, the U.S. Capitol and many other buildings have domes and arches inspired by Roman architecture.

Reading Check **Analyzing** Describe ancient Rome's influences on the modern world.

Roman Influences

NATIONAL GEOGRAPHIC

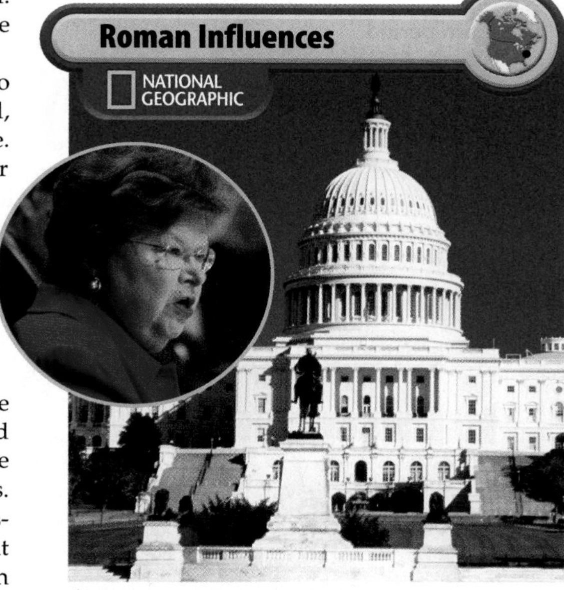

The style of the U.S. Capitol was influenced by Roman architecture. Barbara Mikulski (inset) is a member of the U.S. Senate, which has powers similar to the ancient Roman Senate. ***Place* Who made up the Roman Senate?**

R Reading Strategy

Analyzing Text Structure Ask: Is the text in these two paragraphs persuasive, narrative, or descriptive? *(narrative)* **How do you know?** *(because the events are in chronological order and it is organized like a story with a beginning, a middle, and an end)* OL

D Differentiated Instruction

Advanced Learners Have students research U.S. government organization and compare it to the government organization of the Roman Empire. Then have them complete a Venn diagram to illustrate the similarities and differences. AL

Reading Check **Answer:** Roman law shaped the legal systems of many countries, including the United States; the Latin language became the basis for many modern European languages; Roman styles and features influenced Western architectures.

Caption Answer: rich landowners

Geography and History Activity, URB pp. 11–12

Barbarians Invade the Roman Empire

Objective: Read to learn how attacks by Germanic invaders brought the Western Roman Empire to an end.

Focus: Define the word *barbarian* and identify the names of the Germanic tribes on the map.

Teach: On the board, list the reasons for the decline and fall of the Roman Empire.

Assess: Demonstrate an understanding of the invasions by answering the questions.

Close: Explain how place names in Europe provide evidence of the Germanic invasions.

Differentiated Instruction Strategies

- **BL** List the sequence of events in the article on a time line.
- **AL** Research and write a paper about one of the Germanic tribes.
- **ELL** Define the words *sacked* and *looted*. Explain why the word *vandal* is used today to mean "someone who willfully destroys someone else's property."

R Reading Strategy

Outlining To help students understand the text in this section, have them complete an outline, using the headings from the section as their outline headings. As students read, have them note important details under each outline heading. BL

S Skill Practice

Visual Literacy Ask: In addition to the thick walls, what other feature might have protected the nobles in this castle? *(the water, which would have made it difficult to attack the castle from this side)* OL

D Differentiated Instruction

Visual/Spatial Have students create graphic organizers to depict the feudal system. For example, students might draw a pyramid with the king at the top, the nobles beneath the king, and the peasants at the bottom. OL

Caption Answer:
Its thick walls and small windows would have made it hard for enemies to capture the castle. It also has towers from which people in the castle could fire on enemies.

Expansion of Europe

Main Idea During the Middle Ages, European society, religion, and government underwent great changes.

Geography and You Are there still parts of the world left to explore? Read to learn about changes in Europe, including how Europeans began to explore the far reaches of the world in the 1400s.

After Rome's fall, Europe entered the Middle Ages, a 1,000-year period between ancient and modern times. Christianity strongly influenced society during this period. In the 1300s, though, interest in education, art, and science exploded. Questions began to arise about earlier beliefs and practices. By the 1500s, Europe was experiencing changes that gave birth to the modern period.

Castle Conwy, Wales

NATIONAL GEOGRAPHIC

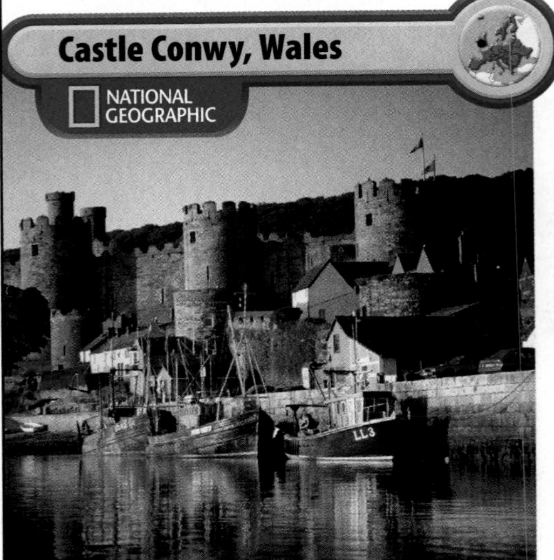

During the Middle Ages, nobles were forced to build thick-walled castles for protection against invaders. ***Place*** **How can you tell that this castle was built for defense?**

A Christian Europe

During the Middle Ages, Christianity held a central place in people's lives. Two separate branches of the religion had formed, though. The Roman Catholic Church, based in Rome, was headed by a powerful **pope.** The Eastern Orthodox Church was centered in the Byzantine Empire. The Roman Catholic Church spread Roman culture and law to the Germanic groups living in western and central Europe. In eastern Europe, the Byzantine Empire passed on Eastern Orthodoxy and Greek and Roman culture to Slavic groups.

The Middle Ages

About A.D. 800, a Germanic king named Charlemagne united much of western Europe. After his death, this empire broke up. At that point, no strong governments existed to help western Europeans withstand invaders. To bring order, a new political and social system arose by the 1000s. Under this system, called **feudalism,** kings gave land to nobles. The nobles in turn provided military service, becoming knights, or warriors, for the king. As romantic as this may sound, life was hard for the masses. Most western Europeans were poor peasants. They farmed the lands of kings, nobles, and church leaders, who housed and protected them but who also limited their freedom.

The Crusades

In feudal times, the Christian faith united Europeans. Yet the religion of Islam, founded in the A.D. 600s by an Arab named Muhammad, was on the rise. Followers of Islam, called Muslims, spread through Southwest Asia to North Africa and parts of Europe. They also gained control of Palestine, alarming Christians who considered this the Holy Land. Beginning in the

Hands-On Chapter Project Step 1

Art as a Reflection of History and Culture

Step 1: Locating Works of Art Groups of students will locate works of art that illustrate various periods in Europe's history.

Essential Question What forces have helped unify Europeans at different times?

Directions Explain that we can learn a great deal about people's ways of living and thinking by studying their art. Organize students into groups and assign each group one or two of the following periods: Greek Empire, Roman Empire, Middle Ages, Renaissance and Reformation, or modern Europe. Tell the groups that they should locate pictures of works of art that were created during their assigned period(s) to use in making presentations about each period. Explain that they should choose examples of art that show how people lived and what was important to them, and that illustrate important events. Remind students to look for unifying forces.

Summarizing Allow students time to share what they learned from this exercise. In section 2 students will make a presentation of their art. OL

(Chapter Project continued in Section 2)

1000s, nobles from western Europe gathered volunteers into large armies to win back the Holy Land. These religious wars, called the Crusades, were only partly successful. Muslims eventually recaptured much of the region.

The Crusades, however, had a major impact on Europeans. Goods began to flow more steadily between Europe and the Muslim lands. This trade benefited European kings, who taxed the goods that crossed their borders. Kings also took over land from nobles who left to fight in the Crusades. As a result, feudalism gradually withered, and Europe's kingdoms grew stronger and larger. Many of them later became modern Europe's **nation-states.** A nation-state is a country made up of people who share a common culture or history. C1

Muslim-Christian conflict arose again in Spain in the late 1400s. Since the A.D. 700s, Muslim groups had controlled parts of Spain. In what came to be known as the Reconquest, Spanish rulers forced out Muslims and united the country in 1492.

Meanwhile, in the 1300s, people all across Europe were battling a frightful disease. The bubonic plague, or Black Death, spread rapidly and killed perhaps a third of Europe's population. One consequence was a shortage of labor. Although the shortage hurt the economy, it helped workers earn higher wages and gain more freedom. In this way, the Black Death became another force that weakened feudalism.

The Renaissance

As parts of Europe recovered from the Black Death, interest in art and learning revived. Ways of thinking changed so much between about 1350 and 1550 that this period is called the Renaissance, from the French word for "rebirth."

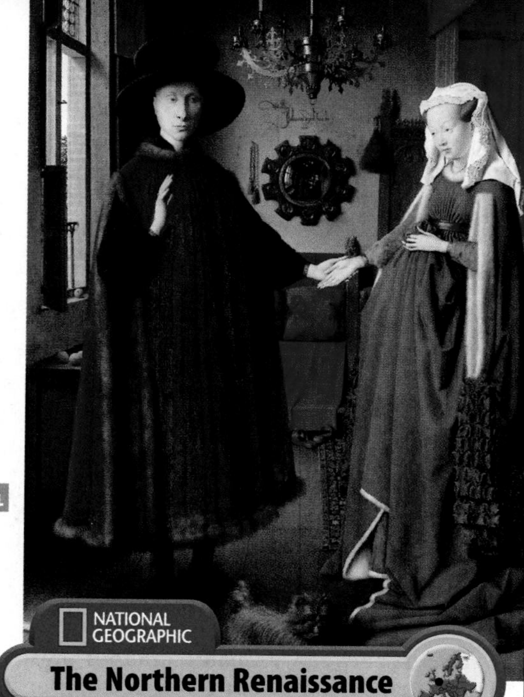

NATIONAL GEOGRAPHIC

The Northern Renaissance

Several great Renaissance artists were from northern Europe, including Jan van Eyck, who painted this portrait of a married couple. ***Location*** **Why did the Renaissance begin in Italian city states?**

The Renaissance thrived in Italian city-states, such as Florence, Rome, and Venice. Merchants in these city-states had gained great wealth through trade with Asia and the Mediterranean world. They then used this wealth to support scholars and artists. Poets, sculptors, and painters, such as Michelangelo and Leonardo da Vinci, created stunning masterpieces. People also took an interest in the cultures of ancient Greece and Rome. C2 Another important element of the Renaissance was humanism, a way of thinking that gave importance to the individual and human society. Humanism held that reason, as well as faith, was a path to knowledge. Over time, Renaissance ideas and practices spread from Italy to other parts of Europe.

C1 Critical Thinking

Determining Cause and Effect Have students create a cause-and-effect chart showing the effects of the Crusades. *(Effects: Trade between Europe and Muslim lands increased, and kings took land from crusading nobles. Both of these effects, in turn, caused kingdoms to grow stronger and feudalism to decline.)* **OL**

C2 Critical Thinking

Making Inferences Ask: Why might people in Italy have had an interest in ancient culture? *(Italy was the center of the Roman Empire, so Italians were surrounded by the ruins and art of ancient Rome.)* **AL**

This **Reading Skill** (Making Inferences) was introduced in this unit.

Caption Answer:
Merchants in Italian city-states acquired great wealth, which they used to support scholars and artists.

Additional Support

FastFacts

Bubonic Plague The bubonic plague was a severe infectious disease caused by *Yersinia pestis*, a bacterium carried by rodents. The plague was transmitted to humans by the bites of fleas that had fed on infected rodents' blood. Symptoms included a sudden onset of fever and chills, headache, nausea and vomiting, and swollen lymph nodes. Black boils often developed in the armpits, neck, and groin, which eventually gave the disease the name "Black Death." Death usually occurred within four to five days after infection, since people had not developed a cure for the plague. There are various theories about where the disease originated and how it reached Europe. It is generally believed that the disease originated in China and was carried by flea-infested rats from one port city to another. The Black Death continued to cycle through parts of Europe for four more centuries before public health and sanitation efforts significantly reduced the rate of infection.

C Critical Thinking

Determining Cause and Effect Ask: How did the Reformation affect religious unity and power in Europe? *(The religious unity of Europe was shattered. This weakened the authority of church leaders and strengthened the power of monarchs.)* OL

W Writing Support

Narrative Writing Have students research a European explorer of this time period and write a children's picture book telling the life story of the explorer. Instruct students to include the most important events in the explorer's life, and encourage them to use literary techniques, such as dialogue and suspense. Have students illustrate their stories and then read them to a class of younger students. OL

Reading Check Answer: It killed up to a third of Europeans, created a shortage of labor that helped workers gain higher wages and more freedoms, and helped bring an end to feudalism.

The Reformation

During the 1500s, the Renaissance idea of humanism led people to think about religion in a new way. Some people felt there were problems in the Roman Catholic Church that needed to be corrected.

In 1517 Martin Luther, a German religious leader, set out to reform, or correct, certain church practices. The pope in Rome, however, did not accept Luther's ideas, and Luther broke away from the Roman Catholic Church. Luther's ideas sparked a religious movement called the Reformation, which led to a new form of Christianity called Protestantism. By the mid-1500s, different Protestant groups dominated northern Europe, while the Roman Catholic Church remained strong in southern Europe.

C Wars between Roman Catholics and Protestants soon swept through Europe. The Reformation thus shattered the religious unity of Europeans. It also strengthened the power of monarchs. As the **authority** of church leaders was challenged, kings and queens claimed more authority for themselves.

European Explorations

W As Europe's kingdoms grew stronger, European seafarers began a series of ocean voyages that led to a great age of exploration and discovery. During the 1400s, Portugal wanted an easier way to get exotic spices from India and other parts of East Asia. Portuguese navigators developed new trade routes by sailing south around the continent of Africa to Asia. Sailing for Spain in 1492, the Italian-born explorer Christopher Columbus tried to find a different route to Asia. Instead of sailing south around the coast of Africa, Columbus attempted to sail west, across the Atlantic Ocean. Columbus's voyage took him to the Americas, continents unknown in Europe at the time.

In the Americas, Spain found gold and other resources and grew wealthy as a result of its overseas expeditions. Its success made other European countries, such as England, France, and the Netherlands, eager to send forth their own explorers. Conquests followed these voyages. Europeans began founding colonies, or overseas settlements, in the Americas, Asia, and Africa. Trade with the colonies brought Europe great wealth and power. Sadly, though, the Europeans often destroyed the local cultures in the lands they claimed.

Reading Check **Determining Cause and Effect** What changes did the Black Death bring to Europe?

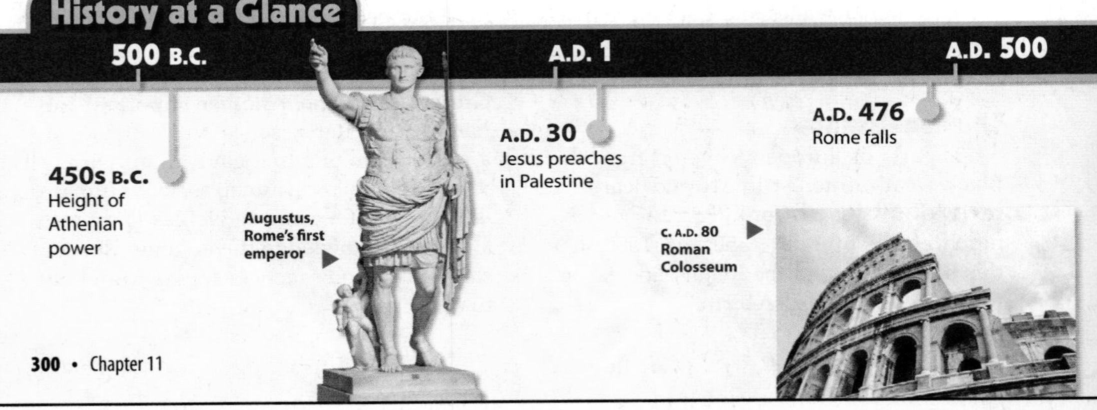

Additional Support

Activity: Economics Connection

Problem Solving Explain to students that Europeans in the 1400s were looking for new trade routes to Asia because transporting goods from Asia had become difficult and more expensive. **Ask: How did European explorers solve the problem of getting goods from Asia?** *(They found new routes around Africa to Asia, and Christopher Columbus tried to sail west to get to Asia.)* Organize students into small groups. Give each group the following scenario: "You have decided to buy a new computer. You can buy the same computer at the same price from a small, neighborhood electronics store, from a large discount store in another city 50 miles away, or from a company on the Internet." Have students list the steps they would need to follow to determine which way of getting the computer would be (a) fastest and (b) least expensive. Make sure they take into account such variables as shipping costs, travel time, and travel costs. Then have each group decide which method of getting the computer they would use. Groups should present their decisions to the rest of the class and explain why they chose that method. AL

Modern Europe

Main Idea **From the 1600s to the 1800s and beyond, new ideas and discoveries helped Europe become a global power.**

Geography and You How would your life be different without computers, cell phones, or other modern technologies? Read on to discover how new technology changed Europe after 1600.

From the 1600s to the 2000s, Europe experienced rapid change. New machines helped economies grow. Powerful new weapons, however, made for deadly wars.

The Enlightenment

After the Renaissance, educated Europeans turned to science as a way to explain the world. Nicolaus Copernicus, a Polish mathematician, concluded that the sun, not the Earth, is the center of the universe. An Italian scientist named Galileo Galilei believed that new knowledge could come from carefully observing and measuring the natural world. These and other ideas sparked a **revolution**, or sweeping change, in the way people thought. During this Scientific Revolution, many Europeans relied on reason, rather than faith or tradition, to guide them. Reason, they believed, could bring both truth and error to light. As a result, the 1700s became known as the Age of Enlightenment.

Englishman John Locke was an important Enlightenment thinker. He said that all people have natural rights, including the rights to life, liberty, and property. He also said that when a government does not protect these rights, citizens can overthrow it. The American colonists later used Locke's ideas to support their war for independence from Britain in 1776.

Inspired by the American example, the people of France carried out their own political revolution in 1789. They overthrew their king, executed him three years later, and set up a republic. The French republic did not last long, however. A brilliant military leader named Napoleon Bonaparte gained power and made himself emperor. Napoleon was a small man with big ambitions. His armies conquered much of Europe, until several countries united to defeat him in 1815.

Political revolutions continued to erupt in Europe in the 1800s. By 1900, most countries had responded by limiting the powers of rulers and guaranteeing at least some political rights to citizens.

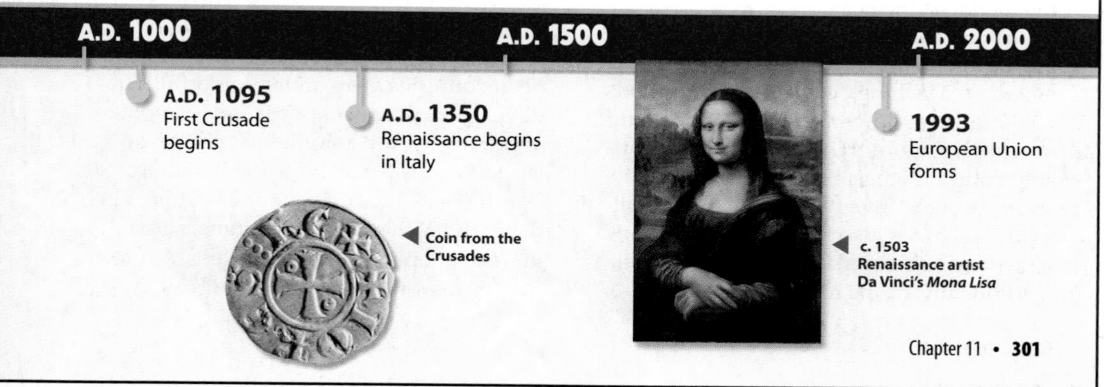

◀ Coin from the Crusades

◀ c. 1503 Renaissance artist Da Vinci's *Mona Lisa*

R1 Reading Strategy

Previewing Have students read the Main Idea and Geography and You. **Ask: What important changes in Europe do you think you will be reading about?** *(new ideas, discoveries, and technologies)* BL

C Critical Thinking

Analyzing Primary Sources Provide students with a copy of the Declaration of Independence and have them read it. Ask them to compare the rights stated in the Declaration of Independence to the rights proposed by John Locke. **Ask: What similarities do you see between John Locke's ideas and the ideas expressed in the Declaration of Independence?** *(Both call for the right to life and liberty, as well as the right to overthrow a government that does not protect people's rights.)* AL

For further practice on this skill (Analyzing Primary Sources), see the **Skills Handbook**.

R2 Reading Strategy

Using Context Clues Have students use context clues to determine the meaning of the word *executed* in the sentence. *(killed)* ELL

Activity: Interdisciplinary Connection

Science Ask: Which areas of study were most affected by the Scientific Revolution? *(Answers may include math, astronomy, physics, chemistry, biology, and medicine.)* Organize students into small groups. Assign each group one or more of the following people to investigate—Nicolaus Copernicus, Andreas Vesalius, William Harvey, Robert Hooke, Francis Bacon, Galileo Galilei, Johannes Kepler, René Descartes, Robert Boyle, Antoine Lavoisier, Marie Lavoisier, Martha Ramsey, Nichole-Reine LePaute, and Isaac Newton. Ask students to conduct research to learn more about each person's contribution to science or math. Students should determine when and where each of these scientists and mathematicians lived and the major discoveries attributed to him or her. Have groups share their findings with the class. As each group presents its research, complete a chart on the board with columns for the scientist's name, dates of birth and death, home country, and major discoveries. Use this chart to discuss the impact of the Scientific Revolution and how certain scientists built on the discoveries of others. OL

C Critical Thinking

Drawing Conclusions **Ask:** **Based on the map, is the European Union becoming more popular or less popular among European nations?** *(It is becoming more popular.)* **OL**

R Reading Strategy

Summarizing Have students write a summary of the text describing the Industrial Revolution. To prevent students from repeating the text word for word, tell them their summaries can be no longer than three sentences. **OL**

Map Skills

Answers:

1. Brussels
2. The euro makes trade among European countries easier.

Skills Practice

Ask: **Which Western European countries are not part of the European Union?** *(Iceland, Switzerland and Norway)*

Additional Support

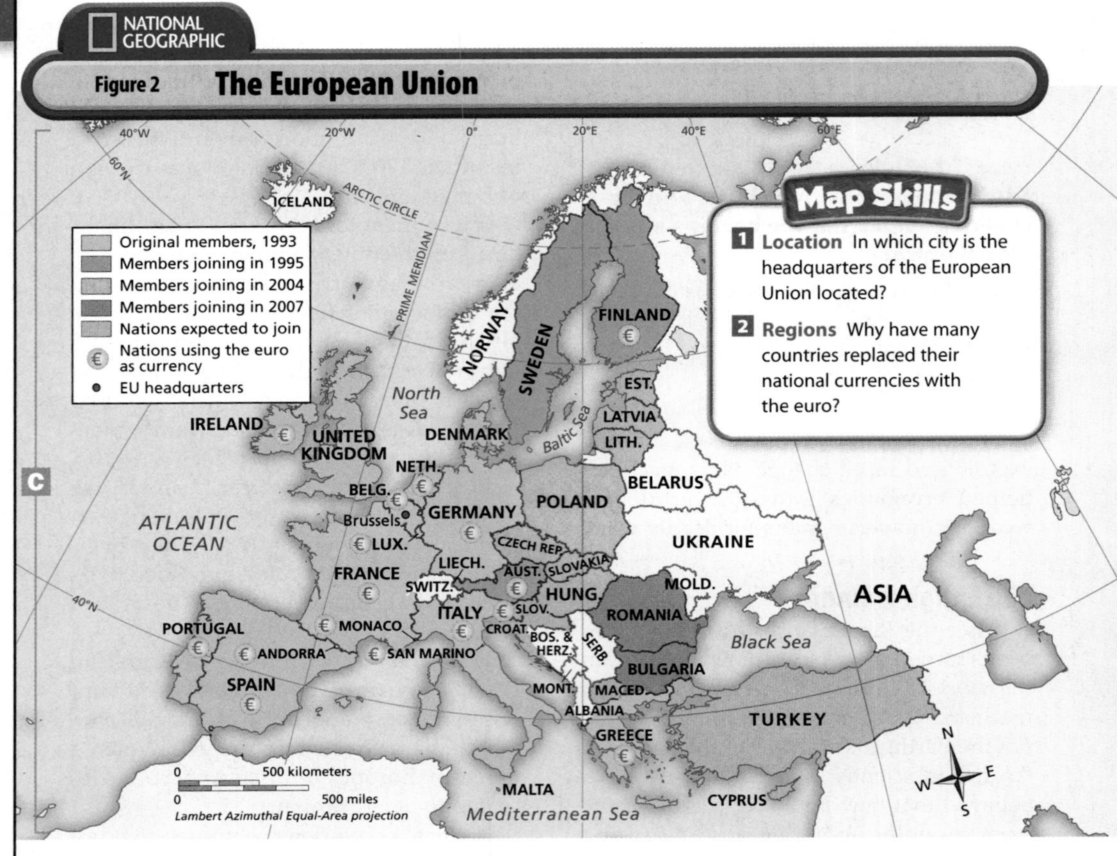

Map Skills

1. **Location** In which city is the headquarters of the European Union located?
2. **Regions** Why have many countries replaced their national currencies with the euro?

Industry and Conflict

Meanwhile, an economic revolution was also transforming Europe. The Industrial Revolution began in Britain. As it spread, it changed the way that people across Europe lived and worked.

Instead of making goods by hand, people began using machines and building factories. Machines could produce goods faster and at lower cost. People could now afford more things, such as comfortable cotton clothes. Travel improved, too, thanks to new inventions such as the railroad. Machines also helped farmers grow more food, which led to population growth. Additionally, farms required less labor.

Many people left farms to find work in cities. Cities became crowded, industries spewed out pollution, and diseases spread. Urban life remained grim for many Europeans until the mid-1800s. In the long run, though, the achievements of the Industrial Revolution benefited most people.

Industrial advances also helped European countries grow more powerful. They developed new weapons and competed aggressively for colonies. Tensions soon led to World War I (1914–1918) and World War II (1939–1945). These devastating conflicts left much of Europe in ruins, with millions of people dead or homeless. A major horror of World War II was the **Holocaust**,

Activity: Technology Connection

Diagramming Explain to students that the Industrial Revolution was possible because of great technological advancements. Timesaving machines included the spinning jenny, the power loom, and the cotton gin. **Ask:** **What machines make your life easier today?** *(Answers may include hair dryers or washing machines.)* **How might new technology help workers?** *(New technology often helps people do their jobs faster and more easily.)* Tell each student to select an invention from the Industrial Revolution. Then have them research to learn more about the invention and use presentation software to describe the invention to the rest of the class. The presentation should include a diagram of the machine with each part labeled. Have students explain how each invention worked and how it saved time or helped people do their jobs more easily. **OL**

the mass killing of 6 million European Jews by Germany's Nazi rulers.

After World War II, the United States and the Soviet Union became rivals in the Cold War. This was not a war of bullets and bombs, but a struggle for world power. Much of Western Europe allied with the United States. Most lands in Eastern Europe allied with the Communist Soviet Union. **Communism** is a system in which the government controls the ways of producing goods.

A New Era for Europe

In 1989 people in Eastern Europe forced several Communist governments from power and set up new democracies. A year later, East and West Germany merged to become one democratic state. Then in 1991, the Soviet Union broke apart.

In 1993 several democracies in Western Europe formed the European Union (EU). The goal of the organization, which now also includes eastern European countries, is a united Europe. The EU allows goods, services, and workers to move freely among member countries. It has also created a common EU **currency** called the euro. Member countries, shown in **Figure 2,** can now trade more easily among themselves because there is no need to exchange, for example, French francs for German marks.

Reading Check **Describing** What was the Age of Enlightenment?

Section 1 Review

Social Studies ONLINE
Study Central™ To review this section, go to glencoe.com.

Vocabulary

1. **Explain** the significance of:
   a. classical
   b. city-state
   c. democracy
   d. republic
   e. emperor
   f. pope
   g. feudalism
   h. nation-state
   i. revolution
   j. Holocaust
   k. communism

Main Ideas

2. **Describing** Describe the political system of ancient Athens.
3. **Explaining** How did the Crusades help lead to the creation of modern Europe's nation-states?
4. **Summarizing** Use a diagram like the one below to summarize the changes brought about by the Industrial Revolution.

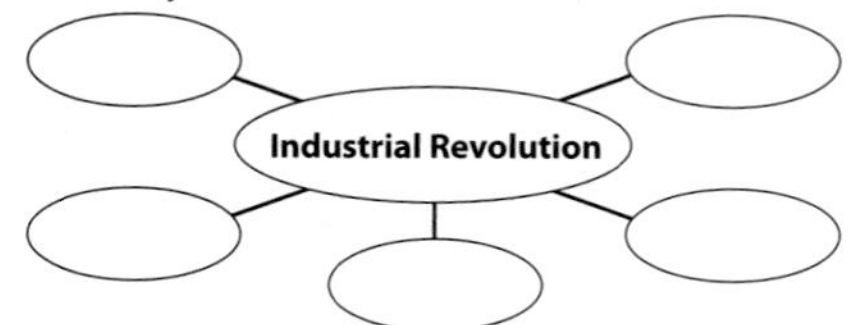

Critical Thinking

5. **Analyzing** How did Rome build a large, strong empire?
6. **Challenge** Which of Europe's revolutions do you think was most important for the creation of modern Europe? Explain your answer.
7. **BIG Idea** Provide an example of how political or social ideas, such as democracy or Christianity, spread in Europe.

Writing About Geography

8. **Using Your FOLDABLES** Use your Foldable to write a summary describing how governments in Europe have changed over time.

D Differentiated Instruction

English Learners Explain to students that the word *mass* has several meanings. In this case, it means "a large number, or amount, of people." **ELL**

Reading Check **Answer:** a time when people began to rely on reason, rather than faith or tradition, to guide them and bring truth and error to light

Assess

Social Studies ONLINE
Study Central™ provides summaries, interactive games, and online graphic organizers to help students review content.

Close

Describing Have each student describe to a partner the important events that took place in ancient, medieval, and modern Europe. **OL**

Answers

1. Definitions for the vocabulary words are found in the section and the Glossary.
2. Ancient Athens was the world's first democracy; citizens shared in running the government.
3. During the Crusades, European kingdoms grew stronger, as kings became wealthy from trade and took land from crusading nobles. Many of these kingdoms later became modern Europe's nation-states.
4. Machines produced goods faster and at lower cost than work done by hand; people could afford more things; travel improved; farmers grew more food with less labor; populations grew; cities became crowded; industries produced pollution; diseases spread; European countries grew more powerful.
5. Roman armies conquered territories throughout the Mediterranean. The Romans then granted citizenship to many conquered peoples. This built a strong empire with loyal members.
6. Answers should show a clear link between the revolution and its impact on modern Europe.
7. Answers should focus on a specific political or social idea and explain how it spread through Europe.
8. Summaries should include the various types of government throughout Europe's history.

Focus

R Reading Strategy

Predicting Ask students to predict what might happen if they moved to a country in which English was not spoken. **Ask:** **How would you feel if you were not allowed to speak English at school?** *(Possible answer: I would be confused at first, because I would not understand what was going on.)* **OL**

For further practice on this skill (Predicting), see the **Skills Handbook**.

Teach

Have students create a T-chart with the headings "For Speaking the Same Language" and "Against Speaking the Same Language." As they read the feature, have them note arguments for and against allowing only the country's official language to be spoken in schools. **OL**

Additional Support

Learning in School: Should All Students Speak the Same Language?

R **In Europe, migration between countries is common. As a result, many students do not speak the local language where they live. Some educators believe that all students should speak the nation's official language in school. For example, in Berlin, Germany, several schools allow only the German language to be spoken during class, on school property, and on school trips. However, others disagree, arguing that students should be allowed to learn in their own languages.**

For Speaking the Same Language

I believe that knowledge of the German language is the key to integration [becoming part of society] and to success both at school and in a future profession. . . . The pupils themselves are very satisfied with [this rule], because they know that speaking correct German increases their opportunities. . . .

When children start school and don't speak the language correctly, they . . . receive worse grades. That continues throughout their schooling and in the end they aren't able to get a vocational [job] training place. That's why we are in favour of introducing language tests starting from the age of four and thereby promoting language skills from kindergarten on.

—Armin Laschet
Minister for Generations, Family, Women, and Integration
North Rhine-Westphalia, Germany

FastFacts

Regional Languages Throughout much of Europe, various groups speak languages that are different from the official languages of their countries. In fact, it is estimated that nearly 40 million people in the European Union speak a regional or minority language. These languages are not simply dialects of the majority language of the country or foreign languages spoken by immigrants. They are distinct languages that have been passed down from generation to generation within the country itself. One example of a regional language is Catalan, a language spoken by about 7 million people in parts of Spain, France, and Sardinia; Another example is Saami, a family of languages spoken in parts of Scandinavia. Experts have identified more than 60 regional or minority languages in the European Union. Some of these languages are spoken by as little as a few hundred people.

Speaking the Same Language

Banning pupils from speaking their [traditional] languages in the schoolyard is not the answer, even if it were workable, which it is not. Other means of developing their linguistic [language] skills, such as pre-school instruction in German, are much more likely to be effective and should be fully supported.

. . . It is perfectly acceptable to ban other languages within the classroom. But outside the classroom pupils should be free to speak whichever language they like. Banning pupils' [traditional] languages sends a message that they are somehow "second class" citizens, which is likely to promote resentment rather than integration. . . .

Many children of immigrants choose to communicate in German in any case. . . .

There also appears to be a fallacy [mistaken belief] that speaking another language somehow [takes away] from pupils' ability with German. This is not the case. Humans have an almost unlimited ability to learn languages and in general there is no reason why the average person cannot master two or more languages.

—David Gordon Smith
Editor, Expatica: Germany

You Be the Geographer

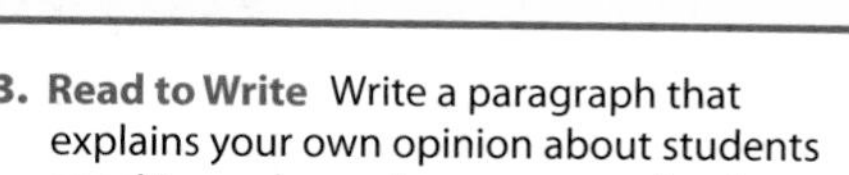

1. **Identifying** What reasons do Laschet and Smith give to support their opinions?
2. **Critical Thinking** What might be some challenges for a student who speaks a different language than that of the other students in his or her class?
3. **Read to Write** Write a paragraph that explains your own opinion about students speaking only one language at school.

Assess/Close

Organize the students into two groups to debate allowing only one language to be used in schools. Have students prepare by finding additional resources in the library or on the Internet. Then have each group present its arguments before another teacher at your school. Ask this teacher to explain which group was more persuasive. **OL**

You Be the Geographer

Answers:

1. Laschet: requiring the use of an official language will help students integrate more quickly and be more successful in school and in the future; Smith: banning students from speaking their traditional languages makes them feel inferior and that other, more effective ways can be used to develop their language skills.
2. It might be difficult for the student to make friends and to understand what is being taught.
3. Answers will vary, but students should give reasons to support their opinions.

Activity: Connecting With the United States

Language Learning in the United States Ask students if they have heard about a similar controversy in the United States. Explain that a great deal of debate takes place over how best to integrate Spanish-speaking students into American classrooms. Although people do not always agree on how best to teach English to Spanish-speaking students, many people do agree that English-speaking students could benefit from learning a second language in elementary school. Dual-immersion programs, which teach English- and Spanish-speaking students in both languages, are becoming more common. **Ask: Do you think dual-immersion programs would be beneficial? Why or why not?** *(Possible answer: Yes, because many students must learn a foreign language in high school, so learning a language in elementary school gives them a head start at a time in their lives when learning a second language is easier.)* **OL**

Focus

Bellringer

Daily Focus Transparency 11-2

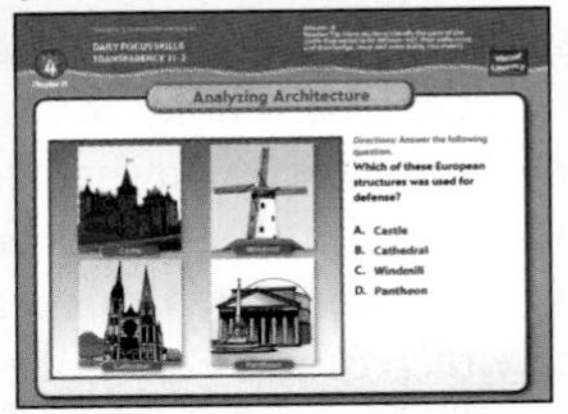

Guide to Reading

Answers to Graphic:

Europe's Population: crowded into a relatively small space; not distributed evenly; many ethnic groups; number of immigrants increasing; overall population decreasing and aging

Section Spotlight Video

To learn more about the cultures and lifestyles of Europe, have students watch the Section Spotlight Video.

Guide to Reading

BIG Idea

Culture groups shape human systems.

Content Vocabulary

- ethnic group *(p. 307)*
- welfare state *(p. 307)*
- fertility rate *(p. 307)*
- urbanization *(p. 308)*
- secular *(p. 310)*

Academic Vocabulary

- bond *(p. 307)*
- attitude *(p. 310)*

Reading Strategy

Organizing Information Use a diagram like the one below to list key facts about Europe's population patterns.

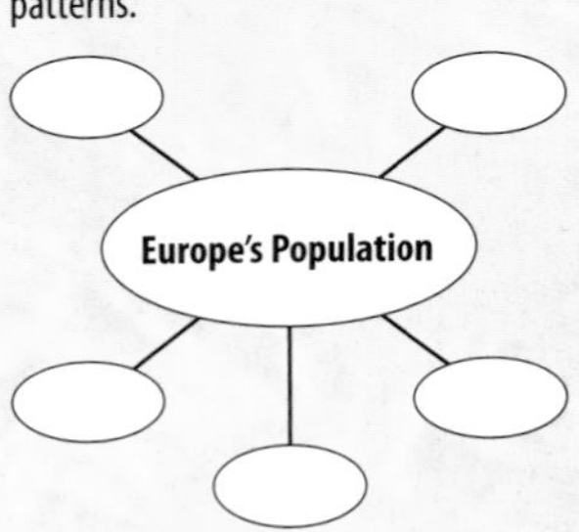

SECTION 2 Cultures and Lifestyles

Picture This Bog snorkeling? For more than twenty years, competitors wearing snorkels and flippers have met in the small town of Powys, Wales, to swim in its slimy bog. The challenge is to swim the fastest without using any standard swimming strokes. The just-for-fun event has attracted swimmers from as far away as South Africa and Australia. Read Section 2 to learn more about the cultures and lifestyles of Europeans.

Decorated in blue paint, this swimmer hopes to win first place.

Resource Manager

R Reading Strategies	C Critical Thinking	D Differentiated Instruction	W Writing Support	S Skill Practice
Teacher Edition • Using Cont. Clues, p. 307 • Questioning, p. 308 • Act. Prior Know., p. 309 • Ac. Vocab., p. 310 • Making Con., p. 311 **Additional Resources** • Guid. Read., URB p. 62 • Cont. Vocab., URB p. 63 • Ac. Vocab., URB p. 65	**Teacher Edition** • Predicting, p. 311 **Additional Resources** • Crit. Think., URB p. 71 • Env. Case Studies, URB p. 13 • Geo. & Econ., URB p. 9 • Quizzes and Tests, p. 122	**Teacher Edition** • Visual/Spatial, p. 307 • Logical/Math., p. 308 • Adv. Learners, p. 310 **Additional Resources** • GeoLab, URB p. 23	**Teacher Edition** • Persuasive Writing, p. 307 **Additional Resources** • Writing Skills, URB p. 77	**Teacher Edition** • Visual Literacy, p. 309 **Additional Resources** • Daily Focus Trans. 11-2 • Reg. Atlas, URB pp. 1–7 • Chart, Graph, and Map Skills, URB p. 69 • Speak/Listen Skills, URB p. 73

Population Patterns

Main Idea **Ethnic differences and population changes pose challenges for Europe.**

Geography and You How do you treat a new person who joins your class? What kind of challenges does he or she face? Read to discover how Europe is responding to its new immigrant populations.

Europe's people are crowded into a relatively small space. The population is not distributed evenly, however, and it continues to undergo change.

A Rich Ethnic Mix

Today Europe is home to many ethnic groups. An **ethnic group** is a group of people with shared ancestry, language, and customs. Europe's ethnic mix has resulted from migrations, wars, and changing boundaries over the centuries. **D**

Many Europeans identify strongly with their particular country or ethnic group. Having a common heritage or culture creates **bonds** among people. National and ethnic loyalties, however, have also led to conflict. In the 1990s, disputes among ethnic groups split Yugoslavia into five separate countries. In some of these new countries, ethnic hatred sparked the worst fighting in Europe since World War II.

Despite divisions, Europeans have a growing sense of unity. They realize that because their countries are linked by geography, cooperation can help bring peace and prosperity. In addition, the people share many values that go beyond ethnic or national loyalties. For example, Europeans value democracy and human rights. They also believe that a government must care for its citizens. Many European countries are **welfare states** in which the government is the main provider of support for the sick, the needy, and the retired.

NATIONAL GEOGRAPHIC

A Changing Population

These schoolgirls in London demonstrate Europe's growing immigrant population and ethnic diversity. ***Movement*** **From where have people immigrated to Europe?**

Population Changes

Because of recent immigration, Europe's population is still undergoing change. Since World War II, many people from Asia, Africa, and Latin America have settled in Europe. Tensions have risen as immigrants and local residents compete for jobs, housing, and social services. As a result, immigrants have not always felt welcome in many places in Europe. **R**

European countries deal with immigrants in various ways. Some want immigrants to adapt quickly, so they require newcomers to learn the national language. Other countries pass laws to keep immigrants from settling within their borders. Still others try to improve educational and job opportunities for newcomers. **W**

You might be surprised to learn that although the number of immigrants is increasing, the region's overall population is decreasing. Europe has a low **fertility rate**, which is the average number of children born to each woman.

Teach

D Differentiated Instruction

Visual/Spatial Have students work in small groups to create a collage entitled "Europe's Ethnic Diversity." Direct students to use magazines and their own artwork to illustrate the various ethnic groups that live in Europe. **OL**

R Reading Strategy

Using Context Clues **Ask: What is an immigrant?** *(a person who comes to a new country from another country)* **BL**

W Writing Support

Persuasive Writing Have students select one of the ways that European countries deal with immigrants. Then have them write a paragraph persuading the reader that this is an effective approach to supporting immigration. **OL**

Caption Answer:
Asia, Africa, and Latin America

Additional Support

Activity: Economics Connection

Predicting Ask: What is happening to the overall population of Europe? *(It is decreasing.)* **What will happen to the workforce if the number of young people decreases?** *(Fewer people will be available to fill positions.)* Tell students to imagine that their class represents the population of a European country. One-third of the class is older and retired from the workforce. Another third is not yet old enough to work. **Ask: What does this mean for the remaining third?** *(A small group must work to provide for the rest of the population.)* Discuss with students the economic issues facing Europe as its population both decreases and ages. **OL**

D Differentiated Instruction

Logical/Mathematical Tell students that in 2005, the population of Europe was estimated at 728 million. Have them calculate what the population will be in 2050 if the population decreases by 10 percent. *(655 million)* OL

R Reading Strategy

Questioning Have students write one question based on each heading within this subsection. Have them next write down what they think the answers will be. After students read the section, have them examine how their questions were answered in the text. BL

Reading Check **Answer:** Ethnic and national loyalties create bonds among people who share a common culture or heritage, but they can also lead to conflict and violence.

Caption Answer:
There will be fewer workers to keep the country's economy growing and to support an aging population.

D As a result, Europe is expected to have 10 percent fewer people by 2050. This is worrisome, because there will be fewer workers to keep Europe's economy growing. Meanwhile, Europeans are living longer because of better health care. As older people increasingly account for a greater share of the population, young workers will face higher taxes to support them.

Reading Check **Making Generalizations** How do national and ethnic loyalties benefit and harm Europeans?

NATIONAL GEOGRAPHIC

European Fashion

With their generally high incomes, many Europeans can afford the latest fashions, like the one worn by this model at a fashion show in Paris. ***Regions*** **How might a shrinking population affect Europe's economy?**

R Life in Europe

Main Idea **European lifestyles today reflect the region's urban society and level of wealth.**

Geography and You Does the idea of living in a city appeal to you? Read to discover how cities play an important part in the lives of Europeans.

Customs, languages, and religions have always differed among Europeans. In recent decades, however, differences in lifestyles among Europe's peoples have lessened as a result of industrial and economic growth, urban growth, and improved standards of living. Today, most Europeans are well-educated city dwellers with comfortable incomes.

Cities

Beginning in the late 1700s, the Industrial Revolution changed Europe from a rural, farming society to an urban, industrial society. Rural villagers moved in large numbers to urban areas. This concentration of people in towns and cities is known as **urbanization.** Many of Europe's cities grew quickly and became some of the world's largest.

Today, three of every four Europeans live in cities. Paris and London rank among the largest urban areas on the globe. The next biggest cities are Milan, Italy; Madrid, Spain; and Berlin, Germany.

Many European cities blend the old and the new. Ancient landmarks often stand near modern highways and skyscrapers. European cities are also crisscrossed by public transportation systems that bring people to jobs and urban attractions. In recent decades, however, more Europeans have bought cars and have chosen to live in suburbs outside the cities.

Additional Support

Teacher Tip

Collaborative Learning Doing research can sometimes isolate students, or cause some to feel like they do all the work. You can help groups work more effectively by asking them to set clear goals and delegate specific responsibilities among all members of the group.

Activity: Collaborative Learning

Describing Ask: What are Europe's largest cities? *(London, Paris, Madrid, Milan, and Berlin)* Have students work in small groups to research a major city in Europe. The city may be one of those listed in the text, or it may be another city of the students' choice. Instruct students to use online and library resources to find the following information about their city: population, major industries, ethnic composition, landmarks, and other cultural and historical points of interest. Tell students to describe their city to the class using a multimedia format that includes maps, photos and music. Have students begin their presentations by showing where their city is located on a map of Europe. OL

Transportation

Most of Europe's transportation systems are government owned. Standards differ from country to country, but overall, Europe boasts one of the world's most advanced transportation networks. The rail system is vast, linking cities and towns across the continent. Trains even travel underwater between England and France via a 31-mile (50-km) tunnel called the Chunnel. France developed the use of high-speed trains, which cause less damage to the environment than most other forms of transportation. High-speed rail lines now operate in a number of European countries.

Highways also allow high-speed, long-distance travel. Cars can zip along Germany's autobahns at more than 80 miles (129 km) per hour. Trucks use the roadways to carry the great majority of freight within Europe.

Canals and rivers are also used to transport goods. The Main-Danube Canal in Germany links hundreds of inland ports between the North Sea and the Black Sea. Europe's long coastline is dotted with other important ports, such as Rotterdam, in the Netherlands. This is one of the busiest ports in the world.

Airports connect European cities too. Planes fly both people and goods to their destinations all around Europe.

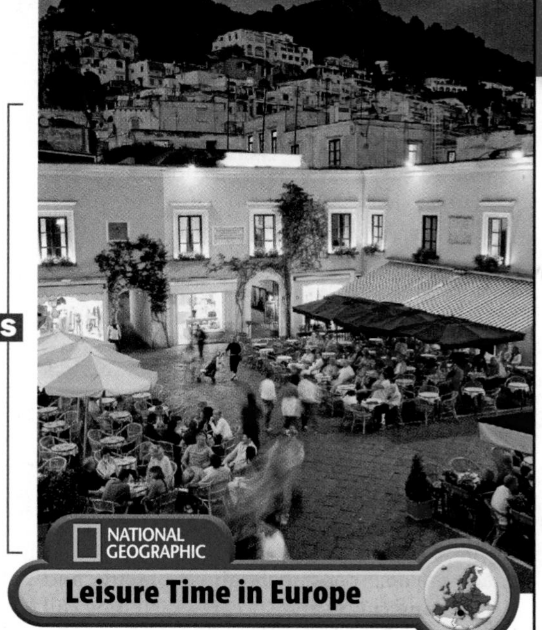

NATIONAL GEOGRAPHIC

Leisure Time in Europe

Europeans enjoy dining with friends at outdoor cafés, such as this one on the island of Capri, Italy. ***Regions*** **What other leisure activities are popular with Europeans?**

Education and Income

Europeans take schooling seriously. They tend to be well educated and have some of the highest literacy rates in the world. More than three-quarters of young people complete high school.

Because of their high levels of education, Europeans earn more money than people in many other parts of the world. There are differences, however, from place to place. Incomes are higher in northern and western Europe than in southern and eastern Europe. Many eastern European countries are still struggling to rebuild economies that were damaged by conflicts or slowed by years of Communist rule. Throughout Europe, service industries, such as banking, provide more jobs than any other economic activity.

Income can also vary greatly within a country. For example, unemployment and poverty are common in southern Italy. Mountains and a lack of natural resources in the area have slowed the development of industry. Workers are better off in northern and central Italy, where rich farmland and modern industries provide many jobs.

Leisure

Their relatively high incomes allow many Europeans to enjoy their leisure time. They have a generous amount of it too!

R Reading Strategy

Activating Prior Knowledge Ask students if they have ever seen a canal. Have those who have seen canals describe them. Have pictures of canals ready to share in case no one has seen one. Then ask students to explain the purpose of canals. *(Canals connect areas that are not linked by natural waterways, and they are often used for transporting goods.)* **BL**

S Skill Practice

Visual Literacy Have students write a paragraph describing the scene in the picture. Instruct them to use adjectives and action verbs in their writing that explain what is happening. **OL**

Caption Answer:
travel, outdoor sports, and spectator sports

Differentiated Instruction

Environmental Case Study, URB pp. 13–16

Traveling Light

Objective: Read to discover the importance of public transit in western Europe.

Focus: Examine the map of rail lines in western Europe and compare it to train use in the United States.

Teach: Discuss why using public transit is better for the environment than using cars.

Assess: Design a city that provides sustainable transportation.

Close: Create a poster of a "sustainable city."

Differentiated Instruction Strategies

BL List the different types of transportation used in western Europe, and give one environmental benefit for each.

AL Research high-speed train use in Europe. List its advantages.

ELL Find pictures of the different types of transportation and label each one.

D Differentiated Instruction

Advanced Learners Have students research how popular sports, such as rugby and soccer, affect the lives of people in Europe. Ask students to compare the sports customs in Europe to those in the United States. **AL**

R Reading Strategy

Academic Vocabulary Ask: **What does "attitudes" mean in this paragraph?** *(feelings or way of thinking about something)* **ELL**

Reading Check Answer: service industries

Caption Answer: ice hockey and skiing

Differentiated Instruction

In a number of European countries, workers receive four weeks of paid vacation each year. Many Europeans use this vacation time to travel. France and Italy are popular vacation spots because of their lively cities, beautiful countryside, mild climate, and fine food.

D Europeans also take full advantage of their natural surroundings. The region's mountains, seas, lakes, and rivers provide great opportunities for recreation. Winter sports such as ice hockey and skiing had their beginnings in Scandinavia about 5,000 years ago. In summer, Europeans lace up their hiking boots, hop on their bikes, or take to the water. Many Europeans are also passionate about playing and watching rugby and soccer, which they call football.

Reading Check **Making Connections** What type of industry provides the most jobs in Europe?

Football in Europe

NATIONAL GEOGRAPHIC

Many Europeans, like these Romanians, enjoy playing soccer. Rules for the game were first established in England in the 1800s. ***Regions*** **What winter sports developed in Europe?**

Religion and the Arts

Main Idea **Religion, especially Christianity, has had an important effect on European society and arts.**

Geography and You If you enjoy creative writing or making art or music, what ideas inspire you? Read on to find out how religion, nature, and other influences shaped the arts in Europe.

As in other parts of the world, religion has shaped European culture, including its arts. Today, though, European art reflects a variety of influences.

Religion

R For centuries, Christianity was a major influence in European life. Since the 1700s, however, European **attitudes** have become more **secular,** or nonreligious. Today many Europeans do not belong to a particular religious group. Still, Christian moral teachings, such as respect for human life and compassion for others, remain core values throughout the region.

Most of Europe's Christians are Roman Catholic. As you can see in **Figure 3,** Roman Catholics are heavily concentrated in the southern part of western Europe and in some eastern European countries. Protestants are dominant in northern Europe. Eastern Orthodox churches are strongest in the southern part of eastern Europe.

Judaism and Islam have also influenced European culture. Judaism, like Christianity, reached Europe during Roman times. Despite eras of persecution, Jews have made major contributions to European life. Today, Jewish communities thrive in all major European cities. Meanwhile, Muslim immigrants are pouring into the region by the thousands.

Leveled Activities

BL Speaking and Listening Skills Activity, URB p. 73

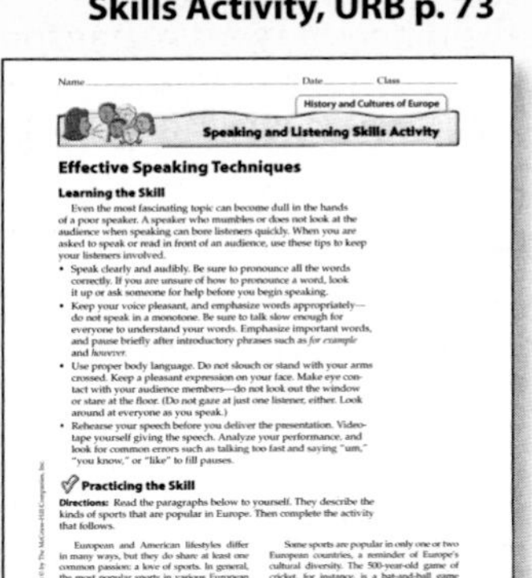

History and Cultures of Europe

Speaking and Listening Skills Activity

Effective Speaking Techniques

OL Chart, Graph, and Map Skills Activity, URB p. 69

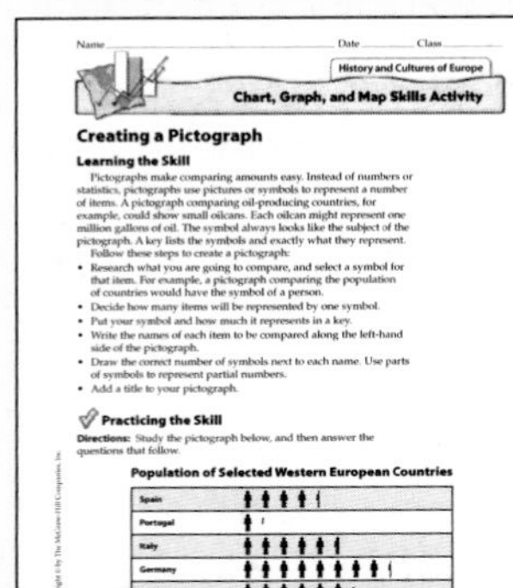

History and Cultures of Europe

Chart, Graph, and Map Skills Activity

Creating a Pictograph

Population of Selected Western European Countries

AL Critical Thinking Skills Activity, URB p. 71

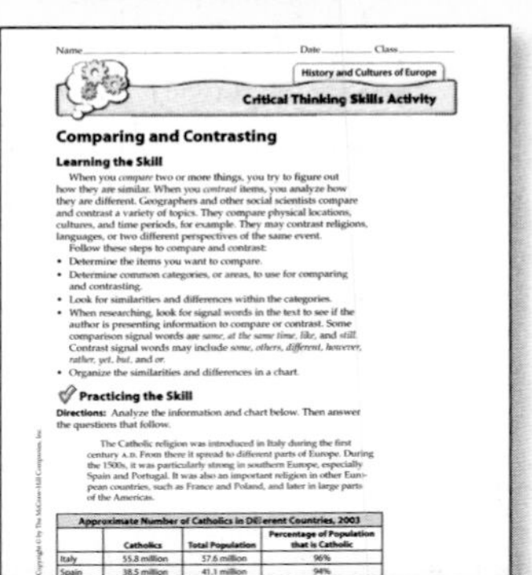

History and Cultures of Europe

Critical Thinking Skills Activity

Comparing and Contrasting

ELL Academic Vocabulary Activity, URB p. 65

For the most part, Europeans of different faiths live together peacefully. In some cases, though, Europe's religious differences have led to violence. For years, hostility between Catholics and Protestants created conflict in Northern Ireland, a part of the United Kingdom. Since 1998, both sides have agreed to share political power, but the situation remains unstable. Religious and ethnic differences were also at the heart of troubles on the Balkan Peninsula. There, Roman Catholic, Eastern Orthodox, and Muslim groups fought over land and political power during the 1990s. **C**

Arts

The arts have flourished in Europe for centuries. In ancient times, the Greeks and Romans constructed stately temples and public buildings with huge, graceful columns. During the Middle Ages, a new style known as Gothic architecture arose. Europeans built majestic churches called cathedrals, designing them with pointed arches and large, stained-glass windows. **R**

Religion also inspired European art, literature, and music. From ancient times to the Middle Ages, artists and writers focused on holy or heroic subjects.

NATIONAL GEOGRAPHIC

Figure 3 **Europe's Religions**

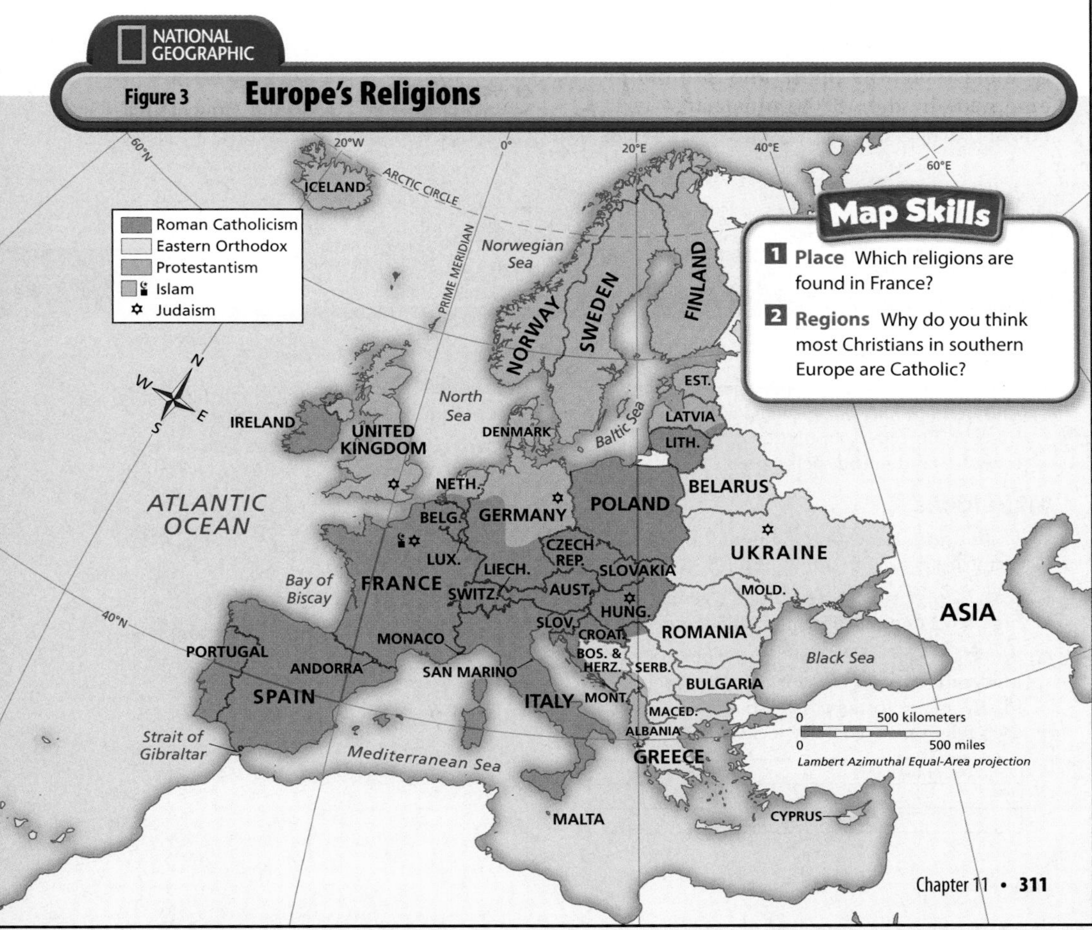

Map Skills

1. **Place** Which religions are found in France?
2. **Regions** Why do you think most Christians in southern Europe are Catholic?

C Critical Thinking

Predicting Ask: Based on this information, do you think religious clashes will continue in Europe? Why? *(Possible answer: yes, because so many different religious groups live in Europe, and because the religious composition is continuing to change; also, because religious groups tend to cluster in neighborhoods where they face challenges as a unified group)* **OL**

For additional practice with this skill (Predicting), see the **Skills Handbook**.

R Reading Strategy

Making Connections Provide students with photographs of Gothic architecture in Europe. Then have them research the library or Internet for examples of this architectural style in the United States. **AL**

Map Skills

Answers:

1. Roman Catholicism, Islam, and Judaism
2. because southern Europe is closer to Rome, the seat of the Roman Catholic Church

Hands-On Chapter Project
Step 2

Art as a Reflection of History and Culture

Step 2: Making the Presentations Groups will present the works of art they chose in Step 1 and explain the significance of each.

Directions Explain that works of art reflect the cultures of the people who created them. Remind students that "culture" has many elements, including language, religion, arts, government, economy, social structure, and daily life. Have each group present the works of art they have chosen for their assigned period(s). The groups should explain the significance of each work and why they chose to include it in their presentation.

Putting It Together Have students discuss what their images reveal about European culture. **OL**

(Chapter Project cont. on the Visual Summary page)

Reading Check **Answer:** For much of Europe's history, artists and writers focused on holy or heroic subjects, and composers wrote pieces to accompany religious services. In eastern Europe, symbolic religious images, or icons, were painted on wood. During the Renaissance, styles changed, but artists continued to create religious art.

Assess

Social Studies ONLINE
Study Central™ provides summaries, interactive games, and online graphic organizers to help students review content.

Close

Summarizing Have students write a paragraph summarizing life in Europe. **OL**

Composers wrote pieces to accompany religious services. In eastern Europe, Christian art included icons, or symbolic religious images painted on wood.

During the 1500s and 1600s, Renaissance artists continued to create religious art, but their art also portrayed life in the everyday world. Renaissance artists tried to make their works more realistic. When you study a painting by Leonardo da Vinci or a statue by Michelangelo, you will see lifelike figures. In the writings of England's William Shakespeare or Spain's Miguel de Cervantes, you will encounter believable characters with timeless problems.

Artistic creativity continued to soar in Europe. In the 1600s and 1700s, new types of music, such as opera and symphony, emerged. In the 1800s, musicians, writers, and artists developed a style known as Romanticism, which aimed to stir strong emotions. This style drew inspiration not from religion but from nature and historical events. Later in the 1800s, the Impressionist movement began. Impressionist painters used bold colors and brushstrokes to create "impressions" of the natural world.

In the 1900s, European artists moved away from portraying the world as it appeared to the human eye. They turned to abstract painting to express feelings and ideas. Architects began to create sleek, modern buildings using materials such as glass and concrete. New kinds of music, such as rock and roll, caught on. Today Europe's artists remain creative and influential.

Reading Check **Analyzing** How has religion influenced the arts in Europe?

Section 2 Review

Social Studies ONLINE
Study Central™ To review this section, go to glencoe.com.

Vocabulary

1. **Explain** how the terms *ethnic group, welfare state, fertility rate, urbanization,* and *secular* relate to Europe's population by writing a sentence containing each word.

Main Ideas

2. **Explaining** How do individual European countries deal with immigration?
3. **Describing** How does Europe's generally high level of education affect life there?
4. **Identifying** Use a chart like the one below to identify Europe's major religions, including the major forms of Christianity, and where each religion is generally located in Europe.

Major Religion	Where Found

Critical Thinking

5. **Challenge** Will immigration benefit Europe in the future? Explain your answer.
6. **Drawing Conclusions** What factors have slowed economic development in certain areas of Europe?
7. **BIG Idea** What factors help unify Europe's different ethnic groups today?

Writing About Geography

8. **Expository Writing** Write a paragraph comparing European and American cultures.

Section 2 Review

Answers

1. Sentences should use vocabulary words according to their definitions in the section and glossary.
2. Some countries require immigrants to learn the national language; others pass laws to keep immigrants out; still others try to help immigrants by improving their educational and job opportunities.
3. Europeans earn more money than people in many other parts of the world and generally have high standards of living and much leisure time.
4. Roman Catholicism: southern part of western Europe and some eastern European countries; Protestantism: northern Europe; Eastern Orthodox: southern part of eastern Europe; Islam: throughout the region; Judaism: major European cities
5. Possible response: Yes, because Europe's overall population is decreasing and more workers will be needed to keep its economy growing and to support its aging population
6. damage from conflicts, Communist rule, mountains, lack of natural resources
7. Europeans share many values that go beyond ethnic loyalties. They also realize that cooperation can help bring peace and prosperity.
8. Paragraphs should compare American culture with European culture.

Visual Summary

Ancient Europe

- The Greek city-state of Athens introduced the world's first democracy.
- Rome influenced later civilizations through its legal system, its language, and its role in the spread of Christianity.
- Invasions by Germanic peoples led to the Roman Empire's decline.

Caesar Augustus

Europe's Expansion

- Christianity shaped Europe's society and culture during the Middle Ages.
- The Renaissance, which began in Italy, brought about a new interest in learning.
- European countries controlled various parts of the world as a result of overseas explorations.

Map of the world, c. 1620

Modern Europe

- Through revolutions people challenged the power of kings and demanded certain rights for citizens.
- As industries grew, many people left rural areas to find work in city factories.
- Two costly world wars led European countries to seek peace and greater unity.

Population Patterns

- Europe is densely populated in many areas.
- Europe's population is aging, and the total population is declining.
- Many people have immigrated to Europe from Asia, Africa, and Latin America.

Playing chess in Prague, Czech Republic

Life and Culture

- Europeans tend to live in urban areas and have relatively high levels of education and income.
- With more leisure time, Europeans enjoy sports such as soccer.
- European society and culture have become more secular.

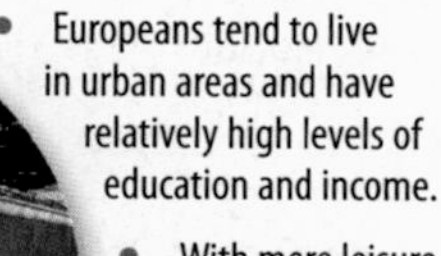

Eurostar train, London

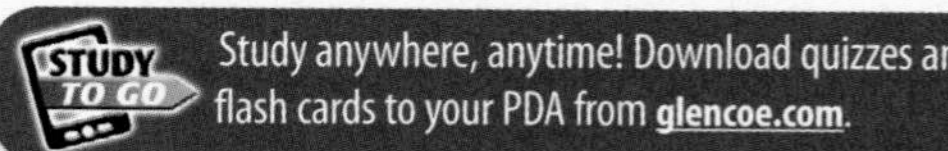

Study anywhere, anytime! Download quizzes and flash cards to your PDA from glencoe.com.

Visual Summary

Classifying Have students create board games that require players to classify facts under the headings "Ancient Europe," "Europe's Expansion," or "Modern Europe." Organize students into small groups and have them use the text to find facts for each category. If needed, have students use a T-chart with the category headings to classify the facts they find before they reproduce them in their games.

Before students begin, have them think about other board games they have played and game shows they have seen on television. Ask them to decide which game format would work best for classifying facts. Supply students with various art and scrap materials to create their boards and game pieces. Also provide them with samples of game instructions to use as models for their own instructions. After students finish creating their games, have each group demonstrate how it is played. Then allow students to play other groups' games. **OL**

Identifying Central Issues Have students read the points under the heading "Population Patterns." **Ask:** **What do you think is the main challenge facing Europe's population?** *(Possible answers include the decline in the total population and its effects on the economy or the impact that an increase in immigration is having in many European countries.)* **OL**

Hands-On Chapter Project
Step 3: Wrap Up

Art as a Reflection of History and Culture

Step 3: Learning From Art Students will synthesize what they have learned in Steps 1 and 2.

Directions Write the Essential Question on the board. Ask students to think about what they have learned from the presentations of European art that might help them answer this question. Create a chart on the board with two columns, "Unifying" and "Divisive." **Ask:** **What events in European history promoted unity? What events were divisive? What aspects of culture were unifying? What aspects caused conflict and division?** As students answer each question, record their ideas under the appropriate column. At the end of the discussion, have students write a few sentences in their journals to answer the Essential Question. **OL**

Answers and Analyses

Reviewing Vocabulary

1. B Students may be confused because three of the answers refer to systems of government discussed in the chapter. *Communism* is a modern form of government in which the state controls the method of producing goods. A *republic* is form of government in which people elect their rulers. Only in *feudalism* was land exchanged for service.

2. C This question presents a challenge because all the answers are titles used for people who govern or lead in some fashion. However, both *emperor* and *king* are titles for secular rulers, while the other two choices, *pope* and *archbishop*, are religious titles. *Pope*, which comes from the Latin *papa*, meaning "father," is the title for the head of the Catholic Church.

3. A One way to remember the definition of *classical* is to consider the meaning of *classic*, which refers to something that endures or is memorable. The influence of Greece and Rome has lasted thousands of years. Hence, their world is called *classical*.

4. D If students read this question carefully, they will realize that they are looking for a term that refers both to government and caring for the needy. Most students will be familiar with the term *welfare*, which has come to mean financial assistance from the government.

5. B The key here is to analyze which terms could impact population growth. The most difficult term is *urbanization rate*, because students may assume that a growing urban area translates into a larger population.

STANDARDIZED TEST PRACTICE

TEST-TAKING TIP

Eliminate answers that do not make sense. For instance, if an answer refers to a region of the world other than Europe, you know it cannot be correct.

Reviewing Vocabulary

Directions: Choose the word(s) that best completes the sentence.

1. In the system known as ______, nobles provided service to a king in exchange for land.

A communism
B feudalism
C a republic
D a city-state

2. The head of the Catholic Church is called the ______.

A emperor
B king
C pope
D archbishop

3. The ______ world refers to ancient Greece and Rome.

A classical
B Hellenistic
C democratic
D dominant

4. In a(n) ______, the government is the main provider of support for the sick, needy, and retired.

A democracy
B corporate donor
C urbanized center
D welfare state

5. Because Europe has a low ______, it is expected to have 10 percent fewer people by 2050.

A urbanization rate
B fertility rate
C ethnic group
D secular group

Reviewing Main Ideas

Directions: Choose the best answer for each question.

Section 1 *(pp. 294–303)*

6. The prosperous Greek city-state of Athens introduced the world's first ______.

A democracy
B artistic thinkers
C free society
D army

7. The ______ resulted in the rise of a new form of Christianity called Protestantism.

A Crusades
B Reformation
C Enlightenment
D Renaissance

Section 2 *(pp. 306–312)*

8. Europe's population shifts may pose challenges because

A few jobs exist for the growing population.
B few people immigrate into the region.
C Europeans are no longer living as long.
D there will be fewer workers to keep Europe's economy growing.

9. Which of the following most clearly explains how European lifestyles reflect the region's level of wealth?

A Europeans are able to enjoy their leisure time.
B Transportation standards vary from country to country.
C More than three-quarters of Europeans complete high school.
D Many eastern Europeans are still struggling from years of Communist rule.

GO ON

Reviewing Main Ideas

6. A Students should realize that there were armies and artistic thinkers in other civilizations prior to Athens. Because there were enslaved people in Athens, it was not a completely free society. This leaves choice A, *democracy*, which was one of Athens' most important contributions.

7. B One of the interesting facts about the Reformation is that its leaders did not originally intend to start a new form of Christianity. Luther merely wanted to reform the Church. Hence, the period is called the Reformation.

Critical Thinking

Directions: Choose the best answer for each question.

10. Which of the following was a result of the Renaissance?

A A revival in art and literature began.

B Workers gained higher wages and more freedoms.

C A new form of Christianity developed.

D Many European countries began to send out explorers.

Base your answer to question 11 on the map below and your knowledge of Chapter 11.

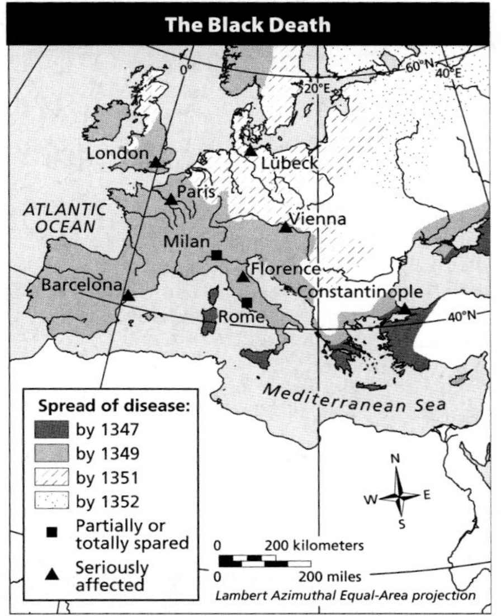

11. Which city was first affected by the Black Death?

A Constantinople

B Paris

C Lübeck

D Barcelona

Document-Based Questions

Directions: Analyze the document and answer the short-answer questions that follow.

In 1215 nobles in England forced King John to sign the Magna Carta. This document gave common people some freedoms and limited the power of the king. It was an important influence in the rise of democratic governments.

> *TO ALL FREE MEN OF OUR KINGDOM*
>
> *we have also granted, for us and our heirs for ever, all the liberties written out below . . .*
>
> *(20) For a trivial offence, a free man shall be fined only in proportion to the degree of his offence. . . .*
>
> *(30) No sheriff, royal official, or other person shall take horses or carts for transport from any free man, without his consent. . . .*
>
> *(40) To no one will we sell, to no one deny or delay right or justice.*
>
> —Magna Carta

12. What does article 20 of the Magna Carta mean? Rephrase it in your own words.

13. What complaints do you think the Magna Carta attempted to fix?

Extended Response

14. Take the role of a citizen of a European country that is not in the European Union but is debating whether to apply for membership. Write a short speech explaining why you think your country should or should not join the EU.

STOP

Social Studies ONLINE

For additional test practice, use Self-Check Quizzes—Chapter 11 at glencoe.com.

Need Extra Help?

If you missed question. . .	1	2	3	4	5	6	7	8	9	10	11	12	13	14
Go to page. . .	298	298	295	307	307	295	300	308	309	299	299	299	299	303

Critical Thinking

10. A If students have trouble with this question, remind them that *Renaissance* means "rebirth." This may help them remember that the Renaissance was a renewal of art and learning.

11. A In order to correctly answer this question, students need to pay attention to what cities lie in what shades or patterns and compare them to the key. Some students may look at the map too quickly and miss *Constantinople*.

Document-Based Questions

12. Possible answer: Free men will not be fined excessively. Students should note the intent of this article is for the punishment to fit the crime.

13. Possible answer: People were being punished excessively; sheriffs, officials, and others were taking horses and carts from people without their consent; people were being denied justice.

Extended Response

14. Answers will vary, but students should consider the benefits of joining the European Union and weigh these against the cost of joining the union for their particular country.

8. D This question includes answers that distract because they relate to population changes. However, most of the statements are simply not true. Europe's population is declining, not growing, more people are immigrating into the region, and Europeans are living longer. Therefore, only choice D is a true statement.

9. A Students may have difficulty choosing the correct answer because all of the answer choices are true statements. However, only answer choice A relates to European lifestyles in a way that reflects the region's level of wealth.

Social Studies ONLINE

Have students visit the Web site at glencoe.com to review Chapter 11 and take the Self-Check Quiz.

Need Extra Help?

Have students refer to the pages listed if they miss any of the questions.

Teach

C Critical Thinking

Comparing and Contrasting Ask: **How does Kade's breakfast compare with breakfasts eaten in the United States?** *(Possible answer: different: American children do not normally drink warm chocolate milk out of bowls; similar: American children often eat some type of bread)* **OL**

R Reading Strategy

Using Context Clues Ask: **Do you think Kade's brother is older or younger than she is? Why?** *(probably younger, because she picks him up from school)* **OL**

TIME JOURNAL

"Hello! My name is Kade.

I am 13 years old and live in Paris, the capital of France. My family moved here from Guinea, a country in Africa. Like other immigrant families, we blend some of our own traditions with France's rich culture. Here's how I spend my day."

8:45 a.m. My mom wakes me up. I sleep late today because school does not start until 10 o'clock on Mondays! (On other days, it begins at 8 o'clock.) I shower and get dressed.

9:15 a.m. I eat breakfast with my parents and little brother and sister. We have warm chocolate milk, which we drink out of bowls. We also have flaky rolls called croissants. Croissants are delicious. I like them best when they are filled with chocolate.

9:40 a.m. I meet my friends and walk to school. We can see the Eiffel Tower from our building.

10:00 a.m. It's the start of a long day—and a long week. Like many French kids, I go to school six days a week. Wednesdays and Saturdays are half days, though. I look forward to them!

10:15 a.m. In history, my first class, we are learning about ancient Greece. Then I study geography. Our geography classroom is decorated with flags from all over the world.

12:00 p.m. In music class, I take an exam on the flute. I hope I did well!

1:00 p.m. It's time for *déjeuner* (day•zhuh•NAY), or lunch. Many students go home for lunch, but I buy my meal in the cafeteria. Today I choose a grapefruit, chicken nuggets, and pasta.

2:00 p.m. I go to the computer lab for technology class. After that, we have a short recess period. My friends and I play dodgeball. I enjoy sports. I think I would like to be a handball instructor one day.

3:00 p.m. In English class, we practice saying sentences that begin with the phrase, "Do you like…?" My English is already strong because we often speak it at home, but this lesson is fun.

4:00 p.m. School is over. I walk back home with my friends. Today, some of them come to my apartment. We watch music videos and listen to CDs. I like most kinds of music, including rock and reggae.

6:00 p.m. My dad will be home from work soon. He designs and sells clothing. My mom is starting to prepare dinner. I help her out by picking up my brother from school.

6:30 p.m. I do my homework.

7:30 p.m. Dinner is ready. We are having rice with fish and vegetables in a spicy sauce. It is a dish that is popular in Guinea. Now my family has brought it to France!

8:30 p.m. I play and watch cartoons with my little brother and sister.

9:30 p.m. I brush my teeth and go to bed. I listen to music until I get sleepy. I use earphones so I do not wake my sister.

ILLUSTRATIONS BY BOOKMAPMAN

BEFORE CLASS Kade meets up with her friends. French students go to school six days a week.

DODGEBALL At Kade's school, this sport is popular at recess. Soccer is still the number one sport in France, as it is in most of Europe.

MAP TIME Kade's teacher checks her work. Geography is a required subject in France, a nation that borders several countries.

316

Additional Support

Additional Statistics You can find data like this and much more in the *CIA World Factbook*. Go to www.cia.gov and follow the link to the *World Factbook*. There you can click on the countries you wish to learn more about.

French Population Statistics

Category	Male	Female
Infant mortality rate	4.71 deaths/1,000 live births	3.69 deaths/1,000 live births
Median age	37.6 years	40.7 years
Population aged 14 and under	5,704,152	5,427,213
Literacy rate	99%	99%
Life expectancy	76.1 years	83.5 years

Source: *CIA World Factbook*, 2006.

BACKPACKED Kade Diallo (kahd dee•AH•low) passes the Eiffel Tower on her way to school. The teen moved to France with her parents and brother and sister in search of better economic opportunities.

What's Popular in France

Cheese France produces 500 different varieties. The average French person eats about 50 pounds of cheese each year.

STEVEN MARK NEEDHAM/PICTUREARTS/NEWSCOM

Cycling Every July, France hosts a three-week, 2,000-mile bicycle race called the Tour de France. More people come to watch the race than any other sporting event in the world.

FRANCK FIFE/AFP/NEWSCOM

Fashion France is home to some of the world's top clothing designers. Styles that start in workrooms here end up in stores all over the world.

Say It in French

France's 60 million people are united by a common language, French. Like English and many other languages, the French language has roots in Latin. Try these simple French phrases.

Hello
Bonjour (bohn•ZHOOR)

Good-bye
Au revoir (oh reh•VWAH)

My name is _______.
Je m'appelle (zhuh mah•PELL) _______.

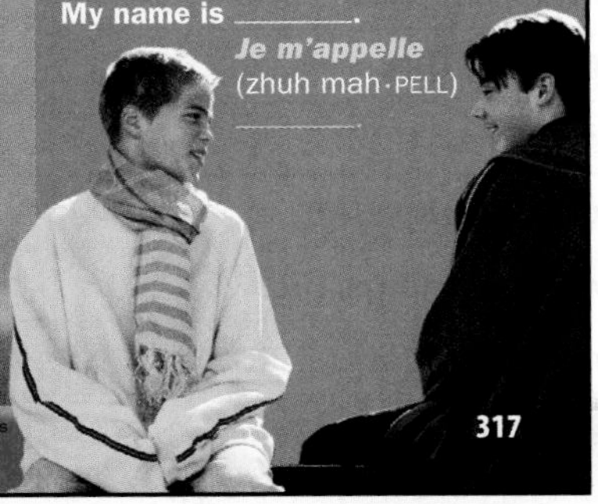

PATRICK SHEANDELL O'CARROLL/GETTY IMAGES

317

What's Popular in France

Fashion Some of the world's most famous fashion designers are from France. One designer, Louis Vuitton, was born in the early 1800s and opened his first store in Paris in 1854. His son, Georges, designed the unique "LV" monogram that decorates the designer's purses and luggage. Today, the designer's line remains popular and is managed by Patrick Louis Vuitton, a fifth-generation Vuitton.

Say It in French

French About 119 million people worldwide speak French fluently or claim it as their first language, about 63 million speak some French, and about 85 million people are learning to speak the language. In fact, French is one of the only languages, other than English, that is spoken on all seven continents. English-speaking people use French nearly every day, often without realizing it. Many "English" words, such as *café*, *lingerie*, *envelope*, and *avalanche*, were borrowed from French.

Activity: Narrative Writing

Writing a Biography Tell students to make lists of their activities for one day, as Kade has done. Then have them use their lists to write a short autobiography entitled "A Day in My Life." Explain to students that their autobiographies can be humorous or informative, but they should follow a chronological order. When students have completed their autobiographies, have pairs of students read what they have written to each other. **OL**

Planning Guide

Key to Ability Levels	
BL Below level	AL Above level
OL On level	ELL English Language Learners

Key to Teaching Resources	
Print Material	DVD
CD-ROM	Transparency

BL	OL	AL	ELL		Resources	Chapter Opener	Section 1	Section 2	Section 3	Section 4	Chapter Assess
					FOCUS						
BL	OL	AL	ELL	Transparency	Daily Focus Skills Transparencies		12-1	12-2	12-3	12-4	
					TEACH						
BL	OL		ELL	Print Material	Guided Reading Activity, URB*		p. 85	p. 86	p. 87	p. 88	
BL	OL	AL	ELL	Print Material	Content Vocabulary Activity, URB*		p. 89	p. 89	p. 89	p. 89	
BL	OL	AL	ELL	Print Material	Academic Vocabulary Activity, URB		p. 91	p. 91	p. 91	p. 91	
BL	OL	AL	ELL	Print Material	Differentiated Instruction Activity, URB		p. 93				
BL	OL	AL	ELL	Print Material	Chart, Graph, and Map Skills Activity, URB		p. 95	p. 95	p. 95	p. 95	
	OL	AL		Print Material	Critical Thinking Activity, URB				p. 97	p. 97	
BL	OL	AL	ELL	Print Material	Speaking and Listening Skills Activity, URB		p. 99				
BL	OL	AL	ELL	Print Material	Writing Skills Activity, URB			p. 103			
BL	OL	AL	ELL	Print Material	School-to-Home Connection Activity, URB*		p. 107	p. 107	p. 107	p. 107	
BL	OL	AL	ELL	Print Material	Regional Atlas Activities, URB		pp. 1–7	pp. 1–7	pp. 1–7	pp. 1–7	
		AL		Print Material	Geography and Economics Activity, URB			p. 9			
	OL	AL		Print Material	Environmental Case Study, URB		p. 13	p. 13	p. 13	p. 13	
BL	OL		ELL	Print Material	Time Line Activity, URB		p. 17	p. 17	p. 17	p. 17	
		AL		Print Material	Enrichment Activity, URB		p. 19	p. 19	p. 19	p. 19	
BL	OL		ELL	Print Material	Reading Skills Activity, URB		p. 25				
BL	OL	AL	ELL	Print Material	Primary Source Readings, URB		p. 29				
	OL	AL		Print Material	World Literature Readings, URB		p. 31				
BL	OL		ELL	Print Material	Reading Essentials and Note-Taking Guide*		p. 79	p. 82	p. 85	p. 88	
	OL	AL		Print Material	TIME Perspectives: Exploring World Issues				pp. 13–16		
	OL			Print Material	Interactive Geography Activity		p. 25	p. 25	p. 25	p. 25	
BL	OL	AL	ELL	Transparency	In-Text Map Overlay and Population Pyramid Transparencies	4A	4A, 4C, 4D	4A, 4C, 4D	4A, 4C, 4D	4A, 4C, 4D	
	OL			Print Material	Foods Around the World		p. 14		p. 16		
BL	OL	AL	ELL	Print Material	Outline Map Resource Book	p. 36					
BL	OL	AL	ELL	Print Material	NGS World Atlas*	✓	✓	✓	✓	✓	

Note: Please refer to the *Unit Resource Book: Europe* for this chapter's URB materials

* Also available in Spanish

- Interactive Lesson Planner
- Interactive Teacher Edition
- Fully editable blackline masters
- Section Spotlight Videos Launch
- Differentiated Lesson Plans
- Printable reports of daily assignments
- Standards Tracking System

Levels: BL	OL	AL	ELL		Resources	Chapter Opener	Section 1	Section 2	Section 3	Section 4	Chapter Assess
					TEACH *(continued)*						
BL	OL	AL	ELL		NGS World Desk Map	✓	✓	✓	✓	✓	✓
BL	OL	AL	ELL		World Literature Library	✓	✓	✓	✓	✓	✓
BL	OL	AL	ELL		Writer's Guidebook	✓	✓	✓	✓	✓	✓
BL	OL	AL	ELL		Vocabulary PuzzleMaker CD-ROM*		✓	✓	✓	✓	✓
	OL	AL			Primary Sources CD-ROM	✓	✓	✓	✓	✓	✓
BL	OL	AL	ELL		StudentWorks™ Plus DVD	✓	✓	✓	✓	✓	✓
BL	OL	AL	ELL		Section Video Program Activities	✓	✓	✓	✓	✓	✓
BL	OL	AL	ELL		World Music: A Cultural Legacy	✓	✓	✓	✓	✓	✓
BL	OL	AL	ELL		Writing Process Transparencies	✓	✓	✓	✓	✓	✓
Teacher Resources					Building Academic Vocabulary	✓	✓	✓	✓	✓	✓
Teacher Resources					Strategies for Success		✓	✓	✓	✓	✓
Teacher Resources					Teacher's Guide to Differentiated Instruction	✓	✓	✓	✓	✓	✓
Teacher Resources					Presentation Plus! DVD	✓	✓	✓	✓	✓	✓
					ASSESS						
BL	OL	AL	ELL		Quizzes and Tests		p. 131	p. 132	p. 133	p. 134	p. 135
BL	OL	AL	ELL		Authentic Assessment With Rubrics		p. 12	p. 12			p. 12
BL	OL	AL	ELL		Standardized Test Practice						p. 45
BL	OL	AL	ELL		*ExamView® Assessment Suite* CD-ROM*		12-1	12-2	12-3	12-4	Ch. 12
BL	OL	AL	ELL		Interactive Tutor Self-Assessment CD-ROM		12-1	12-2	12-3	12-4	
					CLOSE						
BL			ELL		Reteaching Activity, URB*		p. 105	p. 105	p. 105	p. 105	p. 105
BL	OL		ELL		Reading and Study Skills Foldables™	p. 72	p. 72	p. 72	p. 72	p. 72	p. 72
BL	OL	AL	ELL		Graphic Organizer Transparencies and Strategies		✓	✓	✓	✓	
BL	OL	AL	ELL		*Exploring Our World* in Graphic Novel						pp. 41, 49

Integrating Technology

Using the Primary Source Document Library Database

Searching by Keyword, Author, or Title

Technology Product

Glencoe's *American History Primary Source Document Library CD-ROMs* includes more than 200 primary source documents. The documents provide new sources of knowledge that encourage students to think critically about history and historical concepts. The *American History Primary Source Document Library* allows you to

- perform a search based on key words, author names, or titles of documents;
- choose documents from the results list to read and/or listen to;
- utilize **Teaching Strategies, Questions/Answers,** and **Blackline Masters** resources in conjunction with the primary source document to maximize student learning.

Steps

- After launching **Primary Source Document Library CD-ROM**, choose the **Search** button.
- Click on Search icon (binoculars and document) in the Adobe Reader toolbar and enter key words related to an author, title, content, etc.
- Make a selection from the list of documents in the "Results" window.
- Review the **Document Overview** and **Guided Reading Questions** at the top of each document.
- Click on the **User's Guide and Teaching Strategies** link in at the bottom of the bookmarks listed on the left. Select **To the Teacher** and **Teaching Strategies** for teaching suggestions and procedures using the primary source documents.
- Select **Questions/Activities** and **Blackline Masters** for worksheets and organizers.

Social Studies ONLINE

	Student	Teacher	Parent
Beyond the Textbook	●		●
Chapter Overviews	●		●
Concepts in Motion	●		●
ePuzzles and Games	●		●
Literature Connections		●	
Multi-Language Glossaries	●		●
Online Student Edition	●	●	●
Section Videos	●	●	●
Self-Check Quizzes	●		●
Student Web Activities	●		●
Study Central™	●		●
Teaching Today		●	
TIME Current Events	●		●
Vocabulary eFlashcards	●		●
Web Activity Lesson Plans		●	

- **Timed Readings Plus in Social Studies** helps students increase their reading rate and fluency while maintaining comprehension. The 400-word passages are similar to those found on state and national assessments.
- **Reading in the Content Area: Social Studies** concentrates on six essential reading skills that help students better comprehend what they read. The book includes 75 high-interest nonfiction passages written at increasing levels of difficulty.
- **Reading Social Studies** includes strategic reading instruction and vocabulary support in Social Studies content for ELLs and native speakers of English.
- **Content Vocabulary Workout** (Grades 6–8) accelerates reading comprehension through focused vocabulary development. Social Studies content vocabulary comes from the glossaries of Glencoe's Middle School Social Studies texts. www.jamestowneducation.com

NATIONAL GEOGRAPHIC

Index to National Geographic Magazine:

The following articles relate to this chapter:

- "Europe's Big Gamble," Don Belt, May 2004.
- "Prince Charles—Not Your Typical Radical," May 2006.

National Geographic Society Products To order the following, call National Geographic at 1-800-368-2728:

- *National Geographic Atlas of the World* (Book).

Access National Geographic's new dynamic MapMachine Web site and other geography resources at:
www.nationalgeographic.com
www.nationalgeographic.com/maps

Biography  

The following videotape programs are available from Glencoe as supplements to Chapter 12:

- Eiffel Tower (ISBN 1-56-501465-0)
- Mystical Monuments of Ancient Greece (ISBN 0-76-700012-9)

To order, call Glencoe at 1-800-334-7344. To find classroom resources to accompany many of these videos, check the following home pages:

A&E Television: www.aetv.com
The History Channel: www.historychannel.com

GLENCOE BOOKLINK 3

Use this database to search more than 30,000 titles to create a customized reading list for your students.

- Reading lists can be organized by students' reading level, author, genre, theme, or area of interest.
- The database provides Degrees of Reading Power™ (DRP) and Lexile™ readability scores for all selections.
- A brief summary of each selection is included.

Leveled reading suggestions for this chapter:

For students at a Grade 5 reading level:
- ***Scotland,*** by Chris Oxlade and Anita Ganeri

For students at a Grade 6 reading level:
- ***Ireland Is My Home,*** by Gini Holland

For students at a Grade 7 reading level:
- ***Safe Area Gorazde,*** by Joe Sacco

For students at a Grade 8 reading level:
- ***France: City and Village Life,*** by Teresa Fisher

For students at a Grade 9 reading level:
- ***Norway,*** by Mike Hepso

Focus

The Essential Question

As students study the chapter, remind them to consider the chapter-based Essential Question. Answering this question will help them understand the important concepts in the chapter. In addition, the Hands-On Chapter Project relates the content from each section to the Essential Question. The steps in each section build on each other as students progress through the chapter. The Hands-On Chapter Project culminates in the Wrap Up activity on the Visual Summary page.

More About the Photo

Visual Literacy Trafalgar Square in London was originally home to stables. In the 1800s, the area was transformed into a cultural center by British architects. It was officially named Trafalgar Square in 1830 to commemorate the British naval victory over France and Spain in 1805 at the Battle of Trafalgar off Spain's south-west coast. A column and statue in honor of Admiral Nelson, the victor of the battle, was added to the square in 1843. Today, the square plays host to many cultural, artistic, and sporting events and is a popular site for political demonstrations and rallies.

CHAPTER 12

Europe Today

Essential Question

Human-Environment Interaction Europe is one of the economic powerhouses of the world, home to many large companies that sell goods in the United States. Europe is also an important market for goods and services produced in North America, such as movies and computer programs. What factors help make a region an important world economic center?

Teach

The BIG Ideas *As you begin teaching each section, use these questions and activities to help students focus on the Big Ideas.*

Section 

Northern Europe Ask: How might their northern location affect the countries of northern Europe? *(Many of these countries have a cold climate, which would create challenges, such as developing industry and agriculture. The parts of this region with the coldest climates are less densely populated than other parts of Europe.)* Tell students that Section 1 discusses the land, economies, and governments of the countries of northern Europe. Students will also learn about the distinct cultures of this part of Europe. **OL**

Section 

Europe's Heartland Ask: How do resources affect the economy of a country and the way of life of its people? *(Resources affect the development of agriculture and industry and often the types of jobs people have.)* Point out to students that Section 2 discusses the land, economy, and people of Europe's heartland, an area with rich soil and other resources. **OL**

Trafalgar Square, London

BIG Ideas

Section 1: Northern Europe

BIG IDEA Geographers organize the Earth into regions that share common characteristics. The countries of northern Europe have developed diverse economies and high standards of living.

Section 2: Europe's Heartland

BIG IDEA People's actions can change the physical environment. Today the countries of Europe's heartland are agricultural and manufacturing centers.

Section 3: Southern Europe

BIG IDEA Places reflect the relationship between humans and the physical environment. Seas and mountains have influenced where people live and how they work in southern Europe.

Section 4: Eastern Europe

BIG IDEA Geography is used to interpret the past, understand the present, and plan for the future. After changes in government, eastern Europe's economies are struggling to recover.

Summarizing Information Make this Foldable to help you collect information about Europe's people, politics, and economies.

Step 1 Fold the sides of a piece of paper into the middle to make a shutter fold.

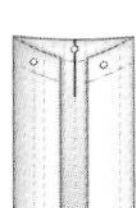

Step 2 Cut each flap at the midpoint to form four tabs.

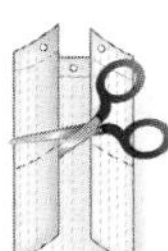

Step 3 Label the tabs as shown.

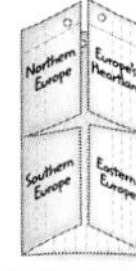

Reading and Writing Use the notes in your Foldable to write a short essay comparing the economies of Europe's four subregions.

To preview Chapter 12, go to glencoe.com.

Previewing the Region

If you have not already done so, engage students in the Regional Atlas and chart activities to help them become familiar with the general content of the region.

Dinah Zike's Foldables

Purpose This Foldable helps students collect information about Europe's people, politics, and economies. Students should gather information based on each of the four subregions. After students read the chapter, they can use the Foldables to write their essays and prepare for assessment.

More Foldables activities for this chapter can be found in *Dinah Zike's Reading and Study Skills Foldables* ancillary.

Introduce students to chapter content and key terms by having them access the Chapter Overview at glencoe.com.

Section 3

Southern Europe Ask: How might being located on the sea affect a country's economy? *(Countries on the sea are often involved in trade, fishing, shipping, and tourism.)* Tell students that in Section 3 they will learn about how location near seas and oceans has affected the countries of southern Europe. **OL**

Section 

Eastern Europe Ask: How might changes in government affect the people of a country? *(A change in government can determine the freedoms and the economic system in a country.)* Tell students that Section 4 describes how changes in government in this region have brought about economic changes and challenges. **OL**

Focus

Bellringer

Daily Focus Transparency 12-1

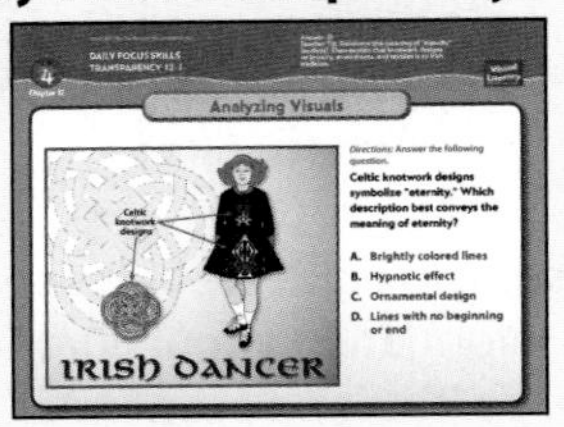

Guide to Reading

Answers to Graphic:

Answers for Ireland and Scandinavia should contain similar information to the following answer for the United Kingdom: **United Kingdom** third most populous country in Europe; most people live in cities; English is the main language, but Welsh and Scottish Gaelic are spoken in some areas; most people are Protestant Christians, but other religions are also practiced, especially by immigrants; known for cricket and rich literature

Section Spotlight Video

To learn more about northern Europe, have students watch the Section Spotlight Video.

Guide to Reading

BIG Idea

Geographers organize the Earth into regions that share common characteristics.

Content Vocabulary

- constitutional monarchy *(p. 322)*
- parliamentary democracy *(p. 323)*
- peat *(p. 325)*
- bog *(p. 325)*
- productivity *(p. 325)*
- geyser *(p. 327)*
- fjord *(p. 327)*
- geothermal energy *(p. 327)*

Academic Vocabulary

- differentiate *(p. 321)*
- document *(p. 322)*
- vary *(p. 326)*

Reading Strategy

Organizing Information Use a graphic organizer like the one below to organize key facts about the people and cultures of northern Europe.

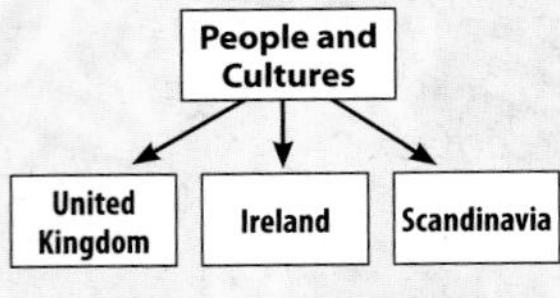

SECTION 1 Northern Europe

Picture This Iceland's huge chunks of moving ice are centuries old. Iceland, however, is not a bitter cold wasteland. It has a relatively mild climate even though it is near the Arctic Circle. The people of Iceland have adjusted to living in this climate and have made efficient use of the country's resources. Learn more about Iceland and other countries of northern Europe by reading Section 1.

▼ A glacial wall in Iceland

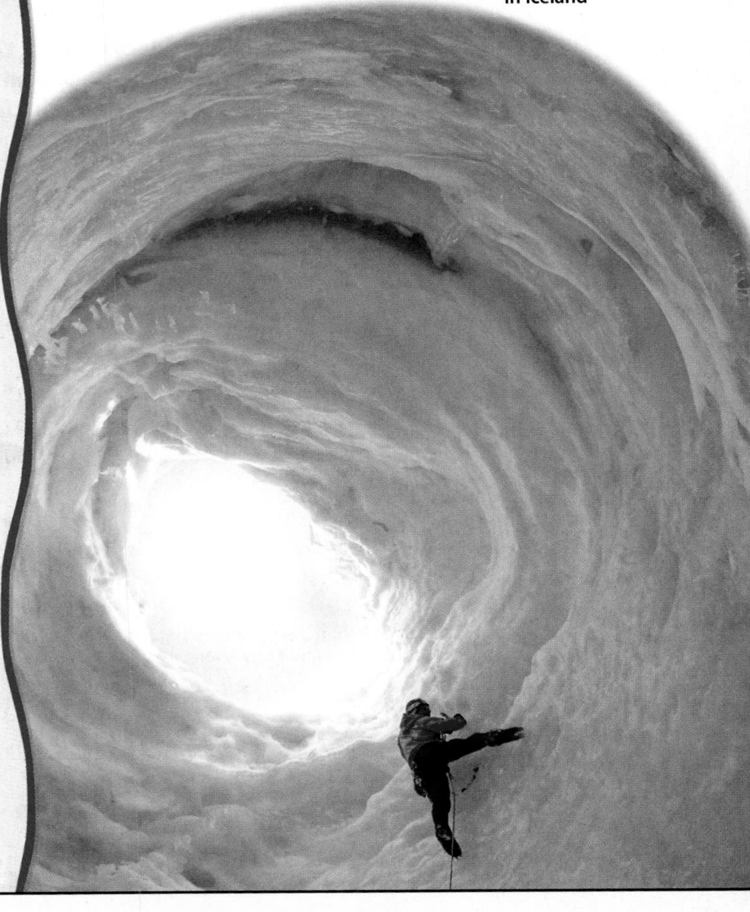

Resource Manager

R Reading Strategies	C Critical Thinking	D Differentiated Instruction	W Writing Support	S Skill Practice
Teacher Edition • Set. a Purp., p. 321 • Using Word Parts, p. 322 • Summarizing, p. 323 • Outlining, p. 325 • Visualizing, p. 327 **Additional Resources** • Guid. Read., URB p. 85 • Cont. Vocab., URB p. 89 • Pri. Source, URB p. 29 • World Lit., URB p. 31	**Teacher Edition** • Analyzing Info., pp. 321, 322 • Det. Cause/Effect, p. 327 **Additional Resources** • Authentic Assess., p. 12 • Quizzes and Tests, p. 131 • Time Line, URB p. 17 • Enrichment, URB p. 19	**Teacher Edition** • Verbal/Linguistic, pp. 323, 325 • Visual/Spatial, p. 325 • Kinesthetic, p. 326 **Additional Resources** • Diff. Instr., URB p. 93 • Reteach., URB p. 105 • School-to-Home Conn., URB p. 107	**Teacher Edition** • Personal Writing, p. 326 • Narrative Writing, p. 328	**Teacher Edition** • Using Geo. Skills, p. 321 **Additional Resources** • Read. Skills, URB p. 25 • Speak./Listen. Skills, URB p. 99 • Chart, Graph, and Map Skills, URB p. 95 • Daily Focus Trans. 12-1 • Reg. Atlas, URB pp. 1–7

The United Kingdom

Main Idea **Once the center of a worldwide empire, the United Kingdom has had a great impact on the rest of the world.**

Geography and You Have you ever seen a picture of Big Ben, the large clock tower located in London? Big Ben is a symbol of the United Kingdom. Read to find out more about this country in the North Atlantic.

It is easy to be confused by the different names for the island nation off the northwest coast of mainland Europe. People sometimes call it Great Britain, the British Isles, or simply England. The true name, though, is the *United Kingdom of Great Britain and Northern Ireland,* or the *United Kingdom.*

The country includes four separate regions, which you can see in **Figure 1.** Three of them—England, Scotland, and Wales—make up the island of Great Britain. The fourth region, Northern Ireland, occupies a corner of the nearby island of Ireland. (The rest of that island is a completely independent country known as the Republic of Ireland.)

All the people of the United Kingdom can be described as British. Sometimes, though, people **differentiate** among them by referring to the English, the Scots, the Welsh, or the Irish.

The Land

Great Britain is separated from the rest of Europe by the English Channel. Historically, this body of water both connected and protected the British. They were close enough to the mainland to share in European culture. At the same time, they were far enough away to be largely safe from foreign invasions and free to develop their own government and economy.

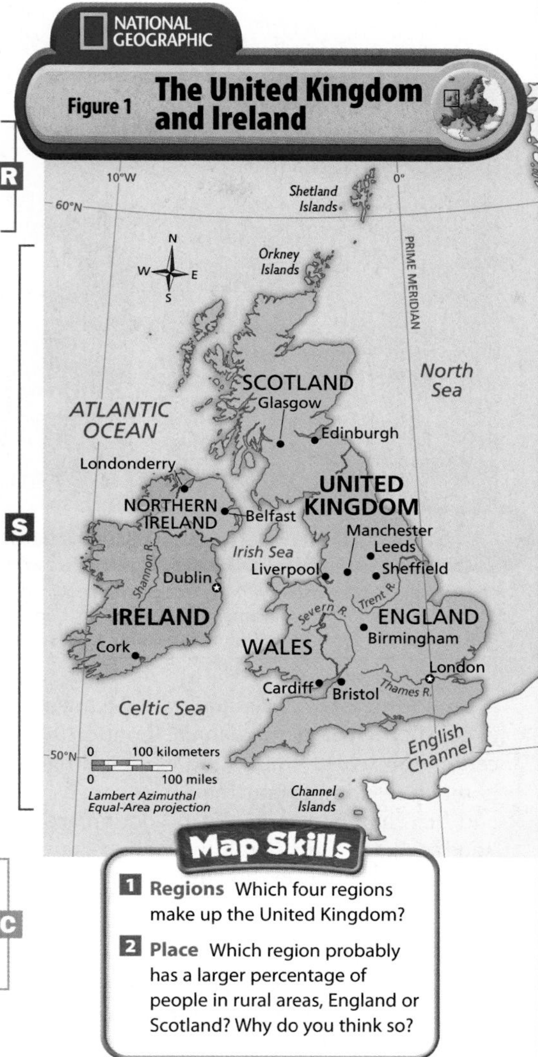

Map Skills

1. **Regions** Which four regions make up the United Kingdom?
2. **Place** Which region probably has a larger percentage of people in rural areas, England or Scotland? Why do you think so?

Rolling fertile plains cover the southern and eastern areas of England. These plains support productive farms. Rough highlands and mountains are found to the north and west in Scotland and Wales. Poor soil and a cold climate make farming difficult in these areas, but many people herd sheep.

Teach

R Reading Strategy

Setting a Purpose Ask students to set a purpose for reading this section by considering the ways a country can have an impact on the world. *(trade, political or military influence, cultural exchange, and so on)* **OL**

C Critical Thinking

Analyzing Information **What are the two different ways that you can refer to a person from Wales?** *(British or Welsh)* **OL**

S Skill Practice

Using Geography Skills **Ask:** **What major bodies of water surround the United Kingdom and Ireland?** *(the North Sea, the English Channel, the Celtic Sea, the Irish Sea, and the Atlantic Ocean)* **OL**

Map Skills

Answers:

1. England, Scotland, Wales, and Northern Ireland
2. Scotland, because Scotland has fewer large cities

Differentiated Instruction

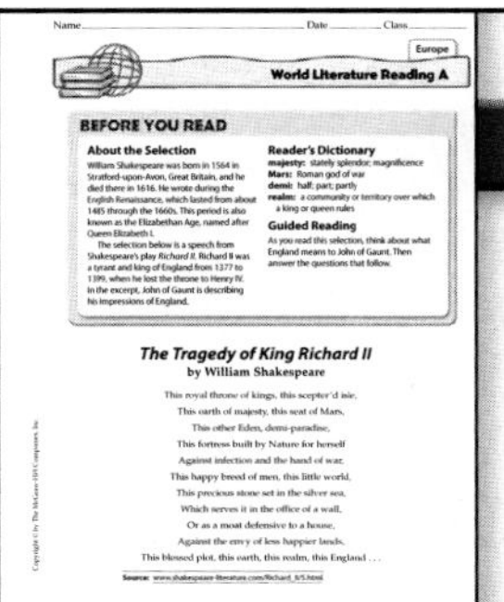
Name Date Class

Europe

World Literature Reading A

BEFORE YOU READ

About the Selection

William Shakespeare was born in 1564 in Stratford-upon-Avon, Great Britain, and he died there in 1616. He wrote during the English Renaissance, which lasted from about 1485 through the 1660s. This period is also known as the Elizabethan Age, named after Queen Elizabeth I.

The selection below is a speech from Shakespeare's play *Richard II.* Richard II was a tyrant and king of England from 1377 to 1399, when he lost the throne to Henry IV. In the excerpt, John of Gaunt is describing his impressions of England.

Reader's Dictionary

majesty: stately splendor; magnificence
Mars: Roman god of war
demi: half; part; partly
realm: a community or territory over which a king or queen rules

Guided Reading

As you read this selection, think about what England means to John of Gaunt. Then answer the questions that follow.

The Tragedy of King Richard II
by William Shakespeare

This royal throne of kings, this scepter'd isle,
This earth of majesty, this seat of Mars,
This other Eden, demi-paradise,
This fortress built by Nature for herself
Against infection and the hand of war,
This happy breed of men, this little world,
This precious stone set in the silver sea,
Which serves it in the office of a wall,
Or as a moat defensive to a house,
Against the envy of less happier lands,
This blessed plot, this earth, this realm, this England . . .

Source: www.shakespeare-literature.com/Richard_II/5.html

World Lit. Readings, URB pp. 31–32

The Tragedy of King Richard II

Objective: To identify metaphors used in *Richard II*

Focus: Write the word *metaphor* on the board, and ask volunteers to define it.

Teach: Read the first line of *Richard II,* and explain the metaphor "royal throne of kings." Have students identify other metaphors in this selection.

Assess: Have students answer the first three literary response questions.

Close: Identify metaphors in the selection from *As You Like It.*

Differentiated Instruction Strategies

BL Give two examples of metaphors used in everyday life.

AL Read other excerpts from one of these plays, and write a few paragraphs explaining the metaphors you find.

ELL Create visual metaphors by using symbols to represent objects.

C Critical Thinking

Analyzing Information Ask: What does the fact that apartments have been built along the Thames, instead of warehouses, suggest about England's economy? *(The country relies less on shipping than it did in the past, and now people live in areas where shipping warehouses once stood.)* OL

R Reading Strategy

Using Word Parts Ask: What noun is contained in the adjective "constitutional"? *(constitution)* What is a monarchy? *(a country that has a monarch—a king or queen)* How could you define the term "constitutional monarchy" by putting these two parts together? *(a country that has a monarch and a constitution)* OL

Caption Answer:
Over the years, nobles took away some of the monarch's powers. Gradually, a law-making body called Parliament arose. Members of Parliament are elected, and the prime minister is the head of government.

NATIONAL GEOGRAPHIC

Government in the United Kingdom

The Palace of Westminster, with the clock tower known as Big Ben, lies in the heart of London. It is home to Parliament, the lawmaking body of the United Kingdom.
Place **How did the United Kingdom become a parliamentary democracy?**

In southeastern England, the Thames (TEHMZ) River helped make London a center for world trade. Today, shipping is much less important than it once was, and the Thames riverbanks in London are lined with apartment buildings rather than warehouses. London, however, remains a world center of finance and business.

The Economy

More than 250 years ago, British inventors and scientists sparked the Industrial Revolution. Today, the United Kingdom is still a major industrial and trading country. Manufactured goods and machinery are its leading exports. New computer and electronics industries, however, are gradually replacing these older industries. Service industries, such as banking and health care, are now a major part of the economy.

Coal once powered the British economy, but oil and natural gas are now the leading energy sources. These fossil fuels come from fields beneath the North Sea. These oil and gas fields meet most of the United Kingdom's energy needs. They also provide fuel exports that give the country a valuable source of income.

Government

The government of the United Kingdom is a **constitutional monarchy.** A king or queen serves as head of state and takes part in ceremonies, but elected officials actively run the government.

The British trace the roots of this form of government to the early 1200s. At that time, nobles forced King John of England to sign the Magna Carta, a **document** that took away some of the king's powers. For example, the king could no longer collect taxes unless a group of nobles agreed. Also, people accused of crimes had a right to fair trials by their peers, or equals.

Hands-On Chapter Project Step 1

Visualizing Europe's Economics

Step 1: Investigating northern Europe Groups of students will plan a bulletin board explaining Europe's economic importance.

Essential Question What factors help make a region an important world-economic center?

Directions Tell students that they will create a bulletin board display that answers the question "Why is Europe important to the world economy?" The display will include information about all of the regions of Europe, starting with northern Europe. Organize the class into groups of three or four students. Tell students to read the text and record important details about that area's economy in a three-column chart, one column each for the United Kingdom, Ireland, and Scandinavia. Have them find photos or other images of northern Europe's agriculture or industries to illustrate these details.

Analyzing Have students answer the following question: What do the economies of the United Kingdom, Ireland, and Scandinavia have in common? OL

(Chapter Project continued in Section 2)

Gradually, a lawmaking body called Parliament arose. In 1628 Parliament decided that King Charles I had misused his power. It forced him to sign the Petition of Right, which said that taxes could be enacted only if Parliament approved. In addition, the king could not imprison people unless they were convicted of a crime. **R** As time passed, more limits were placed on the ruler's authority. The English Bill of Rights, passed in 1689, gave Parliament the power to tax and stated that monarchs could not suspend the laws or form their own armies. That document later helped shape the thinking of the men who wrote the U.S. Constitution.

Today, the United Kingdom is a **parliamentary democracy** as well as a constitutional monarchy. Voters elect members of Parliament, and the leader of the party with the most elected officials becomes prime minister, or head of the government. The prime minister can propose new laws, but only Parliament can put them into **D** action. The prime minister must appear in Parliament regularly to explain and defend his or her decisions. Parliament also has the power to force the prime minister out of office and require new elections. This is a power the U.S. Congress does not have over the U.S. president.

Scotland, Wales, and Northern Ireland have regional legislatures that have control over matters such as health care and education. The Scottish Parliament even has the power to raise or lower taxes in Scotland.

The People

With more than 60 million people, the United Kingdom is the third-most-populous country in Europe. Nearly 9 of every 10 people live in cities. London is by far the largest city, with some 7.6 million residents.

The British people speak English, although Welsh and Scottish Gaelic (GAY·lihk) are spoken in some areas. Most people in the United Kingdom are Protestant Christians. Immigrants from South Asia, Africa, and the Caribbean area, however, practice religions such as Islam, Sikhism, and Hinduism.

In the 1700s and 1800s, when the United Kingdom had a powerful empire, British culture spread to many lands. As a result, the British sport of cricket is now played in Australia, South Asia, and the Caribbean. The English language is spoken in the United States, Canada, South Africa, and a number of other countries. Britain's rich literature of poems, plays, and novels is enjoyed worldwide, too.

Reading Check **Determining Cause and Effect** How has the location of the United Kingdom shaped its history?

Cricket: A British Sport

NATIONAL GEOGRAPHIC

▲ A batsman, or player, hits the ball in a cricket match between England and the South Asian country of Bangladesh. ***Movement*** **How did British sports and culture spread to other lands?**

R Reading Strategy

Summarizing Have students summarize the important British documents discussed in these paragraphs by writing a sentence describing each document. **OL**

D Differentiated Instruction

Verbal/Linguistic Have students role-play the procedures used in a parliamentary democracy. Have students take turns playing the roles of the prime minister, parliament members, and voters. **AL**

Reading Check Answer: The United Kingdom was close enough to mainland Europe to share in its culture but far enough away to develop its own government and economy.

Caption Answer: Britain's powerful empire in the 1700s and 1800s spread British sports and culture.

Differentiated Instruction

Leveled Activities

BL Speaking and Listening Skills Activity, URB p. 99

OL Reading Skills Activity, URB p. 25

AL Primary Source Readings, URB p. 29

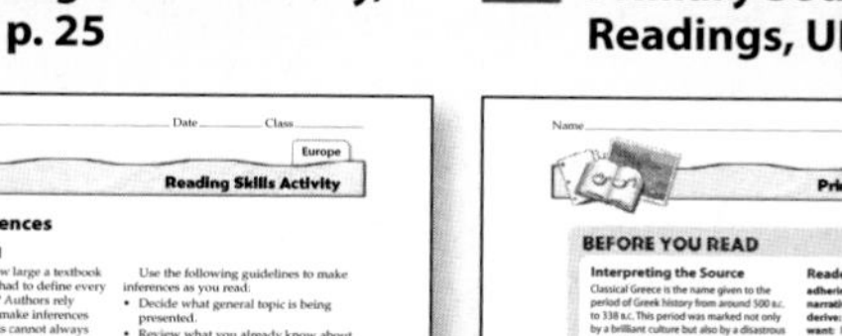

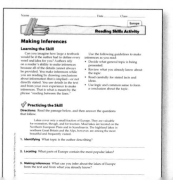

World Literature

Teach

Reading Strategy

Making Inferences Ask: Why were the buildings in Coketown all black? *(because the air pollution coated everything with black smoke and ash)* **Why was the canal black?** *(It was polluted.)* **What did Charles Dickens mean when he wrote, "You saw nothing in Coketown but what was severely workful"?** *(Possible answer: People in Coketown had no life other than work, and factory owners cared only about profits.)*

This Reading Skill (Making Inferences) was introduced in this unit.

Analyzing Literature

Answers:

1. Coketown was dirty and colorless. All the people did the same work, and all the days were exactly like the ones before. It was a very sad place.
2. Answers will vary but should reflect the monotony of work in Coketown and the dreariness of the place.

HARD TIMES

By Charles Dickens

Charles Dickens (1812–1870)

One of Britain's most famous novelists, Charles Dickens, had a difficult childhood because of family financial problems. As a result, Dickens developed a deep sympathy for the lower classes and for the young children who sometimes suffered from society's strict rules. These feelings are evident in many of his books.

Background Information

In *Hard Times*, Charles Dickens explores the problems raised by the Industrial Revolution. His book harshly criticizes the people who promoted this new way of working and the effects it had on the environment. In this passage, Dickens describes an industrial city, which he names Coketown.

Reader's Dictionary

interminable: unending

melancholy: sad

workful: useful

infirmary: hospital

dearest: for the highest price

It was a town of red brick, or of brick that would have been red if the smoke and ashes had allowed it; but as matters stood it was a town of unnatural red and black. . . .

It was a town of machinery and tall chimneys, out of which **interminable** serpents of smoke trailed themselves for ever and ever, and never got uncoiled.

It had a black canal in it, and a river that ran purple with ill-smelling dye, and vast piles of buildings full of windows where there was a rattling and a trembling all day long, and where the piston of the steam-engine worked monotonously up and down, like the head of an elephant in a state of **melancholy** madness. It contained several large streets all very like one another, and many small streets still more like one another inhabited by people equally like one another, who all went in and out at the same hours, with the same sound upon the same pavements, to do the same work, and to whom every day was the same as yesterday and to-morrow, and every year the counterpart [duplicate] of the last and the next. . . .

You saw nothing in Coketown but what was severely **workful**. . . . All the public inscriptions in the town were painted alike, in severe characters of black and white. The jail might have been the **infirmary,** the infirmary might have been the jail, the townhall might have been either, or both, or anything else. . . . What you couldn't state in figures, or show to be purchasable in the cheapest market and salable in the **dearest,** was not [to be found there], and never should be. . . .

From: *Hard Times,* Charles Dickens, New York Books, Inc., n.d.

Analyzing Literature

1. **Making Inferences** How would you describe Coketown?
2. **Read to Write** Suppose you were a person who moved from a farm to work in a factory in Coketown. Write a letter to a family member that contrasts life on the farm with life in the city.

Additional Reading

Review suggested books before assigning them.

Biography: ***Hana's Suitcase*** by Karen Levine is the story of the search by the curator of a Japanese Holocaust education center for information about a mysterious suitcase with the name "Hana Brady" written on it.

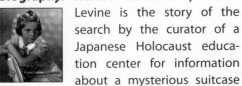

Fiction: ***The Devil and His Boy*** by Anthony Horowitz relates the adventures of 13-year old Tom in sixteenth-century England. Tom gets involved with a troupe of actors and meets William Shakespeare and even Queen Elizabeth.

Nonfiction: ***Searching for Anne Frank: Letters from Amsterdam to Iowa*** by Susan Goldman Rubin is the correspondence between Anne Frank and her American pen-pal, Juanita. The letters highlight the differences in how World War II affected America and Europe.

For further reading, see BookLink 3

The Republic of Ireland R

Main Idea **Ireland is growing economically, but a territorial dispute remains unsettled.**

Geography and You Why do you think Ireland is called the Emerald Isle? Read to find out about Ireland and its resources.

When people speak of Ireland, they usually mean the Republic of Ireland. This is the Catholic country that occupies the southern five-sixths of the island of Ireland. The country won its independence from the United Kingdom in 1922. The British, meanwhile, keep control of Northern Ireland, where most people are Protestants.

The Land

Ireland has the shape of a shallow bowl. The interior is a lowland plain with gently rolling hills. The coastal areas are rocky highlands and towering cliffs.

Ireland's regular rainfall produces lush, green fields. The landscape stays so green year-round that the country is nicknamed the Emerald Isle. Low-lying areas are rich in **peat,** or plants that have partly decayed in water. Peat is dug from **bogs,** or low swampy lands. It is then dried and can be burned for fuel. D1

The Economy

Irish farmers raise sheep and cattle and grow vegetables such as sugar beets and potatoes. Potatoes were Ireland's chief food in the 1800s. When disease destroyed the potato crop in the 1840s, more than one million people died. Another million left for the United States and other countries.

Today, manufacturing employs more of Ireland's people than farming does.

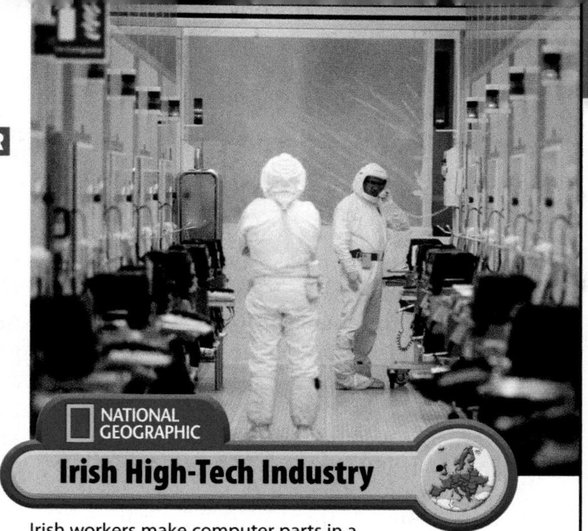

NATIONAL GEOGRAPHIC

Irish High-Tech Industry

Irish workers make computer parts in a laboratory "clean room." ***Place*** **How has Ireland's economy changed in recent years?**

The Irish work in industries that produce clothing, pharmaceuticals, and computer equipment. In recent years, the increased productivity of Irish workers has helped Ireland's economy. **Productivity** is a measure of how much work a person does in a specific amount of time. When workers produce more goods, companies earn higher profits and the workers earn higher incomes.

The People

The Irish trace their ancestry to the Celts, who settled the island hundreds of years ago. Irish Gaelic, a Celtic language, and English are Ireland's two languages. About 60 percent of the Irish live in cities or towns. Nearly one-third live in Dublin, the capital.

The Irish are very proud of their culture. Irish music and folk dancing are performed around the world. Of all the arts, however, the Irish have had their greatest influence on literature. Playwright George Bernard Shaw, poet William Butler Yeats, and novelist James Joyce are some of Ireland's best-known writers. D2

R Reading Strategy

Outlining To help students understand the text in this subsection, have them complete an outline, using the headings from the section as their outline headings. As students read, have them note important details under each outline heading. BL

D1 Differentiated Instruction

Visual/Spatial Have students create colored illustrations or paintings that reflect the landscape of Ireland. Provide students with photos to use as references. OL

D2 Differentiated Instruction

Verbal/Linguistic Have students select a poem by William Butler Yeats to read and study. Then have them perform a reader's theater of the poem for a student audience. AL

Caption Answer:
Ireland's workers have increased their productivity, which has helped the country's economy.

Additional Support

Activity: Interdisciplinary Connection

Music Discuss with students the different types of music they listen to and the instruments that make the music. Then play tapes of Irish music. Ask students to identify any instruments they recognize in the music. Have them compare the Irish music to music they listen to. **Ask:** **Are the Irish rhythms like any you hear in music on the radio?** *(Answers might include folk music or country music.)* **Do you recognize any instruments that you hear played on the radio?** *(Answers might include accordions or fiddles.)* Tell students to work in small groups to compare Irish dancing to American dancing. Provide students with videos of the different dance styles, or have them conduct their own research. Then have them share their observations in a class discussion. OL

W Writing Support

Personal Writing Discuss the conflict in Northern Ireland as a class. Then have students write brief essays describing their feelings about the conflict in Northern Ireland as they explore questions such as: How should conflicts be settled? How might people of different religions work toward peaceful solutions to disagreements? AL

D Differentiated Instruction

Kinesthetic Have students study the scientific reason for the continuous daylight during summer in Scandinavia. Then have students demonstrate this phenomenon using a globe and a light. OL

Reading Check **Answer:** More than a million people died, and a million more left Ireland for the United States and other countries.

Caption Answer:
to the Celts, who settled the island hundreds of years ago

Conflict Over Northern Ireland

The Irish are also strong Catholics, and many of their Catholic neighbors in Northern Ireland would like to unite with them. However, most Protestants in Northern Ireland—who are the dominant group there—wish to remain part of the United Kingdom. This dispute over Northern Ireland has led to violence, especially from W the 1960s to the 1990s. In 1998 leaders of the United Kingdom and the Republic of Ireland met with leaders of both sides in Northern Ireland. They signed an agreement to end the violence, but disputes have since erupted. The future of Northern Ireland remains uncertain.

Reading Check **Identifying Cause and Effect**
What happened as a result of the potato crop failure in the 1840s?

Irish Folk Dance

NATIONAL GEOGRAPHIC

▲ The féis (FESH) is a celebration of Irish culture that includes dances such as the jig, reel, and hornpipe. ***Place*** **To whom do the Irish trace their ancestry?**

Scandinavia

Main Idea The Scandinavian countries have similar cultures and high standards of living.

Geography and You How would you like to live in a place where the sun never sets in midsummer? The Land of the Midnight Sun lies in the far north of Europe. Read on to see how the people there, known as Scandinavians, adapt to their environment.

Scandinavia, the northernmost part of Europe, is made up of five nations: Norway, Sweden, Finland, Denmark, and Iceland. These countries have related histories and, except for Finland, share similar cultures. They also have standards of living that are among the world's highest.

The Land

Although Scandinavia lies north, warm winds from the North Atlantic Current give its southern and western areas a relatively mild climate. Central Scandinavia has long, cold winters and short, warm summers. The northernmost part of Scandinavia near the Arctic Circle, however, D has a very cold climate. Because this rugged area is so far north, there are summer days when the sun never sets. Many people have to darken their windows to sleep. In midwinter, though, these same people may battle depression, because there are days when the sun never rises.

Scandinavia's physical landscape is quite **varied** because of its large size. Many islands dot the jagged coastlines. Lowland plains stretch over Denmark and the southern part of Sweden and Finland. Mountains form a backbone along the border of Norway and Sweden. Forests and lakes cover much of Sweden and Finland. In the far north, above the Arctic Circle, the land is

Additional Support

Activity: Collaborative Learning

Problem-Solving Ask: What is the conflict over Northern Ireland about? *(The Catholics in Northern Ireland would like to unite with the rest of Ireland, but the Protestants in Northern Ireland want to remain part of the United Kingdom.)* Explain that even when countries sign a peace agreement, people may remain angry, and violence can continue. Organize the class into two groups, one group representing supporters of British rule and the other supporters of Irish republican rule in Northern Ireland. Have each group research the conflict and the point of view of their side regarding the conflict. Then have volunteers from each group conduct a mock debate to present the two sides of the issue. OL

barren tundra that remains frozen for most of the year.

Two countries—Iceland and Norway—have special features. The island of Iceland sits in an area of the North Atlantic Ocean where two of Earth's tectonic plates meet. The two plates are pulling away from each other, allowing hot magma to rise to the surface. This creates hot springs and **geysers** (GY·zuhrs), which are springs that shoot hot water and steam into the air. Iceland also has about 200 volcanoes, though many are not active.

Norway, meanwhile, is known for its many beautiful **fjords** (fee·AWRDS), or narrow inlets of the sea. Steep cliffs or slopes surround the fjords, which were carved by glaciers long ago. Fjords provide inland waterways that supply fish for food and export. R

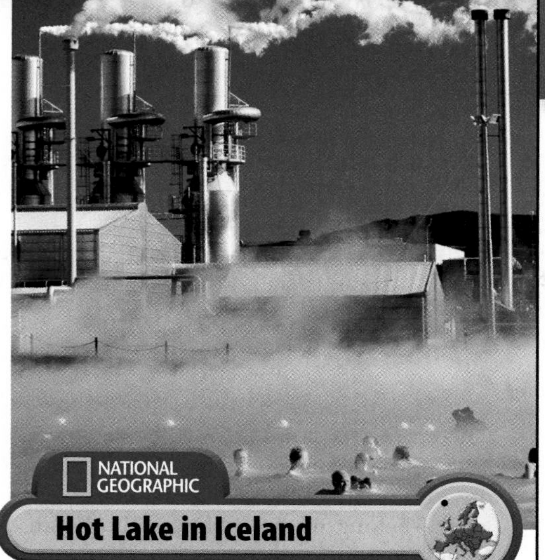

NATIONAL GEOGRAPHIC

Hot Lake in Iceland

People in Iceland swim in a human-made lake. The lake's warm water comes from the nearby plant, which produces energy from hot springs. ***Place*** **Why are hot springs numerous in Iceland?**

The Economies

The countries of Scandinavia are wealthy and prosperous. Their economies are based on a mix of agriculture, manufacturing, and service industries. C Although farmland is limited, most Scandinavian countries produce most of the food they need. Fishing is an important industry, especially in Norway and Iceland.

For energy, Norway relies on its own oil and natural gas, taken from fields under the North Sea. Iceland taps the molten rock beneath its surface to make **geothermal energy.** This is electricity produced by natural underground sources of steam. Iceland also uses hydroelectric power. Finland takes advantage of its fast-running rivers to generate hydroelectric power as well. Sweden uses a combination of nuclear power and oil.

Some Scandinavian countries have abundant mineral and forest resources that support various industries. Sweden has reserves of iron ore that it uses to produce steel for a variety of products, including cars such as Saabs and Volvos. Shipbuilding is important in Finland and Denmark, as are wood and wood product industries in Finland and Sweden.

Denmark plays an important role in world trade. Copenhagen, its capital, sits at the entrance to the Baltic Sea. The largest ships cannot enter that sea because it is not deep enough for them. As a result, many ships stop in Copenhagen, where workers transfer cargoes to other vessels.

People and Culture

Most of the Scandinavian countries are less densely settled than other European countries. Large parts of Scandinavia are located in the cold north or are too mountainous to attract many people. Only Denmark, the smallest of the five countries, has a high population density. Denmark has a mild climate and relatively flat land that supports much agriculture.

R Reading Strategy

Visualizing Tell students that an important reading skill is the ability to visualize descriptions in a text. Read the paragraph aloud, and tell students to make mental pictures of the fjords of Norway as you read. **BL**

C Critical Thinking

Determining Cause and Effect
Ask: How might a mixed economy benefit a country? *(A country with a mixed economy can continue to prosper even when a particular industry or part of the economy has problems.)* **OL**

Caption Answer:
Iceland sits on two tectonic plates that are pulling away from each other, allowing hot magma to rise to the surface and creating hot springs.

FastFacts

- **Hot Springs** Iceland has about 800 hot springs with an average temperature of 167° F (75°C). Some of the springs are geysers, which spout water into the air. The most famous geyser in Iceland, Geysir in Haukadalur, reaches about 180 feet (54.8 m).
- **Volcanoes** The world's largest recorded lava flow occurred in Iceland in 1783. The lava reached 3 cubic miles, and the ash blocked the sunlight and caused a haze to form over Europe and western Asia. The effects of this eruption killed 20 percent of Iceland's population and hundreds of thousands of cattle and sheep.
- **Glaciers** Almost 12 percent of Iceland's land is covered by glaciers. The milder climate of recent years is causing the glaciers to recede.
- **Rivers** Most of Iceland's larger rivers have their source in glaciers, so the water flow is much stronger in the summer when the glaciers melt. The water in almost all of Iceland's rivers and lakes is clean and safe to drink.

W Writing Support

Narrative Writing Have students research the Vikings and create a comic book story about Viking adventures. Provide comic books for students to use as models. When students complete their comic books, have them trade books and read each other's stories. **AL**

Reading Check Answer: oil, natural gas, geothermal energy, hydroelectric power

Assess

Social Studies ONLINE
Study Central™ provides summaries, interactive games, and online graphic organizers to help students review content.

Close

Describing Have students describe to a partner the various industries of northern Europe. **OL**

Section 1 Review

The peoples of Norway, Sweden, Denmark, and Iceland share ethnic ties and speak related languages. They mostly descend from Germanic peoples who settled Scandinavia thousands of years ago. The ancestors of Finland's people, however, probably came from what is now Siberia in Russia. As a result, the Finnish language and culture differ from those of the other Scandinavian countries. Still, Finland shares close historic and religious links to the rest of Scandinavia. For example, most Finns—like most other Scandinavians—belong to the Protestant Lutheran Church.

W During the Middle Ages, Scandinavian sailors and traders known as Vikings raided areas of western Europe and explored the North Atlantic Ocean, even reaching America. They also laid the foundation of the modern nations of Denmark, Norway, Sweden, and Iceland. For several hundred years, Sweden ruled its neighbor, Finland. Finland later was controlled by Russia for many years before gaining independence.

Today, Denmark, Norway, and Sweden are constitutional monarchies with governments similar to that of the United Kingdom. Finland and Iceland are republics with elected presidents. Iceland's parliament, the Althing, first met in A.D. 930, making it one of the oldest surviving legislatures in the world.

The Scandinavian countries take pride in providing extensive services to their citizens. As welfare states, they not only help the needy, but they also offer health care, child care, elder care, and retirement benefits to all. In return for these services, the people pay some of the highest taxes in the world.

Reading Check **Identifying** What energy resources are found in Scandinavia?

Section 1 Review

Social Studies ONLINE
Study Central™ To review this section, go to glencoe.com.

Vocabulary

1. **Explain** the meaning of:
   - a. constitutional monarchy
   - b. parliamentary democracy
   - c. peat
   - d. bog
   - e. productivity
   - f. geyser
   - g. fjord
   - h. geothermal energy

Main Ideas

2. **Summarizing** Use a graphic organizer like the one below to summarize important details about the United Kingdom's government, its history, and how it has influenced governments around the world.

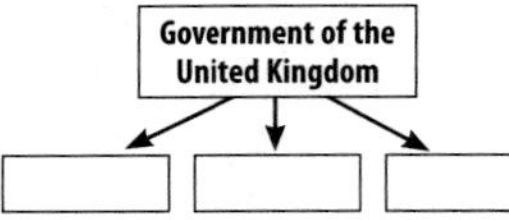

3. **Explaining** Why is the island of Ireland divided, and how has that led to conflict?
4. **Making Generalizations** What do the Scandinavian countries have in common?

Critical Thinking

5. **BIG Idea** Why are the United Kingdom, Ireland, and the countries of Scandinavia considered a subregion of Europe?
6. **Challenge** How are the constitutional monarchies of northern Europe similar to the government of the United States? How are they different?

Writing About Geography

7. **Expository Writing** Write a paragraph comparing the economies of the countries of northern Europe.

Answers

1. Definitions for vocabulary words are found in the section and the Glossary.
2. **Government:** a constitutional monarchy and a parliamentary democracy; prime minister is head of the government; only Parliament can put laws into action; **History:** in the early 1200s nobles forced King John to sign the Magna Carta; Parliament gradually arose as the lawmaking body; the English Bill of Rights limited the ruler's authority; **Influence:** English Bill of Rights influenced the writers of the U.S. Constitution
3. The British kept control of Northern Ireland; the Catholics in northern Ireland would like to unite with the rest of Ireland, while most Protestants wish to remain part of the United Kingdom.
4. a northern location; cold climate; prosperous economies; all but Finland share cultural and ethnic ties and speak related languages
5. because they share a northern location, are influenced by the sea, and have cultural similarities
6. **Similarities:** Constitutions guarantee people's rights, and elected officials run the governments. **Differences:** Constitutional monarchies have a king or queen as the head of state, and the United States does not.
7. Paragraphs will vary, but they should be based on the section.

Guide to Reading

BIG Idea

People's actions can change the physical environment.

Content Vocabulary

- specialization *(p. 330)*
- high-technology industry *(p. 330)*
- bilingual *(p. 332)*
- polder *(p. 332)*
- multinational company *(p. 332)*
- reunification *(p. 336)*
- neutrality *(p. 336)*

Academic Vocabulary

- rely *(p. 330)*
- invest *(p. 335)*

Reading Strategy

Comparing and Contrasting

Use a Venn diagram like the one below to compare and contrast two countries in Europe's heartland.

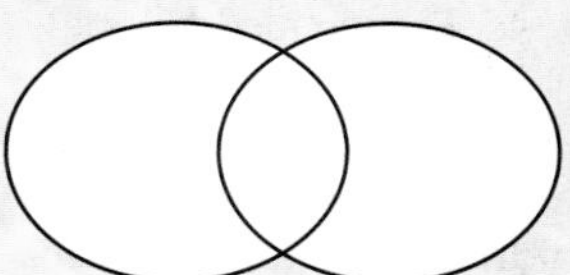

Europe's Heartland

Picture This Mont Blanc, near the French-Italian border, is the highest point in Europe. Glacial hazards and frequent avalanches make hiking and skiing in this area dangerous. Torchlight parades are held to honor those who have lost their lives on the mountain. Mountains in Europe influence how and where people live. Read this section to learn how major landforms affect people living in the heartland of Europe.

Skiers carrying torches descend Mont Blanc

Focus

Bellringer

Daily Focus Transparency 12-2

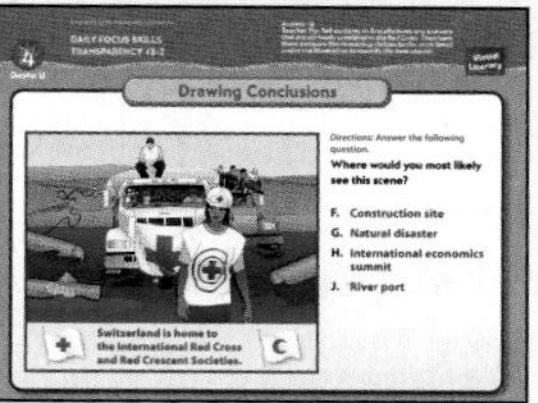

Guide to Reading

Answers to Graphic:

Answers will vary. Possible answer: **France:** French is main language; most people consider themselves Roman Catholic; **Germany:** German is main language; most people are Protestant or Catholic; **Both:** share Northern European Plain; most people live in cities; agriculture and industry are important parts of their economies

Section Spotlight Video

To learn more about Europe's heartland, have students watch the Section Spotlight Video.

Resource Manager

R Reading Strategies	C Critical Thinking	D Differentiated Instruction	W Writing Support	S Skill Practice
Teacher Edition • Monitoring, pp. 330, 332 • Making Connections, p. 332 • Skimming, p. 334 • Using Word Parts, p. 336 **Additional Resources** • Guid. Read, URB p. 86 • Cont. Vocab., URB p. 89 • Ac. Vocab., URB p. 91 • Read. Ess., p. 82	**Teacher Edition** • Making Inferences, pp. 330, 335, 336 • Drawing Con, pp. 332, 336 • Pred. Consequences, p. 333, 337 • Analyzing Info., p. 334 **Additional Resources** • Geo. & Econ., URB, p. 9 • Authentic Assess., p. 12	**Teacher Edition** • Logical/Mathematical, p. 330 • English Learners, p. 331 • Visual/Spatial, p. 335 • Auditory/Musical, p. 335 **Additional Resources** • School-to-Home Conn., URB p. 107 • Reteach., URB p. 105	**Teacher Edition** • Expository Writing, p. 331 **Additional Resources** • Writing Skills, URB, p. 103	**Teacher Edition** • Using Geo. Skills, pp. 333, 334 **Additional Resources** • Chart, Graph, and Map Skills, URB p. 95 • Daily Focus Trans. 12-2 • Reg. Atlas, URB pp. 1–7

Teach

R Reading Strategy

Monitoring Ask: What does "import" mean? *(to bring into a country)* ELL

C Critical Thinking

Making Inferences Ask: What can you infer about the education of French workers from the fact that France has high-tech industries? *(Some of its workers must be highly educated in order to use the sophisticated engineering that goes into making high-tech products.)* OL

D Differentiated Instruction

Logical/Mathematical Have students determine the percentage of the French population that lives in Paris. *(about 16 percent)* OL

Caption Answer:
other landmarks in Paris, such as the Eiffel Tower and Notre Dame Cathedral, as well as Mediterranean beaches, the Alps, and historic castles

France and the Benelux Countries

Main Idea France and the Benelux countries are important cultural, agricultural, and manufacturing centers of Europe.

Geography and You When you think of France, perhaps you picture the Eiffel Tower in Paris. There is, of course, much more to the country, as you will read.

France is in the heart of western Europe. Its three small neighbors to the northeast are known as the Benelux countries. The group name comes from the first syllables of the individual country names—*Be*lgium, the *Ne*therlands, and *Lux*embourg.

France's Land and Economy

France is the second-largest country in Europe. It is slightly smaller than the state of Texas. The landscape in France varies widely. Most of northern France is part of the vast Northern European Plain. In the south, high mountain ranges separate the country from Spain, Italy, and Switzerland. Rivers, such the Seine (SAYN) and the Loire (LWAHR), link France's different regions.

Most of France has a mild or warm climate and rich soil that is ideal for farming. France's agriculture is characterized by **specialization.** This means focusing efforts on certain activities to make the best use of resources. One area of specialization for the French is growing grapes and making wines. Farmers also use the milk of dairy cattle and sheep to produce about 250 kinds of world-famous cheese. France sells these cheeses and other food products to countries that cannot produce them on their own. In turn, France imports goods that it cannot easily make. R

Louvre Museum, Paris

NATIONAL GEOGRAPHIC

The Louvre, in Paris, houses some of the world's most famous paintings and sculptures. ***Place*** **What other attractions in France draw tourists?**

France **relies** on industry as well as agriculture. Workers in traditional industries make cars and trucks, chemicals, textiles, and processed foods. France also has new C **high-technology industries,** which include making computers and other products that require sophisticated engineering. Tourism is an important industry in France. It provides jobs to about 1 in 12 French workers. Millions of people come each year to visit Paris, France's vibrant capital. Other tourists vacation on sunny Mediterranean beaches, ski in the snowy Alps, and tour historic castles called châteaux (sha·TOHZ).

France's People and Culture

Most French trace their ancestry to the Celts, Romans, and Germanic peoples of early Europe. The majority speak French and consider themselves to be Roman Catholic. Islam is France's second religion, because so many people have migrated from Muslim countries in Africa.

D Most of France's 60.7 million people live in urban areas. Almost 10 million make their homes in Paris, one of Europe's largest cities.

Hands-On Chapter Project Step 2

Visualizing Europe's Economics Importance

Step 2: Investigating western Europe Groups of students will prepare the portion of the display illustrating western Europe's economic importance.

Directions Have groups identify three countries in western Europe. Then have them research the five most important imports and exports for each of the three countries. Tell students to use the data to create a visually descriptive bar graph for each country showing the value of these imports and exports in the most recent year for which data is available. Then have students find photos or create illustrations of the products that are imported and exported to accompany the bar graphs on their bulletin board displays.

Drawing Conclusions Have groups write a brief paragraph explaining how western Europe's physical features and resources have influenced the products it imports and exports. OL

(Chapter Project continued in Section 3)

There, people can enjoy museums, universities, fine restaurants, and charming cafes. The Seine River and landmarks like the Eiffel Tower and Notre Dame Cathedral add to the city's beauty.

The French take great pride in their culture, which has greatly influenced the Western world. French cooking and French fashion are admired far and wide. France also boasts famous philosophers, writers, artists, composers, and film directors. **W**

The French Revolution of the late 1700s also influenced the Western world. It brought about the decline of powerful monarchies and the rise of democracies. Today France is a democratic republic with both a president, elected by the people, and a prime minister, appointed by the president. The president has a great deal of power and can even dismiss the legislature, forcing new elections to be held.

The Benelux Countries

The small Benelux countries—Belgium, the Netherlands, and Luxembourg—have much in common. Their lands are low, flat, and densely populated. Most people live in cities, work in businesses or factories, and enjoy a high standard of living. All three nations are also parliamentary democracies with monarchs as heads of state. **D**

Belgium has long been a trade and manufacturing center. With relatively few natural resources of its own, the country imports the raw materials to make and export vehicles, chemicals, and textiles.

TIME GLOBAL CITIZENS

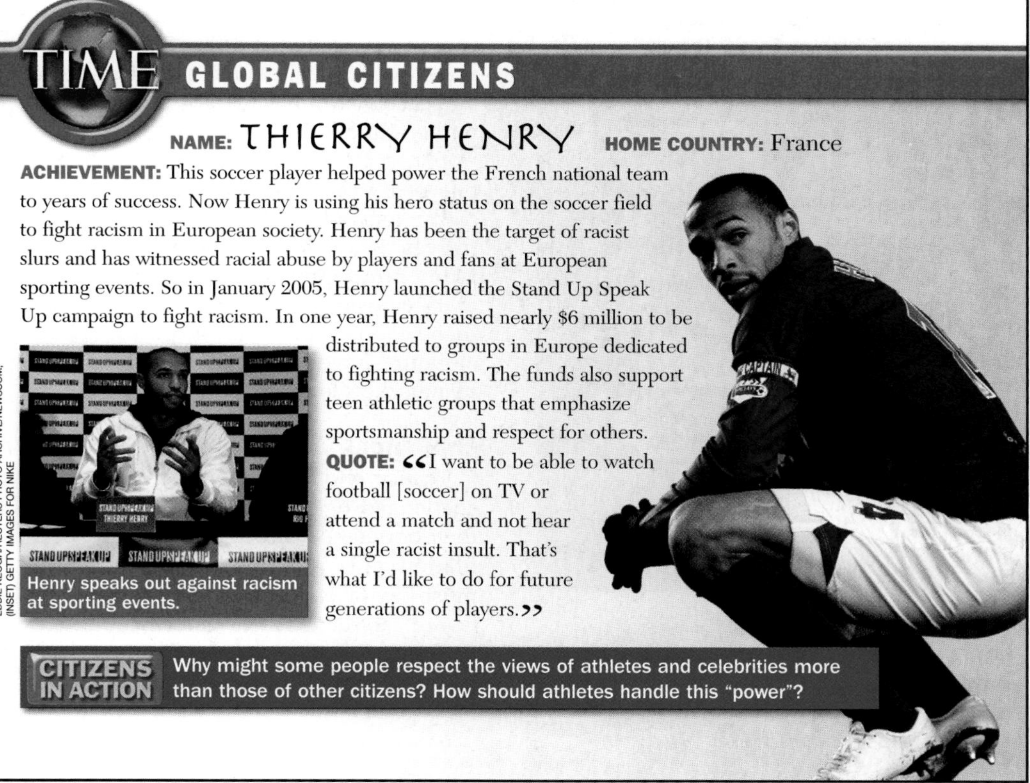

NAME: THIERRY HENRY **HOME COUNTRY:** France

ACHIEVEMENT: This soccer player helped power the French national team to years of success. Now Henry is using his hero status on the soccer field to fight racism in European society. Henry has been the target of racist slurs and has witnessed racial abuse by players and fans at European sporting events. So in January 2005, Henry launched the Stand Up Speak Up campaign to fight racism. In one year, Henry raised nearly $6 million to be distributed to groups in Europe dedicated to fighting racism. The funds also support teen athletic groups that emphasize sportsmanship and respect for others.

QUOTE: "I want to be able to watch football [soccer] on TV or attend a match and not hear a single racist insult. That's what I'd like to do for future generations of players."

Henry speaks out against racism at sporting events.

EDDIE KEOGH/REUTERS PHOTO ARCHIVE/NEWSCOM; (INSET) GETTY IMAGES FOR NIKE

CITIZENS IN ACTION Why might some people respect the views of athletes and celebrities more than those of other citizens? How should athletes handle this "power"?

W Writing Support

Expository Writing Have students research a famous French cook, writer, artist, or fashion designer. Then have them write a brief biography about the person and his or her accomplishments. **OL**

D Differentiated Instruction

English Learners Explain that the word "head" can mean not only the physical head on a person's body, but also the leader of an organization. Ask students which meaning is used in the phrase "heads of state." **ELL**

CITIZENS IN ACTION

Possible Answer:
Answers will vary. Because people admire athletes and celebrities, they may pay more attention to their views. Athletes should handle this power by being careful about what they say about issues.

Additional Support

Activity: Technology Connection

Describing Ask: What are some of France's famous landmarks? *(Answers may include the Seine River, the Eiffel Tower, and Notre Dame Cathedral, as well as other landmarks students might know about.)* Direct students to work with a partner to research a famous French landmark by using Internet search engines to find information from credible sources. After students complete their research, have them use desktop publishing software to create a blog entry about a visit they would like to make to this landmark. Suggest that students include graphics in their blog that are relevant and appealing. Also, remind them that the blog should be free of spelling, punctuation, and grammatical errors. **OL**

R1 Reading Strategy

Monitoring Read this section aloud. **Ask:** **What do dikes do?** *(prevent the sea from flooding the country)* **Why do the people pump the wetlands?** *(to use the soil for farming)* **BL**

C Critical Thinking

Drawing Conclusions **Ask:** **What does tulip production indicate about the Netherlands' climate?** *(It is mild.)* **OL**

R2 Reading Strategy

Making Connections Ask students to name multinational countries that are based in the United States. If they need help, tell them to think of the major beverage and fast-food companies. **OL**

Caption Answer:
vehicles, chemicals, and textiles

Most Belgians live in crowded urban areas. Antwerp is a busy port and the center of the world diamond industry. Brussels is the capital and headquarters of the European Union (EU).

Belgium is made up of three regions—Flanders, Wallonia, and Brussels. In Flanders, to the north and west of Brussels, most people speak Dutch and are known as Flemings. In Wallonia, the areas south and east of Brussels, most people speak French and are known as Walloons. The population of the Brussels region comes from both language groups. As a result, the Brussels region is officially **bilingual,** using two languages. While each region practices self-rule, tensions sometimes arise between Flemings and Walloons.

NATIONAL GEOGRAPHIC

Antwerp's Diamond Trade

▲ Antwerp has been a center of the world's diamond trade for more than 500 years. Some $20 billion in diamond sales occur there annually. ***Movement*** **What goods does Belgium export?**

R1 To the north of Belgium is the Netherlands, whose people are known as the Dutch. About 25 percent of the Netherlands lies below sea level. Without defenses against the sea, high tides would flood much of the country. The Dutch have built dikes, or banks of soil, to control and confine the sea as seen in **Figure 2.** They drain and pump the wetlands dry. Once run by windmills, pumps are now driven by steam or electricity. The drained lands, called **polders,** have rich farming soil.

About 90 percent of the Dutch live in cities and towns. Amsterdam is the capital and largest city. Living in a densely populated country, the Dutch make good use of their space. Houses are narrow but tall, and apartments are often built on canals and over highways. The Dutch work in service industries, manufacturing, and trade. C The major exports of the Netherlands are cheese, vegetables, and flowers. Acres and acres of tulip fields bloom in the spring, and each year the Dutch export about two million tulip bulbs.

Southeast of Belgium lies Luxembourg, one of Europe's smallest countries. Centrally located in Europe, Luxembourg thrives as a center of trade and finance. R2 Many **multinational companies,** or firms that do business in several countries, have their headquarters here. The people of Luxembourg have a mixed French and German background.

Challenges

France and the Benelux countries are challenged by population changes. First, their populations are aging. An aging population puts pressure on workers who must pay taxes to provide retirement and health care benefits for older people. Second, France and the Benelux countries have fairly large African and Asian minority

Differentiated Instruction

Leveled Activities

BL School-to-Home Conn. Act., URB p. 107

School-to-Home Connection Activity

What Do You Know?

AL Geography and Economics, URB p. 9

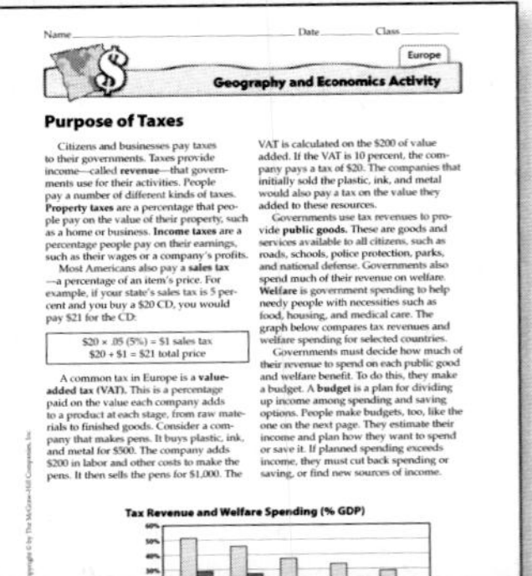
Geography and Economics Activity

Purpose of Taxes

ELL Content Vocabulary Activity, URB p. 89

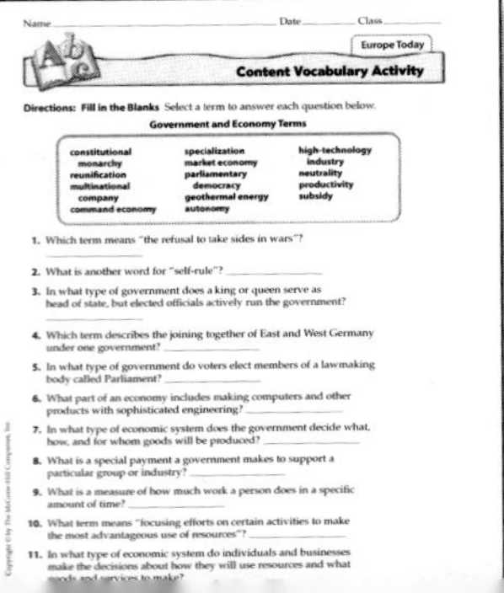
Content Vocabulary Activity

NATIONAL GEOGRAPHIC **Maps In MOtion** See StudentWorks™ Plus or glencoe.com.

Figure 2 **Areas of the Netherlands Reclaimed From the Sea**

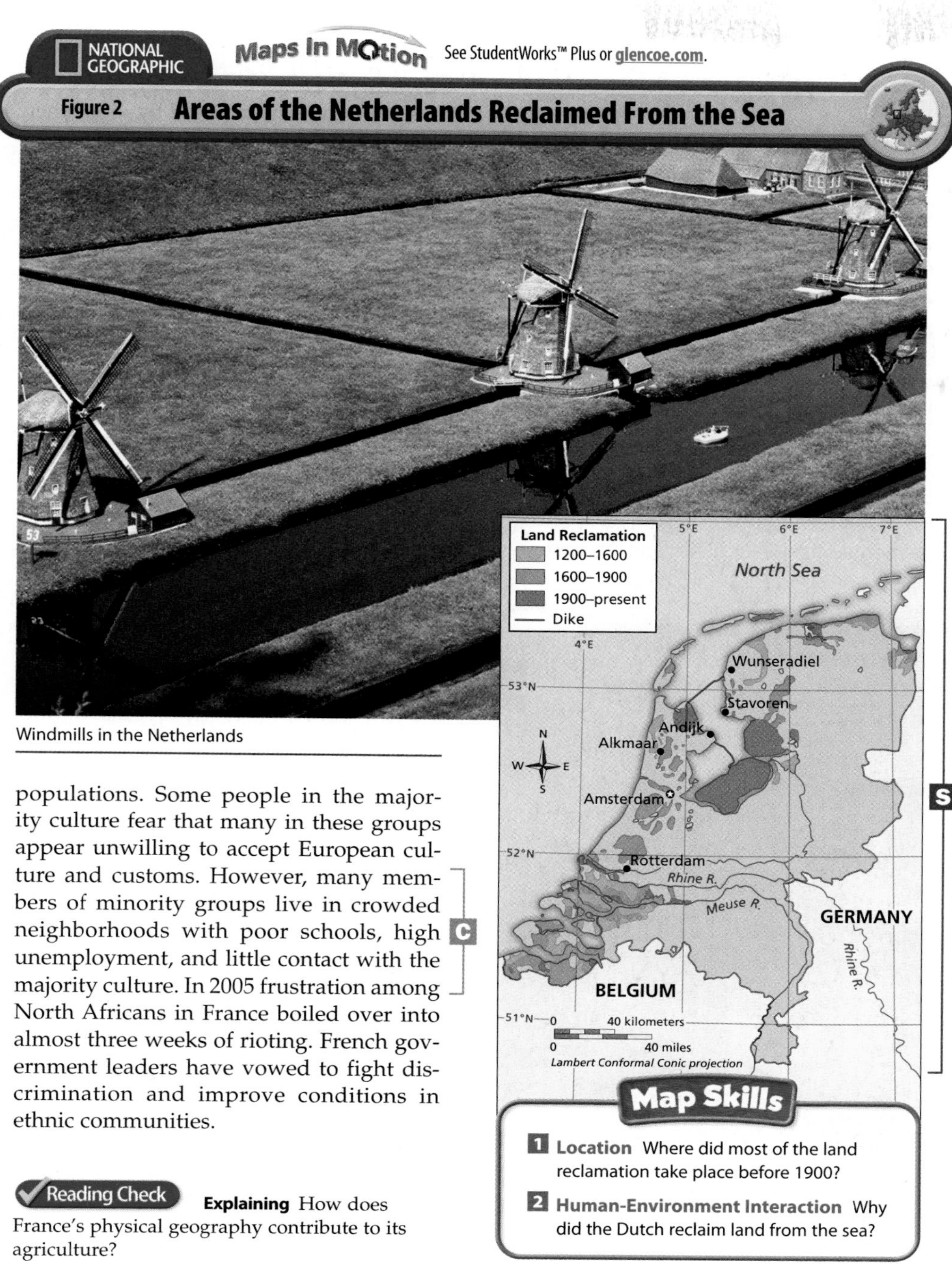

Windmills in the Netherlands

populations. Some people in the majority culture fear that many in these groups appear unwilling to accept European culture and customs. However, many members of minority groups live in crowded neighborhoods with poor schools, high unemployment, and little contact with the majority culture. In 2005 frustration among North Africans in France boiled over into almost three weeks of rioting. French government leaders have vowed to fight discrimination and improve conditions in ethnic communities. **C**

Reading Check **Explaining** How does France's physical geography contribute to its agriculture?

Map Skills

1. **Location** Where did most of the land reclamation take place before 1900?
2. **Human-Environment Interaction** Why did the Dutch reclaim land from the sea? **S**

C Critical Thinking

Predicting Consequences Ask: How might better schools help the people in these neighborhoods? *(Better education might help young people get better jobs and improve their standard of living.)* **OL**

S Skill Practice

Using Geography Skills Ask: How has reclamation affected the amount of available land in the Netherlands? *(It has increased it substantially.)* **OL**

Reading Check Answer: Its mild and warm climates and rich soil are ideal for farming.

Map Skills

Answers:
1. in the southwestern part of the Netherlands
2. to increase the amount of farmland

Additional Support

Activity: Economics Connection

Predicting Ask: What are the major exports of the Netherlands? *(cheese, vegetables, and flowers)* **How might its economy be affected if its dikes were destroyed?** *(The sea would flood the vegetable and flower crops, leaving the country with little to export.)* Discuss with students the importance of exports to a country's economic strength. **Ask: Which economy is generally more stable, one that is based on a single export crop or one that has many different items to export?** *(one that has many different items to export)* **Why?** *(because a country that depends on a single export item puts itself at risk economically if a natural disaster strikes or if demand for that item plummets worldwide)*

R Reading Strategy

Skimming Have students skim through the text under this head looking for words or phrases related to the region's economy. Have them write down any pertinent points for each country. When they are finished, have them compare their notes with a classmate to see if they noted the same things. Then share with the class any additional points you noted as you skimmed the text. **OL**

S Skill Practice

Using Geography Skills Have students use a map or globe to locate the rivers discussed in this section. **OL**

C Critical Thinking

Analyzing Information Ask: How did Germany's location contribute to its involvement in wars? *(Its central location put it in the middle of conflicts in Europe and also gave it the desire to dominate nearby lands.)* **AL**

Caption Answer:
Germany's farms are highly productive, providing enough food to export its surplus, and Germany is also a leading industrial power, producing steel, chemicals, cars, and electrical equipment.

R Germany and the Alpine Countries

Main Idea Germany, Switzerland, and Austria are known for their mountain scenery and prosperous economies.

Geography and You Have you ever found yourself working alongside someone you used to compete against? Germans are in that position now that the two halves of their country are reunited. Read to learn more.

Germany and the Alpine countries—Switzerland, Austria, and Liechtenstein—lie in Central Europe. They all have strong economies and a high standard of living.

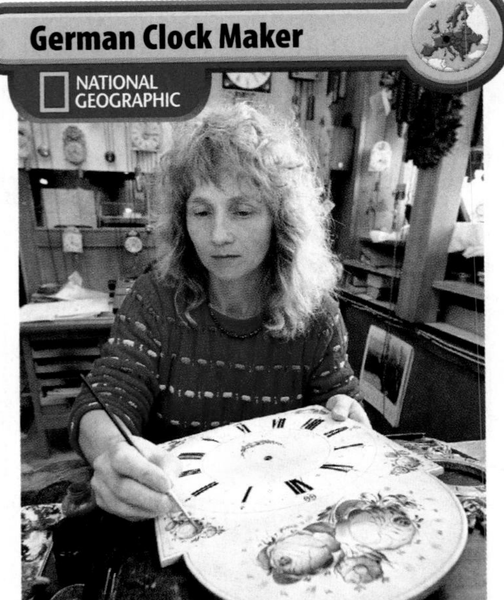

▲ Germany's Black Forest region is famous for its finely crafted clocks, including cuckoo clocks. ***Place*** **Describe Germany's industry and agriculture today.**

Germany's Land

A large country encircled by nine other nations, Germany sits snugly in the heart of Europe. The flat Northern European Plain extends across northern Germany. Rocky highlands, some of which contain rich coal deposits, cover the central part of the country. The majestic Alps rise in the far south. The Alps are famous for their beauty, but many forests on the lower slopes of these mountains are threatened by acid rain.

Rivers have been vital to Germany's economic growth. They are used to transport raw materials to factories and to carry manufactured goods to market. The Danube River, one of Europe's most important waterways, begins in the Black Forest and winds eastward across southern Germany. Another river, the Elbe, flows from the central highlands to the North Sea. S Hamburg, Germany's largest port city, is located on the Elbe River.

The most important of Germany's rivers—the Rhine—actually begins in the Swiss Alps. It then passes through Germany and the Netherlands before spilling into the North Sea. The Rhine is long and deep, allowing oceangoing ships to travel far inland.

History and Government

Germany's central location in Europe has long made it a crossroads for peoples, ideas, and armies. For centuries, Germany was a collection of states that were deeply involved in Europe's wars and religious struggles. C In 1871 these states joined together to form the modern nation of Germany.

During the 1900s, Germany's efforts to dominate Europe helped spark two world wars. Allied countries—the United States, the Soviet Union, the United Kingdom, and France—defeated Germany in World War II.

Differentiated Instruction

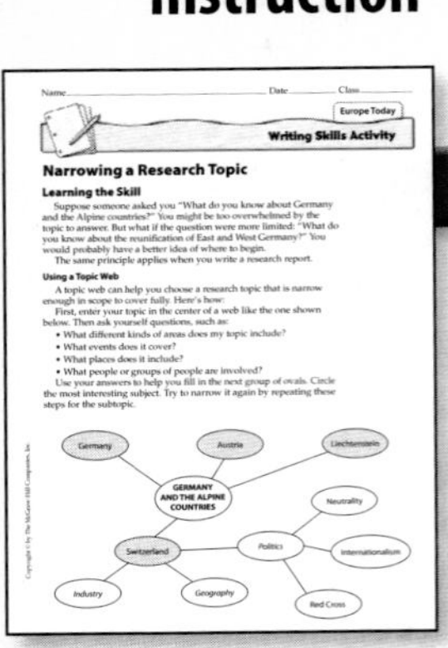
Europe Today
Writing Skills Activity
Narrowing a Research Topic
Learning the Skill

Writing Skills Activity, URB pp. 103–104

Narrowing a Research Topic

Objective: To use a topic web to narrow a research topic

Focus: Copy the sample topic web on the board, and give students time to study it.

Teach: Read aloud the steps for using a topic web, and use the web on the board to illustrate each step.

Assess: Have students use the web to answer the questions.

Close: Tell students to create a new web starting from a different point on the sample web.

Differentiated Instruction Strategies

- **BL** Reduce the web's content so that Switzerland is the center of the web.
- **AL** Create your own topic web, and explain how you would use it to write a research report.
- **ELL** Practice writing research questions that start with the words *who, what, when, where,* and *why.*

In 1945 the Allies divided Germany into four zones of occupation. The Soviet zone later became Communist-ruled East Germany. The three other zones, controlled by the United States, the United Kingdom, and France, became democratic West Germany. After the collapse of communism, the two parts of Germany were reunited in 1990. **D1**

Today, Germany—like the United States—is a federal republic. This means that the national government and state governments share power. An elected president serves as Germany's head of state, but he or she performs only ceremonial duties. The country's chancellor, chosen by parliament, is the real head of government.

Germany's People

Germany has the largest population of the European countries—82.5 million. Nearly 90 percent of the people live in urban areas. **C** The largest city, and the nation's capital, is Berlin. With many museums, concert halls, and theaters, Berlin is a cultural center as well as the seat of government. Germans are proud to have produced many brilliant thinkers and writers, as well as composers such as Johann Sebastian Bach and Ludwig van Beethoven. **D2**

About 90 percent of the country's people are native Germans, and German is the main language. Most of the rest of the population has immigrated from eastern Europe and Turkey. These immigrants came to Germany to find work or to escape political troubles in their homelands. The newcomers include many Muslims and Jews, but most Germans are Protestant or Catholic.

The Economy

Today, Germany is a global economic power and a leader in the European Union. This is due in part to Germany's highly productive agriculture. In the river valleys and plains areas, the fertile land and mild climate are well suited for farming. Germany produces enough food to feed its people and export its surplus.

It is industry, though, that is most responsible for Germany's strong economy. The country is a leading producer of steel, chemicals, cars, and electrical equipment. During the late 1900s, many Western industrialized countries experienced a decline in manufacturing. In Germany, however, the decrease was not dramatic. German firms had **invested** money to research and develop desirable, competitive products.

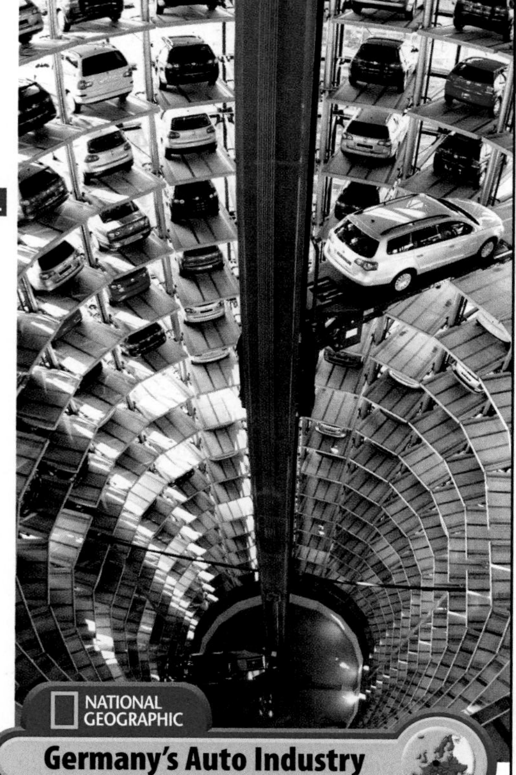

NATIONAL GEOGRAPHIC

Germany's Auto Industry

New cars are placed in a huge storage tower near an automobile plant in Wolfsburg, Germany.
Place **What role does Germany have in the global economy?**

D1 Differentiated Instruction

Visual/Spatial Have students research the territories of East and West Germany. Then have them trace the border between East Germany and West Germany on a current map and identify the major cities that were located in each country. **OL**

C Critical Thinking

Making Inferences Ask: Do you think most of Germany's people work in agriculture? *(no)* **How do you know?** *(because nearly 90 percent live in urban areas)* **OL**

D2 Differentiated Instruction

Auditory/Musical Play selections from the music of Bach and Beethoven. Ask students which selection they like best and why. **AL**

Caption Answer:
It is a global economic power and a leader in the European Union. Its agricultural and industrial sectors are strong; and the country produces well-researched, competitive products.

Additional Support

Activity: Collaborative Learning

Expressing Ask: What happened to Germany after World War II? *(It was divided into four zones that became two separate countries.)* Explain that not only was Germany divided into two parts, but the city of Berlin was also divided—by an actual wall. Organize students into two groups. Have both groups conduct research to learn more about the construction of the Berlin Wall and how it affected people on both sides of the wall. Have one group focus on people in East Berlin and the other on people in West Berlin. Then have both groups work together to write a play about the construction of the wall and its eventual dismantling. Tell students that their plays should portray how the wall affected people's lives, separating friends and family members. When the class finishes preparing their script, have them rehearse the play and present it to a live audience. **OL**

R Reading Strategy

Using Word Parts Explain to students that the prefix *-in* in the word *inefficient* means "not," so *inefficient* means "not efficient." Ask students to think of other words that begin with this prefix, and have them explain the meaning of each term in their own words. **OL**

C1 Critical Thinking

Drawing Conclusions Ask: Why have many international organizations located their offices in Switzerland? *(because Switzerland is a neutral and stable country)* **OL**

C2 Critical Thinking

Making Inferences Ask: Why do many people in Switzerland speak more than one language? *(Because Switzerland is surrounded by countries that speak different languages, Swiss people often must communicate with people who speak various languages.)* **OL**

Caption Answer:
It isolated groups of people, so each community developed unique traditions.

Additional Resources

One of Germany's economic challenges has come as a result of **reunification**, when East and West Germany united under one government in 1990. At the time, workers in East Germany had less experience and less training in modern technology than workers in West Germany. Old and inefficient factories in the east could not compete with the more advanced industries in the west. Many businesses closed, and economic activities in the eastern part of Germany continue to lag behind those in the prosperous west.

The Alpine Countries

The Alpine countries take their name from the Alps of central Europe. These mountainous countries include Switzerland, Austria, and Liechtenstein. Liechtenstein is a tiny country of only 62 square miles (161 sq. km)—smaller than Washington, D.C. The whole population—about 40,000 people—would not even fill a major league baseball stadium.

Switzerland is also a small country, but it is much bigger than Liechtenstein and far more important internationally. The few travel routes that cut through the Alps lie in Switzerland. So for centuries, the Swiss have been "gatekeepers" between northern and southern Europe. That role helped Switzerland decide long ago to practice **neutrality**, or refusal to take sides in wars. As a result, for more than 700 years the Swiss have enjoyed a stable democratic government, even when fighting has raged around them. Today many international organizations, such as the International Red Cross, are based in the Swiss city of Geneva.

Switzerland's geography also affected the growth of individual communities. The rugged mountains isolated groups of people from one another. As a result, each town and city treasures its unique traditions and independence. Today the people of Switzerland represent many different ethnic groups and religions. The country also has not one but four national languages: German, French, and Italian—which are the native tongues of Switzerland's neighbors—and Romansch. Most Swiss speak German, and many speak more than one language.

Although it has few natural resources, Switzerland is a thriving industrial nation. Dams on Switzerland's rivers produce great amounts of hydroelectric power for industries and homes. Using imported materials, Swiss workers make high-quality electronic equipment, chemicals, and other goods. The country is also known for its fine clocks and watches, excellent chocolate and cheeses, and its multipurpose Swiss army

NATIONAL GEOGRAPHIC

Wheels of Swiss Cheese

Fine cheeses may be aged for years before they are ready to eat. Switzerland exports more than 50,000 tons of cheese each year. ***Place*** **How did Switzerland's geography affect its communities?**

FastFacts

Swiss Watches Swiss watches have their origins in Geneva, Switzerland, in the sixteenth century. Religious reforms at the time banned the wearing of jewelry, so jewelry makers needed a new product to make and sell. Their answer was the watch. Mass production of watches, which began in the early twentieth century, made Switzerland the leader in the watch industry. After World War I, the wristwatch was introduced and quickly became popular. Since then, the Swiss have continued to incorporate new technologies, including quartz watches and LED and LCD displays. The quality and popularity of Swiss watches makes them a target for counterfeiters.

knives. A large part of the Swiss economy is dependent upon its banking and other financial services. Because Switzerland's neutrality is honored by other countries, people from around the world consider Swiss banks to be safe and secure. C

East of Switzerland is landlocked Austria. The Alps cover the western three-quarters of Austria, so there is little good farmland. The beautiful mountain scenery does, however, attract many skiers and tourists. The mountains also provide valuable timber and iron ore and, as in Switzerland, fast-moving rivers generate hydroelectric power. With these resources, Austria's factories produce machinery, chemicals, metals, and vehicles. Austria also has strong banking and insurance industries.

The people of Austria mainly speak German and are Roman Catholic. Most Austrians live in cities and towns. Vienna, on the Danube River, is the capital and largest city, and about one-fifth of Austrians live there. Before World War I, Vienna was the heart of the vast Austro-Hungarian Empire that covered much of central and southeastern Europe. Vienna was also a center of culture and learning. Some of the world's greatest composers, including Wolfgang Amadeus Mozart, lived or performed in Vienna. The city's concert halls, historic palaces, and churches continue to draw music lovers and other visitors today.

Reading Check **Contrasting** How do the economies of the western and eastern parts of Germany differ?

C Critical Thinking

Predicting Consequences

Ask: What might happen to Switzerland's banking industry if the country became involved in a war? *(The banking industry would probably suffer because people would feel that Swiss banks were less secure.)*

Reading Check **Answer:** The economy in eastern Germany lags behind that in western Germany because factories in the former East Germany were old and inefficient, and workers there had less training in the use of modern technology.

Section 2 Review

Social Studies ONLINE
Study Central™ To review this section, go to glencoe.com.

Vocabulary

1. **Explain** the significance of the following terms:
   a. specialization
   b. high-technology industry
   c. bilingual
   d. polder
   e. multinational company
   f. reunification
   g. neutrality

Main Ideas

2. **Explaining** How has French culture influenced the world?
3. **Analyzing** Draw a Venn diagram to analyze how agriculture is similar and different in France and Germany.

France | Germany

Critical Thinking

4. **Making Generalizations** How does specialization in French agriculture and food production lead to interdependence with other countries?
5. **BIG Idea** Give three examples of how people in this part of Europe have changed the environment. Explain if you think those changes are positive or negative.
6. **Challenge** Do you think the economic successes of the countries of Europe's heartland can continue in the future? Explain your answer fully.

Writing About Geography

7. **Persuasive Writing** Write a letter to a friend trying to persuade him or her to visit a specific country in Europe's heartland with you. Describe why that country interests you.

Assess

Social Studies ONLINE
Study Central™ provides summaries, interactive games, and online graphic organizers to help students review content.

Close

Comparing and Contrasting Have students create a chart on the board that compares and contrasts the economies of the countries in Europe's heartland. OL

Section 2 Review

Answers

1. Definitions for vocabulary words are found in the section and the Glossary.
2. French cooking and fashion are popular worldwide, and French philosophers, writers, artists, composers, and film directors are also famous.
3. **France:** characterized by specialization, such as cheese and making wine; **Germany:** not as specialized; **Both:** fertile land; produce enough food to export
4. Through specialization France exports its products to other countries and imports from them the products it cannot make.
5. Answers may vary. Possible examples: The Netherlands drains its wetlands, which increases the amount of farmland (positive), but also could have negative environmental effects; France has built housing where many immigrants live, but conditions are crowded; Switzerland has built dams on its rivers to produce hydroelectric power (positive), but this could also have negative environmental effects.
6. Answers will vary, but students should consider the causes and effects of these countries' successes.
7. Answers will vary, but students should support their positions with facts from the chapter.

Focus

Bellringer

Daily Focus Transparency 12-3

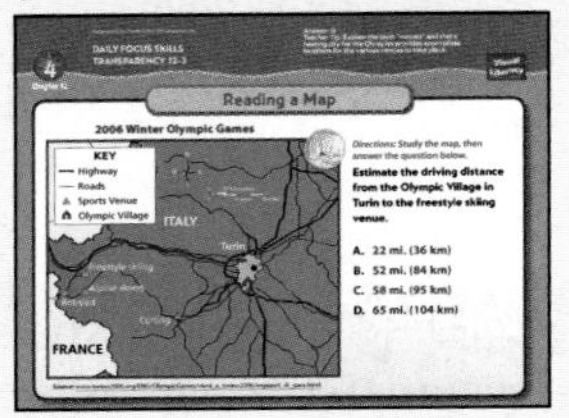

Guide to Reading

Answers to Graphic:

Answers may include:

- Location in southern Europe
- Closeness to the sea/ocean has influenced their histories and economies
- Democratic governments

Section Spotlight Video

To learn more about southern Europe, have students watch the Section Spotlight Video.

Guide to Reading

BIG Idea

Places reflect the relationship between humans and the physical environment.

Content Vocabulary

- dry farming *(p. 339)*
- autonomy *(p. 339)*
- subsidy *(p. 340)*

Academic Vocabulary

- similar *(p. 339)*
- militant *(p. 340)*

Reading Strategy

Making Generalizations Use a diagram like the one below to write three characteristics shared by the countries in this region.

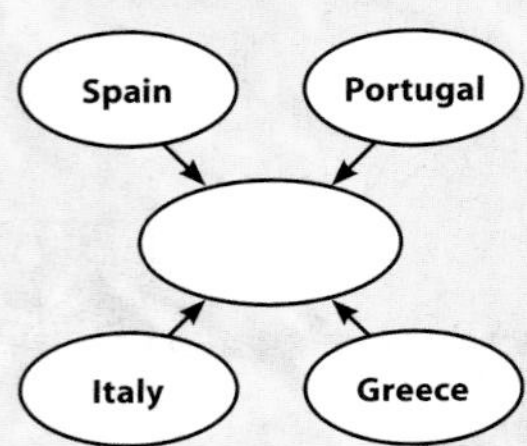

Southern Europe

Picture This Lunchtime lineup! Visit Antiparos, Greece, and you are likely to see octopuses draped over fishing lines to dry in preparation for a later meal. The boneless octopus has a parrot-like beak, a doughnut-shaped brain, eight arms, three hearts, and—it can change colors. Octopuses thrive in the clear, blue waters of the Mediterranean Sea. The sea and the lands surrounding it have supported numerous cultures. Read this section to learn about today's cultures of southern, or Mediterranean, Europe.

Octopuses drying on line, Antiparos, Greece

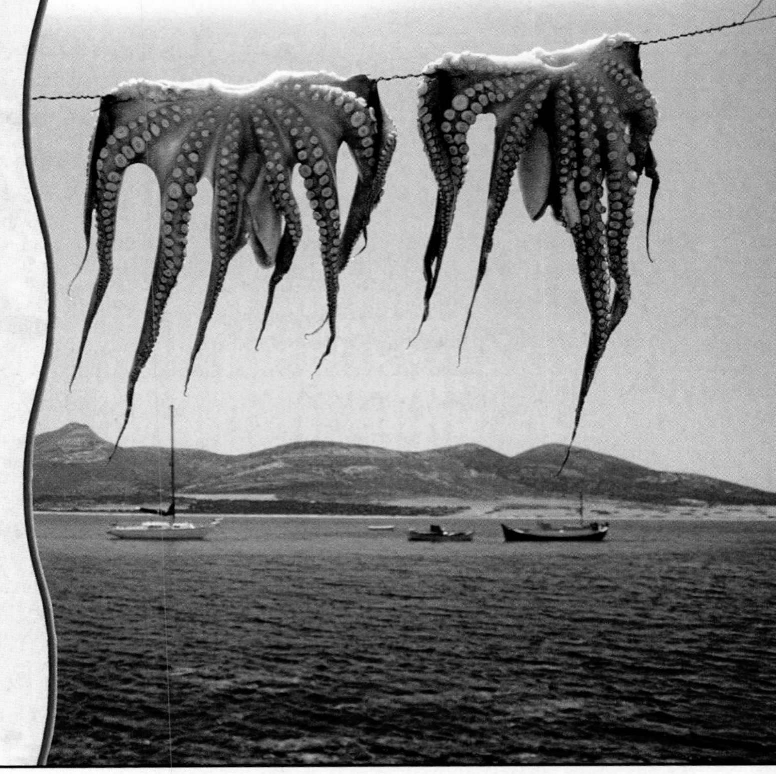

Resource Manager

R Reading Strategies	C Critical Thinking	D Differentiated Instruction	W Writing Support	S Skill Practice
Teacher Edition • Using Context Clues, p. 340 • Previewing, p. 341 **Additional Resources** • Guid. Read., URB p. 87 • Cont. Vocab., URB p. 89 • Ac. Vocab., URB p. 91 • Read. Ess., p. 85	**Teacher Edition** • Pred. Consequences, p. 339 • Det. Cause/Effect, pp. 340, 342 **Additional Resources** • Crit. Think., URB p. 97 • Authentic Assess., p. 12 • Quizzes and Tests, p. 133	**Teacher Edition** • Kinesthetic, p. 341 **Additional Resources** • School-to-Home Conn, URB p. 107 • Reteach., URB p. 105	**Teacher Edition** • Descriptive Writing, p. 339	**Teacher Edition** • Visual Literacy, p. 339 **Additional Resources** • Chart, Graph, and Map Skills, URB p. 95 • Daily Focus Trans. 12-3 • Reg. Atlas, URB pp. 1–7

Spain and Portugal

Main Idea **Spain and Portugal are young democracies with growing economies.**

Geography and You Can you imagine chasing bulls down the main streets of your hometown? People in Pamplona, Spain, do this every year as part of a summer festival. Keep reading to discover more about colorful Spain and its neighbor, Portugal.

Spain and Portugal occupy the Iberian Peninsula in southwestern Europe. They share it with the tiny nation of Andorra, nestled in the Pyrenees Mountains.

Spain

Most of Spain is covered by the Meseta, a dry plateau surrounded by mountain ranges. The reddish-yellow soil there tends to be poor, and rain is scarce. However, crops such as wheat and vegetables are grown by **dry farming.** This technique does not depend on irrigation. Instead the land is left unplanted every few years so that it can store moisture.

Farming is easier in other parts of the country. Northwestern Spain, which borders the Atlantic Ocean, has mild temperatures and plenty of rain. Southern Spain, which borders the Mediterranean Sea, has wet winters and dry summers. In this area, farmers use irrigation to grow citrus fruits, olives, and grapes—Spain's leading agricultural products.

In the late 1900s, Spain's manufacturing and service industries grew rapidly. Today they dominate the economy. Spanish workers produce processed foods, clothing, footwear, steel, and cars. Spain also benefits greatly from tourism. The country's attractions include castles, cathedrals, and

S

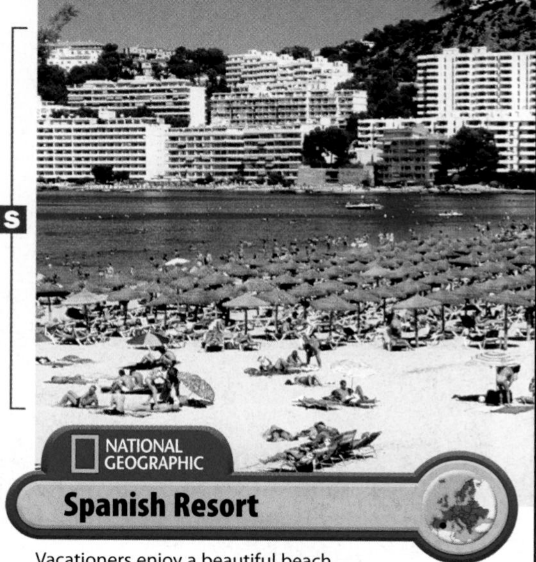

NATIONAL GEOGRAPHIC

Spanish Resort

Vacationers enjoy a beautiful beach in Mallorca, a popular resort island off Spain's Mediterranean coast. ***Human-Environment Interaction*** **Besides tourism, what are Spain's other major industries?**

sunny Mediterranean beaches. Tourists also enjoy Spain's cultural traditions, such as bullfighting and flamenco dancing. W

Most of Spain's people speak Castilian Spanish, the country's official language. Some regions of Spain, however, are home to distinct groups with their own languages. The people of Catalonia, in the northeast, speak Catalan, which is **similar** to an old language of southern France. In the Pyrenees, the Basques speak Euskera, a language unrelated to any other in the world.

After years of rule by a dictator, Spain became a democracy in the late 1970s. In recent times, Spain's democratic government has given the different regions of Spain greater **autonomy,** or self-rule. In the Basque region, though, many people want to be completely separate from Spain. Some Basque separatists have used terrorism to try to achieve this goal. C

Teach

S Skill Practice

Visual Literacy Have students study the photo. **Ask: What might be the purpose of the high-rise buildings in this scene?** *(Possible answer: hotels for tourists)* **OL**

W Writing Support

Descriptive Writing Have students research bullfighting or flamenco dancing. Provide reference materials, videos, and photographs if needed. Then have them write descriptions of these activities. **OL**

C Critical Thinking

Predicting Consequences Ask: What might happen to the tourism industry in Spain if terrorism increases? *(It could decline because tourists might feel that Spain is not a safe place to visit.)* **OL**

Caption Answer:
farming and manufacturing

Differentiated Instruction

Chart, Graph, and Map Skills, URB pp. 95–96

Interpreting a Double-Bar Graph

Objective: To use a double-bar graph to make comparisons

Focus: Draw a double-bar graph on the board that compares two familiar items.

Teach: Review the steps for reading a double-bar graph. Use the languages graph to illustrate the steps.

Assess: Have students use the languages graph to complete the table of languages.

Close: Have students create a double-bar graph using the population and labor force table.

Differentiated Instruction Strategies

BL Choose two different items in the classroom, and count the number of each item. Draw a bar graph that compares the two numbers.

AL Research the population and labor force of Spain and Italy, and add these countries to the double-bar graph.

ELL Ask students the number of languages they speak, and then graph the results.

R **Reading Strategy**

Using Context Clues Ask: What does the word "migrated" mean in this sentence? *(moved from one country or region to another)* **OL**

C **Critical Thinking**

Determining Cause and Effect Ask: How has Portugal's coastal location affected its history and culture? *(It has affected where people live and how they make a living, and helped make Portugal a sea power in the 1500s.)* **OL**

Caption Answer:
The shaky economy is growing stronger, and manufacturing and service industries have become more important than agriculture to Portugal's economy.

Reading Check Answer: Castilian Spanish, Catalan, and Euskera

Harvesting Cork

The bark of a cork oak is stripped and then cut and shaped into corks for bottles (inset). The trees will grow new bark within 10 years. ***Place*** **How have subsidies from the European Union impacted agriculture in Portugal?**

Most of Spain's 43.5 million people live in urban areas. The main cities are Madrid, the capital, and Barcelona, the leading seaport and industrial center. The cities of Seville, Granada, and Córdoba, in the south, show the influence of the Muslims who ruled Spain for much of the Middle Ages.

Most people in Spain today are Roman Catholic. **R** A large number of Muslims from North Africa have migrated to Spain in recent years. Tensions have sometimes developed between the Spanish population and Muslim immigrants. Spain was shaken in 2004 when terrorist attacks by suspected Muslim **militants** killed 191 people on Madrid trains.

Portugal

Spain's smaller neighbor to the west is Portugal. Most of Portugal's land is a low coastal plain split in half by the Tagus River. In both the north and the south, people grow a variety of crops. The most important are grapes used for wine making and oak trees that provide cork. **C** Most Portuguese live in small villages on the coast, near the cities of Lisbon and Porto. Many people earn a living there by fishing in the Atlantic Ocean.

Closeness to the ocean helped Portugal become a sea power during the 1500s. The Portuguese built an empire that included Brazil and parts of Asia and Africa. Today Portugal has a democratic government, and its shaky economy is growing stronger with the help of subsidies from the European Union. **Subsidies** are special payments a government makes to support a group or industry. With this help, manufacturing and service industries have become more important than agriculture to Portugal's economy.

Reading Check **Identifying** What languages are spoken in Spain?

Differentiated Instruction

Leveled Activities

BL Reading Essentials & Note-Taking Guide, p. 85

Chapter 12, Section 3 (Pages 338–342)

Southern Europe

Big Idea

Places reflect the relationship between humans and the physical environment. As you read, complete the diagram below. Write three characteristics shared by Spain, Italy, and Greece.

Spain

Italy

Greece

Notes **Read to Learn**

Spain and Portugal (pages 339–340)

Specifying *What are Spain and Portugal's chief agricultural products?*

Spain:

Spain and Portugal are located on the Iberian Peninsula. A third country, tiny Andorra, is nestled in the Pyrenees Mountains. The Meseta, a dry plateau surrounded by mountains, covers most of Spain. Because little rain falls on the Meseta, farmers use a technique called **dry farming** to grow wheat and vegetables. The land is left unplanted every few years so it can store moisture. The milder climate of southern Spain is good for growing citrus fruits, olives, and grapes.

Manufacturing and service industries dominate the economy. Spain produces foods, clothing, footwear, steel, and cars. Tourism also boosts the economy. Tourists visit Spain's castles, cathedrals, and Mediterranean beaches. They also enjoy Spanish bullfighting and flamenco dancing.

OL Regional Atlas Activity, URB p. 1

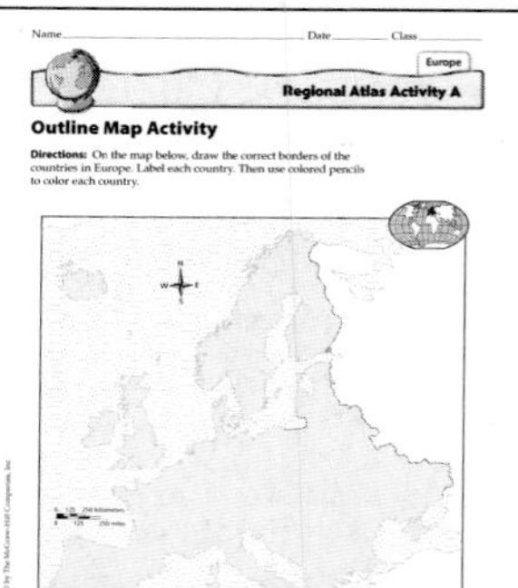

Name
Date
Class
Europe
Regional Atlas Activity A
Outline Map Activity
Directions: On the map below, draw the correct borders of the countries in Europe. Label each country. Then use colored pencils to color each country.

ELL Authentic Assessment, p. 12

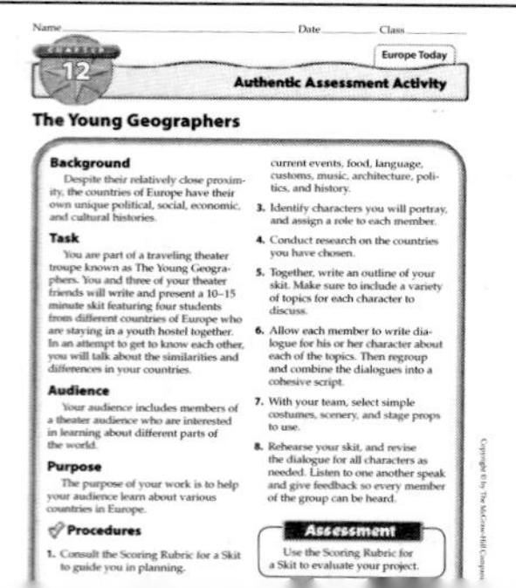

Italy

Main Idea **Italy's north and south form two distinct economic regions.**

Geography and You Do you have a favorite Italian food? When people think of Italy, they often think of delicious pasta. Read to learn what else the country produces.

Italy juts out from Europe into the Mediterranean Sea. The mainland looks like a boot about to kick a triangular football. The "football" is Sicily (SIH·suh·lee), an island that is also part of the country.

In Italy's north, the Alps tower over the broad Lombardy plain. In central and southern areas, the Apennine Mountains form a backbone that stretches into Sicily. Volcanoes also dot the landscape. Throughout history, southern Italy has experienced volcanic eruptions and earthquakes.

The Economy

Since the mid-1900s, Italy has changed from a mainly agricultural country into a leading industrial economy. Most of this growth has taken place in northern Italy. Workers in northern manufacturing cities, such as Milan, Turin, and Genoa, produce cars, technical instruments, appliances, clothing, and high-quality goods. The north's fertile Po River valley is also the country's richest farming region. Farmers there raise livestock and grow grapes, olives, and other crops.

Southern Italy is poorer and less industrialized than northern Italy. Much of the terrain is mountainous, with limited mineral deposits, poor land for farming and grazing, and few navigable rivers. As a result, unemployment is high. Unemployment has led many southern Italians to seek a better life in northern Italy or other parts of Europe.

The People

About 90 percent of Italy's 58.7 million people live in urban areas. In the cities, modern life is mingled with the past. Rome, Italy's largest city, was once the center of the Roman Empire. Today, Rome is Italy's capital and home to the country's democratic republic form of government.

The people of Italy speak Italian, and nearly all are Roman Catholic. In fact, the Roman Catholic Church is based in Rome. The Church rules tiny Vatican City, where the pope and other Church leaders live and work. Although Vatican City is within Rome's boundaries, it is an independent country—the smallest in the world.

Reading Check **Explaining** How do the economies of northern and southern Italy differ?

An Evening in Rome, Italy

NATIONAL GEOGRAPHIC

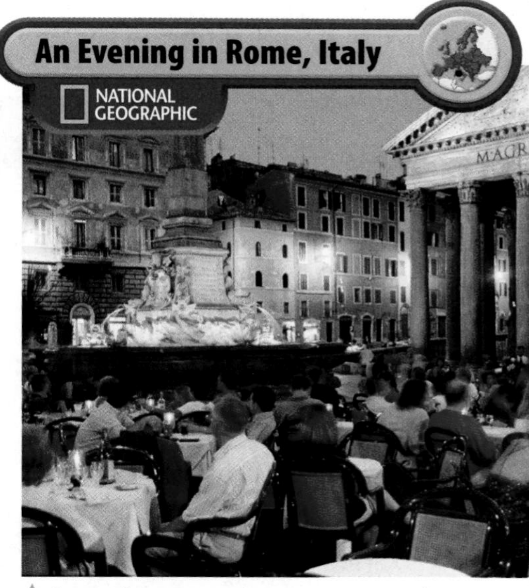

▲ People dine at an outdoor restaurant near the Pantheon, a public building built by the ancient Romans. ***Place*** **What percentage of Italy's people live in urban areas?**

R Reading Strategy

Previewing Have students preview the subsection by reading the Main Idea and looking at the headings and photograph on this page. Ask students to summarize the kinds of information they expect to learn about in this subsection. OL

D Differentiated Instruction

Kinesthetic To help students understand the topography of Italy, have them create salt relief maps of the country using a contour map as a guide. OL

Reading Check **Answer:** The northern area of Italy has developed manufacturing cities and has rich farmland. The southern half has mountainous terrain with limited resources, farmland, or navigable rivers. Hence unemployment there is high.

Caption Answer: about 90 percent

Hands-On Chapter Project Step 3

Visualizing Europe's Economics

Step 3: Investigating Southern Europe Groups of students will prepare the portion of the display illustrating the economic efforts of southern Europe.

Directions Have groups read the section on southern Europe and list important agricultural and industrial products produced in the region. Have the groups select one of the items on their list for further research. Encourage groups to create a diagram, flowchart, or other visual to explain the importance of the item to the region. For example, if a group selects dry farming, their visual could be a diagram of dry farming techniques. If a group selects shipbuilding, their visual could be an annotated drawing of an oil tanker.

Analyzing Have students discuss how the physical features of southern Europe have influenced the kinds of agricultural and industrial products they produce. OL

(Chapter Project continued in Section 4)

C Critical Thinking

Determining Cause and Effect Have students locate Greece on a map. **Ask:** **Why do you think shipping is an important business in Greece?** *(Much of Greece is surrounded by the Mediterranean Sea, and Greece also includes many islands.)* OL

Reading Check **Answer:** The mountains and poor soil in Greece make farming difficult, so many people raise sheep and goats or work in industries like shipping and tourism.

Assess

Social Studies ONLINE
Study Central™ provides summaries, interactive games, and online graphic organizers to help students review content.

Close

Paraphrasing Have students paraphrase the information under each heading in the chapter. OL

Section 3 Review

Greece

Main Idea **Mountains, seas, and islands have shaped Greece's people and economy.**

Geography and You Do you ever go boating or fishing? You will understand why these are popular activities for the Greeks when you read about Greece's geography.

East of Italy, Greece extends from the Balkan Peninsula into the Mediterranean Sea. The country includes not only a mainland, but about 2,000 islands. Like other Mediterranean areas, Greece is often shaken by earthquakes.

Because of mountains and poor, stony soil, agriculture plays a declining role in the Greek economy. In the highlands, people raise sheep and goats. On farms in plains and valleys, farmers grow wheat, olives, and other crops. In recent decades, Greece has developed new industries, such as textiles, footwear, and chemicals. **C** Shipping is a major business. Greece has one of the world's largest shipping fleets, including oil tankers, cargo ships, and passenger vessels. Tourism is another key industry. Each year millions of tourists come to visit historic sites such as the Parthenon, an ancient temple in the city of Athens.

About 60 percent of Greeks are urban dwellers. Nearly a third live in or around Athens, the capital. The Greeks speak a form of Greek similar to that spoken in ancient times. Most of them are Greek Orthodox Christian. Today, Greece is a democratic republic and a member of the European Union.

Reading Check **Explaining** How has geography affected the way Greeks earn a living?

Section 3 Review

Social Studies ONLINE
Study Central™ To review this section, go to glencoe.com.

Vocabulary

1. **Define** *dry farming*, *autonomy*, and *subsidy*, and use each word in a sentence.

Main Ideas

2. **Explaining** How did Portugal benefit from joining the EU?
3. **Identifying** Create a graphic organizer like the one below to identify Italy's agricultural and industrial products.

4. **Comparing and Contrasting** How is Greece similar to and different from the other countries of southern Europe?

Critical Thinking

5. **BIG Idea** Write two generalizations describing the connection between the physical geography of southern Europe and the lives of the region's people.
6. **Challenge** Write a paragraph explaining how countries in southern Europe have worked to improve their economies.

Writing About Geography

7. **Descriptive Writing** Write the text for a travel brochure that encourages visitors to take a cruise that stops in the countries of southern Europe. Describe the landscapes, cities, and activities that visitors could see in those countries.

Answers

1. Definitions for vocabulary words are found in the section and the Glossary.
2. Subsidies from the European Union have helped Portugal's economy.
3. cars, technical instruments, appliances, clothing, high-quality goods, livestock, grapes, olives, and other crops
4. **Similarities:** located on the Mediterranean; tourism is an important industry; democratic government; often shaken by earthquakes; **Differences:** many islands; Greek language; Greek Orthodox Christianity
5. Answers will vary. Possible responses: Because of its southern location, warm climate, and abundance of coastlines, tourism is important in this region. Because much of the region is mountainous with poor soil, agriculture is declining.
6. Paragraphs should include specific examples that reflect the increasing importance of manufacturing and service industries in the region.
7. Answers will vary but should include information from this section about the landscapes, cities, and activities in these countries.

TIME PERSPECTIVES

WHOSE EUROPE IS IT?

As millions of immigrants relocate to Europe, the region's democracies struggle to redefine themselves.

Muslim immigrants gather on Westminster Bridge in London.

People in the United States, a nation formed by immigrants from around the world, understand the concept "out of many, one." Today, the countries of Europe are struggling to comprehend the idea too. For more than 60 years, millions of immigrants—many of them Muslims—have emigrated to some of Europe's oldest democracies.

It has not been easy to get so many different people to respect each other and live together in harmony. In recent years, cultural and religious clashes have developed as immigrants and Europeans struggle to understand each other. As that work continues, there is no doubt that the struggle will have an enormous impact on Europe's future.

BRIAN ATKINSON/ALAMY

Focus

Introducing TIME Perspectives

Ask: Who are immigrants? *(People who move to a new country from another country.)* **What region is the topic of the article?** *(Europe)* Read the title and subtitle aloud to the students. **Ask: What struggles do you think the article will discuss?** *(Answers may include racial, cultural, and economic struggles.)* **OL**

FYI

Read about immigrant rights and cultural differences within the European Union at Europa, the Gateway to the European Union, at http://europa.eu/index_en.htm.

Use the **TIME Perspectives: Exploring World Issues Teacher Guide and Student Activities,** pp. 13–16, to reinforce and extend the concepts in "Whose Europe Is It?"

Additional Support

Background

Immigration from Morocco A large number of immigrants to Europe come from North African nations, such as Morocco. Many of these immigrants have settled in France, which once colonized North Africa. After World War II, European countries, such as France, West Germany, Belguim, and the Netherlands, recruited workers from North Africa, especially Morocco, to help rebuild their war-ravaged economies. Although this openness to immigration ended in the 1970s, many people in North Africa still seek to immigrate to Europe, where there are jobs and a higher standard of living. Today, more than two million people of Moroccan descent live in Europe. Morocco has become a transit point for immigrants from other African nations, such as Senegal, Congo, Liberia, and Nigeria, as they cross the Mediterranean to Europe.

Teach

C Critical Thinking

Making Inferences **Ask:** **What factors contributed to the national identities of European countries in the past?** *(country of origin, race, and religion).* OL

This Reading Skill (Making Inferences) was introduced in this unit.

R Reading Strategy

Summarizing After students read the introductory material, ask them to summarize Europe's immigration trends in three sentences or less. OL

D Differentiated Instruction

Logical/Mathematical Remind students that Germany's population is about 82.5 million. **Ask:** **What percentage of Germany's population is non-German?** *(about 8.5 percent)* OL

INTERPRETING MAPS

Answer:
Albania, Bosnia-Herzegovina, and Macedonia

Additional Support

TIME PERSPECTIVES

EXPLORING WORLD ISSUES

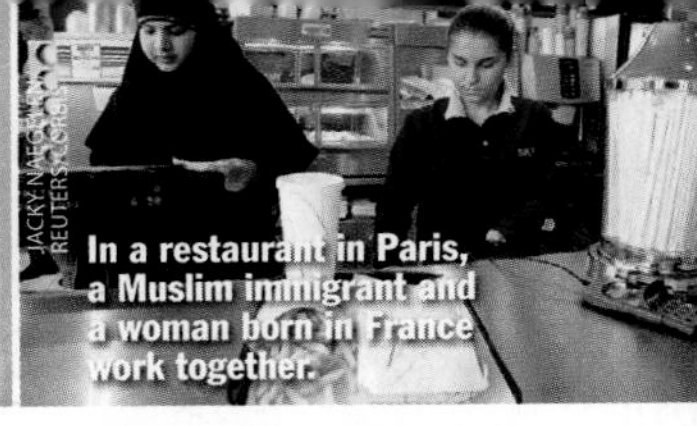
In a restaurant in Paris, a Muslim immigrant and a woman born in France work together.

THE NEW MULTICULTURAL EUROPE

From Paris to Amsterdam and Brussels to Berlin, Europe is changing. Not long ago, most citizens of European countries shared certain characteristics. They were mostly all born in Europe, and the majority of them were white and Christian. These similarities helped create a **national identity** for countries like France, Great Britain, and Germany.

After World War II, many of Europe's immigrants were from countries that had been European colonies, like Algeria, India, and Pakistan. Friendly immigration policies following World War II welcomed the newcomers. Governments also established favorable labor policies in the 1960s that were designed to bring much-needed foreign workers to Europe.

But in recent years, the population of Europe has become more diverse. Millions of immigrants, many of them Muslims from North Africa, Turkey, and Southwest Asia, have left their homelands to start new lives in European nations.

Muslim Populations in European Countries

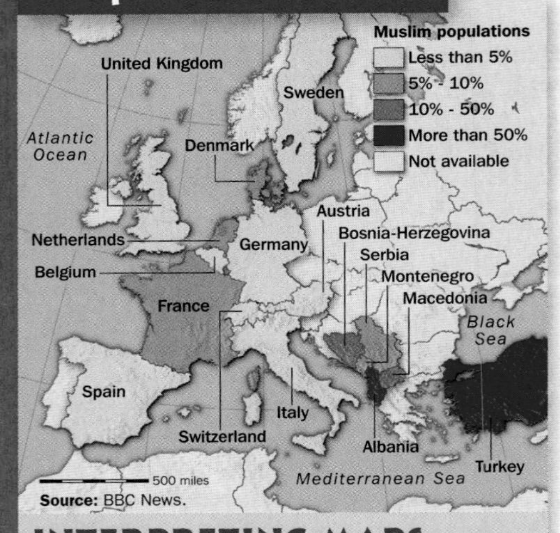

Source: BBC News.

INTERPRETING MAPS

Categorizing Which countries in Europe have the largest Muslim populations?

Creating a New Identity

The number of immigrants living in Europe has greatly increased. In 2006, for example, there were about 7 million non-Germans living in Germany. Many of these immigrants are from Turkey. The large population of immigrants and their offspring have transformed and challenged traditional European beliefs.

Europe's immigrant **populations**, or groups of people, often view the world differently from people who were born in Europe. Many of the differences deal with culture, religious freedom, and the rights of women. At times, these different perceptions have caused conflict and bad feelings between Europe's older populations and its new ones. "We feel unwelcome," said a Muslim immigrant in Denmark. Some of the conflicts have been violent and have had a global impact.

Activity: Connecting With the United States

Making Connections Remind students that the United States has experienced several waves of immigration since its founding. **Ask:** **When did the largest waves of immigration to the United States occur?** *(1840s–1850s and 1880s–1920s)* Divide the class into four groups. Assign each group one of the following groups of immigrants: Irish fleeing the potato famine in the 1840s and 1850s, Germans fleeing economic depression and political unrest from the 1840s to the 1850s, eastern European Jews fleeing persecution during the 1880s to 1920s, or Italians seeking relief from poverty during the 1880s to 1920s. Ask students to research the immigrants they have been assigned, and then present a skit or short play showing the experience of those immigrants in the United States. Encourage students to use costumes and props to make their skits more realistic. Following the skits, lead a discussion on the ways in which the immigrant experience was similar and different among these different groups. OL

Many Turks support their country's proposed admission to the European Union.

Muslims stage a rally to protest the printing of cartoons of the prophet Muhammad.

Danish Prime Minister Fogh Rasmussen, center, discusses the cartoons with a Pakistani diplomat.

When Cultures Collide

Early in 2006, Muslims around the world protested cartoons that were published in Europe. The cartoons showed the Muslim religion's prophet Muhammad in a negative way. They were first published in a newspaper in Denmark and later reprinted in various papers throughout Europe.

Muslims across Europe and the world were angry. They thought the cartoons were disrespectful of their religion, **Islam**. This is because Islam does not allow the publication of any images of Muhammad. **C**

Religion and a Free Press

Anger over the cartoons led thousands of Muslims to protest worldwide. Angry protestors marched in several European cities, including London and Copenhagen. Demonstrations were also held throughout Southwest Asia. Many of the protests turned violent as demonstrators burned Danish flags and set fire to Denmark's embassy in Beirut, Lebanon. The riots killed at least 11 people in Afghanistan.

Denmark's prime minister, Anders Fogh Rasmussen, called the protests a global crisis and called for "calm and steadiness." But Fogh Rasmussen would not apologize for what the newspapers did. Like many European leaders and citizens, Fogh Rasmussen believed in the right of a free press. He defended the newspaper's right to print the cartoons of Muhammad even if their publication caused controversy and protest. **D**

A Search for Common Ground

Learning to live with—and absorb—new ethnic groups is one of the greatest challenges facing Europe. Some experts believe that Turkey's proposed admission to the European Union, or the EU, may help bridge the gap between Muslims and traditional Europeans. Turkey would be the first Muslim country in the EU, a group of European nations that have joined together to solve common problems and create economic opportunities.

Experts believe that the European nations will have to learn to compromise and be tolerant of the cultural and religious differences of all of their citizens. Learning how to do that will be a challenge in a multiethnic Europe.

EXPLORING THE ISSUE

1. **Comparing** How were the opinions of Muslim immigrants and European-born citizens different concerning publishing the cartoons of Muhammad?
2. **Making Inferences** How might Turkey's admission into the EU change the way citizens born in Europe view Muslim immigrants?

TIME PERSPECTIVES

C Critical Thinking

Analyzing Information Provide students with copies of political cartoons. Read the cartoons as a class and analyze each cartoon's message. Ask students if they think the cartoons would offend any particular group. Point out that political cartoons can cause heated debates and offend certain people. **OL**

D Differentiated Instruction

Interpersonal Organize students into small groups. Have the groups analyze the reasons for Prime Minister Rasmussen's refusal to apologize. Then ask them to think about what the outcome might have been if he had apologized. Tell students to consider the effects on the free press as well as ethnic relations. **OL**

EXPLORING THE ISSUE

Answers:

1. Muslim citizens were outraged about the cartoon, while European-born citizens were not offended.
2. Because Turkey is a Muslim country, its admission into the EU might cause European-born citizens to view Muslim immigrants as part of "us" rather than "them."

Differentiated Instruction

Interpreting a Political Cartoon

TIME Perspectives: Exploring World Issues Workbook, p. 15

Interpreting a Political Cartoon

Objective: To interpret a political cartoon

Focus: Show students several political cartoons and explain any symbolism they contain.

Teach: Explain the importance of the caption in interpreting the cartoon.

Assess: Have students read the background information and use it to help them answer the questions about the cartoon.

Close: Ask students if political cartoons are always funny.

Differentiated Instruction Strategies

BL Ask students questions to help them understand each part of the cartoon.

AL Have students draw a political cartoon that answers the Thinking Critically question.

ELL Ask students if their family's immigration experience is reflected in the cartoon.

TIME PERSPECTIVES

C Critical Thinking

Identifying Central Issues
Ask: **Why has the French government banned religious symbols in public schools?** *(It wants to keep the influence of religion away from public schools in order to promote national unity)* Have students debate the issue of sacrificing personal rights for the sake of national unity. **OL**

S Skill Practice

Visual Literacy Have students read the sign the woman is holding in the photo. Ask students to answer the question posed on the sign and tally the responses on the board. Have students analyze the results. **OL**

EXPLORING THE ISSUE

Answers:

1. Relations might deteriorate because Muslims would be offended.
2. Possible answer: France banned all religious symbols so that no one group is discriminated against.

Additional Support

FRANCE'S CLASH OVER SYMBOLS

In January 2004, thousands of Muslim women and men in France took to the streets of Paris to send a message to the French government. Marching hand in hand, many of the women wore head scarves. Some covered their hair with the French flag.

C The protesters were angry over a proposed French law. If passed, the law would stop students from wearing head scarves and other noticeable religious symbols in public schools. French president Jacques Chirac (ZHAHK shee•RAHK) proposed the ban on the head scarves, called ***hijab*** (HEH•JAB), worn by Muslim women and girls. Chirac said the ban was created to make sure French children are not exposed to differences that will "drive people apart." Some Jewish and Christian religious symbols were also included in the proposed ban.

A Heated Debate

Despite the protests, the French government voted the bill into law in 2005. The law continued to be controversial. There are about 5 million Muslims in France, nearly 8 percent of the country's population. Critics of the law say wearing a head scarf in school is a personal choice and a basic right. "The government should not be in the business of telling a woman how to dress," said Salam Al-Marayati, of the Muslim Public Affairs Council.

French officials say the law is not directed against any religion. "The idea is to keep the influence of religion away from public schools," said one French diplomat. "A teacher does not have to know whether students are Muslim, Christian, Jewish, or whatever."

Soon after the ban went into effect, some French Muslims who arrived at school wearing scarves pushed them off their heads when they entered the school grounds. Will cultural differences continue to divide Europe's people? That question remains to be answered by European nations as their populations become more diverse.

S

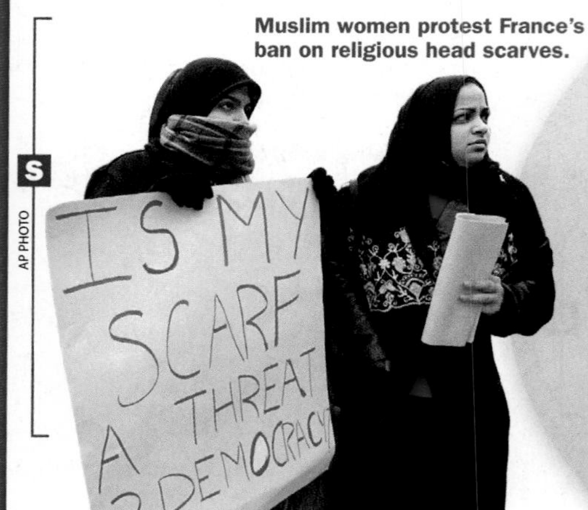

IS MY SCARF A THREAT 2 DEMOCRACY
AP PHOTO

Muslim women protest France's ban on religious head scarves.

EXPLORING THE ISSUE

1. **Predicting** How might the ban on head scarves impact the French government's relations with Muslim countries around the world?
2. **Making Inferences** Why do you think France's law banning *hijab* also forbids the wearing of other religious symbols?

Activity: Connecting With the United States

Analyzing Explain to students that both France and the United States guarantee the right to freedom of religion and speech. **Ask:** **What U.S. document guarantees the freedoms of speech and religion?** *(the United States Constitution, the First Amendment)* Explain to students that governments also have the responsibility of maintaining peace and stability, so some behaviors and types of speech are unlawful. For example, in the United States it is illegal to incite a riot or to conspire to commit a crime. Even religious activities can be outlawed if they harm other people. Have students write a letter to a student in France explaining whether they believe the United States would ever pass a law restricting the wearing of religious symbols in schools. Also have students explain whether they believe such a law would be considered constitutional. **OL**

The EU flag

REVIEW AND ASSESS

UNDERSTANDING THE ISSUE

1. **Making Connections** What might be some reasons that people leave their homeland to live in another country?
2. **Writing to Inform** Write a short article describing the protests of cartoons about Muhammad. Include information about demonstrations around the world.
3. **Writing to Persuade** Write a letter to a friend in Denmark. Convince your friend that newspapers did or did not have the right to publish the cartoons of Muhammad.

INTERNET RESEARCH ACTIVITIES

4. Use Internet resources to find information about the European Union. Read about the EU's three main governing organizations. Choose one and write a brief description of it in your own words.
5. With your teacher's help, use Internet resources to find information about a former European colony such as India, Algeria, or Hong Kong. Read about how the colony was formed and the relationship it had with the colonizing country. Why do you think immigrants from former colonies might want to live in Europe? Write your answer in a 250-word essay.

BEYOND THE CLASSROOM

6. **Research the history of immigration in the United States during the early 1900s.** What were some of the challenges immigrants faced as they settled in the U.S.? Write your answer in an article appropriate for a school newspaper.
7. **Debate the issue.** Debate this resolution: "Wearing a religious head scarf in school is a personal choice and a basic right." A panel of student judges should decide which team has the most compelling arguments.

How the European Union Grew

For nearly 60 years, European nations have been forming an ever-closer economic and political union. Here's a look at the steps they have taken along the way.

- **1948** The Council of Europe is established, creating a forum for Europe's leaders to discuss ways to work together.
- **1951** France, Germany, Italy, the Netherlands, Belgium, and Luxembourg unite their coal and steel industries.
- **1957** The European Economic Community is formed. The EEC is the first step toward a common economic market.
- **1967** EEC merges with other European organizations to form the European Community (EC).
- **1973** The United Kingdom, Denmark, and Ireland join the EC.
- **1981** Greece becomes the EC's tenth member.
- **1991** The Maastricht Treaty creates plans for a common currency and for cooperation in foreign affairs.
- **2002** Most EU members agree to use a common currency, the euro. Britain, Sweden, and Denmark refuse.
- **2004** The EU admits ten new member nations. EU leaders sign a new constitution for Europe. A year later, voters in France and the Netherlands reject it.

Building Time Line Reading Skills

1. **Analyzing Information** How many years does this time line cover? When did Greece join the EC?
2. **Making Inferences** Why do you think European nations cooperated economically before they worked together politically?

Review and Assess

Questions from **Understanding the Issue, Internet Research Activities,** and **Beyond the Classroom** may have more than one correct answer. Pick and choose the two or three activities that work best for your class.

Building Time Line Reading Skills

Answers:

1. 56 years; 1981
2. Possible answer: By cooperating economically, European nations were able to improve their individual economies before handling the more controversial issues regarding political unity.

Close

Ask students to list three facts they learned as a result of reading this article. Have students share their lists with the class. **OL**

Activity: Why It Matters

Defending Explain to students that European efforts to limit immigration in the past three decades have led to an increase in illegal immigration. **Ask: What is illegal immigration?** *(immigrating to another country without the proper visas or permissions, or overstaying a tourist visa in order to work)* Explain that although immigration often puts a strain on society, countries like Spain and Italy need immigrant workers to fill unskilled jobs and to maintain their populations. The nations from which people emigrate may also benefit because emigrants often send money home to help families and communities in their home countries. Divide the class into two teams. Hold a debate and ask one team to argue in favor of relaxing immigration policies in Europe, and the other to argue in favor of stricter immigration laws. Encourage students to consider parallels between immigration issues in Europe and in the United States. Be sensitive to the feelings of immigrants in your class. **OL**

Focus

Bellringer

Daily Focus Transparency 12-4

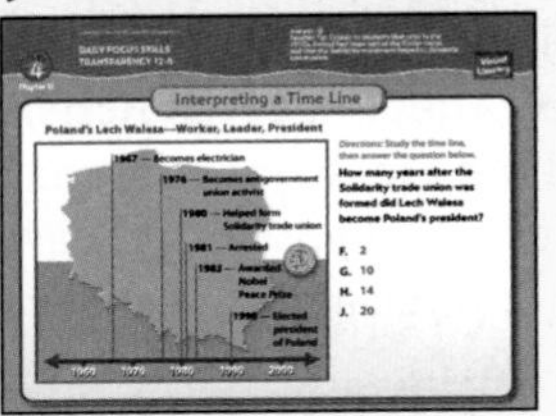

Guide to Reading

Answers to Graphic:

Sample answer provided. Students should provide comparable answers for the other subregions.

Poland, Belarus, Baltic Republics: located in northeastern Europe on or near the Baltic Sea; although the countries are close neighbors, they have distinct histories and cultures.

Section Spotlight Video

To learn more about eastern Europe, have students watch the Section Spotlight Video.

Guide to Reading

BIG Idea

Geography is used to interpret the past, understand the present, and plan for the future.

Content Vocabulary

- command economy *(p. 349)*
- market economy *(p. 350)*
- potash *(p. 350)*
- ethnic cleansing *(p. 356)*

Academic Vocabulary

- income *(p. 350)*
- medical *(p. 356)*

Reading Strategy

Summarizing Use a chart like the one below to summarize key facts about each group of countries.

Country Groups	Key Facts
Poland, Belarus, Baltic Republics	
Czech Republic, Slovakia, Hungary	
Countries of Southeastern Europe	

Section 4 Eastern Europe

Picture This Show your colors! A young person in Kyiv (Kiev), Ukraine, shows his support for the new government of the Orange Revolution. The Orange Revolution took place during the 2004 presidential elections. Orange was the color of the victorious political party. The party chose orange to represent the change in Ukraine's government. Orange represents the changing color of the leaves in autumn—a process that is peaceful and unstoppable. Read this section to learn more about life in eastern Europe today.

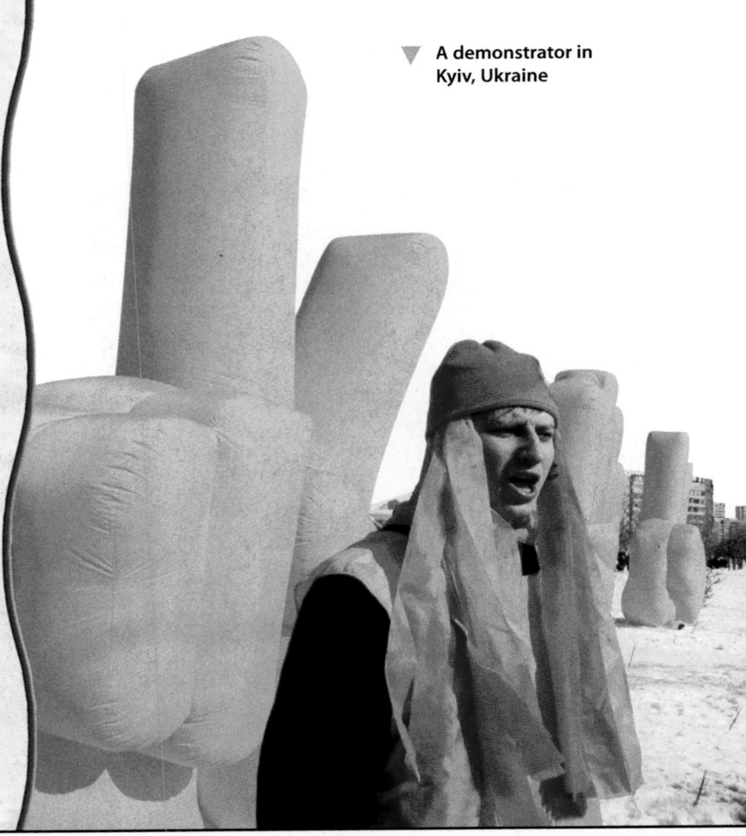

▼ A demonstrator in Kyiv, Ukraine

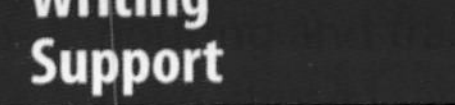

Resource Manager

R Reading Strategies	C Critical Thinking	D Differentiated Instruction	W Writing Support	S Skill Practice
Teacher Edition • Sequencing Info., p. 349 • Visualizing, p. 349 • Academic Vocab., p. 350 • Inferring, p. 352 • Monitoring, p. 355 • Questioning, p. 355 • Act. Prior Know., p. 355 **Additional Resources** • Guid. Read., URB p. 88 • Cont. Vocab., URB p. 89	**Teacher Edition** • Drawing Con., pp. 349, 353 • Making Inferences, p. 350 • Ident. Issues, p. 354 • Analyzing Info., p. 355 **Additional Resources** • Crit. Think., URB p. 97 • Authentic Assess., p. 12 • Enrichment, URB p. 19 • Time Line, URB p. 17	**Teacher Edition** • Special Ed., p. 351 • English Learners, p. 352 • Visual/Spatial, p. 354 **Additional Resources** • School-to-Home Conn., URB p. 107 • Reteach., URB p. 105	**Teacher Edition** • Expository Writing, p. 356	**Teacher Edition** • Using Geo. Skills, pp. 351, 354 • Visual Literacy, pp. 352, 353 **Additional Resources** • Daily Focus Trans. 12-4 • Reg. Atlas, URB pp. 1–7

Poland, Belarus, and the Baltic Republics

Main Idea **Poland and the Baltic Republics have become democratic, while Belarus is still influenced by its Communist past.**

Geography and You How do you feel when someone orders you to do something? The people of Poland, Belarus, and the Baltic states were all under foreign control at one time. Read what happened to these countries.

Poland, Belarus, and the three Baltic Republics—Lithuania, Latvia, and Estonia—are located in northeastern Europe on or near the Baltic Sea. Although they are neighboring countries, they have distinct histories and cultures.

Poland's Land and History

The sizable country of Poland lies east of Germany. The Carpathian Mountains and other highlands rise on its southern and western edges. Most of Poland, however, is a fertile lowland plain, and the majority of its people live there.

Throughout Poland's history, the largely flat landscape made the country an easy target for invading armies. By the 1800s, Poland had fallen victim to stronger neighbors—Germany, Russia, and Austria.

Poland established its independence again after World War I. But in 1939, German troops once more attacked the country, starting World War II. Poles suffered greatly during the war. Warsaw, the capital, was bombed to ashes. R2

Struggle for Freedom

After World War II, a Communist government came to power in Poland. Its leaders set up a **command economy**, in which the government decided what, how, and for whom goods would be produced. Poland's postwar government wanted heavy industry and military goods, so few products were made for consumers. R1 This led to food shortages, causing Poland's people to become dissatisfied and demand huge changes.

The Poles wanted a better life, complete with political liberties and religious freedom. Deeply Roman Catholic, most Poles rejoiced when a Polish church leader was chosen to be the head of the Roman Catholic Church in 1978. Pope John Paul II not only stirred national pride in Poland, but he also encouraged the Poles to resist Communist rule. C

In the 1980s, Polish workers and farmers formed Solidarity, a labor group that supported peaceful democratic change. Communist leaders finally allowed free elections in 1989 that brought about a democracy.

Auschwitz Memorial

Auschwitz was a World War II German prison camp located in Poland. At the camp's entrance was a sign in German that read "Work Sets You Free." Today the camp is a memorial to those who suffered there. ***Movement*** **Why was it easy for armies to invade Poland?**

Social Studies ONLINE
Student Web Activity Visit glencoe.com and complete the Chapter 12 Web Activity about Poland.

Teach

R1 Reading Strategy

Sequencing Information Have students work in pairs to create a graphic organizer that sequences the important events in Poland's history. **OL**

R2 Reading Strategy

Visualizing Ask students to describe the mental pictures created by the phrases "suffered greatly" and "bombed to ashes." **OL**

C Critical Thinking

Drawing Conclusions Ask: How did the election of John Paul II help bring about democratic change in Poland? *(His election stirred national pride, and he encouraged Poles to resist Communist rule.)* **OL**

Caption Answer:
Poland's flat landscape made it easy for armies to invade the country.

Social Studies ONLINE
Objectives and answers to the Student Web Activity can be found at glencoe.com under the Web Activity Lesson Plan for this chapter.

Additional Support

Activity: Economics Connection

Contrasting Ask: What type of economy did Poland have under Communist rule? *(command economy)* **What type of economy does it have now?** *(market economy)* **How is decision making different in these two economic systems?** *(In a command economy, the government decides what, how, and for whom goods will be produced; in a market economy, individuals and businesses make these decisions.)* **Which economic system does the United States have?** *(market economy)* Discuss with students the pros and cons of each system, focusing on how well each system meets people's needs. **OL**

C Critical Thinking

Making Inferences Ask: Why is this type of economic system called a "market" economy? *(because the market—individuals and businesses—make the decisions)*

R Reading Strategy

Academic Vocabulary Tell students to split the word "income" into two parts: "in" and "come." **Ask: How does splitting the word into two parts help define its meaning?** *("Income" is money that "comes in.")* **What word is the opposite of "income"?** *("outgo" or "expense")* **ELL**

Caption Answer:
a labor group that supported peaceful democratic change.

Reading Check Answer: All are located in northeastern Europe, on or near the Baltic Sea, and all were once under Communist rule. However, they speak different languages and follow different religions.

This event helped bring about the fall of Communist governments that had long ruled in eastern Europe.

Poland Today

Poland's democratic leaders quickly moved Poland toward a **market economy.** In this system, individuals and businesses make the decisions about how they will use resources and what goods and services to make. **C**

Economic change caused great hardship at first, and many people lost their jobs. Within a few years, however, the economy began to improve. Agriculture remains important, with Poland among the world's top producers of rye and potatoes. Industries, however, are growing. As Poland's economy changes, more people are moving from rural areas to cities, such as Warsaw and Kraków.

Shipyard in Poland

NATIONAL GEOGRAPHIC

▲ This shipyard in Gdansk, Poland, was the birthplace of the labor group Solidarity in the 1980s. Shipbuilding is still an important industry in Poland today. ***Place*** **What was Solidarity? What was its goal?**

Belarus

East of Poland is Belarus, which also is covered by a lowland plain. Belarus was once part of the Soviet Union, and it still has close ties to Russia. Its leaders favor strong government and a command economy.

Belarus has few resources other than **potash,** a mineral used in making fertilizer. Industries include processing fertilizer and manufacturing trucks, radios, televisions, and bicycles. Government-controlled farms produce vegetables, grain, and other crops.

Most people in Belarus are Eastern Orthodox Slavs. Two-thirds live in cities, such as Minsk, the capital.

The Baltic Republics

The small countries of Lithuania, Latvia, and Estonia lie on the shores of the Baltic Sea. Until 1991, the Baltic Republics were part of the Soviet Union. Today, all three countries have large Russian minority populations. Most people in Estonia and Latvia are Protestant, while Roman Catholics make up the majority in Lithuania.

All three Baltic Republics have seen strong economic growth since the mid-1990s. Their economies are based on dairy farming, beef production, fishing, and shipbuilding. Estonia has done especially well, and its people have the Baltic group's highest average **incomes.** Estonia's major export is telecommunications equipment. **R**

Reading Check **Comparing and Contrasting** What do the Baltic Republics, Belarus, and Poland have in common? How are they different?

Differentiated Instruction

Leveled Activities

BL Reteaching Activity, URB p. 105

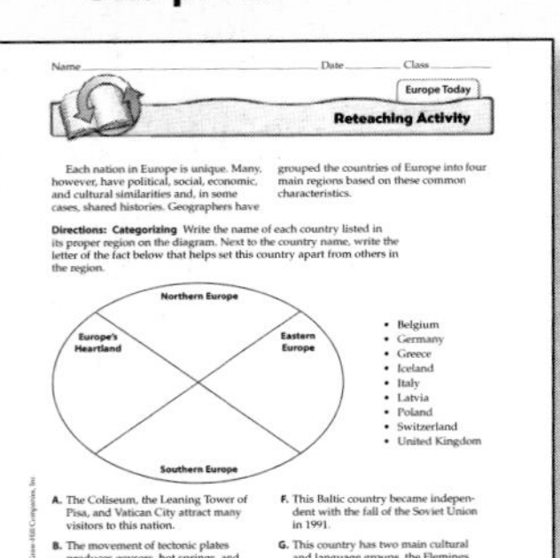

Name______ Date______ Class______

Europe Today

Reteaching Activity

Each nation in Europe is unique. Many, however, have political, social, economic, and cultural similarities and, in some cases, shared histories. Geographers have grouped the countries of Europe into four main regions based on these common characteristics.

Directions: Categorizing Write the name of each country listed in its proper region on the diagram. Next to the country name, write the letter of the fact below that helps set this country apart from others in the region.

- Belgium
- Germany
- Greece
- Iceland
- Italy
- Latvia
- Poland
- Switzerland
- United Kingdom

A. The Coliseum, the Leaning Tower of Pisa, and Vatican City attract many visitors to this nation.

B. The movement of tectonic plates produces geysers, hot springs, and volcanoes on this island.

C. Inventors and scientists from this land sparked the Industrial Revolution.

D. The labor group Solidarity helped bring

F. This Baltic country became independent with the fall of the Soviet Union in 1991.

G. This country has two main cultural and language groups, the Flemings and the Walloons.

H. Millions of tourists visit the historic Parthenon and temple of Apollo at Delphi.

OL Academic Vocabulary Activity, URB p. 91

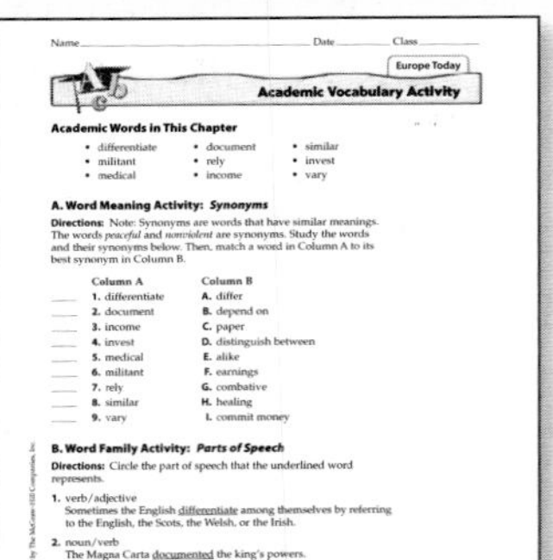

Name______ Date______ Class______

Europe Today

Academic Vocabulary Activity

Academic Words in This Chapter

- differentiate
- militant
- medical
- document
- rely
- income
- similar
- invest
- vary

A. Word Meaning Activity: *Synonyms*

Directions: Note: Synonyms are words that have similar meanings. The words *peaceful* and *nonviolent* are synonyms. Study the words and their synonyms below. Then, match a word in Column A to its best synonym in Column B.

	Column A	Column B
____	1. differentiate	A. differ
____	2. document	B. depend on
____	3. income	C. paper
____	4. invest	D. distinguish between
____	5. medical	E. alike
____	6. militant	F. earnings
____	7. rely	G. combative
____	8. similar	H. healing
____	9. vary	I. commit money

B. Word Family Activity: *Parts of Speech*

Directions: Circle the part of speech that the underlined word represents.

1. verb/adjective
Sometimes the English differentiate among themselves by referring to the English, the Scots, the Welsh, or the Irish.

2. noun/verb
The Magna Carta documented the king's powers.

3. adjective/adverb
Scandinavia has a varied landscape because of its size.

ELL Guided Reading Activity, URB p. 88

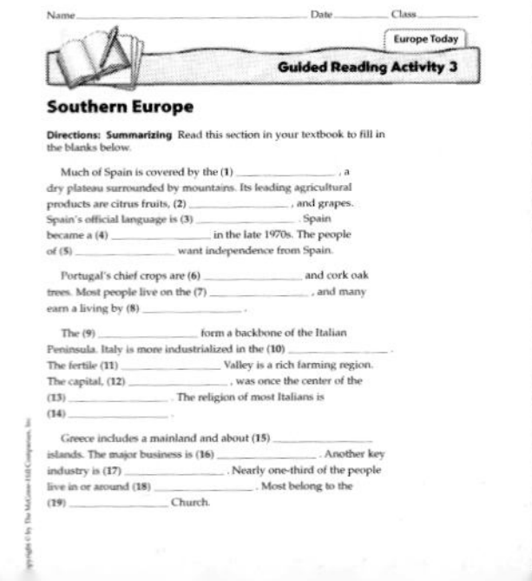

Name______ Date______ Class______

Europe Today

Guided Reading Activity 3

Southern Europe

Directions: Summarizing Read this section in your textbook to fill in the blanks below.

Much of Spain is covered by the (1) ______, a dry plateau surrounded by mountains. Its leading agricultural products are citrus fruits, (2) ______, and grapes. Spain's official language is (3) ______. Spain became a (4) ______ in the late 1970s. The people of (5) ______ want independence from Spain.

Portugal's chief crops are (6) ______ and cork oak trees. Most people live on the (7) ______, and many earn a living by (8) ______.

The (9) ______ form a backbone of the Italian Peninsula. Italy is more industrialized in the (10) ______. The fertile (11) ______ Valley is a rich farming region. The capital, (12) ______, was once the center of the (13) ______. The religion of most Italians is (14) ______.

Greece includes a mainland and about (15) ______ islands. The major business is (16) ______. Another key industry is (17) ______. Nearly one-third of the people live in or around (18) ______. Most belong to the (19) ______ Church.

NATIONAL GEOGRAPHIC

Figure 3 **Language Families of Europe**

Icelandic
ARCTIC CIRCLE
Sami
Norwegian Sea
PRIME MERIDIAN
Swedish
Finnish
Norwegian
Scottish Gaelic
Estonian
North Sea
Danish
Latvian
RUSSIA
Irish
English
Lithuanian
Welsh
English
Dutch
Belorussian
ATLANTIC OCEAN
Flemish
German
Polish
Breton
Ukrainian
Czech
Slovak
Bay of Biscay
French
Moldavian
Hungarian
Galician
Basque
Slovene
Croatian
Romanian
Russian
Portuguese
Bosnian
Black Sea
Spanish
Catalan
Italian
Serbian
Bulgarian
Sardinian
Albanian
Macedonian
ASIA
Greek
Turkish
Mediterranean Sea
Greek

Language Families

Indo-European	Uralic
Germanic	Finnic
Romance	Ugric
Slavic	**Basque**
Baltic	Basque
Greek	**Altaic**
Albanian	Turkish
Celtic	

0 500 kilometers
0 500 miles
Lambert Azimuthal Equal-Area projection

Map Skills

1. **Location** What four language families are found in France?
2. **Regions** Why is the Romance language family dominant in southern Europe?

D Differentiated Instruction

Special Education To help students focus on the areas in the questions, have them place a piece of paper over the eastern and northern portions of Europe, leaving France and the countries beneath it visible. **Ask: What minor language groups are found in Spain?** *(Spanish, Catalan, Basque, and Galician)* BL

S Skill Practice

Using Geography Skills Ask: What language family is dominant in eastern Europe? *(Slavic)* OL

Map Skills

Answers:

1. Celtic, Romance, Basque, and Germanic
2. because Rome once ruled southern Europe and the Romance languages developed from Latin

Teacher Note:
If students struggle with Map Skills question 2, remind them that Romance languages are those based on Latin, the language of ancient Rome.

Hands-On Chapter Project
Step 4

Visualizing Europe's Economics

Step 4: Completing the Display After analyzing eastern Europe, students will complete their bulletin board display.

Directions Tell students that they will complete the research for their bulletin board display and then assemble the display. Have the groups of students skim the information in this section and list the primary industries and economic activities of each eastern European country in a graphic organizer. Then have students find photos or illustrations of eastern Europe's industries. When students have completed their work, have them combine the information they have gathered from all four sections to create their bulletin board display. OL

(Chapter Project cont. on the Visual Summary page)

R Reading Strategy

Inferring **Ask:** Based on what you have read so far in this chapter, do you think the number of countries under Communist rule is increasing or decreasing? *(decreasing)* BL

S Skill Practice

Visual Literacy **Ask:** In what ways does this teenager resemble teenagers in the United States? *(Possible response: Her hair and clothing style are similar, and she has a cell phone, as many American teenagers do.)* OL

D Differentiated Instruction

English Learners Explain to students that the word "backbone" in this sentence does not mean the bone that is in a person's back. Ask students to use context clues to determine the meaning of "backbone" in this sentence. *(the strongest part)* ELL

Caption Answer:
The Czech Republic has a higher standard of living than other eastern European countries.

The Czech Republic, Slovakia, and Hungary

Main Idea **The Czech Republic, Slovakia, and Hungary share common histories but have distinct cultures.**

Geography and You Have you ever ended a close friendship? The Czech and Slovak people shared a country for 75 years, but they divided it into two in 1993. Read to learn about their separate nations and their neighbor, Hungary.

Old and New in Prague

A teenager in Prague, the Czech Republic, talks on her cell phone as she strolls through the city's historic area. ***Regions*** **How does the Czech standard of living compare to that in other eastern European countries?**

In the center of eastern Europe are three landlocked countries: the Czech (CHEHK) Republic, Slovakia, and Hungary. All three were once under Communist rule, but they are now independent democracies.

The Czech Republic

The Czech Republic has a landscape of rolling hills, lowlands, and plains bordered by mountains. Most of the country's people live in cities, such as Prague (PRAHG), the capital. Prague is known for its beautiful historic buildings and monuments.

The Czech people descend from Slavic groups that settled the area in the A.D. 400s and 500s. By A.D. 900, the Czechs had their own kingdom, which became part of Austria's empire in the 1500s. After Austria's defeat in World War I, the Czechs and their Slovak neighbors united to create an independent country.

Czechoslovakia (CHEHK·uh·sloh·VAHK·ee·uh) lasted from 1918 until 1993. In that year, the Czechs and Slovaks decided to settle ongoing disagreements by splitting into the Czech Republic and Slovakia. Today the Czech Republic is a parliamentary democracy.

The Czechs enjoy a high standard of living compared to other eastern Europeans. Although Communists controlled the government for years, the Czechs rapidly moved from a command economy to a free market economy in the 1990s. Today, large fertile areas make the Czech Republic a major agricultural producer. Manufacturing, however, forms the backbone of the country's economy. Factories produce machinery, vehicles, metals, and textiles. The Czech Republic is also known for its fine crystal and beer. Unfortunately, the country's high level of industrialization has caused environmental problems, such as acid rain.

Slovakia

East of the Czech Republic lies its former partner, Slovakia. In northern Slovakia, the Carpathian Mountains dominate the landscape. Rugged peaks, thick forests, and blue lakes make this area a popular vacation spot. In the south, vineyards and farms spread across fertile lowlands near the Danube River.

Differentiated Instruction

Critical Thinking Skills Activity, URB pp. 97–98

Formulating Questions

Objective: Learn to analyze information by formulating questions.

Focus: Write statements about eastern Europe on the board, and have students turn them into questions.

Teach: Read the bulleted list aloud. Then use the title of the passage about Prague to model how to create a question.

Assess: Have students write questions about the passage and then answer them.

Close: Apply this skill to the second passage.

Differentiated Instruction Strategies

- **BL** Ask students to name the 5 "W" question words and use each word in a question.
- **AL** Have students apply this skill to the subsection "The Czech Republic" in the text.
- **ELL** Ask students to define the word "magnificent" and give synonyms for this word.

Independent since 1993, Slovakia is a democracy today. The Slovaks, however, have moved more slowly to a free market economy than the Czechs have. Slovakia has fewer factories than the Czech Republic, and the country is much less industrialized.

The Slovaks also have a language and culture different from the Czechs. While most Czechs are nonpracticing Catholics or are not religious at all, most Slovaks are devout Catholics. Nearly 60 percent of Slovaks live in towns and cities. Bratislava, on the Danube River, is Slovakia's capital. C

Hungary

Hungary is located on a large lowland area south of Slovakia and east of Austria. The capital city, Budapest, straddles Hungary's most important waterway, the Danube River.

The Hungarians are not related to the Slavic and Germanic peoples who live in most of eastern Europe, and the language spoken in Hungary is unique (see **Figure 3**). Their ancestors are the Magyars, who moved into the area from Central Asia about a thousand years ago. Like the Czechs and Slovaks, though, the Hungarians were once part of the Austro-Hungarian Empire. Later, after becoming an independent nation, Hungary too was led by Communists. Today it is a democracy headed by a president.

Hungary has few natural resources besides its fertile land, which is valuable for farming. By importing the necessary raw materials, though, the country began to industrialize after World War II. Today Hungary is an exporter of chemicals, food products, and other goods.

Reading Check **Explaining** Why did Czechoslovakia split into two countries?

Countries of Southeastern Europe

Main Idea **Because of limited natural resources, political upheaval, and ethnic conflict, many countries in southeastern Europe face challenges.**

Geography and You Do you adapt easily to change? The countries of southeastern Europe have been through major political and economic changes in recent times. Read to find out how they have responded.

A dozen or so countries are clustered in southeastern Europe. Ukraine, the largest, lies north of the Black Sea. Romania, Moldova, and Bulgaria are also on or close to the shores of the Black Sea. Their neighbors on the Balkan Peninsula include Albania, Slovenia, Croatia, Bosnia and Herzegovina, Serbia, Montenegro, and Macedonia.

Europe's Breadbasket

NATIONAL GEOGRAPHIC

S

▲ Workers harvest hay on a farm in western Ukraine, an area known for its productive agriculture. ***Human-Environment Interaction*** **What food crops are harvested in Ukraine?**

C Critical Thinking

Drawing Conclusions **Ask:** How does this paragraph help explain why the Czechs and Slovaks would want to have separate countries? *(They have different languages and cultures, including different attitudes toward religion.)* OL

S Skill Practice

Visual Literacy Point out to students that this photo does not show a literal basket of bread. **Ask:** What does the term "breadbasket" mean, and why is this an appropriate title for this photo? *(A breadbasket is a country or region that is an important grower of grain. This is an appropriate title because the photo shows farmers harvesting hay in Ukraine, which is an important grower of grain.)* OL

Reading Check **Answer:** The Czechs and the Slovaks split to settle ongoing disagreements.

Caption Answer:
grains, fruits, and vegetables

Additional Resources

FastFacts

Goulash Food is an important part of Hungary's traditional culture. National dishes include goulash, which is a stew of meat, onions, potatoes, tomatoes, and green peppers. Paprika, a spice made from chili peppers, gives goulash and other Hungarian foods their distinctive flavor.

Hungarian Arts Hungary has produced many famous artists, including the avant-garde painters Lajos Kassák and László Moholy-Nagy, composers Béla Bartók and Franz Liszt, and pianist Annie Fischer.

Nobel Laureates Scholarship and research are important in Hungary, which has the highest number of Nobel prize winners, per capita, of any country in the world.

D Differentiated Instruction

Visual/Spatial Have students create a graphic organizer comparing the two regions of Ukraine, including their industry and the origin of their people. OL

S Skill Practice

Using Geography Skills Ask: What does the map show about employment in eastern Europe compared to the rest of Europe? *(The percentage of workers employed in agriculture is higher in eastern Europe.)* OL

C Critical Thinking

Identifying Central Issues Ask: What issue is creating tensions in Ukraine today? *(Part of the country wants to join the European Union, and part wants closer ties to Russia.)* OL

Map Skills

Answers:

1. Moldova, Romania, and Albania
2. National income is generally lower in countries with a high percentage of agricultural workers.

Additional Support

Teacher Tip

Collaborative Learning Once you have selected groups for a collaborative assignment, discourage students from asking to move to a different group. Remind them that new groups will be formed for future group activities.

With the exception of Albania, these are young countries with newly drawn borders. It is not surprising, then, that many of them are struggling for stability and economic success.

Ukraine

Slightly smaller than Texas, Ukraine is the largest country in all of Europe. It lies on a lowland plain with the Carpathian Mountains rising along its southwestern border. The most important waterway, the Dnieper (NEE·puhr) River, has been made navigable to allow the shipping of goods.

D The Dnieper River divides Ukraine into two regions. To the west, the lowland steppes have rich, black soil that is ideal for farming. Farmers in this "breadbasket of Europe" grow grains, fruits, and vegetables and raise cattle and sheep. The people living here are of Ukrainian descent. To the east of the Dnieper lies a plains area D that has coal and iron ore deposits. Heavily industrialized, this eastern area produces cars, ships, locomotives, and airplanes. Many of the people in eastern Ukraine are of Russian descent.

Ukraine was one of the original republics in the Soviet Union, but it became an independent nation after the Soviet Union dissolved in 1991. Since then, ethnic divisions C have grown sharper. Ethnic Ukrainians in the west want to link the country to western Europe and join the European Union. Ethnic Russians in the east want closer ties to Russia.

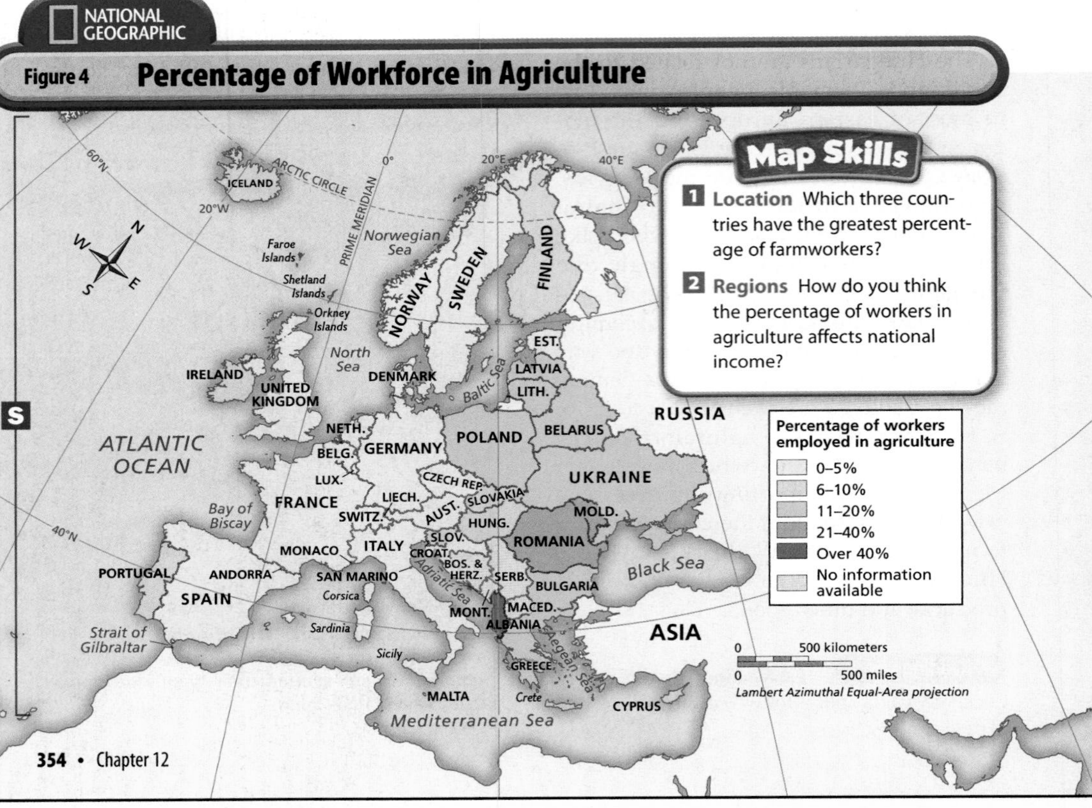

Figure 4 Percentage of Workforce in Agriculture

S

Activity: Collaborative Learning

Applying Ask: What do the colors on the map on this page indicate? *(the percentage of agricultural workers)* Show students other maps that use color to provide information. Organize the class into small groups. Assign each group one or more of the eastern European countries. Have groups research the percentage of workers in industry in their assigned countries, using the *CIA World Factbook* at www.cia.gov. Then have the groups work together to create a map that shows the percentage of workers in industry in each of the countries of eastern Europe. Remind students to include a map legend to explain the colors they use. OL

Romania and Moldova

R1

Unlike other eastern European countries, which ended Communist rule peacefully, Romania drove out the Communists in a bloody revolt in 1989. Soon after, the country fell into a deep economic slump. Romania has a wealth of natural resources, however, and the country is now rebounding. Thanks to deposits of coal, petroleum, and natural gas, industry output is growing. Bucharest (BOO·kuh·REHST), the capital, is the major economic and commercial center in the country. Farming also contributes to the economy, and many Romanians are employed in agriculture, as shown in **Figure 4.** Farmers here grow grains, grapes, and other crops.

As the name *Romania* suggests, the Romans once ruled this region and influenced its culture. The Romanian language, for example, is based on the Latin spoken in ancient Rome. In religion, though, Romanians take after their Slavic neighbors. Many are Eastern Orthodox Christian. R2

Moldova is a small, landlocked country sandwiched between Ukraine on the east and Romania on the west. Moldova's people are mainly Romanian, but Ukrainians and Russians also make up part of the population. Moldova's farms are productive as a result of its fertile soil. Because there are few mineral resources and limited industry, however, Moldova ranks as Europe's poorest country. R3

Bulgaria

Bulgaria lies south of Romania. It is a mountainous country, but people farm in the fertile river valleys between the peaks. Manufacturing employs many people in Sofia, the capital, and other cities. Tourism is growing as visitors seek out Bulgaria's scenic resorts on the Black Sea.

Most of Bulgaria's 7.7 million people trace their ancestry to the Slavs, Turks, and other groups from Central Asia. Most Bulgarians are Eastern Orthodox Christian. A sizable minority are Muslim.

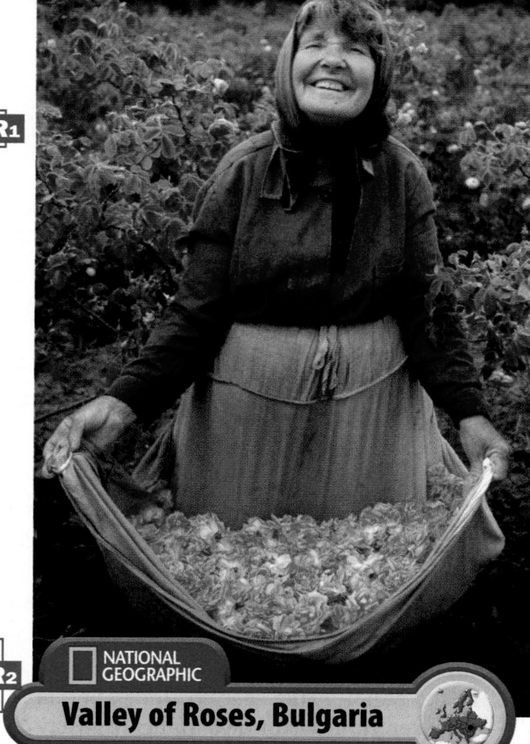

NATIONAL GEOGRAPHIC

Valley of Roses, Bulgaria

A worker holds an apron full of rose blooms gathered at a farm in Bulgaria's famous Valley of Roses. ***Place*** **What are Bulgaria's major economic activities?**

Other Balkan States

To the south and west of Bulgaria, a number of other countries crowd the Balkan Peninsula. Albania, on the Adriatic Sea, is the only country in Europe with a majority Muslim population. It is also unique because farmers outnumber factory workers. With its economy still heavily agricultural, Albania is one of the poorest countries in Europe. C

Other Balkan countries include Slovenia, Croatia, Bosnia and Herzegovina, Macedonia, Serbia, and Montenegro.

R1 Reading Strategy

Questioning Have students work in pairs to create three questions based on the text under the heading "Romania and Moldova." Have pairs exchange questions and answer them. **OL**

R2 Reading Strategy

Activating Prior Knowledge Ask: What other languages are based on Latin? *(Answers may include Spanish, French, and Italian.)* **OL**

R3 Reading Strategy

Monitoring Ask: What does *landlocked* mean? *(surrounded by land)* **BL**

C Critical Thinking

Analyzing Information

Ask: What makes Albania unique in Europe? *(It is the only country with a majority Muslim population, and farmers there outnumber factory workers.)* **OL**

Caption Answer:
tourism, farming, and manufacturing

Activity: Interdisciplinary Connection

Daily Life Ask students to examine the photo of the woman on this page and compare it to the photo of the teenager in Prague from earlier in the section. **Ask: Aside from the age of the people, what differences do you see in the photos?** *(The teenager is in a city, is using a cell phone, and is wearing trendy clothing, while the woman in the photo on this page is on a farm and is wearing traditional clothing.)* Tell students that these two photos demonstrate the diversity of lifestyles in eastern Europe. Have students choose a country in eastern Europe to research more thoroughly. Tell them to focus on information that gives them clues about daily life in that country. Have students use what they learn to write essays in which they describe what daily life is like for young people in that country. **OL**

W Writing Support

Expository Writing Have students write a newspaper article about the current situation in the countries of the former Yugoslavia. Instruct students to answer the 5*W*s in their article—*who, what, when, where,* and *why.* OL

Reading Check Answer: Many of these countries were previously part of a Communist country called Yugoslavia. When communism collapsed, the different ethnic groups of Yugoslavia struggled for power.

Assess

Social Studies ONLINE
Study Central™ provides summaries, interactive games, and online graphic organizers to help students review content.

Close

Categorizing Have students categorize each of the eastern European countries as either mainly agricultural or industrial. OL

None of these nations were even on the map until the 1990s. Before then, they were all part of a Communist country called Yugoslavia.

When communism collapsed in Eastern Europe, the different ethnic groups of Yugoslavia struggled for power. In the early 1990s, four parts of the country—Slovenia, Croatia, Bosnia and Herzegovina, and Macedonia—declared their independence. Meanwhile, another strong part, Serbia, wanted to keep Yugoslavia together under Serbian rule. Serbia's leader used force to try to build power.

The heaviest fighting took place in Bosnia and Herzegovina. There, Serbs carried out **ethnic cleansing**—removing or killing an entire ethnic group—against the Bosnian population. Many people died or became refugees. This and other conflicts left the region badly scarred. Today Serbia has given up hope of reclaiming Yugoslav lands. Montenegro split away from Serbia in 2006, and where Yugoslavia once was, there are now six separate nations.

These Balkan countries were relatively poor during Communist rule, and they continue to be among the poorest in Europe. The mountainous landscape of the Balkan Peninsula makes farming difficult, and there are few natural resources to support economic growth. Ethnic conflict has added to these problems.

Despite these challenges, some countries are moving forward. Slovenia has experienced steady economic growth since it gained independence. Slovenian industries produce machinery, appliances, vehicles, and **medical** supplies. Croatia's economy has also improved, although not as much as Slovenia's.

Reading Check **Explaining** Why have conflicts been fought in the Balkan Peninsula?

Section 4 Review

Social Studies ONLINE
Study Central™ To review this section, go to glencoe.com.

Vocabulary

1. **Explain** the differences between *command economy* and *market economy.* Define *potash* and *ethnic cleansing.*

Main Ideas

2. **Sequencing** List the events that led to democracy in Poland.
3. **Comparing** Create a Venn diagram like the one below to compare the Czech Republic and Slovakia.

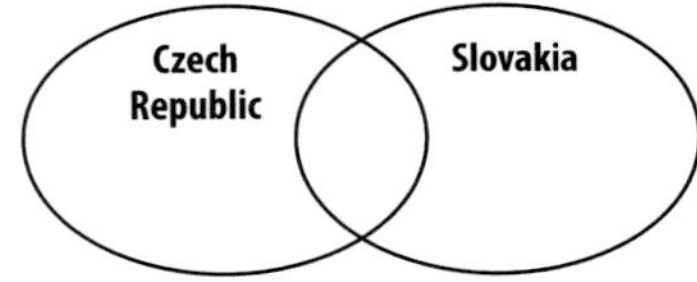

4. **Explaining** Why are many of the countries of southeastern Europe struggling for economic success?

Critical Thinking

5. **BIG Idea** How have eastern Europe's history and physical geography led to differences between that region and other parts of Europe today?
6. **Challenge** Based on what you have read, what do you think will happen politically in Ukraine over the next few years? Why?

Writing About Geography

7. **Using Your FOLDABLES** Use your Foldable to write a paragraph comparing and contrasting conditions in two countries in eastern Europe.

Section 4 Review

Answers

1. Definitions for vocabulary words are found in the section and the Glossary.
2. John Paul II became pope in 1978 and encouraged the Poles to resist Communist rule; Polish workers and farmers formed Solidarity in the 1980s; Communist leaders allowed free elections in 1989 that allowed that allowed democratic government.
3. **Czech Republic:** hills, lowlands, and plains; most people live in cities and are nonpracticing Catholics or not religious at all; moved rapidly to a free market economy; high standard of living; highly industrialized; **Slovakia:** mountainous; 60 percent of people live in cities; most are devout Catholics; moved slowly to a free market economy; less industrialized; **Both:** same country from 1918 to 1993; agriculture is important
4. Most are young countries suffering political upheaval and ethnic conflict. Many were poor under Communist rule and have few natural resources.
5. Under Communist rule, the region developed differently from other parts of Europe. Mountains and physical distance separated the region from the rest of Europe.
6. Answers will vary but should be logical and based on the text.
7. Paragraphs will vary but should compare and contrast the countries.

Visual Summary

Northern Europe

- The United Kingdom is a major industrial and trading country.
- The Republic of Ireland's economy is becoming more industrial.
- Fishing is an important industry in the Scandinavian countries.

Members of the British royal family

France and the Benelux Countries

- France is a world center of art, learning, and culture.
- The Benelux countries are low, flat, and densely populated.

Europe at night

Schoolgirls in France

Germany and the Alpine Countries

- Rivers have been vital to Germany's economic growth.
- The Alps dominate Switzerland, Austria, and Liechtenstein.

Southern Europe

- Spain's historic sites and sunny beaches attract many tourists.
- Most of Italy's industry lies in the northern part of the country.
- Greece consists of a mountainous mainland and more than 2,000 islands.

Eastern Europe

- Poland is a large country with northern plains and southern highlands.
- The Danube River flows through Budapest, Hungary's historic capital.
- Ukrainians disagree on whether to strengthen ties to western Europe or to Russia.
- Ethnic conflict has torn apart Balkan countries in recent years.

Industry in eastern Europe

Fisher in Malta

Study anywhere, anytime! Download quizzes and flash cards to your PDA from glencoe.com.

Visual Summary

Making Inferences Have students study the photos on this page. **Ask:** **If you did not know much about the countries shown in these photos, what inferences might you still be able to make about them?** *(Possible answer: You could infer that the United Kingdom is a monarchy of some kind; you could infer that France has many immigrants or ethnic groups; you could infer that pollution from industry is a problem in eastern Europe; and you could infer that fishing is an important economic activity in Malta.)* **OL**

Distinguishing Fact From Opinion Tell students that although we may be able to make inferences about other countries from photos, we need to be careful not to make *stereotypes*. Explain that a stereotype is an oversimplified idea about a person, group, or country. For example, it is true that fishing is an important economic activity in Malta, but it would be a stereotype to say that all people in Malta fish.

To help students distinguish facts from stereotypes, have each student write three facts and three stereotypes about countries in Europe on a piece of paper. Then have them switch papers with another student and identify the statements as either facts or stereotypes. **OL**

Hands-On Chapter Project
Step 5: Wrap Up

Visualizing Europe's Economics

Step 5: Learning from the Project Students will synthesize what they have learned in Steps 1 through 4.

Directions Write the Essential Question on the board. Encourage students to answer this question by using what they learned while creating their bulletin board display. Begin by asking students to review the industries in the four areas of Europe. Ask volunteers to name European products that people in the United States purchase, such as European cars and clothing. **Ask:** **How does the sale of these goods help U.S. citizens?** *(The availability of European goods creates a wider selection for U.S. consumers.)* **How does the sale of these goods help European citizens?** *(The sale of goods provides jobs and income to European workers.)* **How much do you think people around the world want or need European products?** *(People want European products very much because their products have a reputation for high quality.)* List students' responses on the board, and refer to the Big Ideas from the chapter. Then have students write several sentences in their journal to answer the Essential Question. **OL**

Answers and Analyses

Reviewing Vocabulary

1. B In reviewing the answers, students should be able to immediately eliminate answer choice C, since it is not a form of government. Answer choice A also is incorrect because a dictatorship does not involve elected officials. Students may struggle to choose between the remaining answer choices. Remind them that a monarchy is form of government with a king or queen.

2. C Specialization involves focusing on few activities. Key words in the question might give students clues to the correct answer. For example, the word *certain* carries the idea of "selected" or "special."

3. A Word analysis of the answer choices can help students select the correct answer. The prefix *auto-* means "self," so *autonomy* means "the act of self-rule."

4. D To help students remember the definition for a *command economy,* tell them to think of it as a government commanding, or controlling, a country's economy.

CHAPTER 12

STANDARDIZED TEST PRACTICE

TEST-TAKING TIP

Consider carefully before changing your answer to a multiple-answer test question. Unless you misread the question, your first answer choice is often correct.

Reviewing Vocabulary

Directions: Choose the word(s) that best completes the sentence.

1. In a ______, a king or queen serves as a ceremonial head of state but elected officials actively run the government.

A constitutional dictatorship
B constitutional monarchy
C multinational organization
D parliamentary democracy

2. Focusing on certain economic activities in order to make the most advantageous use of a nation's resources is called ______.

A reunification
B neutrality
C specialization
D productivity

3. A country allowing a region within its borders a certain amount of self-rule is known as ______.

A autonomy
B neutrality
C specialization
D subsidy

4. In a ______, the government decides what, how, and for whom goods will be produced.

A market economy
B parliamentary democracy
C constitutional monarchy
D command economy

Reviewing Main Ideas

Directions: Choose the best answer for each question.

Section 1 *(pp. 320–328)*

5. ______ has been troubled by a history of violence between Catholics and Protestants.

A Finland
B Northern Ireland
C Sweden
D Iceland

Section 2 *(pp. 329–337)*

6. In the Netherlands, wetlands that have been drained, called ______, have rich farming soil.

A Benelux
B chateaus
C polders
D Walloons

Section 3 *(pp. 338–342)*

7. In ______, the southern part of the country is poorer and less industrialized than the northern part.

A Portugal
B Ireland
C Greece
D Italy

Section 4 *(pp. 348–356)*

8. In Eastern Europe, Poland and the Baltic Republics have moved toward democracy and market economies, but ______ maintains a command economy and strong central government.

A Belarus
B Lithuania
C Hungary
D Bosnia

GO ON

Reviewing Main Ideas

5. B Students may recall that part of Ireland is Protestant and part is Catholic. The other choices are the largely Protestant Scandinavian countries.

6. C To help students remember the definition of a polder, tell them that the words *puddle* and *polder* are similar, and both are related to water.

7. D To answer this question correctly, it may help students to remember that Italy is a long country, with southern and northern regions that have different resources.

8. A Students should eliminate answer choice B, because Lithuania is a Baltic Republic with a market economy. Belarus, however, has close ties to Russia and has maintained a command economy.

Critical Thinking

Directions: Choose the best answer for each question.

Base your answers to questions 9 and 10 on your knowledge of Chapter 12 and the map below.

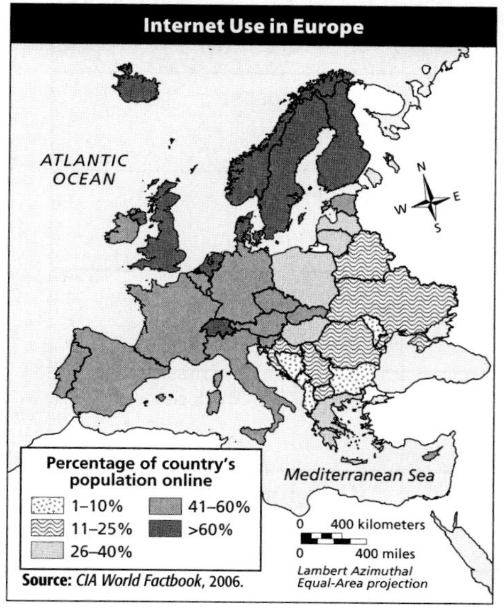

9. Which of the following countries has the lowest percentage of residents online?

A Ukraine
B Czech Republic
C Bulgaria
D Poland

10. In general, which subregion of Europe has the highest percentage of people online?

A Southern Europe
B Northern Europe
C Eastern Europe
D the Balkan countries

Document-Based Questions

Directions: Analyze the document and answer the short-answer questions that follow.

> *Supporters of enlargement [of the European Union] view it as the best way of building economic and political bonds between the peoples of Europe in order to end the divisions of the past.*
>
> *They look forward to sharing the world's largest single market and so to expanding prosperity. . . .*
>
> *Some [critics] contend that the EU decision-making process will become bogged down as the number of countries . . . increases. . . .*
>
> *Expansion is almost certain to continue. Bulgaria and Romania are set to join in January 2007. . . . Talks over Turkey's possible accession [admittance] began in October 2005.*
>
> —BBC News, 2006

11. According to the news article, what are some of the arguments for expansion of the EU? Against expansion?

12. Where are the countries located that are seemingly next in line to join the EU?

Extended Response

13. Imagine you have been invited to be on a panel that is going to pick "Europe's Most Promising Economy of the Future." Prepare a speech in which you nominate a European country for this award. Explain why you believe this country's economy will either grow or remain strong in the future. Be sure to use geographical, population, and economic factors to support your position.

For additional test practice, use Self-Check Quizzes—Chapter 12 at glencoe.com.

Need Extra Help?

If you missed question. . .	1	2	3	4	5	6	7	8	9	10	11	12	13
Go to page. . .	322	330	339	349	326	332	341	350	26	26	355	355	321

Document-Based Questions

11. Arguments for expansion include building economic and political bonds, ending the divisions of the past, sharing the world's largest single market, and expanding prosperity. Arguments against expansion include the possibility that the EU will become so large that decision-making will become a problem.

12. They are all located in southeastern Europe.

Extended Response

13. Answers will vary, but students should support their choice with facts about the country's geography, population, and economy.

Critical Thinking

9. C To answer this question, students need to remember where countries are in Europe. They may need to review a chapter map to do so.

10. B Students need to recall the subregions of Europe and analyze the general composition of each region.

Have students visit the Web site at glencoe.com to review Chapter 12 and take the Self-Check Quiz.

Need Extra Help?

Have students refer to the pages listed if they miss any of the questions.

Unit 5 Planning Guide

UNIT PACING CHART				
	Unit 5	Chapter 13	Chapter 14	Chapter 15
Day 1	Unit Opener	Chapter Opener	Chapter Opener	Chapter Opener
Day 2	Regional Atlas	Section 1	Section 1	Section 1
Day 3	Regional Atlas	You Decide	Section 1	Section 1
Day 4	Reading Social Studies	Section 2	Geography & History	TIME Perspectives
Day 5		World Literature Reading	Section 2	TIME Perspectives
Day 6		Review	Section 2	Section 2
Day 7		Chapter Assessment	Review	Review
Day 8			Chapter Assessment	Chapter Assessment
Day 9			TIME Journal	

Teacher to Teacher

Jeanne Hill
Galaxy Middle School
Deltona, Florida

Create a Hall of Fame Students will create a "Hall of Fame" for the region of Russia. The immense size of Russia is the inspiration for this activity. We use the Geo FastFacts section of the Regional Atlas as a jumping off point. Students work in groups to research the region and select a world record for the Hall of Fame. Their selection can be based on a variety of topics, such as physical features, culture, history, politics, economy, climate, architecture, sports, or recreation. Students' research should include a description and background, pictures, map location, and an explanation of the significance or importance of the topic. Students then create a poster of their Hall of Fame entry to place on the Hall of Fame bulletin board. Next, groups will design and build an award or trophy. Students present their entry at an awards ceremony, with the best entry receiving the award. As an added twist, students can dress for the event and create special envelopes to open to announce the winners.

Author Note

Dear Social Studies Teacher:

There are many stories to be told about the vastness of Russia, but none quite so interesting as those about its rivers. West of the Ural Mountains, Russia's rivers generally flow south into the Black Sea. The Volga—flowing through a large, complex, urban/industrial area—hardly resembles a river any longer. Large dams have been built along its course so that the river valley looks more like a continuous chain of long lakes. Stored water in reservoirs is used by cities, industries, and agriculture, and to generate power. The Dnieper and Don Rivers also have been utilized in this manner. While the Volga River has aided Russia's urban and industrial development, its flow to the Caspian Sea has diminished. Once a fishing port, Astrakhan is now 35 miles (56.3 km) from the edge of the shrinking Caspian. The former Soviet republics of Uzbekistan and Kazakhstan have a similar problem. The decreased water levels of the Syr and Amu Darya Rivers have led to an enormous reduction in the surface area of the Aral Sea. While there are attempts to reverse this trend, it is clear that water needs have outstripped the rivers' ability to provide for the people in that region.

In Siberia, a very different story prevails. The enormous rivers of this area flow northward. When the ice melts in the south during the spring, meltwater has no place to go because the more northern mouths of these great rivers (Yenisey, Ob, Lena, Kolyma) are still frozen. Floodwaters spill over into low-lying areas, creating vast swamps. The West Siberian Plain, for example, which is the largest area of flat land in the world, cannot be farmed. Thus, while rivers play an important role throughout this vast region, their specific impact on physical and human geography varies greatly.

Richard G. Boehm
Senior Author

What Makes Russia a Region?

The three chapters of this unit introduce students to the vast country of Russia. This country has the following characteristics:

- the largest landmass of any country in the world, straddling two continents
- a rich supply of energy resources
- a new government that is still developing democratic reforms
- a new economic system based on free market principles
- environmental problems as a result of former Communist policies
- rich cultural traditions that shape many areas of daily life

NATIONAL GEOGRAPHIC
www.nationalgeographic.com/education

NGS ONLINE This online resource provides lesson plans, atlas updates, cartographic activities with interactive maps, an online map store, and geographic links.

UNIT 5 Russia

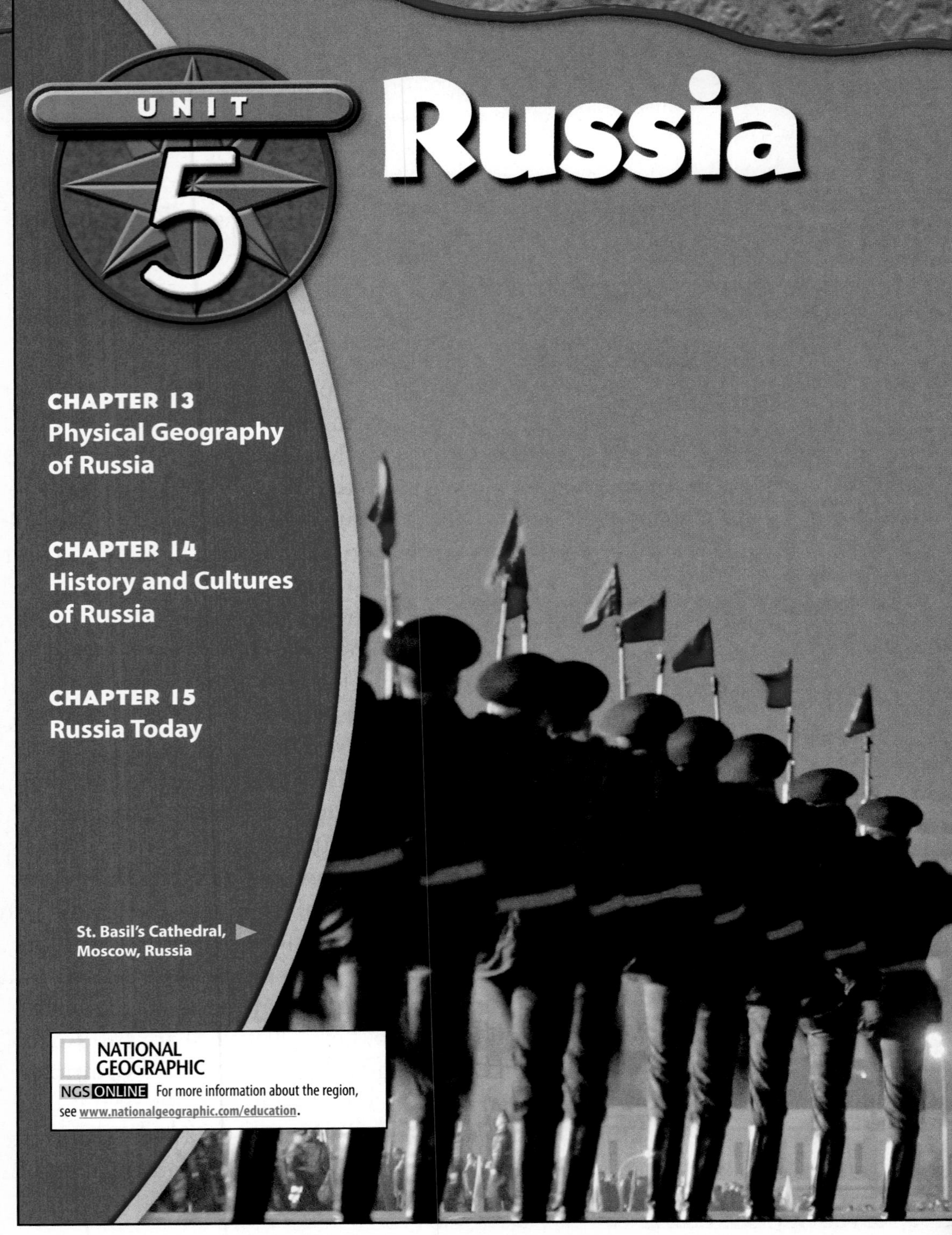

St. Basil's Cathedral, Moscow, Russia

NATIONAL GEOGRAPHIC
NGS ONLINE For more information about the region, see www.nationalgeographic.com/education.

Activity: Launching the Unit

Why Study Russia? Ask: When you think of Russia, what are some of the first things that come to mind? *(Answers might include communism, the Cold War, the size of the country, or cold weather.)* Have students write their ideas in their notebooks. Then explain that some of their ideas may no longer be true of Russia today. For example, if students still associate Russia with communism, explain that Russia has a new government and economic system. Tell students to keep their lists of ideas and check them against the information in this unit to find out if their ideas about Russia are really true. **OL**

Introducing Unit 5

Introduce the Region

Using Maps Have students look at the maps of physical features and economic resources of Russia in the Regional Atlas. Point out that the Ural Mountains divide the European and Asian parts of Russia. **Ask:** **What major rivers are found in European Russia?** *(Volga, Don, N. Dvina, and Ural)* **What major rivers are found in Asian Russia?** *(Ob, Irtysh, Yenisey, and Lena)* Tell students that Lake Baikal is the world's deepest freshwater lake. **Ask:** **Where is this lake located?** *(in southeastern Russia, near the Yablonovyy Range)* **What would you say is Russia's most widespread natural resource?** *(coal)* **Where is most of Russia's commercial fishing found?** *(along the Pacific coast)* **OL**

Unit 5 • 361

More About the Photo

Visual Literacy Red Square, in central Moscow, is bordered by the Kremlin, Lenin's tomb, and St. Basil's Cathedral. St. Basil's Cathedral may be the most recognizable piece of architecture in Russia. It was constructed on the square between 1554 and 1560 by Ivan IV, known as "the Terrible" to commemorate his victories over the Tartars in Kazan. The cathedral consists of a series of chapels, many of them dedicated to saints on whose feast days the tsar had won battles. Each chapel is topped with a colorful onion-shaped dome, which shows the influence of Byzantine architecture in Russia. A Russian legend says that after the cathedral was completed, Ivan the Terrible had the architect blinded so that he could never build anything as wonderful again.

Regional Atlas Activity

Where Is It?

Using a Compass Rose **Ask:** **If you were flying from New York to Vladivostok, which direction would you fly?** *(almost due east or west)* **Where is Russia located in relation to the rest of Europe?** *(east)* **In relation to the rest of Asia?** *(north)* **OL**

How Big Is It?

Math Question Tell students that the total land area of the world is 57,308,738 square miles (148,429,000 sq. km). **Ask:** **About what percent of the world's land is in Russia?** *(about 12 percent)* **OL**

Comparing Population

Ask: **About how many people live in the United States?** *(290 million)* **About how many people live in Russia?** *(140 million)* **Which country is more densely populated? How do you know?** *(the United States, because more than twice the number of people live in about half the amount of land)* **OL**

Regional Atlas

Russia

Where Is It?

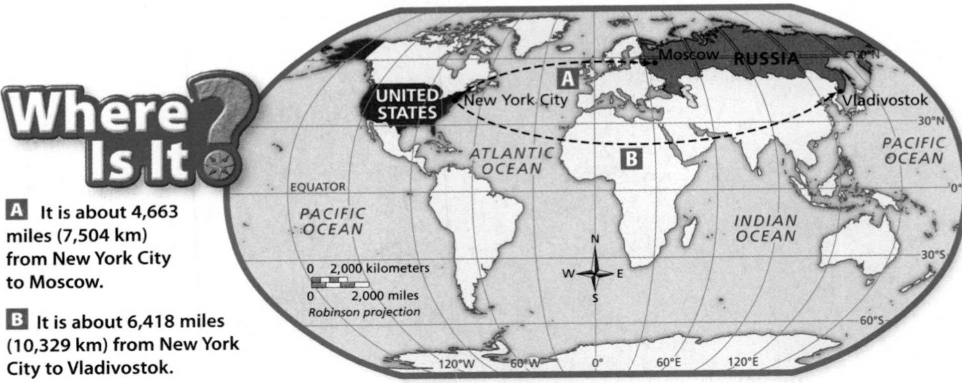

A It is about 4,663 miles (7,504 km) from New York City to Moscow.

B It is about 6,418 miles (10,329 km) from New York City to Vladivostok.

The region of Russia is more than twice the size of the continental United States. Its land area is about 6,592,819 square miles (17,075,322 sq. km). Russia is the third-largest culture region and the largest single country in the world.

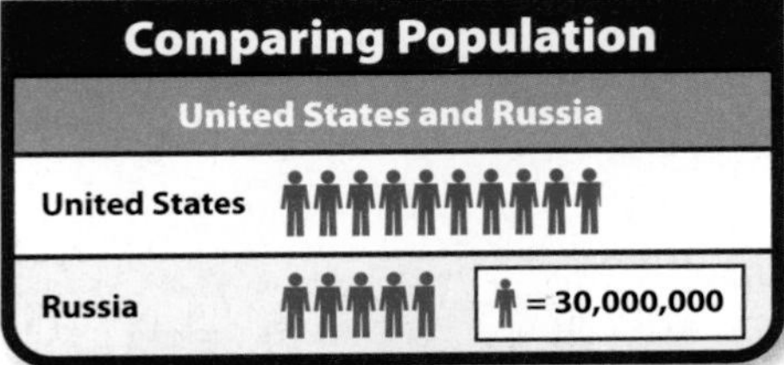

Source: *World Population Data Sheet*, 2005.

Activity: Geographic Theme

Human-Environment Interaction Review with the class how the physical geography of an area can influence how many people live there and what kind of work they do. Ask students to think about how the physical geography of the area where they live has affected the population there. Then have them look at the map that shows the physical features of Russia. **Ask:** **Where do you think most Russians live?** *(Possible answer: Most Russians probably live west of the Ural Mountains, where the land is flatter and there are many waterways.)* **Ask:** **How do you think people who live in different parts of Russia might make their living?** *(Possible answer: People who live near the seas may make their living by fishing; people who live near natural resources may work in industries that use or mine them.)* Have students compare their answers with the population density and economic resources maps in the Regional Atlas. **AL**

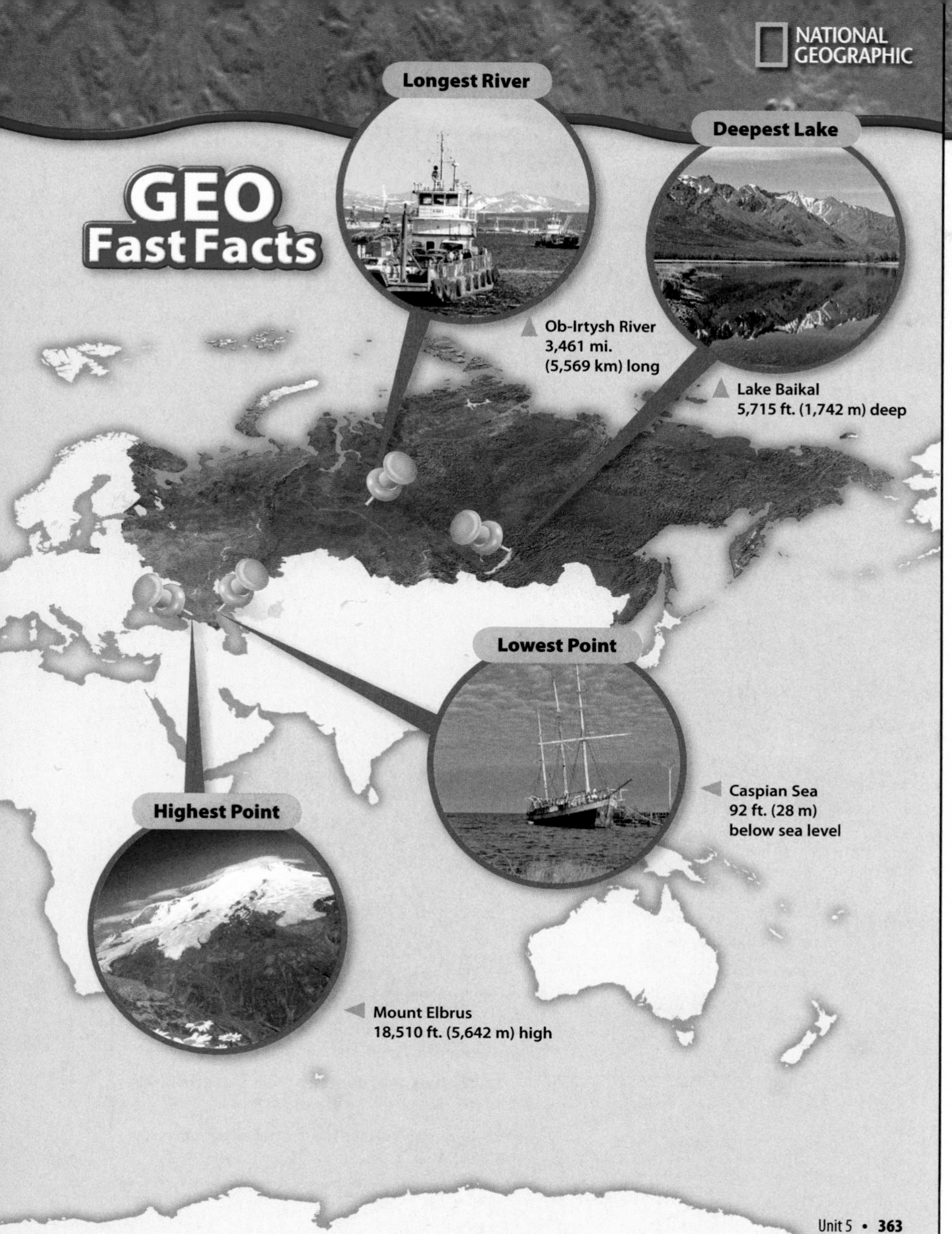

Unit 5 Regional Atlas

Geo Fast Facts

Categorizing Facts Ask: What four features of Russia are highlighted on this map? *(Ob-Irtysh River, Lake Baikal, Mt. Elbrus, and Caspian Sea)* **Into what two categories could you place these features?** *(Answer may include waterways and mountains, or landforms and waterways.)*

Draw a chart on the board with the following headings: landforms, waterways, resources, and cities. Tell students to copy this chart into their notebooks. Then give them time to look through the maps in this unit and note facts that fit into each of the categories on the chart.

Tell students to update their charts with additional facts as they read the chapters in this unit. At the end of each chapter, check to make sure that students are updating their charts. At the end of the unit, draw the chart on the board again and have students use their notes to help you complete this "master" chart. **BL**

FastFacts

- **Kaliningrad** The Kaliningrad region is home to the largest amber mine in the world, containing about 90 percent of the world's amber. Amber is a fossilized resin of conifers, which sometimes encases an insect. The highest-quality amber is crafted into fine jewelry and ornaments.
- **The Arctic Circle** The Northern portions of Russia are within the Arctic Circle. Within this circle, the sun does not set for 24 hours at least once per year. This is sometimes referred to as the "midnight sun." Likewise, the sun does not rise for at least 24 hours at least once per year.
- **Siberian Tigers** This endangered animal still roams in small numbers in eastern Siberia. Estimates differ, but probably only a few hundred Siberian Tigers still exist in the wild. Russia has put conservation programs in place to protect this majestic animal.

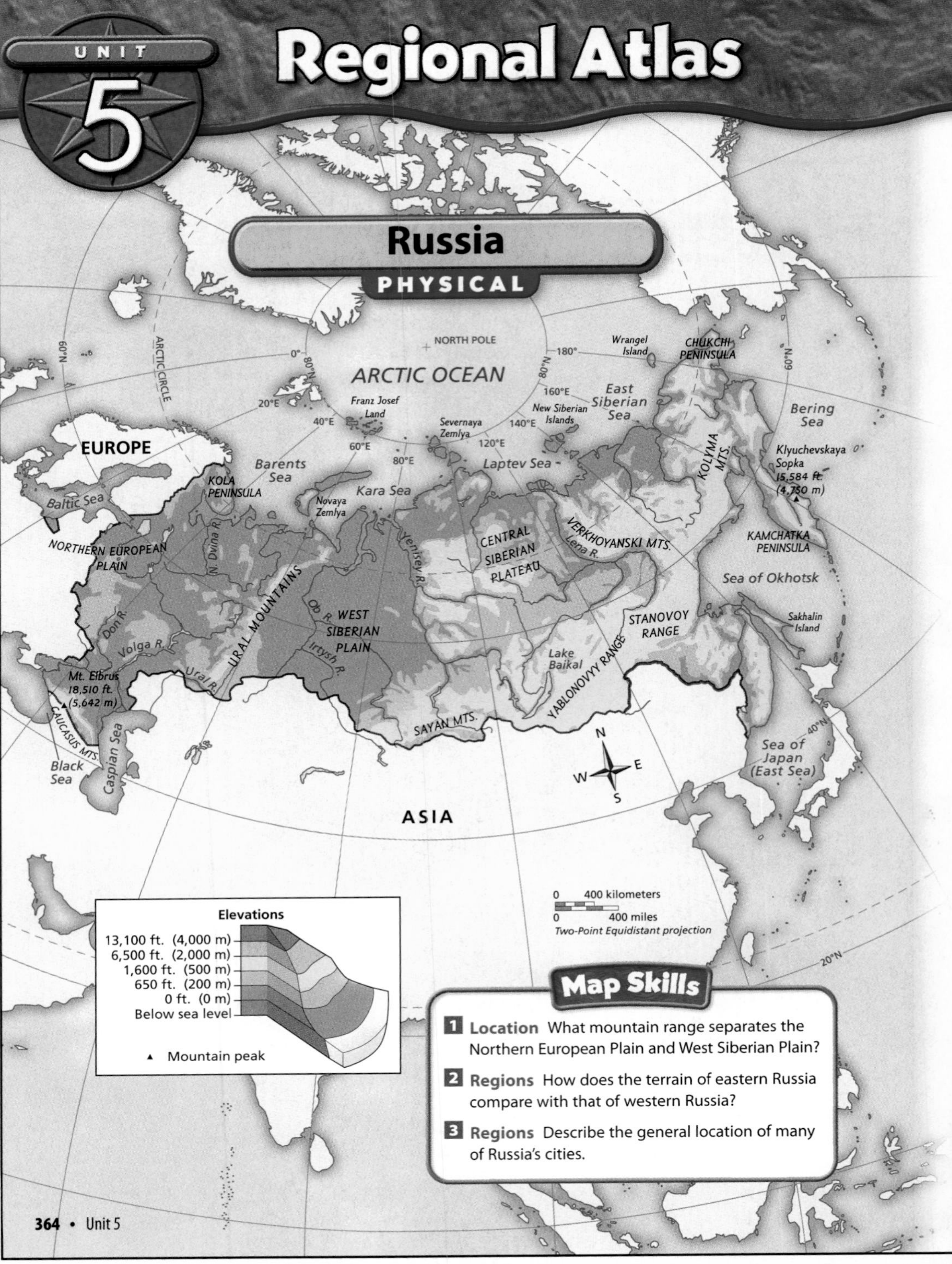

Regional Atlas Activity

Comparing and Contrasting Have students study the physical features of Russia east and west of the Ural Mountains. Then have them work in pairs to create a Venn diagram that lists the similarities and differences between the two regions. After pairs have completed their Venn diagrams, draw a large Venn diagram on the board. Ask volunteers to come to the board and add facts from their own diagrams. **ELL**

FastFacts

The World's Coldest Place The coldest spot outside of Antarctica is in Siberia, in a place called Oymyakon. Temperatures in Oymyakon may drop to as low as –94° F (–70° C) in the winter!

Map Skills

Answers:

1. the Ural Mountains
2. Western Russia is made up of lowlands; in contrast, eastern Russia is more mountainous.
3. mainly to the west and south

Background: Land and Climate

A Country on Two Continents Russia is the largest country in the world, stretching 6,200 miles (9,978 km) from east to west and straddling two continents, Europe and Asia. Most of the country lies in the high latitudes. At the same time, tall mountain ranges block warm air from flowing in from the south. As a result, most of Russia has a cold climate.

The Ural Mountains divide Russia into two parts—European Russia to the west and Asian Russia to the east. Most of European Russia lies on the fertile Northern European Plain. Three-quarters of Russia's population lives here because this part of Russia has the mildest climate. Summers in European Russia are rainy and humid, and winters are snowy and cold.

Asian Russia generally has long, frigid winters and short, cool summers. Siberia, a vast tundra stretching across the northern reaches of Asian Russia, has one of the harshest climates in the world. The land stays frozen here much of the year. Southern Siberia contains the taiga, a huge, dense forest about the size of the continental United States.

NATIONAL GEOGRAPHIC

Unit 5 Regional Atlas

Russia

POLITICAL

National capital
City

0 400 kilometers
0 400 miles
Two-Point Equidistant projection

Country and Capital	Literacy Rate	Population and Density	Land Area	Life Expectancy (Years)	GDP* Per Capita (U.S. dollars)	Television Sets (per 1,000 people)	Flag and Language
RUSSIA Moscow	99.6%	143,000,000 22 per sq. mi. 8 per sq. km	6,592,819 sq. mi. 17,075,322 sq. km	66	$9,800	421	Russian
UNITED STATES Washington, D.C.	97%	296,500,000 80 per sq. mi. 31 per sq. km	3,717,796 sq. mi. 9,629,047 sq. km	78	$40,100	844	English

Sources: *CIA World Factbook*, 2005; Population Reference Bureau, *World Population Data Sheet*, 2005.

For more country facts, go to the **Nations of the World Databank** at glencoe.com.

Countries and flags not drawn to scale

*Gross Domestic Product

Regional Atlas Activity

Hypothesizing Have students study the location of cities in Russia. **Ask:** **Why do you think cities developed in these locations?** *(Possible answers: Most cities are on rivers or are ports on seas; most cities are located in the southern or western part of the country, where the land is less mountainous.)* Have students work in pairs or small groups to research the history of a Russian city. They may use encyclopedias, online resources, or other reference sources. After the groups have finished their research, have them discuss and compare why cities developed in various areas of Russia. **OL**

Map Skills

Skills Practice

Ask: **What cities provide Russia with ports to the Baltic Sea?** *(Kaliningrad and St. Petersburg)* **To the Barents Sea?** *(Murmansk)*

Background: Current Issues

Challenges to Democracy Although Russia now holds free elections, the presidency of Vladimir Putin has severely challenged the country's democratic system. Putin has strengthened the powers of the presidency since taking office in 1999, and his support for democracy and democratic institutions has waned. For example, Putin shut down independent television news networks when they began to criticize his policies. Although free newspapers continue to be published, television news is controlled by the government. Putin has also taken steps to ensure that regional governments will do as he wishes. He organized Russia into seven large districts and installed leaders over these districts who were loyal to him.

In addition to problems at the presidential level, politicians at other levels disregard democratic practices as well. For example, courts often favor the wealthy over the poor. Russians have had little experience with democratic government, and many Russians feel powerless to change the way their government works.

Unit 5 Regional Atlas

Regional Atlas Activity

Classifying Tell students to create a chart with three columns: cities with populations over 5,000,000, cities with populations from 1,000,000 to 5,000,000, and cities under 1,000,000. Have them fill in this chart with the names of the cities found on the population density map, placing each city in the appropriate column. Then have students look at the other maps in the Regional Atlas and list cities found on those maps that are not on the population density map. Ask them to find the populations of these additional cities using online or other reference sources. Then have them use the statistics they have found to list these cities in the appropriate columns on their charts.

Answers:

1. European Russia has a greater number of large cities than Asian Russia.
2. Population density is higher throughout the south.

Skills Practice

Ask: **Which areas of Russia are the most densely populated?** *(the areas around Moscow and along Russia's southern border between the Black and Caspian Seas)*

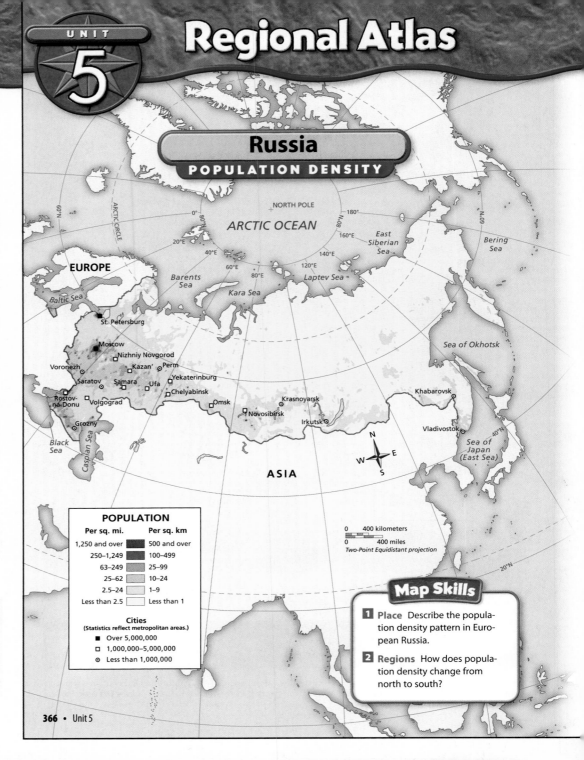

Russia

POPULATION DENSITY

POPULATION

Per sq. mi.	Per sq. km
1,250 and over	500 and over
250–1,249	100–499
63–249	25–99
25–62	10–24
2.5–24	1–9
Less than 2.5	Less than 1

Cities (Statistics reflect metropolitan areas.)

- ■ Over 5,000,000
- □ 1,000,000–5,000,000
- ⊙ Less than 1,000,000

0 400 kilometers
0 400 miles
Two-Point Equidistant projection

Map Skills

1. **Place** Describe the population density pattern in European Russia.
2. **Regions** How does population density change from north to south?

Background: People and Culture

Transportation Challenges Russia is so vast that it has had difficulty developing an effective transportation network. Under Soviet rule, the main form of transportation was railroads. As a result, European Russia's industrial centers and urban areas today are linked by an extensive rail system. The Trans-Siberian Railroad crosses Asian Russia and is the longest railroad in the world. Completion of this railroad in the early 1900s allowed limited access to Siberia's vast natural resources.

In the post-Soviet era, increasing numbers of Russians own cars. However, the system of roads in Russia has not kept pace with car ownership. No highway system links major cities, and existing roads are in poor condition. It is difficult to even get gas along these roads. The government has undertaken a massive project to build a 6,600-mile (10,600-kilometer) highway across the country. When completed, it will be the longest national highway in the world.

Russia
ECONOMIC RESOURCES

NORTH POLE
ARCTIC OCEAN
ARCTIC CIRCLE
EUROPE
Barents Sea
Kara Sea
Laptev Sea
East Siberian Sea
Bering Sea
Sea of Okhotsk
Baltic Sea
Black Sea
Caspian Sea
RUSSIA
Lake Baikal
Sea of Japan (East Sea)
ASIA

Land Use
- Commercial farming
- Subsistence farming
- Livestock raising
- Manufacturing and trade
- Nomadic herding
- Commercial fishing
- Little or no activity

Resources

Bauxite	Natural gas
Chrome	Nickel
Coal	Petroleum
Cobalt	Silver
Copper	Timber
Diamonds	Tin
Gold	Uranium
Iron ore	Zinc
Lead	

0 400 kilometers
0 400 miles
Two-Point Equidistant projection

Map Skills

1 Location In what part of Russia are gold and silver deposits found?

2 Regions Describe the general location of commercial farming areas in Russia.

Regional Atlas Activity

Synthesizing Information Help students synthesize the information in the Regional Atlas maps by playing a location game. Ask students to review the maps and pick a secret location. Then have them write a series of clues that will help others figure out where this secret location is. The clues should come from at least three different maps in the Regional Atlas. Have each student read his or her clues and then have the rest of the class guess that student's location. **OL**

Answers:
1. along the Ural Mountains and in south-central and eastern Russia
2. in the west and south

Background: The Economy

A Changing Economy The economic system in the Russian Federation is in transition. Under Communist rule, the Soviet Union had a command economy in which the central government controlled all aspects of economic life. Russia is now in the process of shifting to a market economy. In this type of economy, individuals make decisions about what to make and how much to charge. To achieve a market economy, the Russian government introduced privatization, or the transfer of businesses and farms from government to private ownership. The government also ended official price controls for goods and services. In this new economy, owners compete for the business of consumers, and people can decide where to work.

The switch to a market economy has not been easy, however. Many businesses that are no longer supported by the government have failed, putting Russians out of work. Many Russians are unable to find jobs that use their skills and education. Prices for many items have risen, making survival difficult for people on fixed incomes.

Why Comparing and Contrasting Is Important

Comparing and contrasting requires students to identify similarities and differences between places, people, or things. Analyzing differences and similarities helps students understand and remember key information about the places, people, or things being compared. Students can learn to identify similarities and differences quickly by looking for words that signal comparisons and contrasts.

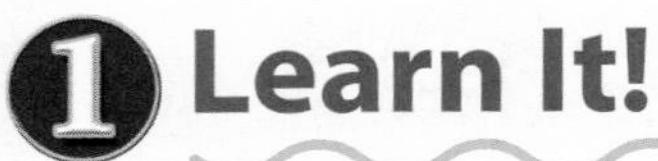

Use a set of common objects to teach how to compare and contrast. For example, use two oranges, and then an orange and a carrot, leaves from two different trees, or two student backpacks. Draw a Venn diagram on the board, and have volunteers list the similarities and differences that they see. BL

Reading Social Studies

Comparing and Contrasting

Reading Skill

When you *compare* people, things, or ideas, you look for the similarities among them. When you *contrast* people, things, or ideas, you identify their differences.

Textbook authors sometimes use this structure to help readers see the similarities and differences between topics.

- Read the following paragraph.
- Then determine how Russia and the United States are similar and how they are different.

> Russia's official name is the Russian Federation. This name reflects the fact that Russia comprises, or is made up of, many different regions and territories. Like the United States, Russia is a federal republic, with power divided between national and regional governments. In the United States, some powers belong to the states, and others belong only to the national government. Some powers are shared by both levels of government. In Russia, the division of powers is less clear because the new Russian government is still developing.
>
> —*from page 409*

In a Venn diagram, differences are listed in the outer parts of the circles. Similarities are described where the circles overlap.

Reading Tip

As you read, look for signal words that show comparisons, such as *similarly, at the same time,* and *likewise*. Contrast signal words include *however, rather,* and *on the other hand.*

The Governments of Russia and the United States

Russia	Similarities	United States
The division of powers between regional governments and the national government is not clear.	• Both countries are federal republics. • Both countries divide power between national and regional governments.	Some powers are given solely to states and solely to the national government, while some powers are shared by both governments.

Reading Strategy — Organizing Information

Comparing and Contrasting Explain to students that another way to see similarities and differences easily is to organize the similarities and differences in a comparison frame. A comparison frame is a chart with a column for each of the subjects that are being compared and a row for each of the areas of comparison. For example, if you are comparing an orange and a carrot, *Orange* and *Carrot* would be the column headings, and *Color* and *Shape* could be two of the row labels. Important facts about each of the areas of comparison are listed in the boxes under each of the column headings. Have students use a comparison frame to compare and contrast two physical features in Russia. ELL

2 Practice It!

Read the following sentences from this unit that describe Russian leaders Ivan IV and Joseph Stalin.

- Draw a Venn diagram like the one shown below.
- List the differences and similarities between the two leaders.

Read to Write Activity

Read and take notes about Russia's physical geography in Chapter 13. Then find similar information about another region in your book. Write an essay that describes the similarities and differences between the two regions.

In 1547 Ivan IV declared himself czar, or emperor. He ruled harshly, using secret police to carry out his will, and earned the name "Ivan the Terrible." By conquering neighboring territories, Ivan expanded his empire south to the Caspian Sea and east past the Ural Mountains.

—*from page 390*

Lenin's policies were later continued by Joseph Stalin, who ruled the Soviet Union after Lenin's death in 1924. A harsh dictator, Stalin prevented the Soviet people from practicing their religions and had religious property seized. His secret police killed or imprisoned anyone who disagreed with his policies.

—*from page 392*

Ivan the Terrible

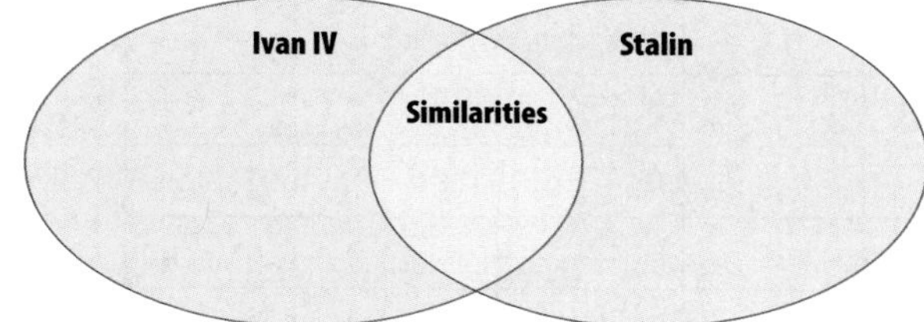

3 Apply It!

As you read Chapters 13, 14, and 15, look for people, things, or ideas that you can compare and contrast. As you read, put notes in a Venn diagram like the one above to help you compare and contrast.

2 Practice It!

Similarities: Both Ivan IV and Stalin ruled the region (Russia or the Soviet Union); both were harsh rulers who used the secret police to punish their opponents.
Differences: Ivan IV ruled in the 1500s; Stalin ruled in the 1900s. Ivan IV wanted to expand his empire, so he conquered neighboring territories; Stalin wanted to prevent the Soviet people from practicing their religions, and he used religious buildings for secular purposes. **OL**

3 Apply It!

As students read this unit, have them use a Venn diagram or a comparison frame to compare and contrast the following: (1) the landforms of eastern and western Russia; (2) life in Russia before and after the Bolshevik Revolution; and (3) the effects of command and market economies in Russia. **OL**

Reading Strategy — Read to Write

Organizing an Essay In a compare and contrast essay, students use two paragraphs to explain the similarities and differences between two items. Have students choose two climate regions in Russia to compare and contrast. Tell them to write a first paragraph that explains how the two regions are similar, using words that indicate similarity, such as *like* or *both*. Then tell them to write a second paragraph about the differences between the two regions. This paragraph should begin with a transition sentence that explains that this paragraph will indicate the differences. The rest of the second paragraph should describe the differences, using words or phrases that contrast the two regions. **AL**

Planning Guide

Key to Ability Levels	
BL Below level	**AL** Above level
OL On level	**ELL** English Language Learners

Key to Teaching Resources	
Print Material	DVD
CD-ROM	Transparency

Levels				Resources		Chapter Opener	Section 1	Section 2	Chapter Assess
BL	OL	AL	ELL						
FOCUS									
BL	OL	AL	ELL	Transparency	**Daily Focus Skills Transparencies**		13-1	13-2	
TEACH									
BL	OL		ELL	Print Material	**Guided Reading Activity, URB***		p. 35	p. 36	
BL	OL	AL	ELL	Print Material	**Content Vocabulary Activity, URB***		p. 37	p. 37	
BL	OL	AL	ELL	Print Material	**Academic Vocabulary Activity, URB**		p. 39	p. 39	
BL	OL	AL	ELL	Print Material	**Differentiated Instruction Activity, URB**			p. 41	
BL	OL	AL	ELL	Print Material	**Chart, Graph, and Map Skills Activity, URB**		p. 43		
	OL	AL		Print Material	**Critical Thinking Activity, URB**		p. 45	p. 45	
BL	OL	AL	ELL	Print Material	**Speaking and Listening Skills Activity, URB**		p. 47		
BL	OL	AL	ELL	Print Material	**Writing Skills Activity, URB**		p. 51		
BL	OL	AL	ELL	Print Material	**School-to-Home Connection Activity, URB***		p. 55	p. 55	
BL	OL	AL	ELL	Print Material	**Regional Atlas Activities, URB**		pp. 1–7	pp. 1–7	
BL	OL	AL	ELL	Print Material	**GeoLab Activity, URB**		p. 23		
BL	OL		ELL	Print Material	**Reading Skills Activity, URB**		p. 25	p. 25	
BL	OL		ELL	Print Material	**Reading Essentials and Note-Taking Guide***		p. 91	p. 94	
	OL			Print Material	**Interactive Geography Activity**		p. 33	p. 33	
BL	OL	AL	ELL	Transparency	**In-Text Map Overlay and Population Pyramid Transparencies**	5	5B	5C–5F	5
BL	OL	AL	ELL	Print Material	**Outline Map Resource Book**	p. 42			
BL	OL	AL	ELL	Print Material	**NGS World Atlas***	✓	✓	✓	
BL	OL	AL	ELL	Print Material	**NGS World Desk Map**	✓	✓	✓	✓
BL	OL	AL	ELL	Print Material	**World Literature Library**	✓	✓	✓	✓
BL	OL	AL	ELL	Print Material	**Writer's Guidebook**	✓	✓	✓	✓
BL	OL	AL	ELL	CD-ROM	**Vocabulary PuzzleMaker CD-ROM***	✓	✓	✓	✓
	OL	AL		CD-ROM	**Primary Sources CD-ROM**	✓	✓	✓	✓
BL	OL	AL	ELL	DVD	**StudentWorks™ Plus DVD**	✓	✓	✓	✓

Note: Please refer to the *Unit Resource Book: Russia* for this chapter's URB materials.

* Also available in Spanish

TeacherWorks Plus
All-In-One Planner and Resource Center

- Interactive Lesson Planner
- Interactive Teacher Edition
- Fully editable blackline masters
- Section Spotlight Videos Launch
- Differentiated Lesson Plans
- Printable reports of daily assignments
- Standards Tracking System

Levels				Resources	Chapter Opener	Section 1	Section 2	Chapter Assess
BL	OL	AL	ELL					
TEACH *(continued)*								
BL	OL	AL	ELL	Section Video Program Activities	✓	✓	✓	✓
BL	OL	AL	ELL	World Music: A Cultural Legacy	✓	✓	✓	✓
BL	OL	AL	ELL	Writing Process Transparencies	✓	✓	✓	✓
Teacher Resources				Building Academic Vocabulary	✓	✓	✓	✓
				Strategies for Success	✓	✓	✓	✓
				Teacher's Guide to Differentiated Instruction	✓	✓	✓	✓
				Presentation Plus! DVD	✓	✓	✓	✓
ASSESS								
BL	OL	AL	ELL	Quizzes and Tests		p. 147	p. 148	p. 149
BL	OL	AL	ELL	Authentic Assessment With Rubrics		p. 13		p. 13
BL	OL	AL	ELL	Standardized Test Practice				p. 49
BL	OL	AL	ELL	*ExamView® Assessment Suite* CD-ROM*		13-1	13-2	Ch. 13
BL	OL	AL	ELL	Interactive Tutor Self-Assessment CD-ROM		13-1	13-2	
CLOSE								
BL			ELL	Reteaching Activity, URB		p. 53	p. 53	p. 53
BL	OL		ELL	Reading and Study Skills Foldables™	p. 74	p. 74	p. 74	p. 74
BL	OL	AL	ELL	Graphic Organizer Transparencies and Strategies		✓	✓	
BL	OL	AL	ELL	*Exploring Our World* in Graphic Novel	p. 65	p. 65	p. 65	

CHAPTER 13

Integrating Technology

Using Study Central: Main Ideas

Technology Product

The Study Central Web site lists the main ideas for each section of a chapter. The main ideas

- highlight key points for students that will be used in other tabs of the Study Central Web site;
- serve as a starting point for class discussions on the focus of each section;
- reinforce section content by having students pose and answer questions based on the main ideas;
- provide practice and review of test taking skills and culminate with section-based activities.

Objectives

The main ideas help students

- build comprehension and study skills;
- enable students to practice developing and answering questions.

Steps

- Locate the Web page for the textbook being studied on the Glencoe Web site glencoe.com.
- Click on **Study Central** under *Textbook Resources.*
- On the Study Central Web site (a new window will have opened), select a chapter and section using the drop-down arrows and click **Enter.**
- Click on the **Main Ideas** tab and then on a Main Idea to engage in a discussion on that topic.
- Have students write and review questions based on the statement, using examples as needed.
- Click on Steps 2 and 3 to discuss the skills involved in answering the questions and to engage students in the activity.
- Discuss the questions again with students to evaluate their answers.

Social Studies ONLINE

	Student	Teacher	Parent
Beyond the Textbook	●		●
Chapter Overviews	●		●
Concepts in Motion	●		●
ePuzzles and Games	●		●
Literature Connections		●	
Multi-Language Glossaries	●		●
Online Student Edition	●	●	●
Section Videos	●	●	●
Self-Check Quizzes	●		●
Student Web Activities	●		●
Study Central™	●		●
Teaching Today		●	
TIME Current Events	●		●
Vocabulary eFlashcards	●		●
Web Activity Lesson Plans		●	

- **Timed Readings Plus in Social Studies** helps students increase their reading rate and fluency while maintaining comprehension. The 400-word passages are similar to those found on state and national assessments.
- **Reading in the Content Area: Social Studies** concentrates on six essential reading skills that help students better comprehend what they read. The book includes 75 high-interest nonfiction passages written at increasing levels of difficulty.
- **Reading Social Studies** includes strategic reading instruction and vocabulary support in Social Studies content for ELLs and native speakers of English.
- **Content Vocabulary Workout** (Grades 6–8) accelerates reading comprehension through focused vocabulary development. Social Studies content vocabulary comes from the glossaries of Glencoe's Middle School Social Studies texts.
www.jamestowneducation.com

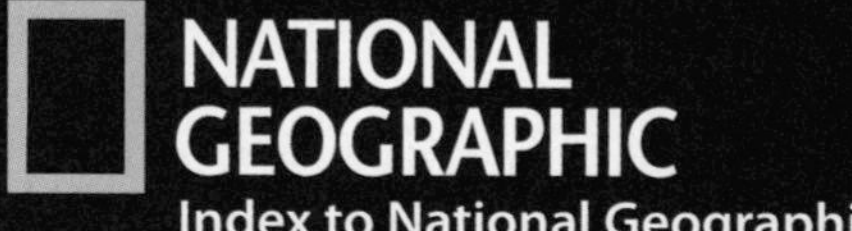

Index to National Geographic Magazine:

The following articles relate to this chapter:

- "Boreal: The Great Northern Forest," by Fen Montaigne, June 2002.
- "Russia's Frozen Inferno" by Jeremy Schmidt, August 2001.

National Geographic Society Products To order the following, call National Geographic at 1-800-368-2728:

- *National Geographic Atlas of the World* (Book).

Access National Geographic's new dynamic MapMachine Web site and other geography resources at:
www.nationalgeographic.com
www.nationalgeographic.com/maps

GLENCOE BOOKLINK 3

Use this database to search more than 30,000 titles to create a customized reading list for your students.

- Reading lists can be organized by students' reading level, author, genre, theme, or area of interest.
- The database provides Degrees of Reading Power™ (DRP) and Lexile™ readability scores for all selections.
- A brief summary of each selection is included.

Leveled reading suggestions for this chapter:

For students at a Grade 5 reading level:

- ***Russia,*** by Elma Schemenauer
- ***Russia,*** by Susan H. Gray
- ***Russian Girl: Life in an Old Russian Town,*** by Russ Kendall

For students at a Grade 6 reading level:

- ***Dropping in on Russia,*** by David C. King
- ***Russia,*** by Kristin Thoennes

For students at a Grade 7 reading level:

- ***Russia,*** by Kremena Spengler

For students at a Grade 8 reading level:

- ***Russia: The Land,*** by Greg Nickles

For students at a Grade 9 reading level:

- ***Russia,*** by Stillman D. Rogers
- ***Russia,*** by Kathleen Berton Murrell

Focus

The Essential Question

As students study the chapter, remind them to consider the chapter-based Essential Question. Answering this question will help them understand the important concepts in the chapter. In addition, the Hands-On Chapter Project relates the content from each section to the Essential Question. The steps in each section build on each other as students progress through the chapter. The Hands-On Chapter Project culminates in the Wrap Up activity on the Visual Summary page.

More About the Photo

Visual Literacy The Nenets reindeer herders have faced many challenges since the 1930s. At that time, Soviet leaders forced the Nenets onto collective farms and established boarding schools for the children of nomadic herders. These children lost much of their parents' culture and language while attending state-run schools. In the 1960s, the collective farms became state-owned farms, and most of the Nenets lost their reindeer and land. However, a few hundred households still herd small groups of reindeer on the Yamal Peninsula.

CHAPTER 13

Physical Geography of Russia

Essential Question

Human-Environment Interaction Russia's vast, cold landscapes include mountain ranges, plains, and evergreen forests. The country is also rich in natural resources, especially those used to create energy. To take advantage of these resources, however, Russia's people must overcome problems created by the country's landforms and climate. How do Russia's location and landforms affect its population and its use of resources?

Teach

The BIG Ideas *As you begin teaching each section, use these questions and activities to help students focus on the Big Ideas.*

Section 

Physical Features Ask: How might a country's physical features affect its economy? *(Possible answer: A country's physical features might affect its economy positively by providing resources to create goods or to sell to other countries, but the physical features may also affect the economy negatively by making farming or travel difficult.)* Explain to students that Russia has many natural resources, but its large size and cold climate make using these resources difficult. Tell them that they will learn more about these challenges in Section 1, which describes Russia's landforms, inland waters, and natural resources. **OL**

Section 

Climate and the Environment Ask: How might the climate of a country affect its economy? *(Climate often determines where people live and what jobs they have, so people in countries with both harsh and mild climates tend to live in the milder climates. Farming is more likely to be an important*

BIG Ideas

Section 1: Physical Features

BIG IDEA Changes occur in the use and importance of natural resources. Russians have used their soil, water, and timber for their own needs. As global demand for energy rises, Russia's rich supply of energy resources will be increasingly important.

Section 2: Climate and the Environment

BIG IDEA People's actions change the physical environment. Because much of Russia has a harsh climate, most Russians live where the climate is milder. The Russian people have adapted to their surroundings, but some of their actions have damaged the environment. Planning is necessary to take advantage of the country's great resources while preserving the environment.

FOLDABLES™ Study Organizer

Organizing Information Make this Foldable to help you organize facts about Russia's physical features, climate, and environment.

Step 1 Fold a piece of 11x17 paper in half.

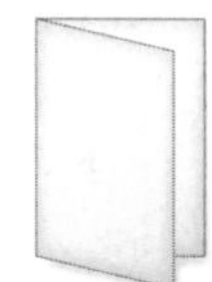

Step 2 Fold the bottom edge up two inches. Glue the outer edges of the tab to create two pockets.

Step 3 Label each pocket as shown. Use these pockets to hold notes taken on index cards or quarter sheets of paper.

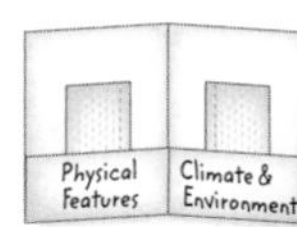

Reading and Writing As you read the chapter, write down facts on separate cards or sheets of paper and place them in the correct pocket. Use your cards to write quiz questions for each section topic.

To preview Chapter 13, go to glencoe.com.

Previewing the Region

If you have not already done so, engage students in the Regional Atlas and chart activities to help them become familiar with the general content of the region.

Dinah Zike's Foldables

Purpose This Foldable helps students organize facts from the chapter. Students should note facts from their reading on index cards and file them in the appropriate pockets in the Foldable. The completed Foldable will help students remember facts and review them for assessment. OL

More Foldables activities for this chapter can be found in *Dinah Zike's Reading and Study Skills Foldables* ancillary.

Social Studies ONLINE

Introduce students to chapter content and key terms by having them access the Chapter Overview at glencoe.com.

industry in milder climates as long as the soil and other conditions are favorable.) Tell students that in Section 2, they will learn about Russia's climate and how it affects where people live. They also will learn about the environmental challenges Russia faces as a result of former government policies. OL

Focus

Bellringer

Daily Focus Transparency 13-1

Guide to Reading

Answers to Graphic:

mountains, plateaus, lowland plains, grassy plains, treeless plains, volcanoes

Section Spotlight Video

To learn more about physical features in Russia, have students watch the Section Spotlight Video.

Guide to Reading

BIG Idea

Changes occur in the use and importance of natural resources.

Content Vocabulary

- fossil fuel *(p. 375)*
- softwood *(p. 375)*
- infrastructure *(p. 375)*

Academic Vocabulary

- benefit *(p. 373)*
- inhibit *(p. 375)*

Reading Strategy

Identifying Use a diagram like the one below to list six of Russia's major landforms.

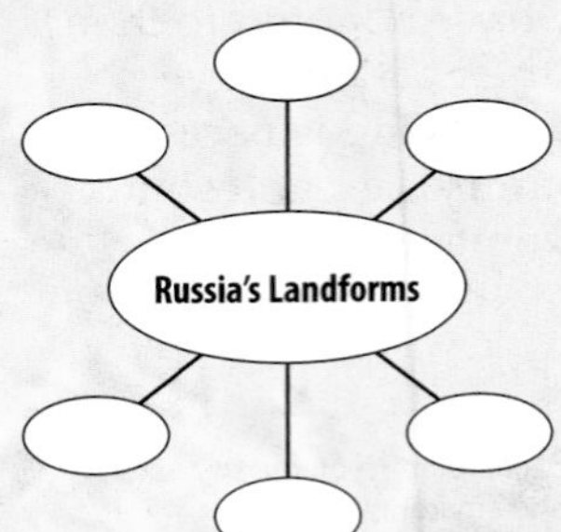

SECTION 1 Physical Features

Picture This The bubbling goo in this volcanic pool is like a pot of boiling soup. Here in far eastern Russia, a huge volcano exploded tens of thousands of years ago. The area now contains cold, rushing rivers, hot springs, and pools filled with steaming, toxic mud. As volcanic gases push their way up through the thick ooze, they create bubbles. The bubbles are evidence that forces under Earth's crust are always in motion. Read this section to learn more about the different types of physical features found in Russia.

▼ Volcanic crater on Kamchatka Peninsula in eastern Russia

Resource Manager

R Reading Strategies	C Critical Thinking	D Differentiated Instruction	W Writing Support	S Skill Practice
Teacher Edition • Setting a Purpose, p. 373 **Additional Resources** • Guid. Read., URB p. 35 • Cont. Vocab., URB p. 37 • Ac. Vocab., URB p. 39 • Read. Ess., p. 91	**Teacher Edition** • Compare/Contrast, p. 374 **Additional Resources** • Crit. Think., URB p. 45 • Authentic Assess., p. 13 • Quizzes and Tests, p. 147	**Teacher Edition** • Below G.L., p. 374 **Additional Resources** • Reteach., URB p. 53	**Teacher Edition** • Expository Writing, p. 375 **Additional Resources** • Writing Skills, URB p. 51	**Teacher Edition** • Using Geo. Skills, p. 373 **Additional Resources** • Chart, Graph, and Map Skills, URB p. 43 • Read. Skills, URB p. 25 • Speak/Listen Skills, URB p. 47 • Daily Focus Trans. 13-1 • Reg. Atlas, URB pp. 1–7

Landforms of Russia

Main Idea **Russia is a huge country with a location and landforms that greatly affect how people live.**

Geography and You If you have ever traveled across the United States, you know that it takes a long time. It would take twice as long to travel across Russia. Read to learn about the landforms of Russia's vast terrain.

Russia is the world's largest country. From east to west, it measures some 6,200 miles (9,980 km). Nearly twice as large as the United States, Russia straddles both Europe and Asia. The Ural Mountains serve as a dividing line between the European and Asian parts of Russia.

A Vast Northern Land

Because of its enormous size, Russia has a long coastline. Russia does not **benefit** from its closeness to the sea, though, because of its northern location. Most of its coast lies along waters that are frozen for much of the year. As a result, Russia has few seaports that are free of ice year-round. Through the Black Sea in the southwest, though, Russian ships have a warm-water route to the Mediterranean Sea.

Russia contains a variety of landforms. Rugged mountains and plateaus lie in the south and east. In the north and west, vast lowland plains reach to the horizon.

European Russia

Most of European Russia lies on the Northern European Plain. This fertile area has Russia's mildest climate, and about 75 percent of Russians live here. Moscow, the capital, and St. Petersburg, a large port city near the Baltic Sea, are located in this region. Much of Russia's agriculture and industry are found on the Northern European Plain.

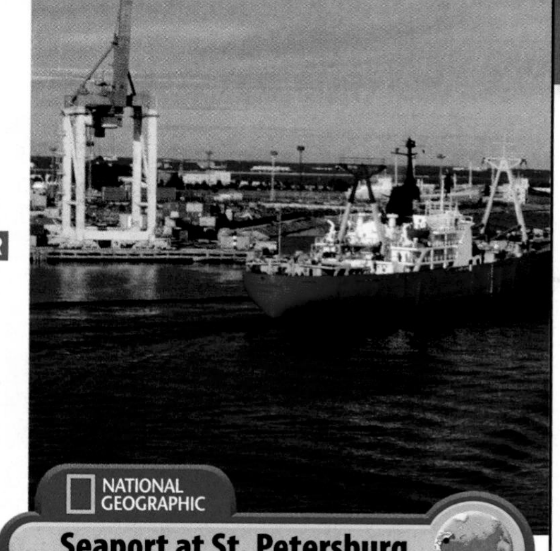

NATIONAL GEOGRAPHIC

Seaport at St. Petersburg

The port at St. Petersburg is one of the busiest in Russia, even though it is frozen three to four months every year. ***Location*** **Which sea provides a warm water outlet for Russian ships?**

Good farmland also lies farther south, along the Volga and other rivers. This area consists of a nearly treeless grassy plain. To the far south of European Russia are the rugged Caucasus Mountains. Located near a fault line, the Caucasus area is prone to destructive earthquakes. Other mountains—the Urals—divide European and Asian Russia. Worn down by erosion, the Urals are not very tall.

Asian Russia

East of the Urals is Asian Russia, which includes Siberia. Northern Siberia has one of the coldest climates in the world. It is a vast treeless plain that remains frozen much of the year. The few people who live here make their living fishing, hunting seals and walruses, or herding reindeer.

Social Studies ONLINE

Student Web Activity Visit glencoe.com and complete the Chapter 13 Web Activity about Siberia.

Teach

R Reading Strategy

Setting a Purpose Have students read the Main Idea. **Ask:** **What do you think you will learn about in this section?** *(Russia's physical features and how these features affect how people live)* Ask students to think of one question they would like to have answered about Russia's physical features. Then tell them to look for the answer as they read the section. **BL**

S Skill Practice

Using Geography Skills Have students locate the Black Sea on a map or globe and trace the route ships would take from this sea to the Mediterranean Sea. **Ask:** **Why do you think the Black Sea is so important to people in Russia?** *(It has ports that are ice free year-round.)* **OL**

Caption Answer:
the Black Sea

Social Studies ONLINE

Objectives and answers to the Student Web Activity can be found at glencoe.com under the Web Activity Lesson Plan for this chapter.

Differentiated Instruction

Chart, Graph, and Map Skills Activity, URB pp. 43–44

Using a Comparison Frame

Objective: Compare and contrast geographic features of the United States and Russia.

Focus: Discuss the difference between "comparing" and "contrasting."

Teach: Have volunteers draw a comparison frame on the board.

Assess: Fill in the empty spaces in the comparison frame using information from the text.

Close: Discuss how a comparison frame helps sort and organize information.

Differentiated Instruction Strategies

BL Ask students to identify the subjects and categories in the comparison frame in the activity.

AL Locate other statistics about the United States and Russia and use a comparison frame to compare and contrast these statistics.

ELL Draw a comparison frame to compare a baseball and a football.

D Differentiated Instruction

Below Grade Level To help students read the graphs more easily, have them use a sheet of notebook paper to cover two graphs and focus on only one graph at a time. **BL**

C Critical Thinking

Comparing and Contrasting

Ask: How are the Caspian Sea and Lake Baikal alike? *(They are two of the largest inland bodies of water in the world, and both are important habitats for fish and other aquatic life.)* **How are they different?** *(The Caspian Sea is a saltwater lake, while Lake Baikal is a freshwater lake.)* **OL**

This Reading Skill (Comparing and Contrasting) was introduced in this unit.

Graph Skills

Answers:

1. United States; Russia
2. natural gas

Reading Check Answer: The Kamchatka Peninsula is mountainous and has many volcanoes.

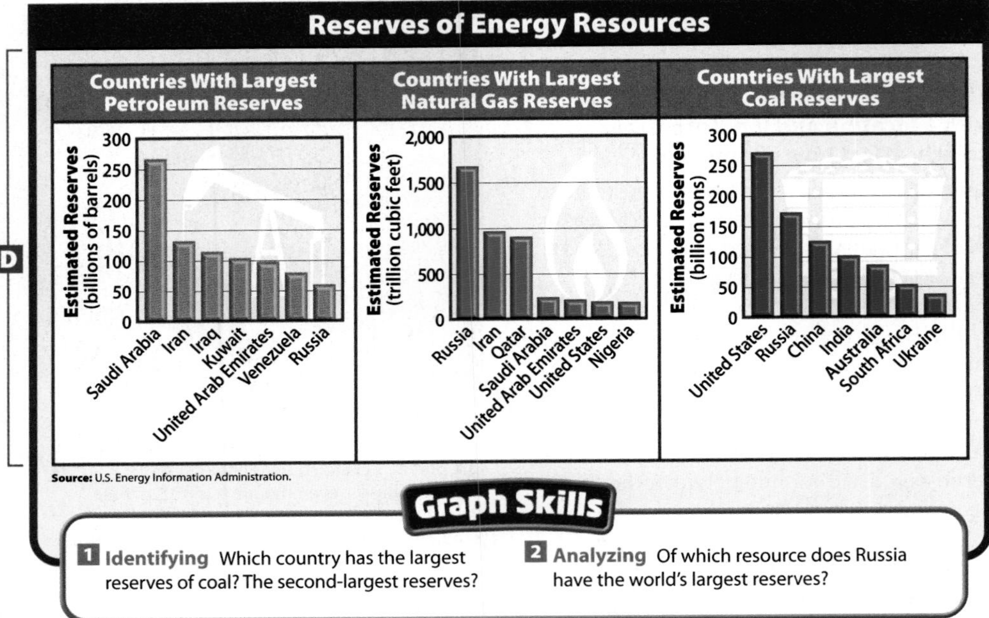

Graph Skills

1. **Identifying** Which country has the largest reserves of coal? The second-largest reserves?
2. **Analyzing** Of which resource does Russia have the world's largest reserves?

To the south of the northern plains area is a region of dense forests where people make their living by lumbering or hunting. Plains, plateaus, and mountain ranges cover the southern part of Siberia.

Mountains also rise on the far eastern Kamchatka (kam·CHAHT·kuh) Peninsula. These mountains are part of the Ring of Fire. This is a region along the rim of the Pacific Ocean where tectonic plates meet and cause Earth's crust to be unstable. As a result, Kamchatka has many volcanoes.

Inland Waters

Russia has many rivers. The Volga is European Russia's major river. Russians have long relied on the Volga for transportation. In Siberia, many rivers begin in mountains in the south and flow north across marshy lowlands, emptying into the frigid Arctic Ocean. The Lena (LEE·nuh), the Yenisey (YIH·nih·SAY), and the Ob' (AWB) are among the longest rivers in the world.

Russia includes or borders many inland bodies of water. Almost the size of California, the Caspian Sea in southwestern Russia is the largest inland body of water in the world. It is actually a saltwater lake that is an important resource for fishing. Major oil and gas deposits are found near or under the Caspian Sea.

In southern Siberia lies Lake Baikal—the world's deepest freshwater lake. The lake holds one-fifth of the world's supply of unfrozen freshwater. Baikal is home to many kinds of aquatic life, including Baikal seals, or nerpa, the only seals that live in freshwater.

Reading Check **Describing** Describe the landforms of the Kamchatka Peninsula.

Hands-On Chapter Project Step 1

Exploring Russian Life Through Posters

Step 1: Planning the Posters Groups of students will do research to plan posters that show how people live in various parts of Russia.

Essential Question How do Russia's location and landforms affect its population and its use of resources?

Directions Remind students that although most Russians live in European Russia, people live all across Russia, even in some of the most inhospitable areas. Organize the class into groups of three to five students. Have each group choose a specific area in Russia to research. Each group should choose a different area. Students may use the textbook, library, and Internet resources. Tell students that they will use what they learn to create a poster that shows how people in that area live. Students should research the types of housing and transportation in the area they have chosen, as well as how people make their living and whether people live primarily in cities or rural areas.

Summarizing After students complete their research, ask each group to describe how location and resources have affected people's choice of housing and transportation in that area. **OL**

(Chapter Project continued in Section 2)

Natural Resources

Main Idea **Although Russia has plentiful resources, many of them are in remote Siberia and are difficult to obtain.**

Geography and You Have you ever worked or played outside in the extreme cold of winter? Read to find out how a cold climate affects Russians' use of resources.

Russia is rich in natural resources. As the graphs on the previous page show, Russia is a leader in reserves of the **fossil fuels**—oil, natural gas, and coal. The country also has major deposits of iron ore, which the Russians have used to develop a large steel industry. Other important metals mined in Russia include copper and gold. W

Russia's other great resource is timber. Trees cover much of Siberia, and Russia produces about a fifth of the world's **softwood.** This wood from evergreen trees is used in buildings and for making furniture.

Russia's large size and cold climate **inhibit,** or limit, humans' ability to use its many resources. Siberia is vast and remote, and its resources are difficult to use because of the area's lack of **infrastructure.** Infrastructure is the system of roads and railroads for transporting materials. W

In addition to transportation difficulties, Siberia's cold climate brings other challenges. Besides trying to stay warm, workers must keep their equipment from freezing. Some advances in technology have made it easier to collect Siberia's resources. For example, a pipeline now carries natural gas from Siberia to Europe.

Reading Check **Explaining** Why are Russia's natural resources difficult to gather?

W Writing Support

Expository Writing Have students write a brief summary of Russia's natural resources. Remind them to read the main idea on this page before writing their summaries. If needed, provide students with a graphic organizer to help them compile facts for their summaries. **OL**

Reading Check **Answer:** Russia is mountainous, the climate is very cold, and there is a lack of infrastructure.

Assess

Social Studies ONLINE
Study Central™ provides summaries, interactive games, and online graphic organizers to help students review content.

Close

Identifying Have students name at least five important natural resources in Russia, including at least one source of energy, one metal, and one other resource. **OL**

Section 1 Review

Social Studies ONLINE
Study Central™ To review this section, go to glencoe.com.

Vocabulary

1. **Explain** the meaning of *fossil fuel, softwood,* and *infrastructure* by using each term in a sentence.

Main Ideas

2. **Comparing and Contrasting** Use a Venn diagram like the one below to compare and contrast physical features in European Russia and Siberia.

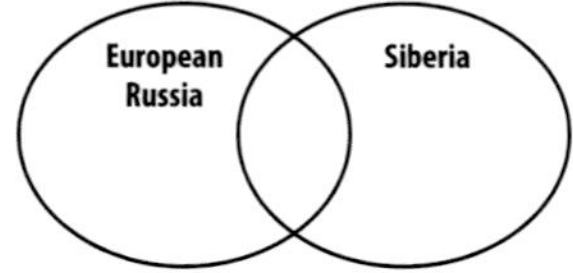

3. **Explaining** Why are Siberia's resources valuable?

Critical Thinking

4. **Analyzing Information** In what part of the country does most of Russia's population live? Why?
5. **BIG Idea** Name some natural resources found in Russia. How do these resources contribute to the Russian and world economies?
6. **Challenge** How might a country's far-north location affect its people and economy? Consider factors such as agriculture and transportation.

Writing About Geography

7. **Expository Writing** Write a paragraph describing what you believe is Russia's most prominent physical feature. Be sure to explain your choice.

Answers

1. Sentences should use vocabulary words according to their definitions in the section and the Glossary.
2. **European Russia:** primarily on the Northern European Plain; Russia's mildest climate; good farmland; Caucasus Mountains to the far south. **Siberia:** cold climate; treeless plain to the north; dense forests, plains, plateaus, and mountain ranges to the south. **Both:** plains, mountains, rivers, and other bodies of water; coastlines that are frozen much of the year
3. Siberia's resources, such as natural gas and timber, are important not only to Russia but also to the rest of the world.
4. Most of the Russian population lives in European Russia, because it has the mildest climate and good farmland.
5. Answers may include coal, iron ore, natural gas, oil, copper, gold, and timber. Russia has used iron ore to build a large steel industry. Coal, natural gas, and oil are important sources of energy and may be sold to other countries. Russia also supplies about a fifth of the world's softwood used in buildings and furniture.
6. As Russia's location illustrates, a country's far-north location can prevent farming and settlement in certain areas. The cold climate in far-north locations also can make it difficult to build roads and railroads.
7. Answers should provide evidence to support the features chosen.

Focus

R Reading Strategy

Previewing Have students read the question in the title. Then have them look at the photos in the feature. **Ask:** **What do you think you will learn about in this feature?** *(Possible answer: the importance of Russia's forests and how using them will impact the environment)* **OL**

Teach

Have students create a graphic organizer like the one below. As they read the feature, have students include the key points supporting and opposing the use of Russia's forests. **OL**

For Development	Against Development
(The trees grow back well; forests are resources that are meant to be used.)	*(Forest use does not provide for long-term economic growth; it destroys the last old-growth forests in Russia and threatens their ecosystems.)*

C Critical Thinking

Analyzing Information **Ask:** **Why is Sedykh a credible source?** *(He is a scientist with the Sukachev Forest Institute.)* **AL**

Additional Support

Russia's Forests: Should They Be Used for Economic Development?

R

The boreal forests are located south of the Arctic Circle. They are found in northern Canada, Europe, and Russia. The forests contain most of the world's unfrozen freshwater. Many species of birds and animals live there or migrate through the forests. The forests are also home to various indigenous peoples. The Russian boreal forest, also known as the taiga, extends about 4,000 miles (6,436 km) across northern Russia. Some Russians want to develop the resources of the forest, such as lumber, oil, and natural gas. Many environmentalists, though, would like to preserve the forest and its biodiversity.

For Development

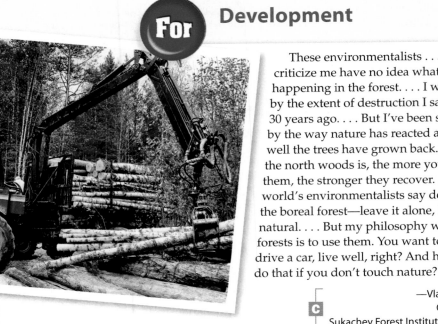

These environmentalists . . . who criticize me have no idea what's really happening in the forest. . . . I was shocked by the extent of destruction I saw here 30 years ago. . . . But I've been surprised by the way nature has reacted and how well the trees have grown back. The law of the north woods is, the more you destroy them, the stronger they recover. . . . The world's environmentalists say don't touch the boreal forest—leave it alone, leave it natural. . . . But my philosophy with the forests is to use them. You want to watch TV, drive a car, live well, right? And how do you do that if you don't touch nature?

C

—Vladimir Sedykh
Chief Scientist
Sukachev Forest Institute, Novosibirsk

FastFacts

Threats to Siberia's Tigers Russia's vast boreal forests are home to the Amur tiger, also known as the Siberian tiger. These shy cats can grow to 11 feet long and 550 pounds. Almost all of their body parts are in demand by makers of traditional Chinese medicines. For example, tiger bone is used to treat rheumatism. That makes Siberian tigers attractive to poachers. Under Soviet rule, the Siberian tiger was protected by law. However, after the fall of communism, logging companies built roads through the taiga to get to valuable timber. Poachers followed. Russia has strict laws protecting the tigers, but these laws are not always enforced. Wildfires set by loggers are another threat because they destroy the tigers' habitat. **OL**

Against Development

C The current economic model of forest use is oriented [directed] mainly towards the export of raw materials and cannot provide long-term economic growth for the region. This model . . . destroys the last old-growth forests in Russia, which have now become the most threatened natural ecosystems. If the current situation does not change, we will lose the most valuable old-growth areas in [the] next 5–10 years. Logging the last European old-growth forests will not solve any social or economical problem in Russia. In its best light it will only postpone the social and economic crash in the forest industry and logging settlements by a matter of several years.

—from *The Last of the Last: The Old-growth Forests of Boreal Europe*
Dmitry Aksenov, Mikhail Karpachevskiy, Sarah Lloyd, and Alexei Yaroshenko

You Be the Geographer

1. **Summarizing** In your own words, summarize the opinion of each writer about how the forest should be used.
2. **Critical Thinking** What argument does Sedykh make to appeal to people who want to live a modern lifestyle?
3. **Read to Write** Do you think developers and environmentalists can work together to use and preserve the boreal forest? Explain your opinion in a one-page essay.

YOU Decide

C Critical Thinking

Identifying Central Issues Ask: There are several arguments presented in this passage. **What is the main argument for this position?** *(The current use of the forests destroys the last old-growth forests in Russia and threatens their ecosystem.)* **OL**

Assess/Close

Ask the class to think of other areas where forests are threatened. *(Answers may include the rain forests of South America and forests in the Pacific Northwest of the United States.)* Lead the class in a discussion of the importance of the world's forests. **OL**

You Be the Geographer

Answers:

1. Sedykh believes that forests are a resource that should be used and will grow back. The other writers believe that using the forests will threaten forest ecosystems and cannot sustain economic growth.
2. He says that it is not possible to have a modern lifestyle without touching nature.
3. Answers will vary but should refer to the arguments in the feature.

Activity: Connecting With the United States

Logging in the United States Ask: In what areas of the United States do you think logging is an important industry? *(the Pacific Northwest, Alaska, West Virginia, the Carolinas)* Explain that one of the most widely used techniques in logging in the United States is clear-cutting. In clear-cutting, loggers remove all the trees in a given area. Sometimes these areas are huge rectangular swaths of forests that stretch down a hillside. Environmentalists argue that clear-cutting destroys animal habitat and leads to increased erosion and flooding. Proponents argue that clear-cutting enables sunlight to reach small plants on the forest floor, encouraging them to grow. They also argue that forests have been able to recover from clear-cutting in the past. Organize students into two groups. Ask one group to research the arguments for clear-cutting, and have the other group research the arguments against this practice. Then have the two groups defend their positions in a debate. **AL**

Focus

Bellringer

Daily Focus Transparency 13-2

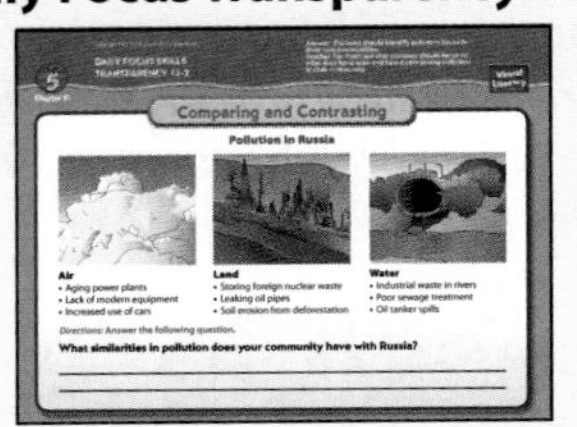

Guide to Reading

Answers to Graphic:

Russia's Climate:
in the high latitudes; much of the country lies inland, away from warm currents; elevations in the far north too low to block Arctic air; mountains in the south and east block warm air from lower latitudes

Section Spotlight Video

To learn more about the climate and environment in Russia, have students watch the Section Spotlight Video.

Resource Manager

R Reading Strategies	C Critical Thinking	D Differentiated Instruction	W Writing Support	S Skill Practice
Teacher Edition • Ac. Vocab., p. 382 **Additional Resources** • Guid. Read., URB p. 36 • Cont. Vocab., URB p. 37 • Ac. Vocab., URB p. 39 • Read. Ess.p. 94	**Teacher Edition** • Det. Cause/Effect, p. 379 **Additional Resources** • Crit. Think., URB p. 45 • Quizzes and Tests, p. 148	**Teacher Edition** • Kinesthetic, p. 380 **Additional Resources** • Diff. Instr., URB p. 41	**Teacher Edition** • Expository Writing, p. 380	**Teacher Edition** • Using Geo. Skills, p. 379 **Additional Resources** • Read. Skills, URB p. 25 • Daily Focus Trans. 13-2 • Reg. Atlas, URB pp. 1–7

Guide to Reading

BIG Idea

People's actions change the physical environment.

Content Vocabulary

- permafrost *(p. 380)*
- taiga *(p. 380)*
- smog *(p. 380)*
- pollutant *(p. 380)*

Academic Vocabulary

- period *(p. 379)*
- decline *(p. 382)*

Reading Strategy

Analyzing Information Use a diagram like the one below to list factors that lead to Russia's cold climate, especially those related to location and landforms.

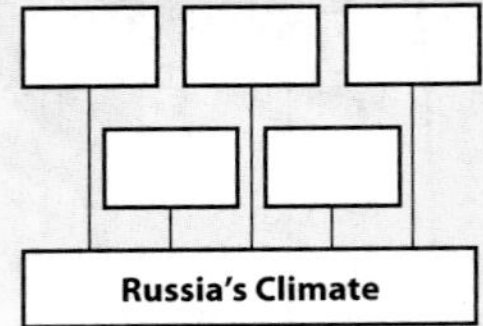

SECTION 2

Climate and the Environment

Picture This For many Russians, ice fishing is a favorite pastime. In this photo, an ice fisher is shielded from the cold winds blowing along the Tom River in Siberia. The fisher must often reach into the icy water and remove slush from the hole to keep it from freezing over. Read this section to learn how Russia's many climate zones have influenced its people.

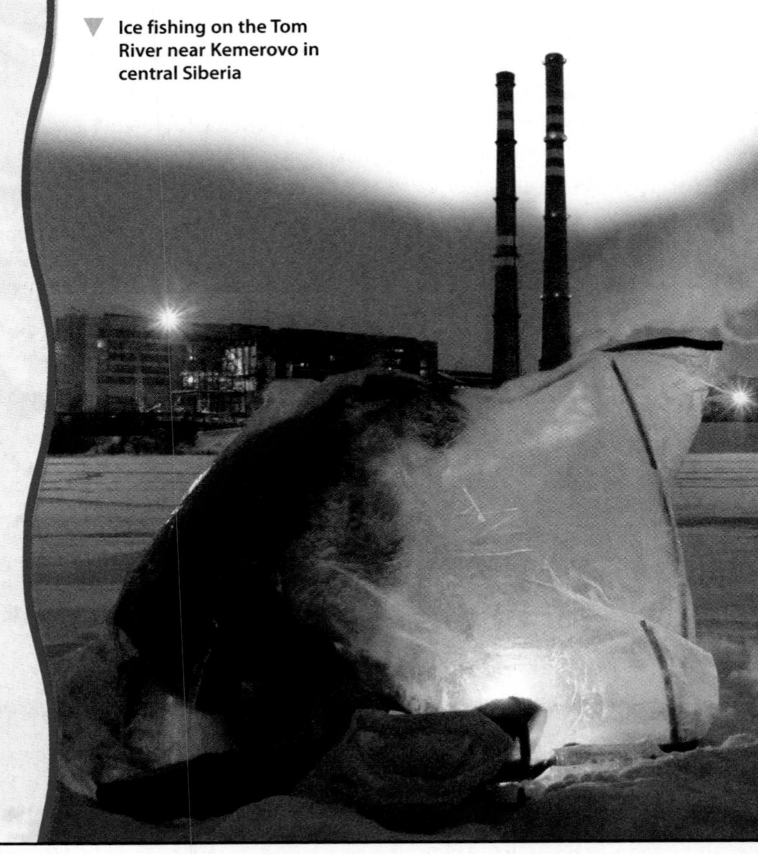

Ice fishing on the Tom River near Kemerovo in central Siberia

A Cold Climate

Main Idea **Russia has a generally cool to cold climate because of its northern location.**

Geography and You Have you ever experienced a winter that was extremely cold and snowy and seemed to go on too long? Read to find out why much of Russia has long, cold winters and short summers.

As **Figure 1** shows, most of Russia lies in the high latitudes. As a result, Russia receives very little of the sun's heat even during summer. In addition, much of Russia lies inland, far from the moist, warm currents of the Atlantic and Pacific Oceans that help moderate temperature in other parts of the world. In Russia's far north, elevations are generally too low to prevent the southerly flow of icy Arctic air. In the country's south and east, tall mountains stop the warm air coming from the lower latitudes. Consequently, Russia has a generally cool to cold climate. Large areas of the country experience only winter- and summerlike conditions. Spring and autumn are simply brief **periods** of changing weather.

NATIONAL GEOGRAPHIC Maps In MOtion See StudentWorks™ Plus or glencoe.com.

Figure 1 **Russia: Climate Zones**

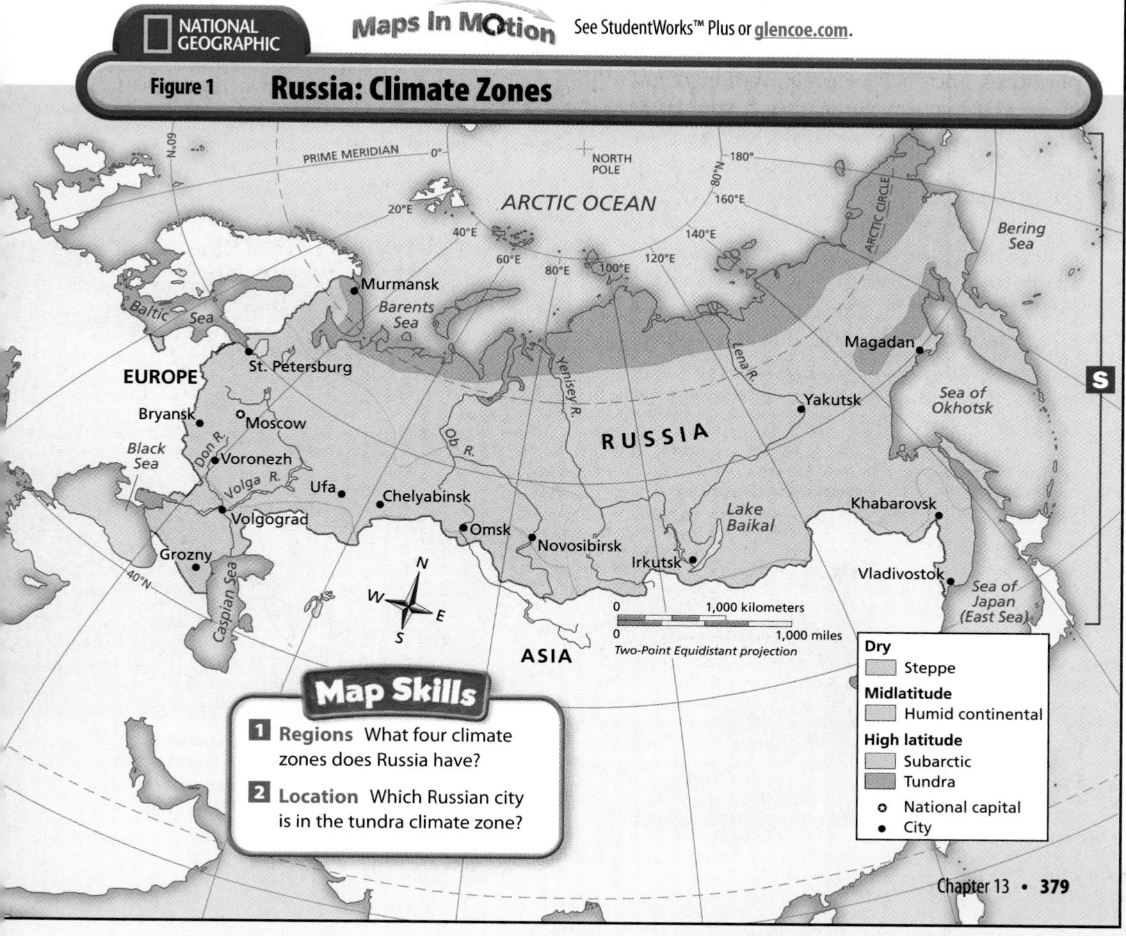

Map Skills

1. **Regions** What four climate zones does Russia have?
2. **Location** Which Russian city is in the tundra climate zone?

Teach

C Critical Thinking

Determining Cause and Effect **Ask:** **How do the warm currents of the Atlantic and Pacific affect climates?** *(They moderate temperatures in other parts of the world besides Russia.)* **OL**

S Skill Practice

Using Geography Skills Have students study the order the climate terms appear in the key and compare this to the way the colors appear on the map. **Ask:** **What patterns do you see?** *(The climates in the legend go from warmer to colder; on the map, the climates get cooler as you go from south to north.)* **OL**

Map Skills

Answers:

1. steppe, humid continental, subarctic, tundra
2. Murmansk

Hands-On Chapter Project Step 2

Exploring Russian Life Through Posters

Step 2: Making the Posters Groups of students will make the posters about life in Russia that they planned in Section 1.

Directions Ask the groups to look for information in this section about the geographic areas they have chosen for their posters. Have students gather all the information they have found in the text and in outside research. Then have them use this information to make posters showing how people live in these regions. Posters may include pictures of typical houses, farms, cars, trains, factories, or other features of Russian life.

Putting It Together Have each group present its poster to the class and explain how the physical features and climate affect how people live there. **OL**

(Chapter Project cont. on the Visual Summary page)

D Differentiated Instruction

Kinesthetic Have students use art materials to create dioramas or other models of Russia's tundra and subarctic zones. Instruct students to use the text to write brief captions describing their models. **OL**

W Writing Support

Expository Writing After reading this subsection, have students write a problem-solution essay about Russia's environmental challenges. Before students write, instruct them to complete a graphic organizer to help plan their writing. **OL**

Reading Check Answer: Mountains in the south and east block warm air from lower latitudes, and the plains in the north do not block cold Arctic air. As a result, Russia's climate is very cold.

Caption Answer:
Because of its high latitude, Russia receives little of the sun's heat, even during summer.

Most of western Russia has a humid continental climate. Summers are warm and rainy, and winters are cold and snowy. Moscow's average July temperature is just 66°F (19°C), while its average January temperature can plunge as low as 16°F (–9°C). The cold winters have played an important role in Russia's history. During World War II, bitter cold halted the German army's advance into Russia. Better-prepared Russian troops soon forced the Germans to retreat.

D In contrast, the northern and eastern areas of Russia have short, cool summers and long, snowy winters. The northern tundra climate zone is so cold that moisture in the soil cannot evaporate. Cold temperatures and lack of precipitation result in **permafrost**, a permanently frozen layer of soil beneath the surface. Only mosses, lichens, and small shrubs can survive in the tundra.

South of the tundra lies the subarctic zone, Russia's largest climate area. Warmer temperatures support a greater variety of vegetation than the tundra does. The **taiga**, the world's largest coniferous forest, stretches about 4,000 miles (6,436 km) across the subarctic zone. This forest is roughly the size of the United States.

Reading Check **Determining Cause and Effect** How do Russia's landforms affect the country's climate?

Russia's Environment

Main Idea **As Russia's economy expanded, the country's environment was poorly cared for.**

Geography and You What might happen if the garbage in your neighborhood was not disposed of properly? Read to learn about Russia's efforts to clean up its environment.

W For most of the 1900s, Russia's leaders stressed economic growth. They ignored the damage this growth caused to the environment. Today, **smog**—a thick haze of fog and chemicals—blankets many of Russia's cities. Factories pour **pollutants**, which are chemicals and smoke particles that cause pollution, into the air. Many Russians suffer from lung diseases and cancer.

Russia's Varying Climates

NATIONAL GEOGRAPHIC

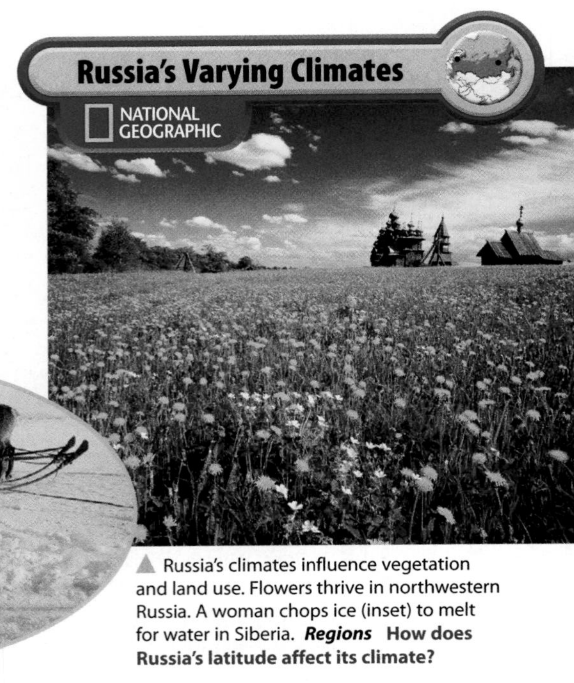

▲ Russia's climates influence vegetation and land use. Flowers thrive in northwestern Russia. A woman chops ice (inset) to melt for water in Siberia. ***Regions*** **How does Russia's latitude affect its climate?**

Differentiated Instruction

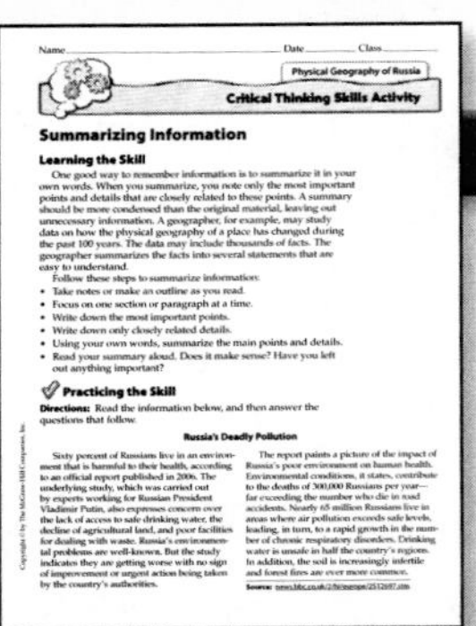

Critical Thinking Activity, URB pp. 45–46

Summarizing Information

Objective: To summarize information about Russia's pollution and the Kamchatka Peninsula

Focus: Ask students how a summary is different from the text it summarizes.

Teach: Have students identify the main points and supporting details as they read.

Assess: Write a one-sentence summary of the passage about Russia's pollution.

Close: Summarize the passage about the Kamchatka Peninsula.

Differentiated Instruction Strategies

- **BL** Have students make an outline of main ideas.
- **AL** Have students write a one-paragraph summary of each passage.
- **ELL** Circle words in each passage that are unfamiliar, and find the definitions of these words before writing the summaries.

Farewell to Matyora

By Valentin Rasputin

And so the village had lived on in its lean and simple way, clinging to its spot on the bluff by the left bank [of the Angara River], greeting and seeing off the years, like the water that joined [the villagers] to other settlements and that had helped feed them since time **immemorial.** And just as the flowing water seemed to have no end or limit, the village seemed ageless: some went off to their Maker, others were born, old buildings collapsed, new ones were built. And the village lived on, through hard times and troubles, for three hundred and more years . . . until the rumor thundered down on them that the village would be no more. A dam was being built downriver on the Angara for a hydroelectric power station, and the waters would rise in the rivers and streams, flooding much land, including, first and foremost, Matyora. Even if you were to pile five islands like Matyora one on top of the other, they would still be flooded and you wouldn't be able to show the spot where people once lived. They would have to move. It wasn't easy to believe that it really would come to pass. . . . A year after the first rumors an evaluating **commission** came by [boat] and began assessing the **depreciation** of the buildings and determining how much money they were worth. There was no more doubt about the fate of Matyora, it was living out its last years. Somewhere on the right bank they were building a new settlement for the . . . state-owned farm, into which they were bringing all the neighboring **kolkhozes,** and some that were not so neighboring, and it was decided, so as not to have to deal with rubbish, to set fire to the old villages.

From: *Farewell to Matyora*, by Valentin Rasputin, translated by Antonina W. Bouis, Evanston, Ill.: Northwestern University Press, 1979.

Analyzing Literature

1. **Identifying Central Issues** What attitude do you think the government has toward the village?
2. **Read to Write** Take the role of a local government official and write an editorial explaining why you either support or oppose the building of the dam.

World Literature

Valentin Rasputin
(1937–)

Born in Siberia, Valentin Rasputin often celebrates the region in his writing. The short novel *Farewell to Matyora* expresses his fear that modern life can erase the traditions of the villagers there.

Background Information

In Soviet times, huge power plants and hydroelectric projects were built to provide energy for heavy industry. Decisions to build factories and power plants were made by the Communist government without consulting the local communities that would be affected by such actions. The government's attempts at modernization often had serious effects on Russia's people.

Reader's Dictionary

immemorial: before memory

commission: official government body

depreciation: lowered value

kolkhozes: government-owned farming villages

Teach

Reading Strategy

Comparing After students have read the excerpt from *Farewell to Matyora*, ask them to draw a Venn diagram to compare and contrast the area as it was before the dam was built with how it would be after the dam was completed. **OL**

This **Reading Skill** (Comparing) was introduced in this unit.

Analyzing Literature

Answers:

1. The government thinks the village is expendable. It thinks of the buildings as simply being in the way of development ("rubbish"). The author probably values the village and its connection to history and traditional ways of life.
2. Answers will vary but should support either modernization efforts or the traditions of the community.

Additional Reading

Review suggested books before assigning them.

Fiction: ***Georgia to Georgia: Making Friends in the U.S.S.R*** by Laurie Dolphin is the story of a boy who travels with his family to the Soviet Republic of Georgia. He makes friends with a Georgian boy and learns a lot about Russian life and customs.

Biography: ***One More Border: The True Story of One Family's Escape from War-Torn Europe*** by William Kaplan and Shelley Tanaka tells the story of one refugee family's journey across Russia to Japan and on to North America to escape the Holocaust during World War II.

Nonfiction: ***Russia: The People*** by Greg Nickles discusses what daily life is like in Russia, including what food Russians eat, what clothes they wear, and what they do for fun.

For further reading, see BOOKLINK 3

R Reading Strategy

Academic Vocabulary **Ask:** What does the word *decline* mean in this sentence? *(decrease)* **ELL**

Reading Check Answer: Russia's government stressed economic growth at the expense of the environment.

Caption Answer: chemicals used in agriculture and industry, and poor sewer systems

Assess

Social Studies ONLINE
Study Central™ provides summaries, interactive games, and online graphic organizers to help students review content.

Close

Describing Have students name the four climate regions in Russia and give a brief description of each one. **OL**

Water Pollution

Water pollution is also a problem. Chemicals used in agriculture and industry often end up in rivers and lakes. Pollution entering Lake Baikal may be causing a **decline** in the populations of some animal species in the area. Another source of water pollution is poor sewer systems. Because of these problems, more than half of Russia's people do not have safe drinking water.

Cleaning Up

Steps have been taken to solve Russia's pollution problems. Other countries are providing Russia with aid to improve sewage systems and clean up heavily polluted sites. Cities are building more efficient power plants that use less energy and burn fuel more cleanly. Still, it will be a long time before Russia has a healthy environment.

Reading Check **Explaining** What government policies harmed Russia's environment?

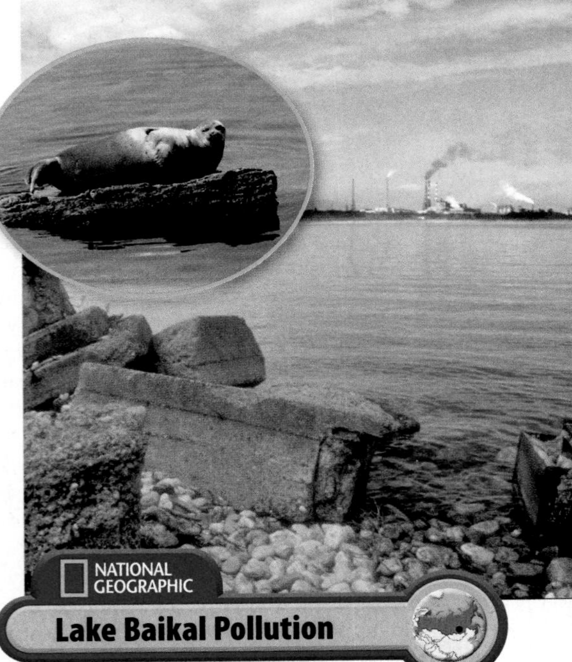

NATIONAL GEOGRAPHIC

Lake Baikal Pollution

Russian industries have polluted their environments, threatening species like the Baikal seal (inset), or nerpa. ***Human-Environment Interaction*** **What are sources of water pollution in Russia?**

Section 2 Review

Social Studies ONLINE
Study Central™ To review this section, go to glencoe.com.

Vocabulary

1. **Explain** the significance of:
   - **a.** permafrost
   - **b.** taiga
   - **c.** smog
   - **d.** pollutant

Main Ideas

2. **Summarizing** Use a chart like the one below to describe characteristics of three major climate zones in Russia.

Climate Zone	Characteristics
Humid Continental	
Tundra	
Subarctic	

3. **Explaining** What steps are being taken to solve Russia's pollution problems?

Critical Thinking

4. **Determining Cause and Effect** How did Russia's climate lead to the defeat of the German army's invasion during World War II?
5. **BIG Idea** How might Russia's vast size, climate, and pollution problems be related?
6. **Challenge** Why do you think the vast wooded areas of the Russian taiga still exist?

Writing About Geography

7. **Use Your FOLDABLES** Use your Foldable to write a letter to a Russian government official explaining why you think improving Russia's environment should be a priority.

Answers

1. Definitions for the vocabulary words are found in the section and the Glossary.
2. **Humid Continental:** warm, rainy summers and cold, snowy winters; **Tundra:** cold temperatures, lack of precipitation, permafrost, limited vegetation; **Subarctic:** warmer temperatures and a greater variety of vegetation than the tundra, world's largest coniferous forest
3. improving sewage systems, cleaning up heavily polluted sites, and construction of more efficient power plants
4. The harsh Russian winter, with its bitter cold temperatures, stopped the advance of the German troops, and the better-prepared Russian troops were able to force the Germans to retreat.
5. Possible response: People who live in cold climates need more energy to heat their homes, and transportation across large regions also requires more energy. The use of many energy sources, like fossil fuels, creates pollution.
6. Possible response: The taiga is so vast that it would take a long time to destroy it all. The taiga is also far away from major population centers and there are few roads or railroads to carry lumber from the remote taiga to mills and markets.
7. Letters will vary but should demonstrate an understanding of the environmental problems facing Russia.

Visual Summary

A Vast Northern Land

- Straddling Europe and Asia, Russia is the world's largest country.
- Most of Russia's long coast lies along waters that are frozen for many months of the year.

Russian icebreaker in the Arctic Ocean

Russia's Landforms

- Northern and western parts of Russia are mostly plains. Eastern and southern areas of the country are covered with mountains and plateaus.
- Inland waterways are important for moving goods through Russia. Many long rivers flow north, however, into the cold Arctic Ocean and freeze in winter.
- Russia has many inland bodies of water, including the Caspian Sea and Lake Baikal.

Natural Resources

- Russia is rich in natural resources, including fossil fuels, metals, and timber.
- Russia's large size and generally cold climate make it difficult for Russians to use their resources.

Climate

- Most of western Russia has a humid continental climate of warm, rainy summers and cold, snowy winters.
- Northern and eastern parts of Russia have cold high latitude climates. The far north of Russia is so cold that moisture in the soil cannot evaporate.
- The country's cold winters helped the Russians defeat German forces during World War II.

Russian coal miner

Environment

- Communist leaders paid little attention to the damage that economic growth was causing to Russia's environment.
- Other countries are providing Russia with aid to clean up heavily polluted areas.

Mount Elbrus

Study anywhere, anytime! Download quizzes and flash cards to your PDA from glencoe.com.

Visual Summary

Visual Literacy Have students study the photos on this page. **Ask: What aspects of Russia's climate and landforms are apparent in the photos?** *(snow, ice, mountains, trees)* **Based on the photos, name two industries in Russia.** *(Answers may include two of the following: shipping, mining, and logging.)* **OL**

Questioning Have students work with a partner to create a board game about Russia's physical geography. Instruct students to use information from this page to create questions for their game. Students should also create an answer key by looking for answers in the chapter, if the answers are not on this page. Encourage students to create rules for moving pieces around the board and to be creative when making the game board. When students finish their games, have them exchange games with another group to play. Make sure they provide the necessary instructions. **OL**

Hands-On Chapter Project
Step 3: Wrap Up

Exploring Russian Life Through Posters

Step 3: Learning From the Posters Students will synthesize what they have learned in Steps 1 and 2.

Directions Write the Essential Question on the board. Encourage students to answer this question by using what they learned while planning and making their posters about life in the different areas of Russia. Review the main geographic regions in Russia. Ask questions such as: How have Russians adapted to climate conditions, such as long, cold winters? How has the distribution of resources affected where people settled in Russia? How do the lifestyles of Russian people compare to your lifestyle? Were you surprised by the similarities or differences? Then have students write a brief paragraph in their journals answering the Essential Question. **OL**

Answers and Analyses

Reviewing Vocabulary

1. C Students can use a process of elimination to answer the question, if they have some knowledge of energy resources. Since the resources listed in the question are not renewable, answer choice B is incorrect. Energy resources are not pollutants. Ores are minerals. Thus, answer choice C is correct.

2. A It is important to note that the question is asking for what Siberia *lacks*, not what it has. Although Siberia's terrain is a barrier to trade, this is not what Siberia *lacks*. A tariff system is not a system of roads and railroads, but a method of taxation. A commercial sector is also not a system of roads and railroads.

3. D Students can remember the definition of *permafrost* by using word analysis. *Perma-* means permanent, and *frost* is frozen moisture. Therefore, the term *permafrost* fits the definition in the question: "a permanently frozen layer of soil."

4. B The taiga is the world's largest coniferous forest, which lies south of the tundra, where vegetation has difficulty growing because of the frozen soil. The remaining choices, *Baikal* and *steppe*, do not relate to forests.

Reviewing Main Ideas

5. B Students may recall from the chapter that most Russians live in the industrialized areas that are in the western portion of the country, closer to Europe.

6. C Many of Russia's valuable resources are in Siberia, which is difficult to access because of its lack of roads and railroads and harsh climate. Answer choices A and B are not locations that are difficult to access, and answer choice D, *south of the Caucasus*, is not part of Russia.

STANDARDIZED TEST PRACTICE

TEST-TAKING TIP

When an answer contains multiple items, such as in question 10, make sure that all the items in the answer are correct.

Reviewing Vocabulary

Directions: Choose the word(s) that best complete the sentence.

1. Russia is among the world's leaders in reserves of ______, which include oil, natural gas, and coal.
- **A** pollutants
- **B** renewable resources
- **C** fossil fuels
- **D** ores

2. Siberia lacks a(n) ______, a system of roads and railroads for transporting materials.
- **A** infrastructure
- **B** trade barrier
- **C** tariff system
- **D** commercial sector

3. In Russia's northern tundra, cold temperatures and lack of precipitation result in a permanently frozen layer of soil beneath the surface called ______.
- **A** taiga
- **B** smog
- **C** steppes
- **D** permafrost

4. Russia has the world's largest coniferous forest called the ______.
- **A** tundra
- **B** taiga
- **C** Baikal
- **D** steppe

Reviewing Main Ideas

Directions: Choose the best answer for each question.

Section 1 *(pp. 372–375)*

5. The great majority of Russians live ______.
- **A** in Siberian Russia
- **B** in European Russia
- **C** east of the Urals
- **D** in Asian Russia

6. Many of Russia's plentiful resources are difficult to obtain because of their location ______.
- **A** in European Russia
- **B** west of the Urals
- **C** in Siberia
- **D** south of the Caucasus

Section 2 *(pp. 378–382)*

7. Russia has a generally ______ climate.
- **A** cool to cold
- **B** warm to hot
- **C** dry to desert
- **D** low latitude

8. Russia's largest climate zone is called the ______ zone.
- **A** tundra
- **B** taiga
- **C** arctic
- **D** subarctic

GO ON

7. A Students might recall the location of Russia, which is mainly in latitudes to the far north. This proximity to the Arctic Circle makes for cooler temperatures than would be present in latitudes closer to the Equator. Therefore, the remaining answer choices are incorrect.

8. D If students picture Russia on a map, they will note that most of it is located just below the Arctic Circle. In analyzing the answer choices, students will see that the term *subarctic* actually means "below the Arctic."

Critical Thinking

Directions: Use the following results of a Russian public opinion survey on the environment to answer questions 9 and 10. Choose the best answer for each question.

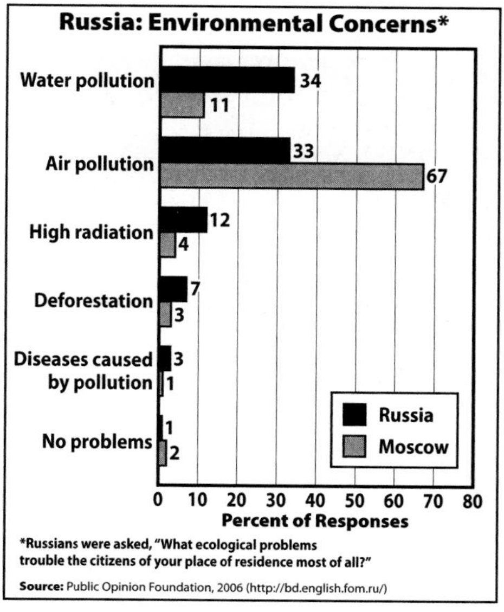

9. Residents of Moscow, Russia's largest city, are more concerned than others about ________.

A high radiation

B water pollution

C air pollution

D ecologically caused diseases

10. Russian citizens living outside of Moscow are almost equally concerned about both ________.

A high radiation and disease

B water and air pollution

C air pollution and high radiation

D water pollution and high radiation

Document-Based Questions

Directions: Analyze the document and answer the short-answer questions that follow.

Mark Sergeev, a Russian poet from the Siberian city of Irkutsk close to Lake Baikal, wrote the following in an essay about the lake.

> *[Native] Siberians have a mystical feeling for [Lake Baikal]. They believe that this is not simply 23 thousand cubic kilometers of water in some enormous stone bowl, but a wizard and healer who should neither be jested with nor enraged. This is why they never call Baikal a lake, only—the sea, or the Old Man, but more often than not they say—He!*
>
> —Mark Sergeev, Irkutsk poet

11. How do native Siberians feel about Lake Baikal? How do they show their feelings?

12. Why might Lake Baikal produce such feelings in the local Siberians?

Extended Response

13. Write an essay describing Asian Russia, including its landforms, waters, climates, and resources. Explain why Asian Russia may play an important role in the country's future economic development in your essay.

STOP

Social Studies ONLINE

For additional test practice, use Self-Check Quizzes—Chapter 13 on glencoe.com.

Need Extra Help?

If you missed question...	1	2	3	4	5	6	7	8	9	10	11	12	13
Go to page...	375	375	380	380	373	375	379	380	380	380	374	374	373

Document-Based Questions

11. Native Siberians believe Lake Baikal is mystical. They show great respect for the lake. They never call Baikal a lake, but refer to it as the sea, or as human.

12. Students may suggest that because Lake Baikal is the deepest lake in the world, and because it is so large, it may seem mysterious to local Siberians. Also, the locals may depend on the lake for their livelihoods, so they would want to treat it with great respect.

Extended Response

13. Students' essays should include accurate descriptions of the region's physical features and climates and should explain that, with its vast spaces and many resources, Asian Russia should be extremely important in Russia's future economy.

Critical Thinking

9. C To answer this question, students must find the longest bar on the graph and note its label to the left. Students should be careful to distinguish the two colors and make sure they focus on the color for Moscow.

10. B The question asks about citizens outside Moscow, so students should focus on the color for Russia, not Moscow. In looking at the graph, students will see that the bars for water and air pollution for Russia are almost equal in length.

Social Studies ONLINE

Have students visit the Web site at glencoe.com to review Chapter 13 and take the Self-Check Quiz.

Need Extra Help?

Have students refer to the pages listed if they miss any of the questions.

Planning Guide

Key to Ability Levels	
BL Below level	AL Above level
OL On level	ELL English Language Learners

Key to Teaching Resources	
Print Material	DVD
CD-ROM	Transparency

Levels					Resources	Chapter Opener	Section 1	Section 2	Chapter Assess
BL	OL	AL	ELL						
FOCUS									
BL	OL	AL	ELL	Transparency	**Daily Focus Skills Transparencies**		14-1	14-2	
TEACH									
BL	OL		ELL	Print Material	**Guided Reading Activity, URB***		p. 59	p. 60	
BL	OL	AL	ELL	Print Material	**Content Vocabulary Activity, URB***		p. 61	p. 61	
BL	OL	AL	ELL	Print Material	**Academic Vocabulary Activity, URB**		p. 63	p. 63	
BL	OL	AL	ELL	Print Material	**Differentiated Instruction Activity, URB**		p. 65		
BL	OL	AL	ELL	Print Material	**Chart, Graph, and Map Skills Activity, URB**			p. 67	
	OL	AL		Print Material	**Critical Thinking Activity, URB**			p. 69	
BL	OL	AL	ELL	Print Material	**Speaking and Listening Skills Activity, URB**		p. 71		
BL	OL	AL	ELL	Print Material	**Writing Skills Activity, URB**			p. 75	
BL	OL	AL	ELL	Print Material	**School-to-Home Connection Activity, URB***		p. 79		
BL	OL	AL	ELL	Print Material	**Regional Atlas Activities, URB**		pp. 1–7	pp. 1–7	
	OL	AL		Print Material	**Geography and History Activity, URB**		p. 11		
	OL	AL		Print Material	**Environmental Case Study, URB**			p. 13	p. 13
BL	OL		ELL	Print Material	**Time Line Activity, URB**		p. 17		p. 17
		AL		Print Material	**Enrichment Activity, URB**			p. 19	
BL	OL	AL	ELL	Print Material	**GeoLab Activity, URB**			p. 23	
BL	OL		ELL	Print Material	**Reading Skills Activity, URB**			p. 25	
BL	OL	AL	ELL	Print Material	**Primary Source Readings, URB**		p. 27		
	OL	AL		Print Material	**World Literature Reading, URB**			p. 31	
BL	OL		ELL	Print Material	**Reading Essentials and Note-Taking Guide***		p. 97	p. 100	
BL	OL	AL	ELL	Transparency	**In-Text Map Overlay and Population Pyramid Transparencies**	5	5A		
	OL			Print Material	**Foods Around the World**			pp. 18–21	
BL	OL	AL	ELL	Print Material	**Outline Map Resource Book**		p. 43		
BL	OL	AL	ELL	Print Material	**NGS World Atlas***	✓	✓	✓	

Note: Please refer to the *Unit Resource Book: Russia* for this chapter's URB materials.

* Also available in Spanish

- Interactive Lesson Planner
- Interactive Teacher Edition
- Fully editable blackline masters
- Section Spotlight Videos Launch
- Differentiated Lesson Plans
- Printable reports of daily assignments
- Standards Tracking System

Levels				Resources	Chapter Opener	Section 1	Section 2	Chapter Assess
BL	OL	AL	ELL					
TEACH *(continued)*								
BL	OL	AL	ELL	NGS World Desk Map	✓	✓	✓	✓
BL	OL	AL	ELL	World Literature Library	✓	✓	✓	✓
BL	OL	AL	ELL	Writer's Guidebook	✓	✓	✓	✓
BL	OL	AL	ELL	Vocabulary PuzzleMaker CD-ROM*	✓	✓	✓	✓
	OL	AL		Primary Sources CD-ROM	✓	✓	✓	✓
BL	OL	AL	ELL	StudentWorks™ Plus DVD	✓	✓	✓	✓
BL	OL	AL	ELL	Section Video Program Activities	✓	✓	✓	✓
BL	OL	AL	ELL	World Music: A Cultural Legacy	✓	✓	✓	✓
BL	OL	AL	ELL	Writing Process Transparencies	✓	✓	✓	✓
Teacher Resources				Building Academic Vocabulary	✓	✓	✓	✓
				Strategies for Success	✓	✓	✓	✓
				Teacher's Guide to Differentiated Instruction	✓	✓	✓	✓
				Presentation Plus! DVD	✓	✓	✓	✓
ASSESS								
BL	OL	AL	ELL	Quizzes and Tests		p. 157	p. 158	p. 159
BL	OL	AL	ELL	Authentic Assessment With Rubrics		p. 14		p. 14
BL	OL	AL	ELL	Standardized Test Practice				p. 53
BL	OL	AL	ELL	*ExamView® Assessment Suite* CD-ROM*		14-1	14-2	Ch. 14
BL	OL	AL	ELL	Interactive Tutor Self-Assessment CD-ROM		14-1	14-2	
CLOSE								
BL			ELL	Reteaching Activity, URB		p. 77	p. 77	p. 77
BL	OL		ELL	Reading and Study Skills Foldables™	p. 76	p. 76	p. 76	p. 76
BL	OL	AL	ELL	Graphic Organizer Transparencies and Strategies		✓	✓	
BL	OL	AL	ELL	*Exploring Our World* in Graphic Novel	pp. 57, 65	pp. 57, 65	p. 65	

Integrating Technology

Using PuzzleMaker™ 3.1 — Online Word Search Puzzles

Technology Product

Glencoe's Vocabulary PuzzleMaker™ 3.1 CD-ROM is an easy-to-use program that lets you create your own puzzles based on the glossary for classroom use. The PuzzleMaker allows you to

- create word search puzzles based on content vocabulary and academic vocabulary that is specific to what is taught in the classroom;
- create online (LAN-based or local area network) or paper word search puzzles.

Objectives

After students complete the word search puzzles, they will be able to

- recall academic vocabulary terms based on the clues provided for a puzzle;
- reinforce their understanding of the vocabulary.

Steps

- Run PuzzleMaker™ 3.1. On the main menu, click on **Create a New Puzzle.**
- Select the *Puzzle Database* for the vocabulary.
- The *PuzzleMaker Wizard* will take you through selecting a puzzle type and grid type.
- Then select one or more chapters from the list. Indicate whether you want the words selected randomly or manually.
- Select the language and words you wish to use within the maximum for the puzzle. Click **Finish.**
- Save your word search puzzle to a location that is easily accessible by your students with PuzzlePlayer™ 3.1, or print copies for your students to complete.
- Use PuzzlePlayer™ 3.1 to review the puzzles after your students have worked on and saved them.

Social Studies ONLINE

	Student	Teacher	Parent
Beyond the Textbook	●		●
Chapter Overviews	●		●
Concepts in Motion	●		●
ePuzzles and Games	●		●
Literature Connections		●	
Multi-Language Glossaries	●		●
Online Student Edition	●	●	●
Section Videos	●	●	●
Self-Check Quizzes	●		●
Student Web Activities	●		●
Study Central™	●		●
Teaching Today		●	
TIME Current Events	●		●
Vocabulary eFlashcards	●		●
Web Activity Lesson Plans		●	

- **Timed Readings Plus in Social Studies** helps students increase their reading rate and fluency while maintaining comprehension. The 400-word passages are similar to those found on state and national assessments.
- **Reading in the Content Area: Social Studies** concentrates on six essential reading skills that help students better comprehend what they read. The book includes 75 high-interest nonfiction passages written at increasing levels of difficulty.
- **Reading Social Studies** includes strategic reading instruction and vocabulary support in Social Studies content for ELLs and native speakers of English.
- **Content Vocabulary Workout** (Grades 6–8) accelerates reading comprehension through focused vocabulary development. Social Studies content vocabulary comes from the glossaries of Glencoe's Middle School Social Studies texts.
www.jamestowneducation.com

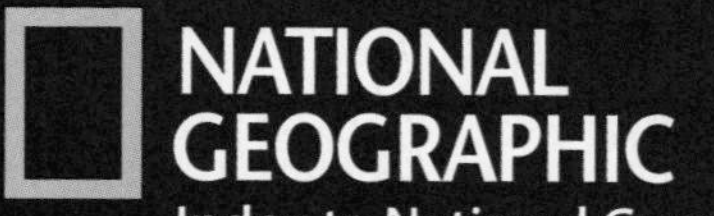

Index to National Geographic Magazine:

The following articles relate to this chapter:

- "Living with the Bomb" by Richard Rhodes, August 2005.
- "Russia Rising," by Fen Montaigne, November 2001.

National Geographic Society Products To order the following, call National Geographic at 1-800-368-2728:

- *National Geographic Atlas of the World* (Book).

Access National Geographic's new dynamic MapMachine Web site and other geography resources at:
www.nationalgeographic.com
www.nationalgeographic.com/maps

Biography

The following videotape programs are available from Glencoe as supplements to Chapter 14:

- Ivan the Terrible (ISBN 0-76-700517-1)
- Joseph Stalin: Red Terror (ISBN 1-56-501820-6)

To order, call Glencoe at 1-800-334-7344. To find classroom resources to accompany many of these videos, check the following home pages:

A&E Television: www.aetv.com
The History Channel: www.historychannel.com

GLENCOE BOOKLINK 3

Use this database to search more than 30,000 titles to create a customized reading list for your students.

- Reading lists can be organized by students' reading level, author, genre, theme, or area of interest.
- The database provides Degrees of Reading Power™ (DRP) and Lexile™ readability scores for all selections.
- A brief summary of each selection is included.

Leveled reading suggestions for this chapter:

For students at a Grade 5 reading level:
- ***Broken Song,*** by Kathyrn Lasky

For students at a Grade 6 reading level:
- ***Russian Girl: Life in an Old Russian Town,*** by Russ Kendall

For students at a Grade 7 reading level:
- ***The People of Russia and Their Food,*** by Ann L. Burckhardt

For students at a Grade 8 reading level:
- ***One Day in the Life of Ivan Denisovich,*** by Aleksandr Solzhenitsyn

For students at a Grade 9 reading level:
- ***Russia Under the Czars,*** by Henry Moscow
- ***The Brothers Karamazov,*** by Fyodor Dostoevsky

Focus

The Essential Question

As students study the chapter, remind them to consider the chapter-based Essential Question. Answering this question will help them understand the important concepts in the chapter. In addition, the Hands-On Chapter Project relates the content from each section to the Essential Question. The steps in each section build on each other as students progress through the chapter. The Hands-On Chapter Project culminates in the Wrap Up activity on the Visual Summary page.

More About the Photo

Visual Literacy The State Historical Museum of Russia was built in the late 1800s. The museum is located at the northern end of Moscow's Red Square, a site of great historical significance. Executions, demonstrations, and riots have taken place there throughout Russia's history. At the other end of Red Square is the Cathedral of St. Basil the Blessed, which is famous for its onion-shaped domes. The tomb of Soviet leader Vladimir Lenin is also located on the square.

CHAPTER 14

History and Cultures of Russia

Essential Question

Movement Today, Russia is the world's largest country. Early in its history, however, it was a small territory on the edge of Europe. Strong rulers gradually expanded Russia's borders. While Russia's government has undergone a number of changes, the country's culture and traditions have remained strong. Why do countries often wish to expand their territory?

Teach

The BIG Ideas *As you begin teaching each section, use these questions and activities to help students focus on the Big Ideas.*

Section 

History and Governments **Ask:** **How can citizens of a country change or influence their government?** *(In a democracy, citizens can vote. In other political systems, citizens may need to participate in protests or revolutions to make changes in government.)* Tell students that Section 1 describes the rise of Russia as a powerful empire, its history as a Communist country, and its recent democratic reforms. Students will learn how the Russian people have changed their governments and how their governments have affected their lives. **OL**

Section 2

Cultures and Lifestyles **Ask:** **How might the climate of a country affect the culture of its people?** *(Possible answer: Climate affects how people live, including the types of housing they live in, their fashions, and their transportation. It also affects the sports people play. For example, people in cold climates probably play more winter*

BIG Ideas

Section 1: History and Governments

BIG IDEA The characteristics and movement of people impact physical and human systems. Russia grew from a small trading center into a large empire. Although Russia's leaders and a few citizens enjoyed great power, most Russians remained poor and had few rights. In time, these conditions led to great changes in Russia's government.

Section 2: Cultures and Lifestyles

BIG IDEA Culture groups shape human systems. The Russian people have created a rich culture that reflects strong national feelings. Cultural traditions have shaped many areas of daily life, such as housing, recreation, and celebrations.

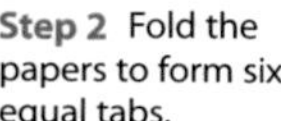

FOLDABLES Study Organizer

Categorizing Information Make this Foldable to help you collect and organize information about Russia's history and cultures.

Step 1 Place three sheets of paper on top of one another about 1 inch apart.

Step 2 Fold the papers to form six equal tabs.

Step 3 Staple the sheets, and label each tab as shown.

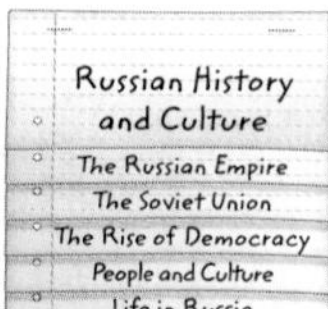

Reading and Writing Use the notes in your Foldable to write a short essay comparing population, culture, and everyday life in Russia and the United States.

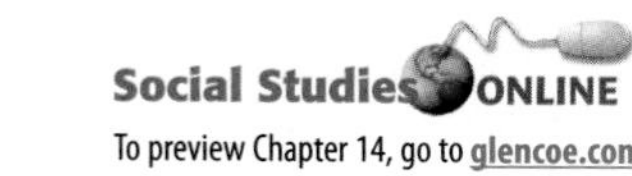

To preview Chapter 14, go to glencoe.com.

State Historical Museum, Moscow, Russia

Previewing the Region

If you have not already done so, engage students in the Regional Atlas and chart activities to help them become familiar with the general content of the region.

FOLDABLES Study Organizer **Dinah Zike's Foldables**

Purpose This Foldable helps students organize information about the history and culture of Russia. Have students note facts from their reading under the appropriate headings on the Foldable. The completed Foldable will help students write their essays and prepare for assessment. **OL**

More Foldables activities for this chapter can be found in *Dinah Zike's Reading and Study Skills Foldables* ancillary.

Social Studies ONLINE

Introduce students to chapter content and key terms by having them access the Chapter Overview at glencoe.com.

sports.) Point out to students that in Section 2, they will learn about Russia's culture, including its ethnic groups, arts, and scientific achievements. They will also learn about everyday life in Russia, as well as the sports and holidays Russians enjoy and the transportation and communications challenges they face. **OL**

Focus

Bellringer

Daily Focus Transparency 14-1

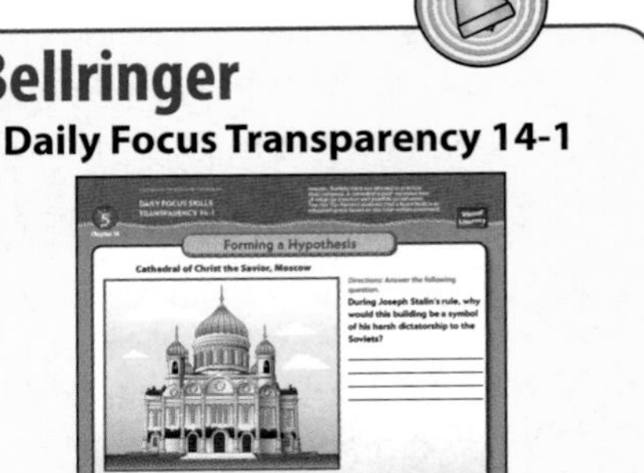

Guide to Reading

Answers to Graphic:

Outlines should follow this pattern:

I. The Russian Empire
- **A.** Russia began as a trade center.
- **B.** Czars created an empire.
- **C.** Suffering led to revolution and a communist state in Russia.

II. The Soviet Union
- **A.** Lenin followed the ideas of Karl Marx to create the Soviet Union.

Section Spotlight Video

To learn more about the history and governments of Russia, have students watch the Section Spotlight Video.

Resource Manager

R Reading Strategies	**C** Critical Thinking	**D** Differentiated Instruction	**W** Writing Support	**S** Skill Practice
Teacher Edition • Questioning, p. 389 • Using Clues, p. 392 • Predicting, p. 393 • Summarizing, p. 394 **Additional Resources** • Guid. Read., URB p. 59 • Cont. Voc., URB p. 61 • Ac. Vocab., URB p. 63 • Read. Ess., p. 97 • Pri. Source, URB p. 27	**Teacher Edition** • Making Inferences, p. 389 • Det. Cause/Effect, pp. 389, 392 • Comparing, p. 391 • Drawing Con., p. 392 **Additional Resources** • Geo. & Hist., URB p. 11 • Authentic Assess., p. 14 • Quizzes and Tests, p. 157	**Teacher Edition** • EL, p. 390 • Adv. Learners, p. 391 • Special Ed., p. 393 **Additional Resources** • Diff. Instr., URB p. 65 • Reteach., URB p. 77 • School-to-Home Conn., URB p. 79	**Teacher Edition** • Persuasive Writing, p. 390 **Additional Resources** • Speak./Listen. Skills, URB p. 71	**Teacher Edition** • Visual Literacy, p. 390 **Additional Resources** • Time Line, URB p. 17 • Daily Focus Trans. 14-1 • Reg. Atlas, URB pp. 1–7

Guide to Reading

BIG Idea

The characteristics and movement of people impact physical and human systems.

Content Vocabulary
- missionary *(p. 389)*
- czar *(p. 390)*
- serf *(p. 390)*
- communist state *(p. 391)*
- collectivization *(p. 392)*
- Cold War *(p. 393)*
- glasnost *(p. 393)*
- perestroika *(p. 393)*
- coup *(p. 394)*

Academic Vocabulary
- convert *(p. 389)*
- release *(p. 391)*
- eliminate *(p. 392)*

Reading Strategy

Outlining Use the model below to make an outline of the section. Use Roman numerals to number the main headings. Use capital letters to list important facts below each main heading.

I. First Main Heading
- A. Key fact 1
- B. Key fact 2

II. Second Main Heading
- A. Key fact 1
- B. Key fact 2

History and Governments

Picture This A giant cat? No, it is actually a miniature city. The highest building in this model of the city of Königsberg stands only 3 feet (91 cm) high. *Königsberg* means "King's Mountain" and was once a German capital. In 1945, during the final days of World War II, German and Soviet armies fought a desperate four-day battle in the city. After the war, the Soviet Union took control of the city and renamed it Kaliningrad. Today, Kaliningrad is part of Russia, which became independent after the Soviet Union's fall in 1991. Read this section to find out more about Russia's history.

▼ Roaming around Königsberg

The Russian Empire

Main Idea **Strong leaders made Russia a vast empire, but widespread suffering eventually led to revolution.** R

Geography and You What causes people to rise up and overthrow their government? Read on to learn about Russia's history up to the time of the Russian Revolution.

Russia today is a vast country, covering millions of square miles and spreading across two continents. This world power, however, began as a small trade center.

Early Russia

Modern Russians descend from Slavic peoples who settled along the rivers of what are today Ukraine and Russia. During the A.D. 800s, these early Slavs built a civilization around the city of Kiev (Kyiv), today the capital of Ukraine. This civilization, called Kievan Rus (KEE·eh·vuhn ROOS), prospered from river trade between Scandinavia and the Byzantine Empire. C1

In A.D. 988 the people of Kievan Rus **converted** to Eastern Orthodox Christianity. **Missionaries**, or people who move to another area to spread their religion, brought this form of Christianity from the Byzantine Empire to Kievan Rus. The missionaries also brought a written language.

In the 1200s, Mongol warriors from Central Asia conquered Kievan Rus. Under Mongol rule, Kiev lost much of its power. Many Slavs moved northward and built settlements. One new settlement was the small trading post of Moscow.

NATIONAL GEOGRAPHIC Maps In MOtion See StudentWorks™ Plus or glencoe.com.

Figure 1 **Expansion of Russia**

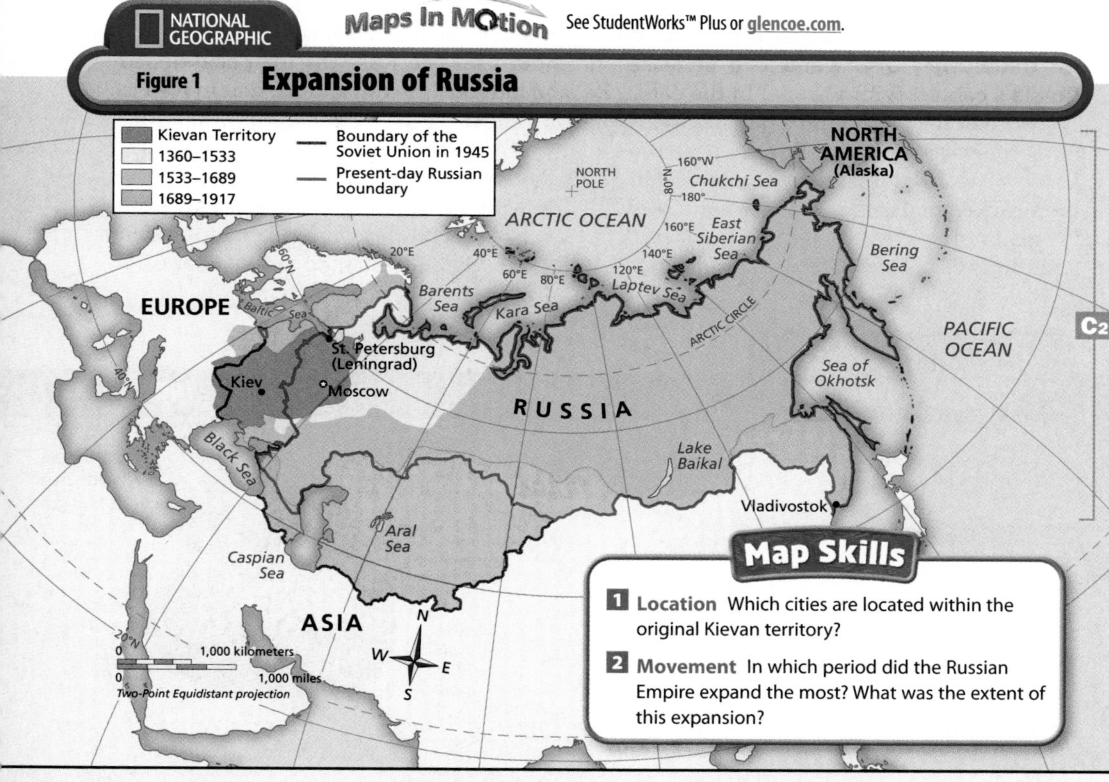

Map Skills

1. **Location** Which cities are located within the original Kievan territory?
2. **Movement** In which period did the Russian Empire expand the most? What was the extent of this expansion?

C2

Teach

R Reading Strategy

Questioning Ask students to think of two questions they would like answered about Russia's history, government, or revolution. Then tell them to look for the answers as they read the section. BL

C1 Critical Thinking

Making Inferences Show the location of the Byzantine Empire on a map. **Ask:** **Why would Kievan Rus have profited from trade between Scandinavia and the Byzantine Empire?** *(because Kiev was located on a river between Scandinavia and the Byzantine Empire)* OL

C2 Critical Thinking

Determining Cause and Effect Remind students that czars ruled Russia from 1547 to 1917. **Ask:** **What effect did the czars have on Russian territory?** *(They expanded it to many times its original size.)* OL

Map Skills

Answers:

1. Kiev, St. Petersburg, Moscow
2. 1689–1917; west into Europe, south and east into Asia, east into North America

Hands-On Chapter Project Step 1

Viewing Russia Through Stamps

Step 1: Identifying Subjects for Stamps Small groups of students will choose appropriate subjects from Russian history and culture to create a series of commemorative stamps.

Essential Question Why do countries often wish to expand their territory?

Directions Have students work in small groups to identify key people and events in the establishment and expansion of Russia. Tell students to list the specific individuals, groups, and developments they find in this section, and then choose three to feature in a series of stamps commemorating Russian history and culture. Direct groups to note details in the text about each of their choices and do research to get additional information and visuals to incorporate into the stamps they will design.

Summarizing Have students write a sentence explaining the historical significance of each subject they have chosen. Groups will identify three additional subjects in Section 2 and then design a series of six commemorative stamps. OL

(Chapter Project continued in Section 2)

D Differentiated Instruction

English Learners Explain to students that the quotation marks around "Ivan the Great" show that this is a nickname. Ask students to find another example of this use of quotations on this page. *("Ivan the Terrible")* **ELL**

S Skill Practice

Visual Literacy Ask students to compare the visuals on this page with the photo of the peasants on the next page. **Ask: How might these photos indicate the differences between Russias' rulers and the peasants?** *(The church and czars were wealthy, while the peasants barely survived.)* **OL**

W Writing Support

Persuasive Writing Ask students to write a letter to Czar Peter the Great to persuade him to make changes to help eliminate poverty in his country. Students should suggest specific changes and indicate how the changes would benefit Russia as a whole. **OL**

It became the center of a new Slavic territory called Muscovy (muh·SKOH·vee). In 1480 Ivan III, a prince of Muscovy, rejected Mongol rule and declared independence. Because he was a strong ruler, Ivan became known as "Ivan the Great."

The Czars

D Muscovy developed into the country known today as Russia. In 1547 Ivan IV declared himself **czar** (ZAHR), or emperor. He ruled harshly, using secret police to carry out his will, and earned the name "Ivan the Terrible." By conquering neighboring territories, Ivan expanded his empire south to the Caspian Sea and east past the Ural Mountains.

The expansion of Russian territory, shown in **Figure 1** on the preceding page, continued under later czars, such as Peter the Great and Catherine the Great. These czars wanted to obtain a warm-water port for trade. They also wanted to increase Russia's contact with Europe. In the early 1700s, Peter the Great built a new capital—St. Petersburg—close to Europe near the Baltic coast. By this time, the Russian Empire extended to the Pacific Ocean. Over the next hundred years, it came to include large parts of Central Asia. As a result, non-Russians, including many Muslims, became part of the Russian Empire.

Through the centuries, Russia remained largely rural and agricultural. The czars, large landowners, and wealthy merchants enjoyed comfortable lives. The majority of **W** Russians, however, were poor peasants. Many were **serfs**, or farm laborers who could be bought and sold with the land. Serfs sometimes revolted, but the czars' armies put down their rebellions.

Revolution

Several times during Russia's history, the country's cold climate and huge size proved to be strong defenses against invasion. In 1812 a French army led by Napoleon Bonaparte invaded Russia. To conquer Russia, the French forces had to march hundreds of miles and capture Moscow. All along the French army's way, the Russian army burned villages and any supplies the French could use. The Russians then abandoned and burned Moscow, and the czar moved to St. Petersburg. Even though they had captured Moscow, French troops had few supplies and were forced to retreat during the brutal Russian winter. Thousands died from the harsh conditions and constant Russian attacks. Russia remained independent.

Differentiated Instruction

Leveled Activities

BL Reteaching Activity, URB p. 77

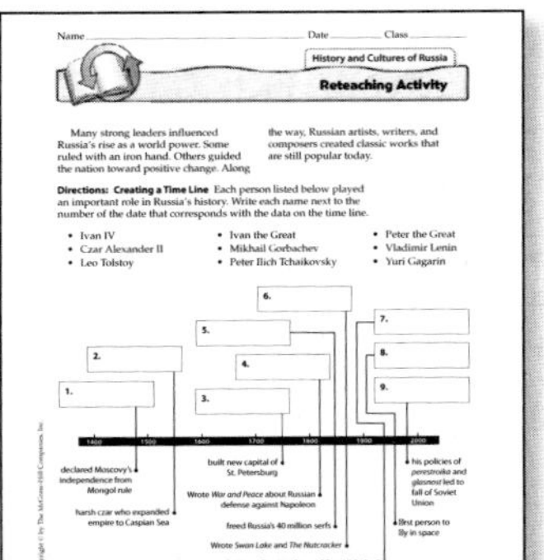

OL Time Line Activity, URB p. 17

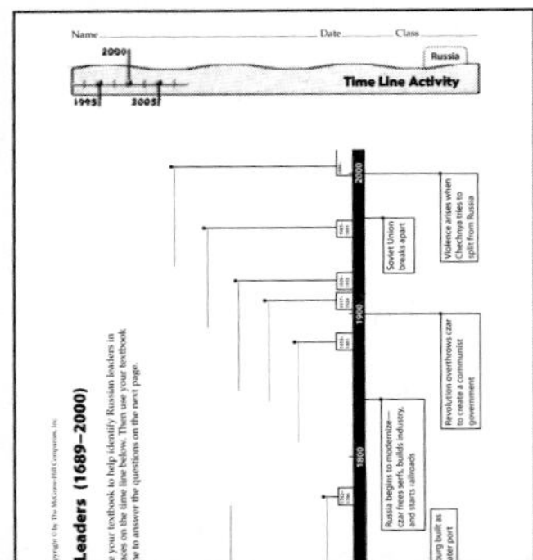

AL Geography and History Activity, URB p. 11

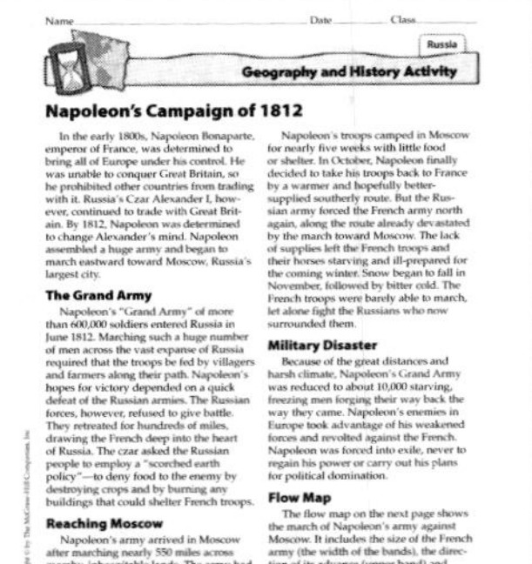

ELL Differentiated Instruction, URB p. 65

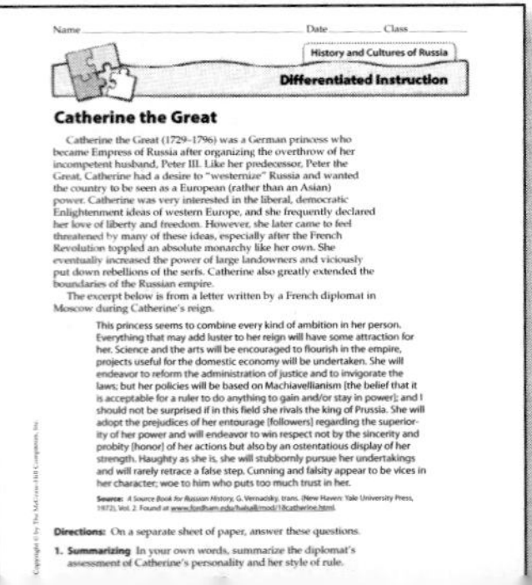

In the late 1800s, Russia entered a period of great change. In 1861 Czar Alexander II freed the country's 40 million serfs. Freedom did not **release** them from poverty, however. Alexander began to modernize Russia's economy, building industries and expanding railroads. Despite these changes, most Russians remained poor, and unrest spread among workers and peasants.

In 1914 Russia joined France and Britain to fight Germany and Austria in World War I. Poorly prepared, Russia suffered military defeats, losing millions of men between 1914 and 1916. Many Russians blamed Czar Nicholas II for the country's poor performance in the war and for food shortages. In early 1917 the people staged a revolution that forced the czar to step down from the throne. Later that year, Vladimir Lenin led a second revolt that overthrew the temporary government. He set about establishing a **communist state** in which the government controlled the economy and society. Fearing invasion, Lenin also moved Russia's capital from coastal St. Petersburg inland to Moscow.

Reading Check **Summarizing** Briefly describe the founding of Kievan Rus and its development into Russia.

The Rise and Fall of Communism

Main Idea **The Communist system controlled many aspects of people's lives, but democratic ideas eventually took hold.**

Geography and You What would it be like if the government told you what job you had to do and also greatly limited the choices of products you could buy in stores? Read to learn about the changes that the Communist government brought to Russia.

Vladimir Lenin and his followers created a new nation called the Union of Soviet Socialist Republics (U.S.S.R.), or the Soviet Union. This nation included 15 republics made up of different ethnic groups. Russia was the largest republic, and the Russian ethnic group dominated the Soviet Union's government.

Lenin followed the ideas of a German political thinker named Karl Marx. Marx believed that industrialization created an unjust system in which factory owners held great power, while the workers held very little. Lenin said that he wanted to make everyone in Soviet society more equal.

Russian peasants, c. 1900

Medal commemorating Trans-Siberian Railroad

D Differentiated Instruction

Advanced Learners Have students use online and library resources to find out more about the revolution that removed Czar Nicholas II from power. Instruct students to create a time line of events before and during the revolution and present their time lines using multimedia software. **AL**

C Critical Thinking

Comparing Ask students to compare industrial society, as described by Marx, to life in Russia before the revolution. **Ask:** **How were the Russian peasants similar to the factory workers Marx described?** *(The peasants were poor and had little power, like the factory workers.)* **OL**

This **Reading Skill** (Comparing) was introduced in this unit.

Reading Check **Answer:** Early Slavs built a civilization around the city of Kiev in the A.D. 800s. After this civilization, Kievan Rus, was conquered by the Mongols, many Slavs moved northward and established a new Slavic territory called Muscovy that developed into the country of Russia.

Primary Source Readings, URB pp. 27–28

The Abdication Speech of Czar Nicholas II of Russia

Objective: To interpret Czar Nicholas II's abdication speech within its historical context

Focus: Tell what you know about the circumstances of the czar's abdication.

Teach: Read Czar Nicholas II's speech, and identify its main ideas.

Assess: Summarize the czar's abdication speech.

Close: Discuss the historical significance of the czar's abdication.

Differentiated Instruction Strategies

BL Write three complete sentences that state the main ideas of the speech.

AL Conduct research to determine the causes and effects of the czar's abdication. Then show them in a cause-and-effect diagram.

ELL Look up the meanings and pronunciations of unfamiliar words in the speech.

R Reading Strategy

Using Context Clues **Ask:** **What does seize mean?** *(to take)* **What clues in the text helped you define this word?** *(Stalin had something done to people's property.)* **OL**

C1 Critical Thinking

Determining Cause and Effect **Ask:** **What was the result of collectivization?** *(The new farms were inefficient and did not produce enough food.)* **OL**

C2 Critical Thinking

Drawing Conclusions **Ask:** **Why does competition help improve the quality of goods?** *(Factories that have competition often need to make better goods in order to attract customers.)* **OL**

CITIZENS IN ACTION

Answer:
Possible answer: Because people may be afraid to criticize the government, or the facts may be carefully hidden.

Additional Support

So he ended private ownership, bringing all farms and factories under the control of the Soviet government. Lenin's policies were later continued by Joseph Stalin, who ruled the Soviet Union after Lenin's death in 1924. A harsh dictator, Stalin prevented the Soviet people from practicing their religions and had religious property seized. His secret police killed or imprisoned anyone who disagreed with his policies.

Agriculture and Industry

Soviet leaders set up a command economy in which the government ran all areas of economic life. They decided what crops farmers should grow and what goods factories should produce.

Leaders also introduced **collectivization**—a system in which small farms were combined into large, factorylike farms run by the government. Government leaders hoped these farms would be more efficient and reduce the need for farmworkers. Thousands of former peasants could then be put to work in factories to increase industrialization.

The Soviet economic plans had mixed success. The new farms were inefficient and did not produce enough food for the Soviet people. Industrial production was more successful. Huge factories produced steel, machinery, and military equipment. Strict government control, however, had drawbacks. The government **eliminated,** or did away with, competition, allowing only certain factories to make certain goods. This led to a lack of efficiency and poor-quality goods.

TIME GLOBAL CITIZENS

NAMES: NIKOLAI AND TATYANA SHCHUR

HOME COUNTRY: RUSSIA

ACHIEVEMENT: As Russia becomes a democracy, this husband-and-wife team is trying to make sure that citizens' rights are protected. In 2002 the couple visited Karabolka, a village near the site of a nuclear plant accident 50 years ago. Many people moved after the accident—but some stayed. For decades, those who remained were not told why so many of them fell mysteriously ill. The Shchurs have forced the government to acknowledge the area's radioactive contamination and to take action. Their dream is to educate a new generation of journalists, teachers, and police with a respect for human rights, including the right to live in an area free of radiation.

QUOTE: Tatyana says, "Nothing will really change until a generation grows up in Russia that is completely free from fear."

YURI KOZYREV FOR TIME (2)

The Shchurs stand by a Russian sign warning of high radiation levels.

CITIZENS IN ACTION Why do you think exposing past government cover-ups might be a difficult task?

Activity: Economics Connection

Drawing Conclusions Explain to students that different economic systems have different goals. Point out that the United States has a market, or free enterprise, system, in which individuals decide what goods and services are produced, how they are produced, and who uses them. The leaders of the Soviet Union set up a command economy, in which the government was in control and made all of the economic decisions. **Ask:** **How might a command economy benefit the people of a country?** *(In the short run, a command economy might benefit a country's people if the government decided to distribute goods and services equally among the people.)* Have students discuss what they think are the pros and cons of market and command systems. Explain that Russia's economic system has changed since the days when it was part of the Soviet Union. Tell students that they will read about these changes later in this section. **OL**

Soviet Power

In 1941, during World War II, Germany invaded the Soviet Union. The Soviets joined Great Britain and the United States to defeat the Germans. About 20 to 30 million Russian soldiers and civilians died in the war. After the war, Stalin wanted to make sure the Soviet Union would not be invaded again. He kept Soviet troops in neighboring eastern European countries and established Communist governments in them.

The Soviet Union and the United States were allies during the war but became bitter rivals after it. From the late 1940s until about 1990, these superpowers, the two most powerful nations in the world, engaged in a struggle for world influence. **D** Because the struggle never became "hot," with actual combat between the two opponents, the conflict became known as the **Cold War**.

Each superpower became the center of a group of nations. Members of each group pledged to come to one another's aid if a member country were attacked by a country from the other group. The United States was the chief member of the North Atlantic Treaty Organization, or NATO, which included most of western Europe's democracies. The Soviet Union led the Warsaw Pact, a group of Communist countries that included most of Eastern Europe.

The Soviet Union and the United States competed to produce military weapons and to explore outer space. With so many resources going to the military, the Soviet people had to endure shortages of basic goods, such as food and cars. By the 1980s, many Soviets were ready for change.

Social Studies ONLINE
Student Web Activity Visit glencoe.com and complete the Chapter 14 Web Activity about the Cold War.

NATIONAL GEOGRAPHIC

Woman in Space

In 1963 Valentina Tereshkova of the Soviet Union became the first woman to travel in space.
Place **With whom did the Soviet Union compete in space exploration?**

Attempts at Reform

In 1985 Mikhail Gorbachev (mih·KAH·eel GAWR·buh·CHAWF) became the Soviet leader. He quickly began a number of reforms in the Soviet Union. Under the policy of **glasnost** (GLAZ·nohst), or "openness," Soviet citizens could say and write about what they thought without fear of being punished. **R** Another policy, known as **perestroika** (PEHR·uh·STROY·kah), or "rebuilding," aimed at boosting the Soviet economy. It gave factory managers more freedom to make economic decisions and encouraged the creation of small, privately owned businesses.

Instead of strengthening the country, Gorbachev's policies made the Soviet people doubt communism even more. Huge protests against Soviet control arose across Eastern Europe. By 1991 all of the region's Communist governments had fallen. Gorbachev hoped that giving some freedoms would win the people's support.

D Differentiated Instruction

Special Education Have students with reading disabilities or visual impairments listen to a recording of this text. Then have them work with a partner to identify the events leading up to the creation of NATO and the Warsaw Pact. **BL**

R Reading Strategy

Predicting After students read the paragraph, ask them to name Gorbachev's two policies *(glasnost* and *perestroika).* Then ask them to predict what they might read in the next paragraph. **OL**

Caption Answer:
The United States

Social Studies ONLINE
Objectives and answers to the Student Web Activity can be found at glencoe.com under the Web Activity Lesson Plan for this chapter.

Activity: Technology Connection

Evaluating Ask: Do you think the Russian government today supports the policy of glasnost as introduced by Gorbachev? *(Answers will vary, but may include that the government has dealt harshly with those who are critical of the government.)* Group students into pairs to investigate the state of glasnost in Russia today. Direct each pair to identify an individual, an issue, or a development related to freedom of speech or the press in Russia. Have students research the topic by finding three reliable articles on the Web, such as those of news organizations. Have pairs share their findings with the rest of the class. **OL**

R Reading Strategy

Summarizing Have students briefly summarize the fall of the Soviet Union. Challenge them to think of three words or phrases that capture the main points of the text and then convert the words or phrases into three complete sentences that summarize the text. If students cannot think of words or phrases, start them off with *hard-line Communists.* OL

Reading Check **Answer:** Gorbachev introduced the policies of glasnost and perestroika. Gorbachev called for these reforms because the Soviet economy was weakening and the Soviet people wanted change.

Assess

Social Studies ONLINE
Study Central™ provides summaries, interactive games, and online graphic organizers to help students review content.

Close

Naming Have students name the rulers and the types of government throughout Russia's history. OL

When Eastern Europeans rejected continued Communist rule, Gorbachev decided not to resort to force. He refused to send troops to Eastern Europe as other Soviet leaders had done in the past.

Collapse of the Soviet Union

As communism ended in Eastern Europe, the Soviet Union faced growing unrest among its ethnic groups. Gorbachev was criticized both by hard-liners who wished to maintain Communist rule as well as by reformers. The hard-liners wanted to stop changes. The reformers, on the **R** other hand, felt that Gorbachev was not making changes fast enough. The reformers were led by a rising politician named Boris Yeltsin (BUHR·YEES YEHLT·suhn). He became the president of Russia, the largest of the Soviet republics.

In August 1991, hard-line Communists attempted a **coup** (KOO), an overthrow of the government by military force. Boris Yeltsin called on the people to resist. When many Russians stood firm, the hard-liners were forced to give up. The coup's failure was the beginning of the end of the Soviet Union. Within a few months, Russia and all of the other Soviet republics declared independence. By the end of 1991, the Soviet Union no longer existed as a nation.

In Russia, Yeltsin had some success in building democracy and a market economy. His successor, Vladimir Putin (vlah·DEE·meer POO·tuhn), however, increased government controls to deal with rising crime and violence. Challenges also came from some ethnic minorities. In the Chechnya (chehch·NYAH) region, a group trying to separate from Russia waged a bloody civil war.

Reading Check **Explaining** What were Gorbachev's reforms? Why were they introduced?

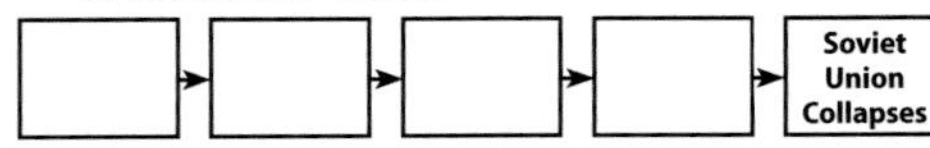

Social Studies ONLINE
Study Central™ To review this section, go to glencoe.com.

Vocabulary

1. **Explain** the significance of:
   a. missionary
   b. czar
   c. serf
   d. communist state
   e. collectivization
   f. Cold War
   g. glasnost
   h. perestroika
   i. coup

Main Ideas

2. **Identifying** What geographic goal drove the czars to expand their empire?
3. **Sequencing** Use a diagram like the one below to list events leading up to the collapse of the Soviet Union.

	→		→		→		→	Soviet Union Collapses

Critical Thinking

4. **Determining Cause and Effect** How did the Soviet Union's involvement in the Cold War affect the Soviet economy?
5. **BIG Idea** How did Russia become a society that included many different ethnic groups?
6. **Challenge** How did the economic systems of the Soviet Union and the United States differ?

Writing About Geography

7. **Using Your FOLDABLES** Use your Foldable to write a summary of how Russia's government changed after World War I.

Answers

1. Definitions for the vocabulary words are found in the section and the Glossary.
2. to obtain a warm-water port for trade and to increase contact with Europe.
3. Gorbachev Introduces Reforms, Communism Ends in Eastern Europe; Ethnic Unrest Grows; Coup by Hard-Line Communists Fails; Soviet Republics Declare Independence
4. Soviets faced shortages of basic goods, such as food and cars, because many resources went to the military.
5. As the Russian Empire expanded, it came to include not only part of Europe and people belonging to various European ethnic groups, but large parts of Central Asia and ethnic groups from those areas.
6. The Soviet Union had a command economy, in which the government controlled the economy and made all economic decisions; the United States has a market, or free enterprise, economy, in which individuals make economic decisions with little interference by the government.
7. Students' summaries should mention the revolution that overthrew the czar and the second revolt, led by Lenin, that established a communist state in which the government controlled the economy and society.

The Longest Railroad

How long does it take to cross the world's largest country? Thanks to the world's longest railroad, you can make the trip in less than a week—barely.

Building the Railroad The Trans-Siberian Railroad starts in Moscow, in western Russia. Nearly 5,800 miles (9,334 km) later, it reaches Vladivostok, on the shores of the Pacific Ocean. Work to build the railroad began in 1891 and was completed in 1901. **D**

The first route crossed Manchuria, a northern part of China. Russian leaders soon feared that Japan would seize Manchuria, however, which would threaten their rail line. As a result, they ordered work on a new route that went north of Manchuria and stayed entirely within Russian land. That route was finished in 1916.

NATIONAL GEOGRAPHIC

The Trans-Siberian Railroad

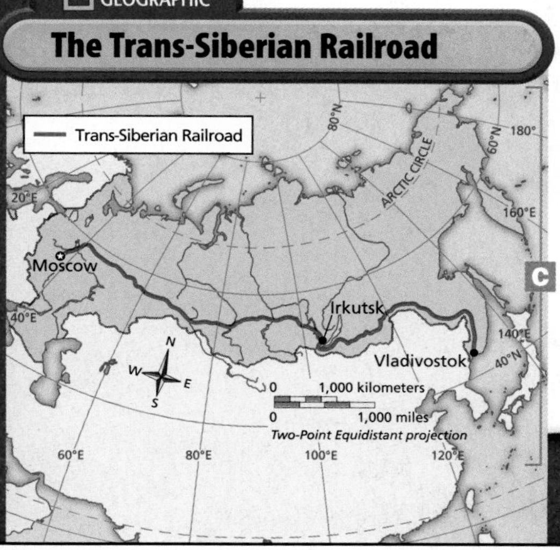

Construction of the railroad was difficult. Track had to be laid across swamps and permafrost and through dense forests and mountains. In eastern Russia, where the railroad crosses many rivers, dozens of bridges had to be built. To keep the railroad running, wells for water and mines to obtain coal and iron were needed.

▲ **A train on the Trans-Siberian Railroad**

The Impact of the Railroad The railroad had a huge impact on Russia. Even today, no highway connects western and eastern Russia. As a result, the railroad is the only land-based route linking these halves of the country. The railroad serves as a vital lifeline for bringing supplies to eastern settlements. It also moves Siberia's timber and mineral resources to factories in the west. **C**

During World War II, the railroad helped save Russia. When Germany invaded western Russia in 1941, the government used the railroad to move equipment from that area into Siberia. There it set up new factories to make the vehicles, weapons, and ammunition needed to continue fighting the war.

Think About It

1. **Human-Environment Interaction** What obstacles did workers building the railroad have to overcome?
2. **Movement** Why was the railroad important during World War II?

Geography & History

D Differentiated Instruction

Logical/Mathematical Have students calculate the number of miles the train travels each day when making the trip from Vladivostok to Moscow, if the train travels the same number of miles each day for seven days. *(about 829 miles per day)* **OL**

C Critical Thinking

Drawing Conclusions Have students compare this map to the maps in the Regional Atlas. **Ask: Why do you think the railroad runs across the southern part of Russia?** *(Southern Russia has a milder climate, is more heavily populated, and has important resources.)* **OL**

Think About It

Answers:

1. They had to overcome swamps, permafrost, dense forests, and mountains, and dig wells and build mines.
2. The railroad helped Russia set up new factories in Siberia during World War II to make vehicles, ammunition, and weapons.

Additional Support

Activity: Connecting With the United States

Comparing and Contrasting Ask: Why did Russia build a railroad linking its western and eastern parts? *(to bring supplies to eastern settlements and ship resources from Siberia to factories in the west)* Tell students that the United States built a transcontinental railroad in the late 1800s. Have students work with partners to research the railroad that linked the eastern and western United States. Have students look for answers to questions such as: Why was a transcontinental railroad needed in the United States? When did construction begin? What difficulties did workers face during construction? When was the project completed? How did the transcontinental railroad affect life in the United States? Direct students to use their findings and the information in this feature to create a chart that compares and contrasts the United States' transcontinental railroad and the Trans-Siberian Railroad. Invite student pairs to share their charts with the rest of the class. **OL**

Focus

Bellringer

Daily Focus Transparency 14-2

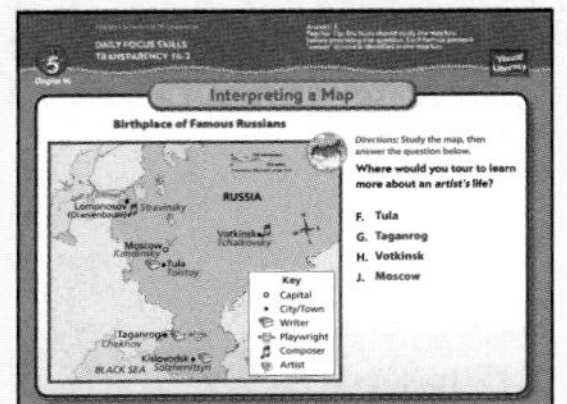

Guide to Reading

Answers to Graphic:

Russian Music and Dance: Folk music influenced many Russian musicians; Russian sense of nationalism reflected in many works; Tchaikovsky wrote famous ballets, such as *Swan Lake* and *The Nutcracker;* Stravinsky wrote *The Firebird Suite* and other works; Bolshoi ballet company in Moscow; Kirov ballet company in St. Petersburg

Section Spotlight Video

To learn more about the cultures and lifestyles of Russia, have students watch the Section Spotlight Video.

Guide to Reading

BIG Idea

Culture groups shape human systems.

Content Vocabulary

- oral tradition *(p. 397)*
- nationalism *(p. 397)*
- autonomy *(p. 399)*

Academic Vocabulary

- promote *(p. 398)*
- primary *(p. 400)*
- exploit *(p. 400)*

Reading Strategy

Summarizing Use a diagram like the one below to list details about Russian music and dance.

SECTION 2

Cultures and Lifestyles

Picture This The model in this photograph is getting ready for Siberian Fashion Week in Krasnoyarsk, Russia. Once a fortress city that protected Siberia from invaders, the city is now home to a festival that highlights the world of beauty. Krasnoyarsk links the eastern and western regions of icy Siberia. In a similar way, Fashion Week combines the artistic traditions of the regions with the business of high fashion. Read Section 2 to learn more about the rich cultures of Russia.

▼ Siberian Fashion Week in Krasnoyarsk, Russia

Resource Manager

R Reading Strategies	C Critical Thinking	D Differentiated Instruction	W Writing Support	 Skill Practice
Teacher Edition • Identifying, p. 397, 400 • Making Conn., p. 399 **Additional Resources** • Guid. Read., URB p. 60 • Cont. Vocab., URB p. 61 • Ac. Vocab., URB p. 63 • Read. Ess., p. 100 • World Lit., URB p. 31	**Teacher Edition** • Making Inferences, p. 399 • Det. Cause/Effect, p. 400 **Additional Resources** • Quizzes and Tests, p. 158 • Env. Case Studies, URB p. 13 • GeoLab, URB p. 23 • Crit. Think., URB p. 69	**Teacher Edition** • Auditory/Musical, p. 397 • Kinesthetic, p. 398 **Additional Resources** • Enrichment, URB, p. 19 • Reteach, URB, p. 77	**Teacher Edition** • Exp. Writing, p. 398 **Additional Resources** • Writing Skills, URB p. 75	**Teacher Edition** • Visual Literacy, pp. 397, 399 **Additional Resources** • Chart, Graph, and Map Skills, URB p. 67 • Read. Skills, URB p. 25 • Daily Focus Trans. 14-2 • Reg. Atlas, URB pp. 1–7

Russia's Cultures

Main Idea **Russia's many ethnic groups and a tradition of great achievements in the arts and sciences contribute to the country's cultures.**

Geography and You Have you ever watched the graceful motions of a ballet dancer? Read to find out how ballet and other arts are an important part of Russia's culture.

Russia has many different ethnic groups and religions. As the Russian Empire expanded, different peoples came under its control. Today dozens of ethnic groups live in Russia. Many of these groups speak their own language and have their own culture. Most people, however, speak Russian, the country's official language.

Russians, or Slavs who descended from the people of Muscovy, are the largest ethnic group. They live throughout Russia, although most Russians live west of the Urals. The next-largest groups include Tatars, who are Muslim descendants of the Mongols, and Ukrainians, who are descendants of Slavs that settled the area around Kiev (Kyiv). Smaller ethnic groups include the Yakut, who herd reindeer and also raise horses and cattle in eastern Siberia. R

Under communism, Russia's people were not allowed to practice religion. The Soviet government officially promoted the position in its schools that there is no god or other supreme being. By the late 1980s, however, the Soviets began to relax their ban on religions. Today, people enjoy religious freedom, and about half of the population practices a faith. Eastern Orthodox Christianity is the country's major religion. Russia also has many Muslims, who live mainly in the Caucasus region. Lesser numbers of Roman Catholics, Protestants, and Jews also live in Russia.

S

Kazan Cathedral

In 1936 Communist leaders destroyed the cathedral that stood on this site in Moscow. It was rebuilt in the 1980s. ***Regions*** **What is Russia's major religion today?**

The Arts

Russia has a rich tradition of literature, art, and music. Early Russians developed a strong **oral tradition**, or passing stories by word of mouth from generation to generation. Later, many writers and musicians drew on these stories or on folk music for their works. The Russian people's strong sense of **nationalism**, or feelings of loyalty toward their country, is reflected in many artistic works.

Russia has long been a center of music and dance. In the late 1800s, Peter Ilich Tchaikovsky (chy·KAWF·skee) wrote some of the world's favorite ballets, including *Swan Lake* and *The Nutcracker.* In the early 1900s, Igor Stravinsky wrote *The Firebird Suite* and other works. Today, the Bolshoi of Moscow and the Kirov of St. Petersburg are among the world's famous ballet companies. D

Teach

R Reading Strategy

Identifying **Ask:** **Name some of the ethnic groups in Russia.** *(Russians or Slavs, Tatars, Ukrainians, and the Yakut)* **OL**

S Skill Practice

Visual Literacy **Ask:** This cathedral looks very different from most cathedrals in Western Europe and the United States. **What feature indicates that this is a religious building?** *(There are crosses on the building.)* **OL**

D Differentiated Instruction

Auditory/Musical Have students listen to a work by Tchaikovsky, preferably a selection from *The Nutcracker* or *Swan Lake.* Ask them to describe the music and explain why it is appropriate for ballet dancing. **OL**

Caption Answer:
Eastern Orthodox Christianity

Differentiated Instruction

Leveled Activities

BL **Chart, Graph, and Map Skills Activity, URB p. 67**

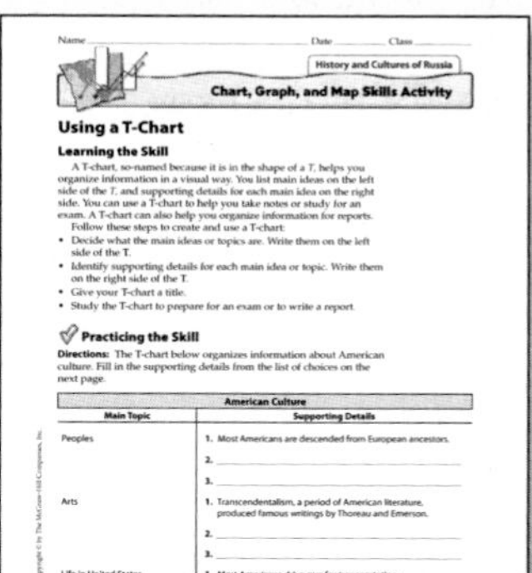

OL **Critical Thinking Activity, URB p. 69**

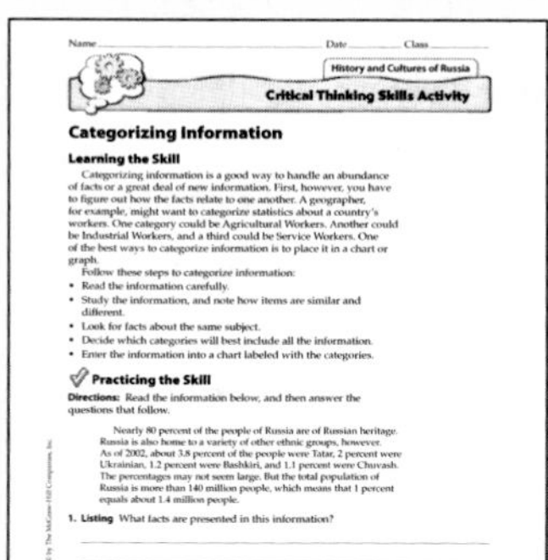

AL **Enrichment Activity, URB p. 19**

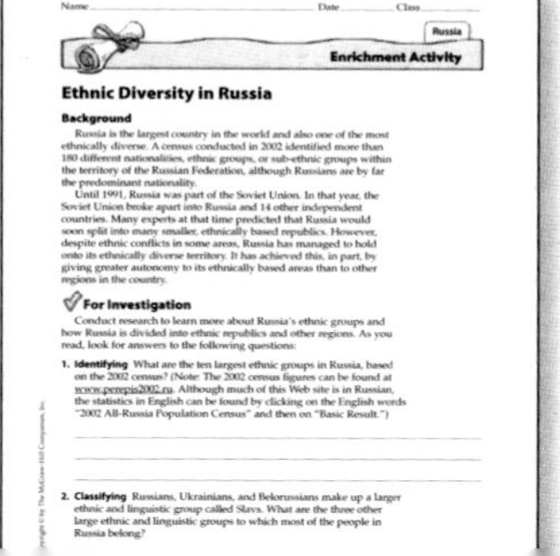

ELL **Guided Reading Activity, URB p. 60**

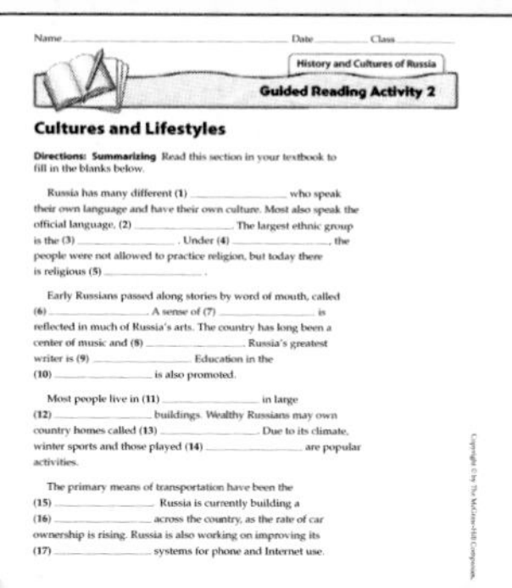

W Writing Support

Expository Writing Have students conduct research to learn more about the life of Solzhenitsyn. Then have them write an essay that explains how Solzhenitsyn's life illustrates the changes in political freedoms in Russia during his lifetime. **AL**

D Differentiated Instruction

Kinesthetic Provide students with photos of Fabergé eggs and art materials. Discuss with students the complexities of the eggs and the difficulties Fabergé probably encountered while making them. Then have students create their own eggs in the Fabergé style. **OL**

Caption Answer:
literature, such as the works of Tolstoy, and music and dance, such as Tchaikovsky's ballets

Reading Check Answer: People in Russia can now practice their religions freely, and about half of the population does so.

The 1800s are often called the "golden age" of Russian literature. During this period, Leo Tolstoy, one of the greatest Russian writers, wrote *War and Peace*. This patriotic novel describes the Russians' defense against the French invasion in 1812.

W During the Soviet era, writers did not enjoy freedom of expression. They were required to **promote** government policies in their works. Alexander Solzhenitsyn (SOHL·zhuh·NEET·suhn), who wrote about the harsh conditions of Communist society, spent time in Russian prison camps before he was forced to leave the country. Russian writers today are generally free to write about any idea or topic. Recently, however, the government placed new limits on freedom of speech.

The visual arts are also an important part of Russian culture. The Hermitage Museum in St. Petersburg has one of the most famous art collections in the world. **D** Among its treasures are the jewel-encrusted Easter eggs crafted by jeweler Peter Carl Fabergé for the czars.

Scientific Advances

For decades, the Soviet Union emphasized education in the sciences. As a result, Russia has many scientists, mathematicians, and doctors. During the Cold War, Russian scientists helped the Soviet Union compete with the United States in space exploration. In 1961 Russian Yuri Gagarin was the first person to fly in space. Since 1998 the Russians have joined with Americans and people from other countries in building the International Space Station.

Reading Check **Explaining** How have religious practices in Russia changed since the fall of communism?

NATIONAL GEOGRAPHIC

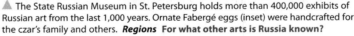

Russian Treasures

▲ The State Russian Museum in St. Petersburg holds more than 400,000 exhibits of Russian art from the last 1,000 years. Ornate Fabergé eggs (inset) were handcrafted for the czar's family and others. ***Regions*** **For what other arts is Russia known?**

Differentiated Instruction

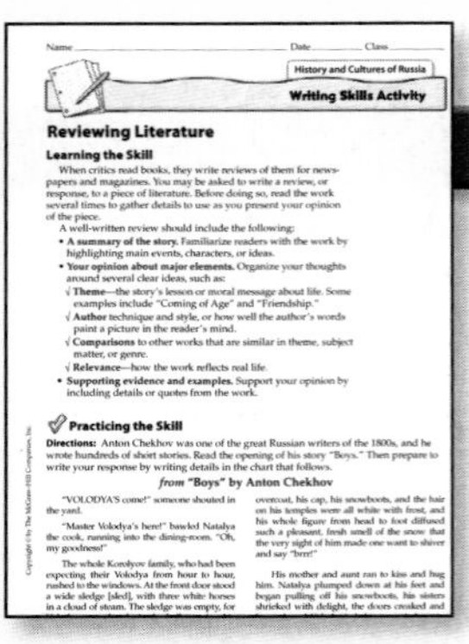

Name ______ Date ______ Class ______

History and Cultures of Russia

Writing Skills Activity

Reviewing Literature

Learning the Skill

When critics read books, they write reviews of them for newspapers and magazines. You may be asked to write a review, or response, to a piece of literature. Before doing so, read the work several times to gather details to use as you present your opinion of the piece.

A well-written review should include the following:

- **A summary of the story.** Familiarize readers with the work by highlighting main events, characters, or ideas.
- **Your opinion about major elements.** Organize your thoughts around several clear ideas, such as:
  - √ **Theme**—the story's lesson or moral message about life. Some examples include "Coming of Age" and "Friendship."
  - √ **Author** technique and style, or how well the author's words paint a picture in the reader's mind.
  - √ **Comparisons** to other works that are similar in theme, subject matter, or genre.
  - √ **Relevance**—how the work reflects real life.
- **Supporting evidence and examples.** Support your opinion by including details or quotes from the work.

Practicing the Skill

Directions: Anton Chekhov was one of the great Russian writers of the 1800s, and he wrote hundreds of short stories. Read the opening of his story "Boys." Then prepare to write your response by writing details in the chart that follows.

from **"Boys" by Anton Chekhov**

"VOLODYA'S come!" someone shouted in the yard.

"Master Volodya's here!" bawled Natalya the cook, running into the dining-room. "Oh, my goodness!"

The whole Korolyov family, who had been expecting their Volodya from hour to hour, rushed to the windows. At the front door stood a wide sledge [sled], with three white horses in a cloud of steam. The sledge was empty, for overcoat, his cap, his snowboots, and the hair on his temples were all white with frost, and his whole figure from head to foot diffused such a pleasant, fresh smell of the snow that the very sight of him made one want to shiver and say "brrr!"

His mother and aunt ran to kiss and hug him. Natalya plumped down at his feet and began pulling off his snowboots, his sisters shrieked with delight, the doors creaked and

Writing Skills Activity, URB pp. 75–76

Reviewing Literature

Objective: To write a review of a short story

Focus: Examine the elements of a well-written review.

Teach: Read the selection, gather details about story elements, and develop opinions about them. Record details and ideas in a chart.

Assess: Use the response planner chart to write a review of the selection.

Close: Share and compare reviews with other readers.

Differentiated Instruction Strategies

BL List the main characters, events, and ideas in the story.

AL Read another work by Chekhov, and write a review of this work.

ELL Write two opinion statements about the selection. Give one detail from the story to support each statement.

Life in Russia

Main Idea **Russian lifestyles are influenced by the region's cold climate and vast area, as well as the country's changing economic system.** R

Geography and You Do you like to celebrate the arrival of spring after a long, cold winter? Read on to find out about Russia's spring festival and other aspects of Russian life. S

While Russia continues to modernize after shedding Soviet control, it faces several challenges. Housing is still in short supply, and transportation and communication networks need updating.

Everyday Life

Most Russians live in cities located west of the Ural Mountains. City residents generally live in large apartment buildings rather than in single-family houses. Housing is scarce and often expensive. For this reason, grandparents, parents, and children frequently share the same apartment or house. Since many Russian mothers work outside of the home, grandparents often help take care of the household. Grandparents may cook, clean, shop, and care for young children in the family.

Middle-class and wealthy Russians may own country homes called dachas (DAH·chuhs). At their country homes, people often tend gardens, growing vegetables that they can either eat or sell in the cities. In rural areas, dachas and other homes are usually built of wood.

In the coldest areas of Russia, people take extra steps to keep their homes warm. For example, some homes in Siberia have three doors at each entrance. This prevents a cold blast of air from rushing in when the outside doors are opened.

NATIONAL GEOGRAPHIC

Family Life in Russia

In Russia it is common for several generations of one family to share a home.
Location **Where do most Russians live?**

Sports and Holidays

It is not surprising that the country's most popular sports are associated with winter or are played indoors. During the Communist era, the Soviet Union placed great emphasis on training world-class athletes. Today, Russian hockey players, figure skaters, and gymnasts are strong competitors in international events.

Russians celebrate several holidays. The newest holiday, Independence Day, falls on June 12 and marks Russia's declaration of **autonomy,** or independence from the Soviet Union. New Year's Eve is one of the most festive holidays. Russian children decorate a fir tree and exchange presents with others in their families. In the spring, Russians celebrate *Maslenitsa.* This weeklong holiday marks the end of winter and includes organized snowball fights, sleigh rides, and parties. Straw dolls that represent winter are burned to signal the beginning of spring. C

R Reading Strategy

Making Connections **Ask:** How do you think climate might affect the daily life of the Russian people? *(Possible answer: People must use reliable transportation to get through snow and ice, and they must heat their homes more frequently and wear warmer clothes.)* OL

S Skill Practice

Visual Literacy **Ask:** How many generations probably live in the home shown in this photo? *(three)* BL

C Critical Thinking

Making Inferences **Ask:** Why do you think Russians celebrate the end of winter? *(Winter is a difficult season in Russia's harsh climate, so people are happy when spring arrives.)* OL

Caption Answer:
in cities located west of the Ural Mountains

Hands-On Chapter Project
Step 2

Viewing Russia Through Stamps

Step 2: Designing Stamps Each group of students will design six stamps commemorating subjects from Sections 1 and 2.

Directions Have each group identify three new aspects of Russian culture. Then have groups design a series of six stamps on the subjects they have chosen from Sections 1 and 2. Remind students that stamps are small and include few, if any, words other than the country's name and amount of postage. Tell students to create simple, clear art to convey the historical or cultural significance of each subject.

Putting It Together Invite each group to present the designs for their stamps to the class. Ask students to explain how their subjects are represented on each of the stamps. OL

(Chapter Project cont. on the Visual Summary page)

R Reading Strategy

Identifying Ask: What is a synonym for extensive? *(vast or widespread)* OL

C Critical Thinking

Determining Cause and Effect
Ask: What is one effect of the increase in car ownership in Russia? *(More highways are being built.)* What else might happen as a result of car ownership? *(People might move out of cities and commute to work, so air pollution might increase.)* OL

Reading Check Answer: *Maslenitsa* celebrates the end of Russia's harsh winter and includes many cold-weather activities.

Assess

Social Studies ONLINE
Study Central™ provides summaries, interactive games, and online graphic organizers to help students review content.

Close

Summarizing Have students summarize Russia's major achievements in the arts and sciences. OL

Transportation and Communications

Russia is so large that people and goods must often be transported over great distances. Railroads were the **primary** means of transportation during the Soviet era and are still important today. The heavily populated area west of the Urals is covered by an extensive railroad network. **R**

This railroad system is linked to the famed Trans-Siberian Railroad, which runs from Moscow in the west to Vladivostok in the east. Completed in the early 1900s, it is the longest rail line in the world. The railroad made it possible for Russians to **exploit**, or use, Siberia's natural resources.

Russia still lacks an effective highway system. No multilane highway system links major cities, and the roads that do exist are in poor condition. There are few gas stations or restaurants along the roads. The government is currently building a 6,600-mile (10,622-km) highway across the country. When completed, it will be the longest national highway in the world.

C One reason that highway improvements are needed is because Russian car ownership is rising. In Soviet times, few families had cars. Now about half of Russian families own a car.

Russia's communications systems also need improvement. For years, telephones were less common in Russia than in most European countries. Since the early 1990s, major improvements have been made that will benefit Russian citizens and the country's economy. New phone lines allow for the rapid transfer of information, making it easier to use the Internet in Russia. Rural areas, however, still have poor phone service.

Reading Check **Making Connections** How does the *Maslenitsa* celebration reflect Russia's culture and environment?

Section 2 Review

Social Studies ONLINE
Study Central™ To review this section, go to glencoe.com.

Vocabulary

1. **Explain** the meaning of *oral tradition, nationalism,* and *autonomy* by using each term in a sentence.

Main Ideas

2. **Identifying** Name and describe four of Russia's ethnic groups.
3. **Organizing** Use a diagram like the one below to list details about Russia's transportation system.

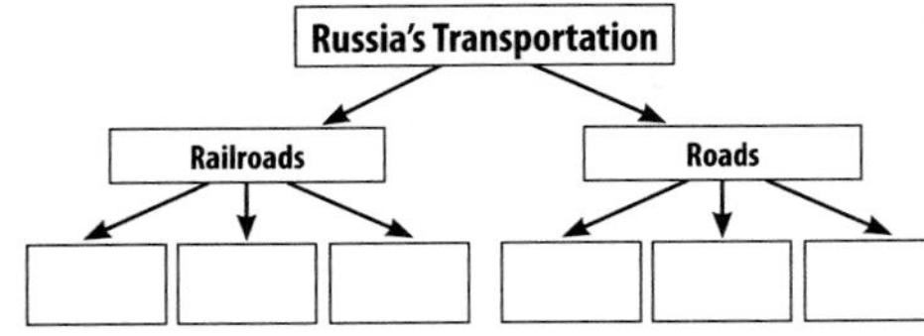

Critical Thinking

4. **Determining Cause and Effect** Why do many grandparents, parents, and children in Russia share the same apartment or house?
5. **BIG Idea** How are Russia's nationalist feelings represented in the country's arts?
6. **Challenge** Why do you think the Soviet Union competed with the United States in the area of space exploration?

Writing About Geography

7. **Expository Writing** Write a paragraph explaining how Russia's cold climate affects Russians' daily lives.

Answers

1. Sentences should use vocabulary words according to their definitions in the section and Glossary.
2. (1) Russians or Slavs—descended from the people of Muscovy; live largely west of the Urals; make up the largest ethnic group; (2) Tatars—Muslim descendants of the Mongols; (3) Ukrainians—descendants of Slavs who settled around Kiev; (4) the Yakut—herd reindeer and raise horses and cattle in eastern Siberia.
3. **Railroads:** main means of transportation in Soviet era; extensive in heavily populated area west of Urals; Trans-Siberian Railroad, the world's longest rail line; **Roads:** no multilane highway system linking major cities; roads in poor condition; cross-country highway now under construction
4. Housing is in short supply and can be expensive.
5. Writers draw on stories from a long oral tradition for their works; musicians draw on Russian folk music.
6. to prove the excellence of Soviet education and to show Soviet advances in scientific research and development
7. Answers may vary but should discuss home construction in the coldest areas, the popularity of winter and indoor sports, and holidays associated with winter, such as New Year's Eve and *Maslenitsa.*

Visual Summary

The Russian Empire

- Russia had its beginnings in small trading centers built by Slavic peoples.
- Rulers known as czars governed the Russian Empire from 1547 to 1917.
- The czars expanded Russian territory to reach from Europe to the Pacific Ocean.
- Revolutions in 1917 overthrew the czar and brought the Communists to power.

Joseph Stalin

Medieval Moscow

The Rise of Democracy

- In 1991 the Soviet Union broke up into Russia and other independent republics.
- Russia has struggled to build a democracy and a market economy.

People and Culture

- Russia has many different ethnic groups.
- Russians practice a number of different religions, but most of the population is Eastern Orthodox Christian.
- Russian artists, musicians, and writers often used themes based on Russian history.

Dacha outside of Moscow

The Soviet Union

- Under the Communist Party, the government ran all areas of economic life.
- After World War II, the Soviet Union and the United States became bitter rivals.

Cold War parade with missiles

Life in Russia

- Most Russians live in apartments in large cities rather than in single-family homes.
- Railroads link heavily populated European Russia with sparsely settled Siberia.
- Russia is working to improve its highway and communications systems.

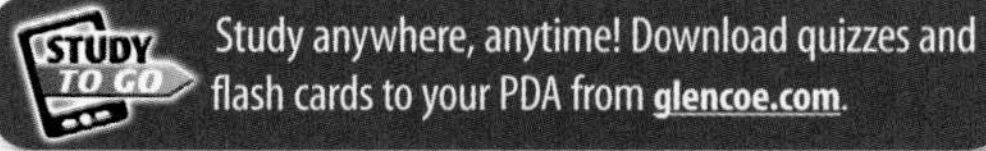

Study anywhere, anytime! Download quizzes and flash cards to your PDA from glencoe.com.

Visual Summary

Sequencing Have students study the text under the first three headings on this page. **Ask:** **In what order is this information presented?** *(chronological order)* Have students use the information under these headings, as well as information from the chapter, to create an illustrated time line of events in Russian history. Tell students to include dates related to the bulleted points under these three headings.

Provide students with pictures, or have them create their own illustrations to add to their time lines. When students complete their work, have them present their time lines to the class and explain how the pictures illustrate the events on the time line. **OL**

Comparing and Contrasting Have students analyze the photo of the dacha on this page. Then have them compare and contrast the dacha to their own home. Encourage students to think about the color of the home, the architectural features, and the location. **OL**

This **Reading Skill** (Comparing and Contrasting) was introduced in this unit.

Hands-On Chapter Project
Step 3: Wrap Up

Viewing Russia Through Stamps

Step 3: Learning from the Project Students will synthesize what they learned in Steps 1 and 2.

Directions Write the Essential Question on the board. Encourage students to answer this question by using what they learned as they planned and designed their stamp series on Russian history and culture. Begin by asking students to describe the subjects they chose for their stamps. List the subjects on the board under the headings "History" and "Culture." Use the list as a springboard to discuss the causes and effects of the expansion of Russia. Ask questions such as: What part did the Mongolians play in the development of Russia? What was Muscovy? How did Ivan the Terrible create an empire? What were the goals of Catherine the Great and Peter the Great in expanding Russian territory? How did Muslims and other non-Russians become part of the empire? What effect did the expansion of Russia have on Russian culture? Next, have students write what they have learned about the Essential Question in their journals. **OL**

Answers and Analyses

Reviewing Vocabulary

1. C This question may challenge students because every answer choice is a group of people. By analyzing the choices, students can narrow down the possibilities. The question asks what the emperors, or rulers, of Russia were called, and answer choices B and D would not fit because they are terms related to religion. The two remaining choices are opposites: serfs were the poor farm workers of the country, and the czars were the rulers.

2. A Students might struggle to choose between answer choices A, *perestroika*, and D, *glasnost*. (The other two choices were not introduced by Gorbachev.) Students need to remember that *perestroika* means "rebuilding," which is what the Soviet economy needed.

3. A The question asks for the term for farm laborers, and if students analyze the answer choices carefully, they will note that answer choices B and C are terms that refer to people based on their religious actions. Of the two remaining choices, *serfs* is the only term that makes sense, since guilds are organizations, not individuals that can be bought and sold.

4. B A close reading of the question will lead students to the correct answer. The question defines the term as "stories passed on by word of mouth." The term *oral* in answer choice B means "by mouth." The question also mentions passing stories on from generation to generation, which indicates tradition.

5. D To help answer the question, students need to look for a term that is a synonym for *independence*, which is what the Russians are celebrating. *Dependence* is an illogical choice, as it is the opposite of independence. *Autonomy* is a synonym for independence, and therefore, choice D is the correct answer.

STANDARDIZED TEST PRACTICE

TEST-TAKING TIP

Read all the choices before choosing your answer. You may overlook the correct answer if you are hasty!

Reviewing Vocabulary

Directions: Choose the word(s) that best completes the sentence.

1. The emperors of Russia were called ______.

A serfs
B converts
C czars
D missionaries

2. Mikhail Gorbachev introduced ______, which was aimed at boosting the Soviet economy.

A perestroika
B collectivization
C Cold War
D glasnost

3. ______ were farm laborers who could be bought and sold with the land.

A Serfs
B Converts
C Missionaries
D Guilds

4. Early Russians developed a strong ______, which means passing stories by word of mouth from generation to generation.

A nationalism
B oral tradition
C autonomy
D glasnost

5. Russia's newest holiday, Independence Day, marks its declaration of ______ the Soviet Union.

A collectivization of
B dependence on
C alliance with
D autonomy from

Reviewing Main Ideas

Directions: Choose the best answer for each question.

Section 1 *(pp. 388–394)*

6. The Russian Empire eventually fell to a revolution due mostly to ______.

A threats from invaders
B widespread hunger and suffering
C outside agitators
D a decline in the military

7. When Communist leaders took control of Russia and renamed it the Soviet Union, they established a ______.

A free market economy
B democratic government
C government controlled economy
D new government controlled by a czar

Section 2 *(pp. 396–400)*

8. The Russian people's sense of nationalism ______.

A has little impact on Russia's arts
B has caused them to avoid foreign art
C is reflected in many artistic works
D is the only topic used in Russian literature

9. Russia's many good hockey players and gymnasts are partly a result of the country's ______.

A high mountains
B many factories and industries
C many professional sports teams
D cold climate

GO ON

Reviewing Main Ideas

6. B To answer this question correctly, it is important that students notice the word *mostly* and look for the *main* cause. Although Russia suffered military defeats in World War I, this was not the primary factor, nor were outside agitators or fear of invasion the underlying causes. The fundamental reason for the revolution was the harsh poverty that people of the country suffered.

7. C Answer choice D can be easily eliminated because Communist party rule ended government by czars. Of the remaining choices, only choice C is a characteristic of a Communist country.

Critical Thinking

Directions: Choose the best answer for each question.

10. Which of the following was a result of perestroika?

A The Soviet economy was weakening.

B The people were ready for change.

C Factory managers gained more freedoms.

D Citizens could say what they thought without punishment.

Base your answer to question 11 on the chart below.

Infant Mortality Rates per 1,000 Live Births

Years	Soviet Union/Russia	United States
1950–1955	97	28
1955–1960	57	26
1960–1965	40	25
1965–1970	32	22
1970–1975	28	18
1975–1980	30	14
1980–1985	26	11
1985–1990	24	10
1990–1995*	21	9
1995–2000	17	8

*After 1991 the Soviet Union collapsed.

Source: http://world.britannica.com/analyst/chrono/table

11. Which of the following statements seems most likely?

A Between 1950 and 2000, medical care decreased in the United States.

B Between 1950 and 2000, infants in the Soviet Union had greater access to hospitals than in the United States.

C Between 1950 and 2000, infants in the Soviet Union had a better chance of surviving than in the United States.

D Between 1950 and 2000, medical care improved in the Soviet Union.

Document-Based Questions

Directions: Analyze the document and answer the short-answer questions that follow.

After it was first adopted in 1918, the constitution of the Soviet Union was rewritten several times. The following is part of the preamble from the 1977 version.

> *The supreme goal of the Soviet state is the building of a classless communist society in which there will be public, communist self-government. The main aims of the people's socialist state are: to lay the material and technical foundation of communism, to perfect socialist social relations and transform them into communist relations, to mould the citizen of communist society, to raise the people's living and cultural standards, to safeguard the country's security, and to further the consolidation of peace and development of international cooperation.*

12. How do you think the Soviet state will "lay the material and technical foundation of communism"?

13. Which parts of the preamble deal directly with Soviet citizens?

Extended Response

14. Citizens of the Soviet Union faced many problems during the period the Communist government was in control. Write an essay in which you explain what you think were the most difficult problems people had to face. Make sure to explain why these problems were worse than others.

Social Studies ONLINE

For additional test practice, use Self-Check Quizzes—Chapter 14 at glencoe.com.

Need Extra Help?

If you missed question...	1	2	3	4	5	6	7	8	9	10	11	12	13	14
Go to page...	390	393	390	397	399	391	392	397	399	393	398	391	391	391

Critical Thinking

10. C Students need to recall that perestroika was a policy related to the economy, eliminating answer choice D. A and B are incorrect because they were not the effects of perestroika, but some of the causes. Answer choice C is correct because perestroika did, indeed, give factory managers more freedom.

11. D The chart shows the infant mortality rate in the United States declining as time passes, which makes answer choice A unlikely. Since the infant mortality rates are higher in the Soviet Union than in the United States, answer choice C is incorrect. Answer choice B does not make sense, because if infants in the Soviet Union had greater access to hospitals, their mortality rate would be lower. Answer choice D is a logical answer because an improvement in medical care should lead to reduced infant mortality.

Document-Based Questions

12. Possible answer: The government will lay the material and technical foundation of communism by controlling the economy.

13. Possible answer: to mould the citizen of communist society; raise living and cultural standards

Extended Response

14. Answers will vary, but could include hunger, shortage of adequate clothing, shelter, and medical care, repressive government, absence of human rights, harsh climate, vast distances, poor economy, and so on.

8. C The Russian people's sense of nationalism, or loyalty to their country, has had a great effect on the arts in Russia. The text discusses how the writers and musicians of Russia drew on oral traditions and folk music for their works. Nationalism has not caused Russians to avoid foreign art, and it is not the only topic of Russian literature.

9. D Students can answer this question with careful analysis of the answer choices and some prior knowledge. Ice is needed to play hockey. Russia's climate makes winter sports, like hockey, popular. Gymnastics is played indoors, and many people in cold climates prefer to stay indoors. High mountains and factories and industries would not influence the development of hockey and gymnastics. Russia does not have many professional sports teams. Therefore, choice D, the cold climate, is the correct answer.

Social Studies ONLINE

Have students visit the Web site at glencoe.com to review Chapter 14 and take the Self-Check Quiz.

Need Extra Help?

Have students refer to the pages listed if they miss any of the questions.

Teach

R Reading Strategy

Making Connections Have students think about their own mealtimes. **Ask: How does the time of Irina's lunch compare to your own?** *(Possible answer: Irina's lunch is later than my lunch.)* **How is Irina's school-day lunch different from yours?** *(Possible answer: Irina eats lunch at home with her mother, while I eat lunch at school.)* **OL**

C Critical Thinking

Making Inferences Ask: What can you infer about Irina's family from the fact that they own a dacha? *(Her family is probably either middle class or wealthy.)*

TIME JOURNAL

"Hello! My name is Irina.

I am 13 years old and I live in Moscow, the capital of Russia, with my parents and little brother, Misha. I go to Moscow School No. 429. This is how I spend a typical day."

7:30 a.m. I wake up and dress quickly in jeans and a sweater. Then I join my parents and Misha in the kitchen and have yogurt for breakfast. (On weekends, I like fried eggs, but today there is not enough time!)

8:00 a.m. My father drives me to school and Misha to kindergarten. In Russia, public schools do not provide buses. After dropping us off, my father will go to his job as a manager at a paper supply company.

8:10 a.m. I arrive at school. School No. 429 is a modern building, but Moscow is a very old city. Some of its buildings are more than 500 years old!

8:30 a.m. Classes begin. One of my first classes of the day is "work study," in which we learn different trades. Right now we are learning to sew clothes. It's interesting, but I don't think it's the right job for me. I would like to be a makeup artist one day.

9:30 a.m. It is time for geography class. I raise my hand to respond to a question, and I answer correctly. This makes me happy because I would like to get a grade of 4 or 5 in this class. A *4* means "very good." A 5 means "excellent."

11:30 a.m. I'm hungry! During a break between classes, I stop in at the canteen (cafeteria) for a small piece of pizza. Later, I will have a bigger lunch at home.

12:30 p.m. In computer class, we log on to the Internet. This is one of my favorite classes.

2:00 p.m. The school day is over, and I take the tram home. The tram is a street car that runs on electricity. Moscow's tramway is more than 100 years old.

R **3:00 p.m.** My mother is home from her job at a print house and Misha is home from school. I help make a lunch of chicken and cold borscht. Borscht is a soup made of beets and other vegetables. It can be served cold or hot.

3:30 p.m. My mother, Misha, and I walk to a large park near our flat, or apartment. There I meet up with my friend Yulia. We roller skate and play with Misha.

5:30 p.m. Back at home, I help do the laundry and dust the flat. When I am done with my chores, I go to my bedroom and start my homework.

7:30 p.m. My father is home, and it is time for a light dinner. Tonight we have a salad made of eggs, cabbage, mayonnaise, and beets. Another dinner I enjoy is pelmeni. It is pieces of meat that are covered in dough and boiled in salty water.

8:00 p.m. I finish my homework and listen to music. I like Russian bands, but I also enjoy American pop music. I listen to it on the radio and on music videos.

10:30 p.m. I go to bed. Tomorrow is Friday, my last day of school for the week. I am looking forward to the weekend! C We will spend it at our dacha, or country cottage. It is in the village of Istra, where my grandparents live. I enjoy spending time with them.

ILLUSTRATIONS BY BOOKMAPMAN

GLOBETROTTING Irina is tested on her geography skills. She got an "excellent"!

COME AND GET IT! Irina helps her mom make dinner. Russians often eat a big lunch and a light supper.

SOAP STORY Blowing bubbles in the park is fun for Irina and her friend Yulia.

404 • Chapter 14

Additional Support

Additional Statistics You can find data like this and much more in the *CIA World Factbook*. Go to www.cia.gov and click on the link to the *World Factbook*. From there you can click on the countries you wish to learn more about.

Communications in Russia

Telephones	Radio and TV	Internet
40.1 million main telephone lines in use	323 AM radio broadcast stations, 1,500 FM radio broadcast stations 62 shortwave radio broadcast stations	1,979,924 Internet hosts (computers connected directly to the Internet)
120 million cellular phone subscribers	7,306 TV broadcast stations	23.7 million Internet users

Source: *CIA World Factbook*, 2006.

TIME JOURNAL

GOING SKATING After school, Irina Timoshenko (uh • REE • nah teem • oh • SHENK • oh) loves to roller skate with her friends. Irina lives in Moscow, Russia's capital, which is filled with parks that are perfect for skating.

JEREMY NICHOLL / POLARIS (4)

What's Popular in Russia

Tea Time Many Russian families drink weak black tea all day long. It is brewed in a pot called a samovar.

BILL ARON / PHOTO EDIT

Steam baths This hot trend is actually an old Russian tradition. At a *banya*, or bath house, a visitor sits in a steam room, then takes an icy cold dip, and finally, receives a gentle massage.

Dachas Many Russian city dwellers—both rich and poor—own cottages, or dachas, in the country. They go on weekends and in summers to relax.

Ballet Russia is home to some of the world's most famous dancers. Moscow's Bolshoi Ballet brought the world *Swan Lake.*

ANATOLY RUKHADZE / ITAR-TASS PHOTOS / NEWSCOM

Say It in Russian

Most of Russia's 140 million people speak the official national language, Russian. Russian is also spoken in Belarus, Kazakhstan, and other nations that were once republics of the Soviet Union. Try saying these phrases in Russian.

Hello
Zdravstvuite (ZDRAHST • vet • yah)

Good-bye
Do svidanja (doh svee • DAH • nee • yah)

My name is ________.
Menya zavut (mee • NYAH zah • VOOT) ________.

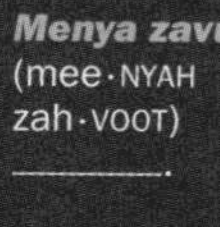

CREATAS / PUNCHSTOCK

What's Popular in Russia

Tea Time The tea pot called a *samovar* is a unique Russian creation. Samovars are metal urns used for brewing and serving tea. Although they are common household items in Russia, they are also regarded as works of art because of their elaborate designs. The city of Tula, near Moscow, is the center of samovar manufacturing.

Say It in Russian

Russian Many ethnic groups in Russia speak languages other than Russian, including Yiddish, Iranian, and Eskimo. In 1993 the Russian government specified in its constitution that all people have the right to retain and speak their native languages. Nonetheless, Russian provides a common language for the country and is the language of government and higher education.

Activity: Expository Writing

Comparing and Contrasting Students will notice similarities and differences between Irina's typical day and their own. Have students write a compare-and-contrast essay to highlight these similarities and differences. First, have students write a paragraph about their typical school day, including information about their families, friends, meals, classes, and after-school activities. Then have them write a second paragraph that compares and contrasts each of these items to similar items in Irina's narrative. Encourage them to end with a concluding sentence that states whether they think their typical day is generally similar to or different from Irina's day. **OL**

Planning Guide

Key to Ability Levels

BL Below level
OL On level
AL Above level
ELL English Language Learners

Key to Teaching Resources

Print Material
DVD
CD-ROM
Transparency

Levels				Resources	Chapter Opener	Section 1	Section 2	Chapter Assess
BL	OL	AL	ELL					
FOCUS								
BL	OL	AL	ELL	Daily Focus Skills Transparencies		15-1	15-2	
TEACH								
BL	OL		ELL	Guided Reading Activity, URB*		p. 83	p. 84	
BL	OL	AL	ELL	Content Vocabulary Activity, URB*		p. 85	p. 85	
BL	OL	AL	ELL	Academic Vocabulary Activity, URB		p. 87	p. 87	
BL	OL	AL	ELL	Differentiated Instruction Activity, URB		p. 89		
BL	OL	AL	ELL	Chart, Graph, and Map Skills Activity, URB		p. 91		
	OL	AL		Critical Thinking Activity, URB			p. 93	
BL	OL	AL	ELL	Speaking and Listening Skills Activity, URB		p. 95		
BL	OL	AL	ELL	Writing Skills Activity, URB			p. 99	
BL	OL	AL	ELL	School-to-Home Connection Activity, URB*		p. 103		
BL	OL	AL	ELL	Regional Atlas Activities, URB		pp. 1–7	pp. 1–7	
		AL		Geography and Economics Activity, URB		p. 9		
	OL	AL		Environmental Case Study, URB		p. 13		
		AL		Enrichment Activity, URB			p. 19	
BL	OL	AL	ELL	GeoLab Activity, URB		p. 23	p. 23	
BL	OL		ELL	Reading Skills Activity, URB		p. 25	p. 25	
BL	OL		ELL	Reading Essentials and Note-Taking Guide*		p. 103	p. 106	
	OL	AL		TIME Perspectives: Exploring World Issues		p. 17		
	OL			Interactive Geography Activity		p. 33	p. 33	
BL	OL	AL	ELL	In-Text Map Overlay and Population Pyramid Transparencies	5	5A–5D	5A–5D	5
	OL			Foods Around the World		pp. 18–21	pp. 18–21	
BL	OL	AL	ELL	Outline Map Resource Book	p. 42			p. 42
BL	OL	AL	ELL	NGS World Atlas*	✓	✓	✓	
BL	OL	AL	ELL	NGS World Desk Map	✓	✓	✓	✓
BL	OL	AL	ELL	World Literature Library	✓	✓	✓	✓
BL	OL	AL	ELL	Writer's Guidebook	✓	✓	✓	✓

Note: Please refer to the *Unit Resource Book: Russia* for this chapter's URB materials.

* Also available in Spanish

- Interactive Lesson Planner
- Interactive Teacher Edition
- Fully editable blackline masters
- Section Spotlight Videos Launch
- Differentiated Lesson Plans
- Printable reports of daily assignments
- Standards Tracking System

Levels				Resources		Chapter Opener	Section 1	Section 2	Chapter Assess
BL	OL	AL	ELL						
TEACH *(continued)*									
BL	OL	AL	ELL		**Vocabulary PuzzleMaker CD-ROM***	✓	✓	✓	✓
	OL	AL			**Primary Sources CD-ROM**	✓	✓	✓	✓
BL	OL	AL	ELL		**StudentWorks™ Plus DVD**	✓	✓	✓	✓
BL	OL	AL	ELL		**Section Video Program Activities**	✓	✓	✓	✓
BL	OL	AL	ELL		**World Music: A Cultural Legacy**	✓	✓	✓	✓
BL	OL	AL	ELL		**Writing Process Transparencies**	✓	✓	✓	✓
Teacher Resources					**Building Academic Vocabulary**	✓	✓	✓	✓
					Strategies for Success	✓	✓	✓	✓
					Teacher's Guide to Differentiated Instruction	✓	✓	✓	✓
					Presentation Plus! DVD	✓	✓	✓	✓
ASSESS									
BL	OL	AL	ELL		**Quizzes and Tests**		p. 167	p. 168	p. 169
BL	OL	AL	ELL		**Authentic Assessment With Rubrics**		p. 15	p. 15	p. 15
BL	OL	AL	ELL		**Standardized Test Practice**				p. 57
BL	OL	AL	ELL		***ExamView® Assessment Suite* CD-ROM***		15-1	15-2	Ch. 15
BL	OL	AL	ELL		**Interactive Tutor Self-Assessment CD-ROM**		15-1	15-2	
CLOSE									
BL			ELL		**Reteaching Activity, URB**		p. 101	p. 101	p. 101
BL	OL		ELL		**Reading and Study Skills Foldables™**	p. 78	p. 78	p. 78	p. 78
BL	OL	AL	ELL		**Graphic Organizer Transparencies and Strategies**		✓	✓	
BL	OL	AL	ELL		***Exploring Our World* in Graphic Novel**	p. 65			p. 65

Integrating Technology

Using CyberScout: Researching Using *Keyword*

Technology Product
CyberScout is a convenient and dynamic search engine that provides several easy ways to locate information outside the McGraw-Hill Learning Network. CyberScout only searches Web sites that have been reviewed by teachers, so the information students find is always appropriate and accurate.

Objectives
After students learn using CyberScout, they will be able to

- research topics and issues in economics using CyberScout;
- exercise research and study skills;
- practice writing skills.

Steps
- From the McGraw-Hill Learning Network home page (www.mhln.com), click on **For Students.**
- Choose **CyberScout** below **Homework Help.**
- Enter a keyword or phrase in the **Keyword** field and click on the **Go** button.
- Click on the link to a Web site of interest.
- Students will be redirected to the Web site in a new window.
- Students navigate through the chosen Web site to gain information on their topic and take notes.

Social Studies ONLINE

	Student	Teacher	Parent
Beyond the Textbook	●		●
Chapter Overviews	●		●
Concepts in Motion	●		●
ePuzzles and Games	●		●
Literature Connections		●	
Multi-Language Glossaries	●		●
Online Student Edition	●	●	●
Section Videos	●	●	●
Self-Check Quizzes	●		●
Student Web Activities	●		●
Study Central™	●		●
Teaching Today		●	
TIME Current Events	●		●
Vocabulary eFlashcards	●		●
Web Activity Lesson Plans		●	

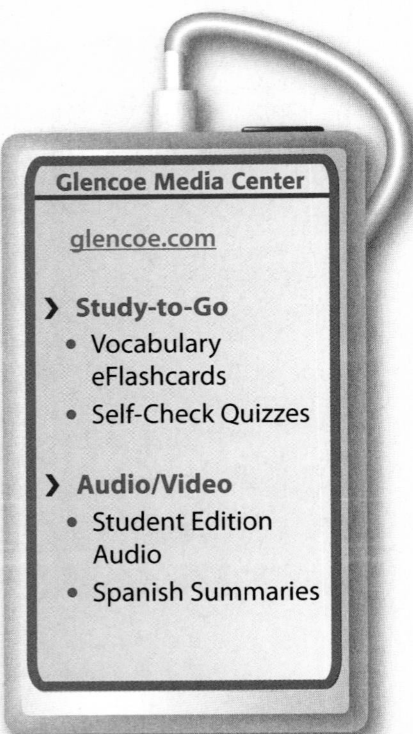

- **Timed Readings Plus in Social Studies** helps students increase their reading rate and fluency while maintaining comprehension. The 400-word passages are similar to those found on state and national assessments.
- **Reading in the Content Area: Social Studies** concentrates on six essential reading skills that help students better comprehend what they read. The book includes 75 high-interest nonfiction passages written at increasing levels of difficulty.
- **Reading Social Studies** includes strategic reading instruction and vocabulary support in Social Studies content for ELLs and native speakers of English.
- **Content Vocabulary Workout** (Grades 6–8) accelerates reading comprehension through focused vocabulary development. Social Studies content vocabulary comes from the glossaries of Glencoe's Middle School Social Studies texts.
  www.jamestowneducation.com

The following videotape programs are available from Glencoe as supplements to Chapter 15:

- Ivan the Terrible (ISBN 0-76-700517-1)
- Joseph Stalin: Red Terror (ISBN 1-56-501820-6)

To order, call Glencoe at 1-800-334-7344. To find classroom resources to accompany many of these videos, check the following home pages:

A&E Television: www.aetv.com
The History Channel: www.historychannel.com

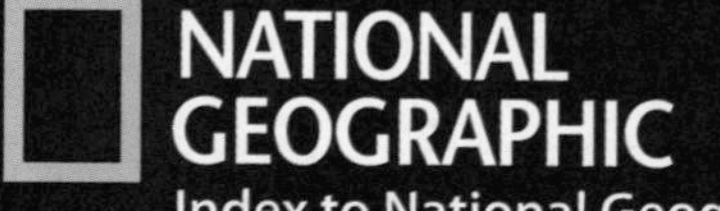

Index to National Geographic Magazine:

The following articles relate to this chapter:

- "How Did It Come to This?" by Andrew Meier, July 2005.
- "Giants Under Siege," by Gleb Raygorodetsky, February 2006.

National Geographic Society Products To order the following, call National Geographic at 1-800-368-2728:

- *National Geographic Atlas of the World* (Book).

Access National Geographic's new dynamic MapMachine Web site and other geography resources at:
www.nationalgeographic.com
www.nationalgeographic.com/maps

Reading List Generator CD-ROM

Use this database to search more than 30,000 titles to create a customized reading list for your students.

- Reading lists can be organized by students' reading level, author, genre, theme, or area of interest.
- The database provides Degrees of Reading Power™ (DRP) and Lexile™ readability scores for all selections.
- A brief summary of each selection is included.

Leveled reading suggestions for this chapter:

For students at a Grade 5 reading level:
- ***Russia,*** by Susan H. Gray

For students at a Grade 6 reading level:
- ***Georgia to Georgia: Making Friends in the U.S.S.R.,*** by Laurie Dolphin

For students at a Grade 7 reading level:
- ***Russia: The People,*** by Greg Nickles

For students at a Grade 8 reading level:
- ***Along the Tracks,*** by Tamar Bergman

For students at a Grade 9 reading level:
- ***Russia,*** by Kathleen Burton Murrell

Focus

The Essential Question

As students study the chapter, remind them to consider the chapter-based Essential Question. Answering this question will help them understand the important concepts in the chapter. In addition, the Hands-On Chapter Project relates the content from each section to the Essential Question. The steps in each section build on each other as students progress through the chapter. The Hands-On Chapter Project culminates in the Wrap Up activity on the Visual Summary page.

More About the Photo

Visual Literacy The people of Russia celebrate May Day on May 1 each year. May Day, a holiday created to honor workers' struggle for an eight-hour work day, originated in the United States. In that country, workers in the late 1700s and early 1800s protested for a shorter working day. In 1890 an international convention in Paris called for workers worldwide to hold demonstrations for an eight-hour work day. Since then, citizens of Russia honor workers by taking time off from work on May Day.

CHAPTER 15

Russia Today

Essential Question

Regions Since the fall of the Soviet Union, Russia has been struggling to build a democracy and a free market economy. It also has sought to regain its influence in world affairs. Such major changes are difficult, however, and the world will watch with great interest as Russia works to become a successful democratic nation. Why is the success of democracy in Russia important to the rest of the world?

406 • Chapter 15

Teach

The BIG Ideas *As you begin teaching each section, use these questions and activities to help students focus on the Big Ideas.*

Section 

A Changing Russia Ask: What challenges might democratic changes bring to a country? *(Answers may include: Various political groups might compete for power, people who were supported by the government might no longer have that support, and elections might not run smoothly.)* Explain to students that Russia has faced many challenges while making a transition from a communist to a democratic form of government. Ask students to think of two or three challenges that Russian citizens have faced in recent years. Tell them that they will learn more about these challenges in this section and in Section 2. **OL**

Section 

Issues and Challenges Ask: What problems might a vast country with many ethnic groups experience as its people change to a democratic government? *(Different ethnic groups might fight for power or decide to break off and claim their independence as a separate nation.)* Point out to students

Section 1: A Changing Russia

BIG IDEA Geographers organize the Earth into regions that share common characteristics. New democratic institutions and a free market economy link the different parts of Russia. These positive changes, however, are threatened by the government's abuse of power, the spread of corruption in business, and a decline in population.

Russians relaxing on May Day holiday, St. Petersburg

Section 2: Issues and Challenges

BIG IDEA Geography is used to interpret the past, understand the present, and plan for the future. The change to democracy and a market economy has been difficult for Russia because of its long history of all-powerful governments. The country also faces challenges from ethnic groups that want independence.

FOLDABLES™ Study Organizer

Organizing Information Make this Foldable to organize information about political and social changes in Russia and other issues in Russia today.

Step 1 Fold a sheet of paper in half from side to side so that the left edge lies about ½ inch from the right edge.

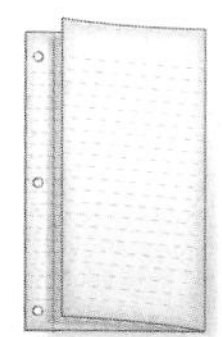

Step 2 Cut the top layer only to make five tabs.

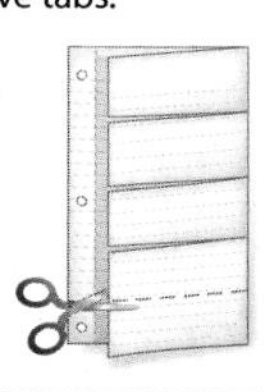

Step 3 Label the Foldable as shown.

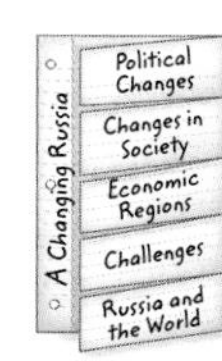

Reading and Writing Use the notes in your Foldable to create an outline showing the major issues facing Russia today.

To preview Chapter 15, go to glencoe.com.

Previewing the Region

If you have not already done so, engage students in the Regional Atlas and chart activities to help them become familiar with the general content of the region.

Dinah Zike's Foldables

Purpose This Foldable helps students organize facts from the chapter as they read. Students should note facts about political and social changes and other issues in Russia under the appropriate tabs on the Foldable. Students can use the Foldable to help them create an outline of the major issues facing Russia and to prepare for assessment. **OL**

More Foldables activities for this chapter can be found in *Dinah Zike's Reading and Study Skills Foldables* ancillary.

Social Studies ONLINE

Introduce students to chapter content and key terms by having them access the Chapter Overview at glencoe.com.

that in Section 2, they will learn more about the political and economic challenges Russia faces, including challenges to its national unity from ethnic groups. **OL**

Focus

Bellringer

Daily Focus Transparency 15-1

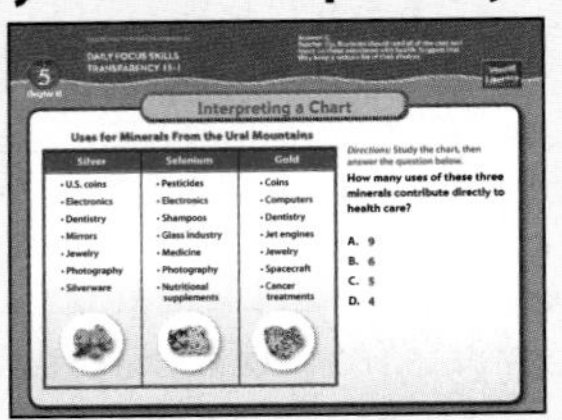

Guide to Reading

Answers to Graphic:

Answers may include:
a new form of government with a new constitution; a change from a command economy to a market economy; political and cultural freedoms

Section Spotlight Video

To learn more about how Russia has changed in recent years, have students watch the Section Spotlight Video.

Resource Manager

R Reading Strategies	C Critical Thinking	D Differentiated Instruction	W Writing Support	S Skill Practice
Teacher Edition • Previewing, p. 411 **Additional Resources** • Guid. Read., URB p. 83 • Cont. Vocab., URB p. 85 • Ac. Vocab., URB p. 87 • Read. Ess., p. 103	**Teacher Edition** • Predicting Consequences, p. 409 • Determining Cause and Effect, p. 411 **Additional Resources** • Geo. & Econ., URB p. 9 • Quizzes and Tests, p. 167 • Geolab, URB p. 23 • Env. Case Study, URB p. 13	**Teacher Edition** • Advanced Learners, p. 409 • English Learners, p. 410 **Additional Resources** • Reteach., URB p. 101 • School-to-Home Conn., URB p. 103	**Teacher Edition** • Expository Writing, p. 410 **Additional Resources** • Authentic Assess., p. 15	**Teacher Edition** • Using Geography Skills, p. 412 **Additional Resources** • Chart, Graph, and Map Skills, URB p. 91 • Speak./Listen. Skills, URB p. 95 • Daily Focus Trans. 15-1 • Reg. Atlas, URB pp. 1–7 • Reading Skills, URB p. 25

Guide to Reading

BIG Idea

Geographers organize the Earth into regions that share common characteristics.

Content Vocabulary

- privatization *(p. 409)*
- middle class *(p. 410)*
- underemployment *(p. 410)*
- pensioner *(p. 410)*
- heavy industry *(p. 411)*
- light industry *(p. 411)*

Academic Vocabulary

- comprise *(p. 409)*
- invest *(p. 410)*
- volume *(p. 411)*

Reading Strategy

Identifying Central Issues Use a diagram like the one below to show three major effects of the fall of communism on Russia.

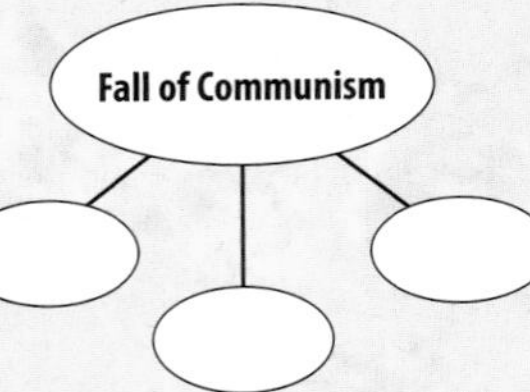

SECTION 1 A Changing Russia

Picture This The figures below are toys, art, and a history lesson all in one! *Matryoshka* dolls, which fit one inside the other, are popular toys and have been hand painted in Russia since the late 1800s. The traditional version of the *Matryoshka* shows a Russian woman wearing a babushka (scarf) and an apron. Here, art becomes history, as the colorful dolls represent Soviet and Russian leaders (from left to right) Mikhail Gorbachev, Boris Yeltsin, and Vladimir Putin. To learn more about recent changes in Russia, read Section 1.

Modern-day *Matryoshka* dolls, St. Petersburg, Russia

Changing Politics and Society

Main Idea **The fall of communism led to great changes in Russia's government, economy, and society.**

Geography and You Can you imagine having to completely change your way of life? Read to learn how Russians faced that situation in the early 1990s.

NATIONAL GEOGRAPHIC

Voting in Russia

Voters in Russia today can choose from many political parties and groups. ***Regions*** **What role did most citizens have in their government when Russia was part of the Soviet Union?**

Russia is still adjusting to the changes that occurred in the 1990s. When communism fell in 1991, Russia was forced to build a new government and economy. These ongoing changes continue to greatly affect the everyday lives of the Russian people.

A New Form of Government

The Communist Party ruled Russia when it was part of the Soviet Union. The Communists did not allow people to challenge their power, and everyday citizens had no voice in choosing their leaders. After the fall of communism, however, Russia became more democratic.

In a 1993 election, Russian voters approved a new constitution and elected members of a legislature to represent them. This new legislature included candidates from many different political parties. Boris Yeltsin, who was Russia's leader when it was a Soviet republic, was elected the first president of Russia. C

Russia's official name is the Russian Federation. This name reflects the fact that Russia **comprises,** or is made up of, many different regions and territories. Like the United States, Russia is a federal republic, with power divided between national and regional governments. In the United States, some powers belong to the states, and others belong only to the national government. Some powers are shared by both levels of government. In Russia, the division of powers is less clear because the new Russian government is still developing.

A New Economic System

As part of the Soviet Union, Russia had a command economy. In a command economy, the central government makes all the economic decisions. Since the fall of communism, Russia has attempted to shift to a market economy. D

To create a market economy, the government introduced **privatization** (PRY·vuh·tuh·ZAY·shuhn). This is the transfer of ownership of businesses from the government to individuals. In the new system, businesses have to compete with one another. As a result, Russian companies have begun to advertise to attract customers. The government has also dropped price controls, which were official prices set for different goods and services. In a market economy, prices result from competition among companies and from what Russian consumers need, want, and are willing to pay.

Teach

C Critical Thinking

Predicting Consequences **Ask:** **What might happen to a country's national unity when people from many parties are elected to its legislature? Why?** *(National unity might suffer because many different parties have many different ideas and agendas, and conflicts are more likely to arise.)* OL

D Differentiated Instruction

Advanced Learners Divide students into two teams, and have them debate a command versus a market economy in a changing country like Russia. Students may use the text and other resources to find evidence to support their arguments. AL

Caption Answer:
They could not challenge their leaders' power or even choose their leaders.

Hands-On Chapter Project Step 1

Launching a New Business

Step 1: Planning the Business Groups of students will create a plan to start a new business in Russia.

Essential Question Why is the success of democracy in Russia important to the rest of the world?

Directions Discuss with students the ways in which Russia's economy is connected with the economies of other countries through international trade. Also discuss how economic and political freedoms support each other. For example, fair courts and strong banks are important for the development of a free market economy. Separate students into groups of four to six. Tell each group that they will make a plan for a business they could start in Russia today. Encourage students to think about businesses that are needed as Russia develops a free market economy. Students might decide to sell something or provide a service, to extract resources, or to transport goods. Have students describe how their business would meet the needs of Russian consumers.

Summarizing Ask students what political or economic institutions their business would rely on in order to succeed. OL

(Chapter Project continued in Section 2)

D Differentiated Instruction

English Learners Read the sentence aloud to students. Ask them to define "consumerism." *(the desire to buy goods)* Ask them to identify the root word in *consumerism*. *(consumer)* Explain that the suffix *-ism* means "a state of being or acting." In this case, "consumerism" means "being a consumer, or purchaser, of goods." **ELL**

W Writing Support

Expository Writing Ask students to write a news article reporting on the changes businesses and workers have endured during the shift from a command economy to a market one. Provide students with business newspaper and magazine articles to use as models. **OL**

Caption Answer:
The middle class is a social group that is neither very rich nor poor, but has enough money to buy some luxury items.

NATIONAL GEOGRAPHIC

Russia's New Economy

Department stores and large discount stores are opening in Russia as the economy grows and people have more money to spend on consumer goods. ***Place*** **What is the middle class?**

Changes in Society

With the end of Communist rule, the government loosened its control on Russian society. Many different political parties were able to organize. Russians were allowed to criticize leaders and their policies. Additionally, the government no longer controlled the content of news reports or books.

Along with political freedom, Russians began to have more contact with other cultures. American and European books, television shows, and CDs became more readily available to Russians. Many people embraced the new ideas, music, and fashions that became available.

D Russia's new economy led to the spread of consumerism—the desire to buy goods. Russians eagerly sought goods they had not been able to buy for years. Businesses prospered, and a Russian **middle class** emerged. This term refers to a social group that is neither very rich nor poor, but has enough money to buy cars, new clothing, electronics, and other luxury items.

W The new economic system gave workers freedom to quit their jobs and seek employment elsewhere. Russians who were willing to take risks could open their own businesses. People also could **invest,** or put money into businesses run by others, in the hope of making even more money. This new economic freedom, however, did not guarantee success. Both new businesses and old businesses, which were no longer supported by the government, failed. Some tried to stay open by firing workers to cut costs. Other businesses simply could not compete and closed, putting more Russians out of work. Some skilled Russian workers still face **underemployment,** which means they are forced to take jobs that require lesser skills than they have. Many people must work second jobs to survive.

The unsettled economy is also difficult for **pensioners** (PEHN·shuh·nuhrs). Pensioners are people who receive regular payments from the government because they are too old or too sick to work. The amount of these payments is usually fixed, or remains the same. When prices rise but the amount of the payments does not increase, it becomes difficult for pensioners to buy goods. These problems caused many Russians to oppose privatization.

Population Changes

Russia's population also has experienced change. During Soviet times, many ethnic Russians moved to other parts of the Soviet Union. When these republics became independent, the ethnic Russians often were no longer welcome. About 3 million of them decided to return to Russia. People of other

Differentiated Instruction

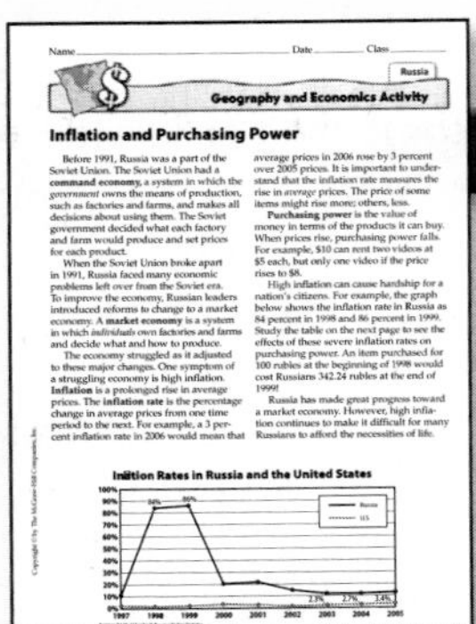

Name______ Date______ Class______

Russia

Geography and Economics Activity

Inflation and Purchasing Power

Before 1991, Russia was a part of the Soviet Union. The Soviet Union had a **command economy,** a system in which the *government* owns the means of production, such as factories and farms, and makes all decisions about using them. The Soviet government decided what each factory and farm would produce and set prices for each product.

When the Soviet Union broke apart in 1991, Russia faced many economic problems left over from the Soviet era. To improve the economy, Russian leaders introduced reforms to change to a market economy. A **market economy** is a system in which *individuals* own factories and farms and decide what and how to produce.

The economy struggled as it adjusted to these major changes. One symptom of a struggling economy is high inflation. **Inflation** is a prolonged rise in average prices. The **inflation rate** is the percentage change in average prices from one time period to the next. For example, a 3 percent inflation rate in 2006 would mean that average prices in 2006 rose by 3 percent over 2005 prices. It is important to understand that the inflation rate measures the rise in *average* prices. The price of some items might rise more; others, less.

Purchasing power is the value of money in terms of the products it can buy. When prices rise, purchasing power falls. For example, $10 can rent two videos at $5 each, but only one video if the price rises to $8.

High inflation can cause hardship for a nation's citizens. For example, the graph below shows the inflation rate in Russia as 84 percent in 1998 and 86 percent in 1999. Study the table on the next page to see the effects of these severe inflation rates on purchasing power. An item purchased for 100 rubles at the beginning of 1998 would cost Russians 342.24 rubles at the end of 1999!

Russia has made great progress toward a market economy. However, high inflation continues to make it difficult for many Russians to afford the necessities of life.

Geography and Economics Activity, URB pp. 9–10

Inflation and Purchasing Power

Objective: To learn how inflation affects purchasing power

Focus: Explain how spreadsheets are used in business.

Teach: Have students read the article and discuss how inflation affects consumers and businesses.

Assess: Have them create a spreadsheet to compute the effect of inflation on one consumer item.

Close: Discuss how spreadsheets are powerful tools for presenting economic information.

Differentiated Instruction Strategies

BL Ask students to explain what information the table and graph in the article provide.

AL Have students research inflation rates in the United States over the past four decades and create spreadsheets to show the change in rates.

ELL Ask students to describe the effect of inflation in their home countries.

ethnic groups also left for Russia to escape hardships in the new republics.

Despite this arrival of immigrants, Russia's population declined from 150 million people in 1991 to 143 million in 2006. This decline is the result of a combination of low birthrates and rising death rates. The life expectancy of men has decreased to 60 years, compared with 74 years for women. These rates are well below those of other developed countries.

The sharp decline in life expectancy is a result of poor nutrition, alcoholism, and drug abuse. Also, pollution has led to more lung diseases. Meanwhile, government spending on health care has dropped.

Reading Check **Comparing** How is Russia's government similar to that of the United States?

Life Expectancies: Russia and Europe

Country	Average Life Expectancy	
	Men	Women
Sweden	78	83
Italy	77	83
France	76	84
Germany	76	82
Poland	71	79
Russia	60	74

Source: *CIA World Factbook*, 2006.

Chart Skills

1. **Identifying** Which country has the highest average life expectancy for women?
2. **Explaining** Why are life expectancies in Russia lower than those in most of Europe?

Russia's Economic Regions

Main Idea **Russia's four economic regions differ in the resources and products they supply.**

Geography and You How does your community contribute to your state's or the nation's economy? Read to learn how Russia's different regions contribute to the Russian economy.

The Moscow Region

Moscow is the political, economic, and transportation center of Russia. A large amount of manufacturing takes place in or near Moscow. Under Soviet rule, most of Russia's factories focused on **heavy industry**, or the production of goods such as machinery, mining equipment, and steel. After communism's fall, more factories shifted to **light industry**, or the production of consumer goods, such as clothing and household products. High technology and electronics industries have also developed in Moscow.

St. Petersburg and the Baltic Region

St. Petersburg and the Baltic region are located in northwestern Russia. St. Petersburg, once Russia's capital, is a major port and cultural center. Well-known for its palaces and churches, St. Petersburg attracts thousands of tourists from around the world each year.

Located near the Baltic Sea, St. Petersburg is an important trading center. A high **volume,** or amount, of goods passes through its port. The city is also a major industrial center. Factories here make machinery, ships, automobiles, and other items. St. Petersburg relies on other regions for food, fuel, and other resources.

R Reading Strategy

Previewing Have students read the Main Idea, then each of the subheads that follow. Have them write one topic sentence that they expect to be addressed in each subhead. **OL**

C Critical Thinking

Determining Cause and Effect

Ask: **What effect has the fall of communism had on factories in Moscow?** *(Factories now focus on light industry instead of heavy industry.)* **OL**

Reading Check **Answer:** Both are federal republics, have constitutions, and allow voters to elect the president and members of the legislature.

Graph Skills

Answers:

1. France
2. poor nutrition, alcoholism, and drug abuse

Differentiated Instruction

Leveled Activities

BL **Reteaching Activity, URB p. 101**

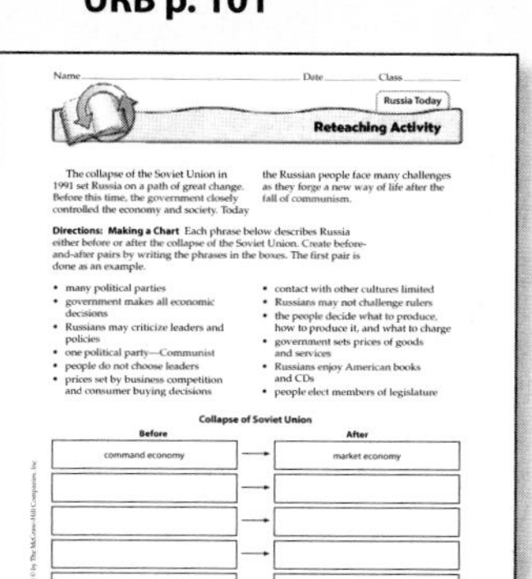

OL **Academic Vocabulary, URB p. 87**

AL **Chart, Graph, and Map Skills, URB p. 91**

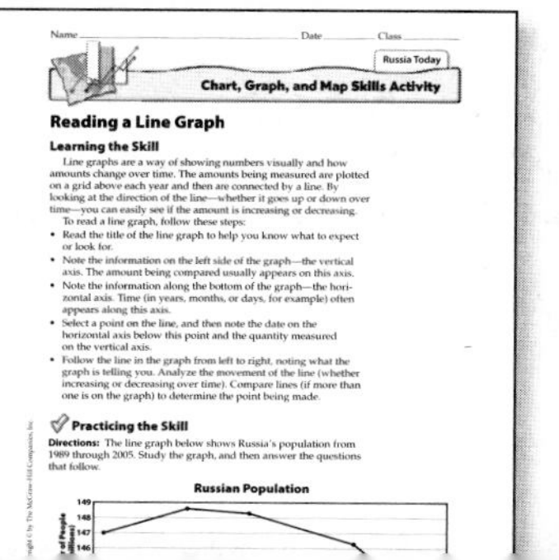

ELL **School-to-Home, URB p. 103**

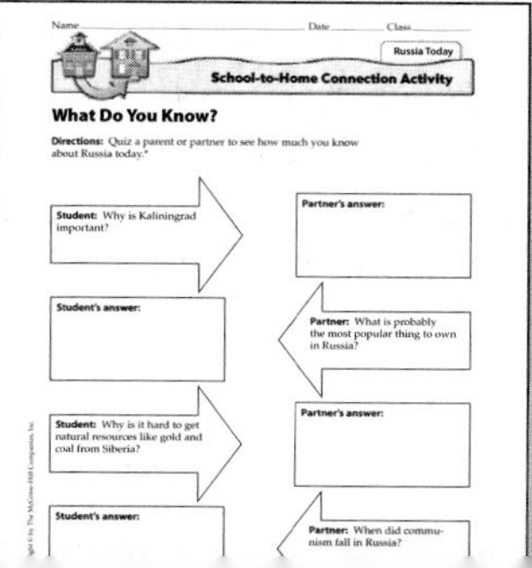

S Skill Practice

Using Geography Skills Have students locate Kaliningrad on a map. Then have them trace the route from Kaliningrad to other major Russian cities, such as St. Petersburg and Moscow. Ask students to speculate what other challenges Kaliningrad might have because of its location besides transportation issues. *(Possible answer: It is vulnerable to actions by surrounding countries and more likely to lose its Russian traditions.)* OL

Reading Check **Answer:** Moscow, St. Petersburg and the Baltic Region, and the Volga and Urals regions are important for manufacturing. The Volga and Urals region is important for agriculture.

Assess

Social Studies ONLINE
Study Central™ provides summaries, interactive games, and online graphic organizers to help students review content.

Close

Stating Have students discuss the challenges facing Russia today. OL

Kaliningrad is another major Russian port along the Baltic Sea. It lies in a small piece of Russian land, about the size of the state of Connecticut, between Poland and Lithuania. This small area of Russia is isolated from the country's main area. Goods shipped to Kaliningrad must cross other countries to reach the nearest inland part of Russia. Kaliningrad is Russia's only port on the Baltic Sea that stays ice-free all year.

The Volga and Urals Region

The Volga and Urals region lies south and east of Moscow. It is a major center of manufacturing and farming. The Volga River is vital to these economic activities. This 2,300-mile (3,701-km) waterway carries nearly half of Russia's river traffic. The Volga River also supplies water for hydroelectric power and for irrigation. Farmers in the region grow large amounts of wheat, sugar beets, and other crops.

The area of the Ural Mountains is a major source for Russian resources. The mountains contain important minerals, including copper, gold, lead, nickel, and bauxite, as well as energy resources.

Siberia

Siberia's cold Arctic winds, rugged landscapes, and frozen ground make it difficult to take advantage of the region's many resources. The lands of Siberia hold valuable deposits of iron ore, uranium, gold, and coal. Timber from the sprawling taiga is also an important resource for Russia. Since resources in other parts of the world are being used up, Russia's economic future may depend on its ability to make use of Siberia's resources.

Reading Check **Categorizing** Which of Russia's economic regions are important for manufacturing? For agriculture?

Social Studies ONLINE
Study Central™ To review this section, go to glencoe.com.

Vocabulary

1. **Explain** the significance of:
   a. privatization
   b. middle class
   c. underemployment
   d. pensioner
   e. heavy industry
   f. light industry

Main Ideas

2. **Describing** Describe some of the freedoms the Russian people gained after the fall of communism.
3. **Explaining** Create a chart like the one below to list at least two ways each economic region contributes to the Russian economy.

Region	Contributions

Critical Thinking

4. **Analyzing Information** Why have some Russians opposed the privatization of industries and businesses?
5. BIG Idea Compare and contrast the cities of Moscow and St. Petersburg in terms of location and economic activity.
6. **Challenge** What might happen to a country if it cannot obtain and make use of its own available resources?

Writing About Geography

7. **Persuasive Writing** Write an editorial to support or oppose the changes that the new democratic Russian government made after the fall of communism.

Answers

1. Definitions for the vocabulary words are found in the section and the Glossary.
2. Possible answers: able to organize political parties, criticize the government, less government control, seek new employment, and own and invest in businesses
3. **Moscow:** heavy industry, light industry, high technology and electronics; **St. Petersburg and the Baltic:** trading, ports, and manufacturing; **the Volga and Urals:** manufacturing, mining and other resources, movement of goods, hydroelectric power, agriculture; **Siberia:** iron ore, uranium, gold, coal, timber
4. Businesses failed. Many people became unemployed, and some remain underemployed. Pensioners lost buying power.
5. **Similarities:** Moscow and St. Petersburg are economic centers that develop heavy industry; **Differences:** Moscow focuses more on light industry, high technology, and electronics; St. Petersburg is a major port.
6. The country would have to import the resources from other countries and would not be able to benefit from using or exporting its own resources.
7. Students should give details and facts from the text to support their argument.

TIME PERSPECTIVES

EXPLORING WORLD ISSUES

RUSSIA'S CHALLENGING ROAD TO DEMOCRACY

Russians are enjoying new freedoms under democracy. But are their freedoms threatened?

Russians attend a political rally.

AP PHOTO

Since the collapse of the Soviet Union in 1991, Russians have worked hard to turn their country into a democracy with a free market system. Today, many Russians have more freedom than ever. As a result of recent reforms, citizens can now own private businesses and elect their leaders.

The new freedoms, however, have also brought new challenges. Corruption has risen among government and private workers. A minority group in Chechnya has carried out terrorist acts that have killed hundreds. As Russia's government combats these challenges, experts wonder if Russia's new freedoms could be lost.

TIME PERSPECTIVES

Focus

Introducing TIME Perspectives

Read the title and subtitle aloud to the students. **Ask: What freedoms might be threatened when a country's government is changed?** *(Answers may include freedom of religion and freedom of speech.)* **What kinds of challenges do you think the article will discuss?** *(Answers may include economic and political challenges.)* **OL**

FYI

Learn about the current status of democracy in Russia at www.freedomhouse.org, the Web site of Freedom House, a nonprofit organization that promotes democratic values around the world.

Use the **TIME Perspectives: Exploring World Issues Teacher Guide and Student Activities,** pp. 17–20, to reinforce and extend the concepts in "Russia's Challenging Road to Democracy."

Additional Support

Background

Executive Power in Russia Under the Russian constitution, the executive branch of government is much stronger than the legislative branch. This gives one person, the president, a great deal of power. Russia has no vice president, and the president nominates the prime minister. The president can also issue decrees without the approval of the legislature. In 2000, President Putin used these powers to group Russia's 89 regions into seven large districts, whose leaders he appointed himself. However, the Russian constitution does limit how long each president can remain in office, as no president can serve more than two consecutive terms.

TIME PERSPECTIVES

Teach

C Critical Thinking

Comparing and Contrasting Ask: **How was life in the Soviet Union different from life in democratic countries, like the United States?** *(The Soviet government did not allow people to choose their jobs or to own property, and the government punished people who spoke against it.)* **OL**

R Reading Strategy

Reading Graphs Ask: **How does the United States rank as one of Russia's export partners?** *(The United States is eighth and last on the graph.)* **OL**

INTERPRETING GRAPHS

Answer: Europe

TIME PERSPECTIVES

EXPLORING WORLD ISSUES

Increased housing construction is a sign of Russia's growing economy.

WOLFGANG KAEHLER/CORBIS

WHERE WILL REFORMS LEAD?

With territory that extends from Europe to Asia, Russia is the largest country in the world. Throughout its history, Russia has faced many great challenges. For centuries Russia was ruled by **czars**, or absolute rulers. In 1922, following a violent revolution, Russia became part of a group of republics called the Union of Soviet Socialist Republics (U.S.S.R.).

The U.S.S.R. had a Communist government that was very powerful and controlling. The U.S.S.R.'s Communist rulers often kept information about the country secret from the outside world. British prime minister Winston Churchill once called the U.S.S.R. "a riddle wrapped in a mystery."

The government controlled nearly every part of Soviet society. It owned all property and businesses and told citizens what they could do for a living and where they would live. Those suspected of disagreeing with the government were sent to labor camps in Siberia, a brutally cold area in eastern Russia. During the Soviet era, millions of people were imprisoned, executed, or tortured.

A New Chapter

Over time, the Soviet Union began to decline under its harsh system. Many citizens were assigned jobs they did not like. Many of those people were uninspired and did not work very hard. As a result, production suffered, and there were all types of shortages, including food and energy.

In the mid-1980s, the Soviet Union's leaders tried to reform the nation's Communist system. They introduced the policies of glasnost and perestroika. *Glasnost* is a Russian word that means "openness." *Perestroika* means "restructuring." Under glasnost, people were allowed to speak their opinions freely for the first time ever. Perestroika gave some of the government's decision-making power to private individuals and businesses.

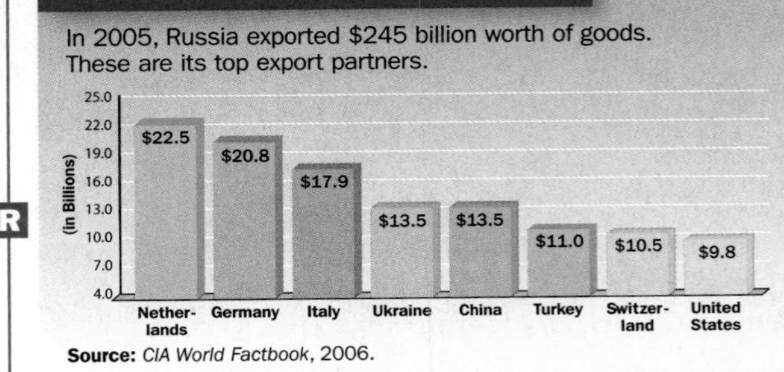

Source: *CIA World Factbook*, 2006.

INTERPRETING GRAPHS

Analyzing Information On what continent are Russia's three top export partners located?

Additional Support

Activity: Connecting With the United States

Analyzing Remind students that under the Soviet system, the government owned all businesses. **Ask:** **What businesses in the United States are owned or controlled by federal, state, or local governments?** *(Possible answers: utilities (in some places), public transportation, the postal service)* Some people believe all businesses should be privately owned, while others believe some services are best provided by the government. Separate students into groups. Have each group make a table listing the pros and cons of government versus private ownership of businesses. **OL**

U.S. president George W. Bush meets with Russian president Vladimir Putin.

Oil wells such as this one dot the Siberian landscape.

A Russian family shops at a modern mall in Moscow.

Not everyone, however, agreed with these reforms. Conservatives who supported the Communist Party and the military tried to take control of the Soviet government. Their attempt failed and eventually led to the Soviet Union's collapse in 1991. Since then, the Russian government and people have been working to change their country into a democracy.

Some of these changes have been successful. Russians now elect their leaders in free and open elections. Under the Soviet system, only members of the Communist Party could vote. Economic reforms have also been introduced to create a free market economy. Russians can now own their own factories, shops, and other businesses. Companies are buying materials to help them grow in the future. As a result of the reforms, the economy has grown. **R**

A Long Road to Democracy

As successful as the economic reforms have been, many experts believe Russia has a long way to go before it has a stable democracy. The reforms have brought freedom, but they have also created new challenges. Criminal gangs and corruption thrive in Russia's open market. Many people must secretly pay officials to get drivers' licenses and permits to build houses and businesses.

Other challenges threaten Russia's security. In Chechnya, an area in southern Russia, rebels have been at war with the government since 1994. The rebels want Chechnya to be an independent nation. They have carried out terrorist attacks against Russia. Hundreds of innocent people, including children, have died.

An Uncertain Future

Some experts think that the challenges Russia faces could weaken the nation's young democracy. They worry that the new freedoms are in danger of being lost as the government works to stop corruption and improve security. Critics of Russia's president Vladimir Putin have complained that, under his leadership, the government has abused **civil liberties**, or individual freedoms, and attacked democratic institutions like the free media. **C**

Is a lasting democracy possible in Russia? The Russian people have a long history of dealing with difficult times and challenges. The future will tell whether history's lessons will be enough to establish democracy in the world's largest country.

EXPLORING THE ISSUE

1. **Making Inferences** How might widespread government corruption threaten democracy in Russia?
2. **Identifying Cause and Effect** How do you think glasnost and perestroika contributed to the collapse of the Soviet Union?

TIME PERSPECTIVES

R Reading Strategy

Taking Notes Tell students to read the first paragraph of the page and write words and phrases that describe Russia's challenges. Then have them repeat the process with the second paragraph. Ask volunteers to share their notes with the class. **BL**

C Critical Thinking

Analyzing Information Ask: Why might the government's actions to stop corruption and improve security threaten people's freedom? *(Possible answer: When government officials and police increase security and law enforcement, their actions can infringe on people's privacy.)* **OL**

EXPLORING THE ISSUE

Answers:

1. Corrupt officials may only take action when citizens pay for it, leaving many citizens' voices unheard.
2. Possible answer: They were admissions that the Soviet system needed to be reformed, which caused people to doubt the system even more.

Differentiated Instruction

Organizing Data

Organizing Data (workbook page thumbnail)

TIME Perspectives: Exploring World Issues Workbook, p. 20

Objective: To learn how to organize data
Focus: Define the terms *glasnost* and *perestroika*.
Teach: Explain that *perestroika* was an economic policy that affected businesses.
Assess: Tell students to place the letter for each statement in the correct circle.
Close: Discuss how this activity helps explain the differences between the two policies.

Differentiated Instruction Strategies

BL Tell students that if a statement seems to fit in both circles, they should put it in the circle that it matches best.

AL Ask students how these reforms helped Russia move toward democracy.

ELL Ask students to give the words for "openness" and "restructuring" in their first language.

R Reading Strategy

Summarizing Ask students to write a three-sentence summary of the reasons for conflict in Chechnya. Ask volunteers to share their summaries. OL

C Critical Thinking

Predicting Consequences

Ask: What might happen if the Chechen rebels continue attacking Russia? *(Possible answer: Russia will increase its military response and attack Chechnya.)* OL

EXPLORING THE ISSUE

Answers:

1. because he views the terrorist attacks as attacks on Russia itself
2. Possible answer: They feel Chechnya should be an independent country, and because Chechens have never accepted Russian rule.

Additional Support

TIME PERSPECTIVES

TERROR IN RUSSIA

In recent years, Russia has suffered a series of deadly terrorist attacks by Chechen rebels. In 2004 terrorists took control of a school and killed more than 300 people, including many children. Other bombings took place at bus and train stations. Altogether, more than 500 people were killed in 2004 as a result of terrorist attacks.

The attacks have shocked and angered the people of Russia. In September 2004, Russians filled the streets of St. Petersburg and Moscow to protest terrorism against their country. Many carried signs with antiterrorism slogans. Some read, "We won't give Russia to terrorists."

The demonstrators believed rebels from Chechnya were responsible for the attacks in 2004. In 2005, however, the violence continued as Chechen rebels set off another bomb in a village in the Caucasus region. The explosion killed 14 people.

Russians protested the terrorist attacks.

A Bitter History

The people of Chechnya want to form their own country. Most Chechens are Muslims, which sets them apart from Russians, who tend to be Christians. Russia first **conquered** Chechnya in 1858, but Chechens never accepted Russian rule. In 1991 Chechnya declared independence, but Russia would not allow it. Russians believe the territory belongs to them. **R** In 1994 Russia went to war against the Chechen rebels. Hundreds of thousands of Chechens died in the fighting.

In 1996 Chechnya won the right to elect its own government, but it remained part of Russia. When Chechen attacks continued, Russian president Vladimir Putin sent troops back into the region in 1999.

Will there be peace? Putin said he would not make deals with terrorists. He said the violence was a "full-scale war." **C** Still, the ongoing hostility puts pressure on Russian and Chechen leaders to find a way to end this deadly conflict.

EXPLORING THE ISSUE

1. **Explaining** Why does Vladimir Putin call the violence a "full scale war"?
2. **Making Inferences** Why might the Chechen rebels feel that Chechnya should be free?

Activity: Collaborative Learning

Identifying Points of View The Russian government has blamed Chechen rebels for terrorist attacks, while the Chechens and members of the Russian media have accused Russian troops of human rights abuses. **Ask: Why do you think the Chechens have resorted to violence to achieve their goals?** *(Possible answer: The Chechens may feel powerless to achieve their goals in any other way.)* Organize the class into two groups. Have one group explore the Chechens' point of view in this conflict, while the other group explores the Russian government's point of view. Tell the groups to find facts to support their point of view in online and other sources. Then have each group present its point of view in a class debate. OL

REVIEW AND ASSESS

A Russian worker produces steel at a metallurgy plant in the Ural Mountains.

AP PHOTO

UNDERSTANDING THE ISSUE

1 **Making Connections** How might glasnost and perestroika have contributed to the creation of new ideas and ways of doing business?

2 **Writing to Inform** Suppose you are a Russian student. Write a letter to an American friend explaining some of the new freedoms that Russian citizens enjoy.

3 **Writing to Persuade** Russia has large amounts of natural resources, like oil and timber, and a well-educated population. Write a brief essay about how these strengths might help Russia build a strong democracy.

INTERNET RESEARCH ACTIVITIES

4 Like today's Russia, the United States had a weak banking system when it was first founded. With your teacher's help, browse the Internet to learn how the U.S. strengthened its early banking system. List ways Russia might learn from the U.S. experience.

5 Important industries in Russia, like steel and manufacturing, need to be modernized. Browse the Internet for information about how Russia plans to update one of these industries. Share your findings with the class.

BEYOND THE CLASSROOM

6 **Visit your school or local library** to learn more about the Soviet Union's labor camps in Siberia. Work in a group to find out what it was like to live in a camp. What hardships did those living in the camps have to endure? Present your findings to your classmates.

7 **Research other nations,** such as Great Britain and Spain, that have had to fight terrorism. What might Russia learn from those nations in dealing with Chechnya? Put your findings in a report.

Russia's Natural Resources

Russia is a vast country that holds many of the world's natural resources. The map shows where some of Russia's resources are located.

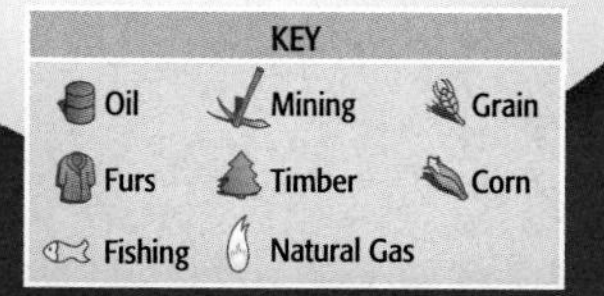

Building Map Reading Skills

1. **Analyzing Information** Based on the map's key, what type of work might prisoners in Siberian labor camps have done?
2. **Drawing Conclusions** Why might Russia want to protect its interests in its southwest?

Review and Assess

Questions from **Understanding the Issue, Internet Research Activities,** and **Beyond the Classroom** may have more than one correct answer. Pick and choose the two or three activities that work best for your class.

Building Map Reading Skills

Answers:

1. mining
2. Important energy resources are in the southwest region. They also needed to preserve access to the Caspian and Black Seas.

Close

Write the following words on the board: *communism, democracy, free market economy, terrorism.* Tell students to write a sentence that includes each word and relays a fact about Russia from the article. For example, "Chechen rebels have committed acts of terrorism against Russia." Ask volunteers to share their sentences. **OL**

Additional Support

Activity: Why It Matters

Evaluating Tell students that the United States and Russia have many goals in common, including reducing the arsenals of nuclear weapons in both countries and around the world. **Ask:** **Why do you think the United States and Russia have unique responsibilities in the area of nuclear technology?** *(Possible answer: Because the United States and the Soviet Union built up their nuclear arsenals during the Cold War, the United States and Russia, as the Soviet Union's successor, must take the lead in promoting nuclear nonproliferation.)* Have students conduct research to learn more about how the United States and Russia are cooperating in this area. Ask them to find answers to such questions as: What steps have both countries taken to reduce their own nuclear arsenals? How does each country feel about other countries developing nuclear technology? Have students summarize what they learn in a brief report. **AL**

Focus

Bellringer
Daily Focus Transparency 15-2

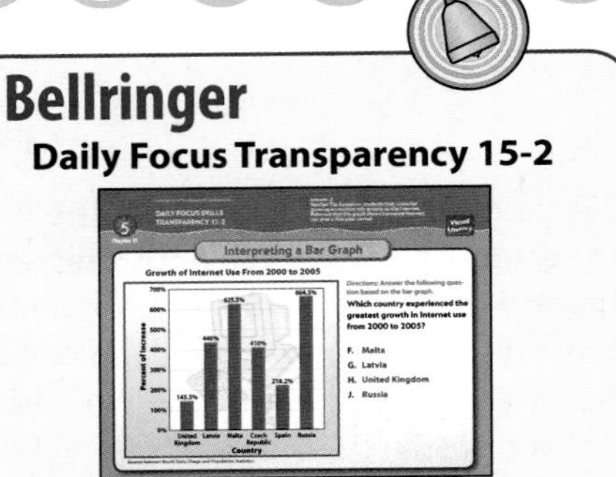

Guide to Reading
Answers to Graphic:

Answers may include:
New businesses have opened; some personal incomes have risen; the country has earned more income on some exports; there is increased crime and corruption; oligarchs have gained control of parts of the country; many Russians remain poor

Section Spotlight Video

To learn more about issues and challenges in Russia, have students watch the Section Spotlight Video.

Guide to Reading

BIG Idea
Geography is used to interpret the past, understand the present, and plan for the future.

Content Vocabulary
- decree *(p. 419)*
- oligarch *(p. 420)*
- deposit insurance *(p. 421)*
- separatist movement *(p. 421)*

Academic Vocabulary
- prior *(p. 419)*
- unify *(p. 421)*
- conduct *(p. 421)*

Reading Strategy
Analyzing Information Use a diagram like the one below to identify the changes, both positive and negative, that have resulted from Russia's switch to a free market economy.

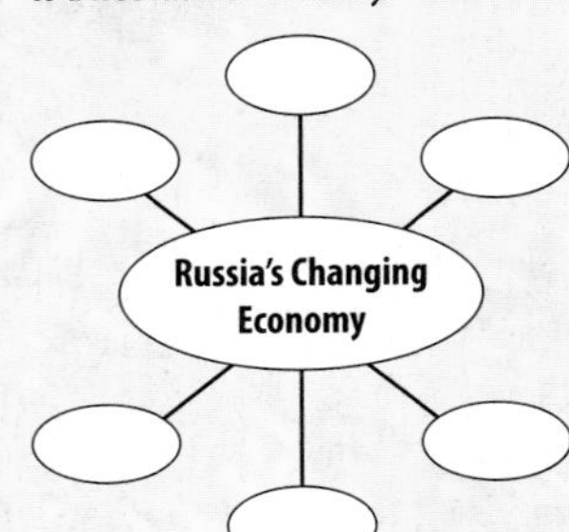

SECTION 2 Issues and Challenges

Picture This What do you think is the most popular possession in Russia? A car? A computer? No, it is most likely a cell phone. The popularity of cell phones has skyrocketed in Russia. Russia has a growing middle class with money to spend. Young business-savvy Russians are starting companies that provide trendy and modern products—like cell phones—to this middle class. As the number of cell phone businesses has increased, so has cell phone use. It is estimated that in 1996, only 10,000 people in Moscow owned cell phones, which cost about $2,000 each! Now 80 million Russians, or about 60 percent of the population, own cell phones, which cost about $100 each. The economy is just one part of Russia that is changing. Read on to learn more about modern Russia's challenges.

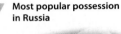

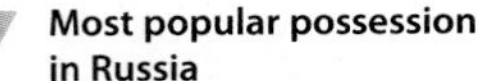
Most popular possession in Russia

Resource Manager

R Reading Strategies
Teacher Edition
- Skimming, p. 419
- Reading Maps, p. 420
- Identifying, p. 422

Additional Resources
- Guid. Read., URB p. 84
- Cont. Vocab., URB p. 85
- Ac. Vocab., URB p. 87
- Read. Ess., p. 106

C Critical Thinking
Teacher Edition
- Comparing and Contrasting, p. 419

Additional Resources
- Crit. Think., URB p. 93
- Quizzes and Tests, p. 168

D Differentiated Instruction
Teacher Edition
- Visual/Spatial, p. 421

Additional Resources
- Diff. Instr., URB p. 89
- Enrichment, URB p. 19
- Reteach., URB p. 101

W Writing Support
Teacher Edition
- Persuasive Writing, p. 420

Additional Resources
- Writing Skills, URB p. 99
- Authentic Assess., p. 15

S Skill Practice
Teacher Edition
- Visual Literacy, p. 421

Additional Resources
- Daily Focus Trans. 15-2
- Reg. Atlas, URB pp. 1–7

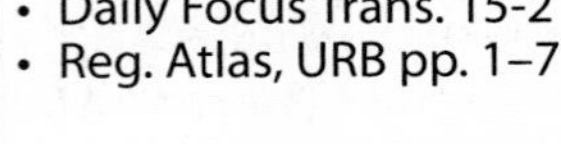

Political and Economic Challenges

Main Idea **Russians face many challenges as they try to build a democracy and a market economy.**

Geography and You Do you think a country needs strong leaders to solve serious problems? Can leaders become too strong? Read to learn about growing challenges to Russia's democracy and free market economy.

Even with its many resources and industrial power, Russia is finding it difficult to make its new government and economy successful. **Prior** to 1991, Russians had little experience with democratic government. Now many political parties compete in free elections. Also, after communism's fall, Russians began to make their own economic decisions.

Roadblocks to Democracy

Becoming truly democratic has not been easy for Russia. Confusion over governmental powers is one problem. For example, the Russian president's power to issue **decrees**—rulings that have the force of law but do not need the approval of the legislature—might make that office too strong.

Since becoming president in 1999, Vladimir Putin has strengthened presidential powers. When people began to criticize government policies, Putin shut down all independent television news networks. Newspapers still remain free, but television news in Russia is subject to government control.

Russia is a federal republic. Power is shared among national, regional, and local governments. To ensure that regional leaders would obey his wishes, Putin organized the country into seven large districts and appointed governors who would support his policies.

Throughout Russian government, many politicians disregard democratic ways. The courts and the legal system often favor rich, powerful citizens. In addition, many Russians still understand little about their government and, therefore, do not know how to make changes in the way it works.

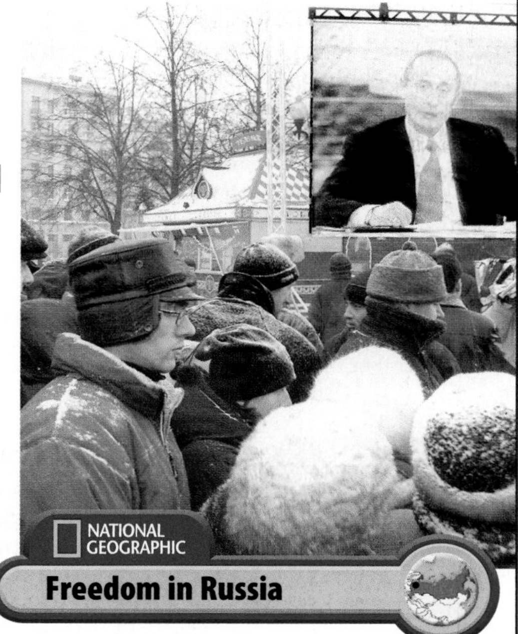

NATIONAL GEOGRAPHIC

Freedom in Russia

Russians gather in central Moscow to watch a televised news conference given by Russian President Vladimir Putin. ***Regions*** **How has Putin responded to criticisms of his rule?**

Social Studies ONLINE

Student Web Activity Visit glencoe.com and complete the Chapter 15 Web Activity about Russia's government.

Teach

R Reading Strategy

Skimming Remind students that skimming involves glancing at the text pages to see what is ahead. The text provides many tools to help a reader skim, such as boldface text and headings. Have students skim this section to see what they might learn. **OL**

C Critical Thinking

Comparing and Contrasting

Ask: **How is Russia's government under Putin different from the U.S. government?** *(The United States has many more states than Russia has districts, and the U.S. president does not appoint governors.)* **OL**

This **Reading Skill** (Comparing and Contrasting) was introduced in this unit.

Caption Answer:
He shut down all independent television news networks.

Social Studies ONLINE

Objectives and answers to the Student Web Activity can be found at glencoe.com under the Web Activity Lesson Plan for this chapter.

Differentiated Instruction

Writing Skills Activity, URB pp. 99–100

Presenting Supportive Evidence

Objective: To use evidence to support an argument

Focus: Describe why proving points is important when writing essays.

Teach: Review the descriptions of different types of evidence that can be used to support a position statement.

Assess: Have students find evidence in the text to support the position in the activity.

Close: Have them write a paragraph that uses evidence to support the statement.

Differentiated Instruction Strategies

BL Ask each student to make and support a position statement about an issue at their school.

AL Ask students to research evidence that *disproves* the position statement in the activity.

ELL Write a statement on the board. Have students provide three examples of how the statement could be proven.

R Reading Strategy

Reading Maps Remind students to review the title and legend on a map before answering questions.
Ask: Which two areas have the lowest per capita income? *(Southern and Volga regions)* OL

W Writing Support

Persuasive Writing Discuss with students the challenges Putin faces while trying to control oligarchs yet maintain a democracy. Have students brainstorm other solutions to the problem besides strengthening government authority. Then have students write a persuasive letter to Putin, describing their solution to the problem and emphasizing how it will promote democracy and a free economy. AL

Map Skills

Answers:
1. Per capita income is much higher in the central region.
2. These are regions that have valuable resources. They also have fewer people to share in the wealth of those regions which makes the per capita income higher.

Shifting to a Market Economy

Russia's shift to a free market economy has brought many positive changes. New companies have been started, and some personal incomes have risen. Higher prices for Russia's oil and natural gas exports have brought the country more income.

Economic success, however, has brought an increase in crime and business corruption. A small group of people, often referred to as oligarchs, control various parts of the economy. An **oligarch** (AH·luh·gahrk) is a member of a small group of rulers that holds great power. In Russia, oligarchs are often corrupt business leaders. Putin has limited the power of some of these oligarchs, but to do so, he has had to strengthen government authority.

Another problem is that the benefits of economic change have not reached all of Russia's people. A few Russians have grown wealthy, but some have become even poorer. There are also strong regional differences in economic success. **Figure 1** shows the average income per capita—or per person—in Russia's seven districts.

NATIONAL GEOGRAPHIC Maps In MOtion See StudentWorks™ Plus or glencoe.com.

Figure 1 Russia's Per Capita Income

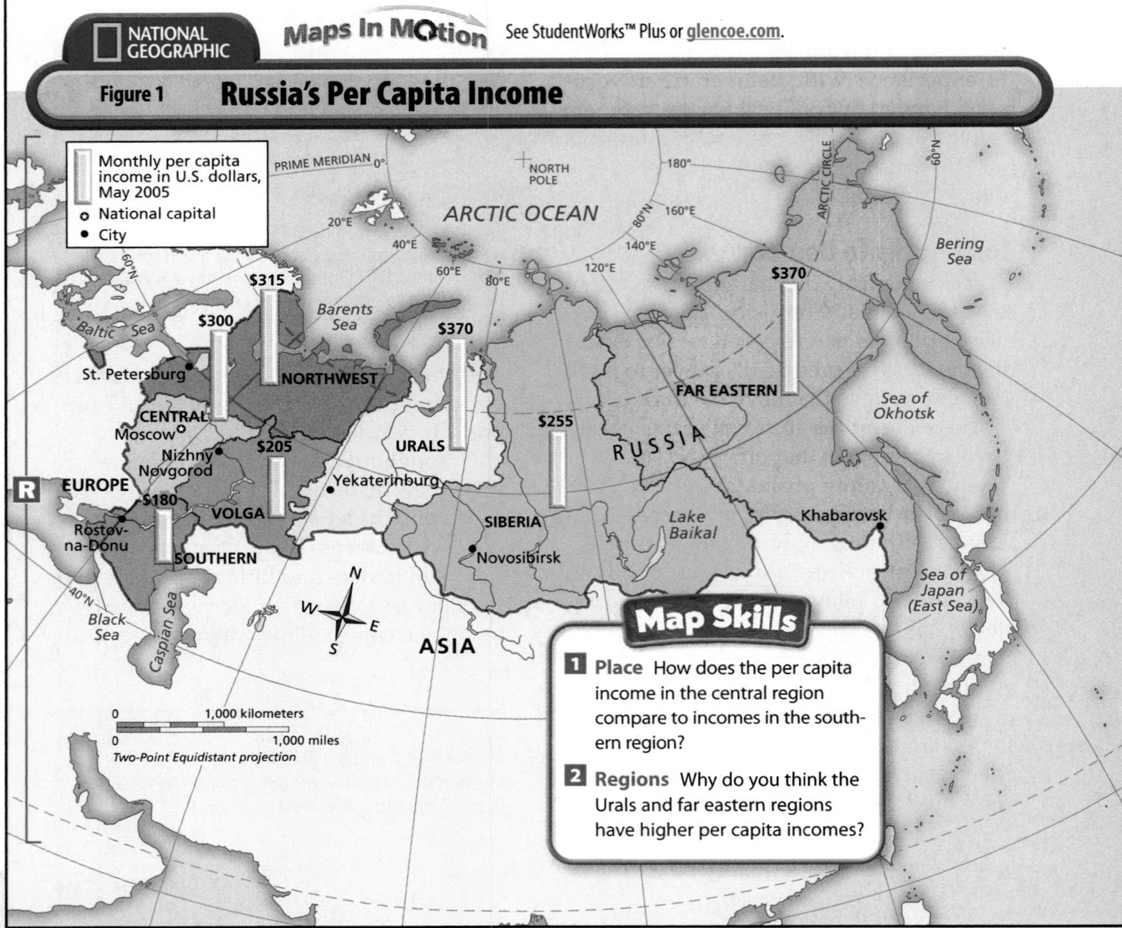

Map Skills

1. **Place** How does the per capita income in the central region compare to incomes in the southern region?
2. **Regions** Why do you think the Urals and far eastern regions have higher per capita incomes?

Hands-On Chapter Project Step 2

Launching a New Business

Step 2: Making a Proposal Each group of students will write a proposal for the business they envisioned in Step 1.

Directions Ask students to search the text for information about how the Russian economy, business, and industry has changed since the fall of communism. Students may want to research real Russian businesses by reading newspaper stories in the library or on the Internet. Have them write a brief business proposal describing what services or goods they would offer and who their customers would be. Encourage students to make their proposals visually appealing with pictures, graphs, and charts.

Putting It Together Have each group present its business idea to the class. Encourage questions about the business plan. OL
(Chapter Project cont. on Visual Summary page)

Monthly incomes in Moscow are much higher compared to other cities and areas of the country.

Russia's banking system also has not been able to fully contribute to economic growth. Banks play a vital role in an economy by collecting people's deposits and lending some of that money to other people. These people borrow the money to buy houses and cars or to start new businesses. All of these actions help create jobs within a region's economy. Greater savings means there is more money to loan, which in turn helps strengthen the economy. If people do not have enough money to deposit into savings, though, banks have fewer funds to lend and the economy suffers.

Many Russians, however, do not trust the country's banks. To encourage people to save their money, the government created a **deposit insurance** system, which will repay people who deposit their money in a bank if the bank goes out of business. Officials hope this system will make people feel safer and more willing to use the banking system.

Challenges to National Unity

While dealing with economic issues, Russians have had to face challenges to their country's political unity. Regional rivalries have increased in recent years. Such resentments have made it difficult to **unify,** or bring together, the country. An even larger challenge is the desire of many ethnic groups to form their own independent countries.

When the Soviet Union fell, several ethnic groups in Russia saw a chance for independence. They launched **separatist movements,** campaigns to break away from the national government and form independent countries. One of the most violent separatist movements began in Chechnya, a Muslim region near the Caucasus Mountains in southern Russia.

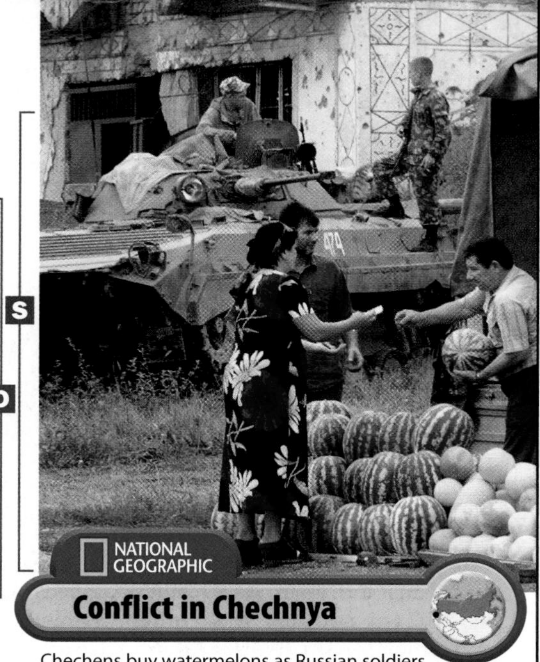

Conflict in Chechnya

Chechens buy watermelons as Russian soldiers guard a shopping area in Grozny, Chechnya's capital. ***Place*** **Why did conflict break out in Chechnya?**

In the early 1990s, Russia's President Boris Yeltsin gave Chechnya more self-rule, but many Chechens (CHEH·chehnz) wanted complete independence from Russia. Yeltsin did not want to allow Chechen separatists to succeed, believing that other regions would also demand independence. In 1994 he sent a large Russian army into Chechnya to crush Chechen forces. Both sides suffered heavy losses.

The Chechen separatists continued to **conduct,** or carry out, terrorist attacks against the Russian government. Truces and agreements between the two sides have failed, and the situation remains unresolved.

Reading Check **Describing** Identify and describe a major challenge to Russian unity.

D Differentiated Instruction

Visual/Spatial Have students create a flowchart or diagram showing the role of banks in a country's economy. Students may use colored markers or pencils to highlight different components of the lending/saving cycle. Instruct students to label their flowchart so others can read it easily. **OL**

S Skill Practice

Visual Literacy **Ask: What are two components of Russia's economy that are evident in this photo?** *(The Russian tank shows the industrial side of the Russian economy, while the farmer shows the agricultural side.)* **OL**

Caption Answer:
The Chechens wanted independence, and Yeltsin would not allow it.

Reading Check **Answer:** Several ethnic groups want their independence from Russia, especially the Chechens. There are also regional rivalries.

Differentiated Instruction

Leveled Activities

BL Content Vocabulary Activity, URB p. 85

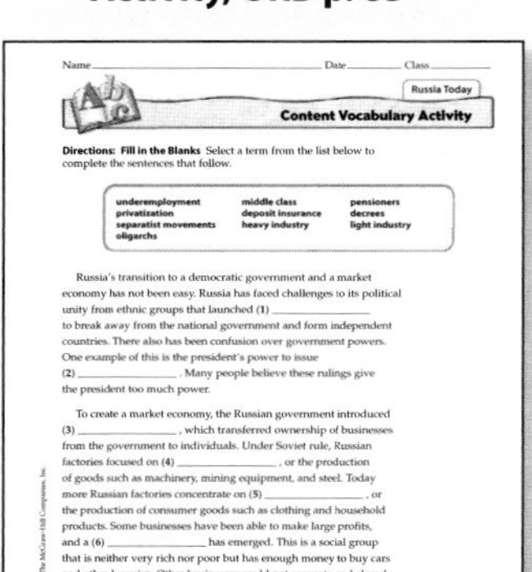

OL Authentic Assessment, p. 15

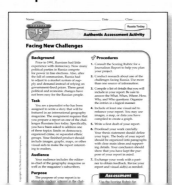

AL Critical Thinking Skills Activity, URB p. 93

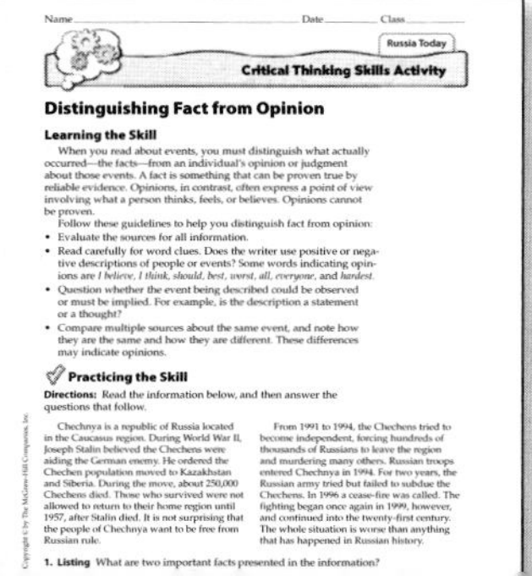

ELL Differentiated Instruction, URB, p. 89

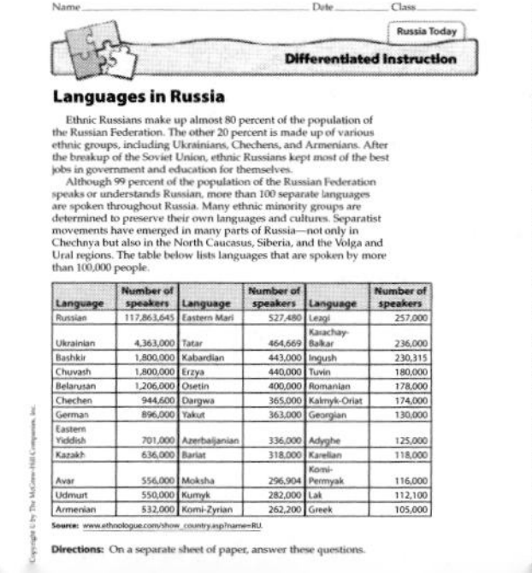

R Reading Strategy

Identifying Ask: What prefix is in the term "pro-Russian?" *(pro-)* **What does the term pro-Russian mean?** *(for Russia)* **Why might a pro-Russian president be a problem for Ukraine?** *(Ukrainians might not want a leader who is influenced by Russian policies.)* OL

Reading Check **Answer:** It wants to strengthen ties with other countries and sees the war in Chechnya as a struggle against terrorism.

Assess

Social Studies ONLINE
Study Central™ provides summaries, interactive games, and online graphic organizers to help students review content.

Close

Summarizing Have students summarize the economic challenges faced by Russia. OL

Russia and the World

Main Idea Although Russia remains a world power, other nations have questioned some of its actions.

Geography and You How do good relations among neighbors build a stronger community? Read to learn about Russia's relations with the rest of the world.

As a major world power, Russia plays an important role in world affairs. In recent years, it has worked to strengthen ties with other countries. Russia sees the war in Chechnya, for example, as a struggle against terrorism. As a result, it agreed in 2002 to support the United States and other NATO (North Atlantic Treaty Organization) countries in fighting global terrorist activities.

Still, the United States and other countries are concerned about President Vladimir Putin's growing power and his declining support for democracy. Meanwhile, Russia has uneasy relations with some of the countries that were once part of the Soviet Union. Some Russian leaders have said they would like to see Russian influence increase, which worries people in these former Soviet countries. In 2004 Putin supported a pro-Russian candidate in Ukraine's presidential election—a position many Ukrainians protested. While other neighboring countries are sometimes unhappy with Russia's actions, they also know they depend on Russia for certain resources, such as oil and natural gas.

Reading Check **Analyzing Information** Why has Russia supported the global war against terrorism?

Section 2 Review

Social Studies ONLINE
Study Central™ To review this section, go to glencoe.com.

Vocabulary

1. **Explain** the meaning of the following terms by using each in a sentence.
   a. decree
   b. oligarch
   c. deposit insurance
   d. separatist movement

Main Ideas

2. **Identifying** Use a diagram like the one below to identify challenges to the growth of democracy in Russia.

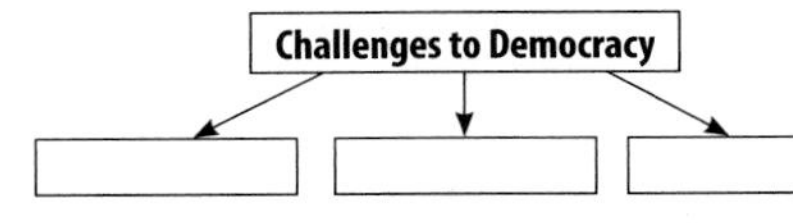

3. **Explaining** Why are some of Russia's neighbors concerned with recent Russian actions?

Critical Thinking

4. **Identifying Cause and Effect** How has the rapid change to a democratic government affected the Russian people's involvement in government? What drawback has this swift change created?
5. **BIG Idea** What factors create challenges to Russian unity?
6. **Challenge** Describe the influence of banking on a country's economy.

Writing About Geography

7. **Using Your FOLDABLES** Use your Foldable to write a paragraph predicting how successful Russia's change to a democracy and free market economy will be. Be sure to support your prediction with facts.

Section 2 Review

Answers

1. Definitions for the vocabulary words are found in the section and the Glossary.
2. Answers may include: presidential power to issue decrees and name regional governors; courts favor rich and powerful citizens; Russians do not understand the new government; corruption in business; separatists movements; and uneasy relations with other nations
3. Other nations depend on Russia for oil and natural gas. Former Soviet countries fear increasing Russian influence.
4. People began to criticize the government openly. Still many people do not understand how their new government works and therefore do not know how to change it.
5. regional rivalries and the desire of ethnic groups to form their own countries
6. Banks collect deposits and lend some of that money to other people. Those people use the money to buy houses and cars and to start new businesses. This creates jobs.
7. Answers should include facts and details from the text to support the student's prediction.

Visual Summary

Communism to Democracy

- After communism's fall, Russia became more democratic.
- Russia is a federal republic, with power divided among national, regional, and local governments.
- Russia has been moving from a command economy to a market economy.

Russia's duma, or parliament, in session

Changes in Society

- Russians now can vote freely and have increased contact with the cultures of other countries.
- The switch to a market economy has benefited some Russians while bringing hardships to others.
- Low birthrates and rising death rates have led to a decline in Russia's population.

Cargo ship on Volga River

Economic Regions

- Moscow, with its many industries, is the economic center of Russia.
- Ports in the St. Petersburg and Baltic region carry on trade between Russia and other countries.
- The Volga and Urals region is a center of manufacturing, mining, and farming.
- Siberia's resources are difficult to tap because of the area's remoteness and harsh climate.

Young Russians playing chess

Challenges

- The increasing power of Russia's president has placed limits on democracy.
- Crime and business corruption have grown in Russia.
- Some ethnic groups want to separate from Russia and form their own countries.

Russia and the World

- Russian leaders have worked to strengthen Russia's ties with the West.
- Russia has uneasy relations with some of the countries that were once part of the Soviet Union.

Vladimir Putin (right) meets with a South African leader

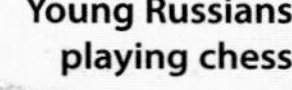

Study anywhere, anytime! Download quizzes and flash cards to your PDA from glencoe.com.

Visual Summary

Distinguishing Fact From Opinion

Ask a volunteer to explain the difference between a fact and an opinion. *(A fact can be proven, whereas an opinion cannot.)* Have students read the bulleted points on this page and study the photos. Then have each student write two facts and two opinions on index cards, one statement per card, using the text for their facts.

Call on students at random to read the statements on their index cards, one at a time. After each statement is read, have the other students vote on whether they believe the statement is a fact or an opinion. Next have the student reading the index card tell whether it is a fact or an opinion. Continue this process until all students have read their index cards. **OL**

Comparing and Contrasting

Ask: How are the economies of the Moscow region and the Volga and Urals region similar? *(Both are industrial centers.)* **OL**

This **Reading Skill** (Comparing and Contrasting) was introduced in this unit.

Hands-On Chapter Project

Step 3: Wrap Up

Launching a New Business

Step 3: Learning From the Proposal Students will synthesize what they have learned in Steps 1 and 2.

Directions Write the Essential Question on the board. Encourage students to answer this question by using what they learned while planning their new Russian businesses. Review the information from the text about the differences between a command economy and a market economy. Discuss with students how market economies and democracies are related. Ask questions such as: Do you believe strong democratic institutions help businesses thrive? Which democratic institutions are most important for the success of new businesses—a fair court system, a strong and honest police force, or the rule of law? How are other nations affected by the changes in Russia's economy and government? Have students finish the project by writing a few sentences in their journal answering the Essential Question. **OL**

Answers and Analyses

Reviewing Vocabulary

1. B In creating a market economy, the Russian government sought to improve the economy. Therefore answer choice A, under-employment, does not work because underemployment is not beneficial to an economy. The government's plan was to promote privatization, or ownership of businesses by individuals instead of the government. Heavy industry and light industry already existed in Russia.

2. C Students might confuse unemployment with underemployment. To make the distinction, explain to students that unemployment relates to the number of people who are not employed, whereas underemployment relates to the use of people's skills. When people are underemployed, their skills are not being used fully.

3. D Students may recognize immediately that answer choice A is incorrect because it is not a person. A pensioner is a person who receives payments from the government, while a separatist is a person who wants to break away from the government. If students do not recall this from their reading, encourage them to use word analysis skills to determine word meanings.

4. A If students struggle, suggest to them that when a government falls, people's reactions usually relate to the government. Careful analysis of the answer choices will help students eliminate choices B and C, which are related to the economy. To select the correct choice from the remaining two, students need to remember that a movement is something that people launch.

STANDARDIZED TEST PRACTICE

TEST-TAKING TIP

Do not pick an answer choice just because it sounds good. Sometimes a choice is meant to sound correct but is not. Read all of the answer choices very carefully before you select the best one.

Reviewing Vocabulary

Directions: Choose the word(s) that best completes the sentence.

1. In order to create a market economy, the Russian government legalized ______ .

A underemployment
B privatization
C heavy industry
D light industry

2. Due to changes in Russia's new economy, many people are ______ , which means they have to take jobs requiring lesser skills than they have.

A unemployed
B privatized
C underemployed
D invested

3. A(n) ______ is a member of a small ruling group that controls great power.

A decree
B pensioner
C separatist
D oligarch

4. When the Soviet Union fell, several ethnic groups in Russia launched ______ .

A separatist movements
B privatization efforts
C light industries
D oligarchies

5. A Russian president may issue ______ , or rulings that have the force of law and do not need the approval of the legislature.

A vetos
B decrees
C opinions
D considerations

Reviewing Main Ideas

Directions: Choose the best answer for each question.

Section 1 *(pp. 408–412)*

6. A new market economy took root in Russia after

A World War II.
B the fall of communism.
C separatist movements.
D a middle class emerged.

7. After the fall of communism, there was a manufacturing shift toward more

A heavy industry.
B oligarchy.
C light industry.
D separatist movements.

Section 2 *(pp. 418–422)*

8. A problem that has accompanied Russia's shift to a free market economy is

A starting up new companies.
B higher prices for gas and oil exports.
C the deposit insurance system.
D the rise of business oligarchs.

9. Other nations in the world have questioned some of Russia's actions, including the

A growing power of the Russian president.
B establishment of free elections.
C creation of a market economy.
D creation of a deposit insurance program.

GO ON

5. B To answer this question correctly, students must think about a president's job. Although presidents might have considerations or opinions, these are things that are not issued formally. Vetoes and decrees are formal functions of a president, but the text did not discuss veto power of Russia's president.

Reviewing Main Ideas

6. B The question is looking for the event that most directly led to the rise of a new market economy. World War II occurred many years prior, and the emergence of a middle class was the result, not the cause, of the new market economy. The rise of the market economy was the direct result of the fall of communism. Therefore, answer choice B is the correct answer.

Critical Thinking

Directions: Base your answers to questions 10 and 11 on the chart below. Choose the best answer for each question.

GNP Per Capita in U.S. Dollars				
Year(s)	Russia	United States	France	Germany
1991	$3,470	$22,340	$20,460	$20,510
1992	2,820	23,830	22,300	23,360
1993	2,350	24,750	22,360	23,560
1994	2,650	25,860	23,470	25,580
1995	2,240	26,980	24,990	27,510
1996	2,410	28,020	26,270	28,870
1997	2,680	29,080	26,300	28,280
1998	2,260	29,240	24,210	26,570
1999	2,250	31,910	24,170	26,620
2000	1,660	34,100	24,090	25,120
2001	1,750	34,280	22,730	23,560

GNP per capita is the dollar value of a country's final output of goods and services in a year (its GNP), divided by its population. It reflects the average income of a country's citizens.

Source: http://world.britannica.com/analyst/chrono/table

10. What happened to Russia's GNP per capita during the period shown?

A It jumped rapidly between 1999 and 2000.

B It rose gradually.

C It declined drastically.

D It grew following 1997.

11. Which nation's GNP per capita increased the most between 1991 and 2001?

A United States

B Germany

C Russia

D France

Document-Based Questions

Directions: Analyze the document and answer the short-answer questions that follow.

"Things Fall Apart–Russia After the Fall of Communism"

The break-up of the USSR and the failures of economic reform have hurt primarily the elderly and the children. In addition, the systems of social services, education, and health care also fell apart. The fabric of society changed with the disappearance of values and morals. Secrecy and [control] were quickly replaced by the power of money. . . . In the past there was a common expression–"Without papers you are a bug, but with papers, you are a man"–which meant that you were constantly required to ask permission from a countless army of [government officials] . . . . Now you cannot expect to be treated with respect unless your pocket is full of a wad of "greens." . . . It doesn't matter if you earned this money by [illegal activities or] selling drugs . . . . Your social status will be much higher than that of an engineer, a professor, or a doctor.

—by Nikolai Zlobin
World Affairs, Winter, 1996

12. According to the writer, who has been most seriously affected by the "new" Russia after the fall of communism? Why?

13. How does the writer feel that Russian society has changed since the breakup of the USSR?

Extended Response

14. Do you believe Russia's transition to a market economy has been good for the country or caused more harm than good? Write a short essay in which you choose one side of the argument. Defend your position by using examples.

Social Studies ONLINE
For additional test practice, use Self-Check Quizzes—Chapter 15 at glencoe.com.

Need Extra Help?

If you missed question...	1	2	3	4	5	6	7	8	9	10	11	12	13	14
Go to page...	409	410	420	421	419	409	411	420	422	420	420	419	419	420

9. A In reviewing the answers, students may see that only one choice, answer choice A, is an action that may cause other countries concern. The other three answer choices are actions that many countries would find favorable in today's political climate.

Critical Thinking

10. C Students can compare the numbers for Russia's GNP and see that only answer C is true.

11. A To answer this question, students need to subtract 1991 income from 2001 income, except for Russia, whose per capita income actually decreased.

Document-Based Questions

12. He states that old people and children have suffered the most, largely due to decreased social services, education, and health care.

13. He believes that morals and values had disappeared in Russia, and that money had become the main factor in society. Power was no longer gained through government connections, but through wealth, no matter how it was earned.

Extended Response

14. Answers will vary but should include the effect of the transition on Russia's population as well as its manufacturing and banking industries.

7. C Students may be able to narrow their answer choices to two by eliminating answer choice B, oligarchy, and D, separatist movements, which do not relate directly to business. Students may have difficulty distinguishing between the two remaining choices. Remind them that light industry is consumer goods, such as clothing, and heavy industry refers to heavy machinery. After the fall of communism, businesses focused more on what consumers want.

8. D Answer choices A and B do not create problems for the country, so they can be eliminated. The deposit insurance system was a response to problems, not a problem itself.

Social Studies ONLINE
Have students visit the Web site at glencoe.com to review Chapter 15 and take the Self-Check Quiz.

Need Extra Help?
Have students refer to the pages listed if they miss any of the questions.

What Is an Appendix?

By definition, an appendix is supplementary material attached to the end of a piece of writing. Students can use the appendix to help them understand the material in their textbook. Explain that students may use an appendix to find out what a word means, how to pronounce a word, or find additional information about a particular word or topic. **Ask: What materials are contained in this appendix?** *(Skills Handbook, Gazetteer, English-Spanish Glossary, Index, and Acknowledgments.)*

Explain what students will learn in the various components of the appendix: the Skills Handbook teaches important social studies skills; the Gazetteer teaches about important geographic locations covered in this textbook; the English-Spanish Glossary defines the vocabulary terms found in this chapter in both English and Spanish; the Index can be used to find the page references where many important topics are covered in the textbook; and the Acknowledgments gives credit to the sources for primary sources, artists and agencies, and photos credits. **BL**

Appendix

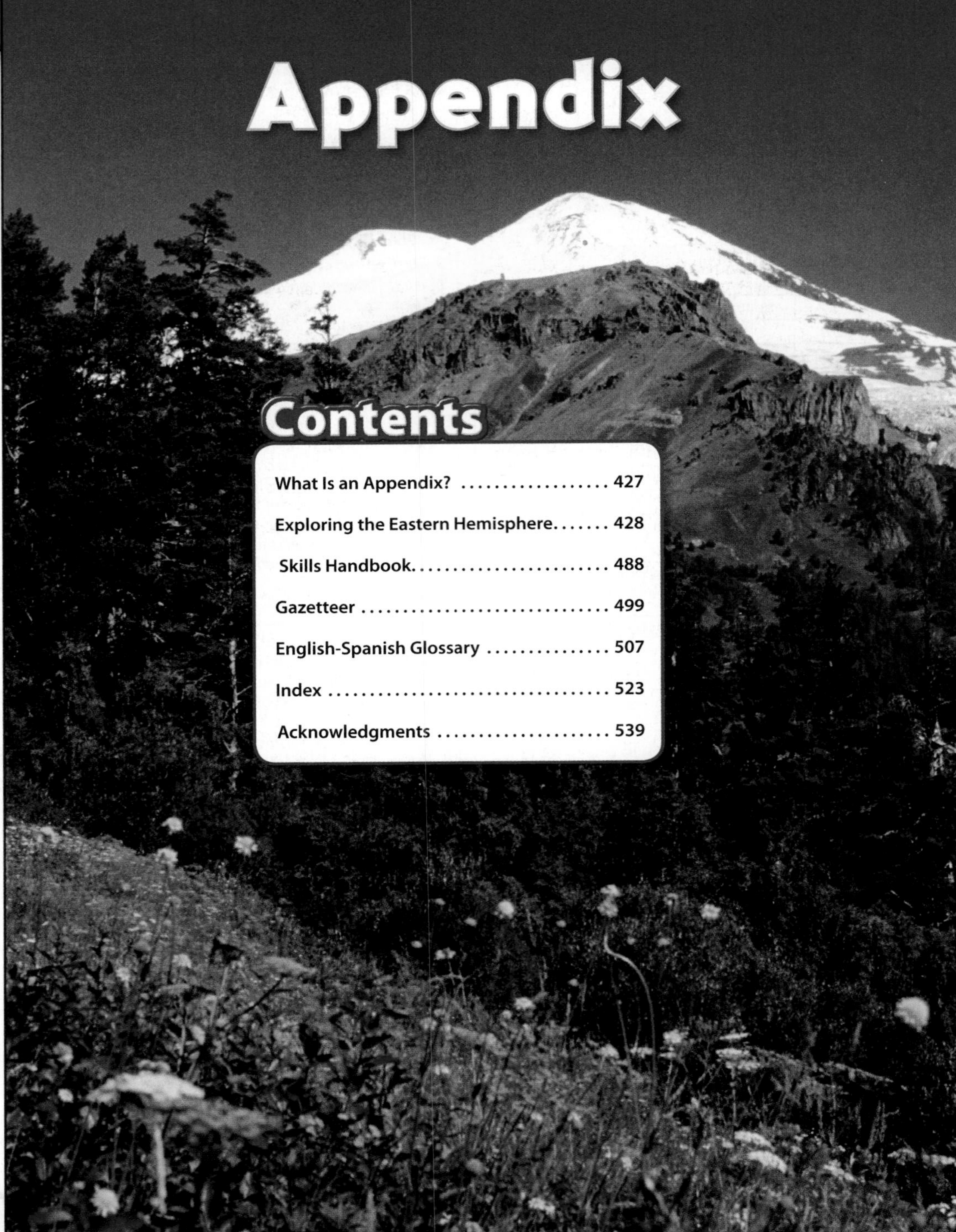

Contents

What Is an Appendix?

What Is an Appendix?

An appendix is the additional material you often find at the end of books. The following information will help you learn how to use the Appendix in *Exploring Our World: People, Places, and Cultures.*

Skills Handbook

The Skills Handbook offers you information and practice using critical thinking and social studies skills. Mastering these skills will help you in all your courses.

Gazetteer

The Gazetteer (GA•zuh•TIHR) is a geographical dictionary. It lists many of the world's largest countries, cities, and important geographic features. Each entry also includes a page number telling where the place is shown on a map in the textbook.

English-Spanish Glossary

A glossary is a list of important or difficult terms found in a textbook. The glossary gives a definition of each term as it is used in the textbook. The glossary also includes page numbers telling you where in the textbook the term is used. Since words may have additional meanings, you may wish to use a dictionary to find other uses for them.

In *Exploring Our World: People, Places, and Cultures,* the Spanish glossary is included with the English glossary. The Spanish term is located directly across from the English term. A Spanish glossary is especially important to bilingual students, or those Spanish-speaking students who are learning the English language.

Index

The Index is an alphabetical listing that includes the subjects of the book and the page numbers where those subjects can be found. The index in this book also lets you know that certain pages contain maps, graphs, photos, or paintings about the subject.

Acknowledgments

This section lists photo credits and literary credits for the book. You can look at this section to find out where the publisher obtained the permission to use a photograph or to use excerpts from other books.

Test Yourself

Find the answers to these questions by using the Appendix on the following pages.

1. What does *famine* mean?
2. Where did you find what the word *famine* means?
3. What is the Spanish word for *availability?*
4. What skill is discussed on page 498?
5. What are the latitude and longitude of Moscow?
6. On what pages can you find information about the government of the United Kingdom?

Appendix

Using an Appendix

Use the descriptions in the student text to explain the sections in the Appendix. Then instruct students to answer the questions at the bottom of the page. Next, discuss the answer to each question. **Ask:** **How can the information in each section help you as you read your textbook?** **OL**

Tell students to write six questions similar to those in **Test Yourself** on a sheet of paper. Students should write the answers on the back of the same paper. Then have students exchange questions and quiz each other. Conclude by having students check their responses. **BL**

Additional Support

Test Yourself Answers

1. severe lack of food
2. in the Glossary
3. *disponibilidad*
4. Interpreting a Population Pyramid
5. 56°N 38°E
6. pages 322–323

Exploring the Eastern Hemisphere

1

2

3

4

Use this handbook to explore other regions of the world.

In *Exploring Our World: People, Places, and Cultures—Western Hemisphere, Europe, and Russia,* you studied several western world regions. Read this special handbook to learn about eastern world regions.

As you read the information, remember what you have already learned about the physical geography, history, culture, and current-day issues of western world regions. Think about how the western world regions are similar to and different from these eastern world regions.

Contents

① Canoeing near Kongou Falls in Gabon
② Strolling in a Japanese garden
③ Harvesting tea in Sri Lanka
④ Traveling across the Nam Song River in Laos

What Makes North Africa, Southwest Asia, and Central Asia a Region?

The countries in this region share the following characteristics:

- vast deserts and dry climates
- the majority of the world's oil and natural gas reserves
- challenges to the environment, including damage to farmland in some areas
- a concentration of population along rivers and in coastal plains
- a predominantly Muslim population, although Jews and Christians also live in the region

NATIONAL GEOGRAPHIC

www.nationalgeographic.com/education

NGS ONLINE This online resource provides lesson plans, atlas updates, cartographic activities with interactive maps, an online map store, and geographic links.

North Africa, Southwest Asia, and Central Asia

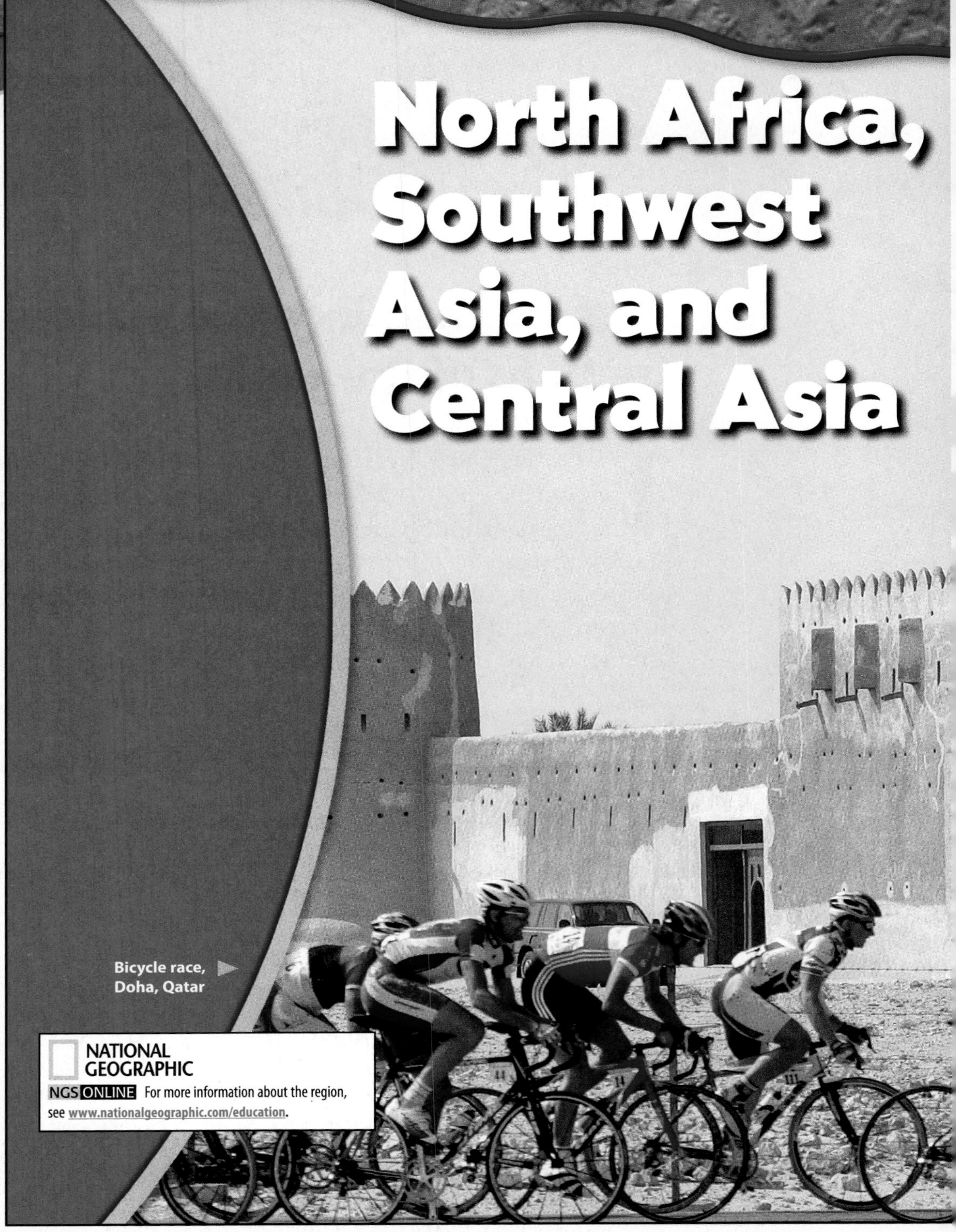

Bicycle race, Doha, Qatar

NATIONAL GEOGRAPHIC

NGS ONLINE For more information about the region, see www.nationalgeographic.com/education.

Activity: Launching the Regional Atlas

Why Study North Africa, Southwest Asia, and Central Asia? Ask: Why do you think the world's attention has been focused on this region so often in recent years? *(Students may answer because of the oil resources in the region or because of the conflicts that have taken place in parts of the region in recent years.)* Tell students that more and more people around the world have begun to study this region in an effort to better understand the reasons for recent conflicts. Have students list questions that they would like to have answered about this region, and then tell them to look for answers to those questions as they study the Regional Atlas. **OL**

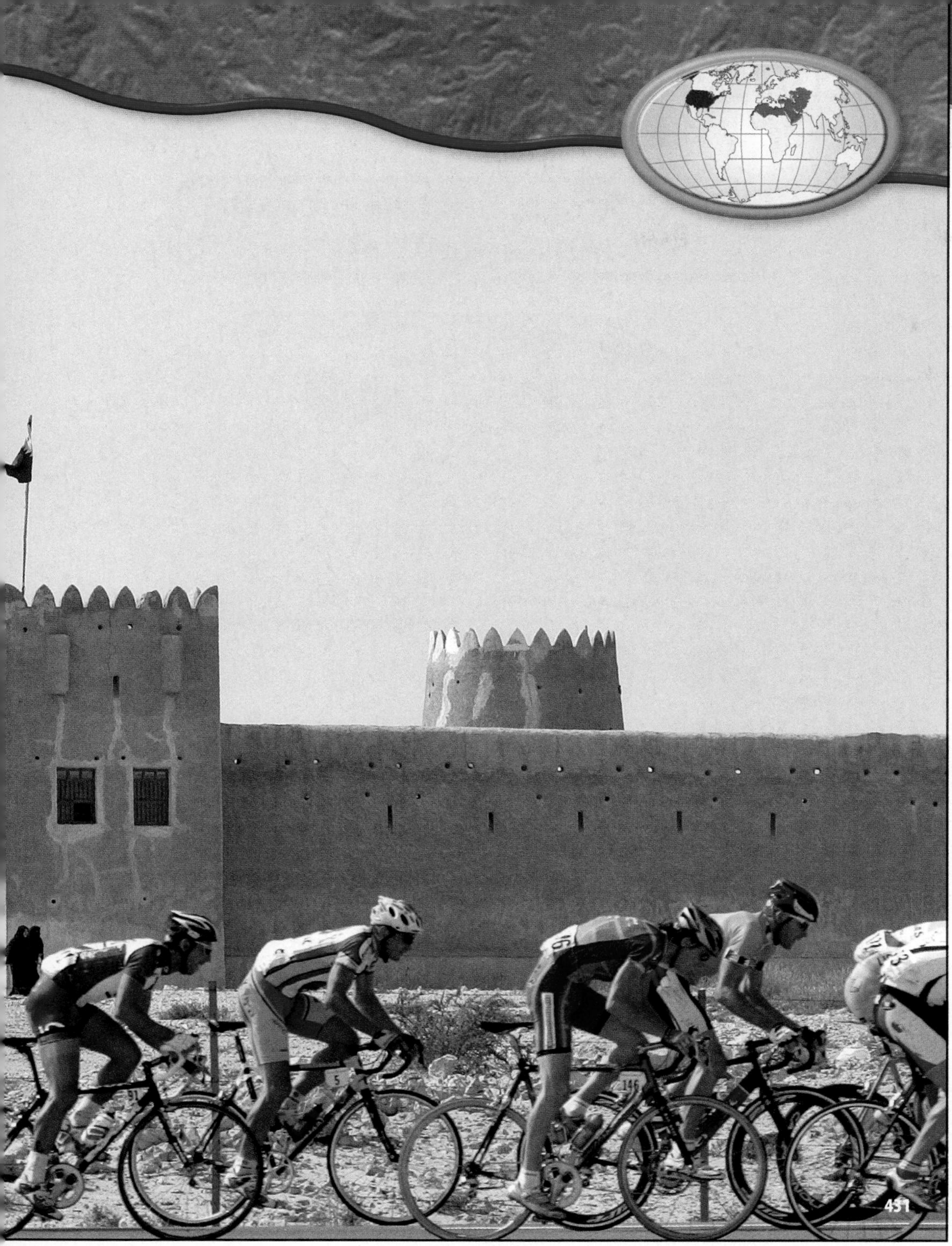

Introduce the Region

Using Maps Have students look at the maps of physical features and economic resources of North Africa, Southwest Asia, and Central Asia in the Regional Atlas. Then display the map overlay transparency for this region. **Ask: How is land used throughout much of North Africa and Southwest Asia?** *(for nomadic herding)* **Ask: What physical feature would account for this type of land use?** *(deserts)* **Ask: Where in the region is land used differently?** *(North of the Arabian Peninsula, in Southwest Asia, the land is used primarily for subsistence farming; in Central Asia, the land is used primarily for raising livestock.)* **OL**

More About the Photo

Visual Literacy Qatar has promoted the sport of cycling in the country, hosting competitions each year. The Tour of Qatar took place from January 31 to February 4th, 2005, in five stages. Seventeen teams of eight riders each competed in the race—including European and Asian teams and for the first time, a team from Qatar.

The riders passed through the town of Al Zubara, 62 miles (100 km) west of Doha, during the fourth stage of the race. Al Zubara is famous for its old fort. Erected in 1938 with circular towers on three of its corners and a rectangular tower on the fourth, it resembles a castle. It was used by the military until the mid-1980s and is now a museum.

Regional Atlas Activity

Where Is It?

Latitude and Longitude Ask students to locate Cairo on the map. **Ask:** **Is Cairo north or south of the Equator?** *(north)* **Is Cairo east or west of the Prime Meridian?** *(east)* **What is the approximate latitude of Cairo?** *(30°N)* **What is the approximate degree longitude of Cairo?** *(30°E)* **What, then, is the absolute location of Cairo?** *(30°N, 31°E)* **OL**

How Big Is It?

Making Connections Have students look in the Regional Atlas and compare this region with Russia. **Ask:** **How does the size of Russia compare to the size of the region of North Africa, Southwest Asia, and Central Asia?** *(They have nearly the same land area.)* **OL**

Comparing Population

Ask: **About how large is the population of Egypt?** *(about 75 million)*
Ask: **What other country in this region has approximately the same population as Egypt?** *(Turkey)* **OL**

Regional Atlas

North Africa, Southwest Asia, and Central Asia

Where Is It?

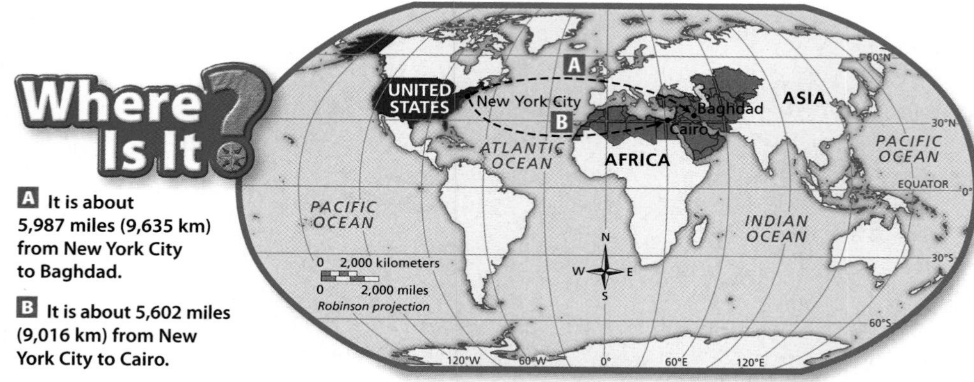

A It is about 5,987 miles (9,635 km) from New York City to Baghdad.

B It is about 5,602 miles (9,016 km) from New York City to Cairo.

How Big Is It?

Together, North Africa, Southwest Asia, and Central Asia occupy almost 6.6 million square miles (17 million sq. km), more than twice the area of the continental United States. At almost 530 million, the population of North Africa, Southwest Asia, and Central Asia is more than one and a half times that of the United States.

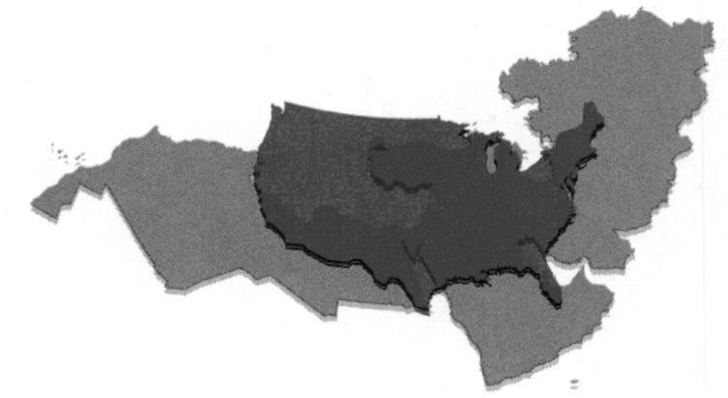

Comparing Population

United States and Selected Countries of North Africa, Southwest Asia, and Central Asia

Country	Population (each figure = 30,000,000)
United States	🧍🧍🧍🧍🧍🧍🧍🧍🧍🧍
Turkey	🧍🧍 and part of a figure
Egypt	🧍🧍 and part of a figure
Iran	🧍🧍 and part of a figure
Afghanistan	🧍
Israel	part of a figure

🧍 = 30,000,000

Source: *World Population Data Sheet*, 2005.

Activity: Geographic Theme

Place Review with the class the concept of place. Remind them that place includes the characteristics that give an area its own special character, including physical features and human characteristics. Ask them to look at the information about Egypt that is found on this page and in the rest of the Regional Atlas. Lead a discussion about what they can learn about Egypt from this information. Then have them work in pairs to study the maps in the Regional Atlas more closely and list physical features and human characteristics of Egypt. *(For example, the Sahara covers most of the country; most people live near the Nile River, where subsistence farming is practiced.)* Have each pair volunteer one characteristic to the class; keep a running list on the board of the characteristics of Egypt that make this place unique. **OL**

NATIONAL GEOGRAPHIC

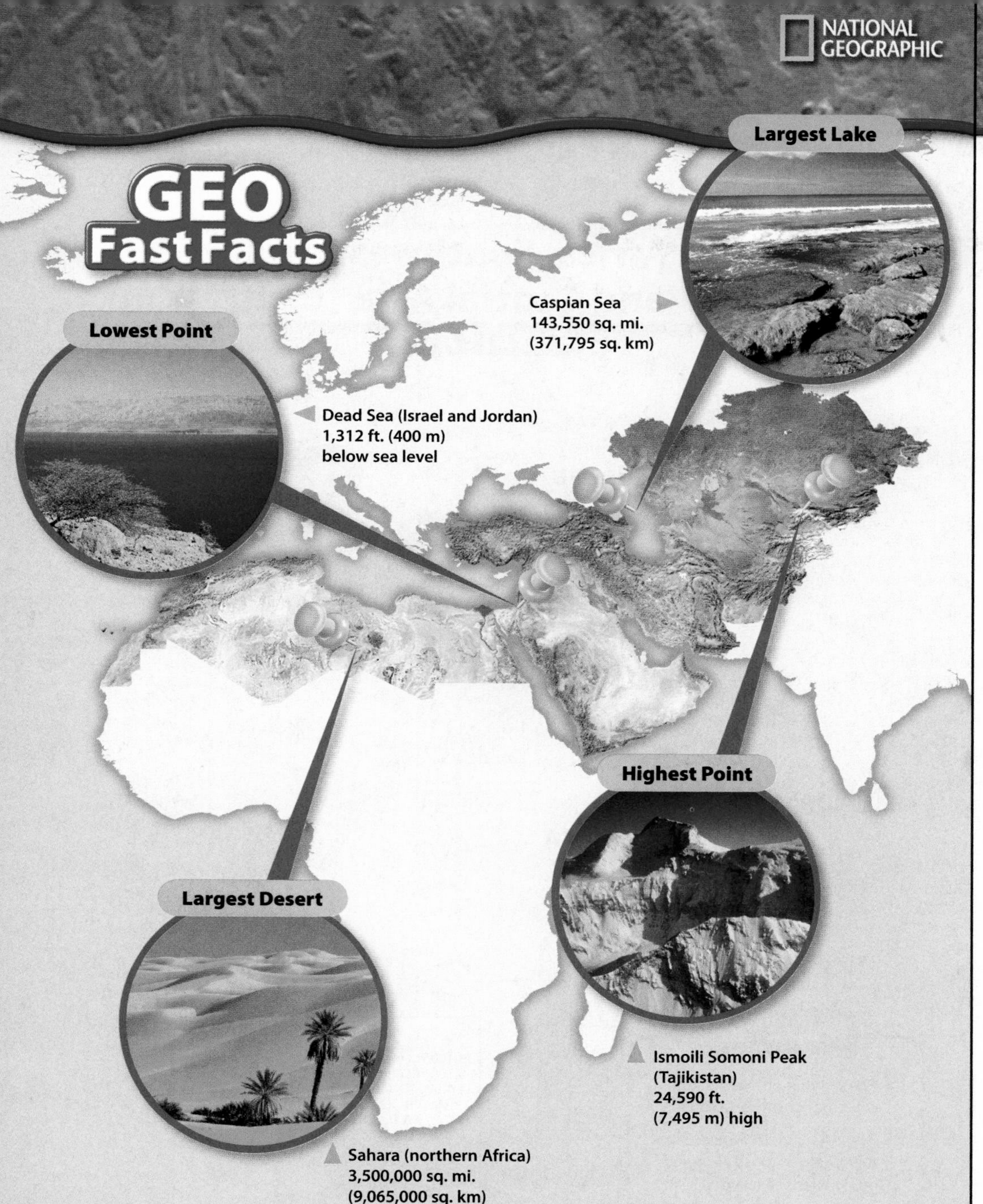

Geo Fast Facts

Identifying Extremes Ask: What four physical features of this region are highlighted on this map? *(its largest lake, largest desert, lowest point, and highest point)* Tell students that three of these features are the "extremes"—or the largest, lowest, and so on—not only in this region, but the entire world. Have students use Internet resources to identify which of the three features on this map are the world extremes. *(lowest point in the world—Dead Sea; largest desert in the world—Sahara; largest lake in the world—Caspian Sea)*

Tell students that this region contains other world extremes, including the longest river in the world—the Nile—and the highest recorded temperature in the world—136°F (58°C) at El Azizia, Libya on September 13, 1922. **OL**

FastFacts

- **Qatar** Al-Jazeera, based in Qatar, was started in 1996 as the first independent Arabic-language television channel. It is unique in the Arab world because it is not run by a government. Although it respects the religion of Islam, it freely criticizes the policies of governments throughout the region.
- **Morocco** On the coast of the Mediterranean Sea lie two cities, Ceuta and Melilla, that are Spanish enclaves within the territory of Morocco. The Spanish government views the cities as somewhere between a standard Spanish city and an autonomous community. Morocco has called for the cities to be integrated into its territory.
- **Egypt** Animals were important in ancient Egyptian culture. In Egyptian art, gods and goddesses were frequently shown with human bodies and the heads of animals. Cats first became domestic pets in ancient Egypt. Bastet, the Egyptian cat goddess, was associated with joy, music, and dancing.
- **Afghanistan** The average life expectancy in Afghanistan is only 42 years—36 years less than the average life expectancy in the United States. More than one in four Afghan children die before their fifth birthday.

Regional Atlas

Regional Atlas Activity

Identifying Have students work in pairs to create matching exercises for other students. First, have them list ten countries from the region in the left-hand column. Then, have them list twelve different physical features found in those countries in the right-hand column. Emphasize that the same physical feature may be found in more than one country, and countries may have more than one of the physical features listed. Finally, have students create a "quiz" by numbering the countries 1–10, and jumbling the physical features in the right-hand column and labeling them A–L. Have pairs exchange quizzes, match the letters of physical features to each country, and return the quizzes for scoring. **AL**

Map Skills

Answers:

1. the Sahara
2. *Possible answer:* This region is largely covered by highlands, as it contains many large mountain ranges and elevations above 1,600 feet (500 m).

Skills Practice

Ask: **What mountain range separates eastern Europe from Asia?** *(the Caucasus Mountains)*

North Africa, Southwest Asia, and Central Asia

PHYSICAL

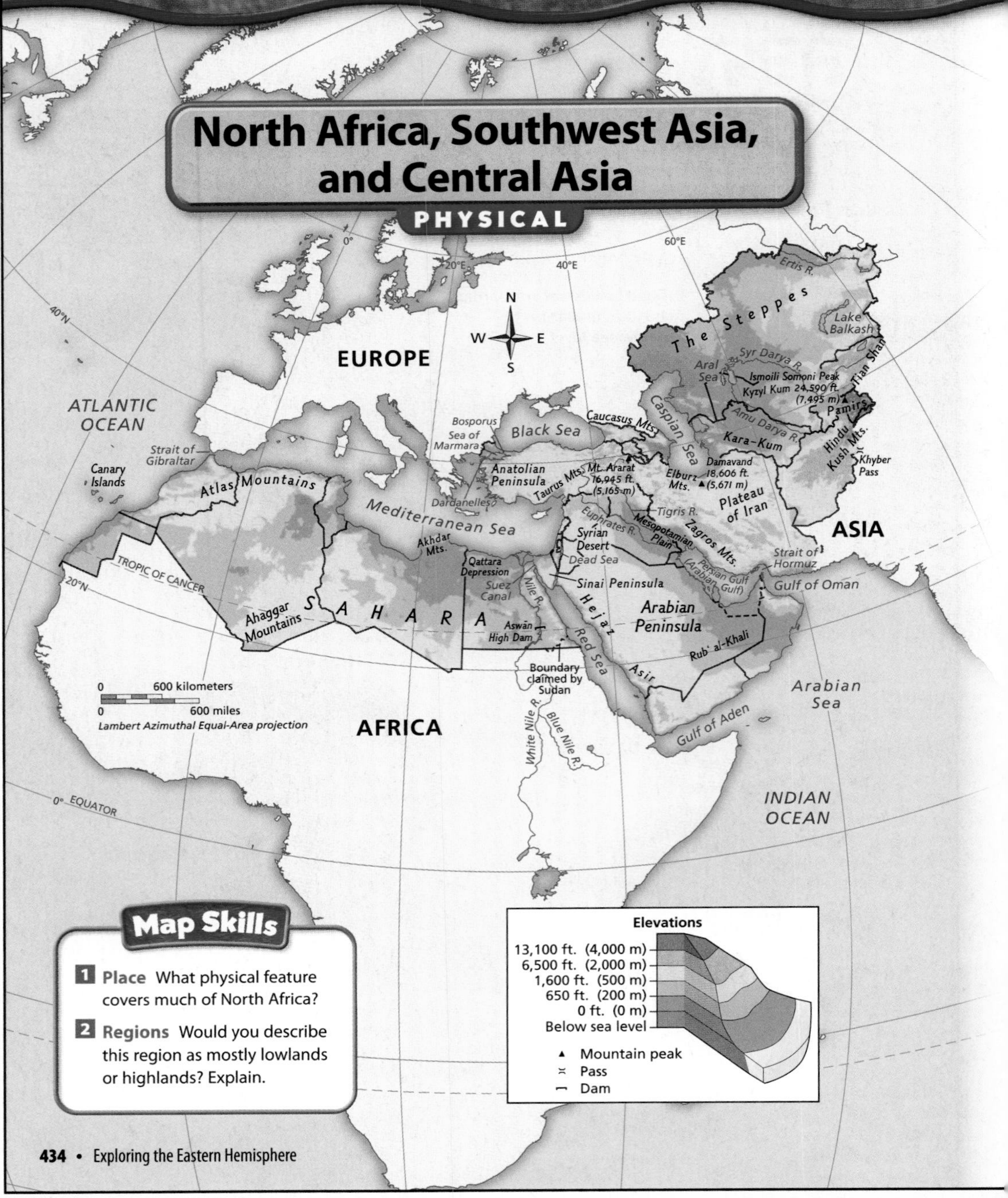

0 600 kilometers
0 600 miles
Lambert Azimuthal Equal-Area projection

Map Skills

1 Place What physical feature covers much of North Africa?

2 Regions Would you describe this region as mostly lowlands or highlands? Explain.

Elevations

13,100 ft. (4,000 m)
6,500 ft. (2,000 m)
1,600 ft. (500 m)
650 ft. (200 m)
0 ft. (0 m)
Below sea level

▲ Mountain peak
Pass
Dam

Background: Land and Climate

A Rugged Landscape The region of North Africa, Southwest Asia, and Central Asia extends from the Atlantic coast of Morocco in northwest Africa to the eastern border of Kazakhstan in Central Asia. Much of this area is characterized by a harsh, dry climate. Major bodies of water, however, border much of the area. The waterways that connect them serve as trade routes and also make farming possible. Many of the coastal areas in the region have Mediterranean climates that are warm and humid.

Much of North Africa and the Arabian Peninsula is covered by dry, hot deserts. Only 3–4 inches (8–10 cm) of rain fall in these areas per year. Central Asia also contains desert areas that receive little rain; these areas have very hot summers but very cold winters. Bordering the deserts throughout Central Asia are dry plains called steppes. In these areas, enough rain falls to support grasses but not trees.

Mountain ranges in much of the region create a rugged landscape. Although many highland areas receive abundant rainfall, the land is too rocky in these areas to support farming.

NATIONAL GEOGRAPHIC

North Africa, Southwest Asia, and Central Asia

POLITICAL

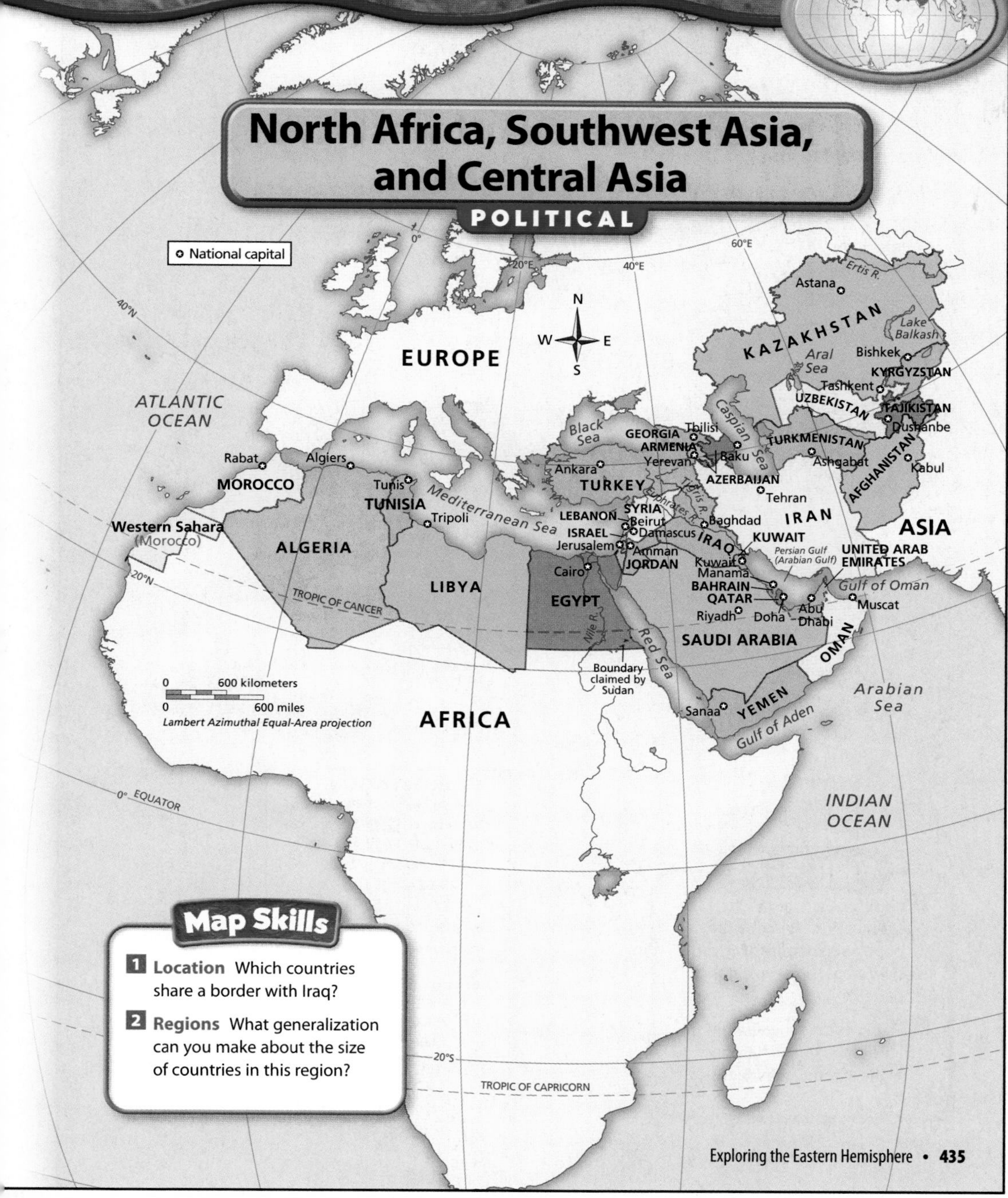

National capital

0 600 kilometers
0 600 miles
Lambert Azimuthal Equal-Area projection

Map Skills

1 Location Which countries share a border with Iraq?

2 Regions What generalization can you make about the size of countries in this region?

Regional Atlas

Regional Atlas Activity

Classifying Point out to students that this region is on two continents—Africa and Asia. Give students a few minutes to study the map on this page. **Ask:** **What countries in the region are in Africa?** *(Egypt, Libya, Tunisia, Algeria, Morocco, and Western Sahara)* **What countries are in Asia?** *(Kazakhstan, Kyrgyzstan, Uzbekistan, Tajikistan, Turkmenistan, Afghanistan, Iran, Azerbaijan, Armenia, Georgia, Turkey, Iraq, Syria, Lebanon, Israel, Jordan, Saudi Arabia, Kuwait, Bahrain, Qatar, United Arab Emirates, Oman, and Yemen)* **What do the names of many of the countries of Central Asia have in common?** *(They end in –stan. The suffix "stan" is Persian for "place of.")* **OL**

Map Skills

Answers:

1. Syria, Jordan, Saudi Arabia, Kuwait, Iran, and Turkey
2. Possible answer: Countries tend to be very large or rather small.

Skills Practice

Ask: **What countries are on the Arabian Peninsula?** *(Kuwait, Qatar, Saudi Arabia, Yemen, Oman, United Arab Emirates)* **What countries are along this region the Caspian Sea?** *(Azerbaijan, Iran, Turkmenistan, Kazakhstan)*

Background: Current Issues

The War on Terror The Islamist terrorist group known as al-Qaeda, led by Osama bin Laden, began attacking American targets in the 1990s. This group launched its most deadly attack on September 11, 2001, when four passenger planes were hijacked. Two planes crashed into the World Trade Center in New York City, one crashed into the Pentagon in Washington, D.C., and one crashed in a rural area of Pennsylvania. The U.S. government responded first by targeting the Islamist government of Afghanistan, known as the Taliban, which protected al-Qaeda. After forcing the Taliban out of Afghanistan, President Bush and U.S. officials turned their attention to Iraq, which they believed possessed dangerous biological and chemical weapons and supported terrorist groups. In March 2003, the United States toppled the Iraqi government and helped begin the long process of rebuilding the country. This task has proved difficult, because American and Iraqi forces have faced armed uprisings and guerrilla attacks.

Regional Atlas

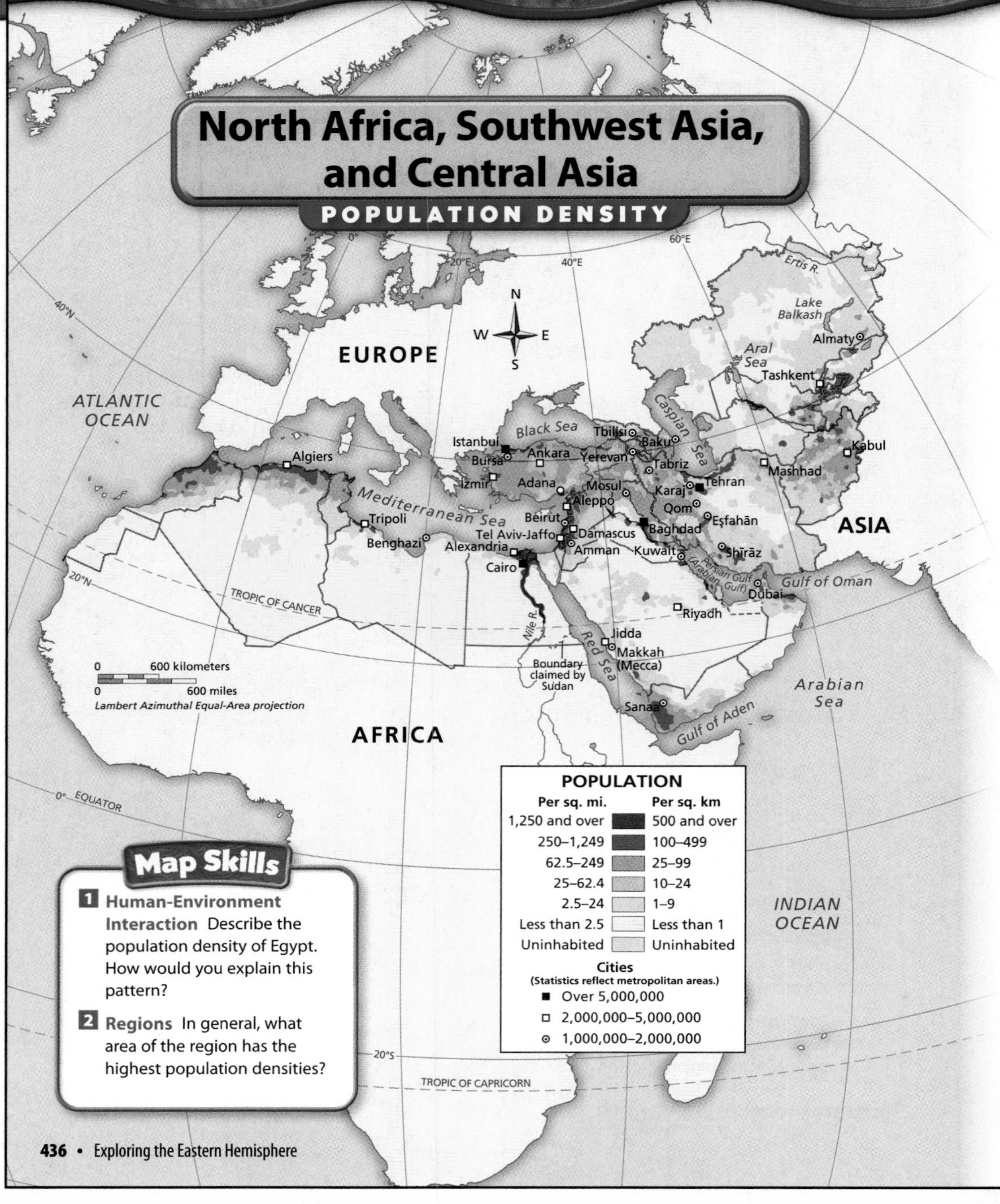

Regional Atlas Activity

Drawing Conclusions Tell students to compare this map to the political map on the previous page. **Ask:** **What parts of this region have the lowest population density?** *(much of North Africa, much of the Arabian Peninsula, much of Iran, and much of Central Asia)* Then have students compare this map to the physical map. **Ask:** **What physical features might account for the low population density in these areas?** *(deserts, mountains, and steppes)* **AL**

Map Skills

Answers:

1. The population density of Egypt is highest along the Nile River, where the land is fertile; other parts of Egypt are desert.
2. Narrow coastal or river plains have the highest population densities.

Skills Practice

Ask: **Where do most people in North Africa live?** *(on the coast of the Mediterranean Sea or Atlantic Ocean or along the Nile River)* **What might be some reasons for the higher population densities of the countries near the Black Sea?** *(This area has a more temperate climate and several rivers, which makes farming possible.)*

Background: People and Culture

Women in the Region Attitudes toward the place of women in society vary across North Africa, Southwest Asia, and Central Asia. In rural areas where people farm to make a living, women have always worked alongside their husbands in the field. In urban areas, however, women have traditionally stayed at home to take care of children and manage households.

In the most traditional countries, women have few rights. In Saudi Arabia, for example, women do not have the right to vote, and cannot travel unless a male relative is with them. While women are allowed to go to university and work, college classes are segregated, and women can work only in professions where they can easily remain separated from men.

Other countries have more modern views regarding the rights of women. In Turkey, for example, women can vote and also be elected to office. Women have served as prime minister in Turkey and Israel. Tansu Çiller served as Turkey's prime minister in the mid-1990s, and Golda Meir served as Israel's prime minister from 1969 to 1974.

NATIONAL GEOGRAPHIC

Regional Atlas

North Africa, Southwest Asia, and Central Asia

ECONOMIC RESOURCES

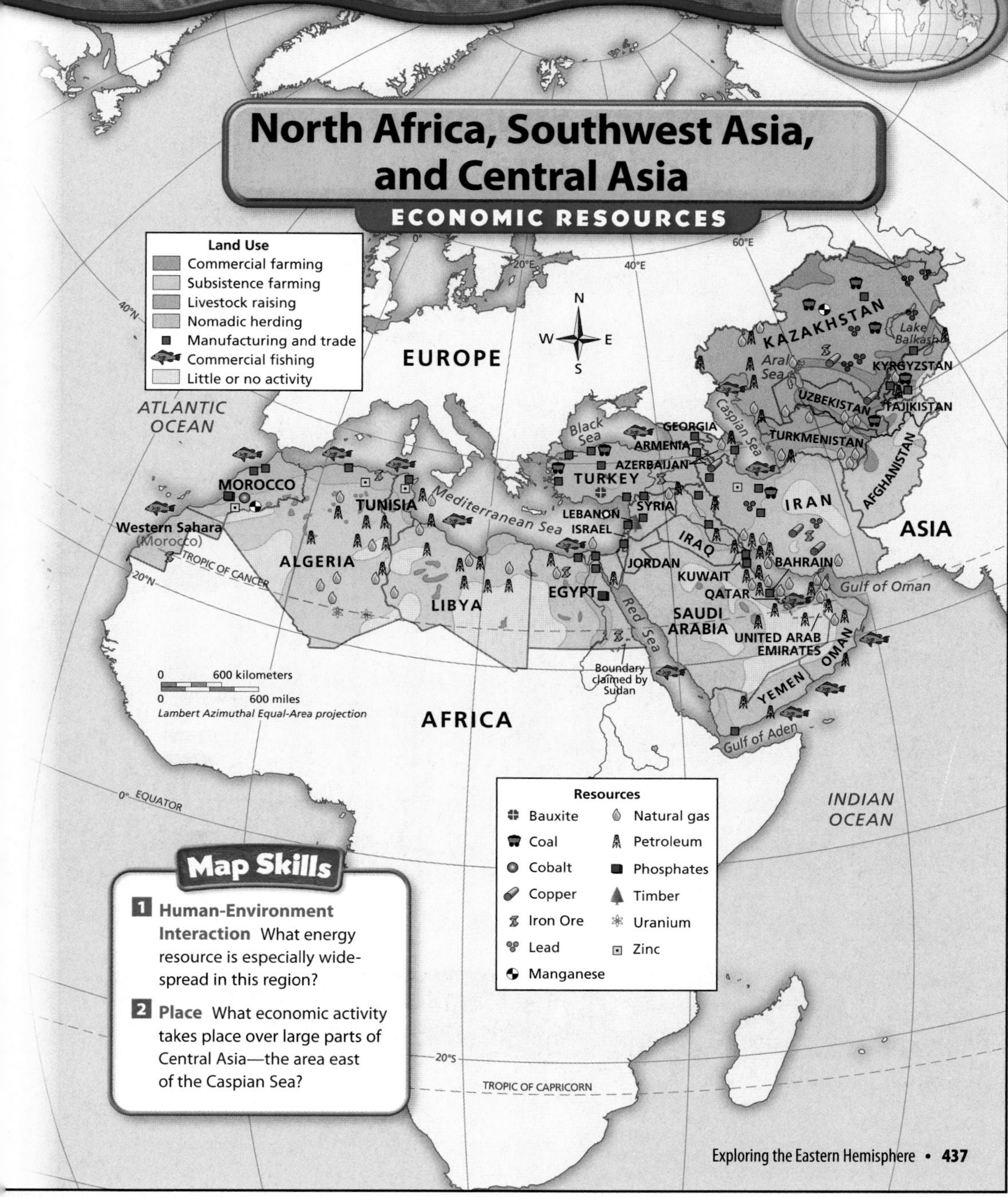

Land Use

- Commercial farming
- Subsistence farming
- Livestock raising
- Nomadic herding
- Manufacturing and trade
- Commercial fishing
- Little or no activity

Resources

Bauxite	Natural gas
Coal	Petroleum
Cobalt	Phosphates
Copper	Timber
Iron Ore	Uranium
Lead	Zinc
Manganese	

0 600 kilometers
0 600 miles
Lambert Azimuthal Equal-Area projection

Map Skills

1 Human-Environment Interaction What energy resource is especially widespread in this region?

2 Place What economic activity takes place over large parts of Central Asia—the area east of the Caspian Sea?

Regional Atlas Activity

Comparing and Contrasting Assign each student or group of students a pair of countries from the region. Have them study the physical features, economic resources, and population density maps in the Regional Atlas. Then ask them to create a Venn diagram that lists the similarities and differences between the two countries. Ask volunteers to share their results with the class. **AL**

Map Skills

Answers:

1. Petroleum is found across much of the region.
2. raising livestock

Skills Practice

Ask: In what area is manufacturing and trade concentrated? *(the northern part of Southwest Asia)* **What economic activity is widespread in Afghanistan?** *(nomadic herding)*

Background: The Economy

The Importance of Oil Several countries in North Africa, Southwest Asia, and Central Asia are among the world's major oil producers. Saudi Arabia, on the Arabian Peninsula, has used the wealth gained from the export of oil to build schools, hospitals, roads, and airports. Oman, in the southeastern corner of the Arabian Peninsula, not only has important oil resources but also has built ports for oil tankers. It guards the Strait of Hormuz, the waterway that oil tankers must use to travel from the Persian Gulf to the Arabian Sea. Kuwait, Bahrain, Qatar, and the United Arab Emirates, all oil-rich countries along the Persian Gulf, have strong economies and provide free services, public education, and health care to their citizens.

In recent years, many oil-producing countries have tried to diversify so that their economies do not rely solely on oil production. Qatar has developed its natural gas industry. Bahrain has become an international banking center. Dubai, in the United Arab Emirates, has a large port and is developing its banking and tourism industries.

Regional Atlas Activity

Comparing and Contrasting.
Ask: What is the population density of Egypt? *(191 people per square mile)* **Of the United States?** *(80 people per square mile)* **How do the land areas and populations of the two countries compare?** *(The land area of the United States is nearly 10 times as large as that of Egypt, while the population of the United States is about 4 times as large.)*

Have students look again at the population density map for Egypt and then consider what they know about the population distribution in the United States. **Ask: How do you think the population distribution in the United States compares to that in Egypt?** *(Answers will vary, but students should recognize that the population in the United States is more evenly distributed than in Egypt, although certain areas have very high population densities—for example, the cities along the east coast—and others have low population densities—for example, the Northern Plains.)* **AL**

FastFacts

Bahrain, an island country in the Persian (Arabian) Gulf, is the smallest Arab country in geographic size. Diving for pearls was Bahrain's main economic activity until the discovery of oil there in the 1930s. Today, as a banking and financial services center, Bahrain relies less on oil than most Gulf countries.

Regional Atlas

North Africa, Southwest Asia, and Central Asia

Country and Capital	Literacy Rate	Population and Density	Land Area	Life Expectancy (Years)	GDP* Per Capita (U.S. dollars)	Television Sets (per 1,000 people)	Flag and Language
AFGHANISTAN Kabul	36%	29,900,000 119 per sq. mi. 46 per sq. km	251,772 sq. mi. 652,086 sq. km	42	$800	14	Dari, Pashto
Algiers ALGERIA	70%	32,800,000 36 per sq. mi. 14 per sq. km	919,591 sq. mi. 2,381,730 sq. km	73	$6,600	107	Arabic
ARMENIA Yerevan	98.6%	3,000,000 261 per sq. mi. 101 per sq. km	11,506 sq. mi. 29,800 sq. km	71	$4,600	241	Armenian
AZERBAIJAN Baku	97%	8,400,000 251 per sq. mi. 97 per sq. km	33,436 sq. mi. 86,599 sq. km	72	$3,800	257	Azerbaijan
Manama BAHRAIN	89.1%	700,000 2,632 per sq. mi. 1,016 per sq. km	266 sq. mi. 689 sq. km	74	$19,200	446	Arabic
Cairo EGYPT	57.5%	74,000,000 191 per sq. mi. 74 per sq. km	386,660 sq. mi. 1,001,445 sq. km	70	$4,200	170	Arabic
GEORGIA Tbilisi	99%	4,500,000 167 per sq. mi. 65 per sq. km	26,911 sq. mi. 69,699 sq. km	72	$3,100	516	Georgian
Tehran IRAN	79.4%	69,500,000 110 per sq. mi. 43 per sq. km	630,575 sq. mi. 1,633,182 sq. km	70	$7,700	154	Persian
UNITED STATES Washington, D.C.	97%	296,500,000 80 per sq. mi. 31 per sq. km	3,717,796 sq. mi. 9,629,047 sq. km	78	$40,100	844	English

*Gross Domestic Product

Countries and flags not drawn to scale

Activity: Using the Chart

Making Graphs Have students use spreadsheet software to create a chart that lists all of the countries in North Africa and their populations. Tell students to total the population figures for each country to find the total population of North Africa. Then have them use the graph function in the spreadsheet software to turn the chart into a circle graph. Have students print their graphs and study them. **Ask: Which country accounts for nearly one-half of the population in North Africa?** *(Egypt)* **Which countries have less than 10% of North Africa's population?** *(Tunisia and Libya)* **OL**

North Africa, Southwest Asia, and Central Asia

Country and Capital	Literacy Rate	Population and Density	Land Area	Life Expectancy (Years)	GDP* Per Capita (U.S. dollars)	Television Sets (per 1,000 people)	Flag and Language
IRAQ Baghdad	40.4%	28,800,000 170 per sq. mi. 66 per sq. km	169,236 sq. mi. 438,319 sq. km	59	$2,100	82	Arabic
ISRAEL† Jerusalem	95.4%	7,100,000 873 per sq. mi. 337 per sq. km	8,131 sq. mi. 21,059 sq. km	80	$20,800	328	Hebrew
JORDAN Amman	91.3%	5,800,000 184 per sq. mi. 71 per sq. km	31,444 sq. mi. 81,440 sq. km	72	$4,500	83	Arabic
KAZAKHSTAN Astana	98.4%	15,100,000 14 per sq. mi. 6 per sq. km	1,049,151 sq. mi. 2,717,289 sq. km	66	$7,800	240	Kazakh, Russian
KUWAIT Kuwait	83.5%	2,600,000 378 per sq. mi. 146 per sq. km	6,880 sq. mi. 17,819 sq. km	78	$21,300	480	Arabic
KYRGYZSTAN Bishkek	97%	5,200,000 68 per sq. mi. 26 per sq. km	76,641 sq. mi. 198,499 sq. km	68	$1,700	49	Kyrgyz, Russian
LEBANON Beirut	87.4%	3,800,000 947 per sq. mi. 365 per sq. km	4,015 sq. mi. 10,399 sq. km	74	$5,000	355	Arabic
LIBYA Tripoli	82.6%	5,800,000 9 per sq. mi. 3 per sq. km	679,359 sq. mi. 1,759,532 sq. km	76	$6,700	139	Arabic
UNITED STATES Washington, D.C.	97%	296,500,000 80 per sq. mi. 31 per sq. km	3,717,796 sq. mi. 9,629,047 sq. km	78	$40,100	844	English

† Israel has proclaimed Jerusalem as its capital, but many countries' embassies are in Tel Aviv. The Palestinian Authority has assumed all governmental duties in non-Israeli-occupied areas of the West Bank and Gaza Strip.

Sources: *CIA World Factbook*, 2005; Population Reference Bureau, *World Population Data Sheet*, 2005.

For more country facts, go to the **Nations of the World Databank** at glencoe.com.

Regional Atlas Activity

Synthesizing Information Assign each student a country in the region. Tell students to study the Regional Atlas maps, as well as the information given in the charts, for their assigned country. Then have them write a "definition" of their country, based on the maps and chart. Give them the following definition as an example:

Israel—country in Southwest Asia, on the Mediterranean Sea; 8,131 square miles, population 7,100,000, capital Jerusalem. **ELL**

FastFacts

Jerusalem The city of Jerusalem, in Israel, has been occupied continuously for nearly 5,000 years. The Old City, in the heart of Jerusalem, is surrounded by walls on four sides and contains four neighborhoods—Jewish, Christian, Armenian, and Muslim. The city contains important holy sites of Jews, Christians, and Muslims.

Activity: Using the Chart

Identifying Central Issues Ask students to check their local newspapers for articles about countries in North Africa, Southwest Asia, and Central Asia for one week. Tell them to either clip or photocopy the articles they find. At the end of the week, have them bring their articles to class, and then use the articles as the basis for a discussion about the issues facing this region. **Ask:** **Which countries in this region received the greatest coverage in the newspapers you read? Why?** *(Answers will vary depending on the week students complete this activity.)* As students identify issues facing countries in the region, list these issues on the board. **Ask:** **How do these issues affect the rest of the world?** *(Answers will vary depending on the issues identified.)* **OL**

Regional Atlas Activity

Drawing Conclusions Have students compare the GDP per capita of Egypt and Saudi Arabia. **Ask:** **What is the GDP per capita of each country?** *(Egypt: $4,200; Saudi Arabia: $12,000)* **What other data indicates that Saudi Arabia is more prosperous than Egypt?** *(Saudi Arabia has a much higher literacy rate—78.8% vs. 57.5%.)* Have students look at the Economic Resources map in the Regional Atlas. **Ask:** **What might account for these differences?** *(Saudi Arabia has much more petroleum.)* **OL**

FastFacts

Istanbul Turkey's largest city, Istanbul, is located in Europe and Asia. Originally built about 657 B.C., it has been known by other names throughout its long history, including Byzantium and Constantinople.

Regional Atlas

North Africa, Southwest Asia, and Central Asia

Country and Capital	Literacy Rate	Population and Density	Land Area	Life Expectancy (Years)	GDP* Per Capita (U.S. dollars)	Television Sets (per 1,000 people)	Flag and Language
Rabat, MOROCCO†	51.7%	30,700,000 178 per sq. mi. 69 per sq. km	172,413 sq. mi. 446,548 sq. km	70	$4,200	165	Arabic
Muscat, OMAN	75.8%	2,400,000 29 per sq. mi. 11 per sq. km	82,031 sq. mi. 212,459 sq. km	74	$13,100	575	Arabic
QATAR, Doha	82.5%	800,000 188 per sq. mi. 73 per sq. km	4,247 sq. mi. 11,000 sq. km	70	$23,200	866	Arabic
SAUDI ARABIA, Riyadh	78.8%	24,600,000 30 per. sq. mi. 11 per sq. km	829,996 sq. mi. 2,149,680 sq. km	72	$12,000	263	Arabic
SYRIA, Damascus	76.9%	18,400,000 257 per sq. mi. 99 per sq. km	71,498 sq. mi. 185,179 sq. km	72	$3,400	68	Arabic
Dushanbe, TAJIKISTAN	99.4%	6,800,000 123 per sq. mi. 48 per sq. km	55,251 sq. mi. 143,099 sq. km	63	$1,100	328	Tajik
Tunis, TUNISIA	74.2%	10,000,000 158 per sq. mi. 61 per sq. km	63,170 sq. mi. 163,610 sq. km	73	$7,100	190	Arabic, French
Ankara, TURKEY	86.5%	72,900,000 244 per sq. mi. 94 per sq. km	299,158 sq. mi. 774,816 sq. km	69	$7,400	328	Turkish
UNITED STATES, Washington, D.C.	97%	296,500,000 80 per sq. mi. 31 per sq. km	3,717,796 sq. mi. 9,629,047 sq. km	78	$40,100	844	English

*Gross Domestic Product

† Morocco claims the Western Sahara area, but other countries do not accept this claim.

Countries and flags not drawn to scale

Activity: Using the Chart

Locating Information Have students work in pairs to create a chart listing the three countries with the highest literacy rates *(Tajikistan, Uzbekistan, Georgia)* and the lowest literacy rates *(Afghanistan, Iraq, Yemen)* in this region. The first column of the chart should list the country names, and the second column should give the literacy rate for each country. Then have students conduct research to find out if the literacy rates for men and women are similar or different in these countries. Tell students that they can find this information online in the *CIA World Factbook* at www.cia.gov. They can click on the link to the *World Factbook*. There they can click on the countries they wish to learn more about. Instruct students to add columns to their chart to record the literacy rates for men and women. **Ask:** **What effect do women's literacy rates have on the overall literacy rates in these countries?** *(In many countries, women's literacy rates are much lower than men's, which lowers the overall literacy rate for the country.)* **AL**

North Africa, Southwest Asia, and Central Asia

Country and Capital	Literacy Rate	Population and Density	Land Area	Life Expectancy (Years)	GDP* Per Capita (U.S. dollars)	Television Sets (per 1,000 people)	Flag and Language
TURKMENISTAN Ashkhabad	98%	5,200,000 28 per sq. mi. 11 per sq. km	188,456 sq. mi. 488,099 sq. km	63	$5,700	198	Turkmen
UNITED ARAB EMIRATES Abu Dhabi	77.9%	4,600,000 143 per sq. mi. 55 per sq. km	32,278 sq. mi. 83,600 sq. km	77	$25,200	309	Arabic
UZBEKISTAN Tashkent	99.3%	26,400,000 153 per sq. mi. 59 per sq. km	172,741 sq. mi. 447,397 sq. km	67	$1,800	280	Uzbek
YEMEN Sanaa	50.2%	20,700,000 102 per sq. mi. 39 per sq. km	203,849 sq. mi. 527,966 sq. km	61	$800	286	Arabic
UNITED STATES Washington, D.C.	97%	296,500,000 80 per sq. mi. 31 per sq. km	3,717,796 sq. mi. 9,629,047 sq. km	78	$40,100	844	English

Sources: *CIA World Factbook*, 2005; Population Reference Bureau, *World Population Data Sheet*, 2005.

For more country facts, go to the **Nations of the World Databank** at glencoe.com.

Regional Atlas Activity

Making Inferences Have students look at the number of television sets per 1,000 people. **Ask: Which country has the highest number of television sets per 1,000 people?** *(Qatar)* **Ask: Why might this country have so many more television sets than others in the region?** *(Possible answers: People in Qatar may be wealthier; the country may have less of a gap between rich and poor; television sets may be inexpensive there; the media may have fewer restrictions there.)* **OL**

Drawing Conclusions Have students look back through the charts and think about what the charts reveal about the standard of living in each country. **Ask: Which country do you think has the lowest standard of living? Why?** *(Possible answer: Afghanistan, because it has the lowest life expectancy and lowest literacy rate and is tied for the lowest GDP per capita, and has the fewest number of television sets per 1,000 people.)* **OL**

FastFacts

The United Arab Emirates (UAE) is a federation of seven states formed in 1971. Although each state maintains a large degree of independence, the UAE is governed by a supreme council of seven emirs, or rulers. The council appoints a prime minister and cabinet to administer the federation.

Activity: Using the Chart

Analyzing Information Tell students to make a list of all of the languages shown on the chart on this page and the previous pages. Next to each language, keep a tally of the number of countries where that language is the official language. **Ask: What is the predominant language in this region?** *(Arabic)* Tell students to find out what the predominant religion is in each of these Arabic-speaking countries. **Ask: What relationship do you see?** *(Most Arabic-speaking countries are predominantly Muslim.)* **OL**

What Makes Africa South of the Sahara a Region?

The countries in this region share the following characteristics:

- a location almost entirely in the Tropics
- the world's fastest-growing and youngest population
- challenges to the environment, especially natural resources and wildlife
- a struggle to improve the quality of life
- political and economic difficulties caused in part by a colonial past

NATIONAL GEOGRAPHIC

www.nationalgeographic.com/education

NGS ONLINE This online resource provides lesson plans, atlas updates, cartographic activities with interactive maps, an online map store, and geographic links.

Africa South of the Sahara

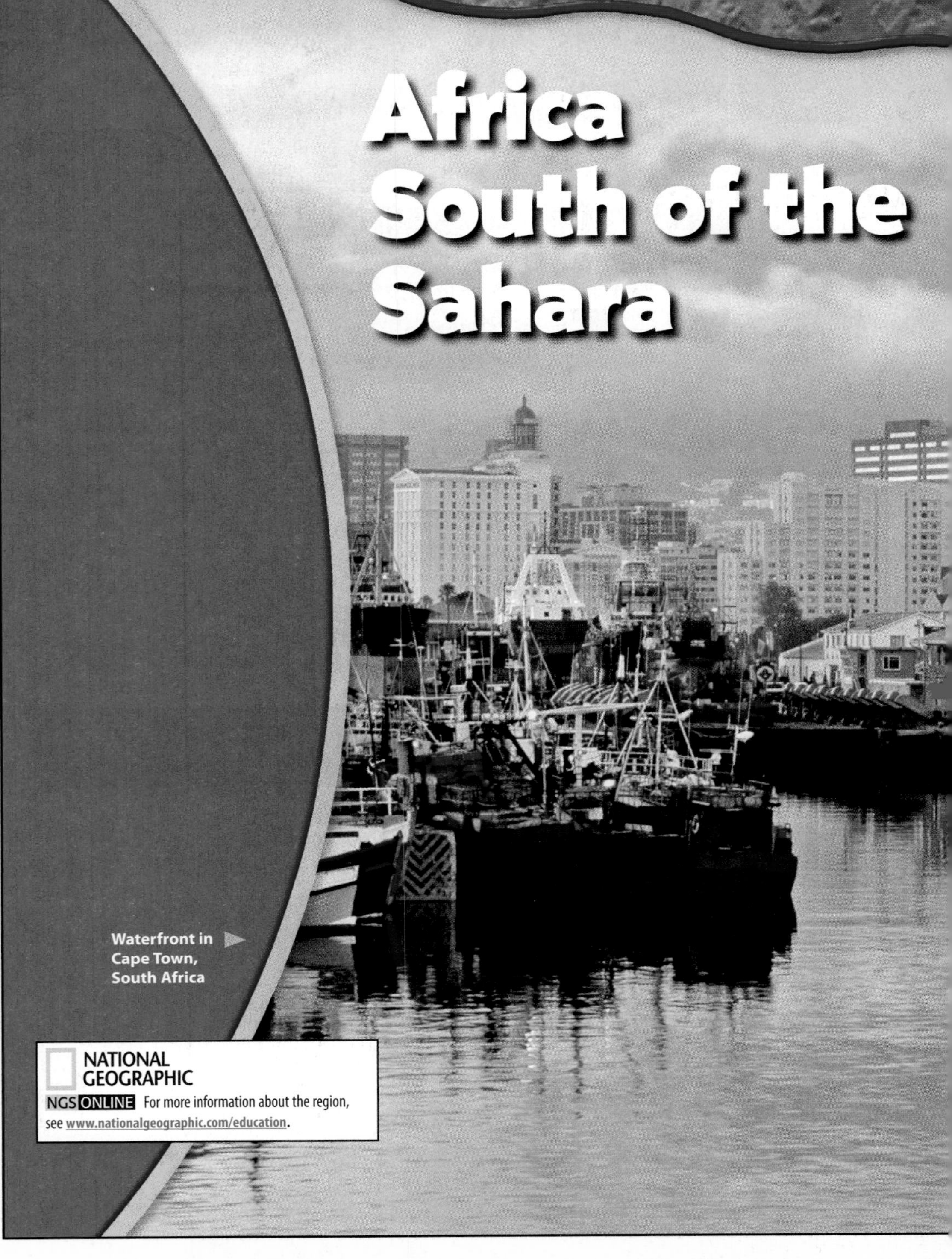

Waterfront in Cape Town, South Africa

NATIONAL GEOGRAPHIC

NGS ONLINE For more information about the region, see www.nationalgeographic.com/education.

Activity: Launching the Regional Atlas

Why Study Africa South of the Sahara? Ask: What challenges do you think Africans face? *(Ethnic divisions have disrupted many countries in recent years. AIDS has reached epidemic proportions in some countries. Developing nations struggle to establish order and economic growth as they compete against more industrialized countries. Traditional values and practices are challenged by the modern world. Some countries are threatened by desertification, habitat loss, and the effects of resource extraction.)* Inform students of these challenges and have them suggest possible solutions. **OL**

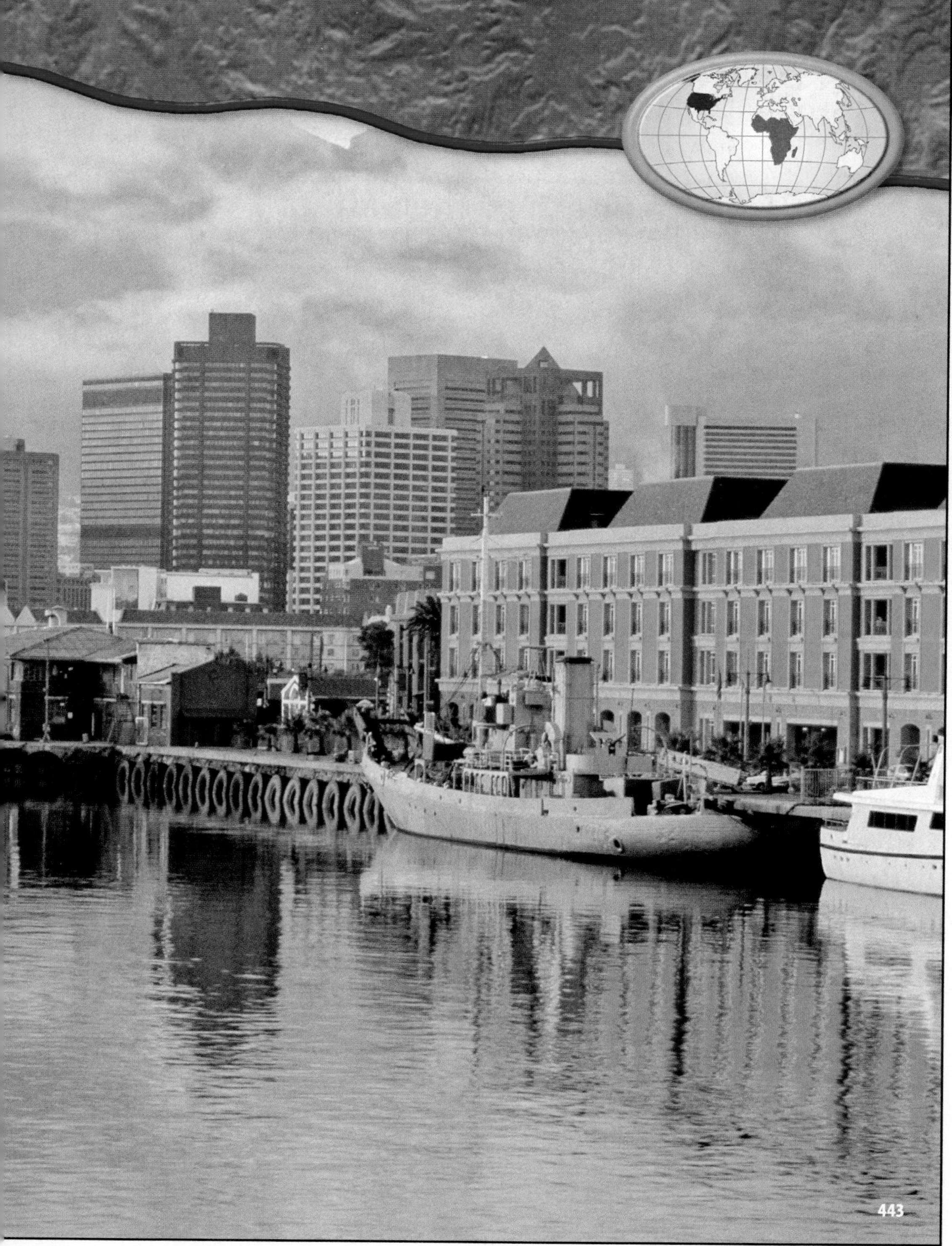

Introduce the Region

Using Maps Have students look at the maps of physical features and political boundaries of Africa south of the Sahara in the Regional Atlas. Then display the map overlay transparency for this region. **Ask:** **What major rivers are found in Africa south of the Sahara?** *(Nile, Congo, Niger)* **Where is Victoria Falls?** *(on the Zambezi River on the border of Zambia and Zimbabwe)* **What countries in the region border the Sahara?** *(Mauritania, Mali, Niger, Chad, Sudan, Eritrea)* **What other deserts are found in the region?** *(Namib and Kalahari deserts)* **What large island is part of Africa south of the Sahara?** *(Madagascar)* **OL**

More About the Photo

Visual Literacy Cape Town, the third-most-populous city in South Africa, is the legislative capital of South Africa. Many government offices, including the parliament, are in Cape Town. The city is a manufacturing center and has a busy port. Victoria Albert Waterfront at Table Bay was the original dock in the city, but it is no longer the main commercial port. However, it still is used by fishing and pleasure boats as well as by smaller cruise ships. This historic harbor and waterfront is a popular tourist destination.

Regional Atlas Activity

Where Is It?

Remembering Directions Using the world map as a base, have students identify the cardinal directions. Ask students to make up a memory aid that will help them remember the location of east and west when they look at a map. You might offer this as a sample:

Right leads us to the east,
but left takes us west,
these directions guide us best.

Have pairs share their ideas. **BL**

How Big Is It?

Math Question Ask: **If Africa south of the Sahara is three times the size of the continental United States, about how big is the land area of the United States? How do you know?** *(about 3.4 million square miles (8.9 million square kilometers); since Africa south of the Sahara is three times larger than the continental United States, divide the land area of the region by 3)* **OL**

Comparing Population

About how many people live in the Democratic Republic of the Congo? *(more than 60 million)* **How many more people live in the United States?** *(about 240 million more people)*

Regional Atlas

Africa South of the Sahara

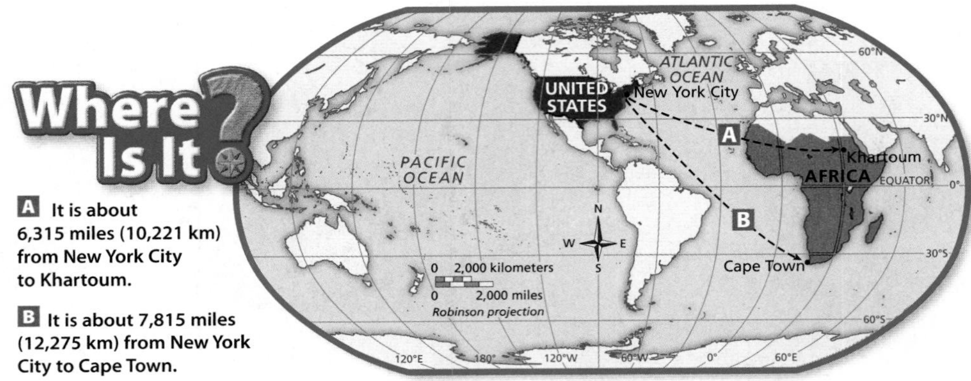

A It is about 6,315 miles (10,221 km) from New York City to Khartoum.

B It is about 7,815 miles (12,275 km) from New York City to Cape Town.

At about 10.3 million square miles (26.8 million sq. km), Africa south of the Sahara accounts for about one-fifth of all the land in the world. The region is three times larger than the United States.

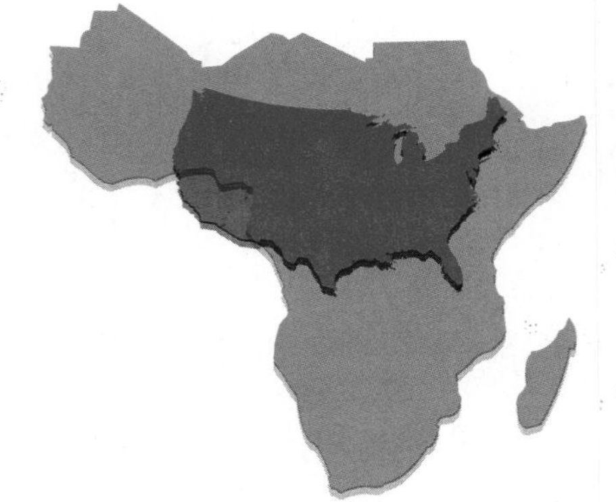

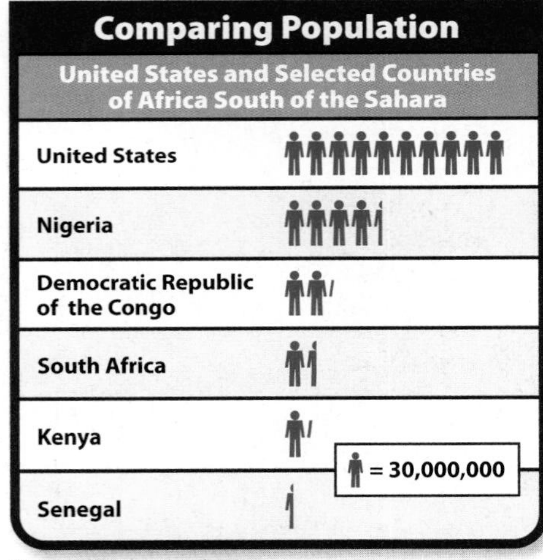

Source: *World Population Data Sheet*, 2005.

Activity: Geographic Theme

Location Demonstrate that students can determine the relative location of two places by comparing their latitude and longitude. Review with the class how to determine a location's latitude and longitude. Then draw circles labeled *Place X* and *Place Y* on the board. Indicate the latitude and longitude of the area covered by the circles by adding the following degrees around each circle: for Place X: 45°N at the top, 70°W to the right, 29°N at the bottom, and 125° W to the left; for Place Y: 30°N at the top, 50°E to the right, 32°S at the bottom, and 15°W to the left. **Ask:** **What is the northern latitude of X?** *(45°N)* **What is the latitude of X on its south?** *(29°N)* **What is the northern latitude of Y?** *(30°N)* **What is the latitude of Y on its south?** *(32°S)* **What is the relative location of X and Y?** *(Y starts just about where X ends.)* Repeat the process for longitude. Help students make a summarizing statement like "X is north and west of Y." Tell students to look at the world map. **Ask:** **What places have we been discussing?** *(the United States, Africa south of the Sahara)* **AL**

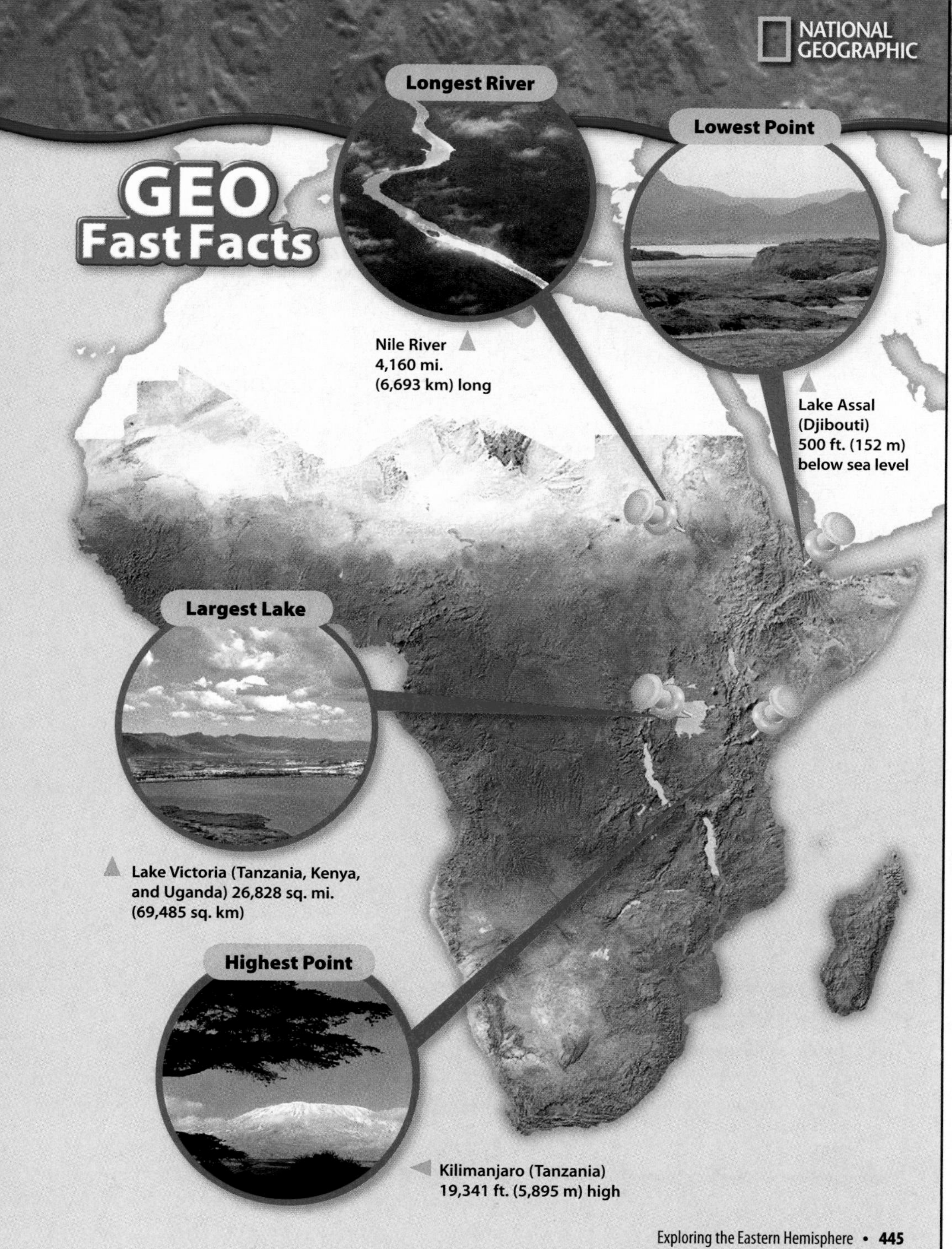

Regional Atlas

Geo Fast Facts

Mapping Interesting Facts

Ask: What categories of information does the Geo FastFacts map show about Africa south of the Sahara? *(its longest river, lowest point, largest lake, highest point)* **What other kinds of information might you like to know about this region?** *(Students may suggest where they could see animals in the wild and if this region contains gold and diamond mines.)*

Distribute outline maps of the region to the class. Explain that students are going to research and record information that they find personally interesting or surprising on the map.

Give students time to write the names of the countries and record the Geo FastFacts on their maps. Students should use library resources to identify at least five items for their maps. Be sure to allow them time to research the locations and place them on their map. Have students share their additions with the class. **OL**

FastFacts

- **Africa** About 90 percent of Africa lies within the Tropics—the largest tropical region of any continent.
- **Chad** The Tibesti Mountains cover an area of more than 50,000 square miles (129,500 sq. km) and reach heights of more than 11,000 feet (3,343 m). One of the world's most rugged and inaccessible places, the Tibesti Mountains have long served as a refuge for desert bandits.
- **Namibia** About 100,000 people in Namibia and southwest Africa speak Khoisan language, which are not related to other languages spoken in Africa. Many Khoisan words contain unusual "click" sounds.
- **Zambia and Zimbabwe** The British explorer, David Livingstone, named Victoria Falls after Queen Victoria. Its original African name, Mosi-oa-Tunya, meant "The Smoke That Thunders."
- **Africa** The Prime Meridian and the Equator meet off the west central coast of Africa, which results in a reading of zero degrees latitude and zero degrees longitude.

Regional Atlas Activity

Synthesizing Information Have students study the physical features of this region. Then have them choose a place or geographic feature shown on the map. Have them describe the relative location of their place or feature. Call on students to share their descriptions. Then have other students try to identify the place or feature. **OL**

Map Skills

Answers:

1. The White Nile and Blue Nile join to form the Nile.
2. *Any three:* Mali, Burkina Faso, Niger, Chad, and Sudan are in the Sahel.

Skills Practice

Ask: **In which parts of Africa is the elevation below 1,000 feet (300 m)?** *(West Africa, especially along the coast, the east African coast)* **About how high are the Tibesti Mountains?** *(13,100 ft.)*

Regional Atlas

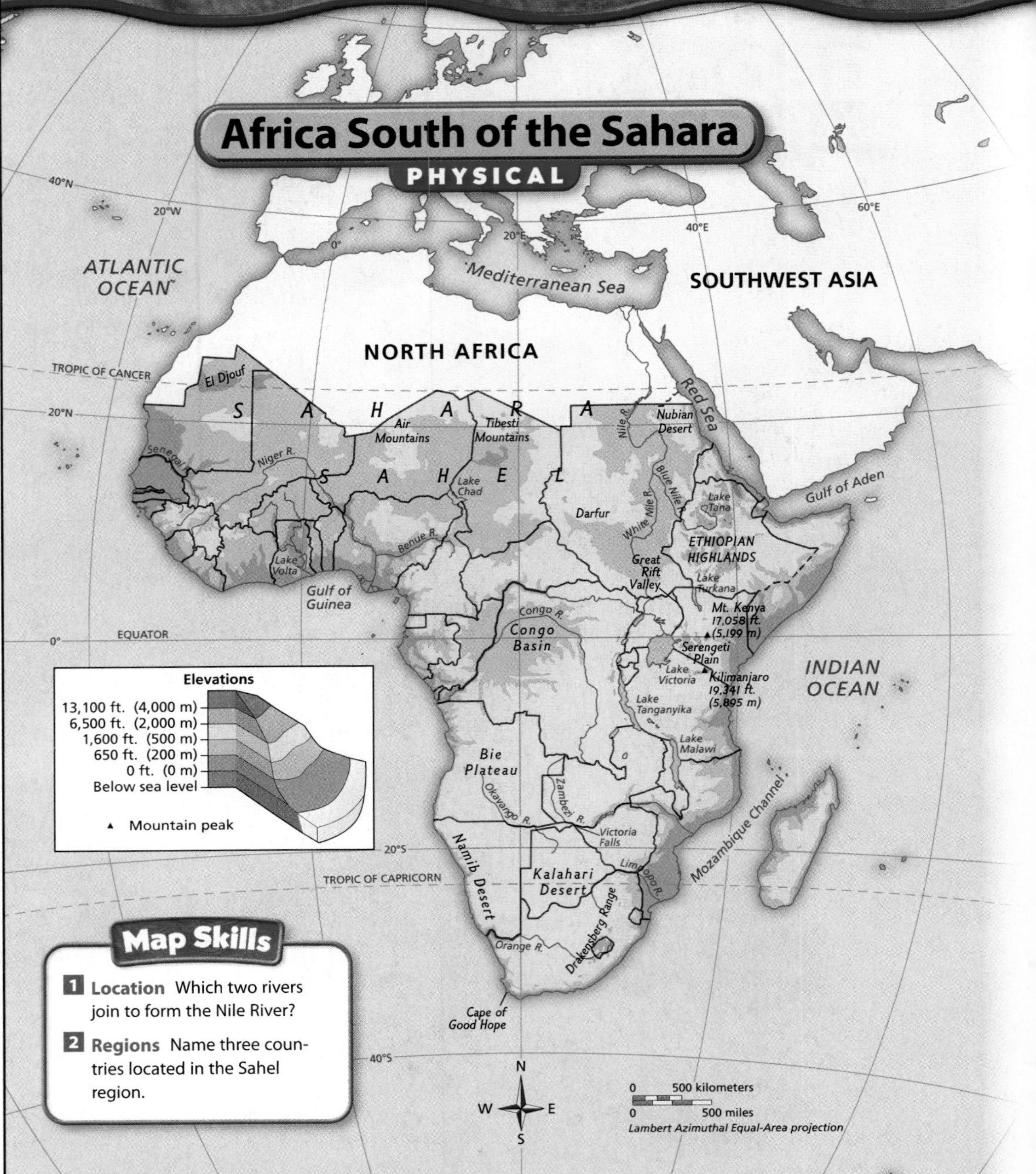

Africa South of the Sahara

PHYSICAL

Map Skills

1. **Location** Which two rivers join to form the Nile River?
2. **Regions** Name three countries located in the Sahel region.

Background: Land and Climate

A Land of Plateaus Africa south of the Sahara has the highest overall elevation of any world region. A narrow band of low plains hugs the Atlantic and Indian Ocean coastlines. Inland, the land rises from west to east in a series of steplike plateaus. Separating the plateaus are steep cliffs. The region has no long mountain ranges and few towering peaks, although Mt. Kenya and Kilimanjaro are exceptions. At 19,340 feet (5,895 m), Kilimanjaro's summit is the highest point on the African continent. Great rivers rise in the interior highlands. Further, the Great Rift Valley slices through eastern Africa like a steep-walled gash in the continent. The valley was formed by movements of the Earth's crust and extends from Mozambique into Southwest Asia.

Africa south of the Sahara has four climate regions. Tropical rain forests lie along the Equator and fill the great basin of the Congo River in central and western Africa. Moving away from the Equator, rain forests give way to the vast grasslands of the savanna. Steppe and desert climates occur in the drier areas and are more common even farther from the Equator.

NATIONAL GEOGRAPHIC

Regional Atlas

Africa South of the Sahara

POLITICAL

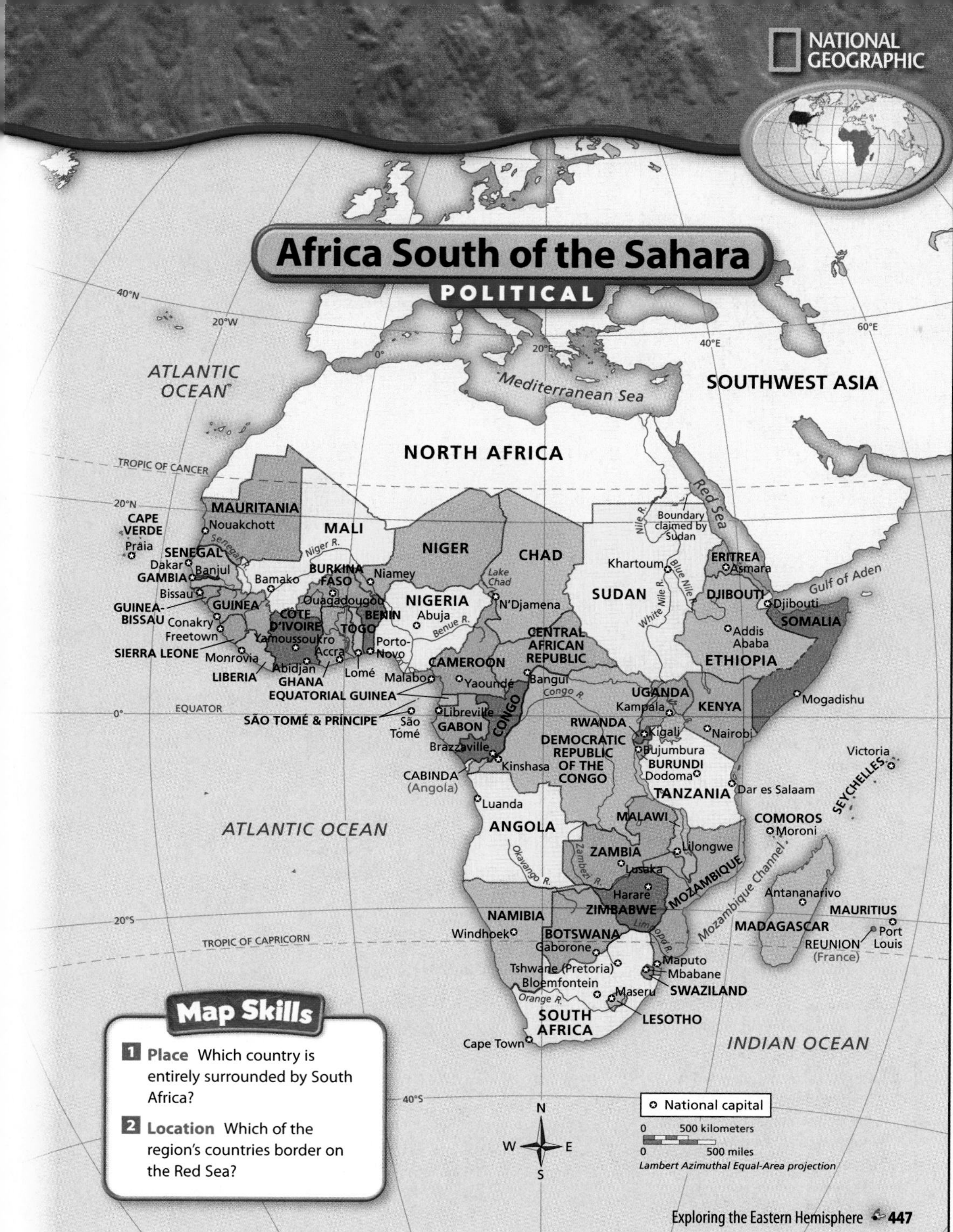

Map Skills

1. **Place** Which country is entirely surrounded by South Africa?
2. **Location** Which of the region's countries border on the Red Sea?

Regional Atlas Activity

Mental Mapping Help students develop a mental map of Africa south of the Sahara by playing a location game. Assign one or more countries to each student. Instruct students to write clues about the locations of the countries they were assigned. (Example: This country is east of Gabon. It borders the Central African Republic. It is west and north of the Democratic Republic of the Congo. It has a coastline on the Atlantic Ocean. Answer—Congo.) Have each student read their clues, one at a time, until a classmate can identify the country. You could also use the clues as part of a team competition. Award points based on the number of clues a team needs to identify the country correctly, with more points received when fewer clues are used. **OL**

Map Skills

Answers:

1. Lesotho is completely surrounded by South Africa.
2. Sudan, Eritrea, Ethiopia, and Djibouti

Skills Practice

Ask: What is the capital of Ethiopia? *(Addis Ababa)* **Which European country has territory in Africa south of the Sahara?** *(France)*

Background: Current Issues

Political Turmoil Today, Africa south of the Sahara struggles with problems that began hundreds of years ago. In the 1400s and 1500s, Europeans began trading with African societies. By the late 1800s, European nations had claimed almost all of Africa as colonies. In the process, they ignored traditional ethnic boundaries and rivalries. Even though most African nations won their independence in the mid-1900s, many countries emerged from colonial rule politically unstable with crippled economies.

Africa has about 2,000 ethnic groups that speak more than 800 different languages. In many cases, diversity was not considered when political boundaries were established. Many countries in the region suffer internal strife because of conflict between ethnic groups. Civil wars have killed or made refugees of hundreds of thousands of people. While many countries are attempting to modernize, many people remain poor, barely making enough to survive each day. Emerging democracies in some countries are hindered by roving bands of warlords and soldiers. Political corruption is a concern in many areas and nations struggle to address public health issues such as the AIDS epidemic.

Regional Atlas

Regional Atlas Activity

Cultural Diversity Assign one or two countries to each student. Direct students to use various reference resources to identify ethnic groups in these countries. Have students write the name of each group on a slip of paper. Post a large wall map of Africa south of the Sahara. Have students read the name of each group and attach it to the appropriate country. As students make their contributions, have students keep a running tally of the number of different groups that live in the region. Use the final total to stimulate discussion about what effects a variety of ethnic groups might have on each country and on the region. **OL**

Map Skills

Answers:

1. The highest concentrations of people live on the coast or near one of the lakes.
2. Population density is low in the northern region because of the Sahara Desert and low in southwestern Africa because the Kalahari and Namib Deserts are there.

Skills Practice

Ask: **Which cities have more than 5,000,000 people?** *(Lagos, Kinshasa-Brazzaville, Johannesburg, Khartoum, Abidjan)* **Compare this map to the physical and the political map. Why do you think Namibia and Botswana are so lightly populated?** *(The terrain includes mountains and the Namib and Kalahari Deserts.)*

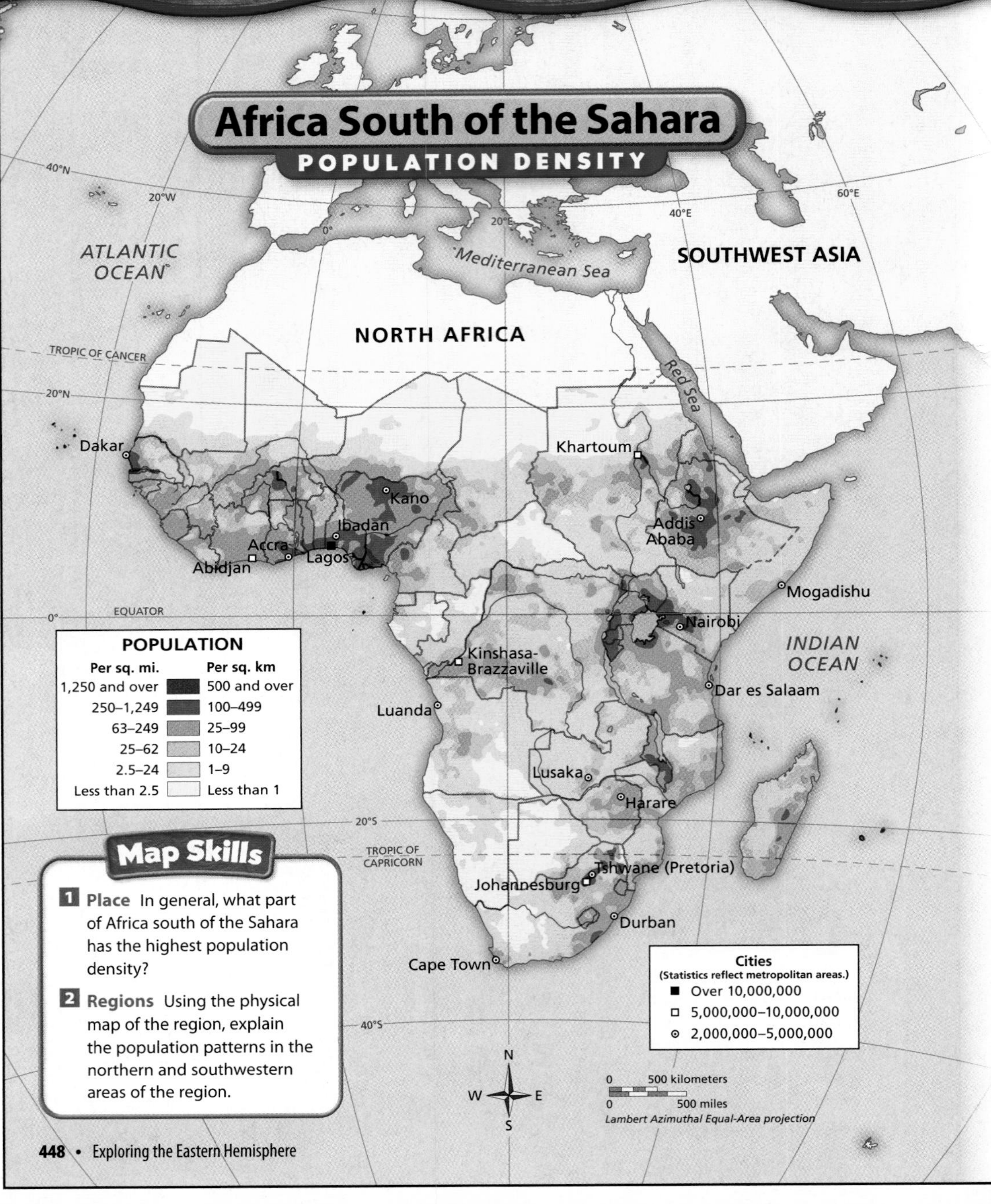

Background: People and Culture

Health Issues Nearly three-fourths of the population of Africa south of the Sahara live in rural areas. Still, African cities are among the fastest-growing urban areas in the world. Large cities in West Africa do not have the infrastructure to support the growing populations. This has created serious health issues for many areas. For example, governments have difficulty providing housing, plumbing, and electricity. In addition, drought and food shortages have created crises in the region. Many cities cannot provide adequate health care to their growing populations. Thousands die each year from illnesses such as malaria and cholera that would be easily treated in the United States. The continuing spread of HIV/AIDS has created an epidemic throughout the entire region.

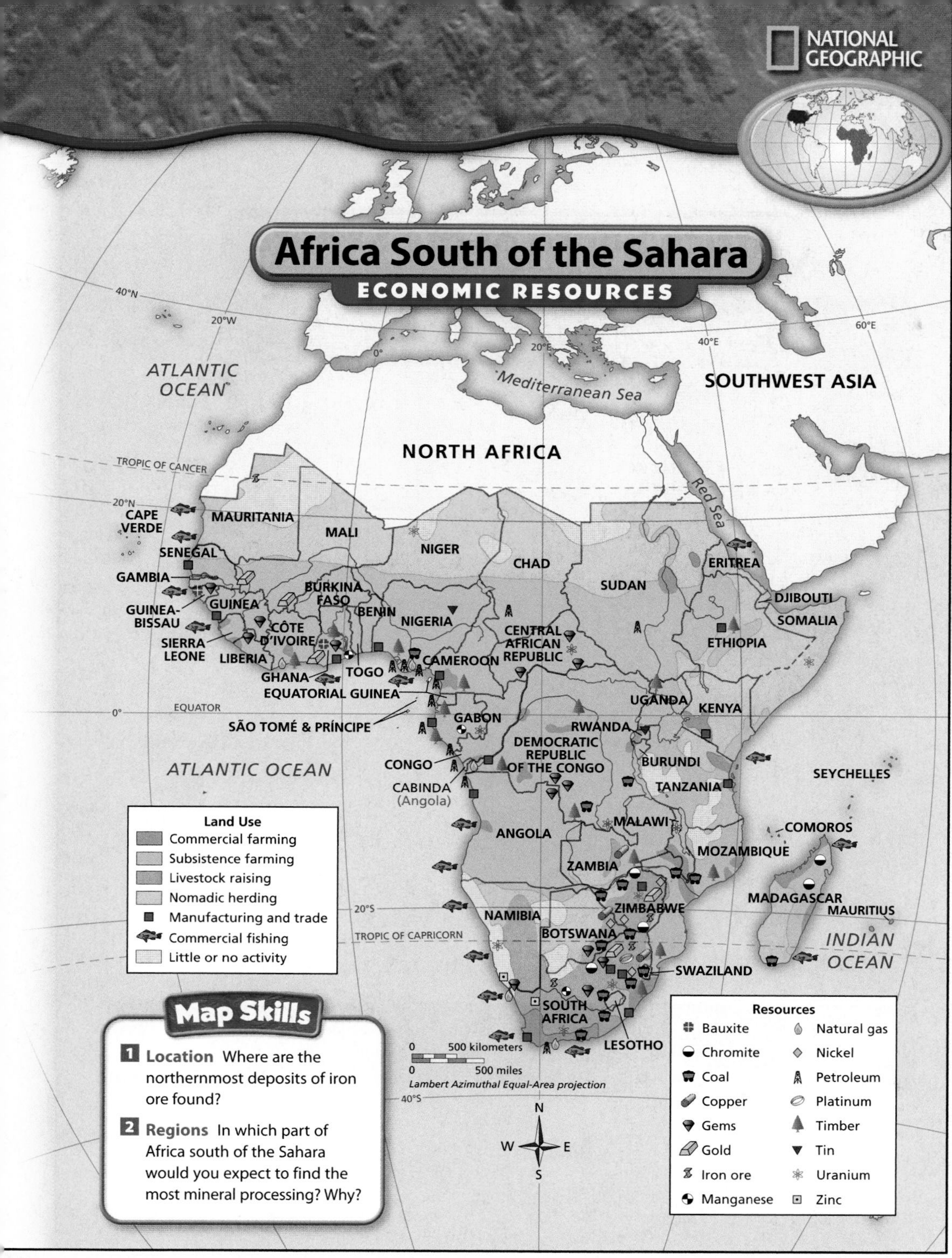

NATIONAL GEOGRAPHIC

Africa South of the Sahara

ECONOMIC RESOURCES

Land Use
- Commercial farming
- Subsistence farming
- Livestock raising
- Nomadic herding
- Manufacturing and trade
- Commercial fishing
- Little or no activity

Resources
- Bauxite
- Chromite
- Coal
- Copper
- Gems
- Gold
- Iron ore
- Manganese
- Natural gas
- Nickel
- Petroleum
- Platinum
- Timber
- Tin
- Uranium
- Zinc

0 — 500 kilometers
0 — 500 miles
Lambert Azimuthal Equal-Area projection

Map Skills

1 Location Where are the northernmost deposits of iron ore found?

2 Regions In which part of Africa south of the Sahara would you expect to find the most mineral processing? Why?

Regional Atlas

Regional Atlas Activity

Economic Resources Allow students to gather facts about the various physical features of Africa south of the Sahara. Students should create a fact sheet for each feature they find. Then set aside one class period or block to discuss the connection between where economic resources are located and the physical features of the area. As you name a physical feature or point to it on a wall map, call on students to volunteer a fact about economic resources there. Repeat for other features. Ask students to discuss the relationship between physical features, economic resources, and the location of cities. **OL**

Map Skills

Answers:

1. The northernmost deposits of iron are in Mauritania.
2. Answers include West Africa and the southern region.

Skills Practice

Ask: **Compare this map to the physical map. What physical feature makes farming difficult in northern Chad?** *(the Sahara)* **How is land used in and around Madagascar?** *(Land uses include commercial and subsistence farming, nomadic herding, commercial fishing, manufacturing, and trade.)*

Background: The Economy

A Struggling Region Africa south of the Sahara is rich in mineral resources, but these resources are not evenly distributed. Nigeria has huge reserves of oil. South Africa has deposits of gold and diamonds, making it the wealthiest country in the region. Overall, however, the region has the lowest standard of living of any in the world. Manufacturing plays only a small role in the region's economy. In the past, colonial rulers used Africa as a source of raw materials and left the continent largely undeveloped. Today the nations in the region are struggling to industrialize. Many people in Africa south of the Sahara still depend on small-scale farming or livestock herding for their livelihoods. Drought is a constant problem for the region's farmers, and many are able to raise only enough food to feed their families.

Regional Atlas Activity

Making Inferences Have students compare the population and density of Cape Verde and Equatorial Guinea. **Ask: What is the population of each country?** *(500,000)* **Why do you think the density is so different?** *(The land area is different. Equatorial Guinea is about seven times larger in size than Cape Verde.)* **How might the population density for these small countries affect living conditions?** *(Cape Verde is much more crowded.)* Now have students compare the land area of Equatorial Guinea with Burundi. *(These countries are relatively similar in land area, but Equatorial Guinea has a larger population.)* **OL**

Drawing Conclusions Have students note the differences in GDP for Cape Verde, Equatorial Guinea, and Burundi and compare them to the GDP of the United States. Then have students analyze the data in the other categories of the Regional Atlas chart. Have students draw a conclusion about reasons for the differences in GDP after comparing the data. *(Compared to the United States, all three countries have a lower GDP. Students may conclude that the data from the chart alone cannot explain the difference in the GDPs.)* **AL**

Regional Atlas

Africa South of the Sahara

Country and Capital	Literacy Rate	Population and Density	Land Area	Life Expectancy (Years)	GDP* Per Capita (U.S. dollars)	Television Sets (per 1,000 people)	Flag and Language
ANGOLA Luanda	42%	15,400,000 32 per sq. mi. 12 per sq. km	481,351 sq. mi. 1,246,693 sq. km	40	$2,100	15	Portuguese
BENIN Porto-Novo	40.9%	8,400,000 193 per sq. mi. 75 per sq. km	43,483 sq. mi. 112,620 sq. km	54	$1,200	44	French
BOTSWANA Gaborone	79.8%	1,600,000 7 per sq. mi. 3 per sq. km	224,606 sq. mi. 581,727 sq. km	35	$9,200	21	English, Setswana
BURKINA FASO Ouagadougou	26.6%	13,900,000 131 per sq. mi. 51 per sq. km	105,792 sq. mi. 274,000 sq. km	44	$1,200	11	French
BURUNDI Bujumbura	51.6%	7,800,000 726 per sq. mi. 280 per sq. km	10,745 sq. mi. 27,829 sq. km	49	$600	15	Kirundi, French
CAMEROON Yaoundé	79%	16,400,000 89 per sq. mi. 34 per sq. km	183,568 sq. mi. 475,439 sq. km	48	$1,900	34	English, French
CAPE VERDE Praia	76.6%	500,000 321 per sq. mi. 124 per sq. km	1,556 sq. mi. 4,030 sq. km	69	$1,400	5	Portuguese
CENTRAL AFRICAN REPUBLIC Bangui	51%	4,200,000 17 per sq. mi. 8 per sq. km	240,533 sq. mi. 622,978 sq. km	44	$1,100	6	French
UNITED STATES Washington, D.C.	97%	296,500,000 80 per sq. mi. 31 per sq. km	3,717,796 sq. mi. 9,629,047 sq. km	78	$40,100	844	English

*Gross Domestic Product

Countries and flags not drawn to scale

Activity: Using the Chart

Analyzing Ask: Which countries do you think are most prosperous? Then assign a country to each student. In two class periods, have students research a variety of other sources to obtain statistical data for each country, such as GDP, GDP per capita, sectors of the economy, and percentages of workers employed in each sector. Students may record this data on index cards. Then, in the next period or block, have students compare and contrast their findings, ranking their countries from most to least prosperous. Post the different countries in that order on a classroom wall. Follow up by asking students to compare the prosperity of Africa south of the Sahara with that of other world regions. **AL**

Africa South of the Sahara

Country and Capital	Literacy Rate	Population and Density	Land Area	Life Expectancy (Years)	GDP* Per Capita (U.S. dollars)	Television Sets (per 1,000 people)	Flag and Language
CHAD N'Djamena	47.5%	9,700,000 20 per sq. mi. 8 per sq. km	495,753 sq. mi. 1,283,994 sq. km	47	$1,600	1	French, Arabic
Moroni COMOROS	56.5%	700,000 813 per sq. mi. 314 per sq. km	861 sq. mi. 2,230 sq. km	60	$700	4	Arabic, French
DEMOCRATIC REPUBLIC OF THE CONGO Kinshasa	65.5%	60,800,000 67 per sq. mi. 26 per sq. km	905,351 sq. mi. 2,344,848 sq. km	50	$700	2	French
REPUBLIC OF THE CONGO Brazzaville	83.8%	4,000,000 30 per sq. mi. 12 per sq. km	132,046 sq. mi. 341,998 sq. km	52	$800	13	French
CÔTE D'IVOIRE Yamoussoukro	50.9%	18,200,000 146 per sq. mi. 56 per sq. km	124,502 sq. mi. 322,459 sq. km	47	$1,500	65	French
DJIBOUTI Djibouti	67.9%	800,000 89 per sq. mi. 34 per sq. km	8,958 sq. mi. 23,201 sq. km	52	$1,300	48	French, Arabic
Malabo EQUATORIAL GUINEA	85.7%	500,000 46 per sq. mi. 18 per sq. km	10,830 sq. mi. 28,050 sq. km	45	$2,700	116	Spanish, French
ERITREA Asmara	58.6%	4,700,000 104 per sq. mi. 40 per sq. km	45,405 sq. mi. 117,598 sq. km	58	$900	16	Afar
UNITED STATES Washington, D.C.	97%	296,500,000 80 per sq. mi. 31 per sq. km	3,717,796 sq. mi. 9,629,047 sq. km	78	$40,100	844	English

Sources: *CIA World Factbook*, 2005; Population Reference Bureau, *World Population Data Sheet*, 2005.

For more country facts, go to the **Nations of the World Databank** at glencoe.com.

Regional Atlas Activity

Making Inferences Ask: What is the GDP per capita of South Africa? *($11,100)* **Of Zimbabwe?** *($1,900)* **What other data indicates that South Africa has a higher standard of living than Zimbabwe?** *(South Africa's life expectancy is higher, and there are more television sets per 1,000 people.)* Have students look at the Economic Resources map in the Regional Atlas. **Ask: What information on this map might account for the differences in GDP?** *(Although both countries are rich in natural resources, Zimbabwe is landlocked and does not have manufacturing and trade centers.)* **OL**

Drawing Conclusions Have students draw conclusions about the continuing influence of European nations on former colonies. Have students locate the Flag and Language column of the Regional Atlas chart. Call on students at random to infer the European power that claimed a particular African country as a colony based on the languages spoken there. **OL**

Activity: Using the Chart

Locating Information Have students examine the entire Regional Atlas chart. **Ask: What questions do you have about these countries?** Have students make a list of questions asked. Then have students research to find answers to their questions. Direct students to appropriate references: encyclopedias, world almanacs, atlases, and reliable online news and information sources. Instruct students to write their questions and the answers or relevant information they have located and the source of the information on index cards. Students may share their findings in a bulletin board display titled *Africa South of the Sahara: Q & A.* Have students post their cards surrounding a map of Africa and use yarn or string as leaders to connect their cards to countries on the map. **OL**

Regional Atlas Activity

Making Predictions Have students look at Nigeria on the Economic Resources map in the Regional Atlas. **Ask: Based on this map, would you expect Nigeria to have a high population density? Why or why not?** *(Answers will vary. A possible answer is that yes, Nigeria will have a high population density because it has two manufacturing centers. Or, no, Nigeria will not have a high population density because most of the land is used for subsistence farming and the area has few natural resources.)* Have students look at Nigeria in the Regional Atlas chart and compare its population density to that of other countries in the region. **Ask: Does Nigeria have a high population density?** *(Yes, it has a high population density compared to other countries in the region and to the United States.)* Have students look at Nigeria on the Population Density map in the Regional Atlas and compare that map to the Economic Resources map. **Ask: Where is Nigeria's population concentrated?** *(around the manufacturing centers)* **OL**

FastFacts

Africa's Coast The coast of Africa appears extensive, but at 18,950 miles (30,497 km) in length, it is actually shorter than the coast of Europe. Few inlets, bays, or gulfs cut into the African continent.

Regional Atlas

Africa South of the Sahara

Country and Capital	Literacy Rate	Population and Density	Land Area	Life Expectancy (Years)	GDP* Per Capita (U.S. dollars)	Television Sets (per 1,000 people)	Flag and Language
ETHIOPIA Addis Ababa	42.7%	77,400,000 182 per sq. mi. 70 per sq. km	426,371 sq. mi. 1,104,296 sq. km	48	$800	5	Amharic
GABON Libreville	63.2%	1,400,000 14 per sq. mi. 5 per sq. km	103,347 sq. mi. 267,667 sq. km	56	$5,900	251	French
GAMBIA Banjul	40.1%	1,600,000 367 per sq. mi. 142 per sq. km	4,363 sq. mi. 11,300 sq. km	53	$1,800	3	English
GHANA Accra	74.8%	22,000,000 239 per sq. mi. 92 per sq. km	92,100 sq. mi. 238,538 sq. km	58	$2,300	115	English
GUINEA Conakry	35.9%	1,600,000 17 per sq. mi. 7 per sq. km	94,927 sq. mi. 245,860 sq. km	49	$2,100	47	French
GUINEA-BISSAU Bissau	42.4%	1,600,000 115 per sq. mi. 44 per sq. km	13,946 sq. mi. 36,120 sq. km	44	$700	information not available	Portuguese
KENYA Nairobi	85.1%	33,800,000 151 per sq. mi. 58 per sq. km	224,081 sq. mi. 580,367 sq. km	47	$1,100	22	English, Kiswahili
LESOTHO Maseru	84.8%	1,800,000 154 per sq. mi. 59 per sq. km	11,718 sq. mi. 30,349 sq. km	35	$3,200	16	Sesotho, English
UNITED STATES Washington, D.C.	97%	296,500,000 80 per sq. mi. 31 per sq. km	3,717,796 sq. mi. 9,629,047 sq. km	78	$40,100	844	English

*Gross Domestic Product

Countries and flags not drawn to scale

Activity: Using the Chart

Comparing Many software programs, including word-processing and spreadsheet programs, will allow you to make charts and then turn those charts into pie, line, or bar graphs. Have students select the GDP per capita for five to eight countries from the region. Students should have a rationale for selecting those countries: for example, comparing the GDP per capita for countries with similar populations or in a specific region of Africa south of the Sahara. Then have students use a software program to chart the GDP for their countries, decide what type of graph would best represent that information, and make a graph. Have students present their graphs to the class. **OL**

Africa South of the Sahara

Country and Capital	Literacy Rate	Population and Density	Land Area	Life Expectancy (Years)	GDP* Per Capita (U.S. dollars)	Television Sets (per 1,000 people)	Flag and Language
LIBERIA Monrovia	57.5%	3,300,000 77 per sq. mi. 30 per sq. km	43,000 sq. mi. 111,369 sq. km	42	$900	26	English
MADAGASCAR Antananarivo	68.9%	17,300,000 76 per sq. mi. 29 per sq. km	226,656 sq. mi. 587,036 sq. km	55	$800	23	French, Malagasy
MALAWI Lilongwe	62.7%	12,300,000 269 per sq. mi. 104 per sq. km	45,745 sq. mi. 118,479 sq. km	45	$600	3	Chichewa
MALI Bamako	46.4%	13,500,000 28 per sq. mi. 11 per sq. km	478,838 sq. mi. 1,240,185 sq. km	48	$900	13	French
MAURITANIA Nouakchott	41.7%	3,100,000 8 per sq. mi. 3 per sq. km	395,954 sq. mi. 1,025,516 sq. km	52	$1,800	95	Arabic
MAURITIUS Port Louis	85.6%	1,200,000 1,523 per sq. mi. 588 per sq. km	788 sq. mi. 2,041 sq. km	72	$12,800	248	Creole, French
MOZAMBIQUE Maputo	47.8%	19,400,000 63 per sq. mi. 24 per sq. km	309,494 sq. mi. 801,586 sq. km	42	$1,200	5	Portuguese
NAMIBIA Windhoek	84%	2,000,000 6 per sq. mi. 2 per sq. km	318,259 sq. mi. 824,287 sq. km	46	$7,300	38	English
UNITED STATES Washington, D.C.	97%	296,500,000 80 per sq. mi. 31 per sq. km	3,717,796 sq. mi. 9,629,047 sq. km	78	$40,100	844	English

Sources: *CIA World Factbook*, 2005; Population Reference Bureau, *World Population Data Sheet*, 2005.

For more country facts, go to the **Nations of the World Databank** at glencoe.com.

Regional Atlas Activity

Analyzing Have students look at the information on the number of television sets per 1,000 people on the Regional Atlas chart. **Ask: What other information given in the chart might have a relationship to the number of television sets in a country?** *(GDP per capita)* **OL**

Drawing Conclusions Have students test their theory by selecting six countries and comparing the number of television sets and GDP per capita. **Ask: Does the number of television sets depend on the GDP?** *(Countries with higher GDPs tend to have more television sets, but it is not a hard and fast rule.)* Have students brainstorm other factors that may influence how many television sets each country may have. *(Examples: how expensive televisions are; access to manufactured products; whether the population has electricity; religious values, etc.)* **OL**

Activity: Using the Chart

Problem Solving Have students examine literacy rates recorded on the Regional Atlas chart. **Ask: What four countries have the lowest literacy rates?** *(Niger, 17.6%; Sierra Leone, 31.4%; Guinea, 35.9%; Somalia, 37.8%)* Ask students to describe what those literacy rates mean in their own words. (Example: In Niger, fewer than one out of five adults can read.) Lead a discussion about what problems a low literacy rate might cause in a country. Then have students research the causes of low literacy rates and what other countries have done to improve their literacy rates. After they have completed their research, have students brainstorm possible solutions for this region. **AL**

Regional Atlas Activity

Synthesizing Organize the class into four groups. Assign several countries to each group. Have groups study the Regional Atlas maps, as well as the information given in the Regional Atlas chart about their countries. Have each group write a one-paragraph description of each of their assigned countries. Then call on each group to read their paragraphs aloud. Ask the other groups to identify the country that is being described. **OL**

Drawing Conclusions Have students study the population density information in the Regional Atlas chart. **Ask: What countries have population densities of lower than 30 per square mile?** *(Botswana, Chad, Gabon, Guinea, Mali, Mauritania, Namibia, Niger)* Have students locate these countries on the Physical map in the Regional Atlas. **Ask: What do many of these countries have in common that may explain their low population densities?** *(Most of them have desert areas within their borders.)* **BL**

Regional Atlas

Africa South of the Sahara

Country and Capital	Literacy Rate	Population and Density	Land Area	Life Expectancy (Years)	GDP* Per Capita (U.S. dollars)	Television Sets (per 1,000 people)	Flag and Language
NIGER Niamey	17.6%	14,000,000 29 per sq. mi. 11 per sq. km	489,189 sq. mi. 1,266,994 sq. km	43	$900	15	French
NIGERIA Abuja	68%	131,500,000 369 per sq. mi. 142 per sq. km	356,668 sq. mi. 923,766 sq. km	44	$1,000	69	English
Kigali RWANDA	70.4%	8,700,000 855 per sq. mi. 330 per sq. km	10,170 sq. mi. 26,340 sq. km	44	$1,300	0.09	Kinyarwanda, English, French
SÃO TOMÉ AND PRÍNCIPE São Tomé	79.3%	200,000 539 per sq. mi. 208 per sq. km	371 sq. mi. 961 sq. km	63	$1,200	229	Portuguese
Dakar SENEGAL	40.2%	11,700,000 154 per sq. mi. 59 per sq. km	75,954 sq. mi. 196,720 sq. km	56	$1,700	41	French
Victoria SEYCHELLES	58%	100,000 575 per sq. mi. 222 per sq. km	174 sq. mi. 451 sq. km	71	$7,800	214	Creole, English
SIERRA LEONE Freetown	31.4%	5,500,000 199 per sq. mi. 77 per sq. km	27,699 sq. mi. 71,740 sq. km	40	$600	13	English
SOMALIA Mogadishu	37.8%	8,600,000 35 per sq. mi. 13 per sq. km	246,201 sq. mi. 637,658 sq. km	47	$600	14	Somali
UNITED STATES Washington, D.C.	97%	296,500,000 80 per sq. mi. 31 per sq. km	3,717,796 sq. mi. 9,629,047 sq. km	78	$40,100	844	English

*Gross Domestic Product

Countries and flags not drawn to scale

Activity: Using the Chart

Synthesizing Have students select a country from the Regional Atlas chart. **Ask: How could you display all the information from the Regional Atlas maps and the Regional Atlas chart for your selected country?** *(make a poster, design a brochure, create a table)* Have students work in pairs. Have each pair determine what product they will produce to synthesize the information from the Regional Atlas. Allow an entire class period for student pairs to create and illustrate their visual. Then, in a second class period, have each pair share the information about their selected country with the rest of the class. **OL**

Africa South of the Sahara

Country and Capital	Literacy Rate	Population and Density	Land Area	Life Expectancy (Years)	GDP* Per Capita (U.S. dollars)	Television Sets (per 1,000 people)	Flag and Language
SOUTH AFRICA Tshwane (Pretoria), Bloemfontein, Cape Town	86.4%	46,900,000 99 per sq. mi. 38 per sq. km	471,444 sq. mi. 1,221,034 sq. km	52	$11,100	138	Afrikaans, English, Zulu
SUDAN Khartoum	61.1%	40,200,000 42 per sq. mi. 16 per sq. km	967,494 sq. mi. 2,505,798 sq. km	57	$1,900	173	Arabic
SWAZILAND Mbabane	81.6%	1,138,000 170 per sq. mi. 66 per sq. km	6,642 sq. mi. 17,203 sq. km	33	$5,100	112	English, siSwati
TANZANIA Dodoma, Dar es Salaam	78.2%	36,500,000 100 per sq. mi. 39 per sq. km	364,900 sq. mi. 945,087 sq. km	44	$700	21	Kiswahili, English
TOGO Lomé	60.9%	6,100,000 278 per sq. mi. 107 per sq. km	21,927 sq. mi. 56,791 sq. km	54	$1,600	22	French
UGANDA Kampala	69.9%	26,900,000 289 per sq. mi. 112 per sq. km	93,066 sq. mi. 241,040 sq. km	48	$1,500	28	English
ZAMBIA Lusaka	80.6%	11,200,000 39 per sq. mi. 15 per sq. km	290,583 sq. mi. 752,606 sq. km	37	$900	145	English
ZIMBABWE Harare	90.7%	13,000,000 86 per sq. mi. 33 per sq. km	150,873 sq. mi. 390,759 sq. km	41	$1,900	35	English
UNITED STATES Washington, D.C.	97%	296,500,000 80 per sq. mi. 31 per sq. km	3,717,796 sq. mi. 9,629,047 sq. km	78	$40,100	844	English

Sources: *CIA World Factbook*, 2005; Population Reference Bureau, *World Population Data Sheet*, 2005.

For more country facts, go to the **Nations of the World Databank** at glencoe.com.

Regional Atlas Activity

Drawing Conclusions Have students examine the information on life expectancy given in the Regional Atlas chart. **Ask: Which countries have a life expectancy of 60 or higher?** *(Cape Verde, 69; Comoros, 60; Mauritius, 72; São Tomé and Principe, 63; Seychelles, 71)* **What do these countries have in common?** *(All of them are islands.)* **Are there any island countries that have lower life expectancies?** *(yes, Madagascar, 55)* **What factors might contribute to a higher life expectancy? To a lower life expectancy?** *(Possible response: Higher life expectancy rates might reflect diet, access to health care and medical information, and type of work. A major factor in low life expectancies in this region is the spread of AIDS. Perhaps the island nations have had less exposure to the disease.)* **OL**

FastFacts

Botswana Botswana suffers from one of the most severe HIV/AIDS epidemics in the world. More than a third of pregnant women are infected with HIV, leading to the potential infection of thousands of infants. The high infection rate among young adults has led to serious and widespread social problems. For example, the United Nations Development Programme has estimated that by 2010, more than one in five Botswana children will be orphaned due to AIDS.

Activity: Using the Chart

Locating Information Have students study the life expectancy information in the Regional Atlas chart. **Ask: Which countries do you think may have been hardest hit by the AIDS epidemic?** *(Students will probably name those countries with the lowest life expectancies.)* Then organize the class into several groups, and assign each group one of these countries. Direct groups to appropriate reference materials to find information on AIDS in their assigned countries, including its prevalence, its effects, programs to prevent it, and access to medical care. Have students write the information they locate on index cards. Have students post their cards around a map of the region and use yarn or string to connect their cards to the countries on the map. **AL**

What Makes South Asia a Region?

The countries in this region share the following characteristics:

- a location on or near the South Asian subcontinent
- a varied landscape, ranging from some of the highest mountain ranges in the world to low-lying coastal areas
- high population densities that have led to environmental challenges in many areas
- seasonal dry and wet monsoon winds in much of the region
- a daily life centered on marriage and family

NATIONAL GEOGRAPHIC

www.nationalgeographic.com/education

NGS ONLINE This online resource provides lesson plans, atlas updates, cartographic activities with interactive maps, an online map store, and geographic links.

South Asia

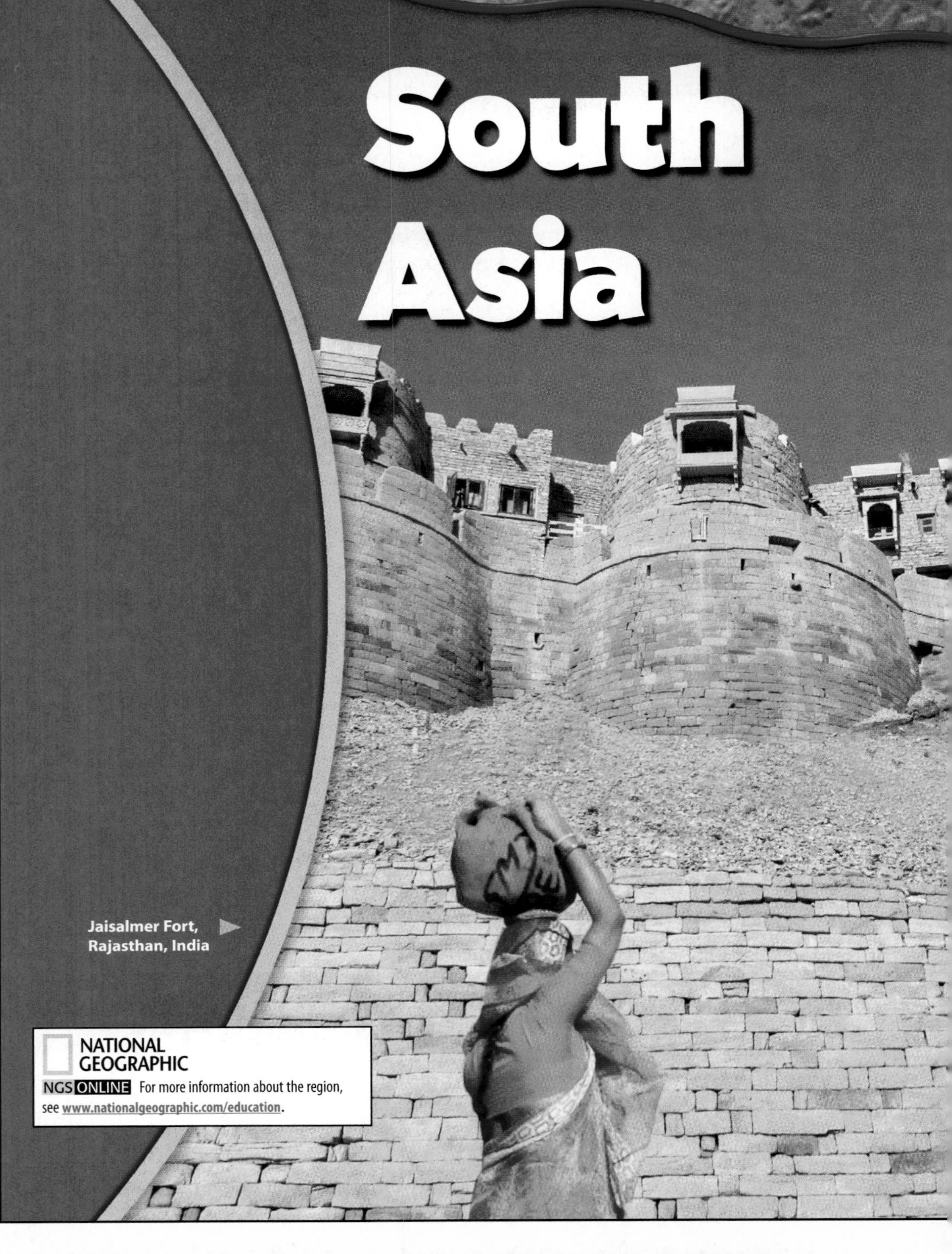

Jaisalmer Fort, Rajasthan, India

NATIONAL GEOGRAPHIC

NGS ONLINE For more information about the region, see www.nationalgeographic.com/education.

Activity: Launching the Regional Atlas

Why Study South Asia? Explain that more than 20% of the world's people live in South Asia, but that the region has only 3% of the world's land. **Ask: How do you think a high population density might affect the people of a region?** *(Students might mention that a high population density can put a strain on food supplies, government services, and natural resources; jobs also might be difficult to find, and there might be inadequate housing, lack of clean water, pollution, and high crime rates.)* Draw a chart on the board with one column labeled *Problem*, another column labeled *Possible Solution*, and a third column labeled *Steps Already Taken*. As students suggest possible problems in the region, list them in the first column. Then have students brainstorm possible solutions. As students work through the Regional Atlas, periodically revisit the chart, listing actual problems in the region and the ways that South Asian countries have tried to solve the problems. **OL**

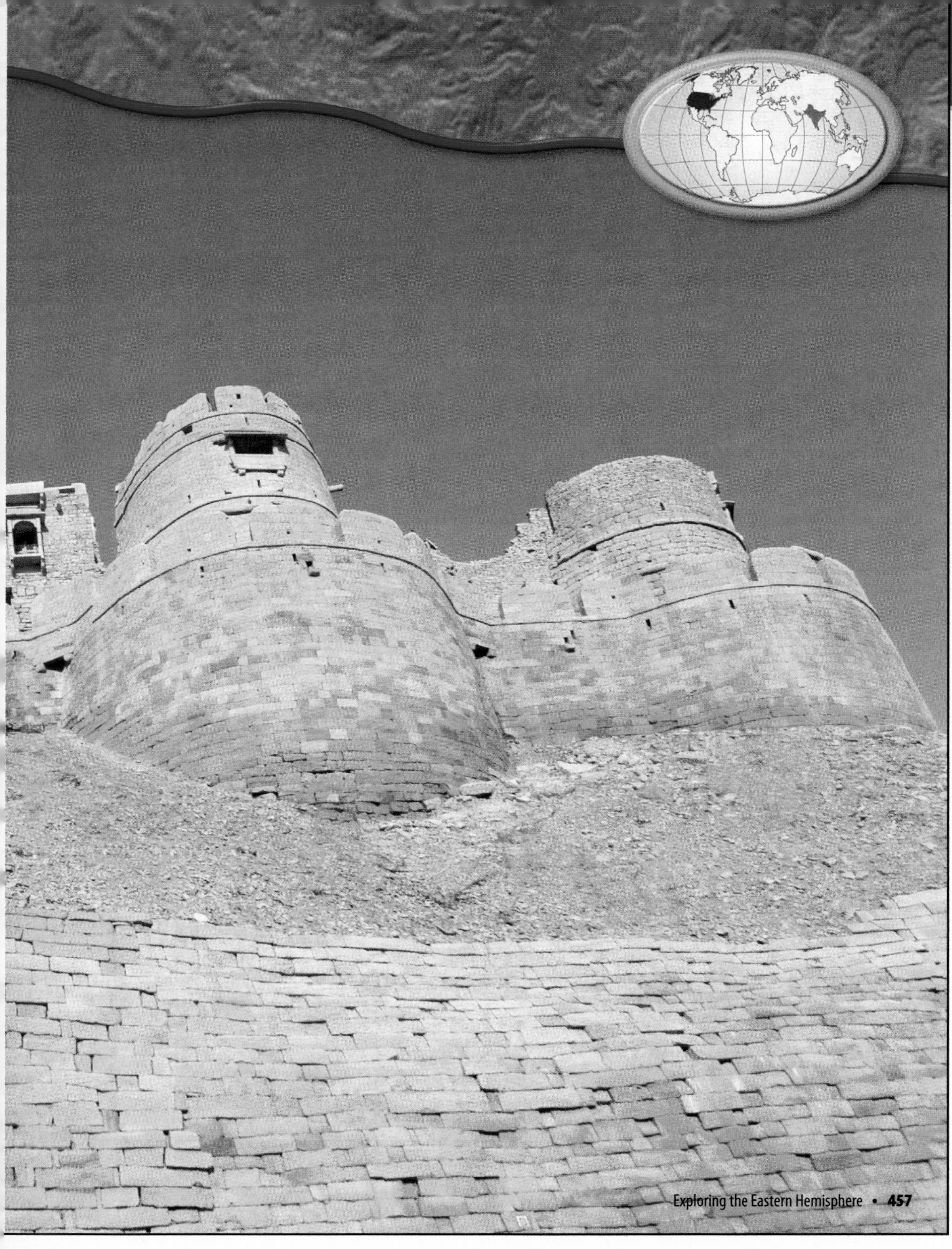

Introduce the Region

Using Maps Have students look at the Physical and Political maps in the Regional Atlas. **Ask:** **What three mountain ranges separate South Asia from the rest of Asia?** *(the Hindu Kush, the Karakoram Range, and the Himalaya)* **In what countries are these mountain ranges located?** *(The Himalaya are in northern India, Bhutan, and Nepal; the Karakoram Range is located primarily in northern India and Pakistan, and the Hindu Kush is in northern Pakistan.)* **What part of South Asia lies in the Tropics?** *(Southern India, Bangladesh, Sri Lanka, and the Maldives)* **What geographic feature of the region might be essential for farming?** *(the many rivers flowing through the region)* **What island nations are located in this region?** *(Sri Lanka and the Maldives)* **OL**

More About the Photo

Visual Literacy The city of Jaisalmer, located in the present-day Indian state of Rajasthan, is known for its massive buildings of yellowish-brown stone. Jaisalmer was founded in 1156 by Rawal Jaisal, the warrior ruler of this historic region. Under his rule, the surrounding region (called the state of Jaisalmer) reached its height of power. Early in the fourteenth century, however, the capital of Jaisalmer was sacked by the emperor of Delhi and subsequently became part of the Mughal Empire. The city is noted for its golden-walled building, the Jaisalmer Fort, shown here. The fort, built in 1156, sits grandly on a hill overlooking the city. It houses the royal palace and several ancient temples, as well as a library called the Gyana Bhandar—A Store of Knowledge—which contains ancient Sanskrit and Prakrit manuscripts. The fort is a major tourist attraction, contributing to Rajasthan's primarily agricultural economy.

Regional Atlas Activity

Where Is It?

Comparing Latitudes **Ask:** **What is the approximate latitude of Islamabad?** *(33°N)* **What is the approximate latitude of Kolkata?** *(28°N)* **How do the latitudes of these cities compare to the latitudes of the southern United States?** *(They are similar, if a little more southern.)* **OL**

How Big Is It?

Math Question Tell students that India has a land area of about 1,269,340 sq. mi. (3,287,575 sq. km). **Ask:** **About what percentage of South Asia's land is found in India alone?** *(about 73%)* **What does this tell you about the size of the other six countries in this region?** *(They are all much smaller than India.)* **OL**

Comparing Population

Ask: **What is the combined population of Pakistan, Nepal, and Sri Lanka?** *(about 210 million)* **How does this compare to India's population?** *(India's population is more than five times as large as the population of these three countries combined.)* **OL**

Regional Atlas

South Asia

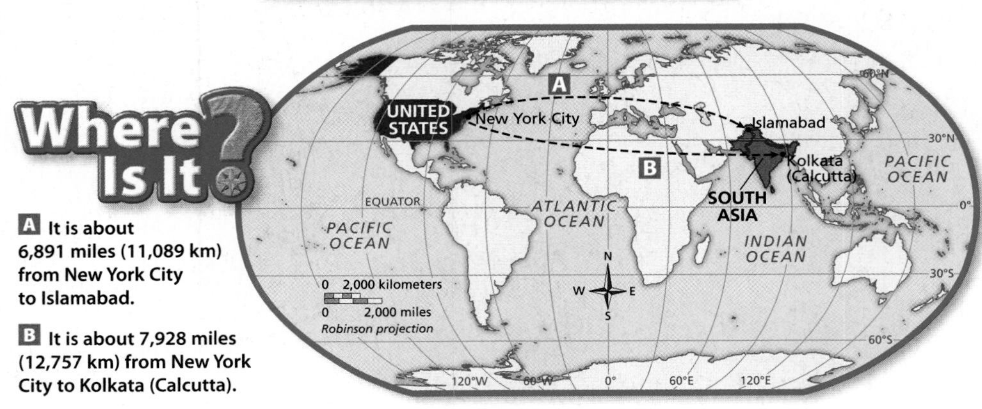

A It is about 6,891 miles (11,089 km) from New York City to Islamabad.

B It is about 7,928 miles (12,757 km) from New York City to Kolkata (Calcutta).

The region of South Asia is more than half the size of the continental United States. Its land area is about 1.7 million square miles (4.5 million sq. km). Though smaller than the United States, South Asia has nearly five times the number of people as the United States and more than one-fifth of the people in the world.

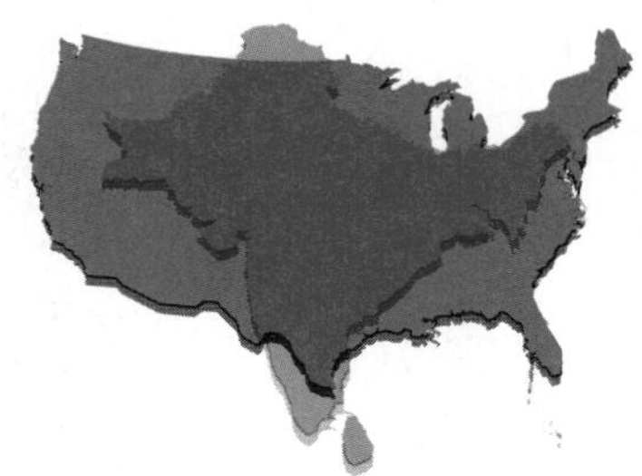

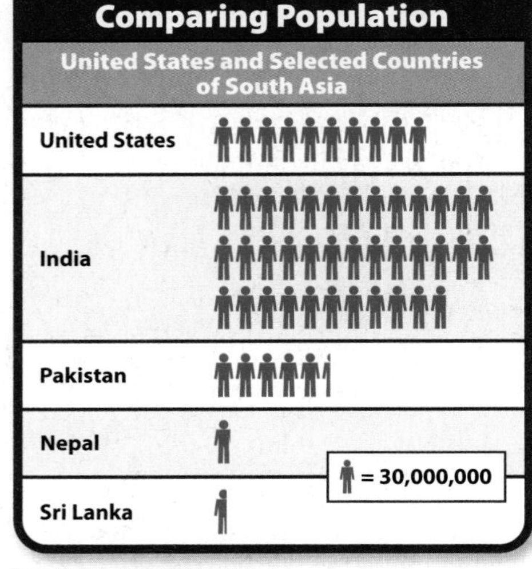

Source: *World Population Data Sheet*, 2005.

Activity: Geographic Theme

Movement Tell students to look closely at the Physical and Political maps in the Regional Atlas. **Ask:** **What physical features of South Asia might limit migration into and out of the region?** *(the high mountains in the north as well as the water separating the island nations of Sri Lanka and the Maldives from the rest of the subcontinent)* **Ask:** **What effect might limited migration have on the peoples in South Asia?** *(Communities would be isolated from outside influences and might develop distinctly different cultures.)* **What countries in the region would be most isolated? Why?** *(Nepal and Bhutan would be most isolated, because they are primarily mountainous countries in the Himalaya.)* **What areas would have been least isolated, and why?** *(Modern-day Pakistan, Bangladesh, and India would have been least isolated, because lower mountains and the Khyber Pass in the northwest, as well as lower mountains on India's eastern border, would have allowed more access to these areas.)* **OL**

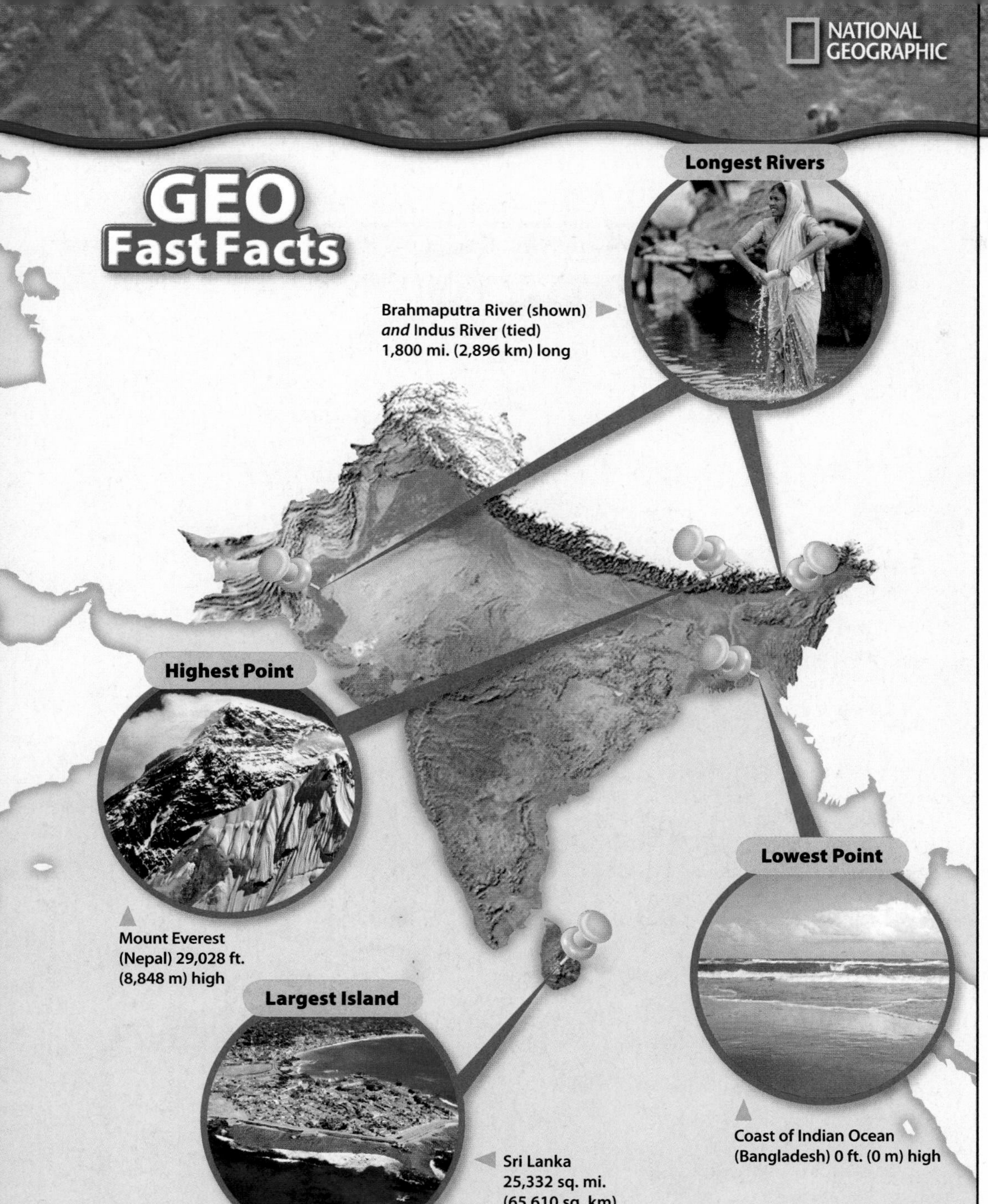

Geo Fast Facts

Creating Posters Ask: What four features of South Asia are highlighted on this map? *(the Brahmaputra and Indus Rivers, Mount Everest, the island of Sri Lanka, and the coast of the Indian Ocean in Bangladesh)* **Why are these four features highlighted?** *(because they are the highest, lowest, longest, or largest in the region)* Point out that Mount Everest is not only the highest point in South Asia, but also the highest point in the world.

Ask students to choose a country in South Asia that they would like to know more about. Tell them to look for special features about that country as they study the Regional Atlas pages. Student should then use Internet sources to create a GEO FastFacts poster about their country. Tell them to include images to illustrate the features they have chosen to highlight. **OL**

FastFacts

- **Mount Everest** The world's highest peak also has been called the "world's highest junkyard." Over many years, Everest's climbers have abandoned tons of supplies and equipment along the mountain's icy slopes. In 1976 the Nepalese government and the Sir Edmund Hillary Himalayan Trust joined forces to establish the Sagarmatha National Park. Located on the Nepalese side of Mount Everest, this park was designated as a UNESCO World Heritage site in 1979. The Nepalese government uses a portion of the site's climbing fees to pay for cleanup efforts.
- **Waves of Destruction** The 2004 Indian Ocean tsunami was one of the most destructive tsunamis in history. The devastation affected people and property in four South Asia countries— Sri Lanka, India, the Maldives, and Bangladesh. Sri Lanka was among the hardest hit. There, the monster waves left more than 30,000 people dead. India reported more than 10,000 people dead. The Maldives were hit by severe flooding and lost more than 80 people. Even faraway Bangladesh reported two tsunami-related deaths.

Regional Atlas

Regional Atlas Activity

Hypothesizing Have students study the Physical map in the Regional Atlas. **Ask: What areas of South Asia would you expect to have the least economic activity? Why?** *(the Thar Desert, as well as the mountain ranges in the north, where little farming, livestock raising, or manufacturing would take place because of the harshness of the climates)* **Where would you expect the land to be put to the most productive use?** *(the river valleys, particularly the deltas where the rivers empty into the Arabian Sea or the Bay of Bengal, where commercial and subsistence farming are likely to take place)* Have students turn to the Economic Resources map in the Regional Atlas and discuss in what ways their hypotheses were correct and in what ways they were incorrect. **OL**

Map Skills

Answers:

1. the Maldives
2. The far north is covered by high mountains; most of the rest of the region is lowland plains.

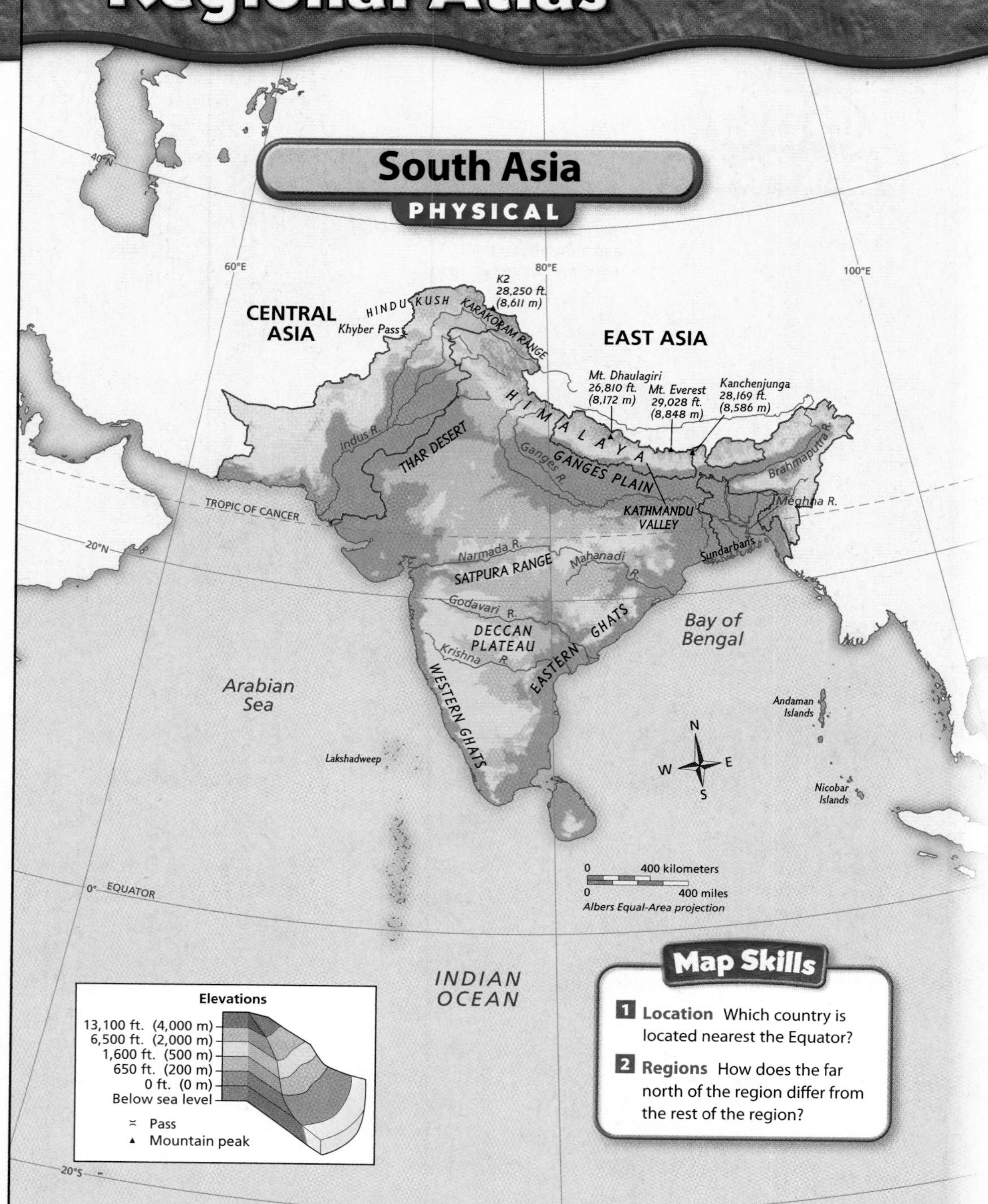

Background: Land and Climate

Towering Mountains The South Asian subcontinent is separated from the rest of Asia by three huge mountain systems—the Hindu Kush, the Karakoram, and the Himalaya. The Himalaya, of which Mount Everest is the tallest peak, is the highest mountain system in the world.

Scientists believe that these mountains were formed about 60 million years ago. At that time, a huge landmass that had broken away from the continent of Africa drifted across the Indian Ocean and collided with Asia to form the Indian subcontinent. The force of the collision created the mountain ranges that now divide the South Asian subcontinent from the rest of Asia. The tectonic plate movements continue to this day; as a result, the mountain ranges grow a little taller each year.

The temperatures above 16,000 feet are always below freezing, so snowcapped mountain peaks are visible all year. Further down the slopes, however, more temperate climates are found.

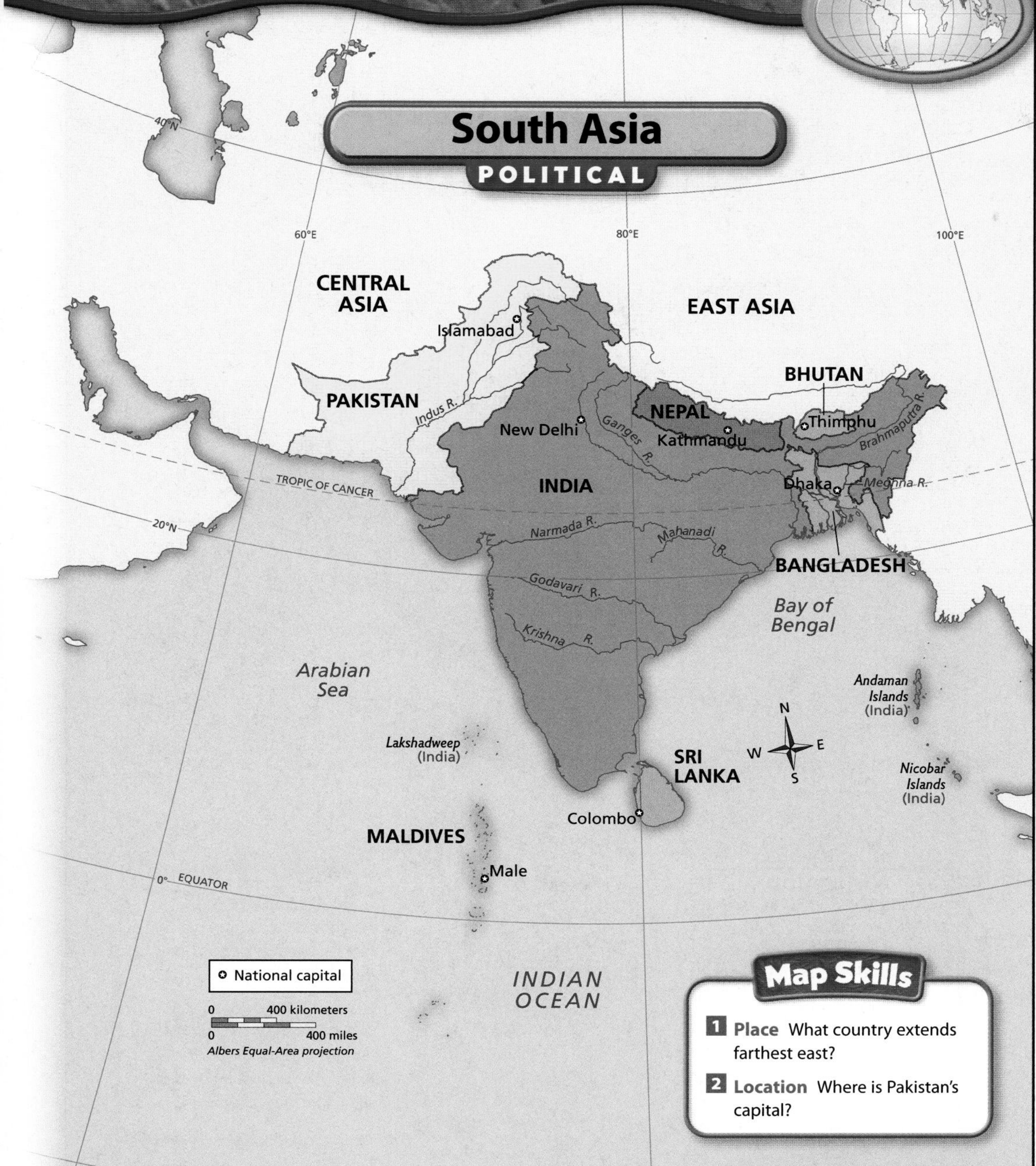

NATIONAL GEOGRAPHIC

Regional Atlas

South Asia
POLITICAL

60°E
80°E
100°E
40°N
20°N
0° EQUATOR
20°S
TROPIC OF CANCER
CENTRAL ASIA
EAST ASIA
PAKISTAN
Islamabad
Indus R.
New Delhi
Ganges R.
NEPAL
Kathmandu
BHUTAN
Thimphu
Brahmaputra R.
INDIA
Dhaka
Meghna R.
Narmada R.
Mahanadi R.
BANGLADESH
Godavari R.
Krishna R.
Bay of Bengal
Arabian Sea
Andaman Islands (India)
Lakshadweep (India)
SRI LANKA
Nicobar Islands (India)
Colombo
MALDIVES
Male
INDIAN OCEAN
N
E
S
W

National capital
0 400 kilometers
0 400 miles
Albers Equal-Area projection

Map Skills

1 **Place** What country extends farthest east?

2 **Location** Where is Pakistan's capital?

Regional Atlas Activity

Synthesizing Information Have students develop flashcards to help them remember information about South Asian nations, including their capitals. Organize students into pairs. Have each pair develop 10 flashcards. Tell students that the front of the flashcard may contain an actual question or it may show a map or other visual for students to identify.

After the pairs have prepared their flashcards, have each pair use the flashcards, first to quiz each other to make sure they have mastered the information on the cards and then to quiz another pair of students in the class. **ELL**

Map Skills

Answers:

1. India extends farthest east.
2. Pakistan's capital, Islamabad, is in the northern part of the country.

Background: Current Issues

Poverty in Bangladesh Bangladesh is one of the most densely populated countries in the world. While although 75% of its people still live in rural areas, Bangladeshis are increasingly moving to the nation's overcrowded cities in search of work. The economy of the country, however, cannot create enough jobs for its 144 million people, and many remain desperately poor. In addition, the nation's farms cannot produce enough food to feed the population. As a result of frequent food shortages, many residents suffer from malnutrition.

To make matters worse, Bangladesh regularly faces serious threats from natural disasters. The nation's location and its low-lying geography make flooding a particular threat. Yearly monsoon rains and powerful cyclones cause frequent floods. Because of the nation's high population density, these floods can kill thousands of people at a time and destroy crops, creating further food shortages.

Regional Atlas Activity

Locating Information Organize students into pairs. Send each pair to appropriate reference sources, such as world almanacs, atlases, or reliable online information sources, to find the populations of the capital cities shown on the Political map on the previous page. Then have them use this information to add any missing cities to the Population Density map, using the appropriate symbols from the map key. **OL**

Map Skills

Answers:

1. Bangladesh has the highest average population density, as the entire country is covered by the highest density level.
2. the Ganges River

Skills Practice

Ask: **Which countries have no cities of a million or more people?** *(Bhutan, Nepal, Maldives, and Sri Lanka)*

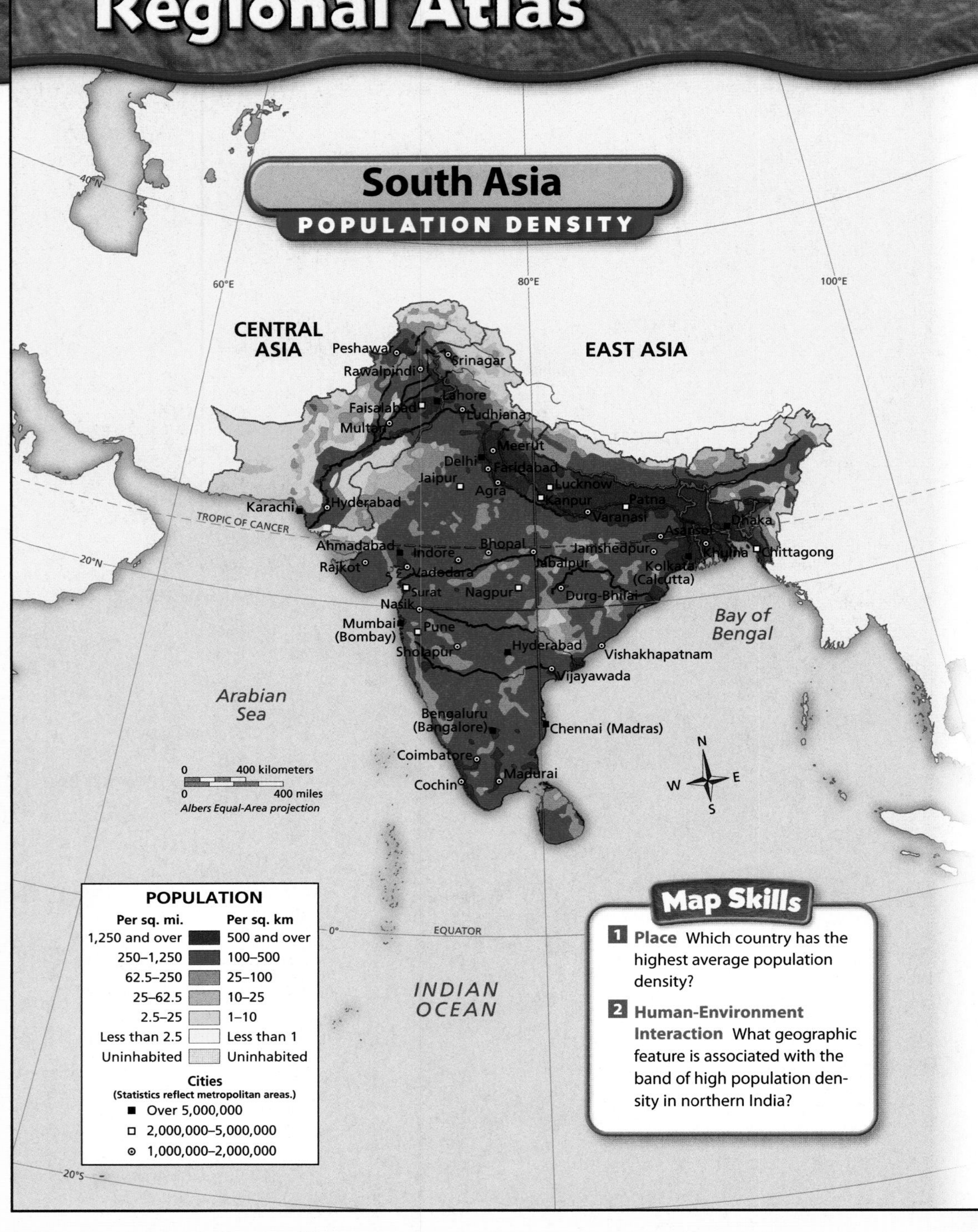

Background: People and Culture

Major World Religions Two major world religions, Hinduism and Buddhism, developed in South Asia. Hinduism is an ancient religion that developed gradually from the mix of beliefs of the peoples living in the region. Hindus believe that all living things have souls, and all souls want to be reunited with Brahman—the eternal spirit. Souls must repeatedly be born into a new body upon dying, a process called reincarnation. As a soul passes through many lifetimes, it becomes increasingly pure before finally reuniting with Brahman.

Buddhism arose in the 500s B.C. from the teachings of a young prince named Siddharta Gautama, who later became known as the Buddha, or "Enlightened One." Buddha taught that people must follow the Eightfold Path in order to end the suffering that comes from being too attached to material things. The steps in the Eightfold Path include thinking clearly, working hard, and showing concern and compassion for all living things. By following this path, people can find nirvana, a state of endless peace and joy.

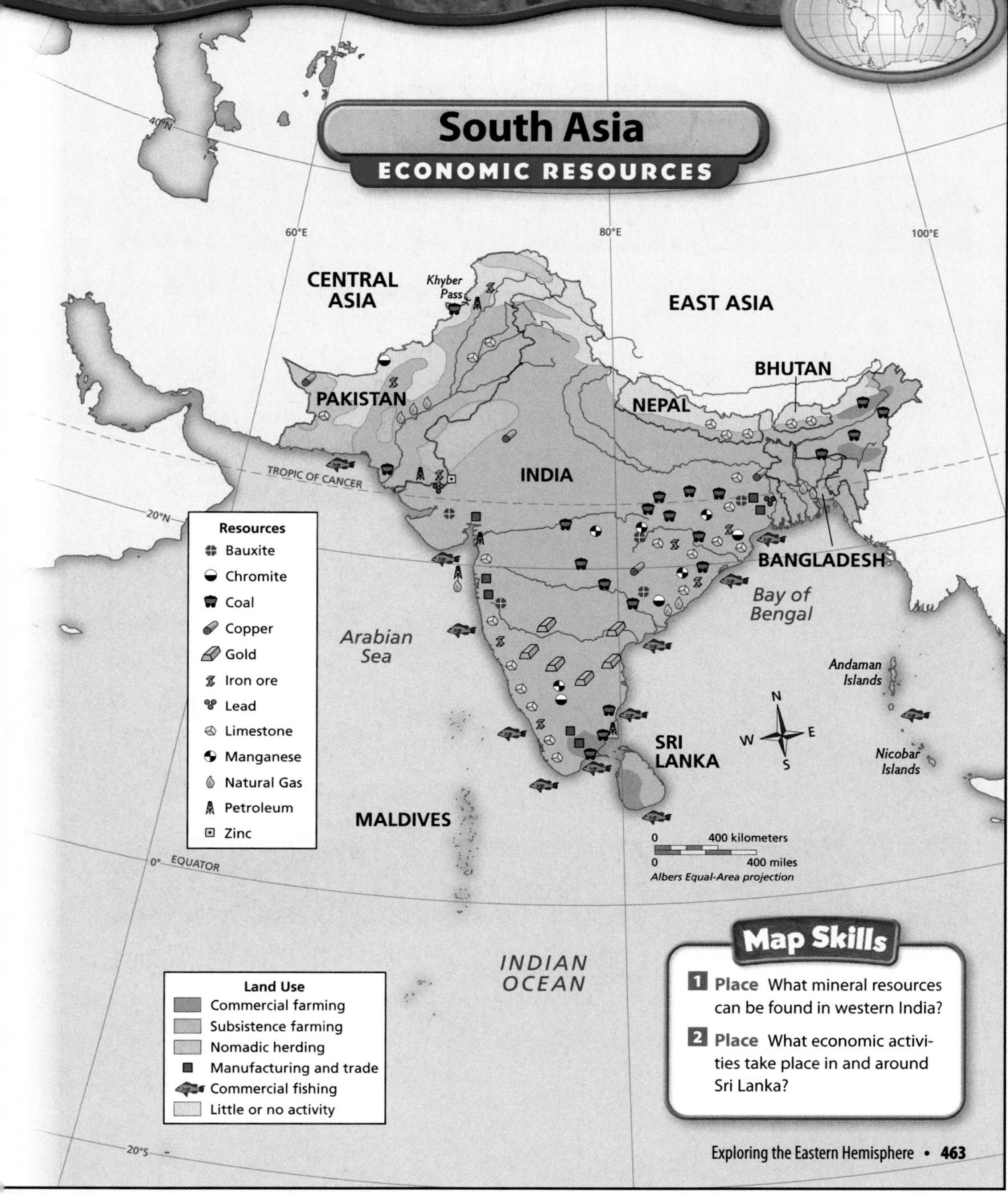

South Asia
ECONOMIC RESOURCES

CENTRAL ASIA
Khyber Pass
EAST ASIA
PAKISTAN
NEPAL
BHUTAN
INDIA
BANGLADESH
Bay of Bengal
Arabian Sea
Andaman Islands
Nicobar Islands
SRI LANKA
MALDIVES
INDIAN OCEAN
TROPIC OF CANCER
EQUATOR

Resources
- Bauxite
- Chromite
- Coal
- Copper
- Gold
- Iron ore
- Lead
- Limestone
- Manganese
- Natural Gas
- Petroleum
- Zinc

Land Use
- Commercial farming
- Subsistence farming
- Nomadic herding
- Manufacturing and trade
- Commercial fishing
- Little or no activity

0 400 kilometers
0 400 miles
Albers Equal-Area projection

Map Skills

1 Place What mineral resources can be found in western India?

2 Place What economic activities take place in and around Sri Lanka?

Regional Atlas Activity

Making Connections Have students compare the Economic Resources map and the Population Density map in the Regional Atlas. **Ask: Which cities in India appear to be manufacturing and trade centers?** *(Madurai, and Mumbai (Bombay), and possibly Kolkata and Ahmadabad)* Have students identify other cities whose economies might rely on particular resources found in South Asia. Then have them use reference sources to verify the importance of these resources to the cities' economies. **OL**

Map Skills

Answers:

1. zinc, iron ore, zinc, petroluem, limestone copper, lead, and bauxite
2. commercial and subsistence farming and fishing

Skills Practice

Ask: In what area of India is the land used for nomadic herding? *(the northwest, around the Thar Desert)* **Where in South Asia is gold found?** *(southern India)*

Background: The Economy

India's Growing Economy After achieving independence from Great Britain in 1947, the Indian government exercised tight control over many aspects of the economy. However, during a period of economic slowdown in the 1970s, the government relaxed its control and moved toward a free market economy, in which businesses are under private ownership. These changes, coupled with the country's huge population growth in recent decades, have made India's economy one of the fastest growing in the world. Agriculture is an important sector in the Indian economy; three out of four Indians are farmers, and more than half the country's land is used for farming. India also mines coal and other mineral resources and exports fish. Industrial goods are produced in factories and in cottage industries, in which people work in their own homes. India's service industries are the fastest-growing sector of the country's economy. This has happened in part because many American businesses hire Indian workers, most of whom are well educated, skilled, and fluent in English—a practice known as outsourcing.

Regional Atlas Activity

Inferring Have students read the languages in the Flag and Language column of the chart. **Ask: What language is an official language in more than one country?** *(English)* **Why do you think English is widely spoken in this region?** *(The British once ruled most of South Asia.)* **OL**

Drawing Conclusions Have students study the flags in the chart. Point out that the flags of Maldives and Pakistan contain crescents. Explain that the crescent is a symbol of Islam. **Ask: What might this indicate about the people of Maldives and Pakistan?** *(They are predominantly Muslim.)* **OL**

Regional Atlas

South Asia

Country and Capital	Literacy Rate	Population and Density	Land Area	Life Expectancy (Years)	GDP* Per Capita (U.S. dollars)	Television Sets (per 1,000 people)	Flag and Language
BANGLADESH Dhaka	43.1%	144,200,000 2,594 per sq. mi. 1,001 per sq. km	55,598 sq. mi. 143,998 sq. km	61	$2,000	7	Bengali
BHUTAN Thimphu	42.2%	1,000,000 55 per sq. mi. 21 per sq. km	18,147 sq. mi. 47,001 sq. km	63	$1,400	6	Dzongkha
INDIA New Delhi	59.5%	1,103,600,000 869 per sq. mi. 336 per sq. km	1,269,340 sq. mi. 3,287,575 sq. km	62	$3,100	75	Hindi, English
MALDIVES Male	97.2%	300,000 2,586 per sq. mi. 1,000 per sq. km	116 sq. mi. 300 sq. km	72	$3,900	38	Maldivian Dhivehi, English
NEPAL Kathmandu	45.2%	25,400,000 447 per sq. mi. 173 per sq. km	56,826 sq. mi. 147,179 sq. km	62	$1,500	516	Nepali
PAKISTAN Islamabad	45.7%	162,400,000 528 per sq. mi. 204 per sq. km	307,375 sq. mi. 796,098 sq. km	62	$2,200	105	Punjabi, Urdu, English
SRI LANKA Colombo	92.3%	19,700,000 778 per sq. mi. 300 per sq. km	25,332 sq. mi. 65,610 sq. km	73	$4,000	102	Sinhala, Tamil, English
UNITED STATES Washington, D.C.	97%	296,500,000 80 per sq. mi. 31 per sq. km	3,717,796 sq. mi. 9,629,047 sq. km	78	$40,100	844	English

*Gross Domestic Product

Countries and flags not drawn to scale

Sources: *CIA World Factbook*, 2005; Population Reference Bureau, *World Population Data Sheet*, 2005.

For more country facts, go to the **Nations of the World Databank** at glencoe.com.

Activity: Using the Chart

Analyzing Ask: Which countries in South Asia do you think are most prosperous, and why? *(Sri Lanka and the Maldives; these two countries have the highest GDP in the region, higher literacy rates than other South Asian countries, and the highest life expectancies)* Direct students to the Economic Resources and Population Density maps in the Regional Atlas. **Ask: What could explain the relative prosperity of Sri Lanka?** *(It has significant land dedicated to commercial farming despite areas of high population density.)* **What other factors not shown on this map might account for their relative prosperity?** *(Answers will vary, but may include historical factors or government decisions.)* Assign groups of students to research possible factors. Have each group present a brief report on the area they researched. Allow enough time to discuss their findings and come to a consensus as a class on what the factors are. **AL**

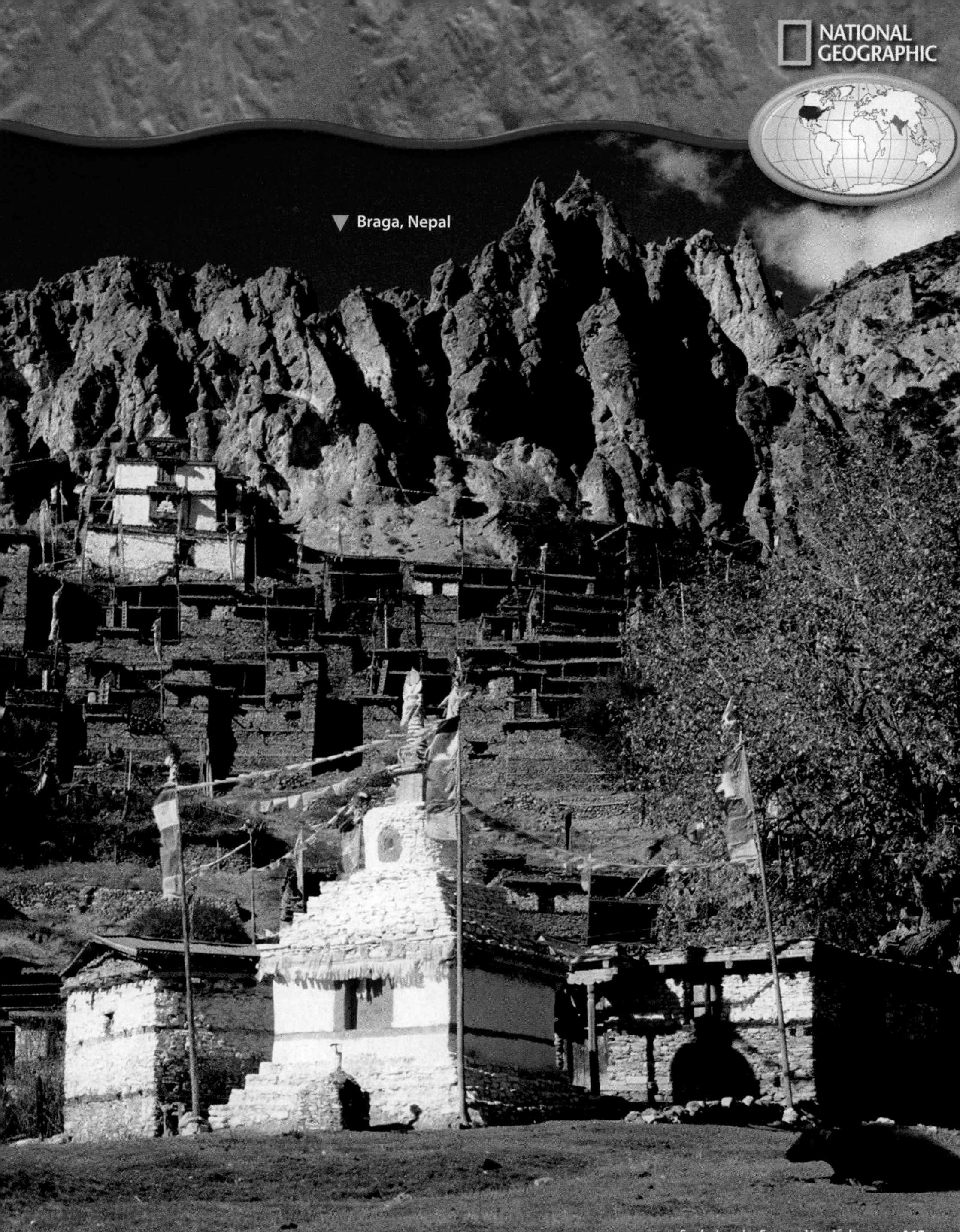

▼ Braga, Nepal

Regional Atlas Activity

Determining Cause and Effect
Have students examine the chart in the Regional Atlas. **Ask:** **Which two countries in South Asia do you think are the poorest? Why?** *(Students probably will mention Bhutan and Nepal, because the GDP per capita in these two countries is the lowest in the region, and their literacy rates and life expectancy are also low.)* **Is there anything on the chart about these two countries that is surprising?** *(Nepal has a relatively high proportion of television sets per 1,000 people, despite its apparent poverty.)* Have students turn to the Economic Resources map in the Regional Atlas. **Ask:** **Using this map, can you determine a cause of the poverty in these two countries?** *(Much of the land in Nepal and Bhutan is used for little or no economic activity; the rest of the land is used for subsistence farming. There are no major natural resources in either country.)* **OL**

More About the Photo

Visual Literacy The white building in this photo is a *chorten*, one form of a Buddhist holy monument called a stupa. Stupas were originally built to house the bodies of Buddha and his associates. Today, they are sometimes used to house sacred texts or commemorate holy sites. The *chorten* is the form of stupa most commonly built by Tibetan Buddhists.

This *chorten* is in Braga, one of Nepal's hillside villages. Nepal's population consists of two main groups: the Indo-Nepalese, who are primarily Hindus, and the Tibeto-Nepalese, some of whom are Buddhists. Buddhism continues to be important in Nepal, in part because Buddha, the founder of Buddhism, was born in present-day Nepal.

What Makes East Asia and Southeast Asia a Region?

The countries in this region share the following characteristics:

- areas of extremely fertile farmland and areas of very high population densities
- a wide variety of climate zones, including cold, tropical, dry, and wet
- some of the most modern and productive economies in the world, as well as some of the world's poorest countries
- some of the world's largest cities
- ethnic groups with rich cultural traditions and heritages
- daily life centered on the family

NATIONAL GEOGRAPHIC

www.nationalgeographic.com/education

NGS ONLINE This online resource provides lesson plans, atlas updates, cartographic activities with interactive maps, an online map store, and geographic links.

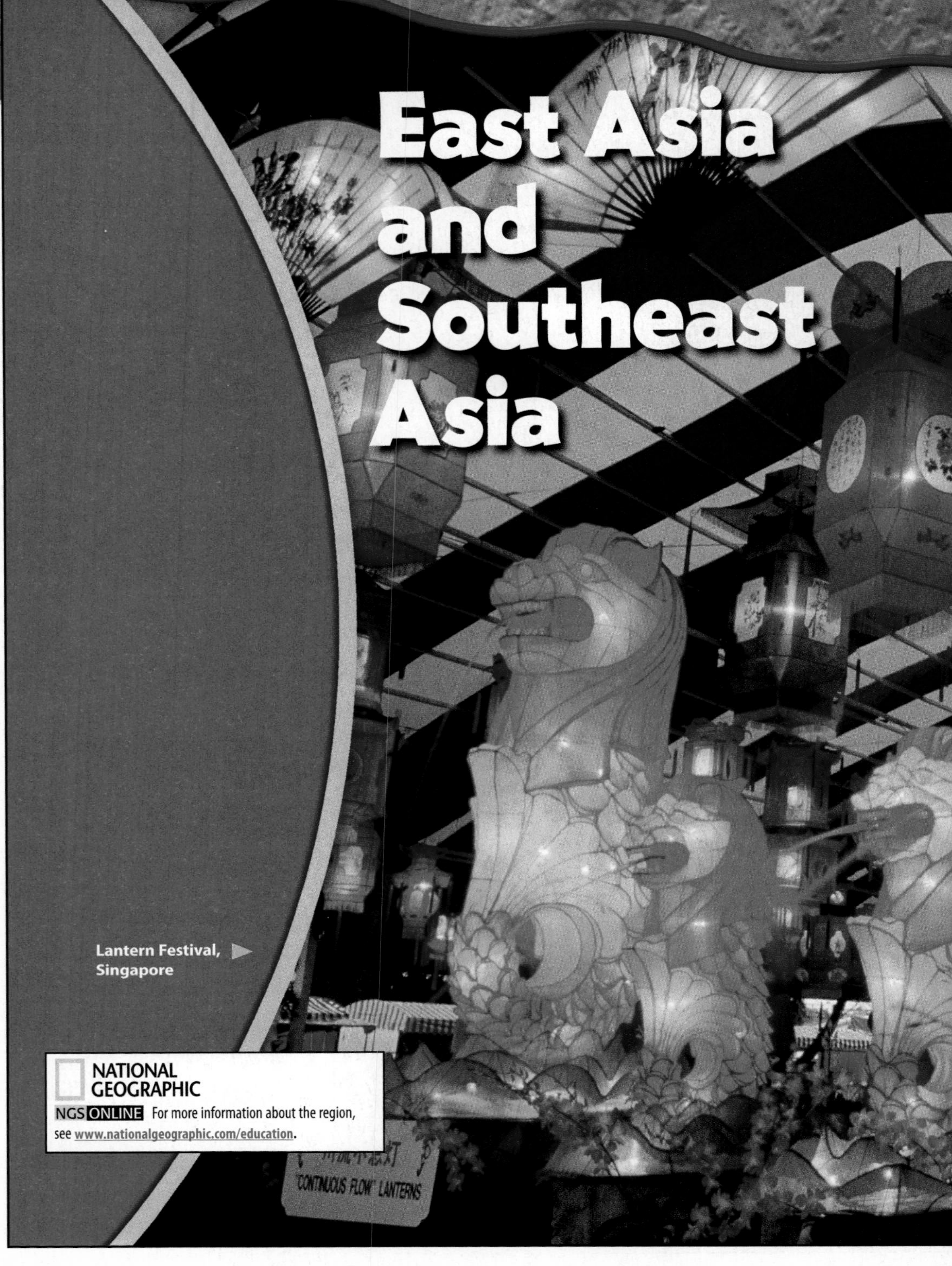

East Asia and Southeast Asia

Lantern Festival, Singapore

NATIONAL GEOGRAPHIC

NGS ONLINE For more information about the region, see www.nationalgeographic.com/education.

Activity: Launching the Regional Atlas

Why Study East Asia and Southeast Asia? Have students name as many of the countries in East Asia and Southeast Asia as they can think of. **Ask:** **What are some things that you associate with East and Southeast Asia?** Explain to students that this region varies in climate, populations, economies, and cultures. Some ideas that students might associate with the region, such as high population densities or particular styles of architecture or dress, might not be true for the entire region. Have students periodically revisit their lists as they read about the region. **OL**

Introduce the Region

Using Maps Have students examine the Physical and Political maps in the Regional Atlas. **Ask:** **What countries are on the Malay Peninsula?** *(Malaysia, Thailand, and Myanmar)* **On what East Asian country's border is the tallest mountain in the world located?** *(Mount Everest is located on the border of China.)* **What are the five main islands of Indonesia?** *(Sumatra, Java, Borneo, Celebes, and New Guinea)* **What countries in this region lie partially or entirely in the Southern Hemisphere?** *(Indonesia and East Timor)* **OL**

More About the Photo

Visual Literacy Throughout the Asian world, lantern festivals accompany the celebration of the Chinese New Year. The Chinese New Year is celebrated with the new cycle of the moon that falls between January 21 and February 19. Each year is named, in sequence, for one of 12 symbolic animals: the rat, ox, tiger, hare, dragon, serpent, horse, ram, monkey, rooster, dog, and boar.

The New Year celebration generally lasts two weeks and ends with the lantern festival. During this festival, merchants hang lighted paper lanterns outside their shops. Many of the lanterns spin from the heat of the candle inside. Children's parades, in which children carry lanterns of various shapes and patterns, are also common.

Regional Atlas Activity

Where Is It?

Relative Location **Ask:** **What is the approximate latitude of New York?** *(40°N)* **What is the approximate latitude of Beijing?** *(40°N)* **What is the approximate longitude of New York?** *(75°W)* **What is the approximate longitude of Beijing?** *(120°E)* **How could you describe Beijing's location relative to New York?** *(Beijing is approximately 195° east of New York.)* **OL**

How Big Is It?

Comparing Have students turn to the country chart in the Regional Atlas. **Ask:** **What is the largest country in this region?** *(China)* **How does the land area of China compare to that of the continental United States?** *(Possible answers: It appears to be similar, or it is slightly smaller than the land area of the continental United States.)* **OL**

Comparing Population

Ask: **Which country in East Asia and Southeast Asia has the largest population?** *(China)* **About how many more people live in China than in the United States?** *(about 1 billion more)* **AL**

Regional Atlas

East Asia and Southeast Asia

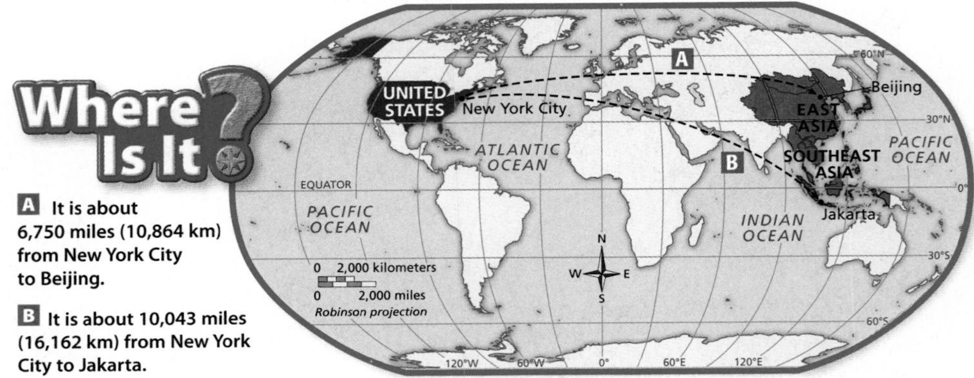

A It is about 6,750 miles (10,864 km) from New York City to Beijing.

B It is about 10,043 miles (16,162 km) from New York City to Jakarta.

The region of East Asia and Southeast Asia is more than two times the size of the continental United States. Its land area is nearly 6.3 million square miles (16.3 million sq. km). With a population of more than two billion people, almost one-third of the people of the world live in the region.

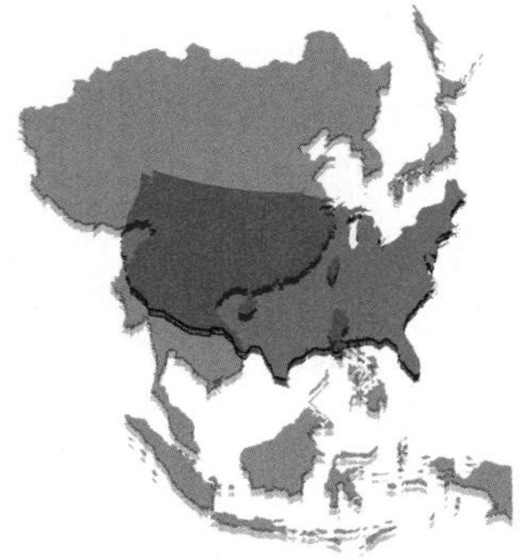

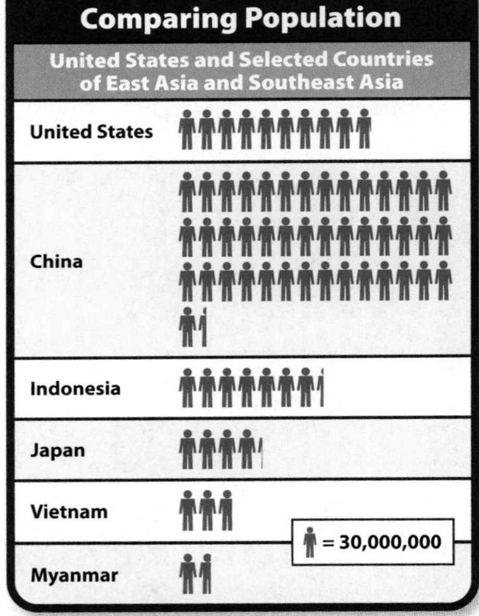

Source: *World Population Data Sheet*, 2005.

Activity: Geographic Theme

Human-Environment Interaction Review with the class how the physical geography of a region can affect population patterns. Have students study the Physical map in the Regional Atlas. **Ask:** **Where do you think most people in this region live?** *(Answers will vary.)* Then have students study the Population Density map and revise their answers if necessary. **Ask:** **How do you think physical geography has affected settlement patterns?** *(Students should mention the rivers and coastal plains that benefit agriculture. They might also mention the higher elevations and deserts in the west that create a harsh terrain.)* **OL**

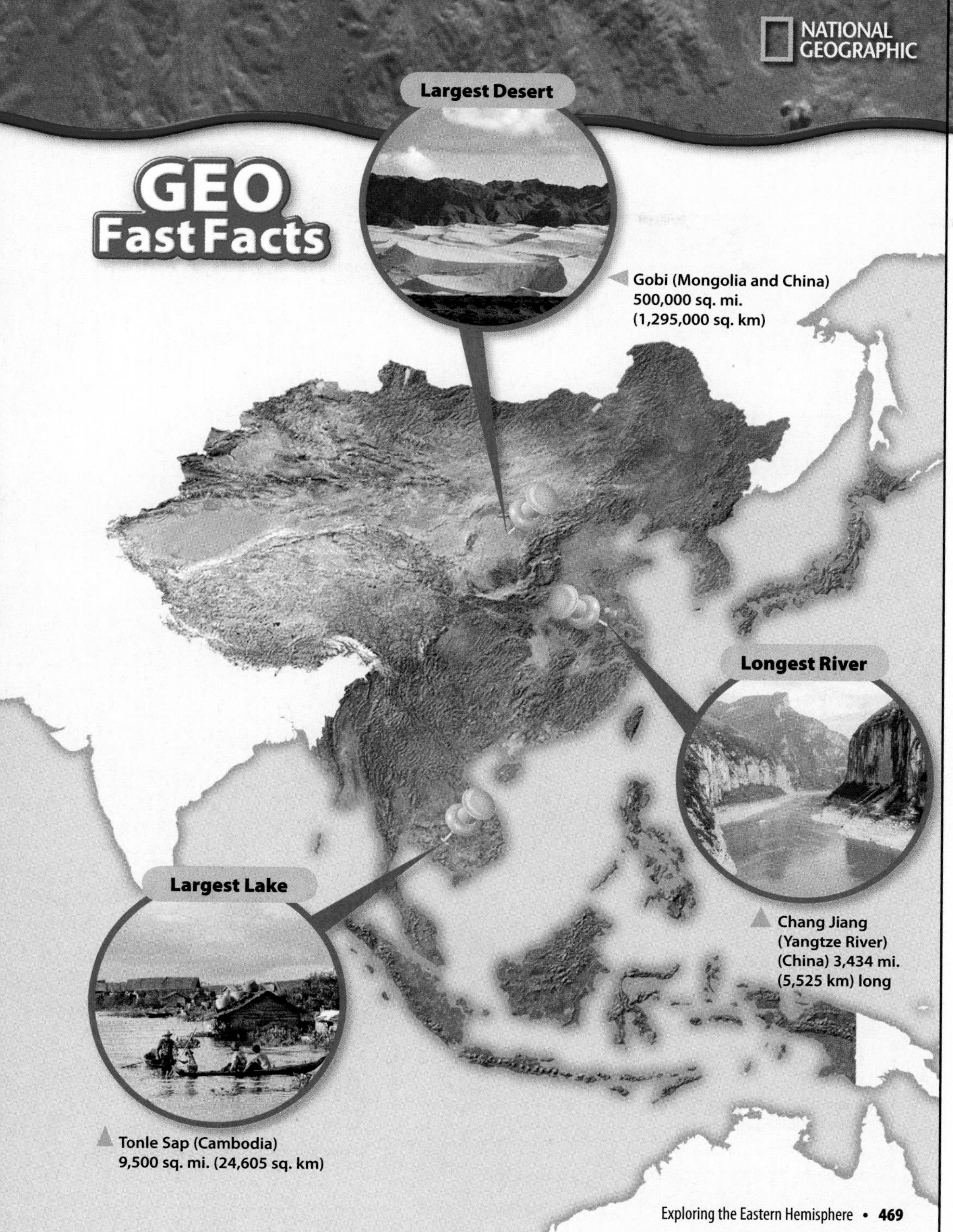

Geo Fast Facts

Categorizing **Ask:** **What types of geographic features are highlighted on this map?** *(a desert, a river, and a lake)*

Have students draw a chart with five columns in their notebooks. Tell them to label the first three columns "Deserts," "Rivers" and "Lakes." Allow each student to choose two more categories to include in his or her chart. Tell students to begin filling in their charts by listing the Geo FastFacts given on this page in the appropriate columns. Then give students time to look through the Regional Atlas and place additional geographic features in their charts.

If time permits, have students choose one of the features and conduct research to learn more about it. Then have students present what they learn in brief reports to the class. **BL**

FastFacts

- **China's One-Child Policy** Beginning in 1979, China began to pressure families to have only one child. One result of this "one-child" policy has been a higher-than-normal ratio of families raising boys as opposed to girls. In China, families sometimes prefer boys to girls because sons are expected to care for their parents in old age.
- **Fuji** Fuji is a celebrated dormant volcano near Tokyo, Japan, and is the highest mountain in Japan. Japanese legend says that Fuji rose from the plain in a single night in 286 B.C. Some religious sects regard the volcano as a sacred place, and thousands of pilgrims visit the numerous shrines and temples on the mountainside each year.
- **Fish in Japan** The Japanese eat more fish than any other people in the world. Sushi, which has become popular in the United States, consists of small rice bundled with raw fish or vegetables and wrapped in seaweed.

Regional Atlas Activity

Making Connections Have students study the elevations displayed on the Physical map. **Ask: How high is the Plateau of Tibet?** *(more than 13,100 feet, or 4,000 m)* Next, have students examine the rivers of the region. **Ask: In what direction does the Chang Jiang (Yangtze River) flow? How do you know?** *(The river flows roughly west to east, because it flows from the higher elevation to the lower elevation and empties into the East China Sea.)* **In what direction does the Irrawaddy River flow? How do you know?** *(It flows roughly north to south, from the higher elevation of the Plateau of Tibet to the Bay of Bengal.)* **AL**

Map Skills

Answers:

1. the Yellow Sea
2. the Plateau of Tibet

Skills Practice

Ask: Which coastal plain in this region is farthest north? *(the Manchurian Plain)* **What island does Indonesia share with another country?** *(New Guinea)*

Regional Atlas

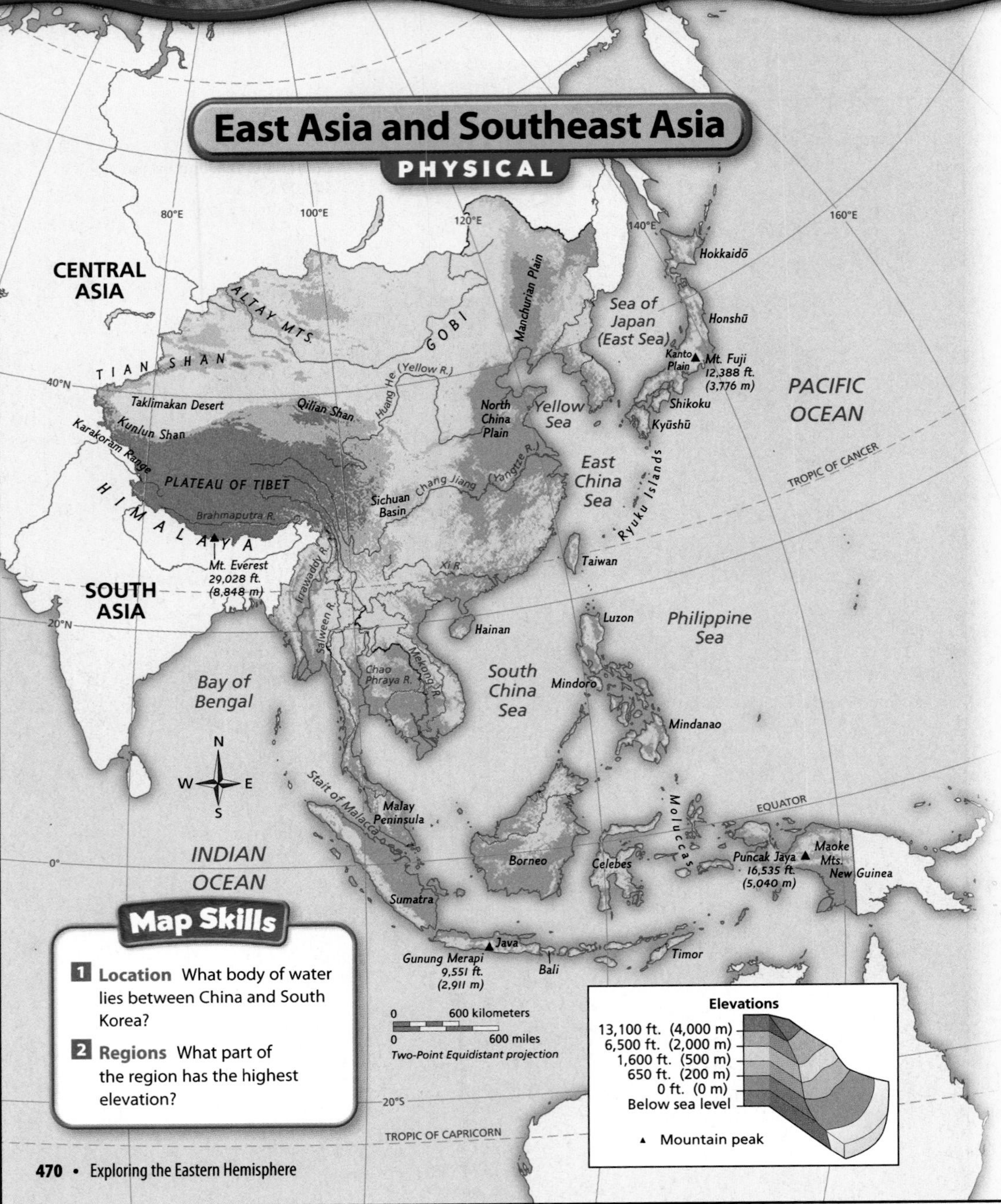

Map Skills

1 Location What body of water lies between China and South Korea?

2 Regions What part of the region has the highest elevation?

Background: Land and Climate

A Land of Contrasts East Asia occupies much of the Asian continent, extending south from Russia's border and inland from the Pacific Ocean to the mountain ranges of the west—the Himalaya, Tian Shan, Altay, and Karakoram. Between the mountains is the Plateau of Tibet. At 15,000 feet, the plateau is so high that it is called the Roof of the World. Further east are East Asia's major lowland areas, the North China Plain and the Manchurian Plain. These fertile areas are home to most of East Asia's people.

Southeast Asia lies south of China and consists of a mainland of peninsulas as well as thousands of islands. The mainland is crossed by mountain ranges running side by side and separated by fertile river plains and deltas, where most Southeast Asians live. The thousands of volcanic islands that are part of the region have rich, fertile farmland. Much of this area is in the Tropics with warm temperatures and rain that falls evenly throughout the year.

East Asia and Southeast Asia
POLITICAL

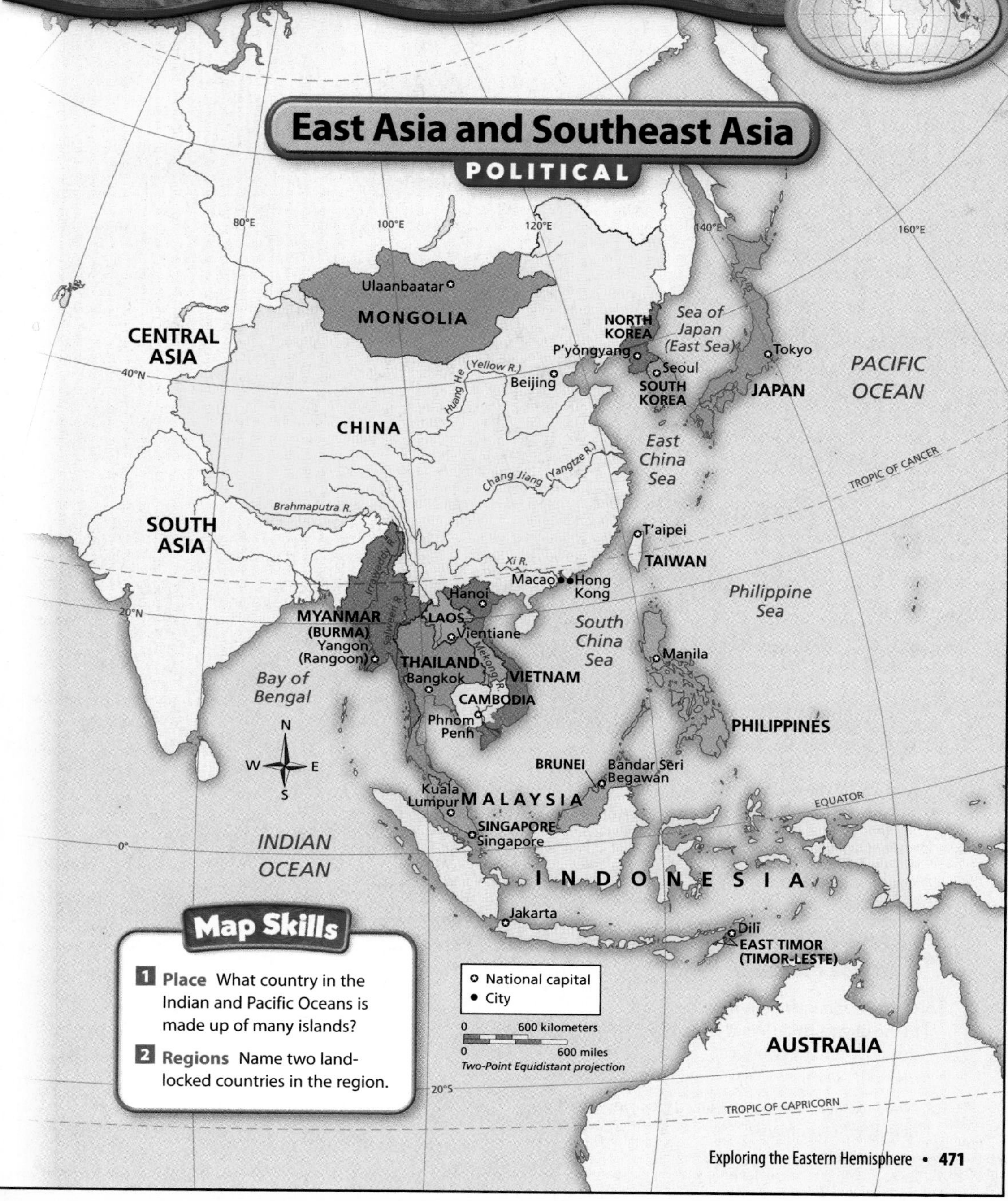

Map Skills

1 Place What country in the Indian and Pacific Oceans is made up of many islands?

2 Regions Name two landlocked countries in the region.

o National capital
• City

0 600 kilometers
0 600 miles
Two-Point Equidistant projection

Regional Atlas Activity

Categorizing Create a three-column chart on the board with the headings "Island," "Peninsula," and "Mainland." Have students compare the Physical and Political maps and then take turns coming to the board to list the countries of East and Southeast Asia under the correct headings. Tell students that a country may be listed under more than one heading. **Ask: What is unusual about Malaysia's location?** *(It is located on the southern end of the Malay Peninsula and also on the island of Borneo.)* **OL**

Map Skills

Answers:

1. Indonesia
2. Mongolia and Laos

Skills Practice

Ask: What body of water separates Japan from North and South Korea? *(the Sea of Japan (East Sea))* **What body of water separates China from the Philippines?** *(the South China Sea)*

Background: Current Issues

Population Growth About one-third of the world's people live in East Asia and Southeast Asia. Poorer countries, such as Cambodia, tend to have have higher birthrates. Wealthier countries, such as Japan, tend to have lower birthrates. In areas with high birthrates, the expanding population places a great strain on resources. Different countries have attempted to deal with these pressures with varying degrees of success. For example, China's government enacted a "one-child" policy in 1979 that encouraged families to have no more than one child. The country's growth rate has slowed as a result, but China's population still grows by millions of people annually, and the country struggles to provide enough opportunities for the young people entering the workforce each year.

Regional Atlas

Regional Atlas Activity

Analyzing Organize the class into groups of four to five students. Have each group study the Population Density map in conjunction with the Political map. **Ask: What two countries do you think have the highest overall population density in the region? What two countries do you think have the lowest population density?** *(Answers will vary.)* Tell students that they need to come to a consensus as a group and be prepared to explain their answers. Then have each group check its answers in the chart pages of the Regional Atlas.

Next, tell the groups to compare the Population Density map to the Physical map. **Ask: How do you think China's physical characteristics affect the patterns of population density in that country?** *(The landscape in the west, including mountains and a high plateau, limits population; the lowlands and rivers closer to the coast encourage settlement there.)* **OL**

Map Skills

Answers:

1. Luzon and Java
2. Eastern Hokkaido and the northern island

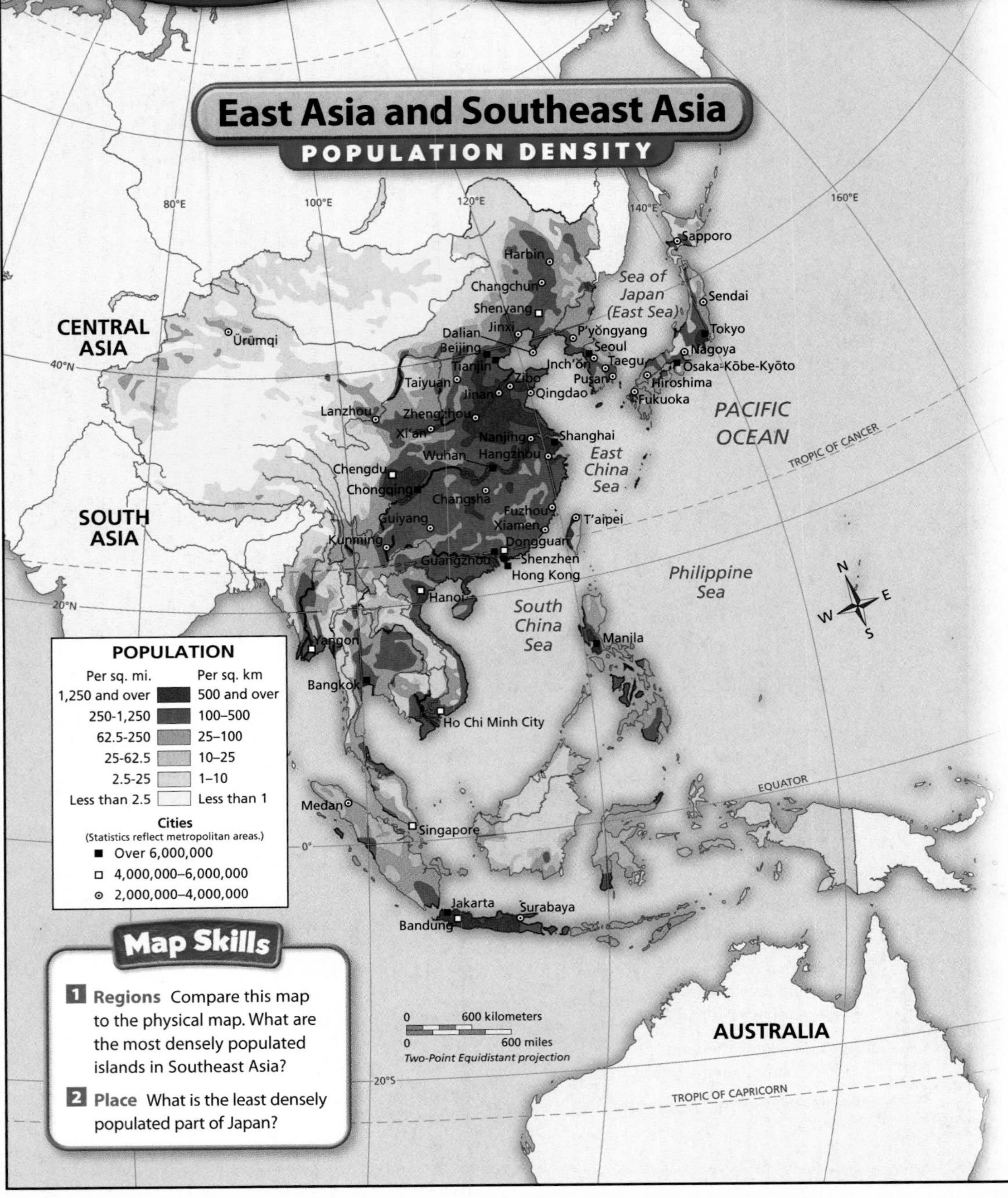

Map Skills

1 Regions Compare this map to the physical map. What are the most densely populated islands in Southeast Asia?

2 Place What is the least densely populated part of Japan?

Background: People and Culture

The Arts Many art forms are popular in East Asia and Southeast Asia. In China, Japan, and Korea, artists paint rugged landscapes that reflect a spiritual reverence for nature. Some of these paintings include poems written in an elegant form of longhand writing called calligraphy.

The architecture of East Asia and Southeast Asia also reflects the region's artistic traditions. In East Asia, for example, buildings called pagodas have a distinctive style. They have tiled roofs that curve up at the edges. Pagodas are used as Buddhist religious temples or as memorials.

The region also has strong literary and theatrical traditions. Japanese haiku is one distinctive form. These are short, structured poems that often reflect a reverence for nature. Puppet plays are popular throughout Southeast Asia. Japan is known for No and Kabuki theater.

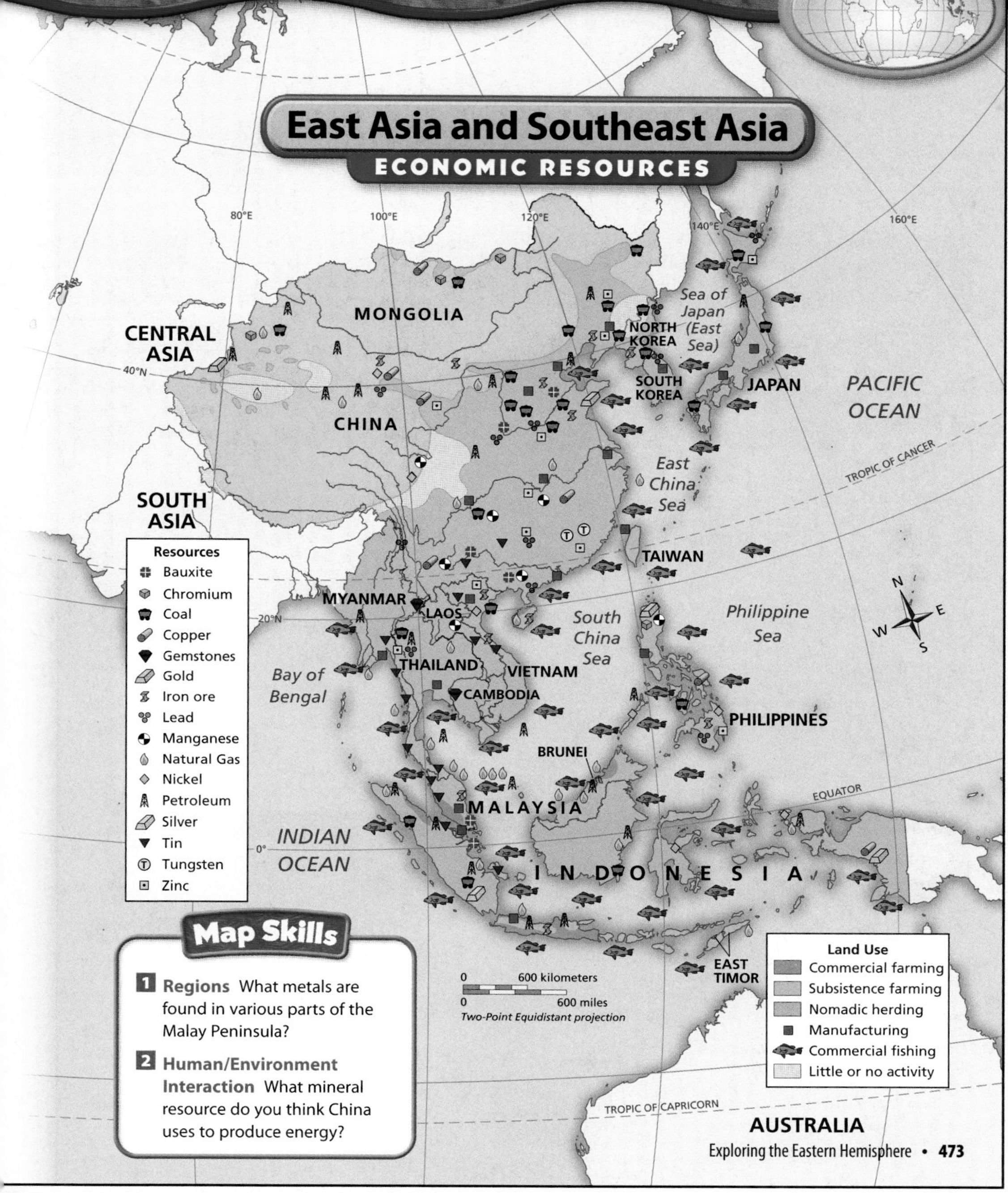

East Asia and Southeast Asia

ECONOMIC RESOURCES

Resources

- Bauxite
- Chromium
- Coal
- Copper
- Gemstones
- Gold
- Iron ore
- Lead
- Manganese
- Natural Gas
- Nickel
- Petroleum
- Silver
- Tin
- Tungsten
- Zinc

Land Use

- Commercial farming
- Subsistence farming
- Nomadic herding
- Manufacturing
- Commercial fishing
- Little or no activity

0 600 kilometers
0 600 miles
Two-Point Equidistant projection

Map Skills

1. **Regions** What metals are found in various parts of the Malay Peninsula?
2. **Human/Environment Interaction** What mineral resource do you think China uses to produce energy?

Regional Atlas Activity

Summarizing Organize the class into four groups and assign each group 4 of the 17 countries in the region, with the exception of China. Then assign China as the fifth country to each group. Have the groups study the Economic Resources map and create a chart listing the resources and types of land use in each assigned country. Have the groups write a brief summary about each country's resources. **OL**

Map Skills

Answers:

1. tin, bauxite, and iron ore
2. coal, because it has abundant reserves of that mineral

Skills Practice

Ask: What is the primary land use in Mongolia? *(nomadic herding)* **In Laos?** *(subsistence farming)*

Background: The Economy

Strong Asian Economies Japan built a modern economy after World War II and is now the world's second-largest economy. Following its lead, several countries in East and Southeast Asia have built strong, modern economies since the 1960s. The economies of South Korea, Taiwan, Singapore, and the Chinese port of Hong Kong are so strong and are growing so quickly that they are sometimes called the "Asian Tigers." The democratic governments of South Korea and Taiwan have supported the development of manufacturing and high-technology industries. Both countries now export cars, computers, and electronics. The economies of the port cities of Hong Kong and Singapore depend in large part on trade. Singapore is a free port where goods can be unloaded, stored, and shipped again without being taxed. This has resulted in a huge amount of goods flowing through that country. China, too, has recently become a major economic power.

Regional Atlas Activity

Synthesizing Help students learn the characteristics of the countries in East Asia and Southeast Asia by playing a game. First, assign each student a country. Then tell them to write a statement about their country from either the maps or the chart in the Regional Atlas. An example might be: My country's capital is Pyongyang.

Start the game by calling on a student to read his or her statement, followed by the question "What country am I?" Allow other students to guess the answer. Then have the first student to answer the question correctly read his or her statement. Continue the game until all students have read their statements. **ELL**

Regional Atlas

East Asia and Southeast Asia

Country and Capital	Literacy Rate	Population and Density	Land Area	Life Expectancy (Years)	GDP* Per Capita (U.S. dollars)	Television Sets (per 1,000 people)	Flag and Language
BRUNEI Bandar Seri Begawan	93.9%	400,000 180 per sq. mi. 72 per sq. km	2,228 sq. mi. 5,570 sq. km	74	$23,600	637	Malay
CAMBODIA Phnom Penh	69.4%	13,300,000 190 per sq. mi. 73 per sq. km	69,900 sq. mi. 181,040 sq. km	56	$2,000	9	Khmer
CHINA Beijing	90.9%	1,303,700,000 353 per sq. mi. 136 per sq. km	3,696,100 sq. mi. 9,572,855 sq. km	72	$5,600	291	Mandarin Chinese
EAST TIMOR (TIMOR-LESTE) Dili	58.6%	900,000 157 per sq. mi. 61 per sq. km	5,741 sq. mi. 14,869 sq. km	55	$400	information not available	Tetum, Portuguese
INDONESIA Jakarta	87.9%	221,900,000 302 per sq. mi. 117 per sq. km	735,355 sq. mi. 1,904,561 sq. km	68	$3,500	143	Bahasa Indonesia
JAPAN Tokyo	99%	127,700,000 875 per sq. mi. 338 per sq. km	145,869 sq. mi. 377,799 sq. km	82	$29,400	719	Japanese
UNITED STATES Washington, D.C.	97%	296,500,000 80 per sq. mi. 31 per sq. km	3,717,796 sq. mi. 9,629,047 sq. km	78	$40,100	844	English

*Gross Domestic Product

Countries and flags not drawn to scale

Activity: Using the Chart

Comparing and Contrasting Organize the class into small groups. Assign each group two countries. Have each group make a poster comparing and contrasting their two countries. Have them begin their poster using the information given in the chart and maps. **Ask: What would you like to know about these countries that is not included on the chart or maps?** Tell groups to consult appropriate reference sources, including encyclopedias, atlases, or reliable online news and information sources, to find more information about their countries. Tell students to include this information on their posters. When students have completed their posters, have each group present its poster to the class. **OL**

East Asia and Southeast Asia

Country and Capital	Literacy Rate	Population and Density	Land Area	Life Expectancy (Years)	GDP* Per Capita (U.S. dollars)	Television Sets (per 1,000 people)	Flag and Language
LAOS, Vientiane	66.4%	5,900,000 65 per sq. mi. 25 per sq. km	91,429 sq. mi. 236,800 sq. km	54	$1,900	10	Lao
MALAYSIA, Kuala Lumpur	88.7%	26,100,000 205 per sq. mi. 79 per sq. km	127,317 sq. mi. 329,750 sq. km	73	$9,700	174	Bahasa Melayu
MONGOLIA, Ulaanbaatar	97.8%	2,600,000 4 per sq. mi. 2 per sq. km	604,826 sq. mi. 1,566,492 sq. km	64	$1,900	58	Khalkha Mongol
MYANMAR, Yangon (Rangoon)	85.3%	50,500,000 193 per sq. mi. 75 per sq. km	261,228 sq. mi. 676,577 sq. km	60	$1,700	7	Burmese
NORTH KOREA, P'yŏngyang	99%	22,900,000 492 per sq. mi. 190 per sq. km	46,541 sq. mi. 120,541 sq. km	71	$1,700	55	Korean
PHILIPPINES, Manila	92.6%	84,800,000 732 per sq. mi. 283 per sq. km	115,830 sq. mi. 299,998 sq. km	70	$5,000	110	Filipino, English
UNITED STATES, Washington, D.C.	97%	296,500,000 80 per sq. mi. 31 per sq. km	3,717,796 sq. mi. 9,629,047 sq. km	78	$40,100	844	English

Sources: *CIA World Factbook*, 2005; Population Reference Bureau, *World Population Data Sheet*, 2005.

For more country facts, go to the **Nations of the World Databank** at glencoe.com.

Regional Atlas Activity

Hypothesizing Ask: What three countries in the region have the highest life expectancy? *(Japan, 82; Singapore, 79; South Korea, 77)* **What three countries have the lowest life expectancy?** *(Laos, 54; East Timor, 55; Cambodia, 56)* **What other data in the chart might help explain the differences in life expectancy among these countries?** *(Students might mention the high GDP per capita of the countries with the highest life expectancy and the low GDP per capita of the countries with the lowest life expectancy.)* **Do you think this fully explains the differences?** *(Students should say no, because some countries with a low GDP per capita have much higher life expectancies than Laos, East Timor, and Cambodia.)* **What other information might be helpful in explaining the differences in life expectancy in this region?** *(Answers might include nutrition, quality of health care, climate, work activities, and so on.)* You can extend this activity by having students do further research into the factors affecting life expectancy in one or more countries. **AL**

Activity: Using the Chart

Making Connections Ask: What country in this region would you like to visit? Tell students that in order to prepare for a trip to that country, they should begin by doing research about the country. Have each student create a list of six to eight questions about the country they would like to visit. Then direct them to appropriate reference materials to find answers. Once students have learned about their countries, have them identify several places within the country that they would like to visit. Tell them to collect as much material as they can about these places. Encourage them to contact tourist offices, research online travel sites, or locate detailed maps to help them find the information they need. Then have students prepare an itinerary for their trip, including the places they will visit and their means of transportation from place to place. Also have them prepare a budget for the trip, including airfare, hotels, meals, and travel costs within the country. At the end of the project, have each student prepare a portfolio of information about traveling to that country. **AL**

Regional Atlas Activity

Identifying Ask students to study the land area column in the chart. **Ask: Which country has the smallest land area?** *(Singapore)* **What is its size?** *(239 square miles or 619 sq. km)* Ask students to study the small map of Singapore in the chart and compare it to the larger maps in the Regional Atlas. Point out that Singapore is a small island off the tip of the Malay Peninsula, but because it is so small, it sometimes appears to be part of the Malay Peninsula on larger maps. **BL**

Regional Atlas

East Asia and Southeast Asia

Country and Capital	Literacy Rate	Population and Density	Land Area	Life Expectancy (Years)	GDP* Per Capita (U.S. dollars)	Television Sets (per 1,000 people)	Flag and Language
SINGAPORE Singapore	92.5%	4,300,000 17,992 per sq. mi. 6,947 per sq. km	239 sq. mi. 619 sq. km	79	$27,800	341	Mandarin
SOUTH KOREA Seoul	97.9%	48,300,000 1,260 per sq. mi. 487 per sq. km	38,324 sq. mi. 99,259 sq. km	77	$19,200	364	Korean
TAIWAN† Taipei	96.1	22,700,000 1,625 per sq. mi. 627 per sq. km	13,969 sq. mi. 36,180 sq. km	76	$25,300	327	Mandarin Chinese
THAILAND Bangkok	92.6%	65,000,000 328 per sq. mi. 127 per sq. km	198,116 sq. mi. 513,118 sq. km	71	$8,100	274	Thai
VIETNAM Hanoi	90.3%	83,300,000 650 per sq. mi. 251 per sq. km	128,066 sq. mi. 331,689 sq. km	72	$2,700	184	Vietnamese
UNITED STATES Washington, D.C.	97%	296,500,000 80 per sq. mi. 31 per sq. km	3,717,796 sq. mi. 9,629,047 sq. km	78	$40,100	844	English

*Gross Domestic Product

† The People's Republic of China claims Taiwan as its 23rd province.

Countries and flags not drawn to scale

Activity: Using the Chart

Locating Information Ask: What country has the lowest population density in East Asia and Southeast Asia? *(Mongolia)* **How does Mongolia's population density compare with that of other countries in the region?** *(Most countries in the region have much higher population densities.)* **What factors do you think may contribute to this difference?** *(Students' answers will vary.)* After discussion, organize the class into small groups and assign each group a topic about Mongolia to research, such as: Mongolia's early history; current government; geography and climate; economy; educational system; religion; or health issues. Have each group use appropriate sources and develop a three-minute class presentation summarizing their topic and analyzing whether the information they have learned helps explain the low population density of Mongolia. **AL**

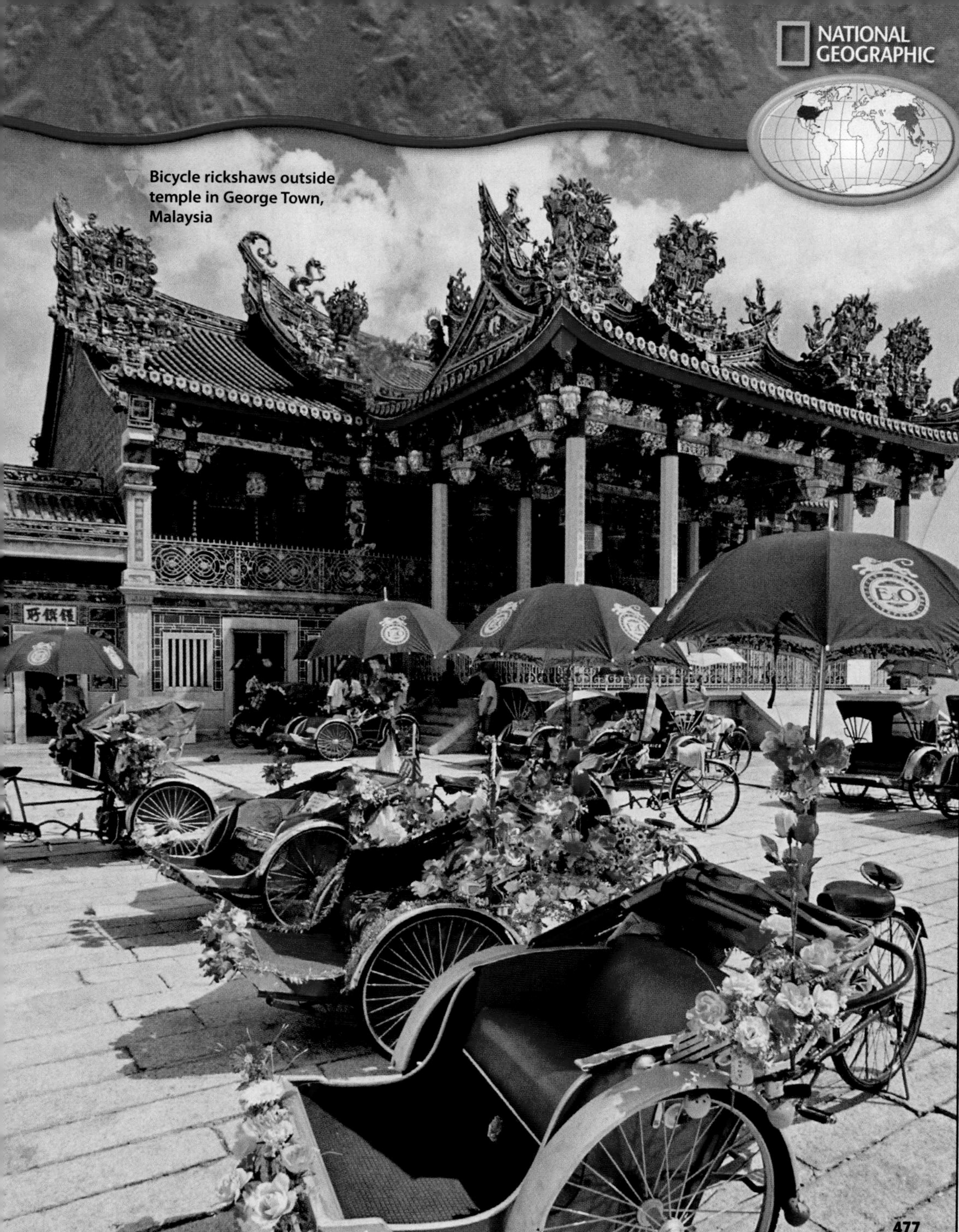

Bicycle rickshaws outside temple in George Town, Malaysia

Regional Atlas Activity

Analyzing Have students study the GDP per capita column in the chart on the previous pages. **Ask: What are the five countries with the highest GDP per capita?** *(Japan, Singapore, Taiwan, Brunei, and South Korea)* Have students research these countries online to determine their major exports as well as new business prospects. Lead a class discussion in which you examine how the economies of these countries might change and how they might influence the U.S. economy. **OL**

More About the Photo

Visual Literacy Rickshaws, or human-powered vehicles for hire, have long been used to transport passengers in many parts of Asia. Today bicyclist-pulled rickshaws, like those shown here are the most common types used. This group of decorated rick-shaws sits in front of Khoo Kongsi Temple in George Town, Penang, Malaysia. The temple was built by Chinese master craftsmen and artisans, and was completed in 1906. The temple is known as one of the finest histori-cal buildings in Malaysia and receives about 800 visitors per day. It was built by the Khoo clan, descendants of seventeenth-century Chinese sailors who settled on the island of Penang. For about 100 years, the temple has been the site of special Khoo clan worship and celebrations.

What Makes Australia, Oceania, and Antarctica a Region?

The countries in this region share the following characteristics:

- a location almost entirely in the Southern Hemisphere, stretching from the Tropics to the South Pole
- unique plants and animals
- environmental challenges, including overgrazing, global warming, and the effects of nuclear testing in the Pacific
- a history of colonization that left some Pacific Island nations with struggling economies
- both modern and traditional ways of life in most countries

NATIONAL GEOGRAPHIC

www.nationalgeographic.com/education

NGS ONLINE This online resource provides lesson plans, atlas updates, cartographic activities with interactive maps, an online map store, and geographic links.

Australia, Oceania, and Antarctica

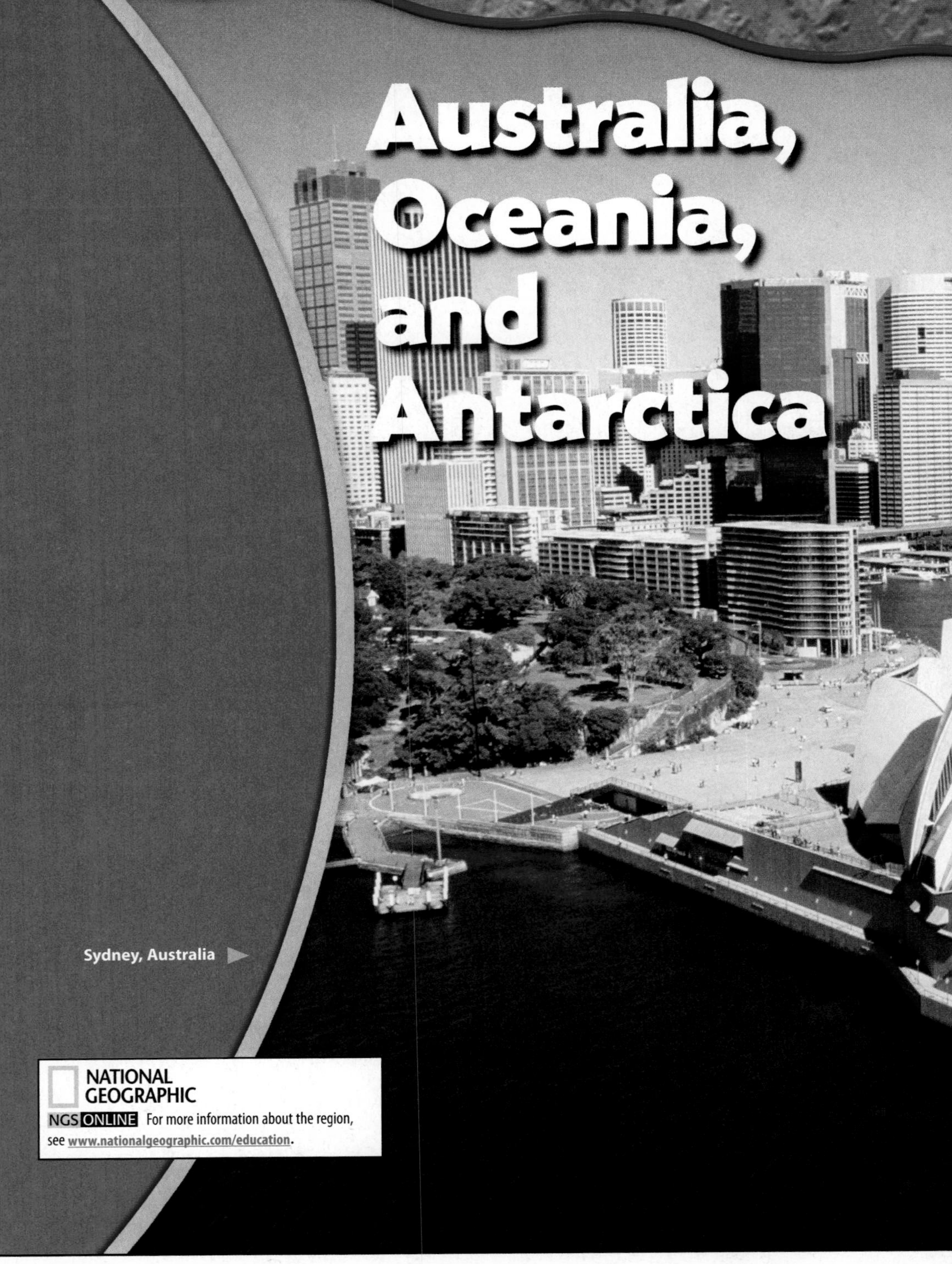

Sydney, Australia

NATIONAL GEOGRAPHIC

NGS ONLINE For more information about the region, see www.nationalgeographic.com/education.

Activity: Launching the Regional Atlas

Why Study Australia, Oceania, and Antarctica? Explain to students that many of the countries in this region are small islands. **Ask: What environmental challenges might countries in this region face?** *(Rising sea levels due to global warming might be a concern for island countries and for the frozen continent of Antarctica. People in the region might be concerned about how the region's unique animals have been affected by human activity.)* Lead in a discussion of the problems associated with global warming and other local environmental challenges. Discuss efforts to deal with these problems. Have students make predictions about the future of this region's environment. **OL**

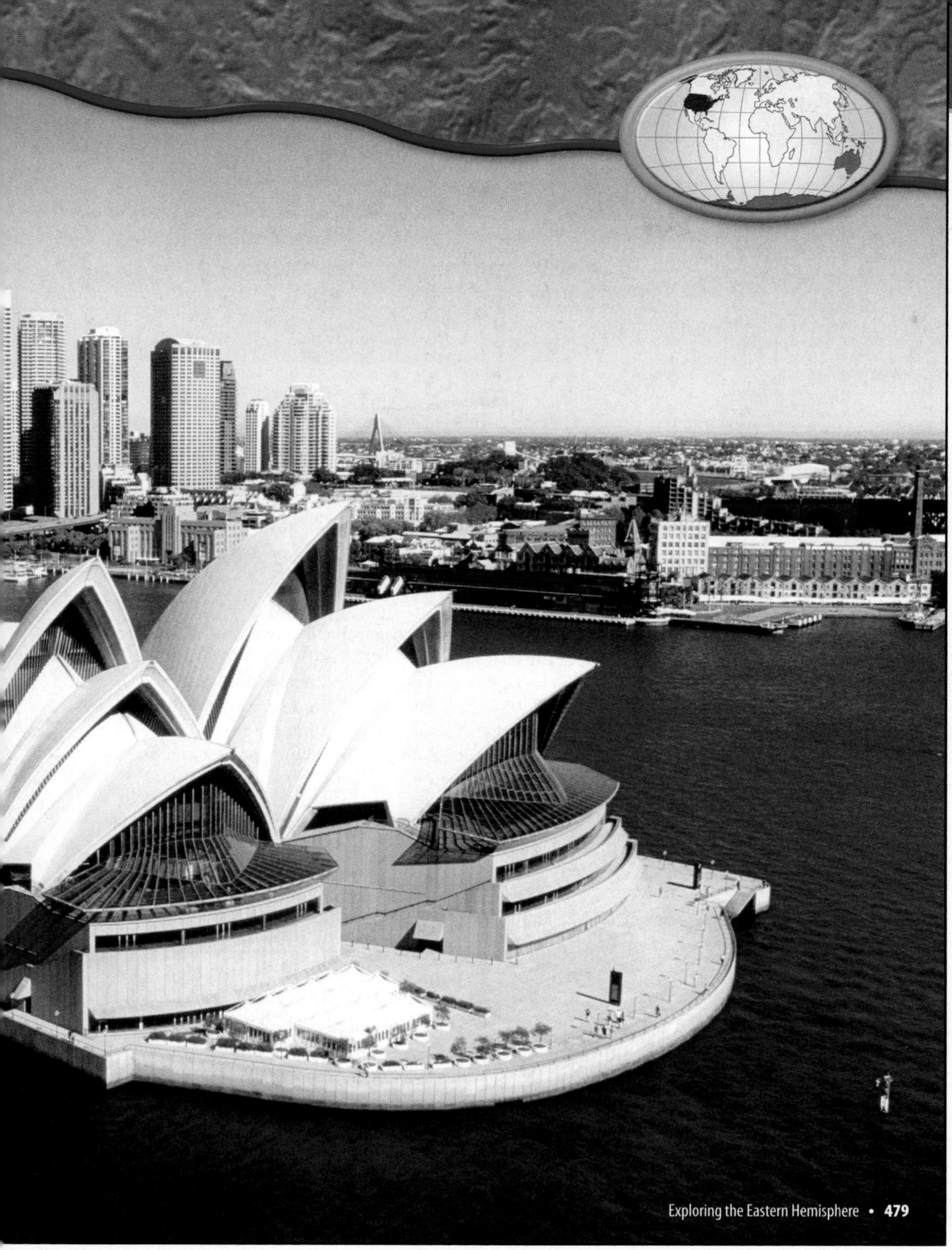

Introduce the Region

Identifying Have students look at the Political map in the Regional Atlas. **Ask: What areas are included in this region?** *(Australia, Antarctica, and large and small islands in the Pacific Ocean)* **Which two continents are located in this region?** *(Antarctica and Australia)* **What do the boxes in the Pacific Ocean mean?** (The boxes drawn around islands are the national boundaries of Pacific Island nations.) **How do Australia and Antarctica differ from Oceania?** *(Australia and Antarctica are much larger than the islands of Oceania.)* **Who controls Antarctica?** *(Antarctica is split into pie-shaped pieces, each controlled by one of seven nations: Chile, Argentina, the United Kingdom, Norway, Australia, France, and New Zealand.)* **OL**

More About the Photo

Visual Literacy Sydney is Australia's largest city and the capital of the state of New South Wales. This view of Sydney captures the traditional and modern architecture of the city, including the beautiful Sydney Harbor, and the internationally famous Sydney Opera House. It is one of the most famous pieces of modern architecture in the world, was designed by Danish architect Jørn Utzon, and was completed in 1973. The beautiful, shell-shaped roofs of the building were designed to be reminiscent of the sails of boats common in the nearby harbor.

Sydney's central business district surrounds the harbor. While tourism is an important industry, Sydney also has service industries, manufacturing, and international commerce. Tourists come to this area for the cultural attractions, the well-preserved historic district, and the magnificent beaches along the coastline.

Regional Atlas Activity

Where Is It?

Identifying Hemispheres Ask: What divides the world into Northern and Southern Hemispheres? *(the Equator)* **What divides the world into Eastern and Western Hemispheres?** *(the Prime Meridian)* **In what hemispheres does the region of Australia, Oceania, and Antarctica lie?** *(Australia, New Zealand, Antarctica, and Papua New Guinea, as well as many smaller islands, are in the Southern Hemisphere; some smaller islands are in the Northern Hemisphere. Antarctica is in both the Eastern and Western Hemispheres; Australia, New Zealand, Papua New Guinea, and many smaller islands are in the Eastern Hemisphere; many of the small islands lie in the Western Hemisphere.)* **OL**

How Big Is It?

Comparing Ask: Which landmass in this region is about the same size as the United States? *(Australia)* **Which landmass is about twice as large as the continental United States?** *(Antarctica)* **What other landmasses exist in this region, and how does their size compare to the size of the United States?** *(Most of the islands of Oceania are tiny compared to the size of the United States, but the continent of Antarctica is almost twice as large.)* **OL**

Comparing Population

Ask: Australia's population is about what percent of the U.S. population? *(a little less than 10%)* **How would you compare the population of New Zealand to the population of Australia?** *(New Zealand's population is just a fraction of Australia's.)* **OL**

Regional Atlas

Australia, Oceania, and Antarctica

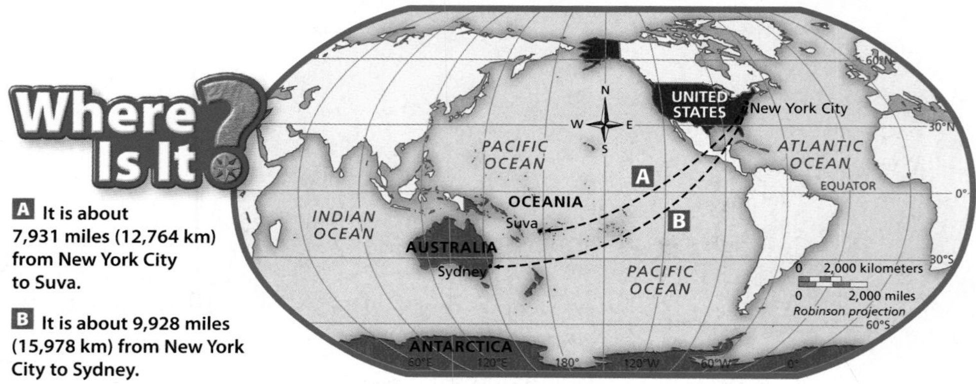

The land area of the region of Australia, Oceania, and Antarctica is about 8.8 million square miles (22.8 million sq. km), and it includes the continents of Australia and Antarctica. With an area of 3.0 million square miles (7.8 million sq. km), Australia is slightly smaller than the continental United States, whereas Antarctica is almost twice as large. The islands of Oceania make up a very small part of the region's land.

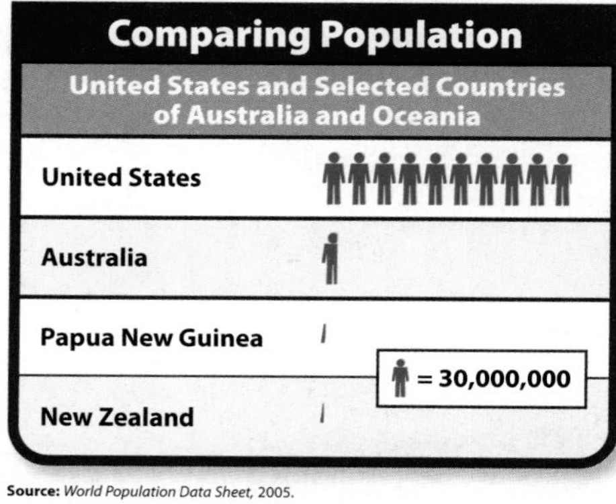

Comparing Population

United States and Selected Countries of Australia and Oceania

United States	10 figures
Australia	1 figure (less than one)
Papua New Guinea	fraction of a figure
New Zealand	fraction of a figure

(1 figure = 30,000,000)

Source: *World Population Data Sheet*, 2005.

Activity: Geographic Theme

Place Ask students to look closely at the Physical map in the Regional Atlas. Tell students that people in Oceania speak more than 1,200 languages. **Ask: Why might people in different parts of Australia and Oceania have developed very different cultures?** *(because the ocean isolated communities from one another)* **Why might people in Papua New Guinea have developed more than 700 languages on that island alone?** *(because communities on the island were isolated from one another by the varied topography of the island, which ranges from coastal plains to high mountain peaks)* Tell students to look for additional reasons for the variety of languages as they study this unit. **OL**

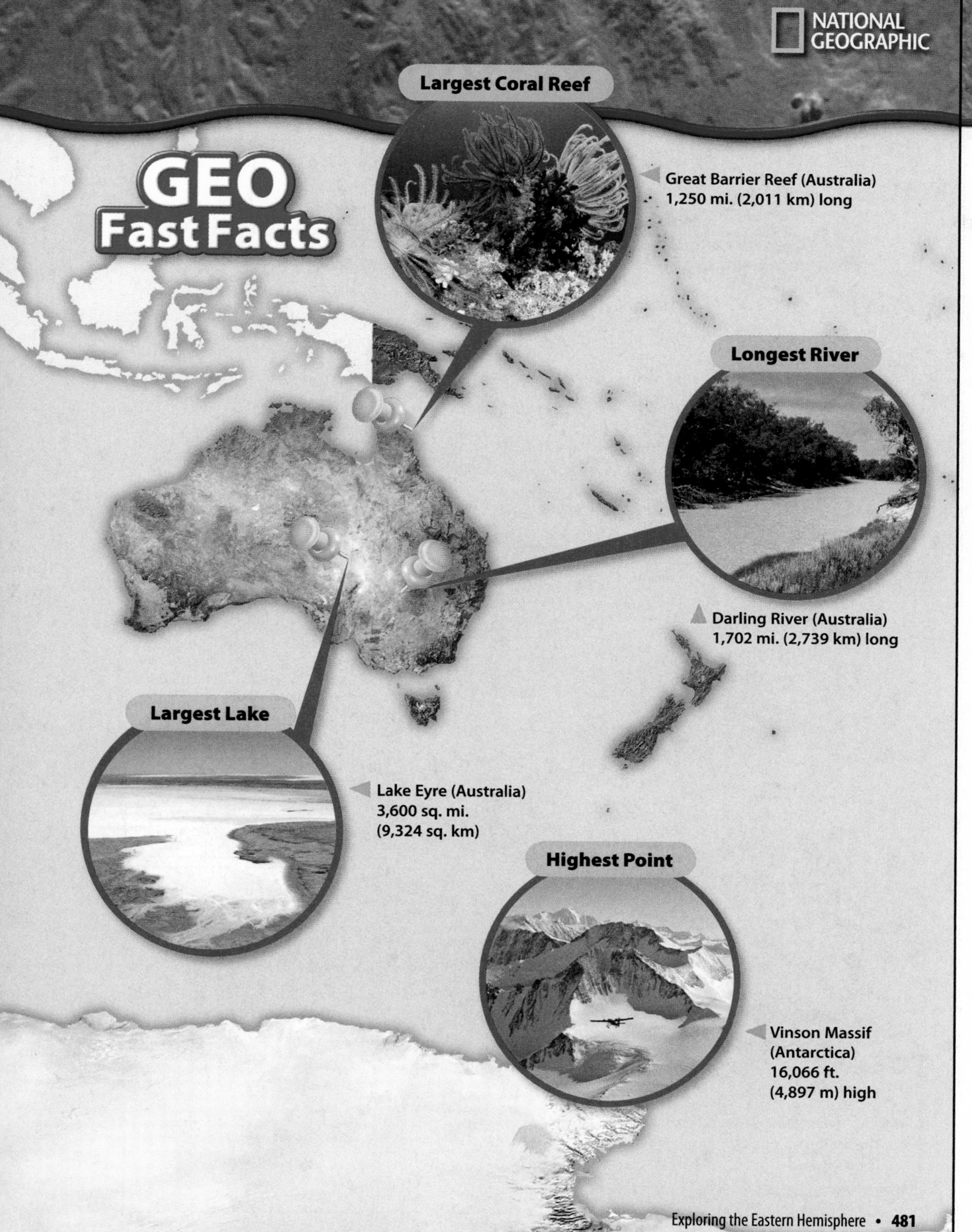

Geo Fast Facts

Charting Physical Features **Ask:** **What four features of Australia, Antarctica, and Oceania are highlighted on this page?** *(the largest coral reef, longest river, highest point, and largest lake)* Draw a chart on the board with the following locations as column headings—Antarctica, New Zealand, Australia, and Papua New Guinea. Have students copy the chart into their notebooks. Then have students list each of the four Geo FastFacts under the correct column head.

Ask: **What other features would you be interested in knowing about?** *(Answers might include longest mountain range, lowest point, smallest island, and so on.)* Have students select the two or three features that most interest them. Have students look through the Regional Atlas and consult appropriate reference materials to determine where the features are located. Then have them add the features to their charts in the appropriate column. Students may need to add more column headings to their charts. **OL**

FastFacts

- **Gondwanaland** Geologist Eduard Suess (1831–1914) proposed that at one time South America, Africa, Australia, and Antarctica as well as the Indian subcontinent formed one supercontinent. He called it Gondwanaland. His work helped lay the basis for tracing the ancient changes in the continents and oceans that created the surface of the Earth that we see today.
- **Bats: The Lonely Mammal** New Zealand is home to many unusual species, including the Kiwi, a prehistoric reptile called a tuatara, and various other reptiles and parrots. However, its only native land mammal is a bat.
- **Antarctica's Ice** Antarctica has about 90% of the world's permanent ice. Scientists estimate that if all of the ice in Antarctica were to melt, the oceans would rise by about 200 feet, flooding a large proportion of the world's land.

Regional Atlas

Regional Atlas Activity

Comparing and Contrasting Have students study the elevations shown on the Physical map. **Ask: Which area has the region's highest elevation?** *(Antarctica)* **How do you know?** *(A large proportion of the continent is shaded orange, indicating an elevation of 6,500 feet or more.)* Assign each student one of the following land areas: Australia, Antarctica, New Zealand, or Papua New Guinea. Tell students to create models of their landmass with modeling clay, paying special attention to the elevations. Have students work together to make certain that their models are constructed using the same elevation scale. **OL**

Map Skills

Answers:

1. in southeastern Australia
2. Mt. Wilhelm; in Papua New Guinea

Skills Practice

Ask: Which deserts are found in Australia? *(Great Sandy Desert, Gibson Desert, Great Victoria Desert)* **Which country generally has a higher elevation, Australia or New Zealand?** *(New Zealand)*

Australia, Oceania, and Antarctica

PHYSICAL

Elevations

13,100 ft. (4,000 m)
6,500 ft. (2,000 m)
1,600 ft. (500 m)
650 ft. (200 m)
0 ft. (0 m)
Below sea level

▲ Mountain peak

0 — 1,000 kilometers
0 — 1,000 miles
Mercator projection

0 — 1,000 kilometers
0 — 1,000 miles
Lambert Azimuthal Equal-Area projection

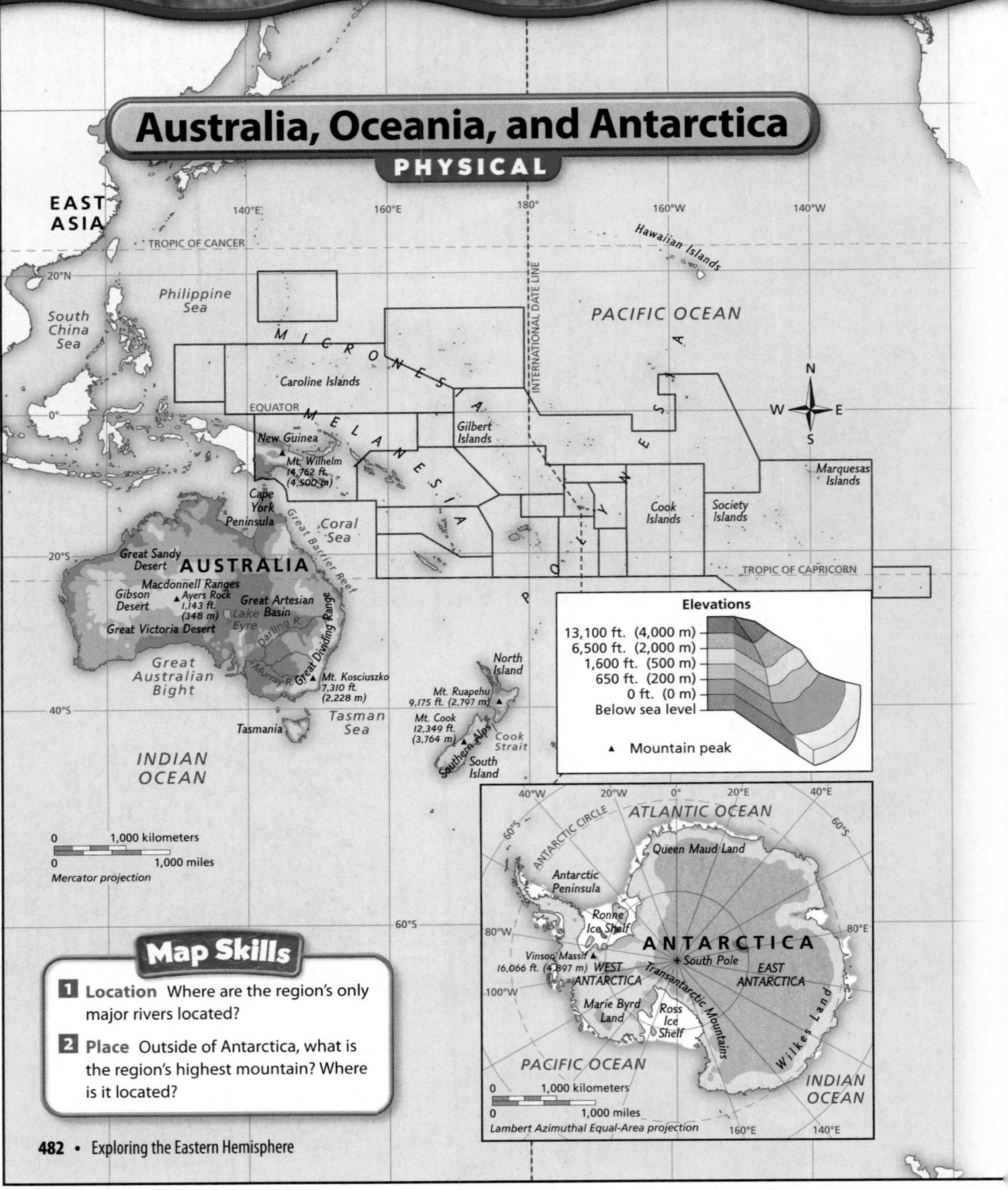

Map Skills

1. **Location** Where are the region's only major rivers located?
2. **Place** Outside of Antarctica, what is the region's highest mountain? Where is it located?

Background: Land and Climate

A Variety of Landforms The landforms of Australia, Oceania, and Antarctica have been shaped over millions of years by plate tectonics, volcanic activity, erosion, and biological processes.

The continent of Australia is mostly flat. Coastal plains in the south and southeast have the nation's best farmland. The Great Dividing Range, the rocky face of a plateau running the length of eastern Australia, separates the coastal plains from the outback in the west.

The thousands of islands of Oceania were formed by three processes. The high islands, formed hundreds of years ago by volcanic activity, have fertile volcanic soil. The low islands were formed by coral, the skeletons of millions of tiny sea animals, and have little soil at all. Continental islands were formed by the rising and folding of rock caused by tectonic activity. They have rugged mountains, plateaus, and valleys.

Antarctica consists of a high plateau in the east, where the South Pole is located, and a group of islands linked by ice in the west. A huge ice cap, 2 miles thick in some places, covers the entire continent.

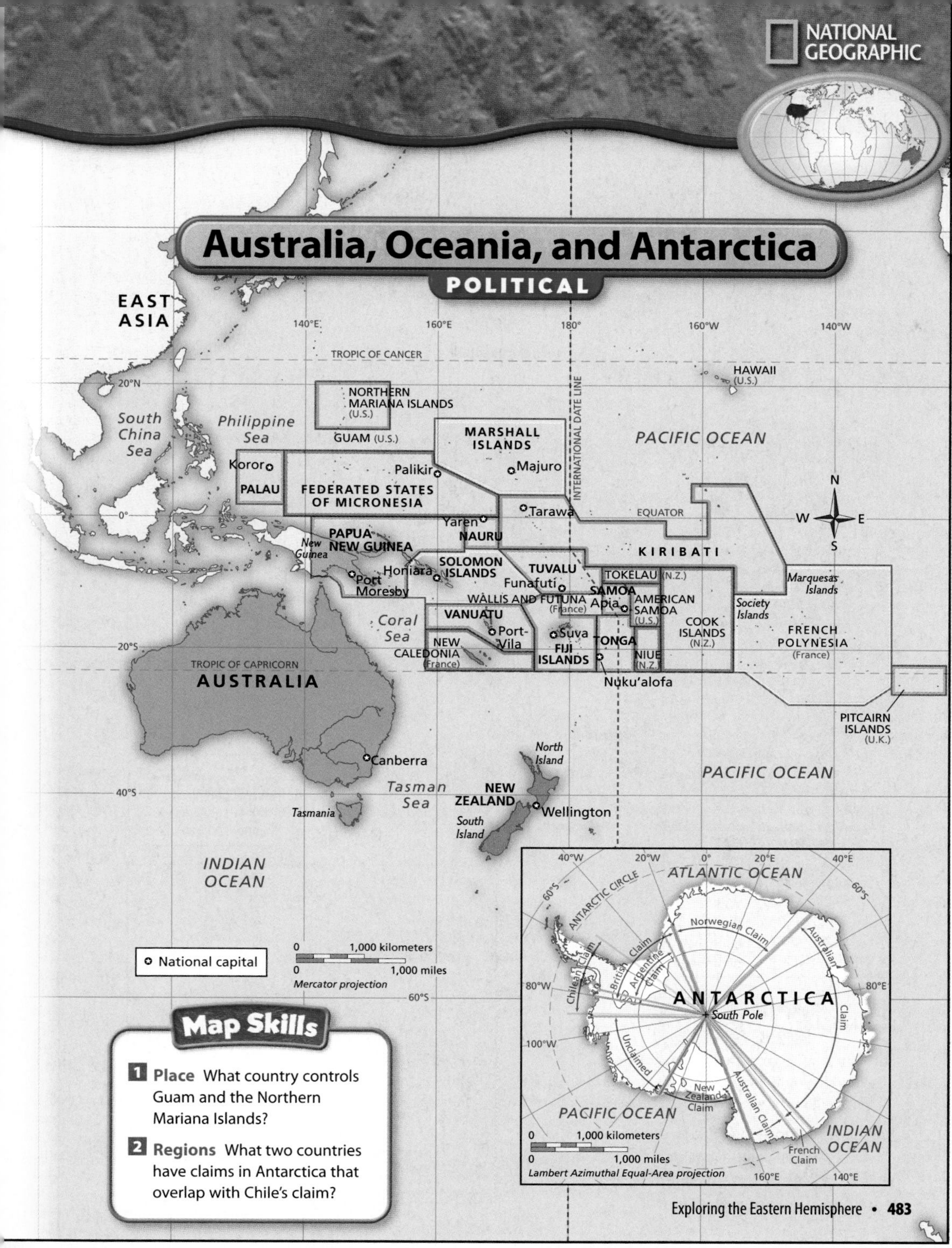

NATIONAL GEOGRAPHIC

Australia, Oceania, and Antarctica

POLITICAL

Map Skills

1. **Place** What country controls Guam and the Northern Mariana Islands?
2. **Regions** What two countries have claims in Antarctica that overlap with Chile's claim?

Regional Atlas Activity

Exploring Political History Point out to students that on the Political map in the Regional Atlas, many of the islands have the initials of another country below the name, which indicates that the island is a territory of that country. **Ask: Which countries have territories in the Pacific islands?** *(Japan, United States, France, the United Kingdom, and New Zealand)* Have students use encyclopedias to compare the political status of Guam, Hawaii, and American Samoa. *(Guam— unincorporated territory of the United States residents are U.S. citizens; Hawaii—a U.S. state; American Samoa—an unincorporated U.S. territory, residents are U.S. nationals, not U.S. citizens)*

Organize students into groups. Assign each group an island or a group of islands. Have students research the history of the island, its form of government, and whether it is ruled by another country. Then have each group present a five-minute oral report to the class. **OL**

Map Skills

Answers:

1. the United States
2. Great Britain and Argentina have overlapping claims with Chile.

Skills Practice

Ask: What is the capital of the Marshall Islands? *(Majuro)* **What is the easternmost island in Oceania?** *(Pitcairn Islands)*

Background: Current Issues

Fragile Environments Some of Australia's economic activities have damaged the environment. Because trees have been cut down for ranches and land has been overgrazed, much of the topsoil has blown away. The continent's unique wildlife also has been threatened by animals brought in from other regions of the world.

In parts of Oceania, nuclear weapons testing has had a devastating impact on the environment. Radiation from the nuclear weapons tests of Western nations in the 1940s caused many island residents to get sick or die. Although the testing was halted, radiation poisoned the land, water, and vegetation.

Antarctica's environment is threatened by global warming. If higher temperatures melt ice, the plants that live on the ice may be lost. This threatens the survival of those animals in Antarctica that depend on the plants for food. Ice melt could also raise sea levels, threatening to flood many low-lying islands and coastal areas around the world.

Regional Atlas

Regional Atlas Activity

Drawing Conclusions Have students look at the Population Density map and the Economic Resources map in the Regional Atlas. **Ask:** **Where are most of Australia's cities located?** *(Most Australian cities are on the southeast coast, although Perth is on the southwest coast.)* **Which of these cities are centers of manufacturing and trade?** *(Perth, Melbourne, Sydney, and Brisbane)* **To what extent do you think the distribution of Australia's natural resources explains the distribution of Australia's population?** *(Many of Australia's natural resources are located along the coasts, which partly explains the concentration of Australia's population there. However, some natural resources are found far inland, where few people live. The low population density in these areas, despite the presence of natural resources, may be explained by the desert and near-desert conditions in the interior of the country.)* **OL**

Map Skills

Answers:

1. Possible answer: Much of central and western Australia is desert.
2. In general, the population density of North Island is higher than that of South Island. This is especially true around the city of Auckland, the largest city in New Zealand.

Australia, Oceania, and Antarctica

POPULATION DENSITY

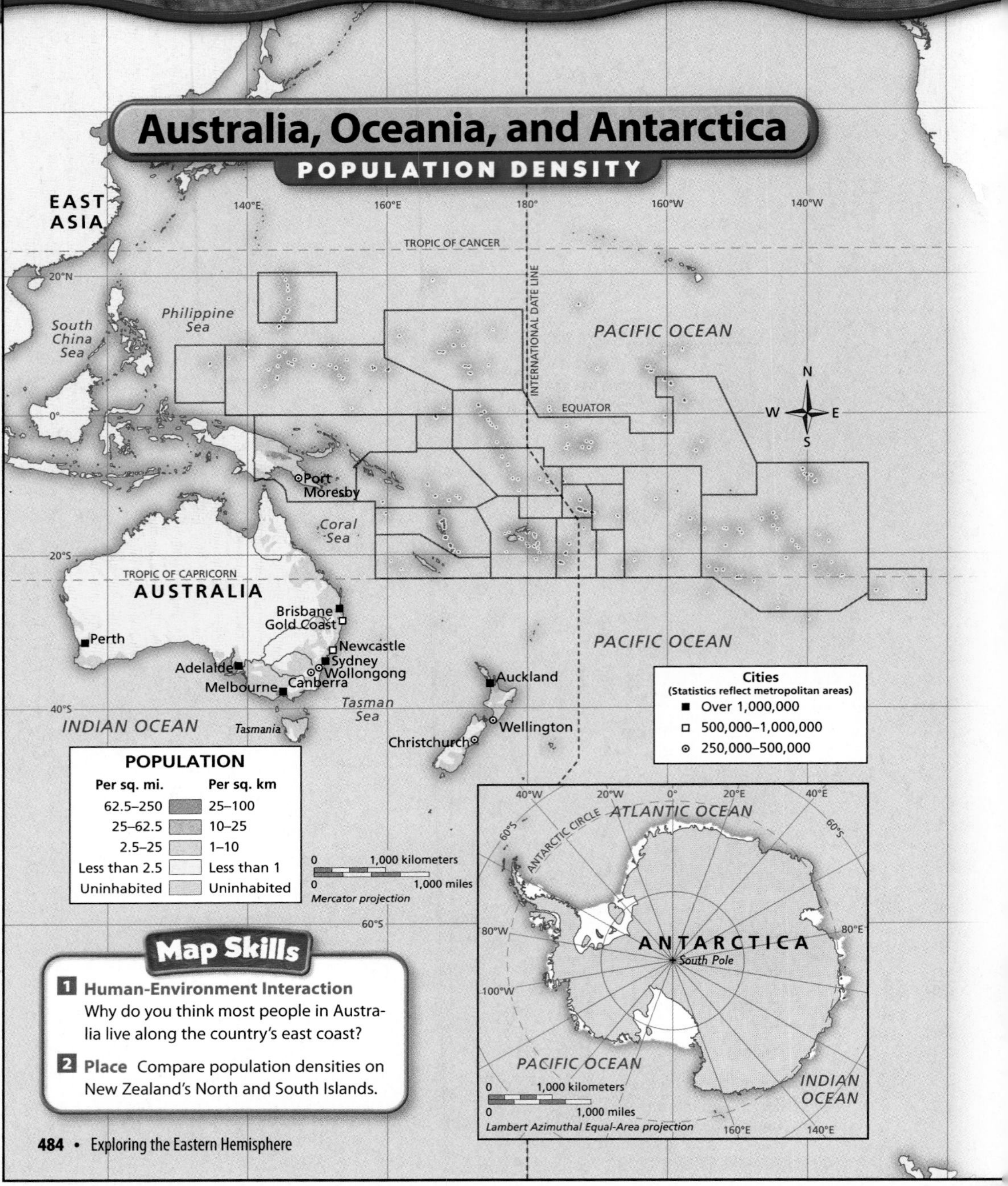

POPULATION

Per sq. mi.	Per sq. km
62.5–250	25–100
25–62.5	10–25
2.5–25	1–10
Less than 2.5	Less than 1
Uninhabited	Uninhabited

Cities
(Statistics reflect metropolitan areas)
- ■ Over 1,000,000
- □ 500,000–1,000,000
- ⊙ 250,000–500,000

Mercator projection

Lambert Azimuthal Equal-Area projection

Map Skills

1 Human-Environment Interaction Why do you think most people in Australia live along the country's east coast?

2 Place Compare population densities on New Zealand's North and South Islands.

Background: People and Culture

Diverse Populations People of European descent, mainly British and Irish, make up more than 90% of Australia's population. People of British descent make up 75% of New Zealand's population. Both countries also have a sizable native population. About 400,000 Aborigines live in Australia, and many Aboriginal languages are still spoken there. In New Zealand, the Maori make up about 13% of the population, and Maori is the official second language of the country. Both countries are becoming more diverse, as Asian and Pacific Islander populations grow.

The peoples of Oceania speak more than 1,200 languages. The largest ethnic groups of Oceania are Melanesians, Micronesians, and Polynesians. However, these groups consist of many smaller groups. Most islands in Oceania also have small populations of European descent. French Polynesia, one of the smaller islands in Oceania, has a large population of European descent—more than a third its total population.

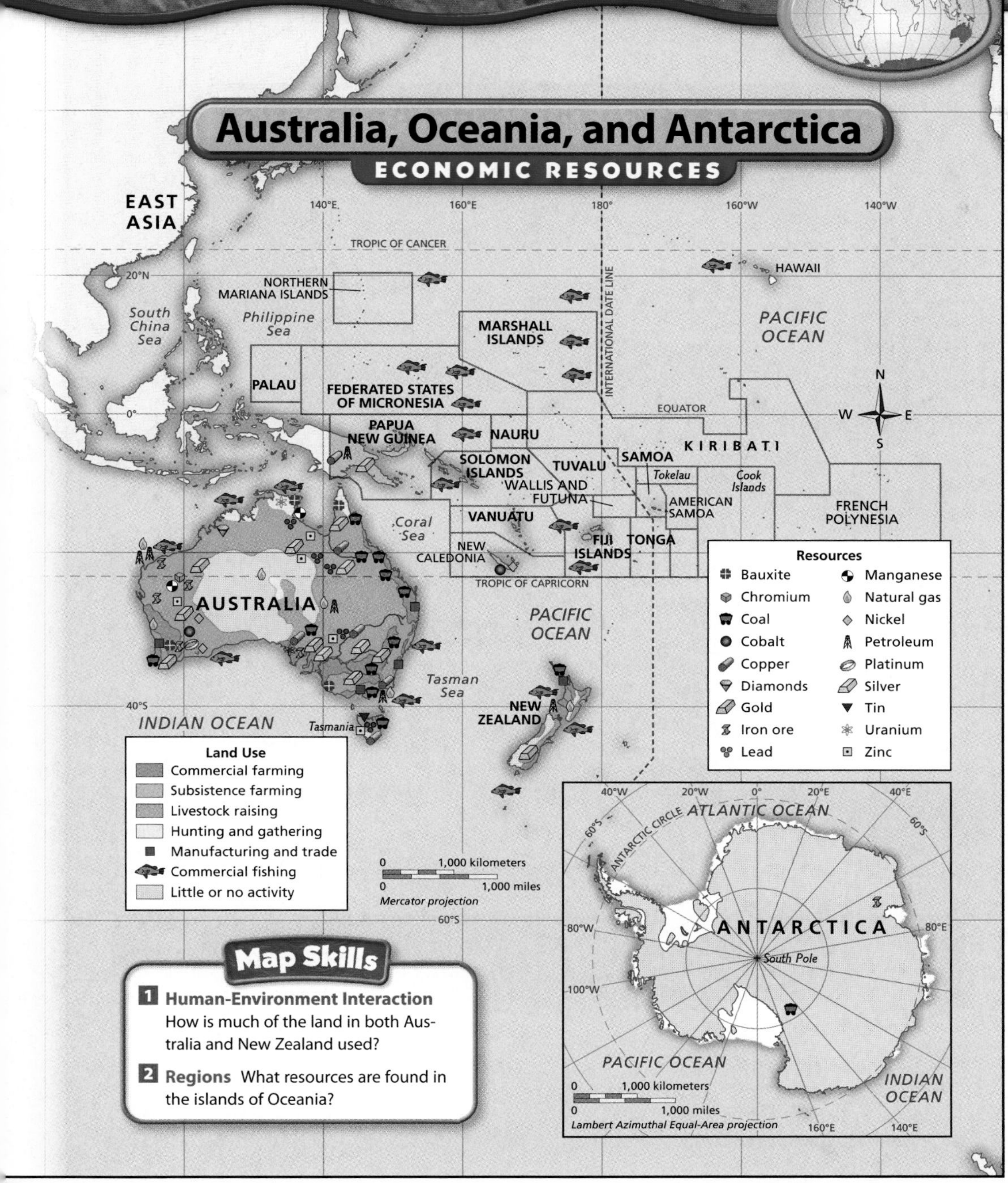

NATIONAL GEOGRAPHIC

Australia, Oceania, and Antarctica

ECONOMIC RESOURCES

Map Skills

1 Human-Environment Interaction How is much of the land in both Australia and New Zealand used?

2 Regions What resources are found in the islands of Oceania?

Regional Atlas Activity

Comparing and Contrasting

Have students study New Zealand and Australia on the Economic Resources map. Draw a Venn diagram on the board to compare the resources of the two countries. Ask student volunteers to come to the board to place the economic resources and types of land use from the map in the appropriate parts of the diagram.

When finished, have students create a Venn diagram in their notebooks comparing the economic resources of Papua New Guinea and New Zealand. **BL**

Map Skills

Answers:

1. It is used for raising livestock.
2. copper, petroleum, cobalt, coal, nickle, and natural gas

Skills Practice

Ask: What are the primary economic activities in Oceania, other than New Zealand? *(commercial fishing and subsistence farming)* **What natural resources are found in Tasmania?** *(tin, zinc, lead, coal, and copper)*

Background: The Economy

Economic Successes and Challenges Australia has a prosperous economy. It benefits from the mining of plentiful natural resources, including gold, diamonds, coal, oil, and natural gas. Some Australians have cattle and sheep ranches in the outback. Farmers are able to grow crops with the help of irrigation techniques.

New Zealand's economy depends in large part on international trade. The main exports are meat and wool. In fact, the country is home to more sheep than people. New Zealand's economy has diversified in recent years, and farmers now produce a variety of agricultural products, including apples, grapes, barley, wheat, corn, and kiwifruit.

Many people in the rest of Oceania live by subsistence farming and fishing. Plantations in countries like Papua New Guinea produce coffee, palm oil, cocoa, and coconut oil for export. In many areas, people still follow traditional ways. The poorest islands in Micronesia and Polynesia depend on foreign aid to survive.

Regional Atlas Activity

Identifying Organize students into pairs. Have each pair create a set of index cards with the name of a country from the region on one side and its capital on the other. Students should take turns quizzing their partners, showing them the country name and asking for the name of the capital.

As students master the capitals of the region, have them show their partners the names of the capitals and ask them to identify the country in which it is located. **BL**

FastFacts

The World's Last Continent

Antarctica was not "discovered" until the early 1800s. In January 1820, two people claimed to have been the first to sight Antarctica. The first was the leader of a Russian expedition. The second was an Englishman. In November of the same year, an American gained conclusive evidence of having seen the mainland. However, these men might not have been the first people to spot Antarctica. A Maori legend tells of a New Zealand Polynesian war canoe under the command of Ui-te-Rangiora that sailed far enough south to have sighted the continent in A.D. 650.

Australia, Oceania, and Antarctica

Country and Capital	Literacy Rate	Population and Density	Land Area	Life Expectancy (Years)	GDP* Per Capita (U.S. dollars)	Television Sets (per 1,000 people)	Flag and Language
AUSTRALIA Canberra	100%	20,400,000 7 per sq. mi. 3 per sq. km	2,988,888 sq. mi. 7,741,184 sq. km	80	$30,700	716	English
FEDERATED STATES OF MICRONESIA Palikir	89.1%	100,000 370 per sq. mi. 143 per sq. km	270 sq. mi. 699 sq. km	67	$2,000	20	English
FIJI Suva	93.7%	800,000 113 per sq. mi. 44 per sq. km	7,054 sq. mi. 18,270 sq. km	68	$5,900	110	English
Tarawa (Bairiki) KIRIBATI	NA	100,000 355 per sq. mi. 136 per sq. km	282 sq. mi. 730 sq. km	63	$800	23	I-Kiribati, English
MARSHALL ISLANDS Majuro	93.7%	100,000 1,449 per sq. mi. 559 per sq. km	69 sq. mi. 179 sq. km	68	$1,600	information not available	Marshallese, English
NAURU Yaren	NA	10,000 1,111 per sq. mi. 435 per sq. km	9 sq. mi. 23 sq. km	61	$5,000	1	Nauruan, English
Wellington NEW ZEALAND	99%	4,100,000 39 per sq. mi. 15 per sq. km	104,452 sq. mi. 270,529 sq. km	79	$23,200	516	English, Maori
Koror PALAU	92%	20,000 112 per sq. mi. 43 per sq. km	178 sq. mi. 461 sq. km	70	$9,000	98	Palauan, English
UNITED STATES Washington, D.C.	97%	296,500,000 80 per sq. mi. 31 per sq. km	3,717,796 sq. mi. 9,629,047 sq. km	78	$40,100	844	English

*Gross Domestic Product

Countries and flags not drawn to scale

Activity: Using the Chart

Locating Information Organize students into pairs. Assign each pair a country in the chart. **Ask: What do you notice about the flag of your assigned country?** *(Answers will vary, but some students may notice that their flag includes the British flag in the upper-left corner.)* Have each pair research the origin of the flag of their assigned country. Tell them to find information such as the year it was created; the meaning of its symbols, colors, and design; its designer; and any other relevant information about the flag's origin. Direct students to appropriate reference sources, including atlases, encyclopedias, and reliable online news and information services. After students have researched their country's flag, have each pair create a poster with a representation of their flag in the center with information about its origin displayed around it. When finished, have each pair of students present their poster to the class. **OL**

Australia, Oceania, and Antarctica

Country and Capital	Literacy Rate	Population and Density	Land Area	Life Expectancy (Years)	GDP* Per Capita (U.S. dollars)	Television Sets (per 1,000 people)	Flag and Language
PAPUA NEW GUINEA Port Moresby	64.6%	5,900,000 33 per sq. mi. 13 per sq. km	178,703 sq. mi. 462,839 sq. km	55	$2,200	13	Melanesian Pidgin
SAMOA Apia	99.7%	200,000 182 per sq. mi. 70 per sq. km	1,097 sq. mi. 2,841 sq. km	73	$5,600	56	Samoan
SOLOMON ISLANDS Honiara	NA	500,000 45 per sq. mi. 17 per sq. km	11,158 sq. mi. 28,889 sq. km	62	$1,700	16	Melanesian Pidgin, English
TONGA Nuku'alofa	98.5%	100,000 345 per sq. mi. 133 per sq. km	290 sq. mi. 751 sq. km	71	$2,300	61	Tongan, English
TUVALU Funafuti	NA	10,000 1,000 per sq. mi. 385 per sq. km	10 sq. mi. 26 sq. km	64	$1,100	9	Tuvaluan
VANUATU Port-Vila	53%	200,000 42 per sq. mi. 16 per sq. km	4,707 sq. mi. 12,191 sq. km	67	$2,900	12	Local Languages, Bislama
UNITED STATES Washington, D.C.	97%	296,500,000 80 per sq. mi. 31 per sq. km	3,717,796 sq. mi. 9,629,047 sq. km	78	$40,100	844	English

Sources: *CIA World Factbook*, 2005; Population Reference Bureau, *World Population Data Sheet*, 2005.

For more country facts, go to the **Nations of the World Databank** at glencoe.com.

Regional Atlas Activity

Synthesizing Information Organize students into pairs. Give each pair a copy of the Regional Atlas chart pages. Leave enough room on the copy for students to add another column on the right-hand side. Tell students to add another column with the heading "Island Region." Then have them look at the Physical map in the Regional Atlas to find the three island regions of Micronesia, Melanesia, and Polynesia. Have students identify the island region of each nation in Oceania by comparing the Physical map to the Political map in the Regional Atlas. Tell pairs to write "Micronesia," "Melanesia," or "Polynesia" for each nation in Oceania in the new column on their chart. **OL**

Activity: Using the Chart

Determining Cause and Effect Ask: Excluding New Zealand, which three countries in Oceania have the highest GDP per capita? *(Palau, $9,000; Fiji, $5,900; and Samoa, $5,600)* **Which three countries have the lowest GDP per capita?** *(Kiribati, $800; Tuvalu, $1,100; and the Marshall Islands, $1,600)*

Ask students what factors shown in the Regional Atlas might be related to the GDP per capita in these countries—in other words, what factors might either have an effect on the GDP per capita or be caused by the GDP per capita. Tell students to use encyclopedias, almanacs, or government Web sites to locate information about these six countries. Have students work in groups to create a chart showing the GDP per capita of the six countries and factors related to the GDP per capita. Have them explain the relationship between the GDP per capita and the other factors in a brief report. **AL**

TEACH

INTRODUCTION

The following **Skills Handbook** offers opportunities to practice individual critical thinking and social studies skills. Students can benefit in multiple ways from completing the lessons. First, being equipped with these skills makes students' reading more meaningful and supports the content of the text. Second, the lessons give students practice in using skills they will need to complete standardized tests successfully because many of these skills are assessed on standardized tests.

You may use the lessons at any point in the text and in any order that you wish. You also can use these lessons as review for students who need extra practice with these skills.

Skills Handbook

Contents

Interpreting Political Cartoons

Skills Handbook

Why Learn This Skill?

Political cartoons express opinions through art. The cartoons appear in newspapers, magazines, books, and on the Internet. Political cartoons usually focus on public figures, political events, or economic or social conditions. This type of art can give you a summary of an event or circumstance, along with the artist's opinion, in an entertaining way. 

1 Learn It!

Follow these steps to interpret political cartoons:

- Read the title, caption, or conversation balloons. They help you identify the subject of the cartoon.
- Identify the characters or people in the cartoon. They may be caricatures, or unrealistic drawings that exaggerate the characters' physical features.
- Identify any symbols. Symbols are objects that stand for something else. An example is the American flag, which is a symbol of our country. Commonly recognized symbols may not be labeled. Unusual symbols might be labeled.
- Examine the actions in the cartoon—what is happening and why?
- Identify the cartoonist's purpose. What statement or idea is he or she trying to express? Decide if the cartoonist wants to persuade, criticize, or just make people think.

2 Practice It!

On a separate sheet of paper, answer these questions about the political cartoon below.

1. What is the subject of the cartoon?
2. What words give clues to the meaning of the cartoon?
3. What item seems out of place?
4. What message do you think the cartoonist is trying to send?

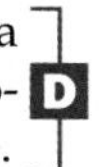

3 Apply It!

Bring a newsmagazine to class. With a partner, analyze the message in each political cartoon you find in the magazine. D

S Skill Practice

Visual Literacy Before the class reads the lesson, distribute copies of two or three political cartoons to small groups of students. Be sure that the selected cartoons contain examples of some of the characteristics described in the lesson: title, caption, conversation balloons, caricatures or exaggerations, and symbols. Have groups compare their cartoons to list the characteristics of cartoons.
Ask: **What is your cartoon's message? What details helped you figure out the message?** *(List group replies on the board, grouping similar responses together.)* OL

D Differentiated Instruction

Visual/Spatial Ask students to choose an issue of importance to them. Tell them to choose a school, community, or national issue. Have students create a cartoon that illustrates their opinions about the issue. Display completed cartoons on a bulletin board. OL

Glencoe Skillbuilder Interactive Workbook CD-ROM, Level 1
This Interactive CD-ROM reinforces student mastery of essential social studies skills.

Additional Support

Skills Practice Answers

Practice It! Answers

1. the history of violent weapons
2. the name of the museum (Weapons of Violence), the signs under the other exhibits (rock, spear, gun, automatic gun)
3. the television set
4. Violence on television is responsible for violence in real life, just as the other weapons in the display are.

Apply It! Answer

Students should use the information under "Learn It!" to help them interpret the cartoons they find in their magazines. Some magazines may not have many cartoons. If this is the case, allow students to share their magazines.

R1 Reading Strategy

Activating Prior Knowledge Ask students what they think would happen if they watch a movie the evening before an important test instead of studying. *(Students likely would perform less well on the test than they would have if they had studied.)* **Ask:** **Why do you think this outcome is likely? On what factors are you basing your predictions?** *(prior experience, experience of others, common sense)* BL

R2 Reading Strategy

Predicting Have students read these questions, then read the first paragraph from a section in their textbooks. Ask them to think about what might happen next. Then have them read the following paragraphs to see if their predictions are true. OL

Glencoe Skillbuilder Interactive Workbook CD-ROM, Level 1
This Interactive CD-ROM reinforces student mastery of essential social studies skills.

Additional Support

Predicting

Why Learn This Skill?

You have probably read about people making difficult decisions based on something they think *might* happen. You will have a better understanding of why people make certain choices when you consider the factors that influenced their decisions.

1 Learn It!

R1 As you read a paragraph or section in your book, think about what might happen next. What you think will happen is your *prediction*. A prediction does not have a correct or incorrect answer. A prediction is an educated guess of what might happen next based on facts.

R2 To make a prediction, ask yourself:

- What happened in this paragraph or section?
- What prior knowledge do I have about the information in the text?
- What similar circumstances do I know of?
- What do I think might happen next?
- Test your prediction: read further to see if you were correct.

Aztec shield

2 Practice It!

To practice the skill, read the following paragraph about the Aztec Empire. Then answer the questions.

In the late 1400s and early 1500s, Spanish explorers arrived in the Americas. They were greatly impressed by the magnificent cities and the great riches of the Native Americans.

In 1519 a Spanish army led by Hernán Cortés landed on Mexico's Gulf coast. He and about 600 soldiers marched to Tenochtitlán, which they had heard was filled with gold.

1. Choose the outcome that is most likely to occur between the Native Americans and the Spaniards.
   - **a.** The Spaniards will conquer the Native Americans.
   - **b.** The Native Americans will conquer the Spaniards.
   - **c.** The two groups will become friends.
2. What clues in the text help you make your prediction?

3 Apply It!

Watch a television show or a movie. Halfway through the show, write down your prediction of how it will end. At the end of the show, check your prediction. Were you correct? What clues did you use to make your prediction?

Skills Practice Answers

Practice It! Answers

1. a
2. The Spaniards were impressed by the great riches of the Native Americans and came to Tenochtitlán because they had heard it was filled with gold. They came with an army of 600 soldiers, so they seem intent on conquering the Native Americans.

Apply It! Answer

Answers will vary; students should have logical arguments to explain their predictions.

Analyzing Library and Research Resources

Why Learn This Skill?

Imagine that your teacher asked you to write a report about the physical geography of Australia using library or Internet resources. Knowing how to choose sources that contain accurate information will help you save time in the library or on the Internet. You will also be able to write a better report.

Learn It!

Not all sources will be useful for your report on Australia's physical geography. Even some sources that involve topics about Australia will not always provide the information you want. In analyzing sources for your research project, choose items that are nonfiction and that contain the most information about your topic.

When choosing research resources, ask these questions:

- Is the information up-to-date?
- Does a book's index have several page references listed for the topic? **C**
- Is the research written in a way that is easy to understand? **R**
- Are there helpful illustrations and photos?

Practice It!

Look at the following list of sources. Which would be most helpful in writing a report on the physical geography of Australia? Explain your choices.

(1) A current travel guide to Australia

(2) A book about Australia's landforms and climates

(3) A children's storybook about an Australian kangaroo

(4) A student's notes on the Internet about a family trip to Australia

(5) A study of the rise and fall of the British Empire

(6) A Web site with physical maps of Australia

(7) A book about Australian government

(8) A geographical dictionary

Apply It!

Go to your local library or use the Internet to create a bibliography of sources you might use to write a report on the physical geography of Australia. Explain why you would choose each source.

Ayers Rock in central Australia

C Critical Thinking

Making Inferences **Ask:** What does having several pages listed for the topic tell you about the book? *(how much information the book has about the topic)* What other parts of the book could you use to make this judgment? *(the table of contents)* **OL**

R Reading Strategy

Reading Secondary Sources
Ask: How could you answer this question about a source? *(Students may say that they could read a few paragraphs or a couple of pages of text to judge the source's readability.)* **OL**

Glencoe Skillbuilder Interactive Workbook CD-ROM, Level 1
This Interactive CD-ROM reinforces student mastery of essential social studies skills.

Skills Practice Answers

Practice It! Answers

Students should indicate that the most helpful would be 2 and 6, because they deal specifically with the physical geography of Australia. However, they might also get some information from 1 and 8.

Apply It! Answer

Encourage students to review each source to evaluate the comprehensiveness and accuracy of the information presented.

R Reading Strategy

Organizing Assign students a section in the textbook and have them look for ideas and facts that are grouped together or have similar characteristics. Tell them to list these characteristics, or categories, as the headings on a chart. Then tell them to look for details as they read and to fill them in under the proper categories on the chart. **OL**

D Differentiated Instruction

Logical/Mathematical Have students study the chart on this page. **Ask: Does the United States export more to, or import more from, these three countries?** *(The United States imports more from these countries.)* **How do you know?** *(The value of U.S. exports to each country is less than the value of exports to the United States from each country.)* **AL**

Glencoe Skillbuilder Interactive Workbook CD-ROM, Level 1
This Interactive CD-ROM reinforces student mastery of essential social studies skills.

Additional Support

Skills Handbook

Interpreting a Chart

Why Learn This Skill?

To make learning easier, you can organize information into groups of related facts and ideas. One way to organize information is with a chart. A chart presents written or numerical information in columns and rows. It helps you to remember and compare information more easily.

1 Learn It!

To organize information in a chart, follow these steps:

- Decide what information you must organize.
- R Identify several major categories of ideas or facts about the topic, and use these categories as column headings.
- Find information that fits into each category, and write those facts or ideas under the appropriate column heading.

2 Practice It!

On a separate sheet of paper, answer the following questions using the chart at the bottom of this page.

1. What type of information does the chart contain?
2. What other related information appears in the chart?
3. Canada also exports clothing and beverages to the United States. Is it necessary to create a new chart to show this information?

3 Apply It!

Create a chart to track your school assignments. Work with five areas of information: Subject, Assignment, Description, Due Date, and Date Completed. Be sure to keep your chart up-to-date.

U.S. International Trade (D)

	Japan	United Kingdom	Canada
Exports to U.S.	Engines, rubber goods, cars, trucks, buses	Dairy products, beverages, petroleum products	Wheat, minerals, paper, mining machines
Value of Exports to U.S.	$138 billion	$51.1 billion	$287.9 billion
Imports from U.S.	Meat, fish, sugar, tobacco, coffee	Fruit, tobacco, electrical equipment	Fish, sugar, metals, clothing
Value of Imports from U.S.	$55.4 billion	$38.6 billion	$211.3 billion

Source: *CIA World Factbook, 2006; United States Census Bureau, Foreign Trade Statistics, 2005.*

Skills Practice Answers

Practice It! Answers

1. exports to the U.S. from Japan, the United Kingdom, and Canada, and imports from the U.S. to these countries
2. the value of these exports and imports
3. No, this information could be added to the list of items under the Canada column heading, in the Exports to the U.S. row.

Apply It! Answer

Check that students have constructed their charts properly with the five areas of information as column headings. Encourage them to keep the chart up-to-date.

Making Comparisons

Why Learn This Skill?

Suppose you want to buy a portable CD player, and you must choose among three models. To make this decision, you would probably compare various features of the three models, such as price, sound quality, size, and so on. After you compare the models, you will choose the one that is best for you. In your studies of world geography, you must often compare countries of the world to identify **C** patterns, make predictions, or make generalizations about regions.

Learn It!

When making comparisons, you identify and examine two or more places, peoples, economies, or forms of government. Then you identify any similarities between two topics, or ways the two topics are alike. **R**

When making comparisons, apply the following steps:

- Decide what topics to compare. Clue words such as *also, as well as, like, same as,* and *similar to* can help you identify when topics are being compared.
- Read the information about each topic carefully.
- Identify what information is similar for both topics.

2 Practice It!

To practice the skill, analyze the information in the chart at the bottom of this page. Then answer these questions.

1. What countries are being compared?
2. What categories for each country are being compared?
3. In what ways are the United States and the United Kingdom similar?
4. Suppose you wanted to compare the two countries in more detail. What other categories might you use?

Apply It!

Think about two sports that are played at your school. Make a chart comparing categories such as where the games are played, who plays them, what equipment is used, and so on.

The United States and the United Kingdom

	United States	United Kingdom
Location	North America	Europe
Language	English	English
Form of Government	Federal republic	Constitutional monarchy
Popular Sports	Baseball, football, basketball	Soccer, rugby, cricket
Popular Foods	Hamburgers, hot dogs	Fish and chips, roast beef

C Critical Thinking

Making Inferences Have students brainstorm some things that geographers might want to compare. *(Answers may include physical features, climates, cultures, economies, and so on.)* **OL**

R Reading Strategy

Activating Prior Knowledge Write the words *cat* and *dog* on the board. **Ask: How are the two animals similar?** *(Both are mammals, have fur and four legs, and are popular pets.)* **How are they different?** *(Cats meow, dogs bark; cats climb trees, dogs do not; cats are felines, dogs are canines; cats are often solitary, dogs like to live in packs.)* Point out to students that the skill of making comparisons includes identifying how things are similar to and different from one another. **BL**

Glencoe Skillbuilder Interactive Workbook CD-ROM, Level 1

This Interactive CD-ROM reinforces student mastery of essential social studies skills.

Skills Practice Answers

Practice It! Answers

1. the United States and the United Kingdom
2. location, language, form of government, popular sports, and popular foods
3. They share the same language (English); they both enjoy various sports.
4. Answers might include ethnic groups, religions, population, land area, and so on.

Apply It! Answer

Answers should show an understanding of the two chosen sports and the similarities and differences between them.

S Skill Practice

Visual Literacy Point out to students that images can be primary sources as well. Have them look through their textbook and identify images that are primary sources, and discuss what aspect of history the images teach us. **OL**

C Critical Thinking

Analyzing Primary Sources Ask students to contribute to a class list of questions to ask about a written primary source document to help them determine its reliability. *(Questions might include who wrote it, what biases the author might have had, what the author's purpose was in writing the document, and so on.)* **AL**

Glencoe Skillbuilder Interactive Workbook CD-ROM, Level 1
This Interactive CD-ROM reinforces student mastery of essential social studies skills.

Additional Support

Analyzing Primary Sources

Why Learn This Skill?

People who study history examine pieces of evidence to reconstruct events. These types of evidence—both written and illustrated—are called *primary sources*. Examining primary sources can help you understand the history of a place.

1 Learn It!

S Primary sources are firsthand accounts that describe a historical event or time period. They can include letters, diaries, photographs and pictures, news articles, legal documents, stories, literature, and artwork.

C Ask yourself the following questions when analyzing primary sources:

- What is the primary source?
- Who created it?
- Where is it from?
- When was it created?
- What does it reveal about the topic I am studying?

Practice It!

The following primary source is from *The Log of Christopher Columbus.* Christopher Columbus reached the new world on October 12, 1492. Columbus's entry explains what occurred when he and his shipmates encountered Native Americans. Read the entry, and then answer the questions that follow.

> *October 12:*
> *The people here called this island* Guanahani *in their language, and their speech is very fluent [easily flowing], although I do not understand any of it. They are friendly . . . people who [bear] no arms except for small spears, and they have no iron. I showed one my sword, and through ignorance he grabbed it by the blade and cut himself. . . .*
> *. . . They traded and gave everything they had with good will, but it seems to me that they have very little and are poor in everything. . . .*
> *This afternoon the people of San Salvador came swimming to our ships and in boats made from one log. They brought us parrots, balls of cotton thread, spears, and many other things. . . . For these items we swapped them little glass beads and hawks' bells.*
>
> —*The Log of Christopher Columbus*

1. Why did Columbus believe that the Native Americans had no knowledge about weapons?
2. Does Columbus fear the Native Americans? Explain.
3. What items did Columbus and his crew exchange with the Native Americans?
4. Why is this reading a primary source?

Apply It!

Find a primary source from your past, such as a photo, newspaper clipping, or diary entry. Explain to the class what it shows about that time in your life.

Skills Practice Answers

Practice It! Answers

1. He saw them bearing only small spears and no iron weapons, and one of the Native Americans grabbed Columbus's sword by the blade and cut himself.
2. No, he refers to them as "friendly" and as giving everything they had with "good will." He allowed them to swim to his ships and trade items.
3. Columbus and his crew exchanged little glass beads and hawks' bells for parrots, balls of cotton thread, spears, and other items.
4. because it is a firsthand account of Columbus's encounter with the Native Americans, from Columbus's own log

Apply It! Answer

Make sure students know that they will share their primary sources on a voluntary basis. Encourage students to respond based on their interests or likes and dislikes, but not to reveal personal information that they may be uncomfortable sharing.

Recognizing Bias

Why Learn This Skill?

If you say, "Cats make better pets than dogs," you are stating a bias. A *bias* is an attitude that favors one way of thinking over another. It can prevent you from looking at a situation in a reasonable or truthful way. C1

Learn It!

Most people have feelings and ideas that affect their point of view on a subject. Their viewpoint, or *bias*, influences the way they interpret events. For this reason, an idea that is stated as a fact may really be only an opinion. Recognizing bias will help you judge the accuracy of what you read.

To recognize bias, follow these steps:

- Identify the speaker or writer and examine his or her views. Why did he or she speak or write about a particular issue?
- Look for language that shows emotion or opinion. Look for words such as *all, never, best, worst, might,* or *should.*
- Examine the information for imbalances. Is it written from one point of view? Does it take into consideration other points of view?
- Identify statements of fact. Factual statements usually answer the *who, what, where,* and *when* questions.
- Does the writer use facts to support his or her point of view?

C2

2 Practice It!

Read the following statement about wildlife in Africa, and answer the questions below.

Mountain gorillas live in the misty mountain forests of East Africa. Logging and mining, however, are destroying the forests. Unless the forests are protected, the gorillas will lose their homes and disappear forever. As a concerned African naturalist, I must emphasize that this will be the worst event in Africa's history.

1. What problem is the speaker addressing?
2. What reasons does the speaker give for the loss of the forests?
3. What is the speaker's point of view, or bias?
4. What words give clues as to the speaker's bias?

Apply It!

Choose a letter from the editorial page of a newspaper. Summarize the issue being discussed and the writer's bias about the issue. Describe a possible opposing opinion and who might have it and why.

Mountain gorilla

C1 Critical Thinking

Analyzing Information Ask: Is this paragraph saying that it is wrong to have opinions? If not, what is the point of the paragraph? *(The paragraph is not warning against having opinions but against allowing opinions to cloud one's judgment.)* **OL**

C2 Critical Thinking

Comparing and Contrasting Distribute copies of two reviews of the same movie, book, television show, or music CD. After students have read both, ask them what biases are revealed in the reviews. Have them identify words and sentences that reveal those biases. **OL**

Glencoe Skillbuilder Interactive Workbook CD-ROM, Level 1

This Interactive CD-ROM reinforces student mastery of essential social studies skills.

Skills Practice Answers

Practice It! Answers

1. the destruction of the gorillas' forest habitat
2. logging and mining
3. The speaker believes that destroying the gorillas' habitat is wrong.
4. The speaker uses emotional language, such as "destroying," "lose their homes," "disappear forever," "concerned," "emphasize," and "worst event in Africa's history."

Apply It! Answer

Summaries and analyses of bias should accurately reflect the letters chosen. Students should also describe an opposing opinion and who might hold this opinion in terms of their age, occupation, and background.

R1 Reading Strategy

Monitoring Ask: Why is a circle graph also called a pie chart? *(because the circle is divided into "slices" or wedge-shaped sections representing parts of the whole)* **What percentage should all of the slices in a circle graph add up to?** *(100 percent)* **BL**

R2 Reading Strategy

Reading Graphs Have students study the circle graph on this page. **Ask: How does this circle graph indicate what each slice represents?** *(by using different colors for each slice and providing a key for those colors)* **How does it indicate the exact percentage that each slice represents?** *(by labeling each slice with a percent)* **ELL**

Glencoe Skillbuilder Interactive Workbook CD-ROM, Level 1

This Interactive CD-ROM reinforces student mastery of essential social studies skills.

Additional Support

Interpreting a Circle Graph

Why Learn This Skill?

Have you ever watched someone serve pieces of pie? When the pie is cut evenly, everyone's slice is the same size. If one slice is cut a little larger, however, someone else gets a smaller piece. A *circle graph* is like a sliced pie. In fact, a circle graph is also called a pie chart. R1 In a circle graph, the complete circle represents a whole group—or 100 percent. The circle is divided into "slices," or wedge-shaped sections representing parts of the whole. R2

1 Learn It!

To read and interpret a circle graph, follow these steps:

- Read the title of the circle graph to find the subject.
- Study the labels or the key to see what each "slice" represents.
- Compare the sizes of the circle slices.

2 Practice It!

Study the circle graph on this page, and answer the following questions.

1. What is the subject of the circle graph?
2. On what do Americans spend most of their incomes?
3. On what do Americans spend the least portion of their incomes?
4. What is the total percentage of income spent on transportation and food?

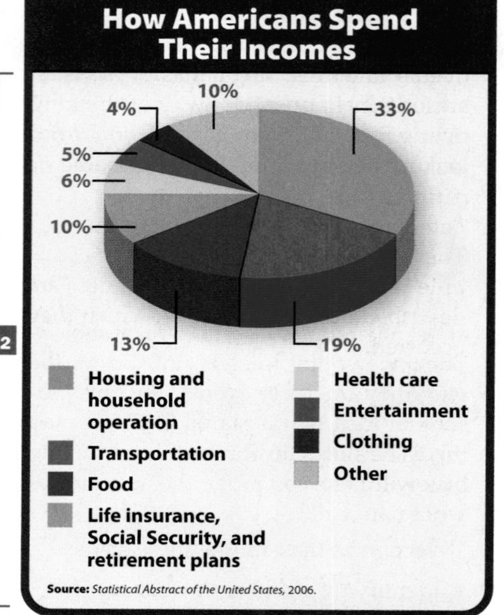

3 Apply It!

Quiz 10 friends about the capitals of India, Pakistan, and Bangladesh. Create a circle graph showing what percentage knew (a) all three capitals; (b) two capitals; (c) one capital; or (d) no capitals.

Skills Practice Answers

Practice It! Answers

1. how Americans spend their incomes
2. housing and household operation
3. clothing
4. 32%

Apply It! Answer

The circle graph should have labels or a key to show what each slice represents. The size of the slices should accurately reflect the percentage of friends in each category, and the percentages should add up to 100 percent.

Sequencing Events

Why Learn This Skill?

Have you ever had to remember events and their dates in the order in which they happened? *Sequencing* means listing facts in the correct order that they occurred. A time line helps you do this. A time line is a diagram that shows how dates and events relate to one another. **D** The years are evenly spaced along most time lines. Events on time lines are described beside the date on which they occurred.

Learn It!

To understand how to sequence events, follow these steps:

- As you read, look for dates or clue words that hint at chronological order, such as *in 2006, the late 1900s, first, then, finally*, and *after*.
- To read a time line, find the dates on the opposite ends of the time line. These dates show the range of time that is covered.
- Note the equal spacing between dates on the time line.
- Study the order of events.
- Look to see how the events relate to one another.

Practice It!

Examine the time line on this page and answer the following questions.

1. When does the time line begin? When does it end?
2. What major event happened in the late 1700s?
3. Did the Civil War begin before or after the United States entered World War I?
4. During what decade did the Cold War end?

Apply It!

List key events from one of the chapters in your textbook that covers the history of a region. Create a time line that lists these events in the order they occurred.

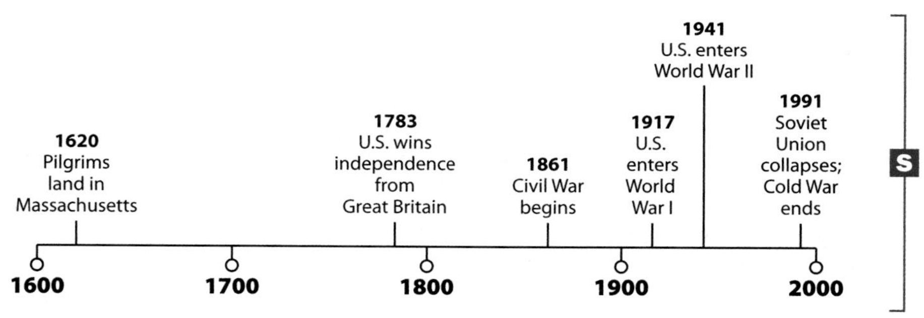

1620 Pilgrims land in Massachusetts
1783 U.S. wins independence from Great Britain
1861 Civil War begins
1917 U.S. enters World War I
1941 U.S. enters World War II
1991 Soviet Union collapses; Cold War ends
1600
1700
1800
1900
2000

S

D Differentiated Instruction

Interpersonal Have students work in small groups to gather information about events in the life of a historical figure, an inventor, or a favorite musical group. Ask them to choose significant events and include them in a time line. Remind students to include the correct time period on the time lines and to place events in chronological order with the proper spacing between events. **AL**

S Skill Practice

Reading a Time Line Have students study the time line on this page.

Ask: **What happened first—the end of the Cold War or the beginning of the Civil War?** *(the beginning of the Civil War)* **During what century did both World Wars take place?** *(the twentieth century or the 1900s)* **OL**

Glencoe Skillbuilder Interactive Workbook CD-ROM, Level 1

This Interactive CD-ROM reinforces student mastery of essential social studies skills.

Skills Practice Answers

Practice It! Answers

1. 1600, 2000
2. The United States won independence from Great Britain.
3. before
4. the 1990s

Apply It! Answer

Time lines should include key events in the history of a region placed in the correct sequence. The time lines should also include clear beginning and end dates and have equal spacing between years.

C Critical Thinking

Drawing Conclusions **Ask:** **If a population pyramid is narrow at the bottom, why does this indicate that the population is declining?** *(because, as older people die, there will be fewer total people)* OL

D Differentiated Instruction

Logical/Mathematical Have students study the population pyramid on this page. **Ask:** **Approximately what percent of Spanish men are 70 and older? Explain.** *(between 11 and 12 percent; men 70–74 are a little more than 4 percent, men 75–79 are between 3 and 4 percent, and men 80+ are a little less than 4 percent)* AL

Glencoe Skillbuilder Interactive Workbook CD-ROM, Level 1
This Interactive CD-ROM reinforces student mastery of essential social studies skills.

Additional Support

Skills Handbook

Interpreting a Population Pyramid

Why Learn This Skill?

A population pyramid shows a country's population by age and gender. Geographers use population pyramids to plan for a country's future needs.

1 Learn It!

A population pyramid is two bar graphs. These bar graphs show the number of males and females living in a region. The number of males and females is given as a percentage along the bottom of the graph. The age range for each group is listed along the left side of the graph.

To interpret population pyramids, follow these steps:

- Look at the bar graphs for the male and female groups.
- Identify, for each group, the bars that indicate the largest percentage and the smallest percentage.
- Find the age range for these groups.
- If a country's population is *growing*, the pyramid will be large at the bottom. This shows that the country's population has a large number of children and young people.

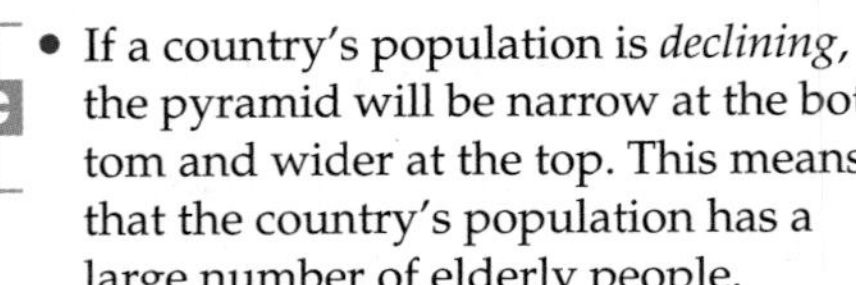

- C If a country's population is *declining*, the pyramid will be narrow at the bottom and wider at the top. This means that the country's population has a large number of elderly people.
- If a country's population is *stable*, the pyramid will have bars with similar lengths over several age ranges.

2 Practice It!

Study the 2007 population pyramid for Spain shown below, then answer the following questions.

1. Which age group makes up the largest portion of Spain's population?
2. Does it appear that Spanish men or Spanish women live longer? Explain.
3. What does the shape of the pyramid tell you about Spain's population?

D

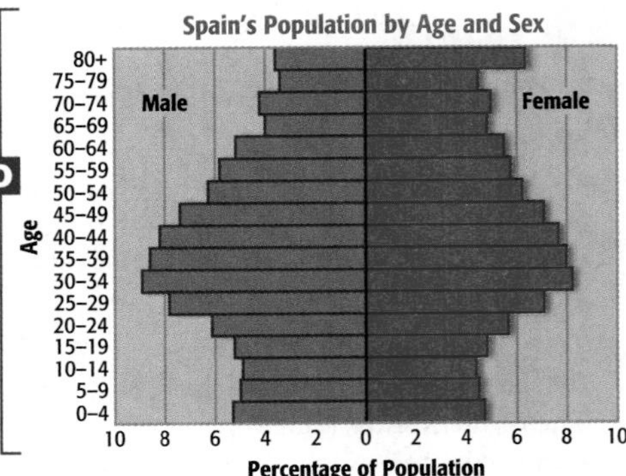

Source: *U.S. Census Bureau, International Data Base.*

3 Apply It!

Find the population pyramids for two countries at www.census.gov/ipc/www/idbpyr.html. Then write a paragraph to describe the similarities and differences between their populations.

Skills Practice Answers

Practice It! Answers

1. 30–34
2. Spanish women; over 6 percent of Spanish women are 80 or older, while less than 4 percent of Spanish men are this old.
3. Its population is probably stable, because the top and bottom sections are about the same.

Apply It! Answer

Have students print the population pyramids for the two countries and submit them with their paragraphs. The paragraphs should accurately describe the similarities and differences between the populations of the two countries, as shown on the population pyramids.

Gazetteer

Gazetteer

A gazetteer (ga•zuh•TIHR) is a geographic index or dictionary. It shows latitude and longitude for cities and certain other places. Latitude and longitude are shown in this way: 48°N 2°E, or 48 degrees north latitude and two degrees east longitude. This Gazetteer lists many important geographic features and most of the world's largest independent countries and their capitals. The page numbers tell where each entry can be found on a map in this book. As an aid to pronunciation, most entries are spelled phonetically.

Abidjan [AH•bee•JAHN] Capital of Côte d'Ivoire. 5°N 4°W (p. RA22)
Abu Dhabi [AH•boo DAH•bee] Capital of the United Arab Emirates. 24°N 54°E (p. RA24)
Abuja [ah•BOO•jah] Capital of Nigeria. 8°N 9°E (p. RA22)
Accra [ah•KRUH] Capital of Ghana. 6°N 0° longitude (p. RA22)
Addis Ababa [AHD•dihs AH•bah•BAH] Capital of Ethiopia. 9°N 39°E (p. RA22)
Adriatic [AY•dree•A•tihk] **Sea** Arm of the Mediterranean Sea between the Balkan Peninsula and Italy. (p. RA20)
Afghanistan [af•GA•nuh•STAN] Central Asian country west of Pakistan. (p. RA25)
Albania [al•BAY•nee•uh] Country on the Adriatic Sea, south of Serbia. (p. RA18)
Algeria [al•JIHR•ee•uh] North African country east of Morocco. (p. RA22)
Algiers [al•JIHRZ] Capital of Algeria. 37°N 3°E (p. RA22)
Alps [ALPS] Mountain ranges extending through central Europe. (p. RA20)
Amazon [A•muh•ZAHN] **River** Largest river in the world by volume and second-largest in length. (p. RA17)
Amman [a•MAHN] Capital of Jordan. 32°N 36°E (p. RA24)
Amsterdam [AHM•stuhr•DAHM] Capital of the Netherlands. 52°N 5°E (p. RA18)
Andes [AN•DEEZ] Mountain system extending north and south along the western side of South America. (p. RA17)
Andorra [an•DAWR•uh] Small country in southern Europe between France and Spain. 43°N 2°E (p. RA18)
Angola [ang•GOH•luh] Southern African country north of Namibia. (p. RA22)
Ankara [AHNG•kuh•ruh] Capital of Turkey. 40°N 33°E (p. RA24)
Antananarivo [AHN•tah•NAH•nah•REE•voh] Capital of Madagascar. 19°S 48°E (p. RA22)
Arabian [uh•RAY•bee•uhn] **Peninsula** Large peninsula extending into the Arabian Sea. (p. RA25)
Argentina [AHR•juhn•TEE•nuh] South American country east of Chile. (p. RA16)
Armenia [ahr•MEE•nee•uh] European-Asian country between the Black and Caspian Seas. 40°N 45°E (p. RA26)
Ashkhabad [AHSH•gah•BAHD] Capital of Turkmenistan. 38°N 58°E (p. RA25)
Asmara [az•MAHR•uh] Capital of Eritrea. 16°N 39°E (p. RA22)
Astana Capital of Kazakhstan. 51°N 72°E (p. RA26)
Asunción [ah•SOON•see•OHN] Capital of Paraguay. 25°S 58°W (p. RA16)
Athens Capital of Greece. 38°N 24°E (p. RA19)
Atlas [AT•luhs] **Mountains** Mountain range on the northern edge of the Sahara. (p. RA23)
Australia [aw•STRAYL•yuh] Country and continent in Southern Hemisphere. (p. RA30)
Austria [AWS•tree•uh] Western European country east of Switzerland and south of Germany and the Czech Republic. (p. RA18)
Azerbaijan [A•zuhr•BY•JAHN] European-Asian country on the Caspian Sea. (p. RA25)

Baghdad Capital of Iraq. 33°N 44°E (p. RA25)
Bahamas [buh•HAH•muhz] Country made up of many islands between Cuba and the United States. (p. RA15)
Bahrain [bah•RAYN] Country located on the Persian Gulf. 26°N 51°E (p. RA25)
Baku [bah•KOO] Capital of Azerbaijan. 40°N 50°E (p. RA25)
Balkan [BAWL•kuhn] **Peninsula** Peninsula in southeastern Europe. (p. RA21)
Baltic [BAWL•tihk] **Sea** Sea in northern Europe that is connected to the North Sea. (p. RA20)
Bamako [BAH•mah•KOH] Capital of Mali. 13°N 8°W (p. RA22)
Bangkok [BANG•KAHK] Capital of Thailand. 14°N 100°E (p. RA27)
Bangladesh [BAHNG•gluh•DEHSH] South Asian country bordered by India and Myanmar. (p. RA27)
Bangui [BAHNG•GEE] Capital of the Central African Republic. 4°N 19°E (p. RA22)
Banjul [BAHN•JOOL] Capital of Gambia. 13°N 17°W (p. RA22)

Barbados [bahr•BAY•duhs] Island country between the Atlantic Ocean and the Caribbean Sea. 14°N 59°W (p. RA15)
Beijing [BAY•JIHNG] Capital of China. 40°N 116°E (p. RA27)
Beirut [bay•ROOT] Capital of Lebanon. 34°N 36°E (p. RA24)
Belarus [BEE•luh•ROOS] Eastern European country west of Russia. 54°N 28°E (p. RA19)
Belgium [BEHL•juhm] Western European country south of the Netherlands. (p. RA18)
Belgrade [BEHL•GRAYD] Capital of Serbia. 45°N 21°E (p. RA19)
Belize [buh•LEEZ] Central American country east of Guatemala. (p. RA14)
Belmopan [BEHL•moh•PAHN] Capital of Belize. 17°N 89°W (p. RA14)
Benin [buh•NEEN] West African country west of Nigeria. (p. RA22)
Berlin [behr•LEEN] Capital of Germany. 53°N 13°E (p. RA18)
Bern Capital of Switzerland. 47°N 7°E (p. RA18)
Bhutan [boo•TAHN] South Asian country northeast of India. (p. RA27)
Bishkek [bihsh•KEHK] Capital of Kyrgyzstan. 43°N 75°E (p. RA26)
Bissau [bihs•SOW] Capital of Guinea-Bissau. 12°N 16°W (p. RA22)
Black Sea Large sea between Europe and Asia. (p. RA21)
Bloemfontein [BLOOM•FAHN•TAYN] Judicial capital of South Africa. 26°E 29°S (p. RA22)
Bogotá [BOH•goh•TAH] Capital of Colombia. 5°N 74°W (p. RA16)
Bolivia [buh•LIHV•ee•uh] Country in the central part of South America, north of Argentina. (p. RA16)
Bosnia and Herzegovina [BAHZ•nee•uh HEHRT•seh•GAW•vee•nuh] Southeastern European country between Croatia, Serbia, and Montenegro. (p. RA18)
Botswana [bawt•SWAH•nah] Southern African country north of the Republic of South Africa. (p. RA22)
Brasília [brah•ZEEL•yuh] Capital of Brazil. 16°S 48°W (p. RA16)
Bratislava [BRAH•tih•SLAH•vuh] Capital of Slovakia. 48°N 17°E (p. RA18)
Brazil [bruh•ZIHL] Largest country in South America. (p. RA16)
Brazzaville [BRAH•zuh•VEEL] Capital of Congo. 4°S 15°E (p. RA22)
Brunei [bru•NY] Southeast Asian country on northern coast of the island of Borneo. (p. RA27)
Brussels [BRUH•suhlz] Capital of Belgium. 51°N 4°E (p. RA18)
Bucharest [BOO•kuh•REHST] Capital of Romania. 44°N 26°E (p. RA19)
Budapest [BOO•duh•PEHST] Capital of Hungary. 48°N 19°E (p. RA18)
Buenos Aires [BWAY•nuhs AR•eez] Capital of Argentina. 34°S 58°W (p. RA16)
Bujumbura [BOO•juhm•BUR•uh] Capital of Burundi. 3°S 29°E (p. RA22)
Bulgaria [BUHL•GAR•ee•uh] Southeastern European country south of Romania. (p. RA19)
Burkina Faso [bur•KEE•nuh FAH•soh] West African country south of Mali. (p. RA22)
Burundi [bu•ROON•dee] East African country at the northern end of Lake Tanganyika. 3°S 30°E (p. RA22)

Cairo [KY•ROH] Capital of Egypt. 31°N 32°E (p. RA24)
Cambodia [kam•BOH•dee•uh] Southeast Asian country south of Thailand and Laos. (p. RA27)
Cameroon [KA•muh•ROON] Central African country on the northeast shore of the Gulf of Guinea. (p. RA22)
Canada [KA•nuh•duh] Northernmost country in North America. (p. RA6)
Canberra [KAN•BEHR•uh] Capital of Australia. 35°S 149°E (p. RA30)
Cape Town Legislative capital of the Republic of South Africa. 34°S 18°E (p. RA22)
Cape Verde [VUHRD] Island country off the coast of western Africa in the Atlantic Ocean. 15°N 24°W (p. RA22)
Caracas [kah•RAH•kahs] Capital of Venezuela. 11°N 67°W (p. RA16)
Caribbean [KAR•uh•BEE•uhn] **Islands** Islands in the Caribbean Sea between North America and South America, also known as West Indies. (p. RA15)
Caribbean Sea Part of the Atlantic Ocean bordered by the West Indies, South America, and Central America. (p. RA15)
Caspian [KAS•pee•uhn] **Sea** Salt lake between Europe and Asia that is the world's largest inland body of water. (p. RA21)
Caucasus [KAW•kuh•suhs] **Mountains** Mountain range between the Black and Caspian Seas. (p. RA21)
Central African Republic Central African country south of Chad. (p. RA22)
Chad [CHAD] Country west of Sudan in the African Sahel. (p. RA22)
Chang Jiang [CHAHNG jee•AHNG] Principal river of China that begins in Tibet and flows into the East China Sea near Shanghai; also known as the Yangtze River. (p. RA29)
Chile [CHEE•lay] South American country west of Argentina. (p. RA16)
China [CHY•nuh] Country in eastern and central Asia, known officially as the People's Republic of China. (p. RA27)
Chişinău [KEE•shee•NOW] Capital of Moldova. 47°N 29°E (p. RA19)
Colombia [kuh•LUHM•bee•uh] South American country west of Venezuela. (p. RA16)

Colombo [kuh•LUHM•boh] Capital of Sri Lanka. 7°N 80°E (p. RA26)
Comoros [KAH•muh•ROHZ] Small island country in Indian Ocean between the island of Madagascar and the southeast African mainland. 13°S 43°E (p. RA22)
Conakry [KAH•nuh•kree] Capital of Guinea. 10°N 14°W (p. RA22)
Congo [KAHNG•goh] Central African country east of the Democratic Republic of the Congo. 3°S 14°E (p. RA22)
Congo, Democratic Republic of the Central African country north of Zambia and Angola. 1°S 22°E (p. RA22)
Copenhagen [KOH•puhn•HAY•guhn] Capital of Denmark. 56°N 12°E (p. RA18)
Costa Rica [KAWS•tah REE•kah] Central American country south of Nicaragua. (p. RA15)
Côte d'Ivoire [KOHT dee•VWAHR] West African country south of Mali. (p. RA22)
Croatia [kroh•AY•shuh] Southeastern European country on the Adriatic Sea. (p. RA18)
Cuba [KYOO•buh] Island country in the Caribbean Sea. (p. RA15)
Cyprus [SY•pruhs] Island country in the eastern Mediterranean Sea, south of Turkey. (p. RA19)
Czech [CHEHK] **Republic** Eastern European country north of Austria. (p. RA18)

Dakar [dah•KAHR] Capital of Senegal. 15°N 17°W (p. RA22)
Damascus [duh•MAS•kuhs] Capital of Syria. 34°N 36°E (p. RA24)
Dar es Salaam [DAHR EHS sah•LAHM] Commercial capital of Tanzania. 7°S 39°E (p. RA22)
Denmark Northern European country between the Baltic and North Seas. (p. RA18)
Dhaka [DA•kuh] Capital of Bangladesh. 24°N 90°E (p. RA27)
Djibouti [jih•BOO•tee] East African country on the Gulf of Aden. 12°N 43°E (p. RA22)
Dodoma [doh•DOH•mah] Political capital of Tanzania. 6°S 36°E (p. RA22)
Doha [DOH•huh] Capital of Qatar. 25°N 51°E (p. RA25)
Dominican [duh•MIH•nih•kuhn] **Republic** Country in the Caribbean Sea on the eastern part of the island of Hispaniola. (p. RA15)
Dublin [DUH•blihn] Capital of Ireland. 53°N 6°W (p. RA18)
Dushanbe [doo•SHAM•buh] Capital of Tajikistan. 39°N 69°E (p. RA25)

East Timor [TEE•MOHR] Previous province of Indonesia, now under UN administration. 10°S 127°E (p. RA27)
Ecuador [EH•kwuh•dawr] South American country southwest of Colombia. (p. RA16)
Egypt [EE•jihpt] North African country on the Mediterranean Sea. (p. RA24)
El Salvador [ehl SAL•vuh•dawr] Central American country southwest of Honduras. (p. RA14)
Equatorial Guinea [EE•kwuh•TOHR•ee•uhl GIH•nee] Central African country south of Cameroon. (p. RA22)
Eritrea [EHR•uh•TREE•uh] East African country north of Ethiopia. (p. RA22)
Estonia [eh•STOH•nee•uh] Eastern European country on the Baltic Sea. (p. RA19)
Ethiopia [EE•thee•OH•pee•uh] East African country north of Somalia and Kenya. (p. RA22)
Euphrates [yu•FRAY•teez] **River** River in southwestern Asia that flows through Syria and Iraq and joins the Tigris River. (p. RA25)

Fiji [FEE•jee] **Islands** Country comprised of an island group in the southwest Pacific Ocean. 19°S 175°E (p. RA30)
Finland [FIHN•luhnd] Northern European country east of Sweden. (p. RA19)
France [FRANS] Western European country south of the United Kingdom. (p. RA18)
Freetown Capital of Sierra Leone. (p. RA22)
French Guiana [gee•A•nuh] French-owned territory in northern South America. (p. RA16)

Gabon [ga•BOHN] Central African country on the Atlantic Ocean. (p. RA22)
Gaborone [GAH•boh•ROH•nay] Capital of Botswana. (p. RA22)
Gambia [GAM•bee•uh] West African country along the Gambia River. (p. RA22)
Georgetown [JAWRJ•TOWN] Capital of Guyana. 8°N 58°W (p. RA16)
Georgia [JAWR•juh] European-Asian country bordering the Black Sea south of Russia. (p. RA26)
Germany [JUHR•muh•nee] Western European country south of Denmark, officially called the Federal Republic of Germany. (p. RA18)
Ghana [GAH•nuh] West African country on the Gulf of Guinea. (p. RA22)
Great Plains The continental slope extending through the United States and Canada. (p. RA7)
Greece [GREES] Southern European country on the Balkan Peninsula. (p. RA19)
Greenland [GREEN•luhnd] Island in northwestern Atlantic Ocean and the largest island in the world. (p. RA6)
Guatemala [GWAH•tay•MAH•lah] Central American country south of Mexico. (p. RA14)

Guatemala Capital of Guatemala. 15°N 91°W (p. RA14)
Guinea [GIH•nee] West African country on the Atlantic coast. (p. RA22)
Guinea-Bissau [GIH•nee bih•SOW] West African country on the Atlantic coast. (p. RA22)
Gulf of Mexico Gulf on part of the southern coast of North America. (p. RA7)
Guyana [gy•AH•nuh] South American country between Venezuela and Suriname. (p. RA16)

Haiti [HAY•tee] Country in the Caribbean Sea on the western part of the island of Hispaniola. (p. RA15)
Hanoi [ha•NOY] Capital of Vietnam. 21°N 106°E (p. RA27)
Harare [hah•RAH•RAY] Capital of Zimbabwe. 18°S 31°E (p. RA22)
Havana [huh•VA•nuh] Capital of Cuba. 23°N 82°W (p. RA15)
Helsinki [HEHL•SIHNG•kee] Capital of Finland. 60°N 24°E (p. RA19)
Himalaya [HI•muh•LAY•uh] Mountain ranges in southern Asia, bordering the Indian subcontinent on the north. (p. RA28)
Honduras [hahn•DUR•uhs] Central American country on the Caribbean Sea. (p. RA14)
Hong Kong Port and industrial center in southern China. 22°N 115°E (p. RA27)
Huang He [HWAHNG HUH] River in northern and eastern China, also known as the Yellow River. (p. RA29)
Hungary [HUHNG•guh•ree] Eastern European country south of Slovakia. (p. RA18)

Iberian [eye•BIHR•ee•uhn] **Peninsula** Peninsula in southwest Europe, occupied by Spain and Portugal. (p. RA20)
Iceland Island country between the North Atlantic and Arctic Oceans. (p. RA18)
India [IHN•dee•uh] South Asian country south of China and Nepal. (p. RA26)
Indonesia [IHN•duh•NEE•zhuh] Southeast Asian island country known as the Republic of Indonesia. (p. RA27)
Indus [IHN•duhs] **River** River in Asia that begins in Tibet and flows through Pakistan to the Arabian Sea. (p. RA28)
Iran [ih•RAN] Southwest Asian country that was formerly named Persia. (p. RA25)
Iraq [ih•RAHK] Southwest Asian country west of Iran. (p. RA25)
Ireland [EYER•luhnd] Island west of Great Britain occupied by the Republic of Ireland and Northern Ireland. (p. RA18)
Islamabad [ihs•LAH•muh•BAHD] Capital of Pakistan. 34°N 73°E (p. RA26)
Israel [IHZ•ree•uhl] Southwest Asian country south of Lebanon. (p. RA24)
Italy [IHT•uhl•ee] Southern European country south of Switzerland and east of France. (p. RA18)

Jakarta [juh•KAHR•tuh] Capital of Indonesia. 6°S 107°E (p. RA27)
Jamaica [juh•MAY•kuh] Island country in the Caribbean Sea. (p. RA15)
Japan [juh•PAN] East Asian country consisting of the four large islands of Hokkaido, Honshu, Shikoku, and Kyushu, plus thousands of small islands. (p. RA27)
Jerusalem [juh•ROO•suh•luhm] Capital of Israel and a holy city for Christians, Jews, and Muslims. 32°N 35°E (p. RA24)
Jordan [JAWRD•uhn] Southwest Asian country south of Syria. (p. RA24)

Kabul [KAH•buhl] Capital of Afghanistan. 35°N 69°E (p. RA25)
Kampala [kahm•PAH•lah] Capital of Uganda. 0° latitude 32°E (p. RA22)
Kathmandu [KAT•MAN•DOO] Capital of Nepal. 28°N 85°E (p. RA26)
Kazakhstan [kuh•ZAHK•STAHN] Large Asian country south of Russia and bordering the Caspian Sea. (p. RA26)
Kenya [KEHN•yuh] East African country south of Ethiopia. (p. RA22)
Khartoum [kahr•TOOM] Capital of Sudan. 16°N 33°E (p. RA22)
Kigali [kee•GAH•lee] Capital of Rwanda. 2°S 30°E (p. RA22)
Kingston [KIHNG•stuhn] Capital of Jamaica. 18°N 77°W (p. RA15)
Kinshasa [kihn•SHAH•suh] Capital of the Democratic Republic of the Congo. 4°S 15°E (p. RA22)
Kuala Lumpur [KWAH•luh LUM•PUR] Capital of Malaysia. 3°N 102°E (p. RA27)
Kuwait [ku•WAYT] Country on the Persian Gulf between Saudi Arabia and Iraq. (p. RA25)
Kyiv [KEE•ihf] Capital of Ukraine. 50°N 31°E (p. RA19)
Kyrgyzstan [KIHR•gih•STAN] Central Asian country on China's western border. (p. RA26)

Laos [LOWS] Southeast Asian country south of China and west of Vietnam. (p. RA27)

La Paz [lah PAHS] Administrative capital of Bolivia, and the highest capital in the world. 17°S 68°W (p. RA16)

Latvia [LAT•vee•uh] Eastern European country west of Russia on the Baltic Sea. (p. RA19)

Lebanon [LEH•buh•nuhn] Country south of Syria on the Mediterranean Sea. (p. RA24)

Lesotho [luh•SOH•TOH] Southern African country within the borders of the Republic of South Africa. (p. RA22)

Liberia [ly•BIHR•ee•uh] West African country south of Guinea. (p. RA22)

Libreville [LEE•bruh•VIHL] Capital of Gabon. 1°N 9°E (p. RA22)

Libya [LIH•bee•uh] North African country west of Egypt on the Mediterranean Sea. (p. RA22)

Liechtenstein [LIHKT•uhn•SHTYN] Small country in central Europe between Switzerland and Austria. 47°N 10°E (p. RA18)

Lilongwe [lih•LAWNG•GWAY] Capital of Malawi. 14°S 34°E (p. RA22)

Lima [LEE•mah] Capital of Peru. 12°S 77°W (p. RA16)

Lisbon [LIHZ•buhn] Capital of Portugal. 39°N 9°W (p. RA18)

Lithuania [LIH•thuh•WAY•nee•uh] Eastern European country northwest of Belarus on the Baltic Sea. (p. RA21)

Ljubljana [lee•oo•blee•AH•nuh] Capital of Slovenia. 46°N 14°E (p. RA18)

Lomé [loh•MAY] Capital of Togo. 6°N 1°E (p. RA22)

London Capital of the United Kingdom, on the Thames River. 52°N 0° longitude (p. RA18)

Luanda [lu•AHN•duh] Capital of Angola. 9°S 13°E (p. RA22)

Lusaka [loo•SAH•kah] Capital of Zambia. 15°S 28°E (p. RA22)

Luxembourg [LUHK•suhm•BUHRG] Small European country between France, Belgium, and Germany. 50°N 7°E (p. RA18)

Macao [muh•KOW] Port in southern China. 22°N 113°E (p. RA27)

Macedonia [MA•suh•DOH•nee•uh] Southeastern European country north of Greece. (p. RA19). Macedonia also refers to a geographic region covering northern Greece, the country Macedonia, and part of Bulgaria.

Madagascar [MA•duh•GAS•kuhr] Island in the Indian Ocean off the southeastern coast of Africa. (p. RA22)

Madrid Capital of Spain. 41°N 4°W (p. RA18)

Malabo [mah•LAH•boh] Capital of Equatorial Guinea. 4°N 9°E (p. RA22)

Malawi [mah•LAH•wee] Southern African country south of Tanzania and east of Zambia. (p. RA22)

Malaysia [muh•LAY•zhuh] Southeast Asian country with land on the Malay Peninsula and on the island of Borneo. (p. RA27)

Maldives [MAWL•DEEVZ] Island country southwest of India in the Indian Ocean. (p. RA26)

Mali [MAH•lee] West African country east of Mauritania. (p. RA22)

Managua [mah•NAH•gwah] Capital of Nicaragua. (p. RA15)

Manila [muh•NIH•luh] Capital of the Philippines. 15°N 121°E (p. RA27)

Maputo [mah•POO•toh] Capital of Mozambique. 26°S 33°E (p. RA22)

Maseru [MA•zuh•ROO] Capital of Lesotho. 29°S 27°E (p. RA22)

Mauritania [MAWR•uh•TAY•nee•uh] West African country north of Senegal. (p. RA22)

Mauritius [maw•RIH•shuhs] Island country in the Indian Ocean east of Madagascar. 21°S 58°E (p. RA3)

Mbabane [uhm•bah•BAH•nay] Capital of Swaziland. 26°S 31°E (p. RA22)

Mediterranean [MEH•duh•tuh•RAY•nee•uhn] **Sea** Large inland sea surrounded by Europe, Asia, and Africa. (p. RA20)

Mekong [MAY•KAWNG] **River** River in southeastern Asia that begins in Tibet and empties into the South China Sea. (p. RA29)

Mexico [MEHK•sih•KOH] North American country south of the United States. (p. RA14)

Mexico City Capital of Mexico. 19°N 99°W (p. RA14)

Minsk [MIHNSK] Capital of Belarus. 54°N 28°E (p. RA19)

Mississippi [MIH•suh•SIH•pee] **River** Large river system in the central United States that flows southward into the Gulf of Mexico. (p. RA11)

Mogadishu [MOH•guh•DEE•SHOO] Capital of Somalia. 2°N 45°E (p. RA22)

Moldova [mawl•DAW•vuh] Small European country between Ukraine and Romania. (p. RA19)

Monaco [MAH•nuh•KOH] Small country in southern Europe on the French Mediterranean coast. 44°N 8°E (p. RA18)

Mongolia [mahn•GOHL•yuh] Country in Asia between Russia and China. (p. RA23)

Monrovia [muhn•ROH•vee•uh] Capital of Liberia. 6°N 11°W (p. RA22)

Monetenegro [MAHN•tuh•NEE•groh] Eastern European country. (p. RA18)

Montevideo [MAHN•tuh•vuh•DAY•OH] Capital of Uruguay. 35°S 56°W (p. RA16)

Morocco [muh•RAH•KOH] North African country on the Mediterranean Sea and the Atlantic Ocean. (p. RA22)

Moscow [MAHS•KOW] Capital of Russia. 56°N 38°E (p. RA19)

Mount Everest [EHV•ruhst] Highest mountain in the world, in the Himalaya between Nepal and Tibet. (p. RA28)

Mozambique [MOH•zahm•BEEK] Southern African country south of Tanzania. (p. RA22)
Muscat [MUHS•KAHT] Capital of Oman. 23°N 59°E (p. RA25)
Myanmar [MYAHN•MAHR] Southeast Asian country south of China and India, formerly called Burma. (p. RA27)

Nairobi [ny•ROH•bee] Capital of Kenya. 1°S 37°E (p. RA22)
Namibia [nuh•MIH•bee•uh] Southern African country south of Angola on the Atlantic Ocean. 20°S 16°E (p. RA22)
Nassau [NA•SAW] Capital of the Bahamas. 25°N 77°W (p. RA15)
N'Djamena [uhn•jah•MAY•nah] Capital of Chad. 12°N 15°E (p. RA22)
Nepal [NAY•PAHL] Mountain country between India and China. (p. RA26)
Netherlands [NEH•thuhr•lundz] Western European country north of Belgium. (p. RA18)
New Delhi [NOO DEH•lee] Capital of India. 29°N 77°E (p. RA26)
New Zealand [NOO ZEE•luhnd] Major island country southeast of Australia in the South Pacific. (p. RA30)
Niamey [nee•AHM•ay] Capital of Niger. 14°N 2°E (p. RA22)
Nicaragua [NIH•kuh•RAH•gwuh] Central American country south of Honduras. (p. RA15)
Nicosia [NIH•kuh•SEE•uh] Capital of Cyprus. 35°N 33°E (p. RA19)
Niger [NY•juhr] West African country north of Nigeria. (p. RA22)
Nigeria [ny•JIHR•ee•uh] West African country along the Gulf of Guinea. (p. RA22)
Nile [NYL] **River** Longest river in the world, flowing north through eastern Africa. (p. RA23)
North Korea [kuh•REE•uh] East Asian country in the northernmost part of the Korean Peninsula. (p. RA27)
Norway [NAWR•WAY] Northern European country on the Scandinavian peninsula. (p. RA18)
Nouakchott [nu•AHK•SHAHT] Capital of Mauritania. 18°N 16°W (p. RA22)

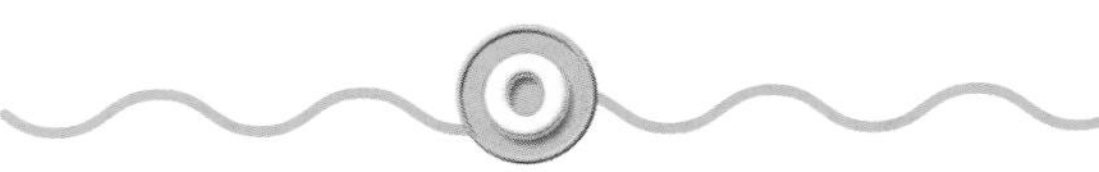

Oman [oh•MAHN] Country on the Arabian Sea and the Gulf of Oman. (p. RA25)
Oslo [AHZ•loh] Capital of Norway. 60°N 11°E (p. RA18)
Ottawa [AH•tuh•wuh] Capital of Canada. 45°N 76°W (p. RA13)
Ouagadougou [WAH•gah•DOO•goo] Capital of Burkina Faso. 12°N 2°W (p. RA22)

Pakistan [PA•kih•STAN] South Asian country northwest of India on the Arabian Sea. (p. RA26)
Palau [puh•LOW) Island country in the Pacific Ocean. 7°N 135°E (p. RA30)
Panama [PA•nuh•MAH] Central American country on the Isthmus of Panama. (p. RA15)
Panama Capital of Panama. 9°N 79°W (p. RA15)
Papua New Guinea [PA•pyu•wuh NOO GIH•nee] Island country in the Pacific Ocean north of Australia. 7°S 142°E (p. RA30)
Paraguay [PAR•uh•GWY] South American country northeast of Argentina. (p. RA16)
Paramaribo [PAH•rah•MAH•ree•boh] Capital of Suriname. 6°N 55°W (p. RA16)
Paris Capital of France. 49°N 2°E (p. RA18)
Persian [PUHR•zhuhn] **Gulf** Arm of the Arabian Sea between Iran and Saudi Arabia. (p. RA25)
Peru [puh•ROO] South American country south of Ecuador and Colombia. (p. RA16)
Philippines [FIH•luh•PEENZ] Island country in the Pacific Ocean southeast of China. (p. RA27)
Phnom Penh [puh•NAWM PEHN] Capital of Cambodia. 12°N 106°E (p. RA27)
Poland [POH•luhnd] Eastern European country on the Baltic Sea. (p. RA18)
Port-au-Prince [POHRT•oh•PRIHNS] Capital of Haiti. 19°N 72°W (p. RA15)
Port Moresby [MOHRZ•bee] Capital of Papua New Guinea. 10°S 147°E (p. RA30)
Port-of-Spain [SPAYN] Capital of Trinidad and Tobago. 11°N 62°W (p. RA15)
Porto-Novo [POHR•toh•NOH•voh] Capital of Benin. 7°N 3°E (p. RA22)
Portugal [POHR•chih•guhl] Country west of Spain on the Iberian Peninsula. (p. RA18)
Prague [PRAHG] Capital of the Czech Republic. 51°N 15°E (p. RA18)
Puerto Rico [PWEHR•toh REE•koh] Island in the Caribbean Sea; U.S. Commonwealth. (p. RA15)
P'yŏngyang [pee•AWNG•YAHNG] Capital of North Korea. 39°N 126°E (p. RA27)

Qatar [KAH•tuhr] Country on the southwestern shore of the Persian Gulf. (p. RA25)
Quito [KEE•toh] Capital of Ecuador. 0° latitude 79°W (p. RA16)

Rabat [ruh•BAHT] Capital of Morocco. 34°N 7°W (p. RA22)
Reykjavík [RAY•kyah•VEEK] Capital of Iceland. 64°N 22°W (p. RA18)

Gazetteer

Rhine [RYN] **River** River in western Europe that flows into the North Sea. (p. RA20)
Riga [REE•guh] Capital of Latvia. 57°N 24°E (p. RA19)
Rio Grande [REE•oh GRAND] River that forms part of the boundary between the United States and Mexico. (p. RA10)
Riyadh [ree•YAHD] Capital of Saudi Arabia. 25°N 47°E (p. RA25)
Rocky Mountains Mountain system in western North America. (p. RA7)
Romania [ru•MAY•nee•uh] Eastern European country east of Hungary. (p. RA19)
Rome Capital of Italy. 42°N 13°E (p. RA18)
Russia [RUH•shuh] Largest country in the world, covering parts of Europe and Asia. (p. RA19, RA27)
Rwanda [ruh•WAHN•duh] East African country south of Uganda. 2°S 30°E (p. RA22)

Sahara [suh•HAR•uh] Desert region in northern Africa that is the largest hot desert in the world. (p. RA23)
Saint Lawrence [LAWR•uhns] **River** River that flows from Lake Ontario to the Atlantic Ocean and forms part of the boundary between the United States and Canada. (p. RA13)
Sanaa [sahn•AH] Capital of Yemen. 15°N 44°E (p. RA25)
San José [SAN hoh•ZAY] Capital of Costa Rica. 10°N 84°W (p. RA15)
San Marino [SAN muh•REE•noh] Small European country located in the Italian peninsula. 44°N 13°E (p. RA18)
San Salvador [SAN SAL•vuh•DAWR] Capital of El Salvador. 14°N 89°W (p. RA14)
Santiago [SAN•tee•AH•goh] Capital of Chile. 33°S 71°W (p. RA16)
Santo Domingo [SAN•toh duh•MIHNG•goh] Capital of the Dominican Republic. 19°N 70°W (p. RA15)
São Tomé and Príncipe [sow too•MAY PREEN•see•pee] Small island country in the Gulf of Guinea off the coast of central Africa. 1°N 7°E (p. RA22)
Sarajevo [SAR•uh•YAY•voh] Capital of Bosnia and Herzegovina. 43°N 18°E (p. RA18)
Saudi Arabia [SOW•dee uh•RAY•bee•uh] Country on the Arabian Peninsula. (p. RA25)
Senegal [SEH•nih•GAWL] West African country on the Atlantic coast. (p. RA22)
Seoul [SOHL] Capital of South Korea. 38°N 127°E (p. RA27)
Serbia [SUHR•bee•uh] Eastern European country south of Hungary. (p. RA18)
Seychelles [say•SHEHL] Small island country in the Indian Ocean off eastern Africa. 6°S 56°E (p. RA22)
Sierra Leone [see•EHR•uh lee•OHN] West African country south of Guinea. (p. RA22)
Singapore [SIHNG•uh•POHR] Southeast Asian island country near tip of Malay Peninsula. (p. RA27)
Skopje [SKAW•PYAY] Capital of the country of Macedonia. 42°N 21°E (p. RA19)
Slovakia [sloh•VAH•kee•uh] Eastern European country south of Poland. (p. RA18)
Slovenia [sloh•VEE•nee•uh] Southeastern European country south of Austria on the Adriatic Sea. (p. RA18)
Sofia [SOH•fee•uh] Capital of Bulgaria. 43°N 23°E (p. RA19)
Solomon [SAH•luh•muhn] **Islands** Island country in the Pacific Ocean northeast of Australia. (p. RA30)
Somalia [soh•MAH•lee•uh] East African country on the Gulf of Aden and the Indian Ocean. (p. RA22)
South Africa [A•frih•kuh] Country at the southern tip of Africa, officially the Republic of South Africa. (p. RA22)
South Korea [kuh•REE•uh] East Asian country on the Korean Peninsula between the Yellow Sea and the Sea of Japan. (p. RA27)
Spain [SPAYN] Southern European country on the Iberian Peninsula. (p. RA18)
Sri Lanka [SREE LAHNG•kuh] Country in the Indian Ocean south of India, formerly called Ceylon. (p. RA26)
Stockholm [STAHK•HOHLM] Capital of Sweden. 59°N 18°E (p. RA18)
Sucre [SOO•kray] Constitutional capital of Bolivia. 19°S 65°W (p. RA16)
Sudan [soo•DAN] East African country south of Egypt. (p. RA22)
Suriname [SUR•uh•NAH•muh] South American country between Guyana and French Guiana. (p. RA16)
Suva [SOO•vah] Capital of the Fiji Islands. 18°S 177°E (p. RA30)
Swaziland [SWAH•zee•land] Southern African country west of Mozambique, almost entirely within the Republic of South Africa. (p. RA22)
Sweden Northern European country on the eastern side of the Scandinavian peninsula. (p. RA18)
Switzerland [SWIHT•suhr•luhnd] European country in the Alps south of Germany. (p. RA18)
Syria [SIHR•ee•uh] Southwest Asian country on the east side of the Mediterranean Sea. (p. RA24)

Taipei [TY•PAY] Capital of Taiwan. 25°N 122°E (p. RA27)
Taiwan [TY•WAHN] Island country off the southeast coast of China; the seat of the Chinese Nationalist government. (p. RA27)
Tajikistan [tah•JIH•kih•STAN] Central Asian country east of Turkmenistan. (p. RA26)

Tallinn [TA•luhn] Capital of Estonia. 59°N 25°E (p. RA19)
Tanzania [TAN•zuh•NEE•uh] East African country south of Kenya. (p. RA22)
Tashkent [tash•KEHNT] Capital of Uzbekistan. 41°N 69°E (p. RA26)
Tbilisi [tuh•bih•LEE•see] Capital of the Republic of Georgia. 42°N 45°E (p. RA26)
Tegucigalpa [tay•GOO•see•GAHL•pah] Capital of Honduras. 14°N 87°W (p. RA14)
Tehran [TAY•uh•RAN] Capital of Iran. 36°N 52°E (p. RA25)
Thailand [TY•LAND] Southeast Asian country east of Myanmar. 17°N 101°E (p. RA27)
Thimphu [thihm•POO] Capital of Bhutan. 28°N 90°E (p. RA27)
Tigris [TY•gruhs] **River** River in southeastern Turkey and Iraq that merges with the Euphrates River. (p. RA25)
Tiranë [tih•RAH•nuh] Capital of Albania. 42°N 20°E (p. RA18)
Togo [TOH•goh] West African country between Benin and Ghana on the Gulf of Guinea. (p. RA22)
Tokyo [TOH•kee•OH] Capital of Japan. 36°N 140°E (p. RA27)
Trinidad and Tobago [TRIH•nuh•DAD tuh•BAY•goh] Island country near Venezuela between the Atlantic Ocean and the Caribbean Sea. (p. RA15)
Tripoli [TRIH•puh•lee] Capital of Libya. 33°N 13°E (p. RA22)
Tshwane [ch•WAH•nay] Executive capital of South Africa. 26°S 28°E (p. RA22)
Tunis [TOO•nuhs] Capital of Tunisia. 37°N 10°E (p. RA22)
Tunisia [too•NEE•zhuh] North African country on the Mediterranean Sea between Libya and Algeria. (p. RA22)
Turkey [TUHR•kee] Country in southeastern Europe and western Asia. (p. RA24)
Turkmenistan [tuhrk•MEH•nuh•STAN] Central Asian country on the Caspian Sea. (p. RA25)

Uganda [yoo•GAHN•dah] East African country south of Sudan. (p. RA22)
Ukraine [yoo•KRAYN] Eastern European country west of Russia on the Black Sea. (p. RA25)
Ulaanbaatar [oo•LAHN•BAH•TAWR] Capital of Mongolia. 48°N 107°E (p. RA27)
United Arab Emirates [EH•muh•ruhts] Country made up of seven states on the eastern side of the Arabian Peninsula. (p. RA25)
United Kingdom Western European island country made up of England, Scotland, Wales, and Northern Ireland. (p. RA18)
United States of America Country in North America made up of 50 states, mostly between Canada and Mexico. (p. RA8)
Uruguay [YUR•uh•GWAY] South American country south of Brazil on the Atlantic Ocean. (p. RA16)
Uzbekistan [UZ•BEH•kih•STAN] Central Asian country south of Kazakhstan. (p. RA25)

Vanuatu [VAN•WAH•TOO] Country made up of islands in the Pacific Ocean east of Australia. (p. RA30)
Vatican [VA•tih•kuhn] **City** Headquarters of the Roman Catholic Church, located in the city of Rome in Italy. 42°N 13°E (p. RA18)
Venezuela [VEH•nuh•ZWAY•luh] South American country on the Caribbean Sea between Colombia and Guyana. (p. RA16)
Vienna [vee•EH•nuh] Capital of Austria. 48°N 16°E (p. RA18)
Vientiane [vyehn•TYAHN] Capital of Laos. 18°N 103°E (p. RA27)
Vietnam [vee•EHT•NAHM] Southeast Asian country east of Laos and Cambodia. (p. RA27)
Vilnius [VIL•nee•uhs] Capital of Lithuania. 55°N 25°E (p. RA19)

Warsaw Capital of Poland. 52°N 21°E (p. RA19)
Washington, D.C. Capital of the United States, in the District of Columbia. 39°N 77°W (p. RA8)
Wellington [WEH•lihng•tuhn] Capital of New Zealand. 41°S 175°E (p. RA30)
West Indies Caribbean islands between North America and South America. (p. RA15)
Windhoek [VIHNT•HUK] Capital of Namibia. 22°S 17°E (p. RA22)

Yamoussoukro [YAH•moo•SOO•kroh] Second capital of Côte d'Ivoire. 7°N 6°W (p. RA22)
Yangon [YAHNG•GOHN] Capital of Myanmar; formerly called Rangoon. 17°N 96°E (p. RA27)
Yaoundé [yown•DAY] Capital of Cameroon. 4°N 12°E (p. RA22)
Yemen [YEH•muhn] Country south of Saudi Arabia on the Arabian Peninsula. (p. RA25)
Yerevan [YEHR•uh•VAHN] Capital of Armenia. 40°N 44°E (p. RA25)

Zagreb [ZAH•GREHB] Capital of Croatia. 46°N 16°E (p. RA18)
Zambia [ZAM•bee•uh] Southern African country north of Zimbabwe. (p. RA22)
Zimbabwe [zihm•BAH•bway] Southern African country northeast of Botswana. (p. RA22)

Glossary/Glosario

- Content vocabulary are words that relate to geography content. They are highlighted yellow in your text.
- Words below that have an asterisk (*) are academic vocabulary. They help you understand your school subjects and are **boldfaced** in your text.

English	Español
absolute location exact spot where a place is found (p. 15)	**ubicación absoluta** punto exacto donde se encuentra un lugar (pág. 15)
***access** a way or means of approach (p. 275)	***acceso** manera o medio de acercamiento (pág. 275)
***accumulate** to increase in amount (p. 48)	***acumular** aumentar en cantidad (pág. 48)
acid rain chemicals from air pollution that combine with precipitation (pp. 64, 171)	**lluvia ácida** sustancias químicas producto de la contaminación ambiental que se mezclan con las precipitaciones (págs. 64, 171)
***adapt** change (p. 125)	***adaptar** cambiar (pág. 125)
***affect** to influence, or produce an effect upon (p. 275)	***afectar** influir o producir un efecto en algo o alguien (pág. 275)
***alter** to change (p. 57)	***alterar** cambiar (pág. 57)
altitude height above sea level (p. 201)	**altitud** altura sobre el nivel del mar (pág. 201)
amendment an addition to a legal document or law (p. 141)	**enmienda** adición a un documento legal o ley (pág. 141)
annex declare ownership of an area (p. 136)	**anexar** declarar posesión de un área (pág. 136)
aquifer underground layer of rock through which water flows (p. 52)	**acuífero** capa de roca subterránea a través de la que fluye agua (pág. 52)
***assemble** put together (p. 235)	***reunir** juntar (pág. 235)
atmosphere layer of oxygen and other gases that surrounds Earth (p. 36)	**atmósfera** capa de oxígeno y otros gases que rodean la Tierra (pág. 36)
***attitudes** a particular feeling or way of thinking about something (p. 310)	***actitudes** sentimientos o maneras de pensar particulares respecto de algo (pág. 310)
***authority** power or influence over others (p. 300)	***autoridad** poder o influencia sobre los demás (pág. 300)
autonomy having independence from another country (pp. 339, 399)	**autonomía** ser independiente de otro país (págs. 339, 399)
***availability** easy or possible to get or use (p. 52)	***disponibilidad** fácil o posible de obtener o usar (pág. 52)
axis imaginary line that passes through the center of Earth from the North Pole to the South Pole (p. 36)	**eje** línea imaginaria que atraviesa el centro de la Tierra desde el Polo Norte al Polo Sur (pág. 36)

B

English	Español
ban legally block (p. 145)	**prohibir** impedir legalmente (pág. 145)

Glossary/Glosario

***benefit** something that does good to a person or thing (pp. 373)

bilingual accepting two official languages; able to speak two languages (pp. 149, 332)

biodiversity variety of plants and animals living on the planet (p. 66)

biome area that includes particular kinds of plants and animals adapted to conditions there (p. 60)

biotechnology study of cells to find ways of improving health (p. 159)

birthrate number of children born each year for every 1,000 people (p. 73)

blizzard severe winter storm that lasts several hours and combines high winds with heavy snow (p. 128)

bog low swampy area (p. 325)

***bonds** a uniting or binding force or influence (p. 307)

brownfield sites that have been abandoned and may contain dangerous chemicals (p. 172)

***beneficio** bien que se hace a una persona o cosa (pág. 373)

bilingüe que acepta dos idiomas oficiales, que puede hablar dos idiomas (págs. 149, 332)

biodiversidad variedad de plantas y animales que viven en el planeta (pág. 66)

bioma área que incluye clases particulares de plantas y animales adaptadas a las condiciones del área (pág. 60)

biotecnología estudio de las células para descubrir maneras de mejorar la salud (pág. 159)

índice de natalidad cantidad de niños nacidos por año cada 1,000 personas (pág. 73)

ventisca tormenta de invierno intensa que dura varias horas y combina vientos y nevadas fuertes (pág. 128)

ciénaga zona pantanosa y baja (pág. 325)

***lazos** fuerza influyente que une o vincula (pág. 307)

zona industrial abandonada sitios abandonados que pueden contener sustancias químicas peligrosas (pág. 172)

C

canopy umbrella-like covering formed by the tops of trees in a rain forest (p. 200)

canyon deep valleys with steep sides (p. 119)

carnival large festival held each spring in countries in Latin America on the last day before the Christian holy period called Lent (p. 224)

cash crop farm product grown for export (p. 211)

caudillo Latin American ruler, often a military officer or wealthy individual ruling as a dictator (p. 213)

century a period of 100 years (p. 16)

city-state independent political unit that includes a city and the surrounding area (p. 295)

civilization highly developed culture (p. 86)

classical referring to the civilizations of ancient Greece and Rome (p. 295)

climate pattern of weather that takes place in an area over many years (p. 56)

climate zone areas that have similar patterns of temperature and rainfall, and may have similar vegetation (p. 59)

bóveda de follaje cubierta en forma de sombrilla, formada por las copas de los árboles en una selva tropical (pág. 200)

cañón valles profundos con laterales de pendientes agudas (pág. 119)

carnaval gran festival que se realiza cada primavera en países de América Latina el día antes del período sagrado cristiano llamado Cuaresma (pág. 224)

cultivo comercial producto agrícola cultivado para la exportación (pág. 211)

caudillo gobernante latinoamericano, a menudo un oficial militar o un hombre rico que gobierna como dictador (pág. 213)

siglo período de cien años (pág. 16)

ciudad-estado unidad política independiente que incluye una ciudad y el área circundante (pág. 295)

civilización cultura con un alto desarrollo (pág. 86)

clásico referente a las civilizaciones de la Grecia y Roma antiguas (pág. 295)

clima conjunto de condiciones atmosféricas que ocurren en una zona durante muchos años (pág. 56)

zona climática áreas que tienen patrones similares de temperatura y precipitaciones, y pueden tener vegetación similar (pág. 59)

Cold War period from about 1947 until 1991 when the United States and the Soviet Union engaged in a political struggle for world influence but did not fight each other (p. 392)

Guerra Fría período desde 1947 hasta 1991, cuando los Estados Unidos y la Unión Soviética se involucraron en una lucha política para influir en el mundo pero sin combatir entre sí (pág. 392)

collection part of the water cycle; process by which streams and rivers carry water that has fallen to the earth back to the oceans (p. 54)

escurrimiento parte del ciclo del agua; proceso en el que los ríos y arroyos llevan el agua que cayó a la tierra, de regreso a los océanos (pág. 54)

collectivization a system in which small farms were combined into huge state-run enterprises with work done by mechanized techniques in the hopes of making farming more efficient and reducing the need for farm workers (p. 392)

colectivización sistema en el que pequeñas granjas se combinaron en grandes emprendimientos controlados por el estado; el trabajo se realizaba con técnicas mecanizadas con la esperanza de que la agricultura fuera más eficiente y que disminuyera la necesidad de empleados (pág. 392)

colony overseas settlement tied to a parent country (p. 136)

colonia asentamiento en el extranjero unido a un país madre (pág. 136)

command economy economic system in which the government decides how resources are used and what goods and services are produced (pp. 240, 349)

economía de mando sistema económico en el que el gobierno decide cómo se usan los recursos y qué bienes y servicios se producen (págs. 240, 349)

***comment** talk about (p. 224)

***comentar** hablar sobre algo (pág. 224)

commonwealth self-governing territory (p. 240)

mancomunidad territorio que se autogobierna (pág. 240)

communism system of government in which the government controls the ways of producing goods (p. 303)

comunismo sistema de gobierno en el que el estado controla los modos de producción de los bienes (pág. 303)

communist state country whose government has strong control over the economy and society as a whole (pp. 215, 391)

estado comunista país cuyo gobierno tiene un fuerte control de la economía y la sociedad como un todo (págs. 215, 391)

community neighborhood (p. 172)

comunidad vecindario (pág. 172)

***complex** highly developed (p. 210)

***complejo** altamente desarrollado (pág. 210)

***comprise** to be made up of (p. 409)

***componer** estar compuesto de (pág. 409)

condensation part of the water cycle; process by which water changes from gas to liquid (p. 54)

condensación parte del ciclo del agua; proceso en el que el agua cambia de la forma gaseosa a la forma líquida (pág. 54)

***conduct** carry out (p. 421)

***conducir** llevar a cabo (pág. 421)

coniferous referring to evergreen trees that have their seeds in cones (p. 285)

coníferas referente a árboles perennes que guardan sus semillas en conos (pág. 285)

conservation careful use of resources to avoid wasting them (p. 66)

conservación uso cuidadoso de los recursos para evitar su derroche (pág. 66)

***considerable** much (p. 200)

***considerable** mucho (pág. 200)

***constant** happening a lot or all the time (p. 47)

***constante** que sucede la mayor parte del o todo el tiempo (pág. 47)

constitutional monarchy form of government in which a monarch is the head of state but elected officials run the government (p. 322)

monarquía constitucional forma de gobierno en la que un monarca es la cabeza del estado pero en el que funcionarios electos controlan el gobierno (pág. 322)

***constrain** limit (p. 117)

***obligar** limitar (pág. 117)

contiguous joined together inside a common boundary (p. 117)

contiguo unidos juntos dentro de una misma frontera (pág. 117)

continent large landmass that rises above an ocean (p. 45)

continente gran masa continental que se alza por encima de un océano (pág. 45)

continental shelf plateau off of a continent that lies under the ocean and stretches for several miles (p. 50)

***convert** change from one to another (p. 389)

cordillera region of parallel mountain chains (p. 118)

core area at the center of the Earth, which includes a solid inner core and a hot liquid outer core (p. 45)

***core** basic or fundamental (p. 141)

coup action in which a group of individuals seizes control of a government (p. 394)

crop rotation changing what crops farmers plant in a field from year to year (p. 65)

crust uppermost layer of the Earth (p. 45)

cultural diffusion process of spreading ideas, languages, and customs from one culture to another (p. 87)

culture way of life of a group of people who share similar beliefs and customs (p. 83)

culture region area that includes different countries that share similar cultural traits (p. 88)

***currency** money (p. 303)

current steadily flowing stream of water in the ocean (p. 57)

czar title given to the emperors of Russia's past (p. 390)

plataforma continental meseta saliente de un continente que se encuentra bajo el océano y se extiende por varias millas (pág. 50)

***convertir** cambiar de una cosa a otra (pág. 389)

cordillera región de cadenas montañosas paralelas (pág. 118)

núcleo área del centro de la Tierra que incluye un núcleo interno sólido y un núcleo externo de líquido caliente (pág. 45)

***esencial** básico o fundamental (pág. 141)

golpe acción en que un grupo de individuos toma el control de un gobierno (pág. 394)

rotación de cultivos cambio en los cultivos que los agricultores plantan en un campo entre un año y el siguiente (pág. 65)

corteza capa superior de la Tierra (pág. 45)

difusión cultural proceso de divulgación de ideas, idiomas y costumbres de una cultura a otra (pág. 87)

cultura estilo de vida de un grupo de personas que comparten creencias y costumbres similares (pág. 83)

región cultural zona que incluye diferentes países que comparten características culturales similares (pág. 88)

***moneda** dinero (pág. 303)

corriente curso de agua que fluye constantemente en el océano (pág. 57)

zar título que recibían los emperadores de Rusia en el pasado (pág. 390)

death rate number of deaths per year out of every 1,000 people (p. 73)

decade a period of 10 years (p. 16)

deciduous trees that lose their leaves in the fall (p. 285)

***decline** a change to a lower state or level (p. 382)

decree order issued by a leader that has the force of law (p. 419)

default failure to make debt payments that are due to a lender (p. 250)

***define** to describe or establish (p. 50)

deforestation cutting down of forests without replanting new trees (p. 65)

democracy form of limited government in which power rests with the people, and all citizens share in running the government (pp. 85, 295)

índice de mortalidad número de muertes por año cada 1,000 personas (pág. 73)

década período de diez años (pág. 16)

caducifolios árboles que pierden sus hojas en otoño (pág. 285)

***descenso** cambio a un nivel o estado inferior (pág. 382)

decreto orden emitida por un líder que tiene el poder de ley (pág. 419)

incumplimiento imposibilidad de realizar los pagos de deuda que se deben a un prestamista (pág. 250)

***definir** describir o establecer (pág. 50)

deforestación destrucción de bosques sin plantar nuevos árboles (pág. 65)

democracia forma de gobierno limitado en el que el poder reside en la gente, y en el que todos los ciudadanos comparten la gestión del gobierno (págs. 85, 295)

deposit insurance government plan that promises to repay people who deposit their money in a bank if the bank should go out of business (p. 421)

seguros de depósito plan del gobierno que promete devolver el dinero a la gente que lo deposita en un banco si éste cierra sus puertas (pág. 421)

developed country country with an economy that has a mix of agriculture, a great deal of manufacturing, and service industries and that is very productive and provides its people with a high standard of living (p. 94)

país desarrollado país con una economía que combina agricultura, manufacturas e industrias de servicio; es muy productivo y proporciona a sus habitantes un nivel de vida alto (pág. 94)

developing country country that has limited industry, where agriculture remains important, incomes are generally low (p. 94)

país en vías de desarrollo país que posee una industria limitada, en el que la agricultura sigue siendo importante y los ingresos son, en general, bajos (pág. 94)

dialect local form of a language that may have a distinct vocabulary and pronunciation (p. 84)

dialecto forma local de un idioma que puede tener un vocabulario y una pronunciación diferentes (pág. 84)

dictatorship form of government in which a leader rules by force and typically limits citizens' freedoms (p. 86)

dictadura forma de gobierno en el que un líder gobierna por la fuerza y, por lo general, limita las libertades de los ciudadanos (pág. 86)

***differentiate** to make or become different in some way (p. 321)

***distinguir, diferenciar** hacer o volver diferente de algún modo (pág. 321)

***distribute** to spread out (p. 56)

***distribuir** dispersar (pág. 56)

***diverse** varied (p. 125)

***diverso** variado (pág. 125)

divide the high point in a landmass that determines the direction rivers flow (p. 120)

divisoria de aguas punto alto de una masa continental que determina la dirección en la que fluye un río (pág. 120)

***document** an important paper (p. 322)

***documento** papel importante (pág. 322)

***dominant** having controlling influence over others (p. 296)

***dominante** que posee influencia controladora sobre los demás (pág. 296)

dominion self-governing country in the British Empire (p. 139)

dominio país con gobierno propio en el Imperio Británico (pág. 139)

drought long period of time without rainfall (p. 126)

sequía período de tiempo largo sin lluvia (pág. 126)

dry farming agriculture that conserves water and uses crops and growing methods suited to semiarid environments (p. 339)

agricultura de secano agricultura que conserva el agua y usa cultivos y métodos de crecimiento apropiados para medios semiáridos (pág. 339)

earthquake sudden and violent movement of the Earth's crust that shakes the land, and can cause great damage (p. 47)

terremoto movimiento sorpresivo y violento de la corteza terrestre que sacude la tierra y puede ocasionar grandes daños (pág. 47)

economic system system that sets rules for deciding what goods and services to produce, how to produce them, and who will receive them (p. 94)

sistema económico sistema que establece las reglas que deciden qué bienes y servicios se producen, cómo producirlos y quién los recibirá (pág. 94)

***economy** way of producing goods (p. 136)

***economía** modo de producción de bienes (pág. 136)

ecosystem place shared by plants and animals that depend on one another for survival (p. 66)

ecosistema lugar compartido por plantas y animales que dependen unos de otros para sobrevivir (pág. 66)

***element** part of something larger (p. 219)

***elemento** parte de algo más grande (pág. 219)

***eliminate** to remove or get rid of (p. 392)

***eliminar** quitar o deshacerse de (pág. 392)

Glossary/Glosario

El Niño weather phenomenon marked by very heavy rains in western South America, often causing flooding; reduced rainfall in Southern Asia, Australia, and Africa; and severe storms in North America; opposite of **La Niña** (p. 58)	**El Niño** fenómeno meteorológico caracterizado por lluvias muy fuertes en la parte occidental de América del Sur, que suelen provocar inundaciones; lluvias reducidas en el sur de Asia, Australia y África, y grandes tormentas en América del Norte; opuesto de **La Niña** (pág. 58)
emigrate to leave a country and move to another (p. 75)	**emigrar** dejar un país y mudarse a otro (pág. 75)
emperor all-powerful ruler (p. 297)	**emperador** gobernante todopoderoso (pág. 297)
empire collection of different territories united under the rule of one government (p. 210)	**imperio** conjunto de diferentes territorios unidos bajo el control de un gobierno (pág. 210)
environment natural surroundings of people (p. 15)	**medio ambiente** entorno natural de las personas (pág. 15)
equinox either of the days in spring and fall in which the noon sun is overhead at the Equator and day and night are of equal length in both the Northern and Southern Hemispheres (p. 38)	**equinoccio** cualquier de los días en primavera y otoño cuando el sol del mediodía está sobre el Ecuador y el día y la noche tienen igual duración en los hemisferios Sur y Norte (pág. 38)
erosion process by which weathered bits of rock are moved elsewhere by water, wind, or ice (p. 48)	**erosión** proceso por el que trozos de roca expuestos a la intemperie se mueven a otros sitios con el agua, el viento o el hielo (pág. 48)
escarpment steep cliff at the edge of a plateau with a lowland area below (p. 194)	**escarpadura** acantilado en gran pendiente en el borde de una meseta con una área de tierra baja debajo (pág. 194)
estuary an area where river currents and ocean tide meet (p. 194)	**estuario** área donde las corrientes del río y la marea del océano se encuentran (pág. 194)
ethnic cleansing forcing people from one ethnic or religious group to leave an area so that it can be used by another group (p. 356)	**limpieza étnica** forzar a la gente de un grupo étnico o religioso a abandonar un área para que la use otro grupo (pág. 356)
ethnic group people with a common language, history, religion, and some physical traits (pp. 84, 307)	**grupo étnico** personas con idioma, historia, religión y ciertas características físicas en común (págs. 84, 307)
evaporation part of the water cycle; process by which water changes from liquid to gas (p. 53)	**evaporación** parte del ciclo del agua; proceso en el que el agua cambia de la forma líquida a la forma gaseosa (pág. 53)
***evolve** develop (p. 147)	***evolucionar** desarrollar (pág. 147)
***exploit** use (p. 400)	***explotar** usar (pág. 400)
export to sell goods or resources to other countries (p. 95)	**exportar** vender bienes o recursos a otros países (pág. 95)

***facilitate** make possible (p. 199)	***facilitar** hacer posible (pág. 199)
famine severe lack of food (p. 73)	**hambruna** falta grave de alimentos (pág. 73)
fault crack in the Earth's crust where two tectonic plates meet; prone to earthquakes (p. 47)	**falla** fractura en la corteza terrestre donde se unen dos placas tectónicas, propensa a los terremotos (pág. 47)
favela an overcrowded city slum in Brazil (p. 247)	**favela** barrio pobre y superpoblado de una ciudad en Brasil (pág. 247)
***feature** a part or detail that stands out (p. 284)	***característica** parte o detalle que se destaca (pág. 284)
federalism form of government in which power is divided between the federal, or national, government and the state governments (p. 140)	**federalismo** forma de gobierno en el que el poder está dividido entre el gobierno federal, o nacional, y los estados (pág. 140)

***fee** payment (p. 239)

fertility rate average number of children born to each woman (p. 307)

feudalism political and social system in which kings gave land to nobles in exchange for the nobles' promise to serve them; those nobles provided military service as knights for the king (p. 298)

***finance** provide funds or capital (p. 95)

***finite** limited in supply (p. 93)

fjord narrow, U-shaped coastal valley with steep sides formed by the action of glaciers (p. 327)

fossil fuel oil, natural gas, or coal, which are an important part of the world's energy supply (p. 375)

free market type of economy in which people are free to buy, produce, and sell with limited government involvement (p. 159)

free trade removal of trade restrictions so that goods flow freely among countries (p. 96)

***cargo** pagos (pág. 239)

tasa de fertilidad cantidad de niños nacidos de cada mujer (pág. 307)

feudalismo sistema político y social en el que los reyes entregaban tierras a los nobles a cambio de su promesa de servirlos; dichos nobles brindaban servicio militar como caballeros del rey (pág. 298)

***financiar** proporcionar fondos o capital (pág. 95)

***finito** limitado en el suministro (pág. 93)

fiordo valle costero angosto y en forma de U con laderas abruptas que se formó por la acción de los glaciares (pág. 327)

combustibles fósiles petróleo, gas natural o carbón, que son una parte importante del suministro de la energía del mundo (pág. 375)

mercado libre tipo de economía en el que las personas son libres para comprar, producir y vender con participación limitada del gobierno (pág. 159)

libre comercio eliminación de restricciones comerciales de modo que los bienes circulen libremente entre los países (pág. 96)

gaucho cowhand in Argentina (p. 249)

gasohol human-made fuel produced from mixing gasoline and alcohol made from sugarcane (p. 195)

***generate** make (p. 147)

Geographic Information System (GIS) combination of computer hardware and software used to gather, store, and analyze geographic information and then display it on a screen (p. 17)

geography study of the Earth and its people (p. 15)

geothermal energy electricity produced by natural underground sources of steam (p. 327)

geyser spring of water heated by molten rock inside the Earth that, from time to time, shoots hot water into the air (p. 327)

glacier giant sheets of ice (p. 119)

glasnost policy of political openness in the Soviet Union that allowed people to speak freely about the country's problems (p. 393)

globalization development of a worldwide culture with an interdependent economy (p. 89)

gaucho vaqueros de Argentina (pág. 249)

gasohol combustible fabricado por el ser humano, producto de la mezcla de gasolina y alcohol hecho de caña de azúcar (pág. 195)

***generar** hacer (pág. 147)

Sistema de Información Geográfica (GIS) combinación de hardware y software para obtener, almacenar y analizar información geográfica y luego exhibirla en una pantalla (pág. 17)

geografía estudio de la Tierra y sus habitantes (pág. 15)

energía geotérmica electricidad producida por fuentes de vapor subterráneas naturales (pág. 327)

géiser fuente de agua calentada por roca derretida dentro de la Tierra que de vez en cuando lanza agua caliente al aire (pág. 327)

glaciar capas gigantes de hielo (pág. 119)

glásnost plan de acción de apertura política en la Unión soviética, que permitió que las personas hablaran libremente sobre los problemas del país (pág. 393)

globalización desarrollo de una cultura amplia mundial con una economía interdependiente (pág. 89)

Global Positioning System (GPS) group of satellites that uses radio signals to determine the exact location of places on Earth (p. 17)

greenhouse effect buildup of certain gases in the Earth's atmosphere that, like a greenhouse, retain the sun's warmth (p. 64)

groundwater water that filters through the soil into the ground (p. 52)

***guarantee** promise (p. 159)

Sistema de Posicionamiento Global (GPS) grupos de satélites que envían señales de radio que registran la ubicación exacta de cada lugar en la Tierra (pág. 17)

efecto invernadero acumulación de ciertos gases en la atmósfera de la Tierra que, al igual que un invernadero, retienen el calor del Sol (pág. 64)

agua subterránea agua que se filtra a través del suelo hacia las profundidades (pág. 52)

***garantizar** prometer (pág. 159)

heavy industry manufacture of goods such as machinery, mining equipment, and steel (p. 411)

hieroglyphics system of writing that uses small pictures to represent sounds or words (p. 209)

high-technology industry areas of business that include making computers and other products with sophisticated engineering (p. 330)

Holocaust mass killing of 6 million European Jews by Germany's Nazi leaders during World War II (p. 302)

hurricane wind system that forms over the ocean in tropical areas and brings violent storms with heavy rains (p. 127)

industria pesada fabricación de bienes como maquinarias, equipo de minería y acero (pág. 411)

jeroglíficos sistema de escritura que usa pequeños dibujos para representar sonidos o palabras (pág. 209)

industria de alta tecnología áreas de negocios que incluyen la creación de computadoras y otros productos con ingeniería sofisticada (pág. 330)

Holocausto asesinato masivo de 6 millones de judíos europeos por parte de los líderes nazis de Alemania durante la Segunda Guerra Mundial (pág. 302)

huracán sistema de vientos que se forma sobre el océano en áreas tropicales y provoca tormentas violentas y fuertes lluvias (pág. 127)

***identical** exactly the same (p. 38)

***impact** effect (p. 279)

import to buy resources or goods from other countries (p. 95)

***income** earned money (p. 350)

indigenous people descended from an area's first inhabitants (p. 149)

infrastructure system of roads and railroads that allows the transport of materials (pp. 375)

***inhibit** limit (p. 375)

interdependence condition that exists when countries rely on each other for ideas, goods, services, and markets (p. 96)

***internal** existing or taking place within (p. 75)

***invest** to lay out money so as to return a profit (pp. 335, 410)

irrigation process of collecting water and distributing it to crops (p. 66)

***idéntico** exactamente lo mismo (pág. 38)

***impacto** efecto (pág. 279)

importar comprar bienes o recursos a otros países (pág. 95)

***ingreso** dinero ganado (pág. 350)

indígenas pueblo descendiente de los primeros habitantes de un área (pág. 149)

infraestructura sistema de carreteras y vías férreas que permiten el transporte de materiales (pág. 375)

***inhibir** limitar (pág. 375)

interdependencia condición que existe cuando los países dependen uno del otro para obtener ideas, bienes, servicios y mercados (pág. 96)

***interno** que existe o sucede dentro de (pág. 75)

***invertir** colocar dinero de manera de obtener una ganancia (págs. 335, 410)

irrigación proceso de recolección de agua y su distribución en los cultivos (pág. 66)

***issue** problem (p. 248)

isthmus narrow stretch of land connecting two larger land areas (p. 193)

***asunto** problema (pág. 248)

istmo extensión estrecha de tierra que conecta dos masas de tierra más grandes (pág. 193)

jade shiny stone that comes in many shades of green (p. 209)

jade piedra brillante de varios tonos de verde (pág. 209)

landlocked having no border with ocean or sea (p. 275)

La Niña weather phenomenon marked by unusually cool waters in the eastern Pacific and low amounts of rainfall there and heavier rains—and a greater chance of typhoons—in the western Pacific; opposite of **El Niño** (p. 58)

***layer** to form by adding layers (p. 64)

leap year year with 366 days, which happens every fourth year to make calendars match Earth's movement around the sun (p. 36)

light industry manufacture of consumer goods such as clothing, shoes, furniture, and household products (p. 411)

literacy rate percentage of people who can read and write (p. 239)

Llanos tropical grasslands that stretch through eastern Colombia and Venezuela (p. 194)

local wind wind pattern typical of a small area (p. 59)

sin salida al mar que no posee fronteras al mar o al océano (pág. 275)

La Niña fenómeno meteorológico caracterizado por aguas inusualmente frías y bajas cantidades de lluvia en el este del Pacífico, y fuertes lluvias (y una mayor posibilidad de tifones) en el oeste del Pacífico; opuesto de **El Niño** (pág. 58)

***hacer capas** formar agregando capas (pág. 64)

año bisiesto año con 366 días, que ocurre cada cuatro años para hacer que los calendarios coincidan con el movimiento de la Tierra alrededor del Sol (pág. 36)

industria liviana fabricación de bienes de consumo como ropas, calzado, muebles y productos para la casa (pág. 411)

tasa de alfabetización porcentaje de personas que saben leer y escribir (pág. 239)

llanos praderas tropicales que se extienden a través del este de Colombia y Venezuela (pág. 194)

viento local patrón de viento típico de un área pequeña (pág. 59)

magma hot melted rock inside the Earth that flows to the surface when a volcano erupts (p. 45)

***maintain** keep up (p. 248)

maize corn (p. 209)

***major** to be great in size or impact (p. 283)

mantle Earth's thickest layer, found between the core and the crust (p. 45)

maquiladora a foreign-owned factory in Mexico where workers assemble parts made in other countries (p. 235)

market economy economic system in which individuals make the decisions about how resources are used and what goods and services to provide (p. 350)

magma roca caliente y derretida dentro de la Tierra que fluye a la superficie durante la erupción de un volcán (pág. 45)

***mantener** conservar (pág. 248)

maíz mazorca y grano (pág. 209)

***principal** grande en tamaño o impacto (pág. 283)

manto capa más gruesa de la Tierra que se encuentra entre el núcleo y la corteza (pág. 45)

maquiladora fábrica de propiedad extranjera en México donde los trabajadores montan piezas hechas en otros países (pág. 235)

economía de mercado sistema económico en el que las personas toman las decisiones sobre cómo se usan los recursos y qué bienes y servicios se proveen (pág. 350)

***media** types of communication such as the Internet, television, and radio (p. 159)

***medical** relating to the science or practice of medicine (p. 356)

megalopolis huge urban area made up of several large cities and nearby communities (p. 117)

mestizo in Latin America, a person of mixed Native American and European heritage (p. 221)

middle class part of society that is neither very rich nor poor but has enough money to buy cars, new clothing, electronics, and luxury items (p. 410)

migrant worker person who earns a living by temporarily moving to a place separate from his or her home in order to work (p. 236)

migration movement of people (p. 219)

***militant** person who uses war or violence to accomplish goals (p. 340)

millennium a period of 1,000 years (p. 16)

missionary person who moves to another area to spread his or her religion (p. 389)

mistral cold, dry winter wind from the north that strikes southern France (p. 287)

monarchy government led by king or queen who inherited power by being born into ruling family (p. 86)

mural large painting on a wall (p. 224)

multinational company company that has locations in more than one country (p. 332)

***medios de comunicación** tipos de comunicación como Internet, la televisión y la radio (pág. 159)

***médico** relativo a la ciencia o la práctica de la medicina (pág. 356)

megalópolis área urbanizada gigantesca compuesta por varias ciudades grandes y comunidades cercanas (pág. 117)

mestizo en América Latina, persona de herencia mixta de nativos americanos y europeos (pág. 221)

clase media parte de la sociedad que no es ni muy rica ni muy pobre, pero que posee suficiente dinero para comprar autos, ropas nuevas, y artículos electrónicos y de lujo (pág. 410)

trabajador migratorio persona que se gana la vida mudándose temporalmente a un sitio alejado de su hogar para poder trabajar (pág. 236)

migración movimiento de personas (pág. 219)

***militante** persona que usa la guerra o la violencia para lograr objetivos (pág. 340)

milenio período de 1000 años (pág. 16)

misionero persona que se muda a otra zona para difundir su religión (pág. 389)

mistral viento invernal, frío y seco, que llega al sur de Francia desde el norte (pág. 287)

monarquía gobierno conducido por un rey o una reina que heredaron el poder al nacer dentro de la familia reinante (pág. 86)

mural pintura grande sobre una pared (pág. 224)

compañía multinacional empresa que tiene ubicaciones en más de un país (pág. 332)

national debt money owed by the government (p. 250)

nationalism feelings of affection and loyalty towards one's country (p. 397)

nation-state country formed of people who share a common culture and history (p. 299)

natural resource material from the Earth that people use to meet their needs (p. 93)

navigable referring to a body of water wide and deep enough for ships to use (pp. 119, 277)

neutrality refusal to take sides in a war between other countries (p. 336)

newly industrialized country country that is creating new manufacturing and business (p. 94)

deuda nacional dinero que el gobierno debe (pág. 250)

nacionalismo sentimiento de afecto y lealtad hacia el propio país (pág. 397)

estado-nación país formado por personas que comparten una historia y una cultura en común (pág. 299)

recurso natural material del planeta Tierra que la gente usa para cubrir sus necesidades (pág. 93)

navegable referente a un cuerpo de agua con anchura y profundidad suficientes para que lo usen barcos (págs. 119, 277)

neutralidad negativa a tomar posición en una guerra entre otros países (pág. 336)

país recientemente industrializado país que está creando nuevos negocios y manufacturas (pág. 94)

newsprint type of paper used for printing newspapers (p. 162)

nonrenewable resource natural resource such as a mineral that cannot be replaced (p. 93)

papel de periódico tipo de papel usado para imprimir periódicos (pág. 162)

recurso no renovable recurso natural, como un mineral, que no se puede reemplazar (pág. 93)

obsidian hard, black, volcanic glass useful for making weapons (p. 209)

***occur** to be found in (p. 50)

oligarch member of a small ruling group that holds great power (p. 420)

oral tradition folktales and other stories that are preserved by being remembered and spoken (p. 397)

orbit specific path each planet follows around the sun (p. 35)

obsidiana vidrio volcánico de color negro y resistente, útil para fabricar armas (pág. 209)

***ocurrir** que se encuentra en algo (pág. 50)

oligarca miembro de un grupo pequeño de gobierno que posee gran poder (pág. 420)

tradición oral relatos tradicionales y otras historias que se preservan mediante la memorización y el recitado (pág. 397)

órbita trayectoria específica que cada planeta sigue alrededor del Sol (pág. 35)

Pampas treeless grassland of Argentina and Uruguay (p. 194)

parliamentary democracy form of government in which voters elect representatives to a lawmaking body called Parliament, and members of Parliament vote for an official called the prime minister to head the government (pp. 141, 323)

***participate** take part in (p. 147)

pass space people can use to travel through a mountain range (p. 277)

peat plants partly decayed in water which can be dried and burned for fuel (p. 325)

pensioner person who receives regular payments from the government because he or she is too old or sick to work (p. 410)

perestroika policy of economic restructuring in the Soviet Union that called for less government control of the economy (p. 393)

***period** a portion of time (p. 379)

permafrost permanently frozen lower layers of soil found in the tundra and subarctic climate zones (p. 380)

pesticide powerful chemicals that kill crop-destroying insects (p. 66)

***physical** related to natural science (p. 15)

pidgin language language formed by combining parts of several different languages (p. 221)

pampas pradera desprovista de árboles en Argentina y Uruguay (pág. 194)

democracia parlamentaria forma de gobierno en la que los votantes eligen representantes para un cuerpo que crea las leyes denominado Parlamento, sus miembros votan a un funcionario llamado primer ministro como jefe del gobierno (págs. 141, 323)

***participar** tomar parte en (pág. 147)

paso lugar que la gente puede usar para viajar a través de una cordillera montañosa (pág. 277)

turba plantas parcialmente descompuestas en agua que pueden secarse y usarse como combustible (pág. 325)

pensionado persona que recibe pagos regulares del gobierno dado que está demasiado anciana o enferma para trabajar (pág. 410)

perestroika política de reestructuración económica en la Unión Soviética que exigía menos control gubernamental de la economía (pág. 393)

***período** lapso de tiempo (pág. 379)

permafrost capas de suelo inferiores que están permanentemente congeladas en la tundra y en las zonas de clima ártico (pág. 380)

pesticidas fuertes sustancias químicas que matan los insectos que destruyen los cultivos (pág. 66)

***físico** relativo a las sciencias naturales (pág. 15)

lengua mixta idioma formado por la combinación de partes de varios idiomas diferentes (pág. 221)

plantation large farm (p. 235)

plantación granja grande (pág. 235)

plate tectonics scientific theory that explains how processes within the Earth form continents and cause their movement (p. 46)

tectónica de placas teoría científica que explica cómo los procesos dentro de la Tierra forman los continentes y causan su movimiento (pág. 46)

plaza public square in Latin American city around which government buildings and major churches were built (p. 233)

plaza lugar público en las ciudades de América Latina alrededor del que se construyeron las iglesias principales y los edificios gubernamentales (pág. 233)

polder reclaimed wetlands that use a system of dikes and pumps to keep out the sea's waters (p. 332)

pólder pantanos recuperados que usan un sistema de diques y bombas para mantener fuera a las aguas marinas (pág. 332)

pollutant chemical and smoke particles that cause pollution (p. 380)

contaminantes sustancias químicas y partículas de humo que provocan contaminación (pág. 380)

pope head of the Roman Catholic Church (p. 298)

papa líder de la Iglesia Católica Romana (pág. 298)

population density average number of people living in a square mile or square kilometer (p. 74)

densidad de población cantidad promedio de personas que viven en una milla cuadrada o un kilómetro cuadrado (pág. 74)

potash mineral salt used in making fertilizer (p. 350)

potasa sal mineral usada en la fabricación de fertilizantes (pág. 350)

prairie rolling inland grassland region with fertile soil (p. 118)

pradera región interna de las llanuras, con pastizales ondulantes y tierras fértiles (pág. 118)

precipitation part of the water cycle; process by which water falls to the Earth as, for example, rain or snow (p. 54)

precipitación parte del ciclo del agua; proceso mediante el que el agua cae a la Tierra, por ejemplo, como lluvia o nieve (pág. 54)

prevailing winds wind patterns that are similar over time (p. 57)

vientos predominantes patrones de viento que se mantienen similares con el paso del tiempo (pág. 57)

***primary** main or most important (p. 400)

***primario** principal o más importante (pág. 400)

***principle** rule or guideline (p. 140)

***principio** regla o pauta (pág. 140)

***prior** earlier in time or order (p. 419)

***precedente** anterior en tiempo u orden (pág. 419)

privatization transfer of ownership of businesses from the government to individuals (p. 409)

privatización transferencia de propiedad de los negocios del gobierno a particulares (pág. 409)

productivity measure of how much work a person produces in a set amount of time (p. 325)

productividad medición de cuánto trabajo produce una persona en una cantidad fija de tiempo (pág. 325)

profit money a business earns after all its expenses are met (p. 159)

ganancia dinero que se gana en un negocio luego de cubrir todos los gastos (pág. 159)

***promote** to put forward (p. 398)

***promover** impulsar (pág. 398)

quota number limit on how many items of a particular product can be imported from a certain nation (p. 95)

cupo límite de la cantidad de artículos de un producto determinado que puede importarse de cierto país (pág. 95)

rain forest dense stand of trees and other growth that receives high amounts of precipitation each year (p. 199)

selva tropical agrupación densa de árboles y otras plantas que reciben grandes cantidades de precipitación cada año (pág. 199)

Glossary/Glosario

rain shadow effect of mountains that blocks rain from reaching interior regions (p. 59)

sombra de lluvia efecto de las montañas que impiden que la lluvia alcance regiones interiores (pág. 59)

refugee person who flees to another country to escape persecution or disaster (p. 76)

refugiado persona que huye a otro país para escapar de la persecución o el desastre (pág. 76)

***regime** government (p. 137)

***régimen** gobierno (pág. 137)

relative location description of where a place is in relation to the features around it (p. 15)

ubicación relativa descripción de dónde está un lugar en relación con las características a su alrededor (pág. 15)

***release** to relieve pressure (p. 45); to set free (p. 391)

***liberar** aliviar la presión (pág. 45); dar la libertad (pág. 391)

***reluctant** hesitant (p. 162)

***reacio** indeciso (pág. 162)

***rely** to depend on (p. 330)

***confiar** depender de (pág. 330)

remittance money sent back home by workers who leave their home country to work in other nations (p. 240)

remesa dinero que envían a su hogar los trabajadores que abandonan su país para trabajar en otras naciones (pág. 240)

renewable resource natural resource that can be replaced naturally or grown again (p. 93)

recurso renovable recurso natural que puede reemplazarse o crecer nuevamente de manera natural (pág. 93)

republic government in which people choose their leaders (p. 296)

república gobierno en el que las personas eligen a sus líderes (pág. 296)

representative democracy form of government in which voters choose leaders who make and enforce the laws (p. 140)

democracia representativa forma de gobierno en el que los votantes eligen a sus líderes para que hagan cumplir las leyes (pág. 140)

***reside** live (p. 194)

***residir** vivir (pág. 194)

***restore** return; to put or bring back into existence or use (p. 126)

***restituir** devolver; restablecer al estado o uso (pág. 126)

***restrict** to limit (p. 169)

***restringir** limitar (pág. 169)

reunification the act of being brought back together (p. 336)

reunificación el acto de ser vuelto a reunir (pág. 336)

***reveal** make known (p. 234)

***revelar** dar a conocer (pág. 234)

revolution one complete circuit around the sun (p. 36); sweeping change (pp. 215, 301)

revolución giro completo alrededor del Sol (pág. 36); cambio radical (págs. 215, 301)

***reverse** opposite (p. 38)

***reverso** opuesto (pág. 38)

rotate to spin on an axis (p. 36)

rotar girar sobre su eje (pág. 36)

***route** journey (p. 119)

***travesía** viaje (pág. 119)

S

secular nonreligious (p. 310)

secular no religioso (pág. 310)

selva Brazilian name for the Amazonian rain forest (p. 247)

selva nombre brasilero para los bosques tropicales del Amazonas (pág. 247)

separatist movement campaign by members of an ethnic group to break away from the national government and form an independent state (p. 421)

movimiento separatista campaña realizada por los miembros de un grupo étnico para separarse del gobierno nacional y formar un estado independiente (pág. 421)

serf farm laborer who could be bought and sold along with the land (p. 390)

siervo labriego que podía comprarse y venderse junto con la tierra (pág. 390)

***shift** to change from one to another (p. 239)

***significant** important (p. 37)

***similar** having qualities in common (p. 339)

sirocco hot winds from Africa that blow across southern Europe (p. 287)

smog thick haze of smoke and chemicals (pp. 64, 380)

sodium nitrate mineral used in fertilizer and explosives (p. 252)

softwood wood of evergreen trees, often used in buildings or making furniture (p. 375)

solar system planets, along with their moons, asteroids and other bodies, and the sun (p. 35)

specialization focusing on certain economic activities to make the best use of resources (p. 330)

***stable** firmly established; not likely to change suddenly or greatly (p. 213)

stock part ownership in a company (p. 159)

***style** form (p. 224)

subregion smaller area of a region (p. 193)

subsidy special payment made by a government to support a particular group or industry (p. 340)

subsistence farm small plot of land on which a farmer grows only enough food to feed his or her family (p. 235)

suburb smaller community just outside a large city (p. 147)

summer solstice day that has the most daylight hours and the fewest hours of darkness (p. 37)

***alternar** cambiar de una cosa a otra (pág. 239)

***significativo** importante (pág. 37)

***similar** que posee cualidades en común (pág. 339)

siroco vientos calientes de África que soplan atravesando el sur de Europa (pág. 287)

smog neblina espesa, resultado de la combinación de humo y sustancias químicas (págs. 64, 380)

nitrato de sodio mineral que se usa en fertilizantes y explosivos (pág. 252)

madera blanda madera de árboles siempre verdes, que se utiliza comúnmente en edificios o muebles (pág. 375)

sistema solar los planetas y sus lunas, los asteroides y otros cuerpos celestes además del Sol (pág. 35)

especialización concentrarse en ciertas actividades económicas para hacer el mejor uso de recursos (pág. 330)

***estable** establecido con firmeza; sin probabilidades de cambiar repentina o ampliamente (pág. 213)

acción parte propietaria en una empresa (pág. 159)

***estilo** forma (pág. 224)

subregión zona más pequeña de una región (pág. 193)

subsidio pago especial hecho por un gobierno para apoyar a un grupo o industria particular (pág. 340)

agricultura de subsistencia parcela de tierra en la cual un granjero cultiva sólo los alimentos suficientes para alimentar a su familia (pág. 235)

suburbio comunidad justo en las afueras de una ciudad grande (pág. 147)

solsticio de verano día que tiene la mayor cantidad de horas de luz diurna y la menor cantidad de horas de oscuridad (pág. 37)

taiga large coniferous forests (p. 380)

tariff tax added to the price of goods that are imported (pp. 95, 170)

***technique** a method of accomplishing something (p. 65)

***technology** the application of scientific discoveries to practical use (p. 73)

terrorism violence used against the people or government in the hopes of winning political goals (p. 137)

***theme** topic (p. 15)

taiga grandes bosques coníferos (pág. 380)

tarifa impuesto agregado al precio de los bienes que se importan (págs. 95, 170)

***técnica** un método para lograr algo (pág. 65)

***tecnología** la aplicación de los descubrimientos científicos a un uso práctico (pág. 73)

terrorismo violencia usada en contra del pueblo o del gobierno con la esperanza de alcanzar metas políticas (pág. 137)

***tema** tópico (pág. 15)

tornado severe windstorm that takes the form of a funnel-shaped cloud and often touches the ground (p. 127)

trade deficit situation that occurs when the value of a country's imports is higher than the value of its exports (p. 170)

trade surplus situation that occurs when the value of a country's exports is higher than the value of its imports (p. 170)

***transform** greatly change (p. 211)

***transport** move (p. 193)

trench deep cut in the ocean floor (p. 50)

tributary small river that flows into a larger river (p. 194)

Tropics area between the Tropic of Cancer and the Tropic of Capricorn, which has generally warm temperatures because it receives the direct rays of the sun for much of the year (pp. 38, 199)

trust territory area temporarily placed under control of another country (p. 197)

tornado intensa tormenta de viento que toma forma de embudo y suele tocar el suelo (pág. 127)

déficit comercial situación que ocurre cuando el valor de las importaciones de un país es mayor que el valor de sus exportaciones (pág. 170)

excedente comercial situación que ocurre cuando el valor de las exportaciones de un país es mayor que el valor de sus importaciones (pág. 170)

***transformar** cambiar mucho (pág. 211)

***transportar** mover (pág. 193)

fosa marina corte profundo en el suelo marino (pág. 50)

tributario río pequeño que fluye dentro de un río más grande (pág. 194)

trópicos área entre el Trópico de Cáncer y el Trópico de Capricornio con temperaturas generalmente cálidas, ya que recibe los rayos directos del Sol durante gran parte del año (págs. 38, 199)

territorio confiado área que se coloca temporalmente bajo el control de otro país (pág. 197)

underemployment situation that arises when a worker must take a job that requires lesser skills than he or she was trained for (p. 410)

***unify** to unite or bring together (p. 421)

***unique** being the only one of its kind (p. 89)

urban climate weather patterns in cities, including higher temperatures and distinct wind patterns, as compared to nearby rural areas (p. 61)

urban sprawl spread of human settlement into natural areas (p. 172)

urbanization growth of cities (pp. 75, 308)

subempleo situación provocada cuando un trabajador debe aceptar un trabajo que requiere menos habilidades que las que él posee (pág. 410)

***unificar** unir o juntar (pág. 421)

***exclusivo** ser el único en su tipo (pág. 89)

clima urbano patrones climáticos de las ciudades, incluyendo temperaturas más altas y patrones de vientos distintos, al compararse con áreas rurales cercanas (pág. 61)

expansión urbana expansión de asentamientos humanos en áreas naturales (pág. 172)

urbanización crecimiento de las ciudades (págs. 75, 308)

***vary** to be different (p. 326)

vaquero Mexican cowhand (p. 234)

***volume** amount (p. 411)

***variar** ser diferente (pág. 326)

vaquero empleado que trabaja con el ganado en México (pág. 234)

***volumen** cantidad (pág. 411)

water cycle system in which water moves from the Earth to the air and back to the Earth (p. 53)

ciclo del agua sistema en el que el agua se mueve de la Tierra hacia el aire y luego de vuelta hacia la Tierra (pág. 53)

Glossary/Glosario

weather changes in temperature, wind speed and direction, and air moisture that take place over a short period of time (p. 56)

weathering process in which rock is broken into smaller pieces by water and ice, chemicals, or even plants (p. 47)

welfare state country where the government is the main provider of support for the sick, needy, and the retired (p. 307)

***widespread** scattered or found in a wide area (pp. 86)

winter solstice day of the year that has the fewest hours of sunlight and the most hours of darkness (p. 38)

clima cambios en la temperatura, velocidad y dirección del viento, y humedad en el aire que duran un período breve (pág. 56)

deterioro por exposición proceso por el cual se rompen las rocas en pedazos más pequeños ocasionado por el agua y el hielo, las químicos o hasta los vegetales (pág. 47)

estado de bienestar país en el que el gobierno es el proveedor principal de ayuda para los enfermos, necesitados y jubilados (pág. 307)

***generalizado** que se distribuye o encuentra en un área amplia (pág. 86)

solsticio de invierno día del año que tiene la menor cantidad de horas de luz diurna y la mayor cantidad de horas de oscuridad (pág. 38)

Index

c=chart	*m=map*
d=diagram	*p=photo*
g=graph	*q=quote*

Index

Index

Index

N

Index

Index

Index

Index

Index

Acknowledgments

Text

51-Mark Twain. *Roughing It.* Harper & Brothers Publishers. Originally published by The American Publishing Company. 1871; **148-**Langston Hughes. "I, Too." In *The Collected Poems of Langston Hughes.* Ed. Arnold Rampersad. New York: Vintage Classics. 1995; **222-**"The Hard-Hearted Son." *Folktales of Mexico.* Ed., Trans. Américo Paredes. The University of Chicago Press. 1970; **324-**Charles Dickens. *Hard Times.* In *The Works of Charles Dickens.* New York: Books, Inc. 1854; **381-**Valentin Rasputin. *Farewell to Matyora.* Trans. Antonina W. Bouis. Evanston, IL: Northwestern University Press. 1991.

Photographs

Cover-(tl) CORBIS, (tc) Alan R. Moller/Getty Images, (c) Bill Bachman/Alamy Images, (r) CORBIS, (bl) Paul Thompson/Alamy Images; **ii–1-**NASA/Photo Researchers; **v-**Paul A. Souders/CORBIS; **vi-**(l) Blaine Harrington III/CORBIS, (r) Pete Oxford/Nature Picture Library; **vii-**Walter Bibikow/Getty Images; **viii-**Peter Guttman/CORBIS; **ix-**Markus Scholz/Peter Arnold, Inc.; **x-**AP Images; **xi-**Lucien Aigner/CORBIS; **xii-**(l) Tim Page/CORBIS, (r) Alfredo Maiquez/Getty Images; **xiii-**Klaus Nigge/National Geographic Image Collection/Getty Images; **11-**Cancan Chu/Getty Images; **12–13-**Gavin Hellier/Getty Images; **14-**John Van Hasselt/CORBIS; **15-**Peter Hulme; Ecoscene/CORBIS; **16-**Michael S. Yamashita/CORBIS; **18-**(t) ThinkStock/SuperStock, (cl) Janet Foster/Masterfile, (cr) Mark Tomalty/Masterfile, (bl) Jurgen Freund/Nature Picture Library, (br) age fotostock/SuperStock; **20-**(t) David Young-Wolff/PhotoEdit, (tc) NOAA/CORBIS, (b) The Photolibrary Wales/Alamy Images, (bc) Martin Harvey/Getty Images; **22-**(t) Dorling Kindersley/Getty Images, (b) Steve Skjold/Alamy Images; **34-**NASA/Roger Ressmeyer/CORBIS; **36-**(l) Andrew Parker/Alamy Images, (r) World Perspectives/Getty Images; **39-**(t) Tony West/CORBIS, (cl) imagebroker/Alamy Images, (cr) Kevin George/Alamy Images, (b) StockTrek/Getty Images; **42–43-**Bill Hatcher/National Geographic Image Collection; **44-**David Parker/Photo Researchers; **46-**Anthony West/CORBIS; **48-**Rafiqur Rahman/Reuters/CORBIS; **49-**Paul Bigland/Lonely Planet Images; **50-**Jimmy Chin/National Geographic Image Collection; **51-**John Lemker/Animals Animals; **52-**(l) Tom Bean/Getty Images, (r) James P. Blair/NGS/Getty Images; **54-**Yves Marcoux/Getty Images; **55-**China Newsphoto/Reuters/CORBIS; **57-**John Maier Jr/Argus Fotoarchiv/CORBIS SYGMA; **61-**AFP/Getty Images; **62-**Peter Arnold, Inc./Alamy Images; **63-**Vince Streano/age fotostock; **64-**Norbert Rosing/National Geographic Image Collection; **67-**(tc) age fotostock, (tr) Tom Uhlman/Alamy Images, (bl) Remi Benali/CORBIS, (br) Greg Stott/Masterfile; **70–71-**ML Sinibaldi/CORBIS; **72-**Keren Su/Getty Images; **74-**(l) Cancan Chu/Getty Images, (r) Greg Elms/Lonely Planet Images; **77-**Wayne R. Bilenduke/Getty Images; **78-**Reuters/Jagadeesh NV; **79-**(tl) Reuters/Bobby Yip, (tr) Danita Delimont/Alamy Images, (b) AP Photo; **80-**Reuters/Gary Hershorn; **81-**Baldev/CORBIS; **82-**Erich Schlegel/Dallas Morning News/CORBIS; **84-**Hideo Haga/HAGA/The Image Works; **86-**North Wind Picture Archives/Alamy Images; **87-**Kevin Lee/Getty Images; **89-**age fotostock/SuperStock; **90-**Charles O. Cecil/Alamy Images; **90–91-**W. Cody/CORBIS; **91-**Sean Sprague/The Image Works; **92-**Frederic J. Brown/AFP/Getty Images; **95-**(l) AP World Wide, (r) George Pimentel/wireimage.com; **97-**(tl) Jamal Said/Reuters/Landov, (cl) Richard I'Anson/Lonely Planet Images, (cr) Tom Hanson/Canadian Press/AP Images, (b) Jerry Alexander/Lonely Planet Images; **100-**(t to b) Creatas/SuperStock, AP Images, Jim Zuckerman/CORBIS, Kurt Scholz/SuperStock, Lisa Englebrecht/Danitadelimont.com, Gary Cook/Alamy Images; **100–101-**(bkgd) NASA; **101-**(t to b) Jose Azel/Getty Images, Macduff Everton/CORBIS, AP Images, ITAR-TASS/Vitaly Belousov/Newscom; **105-**(tl) Timothy O'Keefe/Index Stock Imagery, (tr) Christian Heeb/Aurora Photos, (bl) Jim Wark/Lonely Planet Images, (br) Kevin Horan/Getty Images; **113-**Tim Smith/Getty Images; **114–115-**age fotostock/SuperStock; **116-**Ralph Lee Hopkins/Lonely Planet Images; **117-**aerialarchives.com/Alamy Images; **118-**(l) Paul A. Souders/CORBIS, (r) Sarah Leen/National Geographic Image Collection; **119-**SuperStock; **121-**Richard Olsenius/National Geographic Image Collection; **123-**Mona Reeder/Dallas Morning News/CORBIS; **124-**Steve Terrill/CORBIS; **126-**Liz Condo/AP Images; **127-**Franz Marc Frei/CORBIS; **129-**(t) Paul A. Souders/CORBIS, (cl) Walter Bibikow/Getty Images, (cr) Eric Nguyen/Jim Reed Photography/CORBIS, (b) Robert Harding World Imagery/CORBIS; **132–133-**Gunter Marx Photography/CORBIS; **134-**Mark E. Gibson/CORBIS; **136-**(l) The British Museum/HIP/The Image Works, (r) FPG/Getty Images; **137-**(l) Swim Ink 2, LLC/CORBIS, (r) Tim Brakemeier/dpa/CORBIS; **138-**Joseph Barrak/AFP/Getty Images; **139-**Mary Evans Picture Library; **140-**Najlah Feanny/CORBIS; **142-**Ed Andrieski/AP Images; **142–143-**Photodisc/Getty Images; **143-**Max Whittaker/CORBIS; **144-**Oliver Strewe/Lonely Planet Images; **145-**Bob Daemmrich/The Image Works; **146-**Tony Vaccaro/Getty Images; **148-**(tl) CORBIS, (tr) Lucien Aigner/CORBIS, (b) Bettmann/CORBIS; **149-**Alan Marsh/Getty Images; **151-**(t) Roy Rainford/Robert Harding, (bl) Bettmann/CORBIS, (bc) Hulton Archive/Getty Images, (br) Tim Smith/Getty Images; **154–155-**Aaron Huey/Polaris; **155-**(tcr) Melanie Acevedo, (tr) Ryan Remiorz/AP Images, (bcr) Roy Morsch/age fotostock, (br) Purestock/Alamy Images; **156–157-**Charles O'Rear/CORBIS; **158-**Ed Kashi/CORBIS; **159-**Julia Malakie/AP Images; **161-**Ted Soqui/CORBIS; **163-**AP Photo; **164-**(t) Beth Dixson/Alamy Images, AP Photo; **165-**AP Photo; **166-**AP Photo; **167-**AP Photo; **168-**Bill Brooks/Alamy Images; **169-**Jason Kryk/AP Images; **170-**The Bill and Melinda Gates Foundation; **171-**Evan Vucci/AP Images; **173-**(t) Adam Pretty/Getty Images, (cl) David Leahy/Getty Images, (bl) John and Lisa Merrill/CORBIS, (br) Mark Elias/Bloomberg News/Landov; **176–177-**Stone/Getty Images; **179-**(tr) Jack Novak/SuperStock, (cl) Ken Fisher/Getty Images, (bl) Jeff Rotman/Getty Images, (br) Hubert Stadler/CORBIS; **189-**Tom Cockrem/Lonely Planet Images; **190–191-**Tony Savino/The Image Works; **192-**Jeremy Horner/CORBIS; **193-**Jon Arnold Images/SuperStock; **194-**Kit Houghton/CORBIS; **195-**Pete Oxford/Nature Picture Library; **197-**(t) Media Bakery, (b) The Bridgeman Art Library; **198-**David Lyons/National Geographic Image Collection; **200-**(l) Tui De Roy/Minden Pictures, (r) Brent Winebrenner/LPI; **203-**(tl) SuperStock, (tr) Trevor Smithers ARPS/Alamy Images, (c) Rodrigo Arangua/AFP/Getty Images, (b) Galen Rowell/Odyssey Productions; **206–207-**Danny Lehman/CORBIS; **208-**Carlos Lopez-Barillas/CORBIS; **209-**Robert Frerck and Odyssey Productions; **211-**Werner Forman/CORBIS; **212-**(l) Charles & Josette Lenars/CORBIS, (r) Brooklyn Museum/CORBIS; **213-**(l) Index, Museo de America, Madrid, Spain/The Bridgeman Art Library, (r) Angelo Cavalli/Getty Images; **214-**(l) H.N. Rudd/CORBIS, (r) Jose Fuste Raga/CORBIS; **216-**Tim Page/CORBIS; **216–217-**Getty Images; **217-**Alfredo Maiquez/Getty Images; **218-**Blaine Harrington III/CORBIS; **219-**Tom Cockrem/Lonely Planet Images; **220-**David Dudenhoefer/Odyssey Productions; **221-**(l) Chris Brandis/AP Images, (r) AM Corporation/Alamy Images; **222-**Robert Holmes/CORBIS; **223-**GM Photo Images/Alamy Images; **225-**(tl) Danny Lehman/CORBIS, (tr) Mario Algaze/The Image Works, (bl) Alfredo Dagli Orti/The Art Archive/CORBIS, (br) Adriano Machado/Reuters/CORBIS; **228–229-**Adriana Zehbrauskas/Polaris, (tr) Danita Delimont/Alamy Images, (cr) Ken Welsh/age fotostock, (br) Luc Novovitch/Alamy Images; **230–231-**Chad Ehlers/Getty Images; **232-**Lynsey Addario/CORBIS; **233-**World Pictures/Alamy Images; **234-**Danita Delimont/Alamy Images; **235-**Danny Lehman/CORBIS; **237-**Oswaldo Rivas/Reuters/CORBIS; **238-**(l) Mark Godfrey c. 2004 The Nature Conservancy, (r) Courtesy Marie Claire Paiz; **239-**Alejandro Ernesto/epa/CORBIS; **241-**AP Photo/Dolores Ochoa; **242-**Peter Arnold, Inc./Alamy Images; **243-**(tl) World Picture Library/Alamy Images, (tc) AP Photo/Alberto Cesar-Greenpeace/HO, (tr) Sue Cunningham Photographic/Alamy Images, (b) Reuters/Carlos Barria; **244-**Reuters/Jamil Bittar; **245-**Reuters/Paulo Whitaker; **246-**Roger Ressmeyer/CORBIS; **247-**Paulo Whitaker/Reuters/Landov; **249-**Vanderlei Almeida/AFP/Getty Images; **250-**Eduardo De Baia/AP Images; **251-**Eliseo Fernandez/Reuters/CORBIS; **253-**(t) Marcelo Sayao/epa/CORBIS, (cl) Marco Ugarte/AP Images, (cr) Juan Barreto/AFP/Getty Images, (b) Jeff Greenberg/age fotostock; **256–257-**Roberto Gerometta/Lonely Planet Images; **259-**(tl) Anthony West/CORBIS, (tr) Jon Arnold Images/Alamy Images, (bl) Owen Franken/CORBIS, (br) Walter Bibikow/Getty Images; **269-**Nicole Duplaix/NGS/Getty Images; **271-**Tim Graham/Getty Images; **272–273-**Richard Nebesky/Lonely Planet Images; **274-**Emile Luider/Getty Images; **275-**age fotostock/SuperStock; **276-**(l) Chase Jarvis/Getty Images, (r) Jon Arnold/SuperStock; **277-**Walter Geiersperger/CORBIS; **278-**age fotostock/SuperStock; **279-**(inset) Andra Maslennikov/Peter Arnold, Inc., Ben Osborne/Getty Images; **281-**Sergei Supinsky/AFP/Getty Images; **282-**Fernand Ivaldi/Getty Images; **286-**Raymond Gehman/CORBIS; **287-**George Simhoni/Masterfile; **289-**(tl) John Garrett/CORBIS, (cl cr) age fotostock/SuperStock, (br) Asgeir Helgestad/Nature Picture Library; **292–293-**Hubert Stadler/CORBIS; **294-**David Tomlinson/Lonely Planet Images; **295-**Ted Spiegel/CORBIS; **297-**(l) Matt Houston/AP Images, (r) Royalty-Free/CORBIS; **298-**C. Steve Vidler/eStock Photo; **299-**National Gallery Collection; By kind permission of the Trustees of the National Gallery, London/CORBIS; **300-**(l) Scala/Art Resource, (r) Royalty-Free/Getty Images; **301-**(l) Ashmolean Museum, University of Oxford, UK/Bridgeman Art Library, (r) Rèunion des Musèes Nationaux/Art Resource; **304-**Homer Sykes/Alamy Images; **304–305-**Royalty-Free/CORBIS; **305-**Robert Fried Photography; **306-**Jeff Morgan/Alamy Images; **307-**Gideon Mendel/CORBIS; **308-**Michel Euler/AP Images; **309-**Simeone Huber/Getty Images; **310-**Daniel Mihailescu/AFP/Getty Images; **313-**(t) Art Resource, (cl) The Art Archive, (cr) Jonathan Smith/Lonely Planet Images, (b) Masterfile; **316–317-**Richard Harbus/Polaris; **317-**(tr) Steven Mark Needham/Picturearts/Newscom, (cr) Franck Fife/AFP/Newscom, (br) Patrick Sheandell O'Carroll/Getty Images; **318–319-**Elliot Daniel/Lonely Planet Images; **320-**The Image Bank/Getty Images; **322-**Manfred Gottschalk/Lonely Planet Images; **323-**Jayanta Shaw/Reuters/CORBIS; **324-**(l) General Photographic Agency/Getty Images, (r) Mary Evans Picture Library/The Image Works; **325-**Gideon Mendel/CORBIS; **326-**scenicireland.com/Christopher Hill Photographic/Alamy Images; **327-**Palmi Gudmundsson/Getty Images; **329-**George F. Mobley/National Geographic Image Collection; **330-**Jack Dabaghian/Reuters/CORBIS; **331-**(l) Eddie Koegh/Reuters Photo Archive/Newscom, (r) Getty Images for Nike; **332-**Reuters/Luis D'Orey; **333-**K.M. Westermann/CORBIS; **334-**Winfried Rothermel/AP Images; **335-**Christian Charisius/Reuters/CORBIS; **336-**Martin Ruetschi/epa/CORBIS; **338-**Getty Images; **339-**age fotostock/SuperStock; **340-**(inset) Charles O'Rear/CORBIS, Jose Manuel Ribeiro/Reuters/Landov; **341-**Peter Adams/Getty Images; **343-**Brian Atkinson/Alamy Images; **344-**Jack Naegelen/Reuters/CORBIS; **345–346-**AP Images; **348-**Sergei Supinsky/AFP/Getty Images; **349-**Reuters/Fabrizio Bensch; **350-**Katarina Stoltz/Reuters/CORBIS; **352-**Sean Gallup/Newsmakers/Getty Images; **353-**Peter Turnley/CORBIS; **355-**Robb Kendrick/Getty Images; **357-**(t) Alain Nogues/CORBIS, (cl) Tim Graham/Getty Images, (cr) Bob Stern/The Image Works, (bl) Goddard Space Flight Center Scientific Visualization Studio/NASA, (br) Craig Pershouse/Lonely Planet Images; **360–361-**Viktor Korotayev/Reuters/CORBIS; **363-**(tl) Tkachev Andrei/ITAR-TASS/Landov, (tr) age fotostock/SuperStock, (bl) Konstantin Mikhailov/Nature Picture Library, (br) Roshanak.B/CORBIS; **369-**Novosti/Topham/The Image Works; **370–371-**Maria Stenzel/National Geographic Image Collection; **372-**NGS/Getty Images; **373-**Lee Foster/Lonely Planet Images; **376-**Osetrov Yury/ITAR-TASS/Landov; **376–377-**Karl Weatherly/Getty Images; **377-**Klaus Nigge/NGS/Getty Images; **378-**Rashid Salikhov/EPA/epa/CORBIS; **380-**(l) Maria Stenzel/National Geographic Image Collection, (r) SIME s.a.s/eStock Photo; **381-**(r) Marc Garanger/CORBIS, (b) Wolfgang Kaehler/CORBIS; **382-**(inset) Konstantin Mikhailov/naturepl.com, Chris Niedenthal/Time Life Pictures/Getty Images; **383-**(l) Peter Guttman/CORBIS, (r) Peter Turnley/CORBIS, (b) Wade Eakle/Lonely Planet Images; **386–387-**Mark Sykes/Alamy Images; **388-**Stringer/AFP/Getty Images; **390-**(l) Martin Gray/National Geographic Image Collection, (r) Kremlin Museums, Moscow, Russia/The Bridgeman Art Library;

391-(l) National Geographic Image Collection, (r) Douglas Kirkland/CORBIS; **392-**Yuri Kozyrev for Time; **393-**Central Press/Getty Images; **395-**Markus Scholz/Peter Arnold, Inc.; **396-**Ilya Naymushin/Reuters/CORBIS; **397-**Steve Vidler/SuperStock; **398-**(l) Igor Akimov/ITAR-TASS/Landov, (r) Topham/The Image Works; **399-**REZA/National Geographic Society Image Collection; **401-**(t) Hulton-Deutsch Collection/CORBIS, (cl) Topham/The Image Works, (cr) Marc Garanger/CORBIS, (b) Peter Turnley/CORBIS; **404–405-**Jeremy Nicholl/Polaris; **405-**(tr) Bill Aron/Photo Edit, (cr) Anatoly Rukhadze/ITAR-TASS Photos/Newscom, (br) Creatas/Punchstock; **406–407-**Belinsky Yuri/ITAR-TASS/CORBIS; **408-**Reuters/CORBIS; **409-**Ivan Sekretarev/AP Images; **410-**AP Images; **413-**AP Photo; **414-**Wolfgang Kaehler/CORBIS; **415-**(l c) AP Photo, (r) Peter Blakely/CORBIS SABA; **416-**Smolsky Sergei/ITAR-TASS/CORBIS; **417-**AP Photo; **418-**Richard Nowitz/National Geographic Image Collection; **419-**Reuters/CORBIS; **421-**Khasan Kaziyev/AFP/Getty Images; **423-**(t) Buddy Mays/CORBIS, (cl) Alexey Danichev/AFP/Getty Images, (bl) transit/Peter Arnold, Inc., (br) AP Images; **426-**Wade Eakle/Lonely Planet Images; **428-**(l) Justin Guariglia/National Geographic Image Collection, (t) Michael Nichols/National Geographic Image Collection, (cr) eStock Photo/Picture Finders Ltd., (br) John Elk III/Lonely Planet Images; **430–431-**Tim de Waele/CORBIS; **433-**(tl) Hanan Isachar/CORBIS, (tr) PCL/Alamy Images, (bl) Frank Krahmer/Masterfile Corporation, (br) The Photolibrary Wales/Alamy Images; **442–443-**Jon Arnold Images/Alamy Images; **445-**(tl) Michael Freeman/CORBIS, (tr) Network Photographers/Alamy Images, (cl) Images of Africa Photobank/Alamy Images, (b) David Keaton/CORBIS; **456–457-**Keren Su/CORBIS; **459-**(t) Nature Picture Library/Alamy Images, (cl) DPA/AJI/The Image Works, (bl) Hemis/Alamy Images, (br) David H. Wells/CORBIS; **465-**Eye Ubiquitous/CORBIS; **466–467-**Pixtal/age fotostock; **469-**(t) Dean Conger/National Geographic Image Collection, (bl) Jacques Langevin/CORBIS SYGMA, (br) Keren Su/Lonely Planet Images; **477-**Eye Ubiquitous/CORBIS; **478–479-**R. Wallace/Stock Photos/zefa/CORBIS; **481-**(t) Fred Bavendam/Minden Pictures, (cr) Michael & Patricia Fogden/CORBIS, (bl) R. Ian Lloyd/Masterfile, (br) Gordon Wiltsie/Getty Images; **489-**Jerry Barnett; **490-**Kunsthistorisches Museum, Wien oder KHM, Wien; **491-**Larry Williams/CORBIS; **495-**Michael Nichols/National Geographic Image Collection